CIVILIZATION IN THE WEST

CONTEMPORARY EUROPE
Land Elevation
Feet
Meters
13,123
4,000
6,562
2,000
3,281
1,000
1,640
500
656
200
0
0
Below sea level
Below sea level
0
250
500 mi.
0
250
500 km
30°W
20°W
10°W
0°
70°N
10°E
60°N
50°N
40°N
Arctic Circle
ICELAND
Norwegian Sea
FAROE IS.
SHETLAND IS.
HEBRIDES IS.
ORKNEY IS.
KJØLEN MOUNTAINS
SCANDINAVIAN PEN
NORWAY
SWEDEN
L. Vänern
L. Vättern
Scotland
Northern Ireland
UNITED KINGDOM
BRITISH ISLES
IRELAND
Wales
England
Thames R.
Celtic Sea
North Sea
JUTLAND PENINSULA
DENMARK
ATLANTIC OCEAN
English Channel
NETHERLANDS
RUHR VALLEY
Elbe R.
NORTH E
Oder R.
PO
BELGIUM
GERMANY
Rhine R.
BRITTANY PENINSULA
Seine R.
LUXEMBOURG
CZECH REPUBLIC
SLO
Loire R.
FRANCE
LIECHTENSTEIN
Danube R.
Bay of Biscay
SWITZERLAND
L. Geneva
AUSTRIA
HU
CENTRAL MASSIF
ALPS
SLOVENIA
Drava R.
Garonne R.
Rhône R.
Po R.
Sava R.
CROATIA
PYRENEES
Ebro R.
ITALY
SAN MARINO
BOSNIA & HERZEGOVINA
Duero R.
MONACO
DINARIC A
APENNINES
IBERIAN PENINSULA
ANDORRA
Adriatic Sea
CORSICA
PORTUGAL
Tagus R.
SPAIN
Guadiana R.
Guadalquivir R.
Tyrrhenian Sea
SARDINIA
BALEARIC ISLANDS
SIERRA NEVADA
Strait of Gibraltar
Mediterranean Sea
SICILY
MALTA
AFRICA

30°E
40°E
50°E
60°E
70°E
Barents Sea
KOLA PENINSULA
White Sea
Pechora R.
Ob R.
URAL MOUNTAINS
N. Dvina R.
FINLAND
L. Onega
L. Ladoga
RUSSIA
Gulf of Finland
ESTONIA
L. Peipus
Volga R.
Ural R.
LATVIA
LITHUANIA
EUROPEAN PLAIN
CENTRAL RUSSIAN UPLAND
Oka R.
VOLGA UPLAND
BELARUS
Volga R.
Dnepr R.
Don R.
CASPIAN DEPRESSION
UKRAINE
Dnestr R.
CARPATHIAN MTS.
Siret R.
Prut R.
MOLDOVA
Sea of Azov
Caspian Sea
CAUCASUS
ROMANIA
CRIMEA
TRANSYLVANIAN ALPS
GEORGIA
Black Sea
Danube R.
ARMENIA
BALKAN MTS.
MONTENEGRO
BULGARIA
Bosporus
AZERBAIJAN
BALKAN PENINSULA
TURKEY
GREECE
Dardanelles
ASIA
Aegean Sea
CYPRUS
CRETE

160°W
140°W
120°W
100°W
80°W
60°W
40°W
20°W
ARCTIC OCEAN
Beaufort Sea
Baffin Bay
GREENLAND
ICELAND
Yukon R.
ROCKY MOUNTAINS
NORTH AMERICA
Hudson Bay
Gulf of Alaska
Great Lakes
GREAT PLAINS
Missouri R.
Mississippi R.
APPALACHIAN MTS.
40°N
ATLANTIC OCEAN
Gulf of Mexico
Tropic of Cancer
WEST INDIES
20°N
Caribbean Sea
GUIANA HIGHLANDS
Equator
0°
Amazon R.
AMAZON BASIN
SOUTH AMERICA
ANDES
BRAZILIAN HIGHLANDS
20°S
ATACAMA DESERT
Tropic of Capricorn
Paraná R.
PACIFIC OCEAN
PAMPAS
40°S
PATAGONIA
N
W
E
S
Cape Horn
60°S
Antarctic Circle
Weddell Sea
Ross Sea

20°E
40°E
60°E
80°E
100°E
120°E
140°E
160°E
Laptev Sea
ARCTIC OCEAN
Barents Sea
SCANDINAVIA
Yenisey R.
Lena R.
Ob R.
SIBERIA
URAL MTS.
Volga R.
NORTH EUROPEAN PLAIN
EUROPE
Sea of Okhotsk
Baikal
Amur R.
Aral Sea
ALPS
Danube R.
CAUCASUS MTS.
Caspian Sea
ASIA
GOBI (DESERT)
Black Sea
JAPAN
Sea of Japan
Tigris R.
ZAGROS MTS.
TIBETAN PLATEAU
Mediterranean Sea
Euphrates R.
HIMALAYA MTS.
Huang He R.
Indus R.
East China Sea
Chiang Jiang R.
HARA
ESERT)
Nile R.
ARABIAN DESERT
THAR DESERT
Ganges R.
Tropic of Cancer
Red Sea
Persian Gulf
DECCAN PLATEAU
PACIFIC OCEAN
South China Sea
PHILIPPINES
SUDAN
Arabian Sea
Bay of Bengal
Mekong R.
AFRICA
ETHIOPIAN HIGHLANDS
Zaire R.
Congo R.
CONGO BASIN
Victoria
BORNEO
SUMATRA
INDONESIA
NEW GUINEA
JAVA
INDIAN OCEAN
Zambezi R.
MADAGASCAR
GREAT SANDY DESERT
Tropic of Capricorn
AUSTRALIA
KALAHARI DESERT
GREAT VICTORIA DESERT
Darling R.
Cape of Good Hope
NEW ZEALAND
CONTEMPORARY WORLD
Land Elevation
Feet
Meters
13,123
4,000
6,562
2,000
3,281
1,000
1,640
500
0
0
Below sea level
Below sea level
Ice-covered
0
1,000
2,000 mi.
0
1,000
2,000 km
Robinson Projection
ANTARCTICA

CIVILIZATION IN THE WEST

Seventh Edition

Volume I: To 1715

Mark Kishlansky
Harvard University

Patrick Geary
University of California, Los Angeles

Patricia O'Brien
University of California, Los Angeles

New York San Francisco Boston
London Toronto Sydney Tokyo Singapore Madrid
Mexico City Munich Paris Cape Town Hong Kong Montreal

Senior Acquisitions Editor: Janet Lanphier
Assistant Development Manager: David Kear
Development Editor: Barbara Conover
Executive Marketing Manager: Sue Westmoreland
Supplements Editor: Brian Belardi
Media Editor: Melissa Edwards
Production Manager: Donna DeBenedictis
Project Coordination, Text Design, and Electronic Page Makeup: Elm Street Publishing Services, Inc.
Cover Designer/Manager: John Callahan
Cover Image: The Art Archive/Museo del Prado Madrid/Dagli Orti
Photo Researcher: Vivette Porges
Manufacturing Buyer: Lucy Hebard
Printer and Binder: Quebecor World/Dubuque
Cover Printer: Phoenix Color Corporation

For permission to use copyrighted material, grateful acknowledgment is made to the copyright holders on pp. C-1–C-3, which are hereby made part of this copyright page.

Library of Congress Cataloging-in-Publication Data
Kishlansky, Mark A.
Civilization in the West/Mark Kishlansky, Patrick Geary, Patricia O'Brien.—7ed.
p. cm.
Includes bibliographical references and index.
ISBN 978–0–205–55684–7 (single v. ed.)—ISBN 978–0–205–55685–4 (v. I)—ISBN 978–0–205–55686–1 (v. II)—ISBN 978–0–205–55687–8 (v. A)—ISBN 978–0–205–55688–5 (v. B)—ISBN 978–0–205–55689–2 (v. C)
1. Civilization, Western—History—Textbooks. I. Geary, Patrick J., 1948-II. O'Brien, Patricia, 1945-III.Title.

CB245.K546 2008
909'.09821—dc22

Please visit us at http://www.ablongman.com/kishlansky

ISBN-13: 978–0–205–55684–7 ISBN-10: 0–205–55684–1 (Combined Volume)
ISBN-13: 978–0–205–55685–4 ISBN-10: 0–205–55685–X (Volume I)
ISBN-13: 978–0–205–55686–1 ISBN-10: 0–205–55686–8 (Volume II)
ISBN-13: 978–0–205–55687–8 ISBN-10: 0–205–55687–6 (Volume A)
ISBN-13: 978–0–205–55688–5 ISBN-10: 0–205–55688–4 (Volume B)
ISBN-13: 978–0–205–55689–2 ISBN-10: 0–205–55689–2 (Volume C)
ISBN-13: 978–0–13–600706–7 ISBN-10: 0–13–600706–6 (Advanced Placement* Edition, Since 1300)

2 3 4 5 6 7 8 9 10—QWD—10 09 08

BRIEF CONTENTS

DETAILED CONTENTS

Note: Each chapter ends with Questions for Review, Key Terms, Discovering Western Civilization Online, and Suggestions for Further Reading.

CHAPTER 3
CLASSICAL AND HELLENISTIC GREECE, 500–100 B.C.E. 66

CHAPTER 4
EARLY ROME AND THE ROMAN REPUBLIC, 800–146 B.C.E. 100

CHAPTER 5
IMPERIAL ROME, 146 B.C.E.–192 C.E. 128

CHAPTER 8
THE WEST IN THE EARLY MIDDLE AGES, 500–900 216

CHAPTER 9
THE HIGH MIDDLE AGES 248

CHAPTER 10
THE LATER MIDDLE AGES, 1300–1500 286

CHAPTER 11
THE ITALIAN RENAISSANCE 316

CHAPTER 12
THE EUROPEAN EMPIRES 346

CHAPTER 13
THE REFORM OF RELIGION 378

DOCUMENTS

DOCUMENTS

MAPS

CHRONOLOGIES, GENEALOGIES, AND FIGURES

PREFACE

In planning *Civilization in the West,* our aim was to write a book that students would *want* to read. Throughout our years of planning, writing, revising, rewriting, and meeting together, this was our constant overriding concern. Would students read our book? Would it be effective in conveying information while stimulating the imagination? Would it work for a variety of Western civilization courses with different levels and formats? It was not easy to keep this concern in the forefront throughout the long months of composition, but it was easy to receive the reactions of scores of reviewers to this simple question: "Would students *want* to read these chapters?" Whenever we received a resounding "No!" we began again—not just rewriting but rethinking how to present material that might be too complex in argument or detail or that might simply seem too remote to engage the contemporary student. Although all three of us were putting in long hours in front of computers, we quickly learned that we were engaged in a teaching rather than a writing exercise. And though the work was demanding, it was not unrewarding. We hope that you will recognize and come to share with us the excitement and enthusiasm we felt in creating this text. We have enjoyed writing it, and we want students to enjoy reading it.

From the reactions to our first six editions, they have. We have received literally hundreds of cards and letters from adopters and users of *Civilization in the West.* The response has been both overwhelming and gratifying. It has also been constructive. Along with praise, we have received significant suggestions for making each subsequent edition stronger. Topics such as the Crusades, the Enlightenment, and imperialism have been reorganized to present them more clearly. Subjects such as the ancient Hebrews, Napoleon, and German unification have been given more space and emphasis. New features have been added to freshen the book and keep abreast of current scholarship, and more than 100 excerpts from primary sources are presented to give students a feel for the concreteness of the past. We believe that the seventh edition of *Civilization in the West* not only preserves the much-praised quality of its predecessors but also enhances it.

APPROACH

We made a number of decisions early in the project that we believed contributed to our goal. First, we were *not* writing an encyclopedia on Western civilization. Information was not to be included in a chapter unless it related to the themes of that chapter. There was to be no information for information's sake, and each of us was called upon to defend the inclusion of names, dates, and events whenever we met to critique one another's chapters. We found, to our surprise, that by adhering to the principle that information included must contribute to or illustrate a particular point or dominating theme, we provided as much, if not more, material than books that habitually list names, places, and dates without any other context.

Second, we were committed to integrating the history of ordinary men and women into our narrative. We believe that isolated sections, placed at the end of chapters, that deal with the experiences of women or minority groups in a particular era profoundly distort historical experience. We called this technique *caboosing,* and whenever we found ourselves segregating women or families or the masses, we stepped back and asked how we might recast our treatment of historical events to account for a diversity of actors. How did ordinary men, women, and children affect the course of historical events? How did historical events affect the fabric of daily life for men, women, and children from all walks of life? We tried to rethink critical historical problems of civilization as gendered phenomena. To assist us in the endeavor, we engaged two reviewers whose sole responsibility was to evaluate our chapters for the integration of those social groups into our discussion.

We took the same approach to the coverage of central and eastern Europe that we did to women and minorities. Even before the epochal events of 1989 that returned this region to the forefront of international attention, we realized that in too many textbooks the Slavic world was treated as marginal to the history of Western civilization. Thus, with the help of a specialist reviewer, we worked to integrate more of the history of eastern Europe into our text than is found in most others, and to do so in a way that presented the regions, their cultures, and their institutions as integral rather than peripheral to Western civilization.

To construct a book that students would *want* to read, we needed to develop fresh ideas about how to involve them with the material, how to transform them from passive recipients to active participants. We borrowed from computer science the concept of being "user-friendly." We wanted to find ways to stimulate the imagination of the student, and the more we experimented with different techniques, the more we realized that the most effective way to do this was visually. It is not true that contemporary students cannot be taught effectively by the written word; it is only true that they cannot be taught as effectively as they can by the combination of words and images. From the beginning, we realized that a text produced in full color was essential to the features we most wanted to use: the pictorial chapter openers; the large number of maps; the geographical tours of Europe at certain times in history; and the two-page special feature essays, each with its own illustration.

FEATURES

It is hard to have a new idea when writing a textbook. So many authors have come before, each attempting to do something more effective, more innovative than his or her predecessor. However, we feel that the following features enhance students' understanding of Western civilization.

CHAPTER 21 INDUSTRIAL EUROPE

PORTRAIT OF AN AGE

THE RAILROAD

THE VISUAL RECORD

Arrival of the Normandy Train, Gare Saint-Lazare, 1877

LOOKING AHEAD

618

The Visual Record: Pictorial Chapter Openers

It is probably the case that somewhere there has been a text that has used a chapter-opening feature similar to the one we use here. What we can say with certainty is that nothing else we experimented with, no other technique we attempted, has had such an immediate and positive impact on our readers or has so fulfilled our goal of involving the students in learning as *The Visual Record* pictorial chapter openers.

An illustration—a painting, a photograph, a picture, an artifact, an edifice—appears at the beginning of each chapter, accompanied by text through which we explore the picture, guiding students across a canvas or helping them see in an artifact or a piece of architecture details that are not immediately apparent. It is the direct combination of text and image that allows us to achieve this effect, to "unfold" both an illustration and a theme. In some chapters we highlight details, pulling out a section of the original picture to take a closer look. In others we attempt to shock the viewer into the recognition of horror or of beauty. Some chapter-opening images are designed to transport students back in time, to make them ask the question, "What was it like to be there?" All of the opening images have been chosen to illustrate a dominant theme within the chapter, and the dramatic and lingering impression they make helps reinforce that theme. A *Looking Ahead* section provides a brief overview of chapter coverage and further strengthens the connection between the subject of the opener and the major topics and themes of the chapter.

IMAGE DISCOVERY

Living with the Bomb.
This photo from the early 1950s shows an American family installed in their fallout shelter, intended to protect them from a nuclear blast. These shelters were built below ground or in basements. Note the supplies on hand. From your knowledge of the effects of atomic bombs on Japan, how realistic were people's hopes that radioactive fallout could be avoided? Why were photos like this one common in the 1950s in the United States? Why is this family smiling?

NEW! Image Discovery

Our commitment to using visual materials to enhance learning is seen throughout the book and is reinforced in the seventh edition with a new feature, *Image Discovery.* In *Image Discovery,* students are asked to approach an image as if it were a text. Appearing in each chapter, *Image Discoveries* guide students through suggestive questions to interrogate the image, understand its context, and unpack its multiple meanings.

Map Program

We have taken a similar image-based approach to our *presentation of geography.* When teachers of Western civilization courses are surveyed, no single area of need is cited more often than that of geographical knowledge. Students simply have no mental image of Europe, no familiarity with those geophysical features that are a fundamental part of the geopolitical realities of Western history. We realized that maps, carefully planned and skillfully executed, would be an important component of our text.

Map Discovery

To complement the standard map program of the text, we have two additional map-based features. The first is *Map Discovery.* This feature, which appears two to three times per chapter, offers specially designed maps with supporting caption information and questions designed to engage students in analyzing the map data and making larger connections to chapter discussions. We have found that focusing students' attention on the details of what a map shows and asking them to consider why that information is important is an effective way to strengthen critical thinking skills as well as to expand geographical knowledge.

Population Loss in Germany During the Thirty Years' War
Notice the pattern of population loss during the war. Where was it heaviest? Where was it lightest? Based on the chapter discussion, how might the intervention of Sweden into the war help explain this pattern?

Geographical Tours of Europe

The second map feature is the *Geographical Tours of Europe.* Six times in the book, we pause in the narrative to take a tour of Europe. Sometimes we follow an emperor as he tours his realm; sometimes we examine the impact of a peace treaty; sometimes we follow the travels of a merchant. Whatever the thematic occasion, our intention is to guide the student around the changing contours of the geography of Western history. In order to do this effectively, we worked with our cartographer to develop small, detailed maps to complement the overview map that appears at the beginning of each tour section. We know that only the most motivated students will turn back several pages to locate on a map a place mentioned in the text. Using small maps allows us to integrate maps directly into the relevant text, thus relieving students of the sometimes frustrating experience of attempting to locate not only a specific place on a map but perhaps even the relevant map itself. We have also added labels to all the tour maps and have included in-text references to direct students to relevant maps at specific points in the narrative of the tour. The great number of maps throughout the text, the specially designed geographical tour of Europe feature, and the ancillary programs of map transparencies and workbook exercises combine to provide the strongest possible program for teaching historical geography.

A Closer Look

Another technique we have employed to engage students with historical subjects is the two-page *A Closer Look* special feature that appears in many chapters. *A Closer Look* focuses on an event, phenomenon, or personality chosen to enhance the student's sense that history is something that is real and alive. The features are written more dramatically and sympathetically, with a greater sense of wonder than would be appropriate in the body of the text. The prose style and the accompanying illustration are designed to captivate the reader. To help the student relate personally and directly to a historical event, we have highlighted figures such as Hypatia of Alexandria, Isabella of Castile, and Sigmund Freud.

The West and the Wider World

To engage students with historical subjects, two-page *The West and the Wider World* essays that appear 11 times in the book. These essays focus on instances of dynamic cultural encounters and exchanges between the West and the non-West at different points in history. The topics for this feature were chosen to enhance the student's sense of connections among the events, phenomena, politics, and products of the West and the wider world. At the end of each feature, we have included questions to spark class discussion and to reinforce such connections.

Documents

Civilization in the West contains selections from primary sources designed to stimulate students' interest in history by allowing them to hear the past speak in its own voice. We have tried to provide a mixture of "canonical" texts along with those illustrating the lives of ordinary people in order to demonstrate the variety of materials that form the building blocks of historical narrative. Each selection is accompanied by an explanatory headnote that identifies the author and work and provides the necessary historical context. Following the headnote are two to three *Focus Questions* to guide students' reading and to spark critical thinking. Most of the extracts relate directly to the discussion within the chapter, thus providing the student with a fuller understanding of a significant thinker or event.

Discovering Western Civilization Online

Discovering Western Civilization Online encourages students to further explore Western civilization. These end-of-chapter Website resources link students to documents, images, and cultural sites currently not included in the text.

THE STAINLESS STAR OF WISDOM'S DISCIPLINE

A CLOSER LOOK

Public philosophers were prized citizens of every ancient city. The austere teachers, distinguished by their black robes, were courted by the wealthy as tutors of their sons and by the powerful for the benefit of their wisdom. But in the early fifth century, Alexandria, long famed for its great museum and rival schools, boasted a philosopher with a difference: Hypatia (ca. 370–415), a woman famed for her wisdom and described by one supporter as "mother, sister, teacher, benefactress in all things." Her controversial career and terrible death summarize the complexity and factionalism of late antiquity.

As was the case with many other professional philosophers, Hypatia's father had been a ...

est praise—and her greatest criticism—for her practice of philosophy. Popular teachers are often controversial, and as a pagan, as a woman, and as a philosopher in the turbulent world of late antiquity, Hypatia was the center of more than her share. But philosophers were more than teachers in antiquity. Because of their deep learning, their detachment from the concerns of daily life, and their eloquence, they were allowed and even expected to play a public role, advising, admonishing, and reconciling the powerful.

WORLD TRADE CENTERS

THE WEST AND THE WIDER WORLD

Trade is older than civilization, and almost as old are specialized buildings where trade is carried on. When the World Trade Centers in New York City were destroyed on September 11, 2001, the terrorist attack was aimed at a symbol of American economic power. But like other trade centers throughout the centuries, these buildings contained a truly international community: citizens of eighty countries were among the victims. The tragedy struck at the United States but wounded a global community of business, finance, trade, and civilization.

Specialized buildings for international trade were well established in Asia, Europe, and Africa by the thirteenth century. Merchants needed protection from bandits, judicial organizations ...

The Twin Towers of the World Trade Center.

The Tithe Grange at Provins, France.

Merchant houses on the old wharf of Be...

800 Chapter 26 War and Revolution, 1914–1920

THE TREATY OF VERSAILLES

Of the various treaties negotiating the peace at the end of World War I, the Treaty of Versailles, signed in 1919, was the most important. This treaty dealt with Germany as a defeated nation and was signed in the great Versailles palace outside of Paris in the same location where in 1871 Germany as victor signed a treaty with its defeated enemy, France, at the close of the short Franco-Prussian War (see pp. 694). In the 1919 treaty, the Allies, represented by President Woodrow Wilson of the United States, Prime Minister David Lloyd George of Great Britain, Prime Minister Georges Clemenceau of France, and Prime Minister Vittorio Orlando of Italy, imposed sole blame for the war on Germany and its expansionist aims. According to the treaty, the war was Germany's fault, and Germany must pay reparations for all the destruction of Allied property by its military. Germany lost territories and suffered a greatly reduced military capability. Especially burdensome was article 231 of the treaty, which came to be known as the **War Guilt Clause**, *which spelled out Germany's responsibility and the basis for the need to make restitution.*

Focus Questions

In article 42, for whose benefit were the left and right banks of the Rhine demilitarized? How many different forms of reparation can you identify in the articles cited here? For whose benefit was the German navy scaled back? Examine carefully article 231—the War Guilt Clause. What is your judgment of its validity in light of what you know about the causes of the war?

Part III. Political Clauses for Europe

Article 42. Germany is forbidden to maintain or construct any fortifications either on the left bank of the Rhine or on the right bank to the west of a line drawn 50 kilometers to the east of the Rhine....

Article 45. As compensation for the destruction of the coal-mines in the north of France and as part payment towards the total reparation due from Germany for the damage resulting from the war, Germany cedes to France in full and absolute possession, with exclusive rights of exploita-

Article 89. Poland undertakes to accord freedom of transit to persons, goods, vessels, carriages, wagons, and mails in transit between East Prussia and the rest of Germany over Polish territory, including territorial waters, and to treat them at least as favorably as the persons, goods, vessels, carriages, wagons, and mails respectively of Polish or of any other more favored nationality, origin, importation, starting-point, or ownership as regards facilities, restrictions and all other matters.[2] ...

Part IV. German Rights and Interests Outside Germany

Article 119. Germany renounces in favor of the Principal Allied and Associated Powers all her rights and titles over her overseas possessions. (This renunciation includes Germany's concessions in China.) ...

Part V. Military, Naval, and Air Claims

Article 159. The German military forces shall be demobilized and reduced as prescribed hereinafter.

Questions for Review

Although a standard feature in many texts, the *Questions for Review* in *Civilization in the West* nonetheless are worth noting. They do not provide just a factual review of the chapter. Instead, they prompt students to think critically about the major topics in the chapter and to pull together for themselves some conclusions about the events and peoples of the time.

CHANGES IN THE NEW EDITION

In the seventh edition, we have made significant changes in content and coverage.

NEW! Image Discovery

Appearing in every chapter, new *Image Discovery* features ask students to approach an image as if it were a text. The feature challenges readers to move from a passive mode of information absorption to an active analysis of the visual and material evidence of the past. Through suggestive questions, Image Discoveries guide students to interrogate the image, understand its context, and unpack its multiple meanings. Examples include "A Revolution in Warfare" in Chapter 2, which uses a Corinthian vase depicting hoplites to explore questions of training and warfare; the painting *The Milch Cow* in Chapter 14, which allows for an examination of the politics surrounding the Netherlands in the late sixteenth century; and a photograph in Chapter 28 of Nazi soldiers seizing Jews in Warsaw, which speaks to the experience and expectations of the captured.

Content Updates

The past may not change, but both our understanding of the past and the questions we need to ask about it change constantly. We have taken the opportunity of a new edition to project our history back in time as well as to explore more closely the entangled nature of human history. In the first chapter, a new *The West and the Wider World* feature, confronts the growing consensus that history begins not with Sumer but with the Paleolithic. Here we explore the exciting frontiers of history, genetics, and archaeology that attempt to understand the complex waves of migrations out of Africa that ultimately populated the planet. Elsewhere we explore those extraordinary crossroads of cultural and economic exchange that were trade centers where merchants from Europe, Asia, and Africa have sought the safety and peace necessary to tie together the great civilizations of the world.

Throughout the early chapters we have pruned, eliminating unnecessary and potentially distracting detail while fine tuning content in response to the input from readers and users of previous editions. The addition of the *Image Discovery* feature has provided the opportunity for a broad range of analysis. In some, as in Chapter 3, we ask readers to compare a Hellenistic statue with a classical one; in Chapter 7 we ask them to reflect on how the profession of faith inscribed on Jerusalem's Haram al-Sharif or The Dome of the Rock might be understood as challenging Christian belief. In others, we encourage readers to make use of what they have learned in the text to interpret the images with which they are confronted.

In the middle chapters of the book the authors have continued their efforts to expand the boundaries of Europe and to relate its experiences to those of the wider world. A new feature on the Columbian Exchange highlights the interactive nature of the European encounter with Atlantic populations. It emphasizes the biological and economic impact of discoveries, the disastrous consequences of interchanged diseases, and the enhancements of new products and tools. Pigs and cattle were brought to the new world, potatoes and tomatoes to the old.

Europe's encounters with non-Europeans in the early modern period were not limited to discoveries. The centuries-old struggle between the Ottoman and Holy Roman empires continued deep into the seventeenth century. It reached its apex with the siege of Vienna in 1676—an event that might have transformed European history had it turned out differently. Throughout this section the text has been updated to reflect new historical discoveries and to account for reinterpretations of familiar events. A special effort has been made to enhance sections on the biological sciences.

In the modern chapters, beginning with Chapter 20, attention has been given to updating coverage and information and incorporating the latest bibliographic information. The new *Image Discovery* feature for these chapters (Chapters 20 through 30) includes political cartoons and caricature in understanding how visual images and symbols are a central feature of modern political life beginning in the late eighteenth century. *Image Discovery* has also allowed the authors to interrogate the role of photography in shaping modern consciousness.

One of the great challenges has been the proper inclusion of the United States in the story of *Civilization in the West* from the French Revolution to the war on terrorism. Greater attention to the United States in the story of *Civilization in the West* recognizes the expanding concept of the West as an idea rather than a place. There is expanded treatment of the U.S. role especially in the post–World War II period with the Cold War and the subsequent decline of the Soviet Union. The global context of political, religious, intellectual, and social changes has resulted in increased coverage of Afghanistan, China, South Africa, and India to understand the phenomenon of change in the West. For example, the return of the Taliban changes earlier interpretations about the gains of democratic government in Afghanistan. And the work of Mahatma Gandhi is included in a new way here (in *The West and the Wider World*) to show the influences of ideas in Asia on political discourse in other nations.

The changing nature of ethnicity and nationalism in the contemporary world has required not only updating information but also reconsidering interpretations of the rapid historic changes of the post–Cold War world. Contemporary events such as the trial and death of Saddam Hussein and the civil war in Iraq require new perspectives on the war on terrorism in the final chapter. The chapters that cover the modern period in general are influenced by the weight of contemporary events that continually require reframing and revisiting conclusions.

New West and the Wider World

Two-page *The West and the Wider World* essays explore instances of dynamic cultural encounters and exchanges between the West and the non-West at different points in history. Understanding the importance of viewing the West within this larger context, we have added in this edition six new essays throughout the text: Chapter 1, "The First European Immigrants"; Chapter 10, "World Trade Centers"; Chapter 12, "The Columbian Exchange"; Chapter 16, "The Siege of Vienna"; Chapter 25, "Babylon Discovered"; and Chapter 29, "Mahatma Gandhi's Legacy."

Key Terms and Glossary

In each chapter, key terms are highlighted in boldface type to alert students to principal concepts and events discussed in the chapter. A page-referenced list of the key terms is included at the end of the chapter to help students review the main ideas and events covered in the chapter. A glossary at the end of the book provides definitions for the key terms. In this edition, we have added over 60 new terms.

New Documents

Nine new documents have been added in this edition as well. Chapter 3 now includes an excerpt from Plato's "The Apology" that presents Socrates in his summation to the Athenian jury; Chapter 7 includes Usamah ibn Munqidh's observations in "An Arab in Crusader Jerusalem"; in Chapter 8, Gregory of Tours describes a conflict between two families from Tournai that ultimately destroyed them both; in Chapter 14, in "The Heart and Stomach of a King," Queen Elizabeth rallies her subjects to oppose the invasion of England by the Spanish Armada; Chapter 19 now contains excerpts from Voltaire's great comic novel, *Candide*; the *Treaty of Versailles* is excerpted in Chapter 26; and Chapter 30 now includes both Václav Havel's address to Czechoslovakia from 1 January 1990 and a press release from London Mayor Ken Livingstone regarding his commitment, and that of 21 other mayors from major cities around the world, to reducing greenhouse gases.

New Visual Record Essays

Six new *The Visual Record* pictorial essays were developed for the seventh edition as well. Chapter 3: Classical and Hellenistic Greece, 500–100 B.C.E. opens with a pictorial essay on the Parthenon and Pericles, the man responsible for its construction; Chapter 9: The High Middle Ages, 900–1300 begins with an essay on a portion of the Bayeux tapestry that may well subvert the story of the Battle of Hastings as told by the victors; Chapter 11: The Italian Renaissance opens with an exploration of Leonardo da Vinci's *Last Supper*; Chapter 20: The French Revolution and the Napoleonic Era, 1789–1815 begins with an essay on Jacques-Louis David's *The Oath of the Tennis Court*, which captures the spirit of a key moment in the history of democracy; Chapter 21: Industrial Europe begins with an examination of the transformative power of the railroad as alluded to in Claude Monet's *La Gare Saint-Lazarre*; and Chapter 23: State Building and Social Change in Europe, 1850–1871 opens with an examination of the construction and meaning of London's extraordinary Crystal Palace of 1851.

ACKNOWLEDGMENTS

We want to thank the many conscientious historians who gave generously of their time and knowledge to review our manuscript. We would like to thank the reviewers of the first six editions as well as those of the current edition. Their valuable critiques and suggestions have contributed greatly to the final product. We are grateful to the following:

Achilles Aavraamides, *Iowa State University;* Meredith L. Adams, *Southwest Missouri State University;* Joseph Aieta, III, *Lasell College;* Ken Albala, *University of the Pacific;* Patricia Ali, *Morris College;* Gerald D. Anderson, *North Dakota State University;* Arthur H. Auten, *University of Hartford;* Suzanne Balch-Lindsay, *Eastern New Mexico University;* Sharon Bannister, *University of Findlay;* John W. Barker, *University of Wisconsin;* Patrick Bass, *Mount Union College;* William H. Beik, *Northern Illinois University;* Jean K. Berger, *University of Wisconsin, Fox Valley;* Patrice Berger, *University of Nebraska;* Lenard R. Berlanstein, *University of Virginia;* Raymond Birn, *University of Oregon;* Donna Bohanan, *Auburn University;* Werner Braatz, *University of Wisconsin, Oshkosh;* Thomas A. Brady, Jr., *University of Oregon;* Anthony M. Brescia, *Nassau Community College;* Elaine G. Breslaw, *Morgan State University;* Ronald S. Brockway, *Regis University;* April Brooks, *South Dakota State University;* Daniel Patrick Brown, *Moorpark College;* Ronald A. Brown, *Charles County Community College;* Blaine T. Browne, *Broward Community College;* Susan Carrafiello, *Wright State University;* Kathleen S. Carter, *High Point University;* Robert Carver, *University of Missouri, Rolla;* Edward J. Champlin, *Princeton University;* Stephanie Evans Christelow, *Western Washington University;* Sister Dorita Clifford, BVM, *University of San Francisco;* Gary B. Cohen, *University of Oklahoma;* Robert Cole, *Utah State University;* Jan M. Copes, *Cleveland State University;* John J. Contreni, *Purdue University;* Tim Crain, *University of Wisconsin, Stout;* Norman Delaney, *Del Mar College;* Samuel E. Dicks, *Emporia State University;* Andrew Donson, *University of Massachusetts, Amherst;* Frederick Dotolo, *St. John Fisher College;* Frederick Dumin, *Washington State University;* Janusz Duzinkiewicz, *Purdue University;* Laird Easton, *California State University, Chico;* Brian Elsesser, *Saint Louis University;* Dianne E. Farrell, *Moorhead State University;* Margot C. Finn, *Emory University;* Allan W. Fletcher, *Boise State University;* Luci Fortunato De Lisle, *Bridgewater State College;* Elizabeth L. Furdell, *University of North Florida;* Thomas W. Gallant, *University of Florida;* Bryan Ganaway, *University of Illinois;* Frank Garosi, *California State University, Sacramento;* Lorne E. Glaim, *Pacific Union College;* Joseph J. Godson, *Hudson Valley Community College;* Sue Helder Goliber, *Mount St. Mary's College;* Manuel G. Gonzales, *Diablo Valley College;* David Graf, *University of Miami;* Louis Haas, *Duquesne University;* Eric Haines, *Bellevue Community College;* David Halahmy, *Cypress College;* Paul Halliday, *University of Virginia;* Margaretta S. Handke, *Mankato State University;* David A. Harnett, *University of San Francisco;* Paul B. Harvey, Jr., *Pennsylvania State University;* Benjamin Hett, *Hunter College;* Neil Heyman, *San Diego State University;* Daniel W. Hollis, *Jacksonville State University;* Kenneth G. Holum, *University of Maryland;* Patricia Howe, *University of St. Thomas;* David Hudson, *California State University, Fresno;* Mark M. Hull, *Saint Louis University;* John Hymes, *Horry-Georgetown Technical College;* Charles Ingrao, *Purdue University;* George F. Jewsbury, *Oklahoma State University;* Cynthia Jones, *University of Missouri—Kansas City;* Donald G. Jones, *University of Central Arkansas;* William R. Jones, *University of New Hampshire;* Richard W. Kaeuper, *University of Rochester;* David Kaiser, *Carnegie-Mellon University;* Jeff Kaufmann, *Muscatine Community College;* Carolyn Kay, *Trent University;* John S. Kemp, *Truckee Meadows Community College;* William R. Keylor, *Boston University;* Joseph Kicklighter, *Auburn University;* Charles L. Killinger, III, *Valencia Community College;* Alan M. Kirshner, *Ohlone College;* Charlene Kiser, *Milligan College;* Barbara Klemm, *Broward Community College;* Janilyn M. Kocher, *Richland Community*

College; Alexandra Korros, *Xavier University;* Cynthia Kosso, *Northern Arizona University;* Lara Kriegel, *Florida International University;* Lisa M. Lane, *Mira Costa College;* Lawrence Langer, *University of Connecticut;* David C. Large, *Montana State University;* Catherine Lawrence, *Messiah College;* Bryan LeBeau, *Creighton University;* Erik Lindseth, *Indiana University–Purdue University Indianapolis;* Robert B. Luehrs, *Fort Hays State University;* Donna J. Maier, *University of Northern Iowa;* Margaret Malamud, *New Mexico State University;* Roberta T. Manning, *Boston College;* Lyle McAlister, *University of Florida;* Therese M. McBride, *College of the Holy Cross;* David K. McQuilkin, *Bridgewater College;* Victor V. Minasian, *College of Marin;* David B. Mock, *Tallahassee Community College;* Don Mohr, *University of Alaska–Anchorage,* Robert Moeller, *University of California, Irvine;* Elise Moentmann, *University of Portland;* R. Scott Moore, *University of Dayton;* Ann E. Moyer, *University of Pennsylvania;* Pierce C. Mullen, *Montana State University;* John A. Nichols, *Slippery Rock University;* Thomas F. X. Noble, *University of Virginia;* J. Ronald Oakley, *Davidson County Community College;* Bruce K. O'Brien, *Mary Washington College;* Dennis H. O'Brien, *West Virginia University;* Maura O'Connor, *University of Cincinnati;* Richard A. Oehling, *Assumption College;* James H. Overfield, *University of Vermont;* Catherine Patterson, *University of Houston;* Sue Patrick, *University of Wisconsin, Barron County;* Peter C. Piccillo, *Rhode Island College;* Peter O'M. Pierson, *Santa Clara University;* Alisa Plant, *Tulane University;* Theophilus Prousis, *University of North Florida;* Marlette Rebhorn, *Austin Community College;* Kimberly D. S. Reiter, *Stetson University;* Jack B. Ridley, *University of Missouri, Rolla;* Salvador Rivera, *State University of New York Cobleskill;* Thomas Robisheaux, *Duke University*; Constance M. Rousseau, *Providence College;* Thomas J. Runyan, *Cleveland State University;* John P. Ryan, *Kansas City Community College;* Geraldine Ryder, *Ocean County College;* Joanne Schneider, *Rhode Island College;* Steven Schroeder, *Indiana University of Pennsylvania;* Steven C. Seyer, *Lehigh County Community College;* Lixin Shao, *University of Minnesota, Duluth;* George H. Shriver, *Georgia Southern University;* Ellen J. Skinner, *Pace University;* Bonnie Smith, *University of Rochester;* Patrick Smith, *Broward Community College;* James Smither, *Grand Valley State University;* Sherill Spaar, *East Central University;* Ilicia Sprey, *Saint Joseph's College*; Charles R. Sullivan, *University of Dallas;* Peter N. Stearns, *Carnegie-Mellon University;* Saulius Suziedelis, *Millersville University;* Darryl B. Sycher, *Columbus State Community College;* Roger Tate, *Somerset Community College;* Janet A. Thompson, *Tallahassee Community College;* Anne-Marie Thornton, *Bilkent University;* Donna L. Van Raaphorst, *Cuyahoga Community College;* James Vanstone, *John Abbot College;* George S. Vascik, *Miami University, Hamilton*; Steven Vincent, *North Carolina State University;* Richard A. Voeltz, *Cameron University;* Faith Wallis, *McGill University;* Sydney Watts, *University of Richmond;* Eric Weissman, *Golden West College;* Christine White, *Pennsylvania State University;* Vance Youmans, *Spokane Falls Community College*; William Harry Zee, *Gloucester County College.*

Each author also received invaluable assistance and encouragement from many colleagues, friends, and family members over the years of research, reflection, writing, and revising that went into the making of this text.

Mark Kishlansky thanks Ann Adams, Robert Bartlett, Ray Birn, David Buisseret, Ted Cook, Frank Conaway, Constantine Fasolt, James Hankins, Katherine Haskins, Richard Hellie, Matthew Kishlansky, Donna Marder, Mary Beth Rose, Victor Stater, Jeanne Thiel, and the staffs of the Joseph Regenstein Library, the Newberry Library, and the Widener and Lamont Libraries at Harvard.

Patrick Geary thanks Mary, Catherine, and Anne Geary for their patience, support, and encouragement; he also thanks Anne Picard, Dale Schofield, Hans Hummer, Jared Poley, and Richard Mowrer for their able assistance throughout the project.

Patricia O'Brien thanks Elizabeth Sagias for her encouragement and enthusiasm throughout the project and Robert Moeller for his keen eye for organization and his suggestions for writing a gendered history. She is especially grateful to her assistants Susan Beals and Carolyn Drago for keeping her on track throughout the project.

All the authors thank Janet Lanphier, senior acquisitions editor, Barbara Conover, development editor, and Heather Johnson, project editor at Elm Street Publishing Services, Inc., for producing a beautiful book. Thanks are also due to Melissa Edwards, for her work in producing the media supplements that accompany this volume, and Brian Belardi who worked on the print supplements.

Mark Kishlansky
Patrick Geary
Patricia O'Brien

SUPPLEMENTS

For Qualified College Adopters

- **Instructor's Manual** This thorough instructor's manual includes an introductory essay on teaching Western civilization and a bibliographic essay on the use of primary sources for class discussion and analytical thinking. Each chapter contains a chapter summary, key terms and important geographic locations, discussion questions, and an annotated list of films (not supplied by Longman).
- **Test Bank** This supplement contains more than 1,200 multiple-choice, true/false, and essay questions. Multiple-choice and true/false questions are referenced by topic and text page number.
- **Computerized Test Bank** This flexible, easy-to-master assessment program includes all of the items in the printed test bank and allows instructors to select specific questions, edit them, and add their own items to create exams.
- **Instructor Resource Center (IRC) (www.ablongman.com/irc)** Through the Instructor Resource Center, instructors can log into premium online products, browse and download book-specific instructor resources, and receive immediate access and instructions to installing course management content.
- **Research Navigator and Research Navigator Guide** Research Navigator is a comprehensive website offering EBSCO's ContentSelect Academic Journal & Abstract Database, the *New York Times* Search-by-Subject Archive, *Financial Times* Article Archive and Company Financials, and "Best of the Web" Link Library. The Research Navigator Guide provides your students with access to the Website and includes reference material and hints about conducting online research.
- **Study Card for Western Civilization** Colorful, affordable, and packed with useful information, Longman's Study Cards make studying easier, more efficient, and more enjoyable.
- **Digital Transparency Masters** A set of full-color transparency masters drawn from *Civilization in the West,* Seventh Edition. Available exclusively on the IRC.
- **History Video Program** A list of more than 100 videos from which qualified college adopters can choose. Restrictions apply.
- **History Digital Media Archive CD-ROM** This CD-ROM contains electronic images and interactive and static maps, along with media elements such as video. It is fully customizable and ready for classroom presentation. All images and maps are available in PowerPoint™ as well.
- **Interpretations of the Western World** General Editor Mark Kishlansky has prepared a customizable database of secondary source readings. Selections are grouped topically so that instructors can assign readings that illustrate different points of view about a given historical debate.

For Students

- **Study Guide** Available in two volumes, each chapter in the study guide includes a summary; a timeline activity; map and geography questions; key terms, people, and events; and identification, multiple-choice, and critical-thinking questions.
- ***Western Civilization Map Workbook*** These two volumes test and reinforce basic geography literacy while building critical-thinking skills.
- ***Longman Atlas of Western Civilization*** This 52-page atlas features carefully selected historical maps that provide comprehensive coverage for the major historical periods.
- ***A Short Guide to Writing About History,* Sixth Edition** Written by Richard Marius, late of Harvard University, and Melvin E. Page, Eastern Tennessee State University, and Melvin E. Page, Eastern Tennessee State University, this engaging and practical text helps students get beyond merely compiling dates and facts. Covering both brief essays and the documented resource paper, the text explores the writing and researching processes, identifies different modes of historical writing, including argument, and concludes with guidelines for improving style.

MyHistoryLab (www.myhistorylab.com)

MyHistoryLab provides students with an online package complete with the electronic textbook and numerous study aids. With several hundred primary sources, many of which are assignable and link to a gradebook, pre- and post-tests that link to a gradebook and result in individualized study plans, videos and images, as well as map activities with gradable quizzes, the site offers students a unique, interactive experience that brings history to life. The comprehensive site also includes a History Bookshelf with fifty of the most commonly assigned books in history classes and a History Toolkit with tutorials and helpful links. Other features include gradable assignments and chapter review materials; a Test Bank; and Research Navigator.

MyHistoryKit (www.myhistorykit.com)

MyHistoryKit for Western Civilization is an access-code-protected course-based website that contains a sampling of Longman's premium history content. This website includes practice tests to challenge students' knowledge of the material, flashcards that aid in studying, and media and primary source activities (documents, maps, video and audio clips, and more) that report to an online gradebook. Also included in MyHistoryKit are Research Navigator and Writing About History, both of which provide assistance with and access to powerful and reliable research material.

The Western Civilization Study Site (www.longmanwesterncivilization.com)

Students can take advantage of this open-access online course companion that includes practice tests, Web links, and flash cards that cover the scope of topics covered in a typical Western civilization class.

Longman Library of World Biography Series

Pocket-sized and brief, each biography in the Library of World Biography series relates the life of its subject to the broader themes and developments of the time. Series titles include: ***Ahmad al-Mansur: Islamic Visionary*** by Richard Smith (Ferrum College); ***Alexander the Great: Legacy of a Conqueror*** by Winthrop Lindsay Adams (University of Utah); ***Benito Mussolini: The First Fascist*** by Anthony L. Cardoza (Loyola University); ***Fukuzawa Yûkichi: From Samurai to Capitalist*** by Helen M. Hopper (University of Pittsburgh); ***Ignatius of Loyola: Founder of the Jesuits*** by John Patrick Donnelly (Marquette University); ***Jacques Coeur: Entrepreneur and King's Bursar*** by Kathryn L. Reyerson (University of Minnesota); ***Katô Shidzue: A Japanese Feminist*** by Helen M. Hopper (University of Pittsburgh); ***Simón Bolívar: Liberation and Disappointment*** by David Bushnell (University of Florida); ***Vasco da Gama: Renaissance Crusader*** by Glenn J. Ames (University of Toledo); and ***Zheng He: China and the Oceans in the Early Ming, 1405–1433*** by Edward Dreyer (University of Miami).

Penguin-Longman Partnership

The partnership between Penguin Books and Longman Publishers offers a discount on a wide range of titles when bundled with any Longman history survey textbook. Visit www.ablongman.com/penguin for more information.

ABOUT THE AUTHORS

MARK KISHLANSKY Mark Kishlansky is Frank B. Baird, Jr., Professor of English and European History at Harvard University, where he has taught Western Civilization and courses in the CORE program for general education. He has also been awarded Harvard's Hoopes Prize for undergraduate teaching. Professor Kishlansky served as Associate Dean of the Faculty from 1999–2001. Before joining the Harvard faculty he taught for sixteen years at the University of Chicago where he was a member of the Committee on Social Thought. Professor Kishlansky is a specialist on seventeenth-century English political history and has written, among other works, *A Monarchy Transformed, The Rise of the New Model Army,* and *Parliamentary Selection: Social and Political Choice in Early Modern England.* From 1984–1991 he was editor of the *Journal of British Studies.* He is currently writing a history of the reign of Charles I entitled *The Death of Kings.* He is the General Editor of Pearson Custom Publishing's primary source databases for Western and World Civilization.

PATRICK GEARY Holding a Ph.D. in Medieval Studies from Yale University, Patrick Geary has broad experience in interdisciplinary approaches to European history and civilization. He has served as the director of the Medieval Institute at the University of Notre Dame as well as director for the Center for Medieval and Renaissance Studies at UCLA where he is currently professor of history. He has also held positions at the University of Florida and Princeton University and has taught at the École des Hautes Études en Sciences Sociales in Paris, at the University of Vienna, and at the Central European University in Budapest. He has coordinated and participated in programs for history teachers in Pennsylvania, Florida, and California, and has co-authored a television series on medieval knights. His many publications include *Readings in Medieval History; Before France and Germany: The Creation and Transformation of the Merovingian World; Furta Sacra: Thefts of Relics in the Central Middle Ages;* and *The Myth of Nations: The Medieval Origins of Europe.*

PATRICIA O'BRIEN Between 1995 and 1999, Patricia O'Brien worked to foster collaborative interdisciplinary research in the humanities as director of the University of California Humanities Research Institute. Between 1999 and 2004, she held the position of Dean of the College of Humanities, Arts, and Social Sciences at the University of California, Riverside. She has also held appointments at the University of California, Irvine, Yale University, and at the École des Hautes Études en Sciences Sociales in Paris. Currently Professor O'Brien is the Executive Dean of the UCLA College of Letters and Sciences. Professor O'Brien is a specialist in modern French cultural and social history and has published widely on the history of crime, punishment, cultural theory, urban history, and gender issues. Representative publications include *The Promise of Punishment: Prisons in Nineteenth-Century France;* "The Kleptomania Diagnosis: Bourgeois Women and Theft in Late Nineteenth-Century France" in *Expanding the Past: A Reader in Social History;* and "Michel Foucault's History of Culture" in *The New Cultural History,* edited by Lynn Hunt. Professor O'Brien's commitment to this textbook grew out of her own teaching experiences in large, introductory Western Civilization courses. She has benefited from the contributions of her students and fellow instructors in her approach to the study of Western Civilization in the modern period.

CIVILIZATION IN THE WEST

INTRODUCTION
THE IDEA OF WESTERN CIVILIZATION

The West is an idea. It is not visible from space. An astronaut viewing the blue-and-white terrestrial sphere can make out the form of Africa, bounded by the Atlantic, the Indian Ocean, the Red Sea, and the Mediterranean. Australia, the Americas, and even Antarctica are distinct patches of blue-green in the darker waters that surround them. But nothing comparable separates Europe from Asia, East from West. Viewed from 100 miles up, the West itself is invisible. Although astronauts can see the great Eurasian landmass curving around the Northern Hemisphere, the Ural Mountains—the theoretical boundary between East and West—appear but faintly from space. Certainly they are less impressive than the towering Himalayas, the Alps, or even the Caucasus. People, not geology, determined that the Urals should be the arbitrary boundary between Europe and Asia.

Even this determination took centuries. Originally, Europe was a name that referred only to central Greece. Gradually, Greeks extended it to include the whole Greek mainland and then the landmass to the north. Later, Roman explorers and soldiers carried Europe north and west to its modern boundaries. Asia too grew with time. Initially, Asia was only that small portion of what is today Turkey inland from the Aegean Sea. Gradually, as Greek explorers came to know of lands farther east, north, and south, they expanded their understanding of Asia to include everything east of the Don River to the north and the Red Sea to the south.

Western civilization is as much an idea as the West itself. Under the right conditions, astronauts can see the Great Wall of China snaking its way from the edge of the Himalayas to the Yellow Sea. No comparable physical legacy of the West is so massive that its details can be discerned from space. Nor are Western achievements rooted forever in one corner of the world. What we call Western civilization belongs to no particular place. Its location has changed since the origins of civilization, that is, the cultural and social traditions characteristic of the *civitas*, or city. "Western" cities appeared first outside what Europeans and Americans arbitrarily term *the West*, in the Tigris and Euphrates river basins in present-day Iraq and Iran, a region we today call the Middle East. These areas have never lost their urban traditions, but in time other cities in North Africa, Greece, and Italy adapted and expanded this heritage in different ways. If we focus on this peculiar adaptation and expansion in this book, it is not because of some intrinsic superiority but only because the developments in Europe after the birth of Jesus become more significant than those of Egypt and Mesopotamia for understanding our contemporary culture.

Until the sixteenth century C.E., the western end of the Eurasian landmass—what we think of as western Europe—was the crucible in which disparate cultural and intellectual traditions of the Near East, the Mediterranean, and the north were smelted into a new and powerful alloy. Then "the West" expanded beyond the confines of Europe, carried by the ships of merchants and adventurers to India, Africa, China, and the Americas.

Western technology for harnessing nature, Western forms of economic and political organization, Western styles of art and music are—for good or ill—dominant influences in world civilization. Japan is a leading power in the Western traditions of capitalist commerce and technology. China, the most populous country in the world, adheres to Marxist so-

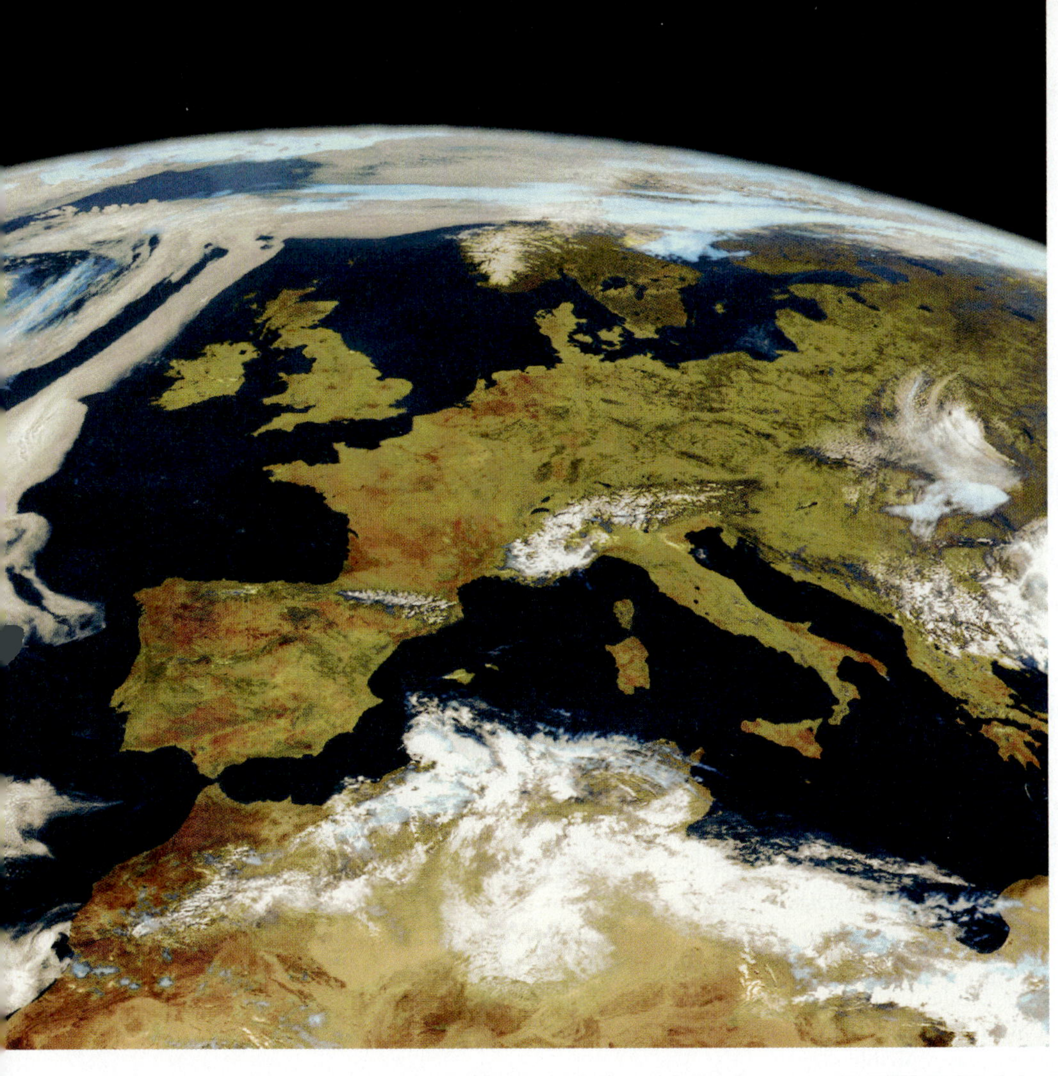

North America seeking a better life but often find poverty, hostility, and racism instead. Finally, the advances of Western civilization endanger our very existence. Technology pollutes the world's air, water, and soil, and nuclear arms threaten the destruction of all civilization. And yet these are the same advances that allow us to lengthen life expectancy, harness the forces of nature, and conquer disease. It is the same technology that allows us to view our world from outer space.

cialist principles—a European political tradition. Millions of people in Africa, Asia, and the Americas follow the religions of Islam and Christianity. Both are monotheistic faiths that developed from Judaism in the cradle of Western civilization.

Many of today's most pressing problems are also part of the legacy of the Western tradition. The remnants of European colonialism have left deep hostilities throughout the world. The integration of developing nations into the world economy keeps much of humanity in a seemingly hopeless cycle of poverty as the wealth of poor countries goes to pay interest on loans from Europe and America. Western material goods lure millions of people from their traditional worlds into the sprawl of third-world cities. Hatred of Western civilization is a central, ideological tenet that inspired the attacks on symbols of American economic and military strength on September 11, 2001, and that fuels anti-Western terrorism around the world. The West itself faces a crisis. Impoverished citizens of former colonies flock to Europe and

How did we get here? In this book we attempt to answer that question. The history of Western civilization is not simply the triumphal story of progress, the creation of a better world. Even in areas in which we can see development—such as technology, communications, and social complexity—change is not always for the better. It would be equally inaccurate, however, to view the course of Western civilization as a progressive decline from a mythical golden age of the human race. The roughly 300 generations since the origins of civilization have bequeathed a rich and contradictory heritage to the present. Inherited political and social institutions, cultural forms, and religious and philosophical traditions form the framework within which the future must be created. The past does not determine the future, but it is the raw material from which the future will be made. To use this legacy properly, we must first understand it, not because the past is the key to the future, but because understanding yesterday frees us to create tomorrow.

CHAPTER 1 THE FIRST CIVILIZATIONS

ÖTZI'S LAST MEAL

TRADITION AND INNOVATION IN PREHISTORIC EUROPE

THE VISUAL RECORD

Most of us never knew our great-grandparents; thus, it seems all the more incredible that we can visit with an ancestor from three hundred generations past—the dawn of civilization. And yet a discovery in the Italian Alps in 1991 has brought us face to face with Ötzi (so-named for the valley where he was found), an ordinary man who faced a cruel death more than five thousand years ago. Ötzi's perfectly preserved body, clothing, tools, and weapons allow us to know how people lived and died in western Europe before it was Europe—before indeed it was the West.

Ötzi was small by modern European standards: he stood at just 5 feet 4 inches. Around 40 years old, he was probably a senior and respected member of his community. Already he was suffering from arthritis, and tattoos on his left wrist, right knee, calves, ankles, and the lumbar region of his spine suggest that, just as in some nomadic societies today, he and his companions used tattooing as a kind of therapy. He probably came from a village below the mountain whose inhabitants lived from hunting, simple agriculture, and goat herding.

One spring day around 3000 B.C.E., Ötzi enjoyed what would be his last meal of meat, some vegetables, and flat bread made of einkorn wheat. He dressed warmly but simply: First, a leather breechcloth secured at his waist with a calfskin belt. Over this he put on a knee-length leather upper garment made of long strips of goatskin sewn together with animal sinews. Below, he protected his legs with leather leggings and slipped his feet into sturdy shoes made of bearskin soles and deerhide tops and lined with soft grasslike socks. On his head was a warm bearskin cap. He was probably in a hurry, and he quickly filled a backpack and took up his usual tools and weapons.

Ötzi traveled light, but he had with him all that he needed to provide for himself. He carried an ax, whose 60-centimeter yew-wood haft ended in a blade of almost pure copper, and a flint knife with an ash-wood handle secured to his belt in a fiber scabbard. In a pouch he carried a tool made of stag antler and limewood with which he could chip new flint tools. He secured his leather backpack on a pack-frame made of a long hazel rod bent into a U shape and reinforced with two narrow wooden slats. Among other things it held birch bark containers, one filled with materials to start a fire, which he could ignite with a flint he carried in his pouch. He also equipped himself with a simple first-aid kit consisting of inner bark from the birch tree, a substance with antibiotic and styptic properties.

For so small a man, Ötzi carried an imposing weapon, but unfortunately for him it was not yet finished. Near his body

■ Ötzi's ax with copper blade.

was found a yew-wood bow almost six feet long and a quiver of arrows. He must have been working on the bow and arrows shortly before he died: the bow's grip was not yet finished and the bow ends had not yet been prepared to attach the bowstring. In a chamois-skin quiver two arrows, equipped with flint heads and fletched with feathers, were ready for use. Twelve other arrow shafts remained unfinished along with his bowstring.

For ten years after the discovery of his body scholars and scientists examined, x-rayed, and studied his remains and speculated on why and how he died. Was he caught by a sudden storm and had he succumbed to hypothermia? Did he fall, injure himself, and die of exposure? And what was he doing so high in the mountains—six hours from the valley where he had his last meal, without adequate food or water—in the first place? For a decade it was thought that the mystery would never be solved. Then, following yet another x-ray of his frozen corpse, the truth came out. A sharp-eyed radiologist saw the telltale shadow of a stone point lodged in his back.

Apparently, Ötzi left the lower villages that fateful spring day frightened and in a great hurry. Alone at an altitude of over 10,000 feet, desperately trying to finish his bow and arrows, he was fleeing for his life, but his luck ran out. Ötzi was shot in the back with an arrow. It pierced his shoulder between his shoulder blade and ribs, paralyzing his arm and causing extensive bleeding. He pulled the arrow out but the flint point remained imbedded, and his efforts only increased the pain and the damage. His simple medical kit was of no help. Exhausted, he lay down in a shallow cleft in the snowy rocks. In a matter of hours he was dead and the snows of centuries quietly buried him.

What does Ötzi's life and death tell us about the story of Western civilization? Although he lived and died at the same time that radically new urban societies and cultures were appearing just east of the Mediterranean, Ötzi still belonged to the Stone Age. His clothing, tools, and weapons all show a perfection of ancient techniques, but nothing innovative. None of his clothing was woven: apparently this basic technology was unknown to his community although it was common in western Asia. The only metal was his precious ax head, and it was of soft copper—Ötzi's society was still ignorant of bronze, a much harder alloy of copper and tin favored in the eastern Mediterranean. And yet, something vital connected Ötzi's world and that distant cradle of civilization: his last meal. Einkorn is not native to western Europe. It originated as a wild grain in the region of the Tigris and Euphrates rivers before being cultivated starting around 10,000 B.C.E. From there, both the grain itself and the technology of its cultivation spread slowly, ultimately reaching Ötzi's world of Alpine villages. If not civilization, then one of the essential components of it had reached this isolated mountain valley. Others would come in the following centuries: weaving, metal working, urbanization, writing, and ways to kill men and women like Ötzi with greater efficiency.

Reconstruction of Ötzi with clothing and equipment.

LOOKING AHEAD

This first chapter begins before Ötzi with the origins of humankind and chronicles the great discoveries that led to the first urban-based civilizations of Mesopotamia and Egypt. It examines as well the **semi-nomadic societies** *that lived on their margins and developed the first great monotheistic religious tradition.*

CHAPTER OUTLINE

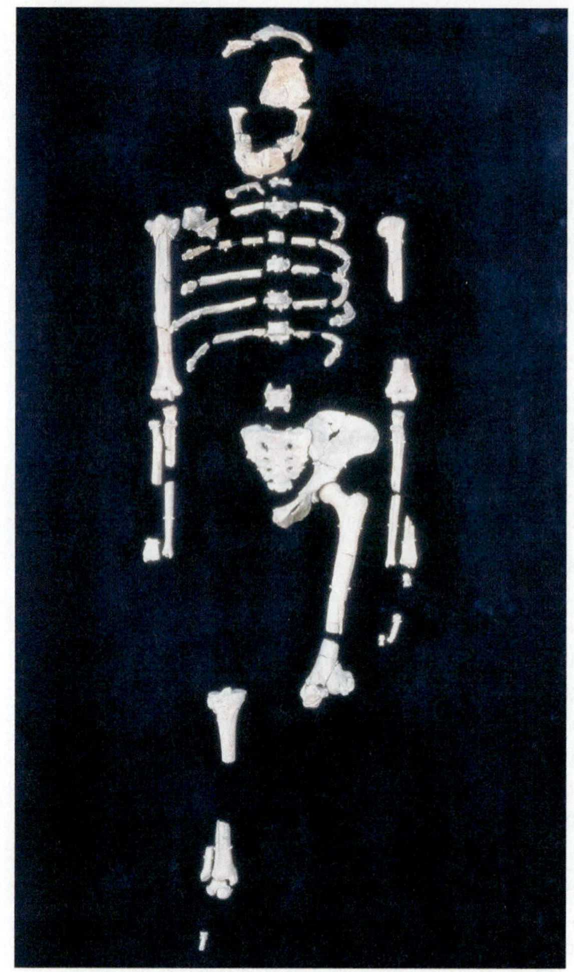

This reconstructed skeleton of a small upright hominid some four million years old is the earliest humanoid thus far discovered.

BEFORE CIVILIZATION

The human race was already ancient by the time that Ötzi died, and civilization first appeared around 3500 years before the Common Era, the period following the traditional date of the birth of Jesus. (Such dates are abbreviated B.C. for "before Christ" or B.C.E. for "before the Common Era"; A.D., the abbreviation of the Latin for "in the year of the Lord," is used to refer to dates after the birth of Jesus. Today, scholars commonly use simply C.E. to mean the Common Era.) The first humanlike creatures whose remains have been discovered date from as long as six and a half million years ago. One of the best-known finds, nicknamed "Lucy" by the scientist who discovered her skeleton in 1974, stood only about four feet tall and lived on the edge of a lake in what is now Ethiopia. Lucy and her band did not have brains that were as well developed as those of modern humans. They did, however, use simple tools such as sticks, bone clubs, and chipped rocks, and they worked together to protect themselves and to find small animals, roots, and berries for food. Lucy lived to a considerable age—she was about 20 when she died. Although small and relatively weak compared with other animals, Lucy's species of creatures—neither fully ape nor human—survived for more than four million years.

Varieties of the modern species of humans, *Homo sapiens* (thinking human), appeared well over 100,000 years ago and spread across the Eurasian landmass and Africa. (See "The First European Immigrants," p. 8.) The earliest humans in Europe, the Neanderthals, differed little from people today. Although the term *Neanderthal* has gained a negative image in the popular imagination, these early humans were roughly the same size and had the same cranial capacity as we. They not only survived but even spread throughout much of Africa, Europe, and Asia during the last great ice age. To survive in the harsh tundra landscape, they developed a cultural system that enabled them to modify their environment. They knew how to make and use stone tools and lived in shelters they built from wood. Customs such as the burial of their dead with food offerings indicate that Neanderthals may have developed a belief in an afterlife. Although a bit shorter and heavier than most people today, they were clearly our close cousins. Nevertheless, DNA studies suggest that Neanderthals are not directly related to modern humans. Their subspecies appears to have been a dead end.

No one knows why or how the Neanderthals were replaced by our subspecies, *Homo sapiens sapiens* (thinking thinking human), around 40,000 years ago. Whatever the reason and whatever the process—extinction, evolution, or extermination—this last arrival on the human scene was universally successful. All humans today belong to this same subspecies. Differences in skin color, type of hair, and build are minor variations on the same theme. The identification of races,

CHRONOLOGY

Before Civilization

ca. 100,000 B.C.E.	*Homo sapiens*
ca. 40,000 B.C.E.	*Homo sapiens sapiens*
ca. 35,000–10,000 B.C.E.	Late Paleolithic era (Old Stone Age)
ca. 8000–6500 B.C.E.	Neolithic era (New Stone Age)
ca. 3500 B.C.E.	Civilization begins

while selectively based on some of these physical variations, is, like civilization itself, a fact not of biology but of culture.

Early *Homo sapiens sapiens* lived in small kin groups of 20 or 30, following game and seeking shelter in tents, lean-tos, and caves. We know little about the organization of this hunter-gatherer society. Although some contemporary historians have suggested that the **Paleolithic era** (ca. 600,000–10,000 B.C.E.) was a peaceful golden age in which women played a dominant role in social organization, no evidence substantiates this theory. Still, Paleolithic people worked together for hunting and defense and apparently formed emotional bonds based on more than sex or economic necessity. The skeleton of a man found a few years ago in Iraq, for example, suggests that although he was born with only one arm and was crippled further by arthritis, the rest of his community supported him and he lived to adulthood. Clearly his value to his society lay in something more than his ability to make a material contribution to its collective life. But even with this cooperation and socialization, life expectancy was very short. Most people died by age 20, but even among those who survived into adulthood, most women were dead by 30 and most men by 40.

The Dominance of Culture

During the time of the upper, or late, Paleolithic era (ca. 35,000–10,000 B.C.E.), **culture**, meaning everything about humans not inherited biologically, was increasingly determinant in human life. Paleolithic people were not on an endless and all-consuming quest to provide for the necessities of life. They spent less time on such things than we do today. Thus they found time to develop speech, religion, and artistic expression. Wall paintings, small clay and stone figurines of female figures, and finely decorated stone and bone tools indicate not just artistic ability but also abstract and symbolic thought. Presumably such figures had religious functions. Hunters may have painted images of animals to ensure that such species of game would always be plentiful. Figures of women may reflect concerns about human and animal fertility.

Paintings: A Cultural Record. The arid wastes of Africa's Sahara may seem an unlikely place to find a continuous record of the civilizing of the West. Yet at the end of the last ice age, around 10,000 B.C.E., much of North Africa enjoyed a mild, damp climate and supported a diverse population of animals and humans. At Tassili-n-Ajjer in what today is Algeria,

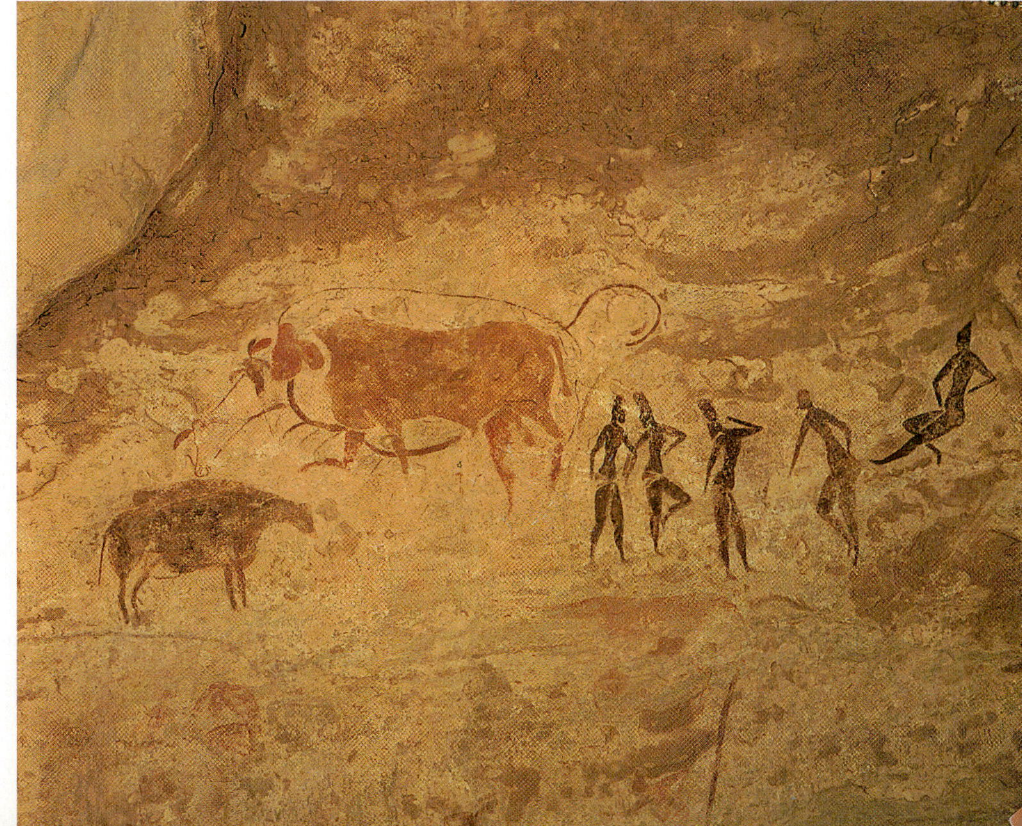

In this cave painting in northern Africa (ca. 5000 B.C.E.), animal magic evokes help from the spirit world in ensuring the prosperity of the cattle herd. A similar ceremony is still performed by members of the Fulani tribes in the Sahel, on the southern fringe of the Sahara.

THE FIRST EUROPEAN IMMIGRANTS

The massive contemporary migrations from Africa to Europe, legal and clandestine, are but the most recent of an ancient tradition: ultimately, Africa is the homeland of all Europeans. But then, it is the homeland of all humans. How Africans came to populate the world is one of the most fascinating and disputed topics of deep history.

The first humanoid (human-like) species appeared in Sub-Saharan Africa over four million years ago and developed a wide variety of physical forms and cultural traditions on that continent. As early as 1.8 million years ago hominids began to migrate from Africa to other parts of the world. In the Republic of Georgia, in China, and in Java, humanoid remains over 1.8 million years old have been discovered; others in Israel are 1.4 million years old, and the earliest humanoid remains found to date in Europe are approximately 800,000 years old. These early peoples lived as scavengers or hunters and gatherers; developed specialized tools they made of stone, wood, and bone; and organized their lives in ways that required cooperation between males and females and thus some social structure.

THE WEST AND THE WIDER WORLD

Some 650,000 years later these early immigrants had developed into a variety of species of humanoids, differing from the Neanderthals of Western Asia and Europe, from smaller species in Asia to more modern species in Africa. But in a fairly short period, everything changed: by 30,000 years ago this heterogeneity disappeared and but one species, the modern human, remained. Surely this was one of the most momentous events in human history. How did it happen? Who were these victorious men and women? How did they replace all of the other species of hominids in Europe, Asia, and the rest of the world? What was the relationship between this human revolution and the environments they came to dominate?

Oldowan tools (2.5–1.4 million years)

Scholars, studying combinations of linguistic, genetic, behavioral, and physical characteristics of human populations, have not determined whether our ancestors developed into modern *homo sapiens* from interspecies mating or if they migrated out of Africa to the rest of the world. Still, their on going debates are among the most exciting at the forefront of history and the life sciences.

One hypothesis suggests that modern humans evolved from widespread populations inhabiting not only Africa but Europe and Asia as well. According to this "multiregional model," favorable genetic variations spread through relatively stable populations—such as that of the Neanderthals. Gradually, individuals with these genetic variations interbred with neighboring populations until the whole world shared the same genetic makeup. In this model, there is no need to postulate migration of populations or a single origin of the new species. Like a human "wikipedia," modern humans are the result of collective genetic

Upper Paleolithic tools (from 90,000 in Africa, from 40,000 elsewhere to 12,000 BP)

contributions by subspecies across the inhabited world.

Supporters of the Replacement, or "Out of Africa," hypothesis suggest on the contrary that modern *homo sapiens* appeared in Africa around 150,000 years ago but remained there until relatively recently—around 40,000 years ago—when they began to migrate into the rest of the world. This new species of humans, with their genetic advantages of greater intelligence and speech capability, displaced or destroyed earlier human species such as the Neanderthals, leaving them as the only ancestors of modern humans. At the same time, they transformed the environment, rapidly driving to extinction megafauna (large animals such as mammoths) that were unprepared for new, more efficient hunting techniques, and beginning a major transformation of the animal and plant populations of the world.

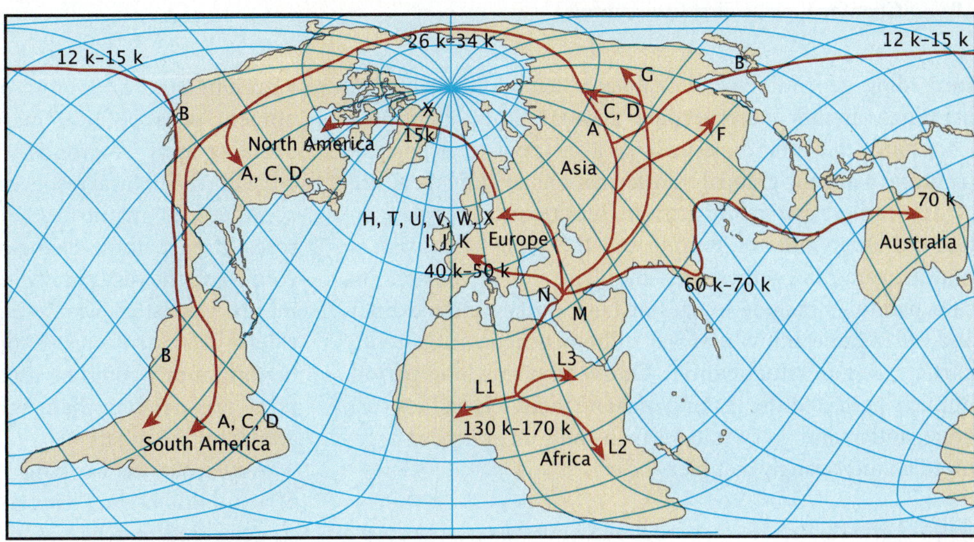

■ DNA migration map (in thousands of years).

But who is correct? The scientists who debate these issues focus on highly technical but vital studies of the archaeology of artifacts that suggest cultural behavior, of fossils, primarily crania (skulls), and most importantly, of DNA. The most useful DNA for these scholars is **mitochondrial DNA (mtDNA)**, that is, the DNA provided only by the mother which does not recombine with the male genome and thus remains very stable across generations. All of these data are subject to differing interpretations.

Can archaeologists pinpoint sharp breaks in cultural traditions that necessarily indicate the arrival of a new species of human in an area? True, the new species of human engaged in startlingly sophisticated behavior: new and complex forms of tools, specialized hunting techniques, broad spectrum exploitation of the environment, exchanges of scarce raw materials over long distances, new and more efficient weapons and weapon systems such as the bow and spear-thrower, and art in the form of wall murals and elaborate figurines. Studies in Europe, in China, and elsewhere, however, dispute the possibility of attributing these innovations to the arrival of a new type of human. After all, these changes occurred across a period of 10,000 to 20,000 years—time enough for a flow of genes and ideas into a region rather than the arrival and triumph of a new species.

Likewise, cranial studies yield ambiguous evidence: most skulls are partial, and—although differences do appear in cranial size and shape—one can find analogies in modern populations, raising the possibility that skulls attributed to different species simply demonstrate the variation within a mixed population. It is often argued that a Neanderthal, properly groomed and dressed, could today be lost in the crowd of any European city.

The most promising area of research is the study of mtDNA. If the multiregional model is correct, one would expect a wide variety of genetic material suggesting lines that reach back to around 1.8 million years ago. Moreover, no one region should show any more variation than another, since the species had multiple points of origin. However, mtDNA studies suggest something quite different. There is extremely little variation in mtDNA. Although it is not quite possible, as some have suggested, to trace all female DNA back to a single "African Eve" who would have lived about 150,000 years ago in what is now Ethiopia, Kenya, or Tanzania, the variation in mtDNA of all living humans is so small that one must assume very few common African ancestors from roughly around this period. Second, African DNA shows the greatest variety on earth, suggesting that modern *homo sapiens* have lived there much longer than anywhere else. Finally, only in Africa has a broad population of megafauna survived, suggesting that as modern humans gradually evolved in Africa, the local large animals gradually developed defensive mechanisms at the same time.

Thus, for the moment at least, the "Out of Africa" hypothesis seems strongest. But was there one migration or many? Did the ancestors of modern Europeans, Asians, Australians, and ultimately Americans follow one route out of Africa or several? Did they eradicate, replace, or indeed absorb the older humans they encountered? These are vital questions of the deep history of the world and they remain to be answered.

QUESTIONS FOR DISCUSSION

What technical background does one need to enter the debate on the origin of modern humans? What are the implications of extending the history of Western civilization to the early Stone Age? How does an understanding of the deep past inform our understanding of the present?

succeeding generations of inhabitants left more than 4000 paintings on cliff and cave walls that date from about 6000 B.C.E. until the time of Jesus. Like a pictorial time line, the paintings show the gradual transformations of human culture.

The earliest cave paintings were produced by people who, like the inhabitants of Europe and the Near East, lived by hunting game and gathering edible plants, nuts, and fruit. The cave paintings include images of huge buffalo, now extinct, and other game animals, as well as human figures apparently participating in ritual dances. Throughout this long period, humans perfected the making of stone tools; learned to work bone, antler, and ivory into weapons and utensils; and organized an increasingly complex society.

Sedentarization. Sometime around 5000 B.C.E., the artists at Tassili-n-Ajjer began to include in their paintings images of domesticated cattle and harness-like equipment. Such depictions are evidence of the arrival in North Africa of two of the most profound transformations in human history: sedentarization, that is, the adoption of a fixed dwelling place, and the agricultural revolution. These fundamental changes in human culture began independently around the world and continued for roughly 5000 years. They appeared first around 10,000 B.C.E. in the Near East, then elsewhere in Asia around 8000 B.C.E. By 5000 B.C.E., the domestication of plants and animals was under way in Africa and in what today is Mexico.

Around 10,000 B.C.E., many hunter-gatherers living along the coastal plains of what is today Syria and Israel and in the valleys and the hill country near the Zagros Mountains between modern Iran and Iraq began to develop specialized strategies that led, by accident, to a transformation in human culture. Near the Mediterranean coast, the close proximity of varied and productive ecosystems—the sea, coastal plains, hills, and mountains—encouraged people to practice what is called **broad-spectrum gathering**. That is, rather than constantly traveling in search of food, people stayed put and exploited the various seasonal sources of food: fish, wild grains, fruits, and game. In communities such as Jericho, people built and rebuilt their mud brick and stone huts over generations rather than moving on, as had their ancestors. In the Zagros region, sedentary communities focused on single, abundant sources of food during specific seasons, such as wild sheep and goats in the mountains in summer and pigs and cattle in the lower elevations in winter. These people also harvested the wild forms of wheat and barley that grew in upland valleys.

Agriculture. No one really knows why settlement led to agriculture, which is, after all, a riskier venture than hunting and gathering. When humans focused on strains of plants and animals with naturally occurring recessive genetic traits that were advantageous to humans, they increased the risk that these varieties might be less hardy than others. Specialization in only a few such species of plants or animals could spell starvation if severe weather caused that crop to fail or if disease destroyed herds. Some scholars speculate that the push to take nature in hand came from population growth and the development of a political hierarchy that reduced the natural breaking away of groups when clans or tribes became too large for the natural resources of an area to support. In settled communities, infant mortality decreased and life expectancy rose. In part, these changes occurred because for the very young and the very old life in a fixed location was less exhausting than constant wandering. The killing of infants and the elderly decreased because young and old members of the tribe or community could be useful in performing simple agricultural tasks rather than being a hindrance to community always on the move.

Archaeologists working in Turkey have found the skeleton of an adult who had lived to maturity, although his legs were so deformed that he never could have walked. That he was supported by his fellows and buried with respect when he died shows that he was valued in spite of his handicap. In a nomadic society, he would never have lived beyond infancy.

Social Organization, Agriculture, and Religion

As population growth put pressure on the local food supply, gathering activities demanded more formal coordination and organization and led to the development of political leadership. This leadership and the perception of safety in numbers may have prevented the traditional breaking away to form other similar communities in the next valley, as had happened when population growth pressured earlier groups. In any case, settlement began to encourage the growth of plants such as barley and lentils and the domestication of pigs, sheep, and goats. People no longer simply looked for these favored species of plants and animals where they occurred naturally. Now they introduced them into other locations and favored them at the expense of plant and animal species not deemed useful. Agriculture had begun.

Control of Nature. The ability to domesticate goats, sheep, pigs, and cattle and to cultivate barley, wheat, and vegetables changed human communities from passive harvesters of nature to active partners with it. The ability to expand the food supply in a limited region allowed the development of sedentary communities of greater size and complexity than those of the late hunter-gatherer period. The peoples of the **Neolithic era**, or New Stone Age (ca. 8000–6500 B.C.E.), organized sizable villages. Jericho, which had been settled before the agricultural revolution, grew into a fortified town complete with ditch, stone walls, and towers sheltering perhaps 2000 inhabitants. Çatal Hüyük in southern Turkey may have been even larger.

The really revolutionary aspect of agriculture was not simply that it ensured settled communities a food supply. The true innovation was that agriculture was portable. For the first time, rather than looking for a place that provided them

■ This terracotta figure from Çatal Hüyük dating to the seventh millennium B.C.E. has been interpreted as a mother goddess giving birth between lions or leopards.

with the necessities of life, humans could carry with them what they needed to make a site inhabitable. This portability also meant the rapid spread of agriculture throughout the region. Farmers in Çatal Hüyük cultivated varieties of plants that came from hundreds of miles away. In addition, the presence there of tools and statues made from stone not obtainable locally indicates that some trading with distant regions was taking place.

Religion. Agricultural societies brought changes in the form and organization of formal religious cults. Elaborate sanctuary rooms decorated with frescoes, bulls' horns, and sculptures of heads of bulls and bears indicate that structured religious rites were important to the inhabitants of Çatal Hüyük. At Jericho, human skulls covered with clay, presumably in an attempt to make them look as they had in life, suggest that these early settlers practiced ancestor worship. In these larger communities the bonds of kinship that had united small hunter-gatherer bands were being supplemented by religious organization, which helped control and regulate social behavior. The nature of this religion is a matter of speculation. Images of a female deity, interpreted as a guardian of animals, suggest the religious importance of women and fertility. An echo of these goddesses appears in a cave at Tassili-n-Ajjer. On one wall, four females and one male appear in a painting with two bulls. The painting may depict a female guardian and her servants or priests.

Around 1500 B.C.E., a new theme appears on the cliff walls at Tassili-n-Ajjer. Now men herd horses and drive horse-drawn chariots. These innovations had only gradually reached the arid world of North Africa. They had developed more than 1500 years before in the Fertile Crescent, the region stretching from the Persian Gulf northwest through Mesopotamia (a name that means "between the rivers"), that featureless desert plain stretching to the marshes near the mouths of the Tigris and Euphrates rivers, and down the Mediterranean coast to Egypt. Chariots symbolized a new, dynamic, and expansive phase in Western culture. Constructed of wood and bronze and used for transport and especially for aggressive warfare, they are symbolic of the culture of early river civilizations, the first civilizations in western Eurasia.

MESOPOTAMIA: BETWEEN THE TWO RIVERS

Need drove the inhabitants of Mesopotamia to create a civilization; nature itself offered little for human comfort or prosperity. The upland regions of the north receive most of the rainfall, but the soil is thin and poor. In the south, the soil is fertile but rainfall is almost nonexistent. There the twin rivers provide life-giving water but also bring destructive floods that usually arrive at harvest time. Agriculture thus is impossible without irrigation. But irrigation systems, if not properly maintained, deposit on the soil harsh chemicals called *alkaloids*, which gradually reduce its fertility. In addition, Mesopotamia's only natural resource is clay. It has no metals, no workable stone, no valuable minerals of use to ancient people. These very obstacles pressed the people to develop cooperative, innovative, and organized measures for survival. Survival in the region required planning and the mobilization of manpower possible only through centralization. Driven by need, they created a civilization.

Until approximately 3500 B.C.E., the inhabitants of the lower Tigris and Euphrates lived in scattered villages and small towns. Then the population of the region, known as Sumer, began to increase substantially. Small settlements became more common; towns such as Eridu and Uruk, in what is now Iraq, began to grow rapidly. The towns developed in part because of the need to concentrate and organize population in order to carry on the extensive irrigation systems necessary to support Mesopotamian agriculture. In most cases, the earlier role of particular villages as important religious centers favored their growth into towns. The towns soon spread their control out to the surrounding cultivated areas, incorporating the smaller towns and villages of the region. They also fortified themselves against the hostile intentions of their neighbors.

Nomadic peoples inhabited the arid steppes of Mesopotamia, constantly trading with and occasionally threatening settled villages and towns. Their menace was as ever-present in Near Eastern history as drought and flood. But nomads were a minor threat compared to the dangers posed by settled neighbors. As population growth increased pressure on the region's food supply, cities supplemented their resources by raiding their more prosperous neighbors. Victims sought protection within the ramparts of the settlements that had grown up around religious centers. As a result, the populations of the towns rose along with their towering temples, largely at the expense of the countryside. Between about 3500 and 3000 B.C.E., the population of Uruk quadrupled, increasing from 10,000 to 40,000. At the same time, the number of smaller towns and villages in the vicinity rapidly decreased. Other Mesopotamian cities developed along the same general lines. The growth of these cities established a precedent that would continue throughout history.

As villages disappeared, large agricultural areas were abandoned. Regions previously irrigated by small natural waterways reverted to desert, while urban centers concentrated water supplies within their districts with artificial canals and dikes. By 3000 B.C.E., the countryside near the cities was intensively cultivated, while outlying regions slipped back into swampland or steppe. The city had become the dominant force in the organization of economy and society.

The Ramparts of Uruk

Cities did more than simply concentrate population. Within the walls of the city, men and women developed new technologies and new social and political structures. They created cultural traditions such as writing and literature. The pride of the first

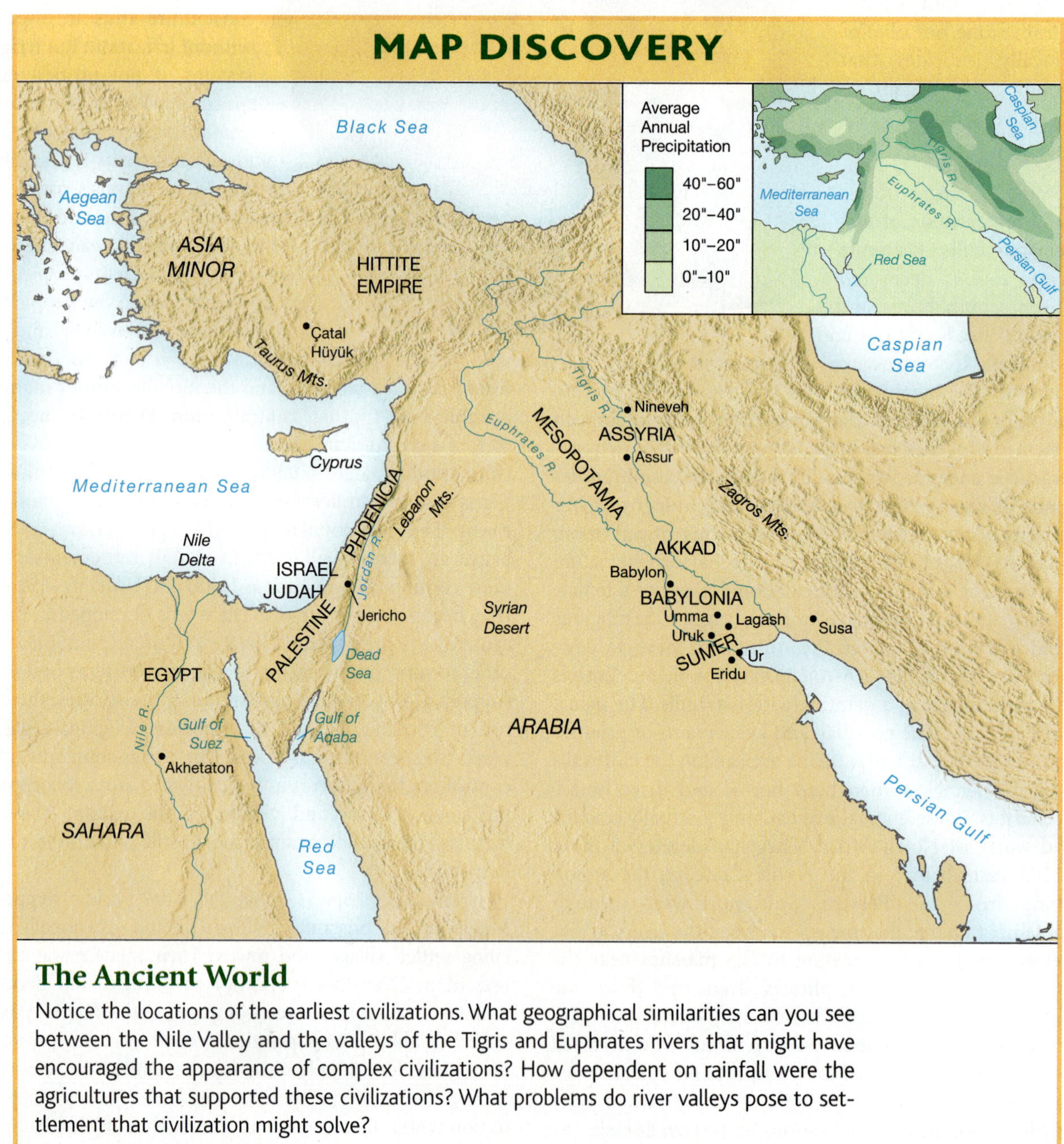

The Ancient World

Notice the locations of the earliest civilizations. What geographical similarities can you see between the Nile Valley and the valleys of the Tigris and Euphrates rivers that might have encouraged the appearance of complex civilizations? How dependent on rainfall were the agricultures that supported these civilizations? What problems do river valleys pose to settlement that civilization might solve?

city dwellers is captured in a passage from the *Epic of Gilgamesh,* the first great heroic poem, which was composed sometime before 2000 B.C.E. In the poem, the hero Gilgamesh boasts of the mighty walls he had built to encircle his city, Uruk:

Go up and walk on the ramparts of Uruk
Inspect the base terrace, examine the brickwork:
Is not its brickwork of burnt brick?
Did not the Seven Sages lay its foundations?

Gilgamesh was justly proud of his city. In his day (ca. 2700 B.C.E.) the walls were marvels of military engineering, and even now their ruins remain a tribute to his age. Archaeologists have uncovered the remains of the ramparts of Uruk, which stretched over five miles and were protected by some 900 semicircular towers. In size and complexity they surpassed the great medieval walls of Paris, which were built some 4000 years later. The protective walls enclosed about two square miles of houses, palaces, workshops, and temples. For the first time, a true urban environment had appeared in western Eurasia, and Uruk was its first city.

Urban Life. Within Uruk's walls, the peculiar circumstances of urban life changed the traditional social structure of Mesopotamia. Urban immigration increased the power, wealth, and status of two groups. In the first group were the religious authorities responsible for the temples. The second group consisted of the emerging military and administrative elites, such as Gilgamesh, who were responsible for the construction and protection of the cities. These two groups probably encouraged much of the migration to the cities. The decision to enter the city was not always voluntary; rather, it was usually forced by the ruling classes, who stood to gain the most from a concentration of population within the walls.

Whether they lived inside the city or on the farmland it controlled, Mesopotamians formed a highly stratified society in which various groups shared unequally in the benefits of civilization. Slaves, who did most of the unskilled labor within the city, were the primary victims of civilization. Most were prisoners of war, but some were people forced by debt to sell themselves or their children. Most of the remaining rural people were peasants whose lives were little better than those of slaves. Having lost their freedom to the religious or military elite, peasants were reduced to working the land of others and depended on markets and prices out of their control. Better off were soldiers, merchants, and workers and artisans who served the temple or palace. At the next level up were landowning free persons. Above all of these were the priests responsible for temple services and the rulers. Rulers included the *ensi,* or city ruler, and the *lugal,* or king, the earthly representative of the

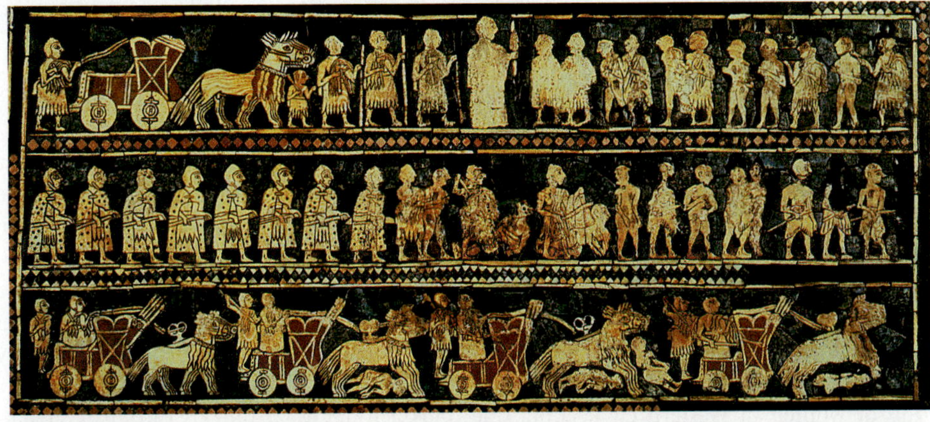

The Standard of Ur, made of shells, lapis lazuli, and limestone, was found at Ur. In the top panel, known as *War,* soldiers and horse-drawn chariots return victorious from battle. In the lower panel, *Peace,* the king celebrates the victory, captives are paraded before him, and the conquered people bring him tribute.

gods. Kings were powerful and feared. The hero of the *Epic of Gilgamesh* is presented as a ruler so harsh that the gods created a wild man, Enkidu, to subdue him.

Women's Status. Urban life also redefined the role and status of women, who in the Neolithic period had enjoyed roughly the same roles and status as men. In cities, women tended to exercise private authority over children and servants within the household, while men controlled the household and dealt in the wider world. This change in roles may have resulted in part from the economic basis of the first civilization. Southern Mesopotamia has no sources of metal or stone. To acquire these precious commodities, trade networks were extended into Syria, the Arabian Peninsula, and even India. The primary commodities that Mesopotamians produced for trade were textiles, and these were largely produced by women captured in wars with neighboring city-states. Their menfolk were normally killed or blinded and used for menial tasks such as milling. The enslaved women employed in urban textile production constituted a dependent female population. Some historians suggest that the disproportionate numbers of low-status women in Mesopotamian cities affected the status of women in general. Although women could own property and even appear as heads of households, by roughly 1500 B.C.E. the pattern of patriarchal households predominated. Although such circumstances may in part explain the position of women in Western civilization, one finds a roughly similar situation in the civilizations of Asia and the Americas. Throughout most of early history, while individual women might at times exercise great power, they did so largely in the private sphere. Public control of the house, the family, the city, and the state was largely in male hands.

Tools: Technology and Writing

Changes in society brought changes in technology. The need to feed, clothe, protect, and govern growing urban populations led to major technological and conceptual discoveries. Canals and systems of dikes partially harnessed water supplies. Farmers began to work their fields with improved plows and to haul their produce to town, first on sleds and ultimately on carts. These land-transport devices, along with sailing ships, made it possible not only to produce a greater agricultural surplus but also to move the surplus to distant markets. Artisans used a refined potter's wheel to produce ceramic vessels of great beauty. Government officials and private individuals began to use cylinder seals, small stone cylinders engraved with a pattern, to mark ownership. Metalworkers fashioned gold and silver into valuable items of adornment and prestige. They also began to cast bronze, an alloy of copper and tin, which came into use for tools and weapons about 3000 B.C.E.

■ The ca. 2700 B.C.E. statues found at the Abu Temple in Tell Asmar are fine examples of the way Sumerian sculpture is typically based on cones and cylinders—arms and legs like pipes, skirts smooth and round, flaring out at their bottoms. Faces are dominated by very large eyes; but, for reasons we might take for granted, artists of many cultures have placed emphasis on eyes.

Pictograms. Perhaps the greatest invention of early cities was writing. As early as 7000 B.C.E., small clay or stone tokens with distinctive shapes or markings were being used to keep track of animals, goods, and fruits in inventories and in bartering. By 3500 B.C.E., government and temple administrators were using simplified drawings—today termed **pictograms**—that were derived from the tokens to help them keep records of their transactions. A scribe molded a small lump of clay into a square. Holding it between his thumb and forefinger, he divided the smooth surface into a series of squares by scratching it with a sharp reed. He then drew his pictograms within each square. In the dry, hot Mesopotamian air, the lumps of clay dried quickly into firm tablets. If accidentally hardened by fire, they became virtually indestructible. Thousands have survived in the ruins of Mesopotamian cities.

Cuneiform. The first tablets were written in Sumerian, a language related to no other known tongue. Each pictogram represented a single sound, which corresponded to a single object or idea. In time, the pictograms developed into a true system of writing. The drawings themselves became smaller and more abstract and were arranged in straight lines. Since the scribe first pressed the triangle-shaped writing instrument into the clay and then drew it across the square, the writing took on its characteristic wedge, or **cuneiform,** shape (from the Latin *cuneus,* wedge). Finally, scribes took a radical step.

Rather than simply using pictograms to indicate single objects, they began to use cuneiform characters to represent concepts. For example, the pictogram for "foot" could also mean "to stand." Ultimately, pictograms came to represent sounds divorced from any particular meaning.

The implications of the development of cuneiform writing were revolutionary. Since symbols were liberated from meaning, they could be used to record any language. Over the next thousand years, scribes used the same symbols to write not only in Sumerian but also in the other languages of Mesopotamia, such as Akkadian, Babylonian, and Persian. The earliest extant clay tablets are little more than lists of receipts. Later, tablets were used to preserve contracts, maintain administrative records, and record significant events, prayers, myths, and proverbs. Writing soon allowed those who had mastered it to achieve greater centralization and control of government, to communicate over enormous distances, to preserve and transmit information, and to express religious and cultural beliefs. Writing reinforced memory, consolidating and expanding the achievements of the first civilization and transmitting them to the future. Writing was power and, for much of subsequent history, a small minority of merchants and elites and the scribes in their employ wielded that power. In Mesopotamia, writing served to increase the strength of the king, the servant of the gods.

Gods and Mortals in Mesopotamia

Uruk had begun as a village like any other. Its rise to importance resulted from its significance as a religious site. A world of many cities, Mesopotamia was also a world of many gods, and Mesopotamian cities bore the imprint of the cult of their gods.

Mesopotamian Divinities. The gods were like the people who worshiped them. They lived in a replica of human society, and each god had a particular responsibility. Every object and element, from the sky to the brick or the plow, had its own active god. The gods had the physical appearance and personalities of humans, as well as human virtues and vices, but always to an exaggerated extent. Like humans, they lived in a stratified society. The hundreds of ordinary divinities were overshadowed by greater gods such as Nanna and Ufu, who were the protectors of Ur and Sippar. Others, such as Inanna, or Ishtar, the goddess of love, fertility, and wars, and her husband Dumuzi, were worshiped throughout Mesopotamia. At the top of the pantheon were the gods of the sky, the air, and the rivers. The sky god was An, whose temple was in Uruk. Enki was god of earth and waters; Enlil was the supreme ruler of the air.

Temples and Rituals. Mesopotamians believed that the role of mortals was to serve the gods and to feed them through sacrifice. By around 2500 B.C.E., although military lords and kings had gained political power at the expense of the temple priests, the priests still controlled a major portion of economic resources. They owned vast estates where peasants cultivated wheat, barley, vegetable gardens, and vineyards and tended flocks of sheep and herds of cattle and pigs. The produce from temple lands and flocks supported the priests, scribes, artisans, laborers, farmers, teamsters, smiths, and weavers who operated the complex religious centers. At Lagash, for example, at a time when the total population was approximately 40,000, the temple of Bau employed more than 1200 workers of various sorts, supervised by an administrator and an inspector appointed by the priests. The temple of Bau was only one of 20 temples in Lagash—and not the largest or most wealthy among them.

The ruins of the Ziggurat of Ur. On top of a main platform 50 feet high, two successively smaller stages were built. The top stage was a temple containing a religious shrine. Ramplike stairways led up to the shrine from the ground.

Temples dominated the city's skyline as they dominated the city's life. Square, rectangular, or oval, they consisted of the same essential elements. Worshipers entered through a vestibule that opened onto a spacious courtyard dominated by an altar. Here sacrifices were offered to the idol of the god. Spreading out from the courtyard was a maze of smaller chambers, which provided housing for the priests and storage facilities for the accumulated offerings brought to feed the god. By around 2000 B.C.E., a **ziggurat**, or tiered tower, dedicated to the god stood near many temples. The great Ziggurat of Ur, for example, measured nearly 2000 square feet at its base and originally stood more than 120 feet high. Ziggurats were constructed of mud bricks and covered with baked bricks set in bitumen, and they often were ornamented with elaborate multicolored mosaics. Today their weathered remains are small hills rising unexpectedly from the Iraqi plain. It is easy to see why people of a later age thought that the people who had built the ziggurats wanted a tower that would reach to heaven—the origin of the biblical story of the Tower of Babel.

Although Mesopotamians looked to hundreds of personal divinities for assistance, they did not attempt to establish personal relationships with their great gods. However, since they assumed that the gods lived in a structured world that operated rationally, they believed that mortals could deal with them and enlist their aid by following the right rituals. Rites centered on the worship of idols. The gods were thought to be present if their idols showed the appropriate features, clothing, ornaments, and equipment, and if they were cared for in the proper manner. The most important care was feeding. At the temple of Uruk, the gods were offered two meals a day, each consisting of two courses served in regal quantity and style. Through the proper rituals, people believed they could buy a god's protection and favor. Still, mortal life was harsh and the gods offered little solace in settling the great issues of human existence. This attitude is powerfully presented in the *Epic of Gilgamesh,* which, while not an accurate picture of Mesopotamian religion, still conveys many of the values of this civilization. In the popular legend, Gilgamesh, king of Uruk, civilizes the wild man Enkidu, who had been sent by the gods to temper the king's harshness. Gilgamesh and Enkidu become friends and undertake a series of adventures. However, even their great feats cannot overcome death. The message is that only the gods are immortal, and that the human afterlife is at best a shadowy and mournful existence. In Mesopotamian society, this earthly life alone was considered worth living, and one had to accomplish all that one could in it.

Sargon and Mesopotamian Expansion

The temple was one center of the city; the palace was the other. As representative of the city's god, the king was the ruler and highest judge. As did people in other strata of society, the king held privileges and responsibilities appropriate to his position. He was responsible for the construction and maintenance of religious buildings and the complex system of canals that maintained the precarious balance between swamp and arid steppe. Finally, he commanded the army, defending his community against its neighbors and leading his forces against rival cities.

Competition and War. The cultural and economic developments of early Mesopotamia occurred within the context of almost constant warfare. From around 3000 B.C.E. until 2300 B.C.E., the rulers of Ur, Lagash, Uruk, and Umma fought among themselves for control of Sumer (their name for the southern region of Mesopotamia). Although their urban and political traditions were similar, the region had no political, linguistic, or ethnic unity. The population was a mixture of Sumerians and Semites—peoples speaking Semitic languages related to modern Arabic or Hebrew—all jealously protective of their cities and gods and eager to extend their domination over their weaker neighbors.

The Akkadian Empire. The extraordinary developments in this small corner of the Middle East might have remained isolated phenomena were it not for Sargon (ca. 2334–2279 B.C.E.), king of Akkad and the most important figure in Mesopotamian history. During his long reign of 55 years, Sargon built on the conquests and confederacies of the past to unite, transform, and expand Mesopotamian civilization. Sargon was the son of a priestess and an unknown father. A

Akkad Under Sargon. Sargon united the entire Mesopotamian region from the sources of the Tigris and Euphrates to the mouth of the Persian Gulf.

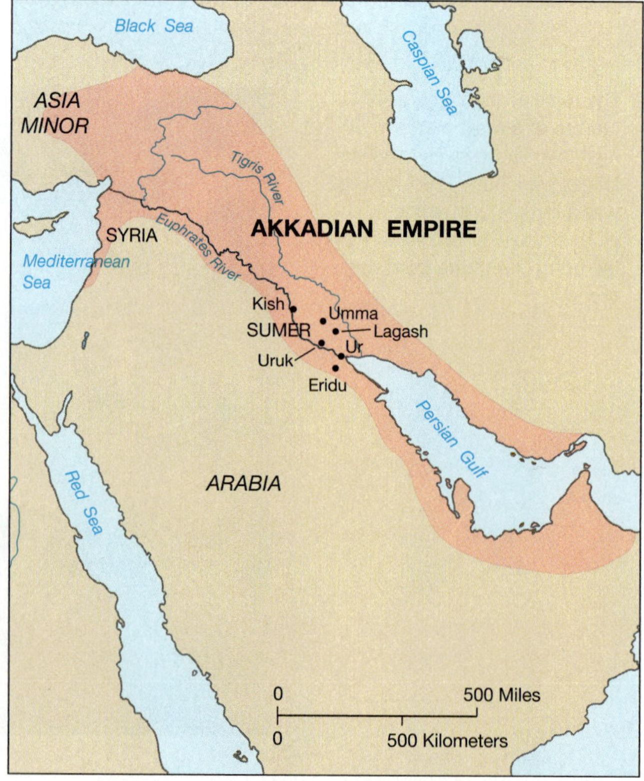

legend similar to that of Moses says that Sargon's mother placed him in a reed basket and set him adrift on the Euphrates. In his youth, he was the cupbearer to the king of Kish. Later, he overthrew his master and conquered Uruk, Ur, Lagash, and Umma, which made him lord of Sumer. Sargon extended his military operations east across the Tigris, west along the Euphrates, and north into modern Syria, thus creating the first great multiethnic empire state in the West.

The Akkadian state, so named by contemporary historians for Sargon's capital at Akkad, consisted of a vast and heterogeneous collection of city-states and territories. Sargon attempted to rule it by transforming the traditions of royal government. First, he abandoned the traditional title of "king of Kish" in favor of "King of the Four Regions," a title emphasizing the universality of his rule. Second, rather than eradicating the traditions of conquered cities, he allowed them to maintain their own institutions but replaced many of their autonomous ruling aristocracies with his own functionaries. He also reduced the economic power of local temples in favor of his supporters, to whom he apparently distributed temple property. At the same time, however, he tried to win the loyalty of the ancient cities of Sumer by naming his daughter high priestess of the moon god Nanna at Ur. He was thus the first in a long line of Near Eastern rulers who sought to unite his disparate conquests into a true state.

Sargon did more than just conquer cities. Although a Semite, he spread the achievements of Sumerian civilization throughout his vast state. In the Akkadian pantheon, Sumerian and Semitic gods were venerated equally, and similar gods from various traditions were merged into the same divinities. Akkadian scribes used cuneiform to write the Semitic Akkadian language, thus continuing the tradition of literate administration begun by the Sumerians. So important did Sargon's successors deem his accomplishments that they ordered him worshiped as a god.

The Akkadian state proved as ephemeral as Sargon's cultural accomplishments were lasting. All Mesopotamian states tended to undergo a rapid rise under a gifted military commander, and then began to crumble under the internal stresses of dynastic disputes and regional assertions of autonomy. Thus weakened, they could be conquered by other expanding states. First Ur, under its Sumerian king and initial law codifier Shulgi (2094–2047 B.C.E.), and then Amoritic Babylonia, under its great ruler Hammurabi (1792–1750 B.C.E.), assumed dominance in the land between the rivers. From about 2000 B.C.E. on, the political and economic centers of Mesopotamia were in Babylonia and in Assyria, the region to the north at the foot of the Zagros Mountains.

■ This bronze head, dating from around 2300 B.C.E., was found at Nineveh. It is sometimes identified as Sargon, king of Akkad. Later invaders mutilated the nose and eyes, apparently making a political statement.

Hammurabi and the Old Babylonian Empire

In the tradition of Sargon, Hammurabi expanded his state through arms and diplomacy. He expanded his power south as far as Uruk and north to Assyria. In the tradition of Shulgi, he promulgated an important body of law, known as the Code of Hammurabi. In the words of its prologue, this code sought

> To cause justice to prevail in the country
> To destroy the wicked and the evil,
> That the strong may not oppress the weak.

Law and Society. As the favored agent of the gods, the king was responsible for regulating all aspects of Babylonian life, including dowries and contracts, agricultural prices and wages, commerce and money lending, and even professional standards for physicians and architects. The code creates a picture of a prosperous society composed of three legally defined social strata: a well-to-do elite, the mass of the population, and slaves. Each group had its own rights and obligations in proportion to its status. Even slaves enjoyed some legal rights and protection, could marry free persons, and might eventually obtain freedom.

Much of the code seeks to protect women and children from arbitrary and unfair treatment. Husbands ruled their households, but they did not have unlimited authority over their wives. Women could initiate their own court cases, practice various trades, and even hold public positions. Upon marriage, husbands gave their fathers-in-law a payment in silver or in furnishings. The father of the wife gave her a dowry over which she had full control. Some elite women personally controlled great wealth.

The law code held physicians, veterinarians, architects, and boat builders to standards of professional behavior. If a physician performed a successful eye operation on a member of the elite, the code specified that he receive ten shekels of silver. If the physician caused the loss of the eye, however, he lost his hand. Builders of houses had to repair any damage caused if their structures collapsed. If a free person died in the collapse, the builder had to pay with his life.

DOCUMENT
Near Eastern Law Codes

The Code of Hammurabi was less a royal attempt to restructure Babylonian society than an effort to reorganize, consolidate, and preserve previous laws in order to maintain the established social and economic order. What innovation it did show was in the extent of such punitive measures as death or mutilation. Penalties in earlier codes had been primarily compensation in silver or valuables. Hammurabi's extensive use of the law of retaliation was an assertion of royal authority in maintaining justice.

Mathematics. Law was not the only area in which the Old Babylonian kingdom began an important tradition. In order to handle the economics of business and government administration, Babylonians developed the most sophisticated mathematical system known prior to the fifteenth century C.E. Babylonian mathematics was based on a numerical system from 1 to 60. (Today we still divide hours and minutes into 60 units.) Babylonian mathematicians devised multiplication tables and tables of reciprocals that allowed quick calculations of all products from 1 to 59 with each of the numbers from 2 to 59. They also devised tables of squares and square roots, cubes and cube roots, and other calculations needed for computing such important figures as compound interest. Babylonian mathematicians developed an algebraic system and solved linear and quadratic equations for such practical purposes as determining the shares of inheritance for several sons or the wages to be paid for a variety of workers employed for several days. Similar tables of coefficients made possible the calculation of areas of various geometric figures, as well as the amounts of standard building materials needed for buildings in such shapes. Although Babylonian mathematicians were not primarily interested in theoretical problems and were seldom given to abstraction, their technical proficiency indicates the advanced level of sophistication with which Hammurabi's contemporaries could tackle the problems of living in a complex society.

THE CODE OF HAMMURABI

The society revealed in the Code of Hammurabi was a complex world of landed aristocrats, merchants, and simple workers and shopkeepers. Its economy functioned on a complex system of credit relationships binding the various members of the society together, as seen in the following selections.

Focus Questions

What occupations were pursued in the Old Babylonian Empire? How did gender and social status affect legal penalties?

If a merchant lent grain at interest, he shall receive sixty *qu* of grain per *jur* as interest [equal to a 20 percent rate of interest]. If he lent money at interest, he shall receive one-sixth shekel six *se* (i.e., one-fifth shekel) per shekel of silver as interest.

If a seignior who incurred a debt does not have the money to pay it back, but has the grain, the merchant shall take grain for his money with its interest in accordance with the ratio fixed by the king.

If a seignior gave money to another seignior for a partnership, they shall divide equally in the presence of god the profit or loss which was incurred.

If a woman wine seller, instead of receiving grain for the price of a drink, has received money by the large weight and so has made the value of the drink less than the value of the grain, they shall prove it against that wine seller and throw her into the water.

If an obligation came due against a seignior and he sold the services of his wife, his son, or his daughter, or he has been bound over to service, they shall work in the house of their purchaser or obligee for three years, with their freedom reestablished in the fourth year.

If an obligation came due against a seignior and he has accordingly sold [the services of] his female slave who bore him children, the owner of the female slave may repay the money which the merchant paid out and thus redeem his female slave.

IMAGE DISCOVERY

Law or Propaganda?

The seven-foot-high diorite stele, dating from about 1750 B.C.E. is inscribed with the law code of Hammurabi. The relief at the top shows Hammurabi adoring the sun god, who was understood to bring injustice to light. How might such a depiction of the law-giving king serve as propaganda to increase the validity of his laws in the eyes of his subjects?

The Hittite Empire. For all its successes, Hammurabi's state was no more successful than those of his predecessors at defending itself against internal conflicts or external enemies. Despite his efforts, the traditional organization inherited from his Sumerian and Akkadian predecessors could not ensure orderly administration of a far-flung collection of cities. Hammurabi's son lost more than half of his father's kingdom to internal revolts. Weakened by internal dissension, the kingdom fell to a new and potent force in Western history, the Hittites.

From their capital of Hattushash (modern Boğazköy in Turkey), the Hittites established a centralized state based on agriculture and trade in the metals mined from the ore-rich mountains of Anatolia and exported to Mesopotamia. Perfecting the light horse-drawn war chariot, the Hittites expanded into northern Mesopotamia and along the Syrian coast. They were able to destroy the Babylonian state around 1600 B.C.E. Unlike the Sumerians and the Semitic nomads, Akkadians, and Babylonians, the Hittites were an Indo-European people, speaking a language that was part of a linguistic family that includes most modern European languages as well as Persian, Greek, Latin, and Sanskrit. The Hittites' gradual expansion south along the coast was checked at the battle of Kadesh around 1286 B.C.E., when they encountered the army of an even greater and more ancient power: the Egypt of Ramses II.

CHRONOLOGY

Between the Two Rivers

ca. 3500 B.C.E.	Pictograms appear
ca. 3000–2316 B.C.E.	War for control of Sumer
ca. 2700 B.C.E.	Gilgamesh
ca. 2334–2279 B.C.E.	Sargon
1792–1750 B.C.E.	Hammurabi
ca. 1600 B.C.E.	Hittites destroy Old Babylonian state
ca. 1286 B.C.E.	Battle of Kadesh

THE GIFT OF THE NILE

Like that of the Tigris and Euphrates valleys, the rich soil of the Nile Valley can support a dense population. There, however, the similarities end. The Nile floodplain, unlike the Mesopotamian one, required little effort to make the land productive. Each year the river flooded at exactly the right moment to irrigate crops and to deposit a layer of rich, fertile silt. North of the last cataracts, the fertile region called Upper Egypt is about eight miles wide and is flanked by high desert plateaus. Near the Mediterranean in Lower Egypt, the Nile spreads across a lush, marshy delta more than 100 miles wide. Egypt knew only two environments, the fertile Nile Valley and the vast wastes of the Sahara surrounding it. This inhospitable and largely uninhabitable region limited Egypt's contact with outside influences. Thus, while trade, communication, and violent conquest characterized Mesopotamian civilization, Egypt knew self-sufficiency, an inward focus in culture and society, and stability. In its art, political structure, society, and religion, the Egyptian universe was static. Nothing was ever to change.

The earliest sedentary communities in the Nile Valley appeared on the western margin of the Nile Delta around 4000 B.C.E. In villages such as Merimda, which had a population of

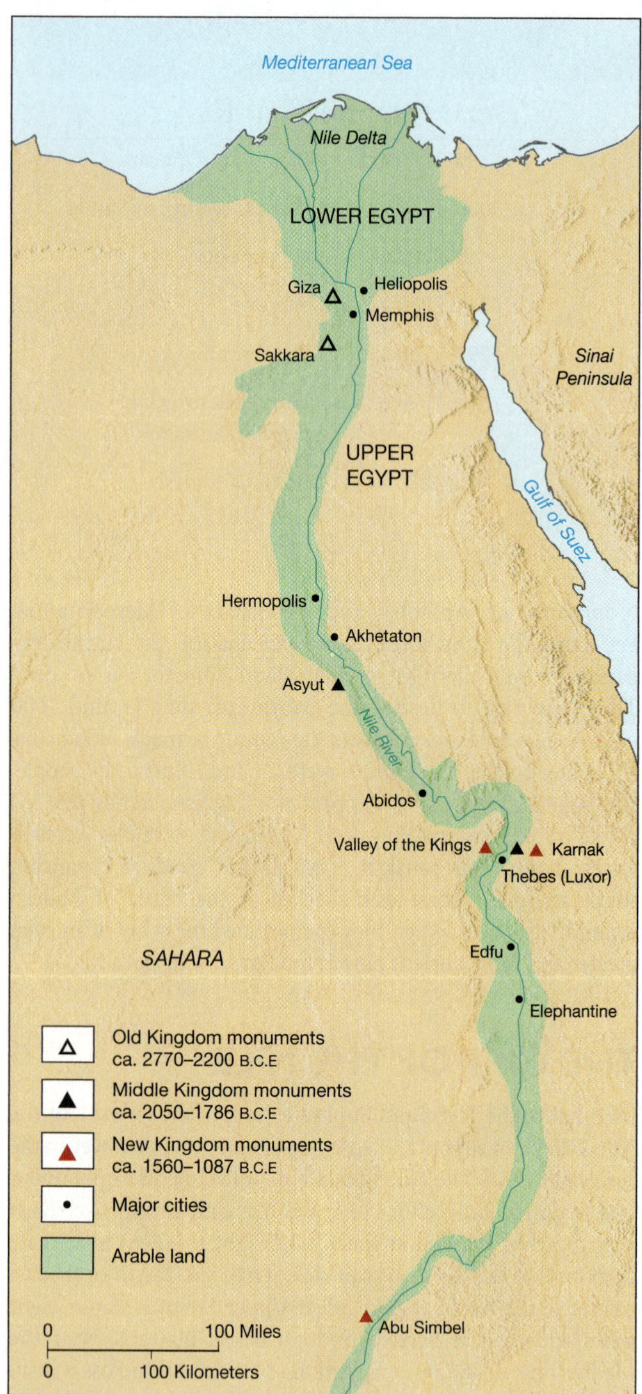

■ Ancient Egypt. The thin strip of rich land bordering the Nile saw the development of an extraordinary civilization that endured for more than 2000 years.

more than 10,000, huts were constructed of poles and adobe bricks and were huddled together near wadis—fertile river beds that were dry except during the rainy season. Farther south, in Upper Egypt, similar communities developed somewhat later but achieved earlier political unity and a higher level of culture. By around 3200 B.C.E., Upper Egypt was in contact with Mesopotamia and had apparently borrowed something of that region's artistic and architectural traditions. During the same period, Upper Egypt developed a pictographic script.

These cultural achievements coincided with the political centralization of Upper Egypt under a series of kings. Probably around 3150 B.C.E., King Narmer or one of his predecessors in Upper Egypt expanded control over the fragmented south, uniting Upper and Lower Egypt and establishing a capital at Memphis on the border between the two regions. For more than 2500 years, the Nile Valley, from the first cataract to the Mediterranean, enjoyed the most stable civilization the Western world has ever known.

Tending the Cattle of God

Historians divide the vast sweep of ancient Egyptian history into 31 dynasties, regrouped in turn into four periods of political centralization: pre- and early dynastic Egypt (ca. 3150–2770 B.C.E.), the Old Kingdom (ca. 2770–2200 B.C.E.), the Middle Kingdom (ca. 2050–1786 B.C.E.), and the New Kingdom (ca. 1560–1087 B.C.E.). The time gaps between kingdoms were periods of disruption and political confusion termed *intermediate periods.* While minor changes in social, political, and cultural life certainly occurred during these centuries, the changes were less significant than the astonishing stability and continuity of the civilization that developed along the banks of the Nile.

God Kings. Divine kingship was the cornerstone of Egyptian life. Initially, the king was the incarnation of Horus, a sky and falcon god. Later, the king was identified with the sun god Ra (subsequently known as Amen-Ra, the great god), as well as with Osiris, the god of the dead. As divine incarnation, the king was obliged above all to care for his people. It was he who ensured the annual flooding of the Nile, which brought water to the parched land. His commands preserved **maat,** the ideal state of the universe and society, a condition of harmony and justice. In the poetry of the Old Kingdom, the king was the divine herdsman, while the people were the cattle of god:

Well tended are men, the cattle of god.
He made heaven and earth according to their desire
and repelled the demon of the waters. . . .
He made for them rulers (even) in the egg,
a supporter to support the back of the disabled.

Unlike the rulers in Mesopotamia, the kings of the Old Kingdom were not warriors but divine administrators. Protected by the Sahara, Egypt had few external enemies and no standing army. A vast bureaucracy of literate court officials and provincial administrators assisted the god-king. They wielded wide authority as religious leaders, judicial officers, and, when necessary, military leaders. A host of subordinate overseers, scribes, metalworkers, stonemasons, artisans, and tax collectors rounded out the royal administration. At the local level, governors administered provinces called *nomes,* the basic units of Egyptian local government.

The great pyramids of Giza built by (left to right) Pharaohs Menkuare (ca. 2533–2525 B.C.E.), Khafre (ca. 2570–2544 B.C.E.), and Khufu (ca. 2601–2528 B.C.E.) of the IV Dynasty were originally only part of funerary complexes that included mortuary temples, procession ways, and other structures intended for the cult of the pharaohs.

Statue of Nedjemu.

Gender and Bureaucracy. Women of ancient Egypt were more independent and involved in public life than were those of Mesopotamia. Egyptian women owned property, conducted their own business, entered legal contracts, and brought lawsuits. They also had an integral part in religious rites. They were not segregated from men in their daily activities and shared in the economic and professional life of the country at every level except one: women apparently were excluded from formal education. The professional bureaucracy was open only to those who could read and write. As a result, the primary route to public power was closed to women, and the bureaucratic machinery remained firmly in the hands of men.

The role of the bureaucracy was to administer estates, collect taxes, and channel revenues and labor toward vast public works projects. The construction projects focused on the king. He lived in the royal city of Memphis in the splendor of a *Per-ao,* or "great house," from which comes the word *pharaoh,* the Hebrew term for the Egyptian king. During the Old and Middle Kingdoms, more imposing than the great house of the living king were the pyramid temple-tomb complexes of his ancestors. The vast size and superb engineering of these structures remain among the marvels of human creation.

The Pyramids. The founder of the Old Kingdom, King Zoser, who was a rough contemporary of Gilgamesh, built the first of the pyramid temples, the Step Pyramid at Sakkara. The pyramid tombs were only part of elaborate religious complexes at whose center were temples housing royal statues. Within the temples, priests and servants performed rituals to serve the dead kings, just as they had served the kings when they were alive. Even death did not disrupt the continuity so vital to Egyptian civilization. The cults of dead kings reinforced the monarchy, since veneration of past rulers meant veneration of the kings' ancestors. The pyramids thus strengthened the image of the living king by honoring the physical remains of his predecessors.

Building and equipping the pyramids focused and transformed Egypt's material and human resources. Artisans had to be trained, engineering and transportation problems solved, quarrying and stone-working techniques perfected, and laborers recruited. In the Old Kingdom, whose population has been estimated at perhaps 1.5 million, more than 70,000 workers at a time were employed in building the great temple-tombs. No smaller work force could have built such a massive structure as the Great Pyramid of Khufu (ca. 2600 B.C.E.), which stood 481 feet high and contained almost six million tons of stone. The pyramids were constructed by peasants working when the Nile was in flood and they could not till

Egyptian Famine

the soil. Although actual construction was seasonal, the work was unending. No sooner was one complex completed than the next was begun.

Feeding the masses of laborers absorbed most of the country's agricultural surplus. Equipping the temples and pyramids provided a constant demand for the highest-quality luxury goods, since royal tombs and temples were furnished as luxuriously as palaces. Thus the construction and maintenance of the vast complexes focused the organization and production of Egypt's economy and government.

Democratization of the Afterlife

In the Old Kingdom, future life was available only through the king. The graves of thousands of his attendants and servants surrounded his temple. All the resources of the kingdom went to maintaining existing cults and establishing new ones. All the wealth, labor, and expertise of the kingdom thus flowed into the temples, reinforcing the position of the king. Like the tip of a pyramid, the king was the summit, supported by all of society.

Decline of Royal Power. Gradually, however, the absolute power of the king declined. The increasing demands for consumption by the court and the cults forced agricultural expansion into areas where returns were poor, thus decreasing the flow of wealth. As bureaucrats increased their efforts to supply the voracious needs of living and dead kings and their attendants, they neglected the maintenance of the economic system that supplied those needs. The royal government was not protecting society; the "cattle of god" were not being well tended. Finally, tax-exempt religious foundations, established to ensure the perpetual cult of the dead, received donations of vast amounts of property and came to rival the power of the king. These removed an ever-greater amount of the country's wealth from the control of the king and his agents. Thus the wealth and power of the Egyptian kings declined at roughly the time that Sargon was expanding his Akkadian state in Mesopotamia. By around 2200 B.C.E. Egyptian royal authority collapsed entirely, leaving political and religious power in the hands of provincial governors.

The Middle Kingdom. After almost 200 years of fragmentation, the governors of Thebes in Upper Egypt reestablished centralized royal traditions, but with a difference. Kings continued to build vast temples, but they did not resume the tremendous investments in pyramid complexes on the scale of the Old Kingdom. The bureaucracy was opened to all men, even sons of peasants, who could master the complex pictographic writing. Private temple-tombs proliferated and with them new pious foundations. These foundations promised eternal care by which anyone with sufficient wealth could enjoy a comfortable afterlife.

The memory of the shortcomings of the Old Kingdom introduced a new ethical perspective expressed in the literature written by the elite. For the first time, the elite voiced the concern that justice might not always be served and that the innocent might suffer at the hands of royal agents. In the story of Sinuhe, a popular tale from around 1900 B.C.E., an official of Amenemhet I (d. 1962 B.C.E.) flees Egypt after the death of his king. He fears that through false reports of his actions he will incur the wrath of Amenemhet's son, Senusert I. Only in his old age, after years of exile and homesickness, does Sinuhe dare to return to his beloved Egypt. There, through the intercession of the royal children, Senusert receives him honorably and grants him the ultimate favor, his own pyramid-tomb. In the "Tale of the Eloquent Peasant," a peasant is constantly mistreated by royal officials. Although he, like Sinuhe, ultimately receives justice, the moral is clear. The state system at times failed in its responsibility to safeguard *maat.* Still, these stories, in the end, reaffirm the existing system.

Egyptian Folk Tale

The Hyksos. The greater access to power and privilege in the Middle Kingdom benefited foreigners as well as Egyptians. Assimilated Semites rose to important administrative positions. By around 1600 B.C.E., when the Hittite armies were destroying the state of Hammurabi's successors, large bands of Semites had settled in the eastern Delta, setting the stage for the first foreign conquest of Egypt. A series of kings referred to by Egyptian sources as "rulers of foreign lands," or *Hyksos,* overran the country and ruled the Nile Valley as far south as Memphis. These foreigners adopted the traditions of Egyptian kingship and continued the tradition of divine rule, even using names compounded with that of the sun god, Ra.

The Hyksos kings introduced their military technology and organization into Egypt. In particular, they brought with them the light horse-drawn war chariot. This mobile fighting platform—manned by warriors armed with bows, bronze

CHRONOLOGY

The Gift of the Nile

ca. 3150–2770 B.C.E.	Predynastic and early dynastic Egypt
ca. 2770–2200 B.C.E.	Old Kingdom
ca. 2600 B.C.E.	Pyramid of Khufu
ca. 2050–1786 B.C.E.	Middle Kingdom
ca. 1560–1087 B.C.E.	New Kingdom
1552–1527 B.C.E.	Ahmose I
1506–1494 B.C.E.	Thutmose I
1494–1490 B.C.E.	Thutmose II
1490–1468 B.C.E.	Hatshepsut
1364–1347 B.C.E.	Amenhotep IV (Akhenaten)
1347–1337 B.C.E.	Tutankhamen
1289–1224 B.C.E.	Ramses II

A HOMESICK EGYPTIAN

The story of Sinuhe, an Egyptian of the Middle Kingdom (ca. 2050–1786 B.C.E.), was among the most popular stories in Egyptian history. Sinuhe fled into exile but, in spite of his prosperity among foreigners, longed for his home. In the following passage, Sinuhe, who has been summoned to return to the pharaoh, tells of his reception.

Focus Questions

What does Sinuhe's behavior in the presence of the pharaoh suggest about how Egyptians regarded their rulers? What gift does the pharaoh offer Sinuhe that was the greatest wish of every ordinary Egyptian?

I found his majesty upon the great throne in a recess of fine gold. When I was stretched out upon my belly, I knew not myself in his presence, although this god greeted me pleasantly. I was like a man caught in the dark: my soul departed, my body was powerless, my heart was not in my body, that I might know life from death.

Then his majesty said: "Lift him up. Let him speak to me." Then his majesty said: "Behold thou art come. Thou hast trodden the foreign countries and made a flight. But now elderliness has attacked thee; thou hast reached old age. It is no small matter that thy corpse be properly buried; thou shouldst not be interred by bowmen. Do not, do not act thus any longer: for thou dost not speak when thy name is pronounced!" Yet I was afraid to respond, and I answered it with the answer of one afraid: "What is it that my lord says to me? I should answer it, but there is nothing that I can do: it is really the hand of a god."

Then his majesty said: "He shall not fear. He has no title to be in dread. He shall be a courtier among the nobles. He shall be put in the rank of the courtiers. Proceed to the inner chambers of the morning toilet, in order to make his position."

There was constructed for me a pyramid-tomb of stone in the midst of the pyramid-tombs. The stonemasons who hew a pyramid-tomb took over its ground-area. The outline draftsmen designed in it; the chief sculptors carved in it; and the overseers of works who are in the necropolis made it their concern. My statue was overlaid with gold, and its skirt was of fine gold. It was his majesty who had it made. There is no poor man for whom the like has been done. So I was under the favor of the king's presence until the day of mooring had come.

swords of a type previously unknown in Egypt, and lances—transformed Egyptian military tactics. These innovations remained even after the Hyksos were expelled by Ahmose I (1552–1527 B.C.E.), the Theban founder of the Eighteenth Dynasty, with whose reign the New Kingdom began.

The Egyptian Empire

Ahmose did not stop with the liberation of Egypt. He forged an empire. He and his successors used their newfound military might to extend the frontiers of Egypt south up the Nile beyond the fourth cataract and well into Nubia, solidifying Egypt's contacts with other regions of Africa. To the east, they absorbed the caravan routes to the Red Sea, from which they were able to send ships to Punt (probably modern Somalia), the source of the myrrh and frankincense needed for funeral and religious rituals. Most important was the Egyptian expansion into Canaan and Syria. There, Egyptian chariots crushed their foes as kings pressed on as far as the Euphrates. Thutmose I (1506–1494 B.C.E.) proclaimed: "I have made the boundaries of Egypt as far as that which the sun encircles."

Thutmose's immediate successors were his children, Thutmose II (1494–1490 B.C.E.) and Hatshepsut (1490–1468 B.C.E.), who married her brother. Such brother-sister marriages, although not unknown in polygamous Egyptian society, were rare. After the death of Thutmose II, Hatshepsut ruled both as regent for her stepson Thutmose III (1490–1468 B.C.E.) and as co-ruler. She was by all accounts a capable ruler, preserving stability and even personally leading the army on several occasions to protect the empire. However, the traditions of male leadership were such that Hatshepsut could not present a public image as a female monarch. In royal inscriptions and in pictures, she had herself portrayed in the formal rigid pose and dress of a king, including a false beard.

In spite of the efforts of Hatshepsut and her successors, the Egyptian Empire was never as grand as its kings proclaimed. Many of the northern expeditions were raids rather than conquests. Still, the expanded political frontiers meant increased trade and unprecedented interaction with the rest of the ancient world. The cargo excavated from the wreck of a ship that sank off the coast of what is now Turkey around 1350 B.C.E. vividly portrays the breadth of international exchange in the New Kingdom. The nationality of the ship, its origins, and its destination are unknown, but it carried a cargo of priceless and exotic merchandise from around the Mediterranean world. From distant Cyprus came copper ingots. Tin ingots probably originated in the Hittite state in what are now parts of Afghanistan and Turkey. In the ship's hold lay numerous jars from Canaan and vases from Greece. When it sank, the ship was carrying Canaanite glass ingots, jewelry, and jars of ointment; ebony from Nubia; pottery from Cyprus; weapons from Egypt, Greece, and Syria; cylinder seals from

Mesopotamia or Syria; raw ivory; and a mass of damaged Egyptian gold jewelry probably intended for scrap.

The lost ship was probably not a merchant vessel in the modern sense; private merchants were virtually unknown in the Egyptian Empire. Instead, most precious commodities circulated through royal ventures or as gifts and tribute. The ship may well have been carrying tribute to the king, for in the New Kingdom as in the Old, the ruler, as the incarnation of the great god Amen-Ra, was the pinnacle of the political and economic order.

■ This painted limestone head of Hatshepsut was originally from a statue. She is shown wearing the crown of Egypt and the stylized beard that symbolized royalty and that was often seen on the statues and death masks of pharaohs.

MAP DISCOVERY

The Egyptian Empire

This map shows the extent of the Egyptian Empire during the New Kingdom. In what directions did Egyptian imperial activities expand the empire? What commercial and strategic advantages did this extension bring?

Religious and Royal Consolidation Under Akhenaten

Religion was both the heart of royal power and its only limiting force. Although the king was the embodiment of the religious tradition, he was also bound by that tradition, as it was interpreted by an ancient and powerful system of priesthoods, pious foundations, and cults. The intimate relationship between royal absolutism and religious cult culminated in the reign of Amenhotep IV (1364–1347 B.C.E.), the most controversial and enigmatic ruler of the New Kingdom, who challenged the very basis of royal religious control. In a calculated break with more than 1000 years of Egyptian religious custom, Amenhotep attempted to abolish the cult of Amen-Ra along with all of the other traditional gods, their priesthoods, and their festivals. In their place he promoted a new divinity, the sun-disk god Aten. Amenhotep moved his capital from Thebes to a new temple city, Akhetaton (near the modern village of Tel al-'Amarna), and changed his own name to Akhenaten ("it pleases Aten").

■ Breaking with ancient tradition of Egyptian portraiture, this statue of the head of Akhenaten, the revolutionary pharaoh who attempted to transform Egyptian religion, depicts the pharaoh with the symbol characteristics of both male and female.

Akhenaten has been called the first monotheist, a reformer who sought to revitalize a religion that had decayed into superstition and magic. Yet his monotheism was not complete. The god Aten shared divine status with Akhenaten himself. Akhenaten attacked other cults, especially that of Amen-Ra, to consolidate royal power and to replace the old priesthoods with his own family members and supporters. In his artistic policies, he broke with the past, but again the break was limited. Official portraiture, which depicted Akhenaten with a long, thin face, a swollen stomach, and large thighs, was no more realistic than the earlier tradition. Instead, Akhenaten appeared as both man and woman, an image of his counterpart Aten, the godhead who was father and mother of all creation.

A New Aesthetic. Still, in attempting to reestablish royal divinity, Akhenaten did temporarily transform the aesthetics of Egyptian court life. Traditional archaic language gave way to the everyday speech of the fourteenth century B.C.E. Wall paintings and statues showed people in the clothing that they actually wore rather than in stylized parade dress. This new style rendered the king at once more human and more divine. It differentiated him from the long line of preceding kings, emphasizing his uniqueness and his royal power.

The strength of royal power was so great that during his reign Akhenaten could command acceptance of his radical break with Egyptian stability. However, his ambitious plan did not long survive his death. His innovations annoyed the Egyptian elite, while his abolition of traditional festivals alienated the masses. His son-in-law, Tutankhamen (1347–1337 B.C.E.), the son of Akhenaten's predecessor, was a child when he became king upon Akhenaten's death. Under the influence of his court advisers, probably inherited from his father's reign, he restored the ancient religious traditions and abandoned the new capital of Akhetaton for his father's palace at Thebes. Something of the relaxed artistic style introduced by Akhenaten survived in the art of Tutankhamen's reign. However, the religious themes and objects found in the young king's tomb show a complete return to the old ways within a few years of Akhenaten's death.

VIDEO
Temple of Karnak

The Hittites. Return to the old ways meant return to the old problems. Powerful pious foundations controlled fully 10 percent of the population. Dynastic continuity ended after Tutankhamen, and a new military dynasty seized the throne. These internal problems provided an opportunity for the expanding Hittite state in Asia Minor (now Turkey) to expand south at the expense of Egypt. Ramses II (1289–1224 B.C.E.) checked the Hittite expansion at the battle of Kadesh, but the battle was actually a draw. Eventually, Ramses and the Hittite king Hattusilis III signed a peace treaty whose terms included nonaggression and mutual defense. Archaeologists have found copies of the treaty, both in Hattushash and in Egypt. Written in Egyptian, Hittite, and the international diplomatic language of Akkadian, the agreement marked the failure of both states to unify the Fertile Crescent.

The mutual standoff at Kadesh did not long precede the disintegration of both Egypt and the Hittite state. Within a century, states large and small along the Mediterranean coast from Anatolia to the Delta and from the Aegean Sea in the west to the Zagros Mountains in the east collapsed or were destroyed in what seems to have been a general crisis of the civilized world. The various raiders, sometimes erroneously called the "Sea Peoples," who struck Egypt, Syria, the Hittite state, and elsewhere were not the primary cause of the crisis. Rather it was internal political, economic, and social strains within both Egypt and the Hittite state that provided the opportunity for various groups—including Anatolians, Greeks, Israelites, and others—to raid the ancient centers of civilization. In the ensuing confusion, the small Semitic kingdoms of Syria and Canaan developed a precarious independence in the shadow of the great powers.

BETWEEN TWO WORLDS

City-based civilization was an endangered species throughout antiquity. Just beyond the well-tilled fields of Mesopotamia and the fertile delta of the Nile lay the world of Semitic tribes of semi-nomadic shepherds and traders. Of course, not all Semites were nonurban. Many had formed part of the heterogeneous population of the Sumerian world. Sargon's Semitic Akkadians and Hammurabi's Amorites created great Mesopotamian states, adopting the ancient Sumerian cultural traditions. Along the coast of Canaan, other Semitic groups established towns that were modeled on those of Mesopotamia and that were involved in the trade between Egypt and the north. But the majority of Semitic peoples continued to live a life radically different from that of the people of the floodplain civilizations. From these, one small group, the Hebrews, emerged to establish a religious and cultural tradition unique in antiquity.

The Hebrew Alternative

Sometime after 2000 B.C.E., small Semitic bands under the leadership of patriarchal chieftains spread into what is today Syria, Lebanon, Israel, and Palestine. These bands lived on the edge of civilization. They crisscrossed the Fertile Crescent, searching for pasture for their flocks. Occasionally they participated in the trade uniting Mesopotamia and the towns of the Mediterranean coast. For the most part, however, they pitched their tents on the outskirts of towns only briefly, moving on when their sheep and goats had exhausted the supply of pasturage. The biblical patriarch Abram was typical of these chieftains. The story of his migration from Ur to Haron and then to Hebron—as described in the Book of Genesis, Chapters 11 and 12—may be the stuff of legend, but it conforms to the general pattern of such wandering groups. Semitic Aramaeans and Chaldeans brought with them not only their flocks and families, but Mesopotamian culture as well.

Mesopotamian Origins. Later Hebrew history records such Mesopotamian traditions as the story of the flood (Genesis, Chapters 6–10), legal traditions strongly reminiscent of those of Hammurabi, and the worship of the gods on high places. Stories such as that of the Tower of Babel (Genesis, Chapter 11) and the Garden of Eden (Genesis, Chapters 2–4) likewise have a Mesopotamian flavor, but with a difference. For these wandering shepherds, urban culture was a curse. In the Hebrew Bible (the Christian Old Testament), the first city was built by Cain, the first murderer. The Tower of Babel, probably a ziggurat, was a symbol not of human achievement but of human pride.

At least some of the wandering Aramaeans, among them perhaps Abram, as the Hebrews later described him, also rejected the gods of Mesopotamia. Religion among these nomadic groups focused on the specific divinity of the clan. In the case of Abram, this was the god El, the highest god of the Canaanites, the inhabitants of the coastal regions that would later be Lebanon, Palestine, and Israel. Abram and his successors were not monotheists. They did not deny the existence of other gods. They simply believed that they had a personal pact or covenant with their own god. According to Hebrew tradition, Abram's god promised him that he would be the father of a great nation and as a sign of this promise changed his name to Abraham.

In its social organization and cultural traditions, Abraham's clan was no different from its neighbors. The independent clans were ruled by a senior male (hence the Greek term *patriarch*—"ruling father"). Women, whether wives, concubines, or slaves, were treated as distinct inferiors, virtually as property. As a nonliterate society, the nomadic people had little access to the learned traditions of the Fertile Crescent. Indeed, nothing marked them for any greatness. They became significant only in retrospect, and not in the Canaan of the patriarchs but in the Egypt of the pharaohs.

Egypt and Exodus. Some of Abraham's descendants must have joined the steady migration from Canaan into Egypt that took place during the Middle Kingdom and the Hyksos period. Although initially they were well treated, after the expulsion of the Hyksos in the sixteenth century B.C.E. many of the Semitic settlers in Egypt were reduced to slavery. According to tradition, around the thirteenth century B.C.E. a small band of Semitic slaves left Egypt for Sinai and Canaan under the leadership of Moses. The memory of this departure, known as the Exodus, became the formative experience of the descendants of those who had taken part and those who later joined them. Moses, a Semite who carried an Egyptian name and who, according to tradition, had been raised in the royal court, was the founder of the Israelite people (so named for Israel, a name given the patriarch Jacob).

A relief on a basalt obelisk (ca. 830 B.C.E.) depicts Jehu, a king of Israel, making obeisance to the Assyrian monarch Shalmaneser III. This is the oldest identified portrait of an Israelite.

During the years that they spent wandering in the desert and then slowly conquering Canaan, the Israelites forged a new identity and a new faith. From the Midianites of the Sinai Peninsula they adopted the god Yahweh as their own. Although composed of various Semitic and even Egyptian groups, the Israelites adopted the oral traditions of the clan of Abraham as their common ancestor and identified his god, El, with Yahweh. They interpreted their extraordinary escape from Egypt as evidence of a covenant with this god, a treaty similar to those concluded between the Hittite kings and their dependents.

The Hebrew tradition of exodus embodied two themes. The first concerns what Yahweh had done: "I am Yahweh your God, who brought you out of Egypt, out of the house of bondage" (Exodus 20:2). The second theme—which is embodied in the Ten Commandments, the basis of Mosaic law—prescribes how Israel should respond. Unlike the conditional laws of Hammurabi's code (if . . . , then . . .) the law of Yahweh was absolute: "Thou shall not. . . ." More than simply commands, the laws were ethical claims made by Yahweh on his people. Thus Yahweh was to be the Israelites' exclusive god; they were to make no alliances with any others. They were to preserve peace among themselves, and they were obligated to serve Yahweh with arms. Finally, each generation was under the moral obligation to renew the covenant as God's chosen people.

Inspired by their new identity and their new religion, the Israelites swept into Canaan. Taking advantage of the vacuum of power left by the Hittite-Egyptian standoff following the battle of Kadesh, they destroyed or captured the cities of the region. In some cases, the local populations welcomed the Israelites, abandoned or overthrew their local leaders, and accepted the religion of Yahweh. In other places, the indigenous peoples were slaughtered, down to the last man, woman, and child.

The Kingdoms of Israel and Judah. From its greatest extent under Solomon, the Kingdom of Israel split into rival northern and southern kingdoms and then progressively lost ground against Assyria and Babylon.

A King Like All the Nations

During its first centuries, Israel was a loosely organized confederation of tribes whose only focal point was the religious shrine at Shiloh. This shrine, in contrast to the temples of other ancient peoples, housed no idols—only a chest known as the Ark of the Covenant, which contained the law of Moses and mementos of the Exodus. At times of danger temporary leaders would head united tribal armies. The power of these leaders, called *judges* in the Hebrew Bible, rested solely on their personal leadership qualities. This charisma indicated that the spirit of Yahweh was with the leader. Yahweh alone was the ruler of the people.

By the eleventh century B.C.E., this disorganized political tradition placed the Israelites at a disadvantage in fighting their neighbors. The Philistines, who dominated the Canaanite seacoast and had expanded inland, posed the greatest threat. By 1050 B.C.E., the Philistines had defeated the Israelites, captured the Ark of the Covenant, and occupied most of their territory. Many Israelites clamored for "a king like all the nations" to lead them to victory. To consolidate their forces, the Israelite religious leaders reluctantly established a kingdom. Its first king was Saul and its second was David.

Davidic Kingship. David (ca. 1000–962 B.C.E.) and his son and successor, Solomon (ca. 961–922 B.C.E.), brought the kingdom of Israel to its peak of power, prestige, and territorial expansion. David defeated and expelled the Philistines, subdued Israel's other enemies, and created a united state that included all of Canaan from the desert to the sea. He established Jerusalem as the political and religious capital. No longer would the Ark of the Covenant rest in the tents of Israel's nomadic ancestors. Solomon went still further, building a magnificent temple complex to house the Ark and to serve as Israel's national shrine. Just as they transformed the worship of Yahweh from rural cult to urban religion, David and Solomon restructured Israel from a tribal to a monarchical society. The old tribal structure remained only as a religious tradition. Solomon centralized land divisions, raised taxes, and increased military service in order to strengthen the monarchy.

The cost of this transformation was high. Originally the kingship was intended to be a holy office instituted by and subordinate to Yahweh, who was understood to have made an everlasting covenant with David as fulfillment of the promise of a nation to Abraham. However, under David, and especially under Solomon, the kingdom grew more tyrannical as it grew more powerful. Solomon behaved like any other king of his time. He contracted marriage alliances with neighboring princes and allowed his wives to practice their own cults. He demanded extraordinary taxes and services from his people to pay for his lavish building projects. When he was unable to pay his Phoenician creditors for supplies and workers, he deported Israelites to work as slaves in Phoenician mines.

THE KINGDOM OF ISRAEL

Hebrew scriptures preserve two accounts of the establishment of the monarchy and the selection of Saul by Samuel as the first king (ca. 1020 B.C.E.). The first, from 1 Samuel 9, is favorable to the monarchy, describing how Saul was privately anointed by Samuel. The second, from 1 Samuel 8, is hostile to the monarchy, suggesting that by desiring a king, the people of Israel were rejecting the traditional leadership of God alone.

Focus Questions

What are the advantages that the author of the first passage sees in kingship? What dangers does the second author think that kings pose to the Israelites?

1 Samuel 9:10

The Lord revealed to Samuel: "Tomorrow about this time I will send to you a man from the land of Benjamin, and you shall anoint him to be prince over my people Israel. He shall save my people from the hand of the Philistines; for I have seen the affliction of my people because their cry has come to me." . . . Then Samuel took a vial of oil and poured it on his head and kissed him and said, "Has not the Lord anointed you to be prince over his people Israel? And you shall reign over the people of the Lord and you will save them from the hand of their enemies round about."

1 Samuel 8

All the elders of Israel gathered together and came to Samuel at Ramah, and said to him . . . "Appoint for us a king to govern us like all the nations." . . . And Samuel prayed to the Lord. And the Lord said to Samuel, "Hearken to the voice of the people in all that they say to you; for they have not rejected you, but they have rejected me from being king over them." . . . So Samuel told all the words of the Lord to the people who were asking for a king from him. He said, "These will be the ways of the king who will reign over you: He will take your sons and appoint them to his chariots and to be his horsemen, and to run before his chariots; and he will appoint for himself commanders of thousands and commanders of fifties, and some to plow his ground and to reap his harvest, and to make his implements of war and the equipment of his chariots. He will take your daughters to be perfumers and cooks and bakers. He will take the best of your fields and vineyards and olive orchards and give them to his servants. He will take the tenth of your grain and of your vineyards and give it to his officers and to his servants. . . . And in that day you will cry out because of your king, whom you have chosen for yourselves; but the Lord will not answer you in that day."

But the people refused to listen to the voice of Samuel; and they said, "No! but we will have a king over us, that we also may be like all the nations, and that our king may govern us and go out before us and fight our battles."

From the Holy Bible, Revised Standard Version.

The Prophets. In order to protect the covenant with Yahweh from the demands of the kings, religious leaders known as *prophets,* operating outside the royal power structures, criticized kings and their professional temple prophets, calling the people of Israel and its leaders to an accounting. They explained historical events in terms of the faithfulness of the Israelites to their covenant with Yahweh. The prophets were independent of royal control and spoke out constantly against any ruler whose immorality compromised the terms of the covenant. They called upon rulers and people to reform their lives and to return to Yahweh. Some prophets were killed. Still they persisted, establishing a tradition of religious opposition to royal absolutism, a tradition that, like monotheism itself, is an enduring legacy.

Exile

Not surprisingly, the united kingdom did not survive Solomon's death. The northern region, demanding that aspirants to the throne should be tested for their faithfulness to Yahweh, broke off to become the kingdom of Israel, with its capital in Shechem. The south, the kingdom of Judah, continued the tradition of David from his capital of Jerusalem. These small, weak kingdoms did not long maintain their independence. Beginning in the ninth century B.C.E., a new Mesopotamian power, the Assyrians, began a campaign of conquest and unprecedented brutality throughout the Near East. The Hebrew kingdoms were among their many victims. In 722 B.C.E., the Assyrians destroyed the kingdom of Israel and deported thousands of its people to upper Mesopotamia. Judah escaped destruction for just over a century by submitting to Assyria and becoming a dependent client state. In 586 B.C.E., the kingdom of Judah was conquered by Assyria's destroyers, the New Babylonian Empire under King Nebuchadnezzar II (604–562 B.C.E.). The temple of Solomon was destroyed, Jerusalem was burned, and Judah's elite were deported to Babylon.

Babylonian Captivity. During their years of exile in Babylon, the Israelites replaced temple worship with an intense study of the **Torah,** or law. In synagogues, or houses of study, the exiles rethought the meaning of their covenant in light of the destruction of their kingdom and the temple.

Increasingly, Yahweh was understood to be not one god among many but rather the one universal God, creator and ruler of the universe. Although Yahweh might be described in human terms, he was so beyond human understanding that he could not be depicted in any image.

Although beyond all earthly powers, Yahweh was believed to have intervened in human history to accomplish his goals. It was understood that he had formed a covenant with Abraham and renewed it with Moses and David. Yahweh was expected to triumph in the future through a servant whose fidelity, sufferings, and humility would be the instruments of that divine triumph. Whether this suffering servant was understood either as an individual or as those exiles that remained faithful to Yahweh, the belief was central to the exilic tradition.

Second Temple Judaism. The Babylonian captivity ended some 50 years later when the Persians, who had conquered Babylonia, allowed the people of Judah to return to their homeland and rebuild their temple. Those who returned did so with a new understanding of themselves and their covenant, an understanding that developed into Judaism. The fundamental figures in this transformation were Ezra and Nehemiah (fifth and fourth centuries B.C.E.). These important Jewish emissaries of the Persian king came to Judaea (formerly the kingdom of Judah) to revive piety by emphasizing the Torah. Ezra and Nehemiah were particularly concerned with keeping Judaism uncontaminated by other religious and cultural influences. They condemned those who had remained in Judaea and who had intermarried with foreigners during the exile. Only the exiles who had remained faithful to Yahweh and who had avoided foreign marriages could be the true interpreters of the Torah. This new, increasingly complex system of separatism and national purity, reinforced through teaching in synagogues, came to characterize the Jewish religion in the postexilic period.

Among its leaders were a group known as Pharisees, zealous adherents to the Torah, who produced a body of oral law termed the **Mishnah,** or second law, by which the law of Moses was to be interpreted and safeguarded. In subsequent centuries this oral law, along with its interpretation, developed into the **Talmud.** Pharisees believed in resurrection and in spirits such as angels and devils, and they held some of the prophetic books to be part of the Torah. A group of conservative, aristocratic priests and landowners called Sadducees opposed what they saw as innovations made by the Pharisees. They accepted only the first five books of the Bible as Torah and rejected such Pharisaic beliefs as resurrection.

Both traditions reinterpreted the covenant tradition within the realities of existence in a small, dependent region within a great empire. The Pharisees and much of the populace believed that a messiah, or savior, would arise as a new David to reestablish Israel's political independence. Among the priestly elite, the hope for a Davidic messiah was seen as more universal: a priestly messiah would arise and bring about the kingdom of glory. Some Jews actively sought political liberation from the Persians and their successors. Others were content to cooperate with a succession of foreign rulers while preserving ritual and social purity and awaiting the messiah. Still others, such as the Essenes, withdrew into isolated communities to await the fulfillment of the prophecies.

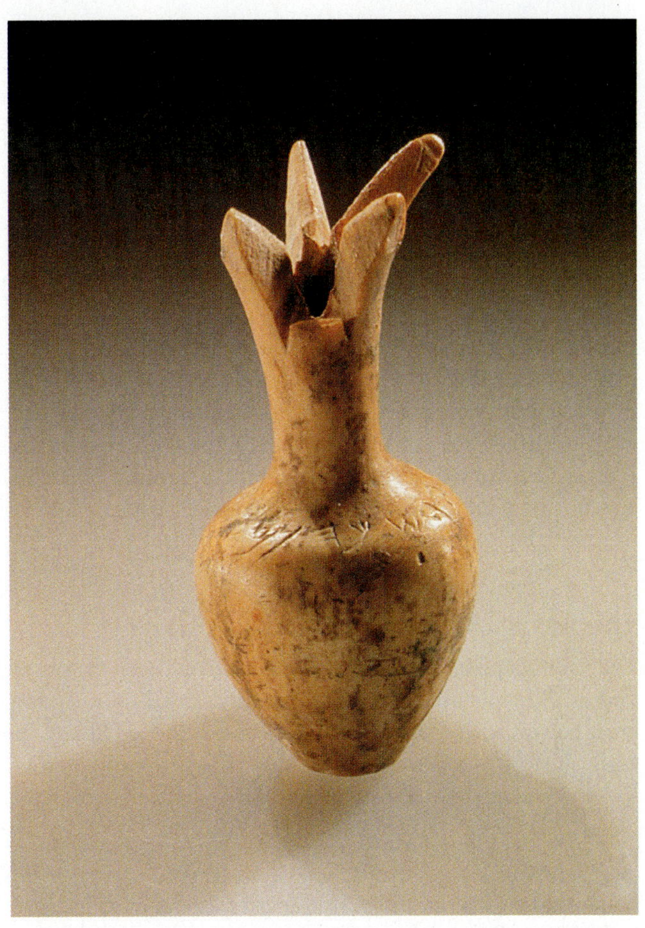

This small ivory pomegranate, a symbol of fertility, may be the only surviving object from Solomon's Temple, although its forged inscription cast its authenticity in doubt. If genuine, it probably decorated the head of a ceremonial scepter used by the temple priest.

CHRONOLOGY

Between Two Worlds

ca. 1050 B.C.E.	Philistines defeat the Israelites
ca. 1000–962 B.C.E.	David, king of Israel
ca. 961–922 B.C.E.	Solomon, king of Israel
722 B.C.E.	Assyrians destroy Kingdom of Israel
604–562 B.C.E.	Nebuchadnezzar II
586 B.C.E.	Nebuchadnezzar II conquers Kingdom of Judah

NINEVEH AND BABYLON

The Assyrian state that destroyed Israel accomplished what no other power had ever achieved. It tied together the floodplain civilizations of Mesopotamia and Egypt. But the Assyrian state was not just larger than the nation-states that had preceded it; it differed in nature as well as in size. Earlier states had allowed conquered areas to preserve their own institutions and cultural traditions while diverting economic resources to the capital. The Assyrian Empire was an integrated state in which conquered regions were reorganized and remade on the model of the central government. By the middle of the seventh century B.C.E., the Assyrian Empire stretched from the headwaters of the Tigris and Euphrates rivers to the Persian Gulf, along the coast from Syria to beyond the Delta, and up the Nile to Thebes. Now the ancient gods of Sumer were worshiped in the sanctuaries of Memphis.

The Assyrian Empire

The Assyrian plain north of Babylonia had long been the site of a small Mesopotamian state threatened by semi-nomads and great powers such as the Babylonians and later the Hittites. Its early history was similar to that of so many earlier Mesopotamian empires. Early expansion soon gave rise to internal revolt and external threats. However, the revolt paved the way for the ascension of Tiglath-pileser III (746–727 B.C.E.), the greatest empire builder of Mesopotamia since Sargon. Tiglath-pileser and his successors transformed the structure of the Assyrian state and expanded its empire. They created a model for empire that would later be copied by Persia and Macedonia. In the sense that the Assyrians not only conquered but created an administrative system by which to rule, theirs was the first true empire.

Empires of the Ancient Near East

■ The Assyrian and New Babylonian Empires. The Assyrians united the two great river valley civilizations of Mesopotamia and Egypt into an enormous empire held together by military force.

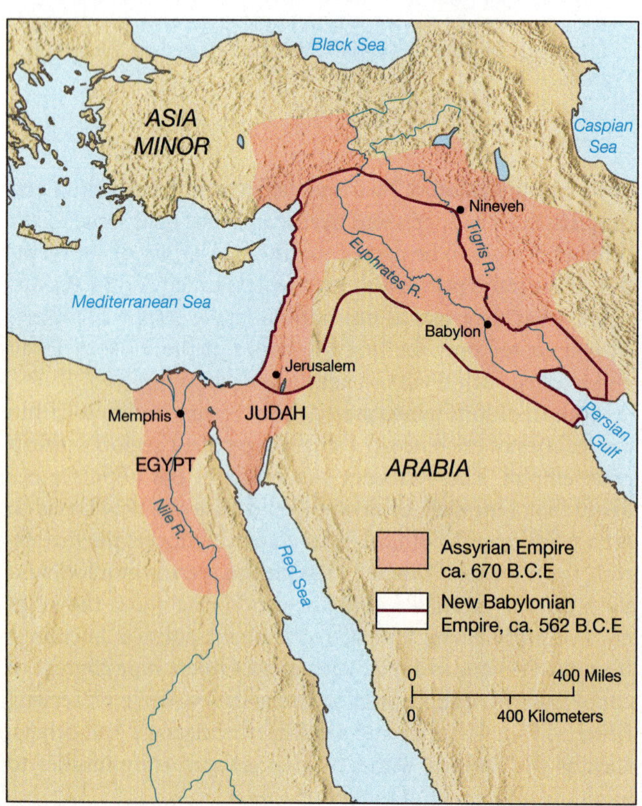

From his palace at Nineveh, Tiglath-pileser combined all the traditional elements of Mesopotamian statecraft with a new religious ideology and social system to create the framework for a lasting multiethnic imperial system. The system rested on five bases: a transformed army, a new military-religious ideology, a novel administrative system, a social policy involving large-scale population movements, and the calculated use of massive terror.

The heart of Tiglath-pileser's program was the most modern army the world had ever seen. In place of traditional armies of peasants and slaves supplied by great aristocrats, he raised professional armies from the conquered lands of the empire and placed them under the command of Assyrian generals. The Assyrian army was also the first to use iron weapons on a massive scale. The bronze swords and shields of their enemies were no match for the stronger iron weapons of the Assyrians. Assyrian armies were also well balanced, including not only infantry, cavalry, and chariots, but also engineering units for constructing the siege equipment needed to capture towns. Warfare had become a science.

In addition to the professional army, Tiglath-pileser created the most developed military-religious ideology of any ancient people. Kings had long been agents of the gods, but Ashur, the god of the Assyrians, had but one command: Enlarge the empire! Thus warfare was the mission and duty of all, a sacred command paralleled through the centuries in the cries "God wills it" of the Christian crusaders and "God is great" of the Muslims.

Tiglath-pileser restructured his empire, both at home in Assyria and abroad, so that revolts of the sort that had nearly destroyed it would be less possible. Within Assyria, he increased the number of administrative districts, thus decreasing the strength of each. This reduced the likelihood of successful rebellions launched by dissatisfied governors. Outside Assyria proper, the king liquidated traditional leaders whenever possible and appointed Assyrian governors or at least assigned loyal overseers to protect his interests. Even then he did not allow governors and overseers unlimited authority or discretion; instead, he kept close contact with local administrators through a system of royal messengers.

In order to shatter regional identities, which could lead to separatist movements, Tiglath-pileser deported and resettled conquered peoples on a massive scale. He sent 30,000 Syrians to the Zagros Mountains and moved 18,000 Aramaeans from the Tigris to Syria. Thousands must have died of exhaustion, hunger, and thirst during the forced marches of men, women, and children. The survivors, cut off from their homelands by

NM's Creative Impulse: Prehistory
history.evansville.net/prehist.html
Prehistoric links.

Rock Art Links—Petroglyphs and Pictographs
www.electronics-ee.com/Art/Art_History/Rock_Art.htm
Online database of links to prehistoric rock art throughout the world.

Çatal Hüyük
catal.arch.cam.ac.uk/catal/catal.html
A site devoted to Çatal Hüyük, one of the earliest settlements to have developed into a sedentary agricultural community.

Prehistoric Cultures
www.d.umn.edu/cla/faculty/troufs/anth1602/
A course Website at the University of Minnesota Duluth that has links to materials on prehistoric cultures around the world.

Mesopotamia

NM's Creative Impulse: Mesopotamia
history.evansville.net/meso.html
A course Website for Mesopotamian history.

ABZU: Guide to Resources for the Study of the Ancient Near East Available on the Internet
www.etana.org/abzu/
A major site for all aspects of Ancient Mesopotamia and Egypt maintained by the Oriental Institute of The University of Chicago.

Mesopotamia (Ur)
www.taisei.co.jp/cg_e/ancient_world/ur/aur.html
The city of Ur reproduced with computer graphics.

Egypt

NM's Creative Impulse: Egypt
history.evansville.net/egypt.html
Award-winning site for Egyptian history.

Survey of Ancient Egypt
www.cofc.edu/~piccione/hist270/index.html
Excellent class Web page on Ancient Egypt.

Egyptian Kings
touregypt.net/kings.htm
A site that provides information on all of the pharaohs.

Giza Plateau Computer Model
www-oi.uchicago.edu/OI/DEPT/COMP/GIZ/MODEL/Giza_Model.html
A site devoted to Giza with a computer model of its pyramids and other monuments.

Israel

The Hebrews: A Learning Module
www.wsu.edu/~dee/HEBREWS/HEBREWS.HTM
An excellent course site devoted to the ancient Hebrews.

The Israel Museum, Jerusalem: Archaeology
www.imj.org.il/eng/archaeology/
Site on early Israel archaeology.

Nineveh and Babylon

The Palace of Ashurnasirpal II
ccat.sas.upenn.edu/arth/asrnsrpl.html
A 3-D animated fly-through of The Palace of Ashurnasirpal II.

Babylon
www.geocities.com/Area51/Cavern/5178/main.html
A tour of Babylon in the year 580 B.C.E.

SUGGESTIONS FOR FURTHER READING

General Reading

Cambridge Ancient History, vol. 1 (Cambridge: Cambridge University Press, 1990). Contains essays on every aspect of ancient civilizations.

William W. Hallo and William Kelly Simpson, *The Ancient Near East: A History* (Fort Worth, TX: Harcourt Brace College Publishers, 1998). A general introduction to early Near Eastern history.

A. Bernard Knapp, *The History and Culture of Ancient Western Asia and Egypt* (Belmont, CA: Wadsworth Publishing Company, 1990). A good general survey of the entire period.

Barbara S. Lesko, ed. *Women's Earliest Records from Ancient Egypt and Western Asia: Proceedings of the Conference on Women in the Ancient Near East* (Atlanta: Scholars Press, 1989). Important collection of essays on all aspects of women in ancient societies.

Donald B. Redford, *Egypt, Canaan and Israel in Ancient Times* (Princeton: Princeton University Press, 1992). A synthesis of the interrelations among three great Near Eastern civilizations.

Before Civilization

Barry Cunliffe, *Prehistoric Europe: An Illustrated History* (Oxford: Oxford University Press, 1997). An engaging introduction to early Europe.

Brian M. Fagan, *People of the Earth: An Introduction to World Prehistory,* 7th ed. (New York: HarperCollins, 1992). Excellent introduction to the prehistory of Europe and Asia.

R. Dale Guthrie, *The Nature of Paleolithic Art* (Chicago: University of Chicago Press, 2005). A comprehensive and challenging reconsideration of prehistoric art that argues for the wide participation of all members of society in the creative process.

Mesopotamia: Between the Two Rivers

Jean Bottero, *Everyday Life in Ancient Mesopotamia* (Baltimore: Johns Hopkins University Press, 2001). Social history of Mesopotamia by a leading expert.

Gwendolyn Leick, *The Babylonians, An Introduction* (New York: Routledge, 2003). General introduction to Babylonian history.

Jane McIntosh and John Weeks, *Ancient Mesopotamia: New Perspectives* (Santa Barbara, CA.: ABC-CLIO, 2005). A comprehensive introduction to Mesopotamian society and culture by an archaeologist.

O. Neugebauer, *The Exact Sciences in Antiquity* (New York: Dover, 1970). A series of technical essays on ancient mathematics and astronomy.

Susan Pollock, *Ancient Mesopotamia: The Eden that Never Was* (Cambridge: Cambridge University Press, 1999). An original introduction to the earliest phase of Mesopotamian history.

The Gift of the Nile

Cyril Aldred, *The Egyptians,* 3rd rev. ed. (New York: Thames & Hudson, 1998). Readable general history of ancient Egypt focusing on culture.

Wolfram Grajetzki, *The Middle Kingdom of Ancient Egypt: History, Archaeology and Society* (London : Duckworth, 2006). An Egyptologist summarizes two centuries of scholarship on this classic period of Egyptian history.

Erik Hornung, *History of Ancient Egypt: An Introduction* (Ithaca, NY: Cornell University Press, 1999). A brief survey of Egypt by a great European scholar.

Ian Shaw, ed. *The Oxford History of Ancient Egypt* (Oxford: Oxford University Press, 2000). Comprehensive collaborative survey of ancient Egypt.

Between Two Worlds

John Curtis, *Ancient Persia* (Cambridge, MA: Harvard University Press, 1990). Brief overview of ancient Iran.

Roland De Vaux, *Ancient Israel: Its Life and Institutions* (Grand Rapids, MI: Wm. B. Eerdmans Publishing Co., 1997). A classic account of religious and social life in ancient Israel.

Henry Jackson Flanders, Robert Wilson Crapps, and David Anthony Smith, *People of the Covenant: An Introduction to the Hebrew Bible,* 4th ed. (New York: Oxford University Press, 1996). A balanced introduction to Hebrew and Jewish history that draws on both Jewish and Christian scholarship.

A. T. Olmstead, *History of Assyria* (Chicago: University of Chicago Press, 1975). The fundamental survey of the Assyrian Empire.

For a list of additional titles related to this chapter's topics, please see http://www.ablongman.com/kishlansky.

CHAPTER 2

EARLY GREECE, 2500–500 B.C.E.

HECUBA AND ACHILLES

THE BIRTH OF GREEK CIVILIZATION

THE VISUAL RECORD

The wrath of the great warrior Achilles is the subject of Homer's *Iliad,* the first and greatest epic poem of Greece, written shortly after 750 B.C.E. Angered by a perceived slight to his honor, Achilles sulks in his tent while the other Achaeans, or Greeks, fight a desperate and losing battle against their enemies, the defenders of the city of Troy. Only after his friend Patroclus is slain by the Trojan prince Hector does Achilles return to the battle to avenge his fallen comrade and propel the Achaeans to victory. Near the end of the epic, after he has slain Hector in hand-to-hand combat, Achilles ties his foe's body to the back of his chariot and drags it three times around Patroclus's tomb to appease his friend's spirit. The gods are horrified at this demeaning treatment of the body of one who had always been faithful in his sacrifices. Zeus, the chief god, sends his messenger Iris to Hector's mourning parents—his father, Priam, king of Troy, and his mother, Hecuba. Iris urges them to ransom their son's body from Achilles. Moved by the message, Priam goes to Achilles' tent to plead for Hector's body. Achilles, moved by pity and grief for his own father and for Patroclus, grants the old king his request, and Priam returns in sorrow to Troy, bearing the body of his son for burial.

The first portions of this episode are brilliantly rendered on the side of the sixth-century B.C.E. *hydria,* or water pitcher, shown here. At the center, Achilles leaps into his chariot. The naked body of Hector stretches below him, and the chariot rushes around the *tumulus,* or burial mound, of Achilles' friend, represented by the white hill to the right. Above it, the small winged spirit of Patroclus watches. In death he is a pale reflection, a shade of his former self, still attired in the clothing and arms of a warrior. But even as Achilles carries out his deed of vengeance, Iris, the winged messenger of Zeus, rushes to Hector's parents, who are shown under a columned portico, which represents Troy. Typically, the artist has taken some liberty with the story. It is not the grieving father the artist has chosen to feature but rather Hecuba, Hector's disconsolate mother. In a vivid manner, totally alien to previous artistic traditions, the Greek artist, like the Greek poet, has captured the essentials of human tragedy.

For all its violent action, the *Iliad* is concerned less with what people do than with how they face the great moments of their life, their time of suffering, their time of death. Hector died well and in so doing won immortal fame from his enemies, the Greeks. Achilles eventually acted well and in his encounter with Priam faced the universal elements of human destiny: life, love, suffering, endurance, and death. Such sentiments, expressed by Homer, became an enduring heritage of Greek civilization and, through it, the civilization of the West. In the small, fragile, and violent communities of Greek speakers spread across the Mediterranean, citizen soldiers first struggled with these and other fundamental issues that have set the agenda for the West to the present day.

LOOKING AHEAD

In this chapter, we will explore the first Greek-speaking societies in the Eastern Mediterranean, their collapse, and then the emergence of a new and powerful form of civilization created in the cities of Archaic Greece.

■ Achilles dishonors the body of Hector while Hecuba looks on in this sixth-century B.C.E. hydria.

CHAPTER OUTLINE

- GREECE IN THE BRONZE AGE TO 800 B.C.E.
  Islands of Peace ▪ Mainland of War ▪ The Dark Age
- ARCHAIC GREECE, 800–500 B.C.E.
  Ethnos and Polis ▪ Technology of Writing and Warfare ▪ Colonists and Tyrants ▪ Gender and Power ▪ Gods and Mortals ▪ Myth and Reason ▪ Investigation and Speculation ▪ Art and the Individual
- A TALE OF THREE CITIES
  Wealthy Corinth ▪ Martial Sparta ▪ Democratic Athens
- THE COMING OF PERSIA AND THE END OF THE ARCHAIC AGE

GREECE IN THE BRONZE AGE TO 800 B.C.E.

Early in the *Iliad* Homer pauses to list the captains and ships of the besieging forces. The roll call of heroes and their homelands is more than a literary device. It is the distant echo of a vanished world, the world of "the goodly citadel of Athens, wealthy Corinth, Knossos, and Gortys of the great walls, and the established fortress of Mycenae." The poet lived in an age of illiterate warrior herdsmen, of impoverished, scattered, and sparsely populated villages. Still, in the depths of this "Dark Age"—roughly from 1200 to 800 B.C.E.—the distant memory of a time of rich palaces, teeming cities, and powerful kings lived on. Homer and his contemporaries could not know that these confused memories were of the last great Bronze Age (ca. 3500–1200 B.C.E.) civilization of the Mediterranean. Still less could they have imagined that at the very time when they were singing of the wrath of Achilles and the lost glory of his age, they were also preparing the foundations of a far greater and lasting civilization, that of classical Greece.

Unlike the rich floodplains of Mesopotamia and Egypt, Greece is a stark world of mountains and sea. The rugged terrain of Greece, only 10 percent of which is flat, and the scores of islands that dot the Aegean and Ionian seas favor the development of small, self-contained agricultural societies. The Greek climate is uncertain, constantly threatening Greek farmers with failure. While the temperature remains fairly constant, rainfall varies enormously from year to year, island to island, valley to valley. Arid summers alternate with cool, wet winters. Greek farmers struggled to produce the Mediterranean triad of grains, olives, and wine, which first began to dominate agriculture around 3000 B.C.E. Wheat, barley, and beans were the staples of Greek life. Chickpeas, lentils, and bread, supplemented with olive oil, wine, and cheese, filled the stomachs of Greek farmers and townspeople. Only on rare holidays did ordinary folk see fish or perhaps some mutton on their tables. When the rains came too soon or too late, even bread and beans might be missing. The constant fluctuations in climate and weather from region to region helped break down the geographical isolation by forcing isolated communities to build contacts with a wider world in order to survive.

Islands of Peace

To Homer, the Greeks were all Achaeans, whether they came from the Greek mainland, the islands in the Aegean Sea, or the coast of Asia Minor. Since the late nineteenth century, archaeologists have discerned three fairly distinct late Bronze Age cultures—the Cycladic, the Minoan, and the Mycenaean—that flourished in the Mediterranean prior to the end of the twelfth century B.C.E.

The Cyclades. The first culture appeared on the Cyclades, the rugged islands strewn across the bottom of the Aegean from the Greek mainland to the coast of Asia Minor. As early as 2500 B.C.E., artisans in small settlements on the islands of Naxos and Melos developed a high level of metallurgical and artistic skill. Veins of lead and silver run through the hills of the Cyclades. Local people perfected techniques of working the metals, methods that later traveled both north to the mainland and south to Crete. The most impressive and enigmatic remains of the **Cycladic culture** (ca. 3000–ca. 1550 B.C.E.) are marble figurines, both male and female, found in large numbers in graves on the mainland, on the islands themselves, and in Asia Minor. These severe geometrical figures presumably had a religious significance that is now unknown.

Cycladic society was not concentrated into towns, nor apparently was it particularly warlike. Many of the largest Cycladic settlements were unfortified. Cycladic religion, to judge from fragments of large clay statues of female figures found in a temple on the island of Ceos, focused on female deities, perhaps fertility goddesses. This early Bronze Age society faded slowly and imperceptibly, but not before influencing its neighbors, especially Crete, the large Mediterranean island to the south. Crete, beginning around 2500 B.C.E., developed a remarkably sophisticated centralized civilization termed Minoan after the legendary King Minos.

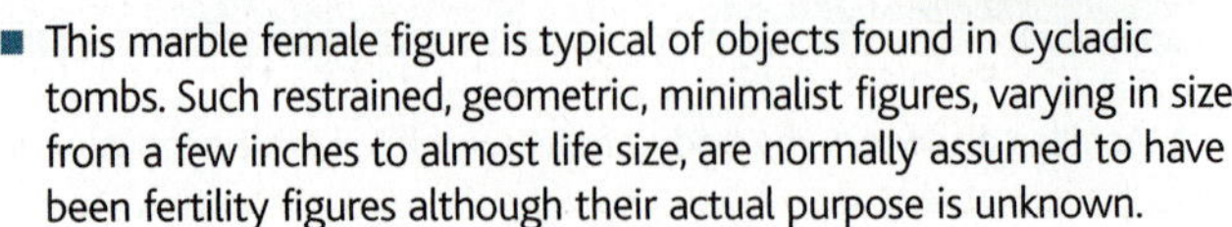

This marble female figure is typical of objects found in Cycladic tombs. Such restrained, geometric, minimalist figures, varying in size from a few inches to almost life size, are normally assumed to have been fertility figures although their actual purpose is unknown.

Minoan Crete. Knowledge of **Minoan civilization** burst upon the modern world suddenly in 1899. In that year the English archaeologist Sir Arthur Evans made the first of a series of extraordinary archaeological discoveries at Knossos, the legendary palace of Minos. Since then, additional centers have been found on the southern and eastern coasts of the island, as well as at Chania in the northwest. Crete's location between the civilizations of the Fertile Crescent and the barbarian worlds of the north and west made the island a natural point of exchange and amalgamation of cultures. Still, during the golden age of Crete, roughly between 2000 and 1550 B.C.E., the island developed unique traditions. Great palace complexes were constructed at Knossos, Phaistos, Hagia Triada, and elsewhere on the island. They appear as a maze of storerooms, workrooms, and living quarters clustered around a central square. The walls of the palaces still display frescoes that present a vivid image of Cretan life in the late Bronze Age. Some frescoes depict crowds of prosperous Cretans watching as court ladies dance under olive trees or as male and female athletes practice the deadly sport of vaulting over the backs of ferocious bulls. Other wall paintings show aristocratic women, elaborately clothed in sumptuous dresses that leave

MAP DISCOVERY

Greece in the Bronze Age

What geographical characteristics distinguished Cycladic, Minoan, and Mycenaean civilizations? Given its location, what older civilizations might have exerted a major influence on the civilization of Crete?

their breasts exposed, engaged in conversation while the athletic spectacle unfurls before them.

Palace bureaucrats, using a unique form of syllabic writing known as Linear A which has never been fully deciphered, controlled agricultural production and distribution as well as the work of skilled artisans in their surrounding areas. A well-maintained road system connected the cities across the island, especially between Knossos, the capital, and Phaistos in the south, which may have been a winter palace. Towns with well-organized street plans, drainage systems, and clear hierarchies of elite and lesser homes dotted the landscape.

Cretan Society and Religion. Like other ancient civilizations, Minoan Crete was a strongly stratified system in which the vast peasantry paid a heavy tribute in olive oil and other produce. Tribute or taxes flowed to local and regional palaces and ultimately to Knossos, which stood at the pinnacle of a four-tier network uniting the island. To some extent, the palace elites redistributed this wealth back down the system through their patterns of consumption. However, the abundance of luxury imports at Knossos, Phaistos, and elsewhere indicates that much of the wealth amassed by the elite was consumed by the great numbers of palace servants and artisans or went abroad to pay for the Egyptian and Syrian luxury goods, Italian metal, and Baltic amber found in abundance in the ruins.

Although the system may have been exploitive, it was not militaristic. None of the palaces or towns of Crete was fortified. The delicate and naturalistic frescoes and statues never depict warriors, weapons, or battles. Nor was the cult of the ruler particularly emphasized. The throne room at Knossos is small, and none of its decorations suggest the sort of royal aggrandizement typical in the Mesopotamian, Hittite, or Egyptian worlds. Its central feature is the modest throne decorated with twin griffins. A key to this unique social tone may be the Cretan religion, and with it the unusually high status of women. Although male gods received veneration, Cretans particularly worshiped female deities, whose cults were centered in some 25 caves scattered across the island. Here and at the palaces, bulls and bulls' horns as well as the double-headed ax, or *labrys*, played an important—if today mysterious—role in the worship of these gods. Chief among the female deities was the mother goddess, who was the source of good and evil. One must, however, be careful not to paint too idyllic an image of Cretan religion. Children's bones found in excavations of the palace of Knossos and elsewhere show knife cuts that are traces of butchering and the removal of slices of flesh.

Although evidence such as the frequent appearance of women participating in or watching public ceremonies and the widespread worship of female deities cannot lead to the conclusion that Minoan society was a form of matriarchy, it does suggest that Minoan civilization differed considerably from the floodplain civilizations of the Near East and the societies developing on the mainland. At least until the fourteenth century B.C.E., Cretan society was unique. Both men and women seem to have shared important roles in religious and public life and together built a structured society without the need for vast armies or warrior kings.

■ The throne room of the Cretan Palace of Minos, in Knossos.

Around 1450 B.C.E., a wave of destruction engulfed all of the Cretan cities except Knossos, which finally met destruction around 1375 B.C.E. The causes of this catastrophe continue to inspire historical debate. Some argue that a natural disaster such as an earthquake or the eruption of a powerful volcano on Thera was responsible for the destruction, but the chronology of the two do not coincide exactly. More likely, given the martial traditions of the continent and their total absence on Crete, the destruction was the work of mainland Greeks taking control of Knossos and other Minoan centers. An Egyptian tomb painting from the fifteenth century B.C.E. graphically illustrates the transition. An ambassador in Cretan dress was overpainted by one wearing a kilt characteristic of that worn by mainland Greeks. Around this same time, true warrior graves equipped with weapons and armor begin to appear on Crete and at Knossos for the first time. Following the violent conquest, only Knossos and Phaistos were rebuilt, presumably by Greek lords who had eliminated the other political centers on the island. A final destruction hit Knossos around 1200 B.C.E.

Mainland of War

The contrast between the islands and the Greek mainland was particularly marked. Around 1600 B.C.E., a new and powerful warrior civilization arose on the Peloponnesus at Mycenae. The only remains of the first phase of this civilization are 30 graves found at the bottom of deep shafts arranged in two circles, but they tell of a rich, powerful, and warlike elite. The

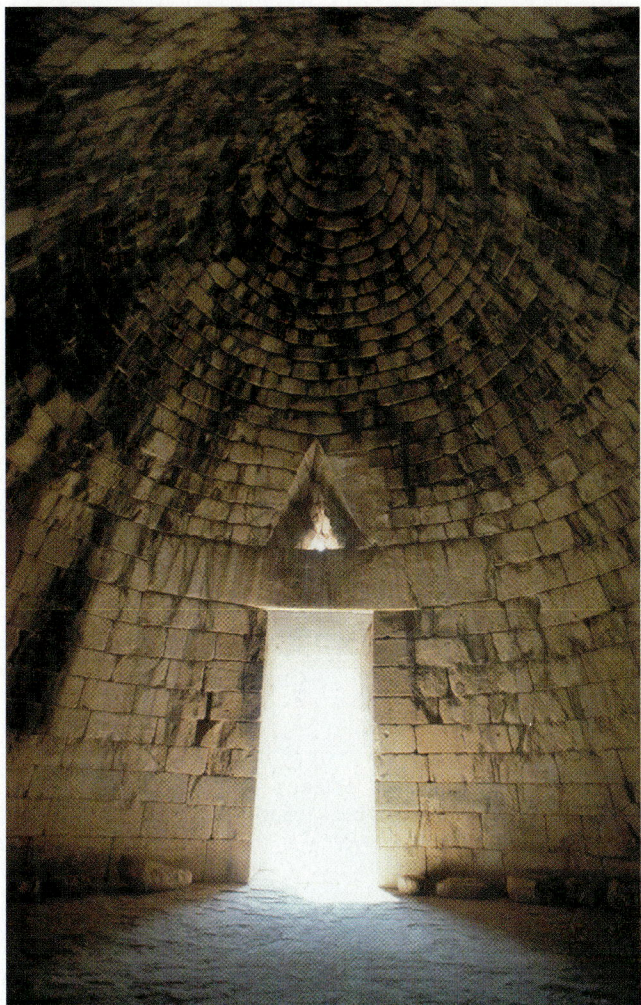

■ Tholos tomb in Mycene.

delicate gold ornaments, bronze swords, spearheads, knives, axes, armor, and utensils that fill the graves emphasize the warrior lives of their occupants. By 1500 B.C.E., mainland Greeks were using huge **tholoi**, or beehive-shaped tombs, for royal burials. These structures were magnificent achievements of architecture and masonry, far beyond anything seen previously in Europe. The largest, found at Mycenae, is 48 feet in diameter and 43 feet from the floor to its vaulted ceiling. This great vault, capped by a stone weighing more than 100 tons, was the largest vault in the world for more than 1600 years, surpassed only by Roman architecture at the height of the Roman Empire. More than 50 such tombs have been found on the Greek mainland, as have the remains of more than 500 villages and great palaces at Mycenae, Tiryns, Athens, Thebes, Gla, and Pylos. The entire civilization, which encompassed not only the Greek mainland but also parts of the coast of Asia Minor, is called **Mycenaean,** although there is no evidence that the city of Mycenae actually ruled all of Greece.

The Mycenaeans quickly adopted artisanal and architectural techniques from neighboring cultures, especially from the Hittites and from Crete. However, the Mycenaeans incorporated the techniques into a distinctive tradition of their own. Unlike the open Cretan palaces and towns, Mycenaean palaces were strongly walled fortresses. From these palaces Mycenaean kings, aided by a small military elite, organized and controlled the collection of taxes and tribute from subordinate towns and rural districts. Through their palace administrators, they controlled the production of bronze, the weaving of woolen cloth, and the extensive maritime trade in agricultural produce with other regions.

Mycenaean administrators also adopted the Linear A script of Crete, transforming it to write their own language, a Greek dialect, in a writing known as **Linear B.** Linear B appears to have been used almost exclusively for record keeping in palaces—indicating amounts of tribute, the organization of workers, and the quantities of weapons, sheep, and slaves engaged in various religious and palace duties.

The Dark Age

■ Dark Age vase, with geometric design typical of artifacts from that era.

Mycenaean domination did not last for long. Around 1200 B.C.E., many of the mainland and island fortresses and cities were sacked and totally destroyed. Centralized government, literacy, urban life—civilization itself—disappeared from Greece for more than 300 years. Why and how this **Dark Age** occurred is one of the great mysteries of world history.

In later centuries the Greeks believed that following the Trojan War, new peoples, especially the Dorians, had migrated into Greece, destroying Mycenae and most of the other Achaean cities. More recently, some historians have argued that catastrophic climatic change, volcanic eruptions, or some other natural disaster wrecked the cities and brought famine and tremendous social unrest in its wake. Neither theory is accurate. No single invasion or natural disaster caused the collapse of the civilizations of late Bronze Age Greece. Mycenaean Greece was destroyed neither by barbarian invaders nor by acts of God. It self-destructed. Its disintegration was part of the widespread crisis affecting the eastern Mediterranean in the twelfth century B.C.E. (see Chapter 1, p. 00). The pyramid of Mycenaean lordship, built by small military elites commanding maritime commercial networks, was always threatened with collapse. Overpopulation, the fragility of the agrarian base, the risks of overspecialization in cash crops such as grain in Messenia and sheep raising in Crete, and rivalry among states all made Mycenaean culture vulnerable. The disintegration of the Hittite Empire and the near-collapse of the Egyptian Empire also disrupted Mediterranean commerce, exacerbating hostilities among Greek states. As internal warfare raged, the delicate structures of elite lordship disappeared in the mutual sackings and destructions of the palace fortresses. The Dark Age poet Hesiod (ca. 800 B.C.E.), though writing about his own time, probably got it about right:

Father will have no common bond with son
Neither will guest with host, nor friend with friend
The brother-love of past days will be gone. . . .
Men will destroy the towns of other men.

CHRONOLOGY

Greece in the Bronze Age

ca. 2500 B.C.E.	Beginning of Minoan civilization in Crete
ca. 2000–1500 B.C.E.	Golden Age of Crete
ca. 1600 B.C.E.	Beginning of Mycenaean civilization in Greece
ca. 1450 B.C.E.	Cretan cities, except Knossos, destroyed
ca. 1375 B.C.E.	Knossos destroyed
ca. 1200–800 B.C.E.	Greek Dark Age
ca. 1200 B.C.E.	Mycenaean sites in Greece destroyed; Knossos destroyed again
ca. 1100–1000 B.C.E.	Writing disappears from Greece

■ A golden funeral mask (ca. 1500 B.C.E.) found in the royal tombs of Mycenae. The mask was once thought to be the likeness of Agamemnon, the king of Mycenae in the Homeric epics.

With the collapse of the administrative and political system on which Mycenaean civilization was built, the tiny elite that had ruled it vanished as well. Some of the rulers probably migrated to the islands, especially Cyprus, and to the eastern Mediterranean. Others took to piracy, alternately raiding the coast from Anatolia to Egypt and serving as mercenaries in foreign armies. What later Greeks remembered as the Trojan War may have been a cloudy recollection of the last raids of freebooters along the edge of the collapsing Hittite Empire. From roughly 1200 until 800 B.C.E., the Aegean world entered what is generally termed the Dark Age, a confused and little-known period during which Greece returned to a more primitive level of culture and society.

A New Material Culture. In the wake of the Mycenaean collapse, bands of northerners moved slowly into the Peloponnesus while other Greeks migrated out from the mainland to the islands and the coast of Asia Minor. As these tribal groups merged with the indigenous populations, they gave certain regions distinctive dialectic and cultural characteristics. Thus the Dorians settled in much of the Peloponnesus, Crete, and southwest Asia Minor. Ionians made Attica, Euboea, and the Aegean islands their home, while a mixed group called Aeolians began to migrate to central and northwest Asia Minor. As a result, from the eleventh century B.C.E., both shores of the Aegean became part of a Greek-speaking world. Still later, Greeks established colonies in what are today Ukraine, Italy, North Africa, Spain, and France. Throughout its history, Greece was less a geographical than a cultural designation. Everywhere in this world, between roughly 1100 and 1000 B.C.E., architecture, urban traditions, and even writing disappeared along with the elites whose exclusive benefit those achievements had served. The Greece of this Dark Age was much poorer, more rural, and more simply organized. It was also a society of ironworkers. Iron began to replace bronze as the most common metal for ornaments, tools, and weapons. At first this was a simple necessity. The collapse of long-distance trade deprived Greeks of access to tin and copper, the essential ingredients of bronze. Gradually, however, the quality of iron tools and weapons

THE RACE OF IRON

Hesiod (fl. ca. 800 B.C.E.), like Homer, is known only from the two poems ascribed to him, "Theogony" and "Works and Days," written at the end of the Dark Ages. In his "Works and Days," he tells of two brothers, himself and Perses, the one just and one unjust, who argue their positions before a group of kings. When the kings find in favor of the unjust brother, Hesiod describes his generation as an Age of Iron, when men lead harsh, brutal lives. And yet he counsels his brother Perses to virtue.

Focus Questions

What are the primary virtues and vices Hesiod sees in his world? What is the role of the gods in enforcing morality?

Thereafter, would that I were not among the men of the fifth generation, but either had died before or been born afterwards. For now truly is a race of iron, and men never rest from labour and sorrow by day, and from perishing by night; and the gods shall lay sore trouble upon them. But, notwithstanding, even these shall have some good mingled with their evils. The father will not agree with his children, nor the children with their father, nor guest with his host, nor comrade with comrade; nor will brother be dear to brother as aforetime. Men will dishonour their parents as they grow quickly old, and will carp at them, chiding them with bitter words, hard-hearted they, not knowing the fear of the gods. They will not repay their aged parents the cost of their nurture, for might shall be their right: and one man will sack another's city. There will be no favour for the man who keeps his oath or for the just or for the good; but rather men will praise the evil-doer and his violent dealing. Strength will be right and reverence will cease to be; and the wicked will hurt the worthy man, speaking false words against him, and will swear an oath upon them. Envy, foul-mouthed, delighting in evil, with scowling face, will go along with wretched men one and all. Bitter sorrows will be left for mortal men, and there will be no help against evil. [. . .] (ll. 170–201)

But you, Perses, listen to right and do not foster violence; for violence is bad for a poor man. Even the prosperous cannot easily bear its burden, but is weighed down under it when he has fallen into delusion. The better path is to go by on the other side towards justice; for Justice beats Outrage when she comes at length to the end of the race. But only when he has suffered does the fool learn this. For Oath keeps pace with wrong judgments. There is a noise when Justice is being dragged in the way where those who devour bribes and give sentence with crooked judgments, take her. And she, wrapped in mist, follows to the city and haunts of the people, weeping, and bringing mischief to men, even to such as have driven her forth in that they did not deal straightly with her. (ll. 212–224)

But they who give straight judgments to strangers and to the men of the land, and go not aside from what is just, their city flourishes, and the people prosper in it: Peace, the nurse of children, is abroad in their land, and all-seeing Zeus never decrees cruel war against them. Neither famine nor disaster ever haunt men who do true justice; but lightheartedly they tend the fields which are all their care. The earth bears them victual in plenty, and on the mountains the oak bears acorns upon the top and bees in the midst. Their woolly sheep are laden with fleeces; their women bear children like their parents. They flourish continually with good things, and do not travel on ships, for the grain-giving earth bears them fruit. (ll. 225–237)

began to improve as smiths learned to work hot iron into a primitive steel.

What little is known of this period must be gleaned from archaeology and from two great epic poems written down around 750 B.C.E., near the end of the Dark Age. The archaeological record is bleak. Pictorial representation of humans and animals almost disappears. Luxury goods and most imports are gone from tombs. Gold ornaments and jewelry are so rare that they may have come from some Mycenaean hoard found by Dark Age Greeks rather than from contemporary artisans. Pottery made at the beginning of the Dark Age shows little innovation, crudely imitating forms of Mycenaean production.

Gradually, beginning in the eleventh century B.C.E., things began to change a bit. New geometric forms of decoration begin to appear on pottery. New types of iron pins, weapons, and decorations appeared that owe little or nothing to the Mycenaean tradition. Cultural changes accompanied these material changes. Around the middle of the eleventh century B.C.E., Greeks in some locations stopped burying their dead and began to practice cremation. Whatever the meaning of these changes, they signaled something new on the shores of the Aegean.

The Evidence of Homer. The two epic poems—the *Iliad* and the *Odyssey*—hint at this something new. The *Iliad* is the older poem, dating probably to the second half of the eighth century B.C.E. The *Odyssey* dates from perhaps 50 years later. Traditionally ascribed to Homer, the epics were actually the work of oral bards, or performers who composed as they chanted, weaving the tale of traditional lines and expressions as they went along.

The world in which the action of the Homeric epics takes place was already passing away when the poems were composed, but the world described is not really that of the late Bronze Age. Although the poems explicitly harken back to the Mycenaean age, much of the description of life, society, and culture actually reflects Dark Age conditions. Thus Homer's heroes were petty kings, chieftains, and nobles, whose position rested on their wealth, measured in land and flocks, on personal prowess, on networks of kin and allies, and on military followings. The Homeric hero Odysseus is typical of the Dark Age chieftains. In the *Iliad* and the *Odyssey* he is king of Ithaca, a small island off the west coast of Greece. He had inherited his kingship from his father, but he derived his real authority from his skills as a speaker and warrior. To the Homeric poets he was "goodly Odysseus" as well as "the man of wiles" and "the waster of cities." He retained command of his men only as long as he could lead them to victory in raids against their neighbors, which formed the most honorable source of wealth. Odysseus describes his departure for home after the fall of Troy with pride:

Iliad

> *The wind that bore me from Ilios brought me . . . to Ismarus, whereupon I sacked their city and slew the people. And from the city we took their wives and much goods, and divided them among us, that none through me might go lacking his proper share.*

When present, the king was judge, gift giver, lawgiver, and commander. But when he was absent, no legal or governmental institutions preserved his authority. Instead the nobility—lesser warriors who were constantly at odds with the king—sought to take his place. In the *Odyssey* only their mutual rivalry saves Odysseus's wife, Penelope, from being forced to marry one of these haughty aristocrats eager to replace the king.

The nobles—warriors wealthy enough to possess horses and weapons—lived to prove their strength and honor in combat against their equals, which was the one true test of social value. The existence of chieftains such as Odysseus was a threat to their

HECTOR AND ANDROMACHE

The Trojan hero Hector is almost as central to the Iliad *of Homer as is Achilles. Unlike the latter, Hector is a dutiful, reliable support to his city and to Andromache, who is not only his wife but his closest and dearest companion. The description of their last meeting is one of the great expressions of the heroic ethos and of the bonds of man and woman in that culture.*

Focus Questions

How would you describe the relationship between Hector and Andromache? What is the ideal future that Hector wishes for his son?

At last his own generous wife came running to meet him,
Andromache, the daughter of high-hearted Eëation. . . .
She came to him there, and beside her went an attendant carrying
the boy in the fold of her bosom, a little child, only a baby,
Hector's son, the admired, beautiful as a star shining. . . .
Andromache, stood close beside him, letting her tears fall,
and clung to his hand and called him by name and spoke to him:
"Dearest, your own great strength will be your death, and you
have no pity on your little son, nor on me, ill-starred, who soon must be your widow." . . .
Then tall Hector of the shining helm answered her: "All these
things are in my mind also, lady; yet I would feel deep shame
before the Trojans, and the Trojan women with trailing garments,
if like a coward I were to shrink aside from fighting. . . .
But it is not so much the pain to come of the Trojans that
troubles me . . . as the thought of you, when some bronze-armored Achaian leads you off, taking away your day of liberty in
tears; and in Argos you must work at the loom of another." . . .
Then taking up his dear son he tossed him about in his arms and
kissed him, and lifted his voice in prayer to Zeus and the other immortals:
"Zeus, and you other immortals, grant that this boy, who is my
son, may be as I am, pre-eminent among the Trojans,
great in strength, as I am, and rule strongly over Ilion;
And someday let them say of him: 'He is better by far than his father,'
as he comes from the fighting; and let him kill his enemy
and bring home the blooded spoils, and delight the heart of his mother."

From the *Iliad* of Homer, Book VI.

honor, and by the eighth century B.C.E., the aristocracy had eliminated kings in most places. Ranking beneath the proud warriors, as a shadowy mass, was the populace. Some of this group, like Odysseus's faithful servants who aided him in defeating his enemies upon his return home, were slaves. Most were shepherds or farmers too mired down in the laborious work of subsistence agriculture to participate in the heroic lifestyle of their social betters. Still, even the populace was not entirely excluded from public life. Odysseus's son Telemachus summoned an assembly of the people to listen to his complaints against the noble suitors of his mother. This does not mean that the assembly was particularly effective. They listened to both sides and did nothing. Still, a time was coming when changes in society would give a new and hitherto unimagined power to the silent farmers and herdsmen of the Dark Age.

From the Bronze Age civilizations, speakers of Greek had inherited distant memories of an original, highly organized urban civilization grafted onto the rural, aristocratic warrior society of the Dark Age. Most importantly, this common, dimly recollected past gave all Greek-speaking inhabitants of the Mediterranean world common myths, values, and identity.

ARCHAIC GREECE, 800–500 B.C.E.

Between roughly 800 and 500 B.C.E., extraordinary changes took place in the Greek world. The descendants of the farmers and herdsmen of Homer's Dark Age brought about a revolution in political organization, artistic traditions, intellectual values, and social structures. In a burst of creativity forged in conflict and competition, they invented politics, invented abstract thought, invented the individual. Greeks of the Archaic Age (ca. 800–500 B.C.E.) set the agenda for the rest of Western history.

The first sign of radical change in Greece was a major increase in population in the eighth century B.C.E. In Attica, for example, between 780 and 720 B.C.E. the population increased perhaps sevenfold. Similar rapid population growth occurred throughout the rest of the Greek world. The reasons for this extraordinary increase are obscure, but it may have resulted from a shift from herding to agriculture. In any case, the consequences were enormous. First, population increase meant more villages and towns, greater communication among them, and thus more rapid circulation of ideas and skills. Second, the rising population placed impossible demands on the agricultural system of much of Greece, overcrowding the land and forcing many farmers into poverty and many others into migration. Third, it led to greater division of labor and, with an increasingly diverse population, to fundamental changes in political systems. The old structure of loosely organized tribes and chieftains became inadequate to deal with the more complex nature of the new society.

The multiplicity of political and social forms developing in the Archaic Age set the framework for the first flowering of Greek culture. Economic and political transformations laid the basis for intellectual advance by creating a broad class with the prosperity to enjoy sufficient leisure for thought and creative activity. At the same time, literacy and local pride allowed the new citizen populations of the Greek cities to participate in intellectual and cultural activities in an unprecedented manner. Finally, maritime relations brought together people and ideas from around the Greek world, cross-fertilizing artists and intellectuals in a way never before seen.

Ethnos and Polis

In general, two forms of political organization developed in response to the population explosion of the eighth century B.C.E. On the mainland and in much of the western Peloponnesus, people continued to live in large territorial units called *ethne* (sing. *ethnos*). In each **ethnos** people lived in villages and small towns scattered across a wide region. Common customs and a common religion focusing on a central religious sanctuary united them. The ethnos was governed by an elite, or **oligarchy** (meaning "rule by the few"), made up of major landowners who met from time to time in one or another town within the region. This form of government, which had its roots in the Dark Age, continued to exist throughout the classical period.

A much more innovative form of political organization, which developed on the shores of the Aegean and on the islands, was the **polis** (pl. *poleis*), or city-state. Initially, *polis* meant simply "citadel." Villages clustered around fortifications, which were both protective structures and cult centers for specific deities. These high, fortified sites—*acropolis* means "high citadel"—were

■ This sixth-century B.C.E. terra cotta figure from Thebes represents a farmer plowing with a yoke of oxen, an essential agricultural activity in Archaic Greece.

MAP DISCOVERY

Greek Cities and Colonies of the Archaic Age

Where are the areas of Greek settlement and major colonies in the Archaic Age? What does the location of Greek settlements tell us about the relationship between Greek culture and geography? What regions of Europe and the Near East lacked Greek colonies? Why?

sacred to specific gods: in Athens and Sparta, to Athena; in Argos and Samos, to Hera; in Corinth and Thermon, to Apollo. In addition to protection, the polis offered a marketplace, or *agora*, where farmers and artisans could trade and conduct business. The rapid population growth of the eighth century B.C.E. led to the fusion of the villages and the formation of real towns. Each town was independent, each was ruled by a monarch or an oligarchy, and each controlled the surrounding region, the inhabitants of which were on an equal footing with the townspeople. At times of political or military crisis, the rulers might summon an assembly of the free males of the community to the agora to participate in or to witness the decision-making process.

Technology of Writing and Warfare

The general model of the polis may have been borrowed from the eastern Mediterranean Phoenicians, the merchant society responsible for much of the contact Greeks of the eighth century B.C.E. had with the outside world. On the other hand, by 800 B.C.E. the Greeks themselves had a permanent trading post at Al Mina on the Syrian coast and thus were in direct contact with the traditions of the Near East. The Phoenicians were certainly the source of an equally important innovation that appeared in Greece at the same time: the reintroduction of writing. The Linear B script, which the Mycenaeans had used exclusively for administrative and bureaucratic purposes, had entirely disappeared, along with the complex palace systems that it had served. Sometime in the eighth century B.C.E., Greeks adopted the Phoenician writing alphabetic system. But this time the purpose was not primarily central administrative record keeping. From the start, this writing system was intended for private, personal use and was available to virtually anyone. In a society fascinated with the oral traditions of the heroic past, it is no surprise that the Greeks radically transformed the Phoenician system, making its Semitic characters into arbitrary sounds and adding vowel notation in order to record poetry. Soon they were using the writing system to indicate ownership of objects, to record religious and secular vows, and even to entertain.

Greek Poetry

Within the polis, political power was not the monopoly of the aristocracy. The gradual expansion of the politically active population resulted largely from the demands of warfare. In the Dark Age, warfare had been dominated by heavily armed, mounted aristocrats who engaged their equals in one-on-one combat. In the Archaic Age, such individual combat between aristocratic warriors gave way to battles decided by the use of well-disciplined ranks of infantrymen called *phalanges* (sing. **phalanx**). Properly disciplined, the phalanx could withstand attacks of better-equipped aristocratic warriors. And, although few Greeks could afford costly weapons, armor, and horses, between 25 and 40 percent of the landowners could provide the shields, lances, and bronze armor needed by the infantrymen, or **hoplites.** These foot soldiers developed their own warrior pride, equal to but differing from that of the aristocrat. In the words of Tyrtaeus, a poet of the mid-seventh century B.C.E., the hoplite was to "stand near and take the enemy, strike with long spear or sword, set foot by foot, lean shield on shield, crest upon crest, helmet on helmet."

The democratization of war led gradually to the democratization of political life. Those who brought victory in the phalanx were unwilling to accept total domination by the aristocracy in the agora. Growing demands of the common people, combined with demographic expansion and economic changes, created enormous social and political tensions throughout the Greek world. The rapid growth of the urban population, the increasing impoverishment of the rural peasantry, and the rise of a new class of wealthy merchant commoners were all challenges that traditional forms of government failed to meet. Everywhere traditional aristocratic rule was being undermined, and cities searched for ways to resolve this social conflict. No one solution

IMAGE DISCOVERY

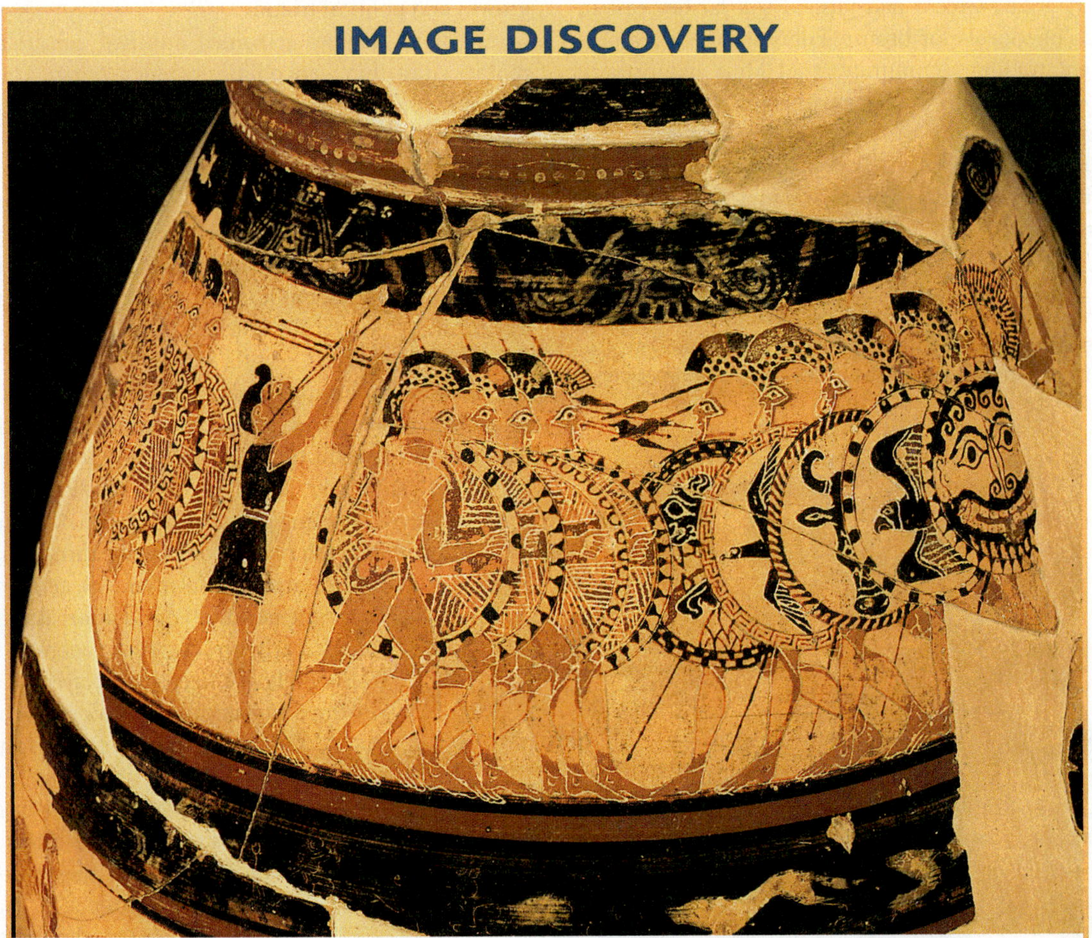

A Revolution in Warfare

A Corinthian vase showing hoplites marching into battle. Look at the weapons, equipment, and organization of the two opposing lines. How would the cost of equipping a hoplite compare with that of a cavalryman? What kind of tactical training and discipline was required in order to ensure success on the battlefield? How might this training and investment carry beyond the battlefield?

emerged, and one of the outstanding achievements of Archaic Greece was the almost limitless variety of political forms elaborated in its city-states.

Colonists and Tyrants

Colonization and tyranny were two intertwined results of the political and social turmoil of the seventh century B.C.E. Population growth, changes in economy, and opposition to aristocratic power led Greeks to seek change externally through emigration and internally through political restructuring.

Late in the eleventh century B.C.E., Greeks began to migrate to new homes on the islands and along the coast of Asia Minor in search of commercial advantages or a better life. Many of these communities, such as Rhodes, Miletus, Ephesus, and Erythrae, probably renewed older Greek traditions from the Mycenaean period. By the eighth century B.C.E., Greeks had pushed still farther east in search of sources for bronze. Euboeans created a permanent trading community at Al Mina in northern Syria, and Greeks established themselves in other eastern towns such as Tarsus.

Ephesus

Beginning around 750 B.C.E., a new form of colonization began in the western Mediterranean. The impetus for this expansion was not primarily trade, but rather the need to reduce the population pressure at home. The first noteworthy colony, Cumae near Naples, was founded by emigrants from Euboea. Soon other cities sent colonists to southern Italy and Sicily. Chalcis founded Messina, Corinth founded Syracuse, and Achaea founded Sybaris, to name a few. Before long, the colonies themselves became mother cities, sending out parties to found still other colonies. Around 700 B.C.E., similar colonies appeared in the northeast in Thrace, on the shores of the Black Sea, and as far away as the mouth of the Don River. Colonists were not always volunteers. At Thera, for example, young men were chosen by lot to colonize Cyrene. The penalty for refusing to participate was death and confiscation of property. According to tradition, Sparta sent illegitimate sons to found Tarentum, and other cities forced political dissidents to emigrate. Usually colonists included only single males, the most volatile portion of the community. Colonies were thus a safety valve to release the pressures of population growth and political friction.

■ Greek commerce expanded along with the colonies. In the painting on the interior of the Arkesilas Cup, dating from around 560 B.C.E., the king of Cyrene, a Greek colony in North Africa, is shown supervising the preparation of hemp, or flax, for export.

Although colonies remained attached culturally to their mother cities, they were politically independent. The men who settled them were warriors as well as farmers or traders, and they carved out their new cities at the expense of the local population. Intermarriage was the norm, but so was the conquest and enslavement of much of the original population, followed by a gradual absorption of natives into Greek civilization.

Colonization relieved some of the population pressure on Greek communities, but it did not solve the problem of political conflict. As opposition to entrenched aristocracies grew, first in Argos, then at Corinth, Sicyon, Elis, Mytilene, and elsewhere, individuals supported by those opposed to aristocratic rule seized power. These rulers were known as **tyrants,** a term that originally meant the same as "king." In the course of the later sixth century B.C.E., tyrant came to designate one who had achieved supreme power without benefit of official position. Often, the rise to power came through popularity with hoplite armies. However, the term tyrant did not carry the negative connotation associated with it today. Early tyrants were generally welcomed by their fellow citizens and played a crucial role in the destruction of aristocratic government and the creation of civic traditions.

Generally, tyrants were motivated not so much by great civic spirit as by the desire to win and maintain power. Still, to this end they weakened the power of entrenched aristocratic groups, promoted the prosperity of their supporters by protecting farmers and encouraging trade, undertook public works projects, founded colonies, and entered marriage alliances with rulers of other cities, which provided some external peace. Although they stood outside the traditional organs of government, tyrants were frequently content to govern through them, leaving magistracies and offices intact but ensuring that through elections these offices were filled with the tyrant's supporters. Thus at

Corinth, Mytilene, Athens, and elsewhere, tyrants preserved and even strengthened constitutional structures as a hedge against the return to power of aristocratic factions.

The great weakness of tyrannies was that they depended for their success on the individual qualities of the ruler. Tyrants tended to pass their powers on to their sons and, as tyrannies became hereditary, cities came to resent incompetent or excessively harsh heirs' arbitrary control of government. The process seldom took more than three generations. As popular tyranny gave way to harsh and arbitrary rule, opposition brought on civil war and the deposition or abdication of the tyrant. Gradually, tyranny acquired the meaning it bears today, and new forms of government emerged. Still, in spite of the bitter memory Greek tyranny left in people's minds, in many cities tyrants had for a time solved the crisis of political order and had cleared the way for broader participation in public life than had ever before been known.

Gender and Power

Military, political, and cultural life in the city-states became more democratic, but the democratization did not extend to women. Greek attitudes toward gender roles and sexuality were rigid. Except in a few cities and in certain religious cults, women played no public role in the life of the community. They were isolated in the portions of the home reserved for them and remained firmly under male control throughout their lives, passing from the authority of their fathers to that of their husbands. Women were to be good mothers and obedient wives, not partners or close friends. For the most part, friendship existed only between members of the same sex, and this friendship was often intensely sexual. Thus bisexuality was the norm in Greek society, although neither Greek homosexuality nor heterosexuality were the same as they are in modern society. Rather, both coexisted and formed part of a sexuality of domination by those considered superior to others in age, rank, or sex. Mature men took young boys as their lovers, helped educate them, and inspired them by word and deed to grow into ideal warriors and citizens. We know less about such practices among women, but teachers such as Sappho of Lesbos (ca. 610–ca. 580 B.C.E.), while themselves married and mothers, formed similar bonds with their pupils, even while preparing them for marriage.

Those women who were in public life were mostly slaves, frequently prostitutes. These ranged from impoverished streetwalkers to *hetairai*—educated, sophisticated courtesans who entertained men at *symposia* (sing. *symposion*), or male drinking parties and banquets, which were the centers of cultural and social life. Many female slaves were acquired by collecting and raising infant daughters who had been abandoned by impoverished families or those who simply did not want any more daughters. Greek society did not condemn or even question infanticide, prostitution, and sexual exploitation of women and slave boys. The practices formed part of the complex and varied social systems of the developing city-states.

Gods and Mortals

The Greeks and their gods were old friends—the gods of Archaic Greece were the same as those of the Mycenaeans. Greeks and gods enjoyed an ambivalent, peculiar, almost irreverent relationship. On the one hand, Greeks made regular offerings to the gods, pleaded with them for help, and gave them thanks for assistance. On the other hand, the gods were thoroughly human, sharing in an exaggerated manner not only human strengths and virtues but also weaknesses and vices.

This sixth-century B.C.E. vase shows a symposium at which three men play cottabos, a drinking game, while two hetairai entertain them with music.

Greeks offered sacrifices to the gods on altars, which were raised everywhere—in homes, in fields, in sacred groves. Normally, the priests responsible for the rituals were laypeople, often political and military leaders, but no group had the sort of monopoly on the cult of the gods enjoyed by Mesopotamian and Egyptian priests. Beginning in the Dark Age, cities dedicated open-air altars to the gods, often on the acropolis. In time, the altars were enclosed within temples. However, unlike the temples of other societies, Greek temples were houses of the gods, not centers of ritual. The earliest temples were constructed of wood or brick. Around 700 B.C.E. the first stone temples appeared, and shortly afterward the Greek temple achieved its classic form. The so-called Doric temple consisted of an oblong or rectangular room covered by a pitched roof and circled by columns. The temples, which housed a statue of the god, were otherwise largely empty. Although dedicated to the gods, temples reflected the wealth and patriotism of the city. They stood as monuments to the human community rather than to the divine.

On special occasions, festivals celebrated at sanctuaries honored the gods of the city with processions, athletic contests, and feasts. Some of the celebrations were local, others involved the whole polis or ethnos, and still others drew participants from all of the Greek world. The two greatest pan-Hellenic (meaning "all Greek," from *Hellas,* the Greek word for Greece) sanctuaries were Olympia and Delphi. Because both were remote from centers of political power, they were insulated from interstate rivalry and provided neutral ground on which hostile neighbors could meet in peace.

Olympia was the main sanctuary of Zeus and had been a cult site since the Bronze Age. Beginning in 776 B.C.E., wars and conflicts were temporarily suspended every four years while athletes from the whole Greek world met at Olympia to participate in contests in honor of Zeus. Initially, the sports included only footraces and wrestling. In the sixth century B.C.E., horse races and other events were added and the games at Olympia grew in importance. (See "A Closer Look: The Agony of Athletics," pp. 52–53.) The religious nature of the contests reduced neither their heated interstate rivalry nor the violence with which they were pursued. Wrestling in particular could be deadly, since matches continued until one participant signaled that he had had enough. Many wrestlers chose death rather than defeat. Victors were seen as the ideals of human society, the perfect triumph of body and soul, and Olympic victors were treated as national heroes. As Greek culture slowly spread throughout the Mediterranean world, so did participation in the Olympics, which continued for more than 1000 years, ending only in C.E. 393.

Delphi, the site of the shrine of Apollo, god of music, archery, medicine, and prophecy, was the second pan-Hellenic cult center. Like Olympia, Delphi drew athletes from the whole Greek world to its athletic contests. However, Delphi's real fame lay in its oracle, or spokeswoman for the god Apollo. From the eighth century B.C.E., before undertaking any important decision such as establishing a colony, beginning a war, or even contracting a marriage, individuals and representatives of distant cities traveled to Delphi to ask Apollo's advice through the oracle. In the turbulent seventh and sixth centuries B.C.E., Apollo was acknowledged as the expert on justice. Through his oracle, petitioners sought purification from the guilt attached to shedding others' blood and reconciliation with their fellow citizens. For a stiff fee, visitors were allowed to address questions to Apollo through a female medium. She entered a trance state and uttered a reply, which lay priests at the shrine then put into verse form and transmitted to the petitioner. The ambiguity of the Delphic replies was legendary. Petitioners had to interpret the answers they received as best they could.

■ A vase painting showing the Pythia, the priestess of Delphi, seated on her tripod. She holds a branch of the laurel plant, which is sacred to her patron, the god Apollo. The petitioner standing at the right will most likely receive an enigmatic reply to his question.

Although gods were petitioned, placated, and pampered, they were not privileged or protected. Unlike the awe-inspiring gods of the Mesopotamians and Egyptians, the traditional Greek gods, inherited from the Dark Age, were represented in ways that showed them as all too human, vicious, and frequently ridiculous. Zeus was infamous for his frequent rapes of boys and girls. His lust was matched only by the fury of his jealous wife, Hera. According to one story, a visitor to Athens asked why its citizens so often used the exclamation "by Zeus." The answer came back, "Because so many of us are." The Greek gods were immortal, superhuman in strength, and able to interfere in human affairs. But in all things, they reflected the values and weaknesses of the Greek mortals, who could bargain with them, appease them, and even trick them.

Religious cults were not under the exclusive control of any priesthood or political group. Thus, there were no official versions of stories of gods and goddesses. This lack of uniformity is evident both from Greek poetry, which often presents contradictory stories of the gods, and from pottery, which bears pictorial versions of myths that differ greatly from written ones. Although centers such as Delphi were universal religious sites, drawing visitors from the whole Greek world and even beyond, no one group or sacred site enjoyed a monopoly on access to the gods. Like literacy and government, the gods belonged to all.

Myth and Reason

The glue holding together the individual and frequently hostile Greek poleis and ethne scattered throughout the Mediterranean was their common stock of myths and a common fascination with the Homeric legends. Stories of gods and heroes, told and retold, were fashioned into *mythoi* (myths, literally, "sayings"), which explained and described the world both as it was and as it should be. Myths were told about every city, shrine, river, mountain, and island. Myths explained the origins of cities, festivals, the world itself. Why are there seasons? Because Persephone, a daughter of Zeus, had been carried off by Hades, god of the dead, and for four months each year she had to dwell in his dark kingdom. What is the place of humans in the cosmos? They stand between beasts and gods because Prometheus tricked Zeus and gave men fire, with which they cook their food and offer the bones and fat of sacrificial animals to the gods. Why is there evil and misfortune? Because, Greek men explained, in revenge for Prometheus's trickery, Zeus offered man Pandora (the name means "all gifts"), the first woman, whose beauty hid her evil nature. By accepting the gift, humans brought evil and misfortune on themselves.

Such stories were more than simply fanciful explanations of how things came to be. Myths sanctioned and supported the authority of social, political, and religious traditions. They presented how things had come to be in a manner that prescribed how they were to remain. The stories of Prometheus and Pandora, for example, defined the ambivalent relationship between gods and humans, the evil nature of women, and the ritual role of fire and sacrifice to the gods.

As important as these myths were, they were not immutable. Archaic Greeks constantly reworked ancient myths, retelling them, adjusting their content and thus their meanings. Pandora began as evil. "Whoever trusts a woman is trusting himself to a thief." But in another version of the myth, Pandora is curious rather than evil. She opens a jar given her by Zeus that contains all evils and thereby unintentionally releases them into the world. As colonists traveled to the far shores of the Mediterranean, their mythic heroes moved with them. New legends told of the travels of Heracles, Apollo, and other gods and heroes to Sicily, Italy, and beyond. In the process of revising and retelling, myths became a powerful and dynamic tool for reasoning about the world.

Archaic Greeks showed a similar combination of veneration and liberty in dealing with the Homeric legends. Young Greeks were urged to model themselves on the example of the ancients, as described in the *Iliad* and the *Odyssey.* Increasingly, however, thoughtful Greeks approached the heroic ideals of these epics with a sense of detachment and criticism. Military values were still important, but the ancient aristocratic values were no longer universally accepted. Some mothers might tell their sons as they marched off to war, "Return with your shield or on it"—that is, victorious or dead—but Archilochus, a seventh-century B.C.E. lyric poet, took a very different view of shields and honor:

> *A perfect shield bedecks some Thracian now;*
> *I had no choice, I left it in a wood.*
> *Ah, well, I saved my skin, so let it go!*
> *A new one's just as good.*

Investigation and Speculation

The new, open examination of traditional values extended into all areas of investigation. By the sixth century B.C.E., a number of Ionian Greeks began to investigate the origins and nature of the universe, not in terms of myth or religion, but by observation and rational thought. Living on the coast of Asia Minor, these Ionians were in contact with the ancient civilizations of Mesopotamia and learned much from the Babylonian traditions of astronomy, mathematics, and science. However, their primary interest went beyond observing and recording to speculating. They were the first philosophers—intellectuals who sought natural explanations for the world around them.

Thales of Miletus (ca. 625–ca. 547 B.C.E.) regarded water as the fundamental substance of the universe. For Anaximander (610–ca. 527 B.C.E.), the primary substance was matter—eternal and indestructible. Anaximenes of Miletus (fl. ca. 545 B.C.E.) regarded air as the primary substance of the universe. Heraclitus of Ephesus (ca. 540–ca. 480 B.C.E.) saw the universe not as one unchanging substance but rather as change itself. For him, the universe is constantly in flux, changing like a flickering fire. One cannot step into the same river twice, Heraclitus taught, because no flowing stream is ever the same from one moment to another. Thus it is with the world. All is constantly in a state of becoming, not in a static state of being; yet this constant change is not random. The cosmic tension between stability and flux is regulated by laws that human reason can determine. The universe is rational.

The significance of such speculative thought was not in the conclusions that were reached, but rather in the method that was employed. The Ionian philosophers no longer spoke in myth but rather in plain language. They reached their conclusions through observation and rational thought in which religion and the gods played no direct role. As significant as their original speculations was the manner in which the philosophers were received. Although as late as the fourth century B.C.E. intellectuals still occasionally fell prey to persecution, by the sixth century B.C.E. much of Greek society was ready to tolerate such nonreligious, rational teaching, which in other times and places would have been thought scandalous or atheistic.

THE AGONY OF ATHLETICS

The Greeks did not play sports. Our word play is related to the Greek word *pais* (child), and there was nothing childish about Greek athletics. The Greek word was *agonia,* and our modern derivation, *agony,* hits closer to the mark. From Homeric times, sports were a deadly serious affair. Poets, philosophers, and statesmen placed athletic victories above all other human achievements. "There is no greater glory for a man, no matter how long his life," proclaimed Homer, "than what he achieves with his hands and feet."

Athletic contests took place within a religious context, honoring the gods but glorifying the human victors. By 500 B.C.E., there were 50 sets of games across the Greek world held at regular intervals. Among the most prestigious contests were the so-called Crown Games at Delphi, Corinth, and Nemea; the most important were those held every four years as part of the cult of Zeus at Olympia. And, the most important event of the Olympic Games was the 192-meter race, or *stade,* from which comes the word *stadium.* So important was victory in this event that the name of the victor provided the basic system of Greek dating. Years were reckoned from the last Olympiad and were recorded as "three years after Epitelidas of Sparta won the stade" (577 B.C.E.) or "the year in which Phanias of Pellene won the stade" (512 B.C.E.). In time, other events were added to the Olympics—other footraces (including one in which the contestants wore armor), throwing of the discus and javelin, the long jump, horse races, and chariot races. The *pankration* combined wrestling and boxing in a no-holds-barred contest. The pentathlon included five events: discus, jumping, javelin, running, and wrestling.

A CLOSER LOOK

The serious nature of sport was equaled by its danger. One inscription from a statue erected at Olympia reads simply, "Here he died, boxing in the stadium, having prayed to Zeus for either the crown or death." The most celebrated pankration hero was Arrichion, who won but died in victory. Although his opponent was slowly strangling him, Arrichion managed to kick in such a way as to horribly dislocate his adversary's ankle. The excruciating pain caused the opponent to signal defeat just as Arrichion died, victorious. The ultimate disgrace was not injury or even death, but defeat. As one contemporary author put it, "In the Olympic Games you cannot just be beaten and then depart, but first of all, you will be disgraced not only before the people of Athens or Sparta or Nicopolis but before the whole world." Greeks did not honor good losers; they honored only winners. As Pindar, the great lyric poet who celebrated victorious athletes, wrote, "As they the losers returned to their mothers no laughter sweet brought them pleasure, but they crept along the backroads, avoiding their enemies, bitten by misfortune."

If failure was bitter, victory was sweet indeed. Victors received enduring fame and enormous fortune. Poets composed odes in their honor, and crowds hurried to meet them on their return home. Most games carried considerable cash prizes. At the four big games, winners received only crowns of olive or laurel leaves, but their home cities gave them more substantial gifts. Athens, for example, paid Olympic victors the equivalent of 500 bushels of grain. This fabulous sum put the winner—for one year at least—in the ranks of the wealthiest Athenians. Most cities granted winners public honors and allowed them to eat at public expense for the rest of their lives. Thus the best athletes were essentially professionals, traveling from game to game. The Thasian boxer and pankratiast Theogenes claimed to have won more than 1300 victories during a professional career that spanned more than two decades. After his death he received the ultimate accolade: he was worshipped in Thasos as a god.

Competition among cities to field winning athletes was as sharp as the competition among the athletes themselves. Cities hired coaches, often themselves former Olympic champions, and actively recruited athletes from rival neighboring cities. The colony of Croton in Italy, for example, won the

Marble relief sculpture of Olympic wrestlers.

stade 44 percent of the time between 588 B.C.E. and 484 B.C.E. Then Croton's leading sprinter, Astylos, was lured to Syracuse and won three races, including the stade, for that city. Croton never again achieved an Olympic victory. Presumably its best athletes had been bought off.

In keeping with the rest of male-dominated Greece, only men were allowed to participate in or attend the Olympic Games. Separate games dedicated to Zeus's wife, Hera, were held for unmarried women at Olympia. Women competed only in footraces over a shortened track. While men competed naked, their bodies rubbed down with olive oil, in the Heraia women wore a short tunic. Victors in the Heraia did not receive the same honors as their male counterparts, but at least one woman found an indirect way to win a victory at the male Olympics. Cynisca, the daughter of a Spartan king, entered a team of horses in the race, encouraged, the story goes, by her brother, who wanted to show that victory in these events "required no excellence but was a victory of money and expense." Whatever her motivation, Cynisca was certainly proud of her achievement. Following the victory won for her by her male driver, she erected a statue of herself at Olympia with an inscription that read:

Sparta's kings were fathers and brothers of mine,
But since with my chariot and storming horses I, Cynisca,
Have won the prize, I place my effigy here
And proudly proclaim
That of all Grecian women I first bore the crown.

The Greeks' passion for games is unique in antiquity, and the progressive interest of Romans and "barbarians" in athletics was a sure sign of their absorption of Greek culture. Perhaps the best explanation of the place of athletics in the Greek world was that the single athlete, standing alone and naked and striving with all his being for excellence, was the purest expression of the individualism that animated Hellenic society.

Art and the Individual

Archaic Greeks borrowed from everywhere and transformed all that they borrowed. Just as they adopted and adapted the Phoenician alphabet and Mesopotamian science, they took Near Eastern and Egyptian painting and sculpture and made them their own. During the Dark Age, the Mycenaean traditions of art had entirely disappeared. Gradually, from the ninth century B.C.E., stylized human and animal figures began to appear within the tightly composed geometric patterns. As Greek traders increased their contacts with the Near East, lions, griffins, and other strange beasts began to appear on vases, jugs, vials, and other pottery containers. But by the eighth century B.C.E., such exotic subjects had given way to the Greek passion for human images taken from their own myths and legends.

The preferred technique was the so-called black figure style, developed first at Corinth. Subjects were painted in black silhouette on red clay, and then details were cut with a sharp point so that the background could show through. As the popularity of the mythic and heroic scenes increased, so too did the artists' technical competence. Unlike Egyptian and Syrian artisans, who were largely content to work within a static tradition of representation, the Greeks competed with one another to overcome technical problems of perspective and foreshortening. They also experimented with techniques of portraying long, complicated narratives on individual vases. Masters of the technique were proud of their skills and eager to proclaim their accomplishments. From the sixth century B.C.E., many of the finest examples were signed—sometimes by both the potter or the owner of the pottery shop and the painter. Such masterpieces celebrated not only the heroes of the past but also the artist as an individual and as the interpreter of culture no less original than the poet.

Greek sculpture underwent a similar dramatic development. The earliest and most common subject of Archaic sculpture was the standing male nude, or **kouros,** figure, which was in wide demand as a grave monument, a statue dedicated to a god, or even a cult statue

CHRONOLOGY

Archaic Greece

ca. 780–720 B.C.E.	Population increase in Greece
776 B.C.E.	First Olympic Games held
ca. 750–700 B.C.E.	Greeks develop writing system based on Phoenician alphabet; Greeks begin colonizing western Mediterranean
ca. 700–500 B.C.E.	Archaic Age of Greece
ca. 700 B.C.E.	First stone temples appear in Greece; Messenian revolt against Sparta
ca. 650 B.C.E.	Cypselus breaks rule of Bacchiads in Corinth; rules city as tyrant
594 B.C.E.	Solon elected chief archon of Athens; institutes social and political reforms
586 B.C.E.	Death of Periander ends tyrants' rule in Corinth
499 B.C.E.	Ionian cities revolt

■ The Calf-Bearer was commissioned for the temple of Athena, which was destroyed by the Persians in 480 B.C.E. when they captured Athens and burned the Acropolis.

of a male deity. In Egypt, seventh-century B.C.E. Greeks had seen colossal statues and had learned to work stone. They brought the techniques home, improved on them by using iron tools (the Egyptians knew only bronze ones), and began to create their own human images. The kouros was a relatively easy figure to carve. Essentially, the sculptor began with a prism-shaped block of stone about 6 feet by 1 foot by 1½ feet. Applying a system of widely accepted ratios, the artist then carved it into a recognizable three-dimensional human form. The rigidly formulaic position of the kouros—standing, arms by the sides, looking straight ahead, left foot extended—followed Egyptian tradition and left little room for originality. Thus sculptors sought to give their statues originality and individuality, not as representations of individuals, but as the creations of the individual sculptors. To this end, they experimented with increasingly natural molding of limbs and body and began signing their works. Thus, as in vase painting, Greek sculpture reflected the importance of the individual, not in its subject matter but in its creator. The widely popular kouros figures left little room for experimentation with more complex problems of composition and action. Their female counterparts, *korai,* followed similarly rigid traditions, to which sculptors added female attributes. In the korai figures it was the clothing rather than the anatomy that allowed some scope to the artist's talents.

The real challenges in sculpture, as in poetry and vase painting, came in the portrayal of narrative in decorations on monuments, primarily temples. Unlike kouroi, which were usually private commissions intended to adorn the tombs of aristocrats, these public buildings were constructed as expressions of civic pride and were accessible to everyone. Here the creativity and dynamism of Greek cities could be paralleled in stone. Figures such as the Calf-Bearer (ca. 590 B.C.E.) and the Rampin Horseman (ca. 560 B.C.E.) from the Athenian acropolis are daring in the complexity of composition and the delicacy of execution. These are statues that tell stories. In the former, a master farmer carries a calf to be sacrificed to Athena. The two gentle heads and the cross formed by the farmer's hands and the calf's legs are individual traits without precedent in ancient art. In the latter, the earliest-known Greek equestrian statue, the rider's head is turned naturally, possibly peeking out from behind the head of his mount. The horseman wears a wreath of parsley, probably an indication that he had won the prize in a race held in connection with a religious feast. Both statues surpass the monotony and anonymity of tradition. Although formally intended for religious purposes, the figures serve not only the gods and the aristocratic elite but the whole community.

■ Assembled fragments of the Rampin Horseman (ca. 560 B.C.E.).

A TALE OF THREE CITIES

The political, social, and cultural transformations that occurred in the Archaic Age took different forms across the Greek world. No community or city-state was typical of Greece. The best way to understand the diversity of Archaic Greece is to examine three very different cities that by the end of the sixth century B.C.E. had become leading centers of Greek civilization. Corinth, Sparta, and Athens present something of the spectrum of political, cultural, and social models of the Hellenic world. Corinth, like many cities, developed into a commercial center in which the assembly of citizens was dominated by an oligarchy. Sparta developed into a state in which citizenship was radically egalitarian but restricted to a small military elite. In Athens, the Archaic Age saw the foundations of an equally radical democracy.

Wealthy Corinth

Corinth owed its prosperity to its privileged site, dominating both a rich coastal plain and the narrow isthmus connecting the Peloponnesus to the mainland. In the eighth century

■ This archaic Kouros statue from Anavysos shows its Egyptian origins, but style is already considerably changed.

B.C.E., as Greeks turned their attention to the west, Corinthians led the way. Corinthian pottery appeared throughout western Greece and southern Italy. Corinthian trade led to colonization, and settlers from Corinth founded Syracuse and other cities in Sicily and Italy. The colonies reduced the population pressure on the city and provided markets for its grain and manufactured goods, primarily pottery and textiles. Even more important to Corinthian prosperity was its role in the transport of other cities' products from east to west. By carrying goods across the isthmus and loading them onto other ships, merchants could avoid the long, dangerous passage around the Peloponnesus. Duties imposed on other cities using this unique passage added to Corinthian wealth from agriculture and its own commerce.

Social Tensions. Until the middle of the seventh century B.C.E., Corinth and its wealth were ruled in typical Dark Age fashion by an aristocratic clan known as the Bacchiads. There were approximately 200 members of this clan, all of whom claimed descent from the mythical hero Heracles. Corinth began its rise under this aristocratic rule, and individual Bacchiads led colonizing expeditions to Italy and Sicily. However, the increasing pressures of population growth, rapidly expanding wealth, and dramatic changes in the economy produced social tensions that the traditional aristocratic rulers were unable to handle. As in cities throughout the Greek world, the tensions led to the creation of a new order.

The early history of Corinth is obscure, but apparently around 650 B.C.E. a revolution led by Cypselus (ca. 657–627 B.C.E.), whose mother had been a Bacchiad and who was supported by non-Bacchiad aristocrats and other Corinthians, broke the Bacchiads' grip on the city. The revolution led to the establishment of Cypselus as tyrant. Cypselus and his son Periander (ca. 627–586 B.C.E.) seem to have been generally popular with most Corinthians. As Periander himself said, "The safety of the tyrant is better guarded by the goodwill of the citizens than by the spears of a bodyguard."

Corinth Under Its Tyrants. In Corinth, as in many other cities, the tyrants restructured taxes, relying primarily on customs duties, which were less of a burden on the peasantry. Around 600 B.C.E., Periander began construction of a causeway across the isthmus on which ships could be hauled from the Aegean to the western Mediterranean. In this way, merchant vessels (and warships) could enter the Gulf of Corinth without having to unload. The causeway eventually became a major source of Corinth's wealth. Under the leadership of Periander, the Corinthian fleet developed into the most powerful naval force in the Adriatic and Aegean seas. Periander also attacked conspicuous consumption on the part of the aristocracy. He forbade women to wear expensive clothes and jewelry. He introduced laws against idleness and put thousands of Corinthians to work in extensive building programs. He erected temples and sent colonists to Italy. Under its tyrants, Corinth led the Greek world in the production of black figure pottery, which spread throughout the Mediterranean. A great seaport, Corinth also became known as a center of prostitution, and a popular saying ran, "Not every man has the luck to sail to Corinth," implying both that not everyone would be fortunate enough to enjoy its pleasures and that not everyone had the luck to survive such a trip without considerable expense.

The tyrants also laid the foundation for broader political participation. Cypselus divided the population into eight tribes, based not on traditional ethnic divisions but on arbitrary groupings by region. All of Corinth was divided into three large regions. The population of each region was distributed among each of the eight tribes. This assignment prevented the emergence of political factions based on regional disputes. Ten representatives from each tribe formed a council of 80 men. Under the tyrants, the council was largely advisory and provided a connection between the autocratic rulers and the citizens.

In Corinth as elsewhere, the strength or weakness of tyranny rested on the abilities and personality of individual tyrants. The benefits they brought their cities could not entirely overcome the negative impression made by the arbitrary nature of their rule. Thus their popularity declined rapidly. Cypselus had been a beloved liberator. His son Periander, in spite of his accomplishments, was remembered for his cruelty and violence. To later Greeks, Periander was the originator of the brutal, arbitrary rule later considered typical of repressive tyranny. Shortly after Periander's death in 586 B.C.E., a revolt killed his successor and tyranny in Corinth ended.

Oligarchy. The new government continued the tribal and council system established by Cypselus. From the sixth century B.C.E. until its conquest by Macedonia in 338 B.C.E., Corinth was ruled by an oligarchy. Although an assembly of the *demos,* or adult males, met occasionally, actual government was in the hands of eight deliberators, or *probouloi,* and nine other men from each tribe, who together formed the council of 80. How council members and probouloi were selected is unknown. Presumably they were elected for very long periods, if not for life, and the council tended to be self-perpetuating. Still, the oligarchs who made up the council avoided the exclusive and arbitrary tendencies that had destroyed both the Bacchiads and the tyrants. They were remarkably successful in maintaining popular support among the citizens and provided a reliable and effective government. Thus Corinth flourished, a city more open to commerce and wealth than most, moderate in its political institutions, and eager for stability. As one fourth-century B.C.E. poet wrote:

[There] lawfulness dwells, and her sister,
Safe foundation of cities,
Justice, and Peace, who was bred with her;
They dispense wealth to men.

Martial Sparta

At the beginning of the eighth century B.C.E., the Peloponnesus around Sparta and Laconia faced circumstances similar to those of Corinth and other Greek communities. Population growth,

TWO FACES OF TYRANNY

The spectrum of tyrannies in Archaic Greece is shown in the lives of Periander of Corinth and Peisistratus of Athens. The description of Periander is that of Herodotus; the description of Peisistratus comes from the Athenian Constitution, *one of more than a hundred constitutions compiled by Aristotle and his students between 328 and 325 B.C.E. as part of the research for his* Politics.

Focus Questions

What were the primary issues that caused tension within the Corinth of Periander and the Athens of Peisistratus? What different routes did Periander and Peisistratus take to eliminate these tensions?

Now Periander at the first was of milder mood than his father; but after he had held converse by his messengers with Thrasybulus the despot of Miletus, he became much more blood-thirsty than Cypselus. For he sent a herald to Thrasybulus and enquired how he should most safely so order all matters as best to govern his city. Thrasybulus led the man who had come from Periander outside the town, and entered into a sown field; where, while he walked through the corn and plied the herald with still-repeated questions about his coming from Corinth, he would ever cut off the tallest that he saw of the stalks, and cast away what he cut off, till by so doing he had destroyed the best and richest of the crop; then, having passed through the place and spoken no word of counsel, he sent the herald away. . . . But Periander understood what had been done, and perceived that Thrasybulus had counseled him to slay those of his townsmen who stood highest, and with that he began to deal very evilly with his citizens. For whatever act of slaughter or banishment Cypselus had left undone, that did Periander bring to accomplishment.

From Herodotus, *The Histories,* Book V, Chapter 92.

The factions were three: one was the part of the Men of the Coast . . . and they were thought chiefly to aim at the middle form of constitution; another was the party of the Men of the Plain, who desired the oligarchy . . . third was the party of the Hillmen, which had appointed Peisistratus over it, as he was thought to be an extreme advocate of the people. And on the side of this party were also arrayed, from the motive of poverty, those who had been deprived of the debts due to them, and, from the motive of fear, those who were not of pure descent. . . . Peisistratus inflicted a wound on himself with his own hand and then gave out that it had been done by the members of the opposite factions, and so persuaded the people to give him a bodyguard. . . . He was given the retainers called Club-Bearers, and with their aid he rose against the people and seized the Acropolis. . . .

Peisistratus's administration of the state was . . . moderate, and more constitutional than tyrannic; he was kindly and mild in everything, and in particular he was merciful to offenders, and moreover he advanced loans of money to the poor for their industries, so that they might support themselves by farming. In doing this he had two objects, to prevent their stopping in the city and make them stay scattered about the country and to cause them to have a moderate competence and be engaged in their private affairs, so as not to desire nor to have time to attend to public business.

From Aristotle, *Athenian Constitution.*

increasing disparity between rich and poor, and an expanding economy created powerful tensions. However, while Corinthian society developed into a complex mix of aristocrats, merchants, artisans, and peasants ruled by an oligarchy, the Spartan solution consisted of a rigid three-tiered social structure. By the end of the Archaic Age, a small, homogeneous class of warriors called *homoioi,* or equals, ruled a vast population of state serfs, or *helots,* and dominated the *perioeci,* or citizens of conquered coastal cities. The three classes lived in mutual fear and mistrust. Spartans controlled the helots through terror and ritual murder. The helots in turn were "an enemy constantly waiting for the disasters of the Spartans." Perioeci exercised limited autonomy, but Sparta firmly controlled their foreign policy and could execute troublesome perioeci. Yet, throughout antiquity the Spartans were the Greeks most praised for their courage, simplicity of life, and service to the state.

Plutarch on Life in Sparta

Messenia. War was the center of Spartan life, and war lay at the origin of the Spartans' extraordinary social and political organization. In the eighth century B.C.E., the Spartans conquered the fertile region of Messenia and compelled the vanquished Messenians, whom they turned into helots, to turn over one-half of their harvests. The spoils were not divided equally but went to increase the wealth of the aristocracy, thus creating resentment among the less privileged. Early in the seventh century B.C.E., the Spartans attempted a similar campaign to take the plain of Thyreatis from the city of Argos. This time they were not so fortunate; they were defeated, and resentment of the ordinary warriors toward their aristocratic leaders flared into open conflict. The Messenians seized upon this moment to revolt, and for a time Sparta was forced to fight at home and abroad for its very existence. In many cities, such crises gave rise to tyrants. In Sparta, the crisis led to radical political and social reforms that transformed the polis into a unique military system.

Reforms of Lycurgus. The Spartans attributed these reforms to the legendary lawgiver Lycurgus (seventh century B.C.E.). Whether or not Lycurgus ever existed and was responsible for all of the reforms, these saved the city and ended its internal tensions but only by abandoning the mainstream of Greek development. Traditionally, Greeks had placed personal honor above communal concerns. During the crisis of the second Messenian war, Spartans of all social ranks were urged to look not to individual interest but to **eunomia,** good order and obedience to the laws, which alone could unite Spartans and bring victory. Faced with certain defeat as the only alternative, Spartans answered the call and became the first Greeks to elevate duty and patriotism above individual interest. United, the Spartans crushed the Messenians. In return for obedience, poor citizens received equality before the law and benefited from a land distribution that relieved their poverty. Conquered land, especially that in Messenia, was divided and distributed to Spartan warriors. However, the warriors were not expected to work the land themselves. Instead, the state reduced the defeated Messenians to the status of helots and assigned them to individual Spartans. While the system did not erase all economic inequalities among the Spartans (aristocrats continued to hold more land than others), it did decrease some of the disparity. It also provided a minimum source of wealth for all Spartan citizens and allowed them to devote themselves to full-time military service.

The land reform was coupled with a political reform that incorporated elements of monarchy, oligarchy, and democracy. The state was governed by two hereditary kings and a council of elders, the *gerousia.* The two royal families probably represented the combination of differing groups that had formed the Spartan polis at some earlier date. Their authority in peacetime was limited to familial and religious affairs. In war, they commanded the army and held the power of life and death.

In theory at least, the central institution of Spartan government was the gerousia, which consisted of 30 men at least 60 years of age and included the two kings. The gerousia directed all political activity, especially foreign affairs, and served as the high court. Members were elected for life by the assembly, or *apella,* which consisted of all equals over the age of 30 and which approved decisions of the gerousia. However, this approval, made by acclamation, could easily be manipulated, as could the course of debate within the gerousia itself. Wealth, cunning, and patronage were more important in directing the Spartan state than were its formal structures.

Actual administration was in the hands of five magistrates termed *ephors.* Ephors were not members of the gerousia and often came from fairly obscure backgrounds. However, their powers were extremely broad. They presided over joint sessions of the gerousia and apella. They held supreme authority over the kings during wartime and acted as judges for noncitizens. Finally, the ephors controlled the *krypteia,* or secret police, a band of youths who practiced state terrorism as part of their rite of passage to the status of equal. On the orders of the ephors, the krypteia assassinated, intrigued, arrested powerful people, and terrorized helots. Service in this corps was considered a necessary part of a youth's education.

Social Control. The key to the success of Sparta's political reform was an even more radical social reform that placed everyone under the direct supervision and service of the state from birth until death. Although admiring aristocratic visitors often exaggerated their accounts of Spartan life, the main outlines are clear enough. Eunomia was the sole guiding principle, and service to the state came before family, social class, and every other duty or occupation.

Spartan equals were made, not born. True, only a man born of free Spartan parents could hope to become an equal, but birth alone was no guarantee of admission to this select body or even of the right to live. Elsewhere in Greece, parents were free to decide whether children should be raised or abandoned. In Sparta, public officials examined infants and decided whether they were sufficiently strong to be allowed to live or should be exposed on a hillside to die. From birth until age 7, a boy lived with his mother, but then he entered the state education system, or *agoge,* living in barracks with his contemporaries and enduring 13 years of rigorous military training. Harsh discipline and physical deprivation were essential parts of this training, which was intended to teach men to endure pain and to conquer in battle.

At age 12, training with swords and spears became more intense, as did the rigors of the lifestyle. Boys were given only a single cloak to wear and slept on thin rush mats. They were encouraged to supplement their meager diet by stealing food, although if caught they were severely whipped, not for the theft but for the failure. All of these abuses they were expected to endure in silence.

Much of the actual education of the youths was entrusted to accomplished older warriors, who selected boys as their homosexual lovers. Such relationships between youths and adults were the norm throughout Greece, although in Sparta they were more important than elsewhere. Not only did

■ A bronze statuette from ca. 500 B.C.E. depicting a young Spartan woman competing in a footrace such as those of the Heraia Games, dedicated to the goddess Hera. Such games took place outside of the Olympic Games.

the lover serve as tutor and role model, but in time the two became a fighting team, each inspiring the other to show the utmost valor. Ultimately, the older warrior would even help his young lover select a wife.

At age 20, Spartan youths were enrolled in the krypteia. Each was sent out into the countryside with nothing but a cloak and a knife and forbidden to return until he had killed a helot. This finishing school for killers kept helots in a constant state of terror and gave ephors a deadly efficient mechanism for enforcing their will.

If a youth survived the rigors of his training until age 30, he could at last be incorporated into the rank of equals, provided he could pass the last test. He had to be able to furnish a sufficient amount of food from his own lands for the communal dining group to which he would be assigned. The food might come from inherited property or, if he had proved himself an outstanding warrior, from the state. Those who passed the final qualification became full members of the assembly, but they continued to live with the other warriors. Now they could marry, but family life in the usual sense was nonexistent. To symbolize the furtive nature of marriage, the prospective groom acted out a ritual abduction of his bride. Thereafter he would slip out occasionally at night to sleep with her.

Although their training was not as rigorous as the education of males, Spartan women were given an upbringing and allowed a sphere of activity unknown elsewhere in Greece. Girls, like boys, were trained in athletic competition and, again like them, competed naked in wrestling, footraces, and spear throwing. This training was based not on a belief in the equality of the sexes but simply on the desire to improve the physical stamina and childbearing ability of Spartan women. Women were able to own land and to participate widely in business and agricultural affairs; since men were entirely involved in military pursuits, women were expected to look after economic and household affairs. When a foreign woman commented that Spartan women were the only women who could rule men, a Spartan wife replied, "With good reason, for we are the only women who bring forth men."

Few Lacedaemonians (as Spartans were also called) ever became equals. Not only were there far more helots than Spartans, but many inhabitants of the region, termed *perioikoi,* or peripherals, although they were free citizens of their local communities, were not allowed into the agoge. Others were washed out, unable to endure the harsh life, and still others lacked the property qualifications to supply their share of the communal meals. Thus, for all the trappings of egalitarianism, equality in Sparta was the privilege of only a tiny minority.

The total dedication to military life was reinforced by a deliberate rejection of other activities. Prior to the eighth century B.C.E., Sparta had participated in the general cultural and economic transformations of the Greek world. Legend even made Sparta the birthplace of music. However, from the time of the second Messenian war, Sparta withdrew from the mainstream of Greek civilization. Equals could not engage in crafts, trade, or any other forms of economic activity. Because Sparta banned silver and gold coinage, it could not participate in the growing commercial network of the Greek world. Although a group of free citizens of subject towns could engage in such activities, the role of Sparta in the economic and cultural life of Greece was negligible after the seventh century B.C.E. Militarily, Sparta cast a long shadow across the Peloponnesus and beyond, but the number of equals was always too small to allow Sparta both to create a vast empire and to maintain control over the helots at home. Instead, Sparta created a network of alliances and nonaggression pacts with oligarchic neighbors. In time this network came to be known as the Peloponnesian League.

Democratic Athens

Athens enjoyed the advantage neither of a strategic site such as Corinth's nor of the rich plains of Sparta. However, the "goodly citadel of Athens" was one of the few Mycenaean cities to have escaped destruction at the start of the Dark Age. Gradually, Athens united the whole surrounding region of Attica into a single polis, by far the largest in the Greek world. Well into the seventh century B.C.E., Athens followed the general pattern of the polis seen in Corinth and Sparta. Like other Dark Age communities, Athens was ruled by aristocratic clans, particularly the Alcmaeonids. Only the members of the clans could participate in the *areopagus,* or council, which they entered after serving a year as one of the nine *archons,* magistrates who were elected yearly. Until the seventh century B.C.E., Athens escaped the social pressures brought on by population growth and economic prosperity that led to civil strife, colonialism, and tyranny elsewhere. This good fortune was due largely to its relative abundance of arable land and its commercial prosperity, based on the export of grain.

Social Tensions. By the late seventh century B.C.E., however, Athens had begun to suffer from the same class conflict that had shaken other cities. Newly rich merchants and artisans of the middle classes resented the aristocratic monopoly on political power. Poor farmers were angry because, far from participating in the growing prosperity, they were being forced into debt to the wealthy. When they were unable to pay their debts, they or their children were sold as slaves by their creditors. Sometime around 630 B.C.E., an aristocrat named Cylon attempted to seize power as tyrant. His attempt failed, but when he was murdered by one of the Alcmaeonids, popular revulsion drove the Alcmaeonids from the city. A decade of strife ensued as aristocratic clans, wealthy merchants, and farmers fought for control of the city. Violence between groups and families threatened to tear the community apart.

Reforms of Solon. In 621 B.C.E., the Athenians granted a lawgiver, Draco, extraordinary powers to revise, systematize, and commit to writing traditional laws concerning vengeance and homicide. His restructuring of procedures for limiting vengeance and preventing bloodshed was harsh enough to add the term *draconian* to the Western legal vocabulary. When asked why death was the most common penalty he imposed, Draco explained that minor offenses merited death and he knew of no more severe penalty for major ones. Still, these measures did nothing to solve the central problems of political control. Finally, in 594 B.C.E., Solon (ca. 630–ca. 560 B.C.E.), an aristocratic merchant, was elected chief archon and charged with restructuring the city's government. Solon based his reform on the ideal of eunomia, as had the Spartans, but he followed a very different path to secure good order.

In Sparta, Lycurgus had begun with a radical redistribution of land. In Athens, Solon began with the less extreme measure of eliminating debt bondage. Athenians who had been forced into slavery or into sharecropping because of their debts were restored to freedom. A law forbade mortgaging free men and women as security for debts. Athenians might be poor, but they would be free. Free peasantry formed the basis of Athenian society throughout its history. Solon also reorganized the rest of the social hierarchy and broke the aristocracy's exclusive control of the areopagus by dividing the society into four classes based on wealth rather than birth and opening the post of archon to the top two classes.

Although Solon's reforms established the framework for a resolution of Athens's social tensions, they did not entirely succeed. Solon himself did not consider his new constitution perfect, only practical. Asked if he had given the Athenians the best laws that he could give them, he answered, "The best that they could receive." Resistance from the still-powerful aristocracy prompted some Athenians to urge Solon to assume the powers of a tyrant in order to force through his reforms. He refused, but after his death, Peisistratus (d. 527 B.C.E.), an aristocrat strongly supported by the peasants against his own class, hired a mercenary force to seize control of the city. After two abortive attempts, Peisistratus ruled as tyrant from 545 B.C.E. until his death.

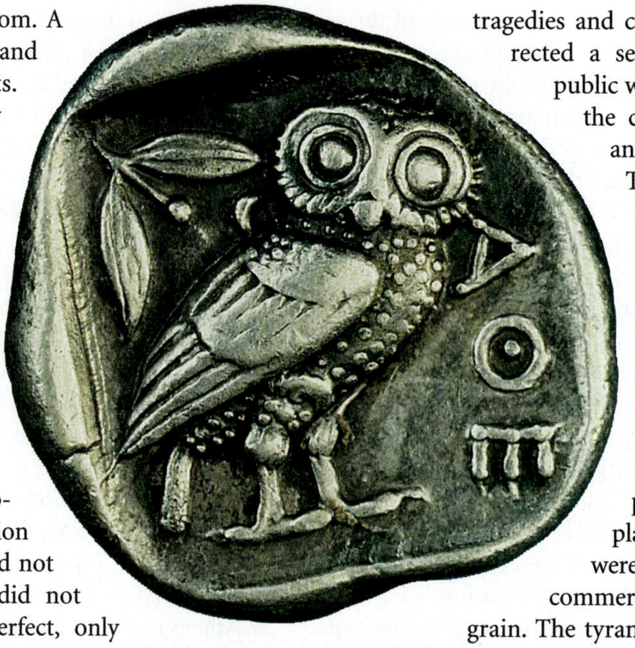

■ An Athenian silver coin called a *tetradrachm,* dating from the fifth century B.C.E. The owl is the symbol of the goddess Athena.

Athenian Tyranny. With his bodyguard firmly established on the acropolis, Peisistratus might have governed the city, for a while at least, as an absolute tyrant. Instead, he—and later his sons Hipparchus (d. 514 B.C.E.) and Hippias (d. 490 B.C.E.), who succeeded him until 510 B.C.E.—continued to rule through Solon's constitution but simply ensured that the archons elected each year were their agents. Thus the Athenian tyrants strengthened Solon's constitution even while they further destroyed the powers of the aristocracy.

Peisistratus and his sons drew their support from the demos—the people at large—rather than from an aristocratic faction. They claimed divine justification for their rule and made a great show of devotion to the Athenian gods. At one point, Peisistratus even dressed a very tall, beautiful girl to look like the goddess Athena, patron of the city, and had her driven into town in a chariot while heralds went before her announcing that Athena herself was supporting him. He also promoted annual festivals, and in so doing began the great tradition of Athenian literature. At the festival of Athena, professional reciters of *rhapsoidiai* (epic poetry) recited large portions of the *Iliad* and the *Odyssey.* During a festival in honor of Dionysus, actors performed the first tragedies and comedies. The tyrants also directed a series of popular nationalistic public works programs that beautified the city, increased national pride, and provided work for the poor. They rebuilt the temple of Athena on the acropolis, for which both the statues of the Rampin Horseman and the Calf-Bearer were commissioned. The tyrants also constructed a system of terracotta pipes by which clear mountain water was brought into the agora, and they built public halls and meeting places. These internal measures were accompanied by support for commerce and export, particularly of grain. The tyrants introduced the silver "owl" coin, which became the first international Greek currency. Soon Athens, trading in grain as far away as the Black Sea, was challenging Corinth as the leading commercial power.

Peisistratus was firm. His sons were harsh. Still, even they enjoyed the support of the majority of the citizens of both popular and aristocratic factions. Only after the assassination of Hipparchus did Hippias become sufficiently oppressive to drive his opponents into exile. Some of these exiles obtained the assistance of Sparta and returned to overthrow Hippias in 510 B.C.E. Hippias's defeat ended the tyrants' rule in Athens and won for Sparta an undeserved reputation as the opponent of all tyranny.

Athenian Democracy. Following the expulsion of Hippias, some aristocrats attempted to return to the "good old days" of aristocratic rule. However, for more than 80 years, Athenians had been accustomed to Solon's constitution and were unwilling to give it up. Moreover, the tyrants had created a fierce sense of nationalistic pride among all ranks of Athenians, and most were unwilling to turn over the government to only a few. Thus, when the aristocrats made their bid to recover power, their primary opponent, Cleisthenes (ca. 570–ca. 507 B.C.E.), "made the demos his faction" and pushed through a final constitutional reform that became the basis for Athenian **democracy.**

The essence of Cleisthenes' reform lay in his reorganization of the major political units by which members of the council were selected. Previously, each citizen had belonged to 1 of 4 tribes, further broken down into 12 brotherhoods, or *phratries,* which were administrative and religious units. In a manner similar to that of Cypselus in Corinth, Cleisthenes reshuffled these phratries into 30 territorial units, or *trittyes,* comprising urban, inland, or coastal regions. The 30 units in turn were grouped into 10 tribes, each consisting of 1 unit from each of the urban, inland, and coastal regions. The tribes elected the members of the council, military commanders, jurors, and magistrates. Cleisthenes also reorganized local governance by creating *demes* or local councils governing several settlements, a village, or a district of a city. As in Corinth, this reorganization destroyed the traditional kin-based social and political pattern and integrated people of differing social, economic, and regional backgrounds. Aristocrats, merchants, and poor farmers had to work together to find common ground for political action, both regionally and nationally. With this new, integrated democracy and its strong sense of nationalism, Athens emerged from the Archaic Age as the leading city of the Hellenic world.

Neither Corinth, Sparta, nor Athens was a typical Archaic Greek city—there was no such thing. However, each faced similar problems: deep conflict between old aristocratic families and the wider society, growing population pressure, and threats from within and without. Their solutions—a period of tyranny in Corinth and Athens followed by oligarchy in the former and radical democracy in the latter or, in the case of Sparta, the creation of a small but egalitarian military elite—suggest the spectrum of alternatives from which cities across the Greek world sought to meet these challenges.

THE COMING OF PERSIA AND THE END OF THE ARCHAIC AGE

By the end of the sixth century B.C.E., the products of Greek experimentation were evident throughout the Mediterranean. Greek city-states had resolved the crises of class conflict. Greek merchants and artisans had found ways to flourish despite poor soil and uncertain climate. Greek philosophers, poets, and artists had begun to celebrate the human form and the human spirit. Still, these achievements were the product of small, independent, and relatively weak communities on the fringe of the civilized world. The Greeks' insignificance and isolation had kept them out of the sphere of interest of the great floodplain empires to the east.

In the second half of the sixth century B.C.E., all this changed. The Persian Empire, under its dynamic king, Cyrus II, began a process of conquest and expansion west into Asia Minor. Cyrus granted the provinces of his empire great autonomy and preserved local forms of government wherever possible, being care-

MAP DISCOVERY

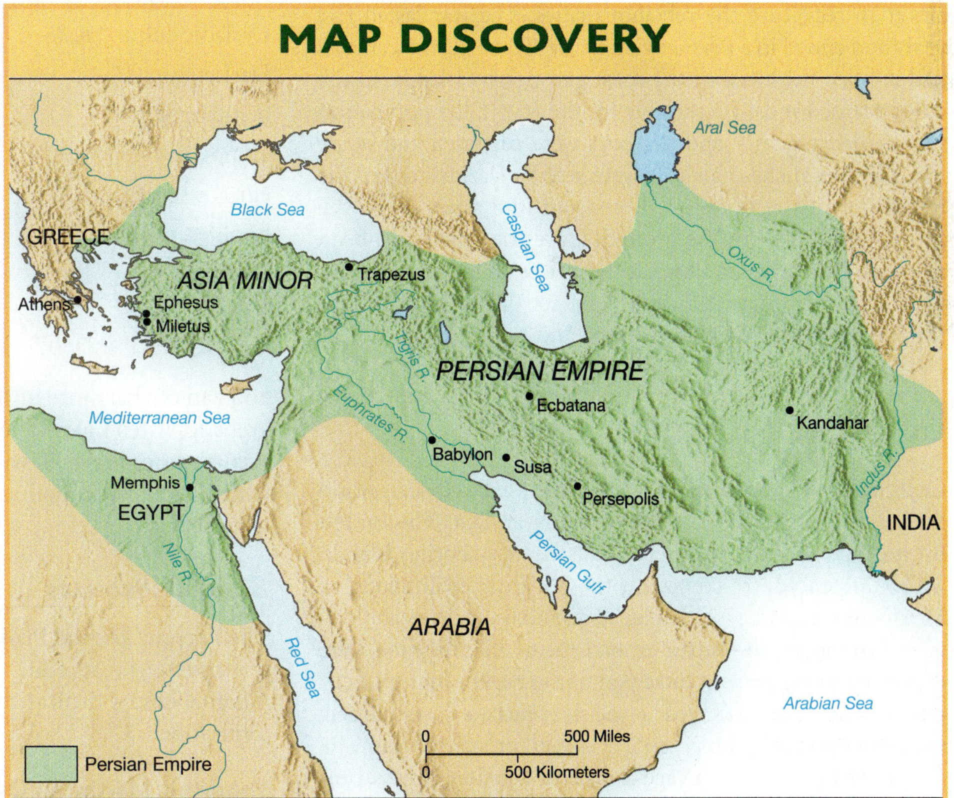

The Persian Empire, ca. 500 B.C.E.

Examine the extent of the Persian Empire. Which ancient civilizations that you have studied so far were incorporated into the Persian Empire? What effects on cultural and economic exchange can you imagine to have resulted from this territorial conquest?

ful only to impose governors, or *satraps,* loyal to him and his Achaemenid dynasty. In keeping with this tradition, when he absorbed Ionia and the kingdom of Lydia on the coast of Asia Minor, he put tyrants loyal to Persia to rule over the Greek communities, and for a few decades these centers of Greek culture and thought accepted foreign control. In 499 B.C.E., the passion for democracy that had swept much of mainland Greece reached Ionia. Cities such as Miletus, Ephesus, Chios, and Samos revolted, expelled their Persian-appointed tyrants, established democracies, and sent ambassadors to the mainland to seek assistance. Eretria and Athens, two mainland cities with Ionian roots, responded, sending ships and men to aid the Ionian rebels. Athenian interests involved more than simple solidarity with their Ionian cousins. Athens depended on grain from the Black Sea region and thus had direct interest in that area. The success of the revolt was short-lived. The puny Greek cities were dealing with the largest empire the West had yet known. By 500 B.C.E., the Persian Empire included Asia Minor, Mesopotamia, Palestine, and Egypt, uniting all the peoples from the Caucasus to the Sudan.

The giant Persian Empire responded slowly, but with force, to the Greek revolt. King Darius I (522–486 B.C.E.) gathered a vast international force from throughout his empire and set about to recapture the rebellious cities. The war lasted five years and ended in a Persian victory. By 494 B.C.E., the Persians had retaken the cities of the coast and nearby islands. In the cities deemed most responsible for the revolt, the population was herded together and the boys were castrated and made into royal eunuchs. The girls were sent to Darius's court, the remainder of the population was sold into slavery, and the towns were burnt to the ground. Once the rebels had been disposed of, Darius and his vast armies, with the same meticulous planning and deliberate pace, set out to punish their supporters on the mainland, Eretria and Athens.

CONCLUSION

Civilization developed much later in the Mediterranean world than it had in the floodplains of the Near East. The earliest Bronze Age societies of Greece and the neighboring islands, while influenced by contact with the great civilizations of Mesopotamia and Egypt, developed distinctive societies and cultures tied closely to the sea around them. Still, they too were caught up in the general cataclysm of the twelfth century B.C.E. Out of the ruins emerged a society much less centralized, wealthy, or powerful but possessing an extraordinary dynamism.

The Archaic Age was an age of experimentation. Greeks, propelled by demographic and political pressures and inspired by the legends of vanished heroes, began in the eighth century B.C.E. to recast traditions and techniques acquired from their ancient neighbors into new forms. The multiplicity of independent communities, their relative isolation, and their differing traditions created a wide spectrum of political forms, social structures, and cultural values. And yet, from Sicily to Asia Minor, Greeks felt themselves united by a common language, a common cultural heritage, and a common commitment to individual freedom within the community, whether that freedom was protected within a monarchy, a tyranny, an oligarchy, or a democracy. That commitment to freedom, fostered in the hoplite ranks, protected in the assembly, and increasingly expressed in poetry and sculpture, hung in the balance as Darius and the Persians marched west.

QUESTIONS FOR REVIEW

1. What social and geographic factors shaped Greek culture in the age of the *Iliad* and the *Odyssey?*
2. What social forces spurred colonization, and what impact did colonization have on Archaic Greek civilization?
3. What do the gods, myths, and art of the Greek people reveal about their lives?
4. How did the Corinthian, Spartan, and Athenian cultures differ, and why did these city-states evolve in such different directions?

KEY TERMS

colonization, *p. 48*	Linear B, *p. 41*
Cycladic culture, *p. 38*	Minoan civilization, *p. 39*
Dark Age, *p. 41*	Mycenaean, *p. 41*
democracy, *p. 61*	oligarchy, *p. 45*
ethnos, *p. 45*	phalanx, *p. 47*
eunomia, *p. 58*	polis, *p. 45*
hoplites, *p. 47*	tholoi, *p. 41*
kouros, *p. 55*	tyrants, *p. 48*

DISCOVERING WESTERN CIVILIZATION ONLINE

You can obtain more information about early Greece at the Websites listed below. See also the Companion Website that accompanies this text, www.ablongman.com/kishlansky, which contains an online study guide and additional resources.

General Websites

The Perseus Digital Project
www.perseus.tufts.edu/
A digital library dedicated to all aspects of ancient Greek civilization.

Thomas R. Martin, An Overview of Classical Greek History
www.perseus.tufts.edu/cgi-bin/ptext?doc=1999.04.0009
This page of The Perseus Digital Project includes an extremely detailed outline of Greek history up to the death of Alexander, with wonderful links to other sources.

NM's Creative Impulse: Greece
history.evansville.net/greece.html
Links to Greek history and civilization.

Greece in the Bronze Age

Palace of Knossos in Minoan Crete
www.dilos.com/region/crete/kn_01.html
A site devoted to the city of Knossos.

Bureaucrats and Barbarians
www.wsu.edu/~dee/MINOA/CONTENTS.HTM
A site devoted to Minoan and Mycenean civilizations.

Archaic Greece

The Ancient Greek World Index
www.museum.upenn.edu/Greek_World/Index.html
A comprehensive site dedicated to ancient Greece from the University of Pennsylvania Museum.

The British Museum Compass
www.thebritishmuseum.ac.uk/compass/
Search the British Museum Collection, which includes Greek antiquities.

Educated Women in Ancient Society
w3.arizona.edu/~ws/ws200/fall97/grp3/grp3.htm
A site devoted to elite women in Greece and their education.

Classical Myth: The Ancient Sources
web.uvic.ca/grs/bowman/myth/
A site devoted to classical mythology with iconography of Greek mythical figures.

A Tale of Three Cities

The Ancient City of Athens
www.Indiana.edu/~kglowack/athens/
A site dedicated to ancient Athens including architecture and sources.

Everything Spartan, Lakonian, and Messenian
www.geocities.com/Athens/Aegean/7849
A site dedicated to Sparta.

The Aegean Map of Greece
www.agn.gr/hellas/map.htm
A Greek government site with an interactive map of Greek locations including historical and modern information.

The Coming of Persia

Internet Ancient History Sourcebook: Persia
www.fordham.edu/halsall/ancient/asbook05.html
A site devoted to sources of ancient Persian history.

SUGGESTIONS FOR FURTHER READING

General Reading

John Boardman, Jasper Griffin, and Oswyn Murray, *Greece and the Hellenistic World* (Oxford: Oxford University Press, 1988). An excellent collection of essays on Greek civilization by British scholars.

S. B. Pomeroy, et. al. *Ancient Greece: A Political, Social, and Cultural History* (Oxford: Oxford University Press, 1998). An important introduction to Greek society and culture.

Greece in the Bronze Age to 800 B.C.E.

Trevor Bryce, *Trojans and Their Neighbours: An Introduction* (London and New York: Routledge, 2006). This comprehensive history of Troy places the ancient city in the context of the eastern Mediterranean during the Bronze Age and beyond.

M. I. Finley, *Early Greece: The Bronze and Archaic Ages,* 2d ed. (New York: W. W. Norton, 1982). A very readable overview by a leading Greek historian.

O. Krzyszkowska and L. Nixon, eds., *Minoan Society* (Bristol: Bristol Classical Press, 1983). An excellent collection of essays on early Crete.

Susan Langdon, ed. *New Light on a Dark Age: Exploring the Culture of Geometric Greece* (Columbia, MO: University of Missouri Press, 1997). Essays on every aspect of society and culture in Dark Age Greece.

N. K. Sandars, *The Sea Peoples* (New York: Thames & Hudson, 1985). A survey of the controversy over the crisis of the twelfth century B.C.E.

William Taylour, *The Mycenaeans* (London: Thames & Hudson, 1990). General overview of Mycenaean civilization and daily life based on archaeology.

Archaic Greece, 800–500 B.C.E.

John Boardman, *The Greeks Overseas* (New York: Thames & Hudson, 1982). A description of varieties of Greek involvement abroad and their effects on Greece by a distinguished archaeologist.

———, *Greek Sculpture: Archaic Period* (New York: Thames & Hudson, 1985). A well-illustrated survey of early Greek sculpture.

Vincent Farenga, *Citizen and Self in Ancient Greece: Individuals Performing Justice and the Law* (Cambridge and New York : Cambridge University Press, 2006). A study of Greek justice from the Dark Ages to the Classical Period.

A. J. Graham, *Colony and Mother City in Ancient Greece* (Chicago: Ares, 1983). A synthetic look at Greek colonies.

Catherine Morgan, *Early Greek States Beyond the Polis* (New York: Routledge, 2003). A reevaluation of the relationship between ethne and polis in the Archaic period.

S. B. Pomeroy, *Families in Classical and Hellenistic Greece: Representation and Realities* (Oxford: Oxford University

Press, 1999). A history of the family in Greece by a leading feminist historian.

Anthony Snodgrass, *Archaic Greece: The Age of Experiment* (Totowa, NJ: Biblio Distribution Center, 1980). An excellent survey of the creative achievements of the Archaic period.

Mark Stansbury-O'Donnell, *Vase Painting, Gender, and Social Identity in Archaic Athens* (New York: Cambridge University Press, 2006). A study of the audience for archaic Greek vase painting that explores ages, genders, and perspectives of the various segments of society that came into contact with these objects.

Christopher Tadgell, *Hellenic Classicism: The Ordering of Form in the Ancient Greek World* (New York: Whitney Library of Design, 1998). A survey of Greek art and architecture to the construction of Athens's Acropolis.

A Tale of Three Cities

Maria Brosius, *Women in Ancient Persia, 559–331 B.C.* (Oxford: Clarendon Press, 1996). Essays on all aspects of women in the Persian Empire.

Paul Cartledge, *Sparta and Lakonia: A Regional History 1300–362 B.C.*, 2nd Ed. (New York: Routledge, Chapman & Hall, 2002). The best survey of Spartan history.

J. B. Salmon, *Wealthy Corinth: A History of the City to 338 B.C.* (New York: Oxford University Press, 1984). A comprehensive history of early Corinth.

David Whitehead, *The Demes of Attica (ca. 508–250 B.C.)* (Princeton, NJ: Princeton University Press, 1986). An excellent study of Athenian politics and society.

For a list of additional titles related to this chapter's topics, please see http://www.ablongman.com/kishlansky.

CHAPTER 3

CLASSICAL AND HELLENISTIC GREECE, 500–100 B.C.E.

PERICLES BUILDS HIS PARTHENON

POLITICS, ART, AND EMPIRE

THE VISUAL RECORD

The temple dedicated to the Virgin Athena, or Athena Parthenos, is both a timeless work of the highest human artistic achievement and a monument to a fateful moment in the history of Athens and the life of the man who caused it to be built—Pericles. Look at what remains today after almost 2500 years. Even in its half-ruined state, the result of an explosion in 1687, its perfect Doric lines continue to awe, just as they did when it was first built. The Parthenon was an instant success, immediately recognized as the most perfect building in the Mediterranean world. It is a rectangle, measuring 228 by 101.4 feet at the base. Two internal tiers of Doric columns and external columns 6.2 feet in diameter and 34.1 feet in height support the roof, while a frieze of 92 marble panels running around the building represents mythical battles between the gods and giants; equally mythical battles between the Athenians and the Amazons; the sack of Troy; and a battle between the legendary Lapiths and half-man half-horse centaurs. Around the interior cella, which housed a monumental statue of Athena, was portrayed the procession held every four years to honor the goddess, during which daughters of Athenian aristocrats presented the statue of the goddess with a new ceremonial dress. On the eastern pediment was a frieze that depicted the birth of Athena; on the west, the battle for the City of Athens between the goddess and Poseidon, god of the sea.

The Parthenon is constructed entirely of marble quarried on Mount Pentelicus, eleven miles from Athens; it is streaked with iron ore, giving it a luminous glow in the Greek sunlight. In all, the temple is the most sumptuously decorated Greek temple known—not surprising, for it was both a temple and a treasury, a treasury holding the accumulated wealth of the Athenian Empire.

If it is a paradox that a league designed to keep Greek cities free had become the means of their enslavement, it is also a paradox that Athens, the most assertive democracy in the ancient world, was effectively ruled at its height by a single man—Pericles—although he held no formal office. A consummate insider and populist leader, Pericles laid the groundwork for the construction of the Parthenon in 449 B.C.E., when he successfully pushed through a law allowing Athens to take the enormous sum of 9000 talents from the treasury of the Delian League, originally a defensive alliance of free cities, to rebuild Athenian temples. The funds had been collected to help the League protect Greek cities from Persia, but the Persian threat was no more; Athens had managed to turn the League into an empire, and the annual contributions of its members into tribute. As president of the commission responsible for constructing the great ivory-and-gold statue of Athena that stood in the center of the Parthenon, Pericles won widespread political support for these and other vast public works projects that gave employment to thousands of Athenians.

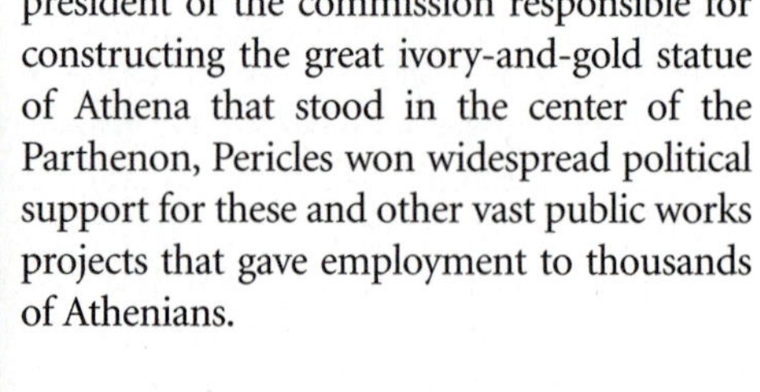

■ Pericles, Athenia statesman and the force behind the construction of the structures on the Acropolis, including the Parthenon.

■ The Parthenon is a timeless work of artistic perfection.

Not everyone was entirely happy with Pericles and his de facto control of the Athenian state. Although his popularity made Pericles a difficult target, both Aspasia, his confidant, advisor, and mistress, who was perhaps the most brilliant and public woman of her day, and his close friend Phidias, the great sculptor responsible for the statue of Athena, were accused of criminal conduct. Aspasia, charged with corrupting Athenian women, was acquitted, but Phidias, charged with embezzling gold intended for the statue of Athena as well as with behaving with impiety, died in prison. Opponents in the ecclesia or assembly began to demand that Pericles himself stand trial for misappropriation of public funds. His desire to turn public attention away from his public works on the Acropolis may have influenced him to pursue an increasingly aggressive foreign policy with the only great power not under Athens's control: Sparta. In 431, the year after he completed the Parthenon, Pericles led Athens into the Peloponnesian War, a war that would destroy the economic, political, and civic foundations on which the Parthenon had been built.

Look again at this magnificent ruin. Never has artistic perfection come at so high a cost.

LOOKING AHEAD

As this chapter will show, the Greek victory over Persian forces in 490 B.C.E. set the stage for an extraordinary flowering of political and cultural production but also a deadly rivalry between Athens and Sparta, the leaders of the victorious Greeks. Democratic Athens transformed its wartime alliance into an empire, and little more than a generation after Athenian and Spartan troops had faced the Persians, they fought each other in a long and futile war. This left the Greek world exhausted and easy prey for the ambitious Macedonian dynasty, which nevertheless spread Greek culture through the Eastern Mediterranean and western Asia.

WAR AND POLITICS IN THE FIFTH CENTURY B.C.E.

The vast Persian army moving west in 490 B.C.E. threatened the fruits of three centuries of Greek political, social, and cultural experimentation. The shared ideal of freedom within community and the common bond of language and culture seemed no basis on which to build an effective resistance to the great Persian Empire. Moreover, Darius I was not marching against the Greeks as such. Few Greek states other than Athens had supported the Ionians against their Persian conquerors. Many Greeks saw the Persians as potential allies or even rulers preferable to the more powerful Greek neighbors and rivals within their own states. Separated by political traditions, intercity rivalries, and cultural differences, the Greeks did not feel any sense of national or ethnic unity. Particular interest, rather than patriotism or love of freedom, determined which cities opposed the Persian march. In the end, only Eretria, a badly divided Athens, and the small town of Plataea were prepared to refuse the Persian king's demand for gifts of earth and water, the traditional symbols of submission.

The Persian Wars

Initially, the Persian campaign followed the pattern established in Ionia. In the autumn of 490 B.C.E., Darius quickly destroyed the city of Eretria and carried off its population in captivity. The victorious Persian forces, which some estimates place as large as 20,000 infantrymen and mounted archers, then landed at the Bay of Marathon, one of the few locations in Attica where horses could pasture that late in the year. Even with approximately 600 Plataeans, the total Athenian force was no more than half that of its enemies, but the Greeks were better armed and commanded the hills facing the Marathon plain on which the Persian troops had massed. The Athenians also benefited from the leadership of Miltiades (ca. 544–489 B.C.E.), an experienced soldier who had served Darius and who knew the Persian's strengths and weaknesses. For more than a week the two armies faced each other in a battle of nerves. Growing dissension in the Athenian ranks finally led the Greek generals to make a desperate and unexpected move. Abandoning the high ground, the Athenian hoplites rushed in disciplined phalanxes over almost a mile of open fields and then attacked the amazed Persian forces at a run. Although the Persians broke through the center of the Greek lines, the Athenians routed the Persian flanks and then turned in, enveloping the invaders in a deadly trap. In a few hours it was all over. Six thousand Persians lay dead, while only 192

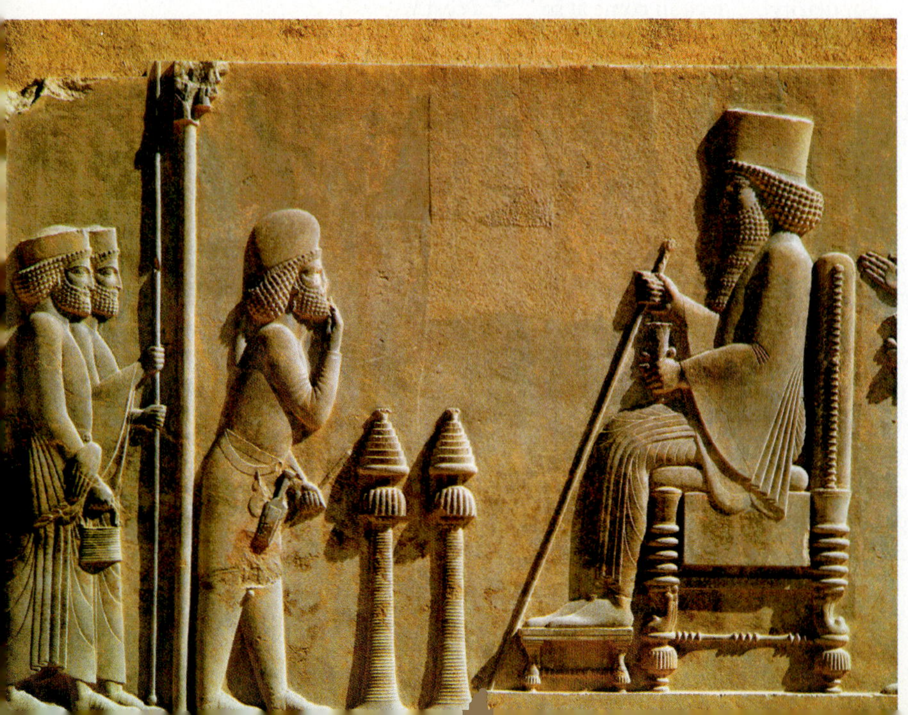

Darius the Great is seated on his throne in his reception chamber while an audience of delegates from provinces around his mighty empire approach him to bring him tribute. This particular dignitary is raising one hand to his mouth as a token of respect and honor and with the other hand he holds his staff of office showing that he was a commander and prime minister of the Medes, as seen by his round cap and uniform. Behind him are two Persian attendants holding a spear and a container of incense.

Athenians were buried in the heroes' grave that still marks the Marathon plain. The Persians retreated to their ships and sailed for the Bay of Phalerum near Athens, hoping to attack the city itself before its victorious troops could return. However, the Athenians, though exhausted from the battle, rushed the 23 miles home in less than eight hours, beating the Persian fleet. When the Persians learned that they had lost the race, they turned their ships for Asia.

The almost miraculous victory at Marathon had three enormous consequences for Athens and for Greece in general. First, it established the superiority of the hoplite phalanx as the finest infantry formation in the Mediterranean world. Not only Athenians but all Greeks were thereafter convinced of the superiority of their soldiers. Second, Greeks expanded this belief in military superiority to a faith in the general superiority of Greeks over the barbarians (those who spoke other languages). Finally, by proving the value of the citizen army, the victory of the Athenians solidified and enhanced the democratic reforms of Cleisthenes.

Common citizens were determined that the victory won by the hoplite phalanx at Marathon should not be lost to an aristocratic faction at home. To guard against this danger, the Athenian assembly began to practice **ostracism**, a ten-year exile without loss of property, imposed on those who threatened to undermine the constitution of Cleisthenes. Each year every Athenian citizen had the opportunity to write on a potsherd (in Greek, *ostrakon*) the name of the man he most wished to leave Attica. If at least 6000 citizens voted, the state sent the individual receiving the most votes into temporary exile. No charges or accusations had to be made, much less proven. Anyone who had offended the Athenians or who, by his prominence, seemed a threat to democracy could be ostracized. Aristides (ca. 530–ca. 468 B.C.E.), known as "The Just" and a hero of the battle of Marathon, was ostracized in 482 B.C.E. During the vote, an illiterate farmer, taking him for an ordinary citizen, approached Aristides and asked him to write the name Aristides on a potsherd for him. When asked if Aristides had done him any wrong, the farmer replied, "None at all, nor do I know him. I am just tired of hearing everyone call him 'The Just.'" Aristides complied and, gaining the most votes, sadly left Attica.

This ostrakon was found in the Athenian agora. It was used to cast a vote to choose a person who would be ostracized—banished from Athens for a period of ten years. The name on the first line is Themistocles.

At the same time, Athenians also began to select their chief officers not simply by direct election but by lot. This practice

The Persian Wars. Greeks fought on both sides in the Persian Wars, while many others remained neutral.

prevented any individual from rising to power by creating a powerful faction. Themistocles (ca. 528–462 B.C.E.), the son of a noble father and a non-Greek mother, took the lead in using the tools of ostracism and selection by lot to hold the aristocratic factions at bay. He also used his influence to convince Athens to fortify its harbor at Piraeus and to invest in a powerful fleet as protection against the inevitable return of the Persians.

Thermopylae and Salamis

Occupied by problems elsewhere in their vast empire and by the unexpected death of Darius I in 486 B.C.E., the Persians paid little attention to Greece for six years. After Darius's death, his son Xerxes (486–465 B.C.E.), probably more interested in securing the western frontier of his empire than in avenging his father's loss at Marathon, began to amass foodstuffs, weapons, and armies for a land assault on his Greek enemies. In response to these preparations, Greek cities began to close ranks against the invaders. Still, however, many Greek communities saw their neighbors as greater threats than the Persians. Some states—including Thebes, Argos, and Thessaly—more or less willingly allied with the Persians against Athens or Sparta. More distant cities such as Syracuse refused assistance except on their own terms, and north of the Peloponnesus only Athens, Plataea, and a few other small states were willing to fight. Sparta was prepared to defend itself and its league but was not interested in campaigns far from home. Finally, in 481 B.C.E., when the Persian invasion was imminent, representatives of what a contemporary called "the Greeks who had the best thoughts for Greece" met in Sparta to plan resistance. The allies agreed that the Spartans would take command of the combined land and sea forces, which probably totaled roughly 35,000 helots, 5000 hoplites, and 378 ships.

■ Glazed brick panels from the Palace of Darius I (521–486 B.C.E.) showing members of his elite guard of "immortals," so-called because their number was always maintained at 10,000.

Although larger than the troops mustered by Athens against Darius, the Greek forces were puny compared with Xerxes' estimated 200,000 infantry and 1000 light, highly maneuverable Ionian and Phoenician ships. The Spartan commanders sought a strategic point at which the numerical superiority of the Persian forces would be neutralized. The choice fell on the narrow pass of Thermopylae and the adjacent Euboean strait. While a select force of hoplites held the pass, the Greek fleet, following a strategy devised by Themistocles, harried the larger Persian one. Neither action produced a Greek victory, but none could have been expected.

At Thermopylae, the Greeks held firm for days against wave after wave of assaulting troops ordered forward by an amazed and outraged Xerxes. Finally, Greek allies of the Persians showed them a narrow mountain track by which they were able to attack the Greek position from the rear. Seeing that all was lost, the Spartan king Leonidas (490–480 B.C.E.) sent most of his allies home. He and his 300 Spartan equals then faced certain death with a casual disdain characterized by the comment made by one Spartan equal. Told that when the Persians shot their arrows, they were so numerous that they hid the sun, the Spartan replied, "Good. If the Persians hide the sun, we shall have our battle in the shade." The epitaph raised later by the Spartan state to Leonidas and his men read simply, "Go tell the Spartans, you who read: we took their orders, and are dead." Dead they were, but they had bought precious time for the Greek allies.

While the Persian troops were blocked at Thermopylae, their fleet was being battered by fierce storms in the Euboean straits and harassed by the heavier Greek ships. Here the Greeks learned that, in close quarters, they could stand up to Xerxes' Phoenician navy. This lesson proved vital a short time later. While the Persian army burned Athens and occupied Attica, Themistocles lured the fleet into the narrow strait between Salamis and the mainland. There the slower Greek vessels bottled up the larger and vastly more numerous enemy ships and cut them to pieces.

After Salamis, Xerxes lost his appetite for fighting Greeks. Without his fleet, he could not supply a vast army far from home in hostile territory. Leaving a force to do what damage it could, he led the bulk of his forces back to Persia. At Athenian urging, the Greek allies under Leonidas's kinsman Pausanias (d. ca. 470 B.C.E.) met the Persians at Plataea in 479 B.C.E. Once more, hoplite discipline and Greek determination meant more than numerical superiority. That night the Spartan king dined in the splendor of the captured tent of the defeated Persian commander. Athenian sea power and Spartan infantry had proven invincible. Soon the Athenians were taking the offensive, liberating the Ionian cities of Asia Minor and, in the process, laying the foundations of an Athenian Empire every bit as threatening to their neighbors as that of Xerxes.

The Athenian Empire

Sparta, not Athens, should have emerged as the leader of the Greek world after 479 B.C.E. The Spartans, after all, had provided the crucial military force and leadership, and Sparta had emerged unscathed from the Persian wars. However, the constant threat of a helot revolt and the league members' desire to go their separate ways left Sparta too preoccupied with internal problems to fill the power vacuum left by the Persian defeat. Nor did Spartan values encourage international ambitions. Sparta's militarism at home did not translate into military expansion abroad.

Athens, on the other hand, was only too ready to take the lead in bringing the war home to the Persians. With Sparta out of the picture, the Athenian fleet was the best hope of liberating the Aegean from Persians and pirates. Athenian propaganda emphasized the Persian menace and Ionian solidarity.

The Delian League. In 478 B.C.E. Athens accepted control of what historians have come to call the **Delian League,** after the island of Delos, a religious center that housed the league's treasury. Athens and some of the states with navies provided ships; others contributed annual payments to the league. Initially, the league pursued the war against the Persians, not only driving them back along the Aegean and Black seas, but also supporting rebels in the Persian Empire as far away as Egypt. At the same time, Athens hurriedly rebuilt its defensive fortifications, a move correctly interpreted by Sparta and other states as directed more against them than against the Persians.

Athens's domination of the Delian League ensured its prosperity. Attica, with its fragile agriculture, depended on Black Sea wheat, and the league kept these regions under Athenian control. Since Athens received not only cash "contributions" from league members but also one-half of the spoils taken in battle, the state's public coffers were filled. The new riches made possible the reconstruction of the city that had been burned by the Persians into the most magnificent city of Greece.

The league was too vital to Athenian prosperity to stand and fall with the Persian threat. The drive against the Persian Empire began to falter after a league expedition to Egypt in 454 B.C.E. ended in total defeat. Discouraged by this and other setbacks, the Athenian Callias, acting for the league, apparently concluded a treaty of peace with Persia in 449 B.C.E., making the alliance no longer necessary. For a brief moment it appeared that the Delian League might disband. But it was too late. The league had become an empire, and Athens's allies were its subjects.

Athenian Imperialism. The Athenian Empire was an economic, judicial, religious, and political union held together by military might. Athens controlled the flow of grain through the Hellespont to the Aegean, ensuring its own supply and heavily taxing cargoes to other cities. Athens controlled the law courts of member cities and used them to repress anti-Athenian groups. Major cases were brought to Athens itself, where large, politicized, democratic juries ensured that the Athenian demos, or people, would emerge as winners. Everywhere the goddess Athena received official worship as the patroness of Ionia. The goddess, through her temples, was viewed as the owner of great amounts of land leased out to Athenians. Rich and poor citizens alike acquired territory throughout the empire. The rich took over vast estates confiscated from local opponents of Athenian dominance, while the poor replaced hostile populations in the colonies.

Control over the empire depended on the Athenian fleet to enforce cooperation. Athenian garrisons were established in each city, and "democratic" puppet governments ruled according to the wishes of the garrison commanders. Revolt, resignation from the league, or refusal to pay the annual tribute resulted in brutal suppression. The whole population of one rebellious city in Euboea was expelled and replaced with Athenian colonists. Athens sold the population of another city into slavery. Persian tyranny had hardly been worse than Athenian imperialism.

Private and Public Life in Athens

During the second half of the fifth century B.C.E., Athens, enriched by tribute from its more than 150 subject states, was a vital, crowded capital drawing merchants, artisans, and laborers from throughout the Greek world. At its height, the total population of Athens and surrounding Attica numbered perhaps 350,000, although probably fewer than 60,000 were citizens, that is, adult males qualified to own land and participate in Athenian politics.

THE TWO FACES OF ATHENIAN DEMOCRACY

Early in the Peloponnesian War, Thucydides summarizes the virtues of Athenian democracy in the speech he ascribes to Pericles in honor of those who died in the first year of the war. By 416 B.C.E., the sixteenth year of the Peloponnesian War, Athenian imperialism no longer even paid lip service to the ideals of democracy or freedom. Thucydides illustrates this in his reconstructed debate between representatives of the Spartan colony of Melos, which had attempted to remain neutral, and representatives of the Athenians, who demanded their surrender and enslavement.

Focus Questions

What limits did the Athenians place on the ideal of democracy? How did the Athenians justify violence to maintain their empire?

Pericles' Funeral Oration

Our constitution is called a democracy because power is in the hands not of a minority but of the whole people. When it is a question of settling private disputes, everyone is equal before the law; when it is a question of putting one person before another in positions of public responsibility, what counts is not membership of a particular class, but the actual ability which the man possesses. No one, so long as he has it in him to be of service to the state, is kept in political obscurity because of poverty.

The Melian Debate

ATHENIANS: You know as well as we do that, when these matters are discussed by practical people, the standard of justice depends on the equality of power to compel and that in fact the strong do what they have the power to do and the weak accept what they have to accept.

MELIANS: And how could it be just as good for us to be the slaves as for you to be the masters?

ATHENIANS: You, by giving in, would save yourselves from disaster; we by not destroying you, would be able to profit from you.

MELIANS: So you would not agree to our being neutral, friends instead of enemies, but allies of neither side?

ATHENIANS: No, because it is not so much your hostility that injures us; it is rather the case that, if we were on friendly terms with you, our subjects would regard that as a sign of weakness in us, whereas your hatred is evidence of our power.

Ultimately the Melians rejected Athens's demands, and shortly after the Athenians captured the city, they executed all the men and sold the women and children as slaves.

From Thucydides, *History of the Peloponnesian War.*

Slaves. Over one-quarter of the total population were slaves. Ever since the reforms of Solon had prohibited debt bondage, great landowners, unable to force ordinary free men to work their estates, had turned to slave labor. Slaves were also vital in mining and other forms of craft and industrial work. In addition, most citizen households, even modest ones, boasted at least one or two domestics.

Greek slaves were not distinguished by race, ethnicity, or physical appearance. Anyone could become a slave. Prisoners of war, foreigners who failed to pay taxes, victims of pirate raids—all could end up on the auction blocks of the ancient world. Slaves were as much the property of their owners as land, houses, cattle, and sheep. Many masters treated their slaves well. After all, the cost of a slave was higher than the annual wage of a skilled free man. However, beatings, tattooing, starvation, and shackling were all common means of enforcing obedience. The bodies of male and female slaves were always at the disposition of their masters, who could use them as they wanted or hand them over to others.

Aristotle on Slavery

Still, the variety of slave experience was enormous. Rural slaves generally fared worse than urban ones, and those who worked the mines led the most appalling lives; they literally were worked to death. Others worked side by side with their masters in craft shops or even set up their own businesses, from which they were allowed to keep some of their profit to ultimately purchase their freedom. One slave left an estate worth more than 33,000 drachmas (the equivalent of 165 years' salary for an ordinary free man), which included slaves of his own!

Metics. Roughly half of Athens's free population were foreigners—metoikoi, or **metics.** These were primarily Greek citizens of the tributary states of the empire, but they might also be Lydians, Phrygians, Syrians, Egyptians, Phoenicians, or Carians. The number of metics increased after the middle of the fifth century B.C.E., both because of the flood of foreigners into the empire's capital and because Athenian citizenship was restricted to persons with two parents who were of citizen families. Under these rules, neither Cleisthenes, the great reformer of the sixth century B.C.E., nor Themistocles, the architect of the victory against Persia, both of whose mothers had been foreigners, could have been Athenian citizens.

Metics could not own land in Attica, nor could they participate directly in politics. They were required to have a citizen protector and to pay a small annual tax. Otherwise, they were free to engage in every form of activity. Metics participated in commerce, manufacturing, banking, and skilled crafts. Educated metics also contributed to the intellectual and cultural life of the city. The great historian of the Persian wars, Herodotus, was a foreigner from Halicarnassus.

On this fifth-century B.C.E. Athenian vase women are depicted making preparations for a wedding.

Women. More than half of those born into citizen families were entirely excluded from public life. These were the women, who controlled and directed the vital sphere of the Athenian home but who were considered citizens only for purposes of marriage, transfer of property, and procreation. During the Archaic period, aristocratic women had enjoyed some independence. However, the triumph of democracy reduced the public role of all women to that of breeder and property conduit. From birth to death, every female citizen lived under the protection of a male guardian, either a close relative such as a father or brother, or a husband or son. Women spent almost their entire lives in the inner recesses of the home, emerging only for funerals and a very few religious festivals. Fathers arranged marriages, which were contracted to produce legitimate children and acquire wealth through dowries. A wife had no control over her dowry, which passed to her son. In the event of divorce or the death of her husband, the woman and her dowry returned to her father. Should a woman's father die without a will or an heir, his closest male relative could demand her as his wife and thus claim the inheritance, even if the woman was already married to someone else.

An honorable Athenian woman stayed at home and managed her husband's household. Wealthy women directed the work of servants and slaves. In modest homes, women were expected to participate along with the slaves in domestic chores such as spinning and in rearing children. Only the poorest citizens sent their wives and daughters to work in the marketplace or the fields. Even the most casual contact with other men was strictly forbidden without permission, although men were expected to engage in various sorts of extramarital affairs. In the words of one Athenian male, "Hetairai we have for our pleasure, mistresses for the refreshment of our bodies, but wives to bear us legitimate children and to look after the house faithfully."

Within the home, Athenian women were vital, if subordinate, partners. The household, as Athenians never tired of repeating, was the foundation of all society. Thus the role of women was indeed important. The public sphere was entirely closed to them, although even some men realized the potential for resentment. A woman in one of Euripides' tragedies describes her status:

We women are the most unfortunate creatures.
Firstly with an excess of wealth it is required
For us to buy a husband and take for our bodies
A master; for not to take one is even worse. . . .
What they say of us is that we have a peaceful time
Living at home, while they do the fighting in war.
How wrong they are! I would very much rather stand
Three times in the front of battle than bear one child.

Male control over women may have resulted in part from fear. Women were identified with the forces of nature, which included both positive forces such as fertility and life and negative forces such as chaotic irrationality, which threatened civilization. These two poles were epitomized by the cult of Dionysus. He was the god of wine, life blood, and fertility, but he was also the deity whose female devotees, the maenads, were portrayed as worshiping him in a state of frenzied savagery that could include tearing children and animals limb from limb.

Freedom in Community. The male citizens of fifth-century B.C.E. Athens were free to an extent previously unknown in the world. But Athenian freedom was freedom in community, not freedom from community. The essence of their freedom lay in their participation in public life, especially self-government, which was their passion. This participation always occurred within a complex network of familial, social, and religious connections and obligations. Each person belonged to a number of groups: a deme, a tribe, a family, various religious associations, and occupational groups. Each of these communities placed different and even contradictory demands on its members. The impossibility of satisfying all of the demands, of responding to the special interests of each, forced citizens to make hard choices, to set priorities, and to balance conflicting obligations. This process of selection was the essence of Athenian freedom, a freedom that, unlike that of the modern world, was based not on individualism but on a multitude of collectivities. The sum of the overlapping groupings was Athenian society, in which friends and opponents alike were united.

Unity did not imply equality. Even in fifth-century B.C.E. Athens, not all Athenians were socially or economically equal. Most were farmers who looked to military service as a means of increasing their meager income. Others engaged in trade or industry, although metics, with their commercial contacts in their cities of origin, dominated much of such activities in Athens. However, the aristocracy was still strong, and most of the popular leaders of the century came from the ranks of old wealth and influence. They used their wealth to attract supporters from the poorer ranks of the citizenry. Still, sovereignty lay not with these aristocrats but with the demos—the people.

In theory, the adult male citizens of Athens were Athens's sovereigns. Since the time of Solon, they had formed the **ekklesia**, or assembly. On particularly solemn occasions, as many as 6000 citizens might convene in the *pnyx*, the meeting place of the assembly. They also made up the large juries, always composed of several hundred citizens, who decided legal cases less on law than on the political merits of the case and the quality of the orators who pleaded for each side. Such large bodies were too unwieldy to deal with the daily tasks of government. Thus, control of those tasks fell to the council, or *boule*, composed of 500 members selected by lot by the tribes; the magistrates, who were also chosen by lot; and ten military commanders or generals, the only major officeholders elected rather than chosen at random.

Demagogues. Paradoxically, the resolute determination of Athenian democrats to prevent individuals from acquiring too much power helped to create a series of extraconstitutional power brokers. Since most offices were filled by lot and turned over frequently, real political leadership came not from officeholders but from generals and from popular leaders. These so-called **demagogues**, while at times holding high office, exercised their power through their speaking skills, informal networks, and knowledge of how to get things done. They acquired that knowledge through their willingness to serve for long periods in various capacities on committees, as unpaid government workers, and in minor elected offices. Demagogues tended to be wealthy aristocrats who could afford to put in the time demanded by the largely voluntary services. Governing an empire demanded skill, energy, and experience, but Athenian democracy was formally run by amateurs. Small wonder that the city's public life was dominated by the popular leaders.

Although many demagogues competed for power and attracted the support of the people, the Athenian demos was not kind to its heroes. Ten years after the Greek victory at Salamis in 480 B.C.E., Athens ostracized Themistocles, whose leadership there had saved Athens. Mistrusted by many of his co-citizens, he ended his days, ironically, in the service of the Persian king. Cimon (ca. 510–451 B.C.E.), the son of the Marathon hero Miltiades, helped destroy Themistocles and succeeded him as the most influential leader of the city. As long as he lavished his wealth on the populace and led Athenian armies to victory against the Persians, Cimon remained popular. He also fought to hold the Athenian Empire together when the island of Thasos attempted to secede in 465 B.C.E. However, his luck ran out three years later. In 462 B.C.E., Cimon led an army to assist Sparta in suppressing a revolt of its helots. The Spartans, fearing that he was actually planning to plot with the helots against them, sent him and his army home in disgrace. This disgrace was fatal, and Athens ostracized Cimon upon his return.

For the next 30 years, one individual dominated Athenian public life: the general Pericles (ca. 495–429 B.C.E.). Although not an original thinker, he was a great orator and a successful military commander who proved to be the man most able to win the confidence of Athens and to lead it during the decades of its greatest glory. The Athenian political system of radical democracy reached its zenith under the leadership of Pericles, even while its imperial program drew it into a long and fatal war against Sparta, the only state powerful enough to resist it.

Pericles and Athens

Pericles was descended from the greatest aristocratic families of Athens. Nevertheless, as one ancient author put it, he "took his side, not with the rich and the few, but with the many and the poor." Pericles acquired intimate knowledge of government through long service on various public works projects, projects that provided lucrative income to poorer citizens who had supplemented their incomes as oarsmen before being idled by the peace of Callias of 449 B.C.E. As we know from The Visual Record (pp. 66–67) Pericles was also president of the commission responsible for constructing the great ivory-and-gold statue of Athena that stood in the Parthenon, the main temple in Athens. He also served on the commission that built the Lyceum, the city exercise center, and the Parthenon itself. The enormous projects won him a large popular following while giving him an intimate knowledge of public finance and the details of Athenian government. He enhanced his position further through his great powers of persuasion. His speaking ability was described by an opponent, Thucydides, son of Melesias (d. ca. 410 B.C.E.). When asked by the king of Sparta whether he or Pericles was the better wrestler, Thucydides was said to have replied that while he could throw Pericles, the latter was so eloquent that he could easily convince those who had seen him thrown that he had not fallen but rather had won the match.

Pericles never ruled Athens. As a general he could only carry out the orders of the ekklesia and the boule, and as a citizen he could only attempt to persuade his fellows. Still, he was largely responsible for the extension of Athenian democracy to all free citizens. Under his influence, Athens abolished the last property requirements for office holding. He convinced the state to pay those who served on juries, thus making it possible for even the poorest citizens to participate in this important part of Athenian government. But he was also responsible for a restriction of citizenship to those whose mothers and fathers had been Athenians. Such a law would have denied citizenship to many of the most illustrious Athenians of the sixth century B.C.E., including his own ancestors. By adopting such a measure, Athens was closing the door to persons of talent and energy who might have been of great service to the city in the future. The law also prevented citizens of Athens's subject states from developing a real stake in the fate of the empire.

Pericles had been an opponent of the aristocratically oriented Cimon at home and disputed Cimon's foreign policy, which saw Athens and Sparta as "yoke mates" against Persia. Pericles had little fear of Persia but mistrusted Sparta. This policy ultimately drew Athens into deadly conflict with Sparta. The first clash between the two great powers came around 460 B.C.E. Megara, which lay between the Peloponnesus and Attica, withdrew from the Spartan alliance and sought Athens's assistance against nearby Corinth in a border dispute. The Athenians, eager to add Megara to their empire, went to their assistance. Soon Sparta and Aegina entered the fray, but Athens emerged victorious, checking Sparta and absorbing Megara, Aegina, and Boeotia. However, in 446 B.C.E., after the Athenian defeat in Egypt, Megara and Boeotia rebelled, and Sparta invaded the disputed region. Unable to face this new threat at home after their disastrous loss abroad, in 445 B.C.E. the Athenians, under the leadership of Pericles, concluded a peace treaty with Sparta whereby Athens abandoned all of its continental possessions. The treaty was meant to last for 30 years. It held for 14.

The two great powers were eager to preserve the peace, but the whole Greek world was a tinderbox ready to burst into flame. The spark came from an unexpected direction. In 435 B.C.E., Corinth and its colony Corcyra on the Adriatic Sea came to blows, and Corcyra sought the assistance of Athens. Athens had never had much interest or involvement in the west, but it did not want the Corinthian fleet, vital to the Spartan alliance, augmented by absorbing the ships of Corcyra. Therefore the Athenians agreed to a defensive alliance with Corcyra and assisted it in defeating its enemy. The assistance infuriated Corinth, an ally of Sparta, and in 432 B.C.E. the Corinthians convinced the Spartans that Athenian imperial ambitions were insatiable. In the words of the great historian of the war, Thucydides (d. ca. 401 B.C.E.), "What made war inevitable was the growth of Athenian power and the fear which this caused in Sparta." The next year, Sparta invaded Attica. The Peloponnesian War, which would destroy both great powers, had begun.

■ Corinthian olpe with animal decoration, 600 B.C.E.

The Peloponnesian War

The Peloponnesian War was actually a series of wars and rebellions. Athens and Sparta waged two devastating ten-year wars, from 431 B.C.E. to 421 B.C.E. and then again from 413 B.C.E. to 404 B.C.E. At the same time, cities in each alliance took advantage of the wars to revolt against the great powers, eliciting terrible vengeance from both Athens and Sparta. Within many of the Greek city-states, oligarchs and democrats waged bloody civil wars for control of their governments. Moreover, between 415 and 413 B.C.E., Athens attempted to expand its empire in Sicily, an attempt that ended in disaster. Before it was over, the Peloponnesian War had become an international war, with Persia entering the fray on the side of Sparta. In the end, there were no real victors, only victims.

Initially, Sparta and Athens both hoped for quick victory. Sparta's strength was its army, and its strategy was to invade Attica, devastate the countryside, and force the Athenians into an open battle. Given the Spartan infantry's strength, numbers, and skill, such a battle could only end in an Athenian defeat. Pericles urged Athens to adopt a strategy of conserving its hoplite forces while exploiting its naval strength. Athens was a naval power and, with its empire and control of Black Sea grain, could hold out for years behind its fortifications, the great wall linking Athens to its port of Piraeus. At the same time, the Athenian fleet could launch raids along the coast of the Peloponnesus, thus bringing the war home to the Spartans. Pericles hoped in this way to outlast the Spartans. In describing the war, Thucydides uses the same word for "survive" and "win."

The Archidamian War. The first phase of the war, called the Archidamian War after the Spartan king Archidamus (431–427 B.C.E.), was indecisive. Sparta pillaged Attica but could not breach the great wall or starve Athens. In 430 B.C.E., the Spartans received unexpected help in the form of plague, which ravaged Athens for five years. By the time it ended in 426 B.C.E., as much as one-third of the Athenian population had died, including Pericles. Still Athens held out, establishing bases encircling the Peloponnesus and urging Spartan helots and allies to revolt. At Pylos in 425 B.C.E., the Athenian generals Cleon and Demosthenes captured a major force of Spartan equals. The Spartans offset this defeat by capturing the city of Amphipolis on the northern Aegean. The defeated Athenian commander, Thucydides, was exiled for his failure and retired to Spartan territory to write his great history of the war. Exhausted by a decade of death and destruction, the two sides contracted peace in 421 B.C.E. Although Athens was victorious in that its empire was intact, the peace changed nothing and tensions festered for five years.

MAP DISCOVERY

The Delian League and the Peloponnesian War

When Athens turned the Delian League into its own empire, the resulting war pitted the Attica city-state against the combined forces of Sparta and Persia. Examine the extent of the Delian League, Sparta and its allies, and the neutral states. Why would Sparta and its allies feel threatened strategically and economically by the Delian League? Why was an alliance with Persia a vital part of Spartan strategy? What threats faced those states that remained neutral?

Alcibiades and the Sicilian Expedition. After the peace of 421 B.C.E., Pericles' kinsman Alcibiades (ca. 450–404 B.C.E.) came to dominate the demos. Well spoken, handsome, and brave—but also vain, dissolute, and ambitious—Alcibiades led the city into disaster. Although a demagogue who courted popular support, he despised the people and schemed to overturn the democracy. His personal life, perhaps typical of privileged young Athenian aristocrats, had little room for the traditional religious or patriotic values of the city. In 415 B.C.E. he urged Athens to expand its empire west by attacking Syracuse, the most prosperous Greek city of Sicily, which had largely escaped the devastation of the Archidamian War. The expedition went poorly and Alcibiades, accused at home of having profaned one of the most important Athenian religious cults, was ordered home. Instead, he fled to Sparta, where he began to assist the Spartans against Athens. The Sicilian expedition ended in disaster. Athens lost more than 200 ships and 50,000 men. At the same time, Sparta resumed the war, this time with naval support provided by Persia.

Suddenly Athens was fighting for its life. Alcibiades soon abandoned Sparta for Persia and convinced the Athenians that if they abandoned their democracy for an oligarchy, Persia would withdraw its support of Sparta. In 411 B.C.E., the desperate Athenian assembly established a brutal oligarchy controlled by a small faction of antidemocratic conspirators. Alcibiades' promise proved hollow, and the war continued. Athens reestablished its democracy, but the brief oligarchy left the city bitterly divided. The Persian king renewed his support for Sparta, sending his son Cyrus (ca. 424–401 B.C.E.) to coordinate the war against Athens. Under the Spartan general Lysander (d. 395 B.C.E.), Sparta and its allies finally closed in on Athens. Lysander captured the Athenian fleet in the Hellespont, destroyed it, killed 3000 Athenian prisoners, and severed Athens's vital grain supply. Within months Athens, entirely cut off from the outside world, was starving. In 404 B.C.E., Sparta accepted Athens's unconditional surrender. Athens's fortifications came down, its empire vanished, and its fleet, except for a mere 12 ships, dissolved.

The Peloponnesian War showed not only the limitations of Athenian democracy but the potential brutality of oligarchy as well. More ominously, it demonstrated the catastrophic effects of disunity and rivalry among the Greek cities of the Mediterranean.

■ This bust of Socrates portrays him with the traditional beard of the philosopher. His features display the tradition that this man, whose thoughts were the most beautiful, was nevertheless of remarkably homely appearance.

ATHENIAN CULTURE IN THE HELLENIC AGE

Most of what we today call Greek is actually Athenian: throughout the Hellenic or Classical age (the fifth and early fourth centuries B.C.E., as distinct from the Hellenistic period of roughly the later fourth through second centuries B.C.E.), the turbulent issues of democracy and oligarchy, war and peace, hard choices and conflicting obligations found expression in Athenian culture even as the glory of the Athenian Empire was manifested in art and architecture. The great dramatists Aeschylus, Sophocles, and Euripides were Athenian, as were the sculptor Phidias, the Parthenon architects Ictinus and Callicrates, and the philosophers Socrates and Plato. To Athens came writers, thinkers, and artists from throughout the Greek world.

The Examined Life

A primary characteristic of Athenian culture was its critical and rational nature. In heated discussions in the assembly and the agora, the courtroom and the private symposion, Athenians and foreigners drawn to the city no longer looked to the myths and religion of the past for guidance. Secure in their identity and protected by the openness of their radical democracy, they began to examine past and present and to question the foundations of traditional values. From that climate of inquiry emerged the traditions of moral philosophy and its cousin, history. The Ionian interest in natural philosophy—the explanation of the universe in rational terms—continued throughout the fifth century B.C.E. But philosophers began also to turn their attention to the human world, in particular to the powers and limitations of the individual's mind and the individual's relationship with society. By the end of his life, the philosopher Heraclitus (see Chapter 2, p. 51) had become intrigued with the examination of the rational faculties themselves

THE UNEXAMINED LIFE IS NOT WORTH LIVING

Plato's Apology *presents Socrates in his summation to the Athenian jury in which he reflects on possible punishments that he might recommend and rejects the possibility of going quietly into exile.*

Focus Questions

What did Socrates' fellow Athenians find so disturbing about his practice of questioning people's assumptions? Why was constant questioning so essential to Socrates?

Perhaps someone may say, "But surely, Socrates, after you have left us you can spend the rest of your life in quietly minding your own business." This is the hardest thing of all to make some of you understand. If I say that this would be disobedience to God, and that is why I cannot "mind my own business," you will not believe me—you'll think I'm pulling your leg. If on the other hand I tell you that to let no day pass without discussing goodness and all the other subjects about which you hear me talking and examining both myself and others is really the very best thing that a man can do, and that life without this sort of examination is not worth living, you will be even less inclined to believe me. Nevertheless that is how it is, gentlemen, as I maintain; though it is not easy to convince you of it.

From Plato, *The Last Days of Socrates* (Harmondsworth: Penguin, 1954), p. 63.

rather than what one could know with them. In part, this meant a search for personal, inner understanding that would lead to proper action within society—in other words, to the search for ethics based on reason. In part, too, such an inquiry led to a study of how to formulate arguments and persuade others through logic.

The Sophists. In the political world of fifth-century B.C.E. Athens, rhetoric—the art of persuasion—was particularly important because it was the key to political influence. Ambitious would-be successors to Pericles and Alcibiades were prepared to pay well to learn the art of persuasion. Teachers called **Sophists** ("wise people") traveled throughout Greece offering to provide an advanced education for a fee. Although the sophistic tradition later gained a negative reputation, teachers such as Gorgias (ca. 485–ca. 380 B.C.E.) and Protagoras (ca. 490–421 B.C.E.) trained young men not only in the art of rhetoric but also in logic. By exercising their students' minds with logical puzzles and paradoxical statements, the Sophists taught a generation of wealthy Greeks the powers and complexities of human reason.

Socrates. The teacher Socrates (ca. 470–399 B.C.E.) was considered by many of his contemporaries as but one more Sophist, but he himself reacted against what he saw as the amoral and superficial nature of sophistic education. Although as a young man he had been interested in natural philosophy, he abandoned that tradition in favor of the search for the moral self-enlightenment urged by Heraclitus. "Know thyself" was Socrates' plea. An unexamined life, he argued, was not worth living. Socrates refused any pay for his teaching, arguing that he had nothing to teach. He knew nothing, he said, and was superior to the Sophists only because he recognized his ignorance while they professed wisdom.

Socrates' method infuriated his contemporaries. He would approach persons with reputations for wisdom or skill and then, through a series of disarmingly simple questions, force them to defend their beliefs. The inevitable result was that in their own words the outstanding Sophists, politicians, and poets of the day demonstrated the inadequacy of the foundations of their beliefs. While his opponents were left in confusion and outrage, Socrates' young followers, who included many of the sons of the aristocracy, delighted in seeing their elders so humiliated and embarrassed.

Since Socrates refused to commit any of his teaching to writing, we have no direct knowledge of the content of his instruction. We know of him only from the conflicting reports of his former students and opponents. One thing is certain, however. While demanding that every aspect of life be investigated, Socrates never doubted the moral legitimacy of the Athenian state. Condemned to death in 399 B.C.E. on the trumped-up charges of corrupting the morals of the Athenian youth and introducing strange gods, he rejected the opportunity to escape into exile. For 70 years, he argued, he had accepted the laws of Athens. Now he must accept their sentence, for by rejecting the laws of the city, he would in fact be guilty of the charges against him. Rather than reject Athens and its laws, he drank the fatal potion of hemlock given him by the executioner.

Understanding the Past

The philosophical interest in human choices and social constraints found an echo in the historical writing of the age. In particular, two writers established the spectrum of how to understand the past.

Herodotus. The earliest was Herodotus (ca. 484–ca. 420 B.C.E.), the first historian. He was one of the many foreigners who found in Athens the intellectual climate and audience he needed to write an account of the Persian Wars of the preceding generation. His book of "inquiries" (in Greek, *historia*), into the origins and events of the conflict between Greeks and Persians is the first true history. Herodotus had traveled widely in the eastern Mediterranean, collecting local stories and visiting famous temples, palaces, and cities. In his study he presents a great panorama of the civilized world at the end of the sixth century B.C.E. His descriptions range from the peoples of the Persian Empire to the construction of the great pyramids. The story builds gradually to the heroic clash between the ancient civilizations of the East and the Greeks. Herodotus did not hesitate to repeat myths, legends, and outrageous tales. His faith in the gods was strong, and he believed that the gods intervened in human affairs. Still, he was more than just a good storyteller or a chronicler of legends. Often, after reporting conflicting accounts, he would conclude, "Both stories are told and the reader may take his choice between them." In other cases, after recounting a particularly far-fetched account heard from local informants, he would comment, "Personally, I think this story is nonsense."

Herodotus, *Histories*

As he explained in his introduction, Herodotus's purpose in writing was twofold. First, he sought to preserve the memory of the past by recording the achievements of both Greeks and Easterners. Second, he set out to show how the two came into conflict. It was the desire to explain, to go beyond mere storytelling, that earned Herodotus the designation of "the father of history." Still, his understanding of cause and effect was fairly simple. He believed that wars arose from grievances and retribution. Thus the Persian Wars appear rather like large-scale feuds, the origins of which are lost in myth. At the same time, Herodotus was less interested in the mythic dimensions of the conflict than in the human, and his primary concern was the action of individuals under the press of circumstances. Ultimately, the Persian Wars became for Herodotus the conflict between freedom and despotism, and he described with passion how different Greek states chose between the two. The choice, as he phrased it, was "to live in a rugged land and rule or to cultivate rich plains and be slaves."

Thucydides. The story of the Peloponnesian War was recorded by a different sort of historian, one who focused more narrowly on the Greek world and on political power. Through oral interviews and reading, Herodotus painstakingly recovered information about the events he described. Thucydides had been an Athenian general and a major actor in the first part of the Peloponnesian War. He began his account at the very outbreak of the conflict, thus writing a contemporary record of the war rather than a history of it. As Herodotus is called the father of history, Thucydides might be called the first political scientist.

Thucydides on Athens

Neither myth nor religion nor morality takes center stage in Thucydides' account of what he saw from the outset to be "a great war and more worth writing about than any of those which had taken place in the past." For him, the central subject was human society in action. His passion was the open, self-conscious political life characteristic of the Greek polis, and his view of the give-and-take of politics shows a strong debt to the sophistic tradition. Thucydides viewed the Greek states as acting out of rational self-interest. His favorite device for showing the development of such policies was the political set speech, in which two opposing leaders attempt to persuade their fellow citizens on the proper course of action. Thucydides was seldom actually present at the events he described. Even when he was, he could not have transcribed the speakers' exact words. Rather, he attempted to put into the mouths of the speakers "whatever seemed most appropriate to me for each speaker to say in the particular circumstances." Although ficti-

GREEKS AND BARBARIANS

Herodotus was unique among classical authors in his refusal to consider Greek customs superior to those of non-Greeks. In the passage that follows, he tells a story to prove his point.

Focus Questions

What is Darius trying to teach his subjects in this story?
How would such an attitude assist in ruling a vast empire?

If it were proposed to all nations to choose which seemed best of all customs, each, after examination made, would place its own first; so well is each persuaded that its own are by far the best. It is not therefore to be supposed that any, save a madman, would turn such things to ridicule. I will give this one proof among many from which it may be inferred that all men hold this belief about their customs: When Darius was king, he summoned the Greeks who were with him and asked them what price would persuade them to eat their fathers' dead bodies. They answered that there was no price for which they would do it. Then he summoned those Indians who are called Callatiae, who eat their parents, and asked them (the Greeks being present and understanding by interpretation what was said) what would make them willing to burn their fathers at death. The Indians cried aloud, that he should not speak of so horrid an act. So firmly rooted are these beliefs; and it is, I think, rightly said in Pindar's poem that use and wont is lord of all.

From Herodotus, *The Histories*, Book III.

tious by modern standards, the speeches penetrate the heart of the tough political choices facing the opposing forces. That hard-nosed approach to political decisions continues to serve as a model to historians and practitioners of power politics.

Still, morality is always just below the surface of Thucydides' narrative. Even as he unflinchingly chronicles the collapse of morality and social order in the face of political expediency, he recognizes that the process will destroy his beloved Athens. In his account of the second phase of the war, Athens acts with the full arrogance of a tyrant. Its overwhelming pride leads it to attack and destroy its weaker neighbors and ultimately to invade Sicily, with all the disastrous consequences of that campaign. Thucydides showed that the consequences of political self-interest, devoid of other considerations, follow their own natural course to disaster and ruin. In the later, unfinished chapters (Thucydides died shortly after Athens's final defeat), the Peloponnesian War takes on the characteristics of a tragedy. In those chapters, Thucydides, the ultimate political historian, shows the deep influence of the dominant literary tradition of his day, Greek drama.

Athenian Drama

Since the time of its introduction by Peisistratus in the middle of the sixth century B.C.E., drama had become popular not only in Athens but throughout the Greek world. Plays formed part of the annual feast of Dionysus and dealt with mythic subject matter largely taken from the *Iliad* and the *Odyssey.* As the dramatist Aeschylus said, "We are all eating crumbs from the great table of Homer." Three types of plays honored the Dionysian festival. Tragedies dealt with great men who failed because of flaws in their natures. Their purpose was, in the words of the philosopher Aristotle, to effect "through pity and terror the correction and refinement of passions." Comedies were more directly topical and political. They parodied real Athenians, often by name, and amused even while making serious points in defense of democracy. Somewhere between tragedies and comedies, satyr plays remained closest to the Dionysian cult. In them lecherous drunken satyrs—mythical half-man, half-goat creatures—interact with gods and men as they roam the world in search of Dionysus.

Aeschylus. Athenian drama became more secular and less mythic as dramatists began to deal with human topics explosive in their immediacy and timeless in their portrayal of the human condition. Only a handful of the hundreds of Greek plays written in the fifth century B.C.E. survive. The first of the great Athenian tragedians whose plays we know is Aeschylus (525–456 B.C.E.), a veteran of Marathon and an eyewitness of the battle of Salamis. His one surviving trilogy, the *Oresteia,* traces the fate of the family of Agamemnon, the Greek commander at Troy. The three plays of the trilogy explore the conflicting obligations of filial respect and vengeance, which ultimately must be settled by rational yet divinely sanctioned law. Upon his return from Troy, the victorious Agamemnon is murdered by his unfaithful wife Clytemnestra. Orestes, the son, avenges his father's murder by murdering Clytemnestra, but in so doing incurs the wrath of the Furies, avenging spirits who pursue him for killing his mother. The conflict of duties and loyalties cannot be resolved by human means. Finally, Orestes arrives at the shrine of Apollo at Delphi, where the god purifies him from the pollution of the killing. Then, at Athens, Athena rescues Orestes, creating the Athenian law court and transforming the Furies into the Eumenides, the kindly guardian spirits of Athens.

Sophocles. The mature plays of Aeschylus's younger contemporary, Sophocles (496–406 B.C.E.), are tragedies in which religion plays a less important role. Instead, Sophocles sought to express human character. He shows how humans make decisions and carry them out, constrained by their pasts, their weaknesses, and their vices, but free nonetheless. Sophocles' message is endurance, acceptance of human responsibility and, at the same time, acceptance of the ways of the gods, who overrule people's plans. The heroine of *Antigone* is the sister of Polynices, exiled son of King Oedipus of Thebes. Polynices has died fighting his city and Creon, its new ruler, commands under penalty of death that Polynices' body be left unburied. This would mean that his soul would never find rest, the ultimate punishment for a Greek. Antigone, with a determination and courage equal to her love for her brother, buries Polynices and is entombed alive for her crime. Here the conflict between the state, which claims the total obedience of its people, and the claims of familial love and religious piety meet in tragic conflict. Creon, warned by a prophet that he is offending heaven, orders Antigone's release, but it is too late. Rather than wait for death, she has already hanged herself.

Sophocles, *Antigone*

Euripides. Sophocles was the most successful of the fifth-century B.C.E. tragedians, and in the next century his plays came to be considered the most "classic" of the tragedies. His younger contemporary, Euripides (485–406 B.C.E.), was far more original and daring in his subject matter and treatment of human emotions. Unlike the stately dramas of Aeschylus and the deliberate progressions of Sophocles, Euripides' plays abound in plot twists and unexpected, violent outbursts of passion. His characters are less reconciled to their fates and less ready to accept the traditional gods:

> *Does someone say that there are gods in heaven?*
> *There are not, there are not—unless one chooses*
> *To follow old tradition like a fool.*

Euripides' women were often wronged and seldom accepted their lot. Medea, the central figure of his most famous tragedy, made it possible for the adventurer Jason to complete his quest for the mythical Golden Fleece. Abandoning her land in the east, she returns with the hero, bears his children, and settles with him at Corinth. Jason hopes to marry the daughter of the king but must send Medea away. He tries to reason with her and she pretends to agree. Instead, she murders the Corinthian princess and her own children by Jason before escaping in a magical chariot drawn by dragons. Passion, not reason, rules Euripides' world.

Greek Comedy. Neither passion nor reason but politics rules the world of Greek comedy. Rather than the timelessness of the human condition, Athenian comic playwrights focused their biting satire on the political and social issues of the moment. Notably, the comic genius Aristophanes (ca. 450–ca. 388 B.C.E.) used wit, imagination, vulgarity, and great poetic sensitivity to attack everything that offended him in his city. In his plays he mocks and ridicules statesmen, philosophers, rival playwrights, and even the gods. His comedies are full of outrageous twists of plot, talking animals, obscene jokes and puns, and mocking asides. Yet Aristophanes was a deeply patriotic Athenian, dedicated to the democratic system and equally dedicated to the cause of peace. In his now lost *Babylonians,* written around 426 B.C.E. as Athenians struggled to recover from the plague and Cleon continued to pursue the bloody war against Sparta, he mocks Cleon and the Athenian demagogues while portraying the cities of the Delian League as slaves forced to grind grain at a mill. In *Lysistrata,* written in 411 B.C.E. after Athens had once more renewed the war, the women of Greece force their men to make peace by conspiring to refuse them sex as long as war continues. Through the sharp satire and absurd plots of his plays, Aristophanes communicates his sympathy for ordinary people, who must match wits with the charlatans and pompous frauds who attempt to dominate Athens's public life.

Art and the Human Image

The humanity in Greek drama found its parallel in art. In the late sixth century B.C.E., a reversal of the traditional black figure technique had revolutionized vase painting. Artists had begun to outline scenes on unfired clay and then fill in the background with black or brown glaze. The interior details of the figures were also added in black. The result was a much more lifelike art, a lighter, more natural coloring, and the possibility of more perspective, depth, and molding. The drinking cup shown below, signed by Douris, one of the finest fifth-century B.C.E. vase painters, exemplifies that fluidity and naturalness. The subject matter is erotic: a mature man is offering a handsome youth money for sex. The execution is masterful. The two figures interact and yet balance each other, exactly filling the circular space of the cup's interior. Douris has captured the animation of the two figures' faces and their naturally expressive gestures as they bargain, as well as the fine detail of their musculature and clothing.

Sculpture reflected the same development toward balance and realism contained within an ideal of human form. The finest bronzes and marbles of the fifth century B.C.E. show freestanding figures whose natural vigor and force, even when they are engaged in strenuous exertion, are balanced by the placidity of their faces and their lack of emotion. The tradition established by the Athenian sculptor Phidias (ca. 500–ca. 430 B.C.E.) sought a naturalism in the portrayal of the human figure, which remained ideal rather than individual. Even explicitly commemorative statues, dedicated for victories in

■ A fifth-century B.C.E. drinking cup in terracotta from Attica in Greece. The cup, depicting a man and a youth, is signed by Douris. More than 200 extant vases are ascribed to him.

■ The ruins on the Acropolis of Athens are dominated by the Parthenon (center). At the left is the temple of Athena as Victory.

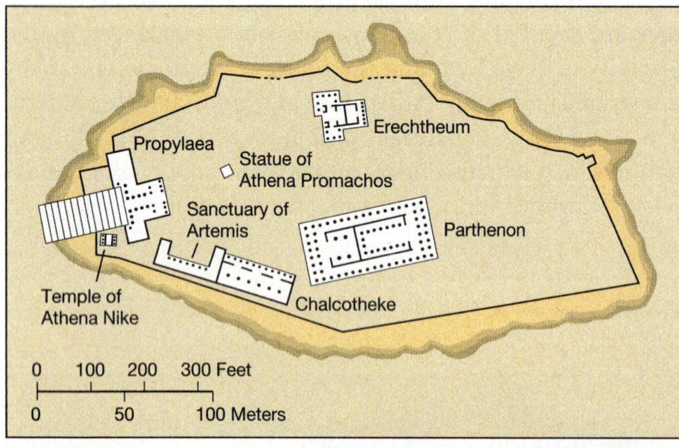

■ The fifth-century temples on Athens's acropolis form the greatest architectural and sculptural composition of antiquity.

games or battle, showed people as they participated in the larger context of humanity.

The greatest sculptural program of the fifth century B.C.E. was that produced for the Athenian acropolis. With vast funds taken from the Delian League's treasury at his disposal, Pericles transformed the Athenian acropolis into the greatest complex of buildings in the ancient world. A first-century C.E. author who had visited all the great cities of the Mediterranean remarked, "They seem to have within them some everlasting breath of life and an ageless spirit intermingled with their composition."

The acropolis complex was so designed that a visitor was guided to see it in the proper order and perspective. One entered through the monumental Propylaea, or gateway, a T-shaped structure approached by a flight of steps. From the top of the steps, one could glimpse both Phidias's great bronze statue of Athena Promachos in the center of the acropolis and, to the right, the Parthenon, with its magnificent friezes. As visitors entered the acropolis itself, they passed on the right the small temple of Athena as Victory. This small temple, built slightly later than the Parthenon, looks out toward Salamis. It was constructed in the Ionic style or order, an architectural tradition distinguished chiefly by the simple but fluid patterns of flowers and scrolls on its capitals, patterns borrowed from Oriental architecture. Continuing on the Sacred Way, one saw on the left the delicate Ionic Erechtheum, which housed the oldest Athenian cults. On the right, visitors were overawed by the Parthenon, a monument as much to Athens as to Athena.

Even today, the ruined temple seems a rectangular embodiment of order, proportion, and balance, an effect achieved through irregularity, illusion, and variation. The Parthenon is the most perfect example of the Doric order, an austerely beautiful building tradition reminiscent of earlier wooden structures. Every surface, from the floor to the columns to the horizontal beams, curves slightly. The spacing of the columns varies, and each column leans slightly inward. Those at the rear are larger than those at the front to compensate for the effect of viewing them from a greater distance. Just as the idealization of Athenian statues leaves the viewer with the impression of seeing a perfect individual, the illusion of flatness, regularity, and repetition in the Parthenon is the intended effect of an optical illusion.

An illusion, too, was the sense of overwhelming Athenian superiority and grandeur the acropolis was intended to convey. By the time the Erechtheum was completed in 406 B.C.E., the Athenian Empire was all but destroyed, the city's population devastated, and its democracy imperiled. Two years later Athens surrendered unconditionally to Sparta.

The intellectual and artistic accomplishments of Athens were as enduring as its empire proved ephemeral. Writers and artists alike focused their creative energies on human existence, seeking a proper proportion, order, and meaning, a blend of the practical and the ideal, which Athens's political leaders tragically lacked.

FROM CITY-STATES TO MACEDONIAN EMPIRE, 404–323 B.C.E.

The Peloponnesian War touched every aspect of Greek life. The war brought changes to the social and political structures of Greece by creating an enduring bitterness between elites and populace and a distrust of both democracy and traditional oligarchy. The mutual exhaustion of Athens and Sparta left a vacuum of power in the Aegean. Finally, the war raised fundamental questions about the nature of politics and society throughout the Greek world.

Politics After the Peloponnesian War

Over the decades-long struggle, the conduct of war and the nature of politics had changed, bringing new problems for victor and vanquished alike. Lightly armed professional mercenaries willing to fight for anyone able to pay them gradually replaced hoplite citizen soldiers as the backbone of the fighting forces. Just as the rise of hoplite phalanxes in the sixth century B.C.E. had weakened oligarchies, the rise of the poorer warriors weakened the political importance of hoplites in favor of those who could pay and outfit rootless mercenaries. The rise of mercenary armies meant trouble for democracies such as Athens, as well as for Sparta with its class of equals.

As war became professional and protracted, it became more brutal. When the Spartans and their band of allies captured Plataea in 427 B.C.E., they slaughtered all the men, enslaved the women, and razed the city. Despite Cleon's urgings, Athens refused to treat Mytilene in the same way when it captured that city in the same year. But by 416 B.C.E., when Athens captured Melos, it did not hesitate to treat Melos's citizens as Sparta had dealt with those of Plataea. Lysander's slaughter of Athenian prisoners of war in 405 B.C.E. was business as usual. The moment of Greek unity experienced during the second Persian War was forgotten in the horrors of the Peloponnesian conflict.

Spartan Imperialism. Victory left Sparta no more capable of assuming leadership in 404 B.C.E. than it had been in 478 B.C.E. Years of war had reduced the population of equals to less than 3000. The city could no longer maintain its traditional isolation from the outside world. Sparta could not control the Greek world without a powerful fleet, but ships and crews were costly and could be maintained only by taxing its empire or by accepting subsidies from Persia. Greedy and ambitious Spartans began to accumulate much of the wealth that poured in as booty and tribute from throughout the Aegean, while other equals lost the land they needed to maintain their place in society.

The Spartans also proved extremely unpopular imperialists. As a reward for Persian assistance, Sparta returned the Ionian cities to Persian control. Elsewhere it established hated oligarchies to rule in a way favorable to Sparta's interests. In Athens, a brutal tyranny of 30 men took control in 404 B.C.E. With Spartan support, they executed some 1500 democratic leaders and forced 5000 more into exile. The Thirty Tyrants evoked enormous hatred and opposition. Within a year the exiles recaptured the city, restored democracy, and killed or expelled the tyrants.

Similar opposition to Spartan rule emerged throughout the Greek world, shattering the fragile peace created by Athens's defeat. For more than 70 years it boiled in constant warfare. Mutual distrust, fear of any city that seemed about to establish a position of clear superiority, and the machinations of the Persian Empire to keep Greeks fighting each other produced a constantly shifting series of alliances.

Thebes. Persia turned against its former ally when Sparta supported an unsuccessful attempt by Cyrus to unseat his brother Artaxerxes II. Soon the unlikely and unstable alliance of Athens, Corinth, Argos, Thebes, and Euboea, financed by Persia, entered a series of vicious wars against Sparta. Rapidly shifting alliances and mutual hostility ensured that there was no real victor. The first round ended in Spartan victory due to the shifting role of Persia, whose primary interest was the continued disunity of the Greeks. By 377 B.C.E., however, Athens had reorganized its league and with Thebes as ally was able to break Spartan sea power. The decline of Sparta left a power vacuum soon filled by Thebes. Athens, concerned by the new threat, shifted alliances, making peace with its old enemy. However, Spartan military fortunes had so declined that when Sparta attacked the Thebians in 371 B.C.E., its armies were destroyed and Spartan power was broken. The next year Thebes invaded the Peloponnesus and freed Messenia, the foundation of Sparta's economic prosperity. Sparta never recovered. Deprived of its economic base, its body of equals reduced to a mere 800, and its fleet gone, Sparta never regained its historic importance.

Theban hegemony was short-lived. Before long the same process of greed, envy, and distrust that had devastated the other Greek powers destroyed Thebes. In 355 B.C.E., when Thebes attempted to conquer the small state of Phocis, its enemies seized Delphi and used the vast treasure that had accumulated there over the years as gifts to Apollo to hire mercenaries. The professional soldiers wore down the Theban forces over the course of ten years. During the same time, Athens's reconstituted league disintegrated as members opposed Athenian attempts once more to convert a free association of states into an empire. By the 330s B.C.E., all of the Greek states had proven themselves incapable of creating stable political units larger than their immediate polis.

Philosophy and the Polis

The failure of Greek political forms, oligarchy and democracy alike, profoundly affected Athenian philosophers. Plato (ca. 428–347 B.C.E.), an aristocratic student of Socrates, grew up during the Peloponnesian War and had witnessed the collapse of the empire, the brutality of the Thirty Tyrants, the execution of Socrates, and the revival of the democracy and its imperialistic ambitions. From these experiences he developed a hatred for Athenian democracy and a profound distrust of ordinary people's ability to tell right from wrong. Disgusted with public life, Plato left Attica for a time and traveled in Sicily and Italy, where he encountered different forms of government and different philosophical schools. Around 387 B.C.E., he returned to Athens and opened the Academy, a school to provide Athenian youth with what he considered to be knowledge of what was true and good for the individual and the state.

■ This bronze statue of a Greek warrior found in the sea near Riace, Italy, dates from c.a. 450 B.C.E. and demonstrates classical Athenian mastery of human portrayal.

Platonic Forms. Plato chose a most unlikely literary form for transmitting his teachings. He used dialogue, in the form of discussions between his teacher, Socrates, and a variety of students and opponents, to develop his ideas. While Plato shared with his mentor the conviction that human actions had to be grounded in self-knowledge, Plato's philosophy extended much further. His arguments about the inadequacy of all existing forms of government and the need to create a new form of government through the proper education of elite philosopher rulers were part of a complex understanding of the universe and the individual's place in it.

Plato argued that true knowledge is impossible as long as it focuses on the constantly changing, imperfect world of everyday experience. Human beings can have real knowledge only of that which is eternal, perfect, and beyond the experience of the senses—the realm of what Plato called the **Forms.** According to Plato, when people judge that individuals or actions are true or good or beautiful, they do so not because those particular persons or events are truly virtuous, but because they recognize that they participate in some way in the Idea, or Form, of truth or goodness or beauty. Consistent with Socrates' insistence on looking within oneself, Plato argued that people recognize these Forms, not in the object itself, but within their memories of a previous existence when their spirits or souls had direct contact with the universe of the Forms. Thus for Plato all knowledge was recollection, and everything existed only to the extent to which it participated in the Forms.

According to Plato, the evils of the world, and in particular the vices and failures of government and society, result from ignorance of the truth. He believed that most people live as though chained in a cave in which all they can see are the shadows cast on the walls by a fire. In their ignorance, they mistake the flickering, imperfect images for reality. Plato said their proper ruler must be a philosopher, one who was not deceived by the shadows. He believed the philosopher's task was to break their chains and turn them toward the source of the light so that they could see the world as it really was. Ultimately, the philosopher would lead them from the cave to see the real source of light—the sun outside. Truth would make them free.

Aristotelian Empiricism. Plato's idealist view (in the sense of the Ideas, or Forms) of knowledge dominated much of ancient philosophy. His greatest student, Aristotle (384–322 B.C.E.), however, rejected this view in favor of a philosophy rooted in the natural world. Aristotle came from a medical family of northern Greece and, although a student in Plato's Academy for almost 20 years, he never abandoned observation for speculation. Systematic investigation and explanation characterize Aristotle's vast work, and his interests ranged from biology to statecraft to the most abstract philosophy. In each field, he employed essentially the

Aristotle, *Poetics*

■ A Roman copy of a Greek statue of Aristotle. Aristotle himself left directions for a statue in his will. Later statues of the philosopher were popular fixtures in Roman gardens. Typically he was portrayed with an undraped right arm.

same method, which came to be known as **empiricism.** He observed as many individual examples of the topic as possible and from those specific observations extracted general theories. His theories—whether on the nature of matter, the species of animals, the working of the human mind, ethics, or the proper form of the state—are distinguished by clarity of logical thinking, precision in the use of terminology, and respect for the world of experience.

Aristotle brought this approach to the question of life in society. He defined humans as "political animals," that is, animals particularly characterized by life in the polis. He analyzed more than 150 city constitutions to learn what contributed to their successes and failures. Unlike Plato, he did not regard any particular form of government as ideal. Rather, he concluded that the type of government ultimately mattered less than the balance between narrow oligarchy and radical democracy. Consistent with his belief that "virtue lies in a mean," he advocated governments composed of citizens who were neither extremely wealthy nor extremely poor. Moderation was the key to stability and justice.

Aristotle's teaching had little effect on his most famous student, Alexander, the son of King Philip of Macedon. Nor apparently did Aristotle's firsthand observation of this traditional hereditary monarchy in northern Greece influence the philosopher's understanding of the realities of Greek politics. Yet, during the very years that Aristotle was teaching, the vacuum created by the failure of the Greek city-states was being filled by the dynamic growth of the Macedonian monarchy that finally ended a century of Greek warfare, and with it the independence of the Greek city-states.

The Rise of Macedon

The polis had never been the only form of the Greek state. Alongside the city-states of Athens, Corinth, Syracuse, and Sparta were more decentralized ethne ruled by traditional hereditary chieftains and monarchs. Macedonia, in the northeast of the mainland, was one such ethnos. Its kings, chosen by the army from within a royal family, ruled in cooperation with nobles and clan leaders. Kings enhanced their position by marrying a number of wives from among the families of powerful supporters and allies. The Macedonian people spoke a Greek dialect, and Macedonian kings and elite identified with Greek culture and tradition. However, constant rivalry for the throne, relative impoverishment, and loose organization prevented the Macedonians from playing much of a role in the events and achievements of the fifth and sixth centuries B.C.E. Macedonia had, however, long served as a buffer between the barbarians to the north and the Greek mainland, and its tough farmers and pastoralists were geared to constant warfare. As Athens, Sparta, and Thebes fought each other to mutual exhaustion, Macedonia under King Philip II (359–336 B.C.E.) moved into the resulting power vacuum.

Philip was called by a contemporary the greatest man Europe had ever produced. If political acumen and military skill had been the only criteria, he deserved the title. These Philip had in abundance, but his ambition exceeded them both. During his twenties he murdered his way to the throne and set about consolidating his position at home and strengthening his influence abroad through military and diplomatic means. Philip showed a particular genius for rapidly organizing and

This golden gorytos or Scythian-style case for bow and arrows was discovered in a royal Macedonian tomb believed to have been that of Philip III Arrhidaeus, the physically and mentally incompetent half brother of Alexander the Great who succeeded him briefly before his assassination in 317 B.C.E. However, since it was found near the remains of Philip's powerful Queen Eurydice who had a military upbringing, it may have been the property of this warrior queen rather than that of her weak husband.

leading armies and for conducting complex multiple campaigns each year. He secured his borders against northern barbarians and captured the northern coast of the Aegean, including the gold and silver mines of Mount Pangaeus, which gave him a ready source of money for his campaigns. Then he turned his attention to the south.

Philip intervened in the war between Thebes and Phocis and in 346 B.C.E. ended that conflict by forcing himself into the center of Greek affairs. From then on, he was relentless in his efforts to swallow up one Greek state after another. In spite of the powerful oratory of the Athenian statesman Demosthenes (384–322 B.C.E.), who recognized Philip's threat, the Greek states resisted uniting against Philip, and one by one they fell. In 338 B.C.E., Philip achieved a final victory at Chaeronea and established a new league, the League of Corinth. However, unlike all those that had preceded it, this league was no confederation of sovereign states. It was an empire ruled by a king and supported by wealthy citizens whose cooperation Philip rewarded well. The new model of government, a monarchy drawing its support from a wealthy elite, became a fixture of the Mediterranean world for more than 2000 years.

Philip's success was based on his powerful military machine, which combined both Macedonian military tradition and the new mercenary forces that had emerged over the past century in Greece. The heart of his army was the infantry, which was trained in the use of pikes some 14 feet long—4 feet longer than those of the Greek hoplites. Tribesmen from the Macedonian hills formed the core of the fighting force. Allies and Greek mercenaries, paid for with Mount Pangaeus gold, could swell their ranks to armies of more than 40,000. Macedonian phalanxes moved forward in disciplined ranks, pushing back their foes, whose shorter lances could not reach the Macedonians. When the enemy was contained, the Macedonian cavalry charged from the flank and cut them to pieces. The cavalry, composed of nobles and tribal chieftains, lived in close proximity to the king and felt tremendous personal loyalty to Philip. Known as the Royal Companions, they were the elite of Macedon and the greatest beneficiaries of Philip's conquests.

No sooner had Philip subdued Greece than he announced a campaign against Persia. He intended to lead a combined Greek force in a war of revenge and conquest to punish the great empire for its invasion of Greece 150 years earlier and its subsequent involvement in the Greek world. Before he could begin, however, he met the fate of his predecessors. At the age of 46 he was cut down by an assassin's knife, leaving his 20-year-old son, Alexander (336–323 B.C.E.), to lead the expedition. Within 13 years Alexander, who came to be known as Alexander the Great, had conquered the world.

The Empire of Alexander the Great

Alexander was less affected by his teacher, the philosopher Aristotle, than he was by the poet Homer. Envisioning himself a new Achilles, Alexander sought to imitate and surpass that legendary warrior and hero of the *Iliad.* Shortly after moving his troops across the Hellespont from Europe to Asia, Alexander visited Troy, where he lay a wreath on the supposed tomb of his hero and took from a temple weapons said to have belonged to Achilles. Those he carried before him in all of his battles.

Alexander's Conquests. Alexander's military genius, dedication to his troops, reckless disregard for his own safety, and ability to move both men and supplies across vast distances at great speed inspired the war machine developed by Philip and led it on an odyssey of conquest that stretched from Asia Minor to India. In 334 B.C.E., the first year of his campaign,

Plutarch on Alexander the Great

Alexander captured the Greek cities of Asia Minor. Then he continued east. At Gordium, according to legend, he confronted an ancient puzzle, a complex knot tied to the chariot of the ancient king of that city. Whoever could loosen the knot, the legend said, would become master of Asia. Alexander solved that puzzle, as he did all of his others, with his sword. Two months later he defeated the Persian king Darius III at Issus and then headed south toward the Mediterranean coast and Egypt. After his victories there, he turned again to the north and entered Mesopotamia. At Gaugamela in 331 B.C.E., he defeated Darius a second, decisive time. Shortly afterward, Darius was murdered by the remnants of his followers. Alexander captured the Persian capital of Persepolis, with its vast treasure, and became the undisputed ruler of the vast empire.

The conquest of Persia was not enough. Alexander pushed on, intending to conquer the whole world. His armies marched east, subduing the rebellious Asian provinces of Bactria and Sogdiana. He negotiated the Khyber Pass from what is now Afghanistan into the Punjab, crossed the Indus River, and defeated the local Indian king. Everywhere he went he reorganized or founded cities, entrusting them to loyal Macedonians and other Greeks and settling them with veterans of his campaigns, and then pushed on toward the unknown. Beyond the Hydaspes River, in what is now Pakistan, his Macedonian warriors finally halted. Worn out by years of bloody conquest and exhausting travel, they refused to go farther, even if Alexander himself were to lead them. "If there is one thing above all others a successful man should know," their spokesman told him, "it is *when to stop*." Furious but impotent, Alexander turned south, following the Indus River to its mouth in the hope that it might turn out to be an extension of the Nile encircling the earth. Upon reaching the Indian Ocean he at last turned west, leading his army across the barren Gedrosian desert and finally back to Persepolis in 324 B.C.E. No mortal had ever before accomplished such a feat. Even in his own lifetime, Alexander was venerated as a god.

Binding Together an Empire. Alexander is remembered as a greater conqueror than ruler, but his plans for his reign, had

MAP DISCOVERY

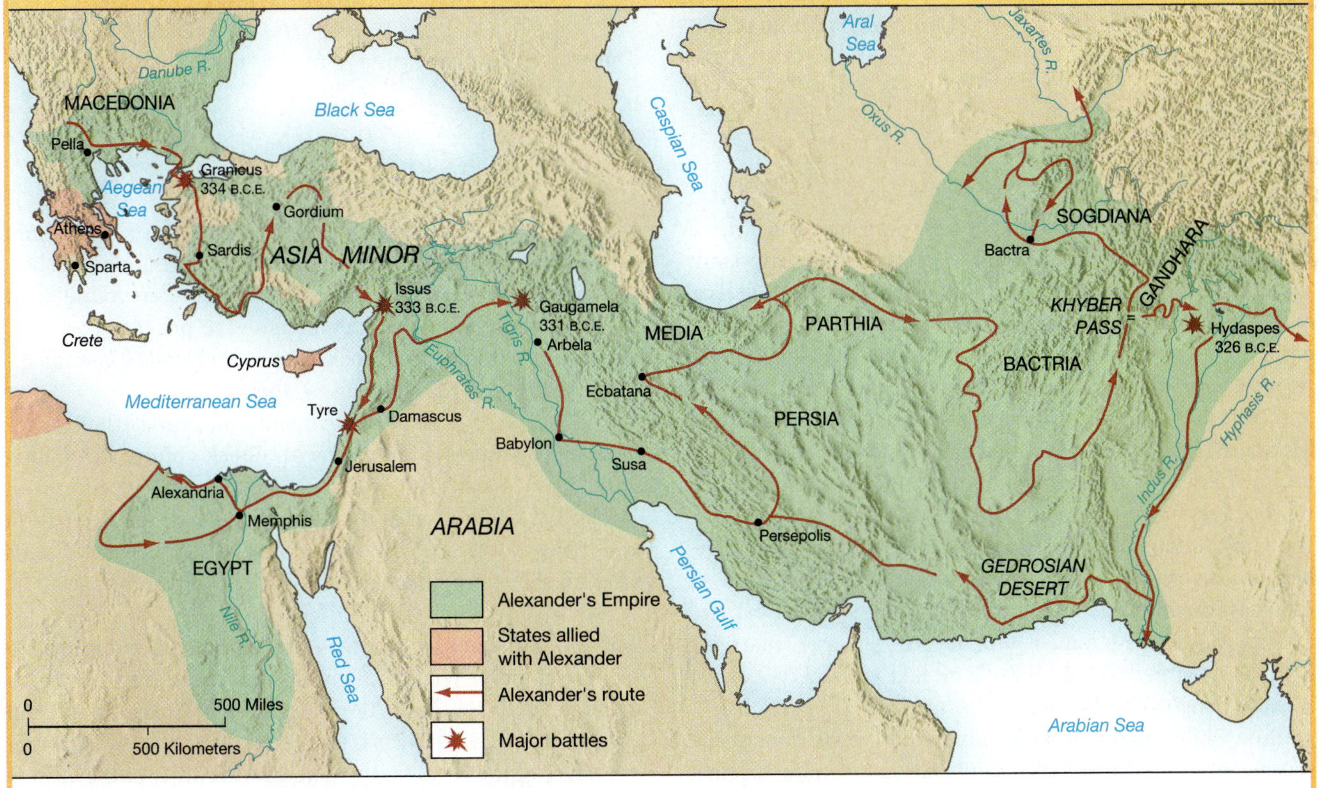

The Empire of Alexander the Great

Compare the Empire of Alexander with the empires of Akkadia (p. 16), Egypt (p. 24), and Persia (p. 61). How do you account for the specific areas Alexander chose to conquer? Based on information presented in this chapter, what lasting effects remained in this region?

ALEXANDER CALLS A HALT

The second-century C.E. historian Arrian, drawing on earlier accounts and his own sense of Alexander, recreates the exchange between Alexander and his trusted officer Coenus, which led Alexander at last to abandon his relentless easterly march of conquest.

Focus Questions

What is Alexander's motivation in urging his army forward?
Why does Coenus urge a halt?

ALEXANDER: I observe, gentlemen, that when I would lead you on a new venture you no longer follow me with your old spirit. I have asked you to meet me that we may come to a decision together: are we, upon my advice, to go forward, or, upon yours, to turn back? . . . With all that [has been] accomplished, why do you hesitate to extend the power of Macedon—your power—to the Hyphasis and the tribes on the other side? Are you afraid that a few natives who may still be left will offer opposition? . . .

For a man who is a man work, in my belief, if it is directed to noble ends, has no object beyond itself. . . . Our ships will sail round from the Persian Gulf to Libya as far as the Pillars of Hercules, whence all Libya to the eastward will soon be ours, and all Asia too, and to this empire there will be no boundaries but what God Himself has made for the whole world.

COENUS: I judge it best to set some limit to further enterprise. You know the number of Greeks and Macedonians who started upon this campaign, and you can see how many of us are left today. . . . Every man of them longs to see his parents again, if they yet survive, or his wife, or his children. . . . Do not try to lead men who are unwilling to follow you; if their heart is not in it, you will never find the old spirit or the old courage. Consent rather yourself to return to your mother and your home. Once there, you may bring good government to Greece and enter your ancestral house with all the glory of the many victories won in this campaign, and then, should you so desire it, you may begin again and undertake a new expedition against these Indians of the East, or if you prefer, to the Black Sea or to Carthage and the Libyan territories beyond. . . . Sir, if there is one thing above all others a successful man should know, it is when to stop.

From Arrian, *The Campaigns of Alexander,* Book V.

he lived to complete them, might have won him equal fame. Unlike his Macedonian followers, who were interested mainly in booty and power, he recognized that only by merging local and Greek peoples and traditions could he forge a lasting empire. Thus, even while founding cities on the Greek model throughout his empire, he carefully respected the local social and cultural traditions of the conquered peoples. In fact, after his return from India, he executed many Macedonian governors found guilty of misrule or corruption. Alexander enlisted elite units of Persian youths to be trained in Macedonian-style warfare and traditions. At the same time, he encouraged marriages between his companions and the daughters of local elites. In one mass ceremony at Susa, thousands of his warriors married Persian women. Alexander himself led the way, marrying Darius's daughter Stateira, just as he had previously married Roxane, daughter of the king of Bactria.

Even while working to unite Greek and Persian culture and society, Alexander sought to bind his vast empire together through the network of more than 35 cities he created. Like the Greek cities of the Mediterranean world, these were well-located, spacious cities with paved streets, flowing fountains, and impressive architecture. They became trading as well as administrative centers and, thanks to the Greek veterans settled in them, centers of Hellenistic culture. To these cities flocked not only retired soldiers and merchants but also artists, poets, scholars, physicians, and architects. Wherever they were found, their language was Greek, and they became the primary means by which Greek traditions of civilization were blended into the indigenous cultures that surrounded them.

Traditions of Persian government and Zoroastrian toleration and openness combined with Greek culture in exciting and novel ways. But whether Alexander's program of Hellenistic civilization and cultural and social amalgamation could have succeeded is a moot point. In 323 B.C.E., two years after his return from India, he died at Babylon at the age of 32.

The Hellenistic Kingdoms. The empire did not long outlive the emperor. Vicious fighting soon broke out among his generals and his kin. Alexander's wife Roxane and son Alexander IV (323–317 B.C.E.) were killed, as were all other members of the royal family. The various units of the empire broke apart into separate kingdoms and autonomous cities, in which each ruler attempted to continue the political and cultural tradition of Alexander in a smaller sphere. Alexander's empire became a shifting kaleidoscope of states, kingdoms, and cities, dominated by priest-kings, native princelings, and territorial rulers, all vying to enhance their positions while preserving a relative balance of power.

By 275 B.C.E., three large kingdoms dominated Alexander's former domain. The most stable was Egypt, which Ptolemy I (323–285 B.C.E.), one of Alexander's closest followers, acquired upon Alexander's death and which he and his descendants ruled until Cleopatra VII (51–30 B.C.E.) was defeated by the Roman Octavian in 31 B.C.E. In the east, the Macedonian general Seleucus (312–281 B.C.E.) captured Babylon in 312 B.C.E., and he and his descendants—the **Seleucids**—ruled a vast kingdom reaching from what is today western Turkey to Afghanistan. Whittled away in the east by both the Greek kingdom of Bactria and the non-Greek Parthians and in the west by the Greek Attalids in Pergamum, the Seleucid kingdom gradually shrank to a small region of northern Syria before it fell to Rome in 64 B.C.E. Nevertheless, Hellenistic influence remained strong in the East even after the political demise of the kingdom and transmitted Greek culture to India while serving as the conduit for Indian culture into the Mediterranean world. After 50 years of conflict, Antigonus Gonatas (276–239 B.C.E.), the grandson of another of Alexander's commanders, secured Macedon and Greece. His Antigonid successors ruled the kingdom until it fell to the Romans in 168 B.C.E.

Alexander's conquests transformed the political map of southern Europe, western Asia, and Egyptian Africa. They swept away or absorbed old traditions of government, brought Greek traditions of urban organization, and replaced indigenous ruling elites with hellenized dynasties. Within this vast region, rulers encouraged commercial and cultural contact, enriching their treasuries and creating a new form of Greek culture. Still, Alexander's successors never developed the interest or ability to integrate this Greek culture and the more ancient indigenous cultures of their subjects. Ultimately, this failure proved fatal for the Hellenistic kingdoms.

■ Philoxenus, thought to be the originator of the mosaic of the Battle of Issus, emphasized Alexander's gaze, which looks into destiny.

CHRONOLOGY

Classical Greece

525–456 B.C.E.	Aeschylus
ca. 500–ca. 430 B.C.E.	Phidias
496–406 B.C.E.	Sophocles
490 B.C.E.	Battle of Marathon
485–406 B.C.E.	Euripides
ca. 484–ca. 420 B.C.E.	Herodotus
480 B.C.E.	Battles of Thermopylae and Salamis
478 B.C.E.	Athens assumes control of Delian League
ca. 470–399 B.C.E.	Socrates
ca. 460–430 B.C.E.	Pericles dominates Athens
ca. 450–ca. 388 B.C.E.	Aristophanes
431–421; 431–404 B.C.E.	Peloponnesian War
ca. 428–347 B.C.E.	Plato
384–322 B.C.E.	Aristotle
384–322 B.C.E.	Demosthenes
338 B.C.E.	Philip of Macedon defeats Athens
336–323 B.C.E.	Reign of Alexander the Great

THE HELLENISTIC WORLD

Although vastly different in geography, language, and custom, the Hellenistic kingdoms (so called to distinguish them from the Hellenic civilization of the fifth and early fourth centuries B.C.E.) shared two common traditions. First, great portions of the Hellenistic world, from Asia Minor to Bactria and south to Egypt, had been united at various times by the Assyrian and Persian Empires. During these periods they had absorbed much of Mesopotamian civilization, and in particular the administrative traditions begun by the Assyrian Tiglath-pileser. Thus the Hellenistic kings ruled kingdoms already accustomed to centralized government and could rely on the existing machinery of tax collection and administration to control the countryside. For the most part, however, the kings had little interest in the native populations of their kingdoms beyond the amount of wealth that they could extract from them. Hellenistic monarchs remained Greek, and they lavished their attentions on the newly created Greek cities, which absorbed vast amounts of the kingdoms' wealth.

The cities and their particular form of Greek culture were the second unifying factor in the Hellenistic world. In the tradition of Alexander himself, the Ptolemys, Seleucids, and Antigonids founded new cities on the Greek model, cultivated Greek urban culture, and recruited Greeks for their most important positions of responsibility. The Seleucids doubled the number of cities in their vast domain, even replacing the ancient city of Babylon with their capital, Seleucia, on the Tigris. In Egypt, the Ptolemys replaced the ancient capital of Memphis with the new city of Alexandria. These cities became the centers of political control, economic consumption, and cultural diffusion throughout the Hellenistic world.

Urban Life and Culture

The Hellenistic kingdoms lived in a perpetual state of warfare with one another. Kings needed Greek soldiers, merchants, and administrators and competed with their rivals in offering Greeks all the comforts of home. Hellenistic cities were Greek in physical organization, constitution, and language. Each had

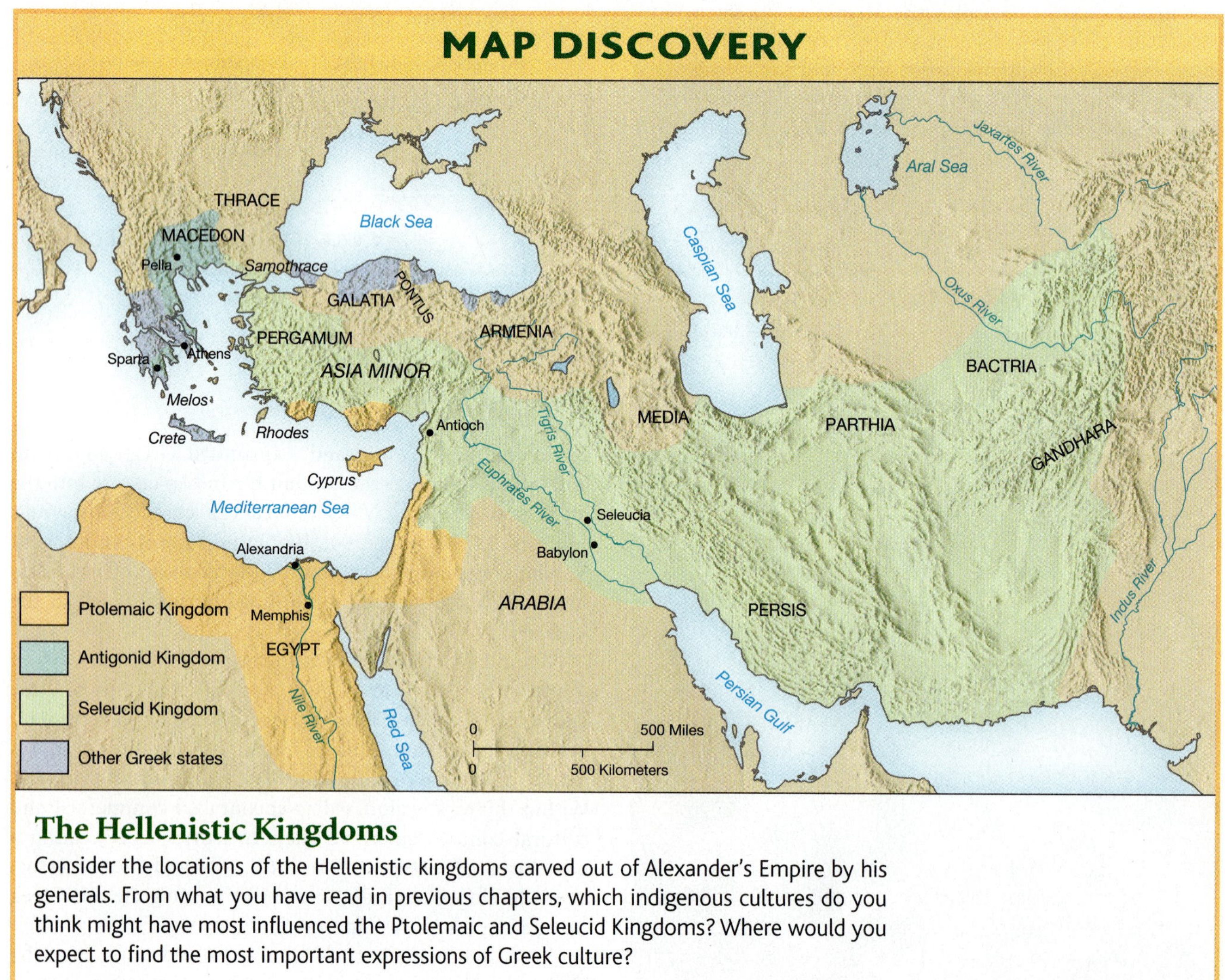

The Hellenistic Kingdoms

Consider the locations of the Hellenistic kingdoms carved out of Alexander's Empire by his generals. From what you have read in previous chapters, which indigenous cultures do you think might have most influenced the Ptolemaic and Seleucid Kingdoms? Where would you expect to find the most important expressions of Greek culture?

an agora, or marketplace, that would not have been out of place in Attica. They boasted temples to the Greek gods and goddesses, theaters, baths, and, most importantly, a *gymnasion,* or combination sports center and school. In the gymnasion young men competed in Greek sports and absorbed Greek poetry and philosophy just as did their cousins on the Peloponnesus. Sophocles' tragedies played to enthusiastic audiences in an enormous Greek theater in what is today Ai Khanoum on the Oxus River in Afghanistan, and the rites of Dionysus were celebrated in third-century B.C.E. Egypt with processions of satyrs, maenads, free wine for all, and a golden phallus 180 feet long. Since the Greeks were drawn from throughout the Greek-speaking world, in time a universal Greek dialect, *koine,* became the common language of culture and business like the Latin of the medieval West, the German of the Habsburg Empire, or basic English in much of the world today.

Greek Heritage in Turkey

For all their Greek culture, Hellenistic cities differed fundamentally from Greek cities and colonies of the past. Not only were they far larger than any earlier Greek cities, but their government and culture were different from those of other cities or colonies. Colonies had been largely independent poleis. The Hellenistic cities were never politically sovereign. The regional kings maintained firm control over the cities, even while working to attract Greeks from the mainland and the islands to them. On the one hand, the policy weakened the political significance of Greek life and culture. Politics was no longer the passion that it had been in the fifth and early fourth centuries B.C.E. In each city, a council elected from among the Greek inhabitants was largely self-governing in domestic matters. However, while the cities were in theory democracies, kings firmly controlled city government, and participation in the city councils and magistracies became the affair of the wealthy.

On the other hand, the Hellenistic cities were much less closed than were the traditional poleis of the Hellenic world. There, citizenship had been largely restricted by birth, and social identity had been determined by deme, tribe, and family. In the new cities of the east, Greeks from all over were welcomed as soldiers and administrators, regardless of their city of origin. By the second century B.C.E., Greeks no longer identified themselves by their city of origin but as "Hellenes," that is, Greeks. Moreover, to a limited extent, native elites could, through the adoption of Greek language, culture, and traditions, become Greek themselves—an achievement that had been impossible for the metics of Athens, Corinth, or Sparta.

Women in Public Life

The great social and geographical mobility possible in the new cities extended to women as well as men. No longer important simply as transmitters of citizenship, women began to assume a greater role in the family, in the economy, and in public life. Marriage contracts, particularly in Ptolemaic Egypt, emphasized the theoretical equality of husband and wife. In one such contract, the wife was granted "mastery in common with [her husband] over all their possessions." The husband and wife were further enjoined to take no concubines or male or female lovers. The penalty for the husband was loss of the wife's dowry; for the wife, the punishment was divorce. Since women could control their own property, many engaged in business and some became wealthy. Wealth translated into civic influence and power. Phyle, a woman of the first century B.C.E. from Priene in Asia Minor, spent vast sums on a reservoir and aqueducts to bring water to her city. She was rewarded with high political office, as was a female archon in Histria on the Black Sea in the second century B.C.E.

The most powerful women in Hellenistic society were queens, especially in Egypt, where the Ptolemys adopted the Egyptian tradition of royal marriages between brothers and sisters. Four of the first eight Ptolemys married sisters in order to eliminate foreign dynastic influences in court. Arsinoë II (ca. 316–270 B.C.E.) ruled as an equal with her brother-husband Ptolemy II (286–246 B.C.E.). She inaugurated a tradition of powerful female monarchs that ended only with Cleopatra VII, the last independent ruler of Egypt, who successfully manipulated the Roman generals Julius Caesar (100–44 B.C.E.) and Mark Antony (81–30 B.C.E.) to maintain Egyptian autonomy.

Just as monarchs competed with one another in creating Greek cities, they vied in making their cities centers of Greek culture. Socially ambitious and newly wealthy citizens supported poets, philosophers, and artists as a means of demonstrating their status. Queens, in particular, patronized poets and dramatists, and cities and wealthy individuals endowed gymnasia and libraries.

Alexandria

The most vibrant center of this rich complex of social change and culture was Alexandria in Egypt. Alexander the Great had founded it after having himself crowned pharaoh in the ancient capital of Memphis in 331 B.C.E. Its location, on a narrow strip of land between Lake Maroetis and the Mediterranean, possessed excellent deep-water harbors, and a healthy climate made it ideally suited to become the major international port of Egypt. After Alexander's death, Ptolemy I made it not only his political and commercial center but the cultural center for Greek art, science, and scholarship for the whole world. He lavished money on its temples and public buildings. He gathered poets, scientists, and scholars from throughout the Greek-speaking world. The heart of his enterprise was the **Museum** (*Mouseion*) or shrine to the Muses—the goddesses of literature, music, and the arts—and closely attached to it, a library in which he sought to collect all the great works of Greek literature and learning.

Descriptions of Alexandria

The Museum and library became a residential research institute in which scholars, scientists, and philosophers, supported by the Ptolemaic rulers, lived, worked, and taught, free of ordinary cares. They saw as their primary task the collection and preservation of all Greek literature and set out to obtain copies of every work. By royal order, ships arriving in Alexandria were boarded and searched for books to copy. Royal agents scoured the book markets of Greece and Asia Minor, paying top prices for rare and obscure texts. Ptolemy III (246–221 B.C.E.) borrowed from Athens the official copies of the tragedies of Aeschylus, Sophocles, and Euripides, in order to correct the copies held by the library. The Athenians required that he leave an enormous deposit for the precious scrolls. However, once having obtained them, Ptolemy decided to keep them in the library and forfeit his security deposit. In time, the library at Alexandria housed half a million book-rolls including all of the great classics of Greek literature. It was the greatest library of the Ancient World.

Generations of poet-scholars spent their careers in the Museum, studying, editing, and commenting on the classics. As in any academic community, not everyone found their work equally valuable. One critic wrote, "In the polyglot land of Egypt many now find pasturage as endowed scribblers, endlessly quarreling in the Muses' birdcage." However, in the process they not only standardized texts but invented such basic aspects of writing as punctuation, accent marks, and new, more flowing forms of handwriting. Their commentaries on sources and their marginal comments became the basis for literary criticism and scholarship. Finally, their patient efforts preserved much of what is known about classical authors.

Hellenistic Literature

Hellenistic writers were not simply book collectors or critics. They developed new forms of literature, including the romance, which often recounted imaginary adventures of Alexander the Great, and the pastoral poem, which the Sicilian Theocritus (ca. 310–250 B.C.E.) developed out of popular shepherd songs. Callimachus (ca. 305–ca. 240 B.C.E.), the cataloger of the library in Alexandria and royal tutor, was the acknowledged (and envied) master of the short, witty epigram. With equal skill he could poke fun at himself as a frustrated lover of boys and parties or move the reader with touching poems about his deceased friends. An erudite and sophisticated author who dismissed weighty literary efforts with the epigram, "Big book, big evil," he nevertheless is credited with more than 800 compositions, including short epics, hymns, lyric poems, epigrams, and occasional poems for his patrons. Little of his poetry survives other than in fragments, and today his poetry seems obscure, artificial, and difficult to appreciate. Throughout antiquity, however, Callimachus was considered a model, more frequently quoted than any other poet but Homer. His influence on Roman poets, including Virgil and Ovid, was enormous.

Alexandria was able to attract the greatest scholars and poets of the Hellenistic world, but its greatest playwright, Menander (342–292 B.C.E.), refused to leave his native Athens for the rewards of Ptolemaic patronage. Menander's gift was that for comedy, but it was a new type of comedy quite removed from the politically biting and often vulgar humor of Aristophanes. Menander wrote with great poetic skill and artistry some hundred wildly complicated, good-natured plays. His characters were stock figures: slaves, freedmen, soldiers, old men, wily shepherds, lovers, and fools. Plots are full of mistaken identities: slaves who turn out to be free-born children kidnapped at birth, and soldiers believed dead who return to disappoint their mourning but greedy heirs. Still, Menander's characters are not simply one-dimensional caricatures. Their ironic portrayal is diffused with sympathy and they are credible as human beings, even if they do not evoke profound psychological study. Menander was a master of the happy ending: families reunite, the lost are saved, and everyone lives happily ever after. In his light comedies, Menander not only provided the plots for virtually every subsequent comedy from the Roman theater to television sit-coms, he also created an enduring sense of what ordinary people, with their foibles and weaknesses, their universality, and, ultimately, their decency, are really like. More than any other ancient

■ This marble relief by the Hellenistic sculptor Archelaos of Priene (ca. 220–159 B.C.E.), depicting the Apotheosis or deification of Homer, shows the three realms of the universe—that of humans, the temple, and the gods—and testifies to the continuing esteem for the Homeric epics throughout the Hellenistic world.

■ The *Nike,* or Winged Victory, is an outstanding example of Hellenistic sculpture. It was found in fragments on the island of Samothrace in the Aegean Sea in 1863. The head and arms were never discovered. The statue is now in the Louvre in Paris.

poet or playwright, he draws a sympathetic image of ordinary men and women.

Architecture and Art

Political rivalry encouraged architectural and artistic rivalry as kings competed for the most magnificent Hellenistic cities. Temples, porticoes, and public buildings grew in size and ornamentation. Architects experimented with multitiered buildings, combining traditional Doric and Ionian orders. In the Seleucid kingdom, the more flamboyant Corinthian order with its luxuriantly foliated capitals was especially popular. The Seleucid king Antiochus IV (176–165 B.C.E.) completed in the Corinthian order the great temple of Olympian Zeus in Athens, which until Roman times was the largest building in Europe.

Mausoleum of Halicarnassus

Hellenistic architects not only developed more elaborate and monumental buildings, they also combined the buildings in harmonious urban ensembles. New cities presented unprecedented opportunities for urban planners, and Hellenistic rulers provided the funds to undertake major urban renewal projects in older cities. In cities such as Rhodes and Pergamum, planners incorporated their constructions into the terrain, using natural hills and slopes to create elegant terraced vistas.

Freestanding statues and magnificent murals and mosaics adorned the public squares, temples, and private homes of Hellenistic cities. While artists continued the traditions of the Hellenic age, they displayed more freedom in portraying tension and restlessness as well as individuality in the human form. Little remains of Hellenistic painting, although Roman mosaics such as that of Alexander at Issus suggest the virtuosity with which mural painters managed multifigure compositions, perspective, and realistic portrayal of landscapes. Sculptors also demonstrated their skill in the portrayal of drapery tightly folded or falling naturally across the human form. The *Nike* (Victory) from Samothrace (ca. 200 B.C.E.) and the Aphrodite from Melos, known more commonly as the Venus de Milo (ca. 120 B.C.E.), are supreme examples of Hellenistic sculptural achievement.

Hellenistic Philosophy

Philosophy, too, flourished in the Hellenistic world, but in directions different from those initiated by Plato and Aristotle, who were deeply committed to political involvement in the free polis. Instead, Cynics, Epicureans, and Stoics turned inward, advocating types of morality less directly related to the state and society. The philosophies appealed to the rootless Greeks of the Hellenistic east who were no longer tied by bonds of religion or patriotism to any community. Each philosophy was as much a way of life as a way of thought and offered different answers to the question of how the individual, cut loose from the security of traditional social and political networks, should deal with the whims of fate.

Cynics. Antisthenes (ca. 450–ca. 350 B.C.E.), a pupil of Socrates, and Diogenes of Sinope (d. ca. 320 B.C.E.), established the Cynic tradition, which taught that excessive attachment to the things of this world was the source of evil and unhappiness. **Cynics** believed that individual freedom came through renunciation of material things, society, and pleasures and that the more one had, the more one would be vulnerable to the whims of fortune. The Cynics' goal was to reduce their possessions, connections, and pleasures to the absolute minimum. "I would rather go mad than enjoy myself," Antisthenes said. The story was told that once, while Diogenes was sunning himself, Alexander the Great came to see the philosopher and, standing before him, offered to do for him anything that he desired. "Stand out of my sun," was Diogenes' reply.

Epicureans. Like the Cynics, the **Epicureans** sought freedom, but from pain rather than from the conventions of ordinary life. Epicurus (341–270 B.C.E.) and his disciples have often been attacked for their emphasis on pleasure. ("You need only possess perception and be made of flesh, and you will see that pleasure is good," Epicurus wrote.) Yet that search for pleasure was not a call to sensual indulgence. Pleasure was to be pursued rationally, with awareness that today's pleasure could mean tomorrow's suffering. The real goal was to reduce desires to those that were simple and attainable. Thus Epicureans urged retirement from politics and retreat from public competition, with concentration instead on friendship and private enjoyment. Epicurus's garden became a tranquil retreat for himself and his disciples. For Epicurus, reason properly applied illuminated how best to pursue pleasure. He believed that the universe was entirely material, consisting of atoms, and that the gods had no interest or role in this world. Thus alone, humans had to search for their pleasure through reason, which would make them free. The traditional image of the Epicurean as an indulgent sensualist is a gross caricature. As Epicurus advised one follower, an Epicurean "revels in the pleasure of the body—on a diet of bread and water."

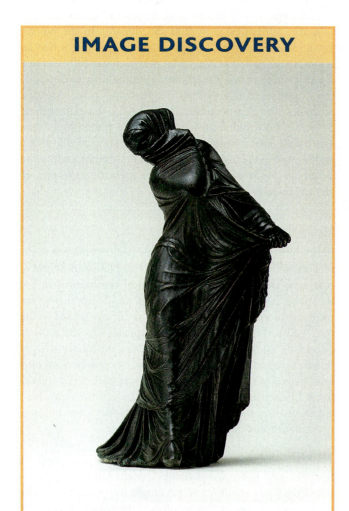

IMAGE DISCOVERY

Portraying the Human Form

A Hellenistic bronze statue of a veiled dancer from the third century B.C.E. Compare this statue with that of the Spartan woman (p. 58) some two hundred years earlier. What technical innovations do you see? How is the human form treated differently? How has the Hellenistic artist changed the treatment of clothing and drapery?

Stoics. The **Stoics** also followed nature, but rather than leading them to retire from public life, it led them to greater participation in it. They believed that just as the universe was a system in which stars and planets moved according to fixed laws, so too was human society ordered and unified. As the founder of Stoicism, Zeno (ca. 335–ca. 263 B.C.E.), expressed it, "All men should regard themselves as members of one city and people, having one life and order." According to the Stoics, every person had a role in the divinely ordered universe, and all roles were of equal value. True happiness consisted in freely accepting one's role, whatever it was, while unhappiness and evil resulted from attempting to reject one's place in the divine plan. Stoic virtue consisted in applying reason to one's life in such a way that one knowingly lived in conformity to nature. Worldly pleasures, like worldly pain, had no particular value. Both were to be accepted and endured.

All three philosophical traditions emphasized the importance of reason and the proper understanding of nature. Hellenistic understanding of nature was one area in which Greek thinkers were influenced by the ancient Oriental traditions brought to them through the conquests of Alexander. Particularly for mathematics, astronomy, and engineering, the Hellenistic period was a golden age.

Mathematics and Science

Ptolemaic Egypt became the center of mathematical studies. Euclid (ca. 300 B.C.E.), whose *Elements* was the fundamental textbook of geometry until the twentieth century, worked there, as did his student Apollonius of Perga (ca. 262–ca. 190 B.C.E.), whose work on conic sections is one of the greatest monuments of geometry. Both Apollonius and his teacher were as influential for their method as for their conclusions. Their treatises follow rigorous logical proofs of mathematical theorems, which established the form of mathematical reasoning to the present day. Archimedes of Syracuse (ca. 287–212 B.C.E.) corresponded with the Egyptian mathematicians and made additional contributions to geometry—such as the calculation of the approximate value of pi—as well as to mechanics, arithmetic, and engineering. Archimedes was famous for his practical application of engineering, particularly to warfare, and legends quickly grew up about his marvelous machines with which he helped Syracuse defend itself against Rome. (See "A Closer Look: Technology and Innovation," pp. 96–97.) Although the rumor that he was on the city's walls was not true, as reported, it was sufficient to cause the Roman fleet to flee in terror. Such stories indicate the esteem with which applied science and its masterminds were held in the Hellenistic world.

Mathematical Astronomy. Many mathematicians, such as Archimedes and Apollonius, were also mathematical astronomers, and the application of their mathematical skills to the exact data collected by earlier Babylonian and Egyptian empirical astronomers greatly increased the understanding of the heavens and earth. Archimedes devised a means of measuring the diameter of the sun, and Eratosthenes of Cyrene (ca. 276–194 B.C.E.) calculated the circumference of the earth to within 200 miles. Aristarchus of Samos (ca. 270 B.C.E.) theorized that the sun and fixed stars were motionless and that the earth moved around the sun. His theory, unsupported by mathematical evidence and not taking into account the elliptical nature of planetary orbits or their nonuniform speeds, was rejected by contemporaries. Hipparchus of Nicea (ca. 146–127 B.C.E.) offered an alternative theory, placing the earth at the center of the universe. Backed by more mathematically acceptable arguments, Hipparchus's system remained, with slight adjustments made 300 years later by Ptolemy of Alexandria, the dominant theory until the sixteenth century.

Medicine. Like astronomy, Hellenistic medicine combined theory and observation. In Alexandria, Herophilus of Chalcedon (ca. 335–ca. 280 B.C.E.) and Erasistratus of Ceos (ca. 250 B.C.E.) conducted important studies in human anatomy. The Ptolemaic kings provided them with condemned prisoners, whom they dissected alive so as to observe the functioning of the organs of the body. The terrible agonies inflicted on their experimental subjects were considered to be justified by the argument that there was no cruelty in causing pain to guilty men while seeking remedies for the innocent. Through his studies, Herophilus recognized the brain as the center of the nervous system and was able to distinguish accurately between motor and sensory nerves. He also produced the first accurate descriptions of such organs as the eye, brain, liver, and salivary glands.

Cultural Resistance

For all of the vitality of the Hellenistic civilization, the cities remained parasites on the local societies. No real efforts were made to merge the two and to develop a new civilization. Some ambitious members of the indigenous elites tried to adopt the customs of the Greeks, while others plotted insurrection. The clearest example of the conflicting tensions was that of the Jewish community. Early in the second century B.C.E., a powerful Jewish faction, which included the High Priest of Yahweh, supported hellenization. With the assistance of the Seleucid king, the faction set up a gymnasion in Jerusalem where Jewish youths and even priests began to study Greek and participate in Greek culture. Some even underwent painful surgery to reverse the effects of circumcision so that they could pass for Greeks in naked athletic contests. The faction's rejection of tradition infuriated a large portion of the Jewish population. When the Seleucids finally attempted to introduce pagan cults into the temple in 167 B.C.E., open rebellion broke out and continued intermittently until the Jews gained independence in 141 B.C.E.

Such violent opposition was repeated elsewhere from time to time, especially in Egypt and Persia, where, as in Judaea, old traditions of religion and monarchy provided rallying points against the transplanted Greeks. In time, the Hellenistic kingdoms' inability to bridge the gap between Greek and indigenous populations proved fatal. In the east, the non-Greek kingdom of Parthia replaced the Seleucids in much of the old Persian Empire. In the west, continuing hostility between kingdoms and within kingdoms prepared the way for their progressive absorption by the new power to the west: Rome.

CONCLUSION

In the fifth century B.C.E., the rugged slopes, fertile plains, and arid islands of the Greek world gave rise to characteristic forms of social, political, and cultural organization that have reappeared in varying forms wherever Western civilization has taken root. In Athens, which emerged from the ruins of the Persian invasion as the most powerful and dynamic state in the Hellenic world, the give-and-take of a direct democracy challenged men to raise fundamental questions about the relationship between individual and society, freedom and absolutism, and gods and mortals. At the same time, the society of free males excluded the majority of its inhabitants—women, foreigners, and slaves—from participation in government and fought a long and ultimately futile war to hold together an exploitive empire.

The interminable wars among Greek states ultimately left the Greek world open to conquest by a powerful semi-Greek monarchy that went on to spread Athenian culture throughout the known world. Freed from the particularism of individual city-states, Hellenistic culture became a universal tradition emphasizing the individual rather than the community of family, tribe, or religious association. Its proponents, except for Alexander the Great, never sought a real synthesis of Greek and barbarian traditions. Such a synthesis would begin only with the coming of Rome.

TECHNOLOGY AND INNOVATION

The Hellenistic world could boast not only sophisticated mathematics and astronomy but also an impressive series of technological inventions: cogged gears, pulley systems, water pumps, the screw, the odometer, the water organ, the water clock, and even a copying machine. If Hellenistic innovators did not actually invent the water mill, they probably worked out ways to make it more efficient.

Hero of Alexandria (first century B.C.E.) invented a sort of steam engine and a box gear system whereby he could multiply a physical force by a factor of 200. Of his many inventions, however, the ones actually developed were tricks such as temple doors that seemed to open on their own, statues that poured out offerings of wine to the gods, and a gadget that offered holy water when a coin was dropped in a slot. Hero's revolutionary, labor-saving devices remained undeveloped ideas; their fate was typical of the most exciting Hellenistic technological discoveries: often the most revolutionary inventions remained theoretical models or were used for the ancient equivalent of magic tricks.

A CLOSER LOOK

It is tempting to argue that that technological progress should have developed in the eastern Mediterranean at the end of the first millennium B.C.E. but that Hellenistic engineers failed to develop the kinds of useful, energy-saving devices that have transformed the modern world. But this argument would be anachronistic. Hellenistic engineers did not fail to develop labor-saving devices because labor saving was never their goal. On the contrary, such an idea would have been seen as socially disdainful and politically dangerous.

Technological innovation requires investment of capital as well as labor. But throughout antiquity, investment in anything other than land, civic projects, or conspicuous consumption was considered ignoble. Regardless of the sources of one's wealth, it was invested in land and slaves as quickly as possible. Only landed wealth could bring social status. Surplus from agriculture could buy prestige through generous public works such as building temples, bridges, or aqueducts that employed vast armies of laborers thus advertising one's wealth and generosity. One's wealth and taste could also be advertised through extraordinary, conspicuous consumption. An investment in new, more efficient means of making money could only be seen as crude. Worse than crude, it was dangerous. The Greek word for making a revolution was *neoterizein,* to innovate. Elites considered that the masses of laborers and slaves had to be kept busy at menial tasks fitting their stations. Idle hands might take up weapons in revolt. Revolutionary labor-saving technology might lead to social and political revolution. However, when confronted with a culturally acceptable need, Hellenistic engineers, supported by monarchs, could put technology to use in remarkably sophisticated ways. Moving water in arid Egypt was one such acceptable need. Warfare was the other.

If the fate of Hero's inventions was typical of most Hellenistic innovations, the fate of Archimedes' discoveries was the exception that proves the rule. Archimedes was primarily celebrated as a mathematician: theory was always valued over the practical in the ancient world. However, he is popularly associated with important inventions in hydraulics and warfare that, whether or not attributable to him, were just the sort of practical innovations rulers could appreciate. The Archimedian screw, a large pipe in which a tightly-fitted screw raised water when turned, solved a constant problem in the ancient world: how to move a great volume of water for irrigation or from mine shafts up a very steep incline. The solution, however, did not result in a great decrease of human or animal labor. Operating the screws required a great deal of labor. Moreover, working the mines drained with the screw and irrigating the fields with the water actually increased rather than decreased the need for unskilled labor.

Military technology was one area in which Hellenistic rulers invested willingly, and here one sees just how innovative the Hellenistic world could be. Hellenistic engineers developed the siege tower, the ram for battering through stout walls and gates, the flame thrower, "machine gun" arrow launchers, and, most importantly, the torsion catapult, a machine that used mechanical energy to throw a great stone with tremendous force.

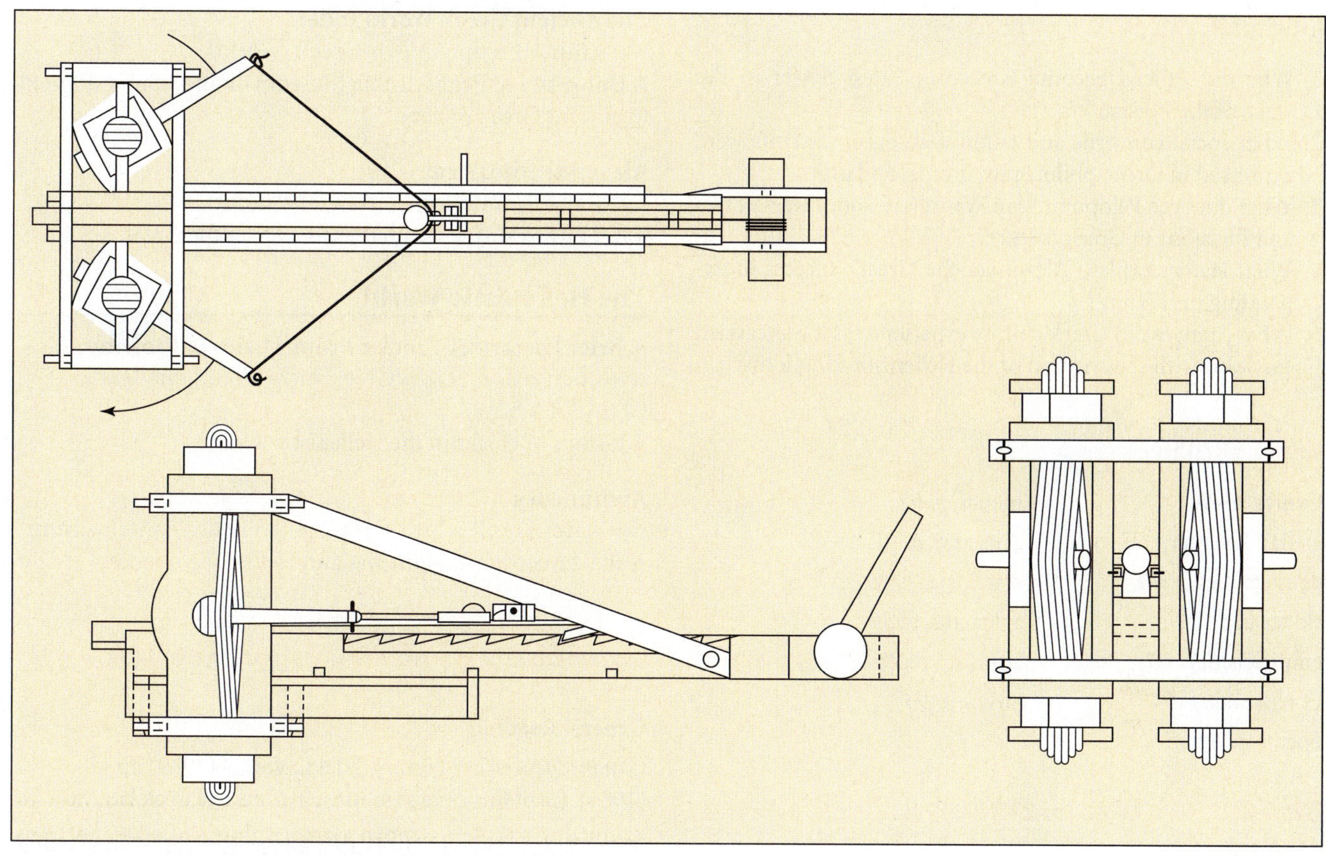

Reconstruction by E. W. Marsden of a stone-throwing torsion catapult introduced circa 270 B.C.E. and described by Hero and Philo.

Although Archimedes is popularly remembered for devising diabolically clever weapons to defend his native Syracuse against the attacking Romans, nowhere was military technology better supported or more systematically pursued than in Ptolemaic Alexandria. Royal research and development teams combined both the theory of mathematics and its practical application in order to design larger and more efficient weapons. Perhaps the most outstanding example of combining scientific, experimental, and mathematical methods for practical results was the design of large torsion catapults capable of hurling massive stones hundreds of yards with great accuracy. Engineers found, through a series of controlled experiments, that the critical variable determining the trajectory of flight was the exact diameter of the holes in the frames of catapults through which passed the twisted cord of animal skin or horse hair that powered the weapon. The heavier the projectile, the thicker and more tightly wound the cord had to be. But how to calculate the proper diameter? Ultimately, the Alexandrine engineers worked out an exact formula: "The weight [of the stone] is first reduced to units, the cube root of this quantity extracted, a tenth of this root added to the root, and the result is the number of digits in the diameter of the opening that receives the skein." Here one has a precise, mathematical formula that solves the real problems faced by Hellenistic rulers: not how to create steam engines or labor-saving devices but how to kill one's enemies with greater efficiency.

QUESTIONS FOR REVIEW

1. Why did Athens become Greece's greatest power in the wake of the Persian Wars?
2. What social concerns and cultural accomplishments were expressed in Greek philosophy, drama, and art?
3. What does the Peloponnesian War reveal about weaknesses and divisions in Greek culture?
4. What factors explain Alexander the Great's success in expanding his empire?
5. What changes did Greek culture experience as it was carried eastward with the creation of the Hellenistic kingdoms?

KEY TERMS

Cynics, *p. 93*
Delian League, *p. 71*
demagogues, *p. 74*
ekklesia, *p. 74*
empiricism, *p. 85*
Epicureans, *p. 94*
Forms, *p. 84*
metics, *p. 72*
Museum, *p. 91*
ostracism, *p. 69*
Seleucids, *p. 89*
Sophists, *p. 78*
Stoics, *p. 94*

DISCOVERING WESTERN CIVILIZATION ONLINE

You can obtain more information about classical and Hellenistic Greece at the Websites listed below. See also the Companion Website that accompanies this text, www.ablongman.com/kishlansky, which contains an online study guide and additional resources.

War and Politics in the Fifth Century B.C.E.

Articles on Ancient Persia
www.livius.org/persia.html
Links to articles on many aspects of ancient Persian history.

The Greeks: Crucible of Civilization
www.pbs.org/empires/thegreeks/
A Public Broadcasting System site devoted to ancient Greece.

The Ancient City of Athens
www.indiana.edu/~kglowack/athens/
An excellent site devoted to Athens.

The Peloponnesian War
www.multimania.com/sdelille/gdpa.html
A site developed by Sven Delille on the Peloponnesian War.

Diotima: Women and Gender in the Ancient World
www.stoa.org/diotima/
A site devoted to women and gender in antiquity.

The Ancient Greek World Index
www.museum.upenn.edu/Greek_World/
A University of Pennsylvania Museum online exhibit devoted to ancient Greek society.

Alexander the Great
history.boisestate.edu/westciv/alexander/
Ellis L. Knox's page devoted to Alexander the Great.

The Hellenistic World

A Brief History of Clocks: From Thales to Ptolemy
www.perseus.tufts.edu/GreekScience/Students/Jesse/CLOCK1A.html
A history of clocks in the Hellenistic world.

Archimedes
www.mcs.drexel.edu/~crorres/Archimedes/contents.html
A site devoted to Archimedes and Hellenistic science.

SUGGESTIONS FOR FURTHER READING

General Reading

Cambridge Ancient History, 2d ed., Vols. 5 (1989) and 7 (1984). Contains essays on most aspects of Greek history.

Pierre Vidal-Naquet, *The Black Hunter: Forms of Thought and Forms of Society in the Greek World* (Baltimore: The Johns Hopkins University Press, 1998). A brilliant exploration of Greek society and politics approached through its margins, its contradictions, and its oppositions.

War and Politics in the Fifth Century B.C.E.

Lindsay Allen, *The Persian Empire* (Chicago: University of Chicago Press, 2005). A comprehensive history of the Persian Empire from its origins to its destruction by Alexander.

Ryan K. Balot, *Greek Political Thought* (Malden, MA: Blackwell Publishers, 2006). Greek political philosophy in its historical context with implications for the twenty-first century.

Sue Blundell, *Women in Ancient Greece* (Cambridge, MA: Harvard University Press, 1995). A good place to start for an understanding of women in classical Greece.

W. R. Connor, *The New Politicians of Fifth-Century Athens* (Indianapolis: Hackett, 1992). Reappraises the demagogues within the context of Athenian political life.

Charles W. Fornara and Loren J. Samons II, *Athens from Cleisthenes to Pericles* (Berkeley: University of California Press, 1991). Detailed survey of the development of Athenian democracy and empire.

Yvon Garlan, *Slavery in Ancient Greece* (Ithaca, NY: Cornell University Press, 1988). A basic study of Greek slavery.

Lisa Kallet, *Money and the Corrosion of Power in Thucydides: The Sicilian Expedition and Its Aftermath* (Berkeley: University of California Press, 2002). A focused study of corruption in a crucial aspect of the Peloponnesian War.

Nigel M. Kennell, *The Gymnasium of Virtue: Education and Culture in Ancient Sparta* (Chapel Hill: University of North Carolina Press, 1995). An investigation of Spartan culture.

Helen King, *Hippocrates' Woman: Reading the Female Body in Ancient Greece* (New York: Routledge, 1998). A study of Greek medical theory concerning women and women's bodies.

P. J. Rhodes, *Ancient Democracy and Modern Ideology* (London: Duckworth Academic, 2003). An essay from a prominent Greek historian exploring the modern uses of Athenian democracy.

Athenian Culture in the Hellenic Age

J. Boardman, *Greek Art,* 3d ed. (New York: Thames & Hudson, 1985). A handbook introduction by period.

W. Burkert, *Greek Religion* (Cambridge, MA: Harvard University Press, 1985). General survey of the topic.

Simon Goldhill, *Reading Greek Tragedy* (New York: Cambridge University Press, 1986). A general introduction to Athenian tragedy.

G. E. R. Lloyd, *Aristotle: The Growth and Structure of His Thought* (New York: Cambridge University Press, 1968). A developmental approach to Aristotle.

C. J. Rowe, *Plato* (New York: St. Martin's, 1984). A good survey of the philosopher's thought.

From City-States to Macedonian Empire, 404–323 B.C.E.

A. B. Bosworth, *Conquest and Empire* (New York: Cambridge University Press, 1988). A scholarly but readable account of Alexander the Great.

J. R. Hamilton, *Alexander the Great* (Pittsburgh: University of Pittsburgh Press, 1973). Still the best biography of Alexander in English.

The Hellenistic World

J. Barnes et al., *Science and Speculation* (New York: Cambridge University Press, 1982). A collection of papers on Hellenistic science.

Andrew Erskine, ed. *A Companion to the Hellenistic World* (Oxford and Malden, MA: Blackwell Publishers, 2003). A comprehensive examination of the Hellenistic world from the death of Alexander to the defeat of Anthony and Cleopatra.

Peter Green, *Alexander to Actium: The Historical Evolution of the Hellenistic Age* (Berkeley: University of California Press, 1990). A broad examination of the Hellenistic period.

Peter Green, ed., *Hellenistic History and Culture* (Berkeley: University of California Press, 1993). A stimulating series of articles and debates on Hellenistic civilization.

For a list of additional titles related to this chapter's topics, please see http://www.ablongman.com/kishlansky.

CHAPTER 4

EARLY ROME AND THE ROMAN REPUBLIC, 800–146 B.C.E.

ETERNAL ROME

FROM VILLAGE TO EMPIRE

THE VISUAL RECORD

Five miles from its mouth, the Tiber River snakes in a lazy S around the first highlands that rise from the marshes of central Italy. The weathered cliffs, separated by tributary streams, look down on the river valley that broadens to more than a mile and a half wide, the first and only natural ford for many miles. Only three promontories, the Capitoline, Palatine, and Aventine, are separate hills. The others, the Quirinal, Viminal, Caelian, Oppian, and Esquiline, are actually spurs of the distant Apennines. Gradually the pastoral villages founded on these hills spread down to the valleys between them, united, and grew to a city whose name for more than 2000 years was synonymous with empire.

Rome wasn't built in a day. The earliest Roman villages were founded on the Palatine—from whose heights the accompanying photograph was taken—which remained throughout Rome's history the favored residential area. Here Latin shepherds first erected their crude huts and republican senators later built their homes. Still later, emperors built their increasingly splendid residences on its slopes until the term *palace* became synonymous with the seat of royalty. The Capitoline with its steep cliffs, which begin at the extreme left of the photograph, served as an acropolis, the religious center of the community. Here was found the Capitol, which contained not only temples but also the state archives and the city mint beside the temple of Juno the Admonisher, Juno Moneta (hence our word *money*). The Capitol, so the Romans thought, was indestructible, and it became a symbol of the eternal city. As Romans established colonies across Italy and throughout the Mediterranean, the colonies too had their hill temples, their so-called capitols.

The area shown in the center of the photograph, between the Palatine and Capitoline, was originally a low, marshy burial ground. In the seventh century B.C.E., Etruscan kings drained the marshes, making it possible to pave the area between the hills and turn it into a public meeting place, or *forum.* The Forum became the heart of the city. Through it ran the Sacred Way, the road that cuts diagonally from left to right in the photograph. At the south end, to the right of the photograph, was the marketplace, which bustled with shops and businesses. To the north, where the domed church of Saints Luca and Magartina now stands, was the *Comitium,* the meeting place of the citizens' assembly. Here the king and, in republican times, the popular assembly conducted political business. Just below it still stands the *Curia,* the meeting place of the Roman Senate, which survived because it was converted into a Christian church in the seventh century C.E.

Here too temples and monuments rose to meet religious and public needs. Perhaps the most ancient structure was the circular temple of Vesta, the hearth goddess, the surviving columns of which can be seen in the lower center of the photograph. In this temple consecrated virgins, the most honored women of Rome, tended the sacred fire, the symbol of the life of Rome. The ruins of the virgins' magnificent residence fill the lower right of the photograph. Just above it stood the royal residence, the *Regia,* which during the republic came to be the quarters of one of Rome's chief priests, the *pontifex maximus.* To the lower right stood the temple to the twin gods Castor and Pollux, who were credited with bringing victory in the early days of the republic against Rome's Latin neighbors. In time, still other temples were built, for honoring the gods and honoring Rome were one.

As Rome grew from a simple city to an empire, the Forum reflected the changes. Simple Etruscan architecture gave way to the Greek style of building. Marble replaced brick and stucco. Near the Curia, a golden milestone marked the point from which all distances were measured and to which all

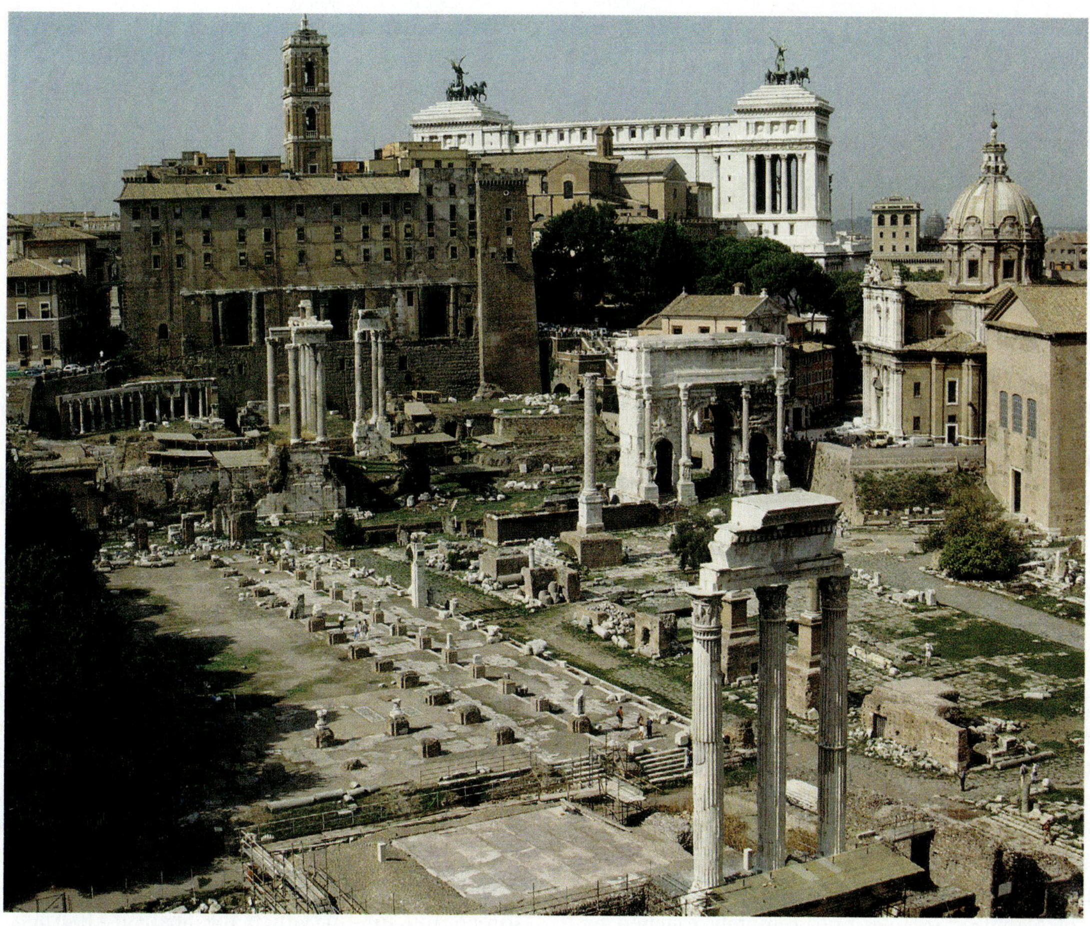

■ The Roman Forum today viewed from the Palatine Hill.

roads of the empire led. The turmoil of the last years of the republic also left its mark. In the center of the picture, the semicircular brown stone ruin is all that remains of the temple of the Divine Julius, erected on the spot where Julius Caesar's remains were cremated after his murder on the Ides of March. After his death, Caesar received divine honors; he was the first Roman to be so treated by his city. Next to the temple stands all that remains of the monumental arch of Caesar's adopted son Octavian, known to history as Augustus, the first and greatest of the Roman emperors.

By the time of Caesar and Augustus, Rome had replaced its Forum, just as it had replaced its republican constitution. Caesar had begun and Augustus had completed new forums, known collectively as the Forum of the Caesars, which lay beyond the trees at the top of the picture. Their successor Trajan (98–117 C.E.) would build a still greater one just beyond it. Still, for centuries of Romans and for the Western societies that succeeded them, the narrow space encompassing the Capitoline, the Palatine, and the Forum was the epicenter of the city and the world.

LOOKING AHEAD

This chapter begins with a survey of the western Mediterranean and charts the gradual expansion of Roman power from but another Italian village at the site of this forum to the dominant power in the western Mediterranean. As its power expanded abroad, social and economic tensions grew at home, and from this tension arose a new culture, deeply indebted to Greek and Etruscan traditions but deeply original in its political forms and social organization.

CHAPTER OUTLINE

- THE WESTERN MEDITERRANEAN TO 509 B.C.E.
  Merchants of Baal ▪ The Western Greeks ▪ Italy's First Civilization
- FROM CITY TO EMPIRE, 509–146 B.C.E.
  Latin Rome ▪ Etruscan Rome ▪ Rome and Italy ▪ Rome and the Mediterranean
- REPUBLICAN CIVILIZATION
  Farmers and Soldiers ▪ The Roman Family ▪ Social Effects of Expansion ▪ Roman Religion ▪ Republican Letters
- THE CRISIS OF ROMAN VIRTUE

THE WESTERN MEDITERRANEAN TO 509 B.C.E.

Civilization came late to the western Mediterranean, carried in the ships of Greeks and Phoenicians. While the great floodplain civilizations of Mesopotamia and Egypt and the Greek communities of the eastern Mediterranean were developing sophisticated systems of urban life and political organization, western Europe and Africa knew only the scattered villages of simple farmers and pastoralists. These populations were the descendants of Neolithic peoples only remotely touched by the developments in the east. The west was, however, rich in metals, and an indigenous Bronze Age culture developed slowly between 1500 and 1000 B.C.E., spreading widely north of the Alps and south into Italy and Spain. By the twelfth century B.C.E., workshops in northern Italy were producing bronze spearheads, swords, and axes both for local use and for export to Crete, Naxos, Corfu, and Mycenae. In addition to finished weapons and other objects, the eastern cities sought in Italy and Spain unworked bronze, silver bullion, tin, and iron.

The western shores of the Mediterranean did not escape the widespread crisis of the twelfth century B.C.E., which transformed so profoundly the established civilizations of Mycenae and the Near East, but its exact effects on the west are unknown. Sometime around the year 1000 B.C.E., a new, distinctive iron-using civilization first appeared in northern Italy. These **Villanovans**—so called for a major archaeological discovery of this civilization at Villanova near Bologna—differed from earlier Italian peoples in their use of iron, in the practice of cremating their dead and burying their ashes in large urns, and in the greater size and complexity of their settlements. No one knows whether the Villanovans were new arrivals in Italy or simply the descendants of previous inhabitants. However, around this time, small groups of warrior peoples did begin to infiltrate Italy from the east and the north, occupying the mountainous terrain of the Apennines and pushing the indigenous society west. These new arrivals shared no common organization or identity, but all spoke related Indo-European languages we call Italic, including Latin. The newcomers were warriors, and their steady progress is marked by the appearance of their distinctive form of burial, in which their dead were cremated and buried with weapons. Like the Dark Age Greeks, these peoples soon developed the art of making iron weapons, which gave them a decided advantage over the older inhabitants of the peninsula. By 800 B.C.E., they were in firm control of the mountainous region of central Italy and threatened the coastal societies of the west and south.

Merchants of Baal

Also around 800 B.C.E., Phoenicians arrived in the west, first as traders and then as colonists. The Phoenicians were known as the best and the most ruthless seafarers of antiquity. Setting out in warships from the regions of Tyre, Sidon, and Byblos, they ventured beyond the Strait of Gibraltar in search of supplies of silver and tin. They established a trading post at Cadiz (*gadir,* "walled place" in Phoenician) at which they could trade with the local inhabitants for silver from the Sierra Morena and for tin, which the Spanish (Iberians) obtained from distant Britain and Ireland. Because sailing vessels hugged the coastline whenever possible rather than braving the open sea, the Phoenicians established a series of bases on the coasts along the route to and from Spain and on the islands of Corsica and Sicily. The bases were established on the islands of Ibiza and Motya in the Mediterranean, at Panormus on Sicily, and at Utica and Carthage on the coast of North Africa, and they provided Phoenician ships on their way to and from Cadiz safe harbor, food, and supplies.

Carthage. The great city of Carthage began as no more than a small anchorage for ships. Gradually, its population grew as overcrowding forced emigration from Tyre. When, in the sixth century B.C.E., Tyre was conquered by Nebuchadnezzar and incorporated into the New Babylonian Empire, Carthage became

The "Benacci Askos" pitcher from ca. 800 B.C.E. is a rare example of Villanovan pottery in the shape of an ox with a horse-shaped handle ridden by a warrior.

an independent city and soon established itself as the center of an expanding Phoenician presence in the western Mediterranean.

The city was perfectly situated to profit from both the land and the sea. Its excellent double harbor, which had attracted the Phoenicians initially, made it an ideal port. Here ships could lie at rest, protected from storms as well as from enemies by a narrow, 70-foot entrance to the sea, which could be closed with iron chains. In good weather, captains could anchor their ships outside the harbor proper along a pier some 300 yards long. The city was equally protected on land. It was situated on a narrow isthmus and surrounded by massive walls more than 40 feet high and 30 feet thick. As long as Carthage controlled the sea, its commercial center was secure from any enemies.

The wealth of Punic (from *Puni,* or *Poeni,* the Roman name for the Carthaginians) commerce was supplemented by the agricultural riches of the surrounding region. The fertile coastal plain produced grain and fruits for export in abundance, while inland the subject native population engaged in cattle raising and sheep-herding for their masters.

Carthaginian Empire. By the middle of the sixth century B.C.E., Carthage was the center of a real empire. But in contrast with the Athenian Empire of the following century, that of Carthage was much more successful at integrating other cities and peoples into its military and thus sharing the burden of warfare. Carthaginian mercenary armies consisted of Libyan light infantry, Numidian cavalry, Spanish hill people, Balearic sling throwers, Gallic infantry, Italians, and often Greeks. Only the fleet was composed primarily of Carthaginians. This multiethnic empire proved far more stable than any of those created by the Greeks, succeeding in victory and withstanding defeat to endure for more than three centuries.

Carthage was governed by a mixed constitution that combined elements of monarchical, aristocratic, and popular rule. The assembly of citizens annually elected the heads of state. In spite of the role of the free citizenry in their selection, however, the officials consistently came from among the wealthy and powerful merchant aristocracy. They presided over the popular assembly and the smaller aristocratic senate and dispensed justice. The officials were assisted in their governmental tasks by "judges," who were a select body of magistrates chosen from the senate and who had broad judicial and administrative responsibility.

As a society of merchants, Carthaginians mistrusted military leaders, and they carefully separated military authority from civil. Generals were elected and served open-ended terms. Because almost all of Carthage's wars were conducted far from home and used mercenaries or citizens of subject cities, selection of commanders was often based more on the aristocracy's concern to avoid giving too much power to ambitious, capable leaders than on the desire to select the best soldiers. Unlike commanders in Greek states, successful Carthaginian generals found themselves more distrusted than honored by their fellow citizens.

Although superficially similar to many Greek cities, the Punic state differed profoundly in the relationship between citizen and state. Compared with that of the Greek states, Punic popular politics has been termed essentially apolitical. In spite of the formal role of the assembly, ordinary citizens had little involvement, and apparently little interest, in government. Unlike the Greeks, they normally did not serve in the military and thus did not develop a sense of solidarity and involvement in the state. According to Aristotle, the aristocracy treated the rest of the population generously, sharing with it profits in the exploitation of its commercial and imperial wealth. Thus the kinds of class pressures that created the Greek tyrants never emerged in Carthage.

The Gods of Carthage. The gods of Carthage were local variations of the Phoenician gods, especially Baal Hammon, the supreme god El of the Semitic world, and the goddess Tanit, a version of the Near Eastern goddess Asherat. Baal Hammon was an awesome figure. Many Greeks equated him not with Zeus but with the more ancient supreme god, Kronos, a cruel tyrant who devoured his children. Tanit, goddess of fertility, assumed an importance equal to that of Baal Hammon, probably under the influence of the indigenous Libyan society. Submission of humans to the will of the gods and the appeasing of the deities through human sacrifice characterized Carthaginian religion.

According to hostile Greek and Roman sources, all Carthaginian citizens were obligated to sacrifice their first-born sons, and the sacrifice of children constituted the most important and, to their Greek and barbarian neighbors, the most repulsive aspect of Punic culture. The basic reliability of the reports was dramatically confirmed in 1922, when archaeologists excavated the sanctuary of Tanit at Salammbo, site of the earliest Punic settlement. It was found to contain urns filled with the remains of hundreds of children. Other similar sacred sites have since been found.

Stable, prosperous, and devout, Carthage was the master of the western Mediterranean. But its dominion was not undisputed. From the sixth century B.C.E., the Punic Empire felt the pressure of ambitious and expansive Greek cities eager to gain a share of the west's riches.

The Western Greeks

The Greek arrival in the west was the result of a much more complex process than the trading policy of the Phoenicians. As we saw in Chapter 2, toward the end of the Dark Age, commerce, overpopulation, and civic tension sent Greek colonists out in all directions. In the eighth century B.C.E., Crete, Rhodes, Corinth, Argos, Chalcis, Eretria, and Naxos all established colonies in Sicily and southern Italy. One of the earliest of these colonies, Cumae on the Bay of Naples, began, like Cadiz, as a trading post. There Corinthians could trade for copper ore from Etruria and Campania.

In the seventh century B.C.E., Syracuse became the greatest city of Sicily and one of the most prosperous cities of the

Greek world. Greek colonies spread slowly up the boot of Italy, known as Greater Greece, in pursuit of trade and arable land. Initially, the expansion posed no problem for the Phoenicians and Carthaginians, who concentrated primarily on the Spanish and African coasts. But by the last quarter of the seventh century B.C.E., the autonomous Greek colonies began to encroach on the Carthaginian Empire's sphere of influence. Around 631 B.C.E., Greeks from Thera founded a colony at Cyrene in North Africa. The Greek city of Phocaea in Asia Minor established a colony at Massilia (Marseille) around 600 B.C.E. and began to trade down the coast of Spain.

Both commercial rivalry and open warfare characterized the relationship between Greeks and Phoenicians in the western Mediterranean. In the course of the sixth century B.C.E., Greeks in Sicily attempted to expel the Phoenicians from the island. In the fifth century B.C.E., Syracuse, under its tyrant Gelon (ca. 540–478 B.C.E.), threatened both Punic and Greek cities on the island. In an attempt to defend its colonies, in 480 B.C.E. Carthage launched an enormous force to support Gelon's Greek enemies. The attack took place, probably not coincidentally, at the same moment that Xerxes invaded Greece. At the battle of Himera—fought, we are told, on the same day as the battle of Salamis—the Syracusans soundly defeated the Carthaginians. The Carthaginian commander, in a fruitless attempt to summon Baal to his aid, is said to have thrown himself into a sacrificial fire and perished.

Gelon's victory at Himera ushered in a period of prosperity and cultural achievement in Sicily only slightly less extraordinary than that which followed the battles of Marathon and Salamis in Greece. The tyrants of Syracuse, enriched with the spoils of victory, created a court whose magnificence, wealth, and generosity won the acclaim of poets and admirers from throughout the Greek world. This prosperity continued after the elimination of the tyranny in midcentury, and in 415 B.C.E. Syracuse was able to withstand Athens's attempt at conquest. (See Chapter 3, p. 76.) A far more serious threat appeared in 410 B.C.E., when a new Carthaginian army arrived in Sicily seeking revenge. The Carthaginians rapidly captured and destroyed Himera, sacrificing 3000 prisoners on the site where the earlier commander had offered himself up and ex-

MAP DISCOVERY

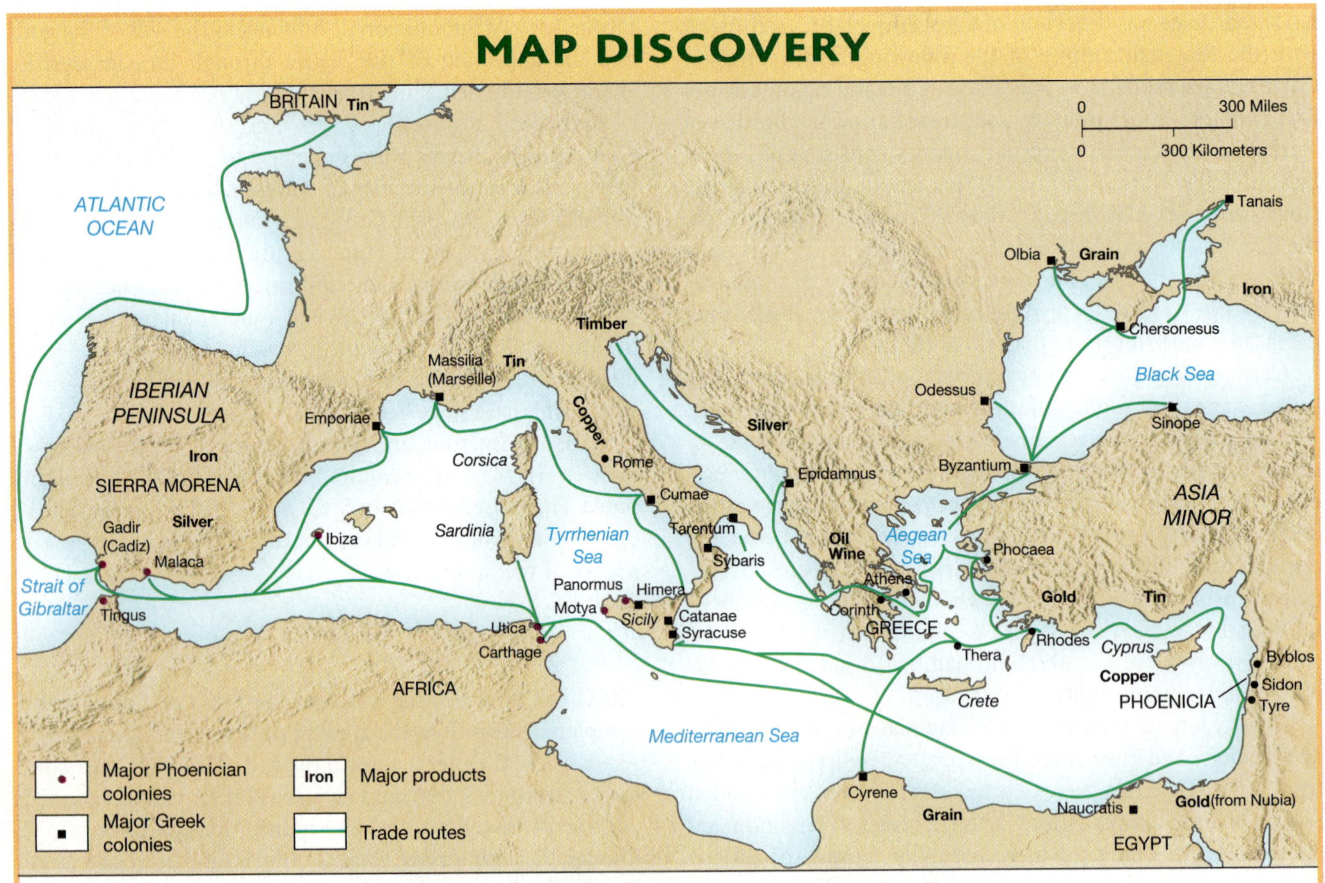

Greek and Phoenician Colonies and Trade

Note the location of the major Phoenician and Greek colonies and the extent of the trade routes to and from these colonies. Where, if at all, did Greek and Phoenician colonies come into close proximity and competition? Did the two systems compete for the same trade goods?

tending the boundaries of Punic Sicily. The invasion initiated a century of inconclusive conflict between Syracuse and Carthage.

Early on in their struggle with the Sicilian Greeks, the Carthaginians found allies in the third major civilization of the west. These were the Etruscans, who in the seventh century B.C.E. dominated the western part of central Italy, known as Etruria. The region today is Tuscany; its name derives from *Tusci*, the Roman name for this early people.

Italy's First Civilization

Etruscan civilization was the first great civilization to emerge in Italy. The **Etruscans** long have been regarded as a people whose origins, language, and customs are shrouded in mystery. Actually, the mystery is more apparent than real. The Greek historian Herodotus thought that the Etruscans had emigrated from Lydia in Asia Minor, and many historians, noting similarities between Etruscan and eastern traditions, subsequently accepted the thesis of eastern origins. A second ancient tradition, reported by the Greek scholar Dionysius of Halicarnassus (ca. 20 B.C.E.), is that the Etruscans did not emigrate from anywhere but rather had always been in western Italy. Recent DNA studies support the former hypothesis; the archaeological record favors the latter.

Etruscan Origins. The earliest materials from Etruscan sites indicate no break with the civilization of pre-Italic Villanovan Italy but rather a gradual development from it. Probably, just as in the Aegean, an indigenous cultural tradition was overwhelmed by the chaos of the twelfth-century B.C.E. crisis and the migration of Indo-Europeans from the north. The tradition shares much with eastern civilizations, such as the importance of underworld gods, fertility cults, and the high status of women. Some scholars even speak of a common Mediterranean civilization submerged for a time but reemerging transformed, centuries later.

■ Etruscan gold jewelry from the seventh century B.C.E., found in a tomb in Cerveteri. Eastern influence is evident in the motif of the Mistress of the Animals and other elements of the design.

The Etruscan language is commonly seen as the second great mystery. Unlike the Minoan writing known as Linear B, which although written in a previously unknown script was found to be early Greek, Etruscan is written in an alphabet derived from that of Greece. Still, despite this derivation, the Etruscan language appears to be unrelated to any other language, and even today some of the extant Etruscan texts remain incompletely deciphered. Bilingual inscriptions and careful analysis, however, have made it possible to read many of the extant Etruscan texts, and in the process the mysteries of the Etruscans have become much less mysterious.

Etruscan civilization coalesced slowly in Etruria over the course of the seventh century B.C.E. from diverse regional and political groups sharing a similar cultural and linguistic tradition. In the mid-sixth century B.C.E., in the face of Greek pressure from the south, 12 of these groups united in a religious and military confederation. Over the next 100 years, the confederation expanded north into the Po Valley and south to Campania, creating a loose Etruscan alliance that included almost all of the peninsula. Cities, each initially ruled by a king, were the centers of Etruscan civilization, and everywhere the Etruscans spread, they either improved upon existing towns or founded new ones. Towns in the north included Bologna, Parma, Modena, Ravenna, Milan, and Mantua; in the south, there were Nola, Nuceria, Pompeii, Sorrento, and Salerno. The Etruscan confederation remained a loose one and, unlike that of the Carthaginians, never developed into a centralized empire. Etruscan kings assumed power in conquered towns, but between the sixth and fifth centuries B.C.E., Etruscan kingship gave way to oligarchic governments, much as Greek monarchies did a bit earlier. In the place of kings, aristocratic assemblies selected magistrates, often paired together or combined into "colleges" to prevent individuals from seizing power. Etruscan institutions provided the foundation for later Roman republican government.

An Archaic Society. The remnants of an ancient civilization, the Etruscans retained throughout their history social and cultural traditions long since vanished from elsewhere in the Mediterranean. Society divided sharply into two classes, lords and servants. The lords' wealth was based on the rich agricultural regions of Etruria, where grain grew in abundance, and on the equally rich deposits of copper and iron. The vast majority of the population were actual slaves, working the lands and mines of the aristocracy.

The aristocrats were aggressive and imaginative landowners. They developed hydraulic systems for draining marshes, produced wine famous throughout the Mediterranean, and put their slaves to work in mines and in smelting. Still, they were largely absentee landlords, spending much of their time in the cities that characterized Etruscan civilization. The cities, with their massive walls, enclosed populations of as great as 20,000. Etruscans built largely with wood, so little remains of their houses, temples, and public buildings. However, their extensive cemeteries have preserved a vivid image of Etruscan life. In the tombs of Caere and other

Etruscan settlements, the dead were buried in family chamber tombs that recall the homes of the living. These tombs were furnished with the wares of everyday life, including benches, beds, ornaments, utensils, and vessels and platters of Etruscan and Corinthian manufacture. The walls of the more sumptuous tombs were decorated with lively, brilliantly colored scenes of feasting, processions, and activities of daily life.

The most striking aspect of Etruscan life to Greek contemporaries and later to Romans was the elevated status of Etruscan women. The decorations and furnishings of tombs, inscriptions, and reports by contemporaries indicate that, as in the much earlier Minoan civilization, women played an active public role in society. Unlike honorable Greek women, Etruscan women took part in banquets, reclining beside their male companions on couches from which they ate. They attended and even occasionally presided over dances, concerts, and sporting events. Women, as wives and mothers, were also active in political life. When a king died, his successor had to be designated and consecrated by the Etruscan queen to establish his legitimacy. Greeks such as Aristotle regarded the public behavior of Etruscan women as lewd. The great philosopher accused them of lying under the same cloak with men at banquets. To Romans, the political role of women such as Tullia, wife of King Lucius Tarquin (Tarquin the Proud), the Etruscan king of Rome, was equally disturbing. The Roman historian Livy (59 B.C.E.–17 C.E.) claims that when Tullia was the first person to acknowledge her husband as king, he was so shocked by this political action that he sent her home. In truth, he was surely grateful.

Etruscans worshiped a variety of gods personifying the sun, the moon, dawn, and the planets Venus and Mars. Many of their gods, under different names, would eventually be appropriated by the Romans. Gods and humans were controlled by nameless powers that were the fates. They also developed highly sophisticated means of divination, or the prediction of the future, through the study of the flights of birds, examination of the internal organs of sacrificed animals, and observation of the patterns of lightning flashes. Etruscans also placed great emphasis on the afterlife, and their tombs took the form of homes of the dead where the deceased, carved in effigy on their sarcophagi or coffins, reclined as though at a festive banquet.

Etruscan Dominance. While the Etruscans were consolidating their hegemony in western Italy, they were at the same time establishing their maritime power. From the seventh to the fifth century B.C.E., Etruscans controlled the Italian coast of the Tyrrhenian Sea as well as Sardinia, from which their ships could reach the coast of what is today France and Spain. Attempts to extend farther south into Greek southern Italy and toward the Greek colonies on the modern French coast brought the Etruscans and the Greeks into inevitable conflict. Etruscan cities fought sporadic sea battles against Greek cities in the waters of Sicily, as well as off the coasts of Corsica and Etruria. Common hostility toward the Greeks as well as complementary economic interests soon brought the Etruscans into alliances with Carthage. Toward the end of the sixth century B.C.E., Etruscan cities—including Rome—signed a series of pacts with Carthage that created military alliances against the Phocaeans and Syracuse. Etruscan fleets were victorious over the Phocaeans, driving them from Corsica, but they were no match for Syracuse. In 474 B.C.E., shortly after the battle of Himera, the Syracusan fleet destroyed that of the Etruscans off Cumae. Cumae marked the beginning of Etruscan decline. Throughout the fifth century B.C.E., Etruscan cities lost control of the sea to the Greeks. Around the same time, Celts from north of the Alps invaded and conquered the Po Valley. And to the south, Etruscans saw their inland territories progressively slipping into the hands of their former subjects, the Romans.

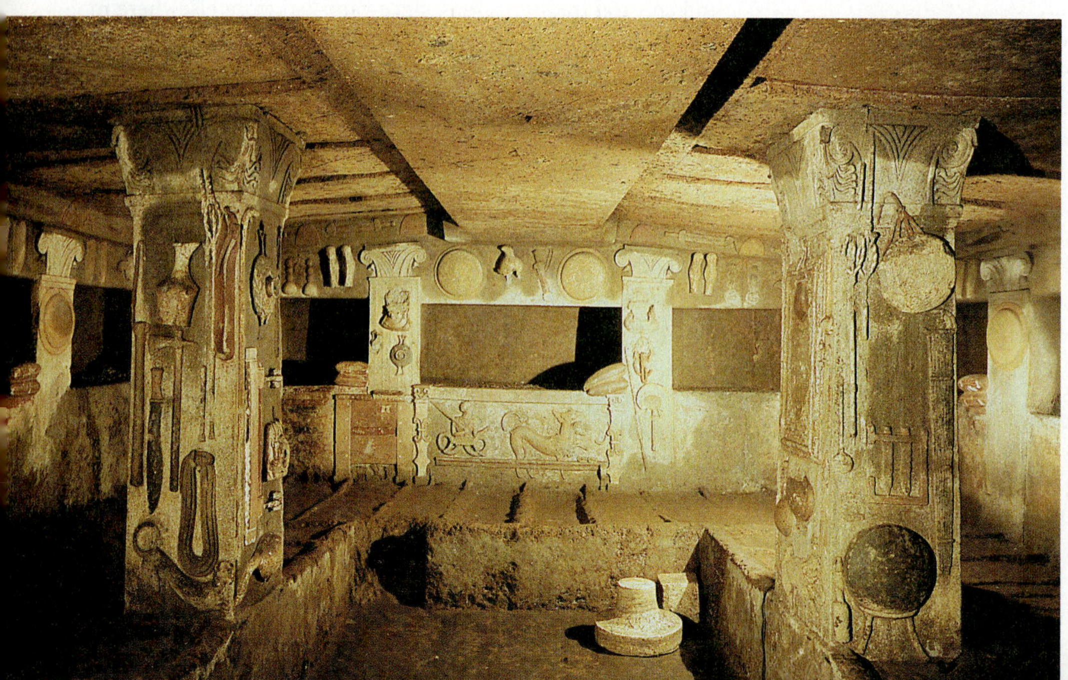

Etruscan tombs were furnished with the familiar objects of everyday life. The square columns of this tomb are adorned with stucco reliefs of cooking utensils, tools, bedding, and weapons. Charon, the guardian of the entrance to Hades, is depicted along with his three-headed dog, Cerberus.

The Romans had learned and profited from their domination by the Etruscans, as well as from their dealings with Greek and Carthaginian civilizations. From those early civilizations on the western shores of the Mediterranean Sea, Rome had begun to acquire the commercial, political, and military expertise to begin its long development from a small city to a great empire.

FROM CITY TO EMPIRE, 509–146 B.C.E.

What manner of people were these who, from obscure origins, came to rule an empire? Their own answer would have been simple: they were farmers and soldiers, simple people accustomed to simple, straightforward actions. Throughout their long history, Romans liked to refer to the clear-cut models provided by their semilegendary predecessors: Cincinnatus the farmer, called away to the supreme office of dictator in time of danger, then returning to his plow; Horatius Cocles, the valiant warrior who held back an Etruscan army on the Tiber bridge until it could be demolished and then, despite his wounds, swam across the river to safety; Lucretia, the wife who chose death after dishonor. These were myths, but they were important myths to Romans, who preferred concrete models to abstract principles.

Later Romans liked to imagine the history of their city as one predestined by the gods for greatness. Some liked to trace the origins of Rome to Romulus and Remus, twin sons of the war god Mars and a Latin princess. According to legend, the children, after having been thrown into the Tiber River, were raised by a she-wolf. Other Romans, having absorbed the Homeric traditions of Greece, taught that the founder of Rome was Aeneas, son of the goddess of love, Aphrodite, and the Trojan Anchises, who had wandered west after the fall of Troy. All agreed that Rome had been ruled by kings who underwent a steady decline in ability and morals until the last, Tarquin the Proud, was expelled by outraged Latins. The legends tell much about the attitudes and values of later Romans. They tell nothing about the origins of the city, its place in the Latin and Etruscan worlds, and its rise to greatness.

■ Ancient Rome. The site of Rome and its seven hills lay between the Etruscan centers of power in the north and those of the Western Greeks in the south.

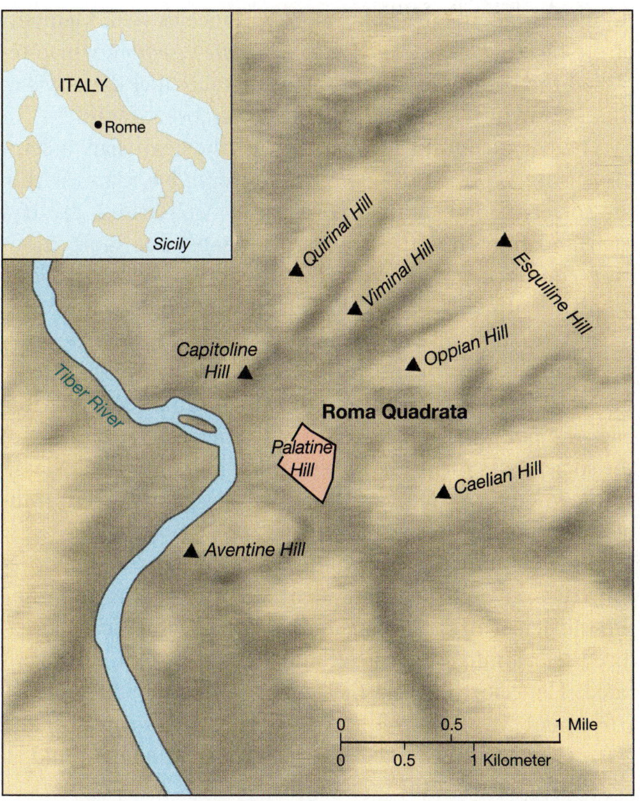

Latin Rome

Civilization in Italy meant Etruria to the north and Greater Greece to the south. In between lay Latium, a marshy region punctured by hills on which a sparse population could find protection from disease and enemies. The population was an amalgam of aboriginal Ligurians and the more recently arrived Latins and Sabines, who lived a pastoral life in small, scattered villages.

The Alban hills south of the Tiber were a center of Latin population. Sometime in the eighth century B.C.E., roughly 40 Latin villages formed a loose confederation, the Alban League, for military and religious purposes. Not long after, in the face of an expanding Etruscan confederation from the north and Sabine penetration from the east, the Albans established a village on the steep Palatine hill to the north. The Palatine was one of several hills overlooking a natural ford on the Tiber; it constituted the first high ground some 14 miles from the sea. The strategic importance of the site, as well as its relatively healthy climate above the disease-ridden marshes, made it a natural location for a settlement. The Alban village, called Roma Quadrata, was soon joined by other Latin and Sabine settlements on nearby hills. By the end of the eighth century B.C.E., seven Latin villages that clustered along the route from the Tiber to Alba had formed a league for mutual defense and shared religious cults.

Early Roman society was composed of households; clans, or *gentes;* and village councils, or *curiae* (sing. *curia*). The male head of each household, the **paterfamilias,** had the power of life and death over its members and was responsible for the proper worship of the spirits of the family's ancestors, on whom continued prosperity depended. Within some villages, families were grouped into gentes, which claimed descent from a semimythical ancestor.

Male members of village families formed councils, which were essentially religious organizations but also provided a forum for public discussion. These curiae tended to be dominated by gentes, but all males could participate, including those who belonged to the **plebs,** that is, families not organized into gentes. Initially the distinction between plebeian families and those families grouped into gentes was one of custom rather than economic, social, or political importance. Only later did the leaders of the gentes call themselves **patricians** ("descendants of fathers") and claim superiority to the plebs.

Important plebeian and patrician families increased their power through a system of clientage, which remained a fundamental aspect of social and political organization throughout Roman history. Clients were free men who depended on the protection of a more powerful individual or family and who owed various services, including political support, in return for the protection.

Villages themselves grouped together for military and voting purposes into ethnic *tribus,* or tribes, each composed of a number of curiae. Each curia supplied a contingent of infantry, and each tribe cooperated to supply a unit of horsemen to the Roman army.

Assemblies of all members of the curiae expressed approval of major decisions, especially declaration of war and the selection of new kings, and thus played a real if limited political role. More powerful although less formal was the role of the Senate (assembly of elders), which was composed of heads of families. The Senate's power derived from the individual importance of its members and from its role in selecting a candidate for king, who was then presented to the assembly of the curiae for approval.

Kings served as religious leaders, the primary means of communication between gods and men. In time, kings attained some political and judicial authority, but throughout the early Latin period, royal power remained fundamentally religious and limited by the Senate, curiae, gentes, and families.

The seven villages that made up primitive Rome developed independently of their Etruscan and Greek neighbors until the middle of the seventh century B.C.E., when the Etruscans overwhelmed Latium and absorbed it into their civilization.

Etruscan Rome

The Etruscans introduced in Latium and especially in Rome their political, religious, and economic traditions. Etruscan city organization partially replaced Latin tribal structures. Etruscan kings and magistrates ruled Latin towns, increasing the power of traditional Latin kingship. The kings not only were religious leaders, directing the cults of their humanlike gods, but also led the army, served as judges, and held supreme political power. In Rome, a series of kings, notably Tarquin the Elder and Servius Tullius, used the city's location on the Tiber ford as a strategic position from which to control Latium to the south. As Latium became an integral part of the Etruscan world, the Tiber became an important commercial route, carrying the agricultural produce of Latium throughout Etruria and bringing to Rome the products of Etruscan and Greek workshops. For the first time, Rome began to enter the wider orbit of Mediterranean civilization. The town's population swelled with the arrival of merchants and artisans.

Urban Growth. As Rome's importance grew, so did its size. Surrounding villages were added to the original seven, as were the Sabine colonies on the Quirinal and Capitoline hills. Etruscan engineers drained the marshes into a great canal flowing to the Tiber, thus opening the lowlands between the hills to settlement. This in turn allowed them to create and pave the Forum. The Etruscans were also builders, constructing a series of vast fortifications encircling the town. Under Etruscan influence, the fortified Capitoline hill, which served much like a Greek acropolis, became the cult center with the erection of the temple to Jupiter, the supreme god; Juno, his consort; and Minerva, an Etruscan goddess of craftwork similar to Athena. In its architecture, religion, commerce, and culture, Latin Rome was deeply indebted to its Etruscan conquerors.

As important as the physical and cultural changes brought by the Etruscans was their reorganization of the society. As in Greece, the restructuring was tied to changes in the military. The Etruscans had learned from the Greeks the importance of hoplite tactics, and King Servius Tullius (578–534 B.C.E.) introduced that system of warfare into Rome, leading to the abolition of the earlier curia-based military and political system in favor of one based only on property holding. Weakening the traditional Latin social units, the king divided Roman society into two groups: the five *classes* and the *infra classem.*

Those landowners wealthy enough to provide armed military service were organized into five *classis* (from which the word *class* is derived), ranked according to the quality of their arms and hence their wealth. Each class was further divided into military units called *centuries.* The military reorganization had fundamental political importance as well. Members of the centuries constituted the *centuriate assembly,* which replaced the older curial assemblies for such vital decisions as the election of magistrates and the declaration of war.

The constitution and operation of the centuriate assembly ensured control by the most conservative forces within the society. Small centuries of wealthy, well-armed cavalrymen and fully armed warriors dominated the more modestly equipped but numerically greater centuries. Likewise, men over the age of 47, though in a minority, controlled more than half of the centuries in each class. Since votes were counted not by individuals but by centuries, this practice ensured within the assembly the domination of the rich over the poor, the elder over the younger. The remainder of the society was the *infra classem,* those literally "under class," who owned no property and were thus excluded from military and political activity.

With the military and political reorganization came a reconstruction of the tribal system. Servius Tullius abolished the old tribal organization in favor of geographically organized tribes into which newcomers could easily be incorporated. Henceforth, while the family remained powerful, involvement in public life was based on property and geography. Latins, Sabines, Ligurians, and Etruscans could all be active citizens of the growing city.

Etruscan terracotta sarcophagus, known as the Sarcophagus of a Married Couple, from Etruria, ca. 510 B.C.E.

Class Divisions. While the old tribal units and curiae declined, divisions between the patricians and the plebeians grew more distinct. During the monarchy the patricians came to compose an upper stratum of wealthy nobles. They owned vast rural estates known as **latifundia** worked by slaves and free tenant farmers who depended on them for survival. They forbade marriage outside their own circle, forming a closed, self-perpetuating group that monopolized the Senate, religious rites, and magisterial offices. Although partially protected by the kings, the plebeians, whether they were rich or poor, were pressed into a second-class status and denied access to political power.

When the Etruscans came to Rome, they found it a small collection of wood and reed villages only beginning to develop into an urban center. In less than two centuries, they transformed it into a prosperous, unified urban center that played an important role in the economic and political life of central Italy. They laid the foundations of a free citizenry, incorporating Greek models of military and social organization. The transformations brought about by the Etruscan kings became an enduring part of Rome. The Etruscans themselves did not. Just as the hoplite revolution in Greece saw the end of most Hellenic monarchies, around the traditionally reported date of 509 B.C.E. the Roman patricians expelled the last king, Tarquin the Proud, and established a republic (from the Latin *res publica*, "public property," as opposed to *res privata*, "private property [of the king"]).

Rome and Italy

Always the moralizers, later Roman historians made the expulsion of King Tarquin the dramatic result of his son's lust. According to legend, Sextus, the son of Tarquin, raped Lucretia, a virtuous Roman matron. She told her husband of the crime and then took her own life. Outraged, the Roman patricians were said to have driven the king and his family from the city. Actually, monarchy was giving way to oligarchic republics across Etruria in the sixth century B.C.E. Rome was hardly exceptional. However, the establishment of the Roman Republic coincided roughly with the beginning of the Etruscan decline, allowing the city of Rome to assert itself and to develop its Latin and Etruscan traditions in unique ways. The development took place within an atmosphere of internal dissension and external conquest.

The Early Republic. The patrician oligarchy had engineered the end of the monarchy, and patricians dominated the offices and institutions of the new republic at the expense of the plebs, who, in losing the king, lost their only defender. Governmental institutions of the early republic developed within this context of patrician supremacy.

Characteristic of republican institutions was that, at every level, power was shared by two or more equals elected for fixed terms. The practice of shared power was intended to ensure that magistrates would consult with each other before making decisions and that no individual could achieve supreme power at any level. Replacing the king were the two consuls, each elected by the assembly for a one-year term. Initially, only the consuls held the **imperium**, the supreme power to command, to execute the law, and to impose the death penalty. Only in moments of grave crisis might a consul, with the approval of the Senate, name a single **dictator** with extraordinary absolute power for a very brief period, never more than six months. In time, other magistracies developed to perform specialized functions including *praetors*, who exercised the imperium, administered justice, and defended the city in the absence of the consuls; *quaestors*, who controlled finances; and *censors*, who assigned individuals their places in society, determined the amount of their taxes, filled vacancies in the Senate, and negotiated contracts for public construction projects. A variety of military commanders directed wars against neighboring cities and peoples under the imperium of the consuls. In all their actions the officeholders consulted with each other and with the Senate, which was composed of roughly 300 powerful former magistrates. The centuriate assembly functioned as the legislative organ of the state, but it continued to be dominated by the oldest and wealthiest members of society.

IMAGE DISCOVERY

Casting a Vote

This Roman coin from the Republican period depicts a voter casting a vote in favor of a new law. Just as today, the images on Roman coins were intended to communicate a message to everyone who used them. What do you think the message of this image was intended to convey?

Patricians, Plebs, and Public Law. During the early republic, wealthy patricians, aided by their clients, monopolized the Senate and the magistracies. Successful magistrates rose through a series of increasingly important offices, which came to be known as the **cursus honorum**, to the position of consul. Censors selected from among former magistrates in appointing new senators, thus ensuring that the Senate would be dominated by the patrician elite. Patricians also controlled the system of priesthoods, positions that were held for life. With political and religious power came economic power. The poorer plebeians in particular found themselves sinking into debt to wealthy patricians, losing their property, and with it the basis for military service and political participation. In the courtroom, in the temple, in the assembly, and in the marketplace, plebeians found themselves subjected to the whims of an elite from which they were excluded.

The plebs began to organize in response to patrician control. On several occasions in the first half of the fifth century B.C.E., the whole plebeian order withdrew a short distance from the city, refusing to return or to serve in the military until conflicts with the patricians were resolved. In time, the plebs created their own assembly, the Council of the Plebs, which enacted laws binding on all plebeians. The council founded its own temples and elected magistrates called *tribunes*, whose persons were declared sacred to the gods. The tribunes protected the plebs from arbitrary patrician power. Anyone harming the tribunes, whether patrician or plebeian, could be killed by the plebs without trial. With their own assembly, magistracies, and religious cults, the plebeians were well on the way to creating a separate republic. The conflict between the plebeians and the patricians, known as the Struggle of Orders, threatened to tear Roman society apart, just as pressure from hostile neighbors placed Rome on the defensive.

Roman preeminence in Latium had ended with the expulsion of the last king. The Etruscan town of Veii just north of the Tiber began launching periodic attacks against Rome. To the south, the Volscians had begun to expand north into the Litis and Trerus valleys. The inability of the patricians to meet the military pressure alone ultimately forced them to compromise with the plebeians. One of the first victories won by the plebs, around 450 B.C.E., was the codification of basic Roman law, the Law of the Twelve Tables, which recognized the basic rights of all free citizens. As important as the specific provisions of the law—which covered private, criminal, sacred, and public matters—was the fact that it was written and posted publicly. Thus anyone, not only patrician magistrates, had access to it. Around the same time, the state began to absorb the plebeian political and religious organizations intact. Gradually, priesthoods and magistracies, and thus the Senate, opened to plebeians. The consulship was the last prize finally won by the plebs in 367 B.C.E. In 287 B.C.E., as the result of a final secession of the plebs, the decisions of the plebeian assembly became binding on all citizens, patrician and plebeian alike.

Political Expansion. Bitter differences at home did not prevent patricians and plebs from presenting a united front against their enemies abroad. External conquest deflected internal hostility and profited both orders. By the beginning of the fourth century B.C.E., the united patrician-plebeian state was expanding its rule both north and south. Roman legions, commanded by patricians but formed of the whole spectrum of property-owning Romans, reestablished Roman preeminence in Latium and then began a series of wars that brought most of Italy under Roman control. In 396 B.C.E., Roman forces captured and destroyed Veii and shortly afterward conquered the rest of southern Etruria. In the south, Roman and Latin forces turned back the Volscians. In 390 B.C.E., Rome suffered a temporary setback at the hands of the Gauls, or Celts, of northern Italy, who raided south and sacked much of the city before being bought off with a large tribute payment. Even that event had a silver lining. The damage to Rome was short-lived, but the Gauls had dealt a deathblow to the Etruscan cities of the north, clearing the way for later Roman conquest. A last-ditch effort by the Latins to preserve their autonomy was crushed in 338 B.C.E.,

THE TWELVE TABLES

The recording of the Twelve Tables in 449 B.C.E. was a great victory for the plebeians, both because it curbed the exercise of arbitrary power by patrician magistrates and because it established the principle of equality before the law.

Focus Questions

What sorts of problems did the law seek to resolve? How did the law regulate and support the importance of the patriarchal family?

Table I. Preliminaries to and Rules for a Trial

If plaintiff summons defendant to court, he shall go. If he does not go, plaintiff shall call witness thereto. Then only shall he take defendant by force.

If defendant shirks or takes to his heels, plaintiff shall lay hands on him. . . .

For a landowner, a landowner shall be surety; but for a proletarian person, let any one who is willing be his protector. . . .

When parties make a settlement of the case, the judge shall announce it. If they do not reach a settlement, they shall state the outline of their case in the meeting place or Forum before noon. . . .

Table III. Execution; Law of Debt

When a debt has been acknowledged, or judgment about the matter has been pronounced in court, thirty days must be the legitimate time of grace. After that, the debtor may be arrested by laying on of hands. Bring him into court. If he does not satisfy the judgment, or no one in court offers himself as surety in his behalf, the creditor may take the defaulter with him. He may bind him either in stocks or in fetters. . . . The debtor, if he wishes, may live on his own. If he does not live on his own, the person [who shall hold him in bonds] shall give him one pound of grits for each day. . . .

Table IV. Rights of Head of Family

Quickly kill . . . a dreadfully deformed child.

Table VI. Guardianship; Succession

Females shall remain in guardianship even when they have attained their majority . . . except Vestal Virgins.

Conveyable possessions of a woman under guardianship of agnates cannot be rightfully acquired by [long-term possession], save such possessions as have been delivered up by her with a guardian's sanction. . . .

Table IX. Public Laws

Laws of personal exception [i.e., bills of attainder] must not be proposed; cases in which the penalty affects the person of a citizen must not be decided except through the greatest assembly and through those whom the censors have placed upon the register of citizens. . . .

Table XI. Supplementary Laws

Intermarriage shall not take place between plebeians and patricians.

and by 295 B.C.E. Rome had secured its rule as far north as the Po Valley. In the south, Roman infantry and persistence proved the equal of professional Greek armies. Rome won a war of attrition against a series of Hellenistic commanders, the last of whom was the Greek king Pyrrhus of Epirus (319–272 B.C.E.). Pyrrhus, regarded as the greatest tactician of his day, won a series of victories that proved more costly to him than to his Roman opponents. In 275 B.C.E., after losing two-thirds of his troops in these "Pyrrhic victories," he withdrew to Sicily. By 265 B.C.E., Rome had absorbed the Hellenistic cities of the south.

The Roman conquest benefited patrician and plebeian alike. While the patricians acquired wealth and power, the plebeians received a prize of equal value: land. After the capture of Veii, for example, the poor of Rome received shares of the conquered land. Since landowning was a prerequisite for military service, the distribution created still more peasant soldiers for further expeditions. Some citizens received land in organized colonies similar to those of Greece, while others received individual plots spread about the conquered territories. Although the constant supply of new land did much to diffuse the tensions between orders, however, it did not actually resolve them. Into the late third century B.C.E., debt and landlessness remained major problems, creating tensions in Roman society. Probably not more than one-half of the citizen population owned land by 200 B.C.E.

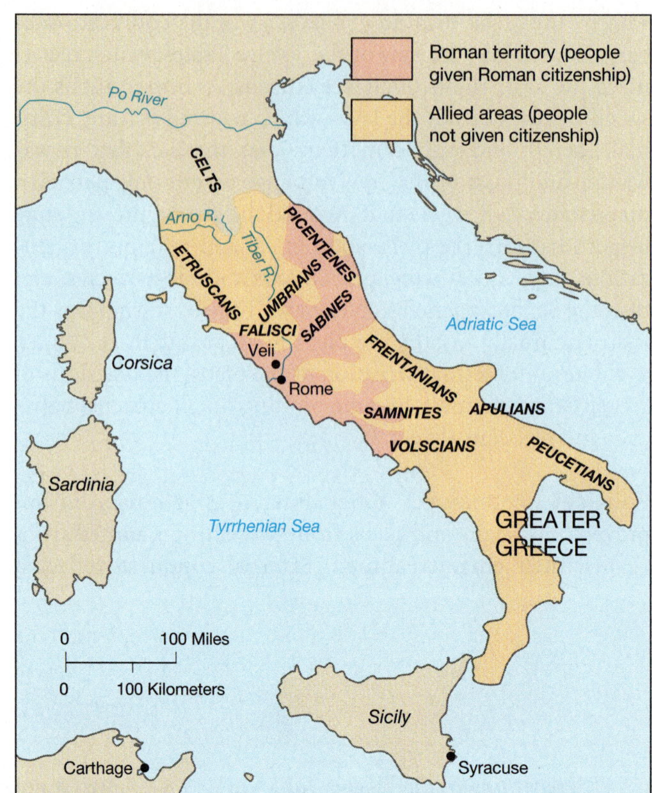

■ Rome in 264 B.C.E. As Rome conquered its neighbors, it either incorporated them directly into its own citizenry or established specific treaties whereby former enemies became Roman allies.

Incorporating the Conquered. The Roman manner of treating conquered populations, radically different from anything existing earlier, also contributed to Rome's success. In war, no one could match the Roman legions for ruthless, thorough destruction. Yet no conquerors had ever shown themselves so generous in victory. After Rome crushed the Latin revolt of 338 B.C.E., virtually all of the Latins were incorporated into the Roman citizenry. Later colonies founded outside Latium were given the same status as Latin cities. Other, more distant conquered peoples were considered allies and were required to provide troops but no tribute to Rome. In time, they too might become citizens. In its wars against the Hellenistic cities of the south, Rome took pains to portray itself as defending Greek civilization against the barbarism of marauding mercenary armies.

The implications of the measures were revolutionary. By extending citizenship to conquered neighbors and by offering the possibility to allies, Rome tied their fate to its own. Rather than potentially subversive subjects, conquered populations became strong supporters. Thus, in contrast to the Hellenistic cities of the east, where Greeks jealously guarded their status from the indigenous population, Rome's colonies acted as magnets, drawing local populations into the Roman cultural and political orbit. In time, a fortunate few who cooperated with Rome might—with luck, talent, and money—share the benefits of Roman citizenship. Greeks were scandalized by the Roman tradition of giving citizenship even to freed slaves. By the end of the fourth century B.C.E., some of the sons of the freedmen were finding a place in the Senate. Finally, in all of its wars of conquest, Rome claimed a moral mandate. Romans went to great lengths to demonstrate that theirs were just wars, basing their claims on alleged acts of aggression by their enemies, on the appeal to Rome by its allies, and, increasingly, on their presenting themselves as the preservers and defenders of Greek traditions of freedom. Both the political and the propagandistic measures proved successful. Between 265 B.C.E. and 91 B.C.E., few serious revolts shook the peace and security of Italy south of the Po.

Benevolent treatment of the conquered spurred further conquest. Since subject cities and peoples did not pay tribute, the only way for Rome to benefit from its conquests or to exercise its authority was to demand and use troops. The troops aided still further conquests, which brought the spoils of war to them as well as to Rome. By 264 B.C.E., all of Italy was united under Roman hegemony. Roman expansion finally brought Rome into conflict with the great Mediterranean power of the west, Carthage.

Rome and the Mediterranean

Since its earliest days, Rome had allied itself with Carthage against the Greek cities of Italy. The zones of interest of the two cities had been quite separate. Carthage was a sea empire, while Rome was a land-based power without a navy. The Greeks, aspiring to power on land and sea, posed a common threat to both Rome and Carthage. However, once Rome had conquered the Greek cities to the south, it became enmeshed in the affairs of neighboring Sicily, a region with well-established Carthaginian interests. There, in 265 B.C.E., a group of Italian mercenary pirates attacked Messina and requested assistance from Rome and Carthage against Syracuse, which came to the defense of Messina. The Roman Senate refused but the plebeian assembly, eager for booty, exercised its newly won right to legislate for the republic and accepted. Shortly afterward the Romans invaded Sicily, and Syracuse turned to its old enemy, Carthage, for assistance. The First Punic War had begun.

The First Punic War. This war, which lasted from 265 to 241 B.C.E., was a costly, brutal, and drawn-out affair that Rome won by dint of persistence and methodical calculation rather than by strategic brilliance. Rome invaded and concluded an alliance with Syracuse in 263 B.C.E. The war rapidly became a sea war. Rome had had little previous naval experience but quickly learned the rules of the game, then rewrote them to its own advantage. Taking a wrecked Carthaginian ship as a model, Roman builders constructed 20 fast ships propelled by roughly 200 oarsmen to ram and sink opposing ships. Rome also built 100 larger ships with crews of 300, manned by Roman allies. Unaccustomed to fighting at sea, Roman engineers turned sea battles into land battles by placing on their ships heavy gangplanks that could be dropped onto enemy ships. The gangplanks were equipped with a heavy iron spike that secured them to the enemy's deck. The gangplanks allowed a contingent of legionnaires to march onto the enemy ship and fight as though on dry land.

With these innovations, the Romans won impressive initial victories but for more than 20 years still could not deliver a knockout blow either in Sicily or in North Africa. Warfare and Mediterranean storms took their toll on opposing fleets. Finally, in 241 B.C.E., Rome forced the Carthaginian commander, Hamilcar Barca (ca. 270–229 B.C.E.), to surrender simply because the Romans could afford to build one more fleet than he. Carthage paid a huge indemnity and abandoned Sicily. Syracuse and Messina became allies of Rome. In a break with tradition, Rome obligated the rest of Sicily to pay a true tribute in the form of a tithe (one-tenth) of their crops. Shortly after that, Rome helped itself to Sardinia as well, from which it again demanded tribute, not simply troops. Rome had established an empire.

During the next two decades, Roman legions kept busy in the north, defeating the Ligurians on the northwest coast, the Celtic Gauls south of the Alps, and the Illyrians along the Adriatic coast. At the same time, Carthage fought a bitter battle against its own mercenary armies, which it had been unable to pay off after its defeat. Carthage then began the systematic creation of an empire in Spain. Trade between Carthage and Rome reached the highest level in history, but trade did not create friendship. The two former enemies maintained a wary peace. On both sides, powerful leaders saw the treaty of 241 B.C.E. as just a pause in a fight to the death.

Securing Western Hegemony. After Hamilcar's death, Carthaginian successes in Spain, led by Hamilcar's son-in-law Hasdrubal (d. 221 B.C.E.) and his son Hannibal (247–183 B.C.E.), finally provoked Rome to war in 218 B.C.E. As soon as the Second Punic War started, Hannibal began an epic march north out of Spain, along the Mediterranean coast, and across the Alps. In spite of great hardships, he was able to transport more than 23,000 troops and approximately 18 war elephants into the plains of northern Italy. (See "A Closer Look: Hannibal's Elephants," pp. 114–115.)

■ A relief of a Roman war galley. The deck is crowded with infantrymen. Galleys were usually rowed by slaves, while the soldiers remained fresh for the task of subduing enemy ships.

HANNIBAL'S ELEPHANTS

A CLOSER LOOK

"What do you get when you cross an Alp with an elephant?" Hannibal hoped that the answer was "Rome." Elephants were the most spectacular, extravagant, and unpredictable element in ancient warfare. Since the time of Alexander the Great, Hellenistic kings and commanders had tried to use the great strength, size, and relative invulnerability of the animals to throw opposing infantry into confusion and flight. Elephants' unusual smell and loud trumpeting also panicked horses not accustomed to the strange beasts, wreaking havoc with cavalry units. Mahouts, or drivers, who were usually Indians, controlled and directed the animal from a seat on the elephant's neck. Normally each elephant carried a small, tower-like structure from which archers could shoot down on the massed infantry. However, as with modern tanks, the primary importance of the beasts was the enormous shock effect created by a charge of massed war elephants. Still, they often created more problems than they solved.

Indian princes had used elephants in warfare for centuries. When Alexander the Great crossed the Indus in 326 B.C.E., the Indian king Porus came close to defeating the Greek conqueror, thanks largely to his more than 200 elephants. In 302 B.C.E., Seleucus I received 500 war elephants from an Indian king as part of a peace treaty. The next year the animals contributed greatly to Seleucus's victory over Antigonus at Ipsus, which made possible the creation of his separatist kingdom in Syria. Thereafter Seleucid kings used elephants as an integral part of their military and even attempted, without much success, to breed elephants in Syria.

The Ptolemys, too, used elephants in Egypt, but lacking access to Indian animals, they had to be content with the smaller African forest elephant. (The great African bush elephant, the largest land animal and a far greater beast than either the forest or the Indian elephant, remained unknown to the Western world until the nineteenth century.) The Ptolemys sent large-scale hunting parties into Ethiopia to capture forest elephants. Captured animals were trained and driven by Indians. In battles between Seleucids and Ptolemys, however, the larger Indian elephants usually brought victory.

The Romans first experienced the terror of elephant charges in their war against Pyrrhus in the south of Italy. They next encountered them in the Punic Wars. The Carthaginians had learned to use elephants around the middle of the third century B.C.E., capturing them in the Atlas Mountains of North Africa and putting them to good use in Spain. When Hannibal decided to invade Italy via the Alps, he naturally wanted to take along the formidable beasts, an objective easier said than done.

In 217 B.C.E., Hannibal set out from Carthago Nova and some weeks later arrived at the Rhone River with an army that included roughly 38,000 infantry, 8000 cavalry, and 37 elephants. Ferrying the pachyderms across the river was a major undertaking, since the frightened animals refused to walk onto rafts. Finally, the Carthaginians lashed together a series of rafts, the first two on dry land, the others forming a pontoon into the river. The sides were piled with earth so that the elephants could not see that they were not walking on dry land. Their Indian mahouts led them a few at a time to the end rafts, which were then cut free and towed across the river by boats. Most of the animals, seeing water on all sides, remained terrified still. Others panicked, upsetting the rafts, falling into the river, and drowning their mahouts. Once in the water, however, most of the elephants were able to swim to the far shore.

As difficult as the river crossing was, it paled in comparison to the problems of crossing the Alps. As Hannibal moved slowly up the valley of the Arc, his troops were under constant harassment from local Celtic tribes eager to ambush them on every occasion. From high up in the passes, the Celts showered down rocks, throwing the pack animals into confusion and causing them to hurl themselves off the narrow paths. Landslides carried away portions of the track and, as Hannibal advanced, the path became too narrow for elephants and eventually even for horses and mules. Engineers had to rebuild paths, taking up valuable time.

Great boulders had to be cleared away by heating them and then pouring vinegar into crevices to cause them to explode. At the top of the pass, new snow forced a three-day halt while a road wide enough for the elephants to descend was constructed down the more precipitous Italian side of the mountain. During this time the elephants were without fodder and suffered enormously. Finally, after 15 days, Hannibal's depleted troops reached the fertile plains of the Po Valley. He had lost almost half of his infantry and cavalry since reaching the Rhone and more than half of his elephants.

Was it worth it? In his first major encounter with the Romans at the Trebia River, Hannibal split his elephants into two groups to protect the wings of his infantry. The beasts were a major factor in the devastating defeat inflicted on the Romans. However, shortly afterward, the cold and snow killed all but one of the animals. This lone survivor became Hannibal's personal command post. The great Punic victories at Lake Trasimene and Cannae were won without the assistance of the pachyderm shock force. In 207 B.C.E., Hannibal's brother Hasdrubal (d. 207 B.C.E.) entered Italy with ten elephants, but at the battle of Metaurus they panicked, stampeded, and did more harm to the Carthaginians than to the Romans.

■ Sculpture of a war elephant with driver and battle tower on its back.

The next time Hannibal faced a Roman army with his full contingent of war elephants was at Zama. There his 80 animals proved a bitter disappointment. Ordered to charge, many of the elephants panicked at the sound of trumpets and horns, wheeled about, and went raging into the massed African cavalry arrayed on the Punic side. Some elephants did charge, but with limited effect. The Romans had learned to take aim at the mahouts, killing them and leaving the animals without direction. The Romans also allowed the elephants to charge past, then attacked their flanks with javelins and their legs with swords. Finally, the Roman commander had taken the precaution of leaving wide paths between his formations. Many of the animals simply charged down these paths and disappeared into the open fields beyond the Roman lines.

The Romans themselves made little use of elephants in warfare. The exotic beasts better suited the inflated egos of eastern kings than the practical minds of Roman generals. The Romans preferred the disciplined advance of a well-trained cohort of Roman legionnaires to the charge of a war elephant. It was with these steadfast and resolute infantrymen, rather than with raging elephants, that they won an empire.

Hannibal's brilliant generalship brought victory after victory to the Carthaginian forces. In the first engagement, on the Trebia River in the Po Valley, the Romans lost 20,000 men, two-thirds of their army. Carthaginian success encouraged the Gauls to join the fight against the Romans. Initially, Italian, Etruscan, and Greek allies remained loyal, but after Rome's catastrophic defeats at Lake Trasimene in Etruria in 217 B.C.E., and especially at Cannae in 216 B.C.E., a number of Italian colonies and allies, particularly the cities of Capua and Syracuse, went over to the enemy. In the east, Philip V of Macedon (238–179 B.C.E.) made a treaty with Carthage in the hope of taking Illyria (today the coast of Croatia) from a defeated Rome.

As commanders chosen by the patrician-dominated Senate failed to stop the enemy, the Roman plebs became increasingly dissatisfied with the way the oligarchy was conducting the war. However, popular pressure to appoint new commanders did little to alleviate the situation. In 217 B.C.E., following the battle of Lake Trasimene, the Senate named the capable general Quintus Fabius Maximus (d. ca. 203 B.C.E.) dictator. He used delaying tactics successfully to slow the Carthaginians, thus earning the nickname *Cunctator*, or Delayer. The popular assembly, impatient for a decisive victory, elected a second dictator, thus effectively canceling the position of Quintus Fabius Maximus. The next year, popular pressure forced the election of Gaius Terentius Varro as consul. Varro quickly led the army to the greatest defeat in Roman history, at Cannae. There Hannibal surrounded and annihilated Varro's numerically superior army.

Three things saved the Roman state. First, while some important allies and colonies defected, the majority held firm. Rome's traditions of sharing the fruits of victory with its allies, extending the rights of Roman citizenship, and protecting central and southern Italy against its enemies proved stronger than the appeals of Hannibal. Although victorious time and again, without local support Hannibal could not hold the terrain and cities he won. Fabius resumed his delaying tactics, and gradually Hannibal's victories slipped from his hands.

The second reason for Rome's survival was the tremendous social solidarity all classes and factions of its population showed during those desperate years. In spite of the internal tensions between patricians and plebeians, their ultimate dedication to Rome never faltered. Much of this loyalty was due to the Roman system of strong family and patronage ties. Kinsmen and clients answered the call of their patriarchs and patrons to bounce back repeatedly from defeat. Roman farmer-soldiers stood firm.

The third reason for Rome's ultimate success was Publius Cornelius Scipio (236–184 B.C.E.), also known as Scipio the Elder, a commander who was able to force Hannibal from Italy. Scipio, who earned the title Africanus for his victory, accomplished this not by attacking Hannibal directly, but by taking the war home to the enemy, first in Spain and then in Africa. His

POLYBIUS COMPARES ROME AND CARTHAGE

In the following abridged selection, the Greek historian Polybius, who was a close friend of the adopted grandson of Scipio Africanus, compares the governments of Rome and Carthage in order to explain Roman victory in the Punic Wars and, more generally, in the creation and establishment of its empire.

Focus Questions

What was Polybius's opinion of popular democracy? What did he see as the advantage of a citizen army?

The constitution of Carthage seems to me to have been well designed at the outset in its most important features. The Carthaginians had kings, the assembly of elders had the powers of an aristocracy, and the people were supreme in such matters as were appropriate, so that the general framework of the state was similar to that of Rome and Sparta. The power and prosperity of Carthage had developed far earlier than that of Rome, and in proportion to this her strength had begun to decline, while that of Rome was at its height, at least so far as her system of government was concerned. Accordingly, at Carthage the influence of the people had already become predominant in the councils of state, while at Rome the Senate still had the decisive voice. This meant that in the one case deliberations were conducted by the masses, and in the other by the most eminent men, with the result that the decisions on public policy made by the Romans proved superior.

Let us now consider differences of detail, such as, in the first place, the conduct of war. In operations at sea the Carthaginians were better trained and equipped, because seamanship had long been their national calling and they occupy themselves with the sea more than any other people; but in military campaigns the Romans train themselves to an altogether higher standard. The reason for this is that they employ foreign and mercenary troops, whereas those of the Romans are citizens and natives of their own country. The Carthaginians depend at all times on the courage of mercenaries to safeguard their prospects of freedom, but the Romans rely on the bravery of their own citizens and the help of their allies. For the Romans, knowing themselves to be fighting for their country and their children, can never weaken in the fury of their struggle, but continue to fight with all their heart and soul until the enemy is overcome.

From Polybius, *The Rise of the Roman Empire.*

victories there drew Hannibal home, where at Zama in 202 B.C.E. the Roman commander destroyed the Carthaginian army. Zama put an end to both the Second Punic War and Carthaginian political power. Saddled with a huge indemnity, forced to abandon all of its territories and colonies to Rome, and reduced to a small portion of the North African coast, Carthage had become in effect a Roman subject.

The Final Destruction. Still, although the defeat was humiliating for Carthage, it was not enough for Rome. While some Roman senators favored allowing Carthage to survive as a means of keeping the Roman plebs under senatorial control, others demanded destruction. Chief among them was the censor Marcus Porcius Cato, known as Cato the Elder (234–149 B.C.E.), who ended every speech with *Delenda est Carthago,* "Carthage must be destroyed." Ultimately, trumped-up reasons were found to renew the war in 149 B.C.E. In contrast to the desperate, hard-fought campaigns of the Second Punic War, the Third Punic War was an unevenly matched slaughter. In 146 B.C.E., Scipio Aemilianus (184–129 B.C.E.), or Scipio the Younger, the adopted grandson of Scipio the Elder, overwhelmed Carthage and sold its few survivors into slavery. As a symbolic act of final destruction, he then had the site razed, plowed, and cursed. Carthage's fertile hinterland became the property of wealthy Roman senators.

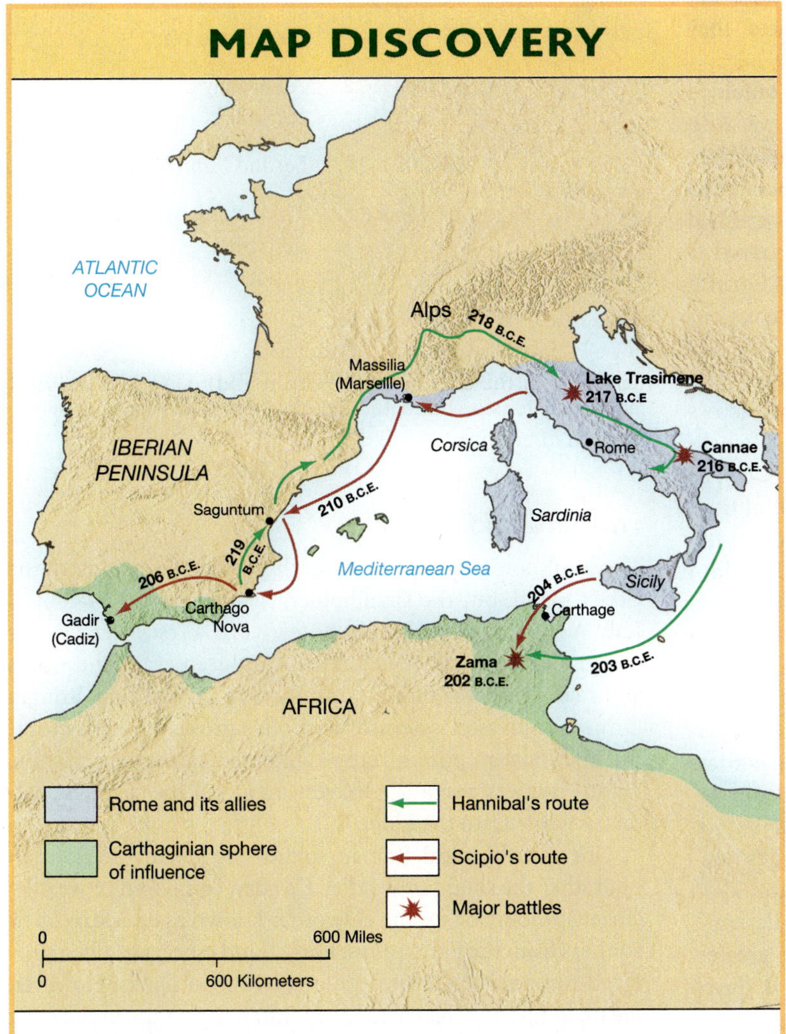

The Punic Wars

What accidents of geography and political expansion made war between Rome and Carthage almost inevitable? What advantages might Hannibal have seen in taking the route he did to attack Rome? What were the long-term effects of Hannibal's route for the inhabitants of the Iberian Peninsula and Gaul? What parts of Carthage's African Empire might have been most attractive to Roman conquerors?

Expansion into the Hellenistic East. In the same year that Carthage was destroyed, Roman armies destroyed Corinth, a second great center of Mediterranean commerce. The victory marked the culmination of Roman imperialist expansion east into the Greek and Hellenistic world that had begun with the conquest of Illyria. The expansion was not simply the result of Roman imperialist ambitions. The Hellenistic states, in their constant warring and bickering, drew Rome into their conflicts against their neighbors. Greek states asked the Roman Senate to arbitrate their disputes. Appealing to Rome's claims as "liberator," cities pressed the Senate to preserve their freedom in the face of aggressive expansion by their more powerful neighbors. In a series of intermittent, uncoordinated, and sporadic engagements, Rome did intervene, though its real focus was on its life-and-death struggle with Carthage.

Roman intentions may not have been conquest, but Roman intervention upset the balance of power in the Hellenistic world. Although Rome became a major player in the eastern Mediterranean more by chance than by design, it rapidly became the winner. The price of Roman arbitration, intervention, and protection was loss of independence. Gradually the Roman shadow fell over the eastern Mediterranean.

The treaty Philip V of Macedon concluded with Carthage during the Second Punic War provided an initial excuse for war, one seized upon more eagerly by the plebeian assembly than by the Senate. Shortly after its victory at Zama, Rome provoked Philip to war and then easily defeated him in 197 B.C.E., proclaiming the freedom of the Greek cities and withdrawing from Greece. In 189 B.C.E., the Seleucid Antiochus III (223–187 B.C.E.) of Syria suffered the same fate, and Rome declared free the Greek cities in Asia Minor he had controlled. The Greeks venerated the Roman commander, Titus Quinctius Flamininus (228–174 B.C.E.), as a god—the first Roman to be accorded this eastern honor. In reality, the control of the cities lay in the hands of local oligarchs favorable to Rome. In 179 B.C.E., Philip's son Perseus (179–168 B.C.E.) attempted to stir up democratic opposition to Rome within the cities. This time Rome responded more forcefully. The Macedonian kingdom was divided into four republics governed by their own senates and magistrates selected from among the local aristocrats. In Epirus, 70 cities were destroyed and 150,000 people sold into slavery. The harsh punishment prompted other Greek cities to react with panic even to the mere threat of Roman retribution. When the citizens of Rhodes heard that the Senate was contemplating declaring war on them, they quickly executed all of their anti-Roman fellows.

The final episode of Rome's expansionist drama unfolded during the Third Punic War. When Rome resumed its war with Carthage in 149 B.C.E., several Greek cities attempted once more to assert their autonomy from the hated oligarchies established by Rome. Retribution was swift. The Roman legions crushed the rebel forces and, as an example to all, Corinth was razed as thoroughly as was Carthage. Vast booty from wealthy Corinth poured into Rome, while the survivors found themselves enslaved in the homes and estates of Roman victors.

By 146 B.C.E., the Roman Republic controlled the whole rim of the Mediterranean from Rhodes in the east across Greece, Dalmatia, Italy, southern Gaul, Spain, and North Africa. Even Syria and Egypt, although nominally independent, had to bow before Roman will. This subjugation had been graphically demonstrated in 168 B.C.E., when the Seleucid Antiochus IV (175–164 B.C.E.) invaded the kingdom of the Egyptian ruler Ptolemy VI (180–145 B.C.E.) and besieged Alexandria. The Ptolemys had long before made a treaty with Rome, and the Senate sent an envoy to Antiochus with written instructions to withdraw at once from Egypt. The king replied that he would like to consult his advisers before making a decision. The Roman envoy immediately drew a circle around Antiochus, ordering him to give an answer before he stepped out of the ring. Such directness was unknown in the world of Hellenistic diplomacy. After a moment's hesitation, the deeply shocked Antiochus replied that he would do whatever the Romans demanded. Perseverance and determination had brought Rome from obscurity to the greatest power the West had ever known. The republic had endured great adversity. It would not survive prosperity.

CHRONOLOGY

The Roman Republic

509 B.C.E.	Expulsion of last Etruscan king; beginning of Roman Republic
ca. 450 B.C.E.	Law of the Twelve Tables
396 B.C.E.	Rome conquers southern Etruria
295 B.C.E.	Rome extends rule north to Po Valley
265–241 B.C.E.	First Punic War
264 B.C.E.	All of Italy under Roman control
218–202 B.C.E.	Second Punic War
149–146 B.C.E.	Third Punic War; Carthage is destroyed

REPUBLICAN CIVILIZATION

Territorial conquest, the influx of unprecedented riches, and exposure to sophisticated Hellenistic civilization ultimately overwhelmed earlier Roman civilization. The civilization had been created by stubborn farmers and soldiers who valued above all else authority, simplicity, and piety. Its unique culture was the source of strength that led Rome to greatness, but its limitations prevented the republic from resolving its internal social tensions and the external problems caused by the burden of empire.

Farmers and Soldiers

The ideal Roman farmer was not the great estate owner of the Greek world, but the smallholder, the dirt farmer of central Italy. A typical farm might be as few as 10 acres worked by the owner and his family. Such farms produced grain and beans and raised hogs for family consumption. In addition, Roman farmers cultivated vineyards and olive groves for cash crops. But the most important crop of Roman farms was citizens. "From farmers come the bravest men and the sturdiest soldiers," wrote Cato the Elder.

Nor was the ideal Roman soldier the gallant cavalryman but rather the solid foot soldier. Cavalry, composed of wealthy citizens who made up the elite order known as **equestrians** or equites (from the Latin *equus,* horse), and especially allies, provided reconnaissance and protected Roman flanks. However, the main fighting force was the infantry. Sometime in the early republic the Greek phalanx was transformed into the Roman legion, a flexible unit composed of 30 companies of 120 men each. Legions maneuvered in three rows of squares of men, each containing 120 soldiers. The first row engaged the enemy, first with javelins and then with short swords. As men in the first row tired, members of the second and eventually the third row could step in to relieve them. Likewise, the whole square could move back in formation, its place taken by a fresh unit that could keep up the pressure on the enemy. Such tactics demanded less virtuoso military ability than solid discipline.

Constant training, careful preparation, and painstaking execution characterized every aspect of Roman military expeditions. Wars were won as much by engineering feats as by feats of arms. Engineers constructed bridges, siege machines, and catapults. By the time of the late republic, Roman armies on the march could construct identical camps each night, quickly building a strong square fort 2150 feet long on each side. Within each camp, every unit had exactly the same location for its quarters, as did the commander and paymaster. The chain of command was rigidly maintained, from the commander—a Roman consul—through military tribunes and centurions, two of whom commanded each company of 120 men. Even the slaughter and the pillage of an enemy city were carried out with firm Roman discipline.

These solid, methodical troops, the backbone of the republican armies that conquered the Mediterranean, were, however, among the victims. The pressures of constant international warfare were destroying the farmer-soldiers whom the traditionalists loved to praise. When the Roman sphere of interest had been confined to central Italy, farmers could do their planting in spring, serve in the army during the summer months, and return home to care for their farms in time for the harvest. When Rome's wars became international expeditions lasting for years, many soldiers, unable to work their lands while doing military service, had to mortgage their farms in order to support their families. When they returned, they often found that during their prolonged absences they had lost their farms to wealthy, aristocratic moneylenders. While aristocrats amassed vast landed estates worked by imported slaves, ordinary Romans and Italians lacked even a family farm capable of supporting themselves and their families. Without land, they and their sons were excluded from further military service and sank into the growing mass of desperately poor, disfranchised citizens.

The Roman Family

In Roman tradition, the paterfamilias was the master of the family—which in theory included his wife, children, and slaves—over whom he exercised the power of life and death. This authority lasted as long as he lived. Only at his death did his sons, even if long grown and married, achieve legal and financial independence. The family was the basic unit of society and of the state. The authority of the paterfamilias was the foundation of the essentially patriarchal society and the key to its success.

Although not kept in seclusion as in Greece, Roman women theoretically never exercised independent power in their male-dominated world. Before marriage, a Roman girl was subject to the authority of her father. When she married, her father traditionally transferred legal guardianship to her husband, thus severing her bonds to her paternal family. A husband could divorce his wife at will, returning her and her dowry to her father. However, wives did exercise real though informal authority within the family. Part of that authority came from their role in the moral education of their children and the direction of the household. Part also came from their control over their dowries. Widows might exercise even greater, if informal, authority in the raising of their children.

Paternal authority over children was absolute. Not all children born into a marriage became members of the family. The Law of the Twelve Tables allowed defective children to be killed for the good of the family. Newborn infants were laid on the ground before the father, who decided whether the child should be raised. By picking up a son, he accepted the child into the family. Ordering that a daughter be nursed similarly signified acceptance. If there were too many mouths to feed or the child was simply unwanted, the father could command that the infant be killed or abandoned. Abandoned children might be adopted by childless couples. Frequently, if they survived at all, it was as slaves or prostitutes.

Nor were all sons born into Roman families. Romans made use of adoption for many purposes. Families without heirs could adopt children. Powerful political and military figures might adopt promising young men as their political heirs. The adopted sons held the same legal rights as the natural offspring of the father and thus were integral members of his family. Some adoptions even took place posthumously. An important Roman might name a younger man as his adopted son in his will.

Slaves, too, were members of the family. On the one hand, slaves were property without personal rights. On the other, they might live and work alongside the free members of the family, worship the family gods, and enjoy the protection and endure the authority of the paterfamilias. In fact, the authority of the paterfamilias was roughly the same over slave and free members of the family. If he desired, he could sell the free members of the family into slavery. Even freed slaves remained obligated to their former owner throughout life. They owed him special respect and could never oppose him in lawsuits or other conflicts, under penalty of returning to servitude.

Slaves in Roman Law

The center of everyday life for the Roman family was the *domus*, the family house, whose architectural style had developed from Etruscan traditions. Early Roman houses, even of the wealthy and powerful, were simple, low buildings well suited to the Mediterranean climate, constructed around an open courtyard, or *atrium*. Cato the Elder described the home of the great general Manius Curius, who had driven Pyrrhus from Italy, as a small, plain dwelling; that simplicity predominated throughout the second century B.C.E. The house looked inward, presenting nothing but blank walls to the outside world. Visitors entered through the front door into the atrium, a central courtyard containing a collecting pool into which rainwater for household use flowed from the roof through terra-cotta drains. Originally, the atrium not only provided sunlight but allowed smoke from the hearth to escape. In niches or on shelves stood wax or terracotta busts of ancestors and statues of the household gods. The walls, constructed of blocks of stone, were often painted in bands of different colors in imitation of polychrome marble. Around the atrium, openings gave onto workrooms, storerooms, bedrooms, offices, and small dining rooms.

■ The garden of one of the most famous houses in Pompeii, the House of the Vettii. The house is named for one of its possible owners, the Vettii brothers, whose signet rings were found during the excavations. The ornate and formal garden would have been glimpsed through the front door of the house, allowing passers-by a glimpse of the wealth and taste of its owners.

Social Effects of Expansion

In the wake of imperial conquests, the Roman family and its environment began to change in ways disturbing to many of the oligarchy. Some women, perhaps in imitation of their more liberated Hellenistic sisters, began to take a more active role in public life. One example is Cornelia, a daughter of Scipio Africanus, who bore her husband 12 children, only three of whom survived to maturity. After her husband's death in 154 B.C.E., she refused to remarry, devoting herself instead to raising her children, administering their inheritance, and directing their political careers.

Some married women, too, escaped the authority of their husbands. Fewer and fewer fathers transferred authority over their daughters to their husbands. Instead, daughters remained under their father's authority as long as he lived. This practice meant that upon the father's death, the daughters became independent persons, able to manage their own affairs without the consent of or interference by their husbands. Although some historians believe that sentimental bonds of affection may have increased between many husbands and wives and between parents and children as legal bonds loosened, it also meant that the wife's relationship to her children was weakened. Roman mothers had never been legally related to their children. Wives and mothers were not fully part of their husband's families. Thus their brothers' families, not their own children, were their natural heirs. Just as adoption created political bonds, marriage to daughters sealed alliances between men. However, when the alliances fell apart or more advantageous ones presented themselves, fathers could force their daughters to divorce their husbands and to marry other men. Divorce became increasingly common in the second century B.C.E. More and more frequently, wives were temporary visitors in their husbands' homes.

Homes grew in size, wealth, and complexity for those who participated in the wealth of empire. With increasing prosperity, the atrium became more elegant, intended to impress visitors with the wealth of the family and its traditions. The water basin became a reflecting pool, often endowed with a fountain and surrounded by towering columns. In many cases a second open area, or *peristyle*, appeared behind the first. The wealthy surrounded the atrium and peristyle with glass-enclosed porticoes and decorated their walls with frescoes, mosaics, and paintings looted from Hellenistic cities of the east. Furniture of fine inlaid woods, bronze, and marble, and eastern carpets and wall hangings increased the exotic luxury of the patrician domus.

Not every Roman family could afford its own domus, and in the aftermath of the imperial expansion, housing problems for the poor became acute. In Rome and other towns of Italy, shopkeepers lived in small houses attached to their shops or in rooms behind their workplaces. Peasants forced off their land and crowded into cities found shelter in multistory apartment buildings, an increasingly common sight in the cities of the empire. In these cramped structures, families crowded into small, low rooms about ten feet square. All the families shared a common enclosed courtyard. The apartment buildings and shops were not hidden away from the homes of the wealthy. In Roman towns throughout Italy, simple dwellings, luxurious mansions, shops, and apartment buildings existed side by side. The rich and the poor rubbed shoulders every day, producing a friction that threatened to burst into flame.

Roman Religion

Romans worshiped many gods, the more the better. Every aspect of daily life and work was the responsibility of individual powers, or *numina.* Every man had his genius or personal **numen**, just as every woman had her *juno.* Each family had its household powers, the *lares familiares,* whose proper worship was the responsibility of the paterfamilias. The *Vesta* was the spirit of the hearth fire. The *lares* were the deities of farmland, the domus, and the guardians of roads and travelers. The *penates* guarded the family larder or storage cupboard. The family spirits exercised a binding power, a *religio,* upon the Romans, and the pious Roman householder recognized those claims and undertook the *officia,* or duties, to which the spirits were entitled.

Those basic attitudes of religion, piety, and office lay at the heart of Roman reverence for order and authority. They extended to other traditional Roman and Latin gods such as Jupiter, the supreme god; Juno, his wife; Mars, the god of war; and the two-faced Janus, spirit of gates and new beginnings. The piety extended also to the anthropomorphic Etruscan gods for whom temples were erected on the Capitoline hill, and to the Greek deities whom the Romans absorbed along with the Hellenic world. Outside the household, worship of the gods and the reading of the future in the entrails of sacrificed animals, the flight of birds, or changes in weather were the responsibilities of colleges of priests. Roman priests did not, as did those in the Near East, form a special caste but rather were important members of the elite who held priesthoods in addition to other public offices. Religion was less a matter of personal relationship with the gods than a public, civic activity binding society together. State-supported cults with their colleges of priests, Etruscan- and Greek-style temples, and elaborate ceremonies were integral parts of the Roman state and society. The world of the gods reflected that of mortals.

As the Roman mortal world expanded, so did the divine. Romans were quick to identify foreign gods with their own. Thus Zeus became Jupiter, Hera became Juno, and Aphrodite became Venus. Whenever possible, Romans interpreted foreign cults in familiar Roman terms. This *interpretatio romana* allowed for the incorporation of conquered peoples into the Roman religious world, which was one with the state. It also made possible the introduction of

This wall painting, completed ca. 50 B.C.E., is the first of a series depicting the initiation of a young bride into the cult of Dionysus. In this picture the bride stands at the left while a young child (perhaps the god himself), assisted by a matron, reads the ritual while a servant pours libations.

In this marble mosaic from Pompeii, a satyr and a maenad, devotees of Dionysus, perform an orgiastic dance as they approach a shrine supporting two vases.

Roman gods into newly conquered regions, where shrines and temples to indigenous gods could be rededicated to the gods of Rome under their local names.

Still, the elasticity of Roman religion could stretch just so far. With the empire came not only the cults of Zeus, Apollo, and Aphrodite to Rome but the cult of Dionysus as well. Unlike the formal public cults of the other Greek deities, which were firmly in the control of authorities, that of Dionysus was largely outside state control. Women, in the tradition of the maenads, controlled much of the ecstatic and overtly sexual rituals associated with the god. Moreover, the rituals took place in secret, open only to the initiates of the god. Following the Second Punic War, the cult of Dionysus, known in Latin as Bacchus, spread rapidly in Italy, drawing thousands of devotees from all social orders. To the members of the oligarchy, everything about the cult seemed to threaten traditional Roman values: it was Greek; it was dominated by women; and most significantly, its rituals were secret. At these rites, or *Bacchanalia,* men and women were rumored to engage in every kind of sexual act. The Roman Senate was ready to believe anything about this rapidly spreading cult. As Titus Livius, or Livy (59–17 B.C.E.), a later Roman moralist and historian, put it:

> The corruption was not confined to one kind of evil, the promiscuous violation of free men and of women; the cult was also a source of false witnesses, forged documents and wills, and perjured evidence, dealing also in poisons and in wholesale murders among the devotees, and sometimes ensuring that not even the bodies were found for burial.

In 186 B.C.E., the Senate decreed the cult of Bacchus a conspiracy and ordered an inquiry. The consul, acting on the dubious testimony of a former prostitute, began a brutal persecution. Rituals were banned, priests and adherents arrested, and rewards offered to informants who provided lurid and fanciful accounts of what had taken place at the Bacchanalia. Panic spread throughout Italy as thousands of devotees fled in fear of their lives. Others took their own lives in despair. Hundreds of people were imprisoned and greater numbers were executed. The Senate ordered all shrines to Bacchus destroyed and Bacchanalia banned throughout Italy. Perhaps more than any other episode, the suppression of the Bacchic cult showed the fear that the oligarchy felt about the changes sweeping Roman civilization.

Republican Letters

As Rome absorbed foreign gods, it also absorbed foreign letters. From the Etruscans the Romans adopted and adapted the alphabet, the one in which most Western languages are written to this day. Early Latin inscriptions are largely funeral monuments, and some public notices such as the no longer extant Law of the Twelve Tables. The Roman high priest responsible for maintaining the calendar of annual feasts also prepared and updated annals—short accounts of important religious and secular events of each year—which he put on public display outside his home. Important treaties, records of booty, and decrees of the Senate found their way onto inscriptions as well. However, prior to the third century B.C.E., apart from extravagant funerary eulogies carefully preserved within families, Romans had no apparent interest in writing or literature as such. The birth of Latin letters began with Rome's exposure to Greek civilization.

Greek Historians of Rome. Early in the third century B.C.E., Greek authors had begun to pay attention to expanding Rome. The first serious Greek historian to focus on the new western power was Timaeus (ca. 356–ca. 260 B.C.E.), who spent most of his productive life in Athens. There he wrote a history of Rome up to the Pyrrhic war, interviewing

Roman and Greek witnesses in order to gain an understanding of the Italian city that had defeated a Hellenistic army. Polybius (ca. 200–ca. 118 B.C.E.), the greatest of the Greek historians to record Rome's rise to power, gathered his information firsthand. As one of a thousand eminent Greeks deported to Rome for political investigation, he became a close friend of Scipio Aemilianus and accompanied him on his Spanish and African campaigns. Polybius became a strong supporter of Roman expansion. For his history of the Punic and eastern wars, in the tradition of Thucydides, Polybius searched for truth in eyewitness testimony, in the writings of earlier authors, and in his own personal experience. Polybius's history is both the culmination of the traditions of Greek historiography and its transformation, since it centers on the rise of a non-Greek power to rule "almost the whole inhabited world."

The Origins of Latin Literature. At the same time that Greeks began to take Rome seriously, Romans themselves became interested in Greece, and in particular in the international Hellenistic culture of the eastern Mediterranean. The earliest Latin literary works were clearly adaptations, if not translations, of Hellenistic genres and texts. Still, they indicated an independence typically Roman. Although Polybius dated the Roman interest in things Greek from the fall of Syracuse in 212 B.C.E., by 240 B.C.E. plays in the Greek tradition were said already to have been performed in Rome. The earliest extant literary works—ironically, in light of the sober image of the Roman farmer-soldier—are the plays of Plautus (ca. 254–184 B.C.E.) and Terence (186–159 B.C.E.), lightly adapted translations of Hellenistic comedies.

Scheming servants, mistaken identities, bedroom farces, young lovers, and lecherous elders make up the plots of the Roman plays. What is most remarkable about the comedies, however, is the extent to which their authors experimented with and transformed Greek literature. Plautus in particular, while maintaining superficially the Greek settings of his plays, actually created a world more Roman than Greek. References to Roman laws, magistrates, clients, and social situations abound, as do humorous derogatory comments on Greek mores. Terence, though remaining closer to Greek models, Romanized his material through the creation of an elegant, natural style. Although criticized by many at the time, his plays rapidly became classics of Latin writing, influencing subsequent generations of Latin authors who worked to create a literary language separate from but equal to Greek.

Determined farmer-soldiers, disciplined by familial obligations and their piety toward the gods and the Roman state, spread Roman rule throughout the Mediterranean world. Confident of their military and governmental skills and lacking pretensions to great skill in arts, literature, and the like, they were eager to absorb the achievements of others, even while adapting them to their own needs.

THE CRISIS OF ROMAN VIRTUE

Rome's rise to world power within less than a century profoundly affected every aspect of republican life. Magistrates operating far from senatorial control in conquered provinces exercised power and found opportunities for enrichment never before seen. Successful commanders, honored and even deified by eastern cities, felt the temptation to ignore the strict requirements of senatorial accountability. There were fortunes to be made in the empire, and those fortunes distanced the oligarchy ever further from ordinary Roman citizens. A cynical saying circulating in the later republic summed up the situation well. During the time of a provincial command, it was said, one had to make three fortunes: the first to pay off the bribes it took to get the office, the second to pay off the jury that would investigate corruption after the command had expired, and the third to live on for the rest of one's life. Thus provincial commanders enriched themselves through extortion, collusion with dishonest government contractors and tax collectors, and wholesale bribe taking. Ordinary citizens, aware of such abuses, felt increasingly threatened by the wealthy and powerful. The old traditions of the farmer-soldier, the paterfamilias, the pious venerator of the gods, and the plain-speaking Latin dissolved before the vast new horizons, previously unimagined wealth, alien culture, and unprecedented opportunities of empire.

In the second century B.C.E., Romans found themselves in a dilemma as the old and the new exerted equal pressures. The tensions led to almost a century of bitter civil strife and ultimately to the disintegration of the republic. The complex

A memorial sculpture of Cato the Elder and his wife. Cato defended the ancient Roman traditions even as he himself was deeply influenced by the changes sweeping Rome.

interaction of the tensions can best be seen in the life of one man, Marcus Porcius Cato.

Cato the Elder is often presented as the preserver of the old traditions, in contrast to Scipio Aemilianus, destroyer of Carthage and proponent of Hellenism in the Roman world. True, as censor fighting against conspicuous consumption and as self-conscious defender of the past, Cato cast himself in the mold of the traditional Roman. And Scipio, with his love of Hellenism and his political career defined more by personal achievement than traditional magistracies, represented a new type of Roman. But if the division between old and new, between Cato and Scipio, had been so clear-cut, the dilemma of republican Rome would not have been so great. As it was, Cato reflected in himself this clash of values. Like the two-faced god Janus, whom he invoked in all his undertakings, Cato was the stern censor, the guardian and proponent of traditional Roman virtue, as well as the new Roman of shrewd business acumen, influence, and power unimaginable to the simple farmers he professed to admire.

Plutarch on Cato the Elder

Cato was born in the Latin town of Tusculum in 234 B.C.E. and grew to maturity on a family estate in Sabine territory. Although he boasted that he had spent his entire youth in frugality, rigor, and industry, his was a moderately wealthy family of Roman citizens. He came of age just at the start of the Second Punic War and distinguished himself in campaigns against Hannibal in Italy and Syracuse in Sicily. In between campaigns he became even more famous for his eloquence in pleading legal cases. His talents, matched by his drive and energy, brought him to the attention of a number of powerful members of the senatorial aristocracy, under whose patronage he came to Rome. There he began to rise through the offices of military tribune, quaestor, and ultimately consul and censor.

The first-generation senator became the spokesman for the traditional values of Rome, for severity and simplicity, for honesty and frugality in private and public life. Never known for his personal charm or tact, Cato was constantly embroiled in controversy. He saved his particular venom for those who enriched themselves with the spoils of conquest, who adopted Greek traditions of culture, and who displayed their new wealth and culture in fine furniture, expensive clothes, and gangs of Greek slaves. He made a great show of his own frugality, glorifying his simple farm life and the care he took in the management of his estates and of his extended familia, and working his fields side-by-side with his slaves. He de-

CATO'S SLAVES

The two sides of Cato's personality are strikingly shown in his treatment of slaves. The following description is within the generally admiring portrait of the old Roman by Plutarch (ca. 46–after 119 C.E.), who leaves it to the reader to decide whether "these acts are to be ascribed to the greatness or pettiness of his spirit."

Focus Questions

How did Cato present himself as a simple farmer? How could he reconcile his treatment of his slaves to his claims to virtue?

He [Cato] himself says that he never wore a suit of clothes which cost more than a hundred drachmas; and that, when he was general and consul, he drank the same wine which his workmen did and that the meat or fish which was bought in the meat-market for dinner did not cost above thirty *asses.* All which was for the sake of the commonwealth, that so his body might be the hardier for the war. Having a piece of embroidered Babylonian tapestry left him, he sold it; because none of his farmhouses were so much as plastered. Nor did he ever buy a slave for above fifteen hundred drachmas; as he did not seek for effeminate and handsome ones, but able sturdy workmen, horse keepers and cow-herds; and these he thought ought to be sold again, when they grew old, and no useless servants fed in the house. In short, he reckoned nothing a good bargain which was superfluous; but whatever it was he bought for a farthing, he would think it a great price, if you had no need of it; and was for the purchase of lands for sowing and feeding rather than grounds for sweeping and watering.

Some imputed these things to petty avarice, but others approved of them, as if he had only the more strictly denied himself for the rectifying and amending of others. Yet certainly, in my judgment, it marks an over-rigid temper for a man to take the work out of his servants as out of brute beasts, turning them off and selling them in their old age, and thinking there ought to be no further commerce between man and man than whilst there arises some profit by it. We see that kindness or humanity has a larger field than bare justice to exercise itself in; law and justice we cannot, in the nature of things, employ on others than men; but we may extend our goodness and charity even to irrational creatures; and such acts flow from a gentle nature, as water from an abundant spring.

From Plutarch, *The Lives of the Noble Grecians and Romans.*

spised senators who were profiting from the expansion of the empire to become involved in trade, and he supported legislation to keep senators out of commerce. In public office Cato was equally frugal, drinking the same cheap wine as his men when on military campaigns and boasting of how little public money he spent. He ridiculed Greek philosophy and education, warning his son that the Romans would be destroyed once they were infected with Greek learning. Cato presented himself as the epitome of the old Roman farmer-soldier, a man of simplicity and traditional values.

Actually, Cato, as much as anyone else, was deeply involved in the rapid changes brought about by the empire. He may have worked along with his slaves and shared their table, but as soon as they grew old he sold them to the state to avoid having to support them, something no conscientious paterfamilias would ever have done. Although he led the battle to prevent senators from participating in commerce, he was perhaps the first of that body to diversify his holdings and investments. He bought up land, hot baths, and mineral deposits. He invested his surpluses in maritime commerce, being careful to use middlemen to circumvent his own laws. He also grew rich through moneylending, not only to merchants but also to slaves. Although he avoided conspicuous consumption himself, as consul and censor he was responsible for many of the sumptuous building projects in Rome through which ordinary Romans first experienced the luxuries of the Hellenistic world. While scorning Greek culture, his extant writings and speeches show how deeply indebted he was to Greek literature. Even in his own day he was called the Roman Demosthenes, and he worked bits of Greek authors' writings even into his attacks on Greek civilization.

Cato was neither unusually duplicitous nor hypocritical. He was simply typical. Many senators agreed with him that the old values were slipping away and with them the foundation of the republic. Many feared that personal ambition was undermining the power of the oligarchy. And yet the same people could not resist exploiting the changed circumstances for their own benefit.

CONCLUSION

Rome had come a long way since its origin as an outpost of the Alban League. At first overshadowed by its more civilized neighbors to the north and south, it had slowly and tenaciously achieved independence from and then domination over its more ancient neighbors. It is difficult to point to specific Roman ideas, institutions, or techniques that made this possible. Virtually all were absorbed or adapted from the Etruscans, Greeks, and others with whom Rome came into contact. Rome's great success was largely due to Roman authoritarianism, as well as to its genius for creative adaptation, flexibility, and thoroughness, and its willingness to give those it conquered a stake in Roman victory. Until the middle of the second century B.C.E., the formula had served the republic well. After the final destruction of Carthage, however, an isolated and fearful oligarchy appeared unwilling or unable to broaden the base of those participating in the Roman achievement. The result was a century of conflict and civil war that destroyed the republican empire.

QUESTIONS FOR REVIEW

1. Why might the Greeks have been surprised by certain characteristics of Carthaginian and Etruscan society?
2. What social, political, and military practices made possible the expansion of Rome from a collection of villages into a power that ultimately destroyed Carthage in the Punic Wars?
3. How were family and household life organized in the domus of the Roman Republic?
4. Why were Romans such as Cato the Elder concerned by the changes that accompanied the expansion of Roman international power?

KEY TERMS

cursus honorum, *p. 110*
dictator, *p. 110*
equestrians, *p. 118*
Etruscans, *p. 105*
imperium, *p. 110*
latifundia, *p. 109*
numen, *p. 121*
paterfamilias, *p. 107*
patricians, *p. 108*
plebs, *p. 108*
Villanovans, *p. 102*

DISCOVERING WESTERN CIVILIZATION ONLINE

You can obtain more information about early Rome at the Websites listed below. See also the Companion Website that accompanies this text, www.ablongman.com/kishlansky, which contains an online study guide and additional resources.

General Websites

Ancient Rome
www.providence.edu/dwc/rome.htm
A course Web page with links to every aspect of Roman history and civilization.

NM's Creative Impulse: Rome
history.evansville.net/rome.html
An excellent Website dedicated to Roman history.

Places to Go: Carthage
www.tourismtunisia.com/togo/carthage/carthage.html
A brief introduction to Carthage designed for tourists but with historical information.

The Etruscan Civilization: Art and Archaeology Links
oncampus.richmond.edu/academics/classics/students/belanger/etruscolnks.html
A site dedicated to Etruscan civilization.

From City to Empire

Frank E. Smitha's World History: The Rise of Ancient Rome
fsmitha.com/h1/ch15.htm
An outline by Frank Smitha of early Roman history beginning with the legendary accounts of Rome's foundation.

The Forum Romanum: History and Religion
library.thinkquest.org/11402/homehis.html
A Thinkquest site on Roman history and religion including links to Roman archaeology.

Republican Civilization

Women's Life in Greece and Rome
www.stoa.org/diotima/anthology/wlgr/
A site devoted to women in Rome and Greece.

Republican Roman Government
www.utexas.edu/depts/classics/faculty/Riggsby/RepGov.html
A detailed explanation of the republican constitution of Rome.

SUGGESTIONS FOR FURTHER READING

Primary Sources

Many of the works of Polybius, Livy, Cato, Caesar, Cicero, and other Roman authors are available in English translation from Penguin Books. The first volume—*Roman Civilization, Selected Readings, Vol. I: The Republic* (1951) by Naphtali Lewis and Meyer Reinhold—contains a wide selection of documents with useful introductions. An excellent selection of Roman historical writing can be found in Ronald Mellor, *The Roman Historians* (New York: Routledge, 1999).

The Western Mediterranean to 509 B.C.E.

Graeme Barker and Tom Rasmussen, *The Etruscans* (Oxford: Blackwell Publishers, 2000). An introduction to Etruscan studies and history.

Serge Lancel, *Carthage: A History* (Oxford: Blackwell Publishers, 1997). A basic introduction.

From City to Empire, 509–146 B.C.E.

Nigel Bagnall, *The Punic Wars* (London: Hutchinson, 1990). Survey of the wars between Rome and Carthage.

Mary Beard and Michael Crawford, *Rome in the Late Republic* (Ithaca, NY: Cornell University Press, 1985). A short interpretive essay on the crisis of the late republic.

John Boardman, Jasper Griffin, and Oswyn Murray, *The Oxford History of the Roman World* (New York: Oxford University Press, 2001). A balanced collection of essays on all aspects of Roman history and civilization.

K. R. Bradley, *Slavery and Society at Rome* (New York: Cambridge University Press, 1994). The place of slavery in the Roman world.

Tim Cornell, *The Beginnings of Rome, 1000–264 B.C.* (New York: Routledge, 1995). A new look at the origins of Rome.

Michael Crawford, *The Roman Republic* (Cambridge, MA: Harvard University Press, 1978). A modern survey of the republican period, emphasizing political history.

P. Matthew Dillon and Lynda Garland, *Ancient Rome: From the Early Republic to the Assassination of Julius Caesar* (London and New York: Routledge, 2005). A survey by two specialists of the republican history of Rome.

Republican Civilization

Geza Alfoldy, *The Social History of Rome* (Berlin: Walter de Gruyter, 1988). A survey of Rome that emphasizes the relationship between social structure and politics.

Erich S. Gruen, *Culture and National Identity in Republican Rome* (Ithaca, NY: Cornell University Press, 1992). Important lectures by a major figure in the field.

———, *The Hellenistic World and the Coming of Rome*, 2 vols. (Berkeley: University of California Press, 1984). A detailed history of the Hellenistic world, presenting Rome's gradual and unintended rise to dominance in it.

Celia E. Schultz, *Women's Religious Activity in the Roman Republic* (Chapel Hill, NC: University of North Carolina Press, 2006). A specialist in Roman religion reevaluates the active roles undertaken by republican-era women in all spheres of religious life.

Callie Williamson, *The Laws of the Roman People: Public Law in the Expansion and Decline of the Roman Republic* (Ann Arbor: The University of Michigan Press, 2005). An analysis of how the expansion of the republic ultimately led to the breakdown of the legal system for Roman conflict resolution and of the republic itself.

The Crisis of Roman Virtue

Alan E. Astin, *Cato the Censor* (New York: Oxford University Press, 1978). An excellent biography of Cato that also analyzes his writings.

Pat Southern, *Pompey the Great* (Stroud, England: Tempus Publishing Ltd., 2002). The most recent biography of the triumvir.

For a list of additional titles related to this chapter's topics, please see http://www.ablongman.com/kishlansky.

CHAPTER 5 IMPERIAL ROME, 146 B.C.E.–192 C.E.

THE ALTAR OF AUGUSTAN PEACE

THE MAKING OF THE ROMAN EMPIRE

THE VISUAL RECORD

The Romans worshipped many gods and goddesses, but in the last century before the common era Pax, the goddess of peace, was almost unknown. Much more familiar was Mars, the god of war. For more than a century, factional strife and then civil had roiled the Roman world and fatally weakened the republic. Finally, in 27 B.C.E., Octavian, known to history as the Emperor Augustus, emerged as the absolute ruler of a Roman world tired of bloodshed. In 13 B.C.E., a grateful (and ingratiating) Senate decreed that Augustus be honored by the construction of an altar dedicated to the new goddess, erected on the field long sacred to her opposite, Mars. Pax was, along with Salus Publica (The Public Good) and Concordia (Harmony) one of Augustus's favorite divinities and the cornerstone of his political program. In return for abandoning all hope of republican government, Augustus promised harmony, prosperity, and, above all, peace. More than any other surviving monument, the Altar of Augustan Peace, in its design and in the ideology of its elaborate carved friezes, embodies Augustus's vision of that peace.

Pax may have been a newcomer to the Roman pantheon, but the altar itself was an intentional anachronism. Its style, a 20-by-24-foot marble rectangle standing more than three feet tall and surrounded on three sides by a U-shaped counter, revived a form common hundreds of years earlier, in what were thought to have been the virtuous days of the Roman Republic. Augustus, whose transformation of the Roman state and society was so radical that it had been rightly termed a revolution, was always careful to present the most daring innovations as restorations of ancient republican tradition.

■ Depiction of Pax on the east (now north) side of the Altar of Peace.

The entrance to the Altar of Peace (Ara Pacis), dedicated in 9 B.C.E.

To reach the altar a visitor must climb a short flight of steps and enter through an enclosure wall erected of massive rectangular slabs of marble, some weighing more than ten tons. The lower course of the external walls is decorated with delicate, intricately intertwined acanthus plants, a symbol of peaceful abundance that came to be intimately associated with Augustan art. The upper course contains exquisitely carved friezes representing Roman past and present as understood by Augustus. A visitor who approached the shrine from the Field of Mars saw on either side of the entryway the stories of the two mythological founders of Rome: Romulus, the abandoned child nursed by the she-wolf, and Aeneas, the legendary Trojan warrior who wandered the Mediterranean in obedience to the gods until he arrived at the site of Rome. On the sides of the wall are images of processions, each involving some 40 or 50 figures rendered in three-quarters life size. On the south, Augustus and his family prepare to celebrate the cult of the goddess of peace. On the north side magistrates and ordinary Roman citizens carry gifts, either to Augustus or to the Augustan Peace — it was really the same thing.

On the far side of the enclosure, the side that was the most visible to passing Romans, the visitor encounters on the right the goddess Roma and on the left the goddess Pax herself. This new divinity did not have a long-established image, so she was represented as a combination of older, better-known goddesses, including Mother Venus, the patroness of Augustus's own family, and Mother Earth. She sits upon a stone ledge amid lush flowers and plants. At her feet a sheep grazes and a cow reclines in the very image of prosperity and contentment. Pax holds two happy infants in her lap who reach up toward her and on whom she gazes with love. Beside her ride allegorical figures of air and water, symbols of fertility and plenty, one on the back of a flying swan, the other on a sea beast.

Domesticity, abundance, fruitfulness, and the simplicity of an earlier time: this is the image of the Augustan Peace that the emperor and his advisors sought to create. This was to be the new reality of Rome restored, a vision so compelling that subsequent generations referred to the empire as the ***Pax Romana.*** And yet, our translation of pax as peace unconsciously accepts Augustus's perspective: to thousands of victims of the empire, a better translation would be pacification. A Roman critic at the end of the first century put it: "They created a desert and called it peace."

LOOKING AHEAD

This chapter explores the consequences of Roman imperial expansion throughout the Mediterranean, the long and violent crises that led to civil war and the end of the republic, and the new forms of government, society, and culture that were imperial Rome.

CHAPTER OUTLINE

THE PRICE OF EMPIRE, 146–121 B.C.E.

Roman victory defeated the republic. Roman conquest of the Mediterranean world and the establishment of the Roman Empire spelled the end of the republican system. Roman society could not withstand the tensions caused by the enrichment of the few, the impoverishment of the many, and the demands of the excluded populations of the empire to share in its benefits. Traditional Roman culture could not survive the attraction of Hellenistic civilization with its wealth, luxuries, and individualistic values. Finally, Roman government could not restrain the ambitions of its oligarchs or protect the interests of its ordinary citizens. The creation of a Mediterranean empire brought in its wake a century of revolutionary change before stable new social, cultural, and political forms emerged in the Roman world.

Winners and Losers

Rome had emerged victorious in the Punic and Macedonian wars but the real winners were the members of the oligarchy—the **optimates,** or "the best," as they called themselves—whose wealth and power had grown beyond all imagining. The optimates included roughly 300 senators and magistrates, most of whom had inherited wealth, political connections, and long-established clientages. Since military command and government of the empire were entrusted to magistrates who were answerable only to the Senate, of which they were members, the empire was essentially their private domain. Their combination of landed wealth, political experience, and social ties placed them at the pinnacle of Roman society.

But new circumstances created new opportunities for many others. Italian merchants, slave traders, entrepreneurs, and bankers, many of lowly origin, poured into the cities of the east in the wake of the Roman legions. The newly enriched Romans constituted a second elite and formed themselves into a separate order, that of the *equites,* or equestrians, distinguished by their wealth and honorific military service on horseback but connected with the old military elite. Since the Senate did not create a government bureaucracy to administer the empire, equestrians became essential to provincial government. Companies of the equestrians became publicans, or tax collectors. They purchased the right to collect rents on public land, tribute, and customs duties from provincials. Whatever they collected beyond the amount contracted for by Roman officials was theirs to keep. Publicans regularly bribed governors and commanders to allow them to gouge the local populations with impunity and on occasion even obtained Roman troops to help them make their collections.

Roman slaves sifting grain. Roman victories in the Punic and Macedonian wars brought a huge influx of slaves from the conquered lands. Slaves were pressed into service on the estates and plantations of wealthy landowners.

Gradually, some of these "new men," their money "laundered" through investments in land, managed to achieve lower magistracies and even move into the senatorial order. Still, the upper reaches of office were closed to all but a tiny minority. By the end of the Punic Wars, only some 25 families could hope to produce consuls.

The losers in the wars included the vanquished, who were sold into slavery by the tens of thousands; the provincials who bore the Roman yoke; the Italian allies who had done so much for the Romans; and even the citizen farmers, small shopkeepers, and free artisans of the republic. All four groups suffered from the effects of empire, and during the next century all resorted to violence against the optimates.

Slave Revolts. The slaves revolted first. Thousands of them, captured in battle or taken after victory, flooded the Italian and Sicilian estates of the wealthy. Estimates vary, but in the first century B.C.E., the slave population of Italy was probably around two million, fully one-third of the total population. Rural slaves on absentee estates enjoyed none of the protections afforded traditional Roman servants. Cato sold off his slaves who reached old age; other masters simply worked them to death. Many slaves, born free citizens of Hellenistic states, found such treatment unbearable. In 135 B.C.E., a small group of particularly badly mistreated slaves in Sicily took up arms against their masters. Soon other slaves joined, ultimately swelling the ranks of the rebels to more than 200,000. It took the Roman state three years to crush the revolt.

A generation later, slaves revolted in southern Italy and, between 104 and 101 B.C.E., again in Sicily. That time the cause was more specific. The Senate had passed a decree freeing enslaved citizens of Roman allies, but Sicilian slave owners blocked implementation of the order in Sicily. The rebel ranks quickly swelled to more than 30,000, and only a full-scale military campaign was able to defeat them.

The most serious slave revolt occurred in Italy between 74 and 71 B.C.E. Gladiators—professional slave fighters trained for Roman amusement—revolted in Capua. Under the competent leadership of the Thracian gladiator Spartacus, more than 100,000 slaves took up arms against Rome. Ultimately eight legions, more troops than had met Hannibal at Zama, were needed to put down the revolt.

All the slave revolts were doomed to failure. The revolutionaries lacked a unified goal, organization, discipline, and strategy. Some wanted freedom to return home. Others sought to establish themselves as autonomous kings with slaves of their own. Still others wanted simply to avenge themselves against their masters. Their desperate struggles proved unequal to the numerical and military superiority of the disciplined legions, and retribution was always terrible. After the defeat of Spartacus, crucified rebels lined the road from Rome to Naples.

Provincial Revolts. Revolts profoundly disturbed the Roman state, all the more because it was not just slaves who revolted. In many cases, poor free peasants and disgruntled provincials rose up against Rome. The most significant provincial revolt was that of Aristonicus, the illegitimate half-brother of Attalus III (ca. 138–133 B.C.E.) of Pergamum, a Roman client state. Attalus had left his kingdom to Rome at his death. In an attempt to assert his right to the kingdom, Aristonicus armed slaves and peasants and attacked the Roman garrisons. The hellenized cities of Asia Minor remained loyal to Rome, but the provincial uprising, the first of many over the centuries, lasted more than three years, from 133 to 130 B.C.E. In 88 B.C.E., Mithridates VI (120–63 B.C.E.), the king of Pontus, led an uprising against Roman soldiers, merchants, businessmen, and publicans in Asia Minor. The revolt spread to Greece, and tens of thousands of Romans died at the hands of poor freemen.

Revolts by slaves and provincials were disturbing enough. Revolts by Rome's Italian allies were much more serious. After the Second Punic War, the allies, on whose loyalty Rome had depended for survival, found themselves badly treated and exploited. Government officials used state power to undermine the position of the Italian elites. At the same time, Roman aristocrats used their economic power to drive the Italic peasants from their land, replacing them with slaves. Some reform-minded Romans attempted to defuse tensions by extending citizenship to the allies, but failure of the effort led to a revolt at Fregellae, south of Rome, in 125 B.C.E. A broader and more serious revolt took place between 91 and 89 B.C.E. after the Senate blocked an attempt to extend citizenship to the allies. During the so-called **Social War** (from *socii*, the Latin word for allies), almost all the Italian allies rose against Rome. The revolts differed from those in the provinces in that the Italian elites as well as the masses aligned themselves against the Roman oligarchy. Even some ordinary Roman citizens joined the rebel forces against the powerful elite.

Optimates and Populares

The despair that could lead ordinary Roman citizens to armed rebellion grew from the social and economic consequences of conquests. While aristocrats amassed vast landed estates worked by cheap slaves, ordinary Romans often lacked even a family farm capable of supporting themselves and their families. Many found their way to Rome, where they swelled the ranks of the unemployed. Huddled into shoddily constructed tenements, they lived off public subsidies. Although many senators bemoaned the demise of the Roman farmer-soldier, few were willing to compromise their own privileged positions to help. In the face of the oligarchy's unwillingness to deal with the problem, in 133 B.C.E. the tribune Tiberius Gracchus (ca. 163–133 B.C.E.) attempted to introduce a land-reform program that would return citizens to agriculture. Gracchus was the first of the **populares,** political leaders appealing to the masses. His motives were probably a mixture of compassion for the poor, concern over the falling numbers of citizens who had the minimum land to qualify for military service, and personal ambition.

■ The tribunes Tiberius Gracchus and Gaius Gracchus, each of whom supported reforms to aid ordinary Romans.

Tiberius Gracchus. During the previous century, great amounts of public land had illegally come into private hands. With the support of reform-minded aristocrats and commoners, Gracchus proposed a law that would limit the amount of public land an individual could hold to about 312 acres. He also proposed establishing a commission to distribute to landless peasants the land recovered by the state as a result of the law. Because many senators who illegally held vast amounts of public land strongly opposed the measure, it faced certain failure in the Senate. Gracchus therefore took it to the plebeian assembly. Since 287 B.C.E., the measures of the assembly had been binding on all society and only the ten elected tribunes could veto its decisions. Here Gracchus's proposal was assured of support by the rural poor, who flocked to Rome to vote for it.

When the aristocratic optimates, hoping to preserve their position, influenced one of the other nine tribunes to oppose the law, Gracchus had the tribune deposed by the assembly, a move that shocked many senators. Senators, bound by custom and tradition, found Gracchus's maneuver to avoid the Senate and his unprecedented deposition of a tribune novel and deeply disturbing. The law passed, and a three-person commission to distribute land was established. However, Gracchus's maneuvering lost him many of his aristocratic supporters, who feared that a popular democracy led by a demagogue was replacing the senatorial oligarchy.

Also in 133 B.C.E., Gracchus introduced another bill that provided that the royal treasury of the kingdom of Pergamum, bequeathed to Rome by Attalus III, be used to help citizens receiving land to purchase livestock and equipment. The law, which challenged the Senate's traditional control over finance and foreign affairs, greatly troubled the conservative elite, but as long as Gracchus held office, he was protected from any sort of attack by the traditional immunity accorded tribunes. It was no secret, however, that the Senate planned to prosecute him as soon as his one-year term expired. To escape that fate, he appealed to the assembly to reelect him for an unprecedented second consecutive term. To his opponents, Gracchus's appeal smacked of an attempt to make himself sole ruler, a democratic tyrant on the Greek model. A group of senators and their clients, led by one of Gracchus's own cousins, broke into the assembly meeting at which the election was to take place and murdered the tribune and 300 of his supporters.

Gaius Gracchus. The optimates in the Senate could eliminate Tiberius Gracchus, but they could not so easily eliminate the movement he had led. In 123 B.C.E., his younger brother, Gaius Sempronius Gracchus (153–121 B.C.E.), became tribune and during his two one-year terms initiated an even broader and more radical reform program. Tiberius had been concerned only about poor citizens. Gaius attempted to broaden the citizenry and to shift the balance of power away from the Senate. Alarmed by the revolt at Fregellae, Gaius attempted to extend citizenship to all Latins and improve the status of Italian allies by giving them the right to vote in the assembly. In order to check the power of senatorial magistrates in the provinces, he transferred to the equestrians the right to investigate provincial corruption. That move brought the wealthy equestrian order into politics as a counterbalance to the Senate. Gaius also improved the supply and distribution of grain in Rome and other Italian cities to benefit the urban poor. He reestablished his brother's land-distribution project, extended participation to Latins and Italians, and encouraged colonization as a means to provide citizens with land. Finally, to protect himself and his party from the anticipated reaction of the Senate and to prepare to avenge his brother's death, Gaius pushed through a law stipulating that only the people could condemn a citizen to death.

Gaius's program was extraordinary for several reasons. In the first place, it was exactly that, a program, the first comprehensive attempt to deal with the problems facing Roman society. Second, it proposed a basic shift of power, drawing the equestrian order for the first time into the political arena opposite the Senate and making the assembly rather than the Senate the initiator of legislation. Finally, it offered a solution to the problem of the allies that, although rejected at the time, was finally adopted some 20 years later. In the short run, however, Gaius's program was a failure. In 121 B.C.E., he was not reelected for a third term and thus lost the immunity of the tribunate. Recalling the fate of his brother, he armed his supporters. Once more the Senate acted, ordering the consul to

THE REFORMS OF TIBERIUS GRACCHUS

In the following passage, the Romanized Greek Appian of Alexandria (ca. 95–ca. 165 C.E.), drawing on earlier but now lost records, describes the positions of the two factions in the dispute over the land reform Tiberius Gracchus introduced in 133 B.C.E.

Focus Questions

How had wealthy Romans acquired vast amounts of public land? Why did the wealthy see Gracchus as so great a threat?

Tiberius Sempronius Gracchus, an illustrious man, eager for glory, a most powerful speaker, and for these reasons well known to all, delivered an eloquent discourse while serving as tribune, lamenting the fact that the Italians, a people so valiant in war and related in blood to the Romans, were declining little by little into pauperism and paucity of numbers without any hope of remedy. He inveighed against the multitude of slaves as useless in war and never faithful to their masters, and adduced the recent calamity brought upon the masters by their slaves in Sicily. . . . After speaking thus he again brought forward the law providing that nobody should hold more than 500 *iugera* of public domain. But he added a provision to the former law, that [two] sons of the occupiers might each hold one-half that amount and that the remainder should be divided among the poor by three elected commissioners, who should be changed annually.

This was extremely disturbing to the rich because, on account of the commissioners, they could no longer disregard the law as they had done before; nor could they buy from those receiving allotments, because Gracchus had provided against this by forbidding such sales. They collected together in groups, and made lamentation, and accused the poor of appropriating their fields of long standing, their vineyards, and their buildings. Some said they had paid the price of the land to their neighbors. Were they to lose the money with the land? Others said the graves of their ancestors were in the ground, which had been allotted to them in the division of their fathers' estates. Others said that their wives' dowries had been expended on these estates, or that the land had been given to their own daughters as dowry. . . . All kinds of wailing and expressions of indignation were heard at once. On the other side were heard the lamentations of the poor—that they were being reduced from competence to extreme poverty, and from that to childlessness, because they were unable to rear their offspring. They recounted the military services they had rendered, by which this very land had been acquired, and were angry that they should be robbed of their share of the common property. . . . Emboldened by numbers and exasperated against each other they kindled incessant disturbances, and waited eagerly for the voting of the new law, some intending to prevent its enactment by all means, and others to enact it at all costs.

take whatever measures he deemed necessary. Gaius and some 3000 of his supporters died.

The deaths of Tiberius and Gaius Gracchus marked a new beginning in Roman politics. Not since the end of the monarchy had a political conflict been decided with personal violence. The whole episode provided a model for future attempts at reform. Reformers would look not to the Senate or the aristocracy but to the people, from whom they would draw their political power. The experience of the Gracchi also provided a model for repression of other reform programs: violence.

THE END OF THE REPUBLIC

With the Gracchi dead and the core of their reforms dismantled, the Senate appeared victorious against all challengers. At home, the masses of ordinary Roman citizens and their political leadership were in disarray. The conquered lands of North Africa and the Near East filled the public coffers as well as the private accounts of Roman senators and publicans. In reality, Rome had solved neither the problem of internal conflict between rich and poor nor that of how to govern its enormous empire. The apparent calm ended when revolts in Africa and Italy exposed the fragility of the Senate's control and ushered in an ever-increasing spiral of violence and civil war.

The Crisis of Government

In 112 B.C.E., the Senate declared war against Jugurtha (ca. 160–104 B.C.E.), a North African client-state king who, in his war against a rival, had killed some Roman merchants in the Numidian city of Cirta. The war dragged on for five years amid accusations of corruption, incompetence, and treason. Finally, in 107 B.C.E., the people elected as consul Gaius Marius (157–86 B.C.E.), a "new man" who had risen through the tribunate, and entrusted him with the conduct of the war. In order to raise an army, Marius ignored property qualifications and enlisted many impoverished Romans and armed them at public expense. Although recruiting of landless citizens had probably taken place before, no one had done it in such an overt and massive manner. Senators looked on Marius's measure with great suspicion, but the poor citizen recruits, who had despaired of benefiting from the land reforms proposed by the Gracchi, looked forward to receiving a grant of land at the end of their military service.

Marius quickly defeated Jugurtha in 106 B.C.E. The next year, Celtic and Germanic barbarians crossed the Alps into Italy and, although technically disqualified from further terms, Marius was elected consul five times between 104 and 100 B.C.E. to meet the threat. During this period he continued to recruit soldiers from among the poor and on his own authority extended citizenship to allies. Marius promised land to his impoverished soldiers, but after his victory in 101 B.C.E. the Senate refused to provide veterans with farms. As a result, Marius's armies naturally shifted their allegiance away from the Roman state and to their popular commander. Soon that pattern of loyalty became the norm. Politicians forged close bonds with the soldiers of their armies. Individual commanders, not the state or the Senate, ensured that their recruits received their pay, shared in the spoils of victory, and obtained land upon their retirement. In turn, the soldiers became fanatically devoted to their commanders. Republican armies had become personal armies, potent tools in the hands of ambitious politicians.

The Civil Wars. The outbreak of the Social War in 91 B.C.E. marked the first use of such armies in civil war. Both Marius and the consul Lucius Cornelius Sulla (138–78 B.C.E.) raised armies to fight the Italians, who were pacified only after Roman citizenship was extended to all Italians in 89 B.C.E. The next year, Mithridates VI (120–63 B.C.E.), the king of Pontus, took advantage of the Roman preoccupation with Italy to invade the provinces of Asia. As soon as the Italian threat receded, Sulla, as the representative of the optimates, raised an army to fight Mithridates. As leader of the populares, who favored reform, Marius attempted to have Sulla relieved of command. Sulla marched on Rome, initiating a bloody civil war. In the course of this war Rome was occupied three times—once by Marius and twice by Sulla. Each commander ordered mass executions of his opponents and confiscated their property, which he then distributed to his supporters.

Ultimately, Sulla emerged victorious and ruled as dictator from 82 to 79 B.C.E., using that time to shore up senatorial power. He doubled the size of the Senate to 600, filling the new positions with men drawn from the equites. He reduced the authority of tribunes and returned jury courts from the equites to the senators. In order to weaken the military power of magistrates, he abolished the practice of assigning military commands to praetors and consuls. Rather, they were to be held by proconsuls, or former magistrates, who would serve for one year as provincial governors.

In 79 B.C.E., his reforms in place, Sulla stepped down to allow a return to oligarchic republican rule. Although his changes bought a decade of peace, they did not solve the fundamental problems dividing optimates and populares. If anything, his rule had proven that the only real political option was a dictatorship by a powerful individual with his own army. During the last generation of the republic, idealists continued their hopeless struggle to prop up the dying republican system, while more forward-thinking generals fought among themselves for absolute power.

Republican Crisis. Marcus Tullius Cicero (106–43 B.C.E.) reflected the strengths and weaknesses of the republican tradition in the first century B.C.E. Although cultivated, humane, and dedicated to the republican constitution, he was also ambitious, blind to the failings of the optimates, a poor judge of character, and out of touch with the political realities of his time. Like Cato in an earlier age, he was a "new man," the son of a wealthy equestrian who provided his children with the best possible education both in Rome and in Athens and Rhodes. In Greece, Cicero developed a lifelong attachment to Stoic philosophy and cultivated the oratory skills necessary for a young Roman destined for public life. After returning to Rome, he quickly earned a reputation for his skills as a courtroom orator.

Cicero identified firmly with the elite, hoping that the republic could be saved through the harmonious cooperation of the equestrian and senatorial orders. Neither group was interested in following his program, but most considered him a safer figure than military strongmen like Sulla, who sought high office. In 63 B.C.E. Cicero was elected consul, the first "new man" to hold the office in more than 30 years. The real threat to the existence of the republic was posed by the ambitions of powerful military commanders—Pompey (106–48 B.C.E.), Crassus (ca. 115–53 B.C.E.), and Julius Caesar (100–44 B.C.E.).

Pompey and Crassus, both protégés of Sulla, rose rapidly and unconstitu-

Marcus Tullius Cicero, the famous statesman and orator, fought throughout his career to save the dying Roman republic.

tionally through a series of special proconsular commands by judicious use of fraud, violence, and corruption. Pompey first won public acclaim by commanding a victorious army in Africa and Spain. Upon his return to Rome in 70 B.C.E., he united with Crassus, who had won popularity for suppressing the Spartacus rebellion. Together they worked to dismantle the Sullan constitution to the benefit of the populares. In return, Pompey received an extraordinary command over all of the coasts of the Mediterranean, in theory to suppress piracy but actually to give him control over all of the provinces of the empire. When in 66 B.C.E. King Mithridates of Pontus again attacked Greece, Pompey assumed command of the provinces of Asia. His army not only destroyed Mithridates but continued on, conquering Armenia, Syria, and Palestine, acquiring an impressive retinue of client kings, and increasing the income from the provinces by some 70 percent.

While Pompey was extending the frontiers of the empire to the Euphrates, Crassus, whose wealth was legendary—"No one should be called rich," he once observed, "who is not able to maintain an army on his income"—was consolidating his power. He allied himself with Julius Caesar, a young, well-connected orator from one of Rome's most ancient patrician families, who nevertheless promoted the cause of the populares. The Senate feared the ambitious and ruthless Crassus, and it was to block the election of Crassus's candidate, Catiline (Lucius Sergius Catilina, ca. 108–62 B.C.E.), to the consulate in 63 B.C.E. that the Senate elected Cicero instead. Catiline soon joined a conspiracy of Sullan veterans and populares, but Cicero quickly uncovered and suppressed the conspiracy and ordered Catiline's execution.

The First Triumvirate. When Pompey returned from Asia in triumph in 62 B.C.E., he expected to find Italy convulsed with the Catiline revolt and in need of a military savior in the tradition of Sulla. Instead, thanks to Cicero's quick action, all was in order. Although he never forgave Cicero for stealing his glory, Pompey disbanded his army and returned to private life, asking only that the Senate approve his organization of the territories he had conquered and grant land to his veterans. The Senate refused. In response, Pompey formed an uneasy alliance with Crassus and Caesar in 60 B.C.E. The alliance was known as the **first triumvirate,** from the Latin for "three men." Caesar was elected consul in 59 B.C.E. and the following year received command of the province of Cisalpine Gaul in northern Italy.

Pompey and Crassus may have thought that this command would remove the ambitious young man from the political spotlight. Instead, Caesar, who has been called, with only some exaggeration, "the sole creative genius ever produced by Rome," used his province as a staging ground for the conquest of a vast area of western Europe to the mouth of the Rhine.

CICERO ON JUSTICE AND REASON

In his De Legibus (On the Laws), *Cicero recast the Stoic tradition of the universal laws of nature into a dialogue modeled on Plato's dialogue by the same name. In it, Cicero defends the belief that true justice must be based on reason, which, accessible to all persons, could be the solution to the evils facing the Roman Republic and a guide in the governance of its empire.*

Focus Questions

How does Cicero distinguish between what is legal and what is just? What does Cicero believe to be the foundation of true justice?

But the most foolish notion of all is the belief that everything is just which is found in the customs or laws of nations. Would that be true, even if these laws had been enacted by tyrants? . . . Justice is one; it binds all human society, and is based on one Law, which is right reason applied to command and prohibition. . . . But if Justice is conformity to written laws and national customs, and if, as the same persons claim, everything is to be tested by the standard of utility, then anyone who thinks it will be profitable to him will, if he is able, disregard and violate the laws. It follows that Justice does not exist at all, if it does not exist in Nature, and if that form of it which is based on utility can be overthrown by that very utility itself. And if nature is not to be considered the foundation of Justice, that will mean destruction of the virtues on which human society depends, for where then will there be a place for generosity, or love of country, or loyalty, or the inclination to be of service to others or to show gratitude for favors received? For these virtues originate in our natural inclination to love our fellow-men, and this is the foundation of Justice. . . . But if the principles of Justice were founded on the decrees of peoples, the edicts of princes, or the decisions of judges, then Justice would sanction robbery and adultery and forgery of wills, in case these acts were approved by the votes or decrees of the populace.

From Marcus Tullius Cicero, *De Re Publica de Legibus.*

His brilliant military skills beyond the Alps and his dedication to his troops made him immensely popular with his legions. His ability for self-promotion ensured that his popularity was matched at home, where the populares eagerly received news of his Gallic wars.

In 53 B.C.E. Crassus died leading an army in Syria, leaving Pompey and the popular young Caesar to dispute supreme power. As word of Caesar's military successes increased his popularity at Rome, Pompey's suspicion of his younger associate also increased. Finally, in 49 B.C.E., Pompey's supporters in the Senate relieved Caesar of his command and ordered him to return to Italy. Return he did, but not as commanded. Rather than leave his army on the far side of the Rubicon River—which marked the boundary between his province of Cisalpine Gaul and Italy—as ordered, he marched on Rome at the head of his legions. This meant civil war, a vicious bloodletting that convulsed the whole Mediterranean world. In 48 B.C.E., Caesar defeated Pompey in northern Greece, and Pompey was assassinated shortly thereafter in Egypt. Still the wars went on between Pompey's supporters and Caesar until 45 B.C.E. when, with all his enemies defeated, Caesar returned to Rome.

The Second Triumvirate. In Rome, unlike Sulla, Caesar showed his opponents clemency as he sought to heal the wounds of war and to undertake an unprecedented series of reforms. He enlarged the Senate to 900 and widened its representation, appointing soldiers, freedmen, provincials, and, above all, wealthy men from the Italian towns. He increased the number of magistracies to broaden participation in government, founded colonies at Carthage and Corinth, and settled veterans in colonies elsewhere in Italy, Greece, Asia, Africa, Spain, and Gaul.

Still, Caesar made no pretense of returning Rome to republican government. In early 44 B.C.E., though serving that year as consul together with his general Mark Antony (Marcus Antonius) (ca. 81–30 B.C.E.), Caesar had himself declared perpetual dictator. The move finally was too much for some 60

The Career of Julius Caesar

Examine the extent of the Roman Empire in ca. 49 B.C.E. and the movement of Julius Caesar's military campaigns. How vital was Gaul to the Roman Empire before Caesar's campaigns? Based on the locations of Caesar's campaigns during the civil war, what can you assume about the center of power of his enemies? What geographical considerations might have led Pompey to seek an alliance with Egypt's Cleopatra?

die-hard republican senators. On 15 March, a group led by two enemies whom Caesar had pardoned, Cassius Longinus and Marcus Junius Brutus, assassinated him as he entered the Senate chamber.

Cicero rejoiced when he heard of the assassination, which was clear evidence of his political naïveté. The republic was dead long before Caesar died, and the assassination simply returned Rome to civil war, a civil war that destroyed Cicero himself. Mark Antony, Marcus Lepidus (d. 12 B.C.E.), another of Caesar's generals, and Caesar's grandnephew and adopted son Octavian (63 B.C.E.–14 C.E.), who took the name of his great-uncle, soon formed a **second triumvirate** to destroy Caesar's enemies. After a bloody purge of senatorial and equestrian opponents, including Cicero, Antony and Octavian set out after Cassius and Brutus, who had fled into Macedonia. At Philippi in 42 B.C.E. Octavian and Antony defeated the armies of the two assassins (or, as they called themselves, liberators), who preferred suicide to capture.

After the defeat of the last republicans at Philippi, the members of the second triumvirate began to look suspiciously at one another. Antony took command of the east, protecting the provinces of Asia Minor and the Levant from the Parthians and bleeding them dry in the process. Lepidus received Africa, and Octavian was left to deal with the problems of Italy and the west.

Initially, Octavian cut a weak and unimposing figure. He was only 18 when he was named adopted son and heir in Caesar's will. He had no military or political experience and was frequently in poor health. Still, he had the magic of Caesar's name with which to inspire the army, he had a visceral instinct for politics and publicity, and he combined these with an absolute determination to succeed at all costs. Aided by more competent and experienced commanders, notably Marcus Agrippa (ca. 63–12 B.C.E.) and Gaius Maecenas (ca. 70–8 B.C.E.), Octavian began to consolidate his power at the expense of his two colleagues.

Lepidus attempted to gain a greater share in the empire but found that his troops would not fight against Octavian. He was forced out of his position and allowed to retire in obscurity, retaining only the honorific title of *pontifex maximus.* Antony, to meet his ever-growing demand for cash, became dependent on the Ptolemaic ruler of Egypt, the clever and competent Cleopatra VII (51–30 B.C.E.). For her part, Cleopatra manipulated Antony in order to maintain the integrity and independence of her kingdom.

Octavian seized the opportunity to portray Antony as a traitor to Rome, a weakling controlled by an eastern woman who planned to move the capital of the empire to Alexandria. Antony, for all his military might, could not attack Italy as long as the despised Cleopatra was with him. Nor could he abandon her without losing her essential financial support. Instead, he tried to lure Octavian to a showdown in Greece. His plan misfired. Agrippa forced him into a naval battle off Actium in 31 B.C.E. in which Antony was soundly defeated. He and his Egyptian queen committed suicide, and Octavian ruled supreme in the Roman Empire.

A Life Worth Leading

Mere survival was a difficult and elusive goal throughout the last decades of the republic. Still, some members of the elite sought more. They tried to make sense of the turmoil around them and formulate a philosophy of life to provide themselves with a model of personal conduct. By now Rome's elite were in full command of Greek literature and philosophy, and they naturally turned to the Greek tradition to find their answers. However, they created from it a distinctive Latin cultural tradition.

The most prominent figure in the late republic was Cicero, who combined his active life as lawyer and politician with an abiding devotion to Stoic philosophy. In the Stoics' belief in divine providence, morality, and duty to one's allotted role in the universe, Cicero found a rational basis for his deep commitment to public life. In a series of written dialogues, Cicero presented Stoic values in a form that created a

CHRONOLOGY

The End of the Republic

135–81 B.C.E.	Revolts against the republic
133–121 B.C.E.	Gracchi reform programs
107 B.C.E.	Gaius Marius elected consul
91–82 B.C.E.	Social War and civil war (Marius vs. Sulla)
82–79 B.C.E.	Sulla rules as dictator
79–27 B.C.E.	Era of civil wars
63 B.C.E.	Cicero elected consul
60 B.C.E.	First triumvirate (Pompey, Crassus, Caesar)
59 B.C.E.	Caesar elected consul
45 B.C.E.	Caesar defeats Pompey's forces
44 B.C.E.	Caesar is assassinated
43 B.C.E.	Second triumvirate (Mark Antony, Lepidus, Octavian)
42 B.C.E.	Octavian and Mark Antony defeat Cassius and Brutus at Philippi
31 B.C.E.	Octavian defeats Mark Antony and Cleopatra at Actium
27 B.C.E.	Octavian is declared Augustus

This mosaic from Pompeii, depicting a human skull above a butterfly that sits on the rim of a wheel, represents how brief and fickle is human life. Above the skull is a level from which the symbols of power (scepter and royal cloak) and of poverty (a beggar's staff and sack) hang in balance. In death everyone is on the same level.

Latin philosophical language freed from slavish imitation to Greek. He also wrote a number of works of political philosophy, particularly *The Republic* and *The Laws,* in conscious imitation of Plato's concern for the proper order of society. The universe, while perhaps not fully intelligible, was nonetheless rational, and reason had to be the basis for society and its laws.

The same concerns for virtue are evident in the writings of two great historians of the late republic, Sallust (86–ca. 34 B.C.E.) and Livy (59 B.C.E.–17 C.E.). Sallust was a supporter of Julius Caesar, who had written his own stylistically powerful histories of the Gallic and civil wars. For Sallust as well as for his younger contemporary, Livy, the chaos of civil war was the direct result of moral corruption and the decline that followed the successes of the empire. For Sallust, the moral failing was largely that of the Senate and its members, who trampled the plebs in their quest for power and personal glory. Livy, who was much more conservative, condemned plebeian demagogues as well as power-hungry senators. Only aristocratic conservatives who, like Cato, had stood for the ancient Roman traditions merited praise. In the second century B.C.E. the Greek historian Polybius had been fascinated with the rise of the Roman Republic to world supremacy. A century later, the Roman historians were even more fascinated with its decline.

A different kind of morality dominated the work of Lucretius (ca. 100–55 B.C.E.), the greatest poet of the late republic. Just as Cicero had molded Stoicism into a Roman civic philosophy, Lucretius presented Epicurean materialist philosophy as a Roman alternative to the hunger for power, wealth, and glory. In his great poem *On the Nature of Things,* Lucretius presented the Epicurean's thoroughly physical understanding of the universe. He described its atomic composition, the evolution of humanity from brutish beginnings to civilization, and the evil effects not only of greed and ambition but also of religion. All that exists is material reality, he believed. He also believed that religion, whether the state-supported cults of ancient Rome or the exotic cults introduced from the east, played on mortals' fear of death, a fear that was irrational emotionalism. "Death is nothing to us," Lucretius wrote. "It is only the natural fulfillment of life."

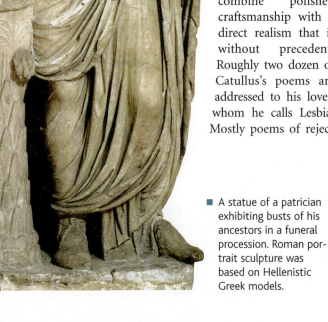

A statue of a patrician exhibiting busts of his ancestors in a funeral procession. Roman portrait sculpture was based on Hellenistic Greek models.

Emotion was precisely the goal of another poetic tradition of the late republic, that of the *neoteric* or new-style poets, especially Catullus (ca. 84–ca. 54 B.C.E.). Avoiding politics or moralistic philosophy, the poets created short, striking lyric poems that, although inspired by Hellenistic poetry, combine polished craftsmanship with a direct realism that is without precedent. Roughly two dozen of Catullus's poems are addressed to his lover, whom he calls Lesbia. Mostly poems of rejection and disillusion, they are both artful and direct, a cry from the heart, but from a very sophisticated heart:

My lady says that she wants to marry no one so much as me,
Not even should Jupiter himself ask her.
So says she. But what a woman says to her eager lover
Should be written in the wind and rushing water.

One of the most striking differences between such Latin poetry and its Greek antecedents is the reality and individuality of the persons and relationships expressed. Lesbia and the other individuals in Catullus's poems are both real people and universal representatives of humanity. Such poetry could exist only because the late republic produced women sufficiently educated and independent to appreciate it.

The same interest in the individual affected the way artists of the late republic borrowed from Greek art. Since Etruscan times, Romans had commemorated their ancestors in wax or wooden busts displayed in the atria of their homes. Hellenistic artists concentrated on the ideal, but Romans cherished the individual. The result was a portraiture that caught the personality of the individual's face even while portraying him or her as one of a type. Statues of the ideal nude, the armored warrior, or the citizen in his simple toga followed the proportions and conventions of Hellenistic sculpture. The heads, however, created in a hard, dry style, are as unique and personal as the characters that live in Catullus's lyric poems. They show the strengths and weaknesses and the stresses and the privileges that marked the last generation of the Roman Republic.

THE AUGUSTAN AGE AND THE *PAX ROMANA*

It took Octavian two years following his victory at Actium in 31 B.C.E. to eliminate remaining pockets of resistance and to work out a system to reconcile his rule with Roman constitutional traditions without surrendering any of his power. That power rested on three factors: his immense wealth, which he used to secure support; his vast following among the surviving elites as well as among the populares; and his total command of the army. His power also rested on the exhaustion of the Roman people, who were eager, after decades of civil strife, to return to peace and stability. Remembering the fate of Julius Caesar, however, Octavian had no intention of rekindling opposition by establishing an overt monarchy. Instead, in 27 B.C.E., as he himself put it in the autobiographical inscription he had erected outside his mausoleum years later, he returned the republic from his own charge to the Senate and the people of Rome. In turn, the Senate decreed him the title of *Augustus,* meaning "exalted."

This decree meant that Augustus, as Octavian was now called, continued to rule no less strongly than before, but he did so not through any autocratic office or title—he preferred to be called simply the "first citizen," or **princeps**—but by preserving the form of the traditional Roman magistracies. For four years, he rested his authority on consecutive terms as consul, and after 23 B.C.E. held a life position as tribune. The Senate granted him proconsular command of the provinces of Gaul, Spain, Syria, and Egypt, which were the major sources of imperial wealth and the locations of more than three-quarters of the Roman army. Later the Senate declared his imperium, or command, of these "imperial"

IMAGE DISCOVERY

Imperial Propaganda

This statue of Augustus found in the villa of his wife Livia at Prima Porta in Rome is a masterpiece of propaganda: Although not a great warrior he is shown in armor with a breast plate covered in mythical figures. In the center of the plate Augustus's stepson receives from a defeated Parthian Roman banners conquered a century earlier. Seated female figures represent conquered Gauls and Iberians, while gods fly above a figure of Earth who cradles two infants. What message would this statue convey to Romans who saw it?

DOCUMENT

Augustus on His Accomplishments

provinces superior to that of any governors of other provinces. Thus Augustus, through the power of the plebeian office of tribune, stood as the permanent protector of the Roman people. As either consul or proconsul, he held the command of the army and the basis of the ancient patrician authority. He was the first and greatest emperor.

The Senate's formalities deceived no one. Augustus's power was absolute. However, by choosing not to exercise it in an absolutist manner, he forged a new constitutional system that worked well for him and for his successors. By the end of his extraordinarily long reign of 41 years, few people living could remember the days of the republic and fewer still mourned its passing. Under Augustus and his successors, the empire enjoyed two centuries of stability and peace, the *Pax Romana.*

The Empire Renewed

Cicero had sought in vain a concord of the orders, a settlement of the social and political frictions of the empire through the voluntary efforts of a public-minded oligarchy. Augustus, however, imposed from above what could not happen voluntarily, reforming the Roman state, society, and culture.

The Senate. Key to Augustus's program of renewal was the Senate, which he made, if not a partner, then a useful subordinate in his reform. He gradually reduced the number of senators, which had grown to more than 1000, to 600. In the process, he eliminated the unfit and incompetent, as well as the impoverished and those who failed to show the appropriate reverence or *pietas* toward the princeps. At the same time, he made membership hereditary, although he continued to appoint individuals of personal integrity, ability, and wealth to the body. Under Augustus and his successors, access to the Senate became easier and more rapid than ever before, and the body was constantly renewed by the admission of wealthy sons of provincials and even of freed slaves. Most conspicuous among the "new men" to enter the Senate under Augustus were the wealthy leaders of Italian cities and colonies. The small-town notables formed the core of Augustus's supporters and worked most closely with him to renew the Roman elite.

Augustus also shared with the Senate the governance of the empire, although again not on equal footing. The Senate named governors to the peaceful provinces, while Augustus named commanders to those frontier imperial provinces where were stationed most of the legions. Senators themselves served as provincial governors and military commanders. The Senate also functioned as a court of law in important cases. Still in all, the Senate remained a creature of the emperor, seldom asserting itself even when asked to do so by Augustus or his successors and competing within its own ranks to see who could be first to do the emperor's bidding. "Men fit for slaves!" was how Augustus's successor Tiberius disgustedly described senators.

The Equites. Augustus undertook an even more fundamental reform of the equites, those wealthy businessmen, bankers, and tax collectors who had vied with the senatorial aristocracy since the reforms of Tiberius Gracchus. After Actium many equites found themselves proscribed—sentenced to death or banishment—and had their property confiscated. Augustus began to rebuild their ranks by enrolling a new generation of successful merchants and speculators, who became the foundation of his administration. Equestrians formed the backbone of the officer corps of the army, of the treasury, and of the greatly expanded imperial administration. The equestrian order was open at both ends. Freedmen and soldiers who acquired sufficient wealth moved into the order, and the most successful and accomplished equestrians were promoted to the Senate. Still, the price for a renewed equestrian order was its removal from the political arena. No longer was provincial tax collection farmed out to companies of equestrian publicans, nor were they allowed a role in executive or judicial deliberations. For most, the changes were a small price to pay for security, standing, and avenues to lucrative employment. Small wonder that emperors often had difficulty persuading the most successful equites to give up their positions for the more public but less certain life of a senator.

The Army. The land crisis had provoked much of the unrest in the late republic, and after Actium, Augustus had to satisfy the needs of the loyal soldiers of his 60 legions. Drawing on his immense wealth, acquired largely from the estates of his proscripted enemies, he pensioned off 32 legions, sending them to colonies he purchased for them throughout the empire. The remaining 28 legions became a permanent professional army stationed in imperial provinces. In time, the normal period of enlistment became fixed at 20 years, after which time Augustus provided the legionnaires with land and enough cash to settle among the notables of their colonies. Augustus also enrolled more than 100,000 noncitizens into auxiliary units stationed in the imperial provinces. Auxiliaries served for 25 years and upon retirement were rewarded with colonies and Roman citizenship. Finally, Augustus established as his personal military force in and around Rome a small, elite unit, the praetorian guard. Initially, the praetorians protected the emperors; in later reigns, they would make them.

The measures created a permanent solution to the problem of the citizen-soldier of the late republic. Veteran colonies—all built as model Roman towns with their central forum, baths, temples, arenas, and theaters as well as their outlying villas and farms—helped Romanize the far provinces of the empire. The colonies, unlike the independent colonies of Greece in an earlier age, remained an integral part of the Roman state. Thus Romanization and political integration went hand in hand, uniting through peaceful means an empire first acquired by arms. Likewise, ambitious provincials, through service as auxiliaries and later as citizens, acquired a stake in the destiny of Rome.

Not every citizen, of course, could find prosperity in military service and a comfortable retirement. The problem of urban poverty in Rome continued to grow. By the time of Augustus, the capital city had reached a population of per-

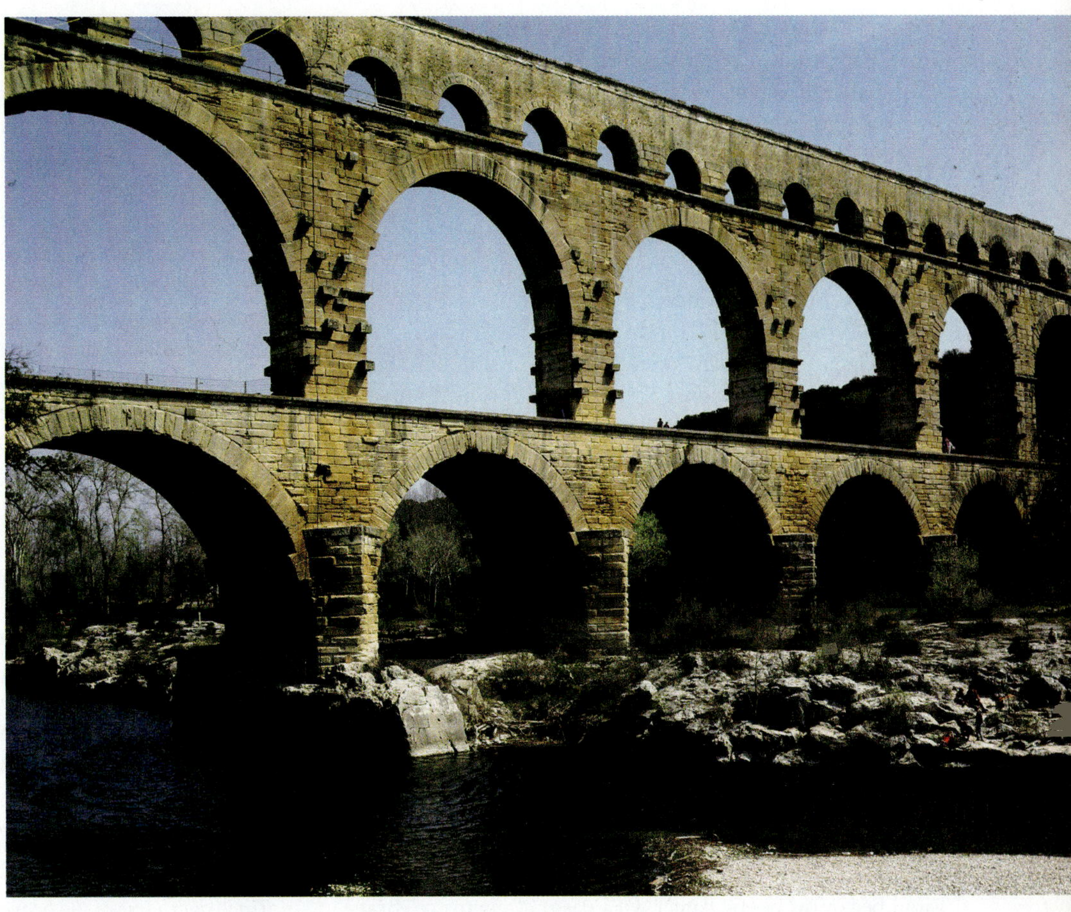

■ The Pont du Gard is part of an aqueduct constructed ca. 50 C.E. to carry mountain water from the source of the river Eure at Uzès to Nîmes some 50 kilometers away. This masterpiece of Roman engineering stands almost 50 meters high and its longest level is 275 meters.

haps 600,000 people. A tiny minority relaxed in comfortable homes built on the Palatine. Tens of thousands more crammed into wooden and brick tenements and jostled each other in the crowded, noisy streets. Employment was hard to find, since free laborers had difficulty competing against slaves. The emperors, their power as tribunes making them protectors of the poor, provided more than 150,000 resident citizens with a basic dole of wheat brought from Egypt. They also built aqueducts to provide water to the city. In addition, the emperors constructed vast public recreation centers. The centers included both the sumptuous baths—which were combination bathing facilities, health clubs, and brothels—and arenas such as colosseums, where 50,000 spectators could watch gladiatorial displays, and the Circus Maximus, where a quarter of the city's population could gather at once to watch chariot races. Such mass gatherings replaced the plebeian assemblies of the republic as the occasions on which the populace could express its will. Few emperors were foolish enough to ignore the wishes of the crowd roared out in the Circus.

Divine Augustus. Augustus's renewal of Rome rested on a religious reform. After the death of Lepidus in 12 B.C.E., he assumed the office of pontifex maximus and used it to direct a reinvigoration of Roman religion. He restored numerous temples and revived ancient Roman cults that had fallen into neglect during the chaos of the civil wars. He established a series of public religious festivals, reformed priesthoods, and encouraged citizens to participate in the traditional cults of Rome.

Augustus's goals in all the religious reforms were twofold. First, after decades of public authority controlled by violence and naked aggression, he was determined to restore the traditions of Roman piety, morality, sacred order, and faith in the relationship between the gods and Roman destiny. A second and equally important goal was Augustus's promotion of his own cult. His adoptive father, Julius Caesar, had been deified after his death, and Augustus had benefited from the association with a divine ancestor. His own genius, or guiding spirit, received special devotion in temples throughout the west dedicated to "Rome and Augustus." In the east, citizens and noncitizens alike worshiped him as a living god. In this manner, the emperor became identical with the state, and the state religion was closely akin to emperor worship. Augustus and virtually all of the emperors after him were worshiped after death as official deities in Rome itself.

Closely related to his fostering of traditional cults was Augustus's attempt to restore traditional Roman virtues, especially within the family. Like the reformers of the late republic, he believed that the declining power of the paterfamilias was at the root of much that was wrong with Rome. To reverse the trend and to restore the declining population of free Italians, Augustus attempted to encourage marriage, procreation, and the firm control of husbands over wives. He imposed penalties for those who chose not to marry and bestowed rewards on those who produced large families. He enacted laws to prevent women from having extramarital affairs and even exiled his own daughter and granddaughter for promiscuity.

Poetry and Patronage. Augustus actively patronized those writers who shared his conservative religious and ethical values and who might be expected to glorify the princeps, and he used his power to censor and silence writers he considered immoral. Chief among the favored were the poets Virgil (70–19 B.C.E.) and Horace (65–8 B.C.E.). Each came from provincial and fairly modest origins, although both received excellent educations. Each lost his property in the proscriptions and confiscations during the civil wars, but their poetry eventually won them the favor of Augustus. In return, through their poetry in praise of the emperor, Horace and Virgil conferred immortality on Augustus.

Horace celebrated Augustus's victory at Actium, his reform of the empire, and reestablishment of the ancient cults that had brought Rome divine favor. In Horace's poems, Augustus is almost a god. His deeds are compared to those of the great heroes of Roman legend and judged superior. Interspersed with the poems praising Augustus are poems of great beauty praising the love of both boys and girls and the enjoyment of wine and music. To Horace, the glories of the new age inaugurated by Augustus with the secular games of 17 B.C.E. included not only the splendor of empire but also the enjoyment of privileged leisure.

Virgil began his poetic career with pastoral poems celebrating the joys of rural life and the bitterness of the loss of lands in the civil wars. By 40 B.C.E. he was turning to greater themes. In his fourth *Eclogue* he announced the birth of a child, a child who would usher in a new golden age. This prophetic poem may have anticipated the birth of a son to Octavian's sister and Mark Antony; it may simply have been an expression of hope for renewal. Later, under the patronage of Maecenas and Augustus, Virgil turned directly to glorify Augustus and the new age. The ultimate expression of this effort was the *Aeneid*, an epic consciously intended to serve for the Roman world the role of the Homeric poems in the Greek.

As he reworked the legend of Aeneas—a Trojan hero who escaped the destruction of the city, wandered throughout the Mediterranean, and ultimately came to Latium—Virgil presented a panoramic history of Rome and its destiny. Unlike the Homeric heroes Achilles and Odysseus, who were driven by their own search for glory, Virgil's Aeneas was driven by his piety, that is, his duty toward the gods and his devotion to his father. Aeneas had to follow his destiny, which was the destiny of Rome, to rule the world in harmony and justice. In the midst of his wanderings, Aeneas (like Odysseus before him) entered the underworld to speak with his dead father. There he saw a vision of Rome's greatness to come. He saw the great heroes of Rome, including Augustus, "son of a god," and he was told of the particular mission of Rome:

Let others fashion in bronze more lifelike, breathing images
Let others (as I believe they will) draw living faces from marble
Others shall plead cases better and others will better
Track the course of the heavens and announce the rising stars.
Remember, Romans, your task is to rule the peoples
This will be your art: to teach the habit of peace
To spare the defeated and to subdue the haughty.

The finest of the poets who felt the heavy hand of Augustus's disfavor was Ovid (43 B.C.E.–17 C.E.), the great Latin poet of erotic love. In *Art of Love* and *Amores*, he cheerfully preached the art of seduction and adultery. He delighted in poking irreverent fun at everything from the sanctity of Roman marriage to the serious business of warfare. In his great *Metamorphoses*, a series of artfully told myths, he parodied the heroic epic, mocking with grotesque humor the very material Virgil used to create the *Aeneid*. By 8 C.E. Augustus had had enough. He exiled the witty poet to Tomis, a miserable frontier post on the Black Sea. There Ovid spent the last nine years of his life, suffering from the harsh climate, the constant danger of nomadic attacks, and, most of all, the pain of exile from the center of the civilization he loved. Exactly what offense he had committed is not clear. Perhaps for Augustus what was most intolerable was that, in spite of the emperor's efforts to foster an immortal poetic tradition glorifying the Roman virtues, Ovid was clearly appreciated by his contemporaries as the greatest poet of the age.

■ A mosaic from North Africa depicting Virgil, flanked by two Muses, writing his *Aeneid*. On his right is Calliope, Muse of Epic Poetry, and on his left is Melpomene, the Muse of Tragedy.

Augustus's Successors

Horace and Virgil may have made Augustus's fame immortal. His flesh was not. The problem of succession occupied him throughout much of his long reign and was never satisfactorily solved. Since the princeps was not a specific office but a combination of offices and honors held together by military might and religious aura, formal dynastic succession was impossible. Instead, Augustus attempted to select a blood relative as successor, include him in his reign, and have him voted the various offices and dignities that constituted his own position.

Unfortunately, Augustus outlived all of his first choices. His nephew and adopted son Marcellus, to whom he married his only child, Julia, died in 23 B.C.E. He then married Julia to his old associate Agrippa and began to groom him for the position, but Agrippa died in 12 B.C.E. Lucius and Gaius, the sons of Julia and Agrippa, also died young. Augustus's final choice, his stepson Tiberius (14–37 C.E.), proved to be a gloomy and unpopular successor but nevertheless was a competent ruler under whom the machinery of the empire functioned smoothly. The continued smooth functioning of the empire even under the subsequent members of Augustus's family—the mad Gaius, also known as Caligula (37–41 C.E.); the bookish but competent Claudius (41–54 C.E.); and initially under Nero (54–68 C.E.)—is a tribute to the soundness of Augustus's constitutional changes and the vested interest that the descendants of Augustus's military and aristocratic supporters had in them. Nero, however, became more than even they could bear.

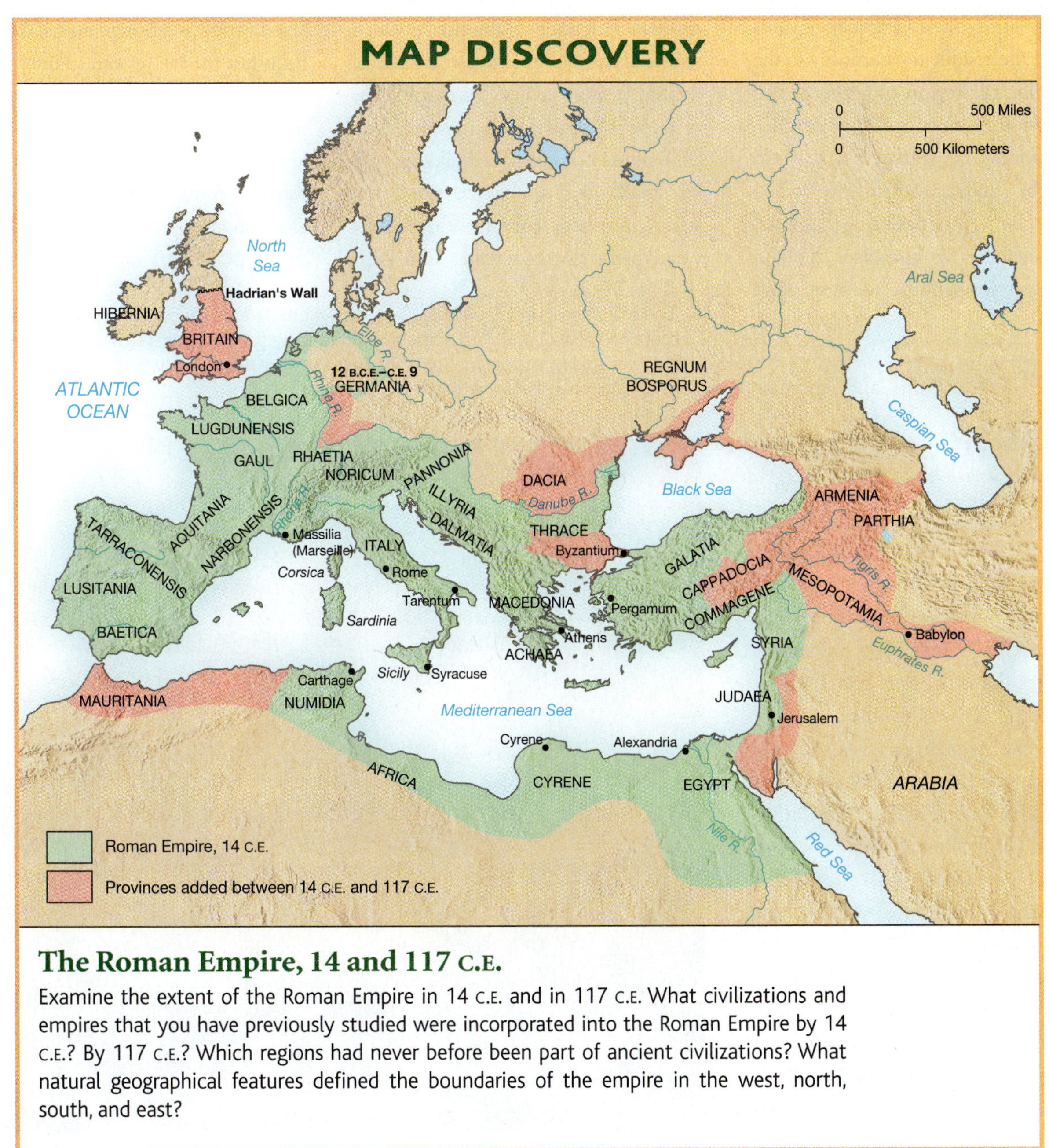

The Roman Empire, 14 and 117 C.E.

Examine the extent of the Roman Empire in 14 C.E. and in 117 C.E. What civilizations and empires that you have previously studied were incorporated into the Roman Empire by 14 C.E.? By 117 C.E.? Which regions had never before been part of ancient civilizations? What natural geographical features defined the boundaries of the empire in the west, north, south, and east?

A DAY IN THE *PAX ROMANA*—HERCULANEUM

A CLOSER LOOK

The street scene in the picture opposite records a moment arrested in time: 24 August 79 C.E. That morning Vesuvius, the great volcano whose summit towers only five miles from the small seaside resort town of Herculaneum. exploded in a tremendous eruption of fire, ash, pumice, and hot gases that rose in a mushroom-like cloud some twelve miles into the atmosphere. Prevailing winds brought the residue down mostly to the east, filling the region of Oplontis and the town of Pompeii with hot ash. But that evening, "a fearful black cloud ripped by sudden bursts of fire" rolled down the mountainside toward Herculaneum. This hot, black cloud—reaching a temperature of more than 750° F—was a wave of ash and pumice mixed with limestone, mud, and rock. Six successive waves swept through the town, burying it more than 65 feet deep. As it cooled into solid rock, it trapped not only stone structures but often even metal, wood, and cloth, preserving them to the present day. As archaeologists patiently chip away the stone, the city reemerges exactly as it was on its final day during the height of the Roman Empire.

Here as nowhere else we can sense what living in the Roman world meant to rich and poor alike. Preserved under the mass of pumice is the Villa of the Papyri, a vast suburban mansion that sprawls 800 feet along the Bay of Naples. Its magnificent peristyle, its fine Greek bronzes and marble busts, its complex aqueduct and hydraulic system, and its marble-floored library containing over 1700 papyrus scrolls, all reflect the extraordinary opulence of the great families, those who benefited most from the *Pax Romana* or Roman peace.

Standing in marked contrast is the cheaply constructed Trellis House. In the 22-foot frontage, tiny inner courtyard, and two dark floors of this house, which sheltered two families, we get a sense of the life of more ordinary urban Italians of the first century of the common era. This flimsy wood-frame building with its small, low rooms averaging ten square feet still contains the simple wood beds, clothes cabinet, and cupboard complete with utensils, glassware, and cups used by the inhabitants. The rope by which the families, too poor to tie into the town's aqueduct, drew water from a well in the courtyard lies coiled around its windlass.

A visitor to Herculaneum can wander the streets and visit the shops exactly as they were on that August day. Wine jugs and a variety of cheeses, nuts, cakes, and fruits line the shelves and countertops of the town's numerous snack bars or wine shops. In the bakeries, ovens almost identical to those used today in nearby Naples produced bread and pastries. Other shops sold vegetables, fruits, grain, and cloth. In small workshops craftsmen

■ One of Pompeii's many *thermopolia*—thought to be food shops or "bars." The terracotta containers (*dolia*) sunk into a masonry counter are believed to have contained hot food that was sold to customers. Some thermopolia have decorated back rooms that may have functioned as dining rooms.

■ A street scene in Herculaneum completely excavated and restored to its appearance on 24 August 79 C.E.

cut gems, made and repaired metal objects, and painted decorative panels for their wealthier neighbors. In all, the tools and merchandise lie as they were left that day by their terrified owners.

Both rich and poor could rub shoulders in either of the town's two bathhouses, one centrally located near the forum, the other near the marina beyond the town walls. There men could exercise or play ball in an open courtyard, then choose a warm or hot bath to be followed by a cold plunge in the *frigidarium.* Similar but smaller facilities were available in the women's portion of the bath. Throughout the building, an elaborate hydraulic system of boilers, pipes, and drains supplied the baths with water at the proper temperature.

Everywhere the spirit of the departed inhabitants lingers in the graffiti written on Herculaneum's walls: "To live is vain" on the wall of a wine shop; professions of undying love or scurrilous attacks on rivals; obscenities in the brothel attached to the suburban bath. Even more eloquent are the silent remains of more than a hundred victims of the disaster, most found near the marina where they fled in a desperate attempt to escape by sea. Even in death, the contrast between rich and poor is striking. Near the marina lay the remains of a wealthy woman about 45 years old, still wearing two gold rings, bracelets, and earrings. Analysis showed her to be tall, well nourished, and in perfect health. Not too far distant were found the remains of a fourteen-year-old slave girl, still cradling the skeleton of a seven-month-old infant who was her charge. The slave had endured a hard life. As an infant she had suffered severe malnutrition, possibly the result of abandonment. Her skeleton also showed the stresses of excessive work for a girl her age. Her owners were certainly getting their money's worth from her.

The streets, buildings, and remains of the inhabitants of Herculaneum strike us with an immediacy often missing in ancient history. Here we observe the ordinary activities of Romans living in a privileged corner of the empire. Their ancestors had survived the turmoil of the republic's collapse. Most lived far removed from the great events of empire and conquest. And yet in their daily lives, their homes, their shops, their luxuries, and their amusements, they show the vitality of Roman civilization, a civilization that ruled the world by the force of its armies but also by the attraction of its culture.

Profligate, vicious, and paranoid, Nero divided his time between murdering his relatives and associates—including his mother, his aunt, his wife, his tutors, and eventually his most capable generals—and squandering his vast wealth on mad attempts to gain recognition as a great poet, actor, singer, and athlete. (When he competed in games, other contestants wisely lost.) Finally, in 68 C.E., the exasperated commanders in Gaul, Spain, and Africa revolted. Once more war swept the empire. Nero slit his own throat (one of his last sentences was "Dead, and so great an artist!"), and in the next year, the "Year of the Four Emperors," four men in quick succession won the office, only to lose their lives just as quickly. Finally, in 70 C.E., Vespasian (69–79 C.E.), the son of a "new man" who had risen through the ranks to the command in Egypt, secured the principate and restored order.

The first emperors had rounded off the frontiers of the empire, transforming the client states of Cappadocia, Thrace, Commagene, and Judaea in the east and Mauritania in North Africa into provinces. Claudius (41–54 C.E.) presided over the conquest of Britain in 43 C.E. The emperors introduced efficient means of governing and protecting the empire, and tied together its inhabitants—roughly 50 million in the time of Augustus—in networks of mutual dependence and common interest. Augustus established peaceful relations with the Parthian Empire, which permitted unhampered trade among China, India, and Rome. In the west, after a disastrous attempt to expand the empire to the Elbe ended in the loss of three legions in 9 C.E., the frontier was fixed at the Rhine. The northern border stopped at the Danube. The deserts of Africa, Nubia, and southern Arabia formed the southern borders of what in the first century C.E. many saw as the "natural" boundaries of the empire.

When Vespasian's troops fought their way into Rome in vicious hand-to-hand street fighting, the populace watched with idle fascination. The violence of 69 C.E., unlike that of the previous century, involved mostly professional legions and their commanders. The rest of the empire sat back to watch. In a few restive regions of the empire, some Gauls, the Batavians along the Rhine, and die-hard Jewish rebels tried to use the momentary confusion to revolt, but by and large the empire remained stable. This stability was the greatest achievement of Augustus and his immediate successors.

The emperors of the Flavian dynasty—Vespasian and his sons and successors Titus (79–81 C.E.) and Domitian (81–96 C.E.)—were stern and unpretentious provincials who restored the authority and dignity of their office, although they also did away with many of the trappings of republican legitimacy that Augustus and his immediate successors had used. They solidified the administrative system, returned the legions to their fairly permanent posts, and opened the highest reaches of power as never before to provincial elites. After the Flavian emperors, the Antonines (96–193 C.E.)—especially Trajan (98–117 C.E.), Hadrian (117–138 C.E.), and Antoninus Pius (138–161 C.E.)—ruled for what has been termed "the period in the history of the world during which the human race was most happy and prosperous"—the **Antonine dynasty.**

Breaking the Peace. Not all was peaceful during this period. Trajan initiated a new and final expansion of the imperial frontiers. Between 101 and 106 C.E. he conquered Dacia (modern Romania). He resumed war with the Parthians, conquering the provinces of Armenia and Mesopotamia by 116 C.E. During the second century, the Palestinian Jews revolted in 115–117 C.E. and again in 132–135 C.E. The emperor Hadrian put down the second revolt and expelled the surviving Jews from Judaea. Along both the eastern and western frontiers legions had to contend with sporadic border incidents. However, within the borders a system of Roman military camps, towns, and rural estates constituted a remarkably heterogeneous and prosperous civilization.

Administering the Empire. The imperial government of the vast empire was as oppressive as it was primitive. Taxes, rents, forced labor service, military levies and requisitions, and outright extortion weighed heavily on its subjects. Still, fewer than 1000 officials ever held direct official command within the empire at any time. The commanders were largely the governors and officials of the senatorial provinces, but even they had little direct control over the daily lives of the governed. The daily exercise of government fell to local elites, the army, and members of the imperial household.

To a considerable extent, the inhabitants of the empire continued to be governed by the indigenous elites, whose cooperation Rome won by giving them broad autonomy. Thus Hellenistic cities managed their own affairs under the supervi-

CHRONOLOGY

The Roman Empire

Julio-Claudian Period	Augustus (27 B.C.E.–14 C.E.)
	Tiberius (14–37 C.E.)
	Caligula (37–41)
	Claudius (41–54)
	Nero (54–68)
Year of the Four Emperors	69 C.E.
Flavian Period, 69–96 C.E.	Vespasian (69–79)
	Titus (79–81)
	Domitian (81–96)
Antonine Period, 96–193	Trajan (98–117)
	Hadrian (117–138)
	Antoninus Pius (138–161)
	Marcus Aurelius (161–180)
	Commodus (180–192)

sion of essentially amateur Roman governors. Local town councils in Gaul, Germany, and Spain supervised the collection of taxes, maintained public works projects, and kept the peace. In return for their participation in Roman rule, the elites received Roman citizenship, a prize that carried prestige, legal protection, and the promise of further advancement in the Roman world.

In those imperial provinces controlled directly by the emperor the army was much more in evidence, and the professional legions were the ultimate argument of imperial tax collectors and imperial representatives, or *procurators.* Moreover, as the turmoil of the Year of the Four Emperors amply demonstrated, the military was the ultimate foundation of imperial rule itself. Still, soldiers were as much farmers as fighters. Legions usually remained in the same location for years, and veterans' colonies sprang up around military camps. The settlements created a strong Roman presence and blurred the distinction between army post and town.

Finally, much of the governing of the empire was done by the vast households of the Roman elite, particularly that of the princeps. Freedmen and slaves from the emperor's household often governed vast regions, oversaw imperial estates, and managed imperial factories and mines. The slaves and former slaves were loyal, competent, and easily controlled. The descendants of the old Roman nobility might look down their noses at imperial freedmen, but they obeyed their orders.

The empire worked because it rewarded those who worked with it and left alone those who paid their taxes and kept quiet. Local elites, auxiliary soldiers, and freedmen could aspire to rise to the highest ranks of the power elite. Seldom has a ruling elite made access to its ranks so open to those who cooperated with it. As provincials were drawn into the Roman system, they were also drawn into the world of Roman culture. Proper education in Latin and Greek, the ability to hold one's own in philosophical discussion, the absorption of Roman styles of dress, recreation, religious cults, and life itself—all were essential for ambitious provincials. Thus, in the course of the first century C.E., the disparate portions of the empire competed not to free themselves from the Roman yoke, but to become Roman themselves.

RELIGIONS FROM THE EAST

The same openness that permitted the spread of Latin letters and Roman baths to distant Gaul and the shores of the Black Sea provided paths of dissemination for other, distinctly un-Roman religious traditions. For many in the empire, the traditional rituals offered to the household gods and the state cults of Jupiter, Mars, and the other official deities were insufficient foci of religious devotion. Many educated members of the elite

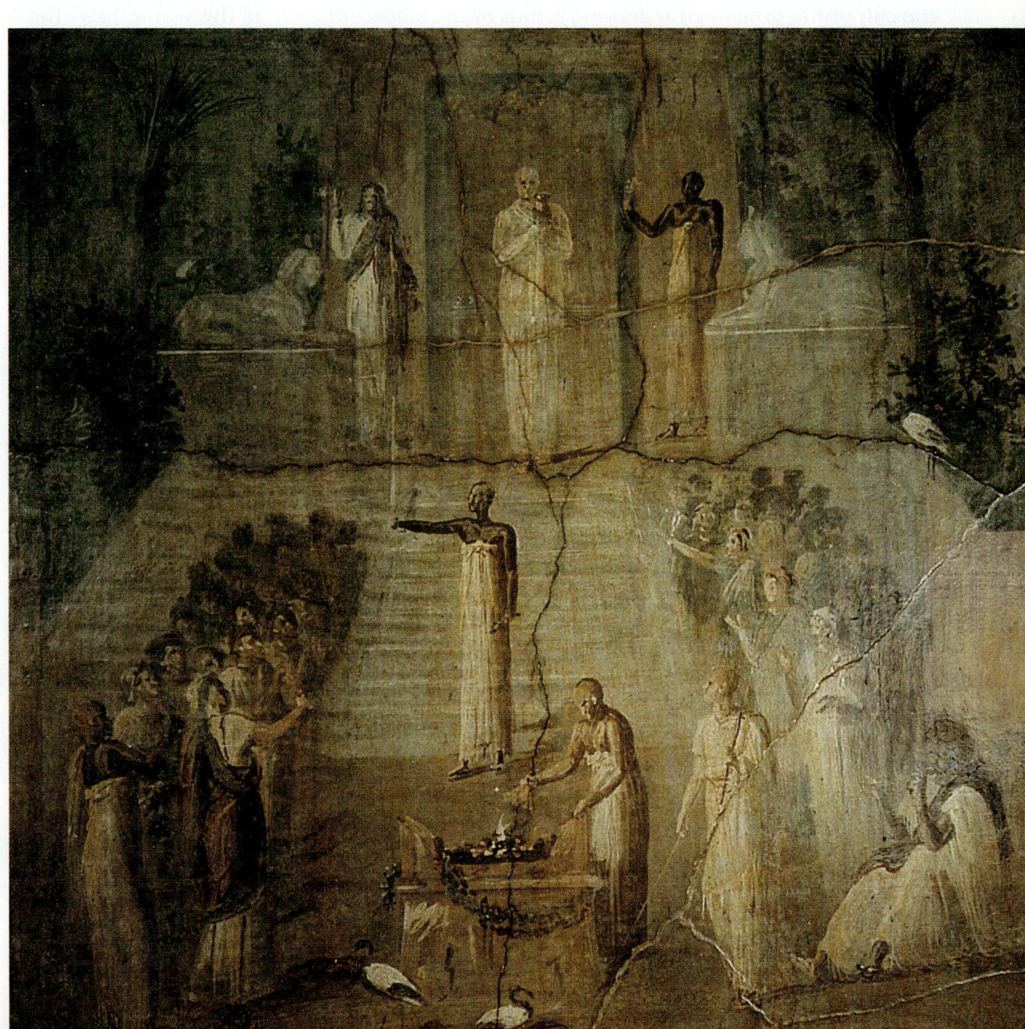

A painting from Herculaneum depicts priests of the cult of Isis, an Egyptian goddess of procreation and birth. By the time of the empire, many Romans had turned from the spiritually unrewarding state religion to eastern mystery cults.

were actually vague monotheists, believing in a supreme deity even while convinced that the ancient traditional cults were essential aspects of patriotism, the cornerstone of the piety necessary to preserve public order. Many others in the empire sought personal, emotional bonds with the divine world.

As noted in Chapter 4, in the second century B.C.E. the Roman world had been caught up in the emotional cult of Dionysus—an ecstatic, personal, and liberating religion entirely unlike the official Roman cults. Again in the first century C.E., so-called **mystery cults**—that is, religions promising immediate, personal contact with a deity that would bring immortality—spread throughout the empire. Some were officially introduced into Rome as part of its open polytheism and included the Anatolian Cybele or great mother-goddess cult, which was present in Rome from the late third century B.C.E. Devotees underwent a ritual in which they were bathed in the blood of a bull or a ram, thereby obtaining immortality. The cult of the Egyptian goddess Isis spread throughout the Hellenistic world and to Rome in the republican period. In her temples, staffed by Egyptian priests, water from the Nile was used in elaborate rites to purify initiates. From Persia came the cult of Mithras, the ancient Indo-Iranian god of light and truth, who, as bringer of victory, found special favor with Roman soldiers and merchants eager for success in this life and immortality beyond the grave. Generally Rome tolerated the alien cults as long as they could be assimilated into, or at least reconciled in some way with, the cult of the Roman gods and the genius of the emperor.

Jewish Resistance

With one religious group such assimilation was impossible. As noted in Chapter 1, the Jews of Palestine had long refused any accommodation with the polytheistic cults of the Hellenistic kingdoms or with Rome. Roman conquerors and emperors, aware of the problems of their Hellenistic predecessors, went to considerable lengths to avoid antagonizing the small and unusual group of people. Judaea was made into a client kingdom under the puppet Herod. Jews were allowed to maintain their monotheistic cult and were excused from making sacrifices to the Roman gods.

The Old City of Jerusalem

Still, the Jewish community remained deeply divided about its relationship with the wider world and with Rome. At one end of the spectrum were the Sadducees. They were willing to work with Rome and even adopt some elements of Hellenism, as long as the services in the temple could continue. At the other end of the spectrum were the Hasidim, who rejected all compromise with Hellenistic culture and collaboration with foreign powers. Many expected the arrival of a messiah, a liberator who would destroy the Romans and reestablish the kingdom of David. One party within the Hasidim were the Pharisees, who practiced strict dietary rules and rituals to maintain the separation of Jews and Gentiles (literally, "the peoples," that is, all non-Jews). The most prominent figure in this movement was Hillel (ca. 30 B.C.E.–10 C.E.), a Jewish scholar from Babylon who came to Jerusalem as a teacher of the law. He began a tradition of legal and scriptural interpretation that, in an expanded version centuries later, became the Talmud. Hillel was also a moral teacher who taught peace and love, not revolt. "Whatever is hateful to you, do not to your fellow man: this is the whole Law; the rest is mere commentary," he taught. He also looked beyond the Jewish people and was concerned with the rest of humanity. "Be of the disciples of Aaron; loving peace and pursuing peace; loving mankind and bringing them near to the Torah."

For all their insistence on purity and separation from other peoples, the Pharisees did not advocate violent revolt against

Spoils from the Temple in Jerusalem, a marble relief from the Arch of Titus. The arch was begun by Titus's father, the emperor Vespasian, to commemorate Titus's victory over the Jews in 78 C.E.

Rome. They preferred to await divine intervention. Another group of Hasidim, the Zealots, were less willing to wait. After 6 C.E., when Judaea, Samaria, and Idumaea were annexed and combined into the province of Judaea administered by imperial procurators, the Zealots began to organize sporadic armed resistance to Roman rule. As ever, armed resistance was met with violent suppression. Throughout the first century C.E., clashes between Roman troops and Zealot revolutionaries grew more frequent and more widespread.

The Origins of Christianity

The already complex landscape of the Jewish religious world became further complicated by the brief career of Joshua ben Joseph (ca. 6 B.C.E.–30 C.E.), known to history as Jesus of Nazareth and to his followers as Jesus the Messiah, or the Christ.

Jesus left no body of sacred texts, and what is known about the man and the first generation of his followers comes from Greek texts written between the middle of the first century and the middle of the second. The texts include gospels, accounts of Jesus' life; letters, or epistles; and historical narratives and visionary writings by his early disciples and their immediate successors. A great number of the documents circulated in the first centuries after Jesus. In time, Christians came to accept a small number, including 4 gospels (out of perhaps 50), some 21 epistles, an account of the early community (the Acts of the Apostles), and 1 book of revelations. The writings, like those that were not ultimately accepted as official or canonical, transmit the memory of Jesus, but they do so in the context of the rapidly developing circumstances and concerns of the first generation of followers of Jesus.

The first three gospels—those of Matthew, Mark, and Luke—are called Synoptic Gospels because they tell essentially the same story. The earliest was probably that of Mark, which the authors of the other two used, along with a now lost collection of the sayings of Jesus, perhaps in Aramaic, the language of Palestinian Jews of the first century. The accounts tell the story of Jesus' teachings largely in the form of parables, or short stories with a moral, and pithy epigrams: "I am the bread of life"; "I am the good shepherd." The Gospel of John was written after the first three and presents differently from the others not only the events in Jesus' life—including some, adding others, and rearranging the chronology—but also a more elaborated image of his teaching, emphasizing the divinity of Jesus and his relationship with God.

The Gospel According to Luke

The historical narrative tradition is represented by the Book of Acts, which is a continuation of the Gospel of Luke and tells about the origins of the Christian church. Much more than simply an account of events, however, it places the developments of the early community within the context of sacred history. It is an account of the working of God through Hebrew and Roman history.

The epistles, written by various followers of Jesus and his immediate followers, are in the form of letters from church leaders to individual communities of believers. Often they are actually sermons or treatises in the form of letters, elaborating on the beliefs and practice of the various communities of followers of Jesus.

Books of revelations such as the canonical Revelation of John were visionary, symbolic literature written in times of crisis or persecution to encourage people to look beyond the sufferings of the present to an anticipated future reward. From such sources, it is difficult to separate the actual historical figure of Jesus from the images of him that developed within the communities in the following century of what have been called *Jesus people.*

Jesus came from Galilee, an area known as a Zealot stronghold. However, while Jesus preached the imminent coming of the kingdom, he did so in an entirely nonpolitical manner. He was, like many popular religious leaders, a miracle worker. When people flocked around him to see his wonders, he preached a message of peace and love of God and neighbor. His teachings were entirely within the Jewish tradition and closely resembled those of Hillel—with one major exception. Whereas many contemporary religious leaders announced the imminent coming of the messiah, Jesus' closest followers began to look to him as the messiah and expected him to liberate the Jewish people.

For roughly three years, Jesus preached in Judaea and Galilee, drawing large, excited crowds. Many of his followers pressed him to lead a revolt against Roman authority and reestablish the kingdom of David, even though he insisted that the kingdom he would establish was not of this world. Other Jews saw his claims as blasphemy and his assertion that he was the king of the Jews, even if a heavenly one, as a threat to the status quo. Jesus became more and more a figure of controversy, a catalyst for violence. Ultimately the Roman procurator, Pontius Pilate, decided that he posed a threat to law and order. Pilate, like other Roman magistrates, had no interest in the internal religious affairs of the Jews. However, he was troubled by anyone who had the potential for causing political disturbances. Pilate ordered Jesus scourged and put to death by crucifixion, a common Roman form of execution for slaves, pirates, thieves, and noncitizen troublemakers.

Spreading the Faith. The cruel death of Jesus ended the popular agitation he had stirred up, but it did not deter his closest followers. They soon announced that three days after his death he had risen and had appeared to them numerous times over the next several weeks. They took his resurrection as proof that he was the messiah and confirmation of his promise of eternal life to those who believed in him. Soon a small group of his followers, led by Peter (d. ca. 64 C.E.), formed another Jewish sect, preaching and praying daily in the temple. New members were initiated into this sect, soon known as Christianity, through baptism, a purification rite in which the initiate was submerged briefly in flowing water. They also shared a ritual meal in which bread and wine were distributed to members. Otherwise, they remained entirely within the Jewish religious and cultural tradition, and hellenized Jews and pagans who wanted to join the sect had to observe strict Jewish law and custom.

Christianity spread beyond its origin as a Jewish sect because of the work of one man, Paul of Tarsus (ca. 5–ca. 67 C.E.), a Pharisee, a follower of the Hillel school, and an early convert to Christianity. Although Paul was an observant Jew, he was part of the wider cosmopolitan world of the empire and from birth enjoyed the privileges of Roman citizenship. He saw Christianity as a separate tradition, completing and perfecting Judaism but intended for the whole world. Non-Jewish converts, he convinced Peter and most of the other leaders, did not have to become Jews. The Christian message of salvation was to be preached to all nations and people of all estates, for "there is neither Jew nor Greek, slave nor free, male or female, for all are one in Christ Jesus."

Paul set out to spread his message, crisscrossing Asia Minor and Greece and even traveling to Rome. Wherever he went, Paul won converts and established churches, called *ecclesiae,* or assemblies. Everywhere Paul and the other disciples went they worked wonders, cast out demons, cured illnesses, and preached. In his preaching and his letters to the various churches he had established, Paul elaborated the first coherent system of theology, or beliefs, of the Christian sect. His teachings, while firmly rooted in the Jewish historical tradition, were radically new: God had created the human race, Paul taught, in the image of God and destined it for eternal life. However, by deliberate sin of the first humans, Adam and Eve, humans had lost eternal life and introduced evil and death into the world. Paul explained that even then God did not abandon his people but began, through the Jews, to prepare for their eventual redemption. That salvation was accomplished by Jesus, the son of God, through his faith, a free and unmerited gift of God to his elect. Through faith, the Christian ritual of baptism, and participation in the church, men and women could share in the salvation offered by God, Paul said.

How many conversions resulted from Paul's theological message and how many resulted from the miracles he and the other disciples worked will never be known. People of the ancient world believed firmly in the power of demons—the supernatural spirits of various types who influenced humans for good or ill. Christian preachers were recognized as having power over spirits, and people who could cast out demons were considered worth listening to. A third factor that certainly played a part in the success of conversions was the courage Christians showed in the face of persecution.

Even the tolerance and elasticity of Rome in accommodating new religions could be stretched only to a point. The Christians' belief in the divinity of their founder was no problem. Their offer of salvation to those who participated in their mysteries was only normal. But their stubborn refusal to acknowledge the existence of the other gods or to participate in the cult of the genius of the emperor was intolerable. Judaism,

PETER ANNOUNCES THE GOOD NEWS

The following passage, attributed to the apostle Peter in the book of Christian Scripture known as the Acts of the Apostles, is probably a close approximation of the earliest Christian preaching. In it, Jesus is presented as the new Moses.

Focus Questions

How does Peter explain Jesus within the Jewish tradition?
How does Peter explain the mission of Jesus?

Men of Israel, why do you stare at us, as though by our own power or piety we had made him [a paralytic who has just been cured] walk? The God of Abraham and of Isaac and of Jacob, the God of our fathers, glorified his servant Jesus, whom you delivered up and denied in the presence of Pilate, when he had decided to release him. But you denied the Holy and Righteous One, and asked for a murderer to be granted to you, and killed the Author of life, whom God raised from the dead. To this we are witnesses. And his name, by faith in his name, has made this man strong whom you see and know; and the faith which is through Jesus has given the man this perfect health in the presence of you all.

And now, brethren, I know that you acted in ignorance, as did also your rulers. But what God foretold by the mouth of all the prophets, that his Christ should suffer, he thus fulfilled. Repent therefore, and turn again, that your sins may be blotted out, that times of refreshing may come from the presence of the Lord, and that he may send the Christ appointed for you, Jesus, whom heaven must receive until the time for establishing all that God spoke by the mouth of his holy prophets from of old.

Moses said, "The Lord God will raise up for you a prophet from your brethren as he raised me up. You shall listen to him in whatever he tells you. And it shall be that every soul that does not listen to that prophet shall be destroyed from the people." And all the prophets who have spoke, from Samuel and those who came afterwards, also proclaimed these days.

You are the sons of the prophets and of the covenant which God gave to your fathers, saying to Abraham, "And in your posterity shall all the families of the earth be blessed." God, having raised up his servant, sent him to you first, to bless you in turning every one of you from your wickedness.

From Acts 3:12–26. The Holy Bible, Revised Standard Version.

■ The baptistry in the Christian Church at Dura-Europos. The architecture of the font is similar to that of a tomb. The room in which the font is constructed is separated from the assembly area of the community. The complex itself was converted from houses.

which accepted the same tenets, was generally tolerated because it was not actively seeking to convert others. Christianity was an aggressive and successful cult, attracting followers throughout the empire. It was viewed not as religion, but as subversion. Beginning during Nero's reign, Roman officials sporadically rounded up Christians, destroyed their sacred Scriptures, and executed those who refused to sacrifice to the imperial genius. But instead of decreasing the cult's appeal, persecution only aided it. For those who believed that death was birth into a new and better life, martyrdom was a reward, not a penalty. Christian men, women, and children suffered willingly, enduring unto death the most gruesome tortures Roman cruelty could devise. The strength of their convictions convinced others of the truth of their religion.

Christian Institutions. As the number of Christians increased in the face of persecution, the organization and teaching of the new faith began to evolve. Initially, the followers of Jesus had assumed that the end of the world was very near, and thus no elaborate organizational structure was needed. As time went on, a hierarchy developed within the various communities established by Paul and the other apostles. The leader of each community was the bishop, an office derived from the priestly leader of the Jewish synagogue who was responsible for both charity and the Torah. Assisted by **presbyters** (priests), deacons, and deaconesses, bishops assumed growing responsibilities as expectations for the Second Coming receded. The responsibilities included presiding over the Eucharist, or ritual meal, that was the center of Christian worship, as well as enforcing discipline and teaching.

In their preaching, bishops connected the texts of the gospels and epistles to the tradition of Jewish Scriptures, explaining that the life of Jesus was the completion and fulfillment of the Jewish tradition. Over centuries, certain gospels, epistles, and one book of revelation came to be regarded as authoritative and, together with the version of Jewish Scripture in use in Greek-speaking Jewish communities, constituted the Christian Bible.

The teaching responsibility of the bishop took on increasing importance in the course of the second and third centuries, as the original Christian message began to be challenged from the outside on moral and intellectual grounds and debated from within by differing Christian interpreters. Hellenistic moral philosophers and Roman officials condemned Christianity as immoral and, because of its rejection of the cult of the emperor and the gods of Rome, atheistic. Neoplatonists found the teachings of Christianity philosophically naive, and they mocked Christian teachers as "wool seekers, cobblers, laundry workers, and the most illiterate and rustic yokels."

Even within the Christian community, different groups interpreted the essential meaning of the new faith in contradictory ways. Monatists, for example, argued that Christians were obligated to fast and abstain from marriage until the Second Coming. Dualist **Gnostics** interpreted the Christian message as a secret wisdom, or *gnosis,* which, combined with baptism, freed men and women from their fates. Jesus, they taught, was no real man but only appeared in human form to impart to select followers the secret wisdom in opposition to Yahweh, the god of the material world.

Bishops took up the challenge of refuting external charges and settling internal debates. They met pagan attacks with their enemies' own weapons, both showing the exemplary morality of Christians by the standards of Stoic ethics and using Neoplatonic philosophical traditions to interpret the Christian message. Their leading role in defending the faith and determining what was correct, or orthodox, belief raised the importance of bishops' authority. By the end of the first century, *episcopal* (from the Greek word for "bishop") authority was understood to derive from their status as successors of the apostles. Bishops of those churches established directly by the apostles in Jerusalem, Antioch, Alexandria, and Rome—

termed *patriarchates*—claimed special authority over other, less ancient communities.

Gradually, the exalted position of the bishop and his assistants led to a distinction between the clergy—that is, those who served at the altar—and the *laity*, the rank and file of Christians. At the same time, women, who had played central roles in Jesus' ministry, were excluded from positions of authority within the clergy. In this process, the Christian community came to resemble closely the Roman patriarchal household, a resemblance that increased the appeal of the new sect to nonbelievers.

Although Christianity spread rapidly throughout the eastern Mediterranean in the first and second centuries, it remained, in the eyes of the empire's rulers, as only a minor irritation, characterized by one cultured senator as "nothing but a degenerate sort of cult carried to extravagant lengths." Its fundamental role in the transformation of the Roman world would not become clear until the third and fourth centuries.

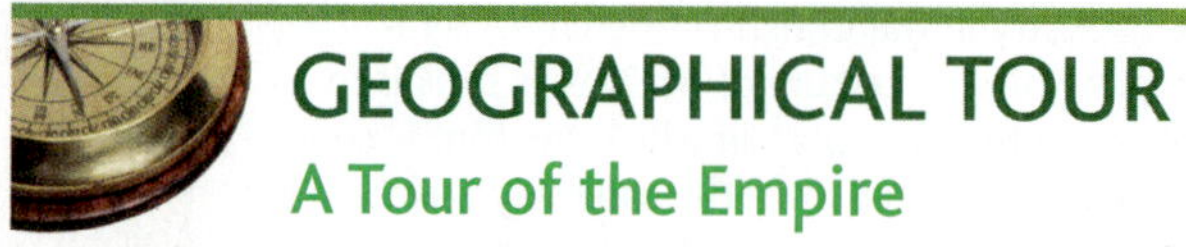

GEOGRAPHICAL TOUR

A Tour of the Empire

Each town in the sprawling empire, from York in the north of Britain to Dura-Europus on the Euphrates, was a center of Roman culture, or *Romanitas*, in provinces still closely tied to local provincial traditions. Each boasted a forum, where locals conducted business and government affairs. Each had an arena for gladiatorial games; baths; a racetrack; and a theater where Greek and Latin plays entertained the populace. Temples to the Capitoline Jupiter and to the deified emperors adorned the cities. Aqueducts brought fresh water from distant springs into the heart of the cities. Local property owners made up the senate or curia of each town in imitation of that of Rome, including both wealthy provincials who had tied their future to Rome and retired veterans whose pensions made them immediately

■ ***Map A. The Roman Empire at the Time of Hadrian.*** Hadrian's empire was a well-ordered world of provinces governed by a vast bureaucracy and held together by a common culture and the power of the imperial army.

■ Bust of the Emperor Hadrian.

part of the local gentry. Local aristocrats competed with each other in their displays of civic duty, often constructing public buildings at their own expense, dedicating statues or temples to the emperor or influential patrons, and endowing games and celebrations for the amusement of their communities.

Connecting the towns was a network of well-maintained roads frequented by imperial administrators, merchants, the idle rich, and soldiers. Beginning in 120 C.E., the roads of the empire saw a most unusual traveler: the emperor Hadrian (117–138 C.E.), who traveled to conduct an extraordinary inspection of the length and breadth of his empire (see **Map A**).

Hadrian, the adopted son and heir of Trajan, had received an excellent Greek education and was an accomplished writer, poet, connoisseur, and critic. Still, he had spent most of his early career as a successful field commander and administrator in Dacia and the lower Danube. Years of military experience in the region had made Hadrian very aware of the potential weaknesses of the vast Roman borders, and his primary interest was to inspect those military commands most critical for imperial stability.

The Western Provinces

Thus Hadrian set out west, traveling first through the provinces of Gaul, prosperous and pacific regions long integrated into the Roman world (see **Map B**). Gaul was known for its good food, its pottery manufacture, and its comfortable, if culturally slightly backward, local elites. Much of Gaul's prosperity came from supplying the legions guarding the Rhine–Danube frontier, and it was across the Rhine toward Germany, where the legions faced the barbarians of "Free Germany," that Hadrian was headed. Legions stationed at Xanten, Cologne, and Trier (see **Map B**) were far removed from the Mediterranean world that formed the heart of the empire. The dark forests, cold winters, and crude life made Germany a hardship post. Hadrian threw himself into the harsh camp life of Germany in order to bolster discipline and combat-readiness. He shared rough field rations, long marches, and simple conditions with his troops, improving their equipment even while demolishing creature comforts such as dining rooms, covered walks, and ornamental gardens erected by their commanders.

From Germany, Hadrian traveled down the Rhine through what is today Holland and then crossed over to Britain. There too defense was uppermost in his mind. Celts from the unconquered northern portion of the island had been harassing the Romanized society to the south. The emperor ordered the erection of a great wall more than 50 miles long across Britain from coast to coast (see **Map A**). The most critical eastern half of this wall, much of which still stands, was built of stone 10 feet thick and 15 feet high, while the western half was constructed of turf. Battlements, turrets, and gates, as well as garrison forts, extended the length of the wall. South of the wall, Roman Britain was studded with hundreds of Roman villas, ranging from simple country farmhouses to vast mansions with more than 60 rooms. More than a hundred towns and villages were large enough to boast walls, ranging from London, with a population of roughly 30,000, to numerous settlements of between 2000 and 10,000.

■ ***Map B. The Provinces of Gaul.*** Gaul was a vast agricultural region supplying legions posted along the Rhine River.

■ ***Map C. Spain.*** Roman Spain was a major source of gold, iron, and tin as well as a vital agricultural region.

■ ***Map D. Asia.*** Asia remained for Rome the center of Hellenistic civilization with its populous cities and vital trade routes.

No sooner had he put things straight in Britain than Hadrian returned to Gaul, paused in Nîmes in the south (see **Map B**), and then headed south toward his native Spain (see **Map C**). By the second century C.E., Spain was even more thoroughly Romanized than most of Gaul, having been an integral part of the empire since the Second Punic War. It was also far richer. Spanish mines yielded gold, iron, and tin, and Spanish estates produced grain and cattle. Since the reign of Vespasian, the residents of Spanish communities had been given some of the rights of Roman citizens, thus making them eligible for military service, a value even greater to the empire than Spain's mineral wealth. Problems with military service brought Hadrian to Spain. The populace was becoming increasingly resistant to conscription, a universal phenomenon, and Hadrian's presence strengthened the efforts of recruiters.

The Eastern Provinces

From Spain, the emperor may have crossed the Strait of Gibraltar (see **Map C**) to deal personally with a minor revolt of Moorish tribes in Mauritania, a constant low-level problem with the seminomadic peoples living on the edge of the desert. In any event, he soon set sail for the provinces of Asia (see **Map D**). There he was in the heart of the Hellenistic world so central to the empire's prosperity. Its great cities were centers of manufacture and its ports the vital links in Mediterranean trade. As in Hellenistic times, the cities were the organizing principle of the region, with local senates largely self-governing and rivalries among cities preventing the creation of any sort of provincial identities. Thus, in Asia, Hadrian worked with individual communities, showering honors and privileges on the most cooperative, checking no doubt on the financial affairs of others, and founding new communities in the Anatolian hinterland. The last activity was particularly important because, for all of the civilized glory of urban Asia, the rural areas remained strongly tied to traditions that neither Greeks nor Romans had managed to weaken. The empire remained composed of two worlds: one urban, hellenized, mercantile, and collaborationist: the other rural, traditional, exploited, and potentially separatist.

In 125 C.E., Hadrian left Asia for Greece (see **Map E**), where he participated in traditional religious rituals. Greek culture continued to be vital for Rome, and by participating in the rituals of Achaea and Athens the emperor placed himself in the traditions of the legendary Heracles and Philip of Macedon. He no doubt also seized the opportunity to audit the accounts of provincial governors and procurators, whose reputation for misuse of their powers was infamous. Finally, in 127 C.E. Hadrian returned to Rome via Sicily (see **Map E**), a prosperous amalgam of Greek and Latin cultures dominated by vast senatorial estates, or latifundia, stopping to climb Mount Etna, it was said, to see the colorful sunrise.

The restless emperor spent less than 12 months in Rome before setting out again, this time for Africa. There, as in Germany, his concern was the discipline and preparedness of

■ ***Map E. Italy and Greece.*** Italy, although economically dependent on the rest of the empire, was the vital center of the empire while Greece was honored more for its glorious past than its present importance.

■ ***Map F. Egypt.*** Throughout the Roman period, Egypt was the breadbasket of the empire, supplying Rome and other cities with essential grain.

the troops guarding the rich agricultural areas and thriving commercial centers of the coast from the marauding nomads on the edges of the desert. Shortly after that, he again went to Athens to dedicate public works projects he had undertaken as well as an altar to himself. Like all emperors in the east, Hadrian was venerated as a living god. From Greece he headed east, again crossing Asia and this time moving into Cappadocia and Syria (see **Map A**). His concern there was again defense, but against a powerful, civilized Parthian Empire, not barbarian tribes. Hadrian renewed promises of peace and friendship with the Parthian king, even returning the latter's daughter, whom Trajan had captured in the last Parthian war.

Moving south, Hadrian stopped in Jerusalem, where he dedicated a shrine to Jupiter Capitolinus on the site of the destroyed Jewish temple before heading to Egypt for an inspection trip up the Nile (see **Map F**). Egypt remained the wealthiest and the most exploited Roman province. Since the time of Augustus, Egypt had been governed directly by the imperial household, its agricultural wealth from the Nile Delta going to feed the Roman masses. At the same time, Alexandria continued to be one of the greatest cultural centers of the Roman world. That culture, however, was a fusion of Greek and Egyptian traditions, constantly threatening to form the basis for a nationalist opposition to Roman administrators and tax collectors. Hadrian sought to defuse the powder keg by disciplining administrators and by founding a new city, Antinopolis, which he hoped would create a center of loyalty to Rome.

Hadrian finally returned to the imperial residence on the Palatine in 131 C.E. He had spent more than ten years on the road, and had no doubt done much to strengthen and preserve the *Pax Romana,* or Roman peace. Still, to the careful observer, the weaknesses of the empire were as evident as its strengths. The frontiers were vast and constantly tested by a profusion of hostile tribes and peoples. Roman citizens from Italy, Gaul, and Spain were increasingly unwilling to serve in such far-flung regions. As a result, the legions were manned by progressively less Romanized soldiers, and their battle readiness and discipline, poorly enforced by homesick officers, declined dangerously. In the more civilized eastern provinces, corrupt local elites, imperial governors, and officials siphoned off imperial revenues destined for the army to build their personal fortunes. Also, in spite of centuries of hellenization and Roman administration, city and countryside remained culturally and politically separated. Early in the second century, such problems were no more than small clouds on the horizon, but in the following century they would grow into a storm that would threaten the very existence of the empire.

THE CULTURE OF ANTONINE ROME

True to Virgil's claim that Rome left it to others to "track the course of the heavens and announce the rising stars," Romans themselves took little interest in natural science. However, they supported Greek science pursued in the east, particularly in Alexandria, where centuries of Greek mathematics, astronomy, and geography came to fruition in the work of Claudius Ptolemaeus (ca. 85–ca.165 C.E.), usually known as Ptolemy. Ptolemy was a cartographer and geographer, but his greatest work was as a mathematician and astronomer.

Building on the work of Hipparchus, Ptolemy developed a complex model for the universe with which to explain the apparent motion of the sun, moon, and planets. Because, as most ancient scientists, he believed the Earth to be the center of the universe, he sought a mathematically correct model to explain the apparent motions of the sun and the moon, which appear to move at varying speeds, and of the planets, which appear to move erratically when observed from Earth. His solution was first to posit a series of eccentric circles around the Earth. The moon, followed by Mercury and Venus, orbits the Earth. The sun, followed by Mars, Jupiter, and Saturn, then circles these inner planets. In order to explain the apparent variations in speed and direction, he posited a series of epicycles: that the planets move in uniform circular motion in a small circle while at the same time moving uniformly on the circumference of a larger circle. The result was a complex series of cycles and epicycles, but the mathematics works quite well. Ptolemy's theory, which he explained in his treatise known from its influential Arabic translation as the *Almagest* (*The Greatest Compilation*), remained the accepted model of the solar system for the next 1400 years.

■ This fifteenth-century Latin translation of the *Almagest* presents Ptolemy's model for the motion of the outer planets, Mars, Jupiter, and Saturn. The complicated cycles and epicycles are necessary to explain the motion of these planets while keeping the Earth at the center of the universe.

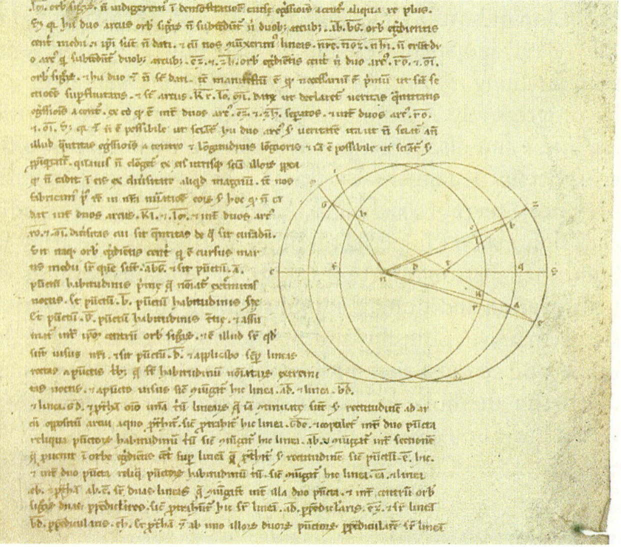

Romans themselves, however, were more interested in how humans should lead their lives than in how the planets moved. Annius Florus, a poet friend of Hadrian, commenting on the emperor's exhausting journeys, wrote:

I do not want to be Caesar,
To walk about among the Britons,
To endure the Scythian hoar-frosts.

To this Hadrian replied:

I do not want to be Florus,
To walk about among taverns,
To lurk about among cook-shops.

Like the other members of his dynasty, Hadrian enjoyed an easy familiarity with men of letters, and like other men of letters of the period, Florus was a provincial, an African drawn from the provincial world to the great capital. Another provincial, Rome's greatest historian, Cornelius Tacitus (ca. 56–ca. 120 C.E.), recorded the history of the first century of the empire. Tacitus wrote to instruct and to edify his generation and did so in a style characterized by irony and a sharp sense of the differences between public propaganda and the realities of power politics. He was also unique in his ability to portray noble opposition to Roman rule. His picture of Germanic and British societies served as a warning to Rome against excessive self-confidence and laxity. Tacitus's contemporaries, Plutarch (ca. 46–after 119 C.E.) and Suetonius (ca. 69–after 122 C.E.), were biographers rather than historians. Plutarch, who wrote in Greek, composed *Parallel Lives,* a series of character studies in which he compared eminent Greeks with eminent Romans. His purpose was to portray public virtue and to show how philosophical principles could be integrated into lives of civic action. Suetonius also wrote biographies, using anecdotes to portray character. Suetonius's biographies of the emperors fall short of the literary and philosophical qualities of Plutarch's character studies and far short of Tacitus's histories. Suetonius delighted in the rumors of private scandals that surrounded the emperors and used personal vice to explain public failings. Still, the portraits Suetonius created remained widely popular throughout the centuries, while Tacitus's histories fell out of fashion.

In the later second century, Romans in general preferred the study and writing of philosophy, particularly Stoicism, over history. The most influential Stoic philosopher of the century was Epictetus (ca. 55–135 C.E.), a former slave who taught that man could be free by the control of his will and the cultivation of inner peace. Like the early Stoics, Epictetus taught the universal brotherhood of humankind and the identity of nature and divine providence. He urged his pupils

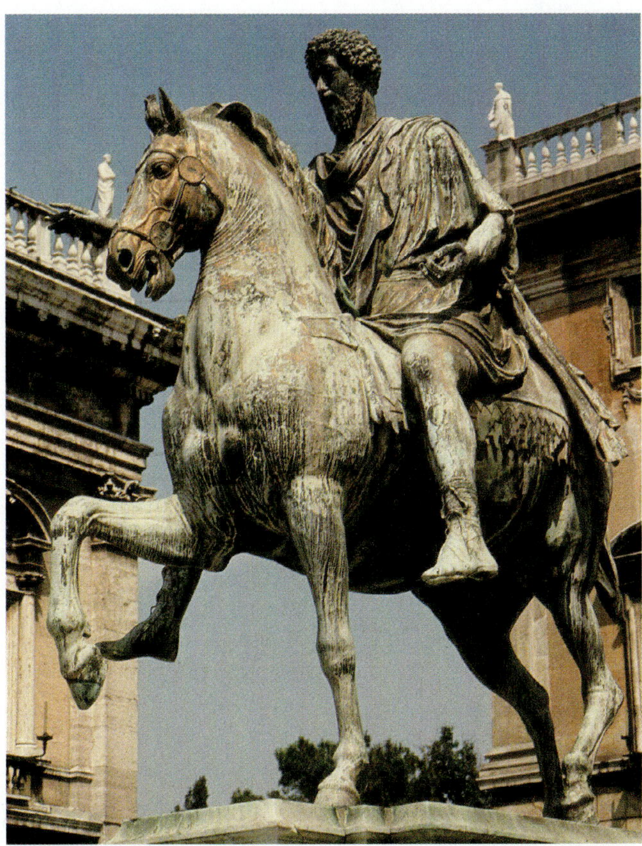

■ This monumental bronze statue of Emperor Marcus Aurelius is the only remaining Roman bronze equestrian statue of an emperor. Surviving because later generations thought it was the first Christian emperor, Constantine, this statue of the emperor stood in front of the Pope's Lateran Palace until the Renaissance.

Juvenal, *Satires*

to recognize that dependence on external things was the cause of unhappiness, and that therefore they should free themselves from reliance on material possessions, public esteem, and all other things prized by the worldly. He taught that individuals would find happiness by adapting themselves to their own particular expression of nature and by accepting with indifference the advantages and disadvantages that the role entailed.

The slave's philosophy found its most eager pupil in an emperor. Marcus Aurelius (161–180 C.E.) reigned during a period when the stresses glimpsed by Hadrian were beginning to show in a much more alarming manner. Once more the Parthians attacked the eastern frontier, while in Britain and Germany barbarians struck across the borders. In 166, a confederation of barbarians known as the Marcomanni crossed the Danube and raided as far south as northern Italy. A plague brought west by troops returning from the Parthian front ravaged the whole empire. Like his predecessor Hadrian, Aurelius felt bound to endure the Scythian hoar-frosts rather than luxuriate in the taverns of Rome. He spent virtually the whole of his reign on the Danubian frontier, repelling the barbarians and shoring up the empire's defenses.

Throughout his reign Aurelius found consolation in the Stoic philosophy of Epictetus. In his soldier's tent at night he composed his *Meditations,* a volume of philosophical musings. Like the slave, the emperor sought freedom from the burden of his office in his will and in the proper understanding of his role in the divine order. He called himself to introspection, to a constant awareness, under the glories and honors heaped upon him by his entourage, of his true human nature: "A poor soul burdened with a corpse."

Aurelius played his role well, dying in what is today Vienna, far from the pleasures of the capital. His Stoic philosophy did not, however, serve the empire well. For all his emphasis on understanding, Aurelius badly misjudged his son Commodus (180–192 C.E.), who succeeded him. Commodus, whose chief interest was in being a gladiator, saw himself as the incarnation of Heracles and appeared in public clad as a gladiator and as consul. As Commodus sank into insanity, Rome was once more convulsed with purges and proscriptions. Commodus's assassination in 192 did not end the violence. The *Pax Romana* was over.

CONCLUSION

The haphazard conquest of the Mediterranean world threw Roman republican government, traditional culture, and antagonistic social groups into chaos. The result was a century and a half of intermittent violence and civil war before a new political and social order headed by an absolute monarch established a new equilibrium. During the following two centuries, a deeply hellenized Roman civilization tied together the vast empire by incorporating the wealthy and powerful of the Western world into its fluid power structure while brutally crushing those who would not or could not conform. The binding force of the Roman Empire was great and would survive political crises in the third century as great as those that had brought down the republic 300 years before.

QUESTIONS FOR REVIEW

1. How were rifts in Roman society widened by Rome's expansion into an empire?
2. In what ways were the life and thought of Cicero indicative of an age characterized by civil conflict and the collapse of republican traditions?
3. How was religious reform an important part of Augustus's efforts to restore stability to Roman society?
4. What did the Flavian and Antonine emperors do to keep Rome's vast empire intact and in relative peace?
5. How did Paul of Tarsus transform the teachings of Jesus of Nazareth from an outgrowth of Judaism into a separate spiritual tradition?

KEY TERMS

Antonine dynasty, *p. 146*
first triumvirate, *p. 135*
Gnostics, *p. 151*
mystery cults, *p. 148*
optimates, *p. 130*
Pax Romana, p. 129
populares, *p. 131*
presbyters, *p. 151*
princeps, *p. 139*
second triumvirate, *p. 137*
Social War, *p. 131*

DISCOVERING WESTERN CIVILIZATION ONLINE

You can obtain more information about imperial Rome at the Websites listed below. See also the Companion Website that accompanies this text, www.ablongman.com/kishlansky, which contains an online study guide and additional resources.

General Websites

Ancient/Classical History with N. S. Gill: The Gracchi
ancienthistory.about.com/cs/gracchi/
An introduction to the Gracchi with links to other sites.

Pompeii Forum Project
www.iath.virginia.edu/pompeii/page-1.html
A great site devoted to the Roman city of Pompeii, which was destroyed by Mount Vesuvius in 79 C.E.

The End of the Republic

History & Literature of the Roman Revolution
johara.web.wesleyan.edu/CCIV274links.html
Jim O'Hara's Web page devoted to the end of the Roman Republic.

The Cicero Home Page
www.utexas.edu/depts/classics/documents/Cic.html
A site dedicated to Cicero, including texts of his orations and a bibliography.

The Vergil Project
Vergil.classics.upenn.edu/
A site dedicated to providing resources and teaching materials on Virgil.

The Augustan Age and the *Pax Romana*

Augustus and the Foundation of the Empire
www.carthage.edu/outis/augustus.html
A Web page devoted to the Emperor Augustus with links to archaeology and art of the Augustan age.

Virtual Tour of Rome
www.geocities.com/Athens/Forum/6946/virtual/virtual.html
A site that provides a virtual tour of the Roman forum.

Roman Imperial Forums
www.capitolium.org/
Over 1000 files on the Roman forums and life in imperial Rome.

The Corinth Computer Project
corinth.sas.upenn.edu/corinth.html
A computer reconstruction of Roman Corinth.

The Bardo Museum
http://homepage.mac.com/melissaenderle/tunisia/bardo.html]
A site dedicated to Northern African mosaics from the second through the fourth centuries in the Bardo Museum near Tunis, Tunisia.

The Dinur Center for Research in Jewish History: Second Temple and Talmudic Era
www.hum.huji.ac.il/dinur/Internetresources/historyresources/second_temple_and_talmudic_era.htm
A site at The Hebrew University of Jerusalem with links to many other sites concerning Judaism and early Christianity.

SUGGESTIONS FOR FURTHER READING

Primary Sources

Major selections of the works of Caesar, Cicero, Tacitus, Plutarch, Suetonius, and Marcus Aurelius are available in English translation from Penguin Books. The second volume by Naphtali Lewis and Meyer Reinhold, *Roman Civilization Selected Readings, Vol. II: The Empire* (1951), contains a wide selection of documents with useful introductions.

The Price of Empire

E. Badian, *Roman Imperialism in the Late Republic* (Ithaca, NY: Cornell University Press, 1968). A study of the contradictory forces leading to the development of the empire.

Mary Beard and Michael Crawford, *Rome in the Late Republic* (Ithaca, NY: Cornell University Press, 1985). An analysis of the political processes of the late republic as part of the development of Roman society, not simply the decay of the republic.

Henrik Mouritsen, *Plebs and Politics in the Late Roman Republic* (Cambridge: Cambridge University Press, 2001). A study of the political role of the masses in the last years of the republic.

The End of the Republic

Robert Gurval, *Actium and Augustus: the Politics and Emotions of Civil War* (Ann Arbor: University of Michigan Press, 1998). Important study of the end of the republic.

A. J. Langguth, *A Noise of War: Caesar, Pompey, Octavian, and the Struggle for Rome* (New York: Simon & Schuster, 1994). The era of the civil wars and the end of the republic.

Ronald Mellor, *Augustus and the Creation of the Roman Empire: A Brief History with Documents* (New York: Palgrave Macmillan, 2006). An introduction with primary sources to the Augustan age.

D. Stockton, *Cicero: A Political Biography* (London: Oxford University Press, 1971). A biography of the great orator in the context of the end of the republic.

The Augustan Age and the *Pax Romana*

J. B. Campbell, *The Emperor and the Roman Army* (New York: Oxford University Press, 1984). Essential for understanding the military's role in the Roman Empire.

Albrecht Dihle, *Greek and Latin Literature of the Roman Empire: From Augustus to Justinian* (New York: Routledge, 1994). A survey of classical literature.

Catharine Edwards and Greg Woolf, ed., *Rome: The Cosmopolis* (New York: Cambridge University Press, 2003). An innovative collection of essays examining the relationship between Rome and its empire.

Karl Galinsky, *Augustan Culture* (Princeton, NJ: Princeton University Press, 1998). An important study of the cultural world of Augustus.

J. E. Lendon, *Empire of Honour: The Art of Government in the Roman World* (Oxford: Oxford University Press, 2001). A provocative study of Roman despotism and the support it enjoyed from the ruling classes of the provinces.

Fergus Millar, *The Emperor in the Roman World* (Ithaca, NY: Cornell University Press, 1992). A study of emperors, stressing their essential passivity by responding to initiatives from below.

Kristina Milnor, *Gender, Domesticity, and the Age of Augustus: Inventing Private Life* (Oxford and New York: Oxford University Press, 2005). Study of how the ideal of female domesticity clashed with the new realities of Augustan society.

D. A. West and A. J. Woodman, *Poetry and Politics in the Age of Augustus* (New York: Cambridge University Press, 1984). The cultural program of Augustus.

Religions from the East

Schuyler Brown, *The Origins of Christianity: A Historical Introduction of the New Testament.* Rev. ed. (Oxford: Oxford University Press, 1993). A balanced and comprehensive introduction to early Christianity.

Ekkehard W. Stegemann and Wolfgang Stegemann, *The Jesus Movement: A Social History of Its First Century* (Minneapolis: Fortress Press, 1999). A new survey of the first century of Christianity.

Robert Turcan, *The Cults of the Roman Empire* (Oxford and Cambridge, MA: Blackwell Publishers, 1996). A comprehensive introduction to the many layers of Roman popular religious cults before the age of Constantine.

A Tour of the Empire

Jane F. Gardner, *Women in Roman Law and Society* (Bloomington: Indiana University Press, 1986). A study of the extent of freedom and power over property enjoyed by Roman women.

Peter Garnsey and Richard Saller, *The Roman Empire: Economy, Society, and Culture* (Berkeley: University of California Press, 1987). A topical study of imperial administration, economy, religion, and society, arguing the coercive and exploitative nature of Roman civilization in relation to the agricultural societies of the Mediterranean world.

Fergus Millar, *Rome, the Greek World, and the East: The Roman Republic and the Augustan Revolution* (Chapel Hill: University of North Carolina Press, 2000). A collection of essays by a leading historian surveying Rome's rise to empire.

For a list of additional titles related to this chapter's topics, please see http://www.ablongman.com/kishlansky.

CHAPTER 6

THE TRANSFORMATION OF THE CLASSICAL WORLD

A BRIDE'S TROUSSEAU

THE SYNTHESIS OF CHRISTIANITY AND THE CLASSICAL TRADITION

THE VISUAL RECORD

Venus, assisted by mythical sea creatures and representations of *erotes,* or cupids, beautifies herself on the central panel of a magnificent silver chest that made up part of a fourth-century Roman bride's trousseau. On the top, the bride, Projecta, and her groom, Secundus, are depicted within a wreath held by two more cupids. Along the base, Projecta, mirroring Venus, completes her own toilette while torchbearers and handmaidens perform for her the tasks of the mythical beings attending to Venus. The iconography as well as the execution of this sumptuous object—composed of solid silver with silver gilt and measuring almost 2 feet by 1 foot—testifies to the high status of the bride and her deep attachment to the ancient classical traditions of Greco-Roman culture. Projecta and Secundus were Roman aristocrats, and their marriage was part of Roman rituals of class, wealth, and power as ancient as the goddess on the marriage chest.

And yet, within the thorough paganism of the symbolism and the lavish expense of the workmanship, the Latin inscription engraved on the rim across the front of the lid confronts the viewer with how utterly changed the Roman world has become. It reads, "Secundus and Projecta, live in Christ." In spite of the elaborate pagan symbolism of the casket, Secundus and Projecta were Christians. Apparently, however, they and their families and friends saw nothing strange or improper about commemorating their marriage in the age-old manner of their pagan ancestors. A bride could live in Christ and still be Venus.

■ Top of the Projecta casket.

tian and pagan symbolism combine in the Projecta casket from the late fourth century.

Such was the world of late antiquity. By the time Projecta married Secundus, the once persecuted Christian sect was not only legal but rapidly on its way to becoming the established religion in the empire. Formerly a religion of Hellenized Jews and freed slaves, it was attracting converts from among the highest classes of Roman society. And yet, while some stern religious teachers might condemn the ancient traditions of Roman religion, and while around the very time of Projecta's marriage the images of divine Victory were being removed from the Roman Senate, aristocratic families, Christian as well as pagan, continued the ancient cultural traditions without a sense of betrayal or contradiction. Rome appeared as eternal and serene as Venus herself.

But the Projecta casket has even more to tell us. It was found, along with more than 60 other exquisite objects and 70 pounds of silver plate, on the Esquiline Hill in Rome, where it had been hastily buried to hide it from some catastrophe. The probable catastrophe is not hard to guess: in 410, when Projecta would have been an elderly woman, the barbarian Visigoths sacked and pillaged Rome for three days, raping Roman women and looting them of such treasures as the marriage chest.

Nevertheless, the barbarians were themselves Christians, while the city of Rome had remained, in spite of exceptions such as Projecta and Secundus, a pagan stronghold. Moreover, the Visigoths were no mere horde but, officially at least, a Roman army reacting in what had become a typical manner to the failure of the state to provide them with what they saw as their due. Such contrasts of paganism and Christianity, of barbarity and Roman culture, were integral parts of a new Roman world, one characterized by radical transformations of Roman and barbarian culture that took place in the two centuries following the death of Marcus Aurelius in 180. Accelerating the process of change and transformation was the combination of events collectively referred to as the *crisis of the third century.*

LOOKING AHEAD

This chapter follows the profound political and social transformations that turned both the Roman Empire and its barbarian neighbors into radically new societies with different political, religious, and social organizations. By the sixth century, Christianity had become the religion of the whole empire, while the eastern half of the empire had become profoundly Hellenized, and the western half had disintegrated into numerous Romano-barbarian kingdoms without losing its close identity with Rome.

CHAPTER OUTLINE

THE CRISIS OF THE THIRD CENTURY

From the reign of Septimius Severus (193–211) to the time of Diocletian (284–305), both internal and external challenges shook the Roman Empire. The empire survived, but its social, political, and economic structures were radically transformed.

Sheer size was a fundamental problem for the empire. Haphazard expansion in many regions—to the north and west, for instance—overextended the frontiers. The manpower and resources needed to maintain the vast territory strained the economic system of the empire. Like a thread stretched to the breaking point, the thin line of border garrisons and forts was ready to snap.

The economic system itself was part of the reason for the strain on resources. For all of its commercial networks, the economy of the empire remained tied to agriculture. To the aristocrats of the ancient world, agriculture was the only honorable source of wealth. Thus the prosperous Roman citizen bought slaves and land, not machinery. The goal of the successful merchant was to liquidate his commercial assets, buy estates, and rise into the leisured landholding elite. As a result, liquid capital, either for investment or for taxation, was always scarce.

Slaves in Roman Law

The lack of sophistication in commercial and industrial business practices characterized the financial system of the empire as well. Government had always been conducted on the cheap. The tax system of the empire had never been very efficient at tapping into the real wealth of the aristocracy. Each city made its own collective assessments. Individuals eager to win the gratitude of their local communities were expected to provide essential services from their own pockets. Even with the vast wealth of the empire at its disposal, the government never developed a system of public debt—that is, a policy of borrowing against future revenues. As a result, the only way to solve short-term cash flow problems was to debase the coinage by using more copper and less silver. This practice became epidemic in the third century, when the price of a bushel of wheat rose more than 200 percent.

The failure of the empire to develop a stable political base complicated its economic problems. In times of emergency, imperial control relied on the personal presence and command of the emperor. As the empire grew, it became impossible for that presence to be felt everywhere. Moreover, the empire never developed either a regular system of imperial succession or an adequate power base. Control of the army, which was the ultimate source of imperial power, was possible only as long as the emperor was able to lead his armies to victory.

Enrich the Army and Scorn the Rest

Throughout much of the late second and third centuries, emperors failed dismally to lead their armies to victory. The pressure on the borders was temporarily halted by Marcus Aurelius, but it resumed under his successors. The barely Romanized provincials in the military bore the brunt of the attacks. When the emperors selected by the distant Roman Senate failed to win victory, front-line armies unhesitatingly raised their own commanders to the imperial office. The commanders, such as the Pannonian general Septimius Severus, set about restructuring the empire in favor of the army. They opened important administrative posts to soldiers, expanded the army's size, raised military pay, initiated expensive building programs in frontier settlements, and in general introduced authoritarian military discipline throughout society. To finance the costly measures, the new military government confiscated senatorial wealth, introduced new forms of taxation, and increasingly debased the coinage.

The Rise of the Military. The old senatorial elite and the people living in the more civilized regions of the empire thought the measures disastrous. Soldiers in the provinces welcomed the changes. With their first rise in real income, soldiers could improve their standard of living while in service and buy their way into provincial elites upon retirement. At long last they were allowed to marry even while on active service. Free-spending soldiers and imperial extravagance helped the bleak settlements on the edges of military camps grow into prosperous cities with all the comforts of the older parts of the empire.

For the first time, capable soldiers could hope to rise to the highest levels of public power regardless of their birth. One extraordinarily successful soldier was Publius Helvius Pertinax. Born the son of a freed slave in the north of Italy (Liguria) in 126, he abandoned a career as a schoolteacher to enter the military. His rise to the top of the military and bureaucratic ladder began in Syria. From Syria he was promoted to a post in Britain. He then returned to the Continent and served in the Danubian region during the Marcomannian

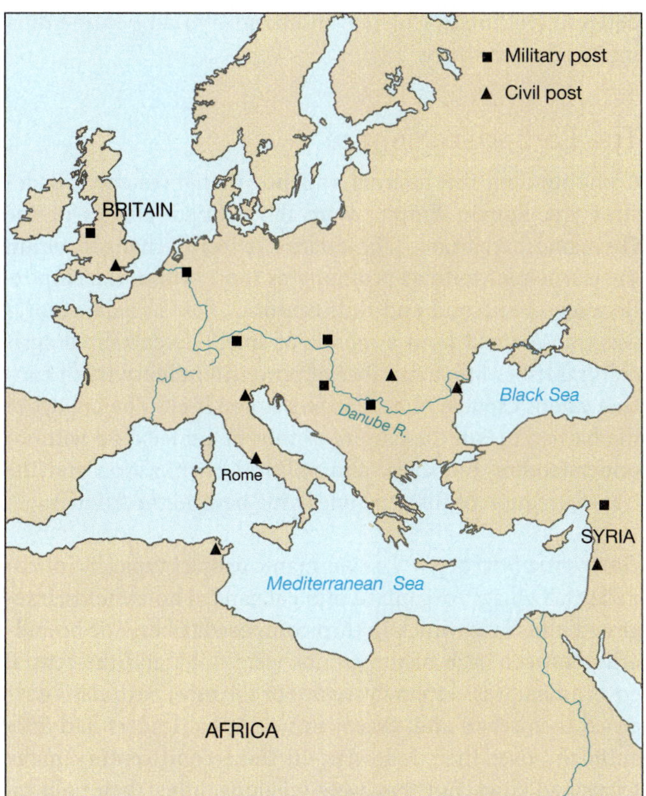

The career of Publius Helvius Pertinax, the first nonsenatorial emperor, shows how political advancement took him to every threatened area of the empire.

wars in both civil and military capacities for approximately ten years. By the time he was 50, his success as a military commander won for him the office of consul. He then held a series of military, civil, and proconsular positions in Syria, Britain, Italy, and Africa before returning to Rome. When the emperor Commodus was murdered in 192, the palace guard proclaimed Pertinax emperor—the first emperor who had not come from the privileged senatorial class.

Economic Disaster. Soon, however, the military control of the empire turned into a nightmare even for the provinces and their armies. Exercising their newly discovered power, armies raised and then destroyed pretender after pretender, offering support to whichever imperial candidate promised them the greatest riches. Pertinax, the first of the soldier-emperors, set the precedent. Less than three months after becoming emperor, he was murdered by his soldiers. The army's incessant demands for higher pay led emperors to lower the amount of silver in the coins with which the soldiers were paid. But the less the coins were worth, the more of them were necessary to purchase goods. And the more that goods cost, the less valuable was the salary of the soldiers. Wages doubled but the price of grain tripled in the third century. Thus soldiers were worse off at the end of the period than at the beginning. Such drastic inflation wrecked the economic stability of the empire and spurred the army on to greater and more impossible demands for raises. Emperors who could not meet the demands were killed by their troops. In fact, the army was much more effective at killing emperors than enemies. Between 235 and 284, 17 of the 20 more or less legitimate emperors were assassinated or killed in civil war.

External Threats. The crisis of the third century did not result only from economic and political instability within the empire. Rome's internal imperial crises coincided with an increase in attacks from outside the empire. In Africa, Berber tribes harassed the frontiers. The Sassanid dynasty in Persia threatened Rome's eastern frontier. When the emperor Valerian (253–260) attempted to prevent the Persian king of kings Shapur I from seizing Roman Mesopotamia and Armenia, he was captured and held prisoner for the rest of his life. Valerian became such a curiosity that after his death his skin reportedly was stuffed and for centuries was kept on display in a Persian temple.

The greatest danger to Rome came not from the south or east but from the west. There, along the Rhine, various Germanic tribes known collectively as the Franks and the Alemanni began raiding expeditions into the empire. Along the lower Danube and in southern Russia, the Gothic confederation raided the Balkans and harassed Roman shipping on the Black Sea.

An Empire on the Defensive

The central administration of the empire simply could not deal effectively with the numerous barbarian attacks. Left on their own, regional provincial commanders at times even headed separatist movements. Provincial aristocrats who despaired of receiving any help from distant Rome often supported the pretenders. One such commander was Postumus, whom the armies of Spain, Britain, and Gaul proclaimed emperor. His nine-year separatist reign (ca. 258–268) was the longest and most stable of that of any emperor, legitimate or otherwise, throughout the entire troubled period.

Tax Burdens. Political and military instability had devastating effects on the lives of ordinary people. Citizenship had been extended to virtually all free inhabitants of the empire in 212, but that right was a formality given simply to enlarge the tax base, since only citizens paid inheritance taxes. In reality, the legal and economic status of all but the richest declined. Society became sharply divided into the privileged **honestiores**—senators, municipal gentry, and the military—and the increasingly burdened **humiliores**—everyone else. The humiliores suffered the most from the tax increases because unlike the honestiores they could neither bribe their way out of them nor intimidate tax collectors with private armies. They were also frequent targets of extortion by the military and of violence perpetrated by bandits.

Banditry. It was the impossible burden of taxation that drove many individuals into banditry. Such crime had long been endemic to the Roman Empire, and slave and peasant bandits, rustlers, and even pirates played an ambivalent role in society. Often they terrorized the countryside, descending from the hills to attack villages or travelers. However, at times they also protected peasants from greedy tax collectors and military commanders. In Gaul and Spain, peasants and local leaders organized armed resistance movements to withstand the exorbitant demands of tax collectors. Although these resistance movements, termed **Bacaudae,** were always ruthlessly crushed, they continued to reappear—a sure sign of the desperation of ordinary people. In the first centuries of the empire, bandits operated primarily in peripheral areas recently and poorly subjugated to Roman rule. In the late second and third centuries they became an increasing problem in Italy itself.

The most famous of the bandits was Bulla the Lucky, who headed a band of more than 600 men and plundered Italy during the reign of Septimius Severus. No simple thief, Bulla was more like a Roman Robin Hood. He often robbed his prisoners of only a portion of their goods, which he distributed to the needy. He detained skilled artisans and made use of their skills, then let them go with a parting gift. On one occasion he captured the centurion charged with hunting him down and, dressed in the official robes of a Roman magistrate, summoned the centurion in his own "court." The centurion, his head shaved like a slave, was brought before Bulla and told: "Carry this message back to your masters: let them feed their slaves so that they might not be compelled to turn to a life of banditry."

Bulla lived and died outside the law, but as the third century progressed, such lawlessness increasingly became the law. The life of Maximinus the Thracian, known as Little Big Man (173–238), typified this change. He began life as a shepherd, then drifted into rustling, but he also protected the local community. Later he entered the Roman army, where his extraordinary physical size and skills caught the attention of Septimius Severus, who promoted him to centurion. Maximinus rose quickly through the ranks and in 235 was proclaimed emperor at Mainz by a mutinous army, which had overthrown the grandson of Septimius Severus. Although Maximinus reigned for only a bit more than two years, his career showed how fluid the boundaries between legitimate violence and banditry had become during the third century.

The Barbarian Menace

Compounding the internal violence that threatened to destroy the Roman Empire were the external attacks of the Germanic barbarians. The attacks reflected changes within the Germanic world as profound as those within the empire. Between the second and fifth centuries the Germanic world was transformed from a mosaic of small, decentralized agricultural tribes into a number of powerful military tribal confederations capable of challenging Rome itself. The impact of the barbarians on the empire cannot be understood without understanding the social and political organization and the transformation of those people living beyond the frontier.

Germanic Society. The Germanic peoples typically inhabited small villages organized into patriarchal households, integrated into clans, which in turn composed tribes. The boundaries between each of the groups were fluid, and the central government was extremely weak. For the most part, clans governed themselves and, except in war, tribal leaders had little authority over their followers. In the second century many tribes had kings, but they were religious rather than political leaders. Germanic communities lived by farming, but cattle raising and especially warfare carried the highest social prestige. Men measured their status by the number of cattle they owned and by their martial ability. Women took care of agricultural chores and household duties.

Warfare defined social groupings and warriors dominated public life. Only within the clan was fighting inappropriate. But rival clans within the same tribe dealt with one another brutally. Conflict took the form of the feud, and each act of aggression was repaid in kind. If an individual within a clan had a grievance with an individual within another clan, all his kinsmen were obliged to assist him. Thus a single incident could result in a continuous escalation of acts of revenge. Murder piled upon murder as sons and brothers retaliated for each act of vengeance.

■ Roman parade mask found at the site of the Battle of Teutoburg Forest (9 C.E.) in which a coalition of Germanic tribes commanded by Arminius, a leader of the Cherusci who had received a Roman education, citizenship, and the rank of equestrian, destroyed three Roman legions and thereby fixed the Roman frontier along the Rhine.

TACITUS ON THE GERMANS

At the end of the first century C.E., Tacitus wrote a brief account of the Germanic peoples living beyond the frontiers, in part to inform Romans about the neighboring people and in part to criticize the morals and practices of Roman society. In general, his information, although selective and filtered through Roman culture, appears quite accurate.

Focus Questions

What, according to Tacitus, are the various types of executive and legislative power among the Germanic peoples? Why was the feud so important in this society?

They pick their kings on the basis of noble birth, their generals on the basis of bravery. Nor do their kings have limitless or arbitrary power, and the generals win favor by the example they set if they are energetic, if they are distinguished, if they fight before the battle-line, rather than by the power they wield. But no one except the priests is allowed to inflict punishment with death, chains, or even flogging, and the priests act not, as it were, to penalize and at the command of the general, but, so to speak, at the order of the god, who they believe is at hand when they are waging war. . . . The nobles make decisions about lesser matters, all freemen about things of greater significance, with this proviso, nonetheless, that those subjects, of which ultimate judgment is in the hands of the mass of people, receive preliminary consideration among the nobles. . . . When the crowd thinks it opportune, they sit down fully armed. Silence is demanded by the priests, who then also have the right of compulsion. Soon the king or the chieftains are heard, in accordance with the age, nobility, glory in war, and eloquence of each, with the influence of persuasion being greater than the power to command. If a proposal has displeased them, they show their displeasure with a roar; but if it has won favor, they bang their *frameae* [spears] together; the most prestigious kind of approval is praise with arms. . . . There is an obligation to undertake the personal feuds as well as the friendships of one's father or blood-relative; but the feuds do not continue without possibility of settlement, for even murder is atoned for by a specific number of cattle and sheep and the entire family accepts the settlement, with advantage to the community, since feuds are the most dangerous when joined with freedom.

From Tacitus, *Germany.*

Clans in other tribes were fair game for raiding and conquering. The wars that resulted formed the normal mechanisms by which wealth circulated among tribes, either as booty or as gifts exchanged to conclude peace. Individuals, clans, and tribes built their reputations on warfare. The more successful a tribe was in warfare, the more clans it attracted and the greater its position became in the barbarian world.

Feuding and Peacemaking. The practice of feuding, especially within the tribe, had enormous costs. Families were decimated, and strong warriors who were needed to defend the tribe from outside attack faced constant danger from members of their own tribe. Thus tribal leaders attempted to reduce hostilities by establishing payments called **wergeld** in place of the blood vengeance demanded in reparation for crimes. Such wergeld, normally paid in cattle or slaves, was voluntary, since the right of vengeance was generally recognized, and the unity of the tribe remained precarious.

Tribes also attempted to reinforce unity through religious cults involving shared myths of common ancestry and rituals intended to underline group cohesion. When not fighting, Germanic warriors spent much of their time drinking beer together at the table of their war leader. Communal beer drinking was also a way of uniting potentially hostile neighbors. Not surprisingly, it could also lead to drunken brawls that reopened the very feuds drinking bouts were intended to end. The feuds could in turn lead to the hiving off of irreconcilable factions, which might in time form their own tribes.

Warrior Bands. In contrast to the familial structure of barbarian society stood another warrior group that cut across kindred and even tribal units. This was the warrior band, called in Latin the *comitatus.* Some young warriors formed personal bonds with particularly able leaders and pledged them absolute loyalty. In return the leaders were obligated to lead their warriors to victory and to share with them the spoils of war. The warrior societies, far from being the basic units of a larger tribal military force, were organized for their own plunder and fighting. While they might be a valuable aid in intertribal warfare, they could also shatter the fragile peace by conducting raids on neighbors, thus bringing whole tribes into internal conflict. Although they were nontribal, successful comitatus could form the nuclei of new tribes. Successful warrior leaders might draw sufficient numbers of followers and conquer so many other groups that in time the band would become a new tribe.

Roman Influence in the Barbarian World

Intratribal and intertribal violence produced a rough equilibrium of power and wealth as long as small Germanic tribes lived in isolation. The presence of the Roman Empire, felt both directly and indirectly in the barbarian world, upset that equilibrium. Unintentionally, Rome itself helped transform the Germanic tribes into the major threat to the imperial system.

The Lure of Roman Culture. The direct presence of Roman merchants extended only about 100 miles beyond the frontiers into "free Germany." However, the attraction of Roman luxury goods and the Romans' efforts to establish friendly Germanic buffer zones along the borders drew even distant tribes into the Roman imperial system. Across the barbarian world, tribal leaders and comitatus leaders sought the prestige that Roman goods brought them. Roman provincial commanders encouraged the leaders to enter into commercial arrangements with the Romans. In exchange for their cattle, which the Romans needed for their troops, the Germanic leaders received gold and grain. The outside source of wealth greatly increased the economic disparity within Germanic society. In addition, some leaders made treaties with Rome, thus receiving the advantage of Roman support, which other tribal leaders lacked. In return for payments of gold and foodstuffs, chieftains of the **federated tribes** agreed to oppose tribes hostile to Rome and to prevent young hotheads of their own tribes from raiding across the frontier. Some chiefs supplied warriors for the Roman army. Others even led their comitatus into Roman service. By the late third century the Roman army included Franks, Goths, and Saxons serving as far away from their homes as Egypt. Such "imperial Germans" moved back and forth between the Roman and barbarian worlds, using each as a foundation for increased power in the other and obscuring the cultural and political differences between the two.

The inherent attraction of Roman material civilization and the Romans' policy of supporting "their" barbarians tended to upset Germanic society and to accentuate political, social, and economic differences within tribal units. That in turn led to the formation of pro- and anti-Roman factions, which further splintered barbarian tribes. New and powerful groups appeared, older tribal units vanished, and new forms of military organization came to predominate.

The West Germanic Revolution. The effects of contact between barbarians and Romans reached far and wide throughout the empire and beyond the frontier. Along the Rhine and Danube, the result was the so-called West Germanic Revolution. In order to survive in a time of constant warfare, tribes had to become armies. The armies needed a united and effective leadership. Among most of the western Germanic peoples, the tradition of the older tribal king was abandoned. A new kind of nonroyal chieftain emerged as the war leader of the people and as the representative of the war god Woden. In the later second and third centuries the turmoil resulted in the formation of new tribes and tribal confederations—the Marcomanni, the Alemanni, and the Franks. By the end of the second century the internal barbarian transformation spilled over into the empire in the form of the Marcomannian wars and the Saxon, Frankish, and Alemannic incursions into the western provinces.

The Gothic Confederation. Around the same time, along the Oder and Vistula rivers to the north, a group later known as the Goths began their slow consolidation around a royal family. The Goths were unique in that their kings exercised more military authority than was usual for a Germanic tribe. The kings formed the nucleus of a constantly changing barbarian group. A Goth was not necessarily a biological descendant of the small second-century tribe living along the shore of the Baltic. Anyone who fought alongside the Gothic king was a Goth.

Between the second and fourth centuries, the bearers of the Gothic royal tradition began to filter to the south and east, ultimately transferring their model of barbarian organization to the area of present-day Kiev in Ukraine. The move was not so much a physical migration of thousands of people across Europe as the gradual confederation under Gothic leadership of various Germanic, Slavic, and Scythian peoples living around the Black Sea. By the early third century, the Gothic confederation was strong enough to challenge Roman supremacy in the region. The first Gothic wars in the east were even more devastating than were the later wars in the west.

THE EMPIRE RESTORED

By the last decades of the third century, the Roman Empire seemed in danger of crumbling under combined internal and external pressure. That it did not was largely due to the efforts of the soldier-emperor Aurelian (270–275), who was able to repulse the barbarians, restore the unity of the empire, and then set about stabilizing the internal imperial structure. Although Aurelian was assassinated, his successors were able to build on his efforts. Restoration came to fruition under Diocletian (284–305), who summed up and solidified the transformations made under his predecessors. However, the restored empire under Diocletian bore little resemblance to the Roman Empire of the first and second centuries.

Diocletian, the God-Emperor

Diocletian, a Dalmatian soldier who had risen through the ranks to become emperor, completed the process of stabilization and reorganization of the imperial system begun by Aurelian. The result was a regime that in some ways increased imperial power and in other ways simply did away with the pretenses that had previously masked the emperor's true position.

No longer was the emperor princeps, or "first citizen." Now he was *dominus,* or "lord," the term of respect used by slaves in addressing their masters. He also assumed the title of *Iovius,* or Jupiter-like, thus claiming divine status and demanding adoration as a living god. Diocletian emphasized the imperial cult and the autocratic power of the emperor, but he did not grasp the power exclusively for himself. He recognized that the empire was too large and complex for one man to rule. To solve the problem, he divided the empire into eastern and western parts, each part to be ruled by both an augustus and a junior emperor, or caesar. Diocletian was augustus in the east, supported by his caesar, Galerius. In the west the rulers were the augustus Maximian and his caesar, Constantius.

The Tetrarchy. In theory the **tetrarchy,** or rule by four, provided for regular succession. The caesars, who were married to daughters of the augusti, were to succeed them. The new system also made revolts and assassinations less likely to be successful, since a person would have to kill all four rulers in order to seize power. Although from time to time subsequent emperors would rule alone, Diocletian's innovation proved successful and enduring. The empire was divided administratively into eastern and western parts until the death of Julius Nepos, the last legitimate emperor in the west, in 480.

The tetrarchy was an attempt to regulate the succession. Here, the emperors Diocletian and Maximian are depicted with their caesars—Constantius of the west and Galerius of the east—who were their respective sons-in-law.

In addition to constitutional reform, Diocletian enacted or consolidated a series of measures to improve the functioning of the imperial administration. He reorganized and expanded the army, approximately doubled the number of provinces, separated their military and civil administration, and greatly increased the number of bureaucrats to administer them. He attempted to stem runaway inflation by increasing the amount of silver in coins and fixing maximum prices and wages throughout the empire. He restructured the imperial tax system, basing it on payments in goods and produce in order to distribute the burden on all citizens more equitably and to avoid the problem of currency debasement.

A Militarized Society. The pillar of Diocletian's success was his victorious military machine. He was effective because, like the barbarian chieftains who had turned their tribes into armies, he militarized society and led that military society to victory. Like Diocletian himself, his soldiers were drawn from marginal provincial regions. They showed tremendous devotion to their god-emperor. By the time of Diocletian's reign, a career such as that of Pertinax (pp. 162–163) had become the rule for emperors rather than the exception.

The career of Aurelius Gaius, an obscure provincial officer, is typical of that of soldiers of Diocletian's army. Gaius was born in a Galatian village in what is today Turkey. Like many other young men from his village, he sought his fortune by entering military service in a Danubian legion that traditionally drew recruits from Galatia. He served in infantry and cavalry units in Pannonia and then in Gaul near Strasbourg, advancing through the ranks from simple recruit to cavalryman, adjutant, and finally centurion in Diocletian's personal guard. He traveled the length and breadth of the empire with Diocletian. Six times he fought outside the empire in campaigns that penetrated the Gothic kingdom, Persia, North Africa, and Numidia.

Compared to that of Pertinax, Gaius's career reflects the differences between successful careers at the end of the second century and those at the end of the third. Unlike Pertinax, Gaius spent his entire career within the military. Diocletian had largely ended the tradition of mixing civil and military offices, a measure that perhaps prevented undue military meddling in civil government but that also cut off most bureaucrats from the army, the real source of power. In addition, Gaius's military service took him to an even wider range of provinces than did that of Pertinax. However, just as remarkable as the regions in which he served are the places he apparently never visited. Except for a short time in Strasbourg, Gaius spent no time in Gaul and never visited Britain. The extreme west of the empire was increasingly irrelevant to the in-

MAP DISCOVERY

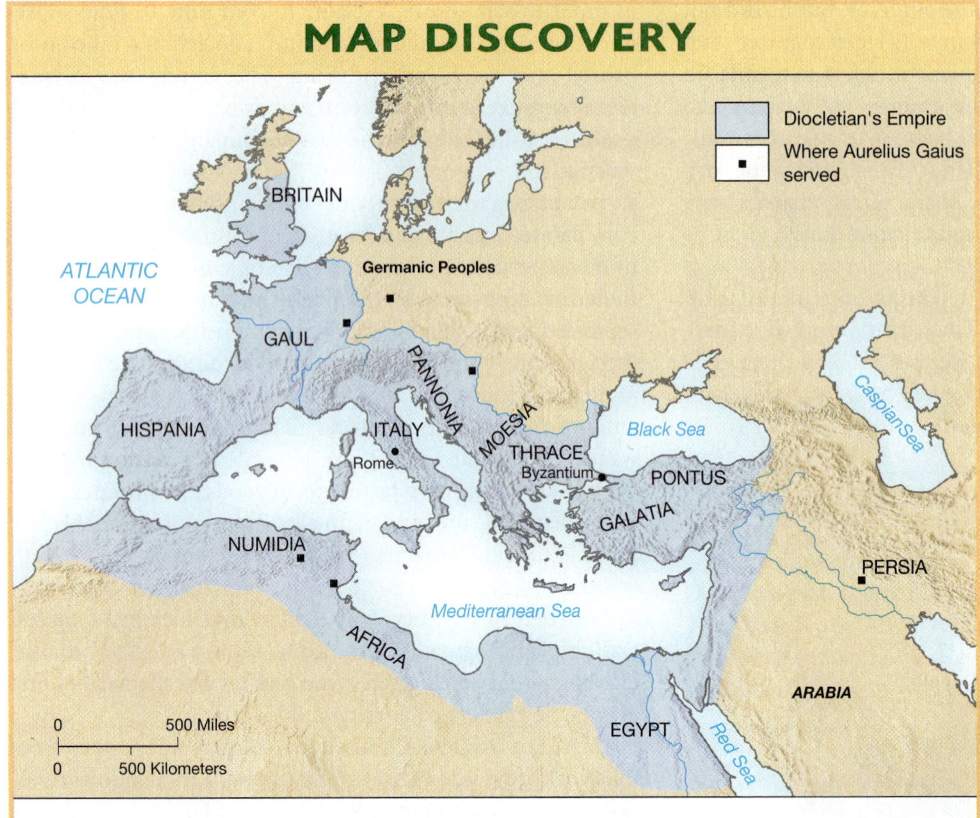

The Empire Under Diocletian

This map shows the extent of the empire in 305, at the end of Diocletian's reign. Compared with the map on page 152, what portions of the empire had been lost or abandoned during his reign? Why? What geographical challenges did the empire's size pose to the emperor? Note where Aurelius Gaius served. What were the troubles and disturbances that influenced his itinerary?

terests of central government. Nor did Gaius visit Italy and Greece, the centers of the old classical world. For him, as for Diocletian, the periphery of the empire had become its center; the center was increasingly marginal to the program of the empire.

Fiscal Reform. Some aspects of Diocletian's program, such as the improvement of the civil administration and the military, were successful. Others, such as the reform of silver currency and wage and price controls, were dismal failures. One effect of the fiscal reforms was to bind **coloni,** or hereditary tenant farmers, to their lands, since they were forbidden to leave the villages where they were registered to pay their taxes. In this practice lay the origins of European serfdom. Another effect was the gradual destruction of the local city councils, since their members—the **decurions**—were held personally responsible for the payment of local assessments, whether or not they could be collected from the other inhabitants. In time this led to the dissolution of local civil government.

All of the measures were designed to marshal the entire population in the monumental task of preserving Romanitas. Central to the task was the proper reverential attitude toward the divine emperors who directed it. One group seemed stubbornly opposed to this heroic effort: the Christians. In 298 an incident occurred that seemed to confirm their subversive attitude. At a sacrifice in the presence of Diocletian, the Roman priests were unable to obtain the desired favorable omens, and they attributed their failure to the presence of Christians, who were crossing themselves to ward off demons. Such blasphemous conduct—it might be compared, for instance, to desecrating the flag at a public assembly—led to the beginning of the Great Persecution, which formally began in 303 and lasted sporadically until 313. Although unevenly pursued across the empire, it resulted in the destruction of churches, the burning of copies of Christian Scriptures, the exclusion of Christians from access to imperial courts, and the torture, maiming, and death of hundreds of Christians who refused to sacrifice to the pagan gods.

Constantine, the Emperor of God

In 305, in the midst of the Great Persecution, Diocletian and his co-augustus Maximian took the extraordinary step of abdicating in favor of their caesars, Galerius and Constantius. The abdication was intended to provide for an orderly succession. Instead, the sons of Constantius and Maximian, Constantine (306–337) and Maxentius (306–312), drawing on the prejudice of the increasingly barbarian armies toward hereditary succession, wrecked the tetrarchy in a struggle to control the empire. In so doing, they plunged the empire once more into civil war as they fought over the western half of the empire.

Victory and Conversion. Victory in the west came to Constantine in 312, when he defeated and killed Maxentius in a battle at the Mulvian Bridge outside Rome. Constantine attributed his victory to a vision telling him to paint ☧ on the shields of his soldiers. For pagans, the symbol indicated the solar

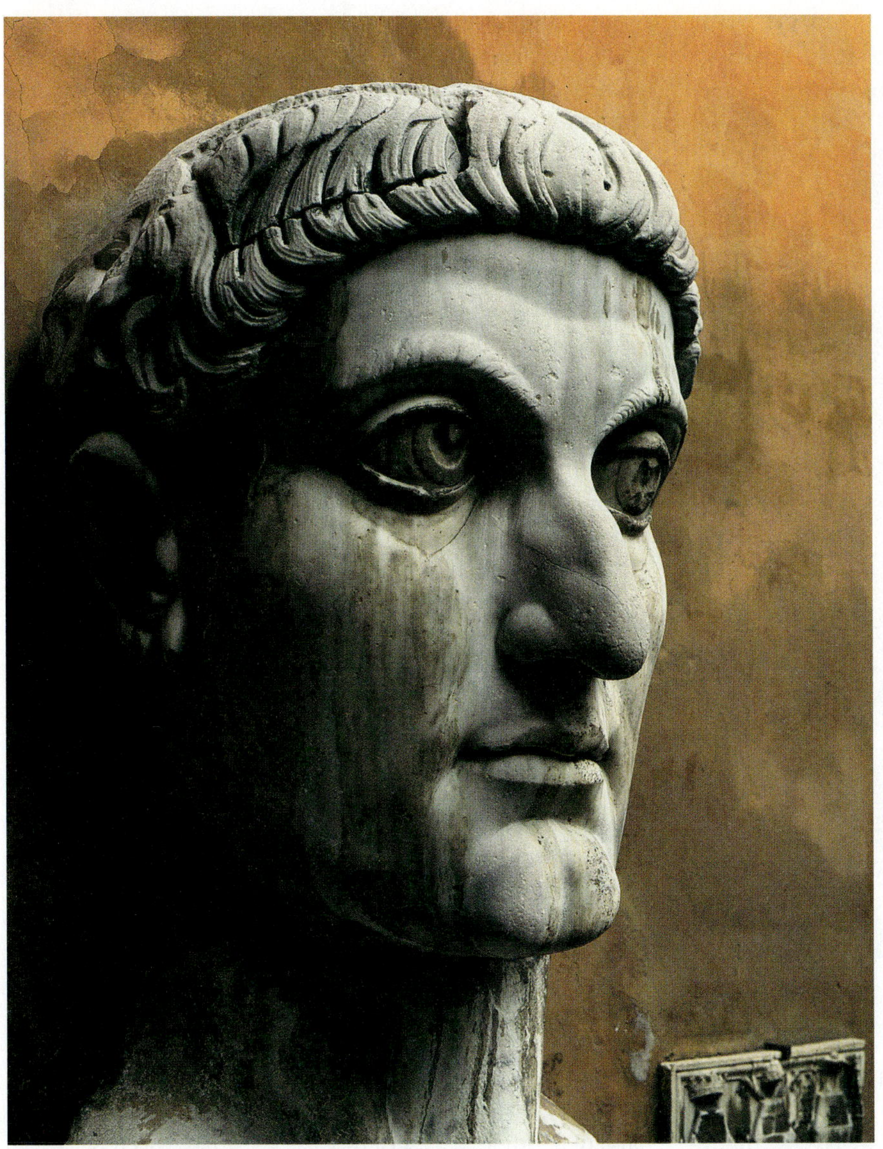

■ This head of Constantine, seven times life size, was part of an immense seated statue intended to portray not the emperor as he was but rather as the divinity that resided in him.

DOCUMENT

Eusebius on Constantine

emblem of the cult of the Unconquered Sun. For Christians, it was the Chi-Rho, formed from the first two letters of the Greek word for Christ. The next year, in Milan, Constantine rescinded the persecution of Christians and granted Christian clergy the same privileges enjoyed by pagan priests. Constantine himself was not baptized until near death, a common practice in antiquity. However, during his reign Christianity grew from a persecuted minority to the most favored cult in the empire.

Constantinople. Almost as important as Constantine's conversion to Christianity was his decision to establish his capital not in Rome, with its strong association with the cult of the traditional gods, or in Milan or Trier, the military capitals of the west, but in Byzantium, a city founded by Greek colonists on the narrow neck of water connecting the Black Sea to the Mediterranean. He transformed and enriched the small town, calling it the New Rome. Later it was known as Constantinople, the city of Constantine. For the next 11 centuries, Constantinople served as the heart of the Roman and then the Byzantine world. From his new city, Constantine began to transform the empire into a Christian state and Christianity into a Roman state religion.

It never will be known just what Constantine's conversion meant to him in personal terms. Its effects on the empire and on Christianity were obvious and enormous. Constantine himself continued to maintain cordial relations with representatives of all cults and to use ambiguous language that would offend no one when talking about "the deity." His successors were less broad-minded. They quickly reversed the positions of Christianity and paganism. In 341 pagan sacrifice was banned, and by 355 the temples had been closed and the death penalty for sacrificing to the gods had been decreed, although not enforced. In 357 the altar of Victory, on which senators had offered incense since the time of Augustus, was removed from the Senate.

The Triumph of Christianity

While paganism was being disestablished, Christianity was rapidly becoming the established religion. Conversion in no way meant a break with the theocratic consolidation initiated by Diocletian. On the contrary, Constantine was one of the most ruthless and ambitious emperors Rome had ever known. He sought in the Christian cult exactly the kind of support Diocletian had looked for in a return to Jupiter and the traditional gods.

Constantine made enormous financial contributions to Christian communities to repay them for their losses during persecutions. He erected rich churches on the model of Roman basilicas, or administrative buildings, and converted temples into Christian places of worship. He gave bishops the authority to act as magistrates within the Christian community. Once the particular objects of persecution, bishops became favored courtiers. Constantine attempted to make himself the de facto head of the Church. He even presided at the council of the

IMAGE DISCOVERY

In the Eye of the Beholder: Jesus or Sun-God?

This mosaic found under St. Peter's Basilica in Rome is believed by many historians to be the earliest representation of Jesus, while others see it as Helios, the sun-god. There are numerous pagan burials under the basilica where, according to tradition, St. Peter was buried after his execution. What elements of this mosaic might suggest that this is an image of Jesus? What elements suggest that it is the pagan sun-god? Might an artist accustomed to depicting pagan gods have used traditional imagery to depict the focus of this new religion's worship?

whole church held in Nicaea in 325. Constantine and his successors, with the exception of his nephew Julian (361–363)—who attempted unsuccessfully both to reestablish paganism and to promote traditional Hellenism—sought to use the cult of the one God to strengthen their control over the empire.

Emperor and Church. Although imperial control over Christianity was strong, it was not total. One of the most powerful Christian successors to Constantine, Theodosius I (347–395), met his match in the person of the equally determined bishop of Milan, Ambrose (339–397). In 390, the emperor, angered by riots in the Greek city of Thessalonica, ordered a general massacre of the population. Ambrose dared to excommunicate, or ban, the emperor from his church in Milan until Theodosius did public penance for his act of brutality. Many people feared that Ambrose would be the next victim of imperial wrath, but finally the emperor acquiesced, acknowledging that even he was subject to the rule of God as interpreted by the bishops. The confrontation between bishop and emperor later became an oft-cited precedent church leaders used to define the relationship between religious and secular authority.

Conversion. Imperial support was essential to the spread of Christianity in the fourth century, but other factors encouraged conversion as well. Christian miracles—particularly that of exorcism, or casting out of demons—won many converts. The ancient world was filled with demons (daimons, supernatural creatures whose power for good or ill no one doubted). Every village had its possessed persons—madmen and women, troubled youths, and hate-filled citizens. Much of traditional pagan ritual was aimed at dealing with the spirits bedeviling such people. Wandering Christian preachers seemed more competent than others to deal with such tormentors, proving that their God was more powerful than the spirits and that their message was worthy of a hearing.

Over the course of the fourth century, the number of Christians rose from 5 million to 30 million. Imperial support, miracles, and preaching could not, by themselves, account for the phenomenal growth. Physical coercion played a large part. The story was told, for example, of the conversion of the town of Gaza under its first bishop, Porphyry, around 400. Although the account is largely fictional, it describes what must have been a fairly typical progression in the process of conversion. Porphyry arrived to find a pagan city. He began to make converts almost at once through the force of his miracles. His prayers to God ended a drought, aided a woman in childbirth, and expelled demons. The eloquence of his preaching struck his opponents dumb. Enormous imperial gifts enriched the local church. Finally, upon imperial command, all of the local temples were destroyed and "a great number" of leading pagans who refused conversion were tortured to death. The remaining pagan population converted.

Spread of Christianity to 300 C.E.

Whether or not the story is true, it illustrates the essential role that naked force often played in the process of conversion. It suited church leaders such as Porphyry who, when questioned about the value of conversions resulting from terror, is said to have quoted St. Paul: "Whether falsely or truly, Christ is preached, and I rejoice in that." Conversion—by whatever method—also suited the emperors, who saw a unified cult as an essential means of bolstering their position.

RELIGIOUS TOLERATION AND PERSECUTION

In 313, Constantine and Licinius met at Milan and agreed on an empire-wide policy of religious toleration. The first selection below is from the "Edict of Toleration" and the so-called Edict of Milan (actually a directive probably issued to eastern governors shortly afterward by Licinius). The second selection, from the Theodosian Code *published by Emperor Theodosius in 395, ends toleration, both of Arianism and of pagan practices, reversing the status of persecutor and persecuted.*

Focus Questions

How do Constantine and Theodosius differ in their attitudes toward religious pluralism? How did the *Theodosian Code* encourage the spread of Christianity?

Edict of Toleration Observing that freedom of worship should not be denied, but that each one should be given the right in accordance with his conviction and will to adhere to the religion that suits his preference, we had already long since given orders both to the Christians . . . to maintain the faith of their own sect and worship. . . .

When I, Constantine Augustus, and I, Licinius Augustus, met under happy auspices in Milan . . . we considered that first of all regulations should be drawn up to secure respect for divinity, to wit: to grant both to the Christians and to all men unrestricted right to follow the form of worship each desired, to the end that whatever divinity there be on the heavenly seat may be favorably disposed and propitious to us and all those placed under our authority. Accordingly, with salutary and most upright reasoning, we resolved on adopting this policy, namely that we should consider that no one whatsoever should be denied freedom to devote himself either to the cult of the Christians or to such religion as he deems best suited for himself, so that the highest divinity, to whose worship we pay allegiance with free minds, may grant us in all things his wonted favor and benevolence.

Theodosian Code *I, 2.* It is Our will that all the peoples who are ruled by the administration of Our Clemency shall practice that religion which the divine Peter the Apostle transmitted to the Romans, as the religion which he introduced makes clear even unto this day. . . . According to the apostolic discipline and the evangelic doctrine, we shall believe in the single Deity of the Father, the Son, and the Holy Spirit, under the concept of equal majesty and of the Holy Trinity.

We command that those persons who follow this rule shall embrace the name of Catholic Christians. The rest, however, whom We adjudge demented and insane, shall sustain the infamy of heretical dogmas, their meeting places shall not receive the name of churches, and they shall be smitten first by divine vengeance and secondly by the retribution of Our own initiative, which we shall assume in accordance with the divine judgment.

X, 2. Superstition shall cease, the madness of sacrifices shall be abolished. For if any man in violation of the law of the sainted Emperor, Our father, and in violation of this command of Our Clemency, should dare to perform sacrifices, he shall suffer the infliction of a suitable punishment and the effect of an immediate sentence.

IMPERIAL CHRISTIANITY

The religion to which Constantine converted had matured institutionally and intellectually since its origins as a reform movement within Judaism. By the late third century, Christian communities existed throughout the empire, each headed by a bishop considered divinely guided and answerable only to his flock and to God. The bishops replaced pagan philosophers as sources of wisdom and authority. (See "A Closer Look: The Stainless Star of Wisdom's Discipline," pp. 178–179.) In the west, the bishop of Rome, termed the *pope,* had acquired the position of first among equals, a position at times acknowledged by the eastern patriarchates as well, out of respect for the successor of Peter and Paul and bishop of the ancient capital. However, the Church as a whole was divided on fundamental questions of belief, and the growing importance of Christianity in the Roman Empire added to the gravity of the divisions. The two most contentious issues were, in the Greek-speaking regions of the empire, the nature of Christ and, in the Latin-speaking provinces, the extent to which individuals could earn their salvation through their own virtue.

Divinity, Humanity, and Salvation

Jesus, the Savior or the "Christ" (the anointed one), was at the heart of Christian belief, but individual Christian communities interpreted the nature of Christ differently as they attempted to reconcile their faith with the intellectual traditions of late antiquity. Christian Scriptures spoke of the Father, the Son, and the Spirit. Yahweh was generally accepted as the Father and Christ as the Son, and the Spirit was understood to be the continuing presence of God sent by Jesus after his resurrection and ascension.

MAP DISCOVERY

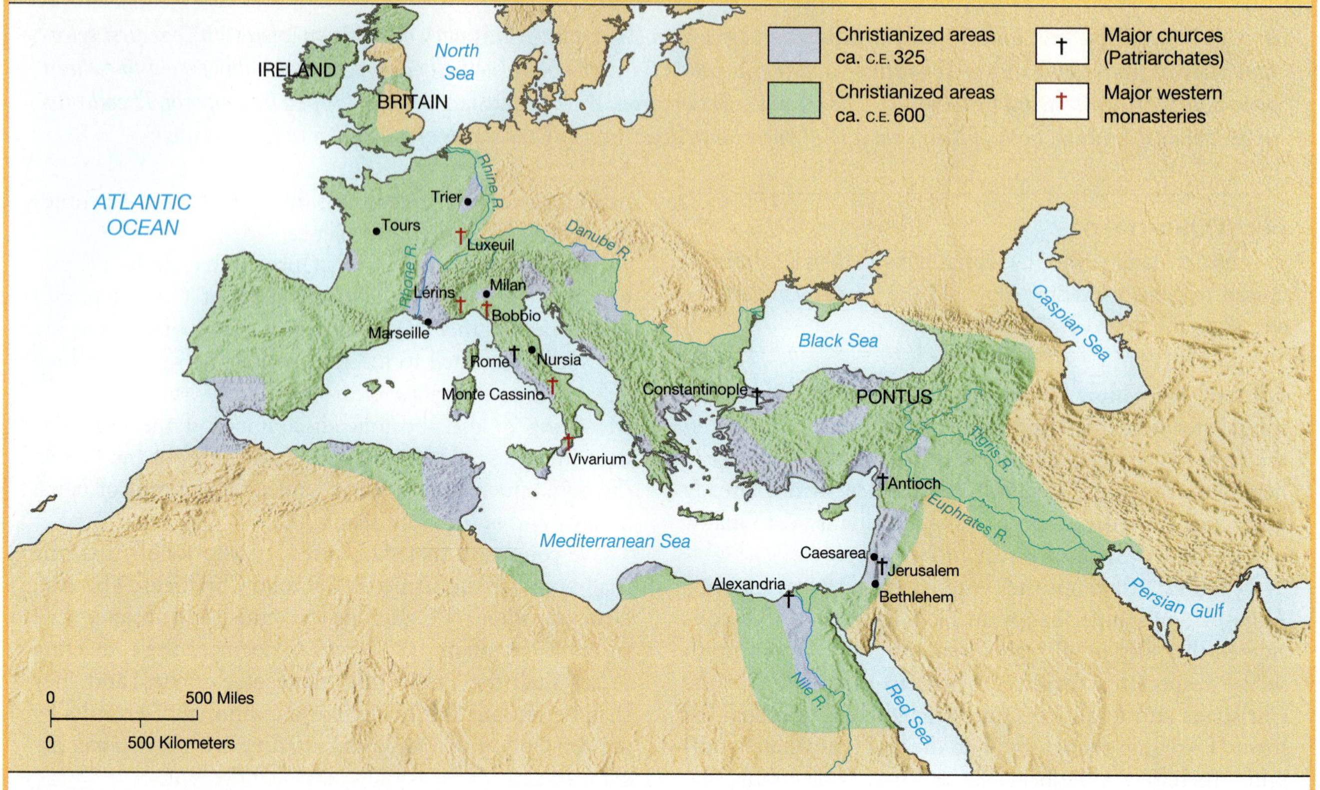

The Spread of Christianity

Examine the regions in which Christianity first became established. What is distinctive about the areas Christianized in the first three centuries of Christendom? What major differences can you detect between Christian centers in the eastern and in the western portions of the Roman Empire? To what extent did Christianity exist outside the empire by 600?

Christology. Generally, Christians saw God as a Trinity, at once one and three. But the relationship among the three was a source of endless debate, particularly for Greek-speaking Christians attempting to reconcile their faith with the Neoplatonic ideas of successive emanations from God to creation. Was Christ just a man, chosen by God as a divine instrument, or was he God, and if so, had he simply appeared to be human? These were not trivial or academic questions for Christians, since the possibility of salvation depended on their answers. Throughout the eastern half of the empire, ordinary people were ready to fight not only with words but even with weapons to defend their positions.

Roman and Christian Views of the Good Life

Throughout the so-called **Christological controversies**—which began in the early third century and continued through the fifth—two extremes presented Christ as either entirely human or entirely God, with centrists attempting to hold a middle ground. At one extreme were the Monarchians, who emphasized the oneness of God by arguing that the three represented three activities although God possessed only one substance, and the Gnostics, who argued that Jesus had only appeared to be human but in reality was only divine. At the other extreme were the **Arians,** who explained that Jesus was a man and not divine.

Origen of Alexandria. The first Christian intellectual to undertake a systematic exposition of the Trinity was the great Alexandrine theologian Origen (185–254). In all of his teachings, Origen moved Christian teaching from a literal to a symbolic understanding of Scripture and gave it a sound philosophical foundation by synthesizing the Neoplatonic tradition with Christianity. His trinitarian teachings insisted on the coeternality of the Son with the Father but, drawing as he did on Neoplatonic ideas of emanations, he seemed to subordinate the Son to the Father and to make the Spirit a creation of the Son. In the generations following Origen, the controversy continued, particularly between those who taught the equality of the persons of the Trinity and those who, like the

Alexandrine theologian Arius (ca. 250–336), insisted that Jesus was not equal to God the Father. By the time of Constantine the issue threatened to destroy the unity of Christianity, and at the emperor's command the bishops of the entire Church assembled at Nicaea in 325 to settle the controversy. At the emperor's urging, the council condemned the teachings of Arius and adopted the term *homoousion,* "of one being," to describe the equality of the Father and the Son.

The Council of Nicaea did not end the Christological controversy. For almost a century, Arians continued to win adherents to their denial of the divinity of Christ, even among the Christian emperors who succeeded Constantine. Before the Arian tradition finally died out within the empire, missionaries spread it to the barbarian Goths beyond the frontiers. Similarly, at the other extreme, Monophysites in Egypt and Syria argued that Christ had only one nature—the divine. A century after Nicaea another council was held at Chalcedon in 451 to resolve the issue. Following the recommendation of the bishop of Rome, Pope Leo I (440–461), the bishops at Chalcedon agreed that in the one God there were three divine persons, the Father, the Son, and the Spirit. However, the second person of the Trinity, the Son, had two natures, one fully human, the other fully divine. The Chalcedon formulation established the orthodox, or "right-believing," position, and the full weight of the imperial machinery worked to impose it on all. In Egypt and Palestine, the decree was greeted with outrage: mobs of monks and laity rioted in the streets to oppose the "unclean synod of Chalcedon."

Salvation. Although a western bishop had provided the formula for Chalcedon, Latin Christians were not as deeply concerned with the Christological debates as were the easterners. For westerners, the great question was less the nature of God than the mechanism of salvation and the role of humans in the salvational process. As the ranks of Christians were swelled by people converting for political or social expediency, two groups, the Donatists and the Pelagians, taught that salvation was the right of only a small, elite minority who held themselves above the imperfect lives of the masses.

The Donatists had developed in North Africa as a response to the political shifts within Christian leadership in the early fourth century. During the last persecutions many Christians and even bishops had collaborated with Roman authorities, handing over sacred Scriptures to be burned. Disturbed by the ease with which the traitors (the English word *traitor* comes from the Latin verb *tradere,* "to hand over") had returned to positions of power in the Church under Constantine and by the growth of political conversions, the Donatists insisted that the Church had to be pure and that its ministers had to be blameless. Thus they argued that baptisms and ordinations performed by the traitors were invalid. The visible Church on earth had to be as perfect as the invisible one, and only the Donatists had preserved this purity. When, not surprisingly, the imperial government rejected the elitist claims and attempted to suppress the sect, the North African Donatists took up arms in a revolt against the imperial system and especially its Orthodox bishops.

The Pelagians also held themselves to a higher standard than that of ordinary Christians, who accepted sin as an inevitable part of human life. Pelagians believed rather that human nature had been so created that people could achieve perfection in this life. Like the Donatists, the Pelagians believed that members of the true Church perfected themselves by the force of their own wills, thus making a radical break with the compromising world in which they lived.

Augustine of Hippo. The primary opponent of both the Donatists and the Pelagians was Augustine of Hippo (354–430), a convert to Christianity who, more than any other individual, set the course of Western Christianity and political philosophy for the next thousand years. Born into a well-off North African family, he was quickly drawn into the good life and upward mobility open to bright young provincials in the fourth century. In his *Confessions,* the first psychological autobiography, Augustine describes how his skills in rhetoric took him to the provincial capital of Carthage and then on to Rome and finally Milan, the western imperial residence, where he gained fame as one of the foremost rhetoricians of the empire.

While in Milan, Augustine came into contact with kinds of people he had never encountered in Africa, particularly Neoplatonists and Christians. The most important was Ambrose, bishop of Milan. The encounter with a spiritual philosophy and a Christianity compatible with it profoundly changed the young professor. After a period of agonized searching, Augustine converted to the new religion. With characteristic enthusiasm, he embraced Christianity as wholeheartedly as he had previously embraced his career. Abandoning his Italian life, he returned to the North African town of Hippo to found a monastery where he could devote himself to reading the Scriptures. However, his neighbors were determined to harness the intellectual talents of their brilliant native son. When their bishop died, they forcibly seized Augustine and made him their bishop.

Augustine spent the remainder of his life as bishop of the small provincial town, but his reputation as spokesperson for the Christian tradition spread throughout the empire. As a professor of rhetoric he had become an expert in debate, and much of his episcopal career was spent in refuting opponents such as Donatists and Pelagians within the Church, as well as dealing with traditional pagans who blamed the problems of the empire on the new religion. Christians, they claimed, had abandoned the traditional gods and the traditional Roman virtues and justice that had made Rome great.

In responding to the attacks, Augustine elaborated a new Christian understanding of human society and the individual's relationship to God, which dominated Western thought for the next 15 centuries. He rejected the elitist attempt of the Donatists and Pelagians to identify the true Church with any earthly community. Likewise he rejected the claim of pagans that the Roman tradition was the embodiment of true virtue.

LOVE IN THE TWO CITIES

Augustine took more than 14 years to write his masterpiece, The City of God. *Initially, he intended to write simply a defense of Christianity from the charge that the disasters of his age, culminating in the sack of Rome in 410, resulted from Rome's abandoning its traditional gods. In time the work grew into a wide-ranging inquiry into the nature of human society. In the following passage, he summarizes his conclusion that human society and divine society are based on fundamentally different foundations.*

Focus Questions

Why, in Augustine's estimation, are all human societies fundamentally flawed? On what does Augustine believe the perfect society should be based?

What we see, then, is that two societies have issued from two kinds of love. Worldly society has flowered from a selfish love which dared to despise God, whereas the communion of saints is rooted in a love of God that is ready to trample on self. In a word, this latter relies on the Lord, whereas the other boasts that it can get along by itself. The city of man seeks the praise of men, whereas the heights of glory for the other is to hear God in the witness of conscience. The one lifts up its head in its own boasting; the other says to God: "Thou art my glory, thou liftest up my head" (Psalm 3:4).

In the city of the world, both the rulers themselves and the people they dominate are dominated by the lust for domination; whereas in the City of God all citizens serve one another in charity, whether they serve by the responsibilities of office or by the duties of obedience. The one city loves its leaders as symbols of its own strength; the other says to its God: "I love thee, O Lord, my strength" (Psalm 17:2). Hence, even the wise men in the city of man live according to man, and their only god has been the gods of their bodies or of the mind or of both, though some of them have reached a knowledge of God, "they did not glorify him as God or give thanks but became vain in their reasonings, and their senseless minds have been darkened. For, while professing to be wise" (that is to say, while glorying in their own wisdom, under the domination of pride), "they have become fools, and they have changed the glory of the incorruptible God for an image made like to corruptible man and to birds and four-footed beasts and creeping things" (meaning that they either led their people, or imitated them, in adoring idols shaped like these things), "and they worshipped and served the creature rather than the Creator who is blessed forever" (Romans 1:21–25). In the City of God, on the contrary, there is no merely human wisdom, but there is a piety which worships the true God as He should be worshipped and has as its goal that reward of all holiness whether in the society of saints on earth or in that of angels of heaven, which is "that God may be all in all" (1 Corinthians 15:28).

From Saint Augustine, *The City of God.*

Instead he argued that the true members of God's elect necessarily coexisted in the world with sinners. No earthly community, not even the empire or the visible Church, was the true "city of God." Earthly society participated in the true Church, the city of God, through the sacraments, and did so quite apart from the individual worthiness of the recipients or even of the ministers of the rites. To believe that the presence of sinners within the Church blocked the plan of salvation or that responsibility for salvation lay with the individual was to deny the omnipotence of God.

According to Augustine, neither the Donatist sect nor the Pelagian community nor even the imperial Church was essential for salvation. Those to be saved were not identified solely with any particular group of Christians. Salvation was free, a gift not earned by virtuous lives but freely granted by God to the elect. In this way, Augustine argued for a distinction between the visible Christian empire and the Christian community. Earlier, the pharisaic Jew Paul had determined that Christianity would survive Judaism even as the latter was being destroyed by Rome. Now Augustine, the Roman rhetorician, determined that Christianity would survive the disappearance of the Roman Empire just as it was disintegrating into barbarian kingdoms. Even as Augustine lay dying in Hippo, the city was under siege by barbarian Vandals.

The Call of the Desert

At the same time that Donatists and Pelagians were attempting to recover the spirit of an earlier, more demanding Christianity, less intellectual but equally determined men and women were searching for a different way of living Christ's message. These were the hermit, monk, and recluse, who taught less by his or her words than by his or her life, a life often so unusual that even the most ignorant and worldly citizen of the late empire could recognize in it the power of God. Beneath the apparent eccentricity, however, lay a fundamental principle: the radical rejection of society's values in favor of absolute dedication to God's.

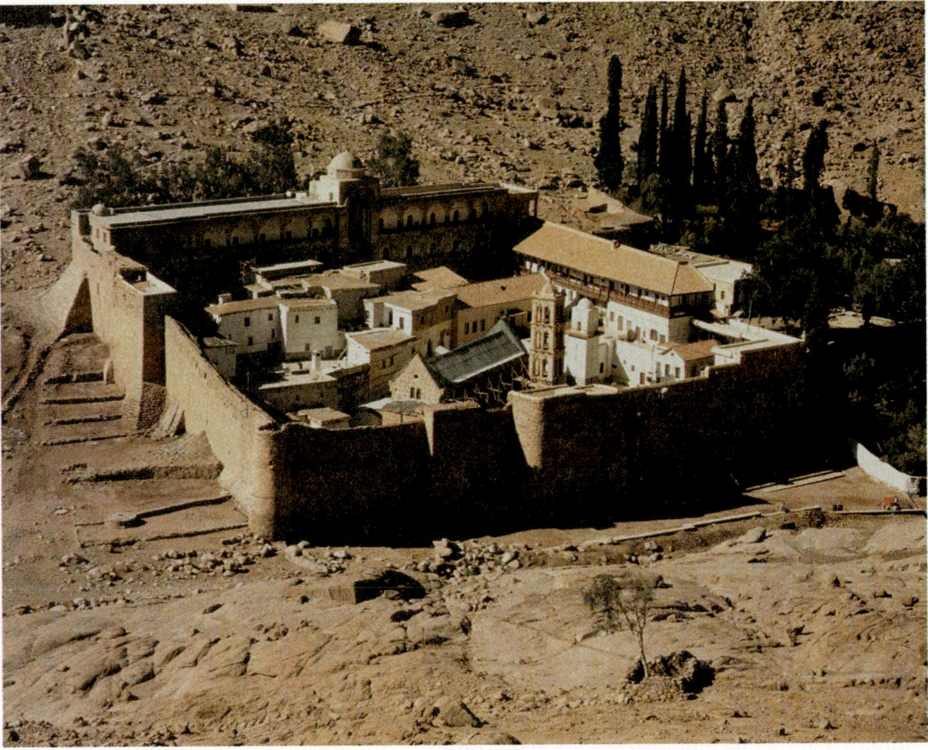

■ The monastery of St. Catherine was constructed between 527 and 565 by order of the Emperor Justinian I. It encloses the Chapel of the Burning Bush, the site where Moses is supposed to have seen the burning bush. The living bush on the grounds is purportedly the original. The site is sacred to three major world religions—Islam, Christianity, and Judaism.

Shortly after the death of Origen in 254, another Egyptian was undertaking a different path to enduring fame. Anthony (ca. 250–355), a well-to-do peasant, heard the Scripture, "Go, sell all you have and give to the poor and follow me." Anthony was uneducated; it was said that he had been too shy as a boy to attend school. The straightforward peasant did exactly what the text commanded. He disposed of all his goods and left his village for the Egyptian desert. There, for the next 70 years, he sought to follow Christ in a life of constant self-mortification and prayer. The dropout from civilization deeply touched his fellow Christians, many of whom were disturbed by the abrupt transformation of their religion from persecuted minority to privileged majority. By the time of his death the monk—the word comes from the Greek *monos*, "alone"—found himself the head of a large, loosely knit community of like-minded persons who looked to him as spiritual father, or abbot. Over the next centuries, thousands rejected the worldliness of civilization and the easy life of the average Christian to lead a monastic life in the wildernesses of the empire.

Monastic Communities

Monasticism took two forms, communal organization or solitary life. Pachomius (ca. 290–346) and Basil the Great (ca. 329–379) in the east and Benedict of Nursia (ca. 480–547) in the west perfected the communal life. Faced with the impossibility of surviving in a harsh environment without cooperation, Egyptian monks banded together into small monastic towns. In these monasteries lived as many as 2000 monks. They placed themselves under the control of the abbot, who served as spiritual guide and administrator of the community. The men and women sought spiritual perfection through physical self-mortification and through the subordination of their own wills to that of the abbot. Monks drank no wine, ate no meat, used no oil. They spent their days in prayer, either communal or individual.

The monastic communities survived by maintaining a symbiotic relationship with the civilized world the monks had sought to escape. Abbots organized their monks into houses according to their various crafts, and the surplus of their gardening, baking, basket making, and the like was sold in the villages and towns of Egypt.

The fame of the religious communities spread throughout the Roman world, carried initially by the local peasants, then by inhabitants of nearby cities who came to see the desert dwellers and ask their advice. Pilgrims from across the empire visited the Egyptian monasteries on their way to and from Jerusalem. Some of the pilgrims returned home with the desire to imitate the Egyptian monks in their native provinces. During the fourth century the monastic tradition spread east to Bethlehem, Jerusalem, Caesarea, and Constantinople and west to Rome, Milan, Trier, Marseille, and Tours. In the following centuries it reached beyond the borders of the empire when Egyptian-style monasticism was introduced into Ireland.

Intellectuals as well as peasants heard the call of monastic life. Chief among the intellectuals was Jerome (ca. 347–420), the greatest linguist of antiquity, who was so impressed by a visit to the monastic communities of the east that he became a priest and founded a monastery in Bethlehem. There he translated the Bible into Latin. The Latin translation, known as the Vulgate, became the standard version of Christian Scripture in the west until the Reformation and, in Roman Catholic countries, until the twentieth century.

In the Greek-speaking world, the definitive form of the monastic community was provided by Basil the Great. Basil had visited the monasteries of Egypt, Palestine, and Syria before founding his own monastery at Pontus near his family estate at Annesi in what is now Turkey. Although he did not write a specific rule for the governance of his monastery, his collection of commentaries and spiritual advice to his followers outlined a form of monastic life in which a day of agriculture, craft work, and care for the sick and the poor was organized within an ordered progression of liturgical prayer. His emphasis on communal life rather than on heroic acts of individual asceticism provided the model for eastern monasticism from his day to the present.

Eastern monastic communities continued active involvement in political and secular affairs. Monasteries provided the early religious training for most religious leaders. Monks and abbots often involved themselves wholeheartedly in the politics of the empire. Rioting of monks in the streets of Constantinople over political issues was a familiar sight for more than a thousand years.

In the west, Benedict of Nursia was as influential in structuring communal religious life as was Basil in the east. Like Anthony before him, Benedict had fled the city for the countryside. In time Benedict became abbot of a small community of monks at Monte Cassino, between Rome and Naples. The rule that he drafted for the governance of his community, while drawn largely from earlier monastic rules circulating in Italy, became the definitive statement of western monasticism. Benedict's rule encouraged moderation and flexibility while emphasizing a life of poverty, chastity, and obedience to an elected abbot. Monks were required to perform some physical labor, and the monastery was intended to be a self-sufficient community. However, the real task of the monks was the continuous praise of God, which consisted of gathering at regular intervals throughout the day and night for communal prayer. Although Benedict lived and died in obscurity, within two and a half centuries his rule became the universal rule for western monasticism.

DOCUMENT
Rule of St. Benedict

Western monasteries, too, provided their share of bishops, but, unlike those in the east, western monks remained more isolated from population centers and from direct involvement in public affairs. Western monasteries were not, however, peripheral to western society and religion. Rather, the rustic communities were centers of religious and economic activity as well as education and learning in the largely rural west. They remained under the authority of the local bishops, who were usually drawn from the lay aristocracy of the empire in the west. Also, western monasteries depended upon the political and economic support that they received from lay patrons.

Solitaries and Hermits

Although Anthony had begun as a hermit, he and most Egyptian monks eventually settled into communal lives. Elsewhere, particularly in the desert of Syria, the model of the monk remained the individual hermit. The Syrian desert, unlike that of Egypt, was particularly suitable for such an ascetic life. There the desert was milder, an individual could find food in wild roots and water in rain pools, and villages were never too far off. Moreover, the life of the wandering hermit was closely connected to traditional semi-nomadic lifestyles in the Fertile Crescent. But the Christian hermits who appeared across Syria in late antiquity were unlikely to be mistaken for Bedouin. The Christian hermits were wild men and women who came down from the mountainsides and galvanized the attention of their contemporaries by their lifestyles. Their lives were characterized by the most extreme forms of self-mortification and radical rejection of civilization. The most famous of the hermits, Simeon Stylites (ca. 390–459), spent 36 years perched at the top of a

■ A gold plaque from a sixth-century Syrian reliquary. The subject is Simeon Stylites on his pillar; the snake represents the vanquished devil. Clients could consult the holy man by climbing up the ladder on the left.

pillar 50 feet high. Two women, Marana and Cyra, lived for 42 years chained in a small open-roofed enclosure.

Such people of God, rejecting civilized life in the most overt and radical ways, nevertheless met very real social and cultural needs of the population. Their lack of ties to human society made them the perfect arbitrators in the constant disputes that threatened to disrupt village life. They were "individuals of power," whose proven ability to cast out demons and work miracles made them ideal community patrons at a time when traditional power brokers of the village were being lured away to imperial service or provincial cities. The greatest of the holy people, like Simeon Stylites, received as visitors not only local peasants but also emperors and empresses who eagerly sought their advice.

Unlike the eastern monks, the Syrian hermits of the fourth and fifth centuries had few parallels in the west. Hermits did inhabit the caves and forests of Italy and Gaul, and pious women found solitude as recluses even in the center of Rome. But the westerners did not establish themselves either as independent sources of religious power or as political power brokers. Their monasticism remained a personal religious commitment. When one Roman woman was asked why she remained shut up in her cell, she replied, "I am on a journey." When asked where she was going, she answered simply, "To God."

A PARTING OF THE WAYS

Those who remained in "the world" at the end of the fourth century could hardly take so serene a view of life. Christians and pagans might differ in their explanations for the ills that had befallen the empire, but none could deny their severity. The vulnerability of the Constantinian system became clear shortly after 376 when the Huns, a nomadic horse-riding people from central Asia, swept into the Black Sea region and threw the entire barbarian world once more into chaos. The Huns quickly destroyed the Gothic confederation and absorbed many of the peoples who had constituted the Goths. Others sought protection in the empire. The Visigoths, as they came to be known, were the largest of the groups, and their fate illustrated how precarious existence could be for all the occupants of the imperial frontier.

Driven from their lands and thus from their food supply, the Visigoths turned to the empire for assistance. But the Roman authorities treated them as brutally as had the Huns, forcing some to sell their children into slavery in return for morsels of dog flesh. In despair the Visigoths rose up against the Romans, and against all odds their desperate rebellion succeeded. They annihilated an imperial army at Adrianople in 378, and the emperor Valens himself was killed. His successor, Theodosius, was forced to allow the Visigoths to settle along the Danube and to be governed by their own leaders despite the fact that they lived within the boundaries of the empire.

Theodosius's treaty with the Visigoths set an ominous precedent. Never before had a barbarian people been allowed to settle as a political unit within the empire. Within a few years the Visigoths were again on the move, traveling across the Balkans into Italy under the command of their chieftain, Alaric (ca. 370–410). In 410 they captured Rome and sacked it for three days, an event that sent shock waves throughout the entire empire. Rome had been sacked before, but ever since the Celtic sack of Rome in 390 B.C.E, the sacking had always been done by Romans. The symbolic effect of the Visigoths' victory far exceeded the amount of real damage, which was relatively light. Only after Alaric's death did the Visigoths leave Italy, ultimately settling in Spain and southern Gaul with the approval of the emperor.

The Barbarization of the West

Rome did not fall. It was transformed. Romans participated in and even encouraged the transformation. Roman accommodation of the Visigoths set the pattern for subsequent settlement of barbarians in the western half of the empire. By this time, barbarians made up the bulk of the imperial army, and commanders themselves were frequently barbarians. However, the barbarian troops had been integrated into existing Roman military structures. Indeed, the so-called imperial Germans had often proven even more loyal to Rome than the Roman provincial populations they were to protect. In the late fourth and fifth centuries, emperors accepted whole barbarian peoples as integral parts of the Roman army and settled them within the empire. Usually the emperors diverted a percentage of tax revenues from the region's estates in order to support these "guests."

The Visigothic kingdom in southern Gaul and Spain was typical in this respect. Alaric's successor, Ataulf, was extremely eager to win the approval of the emperor. He married Galla Placidia, the daughter of Emperor Theodosius and the sister of Emperor Honorius, in a Roman ceremony in Narbonne in 414. Soon afterward he established a government at Bordeaux directed by Gallo-Roman aristocrats. Although his opponents soon assassinated him, his successors concluded a treaty with Constantinople in which the Visigoths were recognized as a legitimate, established political presence within the empire. The so-called kingdom of Toulouse endured for almost a century. South of the Pyrenees, the Gothic kingdom of Toledo continued for almost 300 years.

Salvian, *The Governance of God*

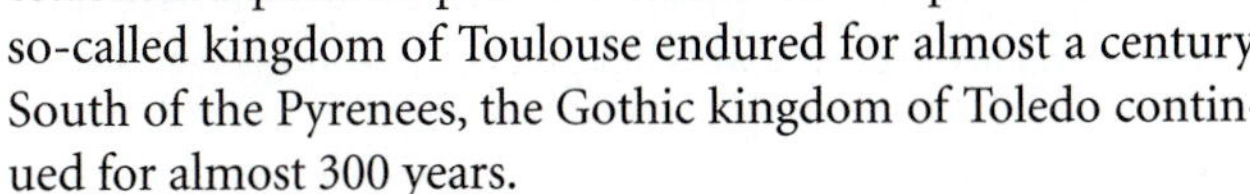

The Visigoths were not the only powerful barbarian people to challenge the empire. The Vandals, who had entered the empire in 406, crossed over into Africa, the richest region of the western empire, and quickly conquered it. Avowed enemies of the empire, the Vandals used their base in North Africa to raid the European coastline and attack Roman shipping. In 455 they sacked Rome much more thoroughly than had the Goths 45 years earlier.

Another threat appeared in the 430s, when the Huns, formerly Roman allies, invaded the empire under their charismatic leader Attila (ca. 406–453). Although defeated in Gaul

THE STAINLESS STAR OF WISDOM'S DISCIPLINE

A CLOSER LOOK

Public philosophers were prized citizens of every ancient city. The austere teachers, distinguished by their black robes, were courted by the wealthy as tutors of their sons and by the powerful for the benefit of their wisdom. But in the early fifth century, Alexandria, long famed for its great museum and rival schools, boasted a philosopher with a difference: Hypatia (ca. 370–415), a woman famed for her wisdom and described by one supporter as "mother, sister, teacher, benefactress in all things." Her controversial career and terrible death summarize the complexity and factionalism of late antiquity.

As was the case with many other professional philosophers, Hypatia's father had been a renowned philosopher before her, specializing in astronomy, mathematics, divination, and Neoplatonic philosophy. Hypatia wrote commentaries on mathematical and astronomical treatises, and she edited and annotated Ptolemy's *Almagest*, the classic textbook of Greek astronomy. However, she won her greatest praise—and her greatest criticism—for her practice of philosophy. Popular teachers are often controversial, and as a pagan, as a woman, and as a philosopher in the turbulent world of late antiquity, Hypatia was the center of more than her share. But philosophers were more than teachers in antiquity. Because of their deep learning, their detachment from the concerns of daily life, and their eloquence, they were allowed and even expected to play a public role, advising, admonishing, and reconciling the powerful.

Hypatia's defenders and detractors came from the ranks of both Christians and pagans. Her former student Synesius of Cyrene, who ended his life as a bishop, was her strongest supporter, describing her as "the lady who rightfully presides over the mysteries of philosophy," while her rival, the pagan philosopher Damascius, considered her a huckstering Cynic ready to teach any philosophy to anyone who wanted

Statue of a woman traditionally believed to be Hypatia of Alexandria.

it. The truth, as usual, was probably somewhere in between, although certainly much of the controversy surrounding her came less from her teaching than from her sex.

Women teachers and philosophers were a comparative rarity, and even for some admirers, her beauty and her independence (she never married) tempted them to expect more from her than philosophy. However, Hypatia forcefully rejected any such advances, insisting that physical attraction had nothing to do with true beauty.

Controversial because of her sex and her teaching, she was even more so because she remained the most publicly admired and consulted pagan philosopher in an increasingly Christian city. Although Christians were in the majority in Alexandria by 400, they were an insecure majority and one prone to violence. Disagreements often ended in street fighting and rioting. To make matters worse, bands of fanatical monks often poured into the city from the nearby desert monasteries to take part in the violent confrontations. In 415, riots broke out as Christians—with the encouragement of the new patriarch, or archbishop, of Alexandria, Cyril (ca. 377–444)—sought to expel the city's large Jewish population. Cyril, always a firebrand and not hesitant to see his supporters turn to violence if it would further his cause, soon ran afoul of the prefect of the city, Orestes, who opposed the violence against the Jews. Monks, in town to support the Christians, accused Orestes of supporting sacrifice to the ancient gods—a capital offense—and one monk attempted to stone the prefect as he rode through the city.

Orestes was exonerated of the charge of paganism, and his supporters quickly arrested the monk who had struck the prefect. After a speedy trial he was tortured to death. Cyril was outraged and appealed to the emperor, claiming that the executed monk was a martyr. But even moderate Christians found Cyril's appeal groundless, and he was forced to abandon it.

When tensions ran high in ancient cities, philosophers often provided the means of breaking an impasse and tipping the scales in one direction or another. It was they who traditionally used their eloquence and wisdom to persuade those in power to act as they should. According to reports, Hypatia, although known as an even-handed teacher of both Christians and pagans, was a close associate of Orestes and was known to have his ear and those of the other members of Alexandria's power elite. The sight of the wealthy and powerful coming and going at her house to seek her advice infuriated Cyril's supporters, who thought that their bishop, not a pagan philosopher, should play the role of guide and advisor in the city. A rumor spread "among the Church people" that she had used her occult wisdom to bewitch Orestes and prevent a reconciliation between the prefect and the patriarch. During the solemn season of Lent, their animosity heightened by the fasting, a mob of monks stopped Hypatia's carriage in the streets, dragged her out, stripped her naked, then took her to a nearby church where they cut her to pieces and threw her remains into a fire.

Hypatia's murder meant more than simply the destruction of a brilliant woman by an ignorant, puritanical mob. It was more than just another violent confrontation between the pagan and Christian worlds. It was the end of a kind of urban culture in which the philosopher, the man or woman of learning, enjoyed a position of public respect and authority. Henceforth, respect and authority would come not from learning but from God.

by a combined army of barbarians under the command of the Roman general Flavius Aetius in 451, they turned toward Italy and penetrated as far as Rome. There they were stopped not by the rapidly disintegrating imperial forces but by the bishop of Rome, Pope Leo I, who met Attila before the city's gates. What transpired between the two is not known, but Attila's subsequent withdrawal from Italy vastly increased the prestige of the papacy. Now not only were popes successors of Saint Peter and bishops of the principal city of the west, but they were replacing the emperor as protector of the city. The foundations of the political power of the papacy were established.

The confederation of the Huns collapsed after the death of Attila in 453, but imperial power did not revive in Italy. A series of incompetent emperors were pushed aside by barbarian generals who assumed power in the peninsula and sought recognition from Zeno, the emperor in the east. However, after the death of the last legitimate western emperor, Julius Nepos, in 480, Zeno conferred the title of patrician on the Ostrogothic king, Theodoric. In 489 Theodoric invaded Italy with imperial blessing and established himself as ruler of Italy.

In Theodoric's kingdom, the Roman and Ostrogothic institutions remained separate, united only at the top in the person of Theodoric. To his barbarians, Theodoric was king; to the Romans, he was patrician and military commander in the west. In reality, imperial presence had ceased to exist in Italy.

In Gaul, between the Seine and the Loire, the Roman general Flavius Aetius and, after his death, the general Syagrius continued to represent some imperial presence. But the armies that Aetius and Syagrius commanded consisted entirely of barbarians—particularly Visigoths and Franks—and they represented the interests of local aristocratic factions rather than those of Constantinople. So thoroughly barbarized had the last Roman commanders become in their military command and political control that the barbarians referred to Syagrius as "king of the Romans." Ultimately, in 486, Syagrius was defeated and replaced by the Frank Clovis, son of his military commander Childeric, probably with the blessing of the emperor.

Britain met a similar fate. Abandoned by Roman legions around 407, the Romano-Celtic population in the province concluded a treaty with bands of Saxons and Angles to protect Britain from other barbarian raiders. As had happened elsewhere in the empire, the barbarians came as federated troops and stayed as rulers. Gradually, during the fifth century, Germanic warrior groups conquered much of the island. The Anglo-Saxons pushed the native inhabitants to the west and the north. There, as the Cornish and the Welsh (in Anglo-Saxon, Welsh means simply "foreigner"), they preserved the Christian religion but largely lost their other Roman traditions.

The New Barbarian Kingdoms

The establishment of barbarian kingdoms within the Roman world meant the end of the western empire as a political entity. However, the emperors of the east and west continued to pretend that all the barbarian peoples, with the exception of the Vandals, were Roman troops commanded by loyal Roman officers who happened to be of barbarian origin. Following the precedent established with the Visigoths, the emperors gave their kings or war leaders official status within the empire as Roman generals or patricians. They generally rewarded their leaders by redirecting to them imperial taxes from areas where they were settled. Occasionally emperors granted them portions of abandoned lands or existing estates. Local Roman elites considered the leaders rude and uncultured barbarians who nevertheless could be made to serve these elites' own interests more easily than better-educated imperial bureaucrats.

DOCUMENT The Rise and Fall of Rome

The Vandals crossed into North Africa from Spain and founded a state centered on Carthage. This mosaic of the late fifth or early sixth century shows a prosperous Vandal lord leaving his villa. His costume is typical of barbarians.

MAP DISCOVERY

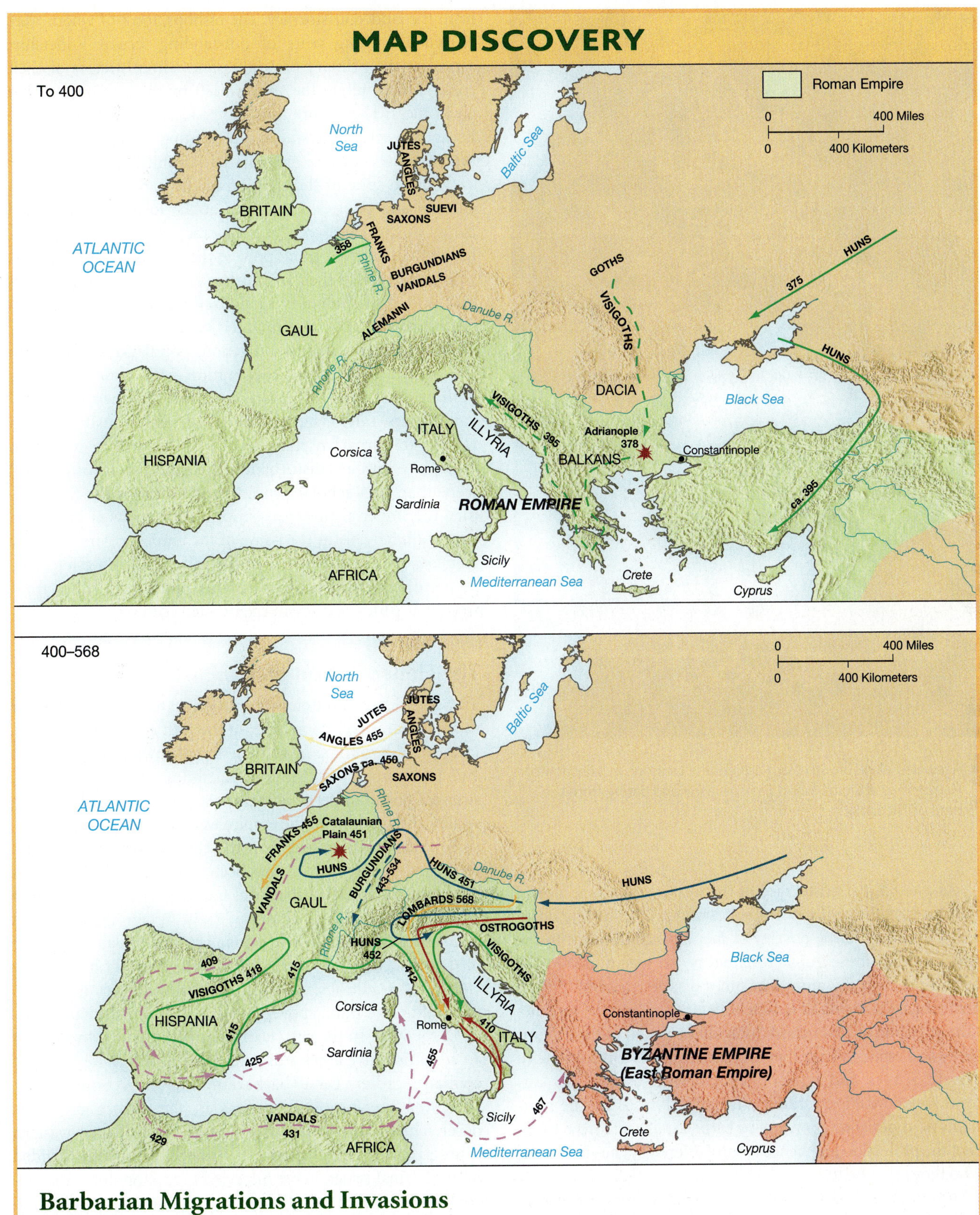

Barbarian Migrations and Invasions

Study these maps of barbarian migrations and invasions. Who were Rome's western neighbors in the fourth century? What effects did the Huns have on barbarian migrations? From these maps, how might you explain the relative stability of the eastern or Byzantine Empire in the sixth century compared with the western?

A jeweled eagle brooch from the Cesena treasure, a collection of Ostrogothic artifacts found near Ravenna and dating from the time of Theodoric.

As a result, the aristocracy of the west, the *maiores,* viewed the decay of the civil government without dismay. The decay was due largely to the poverty of the imperial treasury. In the fifth century, all the public revenues of the west amounted to little more than the annual incomes of a few wealthy private aristocrats. Managing to escape both taxation and the jurisdiction of public officials, those individuals carved out for themselves vast estates, which they and their families controlled with private armies and which they governed as virtually autonomous lordships. Ordinary freemen, pressed by the remnants of imperial taxation and by barbarians, were forced to accept the protection and hence control offered by the aristocrats, who thereby came to control whole villages and districts.

Although during the fifth century the western aristocracy had largely given up on the civil administration, the wealthy landowners increasingly identified with the episcopacy. In Gaul, bishops were regularly selected from members of the greatest Gallo-Roman senatorial families, establishing veritable episcopal dynasties. In Italy and Spain, too, bishops were drawn from the landed aristocracy. The bishops, most of whom were elected after long years of outstanding secular leadership, served as the primary protectors and administrators of their communities, filling the vacuum left by the erosion of other civil offices. They, more than either local civil officials or the Bacaudae, were successful in representing the community before imperial tax collectors or barbarian chieftains.

Thus, in spite of the creation of the barbarian kingdoms, cultural and political leadership at the local level remained firmly in the hands of the aristocracy. Aristocratic bishops, rather than hermits, monopolized the role of mediators of divine power, just as their lay brothers, in cooperation with barbarian military leaders, monopolized the role of mediators of secular power. Barbarian military leaders needed local ties by which to govern the large indigenous populations over whom they ruled. They found cooperation with these aristocrats both necessary and advantageous. Thus, although individual landowners might have suffered in the transition from Roman to barbarian rule, for the most part the transition took place with less disturbance of the local social or political scene than later scholars once thought. During the fifth century the imperial presence simply faded away as barbarian kings came to rule in the name of the emperor. After 480, the emperor resided exclusively in the east. The last western emperors disappeared without serious opposition either from western aristocrats or from their eastern colleagues.

The Hellenization of the East

The eastern half of the empire, in contrast to the west, managed to survive and even to prosper in the fifth and sixth centuries. In the east, beginning in 400, the trends toward militarization and barbarization of the administration were reversed, the strength of the imperial government was reaffirmed, and the vitality and integrity of the empire were restored.

Several reasons account for the contrast between east and west. First, the east had always been more urbanized and civilized than the west. It had an old tradition of civil control that antedated the Roman Empire itself. When the decay of Roman traditions allowed regionalism and tribalism to arise in the west, the same decay brought in the east a return to Hellenistic traditions. Second, the east had never developed the tradition of public poverty and private wealth characteristic of the west. In the east, tax revenues continued to support an administrative apparatus, which remained in the hands of civilians rather than barbarian military commanders. Moreover, the local aristocracies in the eastern provinces never achieved the wealth and independence of their western counterparts. Finally, Christian bishops, frequently divided over doctrinal issues, never managed to monopolize either sacred power, which was shared by itinerant holy men and monks, or secular power, which was wielded by imperial agents. Thus, under the firm direction of its emperors, especially Theodosius and later Zeno, the eastern empire not only survived but prepared for a new expansionist phase under the emperor Justinian.

CONCLUSION

The divergence in religious power between east and west was characteristic of the growing differences between the two halves of the Roman Empire at the close of late antiquity. The profound crises—military, social, and economic—that had shaken the empire and the barbarian world in the course of the third century left the west transformed. The new imperial system, based on an absolute ruler and an authoritarian Christianity, held the Roman world together for a few more centuries. Ultimately, however, the two halves of the old Mediterranean empire drifted in different directions as each formed a new civilization from Roman and indigenous traditions.

The east remained more firmly attached not only to Roman traditions of government but also to the much more ancient traditions of social complexity, urban life, and religious culture that stretched back to the dawn of civilization. The emperors continued to rule from Constantinople for another thousand years, but the extent of their authority gradually shrank to little more than the city itself. Furthermore, their empire was so profoundly Hellenized in nature that it is properly called Byzantine (from the original name of Constantinople) rather than Roman.

The west experienced a transformation even more profound than that of the east. The triple heritage of late Roman political and military forms, barbarian society, and Christian culture coalesced into a new civilization that perhaps was less the direct heir of antiquity than was that of the east, but was all the more dynamic for its distinctiveness. In culture, politics, and patterns of urban and rural life, the west and the east had gone their separate ways, and their paths diverged ever more in the centuries ahead.

QUESTIONS FOR REVIEW

1. How did increasing contact between Roman civilization and the Germanic barbarians transform both?
2. How did Constantine's adoption of Christianity and the movement of his capital to Byzantium contribute to the decline of the western empire?
3. How did different views of the divinity of Christ and the means of salvation divide early Christians?
4. What was the attraction of monasticism, and why did it take so many forms?
5. What were the differences in politics and culture in the eastern and western portions of the empire by the end of the fifth century?

KEY TERMS

Arians, *p. 172*
Bacaudae, *p. 164*
Christological controversies, *p. 172*
coloni, *p. 168*
decurions, *p. 168*
federated tribes, *p. 166*
honestiores, *p. 163*
humiliores, *p. 163*
monasticism, *p. 175*
tetrarchy, *p. 167*
wergeld, *p. 165*

DISCOVERING WESTERN CIVILIZATION ONLINE

You can obtain more information about the transforming Roman world at the Websites listed below. See also the Companion Website that accompanies this text, www.ablongman.com/kishlansky, which contains an online study guide and additional resources.

General Websites

ORB Online Encyclopaedia: Late Antiquity in the Mediterranean
www.nipissingu.ca/department/history/Muhlenberg/orb/LTD.-LATEST.HTM
A guide to late antiquity in the Mediterranean.

The Crisis of the Third Century

Worlds of Late Antiquity
ccat.sas.upenn.edu/jod/wola.html
A comprehensive site dedicated to late antiquity created by James O'Donnell.

The Empire Restored

Diocletian's Palace
www.st.carnet.hr/split/diokl.html
A site devoted to Emperor Diocletian's palace in modern Split.

Imperial Christianity

Resources for Constantine the Great
shsu.edu/~eng_wpf/con-hist.html
Links connecting to sites concerning Constantine.

A Parting of the Ways

A Visual Tour Through Late Antiquity
www.nipissingu.ca/department/history/muhlberger/4505/show.htm
Images of people and places of late antiquity.

SUGGESTIONS FOR FURTHER READING

The Crisis of the Third Century

Peter Brown, *The World of Late Antiquity, A.D. 150–750* (New York: Harcourt Brace Jovanovich, 1971). A brilliant essay on the cultural transformation of the ancient world.

Averil Cameron, *The Later Roman Empire, A.D. 284–430* (Cambridge, MA: Harvard University Press, 1993). An important survey by an authority.

Hans-Werner Goetz, Jorg Jarnut and Walter Pohl, eds., *Regna and Gentes: The Relationship Between Late Antique and Early Medieval Peoples and Kingdoms in the Transformation of the*

Roman World (Leiden, The Netherlands: Brill, 2003). A series of essays on the transformation of the Classical world.

Malcolm Todd, *The Early Germans*, 2d ed. (Oxford: Blackwell Publishers, 2004). A general introduction to pre-Roman Germanic society.

Bryan Ward-Perkins, *The Fall of Rome and the End of Civilization* (Oxford and New York: Oxford University Press, 2005). A very clever if exaggerated revisionist approach to the end of Classical material civilization.

The Empire Restored

T. D. Barnes, *The New Empire of Diocletian and Constantine* (Cambridge, MA: Harvard University Press, 1982). An examination of the transformations brought about under the two great emperors.

Ramsay MacMullen, *Paganism in the Roman Empire* (New Haven, CT: Yale University Press, 1981). A sensible introduction to the varieties of Roman religion in the imperial period.

Imperial Christianity

G. W. Bowersock, *Martyrdom and Rome* (New York: Cambridge University Press, 1995). A new look at Christian martyrdom in antiquity.

Peter Brown, *Authority and the Sacred: Aspects of the Christianisation of the Roman* (Cambridge: Cambridge University Press, 1995). A highly readable account of the emergence of Christianity in the Roman world by the leading historian of late antiquity.

W. H. C. Friend, *The Rise of Christianity* (London: Darton, Longman and Todd, 1984). A panoramic survey of Christianity from its origins to the seventh century.

Noel Lenski, ed., *The Cambridge Companion to the Age of Constantine* (Cambridge and New York: Cambridge University Press, 2006). A collectively authored guide to the fourth century.

A Parting of the Ways

Peter Brown, *The Rise of Western Christendom* (Cambridge, MA: Blackwell Publishers, 1996). A survey of late antiquity by a master scholar and stylist.

Patrick J. Geary, *The Myth of Nations: The Medieval Origins of Europe* (Princeton, NJ: Princeton University Press, 2001). An essay examining the relationship between modern nationalism and ethnic groups in late antiquity.

Judith Herrin, *The Formation of Christendom* (Princeton, NJ: Princeton University Press, 1987). A history of the transformed Mediterranean world, east and west, to 800 from the perspective of a noted Byzantinist.

Herwig Wolfram, *The Roman Empire and Its Germanic Peoples* (Berkeley: University of California Press, 1997). Important general survey of the place of the barbarians in the Roman world.

For a list of additional titles related to this chapter's topics, please see http://www.ablongman.com/kishlansky.

CHAPTER 7

THE CLASSICAL LEGACY IN THE EAST: BYZANTIUM AND ISLAM

FROM TEMPLE TO MOSQUE

THE CONTINUITY OF CIVILIZATION IN THE EASTERN MEDITERRANEAN

THE VISUAL RECORD

First a temple dedicated to the Syriac god Hadad and then to the Roman god Jupiter, later the Christian church of St. John, and finally a mosque, the Great Mosque of Damascus in Syria bears testimony to the great civilizations that have followed one another in the Near East. Like the successive houses of worship, each civilization rose upon the ruins of its predecessor, incorporating and transforming the rich legacy of the past into a new culture. Little of the pagan and Christian structures is visible, although the mosque owes much to both, as does the civilization it represents.

Nothing remains of the pre-Roman structure. In the first century C.E., the Romans rebuilt the temple to include an outer enclosure measuring 1233 by 1000 feet with four monumental gateways. In the interior was a porticoed court marked by four corner towers. Monumental portals, or gateways, in the east and west walls provided access to the inner court through triple doorways. In the center of the court stood a structure housing the statue of Jupiter.

Around the time of Constantine, the temple was converted into a Christian church dedicated to Saint John the Baptist. Apparently, a portion of the interior porticoed court, which measured roughly 517 by 318 feet, was enclosed to provide a space for worshipers. Two of the four towers were raised to serve as bell towers. For a time after Damascus fell to the Arabs in 635, Christians and Muslims shared the church. Initially there were only a few Muslims, who required no more than a small place in the exterior courtyard.

However, the Muslim population of the city grew rapidly, and by 705 Damascus was the capital of a vast, expanding Muslim Empire, which would soon stretch from the Pyrenees to the Indus River. The caliph al-Walid (705–715) wanted a place of prayer befitting his capital's glory. He invited the Christian community to choose a site for another church. When they refused, he expelled them and hired Greek architects to adapt the structure to Muslim worship. They demolished the interior walls of the church, leaving only the ancient walls of the porticoed court and the tower at each of the four corners. The four Christian towers became the first minarets, towers from which Muslim religious leaders call the faithful to prayer five times each day. Within the ancient walls, the court-

■ The interior courtyard of the Great Mosque of Damascus is Roman; the minarets were Roman watchtowers reconfigured into Christian bell towers.

■ The mosque incorporates Roman, Christian, and Islamic elements into a site of worship.

yard was surrounded by porticoes on three sides and by the facade of the sanctuary on the fourth side.

Al-Walid wanted his mosque to be the most magnificent in his empire, and he was determined to employ the finest artists in the world to cover its walls with mosaics. The supreme center of mosaic art was Constantinople, capital of the Byzantine, or eastern Roman, Empire. Although the caliphate and the Byzantine Empire were bitter enemies, the Christian emperor loaned the caliph Byzantine artists to create the mosaics. Even today, the surviving Barada mosaics show Damascus as it appeared to al-Walid's Byzantine artists: a rich, verdant valley of palaces and houses.

The Christian antecedents of the mosque did not entirely disappear. During the preliminary work, an underground chapel was said to have been found, containing a chest with a human head. On the chest was written, "This is the head of John, son of Zacharias." Al-Walid had the sacred relic placed under one of the pillars and a monument erected over it. To this day, the shrine survives in the mosque, a symbol of the links among Judaism, Christianity, and Islam.

This moment of artistic and religious cooperation was brief. Only a few years later, in 717, al-Walid's successor subjected Constantinople to the most fearful siege it would endure for 500 years. Still, the continuity of religious worship and the common taste for classical art show how deeply both the caliphate and the empire were bound together in the common heritage of late antiquity, of which both were the true heirs.

LOOKING AHEAD

This chapter traces the fates of these two heirs of Mediterranean civilization, Byzantium and Islam, from the sixth to the fifteenth centuries. Inspired by central religious visions, they developed their common heritages into religious, artistic, and social forms that contrast with western Europe's path.

CHAPTER OUTLINE

- THE BYZANTINES
  Justinian and the Creation of the Byzantine State ▪ Emperors and Individuals ▪ Families and Villages ▪ A Foretaste of Heaven ▪ Iconoclasm
- THE RISE OF ISLAM
  Arabia Before the Prophet ▪ Muhammad, Prophet of God ▪ The Triumph of Islam ▪ The Spread of Islam ▪ Authority and Government in Islam ▪ Umayyad and 'Abbasid Caliphates ▪ Islamic Civilization
- THE BYZANTINE APOGEE AND DECLINE, 1000–1453
  The Disintegration of the Empire ▪ The Conquests of Constantinople and Baghdad

THE BYZANTINES

At the end of the fifth century C.E., the eastern empire of Theodosius and Zeno had escaped the fate that its western counterpart had suffered at the hands of the Germanic peoples. Wealthier and more urbanized than the west, its population had also been accustomed to centralized government for more than a thousand years. Still, the long-term survival of the eastern empire seemed far from certain. Little unified the empire of Constantinople. The population of the capital split into rival political factions whose violent conflicts often threatened the stability of the government. The rival groups, organized militarily and politically, controlled the Circus, or Hippodrome, where the games and chariot races that were the obsession of the city's population took place. When the two factions joined forces with the army, they were powerful enough to create or destroy emperors. Beyond Constantinople, the empire's population consisted of the more or less Hellenized peoples of Asia Minor: Armenians, Slavs, Arabs, Syrians, Egyptian Copts, and others. Unlike western Europe, the east was still a world of cities, which were centers of commerce, industry, and Hellenistic culture. But the importance of the urban centers began to decline in favor of the rural peasant world, which not only fed the empire and was the source of its great wealth but also provided the generations of tough soldiers necessary to protect the empire from its enemies.

Finally, the eastern empire was more divided than unified by its Christianity. Rivalry among the great cities of Antioch, Alexandria, Jerusalem, Rome, and Constantinople was expressed in the competition among their bishops, or patriarchs. The official "right teaching," or orthodox, faith of Constantinople and its patriarch was bitterly opposed by "de-

■ A mosaic from the church of San Vitale in Ravenna. The emperor Justinian, along with secular and ecclesiastical officials, is shown bringing an offering to the church. The halo around his head signifies the sacred nature of the imperial office.

viant," or heterodox, bishops of other religious traditions, around which developed separatist ethnic political movements. In Syria and Egypt in particular, theological disagreements about the nature of God had become rallying points of political opposition. By the time of Justinian (527–565), emperors were obsessed with maintaining absolute authority and imposing uniformity on their empire.

Justinian and the Creation of the Byzantine State

Strong-willed, restless, and ambitious, Justinian is remembered as "the emperor who never slept." Although his goals were essentially conservative, he transformed the very foundations of the imperial state, its institutions, and its culture. He hoped to restore the territory, power, and prestige of the ancient Roman Empire, but his attempts to return to the past created a new world. With the assistance of his dynamic wife Theodora, his great generals Belisarius and Narses, his brilliant jurist Tribonian, his scientists Anthemius of Tralles and Isidorus of Miletus, and his brutally efficient administrator and tax collector John of Cappadocia, he remade the empire.

Spurred on by the ambitious Theodora, in 532 Justinian checked the power of the Circus factions by brutally suppressing a riot that left 30,000 dead in the capital city. Belisarius and Narses recaptured North Africa from the Vandals, Italy from the Ostrogoths, and part of Spain from the Visigoths, restoring for one last moment some of the geographical unity of the empire of Augustus and Constantine. Tribonian revised and organized the existing codes of Roman law into the Justinian Code, a great monument of Western jurisprudence that remains today the foundation of most of Europe's legal systems.

■ The Eastern Mediterranean. The Arabian Peninsula was peripheral to the Roman and Persian empires until the seventh century when the new Islamic faith suddenly emerged from Arabia to overwhelm its more ancient neighboring empires.

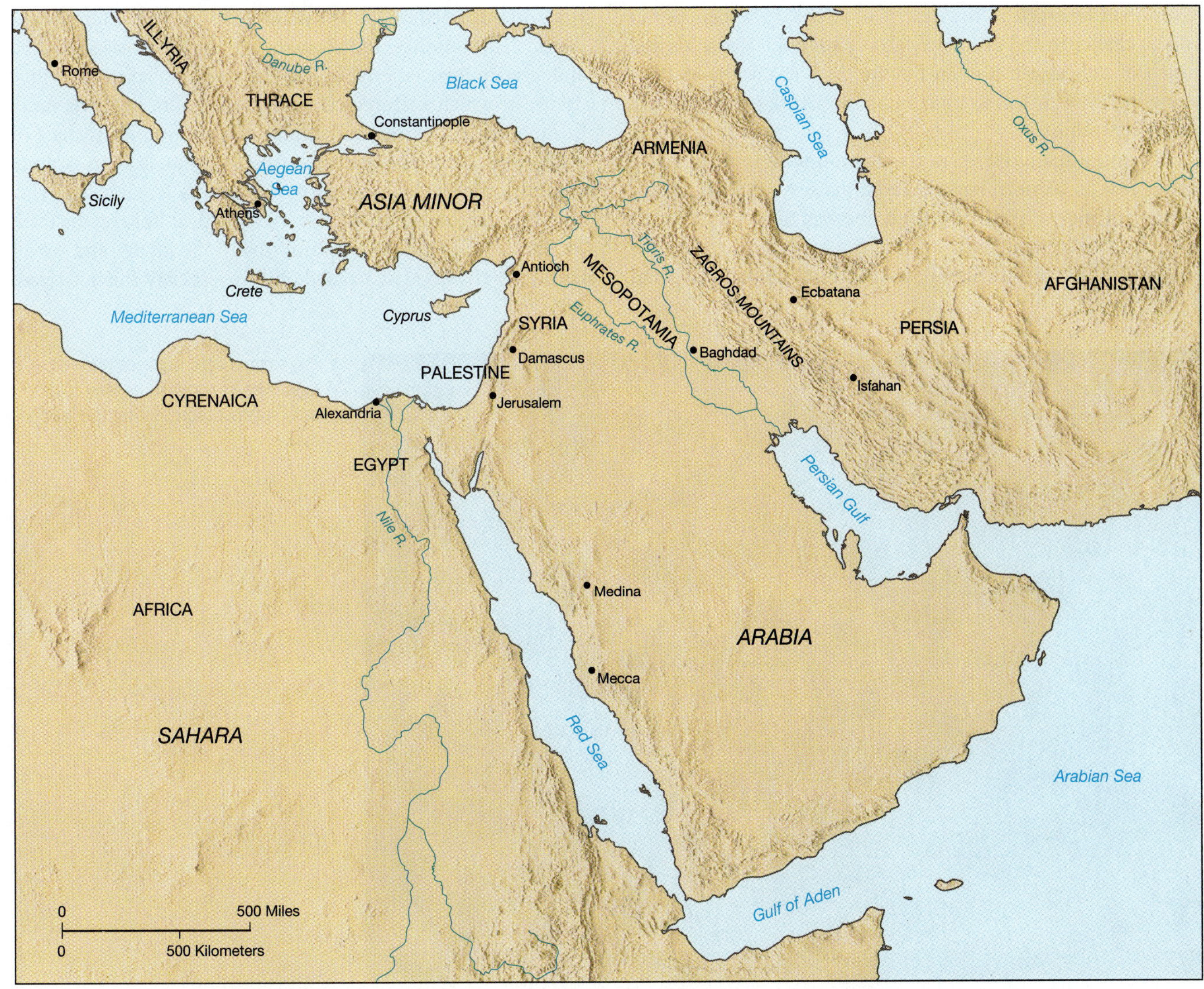

Anthemius and Isidorus combined their knowledge of mathematics, geometry, kinetics, and physics to build the Church of the Holy Wisdom (Hagia Sophia) in Constantinople, one of the largest and most innovative churches ever constructed. The structure was as radical as it was simple. In essence it is a huge rectangle, 230 by 250 feet, above which a vast dome 100 feet in diameter rises to a height of 180 feet and seems to float, suspended in air. As spectacular but not as well appreciated were the achievements of John of Cappadocia, who was able to squeeze the empire's population for the taxes to pay for the conquests, reforms, and building projects. Ultimately, Justinian's spectacular achievements came at too high a price. He left his successors an empire virtually bankrupt by the costs of his wars and his building projects, bitterly divided by his attempts to settle religious controversies, and poorly protected on its eastern border where the Sassanid Empire was a constant threat. Most of Italy and Spain soon returned to barbarian control. In 602 the Sassanid emperor Chosroes II (d. 628) invaded the empire, capturing Egypt, Palestine, and Syria and threatening Constantinople itself. In a series of desperate campaigns, the emperor Heraclius (610–641) turned back the tide and crushed the Sassanids, but it was too late. A new power, Islam, had emerged in the deserts of Arabia. The new power was to challenge and ultimately absorb both the Sassanids and much of the eastern Roman Empire. As a result, the east became increasingly less Roman and more Greek or, specifically, more Byzantine.

For more than 700 years the Byzantine Empire played a major role in Western history. From the seventh through the tenth centuries, when most of Europe was too weak and disorganized to defend itself against the expansion of Islamic states, the Byzantines stood as the bulwark of Christian Europe. When organized government had virtually disappeared in the west, the Byzantine Empire provided a model of a centralized bureaucratic state ruled according to principles of Roman law. When, beginning in the fourteenth century, western Europeans began once more to appreciate the heritage of Greek and Roman art and literature, they turned to Constantinople. There the manuscripts of Greek writers such as Plato and Homer had been preserved and studied and were available to contribute to a rebirth of classical culture in the west. When the Slavic north, caught between the Latin Christians and the Muslims, sought its cultural and religious orientation, it looked to the liturgical culture of Byzantine orthodoxy. Perhaps most importantly, when urban civilization had all but disappeared from the rest of Europe, Greeks and Latins could still look "to the City," *eis ten polin,* or as the Turks pronounced it, *Istanbul.*

Emperors and Individuals

The classic age of Byzantine society, roughly from the eighth through the tenth centuries, has been described as "individualism without freedom." The Byzantine world was intensely individualistic—unlike the Roman, which emphasized public and private associations; unlike the western barbarian kingdoms, in which hierarchical gradations connected everyone, from peasant to king; and unlike the communal society of Islam. But Byzantine individualism did not lead to a great amount of individual initiative or creativity let alone individual freedom of action within the political sphere. Instead, Byzantine individualism meant that individuals and small family groups stood as isolated units in a society characterized,

The magnificent mosaics were covered over to conform to Islamic dictates against representing the human figure.

■ The empress Irene, widow of Leo IV, was the only woman to rule the Byzantine Empire in her own right. As regent during the minority of her son, she reestablished the veneration of icons. In 802 Irene was dethroned and exiled to Lesbos.

until the mid-eleventh century, by the direct relationship between an all-powerful emperor and citizens of all ranks.

Governing Byzantium. In part this individualism resulted from the Byzantine form of government. The Byzantine state was, in theory and often in fact, an autocracy. Since the time of Diocletian, all members of society were subjects of the emperor, who alone was the source of law. How a person became emperor remained, as it had been in the Roman Empire, more a question of military power than of constitutional succession. Although in theory emperors were elected by the senate, army, and people of Constantinople, in practice emperors generally selected their own successors and had them crowned in their own lifetimes.

As long as the empire remained a civilian autocracy, it was even possible for a woman to rule, either as regent for a minor son or as sovereign. Thus Irene (780–802), widow of Leo IV (725–780), ruled as regent for her son Constantine VI (780–797). However, when her son reached his majority, she had him blinded and deposed and ruled alone from 797 to 802, not merely as the *basilissa,* or wife of the emperor, but as the ***basileus,*** or emperor itself. In the eleventh century the empire was ruled for a time by two sisters: Zoe (1028–1034), daughter of one emperor and widow of another, and Theodora (1042–1056), who was dragged out of a church by an enthusiastic mob and proclaimed empress.

Male or female, emperors were above and beyond their subjects, often quite literally. In the tenth century a mechanical throne was installed in the main audience room. The throne would suddenly lift the emperor high above the heads of astonished visitors. Like God the Father, with whom he was closely identified in imperial propaganda, the emperor was separated from the people by an unbridgeable gulf. Thus the traditional corporate bodies of the Roman Empire wasted away or became window dressing for the imperial cult. The senate, which had received the rights and privileges of the Roman Senate in 359, gradually ceased to play any autonomous role. Long before its powers were officially abolished in the ninth century, the senate had become simply a passive and amorphous body of prominent people called upon from time to time to participate in public ceremonies. Such roles were simply part of an elaborate ritual emphasizing the dignity and power of the emperor.

The Circus factions, which in the sixth century had the power to make or break emperors, met the same fate as the corporate bodies of the Roman Empire. From autonomous political groups, the Circus factions gradually became no more than participants in imperial ceremonies, whose role was to praise the emperor by mouthing traditional formulas on solemn occasions.

Bureaucracy and Army. Although the emperor was the source of all authority, the actual administration of the empire was carried out by a vast bureaucracy composed of military and civilian officers. The empire was divided into roughly 25 provinces, or *themes.* The soldiers in each theme, rather than being full-time warriors, were also farmers. Each soldier received a small farm to support himself and his family. Soldiers held their farms as long as they served in the army. When a soldier retired or died, his farm and his military obligation passed to his eldest son. The farmer-soldiers were the backbone of both the imperial military and the economic system. They not only formed a regular, locally based native army, but they also kept much of Byzantine agriculture in the hands of free peasants rather than great aristocrats. The themes were governed by military commanders, or **strategoi**, who presided over both civilian and military bureaucrats. Although virtually all-powerful in their provinces, strategoi could be appointed, removed from office, or transferred at the whim of the emperor.

In contrast to the military command of the themes, the central administration, which focused on the emperor and the imperial family, was wholly civil. The most important positions at court were occupied by eunuchs, castrated men who offered a number of advantages to imperial administration. Eunuchs often directed imperial finance, served as prime ministers, directed the vast bureaucracy, and even undertook military commands. Because they could not have descendants, there was no danger that they would attempt to turn their offices into hereditary positions or that they would plot and scheme on behalf of

MAP DISCOVERY

Byzantine Empire Under Justinian

Examine the boundaries of the Byzantine Empire under Justinian. Why would Justinian have been particularly eager to recover the areas that he reconquered? What problems were posed by the conquest of the Ostrogoths that were not present in the conquest of the Vandals?

their children. Moreover, since the sacred nature of the emperor required physical perfection, eunuchs could not aspire to replace their masters on the throne. Finally, although at times their influence with the emperor made them immensely powerful, eunuchs were at once feared and despised by the general population; there was little likelihood that they would build autonomous power bases outside of imperial favor. The extensive use of eunuchs was one of the keys to the survival of absolutist authority in the empire. While many eunuchs promoted the interests of their brothers and nephews, they were less dangerous than ambitious aristocrats. They preserved imperial authority at a time when both Islamic and Latin states were experiencing a progressive erosion of central power to the benefit of ambitious aristocratic families.

Families and Villages

A godlike emperor and a centralized bureaucracy left little room for the development of the hierarchies of private patronage, lordship, and group action that were characteristic of western Europe. In the Byzantine Empire, aristocrat and peasant were equal in their political powerlessness. Against the emperor and the bureaucracy, no extended kin group or local political unit offered security or comfort. Thus Byzantine society tended to be organized at the lowest level, that of the nuclear family. That structure was imprinted even on the physical landscape of Byzantine cities. Single-family dwellings replaced the public spaces and buildings of antiquity. Public assemblies and communal celebrations either disappeared or were absorbed into the ritual of imperial dignity. Daily life focused on the protective enclosure of the private home, which served as both shelter and workplace. Professional and craft associations continued to exist as they had in antiquity. However, like everything else in Byzantium, they were not autonomous professional groups intended to protect the interests of their members. Instead, they were promoted and controlled by imperial officials in order to regulate and tax urban industry.

Rural Life. The countryside, which was the backbone of Byzantine prosperity into the eleventh century, was also a world with limited horizontal and vertical social bonds. Villages were the basic elements in the imperial system. The village court handled local affairs and tax assessments, but it in turn dealt directly with the imperial bureaucracy. Occasionally villages might unite against imperial tax collectors, but normally villagers dealt with each other and with outside powers as wary individuals. That attitude was an outgrowth of agricultural techniques practiced in Greece and Asia Minor, where a peasant's prosperity depended not on

■ A tenth-century Greek manuscript of the Gospel from Constantinople is decorated with a drawing of laborers in a vineyard. Such illustrated texts often recorded the daily activities of ordinary people, including plowing, fishing, farming, and sheep shearing.

teamwork but rather on individual effort. Most peasants, whether they were landowners, peasant soldiers, or renters on great estates, survived on the labor of their own family and perhaps one or two slaves. In the eleventh century, tax records indicated only three types of peasants, distinguished according to their equipment: those with two yoke of cattle, those with one, and those with none. Large cooperative undertakings as in Islamic lands or the use of communal equipment as became the rule in the West was unknown. Individual families worked their own fields, which were usually enclosed with protective stone or brick walls. Byzantine peasants would have agreed with the neighbor in Robert Frost's poem "Mending Wall," who says, "Good fences make good neighbors."

Urban Life. Like the villages, Byzantine towns were isolated. The mountainous terrain of Greece and Asia Minor contributed to the isolation, cutting off ready overland communication among communities and forcing them to turn to the sea. In this respect Constantinople was ideally situated to develop into the greatest commercial center of the West, at its height boasting a population of more than one million. Because of Constantinople's strategic location on the Bosporus, that slim ribbon of water uniting the Black and Mediterranean seas, all of the products of the empire and those of the Slavic, Latin, and Islamic worlds, as well as Oriental goods arriving overland from central Asia, had to pass through the city. Silks, spices, and precious metals were loaded onto ships at Trebizond and then transported south to Constantinople. Baltic amber, slaves, and furs from the Slavic world were carried down the Dnepr River to the Black Sea and then to Constantinople. There, all goods passing north or south had to be unloaded, assessed, and subjected to a flat import-export tariff of 10 percent.

The empire's cities were centers for the manufacture of luxury goods in demand throughout the Islamic and Christian worlds. The secret of silk manufacture had been smuggled out of China by a Christian monk who had hidden silkworms in his pilgrim's staff during his journey home. (See "The West and the Wider World: Industrial Espionage in the Sixth Century," pp. 194–195.) Imperial workshops in Constantinople and closely regulated workshops in Corinth and Thebes produced fine silks, brocades, carpets, and other luxury products marketed throughout the Mediterranean. The goods were also subject to the state's customary 10 percent tax.

As vital as maritime commerce was to the empire, most Byzantines hated the sea. They feared its pirates and its storms. When they did travel by ship, they prayed to their sacred icons and tried to sail, as one Byzantine put it, "touching the shore with an oar." Moreover, particularly among the elite, commerce was considered demeaning. The story is told that when one ninth-century emperor learned that his wife owned a ship, he ordered it and its cargo burned. Never great mariners, Byzantines were largely content to allow others—first Syrians and Slavs and later Italians—to monopolize the empire's commerce.

A Foretaste of Heaven

The cultural cement that bound emperor and subjects together was **Orthodox Christianity**. The Islamic capture of Alexandria, Jerusalem, and Antioch had removed the centers of regional religious particularism from the empire. The barbarian domination of Italy had isolated Rome and reduced its influence. The two processes left Constantinople as the only remaining patriarchate in the empire and thus the undisputed center of Orthodox Christianity. However, like virtually every other aspect of Byzantine society and culture, the patriarch and the Orthodox faith that he led were subordinated to the emperor.

An Imperial Church. In theory patriarchs were elected, but in reality emperors appointed them. Patriarchs in turn

INDUSTRIAL ESPIONAGE IN THE SIXTH CENTURY

The Emperor Justinian not only laid the political, institutional, and cultural foundations of Byzantium but, in a daring act of industrial espionage and smuggling, he also established what remained for centuries one of its most important export industries: silk manufacture. In the year 950, Bishop Liutprand of Cremona, emissary of the Emperor Otto I to the Byzantine court, was returning home from Constantinople after a humiliating encounter with Emperor Nicephorus when, as a final insult, his baggage was inspected and five valuable pieces of purple silk were confiscated. The German emperor was deemed unworthy of the precious purple cloth. Liutprand fumed and complained but could do nothing. Silk, the most prized cloth in the world, was available only from Byzantium or the Far East. Its manufacture was a closely guarded secret and a state monopoly. But Justinian had stolen the secret in the sixth century, and his Byzantine successors had maintained their monopoly for four hundred years.

THE WEST AND THE WIDER WORLD

Silk is a miracle fabric: a single filament of silk is as strong as steel of the same thickness. It is also much less dense than cotton or wool and much more moisture absorbent, able to take in three times its own weight without appearing damp. It is durable, dyes beautifully, and resists mold and mildew. No wonder it has been a prized commodity for the past five thousand years. However, its production is extraordinary. Silk is produced from the cocoons of silkworm moths. The worms feed on mulberry leaves before spinning their cocoons in one continuous thread that can be as long as 1000 feet. Before the worms can hatch into moths and destroy the cocoon, they are killed with hot air or steam, and the cocoon is softened and unraveled.

This laborious process was first discovered in China, the native habitat of the silkworm, and the Chinese monopolized its production for its first three thousand years. Exports were strictly controlled. Only finished cloth could be exported, and no one was allowed to export eggs, cocoons, or silkworms under penalty of death. Only very gradually did this monopoly break down in Asia. Around 200 B.C.E., Chinese emigrants to Korea brought with them silkworms and mulberry plants and began Korean silk production. Japan and India acquired the secret technology around 300 C.E., but they were as careful as the Chinese to avoid further proliferation of the technique, especially further west.

And the West was mad for silk. Already in antiquity caravan routes along what today is called the Silk Road reached from the western Chinese city of Xian across modern Afghanistan and into modern Iraq and Syria, ending in Damascus. Sea routes also connected Egypt and India through the Red Sea, providing an alternative route for silk to reach the Mediterranean world. Ancient Persians particularly admired the material and even unwove Chinese cloths so they could reuse the precious filaments to reweave them into clothing and textiles of their own. Alexander the Great was so impressed with the splendid silk robes worn by

■ Eastern Han (25–220) tomb decoration showing silk weavers.

the vanquished Persian Emperor Darius III that he demanded vast amounts of the material from the conquered Persians as spoils of war. The Romans first became aware of silk around 50 B.C.E., and the cloth became enormously popular (and enormously expensive). It was literally worth its weight in gold. Aristocratic women and particularly empresses amassed vast quantities of silk shawls and scarves. The conspicuous use of silk was a barometer of Roman morals: severe emperors such as Aurelian forbade his wife to own so much as a single silk shawl, while others like Caligula enjoyed wearing it himself.

But where did silk come from? Although Aristotle was aware that the threads came from the cocoons of the silkworm, Romans had only a vague idea of its origins. Their best guess was that it grew on trees. And they certainly had no means of manufacturing it, being content with importing raw silk and then weaving and dying it according to their own taste. Thus Roman desire for silk was at the mercy of those who controlled the silk route from China and India: their enemies, the Persians.

■ This Byzantine silk cloth, showing a hero or charioteer driving a quadringa (four-horse chariot) was found in Charlemagne's tomb—probably a gift from the Byzantine court to the Frankish emperor.

All this changed around 530 when a group of monks from India appeared before the Emperor Justinian. These men, Nestorian Christians from a region of India that specialized in silk production, explained to the emperor that they could make it possible for the empire to free itself from its dependency on Persia to satisfy its appetite for silk. They revealed to him the origin of silk and the process of recovering it from cocoons. With his encouragement, they returned home and smuggled back to the Empire silkworm eggs and mulberry seeds, according to legend, by hiding them in their hollow walking staffs. Soon, Byzantine silk production was under way, but the Byzantines, in the tradition of the Chinese and Indians before them, maintained silk manufacture as a strictly controlled state monopoly. Silk's beauty, its rarity, and its prestige were too great an economic and political asset to allow uncontrolled production. For centuries, until its monopoly was broken by Muslim silk production in Spain and eventually Italy, silks could be used not simply as commodities but as tools of politics to honor, or to shame, Byzantium's neighbors.

QUESTIONS FOR DISCUSSION

Why do you suppose that Western elites so desired Chinese and Indian silk? Was there a relationship between the expansion of Western religions such as Christianity and Islam into Asia and the end of the Asian silk monopoly?

controlled the various levels of the Church hierarchy, which included metropolitans, bishops, and the local clergy. The ecclesiastical structure reflected the organization of the state bureaucracy, which it reinforced. Local priests were drawn from the peasant society of which they were a part. They were expected to be married and to live much like their neighbors. Bishops, metropolitans, and patriarchs were recruited from monasteries and remained celibate. They were, so to speak, religious "eunuchs" who represented the emperor. In rare instances, a patriarch might threaten to excommunicate an emperor, but such threats could seldom be carried out with impunity. Generally the Church supported the emperor and the imperial cult.

The essence of Orthodox religion was the liturgy, or ceremonies, of the Church, which provided, it was said, a foretaste of heaven. Adoration of God and veneration of the emperor were joined as the cornerstone of imperial propaganda. Ecclesiastical and court processions ensured that everything and everyone were in the proper place and that order and stability reigned in this world as a reflection of the eternal order of the next. This confirmation, in churches and in court, of stability and permanence in the face of possible crisis and disruption calmed and reassured the liturgically oriented society.

The effects of Byzantine ceremonies reached far beyond the Byzantines themselves. According to Russian sources, when the prince of Kiev sent observers to report on the manner of worship in Islamic, Latin, and Greek societies, the effect of the Byzantine liturgy was overpowering: "We knew not whether we were in heaven or on earth, for on earth there is no such splendor or such beauty." So strong was the impression made by the rituals of the Church that the prince decided to invite Byzantine clergy to instruct his people.

Conversion of the Slavs. Whether or not the story is true, the gradual conversion of the Slavs to Orthodox Christianity was a momentous development in European history. In the mid-ninth century, the emperor Michael III sent Cyril (827–869) and Methodius (ca. 826–884), two brothers from Thessalonica, a Greek city with a large Slavic population, to the Slavic kingdom of Moravia in response to a request from the Moravian ruler. Cyril created a Slavonic alphabet in which sacred Scripture and liturgical texts were translated, and for several years the brothers worked to create a Christian Moravian community in the central and southern Balkans. Although they stirred opposition from the pope for their use of the vernacular Slavic language in liturgy and the suspicion of Western political powers, their efforts established an enduring Christian tradition in the Slavic world.

Also during the reign of Michael III the kingdom of the Bulgars entered the Christian community. The Bulgars, an amalgam of south Slavic groups under the leadership of a Turkic elite, had long threatened the empire's northern frontier. In 864, threatened by Serbian enemies to the west and needing the good will of the Byzantines, the Bulgar ruler Boris I agreed to make Christianity the official religion. Initially, he invited missionaries from Rome, but the papacy refused to grant the Bulgar church its own independent head or archbishop. Boris then turned to the patriarch of Constantinople, who proved more accommodating. As a result, the Bulgars adopted the traditions of Greek Christianity. During the next century, as Bulgar power expanded, so too did Christianity, particularly after the Bulgars adopted the Slavic writing and liturgical traditions developed by Cyril and Methodius.

In the late tenth century, Orthodox Christianity became the religion of Russia with the conversion in 988 of Vladimir the Great (956–1015), who married a Byzantine princess and adopted the Slavic liturgical traditions of the Cyrillic tradition.

Iconoclasm

The one aspect of religious life not entirely under imperial control was monasticism. Since the time of the desert fathers, monastic communities had been an essential part of Christianity. From the sixth century on, numerous monastic communities were founded throughout the empire, and by the eleventh century there were at least 300 monasteries within the walls of Constantinople alone. Following the Muslim invasions of the eleventh century, Anatolia became the major center of monastic life outside the city. Monasteries were often wealthy and powerful. Moreover, their religious

In this manuscript illustration, an icon is being destroyed while priests try to persuade Leo V to abandon his iconoclast policies.

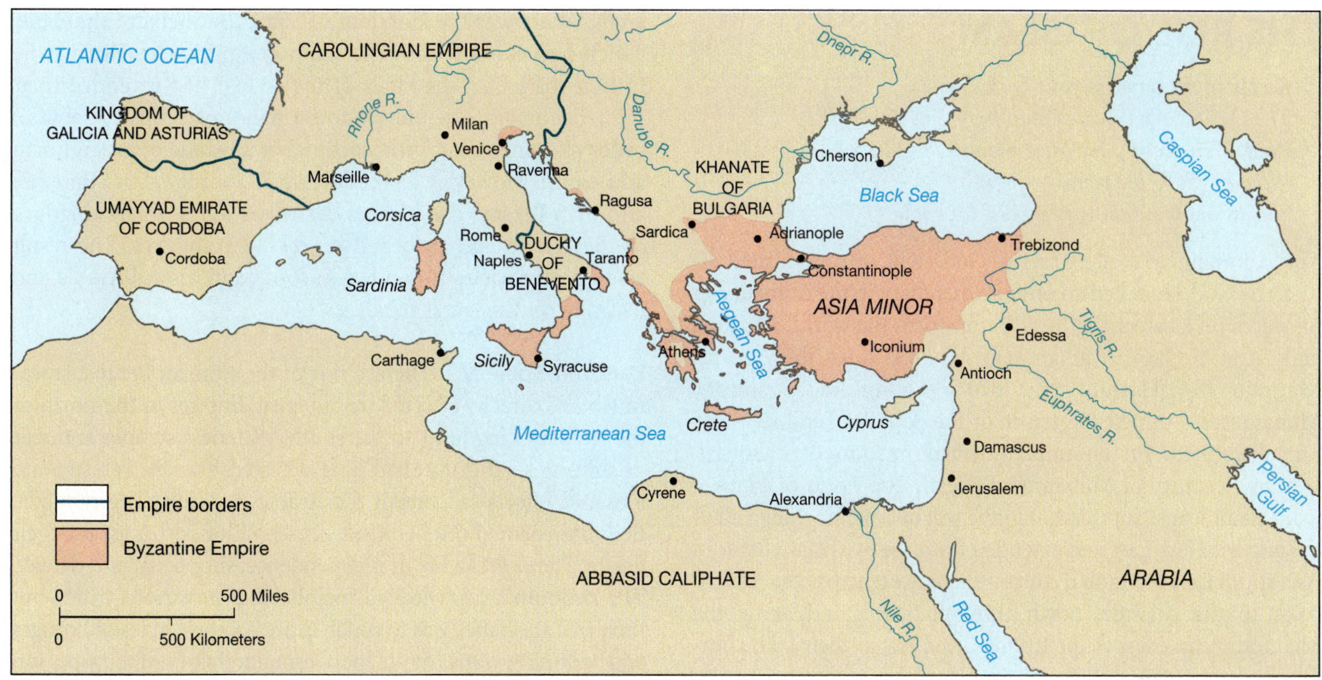

The Byzantine Empire in 814. By the ninth century, the empire had lost all its territories but Asia Minor, Greece, the boot of Italy, and the islands of Sardinia and Sicily.

appeal, often based on the possession of miracle-working religious images, or **icons**, posed an independent source of religious authority at odds with the imperial centralization of all aspects of Byzantine life. To the faithful, icons were not simply representations or reminders of Jesus and the saints: they had a real if intermediary relationship with the person represented, and as such themselves merited veneration and, some argued, adoration.

Beginning with Emperor Leo III, the Isaurian (717–741), the military emperors who had driven back Islam sought to curtail the independence of monastic culture, and particularly the cult of icons that was an integral part of it. The emperors and their supporters, termed **iconoclasts** (literally, "breakers of images"), objected to the mediating role of sacred images in worship. While the iconoclasts may have been influenced by Jewish and Islamic prohibitions of images, they were also fighting the sort of decentralization in religion that the imperial bureaucracy prevented in government. Monasteries, with their miracle-working icons, became the particular object of imperial persecution. Monasteries were closed and their estates confiscated. Monks were forced to marry. Everywhere imperial agents painted over frescoes in churches and destroyed icons, statues, and illustrated manuscripts. The defenders of icons—**iconodules**, or image venerators—were imprisoned, tortured, and even executed. Most bishops, the army, and much of the non-European population of the empire supported the iconoclast emperors, but monks, the lesser clergy, and the majority of the populace—particularly women—violently resisted the destruction of their beloved images.

For more than a century, the iconoclast dispute threatened to tear the empire apart. The first phase, which began in 726, ended in 787 when a council summoned by Empress Irene confirmed the adoration of images. After her deposition in 802, a milder iconoclastic persecution revived until the empress Theodora (842–858), who ruled during the minority of her son, ended the persecution and restored image veneration in 843. Monasteries reopened and regained much of their former wealth and prestige. As images were brought out of hiding and new ones were created, icons resumed their role in the eastern Christian church.

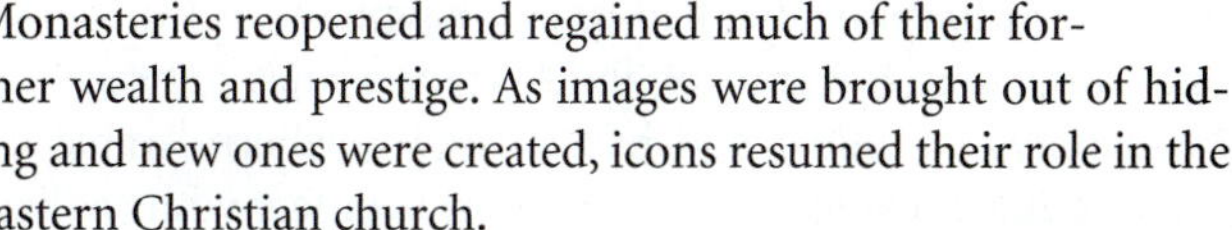

Epitome of the Iconoclastic, 7th Synod

The longest-lasting effect of the iconoclastic struggle was in Byzantium's relations with the west. Christians in western Europe—particularly the popes of Rome—never accepted the iconoclast position. The popes considered the iconoclast emperors heretics and looked increasingly to the Frankish Carolingian family for support against them and the Lombards of Italy. In this manner the Franks first entered Italian politics and began, with papal support, to establish themselves as a rival imperial power in the west, which culminated in the coronation of Charlemagne in 800.

Although Byzantium lost Italy and the city of Rome, the empire survived and even flourished. Between the sixth and ninth centuries, the reduced but still vital Roman Empire in the east developed a distinctive political and cultural tradition based on imperial absolutism and buttressed by a powerful religious tradition and an effective bureaucracy that dealt directly with individual subjects on behalf of the emperor.

THE RISE OF ISLAM

Recite: in the name of your Lord,
The Creator Who created man from clots of blood!
Recite: Your Lord is the Most Bounteous One,
Who taught by the pen,
Taught mankind things they did not know.

This command to recite, to reveal God's will, communicated directly by God, launched an obscure merchant in the Arabian city of Mecca on a career that would transform the world. Through faith, Abu al-Qasim Muhammad ibn 'Abd Allah ibn Abd al-Muttalib ibn Hashim (ca. 570–632)—or more simply, Muhammad—united the tribes of the Arabian Peninsula and propelled them on an unprecedented mission of conquest. Within a century of Muhammad's death, the world of *Islam,* a word that means "submission to the will of God," included all of the ancient Near East and extended from the Syr Darya River in Asia south into the Indian subcontinent, west across the African coast to the Atlantic, north through Spain, and along the Mediterranean coast to the Rhone River. Just as their faith combined elements of traditional Arab worship with Christianity and Judaism, the Arabian conquerors and their subject populations created a vital civilization from a mix of Arabian, Roman, Hellenistic, and Sassanid traditions, a civilization characterized from its inception by a multiplicity of forms in which the various elements were combined with the religious traditions of the prophet Muhammad.

Arabia Before the Prophet

Although Arabs did not appear in written sources as such before the ninth century B.C.E., their ancestors had played an important—if supporting—role in Near Eastern history for thousands of years. In the Egyptian Old Kingdom, the incense trees of southern Arabia had drawn Egyptians to the region, then known as the land of Punt. Trade routes between the Fertile Crescent and Egypt had crossed northern Arabia for just as long, drawing its inhabitants into contact with civilization. By the sixth century C.E., Arabic-speaking peoples from the Arabian Peninsula had spread through the Syrian Desert as far north as the Euphrates.

Between Byzantium and Persia. Those who lived on the fringes of the Byzantine and Sassanid empires had been largely absorbed into the cultural and political spheres of the two great powers. The northern borders of Arabia along the Red Sea formed Roman provinces that even produced an emperor, Philip the Arab (244–249). Hira, to the south of the Euphrates, became a Sassanid puppet principality that, although largely Christian, often provided the Persians with auxiliaries. At times the Sassanid Empire also controlled Bahrain on the Persian Gulf, as well as Yamama and the Yemen, both vital in the spice trade.

Southern Arabia, with a relatively abundant rainfall and fertile soils, was an agricultural region long governed by monarchs. There was the kingdom of Saba, the Sheba of the Bible, which had existed since the tenth century B.C.E. During the fifth century C.E., the kings of the Yemen had extended their influence north over the Bedouin tribes of central Arabia in order to control and protect the caravan trade between north and south. However, in the late sixth century C.E. Ethiopian and then Persian conquerors destroyed the Arabian kingdom of the Yemen and absorbed it into their empires. The result was a power vacuum that left in confusion central Arabia and its trade routes across the deserts.

Bedouin Society. The interior of the Arabian Peninsula was much less directly affected by the great empires to the north or the Arabian kingdoms to the south. Waterless steppes and seas of shifting sand dunes had long defeated Roman, Persian, and Sassanid efforts to control the Arabic Bedouin. The nomadic Bedouin roamed the peninsula in search of pasturage for their flocks. Theirs was a life of independence, simplicity, and danger. The Bedouin acknowledged membership in various tribes, but their real allegiance was to much more narrow circles of lineages and tenting groups. As in the Germanic tribes of Europe, kin relationships rather than formal governmental systems protected individuals through the obligation for vengeance and blood feud. Tribal chieftains, called *sheikhs,* chosen from ruling families, had no coercive power, but served only as arbitrators and executors of tribal consensus. The patriarch of each family held final say over his kin. He could ignore the sheikh and go his own way with his flocks and herds, wives and slaves.

The individual was unimportant in Bedouin society. Private land ownership was unknown, and flocks and herds were often held in common by kindreds. The pastoral economy of the Bedouin provided meat, cheese, and wool. Weapons, ornaments, women, and livestock could be acquired through exchange at the market towns that developed around desert oases. More commonly the goods and women were taken in raids against other tribes, caravans, and settlements or by exacting payments from weaker neighbors in return for protection. Raids, however, yielded much more than mere booty. Often launched in defense of family honor, they were the means of increasing prestige and glory in the warrior society. Prizes won in battle were lightly given away as signs of generosity and marks of social importance.

Some of the Arabs of the more settled south, as well as inhabitants of towns along caravan routes, were Christian or Jewish. As farmers or merchants, those groups were looked down upon by the nomadic Bedouin, most of whom remained pagan. Although they recognized some important gods, and even a high god usually called Allah, Bedouin worshiped local tribal deities often thought of as inhabiting a sacred stone or spring. Worship involved gifts and offerings and played only a small part in nomadic life. Far more important was commitment to the tribe, expressed through loyalty to the tribal cult and through unity of action against rival tribes.

Harams. Rivalry and feuding among tribes could be set aside at a mutually accepted neutral site, which might grow up around a religious sanctuary. A sanctuary, or **haram,** which was often on the border between tribal areas, was founded by a holy man not unlike the Christian holy men of the Syrian Desert. The holy man declared the site and surrounding area neutral ground on which no violence could take place. There, enemies could meet under truce to settle differences under the direction of the holy man or his descendants. Merchant communities sprang up within the safety of the sites, since the sanctuary gave them and their goods protection from their neighbors.

Mecca was just such a sanctuary, around whose sacred black rock, or Ka'bah, a holy man named Qusayy established himself and his tribe, the Quraysh, as its guardians sometime early in the sixth century. In the next century, Mecca grew into an important center under the patronage of the Quraysh, who made it the center of a commercial network. Through religious, diplomatic, and military means they organized camel caravans that could safely cross the desert from Yemen in the south to Iran and Syria in the north. During the early seventh century, when increased hostilities between the Byzantine and Sassanid empires severed the direct trading links between the empires, the Quraysh network became the leading commercial organization in northern Arabia. Still, its effectiveness remained tied to the religious importance of Mecca and the Ka'bah. When Muhammad, a descendant of Qusayy, began to recite the monotheistic message of Allah, his preaching was seen as a threat to the survival of his tribe and his city.

■ Ascent of the Prophet Muhammed on his steed, Buraq, guided by Jibra'il and escorted by angels. A miniature painting from a sixteenth-century manuscript.

Muhammad, Prophet of God

More is known about Muhammad's life than about that of Moses, Jesus, Buddha, or any of the other great religious reformers of history. Still, Muhammad's early years were quickly wrapped in a protective cloak of pious stories by his followers, making it difficult to discern truth from legend. A member of a lesser branch of the Quraysh, Muhammad was an orphan raised by relatives. At about age 20 he became the business manager for Khadijah, a wealthy widow whom he later married. The marriage gave him financial security among the middle ranks of Meccan merchants. During that time he may have traveled to Syria on business and heard the preaching of Christian monks. He certainly became familiar with Judaism through contact with Jewish traders. In his thirties, he began to devote an increasing amount of time to meditation, retiring to the barren, arid mountains outside the city. There, in the month of Ramadan in the year 610, he reported a vision of a man, his feet astride the horizon. The figure commanded: "O Muhammad! Thou art the Messenger of God. Recite!"

Preaching Islam. Khadijah, to whom he confided his revelation in fear and confusion, became his first convert. Within a year he began preaching openly. His early teachings stressed the absolute unity of God, the evils of idolatry, and the threat of divine judgment. Further revelations to Muhammad were copied word for word in what came to be the Qur'an, or Koran. The messages offered Arabs a faith founded on a book. In their eyes, that faith was both within the tradition of and superior to the Christianity and Judaism of their neighbors. The Qur'an was the final revelation and Muhammad the last and greatest prophet. To Muslims—the term *Muslim* means "true believer"—Muhammad is simply the Prophet.

The Holy Qur'an

Muslims believe that Allah's revelation emphasized, above all, his power and transcendence and that the duty of humans is worship. The prayers of Islam, in contrast to those of Christianity and Judaism, are essentially prayers of praise, seldom prayers of petition. The reverential attitude places little premium on scriptural interpretation or theological speculation. Muslims regard the whole Qur'an as the exact and complete revelation of God, literally true, and forming a unified whole, although revelations contained in it came at various times throughout the Prophet's life. It is the complete guide for secular and religious life, the fundamental law of conduct for Islamic society. The Prophet emphasized constantly that he was simply God's messenger and that he merited no special veneration or worship. For this reason, Muslims have always

THE QUR'AN

The following passages from the Qur'an express the central importance of the revelation of Allah, compassion for Jews and Christians as sharers in the belief in the one God, and the condemnation of polytheistic idolaters.

Focus Questions

What are the characteristics of the righteous according to the Qur'an? How does the attitude of Islam differ toward Christians, Jews, and polytheists?

In the name of Allah, the compassionate, the Merciful. This Book is not to be doubted. It is a guide to the righteous, who have faith in the unseen and are steadfast in prayer; who bestow in charity a part of what We give them; who trust what has been revealed to you [Muhammad] and to others before you, and firmly believe in the life to come. These are rightly guided by their Lord; these shall surely triumph.

As for the unbelievers, whether you forewarn them or not, they will not have faith. Allah has set a seal upon their hearts and ears; their sight is dimmed and a grievous punishment awaits them. . . .

Men, serve your Lord, who has created you and those who have gone before you, so that you may guard yourselves against evil; who has made the earth a bed for you and the sky a dome, and has sent down water from heaven to bring forth fruits for your sustenance. Do not knowingly set up other gods besides Him. . . .

Believers, Jews, Christians, and Sabaeans [ancient rulers of Yemen believed to be monotheists]—whoever believes in Allah and the Last Day and does what is right—shall be rewarded by their Lord; they have nothing to fear or to regret. . . .

Yet there are some who worship idols, bestowing on them the adoration due to Allah (though the love of Allah is stronger in the faithful). But when they face their punishment the wrongdoers will know that might is His alone and that Allah is stern in retribution. When they face their punishment the leaders will disown their followers, and the bonds which now unite them will break asunder. Those who followed them will say: "Could we but live again, we would disown them as they have disowned us now."

Thus Allah will show them their own works. They shall sigh with remorse, but shall never come out of Hell.

From Qur'an, sura 2.

rejected the label *Muhammadan,* which nonbelievers often apply to them. Muslims are followers not of Muhammad but of the God of Abraham and Jesus, whom they believe chose to make the final and complete revelation of his power and his judgment through the Prophet.

Initially, such revelations of divine power and judgment neither greatly bothered nor influenced Mecca's merchant elite. Muhammad's earliest followers, such as his cousin 'Ali ibn Abi (ca. 600–661), came from his own clan and from among the moderately successful members of the Meccan community. Elite clans such as the Umayya, which controlled the larger Quraysh tribe, saw little to attract them to the upstart. But soon Muhammad began to insist that those who did not accept Allah as the only God were damned, as were those who continued to venerate the sorts of idols on which Mecca's prosperity was founded. With this proclamation, toleration gave way to hostility. Muhammad and his followers were ostracized and even persecuted.

The Hijra. Around 620, some residents of Medina, a smaller trading community populated by rival pagan, Jewish, and Islamic clans and racked by internal political dissension, approached the Prophet and invited him to govern the community in order to end the factional squabbles. Rejected at home, Muhammad answered their call. On 24 September 622, Muhammad and one supporter secretly made their way from Mecca to Medina. The short journey of less than 300 miles, known as the **Hijra**, was destined to change the world.

The Triumph of Islam

The Hijra marked the beginning of the Islamic dating system in the way that the birth of Jesus began the Christian. The Hijra was the Prophet's first step—or steps—in the shift from preaching to action. He organized his followers from Mecca and Medina into the **Umma**, a community that transcended the old bonds of tribe and clan. He set about turning Medina into a haram like Mecca, with himself as founding holy man and the Umma as his new family. But it was not to be a haram, or indeed a family like any other. Muhammad was seen not merely as a sheikh whose authority rested on consensus but as God's messenger, and his authority was absolute. His goal was to extend that authority far beyond his adopted town of Medina to Mecca, and ultimately to the whole Arab world.

First, he gained firm control of Medina at the expense of its Jewish clans. He had expected the monotheists to embrace his teachings. Instead, they rejected the unlettered Arab's attempt to transform Judaic and Christian traditions into an Arab faith. Rejection was their undoing. The Prophet expelled them in the name of political and religious unity. Those not expelled were executed.

Return to Mecca. Muhammad then used that unified community to attack the Quraysh where they were most vulnerable—in their protection of camel caravans. The inability to destroy the upstarts or protect its trading network cost the Quraysh tribe much of its prestige. More and more members of Meccan families and local tribes converted to Islam. In 629, Muhammad and 10,000 warriors marched on Mecca and captured the city in a swift and largely bloodless campaign.

During the three years between Muhammad's triumphant return to Mecca and his death, Islam moved steadily toward becoming the major force in the Arabian Peninsula. The divine revelations increasingly took on legal and practical dimensions as Muhammad was forced to serve not just as Prophet, but also as political leader of a major political and economic power. The Umma had become a sort of supertribe, open to all individuals who would accept Allah and his Prophet. The invitation extended to women as well as to men.

Women in Early Islam. Islam brought a transformation of the rights of women in Arabian society. That did not mean that women achieved equality with men any more than they did in any premodern civilization, east or west. Women remained firmly subordinate to men, who could have as many as four wives, could divorce them at will, and often kept women segregated from other men. When in public, Islamic women in many regions adopted the Syriac Christian practice of wearing a veil that covered all of the face but the eyes. When they did need to act in public, they did so at a decided disadvantage. In matters of inheritance and in witnessing and giving testimony, women were valued at one-half of a man.

Still, Islamic teachers did not share the common Christian belief that women were the source of evil and sin, the weak temptresses and daughters of Eve. Islam forbade the common pre-Islamic practice of female infanticide. Brides, not their fathers or other male relatives, received the dowry from their husbands, thus making marriage more a partnership than a sale. All wives had to be treated equally. If a man was unable to do so, he had to limit himself to a single wife. Islamic women acquired inheritance and property rights and gained protection against mistreatment in marriage. Although they remained second class in status, at least women had a status, recognized and protected within the Umma.

An Arabian Faith. The rapid spread of Islam within the Arab world can be explained by a number of religious and material factors. Perhaps most attractive, though actually least important, was the sensuous vision of the afterlife promised to believers. Probably more compelling than the description of heaven was the promise of the torments awaiting nonbelievers on the day of judgment. But as central as those otherworldly considerations were, the concrete attractions of Islam in their world were equally important. They included both economic prosperity and the opportunity to continue a lifestyle of raiding and warfare in the name of Allah.

Muhammad won over the leaders of the Quraysh by making Mecca the sacred city of Islam and by retaining the Ka'bah, cleansed of idols, as the center of Islamic pilgrimage.

Arabic manuscripts were decorated with intricate geometric designs. This page from an eighth- or ninth-century copy of the Qur'an illustrates the elegance and formality of the Kufic form of Arabic calligraphy. Vowel marks appear as dots of various colors.

Not unlike the Roman courtiers of Constantine's day who rapidly adopted Christianity, the once disdainful elite now rushed to convert and reestablish their preeminent position within the community. The rapid rehabilitation of old families such as the Umayyads greatly disturbed many of Muhammad's earliest followers, especially those from Medina whose timely invitation had been essential in launching the Prophet's career.

Muhammad's message spread to other tribes through diplomatic and occasionally military means. The divisive nature of Bedouin society contributed to his success. Frequently, factions within other tribes turned to Muhammad for mediation and support against their rivals. In return for his assistance, petitioners accepted his religious message. Since the Qur'an commanded Muslims to destroy idol worship, conversion provided the occasion for holy wars (**jihads**) of conquest and profitable raids against their still-pagan neighbors. Converts showed their piety by sending part of their spoils as alms to Medina. The Qur'an permitted Christians and Jews living under the authority of Islamic communities to continue to practice their faith, but they were forced to pay a head tax shared among members of the Umma.

IMAGE DISCOVERY

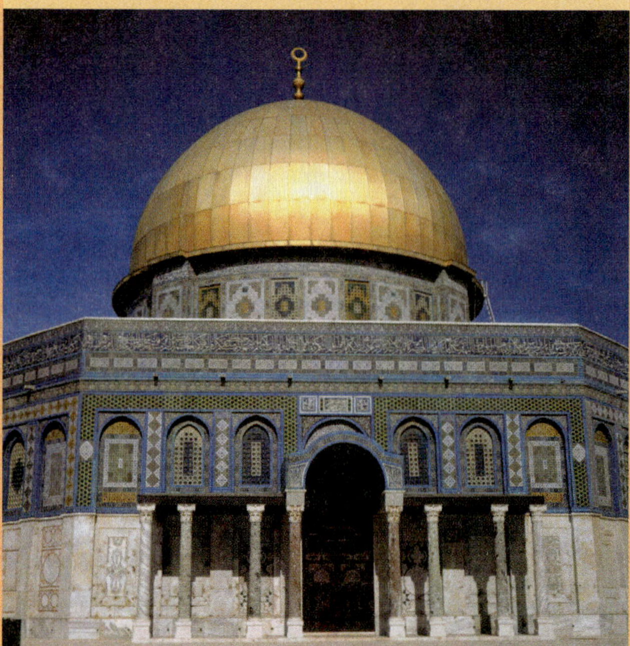

Haram al-Sharif, or the Dome of the Rock: Theology in Stone

Haram al-Sharif, or the Dome of the Rock, is the splendid mosque built on Temple Mount in Jerusalem in 691 following the Muslim conquest of Jerusalem. Its location on the site of the Jewish Temple and its dome that recalls the nearby Christian Church of the Holy Sepulcher built by Constantine connect this Islamic structure with the other great monotheistic faiths. The inscription inside the Dome reads in part, "In the name of God the Merciful, the Compassionate. There is no god but God alone, without partner. Say: He is God, One, God, the Everlasting, who has not begotten and has not been begotten. He is without equal. [Qur'an 112] Muhammad is God's messenger, may God bless him." How does this inscription summarize the essence of Islam and challenge the fundamental tenants of the Christian belief?

The Spread of Islam

Muhammad died in the summer of 632 after a short illness, leaving no successor and no directions concerning the leadership of the Umma. Immediately his closest and most influential followers selected Abu Bakr (632–634), the fourth convert to Islam, to be **caliph**, or successor of the Prophet. Abu Bakr and, after his death two years later, the caliph 'Umar (634–644) faced formidable obstacles. Within the Umma, tensions between the early Medina followers of the Prophet and the Meccan elite were beginning to surface. A more critical problem was that the tribes that had accepted the Prophet's leadership believed that his death freed them from their treaty obligations. Now they attempted to go their own ways.

To prevent the collapse of the Umma, Abu Bakr launched a war of reconversion. Purely by chance, the war developed into wars of conquest that reached far beyond the Arab world. Commanded by Khalid ibn al-Walid (d. 642), the greatest early Islamic general, Muslim forces defeated tribe after tribe and brought them back into the Umma. But long-term survival demanded expansion.

Since Muslims were forbidden to raid fellow believers and raids were an integral part of Bedouin life, the only way to keep recently converted Bedouin in line was to lead them on military expeditions against non-Muslims. Khalid and his armies were people of the desert, and they used the sea of sand as the British Empire would later use the oceans in the nineteenth century. Arab armies could move men and supplies quickly across the arid wastes, crush their enemies, and then retreat back into the desert, beyond the reach of Byzantine and Sassanid forces. Under Abu Bakr, Muslim expansion covered all of Arabia. Under 'Umar, Islam conquered Iran, Iraq, Syria, and Egypt.

The swift and total collapse of the Sassanid Empire and the major portion of the Byzantine Empire astounded contemporaries, not least the Muslims themselves. Their success seemed to be irrefutable proof that Muhammad's message was from God. By 650, Islam stretched from Egypt to Asia Minor, from the Mediterranean to the Indus River.

Of course, other factors contributed to the Muslims' phenomenal success. Protracted wars between the Byzantine and Sassanid empires and internal divisions within the Byzantine world helped. For more than a decade, Egypt, Palestine, and Syria had been under Persian control. Although eventually reconquered by the Byzantine emperor Heraclius, the provinces had not yet recovered from the decades of warfare, and within them a whole generation had grown up with no experience of Byzantine government.

In addition, the reimposed Byzantine yoke was widely resented because of profound cultural differences between Greeks and the inhabitants of Syria, Iraq, and Egypt. Many looked on the Byzantines not as the liberators but as the enemy. Syria and Egypt had always been different from the rest of the Roman world. Although their great cities of Antioch and Alexandria had long been centers of Hellenistic learning and culture, the hinterlands of each enjoyed ancient cultural traditions totally alien to those of their urban neighbors. In Syria, the rural society was Aramaic- and Arabic-speaking; in Egypt, it was Coptic. With the steady decay of urban life and the rising demands on the rural economy, the local traditions rose to greater prominence. Eventually the traditions coalesced around religious customs sustained by liturgies in the vernacular and sharply at odds with the Orthodox Christianity of Constantinople.

The Spread of Islam

The profound cultural, ethnic, and social antagonisms were largely fought out in the sphere of doctrine, particularly over the nature of Jesus the Christ. The form of Christianity that the emperors sought to impose, defined at the Council of Chalcedon in 451, insisted that Jesus was only one person but had two complete natures, one fully human, the other entirely divine. Such a distinction rested less on the language of the New Testament than on the Greek philosophical tradition. To the Syrian and Egyptian communities, that position was heresy. Closer to the Jewish tradition of the transcendence of God, the Syriac and Egyptian Monophysite (meaning "one nature") Christians insisted that Jesus had but a single nature and that it was divine.

The two groups vented their intense hatred of each other in riots, murders, and vicious persecutions directed by zealous emperors. As a result, many Christians of the Near East initially saw as a divine blessing the arrival of the Muslims, whose beliefs about the unity and transcendence of God were close to their own and who promised religious toleration and an end to persecution.

MAP DISCOVERY

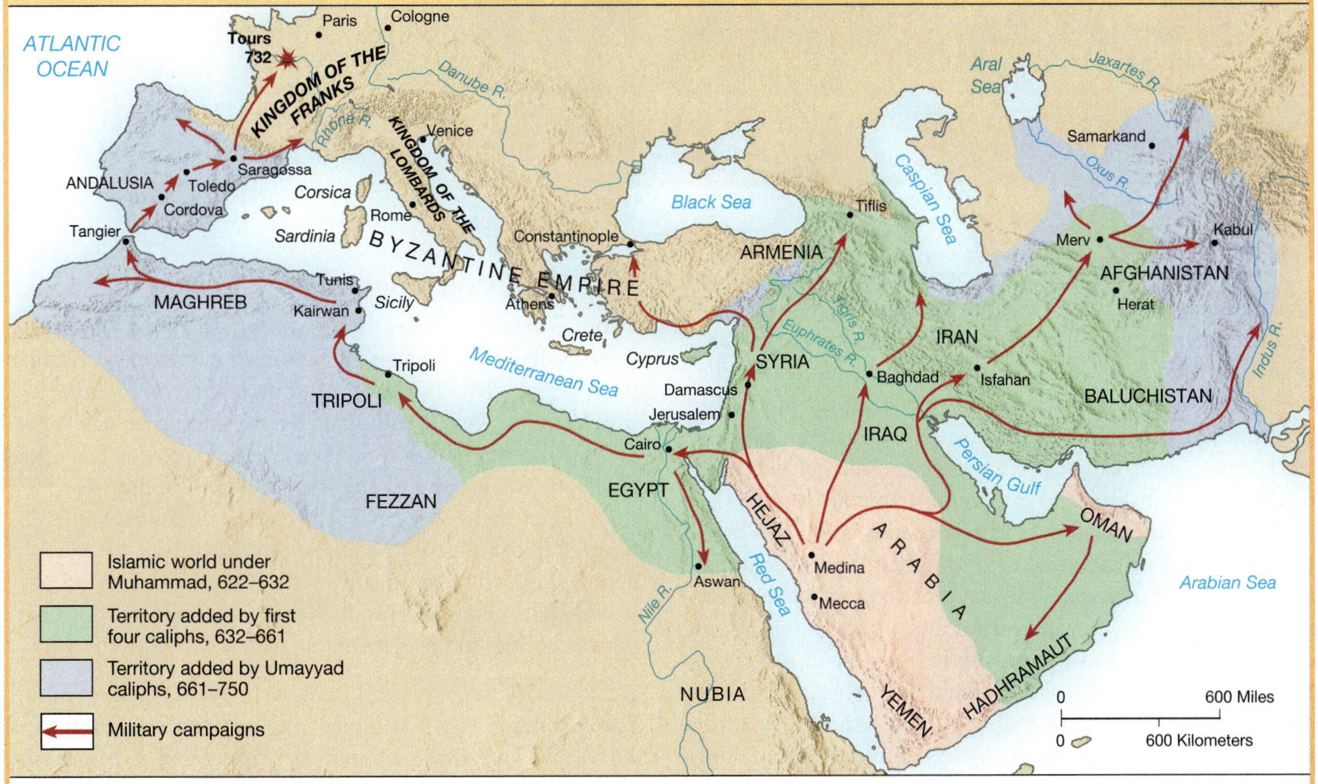

The Spread of Islam

Consider the geographical extent of the Islamic conquest. What trading and cultural networks were united by the spread of Islam? How did the geography of the Islamic world differ from that of its Roman and its Sassanid predecessors? What may have prevented Islam's spread through Asia Minor and up the Iberian peninsula?

A manuscript illustration showing a party of Muslim pilgrims on their way to Mecca. Every able Muslim man is required to make the pilgrimage once in his lifetime.

Many Christians and Jews in Syria, Palestine, Egypt, and North Africa shared the view of the Muslim conquest as liberation rather than enslavement. Jews and Christians may have been second-class citizens in the Islamic world, but at least they had a defined place. Conquered populations were allowed to practice their religion in peace. Their only obligation was to pay a head tax to their conquerors, a burden considerably less onerous than the money exacted by Byzantine tax collectors.

The Byzantines' defeat of the Sassanids indirectly facilitated the Muslims' conquest of Iraq. When the Bedouin realized that the Persians were too weakened to protect their empire against raiders, they intensified their attacks. Soon, recent converts to Islam, too late to profit from the conquests of Syria and Egypt, were spearheading the conquest. By 650 the great Sassanid Empire had disappeared and the Byzantine Empire had lost Egypt, Syria, Mesopotamia, Palestine, portions of Asia Minor, and much of North Africa. During the reigns of Constantine IV (668–685) and Leo III (717–741), Constantinople itself fought for its own survival against besieging Muslim fleets. Although the city itself survived, the Muslim conquests left the once-vast empire a small state reduced to little more than Greece, western Asia Minor, southern Italy, and the Balkans.

Authority and Government in Islam

Conquering the world for Islam proved easier than governing it. What had begun as a religious movement within Arabian society had created a vast multinational empire in which Arabs were a tiny minority. Nothing in the Qur'an, nothing in Arabian experience, provided a blueprint for empire. Thus, the Muslims' ability to consolidate their conquests is even more remarkable than the conquests themselves. Within the first decades following the death of the Prophet, two models of governance emerged, models that continue to dominate Islamic politics to the present.

DOCUMENT
"Instruction" to One's Heirs

The Umma. The first model was that of pre-Islamic tribal authority. The Umma could be considered a supertribe, governed by leaders whose authority came from their secular power as leaders of the superior military and economic elements within the community. The model appealed particularly to Quraysh and local tribal leaders who had exercised authority before Muhammad. The second model was that of the authority exercised by the Prophet. In this model, the Umma was more than a supertribe, and its unity and purity had to be preserved by a religiously sanctioned rule exercised by a member of the Prophet's own family. The second model was preferred by many of the more recent converts to Islam, especially the poor. Governance under each of the two models was attempted successively in the seventh and eighth centuries.

Regardless of their disagreements on the basis of political authority, both groups adopted the administrative systems of their conquered lands. Byzantine and Sassanid bureaucracy and government, only slightly adjusted, became the models for government in the Islamic world until the twentieth century. In Syria and Egypt, Byzantine officials and even churchmen were incorporated into the government, much as had been the case in Europe following the Germanic conquests. For example, John of Damascus (ca. 676–ca. 754), a Christian theologian venerated as a saint, served as the caliph's chief councilor. His faithfulness to the Islamic government and opposition to Byzantine imperial iconoclasm earned him the title of "cursed favorer of Saracens [Muslims]" from the Byzantine emperor.

Likewise, the Muslims left intact the social structures and economic systems of the empires they conquered. Lands remained in the hands of their previous owners. Only state property or, in the Sassanid Empire, that of the Zoroastrian priesthood became common property of the Muslim community. The monastery of Saint Catherine on Mount Sinai, founded by the emperor Justinian around 540, for example, survived without serious harm and still shelters Orthodox monks today.

The Last Orthodox Caliphs. The division of the spoils of conquest badly divided the Umma and precipitated the first crises in the caliphate. Under 'Umar, two groups received most of the spoils of the conquests. First were the earliest followers of the Prophet, who received a disproportionate share of revenues. Second were the conquerors themselves, who were often recent converts from tribes on the fringes of Arabia. After 'Umar's death, his successor, 'Uthman (d. 656), a member of the powerful Umayya clan of Mecca, attempted to consolidate control over Islam by the Quraysh elite. He began to reduce the privileges of early converts in favor of the old Meccan elite. At the same time, he demanded that revenue from the provinces be sent to Medina. The result was rebellion, both within Arabia and in Egypt. 'Uthman's only firm support lay in distant Syria, ruled by members of his own clan. Abandoned at home and abroad, he was finally murdered as he sat reading the Qur'an in his home.

In spite of 'Uthman's unpopularity, his murder sent shock waves throughout the Umma. The fate of his successor, Muhammad's beloved son-in-law and nephew 'Ali (656–661), had an even more serious effect on the future of Islam. Although chosen as fourth caliph, 'Ali was immediately charged with complicity in 'Uthman's murder and strongly opposed by the Umayyad commander of Syria. To protect himself, 'Ali moved the caliphate from Arabia to Iraq. There he sought the support of underprivileged recent converts by stressing the equality of all believers and the religious role of the caliph, who was to be less governor and tax collector than spiritual guide of Islam.

'Ali's spiritual appeal could not make up for his political weakness. At home and abroad, his support gradually crumbled as the Quraysh and their Syrian supporters gained the upper hand. In 661, 'Ali was murdered by supporters of his Umayyad rivals. Still, the memory of the "last orthodox caliph" remained alive in the Islamic world, especially in Iraq and Iran. Centuries later, a tradition developed in Baghdad that legitimate leadership of Islam could come only from the house of 'Ali. Adherents of the belief developed into a political and religious sect known as Shi'ism. Although frequently persecuted as heretical by the majority of Muslims, **Shi'ites** remain a potent minority within the Islamic world today.

Umayyad and 'Abbasid Caliphates

The immediate effect of 'Ali's death, however, was the triumph of the old Quraysh and in particular the Umayyads, who established at Damascus in Syria a caliphate that lasted a century. The Umayyads ruled as secular leaders, attempting to unite the Islamic Empire through an appeal to Arab unity. Profits from the state went entirely to the Quraysh and mem-

The terrifying weapon known as Greek fire is turned on an enemy during a naval battle. This early example of chemical warfare was a mixture of unknown ingredients that ignited and burned furiously when it came into contact with water. The sailors in the illustration are using it like a flame thrower.

bers of Arabian tribes that formed the backbone of the early Umayyad army, monopolized high administration, and acquired rich estates throughout the empire.

Umayyad Caliphate. The Umayyads extended the Islamic Empire to its farthest reaches. In the north, armies from Syria marched into Anatolia and were stopped only in 677 by the Byzantine fleet before Constantinople itself. In the east, Umayyad armies pressed as far as the Syr Darya River on the edge of the Chinese T'ang Empire. In the south and southwest, Umayyad progress was even more successful. After the conquest of the Mediterranean coast of Africa, the general Tariq ibn Ziyad (d. ca. 720) in 711 crossed the strait separating Morocco from Spain near the Rock of Gibraltar. (The name comes from the Arabic *jabal Tariq,* "Tariq's mountain.") He quickly conquered virtually the entire peninsula. Soon raiding parties had ventured as far north as the Loire Valley in what today is France. There they were halted by the Frankish commander Charles Martel near Poitiers in 732. Much of Spain, however, remained part of the Dar al-Harab (the House of Islam) until 1492.

The Umayyad caliphate's external success failed to extend to its dealings with the internal tensions of the Umma. The Umayyads could not build a stable empire on the twin foundations of a tiny Arabian elite and a purely secular government taken over from their Byzantine predecessors. Arabs, as well as Jews, Zoroastrians, and Christians, converted in great numbers. Not all Muslim commanders looked favorably on such conversions. Far from practicing "conversion by the sword," Muslim leaders at times even discouraged the spread of Islam among the non-Arabs they had conquered. The reason was simple. Christians and Jews had to pay the head tax imposed upon them. If they converted, they no longer paid the tax. In time, the growing population of non-Arab Muslims began to demand a share in the empire's wealth.

The 'Abbasid Revolution. Not only were the numbers of Muslims increasing, so also was their fervor. Growing numbers of devout Muslims—Arabs and non-Arabs alike—were convinced that leadership had to be primarily spiritual and that the spiritual mandate was the exclusive right of the family of the Prophet. Ultimately, a coalition of dissatisfied Persian Muslims and Arabian religious reformers united under the black banners of the descendants of Muhammad's paternal uncle, 'Abbas (566–ca. 653). In 750 the group overthrew the Umayyads everywhere but in Spain and established a new caliphate in favor of the 'Abbasids.

With the fall of the Umayyad caliphate, Arabs lost control of Islam forever. The 'Abbasids attempted to govern the empire according to religious principles. The principles were found in the Qur'an and in the **sunnah**, or practices established by the Prophet, and preserved first orally and then in the **hadith**, or traditions, which were somewhat comparable to the Christian Gospels. The new empire was to be a universal Muslim commonwealth in which Arabs had no privileged position. "Whoever speaks Arabic is an Arab," ran a popular saying. The 'Abbasids had risen to power as "the group of the saved," and they hoped to make the moral community of Islam the cornerstone of their government, with obedience to 'Abbasid authority an integral part of Islamic belief.

The institutional foundations of the new caliphate, however, like those of the Umayyads, remained firmly in the ancient empires they had conquered. The great caliph Mansur (754–775) moved the capital from Damascus to Baghdad, an acknowledgment of the crucial role of Iraqi and Iranian military and economic strength. The city, a few miles from the ruins of Ctesiphon on the Tigris River, was largely constructed from building stones hauled by slaves from the old city to the new. In the same manner, the 'Abbasids constructed an autocratic imperial system on the model of their Persian predecessors. With their claims to divine sanction as members of the "holy family" and their firm control of the military, increasingly composed of slave armies known as Mamluks, the 'Abbasids governed the Islamic Empire at its zenith.

Division and Revolt. Ultimately, however, the 'Abbasids were no more successful than the Umayyads in maintaining authority over the whole Muslim world. By the tenth century, local military commanders, termed **emirs**, took control of provincial governments in many areas while preserving the fiction that they were appointed by the 'Abbasid caliphs. The caliphs maintained the symbolic unity of Islam while the emirs went their separate ways. The majority of Muslims accepted the situation as a necessary compromise. In contrast to the **Shi'ites,** who continued to look for a leader from the family of 'Ali, the **Sunnis**, as they came to be known, remain to the present the majority group of Muslims. The Sunnis had no fixed theory of government or succession to the caliphate. Instead, they accepted the events of history in a practical manner, secure in the truth of the hadith: "My Umma will never agree upon an error."

In the west, the 'Abbasids could not maintain even a facade of unity. Supporters of 'Ali's family had never accepted the 'Abbasid claims that they were the legitimate spiritual leaders of the Islamic community. The Shi'ites launched sporadic revolts and separatist movements. The most successful was that of 'Ubayd Allah the Fatimid (d. 934), who claimed to be the descendant of 'Ali and rightful leader of Islam. In 909, with the support of North African seminomadic Berbers, he declared himself caliph in defiance of the 'Abbasids at Baghdad. In 969, 'Ubayd's Fatimid successors conquered Egypt and established a new city, Cairo, as the capital of their rival caliphate. By the middle of the eleventh century, the Fatimid caliphate controlled all of North Africa, Sicily, Syria, and western Arabia.

In Umayyad Spain, although the Muslim population remained firmly Sunni, the powerful emir 'Abd ar-Rahman III (891–961) took a similar step. In 929 he exchanged his title for that of caliph, thus making his position religious as well as secular. Everywhere the political and religious unity of Islam was being torn apart.

The Turks. The arrival in all three caliphates of Muslim peoples not yet integrated into the civilization of the

Mediterranean world accelerated the disintegration. From the east, Seljuk Turks, long used as slave troops, entered Iraq and in 1055 conquered Baghdad. Within a decade they had conquered Iran, Syria, and Palestine as well. Around the same time, Moroccan Berbers conquered much of North Africa and Spain, while Bedouin raided freely in Libya and Tunisia. The invasions by Muslims from the fringes of the Islamic commonwealth had catastrophic effects on the Islamic world. The Turks, unaccustomed to commerce and to the administrative traditions of the caliphate, divided their empire among their war leaders, displacing traditional landowners and disrupting commerce. The North African Berbers and Bedouin destroyed the agricultural and commercial systems that had survived successive Vandal, Byzantine, and Arabian invasions.

Islamic Civilization

The Islamic conquest of the seventh century brought peace to Iraq and Iran after generations of struggle and set the stage for a major agricultural recovery. In the tradition of their Persian predecessors, the caliphs organized vast irrigation systems, which made Mesopotamia the richest agricultural region west of China. Peasants and slaves raised dates and olives in addition to wheat, barley, and rice. Sophisticated hydraulics and scientific agriculture brought great regions of Mesopotamia and the Mediterranean coast into cultivation for the first time in centuries.

By uniting the Mediterranean world with Arabia and India, the ʻAbbasid Empire created the greatest trade network ever seen. Muslim merchants met in busy, bustling ports on the Persian Gulf and the Red Sea. There they traded silk, paper, spices, and horses from China for silver and cotton from India. Gold from the Sudan was exchanged for iron from Persia. Carpets from Armenia and Tabaristan, in what is now Iran, were traded, and from western Europe came slaves. Many of the luxury goods found their way to Baghdad, known as the marketplace for the world.

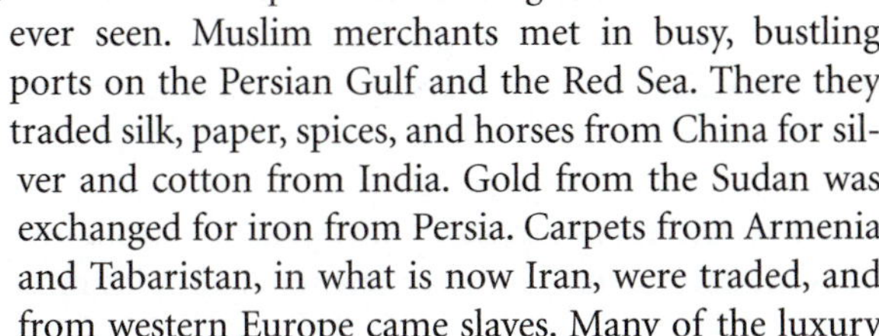

Trade Routes in the Medieval Islamic World

Baghdad and other Muslim cities were marketplaces for ideas as well as for merchandise. Within a few generations, descendants of Bedouin established themselves in the great cities of the ancient Near East and absorbed the traditions of Persian, Roman, and Hellenistic civilizations. However, unlike the Germanic peoples of western Europe, who quickly adopted the Latin language and Roman Christianity, the Muslims recast Persian and Hellenistic culture in an Arabic form. Even in Iran, where Farsi, or Persian, survived as the majority language, Arabic vocabulary and structure transformed the traditional language.

As desert conquerors, the Arabs might have been expected to destroy or ignore the heritage of Persian and Hellenistic culture. Instead, they became its protectors and preservers.

Science and Faith. Islamic intellectuals synthesized and expanded Greek, Persian, and Indian traditions of astronomy and mathematics and sought to find the proper balance between science and faith. As early as the eighth century, caliphs collected Persian, Greek, and Syriac scientific and philosophical works and had them translated into Arabic. Because of the need to establish hours for prayer, Islamic scholars were particularly interested in practical aspects of astronomy and devices for determining time such as the astrolabe, which allows one to determine the time of day or night as well as to determine the exact time of sunrise and sunset and to solve various astronomical problems. Muslim scholars beginning with Ibrahim al-Fazari in ca. 771 perfected the astrolabe, and Islamic treatises and star tables, the most accurate ever devised, were disseminated both west across Europe and east as far as China.

Abu Ja'far Muhammad ibn Musa Al-Khwarizimi (790–850), known as the father of algebra, developed the so-

■ Muslim astronomers made many advances. They perfected the astrolabe, an instrument used to observe and calculate the positions of heavenly bodies.

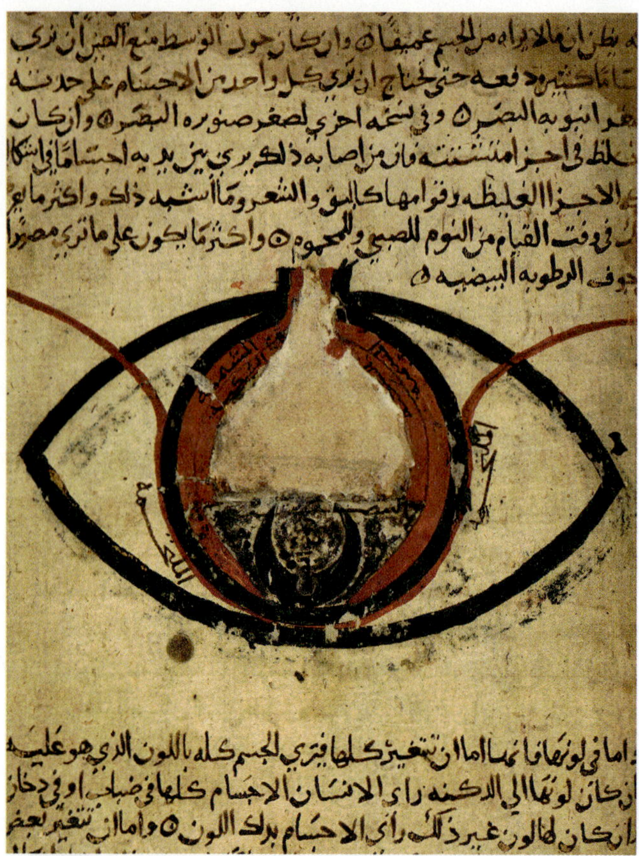

■ Depiction of the anatomy of the eye in a twelfth-century Islamic medical treatise.

lution to quadratic equations and wrote treatises that remained fundamental in the East and the West well into the Renaissance. Muslim intellectuals also introduced the so-called Arabic numerals from India and by the tenth century had perfected the use of decimal fractions. Later Muslim mathematicians such as Omar Khayyam (1048–1122) and Ghiyath al'Din Jamshid Mas'ud al 'Kashi (1390–1450) investigated complex mathematical problems and developed mathematical concepts not surpassed until the nineteenth century.

Medicine was perhaps the area in which Muslims made the greatest contributions in both theory and practice. Charity is fundamental to Islam, and across the Islamic world hospitals were established where the sick could be cared for without cost. Al-Razi (864–930), an Iranian physician who became the head of the hospital in Baghdad, wrote a comprehensive medical encyclopedia that became a standard text, East and West. The Persian physician Ibn Sina (980–1037), known in the West as Avicenna, was perhaps the greatest of the classical Islamic physicians. He was the first to recognize the contagious nature of tuberculosis, the value of anesthetics, and the advantages of experimenting with new drugs on animals before administering them to humans. His *Encyclopedia* covered such topics as surgical removal of cancers, the importance of hygiene, and the uses of more than 700 specific drugs.

Islamic intellectuals also applied ancient learning to questions of Islamic faith. Legal scholars concerned with the authenticity of hadith used Greek rationalist methods to distinguish genuine from spurious traditions. Religious mystics called Sufis blended Neoplatonic and Muslim traditions to create new forms of religious devotion. Abu Hamid Al-Ghazali (1058–1128) combined his deep knowledge of neo-Platonism, law, mathematics, and science with his deep spiritual attachment to Islamic mysticism to produce powerful critiques of what he took to be the excesses of rational science.

Philosophy. Although most Islamic scientists were professional physicians, astronomers, or lawyers, they were also deeply concerned with abstract philosophical questions, particularly those raised by the works of Plato and Aristotle, which had been translated into Arabic. Many sought to reconcile Islam with that philosophical heritage in the same manner that Origen and Augustine had done for Christianity. Ya'qub al-Kindi (d. 873), the first Arab philosopher, noted that "The truth . . . must be taken wherever it is to be found, whether it be in the past or among strange peoples." Ibn Sina, in addition to writing on science and medicine, attempted to synthesize Aristotelian thought into a Neoplatonic view of the universe. In the next century, the Cordoban philosopher Ibn Rushd (1126–1198), called Averroës in the West, went still further, teaching an authentic Aristotelian philosophy stripped of Neoplatonic mystical trappings. His commentaries on Aristotle were enormously influential even outside the Islamic world. For Christian philosophers of the thirteenth century, Averroës was known simply as "the Commentator."

The Islamic world also produced important Jewish scientists, physicians, and scholars, the most significant of whom was Moses Maimonides (1135–1204). Born in Islamic Spain, he migrated to Morocco, Palestine, and eventually Egypt where he became a successful physician. He wrote important texts in Arabic and Hebrew on Jewish law, but his most influential work was *The Guide to the Perplexed,* an Arabic treatise in which he attempts to reconcile Aristotelian and Neoplatonic philosophy to sacred Scripture. His rationalistic approach drew both criticism and praise from within the Jewish, Christian, and Islamic worlds and had a lasting effect on philosophers and thinkers in all three traditions.

Christian Invasion. At the same time that Muslim thought and culture were at their most creative, Islam faced invasion from a new and unaccustomed quarter: Constantinople. In the tenth and early eleventh centuries, the Byzantines pressed the local rulers of northern Syria and Iraq in a series of raids that reached as far as the border of Palestine. At the end of the eleventh century, western Europeans, encouraged and supported by the Byzantines, captured Jerusalem and established a Western-style kingdom in Palestine that survived for over a century. Once more, Constantinople was a power in the Mediterranean world.

The revelations to the prophet Muhammad led to one of the greatest transformations the world has ever known. Islam

AN ARAB'S VIEW OF WESTERN MEDICINE

As heirs to the great medical learning of Hellenistic civilization, Easterners, Muslim and Christian alike, had nothing but contempt for Western medical and surgical practices, especially as employed by crusaders. Even if exaggerated, the following description written by Usama ibn Munqidh, a highly educated and cultured twelfth-century emir (military commander) who had firsthand knowledge of Latin crusaders, conveys the gulf that separated Arabian and Western medical practice.

Focus Questions

What hints does the text give about peaceful interactions between Christians and Muslims? Do you suppose that Tabit might be exaggerating in his report of crusader practice?

The ruler of Munaitira [a crusader fortress in what is now Lebanon] wrote to my uncle asking him to send a doctor to treat some of his followers who were ill. My uncle sent a Christian called Tabit. After only ten days he returned and we said, "You cured them quickly!" This was his story: "They took me to see a knight who had an abscess on his leg, and a woman with consumption. I applied a poultice to the leg, and the abscess opened and began to heal. I prescribed a cleansing and refreshing diet for the woman. Then there appeared a Frankish doctor, who said: 'This man has no idea how to cure these people!' He turned to the knight and said: 'Which would you prefer, to live with one leg or to die with two?' When the knight replied that he would prefer to live with one leg, he sent for a strong man and a sharp axe. They arrived, and I stood by to watch. The doctor supported the leg on a block of wood, and said to the man: 'Strike a mighty blow, and cut cleanly!' And there, before my eyes, the fellow struck the knight one blow, and then another, for the first had not finished the job. The marrow spurted out of the leg, and the patient died instantaneously. Then the doctor examined the woman and said: 'She has a devil in her head who is in love with her. Cut her hair off!' This was done, and she went back to eating her usual Frankish food, garlic, and mustard, which made her illness worse. 'The devil has got into her brain,' pronounced the doctor. He took a razor and cut a cross on her head, and removed the brain so that the inside of the skull was laid bare. Then he rubbed [it] with salt; the woman died instantly. At this juncture, I asked whether they had any further need of me, and as they had none I came away, having learnt things about medical methods that I never knew before."

From *Arab Historians of the Crusades,* selected and translated from the Arabic sources by Francesco Gabrielli, translated by E. Costello.

forged a united Arabian people who went on to conquer more of Asia, Africa, and Europe than had any military empire in history. The conquest in the name of Allah created a vast religious and commercial zone in which ideas and cultures flowed as freely as silks and spices. The Arabians soon lost political control of the Islamic movement, but their religious tradition and its emphasis on worship of the one God remains an enduring legacy in world civilization.

THE BYZANTINE APOGEE AND DECLINE, 1000–1453

During the tenth and eleventh centuries, Byzantium dominated the Mediterranean world for the last time. Imperial armies under the Macedonian dynasty (867–1059) began to recover some lands lost to Islam during the previous two centuries. Antioch was retaken in 969, and for more than a century Byzantine armies operated in Syria and pushed to the border of Palestine. By the middle of the eleventh century, Armenia and Georgia, which had formed independent principalities, had been reintegrated into the empire. To the west, Sicily remained in Muslim hands, but southern Italy, which had been subject to Muslim raids and western barbarian occupation, was secured once more. Byzantine fleets recaptured Crete, cleared the Aegean of Muslim pirates, and reopened the vital commercial sea routes. To the north, missionaries spread Byzantine culture as well as the Christian religion among the Slavic peoples beyond the frontiers of the empire. In 1018, Basil II (976–1025) destroyed the Bulgarian kingdom and brought peace to the Balkan peninsula.

The conquests of the Macedonian dynasty laid the foundation for a short-lived economic prosperity and cultural renaissance. Conquered lands, particularly Anatolia, brought new agricultural wealth. Security of the sea fostered a resurgence of commerce, and customs duties enriched the imperial treasury. New wealth financed the flourishing of Byzantine art and literature. However, just as in the spheres of Byzantine liturgy and court ceremonial, the goal of Byzantine art was to reflect not the transient "reality" of the world but rather the permanent, classic values inherited from the past. The language, style, and themes of classical Greek literature, philosophy, and history completely dominated Byzantine culture. Only in rare works, such as the popular epic *Digenis Akrites,* does something of the flavor of popular Byzantine life appear. The title of the work means

CHRONOLOGY

The Byzantine Empire and the Rise of Islam

527–565	Reign of Justinian
610	Muhammad's vision
622	The Hijra, Muhammad's journey from Mecca to Medina
717	Muslim advance halted at Constantinople
726–787	First phase of iconoclast dispute
750	'Abbasids overthrow Umayyads; take control of Muslim world
802–843	Second phase of iconoclast dispute
843	Empress Theodora ends iconoclast persecution; restores image veneration
867–1059	Macedonian dynasty rules Byzantine Empire; begins recovering lands from Muslims
1054	Schism splits churches of Rome and Constantinople
1071	Robert Guiscard captures Sicily and southern Italy; Battle of Manzikert; Seljuk Turks defeat Byzantines
1099	First Crusade establishes Latin kingdom in Jerusalem
1221	Chingis Khan leads Mongol army into Persia
1453	Constantinople falls to Ottomans

roughly "the border defender born of two peoples," for the hero, Basil, was the son of a Muslim father and a Christian Greek mother. The epic consists of two parts, one describing the exploits of the hero's father, a Muslim emir or general, and the other describing the exploits of the hero, Digenis Akrites, as he fights both Muslims and bandits. The portrayals of the hero's battles, his encounters with wild beasts and dragons, and his heroic death, as well as descriptions of his intelligence, learning, and magnificent palace, are at once part of the Western epic tradition and a reflection of life on the edge of the empire.

Another picture of Byzantine life was created by cultivated authors who were able to master completely their ancient models and to fashion within these inherited forms of literature compelling works of enduring value. One such author was the historian and imperial courtier Michael Psellus (1018–ca. 1078). His firsthand descriptions of rampaging mobs in Constantinople, hounding their enemies "like wild beasts," his acute analyses of imperial politics, and his descriptions of the inner workings of court intrigues bring to life Byzantine society at its height.

The Disintegration of the Empire

In all domains, however, the successes of the Macedonian emperors set the stage for serious problems. Rapid military expansion and economic growth allowed new elites to establish themselves as autonomous powers and to position themselves between the imperial administration and the people. The constant demand for troops always exceeded the supply of traditional salaried soldiers. In the eleventh century, emperors began to grant imperial estates to great magnates in return for military service. The grants, termed *pronoia,* often included immunity from imperial taxation and the right to certain administrative activities traditionally carried out by the central government. The practice created in effect a largely independent landed military aristocracy that stood between the peasantry and the imperial government. The policy weakened the centralized state and reduced its income from taxes.

Internal Conflict. As generals became dissatisfied with the civilian central administration, they began to turn their armies against the emperors, launching more than 30 revolts in as many years. To defend itself against both the Muslims without and the generals within, the central government had to spend vast sums on mercenary armies. The armies, composed largely of Armenians, Germans, and Normans, soon began to plunder the empire they were hired to protect. Further danger came from other, independent Normans who, under their commander, Robert Guiscard (ca. 1015–1085), conquered Byzantine Bari and southern Italy and then Muslim Sicily. Soon Guiscard was threatening the empire itself. The hostility between military aristocracy and imperial administration largely destroyed the tradition of civilian government.

Under increasing pressure from local magnates on the one hand and desperate imperial tax collectors on the other, villages began to make deals with powerful patrons who would represent them in return for the surrender of their independence. Throughout the eleventh and twelfth centuries, the Byzantine peasantry passed from the condition of individualism without freedom to collectivism without freedom. Through the same process, landlords and patrons acquired the means to exercise a political role, which ended the state's monopoly on public power.

A TURKISH GUEST IN CONSTANTINOPLE

Anna Comnena (1083–1148), daughter of the Emperor Alexius I (1048–1118), wrote The Alexiad, *a vivid history of her father's reign. Anna was highly educated and extremely shrewd: she understood well that the only hope for the beleaguered empire was cunning and diplomacy. In the following passage she explains how Emperor Alexius tricked Abul-Kasim, the powerful Turkish governor of Nicaea, who was under threat from a rival Muslim army.*

Focus Questions

Why would the emperor offer peace to a sworn enemy? How does Alexius use Byzantium's past to impress his guest?

The emperor, expert in winning the heart of a man and softening the hardest nature, at once sent Abul-Kasim a letter in which he advised him to make terms with himself (the emperor); by doing this he would relieve himself of much labor and enjoy instead liberal gifts and honors. . . . A treaty of peace was concluded between them, but Alexius was eager to obtain a further advantage, and since there was no other way of achieving his goal, invited the Turk to the capital. . . . Abul-Kasim accepted the offer and was welcomed in the capital with every mark of friendship. Now the Turks who controlled Nicaea had also occupied Nicomedia and the emperor wished to eject them; in order to do so, he thought it essential to build a second stronghold by the sea while the 'love-scene' was being played out in Constantinople. All the construction materials needed for the building of this fortress, together with the architects, were put on board transport ships. Eustathios, who was responsible for the building, was to receive in the most friendly fashion any Turks who happened to pass that way, supplying their needs with the utmost generosity, and inform them that Abul-Kasim knew of the project; all ships were to be barred from the coastal areas of Bithynia to prevent him from finding out what was happening. Every day the emperor continued to give Abul-Kasim presents of money, to invite him to the baths, to horse races and hunts, to sight-seeing tours of the commemorative columns set up in public places; to please him the charioteers were ordered to organize an equestrian display in the theater built long ago by Constantine the Great—all in order to waste time and allow the builders a free hand. When the fortress was finished and his aim achieved, Alexius presented the Turk with more gifts, honored him with the title of Venerable, and sent him with every sign of courtesy back over the sea. When Abul-Kasim eventually heard about the building, although he was deeply distressed, he pretended ignorance and maintained a complete silence on the subject.

From *The Alexiad of Anna Comnena*, edited and translated by E. R. A. Sewter. Harmondsworth: Penguin, 1969.

Commercial Threats. At the same time that civil war and external pressure were destroying the provincial administration, Byzantine disdain for commerce was weakening the empire's ability to control its income from customs duties. Initially the willingness to turn over commerce to Italians and others posed few problems. Those engaged in commerce were for the most part citizens of the empire and were in any case subject to the 10 percent tariff. However, in the tenth and eleventh centuries, merchants of Amalfi, Bari, and then Venice came to dominate Byzantine commerce. Venetian merchant fleets could double as a powerful navy in times of need, and by the eleventh century the Venetians were the permanent military and commercial power in the Mediterranean. When Robert Guiscard and his Normans threatened the empire, the emperors had to turn to the Venetians for protection and were forced to cede them major economic privileges. The Venetians acquired the right to maintain important self-governing communities in major ports throughout the empire and were allowed to pay tariffs lower than those paid by the Byzantines.

In 1071, the year that Robert Guiscard captured the last Byzantine city in Italy, the empire suffered an even more disastrous defeat in the east. At Manzikert in Anatolia, the emperor Romanus IV (1067–1071) and his unreliable mercenary army fell to the Seljuk Turks, who captured Romanus. The defeat at Manzikert sealed the fate of the empire. Anatolia was lost and the gradual erosion of the empire in both the west and the east had begun.

The Conquests of Constantinople and Baghdad

At the end of the eleventh century, the Comnenian dynasty (1081–1185) briefly halted the political and economic chaos of the empire. Rather than fighting the tendency of the centralized state to devolve into a decentralized aristocratic one, Alexius I Comnenus (1081–1118) tied the aristocracy to his family, thus making it an instrument of imperial government. In the short run the process was successful. Still, by the late twelfth century, the empire was a vulnerable second-rate power caught between Latin Europe and Islam.

Initially, the Christian West was a more deadly threat than the Islamic East. In the eleventh century, after more than 500 years of economic and political weakness, western Europe was beginning to reach parity with Byzantium. Robert Guiscard and his Normans, who had conquered Sicily and southern Italy, were typical examples of the powerful, militaristic aristocracy developing in the remains of the old western empire.

Dangers from the West. The military threat from the West was paralleled by a religious one. In the centuries during which Rome had been largely cut off from Constantinople, Western Christianity had developed a number of rituals and beliefs differing from Orthodox practice. The parting of the ways had already appeared during the iconoclastic controversies of the eighth and ninth centuries. In the eleventh century, it was directed by an independent and self-assertive papacy in Rome, which claimed supreme authority throughout Christendom.

Disagreements between the patriarchs of Constantinople and the popes of Rome prevented cooperation between the two Christian worlds and led to further deterioration of relationships between Greeks and Latins. The disagreements came to a head in 1054, when the papal representative, or legate, Cardinal Humbert (ca. 1000–1061), met with the patriarch of Constantinople, Michael Cerularius (ca. 1000–1059), to negotiate ecclesiastical control over southern Italy and Sicily. Humbert was arrogant and demanding, Cerularius haughty and uncompromising. Acting beyond his authority, Humbert excommunicated the patriarch and all his followers. The patriarch responded in kind, excommunicating Humbert and all connected with him. The formal excommunication was finally lifted in the 1960s, but the schism, or split, between the churches of Rome and Constantinople continues today.

Excommunication was probably the least of the dangers the Byzantines faced from the West. The full fury of the Western society reached the empire when, after the defeat at Manzikert, the emperor Alexius called on Western Christians for support against the Muslims. To his horror, adventurers of every sort eager to conquer land and wealth in the name of the cross flooded the empire. In the penetrating and often cynical biography of her father, Alexius's daughter Anna (ca. 1083–1148) describes how, as quickly as possible, Alexius hurried the crusaders (from the Latin *cruciata*, "marked with a cross") on to Palestine before they could turn their violence against his empire. Even while recognizing that the crusaders were uncouth and barbarous, the Byzantines had to admit that the Latins were effective. Despite enormous hardships, the First Crusade was able to take advantage of division in the Muslim world to conquer Palestine and establish a Latin kingdom in Jerusalem in 1099.

The Sack of Constantinople. The crusaders' initial victories and the growth of Latin wealth and power created in Constantinople a temporary enthusiasm for western European styles and customs. The Byzantines soon realized, however, that the Latin kingdom posed a threat not only to Islam but to themselves as well. While crusaders threatened Byzantine

AN ARAB IN CRUSADER JERUSALEM

The contrast between mutual respect and intolerance is captured in this account by Usamah ibn Munqidh, a highly educated and cultured twelfth-century emir (military commander) who had intimate experience of life in the Latin Kingdom of Jerusalem and friends among its defenders.

Focus Questions

To what does Usamah attribute the intolerance of the Christian? What does the reaction of the other Christian Templars suggest about the relationship between Christians and Muslims in twelfth-century Jerusalem?

Everyone who is a fresh emigrant from the Frankish lands is ruder in character than those who have become acclimatized and have held long association with the Moslems. Here is an illustration of their rude character.

Whenever I visited Jerusalem, I always entered the Aqsa Mosque, beside which stood a small mosque which the Franks had converted into a church. When I sued to enter the Aqsa Mosque, which was occupied by the Templars, [Christian Warrior monks] who were my friends, the Templars would evacuate the little adjoining mosque so that I might pray in it. One day I entered this mosque, repeated the first formula, "Allah is great" and stood up in the act of praying, upon which one of the Franks rushed on me, got hold of me and turned my face eastward, saying "This is the way thou shouldst pray!" A group of Templars hastened to him, seized him and repelled him from me. I resumed my prayer. The same man, while the others were otherwise busy, rushed once more on me and turned my face eastward, saying, "This is the way thou shouldst pray!" The Templars again came in to him and expelled him. They apologized to me, saying, "This is a stranger who has only recently arrived from the land of the Franks and he has never before seen anyone praying except eastward." Thereupon I said to myself, "I have had enough prayer." So I went out, and have ever been surprised at the conduct of this devil of a man, at the change in the color of his face, his trembling, and his sentiment at the sight of one praying towards the qiblah [the direction of the Ka'bah in Mecca].

From James Kritzeck, ed., *Anthology of Islamic Literature from the Rise of Islam to Modern Times* (New York: Mentor Books, 1964), p. 194.

territories, Venetian merchants imposed a stranglehold on Byzantine trade. Anti-Latin sentiment reached the boiling point in 1183. In the riots that broke out in that year, Italians and other westerners in Constantinople were murdered and their goods seized. Just 21 years later, in 1204, a wayward crusade, encouraged by Venice, turned aside from its planned expedition to Palestine to capture a bigger prize—Constantinople. After pillaging the city for three days—the Byzantine survivors commented that even the Saracens would have been less cruel—the westerners established one of their own as emperor and installed a Venetian as patriarch.

The Byzantines did manage to hold onto a portion of their empire centering on Nicaea, and before long the Latins fell to bickering among themselves. In 1261 the ruler of Nicaea, Michael Palaeologus (ca. 1224–1282), recaptured Constantinople with the assistance of the Genoese and had himself crowned emperor in the Hagia Sophia. Still, the empire was fatally shattered, its disintegration into autonomous lordships complete. The restored empire consisted of little more than the district around Constantinople, Thessalonica, and the Peloponnesus. Bulgarians and Serbs had expanded far into the Greek mainland. Most of the rich Anatolian regions had been lost to the Turks, and commercial revenues were in the hands of the Genoese allies. The restored empire's survival for almost 200 years was due less to its own prerogative than to the internal problems of the Islamic world.

Eastern Conquests. The caliphs of Baghdad, like the emperors of Constantinople, succumbed to invaders from the barbarous fringes of their empire. In 1221, the Mongol prince Temujin (ca. 1162–1227), better known to history as Chingis Khan or "Universal Ruler," led his conquering army into Persia from central Asia. From there, a portion of the Mongols went north, invading Russia in 1237 and dividing it into small principalities ruled by Slavic princes under Mongol control. In 1258, a Mongol army captured Baghdad and executed the last ʻAbbasid caliph, ending a 500-year tradition. The Mongol armies then moved west, shattering the Seljuk principalities in Iraq, Anatolia, and Syria and turning back only before the fierce resistance of the Egyptian Mamluks.

From the ruins of the Seljuk kingdom arose a variety of small Turkish principalities, or emirates. After the collapse of the Mongol Empire, one of these emirates, the Ottoman, began to expand at the expense of both the weakened Byzantine and the Mongol-Seljuk empires. In the next centuries the Ottomans expanded east, south, and west. Around 1350, they crossed into the Balkans as Byzantine allies but soon took over the region for themselves. By 1450, the Ottoman stranglehold on Constantinople was complete. The final scene of the conquest, long delayed but inevitable, occurred three years later.

For Greeks and for Italian intellectuals of the Renaissance, the conquest of Constantinople by the Ottomans was the end of an imperial tradition that reached back to Augustus. But Mehmed the Conqueror (1452–1481) could as easily be seen as its restorer. True, the city was plundered by the victorious army. But plunder was simply the way of war in the fifteenth century. The city, its palaces, and its religious edifices fared

The Ottoman Empire, ca. 1450. By the mid-fifteenth century the Ottoman Empire had absorbed virtually all of the Byzantine Empire.

Kemha Caftan of Mehmed the Conqueror.

better under the Turks than they had under their previous Christian conquerors. Once more Constantinople, for centuries a capital without a country, was the center of a great Mediterranean empire. In the following centuries, Ottoman rule stretched from the gates of Vienna to the Caspian Sea and from the Persian Gulf to the Strait of Gibraltar. The legacy of absolutism, of imperial government, and of cultural pluralism inherited from Sassanid Persia and imperial Rome survived until the beginning of the twentieth century.

Nestor-Iksander on the Fall of Constantinople

CONCLUSION

Although often deadly enemies, both the Byzantine and the Islamic worlds were genuine heirs of the great eastern empires of antiquity. The traditions of the Assyrian, Alexandrian, Persian, and Roman empires lived on in their cities, their bureaucracies, and their agricultural and commercial systems. Both also shared the monotheistic religious tradition that had emerged from Judaism. In their schools and libraries, they preserved and transmitted the literary and scientific heritage of antiquity. Through Islam, the legacy of the West reached the Far East. Through Byzantium, the peoples of the Slavic world became heirs of the caesars. The inhabitants of western Europe long viewed the two great civilizations with hostility, incomprehension, and fear. Still, in the areas of culture, government, religion, and commerce, the West learned much from its eastern neighbors.

QUESTIONS FOR REVIEW

1. In what ways was Byzantine society characterized by individualism without freedom?
2. How and why did Muhammad both break from tribal and clan traditions and build upon them in creating Islam?
3. How did conflicts within Islam after Muhammad's death divide it spiritually but also contribute to Islam's expansion across Africa and Spain?
4. How did the rapid expansion of Byzantium under the Macedonian dynasty contribute to the empire's slow collapse?

KEY TERMS

basileus, p. 191	icons, *p. 197*
caliph, *p. 202*	jihads, *p. 202*
emirs, *p. 206*	Orthodox Christianity, *p. 193*
hadith, *p. 206*	Shi'ites, *p. 205*
haram, *p. 199*	strategoi, *p. 191*
Hijra, *p. 200*	sunnah, *p. 206*
iconoclasts, *p. 197*	Sunnis, *p. 206*
iconodules, *p. 197*	Umma, *p. 200*

DISCOVERING WESTERN CIVILIZATION ONLINE

You can obtain more information about the classical legacy in the East at the Websites listed below. See also the Companion Website that accompanies this text, www.ablongman.com/kishlansky, which contains an online study guide and additional resources.

The Byzantines

Byzantium: Byzantine Studies on the Internet
www.fordham.edu/halsall/Byzantium/
A major site with links to every aspect of Byzantine civilization maintained by Paul Halsall.

NM's Creative Impulse: Byzantium
history.evansville.net/byzantiu.html
An excellent guide to Byzantine studies on the Web.

Medieval Sourcebook: The Institutes of Justinian, 535 C.E.
www.fordham.edu/halsall/basis/535institutes.html
www.fordham.edu/halsall/source/corpus1.html
Extensive selections from the *Institutes*, a digest of laws and legal opinions designed for law students. The *Institutes*, the *Codex Justinianus*, and the *Digest* were part of the *Corpus Iurus Civilis* (Body of Civil Law) issued under Justinian. This codification of Roman law stands as a great monument of Western jurisprudence.

The Rise of Islam

IslamiCity.com—Education
Islamicity.com/education/ihame/default.asp?Destination=/education/ihame/1.asp
A site for Islamic history maintained by IslamiCity, dedicated to advancing Islamic information, fostering community, and educating people about Islam.

Internet Islamic History Sourcebook
www.fordham.edu/halsall/islam/islamsbook.html
Paul Halsall's site dedicated to sources on Islamic history and culture.

About Islam and Muslims
www.ummah.org.uk/what-is-islam/index.html
A site devoted to explaining Islam maintained by the UNN Islamic Society.

Welcome to Isfahan!
isfahan.apu.ac.uk/isfahan.html
A site devoted to eleventh-century Isfahan, capital of medieval Persia.

The Metropolitan Museum of Art: Islamic Art
metmuseum.org/collections/department.asp?dep=14
A guide to New York's Metropolitan Museum Islamic collection.

The Byzantine Apogee and Decline

The Glory of Byzantium
metmuseum.org/explore/Byzantium/byzhome.html
A site dedicated to Byzantine art and history at the Metropolitan Museum of Art.

Church History with a Focus on Orthodoxy
aggreen.net/church_history/c_histry.html
A site dedicated to Orthodox Christianity with links to Byzantine history and culture.

SUGGESTIONS FOR FURTHER READING

The Byzantines

Jonathan Harris, *Byzantium and the Crusades* (London and New York: Hambledon and London, 2003). A new treatment of relations between Byzantium and western Europe.

Alexander P. Kazhdan, ed., *The Oxford Dictionary of Byzantium* (New York: Oxford University Press, 1991). Standard reference for Byzantine history and culture.

Alexander Kazhdan and Giles Constable, *People and Power in Byzantium* (Washington, DC: Dumbarton Oaks, 1982). An imaginative and controversial analysis of Byzantine culture by a Russian Byzantinist and a Western medievalist.

Michael Maas, ed. *The Cambridge Companion to the Age of Justinian* (Cambridge, MA: Cambridge University Press, 2005). A collectively authored introduction to the early Byzantine Empire.

Cyril Mango, *Byzantium: The Empire of New Rome* (New York: Scribner's, 1980). An imaginative and provocative reevaluation of the Byzantine world.

Dimitri Obolensky, *Byzantium and the Slavs* (Crestwood, NY: St. Vladimir's Seminary Press, 1994). A survey of the Byzantine Empire's relations with eastern Europe.

Warren T. Treadgold, *A Concise History of Byzantium* (New York: St. Martin's Press, 2001). An up-to-date survey of Byzantine history.

The Rise of Islam

Aziz Al-Azmeh, *Arabic Thought and Islamic Societies* (London: Routledge, Chapman & Hall, 1986). A demanding but valuable introduction to Islamic intellectual history.

Mahmoud M. Ayoub, *Islam: Faith and History* (Oxford: Oneworld Publications, 2005). A survey of Islam from its origins to the present from a personal perspective.

Albert Hourani, *A History of the Arab Peoples* (New York: Warner Books, 1992). A clear, thoughtful survey of Arab history for nonspecialists.

Robert G. Hoyland, *Arabia and the Arabs: From the Bronze Age to the Coming of Islam* (New York: Routledge, 2001). A comprehensive survey of the early history of Arabia.

Bernard Lewis, *Islam in History: Ideas, People, and Events in the Middle East* (Chicago: Open Court, 1993). Broad synthesis of Islam.

Bernard Lewis, *The Muslim Discovery of Europe* (New York: W. W. Norton, 1985). Views of the West by Muslim travelers.

Bernard Lewis, ed., *Islam and the Arab World* (New York: Knopf, 1976). An illustrated collection of essays on Islamic history and culture.

Fatima Mernissi, *Women and Islam: An Historical and Theological Enquiry* (Oxford: Basil Blackwell, 1991). Sympathetic study of women in Islam.

Roy P. Mottahedeh, *The Mantle of the Prophet: Religion and Politics in Iran* (New York: Simon and Schuster, 1985). An important introduction to the social values and structures of western Iran and southern Iraq in the tenth and eleventh centuries.

G. E. Von Grunebaum, *Classical Islam: A History, 600–1258* (Chicago: Aldine, 1970). A general introduction to early Islamic history.

The Byzantine Apogee and Decline, 1000–1453

Michael Angold, *The Byzantine Empire, 1025–1204* (White Plains, NY: Longman, 1997). A solid survey of the Byzantine Empire prior to the capture of Constantinople by the Latins.

P. M. Holt, *The Age of the Crusades: The Near East from the Eleventh Century to 1517* (White Plains, NY: Longman, 1986). An excellent survey of the political history of the Near East in the later Middle Ages.

Bissera V. Pentcheva, *Icons and Power: the Mother of God in Byzantium* (University Park, PA: Pennsylvania State University Press, 2006). An analysis of the centrality of the cult of the Virgin in Byzantine public life and imperial ideology.

For a list of additional titles related to this chapter's topics, please see http://www.ablongman.com/kishlansky.

CHAPTER 8 THE WEST IN THE EARLY MIDDLE AGES, 500–900

THE CHAPEL AT THE WATERS

THE WESTERN EMPIRE REBORN

THE VISUAL RECORD

The Palatine Chapel in Aachen, now a German city near the Belgian border, expresses a fascination with the traditions of the Roman past infused with the creativity of a new epoch. These two strands of tradition and change describe Europe during the early Middle Ages, generally the period between 500 and 900. Aachen was a favorite residence of the Frankish king Charles the Great, or Charlemagne (768–814), who often went there to enjoy its natural hot springs. In time it came to be his primary residence and the capital of his vast kingdom, which stretched from central Italy to the mouth of the Rhine River. Around 792, Charlemagne, a descendant of barbarian warriors, commissioned an architect to design a palace as complex as his residence—one that would rival the great Roman and Byzantine buildings of Italy and Constantinople.

Royal agents scoured Europe for Roman ruins from which columns, precious marble, and ornaments could be salvaged and reused. From the ancient stones, masons raised a complex of audience rooms, royal apartments, baths, and quarters for court officials. The whole ensemble was intentionally reminiscent of the Lateran Palace in Rome, which had been the residence of the emperors before being given to the popes.

The central building of Charlemagne's palace complex was the chapel, a symmetrical octagon 300 feet on its principal axes, modeled on San Vitale in Ravenna. The choice of model was significant. Ravenna had been the former capital of Roman Italy and of Theodoric the Great, the Ostrogothic king whom Charlemagne greatly admired. Although modeled on Roman buildings, the Palatine Chapel was admirably suited to the glorification of Charlemagne.

The building was divided into three tiers. The first tier on the ground floor held the sanctuary, where priest and people met for worship. The topmost tier, supported by ancient Roman pillars shipped to Aachen from Rome and Ravenna, represented the heavens. Between the two was a gallery connected by a passage to the royal residence. On this gallery sat the king's throne. From his seat, Charlemagne could look down upon the religious services being conducted below. Looking up to where he sat, worshipers were constantly reminded of the king's intermediary position between ordinary mortals and God.

The architectural design boldly asserted that Charlemagne was more than a barbarian king. By 805, when the chapel was dedicated, he had made good this assertion. As a contemporary chronicler wrote while in Rome in the year 800:

> On the most holy day of Christmas, when the king rose from prayer in front of the shrine of the blessed apostle Peter to take part in the Mass, Pope Leo placed a crown on his head, and he was hailed by the whole Roman people. . . . He was now called Emperor and Augustus.

Thus, to Charlemagne and to his supporters, the coronation ceremony revived the Roman Empire in the west. Charlemagne, with his vast empire and his imperial palace, was a true successor of the ancient Roman emperors. Like his chapel in Aachen (long after known as Aix-la-Chapelle, "the chapel at the waters"), the empire was built on the remains of Roman tradition, onto which was grafted a vigorous tradition of Germanic kinship and society. According to the Byzantines, who looked on Charlemagne and his imperial coronation with alarm, the western empire could not be revived because it had never really ended. According to them, the death in 480 of the last western emperor, Julius Nepos, had ended the division of the empire and since then the Byzantine emperors had pretended that they ruled both east and west. Charlemagne's claims, made through the ceremony in Rome and more subtly in the imperial architecture of his palace, represented to them not a revival of the empire but a threat to its existence.

LOOKING AHEAD

This chapter will trace western Europe's progress toward Aachen, exploring the spectrum of barbarian successor states before concentrating on the unique blend of Roman, Christian, and Frankish institutions and culture that culminated in the Carolingian Empire, an empire whose legacy endured long after its unity dissolved into competing kingdoms and lordships.

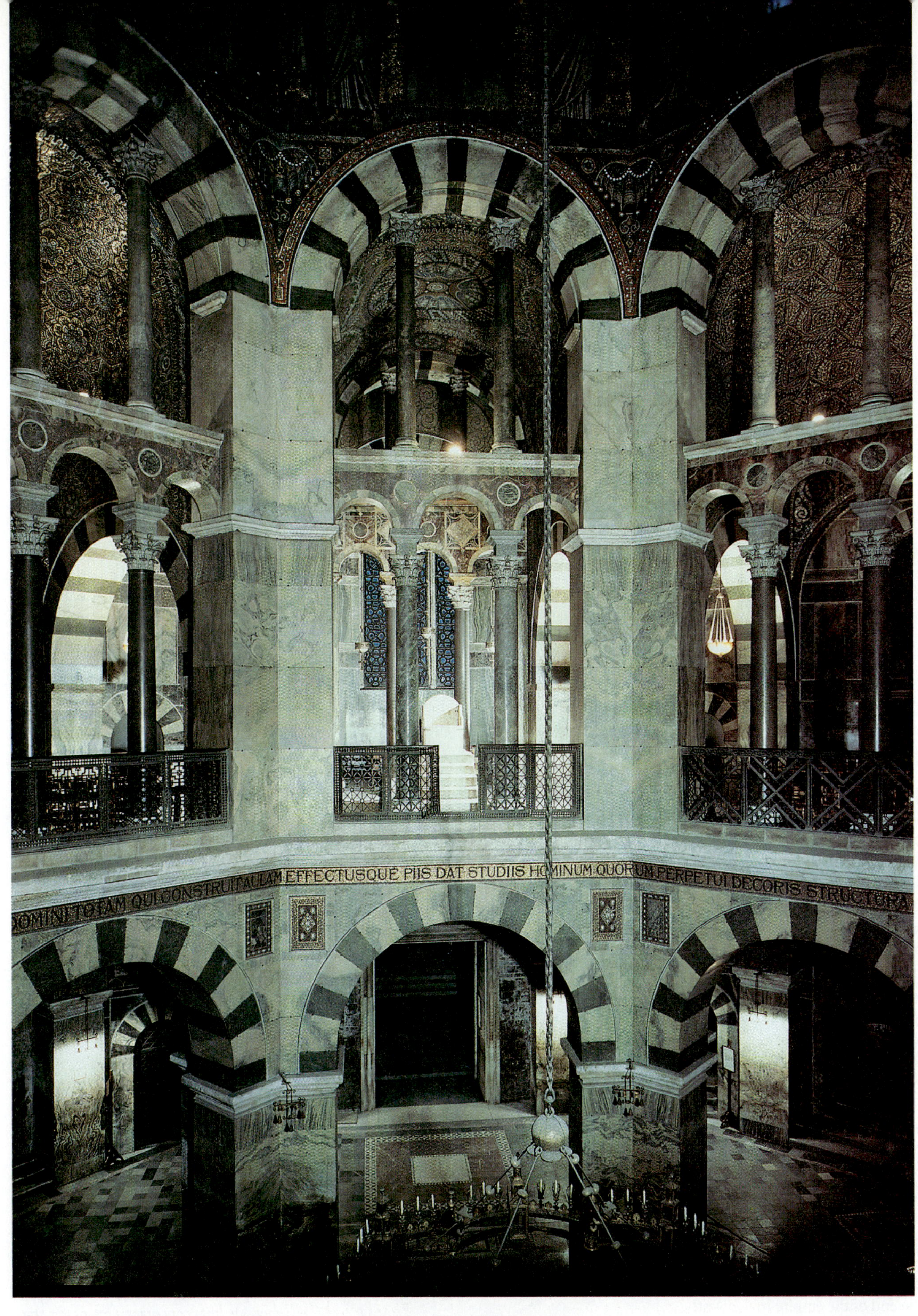

■ The interior of Charlemagne's chapel at Aachen looking across to the royal throne.

CHAPTER OUTLINE

THE MAKING OF THE BARBARIAN KINGDOMS, 500–750

The existence of a united empire had long been but a dream. In the year 500, Emperor Anastasius I (491–518) could delude himself that he ruled the whole empire of Augustus, Diocletian, and Constantine, both east and west. Never mind that in the east war against the Persians dragged on. Never mind that along the northern border of the empire the Bulgarians, a new multiethnic barbarian confederation, had begun to conduct raids into the Balkans. Neither of the conflicts, Anastasius contended, threatened the stability of the empire. In the west, the governor who ruled Italy had sworn that he "rejoiced to live under Roman law, which we are prepared to defend by arms." The king of the once troublesome Vandals had concluded a marriage alliance with the Italian governor and seemed ready to accept Roman statecraft. Beyond the Alps a Roman officer, called a *patrician,* ruled the regions of the upper Rhone River, and a consul controlled Gaul. In Aquitaine and Spain, legitimate, recognized officers of the empire ruled both Romans and barbarians. What need was there to speak of the end of the empire in the west?

Imperial unity was more apparent than real. The Italian governor was the Ostrogothic king Theodoric the Great (493–526), whose Roman title meant less than his Ostrogothic army. The patrician was the Burgundian king Gondebaud (480–516). The Roman officer in Aquitaine and Spain was the Visigothic king Alaric II (485–507), and the Gallic consul was the Frankish king Clovis (482–511). Each of the rulers courted imperial titles and recognition, but not one of them regarded Anastasius as his sovereign. In Britain, the chieftains of the Anglo-Saxons did not even bother with the charade of imperial recognition. Within each barbarian kingdom in the west, the process of merging barbarians and Romans into new political and social entities had begun. No longer were east and west a united empire. The west had gone its own way.

Italy: From Ostrogoths to Lombards

In the early sixth century, all of the Germanic peoples settled within the old Roman Empire acknowledged the Goths as the most successful of the "blond-haired peoples," as the Romans called the barbarians. The Ostrogoths had created an Italian kingdom in which Romans and barbarians lived side by side. The Visigoths ruled Spain and southern Gaul by combining traditions of Roman law and barbarian military might. Yet neither Gothic kingdom endured for more than two centuries.

The Ostrogothic Kingdom. Theodoric the Ostrogoth was the most cultivated, capable, and sophisticated barbarian ruler. He was also the most powerful. Burgundians, Franks, Visigoths, and Alemanni looked to him for leadership and protection. Theodoric's success was the result of his deep understanding of Roman and barbarian traditions. As a teenage hostage in Constantinople, he had learned to understand and admire Roman ways. In Italy, he put his knowledge of Roman law and governance to good use, establishing a dual government that respected both the remains of Roman civil administration and Gothic military organization. As theoretical representative of the Byzantine emperor, Theodoric governed the Roman population through the traditional Roman bureaucracy. As hereditary king he led his Ostrogoths, a small but powerful military minority.

Religion as well as government divided Italy's population. The Ostrogoths were Arians, while the majority of the Romans were Orthodox Christians. Initially, Theodoric made no effort to interfere with the religion of his

■ A golden solidus coin minted under Theodoric in Ravenna but bearing the portrait of the Emperor Anastasius. Although the obverse bears the monograph of Theodoric, the iconography maintains the fiction of the subordination of the Gothic ruler to the Emperor.

MAP DISCOVERY

The Barbarian Kingdoms, ca. 526

Examine the locations of barbarian kingdoms in the sixth century. What strategic geographical advantages did the Ostrogothic kingdom hold that allowed Theodoric the Great to play a dominant role in the West? How did the relative isolation of the Kingdom of the Franks aid its future development? Which barbarian kingdoms were in a position to absorb the most Roman traditions? Which the least?

subjects. This religious toleration attracted to his government outstanding Roman intellectuals and statesmen. Boethius (480–524), while serving in Theodoric's government, was also trying to synthesize the philosophical traditions of Plato and Aristotle. Cassiodorus (ca. 490–ca. 585), a cultivated Roman senator, served as Theodoric's secretary and held important positions in his government before retiring to found monasteries, where he and his monks worked to preserve the literary and philosophical traditions of Rome.

What might have been the fate of Italy and the west had Theodoric's kingdom survived the sixth century is a matter of speculation. Tensions grew between Ostrogoths who feared that their children were abandoning Gothic traditions, and Romans who still looked to Constantinople for protection.. The early atmosphere of toleration soured into suspicion. Boethius himself was accused of treason and executed. Following Theodoric's death in 526, internal conflict over the succession paved the way for a protracted and devastating invasion, which destroyed not only the Ostrogothic kingdom but also much of what remained of Roman Italy. The destructive new invaders were not another barbarian tribe but the civilized Byzantines.

Italy was simply too close to Constantinople and too important for the ambitious Emperor Justinian I (527–565) to ignore. Encouraged by his easy victory over the Vandals, he sent an army into Italy, where he anticipated an easy reconquest of the peninsula (see p. 189). Instead he got almost 20 years of vicious warfare. Not only were the Goths more formidable foes than he had expected, but when Roman tax collectors arrived with the Roman armies, Justinian found that the Italian people did not greet their "liberators" with open arms. In addition, in the midst of the reconquest, a new and terrible disease appeared throughout the Mediterranean world. The plague killed about one-third of Europe's population in the next two centuries.

Lombard Conquest. The destruction of Italy by war and disease paved the way for its conquest by the **Lombards**. As allies in Justinian's army, some members of the Germanic tribe from along the Danube had learned firsthand of the riches of Italy. In 568 the Lombard people left the Carpathian basin to their neighbors, the Avars, and invaded the exhausted and war-torn Italian peninsula. By the end of the sixth century, the Ostrogoths had disappeared and the Byzantines retained only the boot of Italy and a narrow strip stretching from Ravenna to Rome. The Byzantine presence in Rome was weak. By default, the popes—especially Gregory the Great (590–604)—became the defenders and governors of the city. Gregory organized the resistance to the Lombards, fed the population during famines, and comforted his people throughout the dark years of plague and warfare. As a vigorous political and spiritual leader, he laid the foundations of the medieval papacy.

The Lombards had little use for Roman administrative tradition. Instead they divided Italy into military districts under the control of dukes whose authority replaced that of Roman bureaucrats. Still, they largely eliminated the Roman tax system under which Italians had long suffered. Moreover, they were less concerned with preserving their own cultural traditions than were the Ostrogoths, even in the sphere of religion. Initially many Lombards were Arians, but in the early seventh century the Lombard kings and their followers accepted Orthodox Christianity. The conversion paved the way for the unification of the society. Italy may have been less civilized under the Lombards than under the Goths or Romans, but life for the vast majority of the population was probably better than it had been for centuries.

Visigothic Spain: Intolerance and Destruction

Rather than accepting a divided society (as did the Ostrogoths) or merging into an orthodox Roman culture (as did the Lombards), the Visigoths of Gaul and Spain sought to unify the indigenous population of their kingdom through law and religion. Roman law deeply influenced Visigothic law codes and formed an enduring legal heritage for the West. Religious unity was a more difficult goal. The kings' repeated attempts to force conversion to Arianism failed and created tension and mistrust. That mistrust proved fatal. In 507 Gallo-Roman aristocrats supported the Frankish king Clovis in his successful conquest of the Visigothic kingdom of Toulouse. Defeat drove the Visigoths deeper into Spain, where they gradually forged a unified kingdom based on Roman administrative tradition and Visigothic kingship.

Spain was a rich country, and its Visigothic kings profited accordingly. Cordoban leather, olive oil, and grain cultivated on vast estates still owned by the Romans were exported throughout the known world. Greek, Jewish, and Syrian merchants crowded into the ports of the kingdom and carried its products as far as Ireland to the northwest and Palestine in the east. The prosperity benefited Spain's rulers, filling royal coffers with gold, since some of the Roman tax system survived. Both the Franks to the north and the Muslims to the south eyed Spain's riches greedily.

Conversion and Intolerance. The long-sought religious unity was finally achieved when King Recared (586–601) and the Gothic aristocracy embraced Orthodox Christianity. The conversion further blurred the differences between Visigoths and Roman provincials in the kingdom. It also initiated an unprecedented use of the Church and its ideology to strengthen the

This gilded copper plate, one of the Lombard treasures, was part of a helmet decoration. The Lombard king Agilulf (590–615) is shown receiving tribute from his conquered subjects. On either side of the king are winged victories carrying signs saying VICTURIA.

monarchy. Visigothic kings modeled themselves after the Byzantine emperors, proclaimed themselves new Constantines, and used Church councils—held regularly at Toledo—as governing assemblies. Still, Visigothic distrust, which was directed toward anyone who was different, continued. It focused especially on the considerable Jewish population, which had lived in Spain since the diaspora, or dispersion, in the first century of the Roman Empire. Almost immediately after Recared's conversion, he and his successors began to enact a series of anti-Jewish measures, culminating in 613 with the command that all Jews accept baptism or leave the kingdom. Although the mandate was never fully carried out, the virulence of the persecution of the Jews grew through the seventh century. At the same time, rivalry within the aristocracy weakened the kingdom and left it vulnerable to attack from without.

Islamic Conquest. In 711, Muslims from North Africa invaded and quickly conquered the Visigothic kingdom. While some remnants of the Visigoths held on in small kingdoms in the northwest, most of the population quickly came to terms with the new masters. Jews rejoiced in the religious toleration brought by Islam, and many members of the Christian elite converted to Islam and retained their positions of authority under the new regime. (See "A Closer Look: The Jews in the Early Middle Ages," pp. 222–223.)

The Anglo-Saxons: From Pagan Conquerors to Christian Missionaries

The motley collection of Saxons, Angles, Jutes, Frisians, Suebians, and others who came to Britain as federated troops and stayed on as rulers did not coalesce into a united kingdom until almost the eleventh century. Instead, the Germanic warriors carved out small kingdoms for themselves, dominating the Romanized Britons or driving them into Wales. Although independent, the little kingdoms—varying from 5 to as many as 11 at different times—maintained some sort of identity as a group. The king of the dominant kingdom received recognition from his Saxon, and some Briton, neighbors. Other kings looked to him as first among equals and sought his advice and influence in their dealings with one another. Unlike the Goths, none of those peoples had previously been integrated into the Roman world. Thus, rather than fusing Roman and Germanic traditions, they eradicated the former. Urban life disappeared, and with it the Roman traditions of administration, taxation, and culture.

Aristocratic Society. In their place developed a world whose central values were honor and glory, whose primary occupation was fighting, and whose economic system was based on plunder and the open-handed distribution of riches. It was a society dominated by petty kings and their aristocratic war leaders. The invaders were not, like the Goths, just a military elite. They also included free farmers who replaced or absorbed the Romanized British peasantry, introducing their language, agricultural techniques, social organization, and folkloric traditions to the southeastern part of the island. The ordinary settlers, much more than the kings and aristocrats, were responsible for the gradual transformation of Britain into England—the land of the Angles.

■ The elaborate helmet of a seventh-century Anglo-Saxon king, recovered from his ship burial at Sutton Hoo on the southeast coast of England, shows the wealth and culture of these rulers.

Conversion. The Anglo-Saxons were pagans, and although Christianity survived, the relationship between conquered and conquerors did not provide a climate conducive to conversion. Christianity came instead from without. The conversion of England resulted from a two-part effort. The first originated in Ireland, an island that had never been part of the Roman Empire and thus had never adapted the forms of urban life and centralized, hierarchical government or religion characteristic of Britain and the Continent. In the fifth century, merchants and missionaries introduced to Ireland an eastern, monastic form of Christianity, which was adapted easily

THE JEWS IN THE EARLY MIDDLE AGES

A CLOSER LOOK

The intolerance and persecution of Jews by the Visigoths was the exception rather than the rule in early medieval Europe. Since the diaspora, Jews had settled throughout the West, primarily in towns. Rome, Ravenna, and Pavia all had important Jewish communities. In the Frankish kingdom, Jews were particularly numerous in the southern cities of Lyon, Vienne, Arles, Marseille, and Narbonne, although Jewish communities could also be found in more northern towns such as Orléans, Soissons, Nantes, Aachen, and Frankfurt. In contrast to later practice, Jews appeared no different from their Christian neighbors. They spoke the same language, wore no distinctive clothing, and occupied no designated section of town or ghetto. Although they worshiped in their synagogues and studied in their yeshivas, they otherwise were very much integrated into the fabric of society.

Some Jews owned rural estates, where they cultivated vineyards and farms alongside their Christian neighbors. Jewish farmers and landowners were particularly common in the areas of Vienne, Mâcon, and Arles, where they appear in records of land transactions buying, selling, and exchanging property with individuals and Christian churches. However, most Jews were merchants or practiced other urban professions such as goldsmithing and medicine. Some acted as tax collectors and emissaries for lay and ecclesiastical lords. The reasons for the specializations were obvious. First, Jewish communities in the West maintained ties with other Jews in the Byzantine and Muslim worlds, exchanging letters on religious and legal affairs and traveling back and forth. Second, sporadic attacks on Jews did occur. In the sixth century, for example, the Frankish king Chilperic (561–584) attempted to force Jews in his kingdom to be baptized. Thus Jews concentrated in occupations that allowed them to move easily and quickly in time of danger. Finally, the lack of interest on the part of their Christian neighbors in trade and the disappearance of Syriac and Greek merchants in the seventh century left long-distance commerce almost entirely in the hands of Jews. Royal documents speak frequently of "Jews and other merchants," possibly implying that Gentile merchants were an unimportant minority.

Jewish merchants traveled widely—from Scandinavia to Iran, India, and even as far as China—exporting Western slaves, furs, and weapons and returning with such exotic luxuries as spices and silks. Trade was important to Western monarchs, not only for supplies of luxuries but also for the tariff income it provided. In the ninth century, Jewish merchants were so vital to the empire of Louis the Pious that he granted them special privileges and took them under his royal protection. A palace official, the master of the Jews, was responsible for protecting the Jews throughout the empire, and appeals against them to the king usually were settled in the Jews' favor. Not everyone was equally pleased with the tolerance shown this non-Christian minority. Bishop Agobard of Lyon (799–840) complained bitterly to Louis about his policy of tolerance. The bishop was particularly disturbed by the fact that, while few Jews could be persuaded to convert, in the area of Lyon many Christians found the sermons of rabbis preferable to those of their priests and conversions to Judaism were becoming frequent.

The most celebrated conversion was that of Bodo, a young Frankish aristocrat raised in Louis's palace and educated in his school. In 838, while on what he pretended was a pilgrimage to Rome, he converted to Judaism, sold his entourage into slavery, married a young Jewish woman, and fled to Saragossa in Muslim Spain. From there he wrote scathing attacks on the immorality and doctrinal ignorance of the Christian clergy he had known in Aachen. Fourteen clerics there, he claimed, held 14 different opinions on their faith. Disgusted by what he con-

Image of a Jewish tax collector from an early medieval Hebrew manuscript.

sidered to be the ignorance and idolatry of Christianity, he saw his conversion as a return to the worship of the one true God.

Christian churchmen were scandalized by Bodo and embarrassed by their inability to convert Jews through peaceful persuasion, but they were powerless to do anything about the situation. Traditional Christian doctrine asserted that the conversion of the Jews would be one of the signs of the end of the world. Until then they had the right to toleration. Moreover, the early medieval world was one of many peoples, laws, and traditions. In a society in which different people in the same towns, and even the same households, might live according to Roman, Frankish, Gothic, or Burgundian law, Jews were but one more group with a distinct identity. Kings refused to limit the civil and religious rights of their Jewish subjects, forbade Christians to baptize Jewish slaves, and in general protected them as valued members of society.

to the rural, tribal organization of Irish society. Although Irish Christianity was entirely Orthodox in its beliefs, the isolation of Ireland led to the development of numerous practices at odds with those common to Constantinople and Rome. Thus, while Ireland had important bishops, the most influential churchmen were powerful abbots of strict, ascetic monasteries, closely connected with tribal chieftains, who directed the religious life of their regions. Around 565 the Irish monk Columba (521–597) established a monastery on the island of Iona off the coast of Scotland. From there, wandering Irish monks began to convert northern Britain.

The second effort at Christianizing Britain began with Pope Gregory the Great. In 596 he sent the missionary Augustine (known as Augustine of Canterbury to distinguish him from the bishop of Hippo) to attempt to convert the English. Augustine arrived in the southeast kingdom of Kent, where the pagan King Ethelbert—encouraged by his wife Bertha, a Christian Frankish princess—gave him permission to preach. Augustine laid the foundations for a hierarchical, bishop-centered church based on the Roman model. In time, Ethelbert and much of his kingdom accepted Christianity, and Augustine was named Archbishop of Canterbury by the pope. Augustine had similar success in nearby Essex and established a second bishopric at London shortly before his death in 604.

As Irish missionaries spread south from Iona and Roman missionaries moved north from Canterbury, their efforts created in England two opposing forms of Orthodox Christianity. One was Roman, episcopal, and hierarchical. The other was Celtic, monastic, and decentralized. Each had its own calendar of religious feasts and its own rituals. The differences posed serious problems since they existed not only in the same society but sometimes even within the same family. For example, a wife who followed Roman custom might be fasting and abstaining from meat during the season of penance that preceded Easter, while her husband, who followed the Celtic calendar—according to which Easter came earlier—was already feasting and celebrating. It was precisely that situation that led King Oswy of Northumbria (d. 670) to call an episcopal meeting, or **synod,** in 664 at Whitby to settle the issue. After hearing arguments from both sides, Oswy ac-

TWO MISSIONARIES

Bede (ca. 672–735) described in detail the two missionary movements in England. The first, led by Augustine of Canterbury, represented Roman traditions to which Bede himself was firmly attached. The second, led by Aidan (d. 651), represented the Irish traditions Bede opposed. And yet he wrote vivid and contrasting descriptions of the character and styles of the two men.

Focus Questions

How did the tactics of Augustine and Aidan differ in their missionary activities? How might one explain the behavior of the Roman missionary Augustine?

Those [British bishops] summoned [by Augustine] to this council first visited a wise and prudent hermit and enquired of him whether they should abandon their own Traditions and Augustine's demand. He answered: "If he is a man of God, follow him." "But how can we be sure of this?" they asked. "Our Lord says, Take my yoke upon you and learn of Me, for I am meek and lowly of heart," he replied. "Therefore if Augustine is meek and lowly in heart, it shows that he bears the yoke of Christ himself, and offers it to you. But if he is haughty and unbending, then he is not of God, and we should not listen to him. Arrange that he and his followers arrive first at the place appointed for the conference. If he rises courteously as you approach, rest assured that he is the servant of Christ and do as he asks. But if he ignores you and does not rise, then, since you are in the majority, do not comply with his demands."

The Bishops carried out his suggestion, and it happened that Augustine remained seated in his chair. Seeing this, they became angry, accusing him of pride and taking pains to contradict all that he said . . . saying among themselves that if he would not rise to greet them in the first instance, he would have even less regard for them once they submitted to his authority.

Later, Bede describes Aidan's approach to spreading the word of God:

He never sought or cared for any worldly possessions, and loved to give away to the poor who chanced to meet him whatever he received from kings or wealthy folk. Whether in town or country, he always traveled on foot unless compelled by necessity to ride; and whatever people he met on his walks, whether high or low, he stopped and spoke to them. If they were heathen, he urged them to be baptized; and if they were Christians, he strengthened their faith, and inspired them by word and deed to live a good life and to be generous to others. . . . He cultivated peace and love, purity and humility; he was above anger and greed, and despised pride and conceit; he set himself to keep as well as to teach the laws of God, and was diligent in study and prayer. He used his priestly authority to check the proud and powerful.

From Bede, *A History of the English Church and People.*

FROM SLAVE TO QUEEN

Queen Balthild (d. ca. 680), an Anglo-Saxon woman captured and sold into slavery in Francia, became the wife of Clovis II, king of Neustria and Burgundy (639–657). Her career, including her regency for her son Clothar III and her eventual forced retirement to the monastery she had founded at Chelles, is typical of the complex role and reputation early medieval queens enjoyed. This laudatory account, which was probably written by a nun at Chelles, hints that Balthild had been forced into the convent by those opposed to her political role.

Focus Questions

What roles of a queen does this passage illustrate? What reforms did Balthild attempt to introduce in Frankish society?

Divine providence called her from across the seas. She, who came here as God's most precious and lofty pearl, was sold at a cheap price. Erchinoald, a Frankish magnate and most illustrious man, acquired her, and in his service the girl behaved most honorably. She gained such happy fame that, when the said lord Erchinoald's wife died, he hoped to unite himself to Balthild, that faultless virgin, in a matronal bed. But when she heard this, she fled and most swiftly took herself out of his sight. Thereafter it happened, with God's approval, that Balthild, the maid who escaped marriage with a lord, came to be espoused to Clovis, son of the former king Dagobert. Thus by virtue of her humility she was raised to a higher rank.

She acted as a mother to the princes, as a daughter to priests, and as a most pious nurse to children and adolescents. She distributed generous alms to everyone. She guarded the princes' honor by keeping their intimate counsels secret. In accordance with God's will, her husband King Clovis migrated from the body and left his sons with their mother. Immediately after him her son Clothar took up the kingdom of the Franks, maintaining peace in the realm. Then, to promote peace, by command of Lady Balthild with the advice of the other elders, the people of Austrasia accepted her son Childeric as their king and the Burgundians were united with the Franks. And we believe, under God's ordinance, that these three realms then held peace and concord among themselves because of Lady Balthild's great faith. She proclaimed that no payment could be exacted for receipt of a sacred rank. Moreover, she ordained that yet another evil custom should cease, namely that many people determined to kill their children rather than nurture them, for they feared to incur the public exactions which were heaped upon them by custom, which caused great damage to their affairs.

It was her holy intention to enter the monastery of religious women which she had built at Chelles. But the Franks delayed much for love of her and would not have permitted this to happen except that there was a commotion made by the wretched Bishop Sigobrand whose pride among the Franks earned him his mortal ruin. Indeed, they formed a plan to kill him against her will. Fearing that the lady would act heavily against them, and wish to avenge him, they suddenly relented and permitted her to enter the monastery.

From *The Life of the Blessed Queen Balthild.*

cepted the customs of the Roman Church—allying himself and ultimately all of Anglo-Saxon England with the centralized, hierarchical form of Christianity, which could be used to strengthen his monarchy.

During the century and a half following the Synod of Whitby, Anglo-Saxon Christian civilization blossomed. Contact with the Continent, and especially with Rome, increased. The monasteries of Monkwearmouth and Jarrow became centers of learning, culminating in the writings of Bede (673–735), the greatest scholar of his century. Bede's knowledge of natural science, rhetoric, chronology, Scripture, and especially history spread his fame throughout the West. His history of the English church and people is the finest historical work of the early Middle Ages.

Anglo-Saxon Missionaries. By the eighth century, England was no longer a mission land but had itself begun to send out Christian missionaries. From around 700, descendants of the Anglo-Saxon conquerors started traveling to "Old Saxony" (the region of the continent from which their ancestors had originally come), as well as to other parts of the Germanic world, to convert their still-pagan cousins. Until the late eighth and ninth centuries, when new waves of Germanic invaders known as Vikings began to destroy Anglo-Saxon civilization, England furnished the Continent with many of its leading thinkers and scholars.

The Franks: An Enduring Legacy

The name Frank means "fierce" or "free." In fact, in their early history most Franks were virtual slaves of the Romans. In the fourth century C.E., various small Germanic tribes along the Rhine River coalesced into a loose confederation known as the Franks. A significant group of them, the Salians, made the mistake of attacking Roman garrisons and were totally defeated. The Romans resettled the Salians in a largely abandoned

FEUDING IN THE FRANKISH KINGDOM

Violent self-help was considered a normal and legitimate means of settling disputes in the barbarian successor kingdoms, and rulers could do little about such feuds unless they grew seriously out of hand. In the following passage, Bishop Gregory of Tours describes such an escalating conflict that ultimately destroyed two families.

Focus Questions

If marriages were often intended to create alliances between rival families, what were the dangers that such marriages might bring? What threats did feuds pose to wider society? Was Fredegund's "solution" the only one possible in such a society?

An altercation now arose between certain Franks in Tournai. The immediate cause was that the son of one of them angrily and repeatedly rebuked the son of another, who had married his sister, for neglecting his wife and going after loose women. The young man at fault took no notice. The ill-feeling reached such a pitch that the girl's brother attacked his brother-in-law and killed him, with some of his relations. Then the brother in his turn was murdered by those who had supported his brother-in-law. In the end not a single member of either family remained alive, except one survivor for whom there was no opponent left. The next thing which happened was that the relations of each of the two families started quarrelling with each other. They were warned by Queen Fredegund on a number of occasions to give up their feud and to make peace once more, for if the dispute continued it would become a public nuisance of considerable dimensions. This attempt at reconciliation by soothing talk was not a success, and in the end Fredegund silenced both sides by the axe.

From Gregory of Tours, *The History of the Franks.*

region of what is now Belgium and Holland. There they formed a buffer to protect Roman colonists from other Germanic tribes and provided a ready supply of recruits for the Roman army. During the fourth and fifth centuries, the Salian Franks and their neighbors assumed an increasingly important role in the military defense of Gaul and began to spread out of their "reservation" into more settled parts of the province. Although many high-ranking Roman officers of the fourth century were Franks, most were neither conquerors nor members of the military elite but rather soldier-farmers who settled beside the local Roman peoples they protected.

In 486, Clovis, leader of the Salian Franks and commander of the barbarized Roman army, staged a successful coup (possibly with the approval of the Byzantine emperor), defeating and killing Syagrius, the last Roman commander in the west. Although Clovis ruled the Franks as king, he worked closely with the existing Gallo-Roman aristocracy as he consolidated his control over various Frankish factions and over portions of Gaul and Germany held by other barbarian kingdoms. Clovis's early conversion to Orthodox Christianity helped ensure the effectiveness of the Gallo-Roman cooperation. The king's baptism convinced many of his subjects to convert as well, paving the way for the assimilation of Franks and Romans into a new society. The Frankish society became the model for European social and political organization for more than a thousand years.

The mix of Frankish warriors and Roman aristocrats spread rapidly across western Europe. Clovis and his successors absorbed the Visigothic kingdom of Toulouse, the Thuringians, and the kingdom of the Burgundians. They also

This sword hilt decorated with gold and enamel from the tomb of the Frankish king Childeric shows the wealth of Frankish military leaders in Roman service at the end of the fifth century.

expanded Frankish hegemony through what is now Bavaria and south of the Alps into northern Italy. Unlike other barbarian kingdoms such as those of the Huns or Ostrogoths, which evaporated almost as soon as their great founders died, the Frankish synthesis was enduring. Although the dynasty established by Clovis—called the **Merovingian** after a legendary ancestor—lasted only until the mid-eighth century, the Frankish kingdom was the direct ancestor of both France and Germany.

After Clovis's death in 511 his Germanic warriors, Roman advisors, and his heirs agreed to divide his kingdom among his four sons. For the next 200 years, the heart of the Frankish kingdom—the region between the Rhine and Loire rivers—was often divided into the kingdoms of Neustria, Burgundy, and Austrasia, each ruled by a Merovingian king. The outlying regions of Aquitaine and Provence to the south and Alemania, Thuringia, and Bavaria to the east were governed by Frankish dukes appointed by the kings. Still, the Frankish world was never as divided as Anglo-Saxon England. In the early eighth century, a unified Frankish kingdom reemerged as the dominant force in Europe.

With the establishment of the barbarian kingdoms, the theoretical unity of the western empire was forever destroyed. Within each of these smaller polities, rulers and ruled began forging from their complex Roman and Germanic traditions a new cultural synthesis.

LIVING IN THE NEW EUROPE

The substitution of Germanic kings for imperial officials made few obvious differences in the lives of most inhabitants of Italy, Gaul, and Spain. The vast majority of Europeans were poor farmers whose lives centered on their villages and fields. For those people the seasons in the agricultural year, the burdens of rent and taxation, and the frequent poor harvests, food shortages, famines, and epidemics were more important than empires and kingdoms. Nevertheless, fundamental if imperceptible changes were transforming ordinary life. The changes took place at every level of society. The slaves and semi-free peasants of Rome gradually began to form new kinds of social groups and to practice new forms of agriculture as they merged with the Germanic warrior-peasants. Elite Gallo-Roman landowners came to terms with their Frankish conquerors, and the two groups began to coalesce into a single unified aristocracy. In the same way that Germanic and Roman societies began to merge, Germanic and Roman traditions of governance united between the sixth and eighth centuries to create a powerful new kind of medieval kingdom.

Creating the European Peasantry

Three fundamental changes transformed rural society during the early Middle Ages. First, Roman slavery virtually disappeared. Second, the household emerged as the primary unit of social and economic organization. Third, Christianity spread throughout the rural world.

Economics, not ethics, destroyed Roman slavery. In the kind of slavery typical of the Roman world, large gangs of slaves were housed in dormitories and directed in large-scale operations by overseers. That form of slavery demanded a highly organized form of estate management and could be quite costly, since slaves had to be fed and housed year round. Since slaves did not always reproduce at a rate sufficient to replace themselves, the supply had to be replenished from elsewhere. However, as the empire ceased to expand, the supply of fresh slaves dwindled. As cities shrank, many markets for agricultural produce disappeared and market-oriented, large-scale agriculture became less profitable. From the sixth through the ninth centuries, enterprising landlords in the west sold off some of their slaves to the east, particularly to the Muslims, while establishing other slave families on individual plots of land. The slaves and their descendants cultivated the plots, made annual payments to their owners, and cultivated the undivided portions of the estate, the fruits of which went directly to the owner. Thus slaves became something akin to sharecroppers. Gradually they began to intermarry with colons and others who, though nominally free, found themselves in an economic situation much like that of slaves. By the ninth century, the distinction between slaves who had acquired traditional rights to their farms, or **manses,** and free peasants who held and worked manses belonging to others was blurred. By the tenth and eleventh centuries, peasant farmers throughout much of Europe were subject to the private justice of their landlords, whether their ancestors had been slave or free. Although they were not slaves in the classical sense, the peasantry had fused into a homogeneous unfree population.

Social Conditions in the 9th Century

Rural Households

The division of estates into separate peasant holdings contributed to the second fundamental transformation of European peasant society: the formation of the household. Neither the Roman tradition of slave agriculture nor the Germanic tradition of clan organization had encouraged the household as the basic unit of society. When individual slaves and their spouses were placed on manses, which they and their children were expected to cultivate, the household became the basic unit of Western economy.

However, the household was more than an economic unit. It was also the first level of government. The head of the household, whether slave or free, male or female—women, particularly widows, were often heads of households—exercised authority over its other members. That authority made the householder a link in the chain of the social order, which stretched from the peasant hovel to the royal court.

The Peasantry. Peasant life centered on the house, the village, and the field. In the Mediterranean area, peasants constructed their houses of fieldstone. In the north, they built their houses of wood. Often the structures consisted simply of two or three rooms shared by both the human and animal members of the household. Archaeologists can often distinguish the areas of human and animal habitation in such houses only by the relatively higher frequency of animal dung in one section than in another. The hovel was heated by the body warmth of the cattle and sheep and by a hearth fire. Smoke escaped not through a chimney, but through a hole in the roof.

The rhythm of peasant life was tied to the agricultural cycle, which had changed little since antiquity. January and February were the dormant months, when the family huddled together from the cold and tried to survive on the previous harvest. They lived on coarse bread made from the previous year's grain, onions and leeks, and nuts gathered from the forest. They drank wine or, in the north, a thick beer, which was a major source of protein. On special occasions they might enjoy a bit of pork. In March, they trimmed the vines for the growing season. Cattle were put out to pasture in April. In May, peasants cut the fodder needed by the lord's horses. June meant plowing, July haying, and August harvesting. In September and October, grapes were harvested and winter grain (an innovation of perhaps the eighth century) was planted. In November, the new wine was stored in barrels, the grain was milled, and the pigs (the primary source of meat for peasants) were allowed into the forest to gorge themselves on nuts and grubs. December was slaughter month, and then the family faced another winter. Although women and men worked together on the harvest, normally peasants divided labor into male and female tasks. Husbands and sons tended to the work in the fields. Wives and daughters cared for chickens, prepared the dark bread that was the staple of the peasant diet, and spun and wove wool and flax to make clothing.

Agriculture. Occasionally, peasants used new tools or technical innovations in their labor. Some lords established water mills for grinding grain on their estates. Here and there, peasants used heavy plows capable of cutting and turning the heavy clay soil of northern Europe. Some farsighted lords had their peasants fertilize the fields with lime to restore the soil, but ninth-century peasants resented the extra labor that this recent innovation required. Technological progress was sporadic and uneven, and agricultural returns were correspondingly low.

In fact, returns were much lower than they had been in antiquity. Careful Roman landlords, using better tools and coordinating the work of their slaves more efficiently, were accustomed to harvesting eight times as much grain as they had sown. Frankish estates were doing well if they recorded harvests of three or four to one. In some years, no more grain was harvested than the seed necessary to plant the following June. Peasants had to choose between starving through the winter or eating the seed and starving the following year. Actually, the choice was not theirs, but rather that of their aristocratic lords, whose noble lifestyle they were forced to support.

Christianity. Peasant culture, like peasant society, experienced a fundamental transformation during the early Middle Ages. During this period the peasantry became Christian. In antiquity, Christianity had been an urban phenomenon. The term for the rural population—pagans, that is, the inhabitants of the countryside (*pagus*)—had long been synonymous with "unbelievers." The spread of Christianity throughout the rural world began in earnest in the sixth century, when bishops and monks began to replace the peasants' traditional agrarian cults with Christian feasts, rituals, and beliefs. In sixth-century Gaul, for example, peasants regularly held a three-day celebration beside a mountain lake into which they threw food and valuable objects as an offering to the local god. The local bishop was unable to convince them to abandon the practice. Instead, he built a church on the spot in honor of Saint Hilary of Poitiers. The church contained relics of the saint. Peasants

■ "The labors of the months" was a popular motif in medieval art. This illustration from the *Astronomical Notices* was found in Salzburg. The annual round of agricultural tasks, such as sowing, reaping, and grape picking, is depicted along with scenes of hunting and hawking.

continued to travel to the lake to celebrate the feast, but the new purpose of the feast was to honor Saint Hilary.

Christianity penetrated more deeply into rural society with the systematic establishment of parishes, or rural churches. By the ninth century, the parish system began to cover Europe. Bishops founded parish churches in the villages of large estates, and owners were obligated to set aside one-tenth of the produce of their estates for the maintenance of the parish church. The priests who staffed the churches came from the local peasantry and received a basic education in Latin and in Christian ritual from their predecessors and from their bishops. The continuing presence of priests in each village had a profound effect on the daily lives of Europe's peasants. Christian ritual came to be a regular part of peasant life.

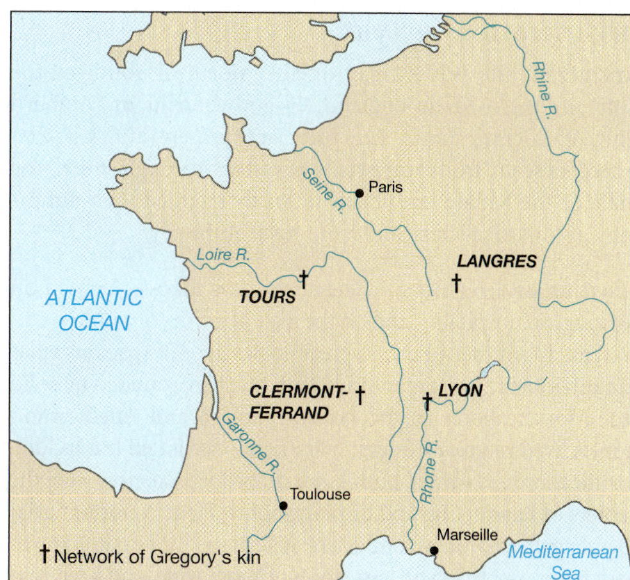

The Episcopal Kin of Gregory of Tours. Typical of Gallo-Roman aristocrats, Gregory's position was reinforced by kinship ties with important people throughout Gaul.

Creating the European Aristocracy

At the same time that a homogeneous peasantry was emerging from the blend of slaves and free farmers, a homogeneous aristocracy was evolving out of the mix of Germanic and Roman traditions. In Germanic society, the elite had owed its position to a combination of inherited status and wealth, perpetuated through military command. Families who produced great military commanders were thought to have a special war-luck granted by the gods. The war-luck bestowed on men and women of those families a near-sacred legitimacy.

That legitimacy made the aristocrats largely independent of their kings. In times of war, kings might command, but otherwise, the extent to which they could be said to govern aristocrats was minimal. The earliest Frankish laws, which prescribe wergeld, or payments, for offenses in place of unlimited blood feuds do not mention aristocrats. The reason is probably that the kings had no recognized authority to command aristocrats to forego their right to settle disputes among themselves. The freedom of the aristocracy meant freedom from royal governance.

The Roman aristocracy was based on inheritance of land rather than on leadership. During the third and fourth centuries, Roman aristocrats' control of land extended over the persons who worked that land. At the same time, great landowners were able to free themselves from provincial government.

Like their Germanic counterparts, Roman aristocrats acquired a sacred legitimacy, but within the Christian tradition. They monopolized the office of bishop and became identified with the sacred and political traditions associated with the Church. The family of the Gallo-Roman bishop and historian Gregory of Tours (539–594) exemplifies that aristocratic tradition. By the time he took office in 573, 13 of the previous 18 bishops of Tours had come from his family. In addition, he was related to generations of bishops from Langres, Lyon, Clermont-Ferrand, and elsewhere.

Gregory of Tours

In Spain and Italy, the religious differences separating Arians and Orthodox Christians impeded the fusion of the Germanic and Roman aristocracies. In Gaul, the conversion of Clovis and his people facilitated the rapid blending of the two worlds. North of the Loire River, where most of the Franks had settled, Roman aristocrats soon became Franks. By the mid-sixth century, the descendants of Bishop Remigius of Reims, who had baptized Clovis, had Frankish names and considered themselves Franks. Still, the Roman aristocratic tradition of great landholders became an integral part of the identity of the Frankish elite.

In the late sixth century, the northern Frankish aristocracy found its own religious identity and legitimacy in the Irish monasticism introduced by Saint Columbanus (543–615) and other wandering monks. At home in Ireland, the monks had been accustomed to working not with kings, but with leaders of clans. In Gaul the monks worked closely with the Frankish aristocrats, who encouraged them to build monasteries on the aristocrats' estates. Eventually the monasteries amassed huge landholdings and became major economic and political centers headed by aristocrats who had abandoned secular life for the cloister. The abbots and abbesses who headed the monasteries were venerated after their deaths as saints and miracle workers. Their descendants drew on the inherited prestige of being members of the "family of saints" in the same way that earlier aristocrats had claimed legitimacy as carriers of war-luck.

South of the Loire River, conditions were decidedly different. Here Irish monasticism was less important than episcopal office. The few Frankish and Gothic families who had settled in the south were rapidly absorbed into the Gallo-Roman aristocracy, which drew its prestige from control of local religious and secular power. Latin speech and Roman culture distinguished them as "Romans," regardless of their ancestry.

Aristocratic Lifestyle

Aristocratic life was similar whether north or south of the Loire, in Anglo-Saxon England, Visigothic Spain, or Lombard Italy. Aristocratic family structures were loosely knit clans that traced descent from important ancestors through either the male or the female line. Clans jealously guarded their autonomy against rival clans and from royal authority.

Feasting and Fighting. The aristocratic lifestyle focused on feasting, on hospitality, and on the male activities of hunting and warfare. In southern Europe, great nobles lived in spacious villas (an inheritance of Roman tradition), often surrounded by solid stone fortifications. In the north, Frankish and Anglo-Saxon nobles lived in great wooden halls, richly decorated but lacking fortifications. In winter, both kinds of lordly residences were the centers of banqueting and drinking bouts. Here important aristocrats gathered their supporters; entertained them at extravagant banquets; fed them vast stores of food, wine, and beer; and lavished on them gifts of jewelry, weapons, and fine horses. At the nobles' residences they received their rivals, planned their alliances, and settled their disputes.

During the fall and winter months, aristocratic men spent much of their time hunting deer and wild boar in their forests. Hunting was not merely sport. Essentially it was preparation for war, the activity of the summer months. As soon as the snows of winter began to melt and roads became passable, aristocrats gathered their retainers and marched to war. The enemy varied. It might be rival families with whom feuds were nursed for generations. It might be raiding parties from a neighboring region. Or the warriors might join a royal expedition led by the king and directed against a rival kingdom. Whoever the enemy, warfare brought the promise of booty and, as important, glory.

Women in Aristocratic Society. Within the aristocratic society, women played a wider and more active role than had been the case in either Roman or barbarian antiquity. In part, women's new role was due to the influence of Christianity, which recognized the distinct—although always inferior—rights of women. Christianity fought against the barbarian tradition of allowing chieftains numerous wives and recognized women's right to lead a cloistered religious life. In addition, the combination of Germanic and Roman familial traditions permitted women to participate in court proceedings, to inherit and dispose of property, and, if widowed, to serve as tutors and guardians for their minor children. Finally, the long absence of men at the hunt, at the royal court, or on military expeditions left wives in charge of the domestic scene for months or years at a time.

The religious life in particular opened to aristocratic women possibilities of autonomy and authority previously unknown in the West. Women administered large and wealthy institutions and even exercised such authority over mixed monasteries, in which men and women lived in separate quarters but recognized the rule of the abbess. For example, Saint Hilda of Whitby (614–680), an Anglo-Saxon princess, established and ruled a religious community that included both women and men. The community was one of the most important in England. Five monks of Whitby later became bishops, and kings and aristocrats regularly traveled to the monastery to ask Hilda's advice. It was in Hilda's community that the Synod of Whitby took place, and Hilda played an active role advising the king and assembled bishops.

Governing Europe

The combination in the early Middle Ages of the extremes of centralized Roman power and fragmented barbarian organization produced a wide variety of governmental systems. At one end of the spectrum were the politically fragmented Celtic and Slavic societies. At the other end were the Frankish kingdoms that descendants of Clovis, drawing on the twin heritages of Roman institutions and Frankish tradition, attempted to rule.

Kings and Aristocrats. Rulers and elites both needed and feared each other. Kings had emerged out of the Germanic aristocracy and could rule only in cooperation with aristocrats. Aristocrats were primarily concerned with maintaining and expanding their own spheres of control and independence. They perceived royal authority over them or their dependents as a threat. Still, they needed kings. Strong kings brought victory against external foes and thus maintained the flow of booty to the aristocracy. Aristocrats in turn redistributed the spoils of war among their followers to preserve the bonds of warrior society. Thus, under capable kings aristocrats were ready to cooperate, not as subjects but as partners.

As the successors of Germanic war leaders and late Roman generals, kings were primarily military commanders. During campaigns and at the annual **Marchfield,** when the free warriors assembled, the king was all-powerful. At those times he could cut down his enemies with impunity. At other times, the king's role was strictly limited. His direct authority extended only over the members of his household and his personal warrior band.

Royal Justice. The king's role in administering justice was similarly ambivalent. He was not the source of law, which was held to be simply the customs of the past, nor was he responsible for enforcing that customary law. Enforcement was the duty of individuals and families. Only if they desired did people bring their grievances to the king or his agents for arbitration or judgment. However, even though kings could not formally legislate, they effectively molded law and legal procedure by collecting, selecting, clarifying, and publishing customary laws. Again Clovis presents a model for such legislative activity in the compilation of Salic law made during his reign. Anglo-Saxon and Visigothic kings of the seventh through tenth centuries did the same.

As heirs of Roman governmental tradition, kings sought to incorporate the traditions into their roles. By absorbing the remains of local administration and taxation, kings acquired nascent governmental systems. Through the use of written documents, Roman scribes expanded royal authority beyond

This scene is from the lid of the Franks Casket, a whalebone box that was made in the north of England at the beginning of the eighth century. The carving depicts Egil the Archer defending his home. The other sides of the box are carved with a mixture of Christian and pagan scenes.

the king's household and personal following. Tax collectors continued to fill royal coffers with duties collected in markets and ports.

Finally, by assuming the role of protector of the Church, kings acquired the support of educated and experienced ecclesiastical advisers and the right to intervene in disputes involving clergy and laity. Further, as defenders of the Church, kings could claim a responsibility for the preservation of peace and the administration of justice—two fundamental Christian (but also Roman) tasks. Early medieval kings had no fixed capitals from which they governed. Instead they were constantly on the move, supervising their kingdoms and consuming the produce of their estates. The arrival of the king and his entourage was a major event long remembered in a region. A chronicler writing years later recalled the arrival in Burgundy (eastern France) of the Frankish king Dagobert I (623–638): "The profound alarm that his coming caused among the Burgundian bishops, magnates and others of consequence was a source of general wonder; but his justice brought great joy to the poor."

Royal Administration. Since kings could not be everywhere at once, they were represented locally by aristocrats who enjoyed royal favor. In the Frankish world, the favorites were called *counts* and their districts *counties.* In England, royal representatives were termed *ealdormen* and their regions were known as *shires.* Whether counts or ealdormen, the representatives were military commanders and judicial officers drawn from aristocratic families close to the king. Under competent and effective kings, partnership with these aristocratic families worked well. Under less competent rulers and during the reigns of minors, the families often managed to turn their districts into hereditary, almost autonomous regions. The same thing happened when rival members of the royal house sought supporters against their cousins and brothers. The sphere of royal authority shrank or expanded, in large measure in response to the individual qualities of the king. The personality of the king mattered far more than the institution of kingship did.

Thus, at both ends of the social spectrum, Germanic and Roman traditions and institutions were combining to create a new society, organized not by nationality or ethnicity but by status and united by shared religious values and political leadership.

THE CAROLINGIAN ACHIEVEMENT

The Merovingian dynasty initiated by Clovis presided over the synthesis of Roman and Germanic societies. It was left to the Carolingians who followed to forge a new Europe. In the seventh century, members of the new aristocracy were able to take advantage of royal minorities and dynastic rivalries to turn themselves into virtual rulers of their small territories. By the end of the century, the kings had become little more than symbolic figures in the Frankish kingdoms. The real power was held by regional strongmen called *dukes.* The most successful of the aristocratic factions was that led by Charles Martel (ca. 688–741) and his heirs, known as the Carolingians.

Charles Martel. The family had risen to prominence in the seventh century in Austrasia by controlling the office of mayor of the palace, the highest court official who advised the king as spokesman for the aristocracy. The Carolingians increased their influence by marrying their sons to daughters of other aristocratic families. In the late seventh century they extended their control to include Neustria and Burgundy as well as

Austrasia. By the second quarter of the eighth century Charles Martel, while not king, was the acknowledged ruler of the Frankish kingdom.

Charles Martel was ruthless, ambitious, and successful. He crushed rivals in his own family, subdued competing dukes, and united the Frankish realm. He was successful in part because he molded the Frankish cavalry into the most effective military force of the time. His heavily armored mounted warriors were extremely effective but also costly. Martel financed them with property confiscated from his enemies and from the Church. In return for oaths of absolute fidelity, he gave his followers (or **vassals**) estates, which they held as long as they served him faithfully. With his new army he practiced a scorched-earth policy against his opponents that left vast areas of Provence and Aquitaine desolate for decades.

Charles Martel looked beyond military power to the control of religious and cultural institutions. He supported Anglo-Saxon missionaries, such as Boniface (ca. 680–755), who were trying to introduce on the Continent the Roman form of Christianity they knew in England. The hierarchical style of Christianity served Carolingian interests in centralization—especially since Charles appointed his loyal supporters as bishops and abbots. Missionaries and Frankish armies worked hand in hand to consolidate Carolingian rule.

The ecclesiastical policy that proved most crucial to later Carolingians was Charles's support of the Roman papacy. Charles caught the attention of Pope Gregory III (731–741) in 732, after defeating a Muslim force near Tours that had attempted to continue the northward expansion of Islam. A few years later, when the pope needed protection from the Lombards to maintain his central Italian territories, he sought and obtained help from the Frankish leader.

Pippin III. The alliance with the papacy solidified during the lifetime of Charles's son Pippin III (ca. 714–768). Pippin inherited his father's power. However, since he was not of the royal Merovingian family, he had no more right to supreme authority than did any other powerful aristocrat. Pippin needed more than the power of a king: he needed the title. No Frankish tradition provided a precedent by which a rival family might displace the Merovingians. Pippin turned instead to the pope. Building on his increasingly close relationship with the papacy and the Frankish church dominated by his supporters, Pippin sought legitimacy in religious authority. In a carefully orchestrated exchange between Pippin and Pope Zacharias (741–752), the latter declared that the individual who exercised the power of king ought also to have the title. Following the declaration, the last Merovingian was deposed, and in 751 a representative of the pope anointed Pippin king of the Franks.

The alliance between the new dynasty and the papacy marked the first union of royal legitimacy and ecclesiastical sanction in European history. Frankish, Gothic, and Anglo-Saxon kings had been selected on the basis of secular criteria. Kings combined royal descent with military power. Now the office of king required the active participation of the Church. The new Frankish kingship led Europe into the first political, social, and cultural restructuring of the West since the end of the Roman Empire.

Charlemagne and the Renewal of the West

Pippin's son Charlemagne was the heir of the political, religious, and social revolutions begun by his grandfather and father. Charlemagne was a large man, more than six feet tall,

IMAGE DISCOVERY

Equestrian Emperors

This equestrian statue of a Carolingian ruler is thought to be either Charlemagne or, more probably, his grandson Charles the Bald. Compare this statue with that of the Emperor Marcus Aurelius on page 157. How does this depiction of the Frankish ruler summarize Carolingian ideas of renaissance in culture and government? What differences do you see between the Carolingian and Roman representations of power?

CHARLEMAGNE AND THE ARTS

According to Charlemagne's biographer Einhard (ca. 770–840), the emperor not only fostered education for others but himself took an active interest in studies. In the following passage Einhard describes the king's own educational program, the breadth of his interests, and the mixed results he achieved. The description should be read with some caution, however. For example, Charlemagne's interest in astronomy and his practice of keeping writing materials in his bed (presumably to record his dreams) may be more of an indication of his interest in astrology and divination than of his interest in the liberal arts.

Focus Questions

Why did Charlemagne place such importance on education? What areas of study were particularly important for such a king?

Charles had the gift of ready and fluent speech, and could express whatever he had to say with the utmost clearness. He was not satisfied with command of his native language merely, but gave attention to the study of foreign ones, and in particular was such a master of Latin that he could speak it as well as his native tongue; but he could understand Greek better than he could speak it. He was so eloquent, indeed, that he might have passed for a teacher of eloquence. He most zealously cultivated the liberal arts, held those who taught them in great esteem, and conferred great honors upon them. He took lessons in grammar of the deacon Peter of Pisa, at that time an aged man. Another deacon, Albin of Britain, surnamed Alcuin, a man of Saxon extraction, who was the greatest scholar of the day, was his teacher in other branches of learning. The King spent much time and labor with him studying rhetoric, dialectics, and especially astronomy; he learned to reckon, and used to investigate the motions of the heavenly bodies most curiously, with an intelligent scrutiny. He also tried to write, and used to keep tablets and blanks in bed under his pillow, that at leisure hours he might accustom his hand to form the letters; however, as he did not begin his efforts in due season, but late in life, they met with ill success.

From Einhard, *The Life of Charlemagne.*

with piercing eyes, a robust physique, and a restless spirit. To his intimates, he was a generous lord constantly surrounded by friends, whether at table consuming wine and roast meat, in the baths in Aachen (where he often swam with more than a hundred courtiers), or on the march with his Frankish army. To his enemies, he was the man of iron—the grim and invincible warrior clad head to foot in steel, sweeping all before him. He was a conqueror, but he was also a religious reformer, a state builder, and a patron of the arts. As the leader of a powerful, united Frankish kingdom for more than 40 years, Charlemagne changed the West more profoundly than anyone since Augustus.

Almost every spring, Charlemagne assembled his Frankish armies and led them against internal or external enemies. He subdued the Aquitainians and Bavarians. He conquered the kingdom of the Lombards and assumed the title of King of the Lombards. He crushed the Saxons, annexed the Spanish region of Catalonia, and destroyed the vast Pannonian kingdom of the Avars. In wars of aggression, his armies were invincible. The heavy cavalry first employed by Charles Martel simply mowed down the more lightly armored and equipped enemy. Moreover, Charlemagne's logistical support was unmatched in the early Middle Ages. His ability to ship men and supplies down the Danube River enabled him to capture the enormous hoard of gold the Avars had amassed from raids and annual payments by the Byzantines. As Einhard, Charlemagne's counselor and adviser, boasted, "These Franks, who until then had seemed almost paupers, now discovered so much gold and silver in the palace and captured so much previous booty in their battles, that it could rightly be maintained that they had in all justice taken from the Huns [Avars] what these last had unjustly stolen from other nations."

Einhard, *Life of Charlemagne*

War booty fueled Charlemagne's renewal of European culture. As a Christian king, he considered it his duty to reform the spiritual life of his kingdom and to bring it into line with his concept of the divinely willed order. To achieve this goal he needed a dedicated and educated clergy. In the previous three centuries, secular schools had disappeared and Frankish monasteries had ceased to be centers of learning. Most of the native clergy were poorly educated and indifferent in their observance of the rules of religious life.

The Carolingian Renaissance

Creating a reformed, educated clergy was an effort every bit as complex and demanding as organizing the army. Charlemagne recruited leading intellectuals from England, Spain, Ireland, and Italy to the royal court to lead a thorough educational program. The architect of his cultural reform, Alcuin of York (ca. 732–804), directed a school for young lay and ecclesiastical aristocrats in the king's palace and encouraged the king to finance a

MAP DISCOVERY

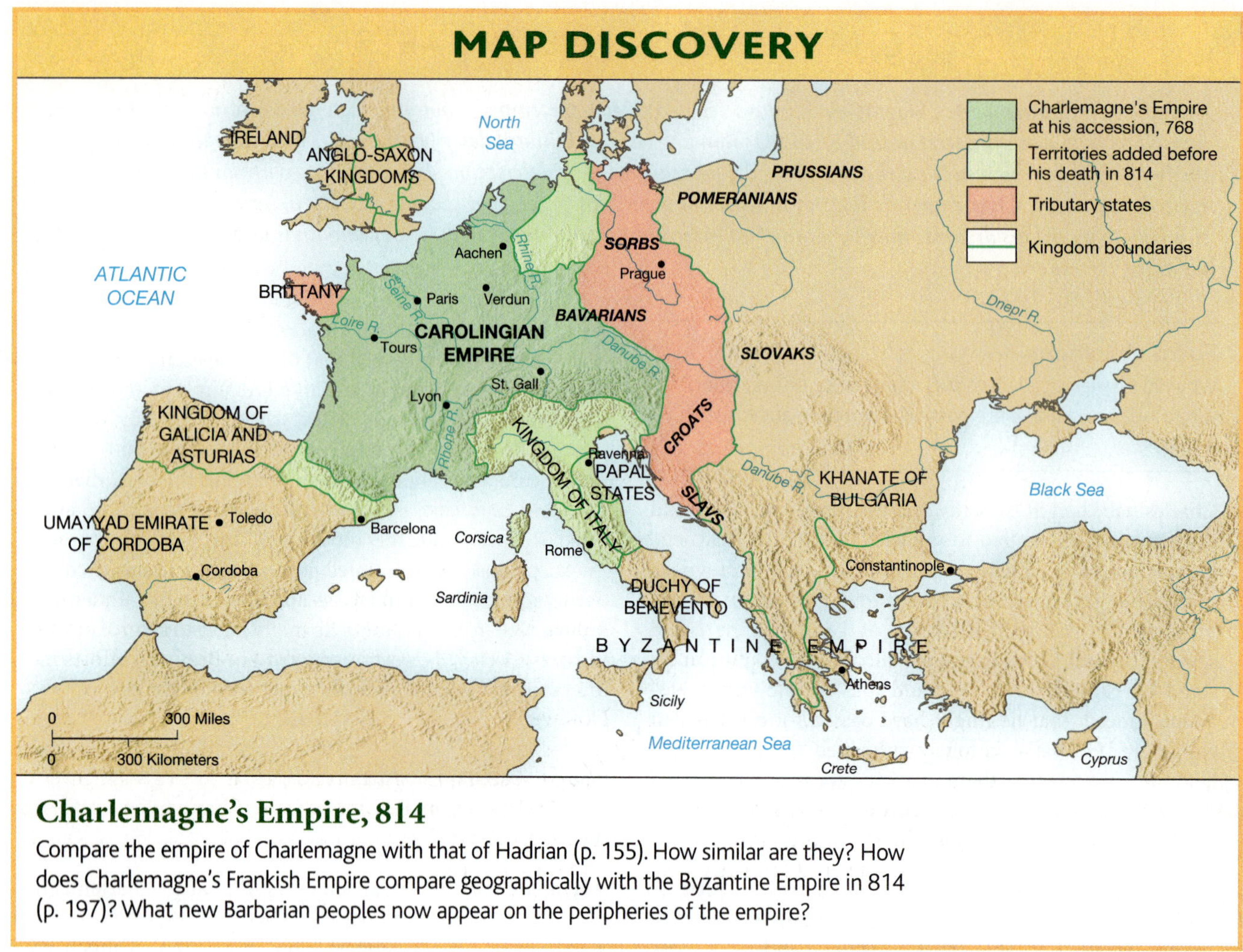

Charlemagne's Empire, 814

Compare the empire of Charlemagne with that of Hadrian (p. 155). How similar are they? How does Charlemagne's Frankish Empire compare geographically with the Byzantine Empire in 814 (p. 197)? What new Barbarian peoples now appear on the peripheries of the empire?

wide variety of educational programs. Charlemagne supported schools in great monasteries such as Fulda and St. Gall for the training of young clerics and laymen.

The schools needed books. Charlemagne's educational reformers scoured Italy for fading copies of works by Virgil, Horace, and Tacitus with the same determination that his builders hunted for antique marbles and columns for his chapel. Alcuin and others corrected and copied classical texts corrupted by generations of haphazard transmission. The earliest extant manuscripts of virtually all the classics of Roman antiquity date from the late eighth or early ninth century. Caroline **minuscule**—the new style of handwriting developed to preserve the texts—was so clear and readable that during the Renaissance, humanists (mistakenly thinking that these manuscripts dated from Roman times) adopted it as their standard script. It remains essentially the form of printing common today—this book is printed in a version of Caroline minuscule.

The first decades of educational reform produced little that was new, but the reformers of this era laid the necessary foundation for what has been called the **Carolingian Renaissance.** Their successors in the ninth century built on that foundation to make creative contributions in theology, philosophy, historiography, and, to some extent, literature. For the first time since Augustine, the West produced a really first-class theologian and philosopher, John Scotus Erigena (ca. 810–ca. 877), who mastered Greek and created a unique and influential synthesis of Neoplatonic philosophy.

The pursuit of learning was not a purely clerical affair. In the later ninth century, great aristocrats were highly literate and collected their own libraries. Count Everard of Friuli, who died in 866, left an estate that included more than 50 books, among them works by Augustine, histories, biographies of saints, and seven law books. Elite women participated fully in the Carolingian Renaissance. One example is the noblewoman Dhuoda, who composed a manual of instruction for her son. Her writings show her to have been a woman of deep piety and learning familiar with the Bible and the works of Augustine, Gregory the Great, other theologians, and some classical authors.

Educational reform went hand in hand with reform of ecclesiastical institutions. Charlemagne and his son Louis the

Pious (814–840) worked to establish the Benedictine rule as the norm for monastic life. They also tried to ensure that parish clergy were competent and committed to serving the needs of the people. The goal was the formation of a purified and organized clergy performing its essential role of celebrating Christian ritual and praying for the Frankish king. At the same time, the monasteries were to provide competent clerics to serve the royal administration at every level. The reforms were expensive. The fiscal reorganization of ecclesiastical institutions was as far-reaching as their cultural reform. For the first time, Frankish synods, or councils, made tithing mandatory, specifying that one-tenth of all agricultural harvests was to go to the maintenance of church buildings, the support of the clergy, and the care of the poor. Monasteries grew rich with donations of land and slaves captured in battle. Monastic estates were reorganized, records of dues and revenues revised for greater efficiency, and dependent workers shifted around to maximize productivity.

Carolingian Government

Charlemagne well knew that conquest alone could not unify his enormous kingdom with its vast differences in languages, laws, customs, and peoples. The glue that held it together was loyalty to him and to the Roman Church.

Local Governance. In the tradition of his father and grandfather, Charlemagne appointed counts throughout Europe. The counts were members of the great Frankish families who had been loyal to Charlemagne's family for generations. Thus he created what might be termed an *imperial aristocracy*—truly international in scope. The counts supervised the royal estates in their counties and each spring led the local military contingent, which included all the free men of the county. Counts also presided over local courts, which exercised jurisdiction over the free persons of the county. The king maintained his control over the counts by sending teams of emissaries, or **missi dominici,** composed of bishops and counts to examine the state of each county.

The Carolingian Church. Charlemagne recognized that while his representatives might be drawn from Frankish families, he could not impose Frankish legal and cultural traditions on all his subjects. The only universal system that might unify the kingdom was Roman Christianity. Unity of religious practices, directed by the reformed and educated clergy, would provide spiritual unity. Furthermore, since the clergy could also participate in the administration of the kingdom, they could guarantee administrative unity as well. Carolingian monarchs did not intend the enriched and reformed Church to be independent of royal authority; rather it was to be an integral part of the Carolingian system of government. However, at least some of the educated clerics and lay aristocrats who participated in the system formed a clear political ideology based on Augustinian concepts of Christian government. They attempted to educate Charlemagne and his successors about the duties of a king: maintaining peace and providing justice.

GENEALOGY

The Carolingian Dynasty

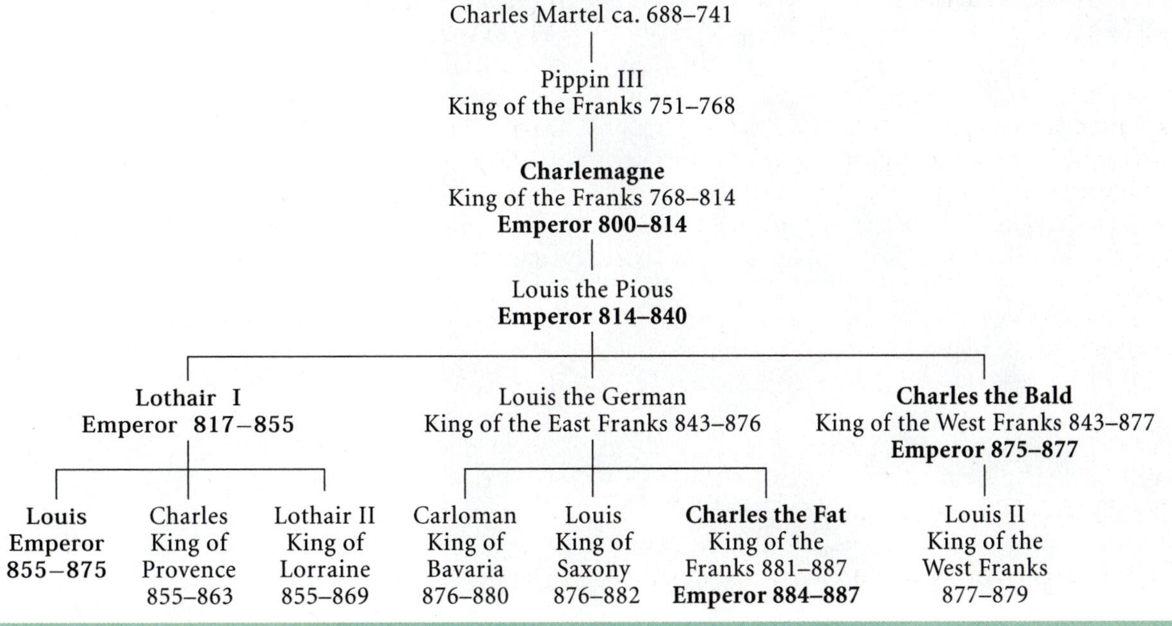

The Court. The mobile palace was the center of Carolingian government. It included the royal household and ecclesiastical and secular aristocrats who directed the various activities of the central administration. Within this palace the king held his own court. There, too, clerics maintained written records, produced official records of royal grants or decisions called **diplomas,** and prepared **capitularies,** which were written instructions for the implementation of royal directives at the local level.

Carolingian government was no modern bureaucracy or state system. The laymen and clerics who served the king were tied to him by personal oaths of loyalty rather than by any sense of dedication to a state or nation. Still, the attempts at governmental organization were far more sophisticated than anything that the West had seen for four centuries or would see again for another four. The system of counts and missi provided the most effective system of government prior to the thirteenth century and served as the model for subsequent medieval rulers.

The Imperial Coronation. The size of Charlemagne's Empire approached that of the old Roman Empire in the West. Only Britain, southern Italy, and parts of Spain remained outside Frankish control. With the reunification of most of the West and the creative adaptation of Roman traditions of culture and government, it is not surprising that Charlemagne's advisers began to compare his empire to that of Constantine. The comparison was accentuated by Charlemagne's conquest of Lombard Italy and his protection of Pope Leo III—a role traditionally played by the Byzantine emperors. At the end of the eighth century, the throne in Constantinople was held by a woman. Irene (752–802) was powerful and capable, but Western male leaders considered her unfit for such an office by reason of her sex. All those fac-

The Book of Kells, which contains the four Gospels and explanatory material was executed ca. 800 by Celtic monks, possibly at the island monastery of Iona off the coast of Scotland. It exemplifies the extraordinary geometric style of Insular art common to Ireland and Britain in the early Middle Ages. This full-page illustration represents Christ enthroned and attended by angels. Compare this artistic style to that of the Utrecht Gospels on page 237.

tors finally converged in one of the most momentous events in Western political history: Charlemagne's imperial coronation on Christmas Day in the year 800.

Historians debate the precise meaning of the event, particularly since Charlemagne was said to have remarked afterward that he would never have entered St. Peter's Basilica in Rome had he known what was going to happen. Presumably he meant that he wished to be proclaimed emperor by his Frankish people rather than by the pope, since this is how he had his son Louis the Pious acclaimed emperor in 813. Moreover, Charlemagne apparently saw his title of emperor more as a reflection of his accomplishments than as a political title indicating the foundation of his authority.

Nevertheless, the imperial coronation of 800 subsequently took on great significance. Louis attempted to make his imperial title the sole basis for his rule, and for the next thousand years Germanic kings traveled to Rome to receive the imperial diadem and title from the pope. In so doing, they inadvertently strengthened papal claims to enthrone—and at times to dethrone—emperors.

■ The Twenty-third Psalm from the Utrecht Psalter, Rheims, made in about 820. The imagery of the drawings in red-brown ink and the arrangement of the script on the page recall models from late antiquity.

Carolingian Art

The same creative adaptation of the classical heritage that gave birth to a new Western empire produced a new Western art. The artistic traditions of the barbarian world consisted almost entirely of the decoration of small, portable objects such as weapons, jewelry, and, after conversion, manuscripts. Although some Mediterranean motifs penetrated northward, barbarian art was essentially nonrepresentational and consisted primarily of elaborate interlaced geometric forms of great sophistication and fine craftsmanship. When animal and human forms did appear, as in the Lindisfarne Gospels, produced around 700, or in the magnificent Book of Kells, created by Irish monks around a century later, they were transformed into intricate patterns of decoration.

For Charlemagne and his reformers, such abstract art was doubly inappropriate. Not only was it too distant from the Roman heritage that they were trying to emulate, but it could not be used for instruction or propaganda. Therefore, Charlemagne invited Italian and Byzantine artists and artisans to his kingdom to teach a form of representational art that would educate as well as decorate. However, the southern traditions were no more slavishly followed by northern artists than were Roman political traditions by Charlemagne's government.

Instead, the artistic styles from the east were transformed. The synthesis of Mediterranean and northern artistic traditions produced a dynamic, plastic style of representation in which figures seem intensely alive and active. The figures—which appear in manuscript illuminations, frescoes, ivories, and bas-reliefs—are often arranged in narrative cycles that engage the mind as well as the eye. The Utrecht Psalter is the consummate masterpiece of this tradition. Each psalm is accompanied by a crowded, complex visual interpretation of the text in which verbal and visual metaphors move from scene to scene. In its arrangement and use of classical allusions, the whole work is clearly intended to echo classical antiquity. And yet the execution breathes with a dramatic vision and reality beyond that of any of its numerous classical models and is fully equal to the religious themes it represents. In art, as in every other sphere, the Carolingian rebirth was actually a new birth.

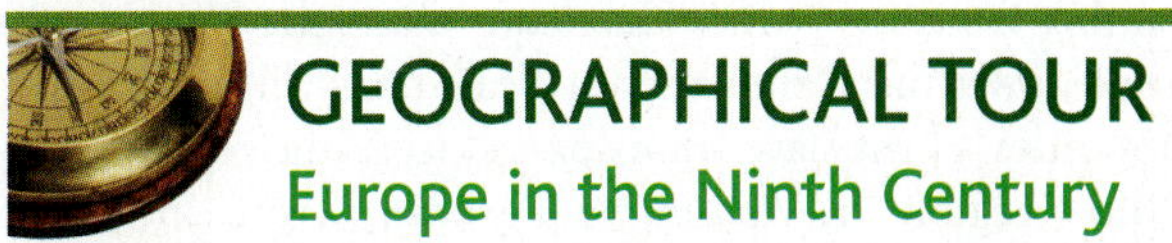

GEOGRAPHICAL TOUR

Europe in the Ninth Century

The Carolingian Empire stretched from the Baltic Sea to the Adriatic and linked, through a network of commerce and exchange, the Germanic and Slavic worlds of the north, the Islamic world of Spain and the Near East, and the Mediterranean world of Byzantium (see **Map A**). Carolingian kings rebuilt roads, bridges, and ports to facilitate trade. Charlemagne also reformed Western currency,

■ **Map A. Europe in the Ninth Century.** In the course of the ninth century, individual kingdoms developed across Europe.

abandoning gold coinage in favor of the more easily obtainable and liquid silver.

Silver was the medium of exchange at the northern ports of Durstede near the mouth of the Rhine and Quentovic near what is now Etaples. It was here that Frankish merchants haggled with Anglo-Saxon and Danish traders over cloth, furs, and amber from the Baltic. Merchants along the Slavic frontier and down the Danube River dealt primarily in human commodities. Great slave trains passed from the regions into the Rhine region. In Verdun, young boys were castrated at "eunuch factories" before being sent down the Rhone River to the cities of lower Provence, where they were sold to Muslim agents from Spain and North Africa. Jewish and Greek merchants supplied the Frankish church and aristocracy with luxury goods from Constantinople and the east. The travels of a merchant in the early ninth century might begin with a short trip from Quentovic to the English coast and then continue clockwise around the Frankish world (see **Map A**).

England

A continental visitor in England (see **Map B**) would be well treated. In 796 Charlemagne had written to King Offa of Mercia (757–796), offering English merchants protection in his kingdom and agreeing that "our men, if they suffer any injustice in your dominion, are to appeal to the judgment of your equity, lest any disturbance should arise." Offa, the only king Charlemagne referred to as "brother," ruled a prosperous kingdom in southern England and was acknowledged as a leader by other Anglo-Saxon rulers. His success was based partly on his military actions against the Welsh. He had led raids deep into Wales and had constructed a great dike 25 feet high and 150 miles long along the entire length of the Welsh frontier. Charlemagne's letter indicates, though, that Mercia's prosperity was also based on extensive trading with the Continent, a trade in which Anglo-Saxon woolens and silver were exchanged for wine, oil, and other products of the Continent.

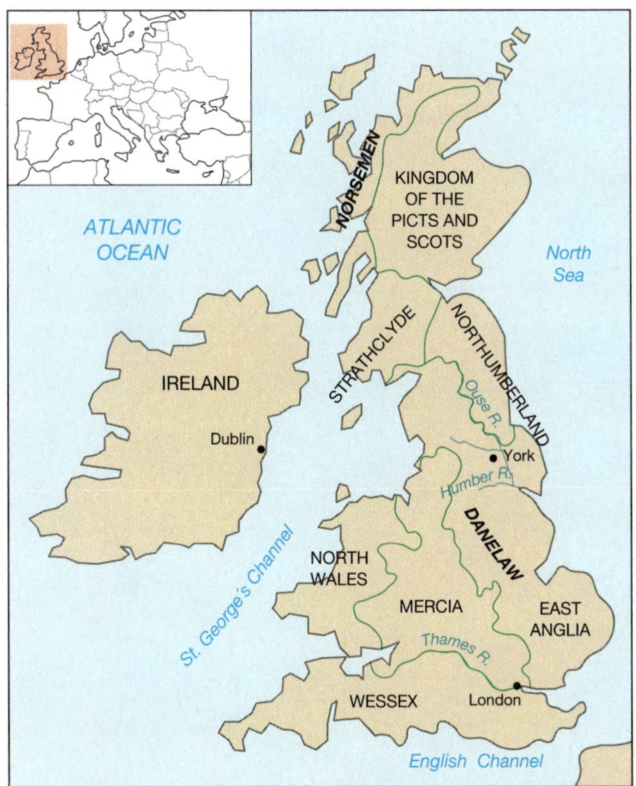

■ **Map B. England.** Anglo-Saxon England was divided into a shifting number of small kingdoms ruled by rival dynasties.

Mercian supremacy did not last beyond the rule of Offa. In the constant warfare among Anglo-Saxon kingdoms during the first half of the ninth century, Mercia fell to Wessex (see **Map B**). The cycle of rise and fall of little kingdoms might have continued had the Vikings not come onto the scene. The Scandinavian raiders had been harassing the coast since 786. They did not pose a serious threat to England, however, until 865, when a great Viking army interested in conquest landed north of the Humber River. All but one of the Anglo-Saxon kingdoms were destroyed. Three kings were killed and a fourth was forced to abdicate.

King Alfred. The surviving king, Alfred of Wessex (870–899), reorganized his army, established a network of fortifications, created a navy, and thus temporarily halted the Viking conquest. Still, he realized that his military achievement could be consolidated only by the transformation of his political base. Few of Alfred's contemporaries saw him as the savior of England. He had first to win the loyalty of people in his own kingdom and then attract that of Anglo-Saxons outside his kingdom.

Alfred won support by reforming the legal and cultural foundations of his kingdom. His legal reforms aimed to reassure subjects of the various Anglo-Saxon kingdoms of equal treatment. At the same time, they emphasized the importance of oaths of loyalty and the gravity of treason. Alfred further reassured Anglo-Saxon nobles by arranging marriage alliances with influential noble families. Finally, Alfred inaugurated a religious and cultural program to extend literacy and learning so that his people might better understand and follow God's word. Alfred and his reformers used the vernacular Anglo-Saxon because at that time Latin was almost entirely unknown in England. Alfred encouraged the translation of the greatest books of the Christian tradition into Anglo-Saxon. He even translated some of the books himself.

By the time Alfred died in 899, southern England was united under Wessex leadership. Eastern England north of the Thames River was occupied and colonized by Danes. In this region, known as the Danelaw (see **Map B**), the Vikings settled as farmers and slowly merged with the local population.

Scandinavia

Scandinavians in England were merchants as well as raiders. They traded furs, amber, and fish for English silver and cloth. A merchant interested in the northern trade might depart England from the town of York and travel down the Ouse and Humber rivers to the North Sea (see **Map B**). To make the passage, a merchant might sail with a Scandinavian Viking in his longboat. The magnificent ships, more than 70 feet long, were fast, flexible, and easily maneuvered. They allowed Scandinavians to cross the ocean to America and to navigate the shallow rivers of Europe. A merchant's journey would begin with passage across the English Channel, followed by a two-day sail north along the coast of the Jutland Peninsula to the mouth of the Eider River (see **Map C**). From there merchants could take advantage of the newly established trade

■ Viking ships such as this magnificent example from Gokstad built around 900 allowed Scandinavians to cross open seas and navigate shallow rivers with equal ease.

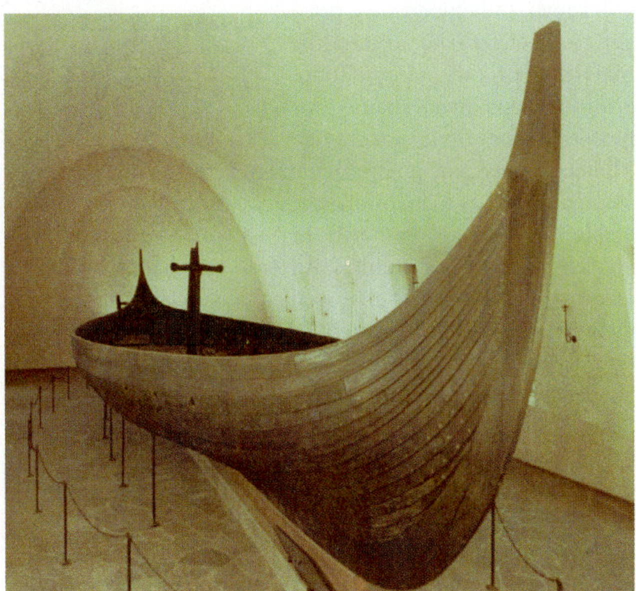

route that crossed the Jutland Peninsula to Hedeby at the head of the Slie Fjord on the Baltic Sea, thus avoiding the long and dangerous sea voyage around the Skaw, the northernmost point of the Jutland Peninsula. After a few days a serious trader would press on, passing the Swedish archipelago, out past the islands of Oland and Gotland, through the narrow strait where Stockholm now stands, to Birka, the greatest port of Scandinavia (see **Map C**). In Birka, Danes, Swedes, Franks, Frisians, Anglo-Saxons, Balts, Greeks, and Arabs met and carried on their international trade.

Like England, Scandinavia had long been an area of Frankish commercial and political interest. The Saxons had previously formed a buffer between the Scandinavians and the Frankish world, but Charlemagne's conquests had brought the two societies into direct contact.

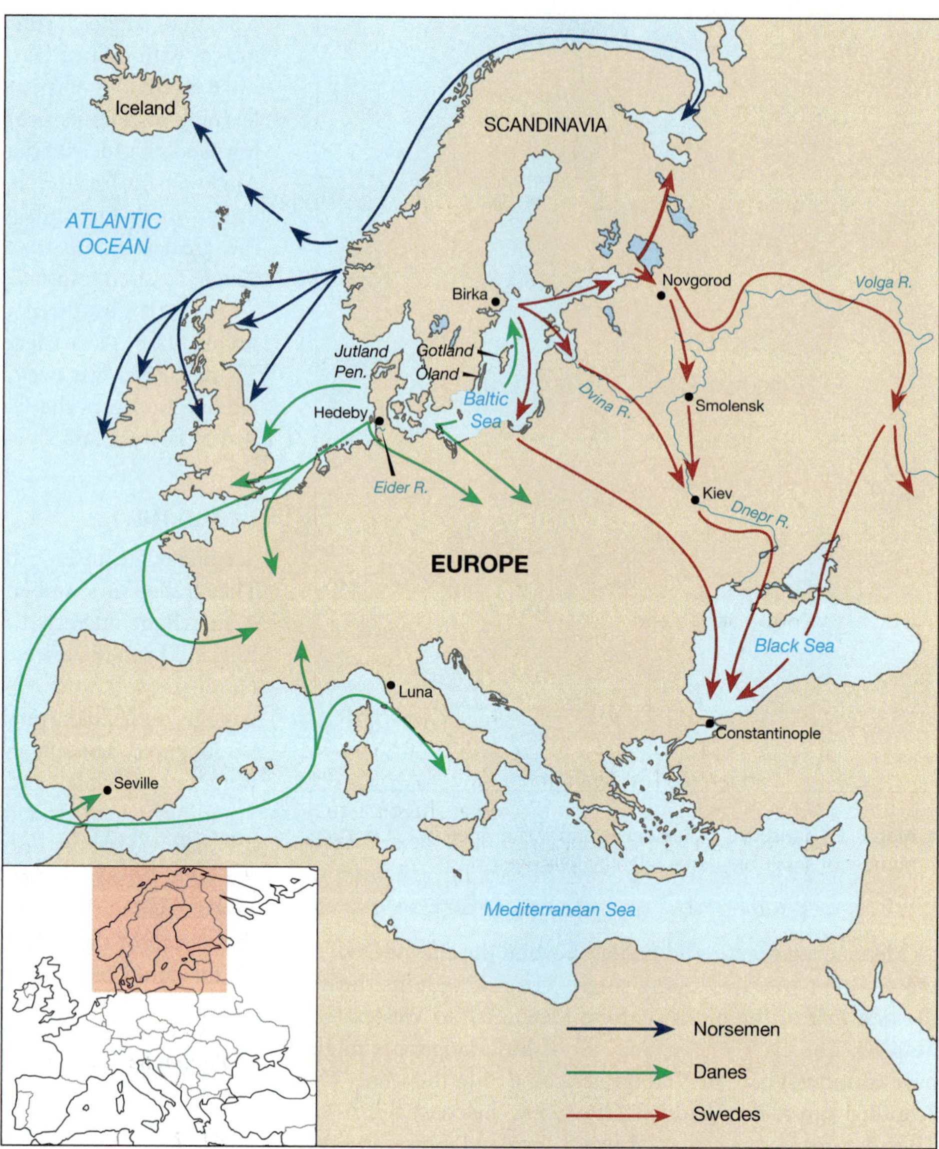

■ **Map C. Scandinavia.** Fleeing political consolidation at home, Scandinavian Vikings raided and settled into Russia and Ukraine, west to Iceland and the British Isles, down the Atlantic coast, and even into the Mediterranean.

Norse Society. Scandinavian society resembled the Germanic society of the first century. It was composed of three social classes. At the top were wealthy chiefs, or *jarlar* (earls), who had numerous servants, slaves, and free retainers. At the bottom were *thralls,* or bondsmen. In between were peasant freeholders, who formed the majority of the population. Scandinavians lived mainly for personal glory and war booty. Military ability and political cunning were equally prized, in women as well as men. In that society, women enjoyed considerable freedom and authority that shocked more "civilized" observers from other cultures. An Arab merchant who visited Hedeby in 950 reported that women could claim the right to divorce whenever they wanted. In the ninth century, however, internal developments began to threaten the traditional independence of Scandinavian men and women, and this led in part to the Scandinavian expansion into the rest of Europe.

Royal Consolidation. Scandinavian kings were traditionally selected by groups of earls; they exercised positions more as firsts among equals than as rulers. Around the end of the eighth century, however—possibly in imitation of Frankish and Anglo-Saxon royalty—Scandinavian kings began to consolidate power at home and to look to the wealthy Anglo-Saxon and Frankish worlds as sources of booty and glory. Earls and royal pretenders, threatened or displaced by the kings, also began to go "viking," or raiding, in order to replace abroad what they had lost at home.

Vikings. The directions in which Northmen went viking depended on the regions of Scandinavia from which they came. Swedes looked east, trading with the Slavic world and Byzantium. Norwegians looked to Ireland and Scotland, and later to Greenland, Iceland, and North America. The Danes tended to focus on England and the Frankish Empire (see **Map C**).

Swedish merchant Vikings, known as Varangians or the Rus', traveled down the Volga, Dvina, and Dnepr rivers as far as the Black and Caspian seas in search of furs and slaves (see **Map C**). There they met the trading routes of the Byzantine Empire and the caliphate of Baghdad. Rus'-fortified trading settlements at Novgorod, Smolensk, and Kiev (see **Map C**) became the nuclei of a Slavic-Scandinavian political unit to which the Rus' eventually gave their name: Russia. In the early 860s, the Slavic tribes around Novgorod had accepted the Varangian chief Ryurik as ruler. The House of Ryurik was beginning to spread its control over other nearby communities. In 882, members of the family captured Kiev and united the two towns. Although the merchant would have had no way of knowing it, this was the beginning of the creation of a Russian Empire.

Norwegians began their viking in Europe's western islands in the late eighth century. Ireland, which until then had been undisturbed by either Roman or Germanic invaders, was the first victim. Norwegians also raided south along the coast of the Frankish kingdom, Spain, and even into the Mediterranean region, where they raided Provence, North Africa, and Italy (see **Map C**). In Italy, a wily Norwegian plundered the city of Luna (which he mistook for Rome) by a ruse so bold that it captured the imagination of even the Franks. Unable to take the town by storm, the commander had his men inform the Italians that the Norwegian leader had died. Since he had been a Christian, they wanted him to receive a Christian burial. When the chieftain's body was brought into the city by his "mourning" followers, he suddenly rose from the dead and killed the bishop, and then he and his men sacked the town.

The political consolidation in Norway under Harold Finehair (860–933) culminated in 872 and led more Norwegians to go viking. Earls who objected to Harold's consolidation went abroad to maintain their freedom. Some settled in the Faroe Islands, while others colonized Iceland. The southernmost Scandinavians, the Danes, were most intimately familiar with the Frankish and Anglo-Saxon realms. During the reigns of Charlemagne's successors, Danish viking progressed from scattered raids against wealthy monasteries or trading towns such as Durstede to organized expeditions and finally to massive conquests. Some of the Vikings, led by Danish kings, colonized whole areas, such as Northumbria and the region of the mouth of the Seine River. It was this region that later became known as Normandy—land of the Northmen.

The Slavic World

A merchant in Scandinavia might join an expedition of Swedish Rus' to cross the Baltic Sea and enter the Slavic world (see **Map D**) in search of ermine and slaves. The Carolingians' effects were felt, both in merchant activity and in the presence of imperialist armies and missionaries. The Slavic world of the ninth century was a rapidly changing amalgam of Germanic and Slavic peoples whose ultimate orientation—north to Scandinavia, east to Constantinople, or west to Aachen—was an open question.

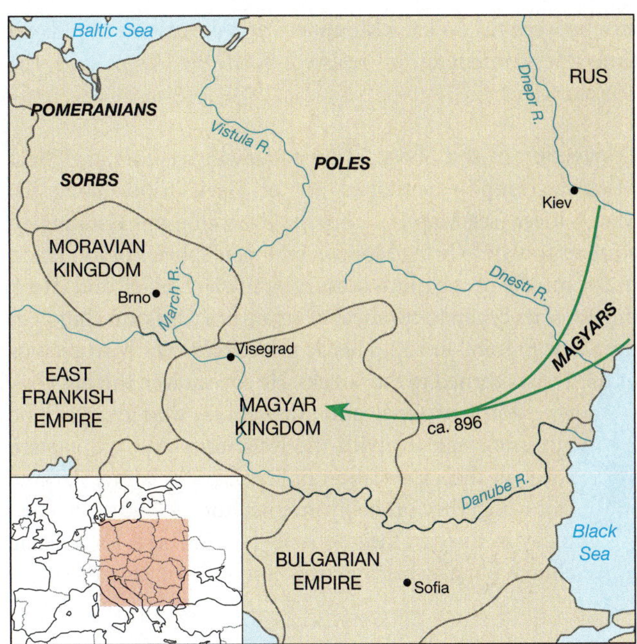

■ **Map D. The Slavic World.** In the ninth century, new kingdoms appeared in the Slavic world under the influence of Vikings, Franks, Byzantine missionaries, Magyar raiders, and local chieftains.

Slavic Origins. In antiquity and the early Middle Ages, distinctions between Slavic, Scythian, and Germanic peoples were hazy. These peoples often made up large portions of steppe confederations such as the Huns and, later, the Avars. In the sixth century, a distinct Slavic identity began to coalesce on the Byzantine frontier, and Slavic tribes had begun to filter both east and west. In the seventh century, a Frank named Samo (d. ca. 660) organized a brief but powerful confederation of Slavs in the

■ **Map E. Spain.** Under the Umayyad emirs, Spain prospered as a center of agriculture, trade, and mixed Islamic, Jewish, and Christian cultures.

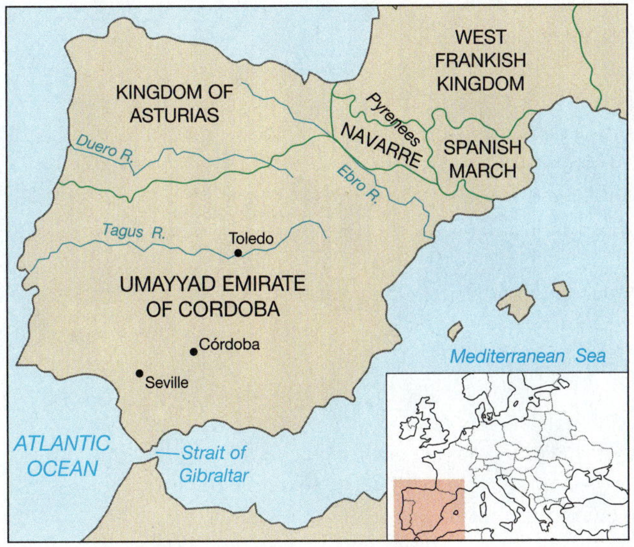

area between the Sudeten Mountains and the eastern Alps. For a time the confederation resisted both the Avars and the Merovingians.

Conversion of the Slavs. In the following century, the Great Moravian Empire developed out of Slavic tribes along the March River (see **Map D**). Both the Byzantine and Carolingian empires sought to bring Moravia into their spheres of influence. In the middle of the ninth century, Frankish, Italian, and Greek missionaries began to compete to organize a Christian church in the Slavic Empire. In 852, a Slavic prince particularly suspicious of the Franks turned to the Greeks. He encouraged the missionary efforts of Cyril and Methodius, who enjoyed the encouragement of both the Byzantines and the papacy. Through their translation of liturgical texts into Slavonic (for which they probably invented the Cyrillic script used today in Russia), they not only laid the basis for a Slavic church but also began a tradition of Slavic literacy.

Vladimir of Kiev's Acceptance of Christianity

The promising beginning made by the two missionary brothers was short-lived, since the Franks feared an independent Slavic church. In 864, the Carolingian king Louis the German (843–876) conquered Moravia. Methodius, who had been appointed archbishop of Moravia and Pannonia by the pope, was imprisoned in a German monastery for the rest of his life. The Frankish hegemony lasted only a few decades. In 895 a new steppe people, the Magyars, or Hungarians, swept into Pannonia, as had the Huns and Avars before them. The new invaders destroyed the Franks' puppet Moravian Empire and split the Slavic world in two. The south Slavs in what is now the Balkans were cut off from the northern Slavs in what is now Poland, Russia, and Ukraine.

The Magyar kingdom (see **Map D**) proved a greater threat to the Franks than the Slavs or Avars. The Magyars not only conquered Pannonia as far as the Enns River, they also raided deep into the Carolingian Empire. For 50 years, swift bands of Magyar horsemen crossed the Alps and pillaged the Po Valley,

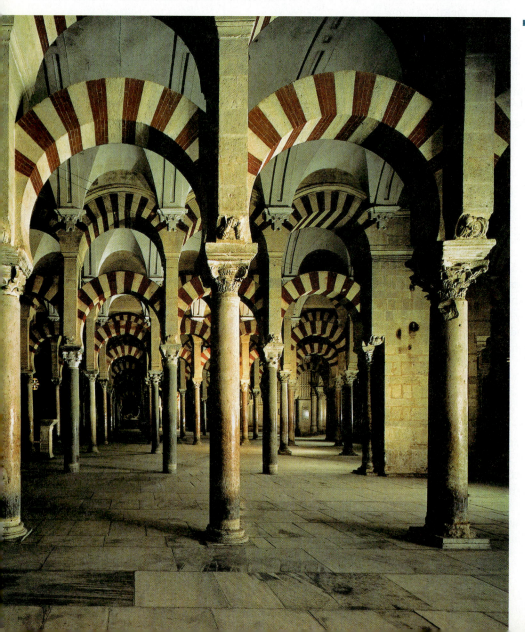

The Mosque of Córdoba, completed in 790, synthesizes Roman, Visigothic, and Islamic architecture.

terrorizing the eastern portions of the empire and even striking as far west as modern Burgundy.

Muslim Spain

The Slavic world was in contact not only with the Christian societies of Byzantium and the West. Muslim merchants used Arab gold to buy furs and slaves from Rus' traders at settlements along the Dnepr River (see **Map D**). A Spanish merchant might depart from Kiev and, to avoid the Magyars, travel down the Dnepr to the Black Sea past Constantinople, and then across the length of the Mediterranean to Al-Andalus, as the Muslims called Spain (see **Map E**). After the disintegration of the Umayyad caliphate (see p. 206), the last Umayyad, 'Abd ar-Rahman I (731–788), made his way to Spain, where in 756 he established an independent emirate. Under the centralized control of the Umayyad emirs, the economic and cultural life of urban Spain, which had stagnated under the Visigoths, experienced a renaissance as vital as that taking place across the Pyrenees in the Frankish Empire.

The Mosque of Córdoba, begun by 'Abd ar-Rahman I in 784 and completed by his son Hisham I in 790, exemplifies this cultural revival (see **Map E**). The building is a veritable forest of columns, overlapping arches, and ribbed cupola, as shown in the photograph opposite. The mosque is, like the emirate itself, a cultural blend incorporating earlier Roman, Early Christian, and Visigothic constructions to create one of the greatest architectural monuments of the world.

The Umayyad Emirate. To secure the emirate, 'Abd ar-Rahman and his successors had to overcome internal division and external aggression. The Spanish population included an elite minority of Arabs, recently arrived Syrians, North African Berbers, converted Spaniards, Christian Spaniards, and Jews. In addition, Frankish aggression and Scandinavian Vikings continually harassed Al-Andalus.

In the short run, 'Abd ar-Rahman secured control by brute force. Relying on a professional army composed mainly of slaves, the emirs crushed revolts mounted by various Muslim factions. They strengthened a series of semiautonomous districts, or marches, commanded by military governors as buffers against the Frankish kingdom to the north. Finally, they established a line of guard posts along the coast to protect themselves against the Northmen.

In the long run, the emirs sought stability in religion and law. They presented themselves as the champions and protectors of Islam, assuming in 926 the titles of "caliph," "commander of the believers," and "defender of the religion of God." In this way they built a religious foundation for their rule. Likewise, they cultivated the study and application of Islamic law as a source of justice and social order.

The economic prosperity of Al-Andalus was based on an enlightened system of agriculture that included the introduction of oranges, rice, sugarcane, and cotton from the eastern Mediterranean. Complementing agriculture was a renewed urban life bolstered by vigorous trade to the north, east, and south. From the later ninth century, the trade was supplemented by raiding expeditions into Italy and southern Gaul. In the ninth and tenth centuries, Spain was the most prosperous region of Europe and one of the wealthiest areas of the Muslim world.

In that climate of security and prosperity developed the most sophisticated and refined culture in the West. Arabic poetry and art developed in a manner exactly the opposite of that in the Carolingian world. Poetry, visual art, and architecture deemphasized physical forms and encouraged abstraction and meditation. Meditation drew the individual away from the reality of objects and images toward the unseen divinity. Such abstract, contemplative art did not develop in Western Christendom for centuries.

AFTER THE CAROLINGIANS: FROM EMPIRE TO LORDSHIPS

Alien, dynamic, and potentially threatening neighbors surrounded the Carolingian kingdom. To the west was Anglo-Saxon England; to the east were the Slavic and Byzantine worlds. Scandinavia lay to the north, and Al-Andalus threatened to the south. In the later ninth and tenth centuries, the Frankish kingdom collapsed, owing in part to the actions of the neighbors but primarily to the kingdom's own internal weaknesses.

Charlemagne, despite his imperial title, had remained dependent on his traditional power base, the Frankish aristocracy. For them, learned concepts of imperial renovation meant little: they wanted wealth and power. Under Charlemagne, the empire's prosperity and relative internal peace had resulted largely from continued successful expansion at the expense of neighbors. Its economy had been based on plunder and the redistribution of booty among the aristocracy and wealthy churches. As wars of conquest under Charlemagne gave place to defensive actions against Magyars, Vikings, and Saracens, the supply of wealth dried up. Aristocratic supporters had to be rewarded with estates within the empire. Aristocrats thus became enormously wealthy and powerful. Count Everard, whose library was mentioned earlier (p. 234), left his sons estates scattered from Friuli in northern Italy to what is now Belgium.

Disintegration of the Empire

Competition among Charlemagne's descendants as well as grants to the aristocracy weakened central authority. By fate rather than by design, Charlemagne had bequeathed a united empire to his son Louis the Pious (814–840). Charlemagne had intended to follow Frankish custom and divide his estate among all his sons, but only Louis survived him. Louis's three sons, in contrast, fought one another over their inheritance. Finally, in the Treaty of Verdun concluded in 843, they divided the empire among them. The eldest son, Lothair (840–855), who inherited

MAP DISCOVERY

The Division of Charlemagne's Empire

Consider how Charlemagne's grandsons divided his empire. What major symbolic locations remained in the kingdom of Emperor Lothair? Do the kingdoms of Kings Charles and Louis appear more culturally and ethnically homogeneous than that of their brother? Into what states would their two kingdoms eventually develop?

his father's imperial title, received an unwieldy middle portion that stretched from the Rhine River south through Italy. Louis the German (840–876) received the eastern portions of the empire. The youngest son, Charles the Bald (840–877), was allotted the western portions. In time, the western kingdom became France and the eastern kingdom became the core of Germany. The middle kingdom, which included what are now Holland, Belgium, Luxembourg, Lorraine (or Lotharingia, from *Lothair*), Switzerland, and northern Italy, remained a disputed region into the twentieth century.

The disintegration of the empire meant much more than its division among Charlemagne's heirs. In no region were his successors able to provide the degree of peace and public control that he had established. The Frankish armies, designed for wars of aggression, were too clumsy and slow to deal with the lightning raids of Northmen, Magyars, and Saracens. The attacks could only be countered by locally organized and led forces, and the aristocrats who were successful in defending their regions gained prestige and power at the expense of the kings. The constant need to please aristocratic supporters made it impossible for kings to prevent aristocrats from attracting other warriors into their personal vassalic followings or from absorbing free peasants and churches into their economic and political spheres. Increasingly, the magnates were able to transform the offices of count and bishop into inherited familial positions. They also determined who would reign in their kingdoms and sought kings who posed no threat to themselves.

Most aristocrats saw this greater autonomy as their just due. Only dukes, counts, and other local lords could organize resistance to internal and external foes at the local level. They needed both economic means and political authority to provide protection and maintain peace. These resources could be acquired only at the expense of royal power. Thus, during the late ninth and tenth centuries, much of Europe found its equilibrium at the local level as public powers, judicial courts, and military authority became the private possession of wealthy families. Charlemagne's Empire had become a patchwork of local lordships.

Emergence of France and Germany

Ultimately, new royal families emerged from among the local leaders. The family of the counts of Paris, for example, gained enormous prestige from the fact that they had led the successful defense of the city against the Vikings from 885 to 886. For a time, they alternated with Carolingians as kings of the West Franks. After the ascension of Hugh Capet in 987, they entirely replaced the Carolingians.

In a similar manner, the eastern German kingdom, which was divided into five great duchies, began to elect non-Carolingians as kings. In 919, the dukes of the region elected as their king Duke Henry of Saxony (919–936), who had proven his abilities fighting the Danes and Magyars. Henry's son, Otto the Great (936–973), proved to be a strong ruler who subdued the other dukes and definitively crushed the Magyars. In 962, Otto was crowned emperor by Pope John XII (955–964), thus reviving the empire of Charlemagne, although only in its eastern half. However, the dukes of the eastern kingdom chafed constantly at the strong control the Ottonians attempted to exercise at their expense. Although the empire Otto reestablished endured until 1806, he and his successors never matched the political or cultural achievements of the Carolingians.

By the tenth century, the early medieval kingdoms, based on inherited Roman notions of universal states and barbarian traditions of charismatic military leadership, had all ended in failure. After the demise of the Carolingian Empire, the West began to find stability at a more local but also more permanent level. The local nature of Western society did not mean, however, that the Roman and Carolingian traditions were forgotten. Carolingian religious reform, classical learning, and political ideology were preserved in the following centuries.

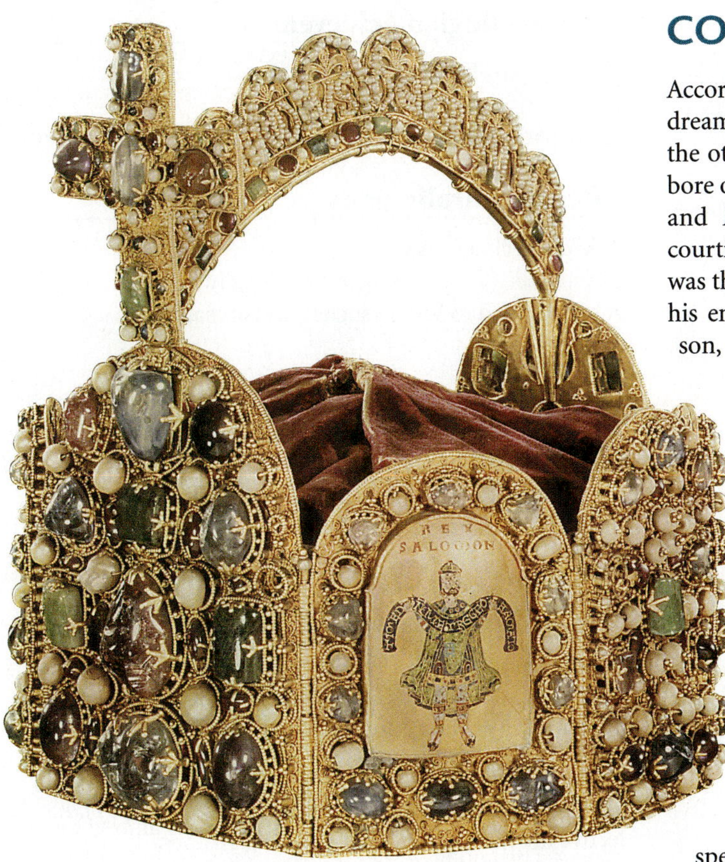

■ This magnificent jeweled crown was made for Otto I. The small portrait represents King Solomon.

Cluny

Church reform took on new life in 909 with the foundation of the monastery of Cluny in eastern France. Cluniac monks, drawn from the lesser aristocracy, were God's shock troops, fighting evil with their prayers with the same vigor that their secular cousins exhibited in fighting the enemy with their swords. Cluny, inspired by the monastic program of Louis the Pious and granted immunity from secular interference, became the center of an extraordinary expansion of Benedictine monasticism throughout the West.

The revival of classical learning begun in Carolingian schools, although hampered by the new wave of invasions that began in the later ninth century, continued in centers such as St. Gall, Auxerre, and Corvey. During the late ninth and tenth centuries, Western Christian civilization spread north and east. By the year 1000, Scandinavia, Poland, Bohemia, and even Hungary had become Christian kingdoms with national churches whose bishops were approved by the pope. Among the aristocracy, just as all restraints on the warrior elite seemed to have been thrown off, a gradual process of transformation of their material and mental world began. Encouraged by Cluniac monasticism and by episcopal exhortations, nobles began to consider limiting their violence against one another and placing it instead in the service of Christendom.

CONCLUSION

According to a ninth-century legend, Charlemagne once dreamed that he was visited by a sword-carrying spirit from the other world. The sword, a gift to the emperor from God, bore on its blade four Germanic words: *Rhat, Radoleiba, Nasg,* and *Enti.* The next day Charlemagne explained to his courtiers that the dream was a prophecy of the future. *Rhat* was the assistance God had given Charlemagne in conquering his enemies. *Radoleiba* indicated how, under Charlemagne's son, all of that would quickly dissipate. *Nasg* foretold the greed of his grandsons, who would allow their followers to plunder the Church and spread poverty through the land. *Enti* indicated the end, either of his royal family or of the world.

The anonymous author of the legend recognized that although the Magyar, Viking, and Saracen raids contributed to the disintegration of the Carolingian Empire, their role was secondary. The internal dynamics of the Frankish world and its unresolved social and political tensions were the essential causes for the collapse of the Carolingian synthesis.

In the long run, however, the Carolingian synthesis left a powerful and enduring legacy. At the start of the Middle Ages in the West, a variety of Germanic kingdoms experimented with a whole spectrum of ways to reconcile the twin elements of barbarian and Roman tradition. The Ostrogoths attempted to preserve the two as separate entities and soon vanished. The Visigoths sought unification through coercion and found themselves isolated and weakened. In England, Germanic invaders sought to replace Roman traditions entirely. Only the Franks found a lasting means of amalgamating Roman and Germanic societies.

The key elements of the synthesis were Orthodox Christianity, Roman administration, and Frankish military kingship. Between 500 and 800, the three elements coalesced into a vital new civilization. Although the political structure created by Charlemagne did not survive his grandsons, the Frankish model proved enduring in every other respect. The cultural renaissance laid the foundation of all subsequent European intellectual activities. The alliance between Church and monarchy provided the formula for European kings for almost a thousand years. The administrative system with its central and local components, its counts and its missi, its diplomas and capitularies, provided the model for later medieval government in England and on the Continent. The idea of the Carolingian Empire, the symbol of European unity, has never entirely disappeared from the West.

QUESTIONS FOR REVIEW

1. What social and political forces encouraged division within the various Gothic, Anglo-Saxon, and Frankish kingdoms?

2. How did the household and the parish provide new units for organizing European society?
3. How did the aristocracy evolve out of Germanic and Roman traditions, and how was the aristocracy both a support and a threat to the kingdoms of the early Middle Ages?
4. What were Charlemagne's achievements?
5. Why did Charlemagne's Empire not outlive him for long?

KEY TERMS

capitularies, *p. 236*
Carolingian Renaissance, *p. 234*
diplomas, *p. 236*
Lombards, *p. 220*
manses, *p. 227*
Marchfield, *p. 230*
Merovingians, *p. 227*
minuscule, *p. 234*
missi dominici, *p. 235*
synod, *p. 224*
vassals, *p. 232*

DISCOVERING WESTERN CIVILIZATION ONLINE

You can obtain more information about the West in the early Middle Ages at the Websites listed below. See also the Companion Website that accompanies this text, www.ablongman.com/kishlansky, which contains an online study guide and additional resources.

General Websites

The Labyrinth: Resources for Medieval Studies
www.georgetown.edu/labyrinth/labyrinth-home.html
Labyrinth is the central Website for all medieval studies.

The Making of the Barbarian Kingdoms

Anglo-Saxon History: A Select Bibliography
www.wmich.edu/medieval/research/rawl/keynesbib/home.htm
A comprehensive bibliographical site on Anglo-Saxon civilization created and maintained by Simon Keynes.

Medieval Art at the Metropolitan Museum
metmuseum.org/collections/view50.asp?dep=17
A look at some of the Metropolitan Museum's collection of medieval art, including migration-period jewelry.

Living in the New Europe

Wharram Percy: The Lost Medieval Village
loki.stockton.edu/~ken/wharram/wharram.htm
A site devoted to exploring a lost medieval village from Roman times to the High Middle Ages.

The Carolingian Achievement

Carolingian Writing Centers
ccat.sas.upenn.edu/jod/map.html
A site with links to centers of Carolingian renaissance culture.

After the Carolingians

Viking Archaeology
bubl.ac.uk/link/v/vikingarchaeology.htm
A site devoted to Viking society and archaeology.

Kingship
ishi.lib.berkeley.edu/history155/slides/kingship/index.html
Interactive explorations of ninth- through eleventh-century images of kings.

SUGGESTIONS FOR FURTHER READING

The Making of the Barbarian Kingdoms, 500–750

James Campbell, ed., *The Anglo-Saxons* (Oxford: Phaidon, 1982). A collection of essays on Anglo-Saxon England by an outstanding group of archaeologists and historians.

Rosamond McKitterick, ed. *The Early Middle Ages: Europe 400–1000* (New York: Oxford University Press, 2001). A collective introduction to early medieval history.

Thomas F. X. Noble, *From Roman Provinces to Medieval Kingdoms* (London and New York: Routledge, 2006). A selection of the most important recent investigations into the current topics of debate regarding the early Middle Ages.

Walter Pohl, ed. with Helmut Reimitz, *Strategies of Distinction: The Construction of Ethnic Communities, 300–800* (Leiden, The Netherlands: Brill, 1998). An important collection devoted to early medieval ethnicity.

Chris Wickham, *Framing the Early Middle Ages: Europe and the Mediterranean 400–800* (Oxford and New York: Oxford University Press, 2005). A massive and important study of local communities in late antiquity.

Ian Wood, *The Merovingian Kingdoms 450–751* (London: Longman, 1994). Excellent survey of early Frankish history with an emphasis on government.

Living in the New Europe

Lisa M. Bitel, *Women in Early Medieval Europe, 400–1100* (Cambridge: Cambridge University Press, 2002). A valuable current survey of women in the early Middle Ages.

Julia Bolton Holloway, Constance S. Wright, and Joan Bechtold, *Equally in God's Image: Women in the Middle Ages*

(New York: P. Lang, 1990). Studies on medieval women from the end of antiquity to the Renaissance.

Julia M. H. Smith, *Europe after Rome: A New Cultural History 500–1000* (Oxford and New York: Oxford University Press, 2005). An examination of early medieval culture.

The Carolingian Achievement

Rosamond McKitterick, *The Frankish Kingdoms Under the Carolingians, 751–987* (New York: Longman, 1983). A very detailed study of Carolingian history with an emphasis on intellectual developments.

Rosamond McKitterick, ed., *The New Cambridge Medieval History, c. 700–c. 900, vol. II* (Cambridge: Cambridge University Press, 1995). An excellent collective history of all aspects of Europe in the eighth and ninth centuries.

Janet L. Nelson, *The Frankish World, 750–900* (London: Hambledon Press, 1996). An excellent and balanced survey.

Pierre Riche, *The Carolingians: A Family Who Forged Europe* (Philadelphia: University of Pennsylvania Press, 1993). A general summary of Carolingian history by a leading French scholar.

Adriaan Verhulst, *The Carolingian Economy* (Cambridge and New York: Cambridge University Press, 2002). The first comprehensive examination of early medieval economic history in decades.

Geographical Tour: Europe in the Ninth Century

Paul M. Barford, *The Early Slavs: Culture and Society in Early Medieval Eastern Europe* (Ithaca, NY: Cornell University Press, 2001). An introduction to eastern Europe in the Early Middle Ages.

Roger Collins, *Early Medieval Spain: Unity in Diversity, 400–1000* (New York: St. Martin's Press, 1983). A balanced survey of Visigothic and Islamic Spain.

F. Donald Logan, *The Vikings in History* (New York: HarperCollins, 1991). General introduction to the Vikings.

Peter Sawyer, *The Age of the Vikings* (New York: St. Martin's Press, 1971). A good introduction to Scandinavian history.

After the Carolingians: From Empire to Lordships

Georges Duby, *The Early Growth of the European Economy: Warriors and Peasants from the Seventh to the Twelfth Century* (Ithaca, NY: Cornell University Press, 1974). An imaginative survey of the economic and social forces forming in Europe in the early Middle Ages.

Heinrich Fichtenau, *Living in the Tenth Century: Studies in Mentalities and Social Orders* (Chicago: University of Chicago Press, 1990). A brilliant evocation of the quest for order on the Continent following the dissolution of the Carolingian Empire.

Timothy Reuter, *Germany in the Early Middle Ages, 800–1056* (New York: Longman, 1991). A readable, original survey of early German history by a British scholar thoroughly knowledgeable about current German scholarship.

For a list of additional titles related to this chapter's topics, please see http://www.ablongman.com/kishlansky.

CHAPTER 9

THE HIGH MIDDLE AGES

HAROLD, KING OF THE ENGLISH

SUBVERTING THE MASTER NARRATIVE

A few decades after William the Conqueror's victory at Hastings in 1066, his half brother, Bishop Odo of Bayeux (ca. 1036–1097), commissioned a great tapestry recording the Norman version of the conquest. An unknown artist, probably an Anglo-Saxon, sketched the cartoon, drawing on models taken from Anglo-Saxon and Carolingian manuscript illumination, but also incorporating images known from more exotic Byzantine and Eastern silks. The women who actually embroidered the tapestry, a strip of linen 230 feet long and 20 inches high, are unknown, but they may well have been Anglo-Saxon nuns—daughters, sisters, and widows of those who lost the field that day at Hastings.

THE VISUAL RECORD

Using techniques familiar to modern film makers—such as jump cuts, flashbacks, close-ups, panoramas, and decomposing movement into freeze-frames—the artist and embroiderers vividly present life in eleventh-century warrior society. It is a masculine society: of the 623 people represented, only six are women. We see peasants working the fields, and craftsmen felling trees and building ships for William's Channel crossing. We see cities, palaces, and churches. We see cooking and banqueting, hunting, traveling, and of course we see fighting and dying. The artists accurately render clothing, armor, and even hairstyles. But the tapestry is not simply a naïve piece of artistry; it is a masterpiece of propaganda.

When King Edward the Confessor (1042–1066) died, three claimants disputed the succession. Anglo-Saxon sources insist that Edward and his nobles chose Earl Harold Godwinson (ca. 1022–1066), the son of the most powerful man in England. King Harold Hardrada of Norway, (1015–1066), a man whose early life as a Viking, as a mercenary in the service of Kiev, and as a commander in Byzantium's elite Varangian Guard fighting in far-off Syria and Africa was already the stuff of legend, claimed the throne by right of inheritance. William, the Duke of Normandy, insisted that King Edward had designated him and that years before, when Harold Godwinson had been shipwrecked on the Norman coast and befriended by the duke, he had sworn an oath to assist William in gaining the crown. This is the scene presented in the panel below. Harold's death, portrayed in the panel opposite, suggests divine vengeance for his perjury. The message is clear. William was the rightful heir and Harold, by his perfidy, merited his tragic fate.

And yet the artists who executed the tapestry for their Norman lord may have subtly introduced a different reading into the story of Harold. He was, after all, a hero to the surviving

Harold as King, as depicted on the Bayeux Tapestry.

■ The death of Harold, as depicted on the Bayeux Tapestry.

English. Harold lost his crown and his life at Hastings, but in part because his army was exhausted. Having defeated and killed Harold Hardrada just three weeks before in the North, he then rushed to meet William's invading forces in the south. Nothing in the tapestry itself specifically labels him a perjurer or usurper. In the critical scene following his coronation, shown on the opposite page, the legend declares him unambiguously the legitimate king: "Here sits Harold, King of the English." Moreover, in this scene he is acknowledged by representatives of the whole society, that is, the workers, represented by the unarmed man at far left; the fighters, represented by the man holding the sword, and the prayers, present in the person of Stigand, the Archbishop of Canterbury. Perhaps the conquered artists were offering a version of William's triumph and Harold's death that undermined the master narrative as told by the winners.

In its vividness, its political subtlety, and its essential ambiguity, the Bayeux tapestry is a fitting introduction to the world of the High Middle Ages. It is a world of workers, fighters, and prayers. But it is also one of cities, merchants, and scholars. Its culture and religion combined, like the tapestry, the extremes of brutal warfare and subtle artistry.

LOOKING AHEAD

This chapter analyzes the world of William and his successors, but also that of the peasants whose fields and villages were ultimately the source of the king's wealth, the knights and ladies who made up the courts, and the religious reform movements that introduced new values to Europe. It also visits the emerging cities of western and central Europe to understand the rebirth of commerce and trade and with it the urban society and culture it made possible. Finally, it traces the development of medieval monarchies, the new political powers created by men such as William the Conqueror.

CHAPTER OUTLINE

THE COUNTRYSIDE

Between the years 1000 and 1300 Europe's population almost doubled, from approximately 38 million to 74 million. Various reasons have been proposed for the growth. Perhaps the end of the Viking, Magyar, and Saracen raids left rural society in relative peace to live and reproduce. The decline of slavery meant that individual peasant families could live and bear children without constraints imposed by masters. Gradually improving agricultural techniques and equipment lessened somewhat the constant danger of famine. Possibly, too, a slowly improving climate increased agricultural yields. None of the explanations is entirely satisfactory, but whatever the cause of the population growth, it changed the face of Europe.

During the tenth century, the great forests that had covered most of Europe began to be cut back as population spread into the wilderness from the islands of cultivation that had characterized the ninth century. In the north of Germany and in what is now Holland, beginning around 1100, enterprising peasants began to drain marshes—a slow process of creating new land that would continue into the 1900s. The progress was not linear everywhere. In England, for example, forests actually gained on plowland after the Norman Conquest of 1066. However, by the mid-twelfth century, the acrid smoke from slash-and-burn clearing of the forest could be smelled all across Europe.

■ This thirteenth-century manuscript illustration shows a woman protecting her crop of millet (a hardy grain more common than wheat in the Middle Ages) from birds.

The Peasantry: Serfs and Freemen

The peasants who engaged in the opening of the internal frontier were the descendants of the slaves, unfree farmers, and petty free persons of the early Middle Ages. In the east, along the frontier of the Germanic Empire, in the Slavic world, in Scandinavia, in southern Gaul, in northern Italy, and in the reconquered portions of Christian Spain, the peasants were free persons who owned land, entered into contracts with magnates, and remained responsible for their own fates. In the course of the eleventh century, across much of northwestern Europe and in particular in France, the various gradations in social status disappeared and the peasantry formed a homogeneous social category loosely described as serfdom. While **serfs** were not slaves in a legal sense, their degraded status, their limited or nonexistent access to public courts of law, and their enormous dependency on their lords left them in a situation similar to that of those Carolingian slaves who settled on individual farmsteads in the ninth century. Each year, peasants had to hand over to their lords certain fixed portions of their meager harvests. In addition, they were obligated to work a certain number of days the **demesne,** or reserve of the lord, the produce of which went directly to him for his use or sale. Finally, they were required to make ritual payments symbolizing their subordination.

Most peasants led lives of constant insecurity. They were inadequately housed, clothed, and fed; subject to the constant scrutiny of their lords; and defenseless against natural or man-made disasters. Their homes offered little protection from the elements. Most houses were small shacks constructed of mud and wood, with one or two rooms inhabited by the entire family and their most precious domestic animals. Roofs were so low that village gossips would often lift up an eave to listen in on their neighbors—hence the origin of the term *eavesdrop.* The huts must have been extremely dark and sooty. They usually had no windows, and until the sixteenth century they had no chimneys; instead, smoke from the open hearth was allowed to escape through a hole in the roof. It is small wonder that tuberculosis and other lung diseases were endemic.

Across Europe, peasant houses were clustered in villages on manors or large estates. That was due in part to the peasants' need for security and companionship against the dangers and terrors of a hostile world. However, in some parts of Europe the clustering was the result of their lord's desire to keep a close eye on his labor supply. Beginning in the tenth century in central Italy and elsewhere, lords forced peasants to abandon isolated farmsteads and traditional villages and to move into small, fortified settlements. In the new villages peasants were obligated to settle disputes in the lord's court, to grind their grain in the lord's mill, and to bake their bread in the lord's oven—all primary sources of revenue for the lord. At the center of the village was the church, often the only stone or brick building in the village. Until the thirteenth century, even the lord's castle was often simply a wooden structure similar to an American frontier fort. The same sort of monopoly enforced on the lords' mills and ovens applied to the church. Villagers had to contribute a tenth of their revenues to the church and to make donations in order to receive the sacraments. In some villages the payments may have actually gone to the church; usually they went to the lord as well.

Each morning men went out to work in the fields, which surrounded the village. In some villages each peasant householder held thin strips of widely scattered land, while pasturage and woodland were exploited in common. While the arrangement may have been inefficient from the perspective of time lost traveling to work different plots of land, such an open-field system allotted all peasant households a portion of all different sorts of land. In addition, the physical separation of the plots provided families insurance against total loss of crops due to sudden storms or other localized disasters. It also encouraged cooperation in sowing and harvesting since it was more efficient for neighbors holding small plots to share equipment and draft animals. In other villages, each household tended a unified parcel of land. The closed fields generally corresponded with greater divergences in wealth within the village and encouraged more independence.

Agricultural Innovation. Agricultural technology gradually changed the ways that peasants worked their land and the amount of food that they could produce. Traditionally, Europeans had worked their fields with simple plows that broke up light soils but were unable to turn and aerate the heavy clay soils of northern Europe. That kind of work could only be done with hoes and shovels—tedious, backbreaking labor that limited the amount of land that could be cultivated. Increasingly, between the ninth and the twelfth centuries, a new, heavier kind of plow became common in Europe. This more sophisticated tool, which contained a metal coulter to cut the soil and a moldboard to turn it, greatly increased the productivity of agricultural work. However, the equipment not only was expensive but also required large teams of oxen or, more rarely, horses to pull it. Such innovations were possible only when lords were willing to invest in agricultural improvements or when free peasants cooperated with each other and pooled resources. In the course of the High Middle Ages, the plows, a rarity in the Carolingian world, became increasingly common throughout Europe.

With the introduction of new technology for plowing came new systems of crop rotation. For millennia, Europeans had known that farming reduced the fertility of soil and that allowing land to remain fallow improved crop yields. Traditionally, farmers divided their land into two parts, one planted, the other plowed (usually twice) but allowed to remain fallow. Sometime around the eighth century, some peasants began to introduce a **three-field system:** one-third of the land was planted in autumn with wheat or rye, one-third remained fallow, and one-third was planted in spring with barley, rye, or a leguminous crop such as beans or peas that added nutrients to the soil. As that innovation became standard after the year 1000, the result was a greatly increased yield, a minimal increase in labor, and an improved diet.

While the men plowed and worked the fields, the women took charge of the domestic tasks. The tasks included wool carding, spinning, weaving, caring for the family's vegetable garden, bearing and raising children, and brewing the thick, souplike beer that was a primary source of carbohydrates in the peasant diet. During harvest time, women worked in the fields alongside the men.

Beer, black bread, beans, cabbage, onions, and cheese made up the typical peasant fare. Meat was a rarity. Cattle and sheep were too precious to slaughter, and what little meat peasants ate came from the herds of pigs left free to forage in nearby forests for acorns and grubs. Inadequate agricultural methods and inefficient storage systems left the peasantry in constant threat of famine. A bad year could send mobs of desperate peasants roaming the land in search of food. In the mid-eleventh century, the archbishop of Trier was on his way to church with his mounted retinue when he was stopped by a crowd of starving beggars. He offered them money but they refused it, forcing him and his entourage to dismount and watch in disbelief while the crowd ripped the horses apart and devoured them.

Negotiating Freedom. The expansion of arable land offered new hope and opportunities to peasants. As rapid as it was, population growth between the tenth and twelfth centuries did not keep up with the demand for laborers in newly settled areas of Europe. Thus labor was increasingly in demand, and lords were often willing to make special arrangements with groups of peasants in order to encourage them to bring new land under cultivation. From the beginning of the twelfth century, peasant villages acquired from their lord the privilege of dealing with him and his representatives collectively rather than individually. Villages purchased the right to control petty courts and to limit fines imposed by the lord's representative; peasants acquired protection from arbitrary demands for labor and extraordinary taxes.

The good times did not last forever. During the late twelfth and thirteenth centuries, the labor market gradually stagnated. Europe's population—particularly in France, England, Italy, and western Germany—began to reach a saturation point. As a result, lay and ecclesiastical lords found that they could profit more by hiring cheap laborers than by demanding customary services and payments from their serfs. They also found that their serfs were willing to pay for increased privileges.

Peasants could purchase the right to marry without the lord's consent, to move to neighboring manors or to nearby towns, and to inherit. They acquired personal freedom from their lord's jurisdiction, transformed their servile payments into payments of rent for their manses, purchased their own land, and commuted their labor services into annual or even one-time payments. In other words, they began to purchase their freedom. The free peasantry benefited the emerging states of western Europe, since kings and towns could extend their legal and fiscal jurisdictions over the free peasants and their lands at the expense of the nobility. Governments thus encouraged the extension of freedom and protected peasants from their former masters. By the fourteenth century, serfs were a rarity in many parts of western Europe.

This is not to say that the freed serfs and their descendants necessarily gained prosperity. Freedom often meant freedom from the protection that lords had provided. It meant the freedom to fail and even to starve. Nevertheless, free peasants were increasingly able to involve themselves in the emerging world of cash-crop farming and to tie into a growing trend toward agricultural specialization. Northern Germany and Sicily focused on grain production; the river valleys of France and Germany focused on vineyards. Areas around emerging towns concentrated on vegetable gardening to supply produce for the growing urban centers. On the one hand, clever and successful peasants acquired land, employed their own workers, and established a level of wealth equivalent at times to that of the lesser nobility. On the other hand, by the fourteenth century bands of unsuccessful landless and starving peasants, expelled from rented property by lords seeking to cut labor costs, began to roam the countryside, occasionally becoming the source of political and social turmoil.

Even as western serfs were acquiring a precious though fragile freedom, the free peasantry in much of eastern Europe and Spain were losing it. In much of the Slavic world through the eleventh century, peasants lived in large, roughly territorial communes of free families. Gradually, however, princes, churches, and aristocrats began to build great landed estates. By the thirteenth century—under the influences of Western and Byzantine models and of the Mongols, who dominated much of the Slavic world from 1240—lords began to acquire political and economic control over the peasantry. In Hungary during the twelfth century, free peasants and unfree servants merged to form a stratum of serfs subordinated to the emerging landed aristocracy and to the lesser nobility composed of free warriors. A similar process took place in parts of Spain where a power-hungry aristocracy won from ambitious monarchs who needed their support the legal right to mistreat peasants, in effect reducing them to the status of serfs. In all the regions, the decline of the free peasantry accompanied the decline of public authority to the benefit of independent nobles. The aristocracy rose on the backs of the peasantry.

The Aristocracy: Warriors and Heiresses

Beginning in the late tenth century, writers of legal documents began to employ an old term in a novel manner to designate certain powerful free persons who belonged neither to the old aristocracy nor to the peasantry. The term was *miles*. In classical Latin, *miles* meant "soldier." As used in the Middle Ages, we would translate it as "knight." Initially, a knight was simply a mounted warrior—the term said nothing about his social status. Some knights were serfs, and in Germany knights remained a distinctly lower social group well into the thirteenth century. However, in France, northern Italy,

■ This drawing from the mid-twelfth century depicts a Norman knight with full accouterments, including the high saddle and stirrups that allowed him to charge holding the long lance.

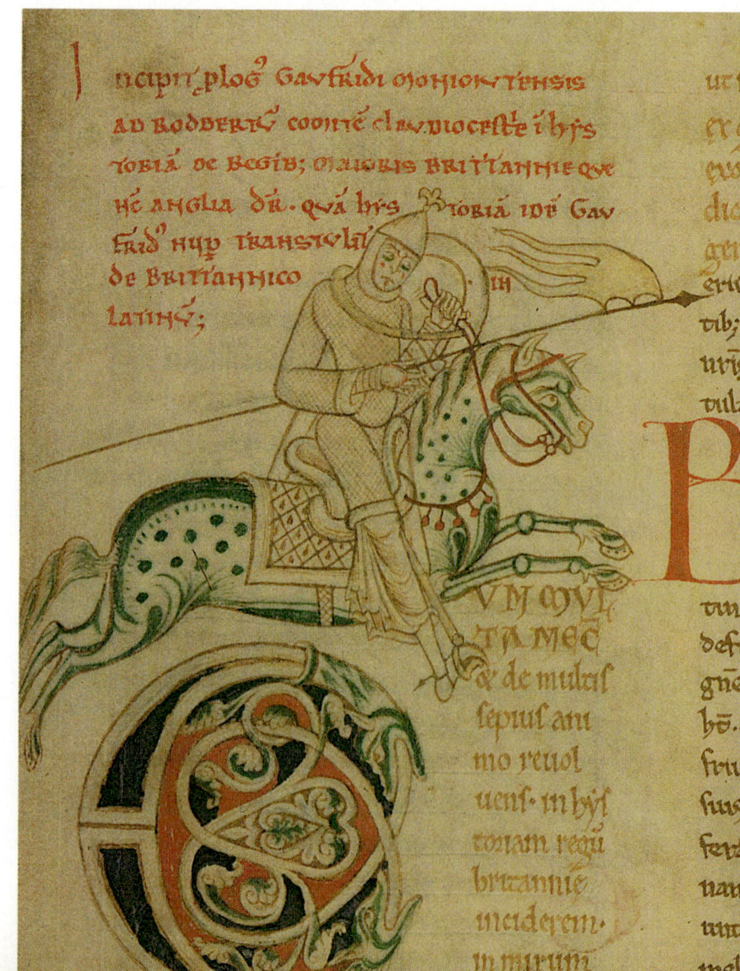

England, and much of Spain, beginning in the eleventh century, the term *knight* (in French, *chevalier;* in Spanish, *caballero*) worked its way up the social ladder. By the end of the twelfth century, even kings such as Richard the Lion-Hearted of England identified themselves as part of a knightly, or *chivalric,* world. A term that originally described a function had come to designate a lifestyle.

The center of that lifestyle was northern France. From there, the ideals of knighthood, or **chivalry,** spread out across Europe, influencing aristocrats as far east as Byzantium. The essence of the knightly lifestyle was fighting. Through warfare that aristocracy had maintained or acquired its freedom, and through warfare it justified its privileges. The origins of the small elite (probably nowhere more than two percent of the population) were diverse. Many were descended from the old aristocracy of the Carolingian age. Inheritance was usually limited to the eldest sons, and daughters were given a dowry but did not share in inheritance. Younger sons had to find service with some great lord or live in the households of their older brothers. Even the eldest sons who became heads of these households could not freely dispose of family property without consulting their kinsmen.

Such noble families, proud of their independence and ancestry, maintained their position through complex kin networks, mutual defense pacts with other nobles, and control of castles. The control gave them the ability to dominate the surrounding countryside. By the twelfth century, nobles lived safely behind castle walls, often even independent of the local counts, dukes, and kings. The lesser nobility absorbed control of such traditionally public powers as justice, peace, and taxation.

A knight receives a token from a lady in this image from a manuscript from ca. 1300 that contains the works of more than 100 German courtly love poets. The ideals of chivalry and courtly love glorified women in literature and song, but in real life the subordinate status of women reflected the values of a martial society.

Aristocratic Education. For the sons of nobles, preparation for a life of warfare began early, often in the entourage of a maternal uncle or a powerful lord. Boys learned to ride, to handle heavy swords and shields, to manage a lance on horseback, and to swing an axe with deadly accuracy. They also learned more subtle but equally important lessons about honor, pride, and family tradition. The feats of ancestors or heroes, sung by traveling minstrels at the banqueting table on long winter nights, provided models of knightly action. In *The Song of Roland*—a legend loosely based on the exploits of a Carolingian count—they learned the importance of loyalty and fierce dedication to duty but also the dangers of pride and reckless faith in one's own sword. In the legends of King Arthur, they learned the disasters that weak leadership could bring to a band of warriors or to a whole country. The culmination of this education for English and French nobles came in a ceremony of knighting. An adolescent from age 16 to 18 received a sword from an older, experienced warrior. No longer a boy, he now became a *youth,* ready to enter the world of fighting for which he had trained.

A youth was a noble who had been knighted but who had not married or acquired land, either through inheritance or as a reward from a lord for service, and thus had not yet established his own house. The length of time one remained a youth varied enormously. It could easily extend into one's thirties or beyond. During this time the knight led the life of a warrior. He joined in promising military expeditions and amused himself with tournaments, mock battles that often proved as deadly as the real thing. A knight could win an opponent's horses and armor as well as renown. Drinking, gambling, and lechery were other common activities. It was an extraordinarily dangerous lifestyle. Many youths did not survive to the next stage in a knight's life—that of acquiring land, wife, honor, and his own following of youths. The basic plot outline of many medieval romances is in essence the dream of every young knight: kill an older opponent, marry his wife, acquire his lands, and found a house.

The period between childhood and maturity was no less dangerous for noblewomen than for men. Marriage was the primary form of alliance between noble houses, and the production of children was essential to the continued prosperity of the family. Thus daughters were raised for dynastic unions, married off at around age 16 and then expected to produce heirs. Given the primitive knowledge of obstetrics, bearing children was even more dangerous than bearing a lance. Many noblewomen died in childbirth, often literally exhausted by frequent successive births. Although occasionally practiced, contraception was condemned both by the Church and by husbands eager for offspring.

In this martial society, the official political and economic status of women declined considerably. Because they were considered unable to participate in warfare, in northern Europe women were also frequently excluded from inheritance, estate management, courts, and public deliberations. This at least was the theory, although we know that many individual women continued to control property, manage estates, and testify in court even in areas where such powers were theoretically forbidden.

Still, the most powerful women were widows who had borne sons and who could play a major part in raising them. Such women were not uncommon. If a noblewoman was able to bear children successfully, she stood an excellent chance of surviving her husband, who was probably at least 15 years her senior and whose military pursuits placed him in constant danger. Such women, experienced in management by years of directing the households of their husbands, well connected by kinship, and experienced in court intrigue from years of attending assemblies in the company of their husbands and sons, could often hold their own with their male counterparts. Their support and alliances were actively sought by aristocrats, kings, and churches.

Land and Loyalty. The noble lifestyle for men and women demanded open-handed generosity to their followers or retainers. Increasingly, codes of aristocratic behavior, courtliness, came to define both a lifestyle appropriate to the aristocracy and a set of values that true nobles were expected to accept. Aristocratic literature, drawing on the poetry of Islamic courts in Muslim Spain as well as on classical literature and indigenous oral traditions, celebrated the value of erotic love in ennobling men and women. The image of the noble lady and her suitor, however, should not be taken as reality: such literature was escape and entertainment, hardly a reflection of the actual relationships between women and men.

To maintain a lifestyle of conspicuous consumption required wealth, and wealth meant land. The nobility was essentially a society of heirs who had inherited not only land but also the serfs who worked their manors. Lesser nobles acquired additional property from great nobles and from ecclesiastical institutions in return for binding contracts of mutual assistance. That tradition was at least as old as the Carolingians, who granted their followers land in return for military service. In later centuries, counts and lesser lords continued the tradition, exchanging land for support. Individual knights became **vassals** of lay or ecclesiastical magnates, swearing fealty or loyalty to the lord and promising to defend and aid him. Normally the oath included serving a certain number of days in the lord's military expeditions, guarding his castles, escorting him, and providing other military services. In some regions, the knight also underwent a ritual of homage whereby he placed his hands in the hands of the lord and acknowledged himself the man (in French, *homme*) of the lord, ready to serve him as far as his freedom permitted. In return the lord swore to protect his vassal and granted him a means of support by which the vassal could maintain himself while serving his lord. Usually the grant, termed a **fief,** was a parcel of productive land and the serfs and privileges attached to it. The vassal and his heirs had the right to hold the fief as long as they were able to provide the service demanded for it. Should they ever be unable to continue or should their lineage die out, the fief returned to the lord.

Individual lords often had considerable numbers of vassals, who might also be the vassals of other lay and secular lords. The networks formed vital social and political structures. In some unusual situations—as in England immediately after the Norman Conquest and in the Latin Kingdom of Jerusalem, founded following the First Crusade in 1099—the structures of lords and vassals constituted systems of hierarchical government. Elsewhere individuals often held fiefs from and owed service to more than one lord; not all of the individuals in a given county or duchy owed their primary obligation to the count or duke. Usually most of a noble's land was owned outright rather than held in fief, thus making the feudal bond less central to a noble's status. As a result, the bonds—anachronistically called **feudalism** by French lawyers of the sixteenth and seventeenth centuries—constituted just one more element of a social system tied together by kinship, regional alliances, personal bonds of fealty, and the surviving elements of Carolingian administration inherited by counts and dukes. Outside Germany, Hungary, and a few regions such as Normandy and Anjou, the society of the eleventh and twelfth centuries was one of intensely local autonomous powers in which public order and political authority were spread more widely than at perhaps any other period in European history.

On Feudal Obligations

The aristocratic domination began to decline from the middle of the twelfth century. Representatives of central authority—counts, dukes, and kings—began to undermine noble autonomy by reasserting traditional public control over justice and warfare. Aided by educated lawyers and financed by taxes on newly emerging towns, the central powers began to mold the chaos of personal ties into a system of hierarchical control, reinterpreting vassalic obligations to incorporate them into mechanisms of royal government.

The economic status of the nobility greatly contributed to the process of centralization. Noble culture demanded ever-increasing expenditures in order to maintain a proper lifestyle, and the revenues from estates were increasingly inadequate to support it. The best source of additional income was paid service in the following of a great lord or a king; from the later twelfth century knights were more likely to fight as paid warriors than as vassals performing their feudal duty. Simple knights and even lords became increasingly common in the royal pay as administrators and judges as well. By the thirteenth century, the old ideal of the independent nobleman living from his own estates and serving his feudal lord for honor and glory was largely a myth. Nevertheless, it was a powerful myth that continued to fascinate and draw Europeans to the imitation of the chivalric lifestyle well into the modern era.

The Church: Saints and Monks

The religious appeals of the peasantry remained those that their pre-Christian ancestors had made: fertility of land, animals, and women; protection from the ravages of climate and the warrior elite; and supernatural cures for the ailments and disabilities of their harsh life. The cultural values of the nobility retained the essentials of the Germanic warrior ethos, including family honor, battle, and display of status. The rural church of the High Middle Ages met the needs of both, although it subtly changed them in the process.

■ This golden reliquary of Saint Fides (Faith) in Conques was the goal of pilgrims from across western Europe.

In the rural world, religion primarily meant action, and the essential religious actions were the liturgical celebrations performed by the clergy. Many of the parish priests who celebrated the Eucharist, performed baptisms, solemnized marriages, and conducted funerals were peasants who had received only rudimentary instruction from their predecessors and whose knowledge of Latin and theology was minimal. But the intellectual factors would become significant only centuries later. The essential qualification was that priests could perform the rites of the Church. What contemporaries complained about was not the clergy's ignorance but its greed and immorality. Ordinary lay people wanted priests who would not extort them by selling the sacraments and would not seduce their wives and daughters. They wanted priests who would not leave the village for months or years at a time to seek clerical advancement elsewhere rather than remaining in the village performing the rituals necessary to keep the supernatural powers well disposed toward men and women in the community.

The most important of the supernatural powers was not some distant divinity but the saints—local, personal, and even idiosyncratic persons. During their lives, saintly men and women had shown that they enjoyed special favor with God. After their deaths, they continued to be the link between the divine and earthly spheres. Through their bodies, preserved as relics in the monasteries of Europe, they continued to live among mortals even while participating in the heavenly court. Thus they could be approached just like local earthly lords and, like them, be won over through offerings, bribes, oaths, and rituals of supplication and submission.

Saints were approached directly. Petitioners pilgrimaged to a saint's tomb and kept vigil there, praying, fasting, and beseeching the saint's protection. The tombs were normally found in monasteries, the "cities of God" that dotted the landscape. As houses of the saints, monasteries orchestrated and controlled the places and times at which the laity could have access to the patrons. As the recipients of gifts to the saints, made in expectation of or in gratitude for supernatural assistance, monastic communities became wealthy and powerful institutions. Every community had its own local saints, either early martyrs of the region or saints whose remains had been transported there. In addition, there were regional and national pilgrimages to saints such as Saint Fides and Saint Denis in France, Saint Stephen in Hungary, and Saint Theodosij in Kiev. (See "A Closer Look: Cathedrals of Light," pp. 256–257.) Finally, there were the great international pilgrimages to Saint James of Compostela in Spain, to the tombs of the martyrs in Rome, and the greatest one of all: to the empty sepulcher of Jesus in Jerusalem.

Monastic Culture. Monasteries did more than orchestrate the cult of the special category of the dead who were the saints. They were also responsible for the cult of the ordinary dead, for praying for the souls of ordinary mortals. In particular, monastic communities commemorated and prayed for those members

CATHEDRALS OF LIGHT

Once the new posterior has been joined
to the anterior
The church flashes with its center made
bright
For bright is that which is brightly cou-
pled with bright
And the noble building flooded by the
new light shines forth
Which has been accomplished in our
time
I Suger, being in charge when it was
being done.

With these verses Suger (1081–1151), abbot of the royal monastery of St. Denis, burial place of French kings (on and off) since the Merovingians, celebrated the first Gothic church and boasted of his own role in constructing it. Although we might think of Gothic architecture as characterized by soaring towers, pointed arches, and flying buttresses, these were but means to an end. Suger's real concern was the flood of light made possible by these new architectural innovations. To Suger and his contemporaries, inspired by Neoplatonic theology, creation and revelation were to be understood as divine illumination, divine wisdom and creation radiating out into the universe. Light then was the fundamental metaphor for God's relationship with humans, and architects sought to bring the experience of this divine radiance into the sacred spaces that were the center of worship.

A CLOSER LOOK

Earlier Romanesque architecture, developed across the centuries from traditions of Roman building, aimed at a different effect: its massive west facades and elaborate sanctuaries, joined by the rhythmic progression of columns supporting massive masonry barrel vaulting, impressed the worshiper with the power and majesty of God. This architecture, too, had overcome impressive technological problems. For centuries, round tunnel or barrel vaults had been used to span relatively small areas such as crypts, while large buildings had wooden roofs supported by rafters. Such construction traditions, reaching back to Rome, had allowed for impressive buildings, but they left them susceptible to fire. The expanded use of barrel vaults made churches fireproof, but the tremendous weight of the vaulting limited the height and width of the nave or main portion of the church. As monasteries and cathedrals were expanded to accommodate ever increasing numbers of worshipers, structural considerations required ever thicker walls, massive galleries above side aisles, and extremely limited window space in order to sustain the growing weight.

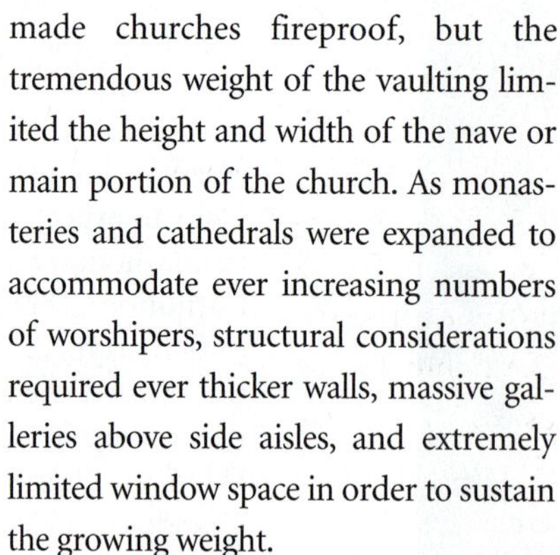

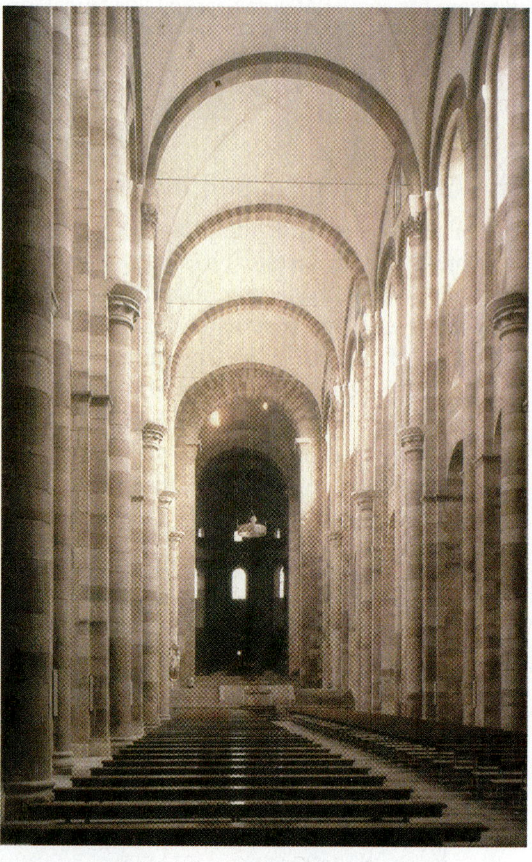

The nave of the Cathedral at Speyer.

Nevertheless the results were impressive. The pilgrimage church of Santiago de Compostela, with its long nave, wide transcept, and long sanctuary, is covered by tunnel vaulting 68 feet in height. The great abbey church of Cluny, rebuilt in the early twelfth century, reached 100 feet from the pavement to the high vault of the nave. The nave of the Cathedral of Speyer, completed in 1137, is the highest of all Romanesque churches, soaring to a height of 107 feet.

Such buildings impressed, but they did not enlighten. And enlightenment, literal and figurative, was exactly what Suger sought in his own reconstruction project. He wanted light everywhere, but he was unwilling to compromise height. Suger, abbot of one of the greatest monasteries in Europe, adviser to kings Louis VI and Louis VII and regent of France while the latter was away on a

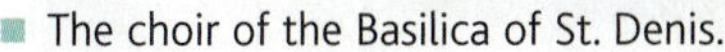

■ The choir of the Basilica of St. Denis.

■ The upper level of the Sainte Chapelle.

crusade, was not going to settle for anything on a small scale. What he sought was a great church that nevertheless had relatively thin walls that could be pierced with windows of stained glass. Although his entire project was never completed, enough remains that one can see his solution. To construct the new choir or posterior of the church, he used a new vaulting technique recently developed in England and France: a framework of diagonal arched ribs carrying the weight of the structure. The systematic use of the ribbed vaults that culminated in a pointed arch allowed thinner exterior walls that could be pierced with large windows. The result, as Suger intended it, was to be a church made up of a thin shell of stone and glass.

St. Denis was a start, but only that. Soon, other techniques were added to the ribbing to carry additional weight from the room without depending on the walls. These were the flying buttresses, already used on some of the larger Romanesque churches. When combined with rib vaults and the pointed arch, this technique made possible the creation of vast, light-filled churches on a scale impossible using earlier techniques. In time, these Gothic structures achieved extraordinary size: the vaults in the naves of the cathedrals of Beauvais and Milan reach 158 feet above the floor. The walls of such cathedrals became frames for massive stained glass windows, flooding the church interior with light and telling the history of the Bible, of the saints, of salvation, in intricate and brilliant images.

But size was never the point of Gothic architecture, and the most perfect realization of Suger's dream of light and illumination is not a great cathedral but a chapel, the Sainte Chapelle, constructed in Paris on the order of King Louis IX of France between 1238 and 1244 to house the relic of the crown of thorns he had received from Jerusalem. Entering the upper chamber of this small church, one realizes Suger's dream fulfilled: the walls had disappeared, replaced with thin ribs of stone that leap toward heaven. Between these ribs are vast areas of stained glass, more than 2700 square feet. To stand in the Sainte Chapelle is indeed to experience the illumination so earnestly sought by Suger.

of noble families who, through donations of land, had become especially associated with the monastic community. Association with such monasteries through gifts and exchanges of property, and particularly through burial in the monastic cemetery, provided noble families the surest means of continuing their honor and prestige into the next world. Across Europe, noble families founded monasteries on their own lands or invited famous abbots to reorganize existing monasteries. The monasteries formed integral parts of the institutional existence of families. They continued the ritual remembrance of the family, providing it with a history and forming an important part of its material as well as spiritual prestige.

Supported by both peasants and nobles, Benedictine monasteries reached their height in the eleventh and twelfth centuries. Within their walls developed a religious culture that was one of the greatest achievements of the Middle Ages. Entry into a monastery was usually reserved for young noble men and women, whose families entrusted them to the monastery at the age of seven. There they were to remain until the end of their lives, first as novices in the religious culture of the monastery and later as mature monks and nuns—the professionals in the dance of medieval religion. The essence of the monastic life was the passionate pursuit of God. The goal was not simply salvation but perfection, and this required discipline of the body through a life of voluntary chastity and poverty and discipline of the spirit through obedience and learning.

The Benedictine's life moved to the rhythm of the divine office, the ancient series of eight hours each day when the monks put aside work, study, or rest and assembled in the monastic church for the communal chanting of prayers, psalms, and hymns. Some of the prayers were fixed. Others varied according to the liturgical calendar and corresponded to the events in the history of salvation and the life of Christ. From matins—recited after midnight—until compline—the last evening prayer—the monks praised God and asked his aid and that of his saints on behalf of themselves, their secular patrons, their families, and all of society.

Proper participation in the communal liturgy required an education closely in tune with the needs of monastic prayer. Its essence was the **lectio divina,** or the process of reading and studying the Old and New Testaments, for which the study of pagan classics and the writings of the Church fathers was essential. Reading and studying were active, physical pursuits. Monks and nuns read out loud, the murmur of their voices filling the monastery even when they read in their own rooms or cells. Study did not mean primarily logical analysis. Rather, it was a system that combined the tools of grammar, memorization, and word association. It emphasized imaginative description, concordance of scriptural passages related only by similar words, and the application of such "scientific" methods as the allegorical meanings of stones, parts of the body, animals, and so on. Such methods were culled from ancient and medieval scientific texts. That study was combined with the allegorical analysis developed by Origen and the early Church fathers to produce a distinctive, nonrational, but extremely powerful form of intellectual and emotional spirituality. Far from denying the physical and erotic side of human nature, the monastic tradition saw in erotic love a metaphor of divine love. The most popular scriptural text in monastic study was the Song of Songs—a remarkable love poem in the Old Testament that never once mentions God.

■ Hildegard of Bingen's fiery vision, as represented by a manuscript illuminator supervised by Hildegard herself.

Monasteries were communities of professional prayers and therein found their social justification. They were also enormously rich and powerful social and political institutions. The monastery of Cluny, in saving souls through prayer, became the first international organization of monastic centers. Cluny had abbeys and dependent communities, called *priories,* throughout Europe. The abbots of Cluny were among the most powerful and influential people in Europe during the eleventh and twelfth centuries—considered as equals with kings, popes, and emperors. In order to remain in form for the strenuous liturgical commemoration of living

VISIONS LIKE A FLAME

In a society that generally took very seriously Saint Paul's admonition that women were "to be silent in the assembly," few women dared to preach or teach, and fewer still were heeded by the rest of society. The great exception in the twelfth century was Hildegard of Bingen (1098–1179), a nun from the Rhine region who spent most of her life in the monastery of Disibodenberg and then in that of Rupertsberg, which she founded in 1150. From earliest childhood she had experienced visions, but only in 1141 did she feel inspired to report them. In time, her extraordinary visions and the religious insights they contained were confirmed by the leading churchmen of her day. After 50 years in the cloister, she set out on preaching missions and for 12 years addressed lay and clerical congregations up and down the Rhine. Her influence reached still farther afield through her letters to emperors, bishops, and popes sternly admonishing them for their failings. The following passage is from her first visionary work, Scivias, *or "Know the Ways," in which she described her first visions.*

Focus Questions

Why do you think Hildegard remained silent for so long about her visions? How did her revelations affect her physically?

In the year 1141 of the incarnation of Jesus Christ the Son of God, when I was forty-two years and seven months of age, a fiery light, flashing intensely, came from the open vault of heaven and poured through my whole brain. Like a flame that is hot without burning it kindled all my heart and all my breast, just as the sun warms anything on which its rays fall. And suddenly I could understand what such books as the Psalter, the Gospel and other catholic volumes both of the Old and New Testament actually set forth; but I could not interpret the words of the text; nor could I divide up the syllables; nor did I have any notion of the cases or tenses.

Ever since I was a girl—certainly from the time I was five years old right up to the present—in a wonderful way I had felt in myself (as I do even now) the strength and mystery of these secret and marvelous visions. Yet I revealed this to no one except for a very few people and the religious who lived in the same community as I; but right up until the time when God in his grace wished it to be revealed, I suppressed it beneath strict silence. The visions which I saw I did not perceive in dreams nor when asleep nor in a delirium nor with the eyes or ears of the body. I received them when I was awake and looking around with a clear mind, with the inner eyes and ears, in open places according to the will of God. But how this could be, it is difficult for us mortals to seek to know.

and dead patrons, Cluniac monks largely abandoned the tradition of manual work, leaving such mundane activities to their thousands of serfs and lay agents.

Monastic Reform. The Cluniac monks' comparative luxury and concentration on liturgy to the neglect of other spiritual activities led some monastic reformers to call for a return to simplicity, separation from the rest of society, and a deeper internal spirituality.

Chief among the reform-minded communities were the Cistercians. In 1098, Robert of Molesme and a small group of monks from the Benedictine monastery of Molesme in France established a new monastery at Cîteaux (Latin *Cistercium*) where they sought to lead a life of strict observance of the rule of Benedict. Under the dynamic leadership of Bernard of Clairvaux (1090–1153), that rigorous, ascetic form of monasticism spread from Ireland to Hungary and by the end of the Middle Ages counted more than 700 houses. Unlike earlier Benedictine monastic movements, the Cistercians established a strict system of control over their far-flung houses through a hierarchy of abbeys emanating from Cîteaux and governed by regular meetings of Cistercian abbots from across Europe. The Cistercians built monasteries in the wilderness and discouraged the kinds of close ties with secular society established by the Cluniacs. They wanted to avoid the crowds of pilgrims and the intense involvement with local affairs that characterized other types of monasticism. Paradoxically, by establishing themselves in remote areas, organizing their estates in an efficient manner, and gaining a great reputation for asceticism, the Cistercians became enormously wealthy and successful leaders in the economic changes taking place in the twelfth and thirteenth centuries.

The rural Church not only served the lay population but worked to transform it. Although monks and bishops were spiritual warriors, most abhorred bloodshed among Christians and sought to limit the violence of aristocratic life. That attitude combined altruistic and selfish motives, since Church property was often the focus of aristocratic greed. The decline of public power and the rise of aristocratic autonomy and violence were particularly marked in southern France. There, beginning in the tenth century, churchmen organized the Peace of God and the Truce of God—movements that attempted to protect peasants, merchants, and clerics from aristocratic violence and to limit the times when warfare was allowed. During the eleventh century, the goals of warfare were shifted from attacks against other Christians to the defense of Christian society. That redirection produced the **Crusades,** religious wars of conquest directed against Europe's non-Christian neighbors.

■ Cluniac and Cistercian Monasteries. Monastic reform spread from eastern France throughout all of western Europe in the tenth through the twelfth centuries.

Crusaders: Soldiers of God

The Crusades left a complex and troubling legacy in world civilization. In order to direct noble violence away from Christendom, in 1095 Pope Urban II (1088–1099) urged Western knights to use their arms to free the Holy Land from Muslim occupation. In return he promised to absolve them from all of the punishment due for their sins in this life or the next. Nobles and commoners alike responded with enormous enthusiasm, and soon gangs of looting peasants and organized bands of noble warriors headed east. The commoners left a swath of destruction in their wake, and few mourned when they were destroyed by the Muslims. The nobles, composed primarily of second sons and lower nobility in search of land and fortune as well as salvation, were remarkably successful. After terrible hardships, the crusaders took Jerusalem in 1099 and established a Latin kingdom in Palestine. For more than two centuries, bands of Western warriors went on armed pilgrimage to defend that precarious kingdom.

The Crusades

The Latin Kingdom of Jerusalem. The Latin kingdom of Jerusalem was the first major experiment in European overseas colonization. Its rulers, a tiny minority of Western knights who established a feudally structured monarchy modeled on the European society they had known, reigned over a vastly larger population of Muslims and Eastern Christians. Although the Christian rulers were not particularly harsh, they made little effort to absorb or even to understand the native population. Crusaders were uninterested in converting Muslims, and their efforts to impose Roman forms of Christian worship and organization alienated the indigenous Christian population of the kingdom. In art, culture, architecture, and social values, the crusaders remained Latins, absorbing only some lessons of military architecture, adopting some of the food and spices, and making some accommodation in their clothing and housing to the climate of the area. Otherwise, the Latin kingdom played a negligible role as a bridge between the Eastern and Western worlds. More pacific contacts in Sicily and Spain were the primary paths of real cultural exchange. The crusaders remained isolated, supported by the regular supplies brought by Italian merchants (for which cities such as Genoa and Pisa obtained valuable economic rights in the kingdom) and by periodic infusions of fighters in the form of individuals or as part of subsequent organized Crusades.

Fulcher of Chartres on the 1st Crusade

POPE URBAN II SUMMONS A CRUSADE

In 1095, Pope Urban II convened a Church council in Clermont, France. The primary focus of the council was to establish peace within the Christian community, but at the same time he launched his appeal for aid to the Byzantine Empire, thus launching what would be the First Crusade. We do not have his exact words, but this version of his sermon was preserved by Fulcher of Chartres, a cleric who participated in the Crusade and who was present at the council.

Focus Questions

What effects does Urban hope the Crusade will have within Christian society? What rewards does he promise those who participate?

Now that you, O sons of God, have consecrated yourselves to God to maintain peace among yourselves more vigorously and to uphold the laws of the Church faithfully, there is work to do. As most of you have been told, the Turks, a race of Persians, who have penetrated within the boundaries of the Byzantine Empire even to the Mediterranean to the Bosporus, in occupying more and more of the lands of the Christians, have overcome them, already victims of seven battles, and have killed and captured them, have overthrown churches, and have laid waste God's kingdom. Concerning this affair I, with suppliant prayer—not I, but the Lord—exhort you, heralds of Christ, to persuade all of whatever class, both knights and footmen, both rich and poor, in numerous edicts, to strive to help expel that wicked race from our Christian lands before it is too late. I speak to those present, I send word to those not here, moreover, Christ commands it. Remission of sins will be granted for going thither, if they end a shackled life either on land or in crossing the sea, or in struggling against the heathen. I, being vested with that gift from God, grant this to those who go. Let those who are accustomed to wage private wars wastefully even against Believers, go forth against the Infidels in a battle worthy to be undertaken now and to be finished in victory. Nor, let those, who until recently existed as plunderers, be soldiers of Christ; not let those who until recently existed as plunderers, against brothers and relations, rightly fight barbarians; now let those who recently were hired for a few pieces of silver, win their eternal reward.

Edward Peters, ed., *The First Crusade: The Chronicle of Fulcher of Chartres and Other Source Materials* (Philadelphia: University of Pennsylvania Press, 1971), pp. 30–31.

The success of the First Crusade eluded subsequent expeditions. Although individuals and small groups of knights constantly undertook armed pilgrimages in fulfillment of personal vows and fought for brief periods, seven more major crusades in all took place between the eleventh and thirteenth centuries. In the middle of the twelfth century, the erosion of the Latin kingdom alarmed Westerners, and the kings of France and Germany, Louis VII and Conrad III, responded to Bernard of Clairvaux's call to take up the cross. The Second Crusade (1145–1149) ended in defeat and disaster at the hands of the Seljuk Turks in Asia Minor.

In 1187, the Kurdish Muslim commander, Saladin, defeated the Latin kingdom at the battle of Hattin and reconquered Jerusalem. Emperor Frederick Barbarossa and the kings of France and England, Philip II Augustus and Richard the Lion-Hearted, responded with the Third Crusade (1187–1192). Frederick drowned in Anatolia, and Richard and Philip quarreled to such a point that Philip abandoned the crusade and returned to France. Richard failed to recapture Jerusalem but signed a peace treaty with Saladin. On his way home, the English king was captured and imprisoned in Austria until his mother, Eleanor, could raise a king's ransom to buy his freedom.

The Fourth Crusade (1201–1204) never even made it to Palestine. It was sidetracked, with Venetian encouragement, into capturing and sacking the Byzantine capital of Constantinople, a disaster that seriously weakened the Byzantine Empire and that remains a major factor in the division between Roman and Orthodox Christianity. The Fifth Crusade (1217–1221), organized by Pope Innocent III and manned primarily by nobles from Austria and Hungary, was unsuccessful. It failed after the crusaders refused an offer by the sultan al-Kamil to exchange the rich seaport of Damietta in return for the holy city of Jerusalem and the rest of the Latin kingdom. Clearly the religious goal of freeing Jerusalem had become less important than economic gain. The Sixth Crusade (1228–1229) was led by the Holy Roman Emperor Frederick II, who regained Jerusalem through a peace treaty with the Muslims. The treaty angered the pope and led to Frederick's excommunication from the Catholic Church. In 1244, the Muslims once again seized Jerusalem. That inspired King Louis IX of France to lead the Seventh Crusade (1248–1254). The Crusade ended when Louis and many of his men were defeated and captured by the Muslims. Louis was freed after a large ransom was paid. In

Geoffrey of Vilhardovin on the 4th Crusade

MAP DISCOVERY

The Crusades

Examine the religious divisions of Europe and the major crusade routes. What different geographical and political obstacles did crusaders face depending on whether they traveled by land or by water? How did the divisions of Christianity and Islam affect the course of the Crusades?

1270, he led the Eighth Crusade against the Muslims. Louis died from a plague soon after arriving in Tunis in northern Africa.

The Mongol Empire. Early in the thirteenth century, hopes for a new ally in the Crusades arose when rumors reached Rome of a powerful empire in the East whose conquests were extending into the 'Abbassid Caliphate. Although Europeans were unsure of just who these people were, they hoped that their leader might be the legendary Prester John, the mythical ruler of a Christian kingdom beyond the edges of civilization. (Actually, these vague rumors of a Christian kingdom were probably distorted accounts of Ethiopia.) The pope as well as the French King Louis IX even sent Franciscan emissaries to try to negotiate an alliance with this new empire to revitalize its efforts to hold onto the Holy Land. What the emissaries found, however, was that this unknown power, far from being the Christian kingdom of legend, was the enormously powerful expansionist empire of the Mongols, who had conquered almost all of China and Central Asia and now were marching west.

The Mongols, like the Huns, Avars, and Magyars before them, were nomadic herdsmen whose loose confederations of clans roamed the steppe lands of northern Asia. The brilliant war leader Temujin (ca. 1167–1227) united the Mongol clans (his title, Chingis Khan, means "universal ruler") and led the Mongols to victory over the ancient Chinese Empire, while others under his command conquered westward. By the reign of Kublai Khan (1216–1294), the Mongol Empire extended from the East China Sea in the east to the Black Sea in the west, creating a vast commercial zone from Hungary to Korea and spanning both ends of the ancient silk route and tying Mediterranean commerce through the Black Sea to the riches of China and India. The Mongol Empire was the first and only world empire to unite Eastern and Central Asia as well as parts of Europe.

The Chinese liked to remind their Mongol lords, "One can conquer the world on horseback, but one cannot govern it on horseback." The conquest was brutal, merciless, and brilliantly successful, but the Mongols had no system with which to rule this vast empire. They were content to leave local governmen-

The Mongol Empire at the End of the Thirteenth Century. Although the Mongol Empire created the largest political unity in world history, it was composed of largely autonomous khanates ruled by different khans who collected taxes and tributes from indigenous authorities.

tal systems intact while collecting taxes and tribute. China continued to be ruled by its vast bureaucracy; Persia by its traditional administration; and Russia by its Christian princes.

In time, the vast empire subdivided into **khanates**, and in each the Mongol rulers came to adopt much of the culture, customs, and religion of the local communities. In China the Great Khan adopted a form of Buddhism while in the west, the Golden Horde became Muslim. So too did Ilkhan Oljeitu (1304–1316), the Khan of Persia, but not before first being baptized with the Christian name of Nicholas (after Pope Nicholas IV) and then becoming a Buddhist, all the while continuing to practice shamanism, and finally trying both Sunni and Shi ʻite sects of Islam. Still, the rulers well into the fourteenth century remained tolerant of all religions and allowed Christian and Muslim missionaries free access to their empire. In the capital of Khanbaliq near modern Beijing, Buddhist Lamas rubbed shoulders with Muslim dignitaries and the first Catholic archbishop, John of Monte Corvino, who was consecrated in 1307. The Great Khan welcomed missionaries of all faiths but had no interest in joining any side in Crusades or wars of religion.

The Crusade as an Ideal. Although military failures, the Crusades appealed particularly to younger sons and knights who hoped to acquire in the east the status that constricting lineages denied them in the west. Other such holy wars were directed against the Muslims in Spain, the Slavs in eastern Europe, and even against heretics and political opponents in France and Italy.

The Crusades—glorified in the nineteenth century by European imperialists, who saw them as the model for Europe's expansion into the east—were brutal and vicious. The crusaders were often motivated as much by greed as by piety. Some began with the wholesale slaughter of Jews in Europe and ended with equally bloody massacres in Palestine. When Jerusalem was taken in 1099, eyewitnesses reported that blood ran ankle deep in the old city. Scalping and headhunting were practiced by both sides, as was the indiscriminate killing of captives. By the end of the thirteenth century, the military failure of the Crusades, the immorality of many of the participants, and doubts about the spiritual significance of such wars contributed to their decline. So too did the rise of centralized monarchies, whose rulers, with few exceptions, viewed the Crusades as wasteful and futile distractions. Although later preachers from time to time urged kings and nobles to take up the cross against the infidel, the age of the Crusades passed with the age of the independent warrior aristocracy.

In the first third of the eleventh century, a French bishop, Adalbero of Laon (d. 1030), described the ideal structure of society as composed of three groups: those who worked, those who fought, and those who prayed. Adalbero identified the workers as the peasants, the fighters as the king, and the prayers as the bishops. Not long afterward, monastic writers adopted but adjusted his schema. The workers remained the peasants, but the fighters became the nobles, and the prayers became the monks. While there were always people who did not fit neatly into any of the systems, in the eleventh and twelfth centuries most Europeans did fall roughly into one of the categories. Peasants, lords, and monks made up the great majority of Europe's population and lived together in mutual dependence, sharing involvement with the rhythm of the agrarian life. From the later part of the twelfth century, however, the rural world became increasingly aware of a different society—the citizens of the growing cities and towns of Europe. The citizens had no place in the simplistic tripartite scheme of Adalbero. They moved to a rhythm different from that of Adalbero's society—commerce and manufacture.

■ Italian Towns and Cities, ca. 1000. The political fragmentation of Italy allowed for the precocious development of autonomous urban life based on trade.

MEDIEVAL TOWNS

For monks, nobles, and peasants, the town was an anomaly—a center of commerce and manufacture populated by people who did not fit well into the traditional social structure that was promoted by representatives of the rural aristocratic order. Towns seemed somehow immoral and perverse, but at the same time fascinating. Monks saw the city as the epitome of evil from which they had fled, and yet in the twelfth century new monasteries were being established in or near towns, while older monasteries established on the outskirts of towns found themselves being incorporated into growing urban areas.

Nobles disdained urban society for its lack of respect for aristocracy and its disinterest in their cult of violence. Still, as rude warriors were transformed into courtly nobles, those nobles were drawn to the luxuries provided by urban merchants and became indebted to urban moneylenders in order to maintain their "gracious" lifestyles.

For many peasants, towns were refuges from the hopelessness of their normal lives. "Town air makes one free," they believed, and many serfs fled the land to try their fortunes in the nearby towns. Clearly, something was very different about the urban communities that emerged, first in Italy, then in the Low Countries and across Europe in the later eleventh and twelfth centuries.

Italian Cities

Urban life had never ceased to be an essential ingredient in Italy, which had maintained its urban traditions and ties with the Mediterranean world since antiquity. Urban populations had shrunk in late antiquity and were dominated by their bishops, who exercised secular and ecclesiastical lordship. However, the towns of the Italian peninsula had continued to play commercial and political roles and to attract not only runaway serfs but even nobles, who maintained fortified towers within the town walls.

The coastal cities of Amalfi, Bari, Genoa, and especially Venice performed important roles in commerce both with the Byzantines and with the new Muslim societies. For Venice, the role was facilitated by its official status as a part of the Byzantine Empire, which gave it access to Byzantine markets. The geographical isolation of most of those cities from prosperous hinterlands gave them an additional advantage as commercial centers. With nothing of their own to trade but perhaps salt and, in Venice, glass, they were forced to serve as go-betweens for the transport of eastern spices, silks, and ivories. The goods were exchanged for western slaves and goods such as iron, timber, grain, and oil. In order to protect their merchant ships, Italian coastal cities developed their own fleets, and by the eleventh century they were major military forces in the Mediterranean. Venice's fleet became the primary protector of the Byzantine Empire and was thereby able to win more favorable commercial rights than those enjoyed by Greek merchants.

Merchants and Capitalists. As the merchants of the Italian towns penetrated the markets at the western end of the great overland spice routes of the Mongol Empire connecting China, India, and central Asia with the Mediterranean, they established permanent merchant colonies in the east. When expedient, they did not hesitate to use military force to win

In this illustration from a fourteenth-century manuscript, the Venetian merchant Marco Polo (1254–1324), with his father and uncle, is seen departing from Venice for points east in 1271. Marco traveled as far as China and did not return home to Venice until 24 years later.

concessions. In 1088, for example, the Venetians sacked the capital of Tunis in North Africa in order to force concessions to their merchants.

The Crusades, armed pilgrimages for pious northern nobles, were primarily economic opportunities for the Italians, who had no scruples about trading with Muslims. Furthermore, only the Italians had the ships and the expertise to transport the crusaders by sea. That mode of transportation offered the crusaders hope of success, since every Crusade but the first, which had followed an overland route, had ended in failure. Moreover, the ships of the Italian cities were the only means of supplying the crusading armies once they were in Palestine. The crusaders paid the Italian merchants handsomely for their assistance. They also granted them economic and political rights in Palestinian port cities such as Tyre and Acre, where both the Venetians and the Genoese had their own quarters governed by their own laws. The culmination of the relationship between the northern crusaders and the Italians was the Fourth Crusade, which, short on funds, was sidetracked by the Venetians into capturing and sacking Constantinople. As noted in Chapter 7 (see pp. 212–213), the Byzantine Empire never recovered from that disaster, and Venice emerged as the undisputed Mediterranean power.

By the thirteenth century, Italian merchants had spread far beyond the Mediterranean. The great merchant banking houses of Venice, Genoa, and later Florence had established offices around the Mediterranean and Black seas; south along the Atlantic coast of Morocco; east into Armenia and Persia; west to London, Bruges, and Ghent; and north to Scandinavia. Some merchants, the Venetian Marco Polo (1254–1324), for example, traded as far east as China and even entered the service of the Great Khan.

The international commercial operations required more sophisticated systems of commercial law and credit than the West had ever known. Italian merchants developed the practices of double entry bookkeeping, limited liability partnership, commercial insurance, and international letters of exchange. Complex commercial affairs also required the development of a system of credit and interest-bearing loans, an idea abhorrent to traditional rural societies. Since usury, or borrowing and lending on credit, was regarded as making money by manipulating time, which belonged only to God, churchmen condemned the practice. They considered it a form of simony, the buying and selling of spiritual goods. In spite of ecclesiastical prohibitions, bankers found ways of hiding interest payments in contracts, thus allowing lender and seller to participate in the growing world of credit-based transactions. Long before the emergence of the Protestant work ethic, Italian capitalists had developed the tools of modern business.

The strength of the Italian towns was that they were able to throw off the rural, aristocratic value system. By the ninth century, even the doge, or duke, of Venice had invested much of his

Medieval Trade Networks

Examine the major trade routes of the High Middle Ages. What commodities and products were plentiful in Europe but scarce in the eastern Mediterranean? What regions were the major wool producers? The major cloth producers? How might silks from the East have arrived in London?

wealth in commercial operations. By the later tenth and eleventh centuries, the passion for commerce had spread from the seacoasts to the towns throughout Italy, and from there to cities such as Marseille, Barcelona, and others in southern Europe.

Urban dwellers generally found nothing ignoble in commerce and banking. By the twelfth century, wealthy citizens, whether descended from successful merchants or from landed aristocrats, were indiscriminately termed *magnates.* The rest of the town's population was called *populars.* The difference between the two was essentially economic. Since commercial activity offered a means of social mobility, the two could act in close accord, particularly when dealing with urban lords or outside powers. In the eleventh and early twelfth centuries, many Italian towns bought off or expelled their traditional lords such as counts and bishops, thus allowing the magnates and populars of the cities to create their own governing institutions or communes.

Communal Government. During the twelfth and thirteenth centuries, Italy played host to a bewildering variety of experiments in self-government as urban populations banded together to take control of their towns from secular and ecclesiastical lords. The relatively small **communes** of citizens (the largest included approximately 100,000 adults) developed a keen sense of patriotism, local pride, and fierce independence reminiscent of the ancient Greek city-states. They manifested that pride in artistic and architectural competition as individual cities and their citizens sought to surpass each other in the construction of beautiful plazas, town halls, and sumptuous urban palaces. The communes also sought to control every aspect of civic life: prices, markets, weights and measures, sanitation, and medical care. Who might wear what forms of dress and jewelry? How many inches of lace might the wife of a merchant wear on her dress? Could an ordinary citizen wear a cloak trimmed with sable? Might Christian women wear earrings, or were those reserved for Jews? Such questions were considered appropriate topics of public legislation.

The unity and patriotism the Italian cities showed the rest of the world were matched in intensity by the violence of their internal disputes. Civil life was intensely partisan as magnates disputed among themselves and with the ordinary populace for control of the town. The conflicts frequently turned violent as citizens took sides on wider issues of Italian and European politics.

Within many towns, the magnates formed their own corporation—the society of knights—to protect their privileged position. Families of nobles and magnates, whose cultural values were similar to those of the rural aristocracy, competed with each other for honor and power. Often they erected lofty towers on their urban palaces, both for prestige and for defense against their neighbors. Feuds fought between noble families and their vassals in city streets were frequent events in Italian towns.

Opposing the magnates were popular corporations—the society of the people—which sought to rein in the violent and independent-minded nobles. The popular organizations could include anyone who was not a member of the society of knights, although in reality they were dominated by the prominent leaders of craft and trade associations, or **guilds.** In many towns, the society of the people was organized both by residential district and by guild and sought to prevent the formation of special interest groups or conspiracies within the commune. To enforce its measures, the society had its own elected officers and its own military, headed by a "captain of the people," who might command as many as 1000 troops against the magnates.

In order to tip the scales in their favor, differing parties frequently invited outside powers into local affairs. The greatest outside contenders for power in the Italian cities were the Germanic Empire and the papacy. Most towns had an imperial faction (named Ghibelline after Waiblingen castle, which belonged to the family of Frederick II) bitterly opposed by a papal faction (in time called Guelph after the Welf family, which opposed Frederick's family). In time, the issues separating Guelphs and Ghibellines changed, and the Guelphs became the party of the wealthy, eager to preserve the status quo, while those out of power rallied to the Ghibelline cause.

In order to maintain civic life in spite of the conflicts, cities established complex systems of government in which officers were selected by series of elections and lotteries designed to prevent any one faction from seizing control. Sovereignty lay with the *arengo,* or assembly, which comprised all adult male citizens enrolled in guilds or corporations. Except in very small communes, that body was too large to function efficiently, so most communes selected a series of working councils. The great council might be as large as 400; an inner council had perhaps 24 to 40 members. Generally, executive authority was vested in consuls, whose numbers varied widely and who were chosen from various factions and classes.

When the consuls proved unable to overcome the partisan politics of the factions, many towns turned to hiring *podestas,* nonpolitical professional city managers from outside the community. The podestas normally were magnates from other communes who had received legal educations and who served for relatively short periods. In Modena, for example, they served for six months. They were required to bring with them 4 judges, 24 cavalrymen, and sergeants and grooms to help maintain order. They could not have any relatives in Modena, could not leave town without permission of the great council, and could not eat or drink with local citizens lest they be drawn into factional conflicts. Their salaries were paid every two months, the last third not being handed over until after a final audit of their term. Only by such stringent means could the commune hope to keep partisan politics from corrupting their podesta.

Northern Towns

The Mediterranean ("mid-earth") Sea was so named because, to the Greeks and Romans, it seemed to be in the middle of the world. In that sense, there were other "mediterranean" seas to the north. The Baltic and North seas and the English Channel tied together the peoples of Scandinavia, Lithuania, northern Germany, Flanders, and England. Scandinavian fish and timber, Baltic grain, English wool, and Flemish cloth circulated around the edges of those lands, linking them in a common economic network. Here, as in the south, there developed urban merchant and manufacturing communities linked by sea routes that were distinguished from the surrounding countryside by the formation of a distinctly urban commercial mentality.

The earliest of those interrelated communities were the cloth towns of Flanders, Brabant, and northern France. Chief among these cloth towns were Ghent, Bruges, Ypres, Flanders, and the wool-exporting towns of England, particularly London. Both Flanders and England had been known for their cloth production since Roman times. In the eleventh century, Flanders, lacking the land for large-scale sheep grazing and facing a growing population, began to specialize in the production of high-quality cloth made from English wool. At the same time England, which experienced an economic and population decline following the Norman Conquest, began to export the greater part of its wool to Flanders to be worked. The production of wool cloth began to develop from a cottage occupation into Europe's first major industry.

Woolen manufacture was a natural for such a transformation. The looms required to manufacture heavy wool cloth were large and expensive, and the skills needed to produce the cloth were complex. The need for water both to power looms and to wash the cloth during production tended to concentrate cloth manufacture along waterways. Finally, as competition increased, only centralization and regulation of manufacture could ensure quality control and thus enhance marketability. Moreover, wool cloth was a necessity of life throughout Europe, and the growing population provided the first large-scale market for manufactured goods since the disintegration of the Roman Empire.

For all of those reasons, by the late eleventh century the traditional image of medieval cloth production had been transformed. No longer did individual women sit in farmhouses spinning and weaving. Now manufacture was concentrated in towns, and men replaced women at the looms. Furthermore, production was closely regulated and controlled by a small group of extremely wealthy merchant-drapiers (cloth makers).

As towns grew, the number and types of jobs grew as well. In this fifteenth-century Flemish manuscript illumination, a master of the dyer's guild supervises as men of the guild dye cloth.

Concentration of capital, specialization of labor, and an increased urban population created vibrant, exciting cities essentially composed of three social orders. At the top were wealthy patricians—the merchant-drapiers. Their agents traveled to England and purchased raw wool, which they then distributed to weavers and other master artisans. The artisans—often using equipment rented from the patricians—carded, dyed, spun, and wove the wool into cloth. Finally, the finished cloth was returned to the patricians, whose agents then marketed it throughout Europe. Through their control of raw materials, equipment, capital, and distribution, the merchant-drapiers controlled the cloth trade, and thus the economic and political life of the Flemish wool towns. Through their closed associations, or guilds, they controlled production and set standards, prices, and wages. They also controlled communal government by monopolizing urban councils. In wealth and power, the merchant-drapiers were almost indistinguishable from the great nobles with whom they often intermarried.

At the bottom of urban society were the unskilled and semiskilled artisans, called *blue nails* because constant work with dye left their fingers permanently stained. Those workers led an existence more precarious than that of most peasants. Employed from week to week, paid barely living wages, and entirely dependent on the woolen industry for their livelihood, they often hovered on the edge of subsistence. In the early fourteenth century, the temporary interruption of grain shipments from northern Germany to Ypres left thousands dead of starvation. Small wonder that from the thirteenth century on, blue nails were increasingly hostile to patricians. Sporadic rebellions and strikes spread across Flanders, Brabant, and northern France. Everywhere they were ruthlessly suppressed. The penalty for organizing a strike was death.

Between the patricians and the workers stood the masters—the skilled artisans who controlled the day-to-day production of cloth and lesser crafts. Masters organized into guilds, with which they regulated every aspect of their trades and protected themselves from competition. The masters often leased their looms or other equipment from the merchant-drapiers and received from them raw materials and wages to be distributed to their workers. If the hope of the common artisan was someday to move up into the rank of master, masters hoped to amass sufficient capital to purchase their own looms and perhaps someday move up into the rank of patrician.

The Fairs of Champagne

Tying together the northern and southern commercial worlds were the great fairs of Champagne. Six times during the year, the towns of Champagne—particularly Troyes and Provins—swelled with exotic crowds of merchants from Flanders, England, Scandinavia, Germany, Brabant, Spain, and Italy. Rich and poor from the surrounding countryside also poured into the towns as merchants from north and south met to bargain and trade under the protection of the local counts.

Medieval Trade Routes and Fairs

Representing Flanders were agents of the merchant-drapiers of each town, whose carefully inspected and regulated products carried the prestige and financial prosperity of their communities. Cloth was known by the name of the town in which it was made, and thus quality control was a corporate rather than an individual issue. From Italy came merchants of the great Italian trading companies to purchase northern cloth for resale throughout the Mediterranean.

Southern merchants brought silks, sugar, salt, alum (a chemical essential in cloth manufacture), and, most important, spices to trade at the fairs. The liberal use of exotic spices may have served as a preservative, but primarily it was part of the conspicuous consumption by which the rich could display their wealth and status.

In addition to the trade in cloth and spices, leather from Spain, iron from Germany, copper and tin from Bohemia, salted or smoked fish and furs from Scandinavia, and local wines, cheeses, and foodstuffs also changed hands under the watchful eyes of fair officials. The officials supervised weights, measures, and currency exchanges. The fair staff also provided courts to settle disagreements among merchants. The great international exchanges connected the financial and marketing centers of the south with the manufacturing and trading communities of the north, tying the north to the south more effectively than any system since the political institutions of the Roman Empire.

Urban Intellectuals

The urban world of the twelfth and thirteenth centuries created forms of religious and cultural expression particularly suited to it. During the eleventh century, cathedrals had become centers of learning as young clerics sought training in schools established by bishops. Initially, the urban schools in Germany, Italy, France, and England were similar to centers of monastic education. However, unlike monks, young men who attended the cathedral schools received an education aimed more at participation in the affairs of the world than in the worship of God. They learned the skills of writing and computation and received the legal training that allowed them to rise to positions of prominence in an increasingly literate and complex urban world. Basic education consisted of the study of the **trivium**—grammar, rhetoric, and logic, the first three of the seven liberal arts, which had formed the basis of Roman liberal education. In some cathedral schools students went on to study the **quadrivium**—the mathematical disciplines of geometry, theory of numbers, astronomy, and musical harmonies. In Italy, students traveled to Ravenna and Bologna to study Roman law.

The Medieval University. In the late eleventh and early twelfth centuries, the pace of urban intellectual life quickened. The combination of population growth, improved agricultural productivity, political stability, and educational interest culminated in what has been called the "renaissance of the twelfth century." In the process developed a uniquely urban cultural and educational institution: the university. Bologna and Paris became the undisputed centers of the new educational movements. Bologna specialized in the study of law. There, from the eleventh century, a number of important teachers began to make detailed, authoritative commentaries on the *Corpus iuris civilis*—the sixth-century compilation of law prepared on the order of the Roman emperor Justinian. In the next century, the same systematic study was applied to Church law, culminating in the *Decretum Gratiani*, or "Concord of Discordant Canons," prepared around 1140 in Bologna by the monk Gratian. The growing importance of legal knowledge in politics, international trade, and Church administration drew students from across Europe to Bologna. There they organized a **universitas,** or guild of students, the first true university. In Bologna, law students, many of them adults from wealthy merchant or aristocratic backgrounds, controlled every aspect of the university, from the selection of administrators to the exact length of professors' lectures. Professors and administrators were firmly subject to the guild's control and were fined if they broke any of the regulations.

North of the Alps, Paris became the center for study of the liberal arts and of theology during the twelfth century. The city's emergence as the leading educational center of Europe resulted from a convergence of factors. Paris was the site of an important cathedral school as well as of a monastic school, that of the Victorines on the left bank of the Seine River. In the twelfth century it became the capital of the French kings, who needed educated clerics, or clerks, for their administrations. Finally, in the early twelfth century, students from across Europe flocked to Paris to study with the greatest and most original intellect of the century, Peter Abelard (1079–1142).

Brilliant, supremely self-assured, and passionate, Abelard arrived in Paris in his early twenties and quickly took the intellectual community by storm. He ridiculed the established teachers, bested them in open debate, and established his own school, which drew the best minds of his day. Abelard's intellectual method combined the tools of legal analysis perfected in Bologna with Aristotelian logic and laid the foundation of what has been called the **Scholastic method.** Logical reasoning, Abelard believed, could be applied to all problems, even those concerning the mysteries of faith.

This illustration from a fourteenth-century manuscript shows Henry of Germany delivering a lecture to university students in Bologna.

So great was Abelard's reputation that an ambitious local cleric engaged him to give private instructions to his brilliant niece, Heloise. Soon Abelard and Heloise were having an affair, and all of Paris was singing the love song he composed for her. When Heloise became pregnant, the two were secretly married, although Heloise protested that their love should not be subject to constraining legal bonds. Although he insisted on marriage, fearing harm to his clerical career, Abelard refused to make the marriage public, preferring to protect his position rather than Heloise's honor. Her outraged uncle hired thugs who broke into Abelard's room and castrated him. After Abelard recovered from his mutilation, he and Heloise each entered monasteries. Abelard spent years as the abbot of a small monastery in Brittany. In 1136 he returned to teach in Paris, where he quickly drew new attacks, this time led by Bernard of Clairvaux, who accused him of heresy. Abelard was convicted by a local council and forced to burn some of his own works. He sought protection from his persecutors in the monastery of Cluny, where he died in 1142.

This fifteenth century image of Abelard and Heloise appears in a manuscript of the popular *Romance of the Rose* which told their story within a long allegorical account of love.

Although Abelard himself met tragedy in his personal and professional lives, the intellectual ferment he had begun in Paris continued long after him. By 1200, education had become so important in the city that the universitas was granted a charter by King Philip Augustus, who guaranteed its rights and immunity from the control of the city. Unlike that at Bologna, the University of Paris remained a corporation of professors rather than of students. It was organized like other guilds into masters; bachelors, who were similar to journeymen in other trades; and students, who were analogous to apprentices.

Students began their studies at around age 14 or 15 in the faculty of arts. After approximately six years they received a bachelor of arts degree, which was a prerequisite for entering the higher faculties of theology, medicine, or law. After additional years of reading and commenting on specific texts under the supervision of a master, students received the title of "master of arts," which gave them the license to teach anywhere within Christian Europe.

Although the years were filled with study, students also enjoyed a spirited life that revolved around the taverns and brothels that filled the student district, or Latin Quarter. Drunken brawls were frequent, and relationships between students and townspeople were often strained because students enjoyed legal immunity from city laws. In 1229, a fight between students and a tavern owner over their bill erupted into general rioting and street battles that left many students and citizens dead or injured. Furious at the government for having sent in soldiers to quell the riot, the masters dissolved the university for six years and threatened never to return to Paris. Masters and students migrated to Oxford, Reims, Orléans, and elsewhere, greatly aiding the development of the other intellectual centers. In 1231, most of the masters' demands were finally met, and many teachers returned to Paris secure in their right of self-governance.

The intellectual life of the universities was in its way as rough-and-tumble as any student brawl. Throughout the thirteenth and fourteenth centuries it was dominated by a pagan philosopher dead for a thousand years. The introduction of the works of Aristotle into the West between 1150 and 1250 created an intellectual crisis every bit as profound as that of the Newtonian revolution of the seventeenth century or the Einsteinian revolution of the twentieth century. For centuries, Western thinkers had depended on the Christianized Neoplatonic philosophy of Origen and Augustine. Aristotle was known in the West only through his basic logical treatises, which in the twelfth century had become the foundation of intellectual work, thanks in large part to the work of Peter Abelard. Logic, or dialectic, was seen as the universal key to knowledge, and the university system was based on its rigorous application to traditional texts of law, philosophy, and Scripture.

■ The Scholastic theologian Thomas Aquinas was influenced by Plato (at lower right) and Aristotle (at lower left), as well as by many early Christian thinkers (shown above him). The Islamic philosopher Averroës is shown lying vanquished at his feet.

The Aristotelian Challenge. Beginning in the late twelfth century, Christian and Jewish scholars in such multicultural centers as Toledo in Spain and Salerno in Sicily began translating Aristotle's treatises on natural philosophy, ethics, and metaphysics into Latin. Suddenly Christian intellectuals who had already accepted the Aristotelian method were brought face to face with Aristotle's conclusions: a world without an active, conscious God; a world in which everything from the functioning of the mind to the nature of matter could be understood without reference to a divine creator. Further complicating matters, the texts arrived not from the original Greek, but usually through Latin translations of Arabic translations. The translations were accompanied by learned commentaries by Muslim and Jewish scholars, especially by Averroës, the greatest Aristotelian philosopher of the twelfth century.

As the full impact of Aristotelian philosophy began to reach churchmen and scholars, reactions varied from condemnation to whole-hearted acceptance. At one extreme, in 1210 Church authorities forbade the teaching of Aristotle's philosophy in Paris, a prohibition the professors ignored. At the other extreme, Parisian scholars such as Siger de Brabant (ca. 1235–ca. 1281) eagerly embraced Aristotelian philosophy as interpreted by Averroës, even when those teachings varied from Christian tradition. To many people, it appeared that there were two irreconcilable kinds of truth, one knowable through divine revelation, the other through human reason.

One Parisian scholar who refused to accept the dichotomy was Thomas Aquinas (1225–1274), a professor of theology and the most brilliant intellect of the High Middle Ages. Although an Aristotelian who recognized the genius of

Averroës, Aquinas refused to accept the possibility that human reason, which was a gift from God, led necessarily to contradictions with divine revelation. Aquinas's great contribution, contained in his *Summa Against the Gentiles* (1259–1264) and in his incomplete *Summa of Theology* (1266–1273), was to defend the integrity of human reason and to reconcile it with divine revelation. Properly applied, the principles of Aristotelian philosophy could not lead to error, he argued. However, human reason unaided by revelation could not always lead to certain conclusions. Questions about such matters as the nature of God, creation, and the human soul could not be resolved by reason alone. In developing his thesis, Aquinas recast Christian doctrine and philosophy, replacing their Neoplatonic foundation with an Aristotelian base. Although not universally accepted in the thirteenth century (in 1277 the bishop of Paris condemned many of his teachings as heretical), in time Aquinas's synthesis came to dominate Christian intellectual life for centuries.

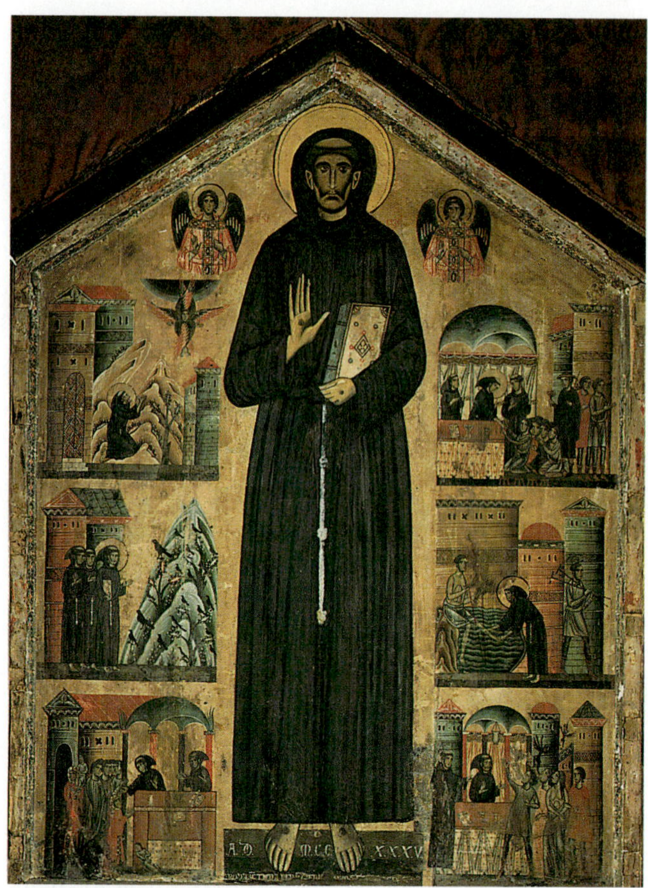

An altarpiece depicting Saint Francis of Assisi with six scenes from his life. His hands show the stigmata—symbolic marks that represent the wounds Christ received on the cross.

Preaching and Poverty. Aquinas was a member of a new religious order, the Dominicans, who along with the Franciscans appeared in response to the social and cultural needs of the new urbanized, monetized European culture. Benedictine monasticism was ideally suited to a rural, aristocratic world; it had little place in the bustling cities of Italy, Flanders, and Germany. In those commercial urban environments, Christians were more concerned with the problems of living in the world than with escaping from it. Lay persons and clerics alike were concerned with the growing wealth of ecclesiastical institutions. Across southern Europe, individual reformers attacked the wealthy lifestyles of monks and secular clergy as un-Christian. Individual monks might take vows of poverty, but monasteries themselves were often very wealthy.

Torn between their own involvement in a commercial world and an inherited Christian-Roman tradition that looked upon commerce and capital as degrading, reformers called for a return to what they imagined to have been the life of the primitive Church, one that emphasized both individual and collective poverty. The poverty movement attracted great numbers of followers, many of whom added to their criticisms of traditional clergy a concern over clerical morality and challenges about the value of sacraments and the priesthood. Although many reformers were condemned as heretics and sporadically persecuted by a new system of Church courts called the Inquisition, their modest lifestyle, their eloquence, and their sharp attacks on church corruption were enormously popular. This heterodox reform movement continued to grow and threatened to destroy the unity of Western Christendom.

The people who preserved the Church's unity were inspired by the same impulses, but they channeled their enthusiasm into reforming the Church from within. Francis of Assisi (1182–1226), the son of a prosperous Italian merchant, rejected his luxurious life in favor of one of radical poverty, simplicity, and service to others. He was a man of extraordinary simplicity, humility, and joy, and his piety was in keeping with his character. As he wandered about preaching repentance, he drew great numbers of followers from all ranks, especially from the urban communities of Italy. Convinced of the importance of obedience, Francis asked the pope to approve the way of life he had chosen for himself and his followers. The pope, recognizing that in Francis the impulses threatening the Church might be its salvation, granted his wish. The Order of Friars Minor, or Franciscans, grew by thousands, drawing members from as far away as England and Hungary.

Francis insisted that his followers observe strict poverty, both individually and collectively. The order could not own property, nor could its members even touch money. Men were expected to beg for food each day for their sustenance. They were to travel from town to town, preaching, performing manual labor, and serving the poor. Francis did not approve of women followers leading such a life but insisted that they pursue radical poverty within cloistered convents that were often within the walls of towns.

In time, the expansion of the order and its involvement in preaching against heresy and in education brought about

SAINT FRANCIS OF ASSISI ON HUMILITY AND POVERTY

By 1223, Francis of Assisi's desire to lead a life of radical poverty and simplicity in conformity with the life of Jesus in the Gospels had inspired thousands to follow his example, and he was obligated to prepare a rule by which his order of Friars Minor would be governed. That simple rule emphasizes his fundamental concerns of humility and poverty.

Focus Questions

How are the friars to provide for the necessities of life according to Francis's rule? How is Francis's form of poverty different from the poverty of the Benedictine tradition?

- This is the rule and way of living of the Minorite brothers: namely to observe the holy Gospel of our Lord Jesus Christ, living in obedience, without personal possessions, and in chastity. Brother Francis promises obedience and reverence to our lord pope Honorius, and to his successors who canonically enter upon their office and to the Roman Church. And the other brothers shall be bound to obey brother Francis and his successors.
- If any persons shall wish to adopt this form of living and shall come to our brothers, they shall send them to their provincial ministers. . . . The ministers shall say unto them the word of the holy Gospel, to the effect that they shall go and sell all that they have and strive to give it to the poor. But if they shall not be able to do this, their good will is enough. . . . And those who have now promised obedience shall have one gown with a cowl, and another, if they wish it, without a cowl. And those who are compelled by necessity, may wear shoes. . . .
- I firmly command all the brothers by no means to receive coin or money, of themselves or through an intervening person. But for the needs of the sick and for clothing the other brothers, the ministers alone and the guardians shall provide through spiritual friends, as it may seem to them that necessity demands.
- Those brothers to whom God has given the ability to labor, shall labor faithfully and devoutly. . . . As a reward, they may receive for themselves and their brothers the necessaries of life, but not coin or money, and this humbly, as becomes the servants of God and the followers of most holy poverty.
- The brothers shall appropriate nothing to themselves, neither a house, nor a place, nor anything; but as pilgrims and strangers in this world, in poverty and humility, serving God, they shall confidently go seeking for alms. Nor need they be ashamed, for the Lord made Himself poor for us in this world. . . .
- I firmly command all the brothers not to have suspicious relations or to take counsel with women. And, with the exception of those whom special permission has been given by the Apostolic Chair, let them not enter nunneries. Neither may they become fellow god-parents with men or women, lest from this cause a scandal may arise among the brothers or concerning brothers.

From *The Rule of St. Francis of Assisi.*

compromises with Francis's original ideals. The Franciscans needed churches in which to preach, books with which to study, and protection from local bishops. Most of the friars accepted the changes. Those friars, the so-called conventuals, were bitterly opposed by the spirituals, or rigorists, who sought to maintain the radical poverty of their founder. In the fourteenth century the conflict led to a major split in the order, and ultimately to the condemnation of the spirituals as heretics.

The order of friars founded by the Castilian Dominic de Guzman (1170–1221) also adopted a rule of strict poverty, but the primary focus of the Dominicans was on preaching to the society of the thirteenth century. While traveling in southern France, Dominic became disturbed at the widespread success of heretical beliefs and the inability of either the regular clergy or monks to combat it by competent preaching. He decided to found a religious order that would outdo the heretics in the severity and simplicity of their lives and would also best them in debate and preaching through a superior education.

The Order of Preachers, as the Dominicans are called, naturally gravitated toward the cities of western Europe, and especially toward its great universities. Dominicans, along with Franciscans, began to formulate for the urban laity of Europe a new vision of Christian society—a society not only of peasants, lords, and monks, but also of merchants, artisans, and professionals. Both Franciscans and Dominicans received enthusiastic support from Europe's laity, particularly in towns, but at the same time they encountered hostility from the diocesan clergy who rightly saw them as spiritual and economic competition. However, protected by reform-minded popes and bishops as well as by powerful lay men and women, they renewed the religious life of Europe, bringing Christianity closer to the common people than ever before.

At the same time, their central organizations and their lack of direct ties to the rural aristocracies made them the favorite religious orders both of the papacy, which used Dominicans to head the Inquisition, and of the increasingly powerful centralized monarchies.

THE INVENTION OF THE STATE

The disintegration of the Carolingian state in the tenth century left political power fragmented among a wide variety of political entities. In general, the entities were of two types. The first, the papacy and the empire, were elective, traditional structures that claimed universal sovereignty over the Christian world, based on a sacred view of political power. The second, largely hereditary and less extravagant in their religious and political pretensions, were the limited kingdoms that arose within the old Carolingian world and on its borders.

The Universal States: Empire and Papacy

The Frankish world east of the Rhine River had been less affected than the kingdom of the West Franks by the onslaught of Vikings, Magyars, and Saracens. The eastern Frankish kingdom, a loose confederacy of five great duchies—Saxony, Lorraine, Franconia, Swabia, and Bavaria—had preserved many of the Carolingian religious, cultural, and institutional traditions. In 919, Duke Henry I of Saxony (919–936) was elected king, and his son Otto I (936–973) laid the foundation for the revival of the empire. Otto inflicted a devastating defeat on the Magyars in 955, subdued the other dukes, and tightened his control over the kingdom. He accomplished that largely through the extensive use of bishops and abbots, whom he appointed as his agents and sources of loyal support. In 951, in order to prevent a southern German prince from establishing himself in northern Italy, Otto invaded and conquered Lombardy. Eleven years later he entered Rome, where he was crowned emperor by the pope.

■ The Empire of Otto the Great, ca. 963. The Ottonian Empire included not only Germany but Slavic lands to the east and disputed regions such as Lorraine to the west.

The Medieval Empire. Otto, known to history as "the Great," had established the main outlines of German imperial policy for the next 300 years, which included conflict with the German aristocracy, reliance on bishops and abbots as imperial agents, and preoccupation with Italy. His successors, both in his own Saxon dynasty (919–1024) and in the succeeding dynasties, the Salians (1024–1125) and the Staufens (1138–1254), continued the tradition. Magnates elected the German kings, who were then consecrated as emperors by the pope. Royal fathers generally were able to bring about the election of their sons, and in this manner they attempted to turn the kingship into a hereditary office. However, the royal families could not manage to produce male heirs in each generation, and thus the magnates continued to exercise real power in royal elections. Because of the elective tradition, German emperors were never able to establish effective control over the German magnates outside their own duchies.

The magnates' ability to expand their own power and autonomy at the expense of their Slavic neighbors to the east also contributed to the weakness of the German monarchy. In the 1150s, for example, Henry the Lion (ca. 1130–1195), duke of Bavaria and Saxony, carved out an autonomous principality in the Slavic areas between the Elbe and the Vistula, founding the major trading towns of Lübeck and Rostock. It was the goal of every great aristocratic family to extend its own independent lordship. In order to counter such aristocratic power, emperors looked to the Church, both for the development of the religious cult of the emperor as "the anointed of the Lord" and as a source of reliable military and political support. While the offices of count and duke had become hereditary within the great aristocracy, the offices of bishop and abbot remained public charges to which the emperor could appoint loyal supporters. Since the ecclesiastics had taken vows of celibacy, the emperor did not fear that they would attempt to pass their offices on to their children. Moreover, churchmen tended to be experienced, educated administrators who could assist the emperor in the administration of the empire. Like the Carolingians, the Saxon and Salian emperors needed a purified, reformed Church free of local aristocratic control to serve the interests of the emperor. The imperial church system was the cornerstone of the empire.

Those laymen the emperor could count on, particularly from the eleventh century on, were trusted household serfs whom the kings used as their agents. Although unfree, the ministerials were entrusted with important military commands and given strategic castles throughout the empire. Despised by the free-born nobility, they tended at first to be loyal supporters of the emperor. In the twelfth century, they took on the chivalric ideals of their aristocratic neighbors and benefited from conflicts between emperor and pope to acquire their autonomy. As old noble families died out, ministerial families replaced them as a new hereditary aristocracy.

Otto the Great had entered Italy to secure his southern flank. His successors became embroiled in Italian affairs until, in the thirteenth century, they abandoned Germany altogether. As emperors, they had to be crowned by the pope. That was possible only if they controlled Rome. Moreover, the growing wealth of northern Italian towns was an important source of financial support if Lombardy could be controlled. Finally, the preoccupation with Italy was a natural outcome of the nature of the empire. Imperial claims to universal sovereignty continued the Carolingian tradition of empire. An imperial office without Italy was unthinkable. Thus the emperors found themselves drawn into papal and Italian politics, frequently with disastrous results. Germany became merely a source of men and material with which to fight the Lombard towns and the pope. From the eleventh through the thirteenth centuries, emperors granted German princes autonomy in return for that support.

The Papacy. The early successes of the imperial program created the seeds of its own destruction. Imperial efforts to reform the Church resulted in a second, competing claimant to universal authority—the papacy. In the later tenth and early eleventh centuries, emperors had intervened in papal elections, deposed and replaced corrupt popes, and worked to ensure that bishops and abbots within the empire would be educated, competent churchmen. The most effective reformer was Emperor Henry III (1039–1056), a devout emperor who took seriously his role as the anointed of the Lord to reform the Church, both in Germany and in Rome. When three rivals claimed the papacy, Henry called a synod that deposed all three and installed the first of a series of German popes. The most effective was Henry's own cousin, Leo IX (1049–1054), who traveled widely in France, Germany, and Italy. Leo condemned simony, that is, the practice of buying Church offices, and fostered monastic reforms such as that of Cluny. He also encouraged the efforts of a group of young reformers drawn from across Europe.

Investiture and Reform. In the next decades, the new, more radical reformers began to advocate a widespread renewal of the Christian world, led not by emperors but by popes. The reformers pursued an ambitious set of goals. They sought to reform the morals of the clergy, and in particular to eliminate married priests. They tried to free churches and monasteries from lay control both by forbidding lay men and women from owning churches and monasteries and by eliminating simony. They particularly condemned **lay investiture,** or the practice by which kings and emperors appointed bishops and invested them with the symbols of their office. Finally, they insisted that the pope, not the emperor, was the supreme representative of God on earth and as such had the right to exercise universal sovereignty. Had not Christ said to Peter, the first bishop of Rome: "To you I shall give the keys of the kingdom of heaven; and whatsoever you shall bind on earth shall be bound also in heaven, and whatsoever you shall loose upon earth will be loosed also in heaven"?

IMAGE DISCOVERY

An Emperor Brought Low

Henry IV kneeling at Canossa to ask Abbot Hugh of Cluny and Countess Matilda of Tuscany to intercede for him with Pope Gregory VII. What does this iconography suggest about the unofficial power wielded by monks and women in the eleventh century? What were the sources of their power?

Every aspect of the reform movement met with strong opposition throughout Europe. However, its effects were most dramatic in the empire because of the central importance there of the Church in the emperor's control of his empire. Henry III's son Henry IV (1056–1106) clashed head-on with the leading radical reformer and former protégé of Leo IX, Pope Gregory VII (1073–1085), over the emperor's right to appoint and to install or invest bishops in their offices.

The investiture controversy changed the face of European political history. The contest was fought not simply with swords but with words. Legal scholars for both sides searched Roman and Church law for arguments to bolster their claims, thus encouraging the revival of legal studies at Bologna. For the first time, public opinion played a crucial role in politics, and both sides composed carefully worded propaganda tracts aimed at secular and religious audiences. Gradually, the idea of the separate spheres of church and state emerged for the first time in European political theory.

The actual course of the conflict was erratic and in the end weakened both the empire and the papacy. In 1075, Henry IV, supported by many German bishops, attempted to depose Gregory. Gregory excommunicated and deposed Henry, freed the German nobility from their obligations to him, and encouraged them to rebel. As anti-imperial strength grew, Henry took a desperate gamble. Crossing the Alps in the dead of winter in 1077, he arrived before the castle of Canossa in northern Italy, where Gregory was staying. Dressed as a humble penitent, Henry stood in the snow asking the pope for forgiveness and reconciliation. As a priest, the pope could not refuse, and he lifted the excommunication. Once more in power, Henry began again to appoint bishops. Again in 1080 Gregory excommunicated and deposed him. This time the majority of the German nobles and bishops remained loyal to the emperor, and Henry marched on Rome. Deserted by most of his clergy, Gregory had to flee to the Normans in southern Italy. He died in Salerno in 1085, his last words being, "I have loved justice and hated iniquity, therefore I die in exile."

Henry did not long enjoy his victory. Gregory's successors rekindled the opposition to Henry and even convinced Henry's own son to join in the revolt. The conflict ended in 1122, when Emperor Henry V (1106–1125) and Pope Calixtus II (1119–1124) reached an agreement known as the Concordat of Worms. The agreement differentiated between the royal and spiritual spheres of authority and allowed the emperors a limited role in episcopal election and investiture. The compromise changed the nature of royal rule in the empire, weakening the emperors and contributing to the long-term decline of royal government in Germany.

The decline that began with the investiture controversy continued as emperors abandoned political power north of the Alps in order to pursue their ambitions in Italy. Frederick I Barbarossa (1152–1190) spent much of his reign attempting to reimpose imperial authority on and to collect imperial incomes from the rich towns of northern Italy. For this he needed the support of the German princes, and he granted them extraordinary privileges in return for their cooperation south of the Alps. In 1156, for example, he gave Henry Jasomirgott (ca. 1114–1177) virtual autonomy in the newly created duchy of Austria. Still, the combined efforts of the Lombard towns and the papacy were too much for Frederick and his armies to win a decisive victory. By the time of Frederick's death in Germany in 1190—he drowned crossing a river while on a crusade—the emperor was more a feudal lord

GENEALOGY

The Saxon, Salian, and Staufen Dynasties

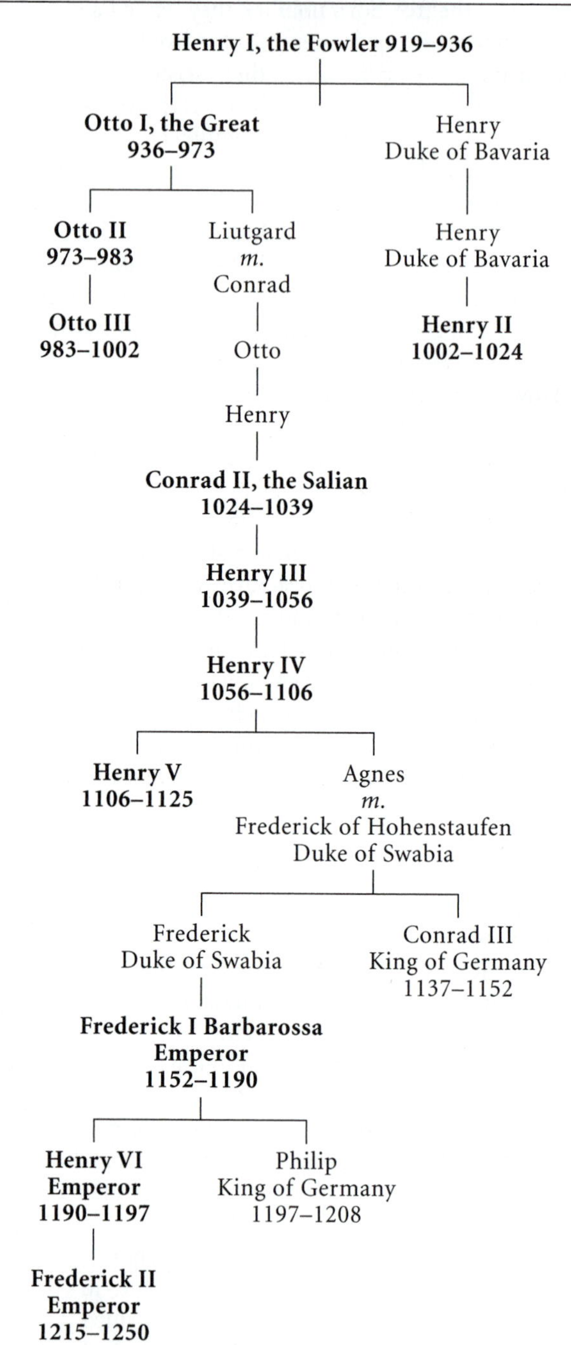

than a sovereign, and in Italy his authority was disputed by the papacy and the towns. Frederick's successors continued his policy of focusing on Italy, with no better success. In 1230, Frederick II (1215–1250) conceded to each German prince sovereign rights in his own territory. From the thirteenth to the nineteenth centuries the princes ruled their territories as independent states, leaving the office of emperor a hollow title.

The investiture controversy ultimately compromised the authority of the pope as well as that of the emperor. First, the series of compromises beginning with the Concordat of Worms established a novel and potent tradition in Western political thought: the definition of separate spheres of authority for secular and religious government. Second, while in the short run popes were able to exercise enormous political influence, from the thirteenth century they were increasingly unable to make good their claims to absolute authority.

The Pinnacle of Papal Power. Papal power was based on more than Scripture. Over the centuries, the popes had acquired large amounts of land in central Italy and in the Rhone Valley that formed the nucleus of the Papal States. Moreover, in every corner of Europe bishops and clergy were, at least in theory, agents of papal programs. The elaboration of systematic canon law encouraged by the papal reformers as a weapon in the investiture controversy created a system of courts and legal institutions more sophisticated than that of any secular monarch. Church courts claimed jurisdiction over all clerics, regardless of the nature of the legal problem, and over all baptized Christians in such fundamental issues as legitimacy of marriages, inheritances, and oaths.

CHRONOLOGY

Prominent Popes and Religious Figures of the High Middle Ages

1049–1054*	Pope Leo IX
1073–1085	Pope Gregory VII
1088–1099	Pope Urban II
1098–1179	Hildegard of Bingen
1119–1124	Pope Calixtus II
1170–1221	Saint Dominic
1182–1226	Saint Francis of Assisi
1198–1216	Pope Innocent III
1225–1274	Saint Thomas Aquinas
1294–1303	Pope Boniface VIII

* Dates for popes are dates of reign.

During the pontificate of Innocent III (1198–1216), the papacy reached the height of its powers. Innocent made and deposed emperors, excommunicated kings, summoned a crusade against heretics in the south of France, and placed whole countries such as England and France under interdict, that is, the suspension of all religious services, when rulers dared to contradict him. Still he found time to support Francis of Assisi and Dominic, and in 1215 to call the Fourth Lateran Council, which culminated the reforms of the past century and had a lasting effect on the spiritual life of clergy and laity alike.

At the council, more than 1200 assembled bishops and abbots, joined by great nobles from across Europe, defined fundamental doctrines such as the nature of the Eucharist, ordered annual confession of sins, and detailed procedures for the election of bishops. They also mandated a strict lifestyle for clergy and forbade their participation in judicial procedures in which accused persons had to undergo painful ordeals, such as grasping a piece of red-hot iron and carrying it a prescribed distance, to prove their innocence. More ominously, the council also mandated that Jews wear special identifying markings on their clothing—a sign of the increasing hostility Christians felt toward the Jews in their midst.

During the thirteenth century, the papacy continued to perfect its legal system and its control over clergy throughout Europe. However, politically the popes were unable to assert their claims to universal supremacy. This lack of success was true both in Italy, where the communes in the north and the kingdom of Naples in the south resisted direct papal control, and in the emerging kingdoms north of the Alps, where monarchs successfully intervened in Church affairs. The old claims of papal authority rang increasingly hollow. When Pope Boniface VIII (1294–1303) attempted to prevent the French king Philip IV (1285–1314) from taxing the French clergy, boasting that he could depose kings "like servants" if necessary, Philip proved him wrong. Philip's agents hired a gang of adventurers who kidnapped the pope, plundered his treasury, and released him a broken, humiliated wreck. He died three weeks later. The French king who had engineered Boniface's humiliation represented a new political tradition much more limited but ultimately more successful than either the empire or the papacy—the medieval nation-state.

The Nation-States: France and England

The office of king was a less pretentious and more familiar one than that of emperor. As the Carolingian world disintegrated, a variety of kingdoms had appeared in France, Italy, Burgundy, and Provence. Beyond the confines of the old Carolingian world, kingship was well established in England and northern Spain. In Scandinavia, Poland, Bohemia, and Hungary, powerful chieftains were consolidating royal power at the expense of their aristocracies. The claims of kings were much more modest than those of emperors or popes. Kings lay claim to a limited territory and, while the king was anointed and thus a "Christus" (from the Greek word for sacred oil), kings were only one of many representatives of God on earth. Finally, kings were far from absolute rulers. During the tenth and eleventh centuries, the powers of justice, coinage, taxation, and military command, once considered public, had been usurped by aristocrats and nobles. Kings needed the support of the magnates, and often—as in the case of France—the dukes and counts were wealthier and more powerful than the kings. Still, between the tenth and fourteenth centuries some monarchies, especially those of France and England, developed into vigorous, powerful, centralized kingdoms. In the process they gave birth to what has become the modern state.

France: Biology, Bureaucracy, and Sanctity. In 987, when Hugh Capet was elected king of the West Franks, no one suspected that his successors would become the most powerful rulers of Europe, for they were relatively weak magnates whose only real power lay in the region between Paris and Orléans. The dukes of Normandy, descendants of Vikings whose settlement had been recognized by Frankish kings, ruled their duchy with an authority of which the kings could only dream. Less than a century later, Duke William of Normandy expanded his power even more by conquering England. In the twelfth century, the English kings ruled a vast collection of hereditary lands on both sides of the English Channel called the Angevin Empire, territories much richer than those ruled by the French king. The counts of Flanders also ruled a prosperous region much better unified than the French king's small territory in the area around Paris. In the south, the counts of Poitou, who were also dukes of Aquitaine, were building up a powerful territorial principality in this most Romanized region of the kingdom. In Anjou, an ambitious aristocratic family consolidated to form a virtually independent principality. Nevertheless, under Hugh's successors, the kingdom of France became the most powerful monarchy in Europe and the center of European learning, architecture, and art.

Biology and bureaucracy created the medieval French monarchy. Between 987 and 1314, every royal descendant of Hugh Capet (after whom the dynasty was called the Capetian) left a male heir—an extraordinary record for a medieval family. During the same period, by comparison, the office of emperor was occupied by men from no fewer than nine families. By simply outlasting the families of their great barons, the Capetian kings were able to absorb lands when other families became extinct. That success was not just the result of luck. Kings such as Robert the Pious (996–1031) and Louis VII (1137–1180) risked excommunication in order to divorce wives who had not produced male heirs. In 1152, Louis had his marriage with the richest heiress of the twelfth century, Eleanor of Aquitaine (1122–1204), annulled, in part because she had given him no sons. With the annulment he also lost the chance to absorb her territories of Aquitaine and Poitou. A few months later Eleanor married Count Henry of Anjou (1133–1189), who two years later became King Henry II of England. Imagine Louis's chagrin when, with Henry, Eleanor produced four sons, in the process making the English kings the greatest magnates in France!

The Capetians' long run of biological luck, combined with the practice of having a son crowned during his father's lifetime and thus being firmly established before his father's death, was only part of the explanation for the Capetian success. The Capetians also wisely used their position as consecrated sovereigns to build a power base in the Île-de-France (the region around Paris) and among the bishops and abbots of the kingdom, and then to insist on their feudal rights as the lords of the great dukes and counts of France. It was this foundation that Philip II (1180–1223), the son of Louis VII by his third wife, used to create the French monarchy.

Philip II was known to posterity as Augustus or "the aggrandizer" because, through his ruthless political intrigue and brilliant organizational sense, he more than doubled the territory he controlled and more than quadrupled the revenue of the

MAP DISCOVERY

The Consolidation of France Under the Capetians

How did the French royal domain compare with the holdings of the English king in France at the end of the twelfth century? What were the major counties that the French monarchy added to its control over the next century? From reading the text, how do you explain the loss of English possessions with the exception of Gascony by 1252?

French crown. Through marriage he acquired Vermandois, the Amienois, Artois, and Valois. He later absorbed Flanders and set the stage for the absorption of the great county of Toulouse by his son Louis VIII (1223–1226) in the aftermath of the Albigensian Crusade launched by Pope Innocent III. Philip's greatest coup, however, was the confiscation of all the continental possessions of the English king John (1199–1216), the son of Henry II and Eleanor of Aquitaine. Although sovereign in England, as lord of Normandy, Anjou, Maine, and Touraine, John was technically a vassal of King Philip. When John married the fiancée of one of his continental vassals, the outraged vassal appealed to Philip in his capacity as John's lord. Philip summoned John to appear before the royal court, and when John refused to do so, Philip ordered him to surrender all of his continental fiefs. That meant war, and one by one John's continental possessions fell to the French king. Philip's victory over John's ally, the emperor Otto IV (1198–1215), at Bouvines in 1214 sealed the English loss of Normandy, Maine, Anjou, Poitou, and Touraine. (See Map Discovery: The Consolidation of France under the Capetians.)

As important as the absorption of the vast regions was the administrative system Philip organized to govern them. Using members of families from the old royal demesne, he set up administrative officials called *baillis* and *seneschals*—salaried nonfeudal agents who collected his revenues and represented his interests. The baillis, who were drawn from common families and who often had received their education at the University of Paris, were the foundation of the French bureaucracy, which grew in strength and importance throughout the thirteenth century. By governing the regions of France according to local traditions but always with an eye to the king's interests, the bureaucrats did more than anyone else to create a stable, enduring political system.

Philip's grandson Louis IX (1226–1270) fine-tuned the administrative machine and endowed it with the aura of sanctity. Louis was as perfect an embodiment of medieval Christian virtue as Saint Francis of Assisi, who died in the year of Louis's coronation. Generous and pious but also brave and capable, Louis took seriously his obligation to provide justice for the poor and protection for the weak. A disastrous Crusade in 1248, which ended in his capture and ransom in Egypt, convinced Louis that his failure was punishment for his sins and those of his government. When he returned to France, he dispatched investigators to correct abuses by baillis and other royal officials and restored property unjustly confiscated by his father's agents during the Albigensian Crusade. In addition, he established a permanent central court in Paris to hear appeals from throughout the kingdom. Although much of the work was handled by a growing staff of professional jurists, Louis often became involved personally. As one of his advisers recalled years later, "In summer, after hearing mass, the king often went to the wood of Vincennes, where he would sit down with his back against an oak, and make us all sit round him. Those who had any suit to present could come to speak to him without hindrance from an usher or any other person."

In 1270 Louis attempted another Crusade and died in an epidemic in Tunis. The good will and devotion that he won from his subjects were a precious heritage that his successors were able to exploit for centuries. When his grandson Philip the Fair (1285–1314) faced the threat of Boniface VIII (see p. 277), he could rely on subjects and agents for whom the king of France, and not the pope, was sovereign.

The growth of royal power transformed the traditional role of the aristocracy. As the power and wealth of kings in-

GENEALOGY

The Capetian Dynasty of France

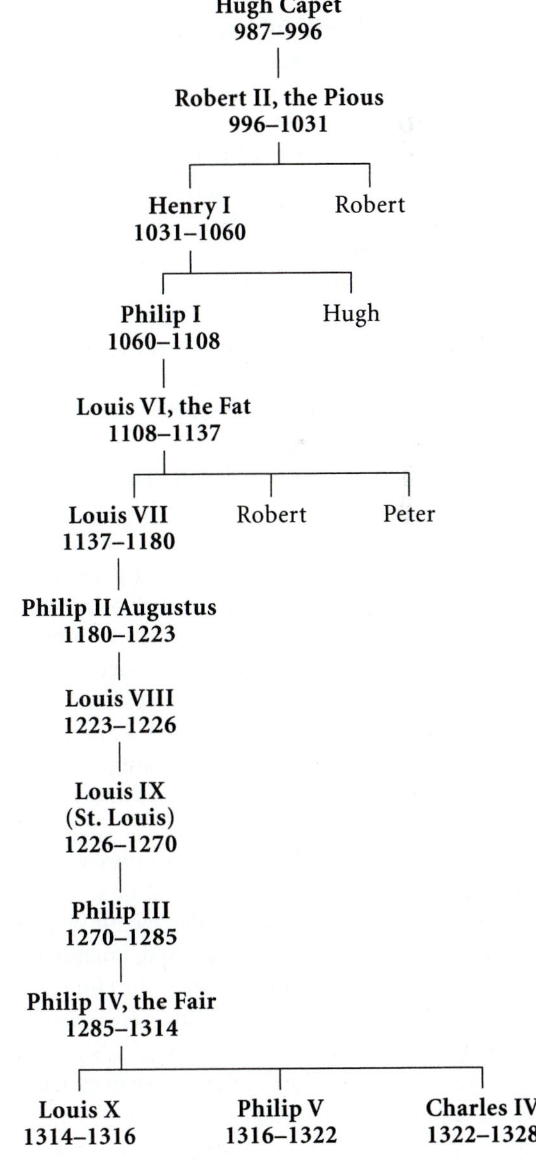

creased, the ability of the nobility to maintain its independence decreased. Royal judges undermined lords' control over the peasantry. Royal revenues enabled kings to hire warriors rather than relying on traditional feudal levies. At the same time, the increasing expenses of the noble lifestyle forced all but the wealthiest aristocrats to look for sources of income beyond their traditional estates. Increasingly they found this in royal service. Thus, in the thirteenth century the nobility began to lose some of its independence to the state.

England: Conquest, Accounting, and Cooperation. A very different path brought the English monarchy to a level of power similar to that of the French kings by the end of the thirteenth century. While France was made by a family and its bureaucracy, the kingdom originally forged by Alfred and his descendants was transformed by the successors of William the Conqueror, using its judges and its people, often in spite of themselves.

When King Edward the Confessor (1042–1066) died, three claimants disputed the succession. Anglo-Saxon sources insist that Edward and his nobles chose Earl Harold Godwinson (ca. 1022–1066) over Duke William of Normandy and the Norwegian king Harold III (1045–1066). However, as we have seen, William insisted that Edward had designated him and that years before, when Earl Harold had been shipwrecked on the Norman coast and befriended by the duke, he had sworn an oath to assist William in gaining the crown. Harold of Norway and William sailed for England. Harold Godwinson defeated the Norwegian's army and killed the king, but he met his end shortly afterward on the bloody field of Hastings, and William secured the throne.

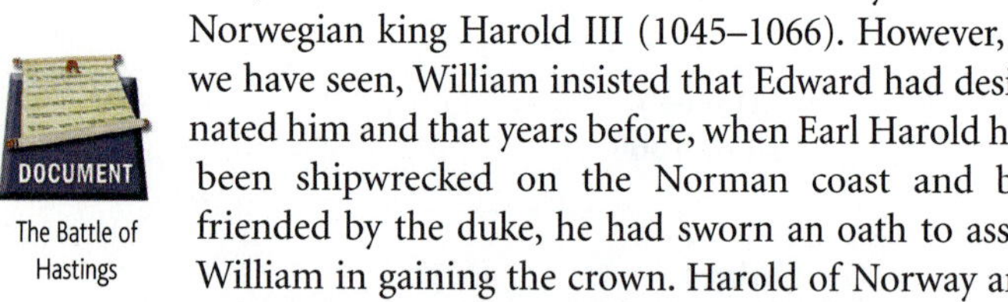

DOCUMENT The Battle of Hastings

William's England was a small, insular kingdom that had been united by Viking raids little more than a century before. Hostile Celtic societies bordered it to the north and west. Still, it had important strengths. First, the king of the English was not simply a feudal lord, a first among equals—he was a sovereign. Second, Anglo-Saxon government had been participatory, with the free men of each shire taking part in court sessions and sharing the responsibilities of government. Finally, the king had agents, or reeves, in each shire (shire reeves, or sheriffs) who were responsible for representing the king's interests, presiding over the local court, and collecting royal taxes and incomes.

The ability to raise money was the most important aspect of the English kingship for William the Conqueror and his immediate successors, who remained thoroughly continental in interest, culture, and language (the first English king to speak English fluently was probably King John). England was seen primarily as a source of revenue. To tap that wealth, the Norman kings transformed rather than abolished Anglo-Saxon governmental traditions, adding Norman feudalism and administrative control to Anglo-Saxon kingship.

William preserved English government while replacing Anglo-Saxon officers with his continental vassals, chiefly Normans and Flemings. He rewarded his supporters with land confiscated from the defeated Anglo-Saxons, but he was careful to give out land only in fief. In contrast to continental practice, where many lords owned vast estates outright, in England all land was held directly or indirectly by the king. Because he wanted to know the extent of his new kingdom and its wealth, William ordered a comprehensive survey of all royal rights. The recorded account, known as the Domesday Book, was the most extensive investigation of economic rights since the late Roman tax rolls had been abandoned by the Merovingians.

Since William and his successors concentrated on their continental possessions and spent little time in England, they needed an efficient system of controlling the kingdom in their absence. To that end they developed the royal court, an institution inherited from their Anglo-Saxon predecessors, into an efficient system of fiscal and administrative supervision. The most important innovation was the use of a large checkerboard, or exchequer, which functioned like a primitive computer to audit the returns of their sheriffs. Annual payments were recorded on long rolls of parchment called *pipe rolls,* the first continuous accounting system in Europe. The use of extensive written records and strict accounting produced the most efficient and prosperous royal administration in Europe.

Almost two decades of warfare over the succession in the first half of the twelfth century greatly weakened royal authority, but Henry II (1154–1189) reestablished central power by reasserting his authority over the nobility and through his legal reforms. Using his continental wealth and armies, he brought the English barons into line, destroyed private castles, and reasserted his rights to traditional royal incomes. He strengthened royal courts by expanding royal jurisdiction at the expense of Church tribunals and of the courts owned by feudal lords.

Henry's efforts to control the clergy led to one of the epic clashes of the investiture controversy. The archbishop of Canterbury, Thomas à Becket (ca. 1118–1170), although a personal friend of Henry who had made him first chancellor and then archbishop, refused to accept the king's claim to jurisdiction over clergy. In spite of his friendship with the king, Becket, who had been educated at Paris, was deeply influenced by the papal reform movement and had a great sense of the dignity of his office. For six years, Becket lived in exile on the Continent and infuriated Henry by his stubborn adherence to the letter of Church law. He was allowed to return to England in 1170, but that same year he was struck down in his own cathedral by four knights eager for royal favor. The king did penance but, unlike the German emperors, ultimately preserved royal authority over the Church.

Henry's program to assert royal courts over local and feudal ones was even more successful, laying the foundation for a system of uniform judicial procedures through which royal justice reached throughout the kingdom: the common law. In France, royal agents observed local legal traditions but sought always to turn them to the king's advantage. In contrast, Henry's legal system simplified and cut through the complex tangle of local and feudal jurisdictions concerning land law. Any free person could purchase, for a modest price, a letter, or writ, from the king ordering the local sheriff to impanel a jury to determine if that person had been recently dispossessed of an estate, regardless of that person's legal right to the property. The procedure was swift and efficient. If the jury found for the plaintiff, the sheriff immediately restored the property, by force if necessary. While juries may not have meted out justice, they did resolve conflicts, and they did so in a way that protected landholders. The writs became enormously successful and expanded the jurisdiction of royal courts into areas previously outside royal jurisdiction.

Henry's son John may have made the greatest contribution to the development of the English state by losing Normandy and most of his other continental lands. Loss of those territories forced English kings to concentrate on ruling England, not their continental territories. Moreover, John's financial difficulties, brought about by his unsuccessful wars to recover his continental holdings, led him to such extremes of fiscal extortion that his barons, his prelates, and the townspeople of

THE GREAT CHARTER

Faced with defeat abroad at the hands of the French King Philip Augustus and baronial revolt at home, in 1215 King John was forced to sign the Magna Carta, the "great charter" guaranteeing the traditional rights of the English nobility. Although a conservative document, in time it was interpreted as the guarantee of the fundamental rights of the English people.

Focus Questions

What protections does the Magna Carta offer women? What protections does the Magna Carta offer in the administration of justice?

John, by the grace of God king of England, lord of Ireland, duke of Normandy and of Aquitaine, and count of Anjou, to his archbishops, bishops, abbots, earls, barons, justiciars, foresters, sheriffs, reeves, ministers, and all his bailiffs and faithful men, greeting. Know that, through the inspiration of God, for the health of our soul and [the souls] of all our ancestors and heirs, for the honour of God and the exaltation of Holy Church, and for the betterment of our realm, by the counsel of our venerable fathers . . . of our nobles . . . and of our other faithful men—

1. We have in the first place granted to God and by this our present charter have confirmed, for us and our heirs forever, that the English Church shall be free and shall have its rights entire and its liberties inviolate. . . . We have also granted to all freemen of our kingdom, for us and our heirs forever, all the liberties hereinunder written, to be had and held by them and their heirs of us and our heirs.
2. If any one of our earls or barons or other men holding of us in chief dies, and if when he dies his heir is of full age and owes relief [that heir] shall have his inheritance for the ancient relief. . . .
6. Heirs shall be married without disparagement.
7. A widow shall have her marriage portion and inheritance immediately after the death of her husband and without difficulty; nor shall she give anything for her dowry or for her marriage portion or for her inheritance—which inheritance she and her husband were holding on the day of that husband's death. . . .
8. No widow shall be forced to marry so long as she wishes to live without a husband; yet so that she shall give security against marrying without our consent if she holds of us, or without the consent of her lord if she holds of another. . . .
12. Scutage or aid shall be levied in our kingdom only by the common counsel of our kingdom, except for ransoming our body, for knighting our eldest son, and for once marrying our eldest daughter; and for these [purposes] only a reasonable aid shall be taken. The same provision shall hold with regard to the aids of the city of London. . . .
17. Common pleas shall not follow our court, but shall be held in some definite place. . . .
20. A freeman shall be amerced for a small offence only according to the degree of the offence; and for a grave offence he shall be amerced according to the gravity of the offence, saving his contentment [sufficient property to guarantee sustenance for himself and his family]. And a merchant shall be amerced in the same way, saving his merchandise; and a villein in the same way, saving his wainage [harvested crops necessary for seed and upkeep of his farm]. . . .
39. No freeman shall be captured or imprisoned or disseised [dispossessed of his estates] or outlawed or exiled or in any way destroyed, nor will we go against him or send against him, except by the lawful judgment of his peers or by the law of the land. . . .
54. No one shall be seized or imprisoned on the appeal of a woman for the death of any one but her husband. . . .

From the Magna Carta.

GENEALOGY

The Norman and Plantagenet Kings of England

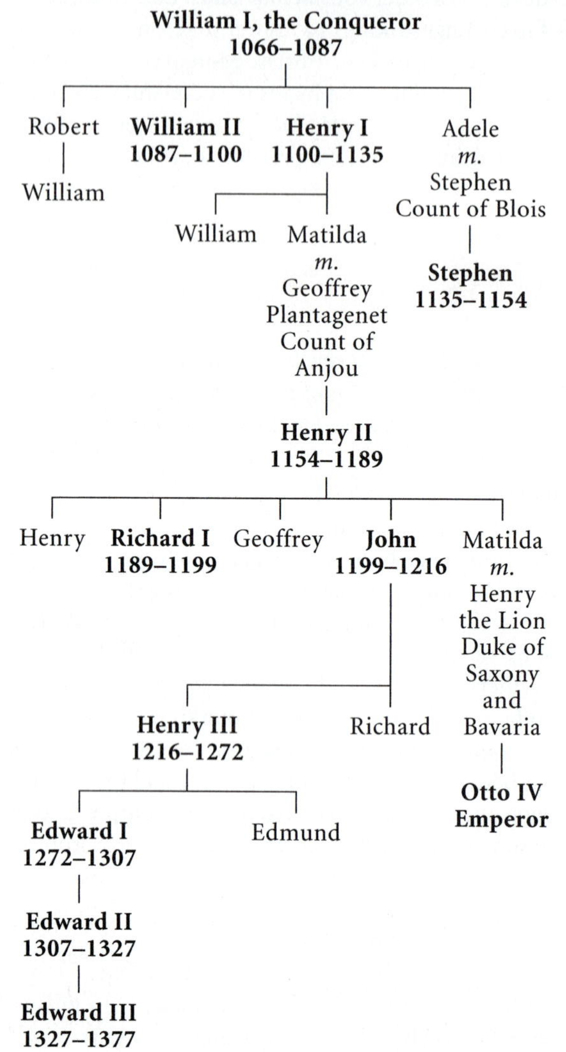

London revolted. In June 1215 he was forced to accept the "great charter of liberties," or **Magna Carta,** a conservative feudal document demanding that the king respect the rights of his vassals and of the burghers of London. The great significance of the document was its acknowledgment that the king was not above the law.

John and his weak, ineffective son Henry III (1216–1272), although ably served by royal judges, were forced by their failures to cede considerable influence to the great barons of the realm. Henry's son Edward I (1272–1307) was a strong and effective king who conquered Wales, defended the remaining continental possessions against France, and expanded the common law. He found that he could turn baronial involvement in government to his own advantage. By summoning his barons, bishops, and representatives of the towns and shires to participate in a "parley" or "parliament," he could raise more funds for his wars. Like similar Spanish, Hungarian, and German assemblies of the thirteenth century, the assemblies were occasions to consult, to present royal programs, and to extract extraordinary taxes for specific projects. They were also opportunities for those summoned to petition the king for redress of grievances. Initially, representatives of the shires and towns attended only sporadically. However, since the growing wealth of the towns and countryside made their financial support essential, the groups came to anticipate that they had a right to be consulted and to consent to taxation.

Through a system of royal courts and justices employing local juries and a tradition of representative parliaments, that forced self-government, coupled with an exacting system of accounting, increased the power of the English monarchy. By 1300, France, with its powerful royal bureaucracy, and England, with its courts and accountants, were the most powerful states in the West.

CONCLUSION

In 1300, Pope Boniface VIII extended a plenary indulgence (the remission of all punishment for people's sins) to those who visited the churches of Rome during that year. It was a jubilee year, an extraordinary celebration to occur once every century. There was much to celebrate. By 1300, Europe had achieved a level of population density, economic prosperity, cultural sophistication, and political organization greater than at any time since the Roman Empire. Across Europe, a largely free peasantry cultivated a wide variety of crops, both for local consumption and for growing commercial markets, while landlords sought increasingly rational approaches to estate management and investment. In cities and ports, merchants, manufacturers, and bankers presided over an international commercial and manufacturing economy that connected Scandinavia to the Mediterranean Sea. In schools and universities, students learned the skills of logical thinking and disputation while absorbing the traditions of Greece and Rome in order to prepare themselves for careers in law, medicine, and government. In courts and palaces, nascent bureaucracies worked to expand the rule of law over recalcitrant nobles, to keep the peace, and to preserve justice. Finally, after almost a thousand years of political, economic, and intellectual isolation, western Europe had become once more a dominant force in world civilization.

QUESTIONS FOR REVIEW

1. How did the different social roles of peasants, knights, and clergymen interact and complement each other?
2. In what ways did life in the urban world pose a threat to the values and priorities of aristocrats and churchmen?

3. How were the pope and the Holy Roman Emperor both dependent on each other and in conflict?
4. Why would Europe's medieval kings ultimately be more successful than the emperor or the papacy in establishing strong, centralized states?

KEY TERMS

chivalry, *p. 253*
communes, *p. 266*
Crusades, *p. 260*
demesne, *p. 250*
feudalism, *p. 254*
fief, *p. 254*
guilds, *p. 267*
khanates, *p. 263*
lay investiture, *p. 275*
lectio divina, *p. 258*
Magna Carta, *p. 282*
quadrivium, *p. 269*
Scholastic method, *p. 270*
serfs, *p. 250*
three-field system, *p. 251*
trivium, *p. 269*
universitas, *p. 269*
vassals, *p. 254*

DISCOVERING WESTERN CIVILIZATION ONLINE

You can obtain more information about the High Middle Ages at the Websites listed below. See also the Companion Website that accompanies this text, www.ablongman.com/kishlansky, which contains an online study guide and additional resources.

General Websites

Medieval Women
georgetown.edu/labyrinth/subjects/women/women.html
Links to resources on medieval women.

Byzantine and Medieval Studies Links
www.fordham.edu/halsall/medweb/
Professor Paul Halsall's links to the medieval world.

The Countryside

Castles on the Web
www.castlesontheweb.com/
An entire Website dedicated to castles, abbeys, and medieval churches.

Medieval Towns

Durham Cathedral & Castle
www.dur.ac.uk/~dla0www/c_tour/tour.html
A virtual tour of Durham's cathedral.

Paris at the Time of Philippe Auguste
www.philippe-auguste.com/uk/index.html
Medieval Paris at the end of the twelfth century.

Medieval Toledo
geocities.com/Athens/Academy/8636/Toledo.html
A site devoted to the city of Toledo in the Middle Ages with an emphasis on its Jewish history links to other related Spanish sites.

The Invention of the State

Les Capetiens-Les Croisades (Capetians to the Crusades)
philae.sas.upenn.edu/French/caroly.html
A hypertext site devoted to Capetian France (in French).

Medieval England
georgetown.edu/labyrinth/subjects/british_isles/england/england.html
The Labyrinth site with links to every aspect of medieval England.

Magna Carta
www.nara.gov/exhall/charters/magnacarta/magmain.html
A site devoted to the Magna Carta, including images of the charter itself.

Virtual Library: History: German History
www.erlangerhistorikerseite.de/heidelberg/gh/e3.html
Links to medieval Germany sites (in German).

SUGGESTIONS FOR FURTHER READING

The Countryside

Robert Bartlett, *The Making of Europe: Conquest, Colonization, and Cultural Change, 950–1350* (Princeton, NJ: Princeton University Press, 1993). A challenging study of European expansion.

R. Howard Bloch, *A Needle in the Right Hand of God: The Norman Conquest of 1066 and the Making and Meaning of the Bayeux Tapestry* (New York: Random House, 2006). An exhaustive and imaginative investigation of the Bayeux Tapestry by a noted medievalist.

Frederic Cheyette, *Ermengard of Narbonne* (Ithaca, NY: Cornell University Press, 2001). An evocative account of Provençal society in the eleventh and twelfth centuries.

Mary C. Erler and Maryanne Kowaleski, *Gendering the Master Narrative: Women and Power in the Middle Ages* (Ithaca, NY: Cornell University Press, 2003). Essays reevaluating women's exercise of power.

John France, *Western Warfare in the Age of the Crusades, 1000–1300* (Ithaca, NY: Cornell University Press, 1999). Warfare in the High Middle Ages.

Peter Lock, *The Routledge Companion to the Crusades* (London and New York: Routledge, 2006). A comprehensive introduction to all aspects of the Crusades—historical, logistical, economic, social, and military.

Richard W. Kauper, *Chivalry and Violence in Medieval Europe* (Oxford: Oxford University Press, 2001). A comprehensive look at the relationship between chivalry and medieval violence.

Jonathan Riley-Smith, ed., *The Oxford Illustrated History of the Crusades* (Oxford: Oxford University Press, 2001). A comprehensive, collectively authored introduction to Crusade history.

Medieval Towns

Barbara A. Hanawalt and Kathryn L. Reyerson, eds., *City and Spectacle in Medieval Europe* (Minneapolis: University of Minnesota Press, 1994). Essays on urban ritual and culture in the Middle Ages.

P. J. Jones, *The Italian City-State: From Commune to Signoria* (Oxford, NY: Clarendon Press, 1997). Major survey of Italian urban history.

Robert S. Lopez, *The Commercial Revolution of the Middle Ages, 950–1350* (New York: Cambridge University Press, 1971). An excellent survey of medieval commercial history.

Joseph H. Lynch, *The Medieval Church: A Brief History* (London and New York: Longman, 1992). A short introduction to medieval Church history.

David Nicholas, *The Growth of the Medieval City* (New York: Addison-Wesley Longman, 1997). A survey of the diversity of medieval urban development from late antiquity to the 1330s.

Norman John Greville Pounds, *The Medieval City* (Westport, CT: Greenwood Press, 2005). Recent introduction to medieval urban history.

The Invention of the State

Robert Bartlett, *England under the Norman and Angevin Kings, 1075–1225* (Oxford: Oxford University Press, 2000). A survey of England from the eleventh to thirteenth centuries.

Thomas N. Bisson, ed., *Cultures of Power: Lordship, Status, and Process in Twelfth-Century Europe* (Philadelphia: University of Pennsylvania Press, 1995). Important collection of essays on medieval lordship.

Jean Dunbabin, *France in the Making, 843–1180* (New York: Oxford University Press, 1985). Good overview of the formation of France.

Horst Fuhrmann, *Germany in the High Middle Ages, c. 1050–1200* (New York: Cambridge University Press, 1986). A fresh synthesis of German history by a leading German historian.

Bernard F. Reilly, *The Medieval Spains* (Cambridge: Cambridge University Press, 1993). Comprehensive survey of the social, political, and cultural history of the medieval Iberian peninsula.

Teofilo F. Ruiz, *From Heaven to Earth: The Reordering of Castilian Society, 1150–1350* (Princeton, NJ: Princeton University Press, 2004). An intelligent examination of the relationship between language and social and political change in Spain.

Joseph R. Strayer, *On the Medieval Origins of the Modern State* (Princeton, NJ: Princeton University Press, 1970). A very brief but imaginative account of medieval statecraft by a leading historian of French institutions.

For a list of additional titles related to this chapter's topics, please see http://www.ablongman.com/kishlansky.

CHAPTER 10

THE LATER MIDDLE AGES, 1300–1500

WEBS OF STONE AND BLOOD

EUROPEAN CIVILIZATION AT THE END OF THE MIDDLE AGES

Like a delicate basket of woven stone, the Gothic vaulting in the choir of Saint Vitus Cathedral in Prague encloses and unifies the sacred space over which it floats. In a similar manner, the great aristocratic families of the fourteenth and fifteenth centuries spun webs of estates, hereditary principalities, and fiefs across Europe. In art as in life, dynamic individuals reshaped the legacy of the past into new and unexpected forms.

THE VISUAL RECORD

In France, where Gothic architecture originated in the twelfth century, architects had long used stone springers and vaults, but only to emphasize verticality and lift the eyes of the faithful to the heavens. Throughout the thirteenth and fourteenth centuries, French architects vied with one another to raise their vaults ever higher but never rethought the basic premise of their design. Peter Parler (1330–1399), the architect of Saint Vitus, approached the design of his cathedral in a novel way. He used intersecting vaults not simply for height but also to bind together the interior space of the edifice in a net of intersecting stone arches. The ability to rethink the architectural heritage of the past marked Peter Parler as the greatest architectural genius of the fourteenth century.

Emperor Charles IV (1355–1378), the head of the most successful web-spinning aristocratic family of the Later Middle Ages, recognized Parler's talent and enlisted him in making his Bohemian capital one of the most splendid cities of Europe.

Along with his innovations in architecture, Peter Parler also opened new directions in sculpture. Again breaking with French tradition, in which sculptors sought to present their subjects as ideal types, Parler concentrated on realism and individual portraiture in his work. The carved heads of Bohemia's kings, queens, prelates, and princes that peer down from the ambulatory of Saint Vitus are real people, with their blemishes, their virtues, and their vices marked in their faces. The interest in the individual was entirely appropriate in the late fourteenth century—a time when kings and peasants, saints and heretics, lords and merchants sought to make their mark by stepping out of their traditional roles. The characters of the age had personalities as marked as those of Parler's individualistic sculptures. Their epithets tell much: John "the Valiant" of Brittany; Philip "the Bold" of Burgundy; his son John "the Fearless"; the Habsburg John "the Parricide"; Charles II "the Bad" of Navarre; Pedro IV "the Cruel" of Aragon; Charles VI "the Mad" of France. Powerful and ambitious men and women fought for political dominance, religious visionaries and preachers announced new

■ The head of Charles IV from St. Vitus Cathedral.

and daring revelations, and thinkers and artists broke with hallowed philosophical and literary traditions. Parler had no doubt about his own importance in that age of individuals. His own portrait bust looks down from the cathedral beside those of kings and queens.

Parler was born into a well-known family of stonemasons near the German town of Württemberg. He learned his craft from his father but at a young age surpassed the elder Parler, not simply in the execution of stone constructions but also in their design. A century earlier, a young man of such recognized talent would almost certainly have gravitated from his native Swabia to France, then the cultural center of Europe. However, although French language, styles, and tradition continued to inspire Europeans everywhere throughout the fourteenth century, by mid-century France was increasingly troubled by dynastic problems, war, economic decline, and the ravages of disease. It was no longer the magnet that drew the greatest artists, architects, and thinkers. Thus, at the age of 23, the brilliant and ambitious young architect looked to the east rather than to the west and cast his lot with the splendid court of Charles IV, king of Bohemia and soon to be Holy Roman Emperor.

■ St. Vitus Cathedral.

Charles invited Parler to complete his great Prague cathedral, which had been begun by a French architect and modeled on the great cathedrals of France. With Charles's patronage, Parler modified the building program to incorporate his original vision of architecture and portraiture. He went on to direct the construction of churches, bridges, and towers in Prague and throughout Bohemia. Within a generation, Parler's students had spread his refinement of Gothic architecture and sculpture throughout the Holy Roman Empire—to Austria, Bavaria, Swabia, Alsace, Poland, and Italy. Parler, the weaver of stone, and Charles, the weaver of politics, were emblematic of their age.

LOOKING AHEAD

This chapter explores the tensions, crises, and creativity of Parler's age. It examines the rise of central Europe as a main stage of cultural and political action, follows the disasters of the Hundred Years' War, the Black Death, and the Great Schism, and reviews the religious, artistic, and literary creativity of the Later Middle Ages.

POLITICS AS A FAMILY AFFAIR

Like those of his architect, Charles's roots were in the Rhineland and his cultural inspiration in France. Between 1250 and 1350, the Luxembourg family greatly expanded its political and geographical powers by involving itself in the dynastic politics of the decaying Holy Roman Empire. At the height of his power, Charles controlled a patchwork of lands that included Luxembourg, Brabant, Lusatia, Silesia, Moravia, Meissen, and Brandenburg. His daughter married Richard II of England. A son succeeded him in Bohemia and another obtained the Hungarian crown.

Such fragmented and shifting territorial bases were typical of the great families of the fourteenth and fifteenth centuries. Everywhere, family politics threatened the fragile institutional developments of the thirteenth century. Aristocrats competed for personal power and used public office, military command, and taxing power for private ends.

The Struggle for Central Europe

In addition to the Luxembourgs, four other similarly ambitious families competed for dominance in the empire. First were the Wittelsbachs, the chief competitors of the Luxembourgs. The Wittelsbachs had originated in Bavaria but had since spread across Europe. In the west the Wittelsbachs had acquired Holland, Hainaut, and Frisia, while in the east they temporarily held Tyrol and Brandenburg. Next were the Habsburgs, allies of the Luxembourgs, who had begun as a minor comital family in the region of the Black Forest. They expanded east, acquiring Austria, Tyrol, Carinthia, and Carniola. The third family, the Premysls, controlled not only Bohemia but also Moravia and a miscellany of lands stretching from Silesia in the north to the Adriatic Sea. Finally, the house of Anjou—French royalty—created a similar eastern network. Charles's son Charles Robert secured election as king of Hungary in 1310. His son Louis (1342–1382) added the crown of Poland (1370–1382). The protracted wars and maneuvers that the families conducted for dominance in the empire resembled nothing so much as the competition that had taken place three centuries earlier for dominance in feudal France.

Eastern Expansion. For more than a century, not only great princes but also monks, adventurers, and simple peasants streamed into the kingdoms and principalities of eastern Europe. Since the early thirteenth century, the Teutonic orders had used the sword to spread Christianity along the Baltic coast. By the early fourteenth century, the knight-monks had conquered Prussia and the coast as far east as the Narva River (now well within Russia), where they reached the borders of the Christian principality of Novgorod. The pagan inhabitants of the regions had to choose between conversion and expulsion. When they fled, their fields were turned over to land-hungry German peasants. Peasants from the Rhineland, Westphalia, and Saxony were able to negotiate advantageous contracts with their new lords, guaranteeing them greater freedom than they had known at home.

By the fifteenth century, religious and secular German lords had established a new agrarian economy, modeled on western European estates, in regions previously unoccupied or sparsely settled by the indigenous Slavic peoples. That economy specialized in the cultivation of grain for export to the west. Each fall, fleets of hundreds of ships sailed from the ports of Gdansk and Riga to ports in the Netherlands, England, and France. Returning flotillas carried Flemish cloth and tons of salt for preserving food to places as far as Novgorod. The influx of Baltic grain into western Europe caused a decline in domestic grain prices and a corresponding economic slump for landlords throughout the fourteenth and fifteenth centuries.

Central European Kingdoms. Farther south, the Christian kingdoms of Poland, Bohemia, and Hungary beckoned different sorts of westerners. Newly opened silver and copper mines in Bohemia, Silesia, southern Poland, and Hungarian Transylvania needed skilled miners, smelters, and artisans. Many were recruited from the overpopulated regions of western Germany. East–west trade routes developed to export those metals, giving new life to the Bohemian towns of Prague and Brno, the Polish cities of Krakow and Lvov, and Hungarian Buda and Bratislava. Trade networks reached south to the Mediterranean via Vienna, the Brenner Pass, and Venice. To the north, trade routes extended to the Elbe River and the trading towns of Lübeck and Bremen. The Bavarian towns of Augsburg, Rothenburg, and Nuremberg flourished at the western end of the network. To the east, Lvov became a great trading center connecting southern Russia with the west.

The wealth of eastern Europe, its abundant land, and its relative freedom attracted both peasants and merchants. The promise of profitable marriages with eastern royalty drew ambitious aristocrats. Eastern nobles preferred the westerners to German aristocrats since the former lacked strong local authority to challenge the nobility's position in the eastern king-

MAP DISCOVERY

Central and Eastern Europe, ca. 1378

Examine this complex map of rival dynasties in fourteenth-century Europe. How do you explain the discontinuous territorial holdings of these great competing families? To what extent could the regions of the Holy Roman Empire be considered a state in 1378? Based on the text discussion, where might the Habsburgs be expected to extend and consolidate their power in the east?

doms. For the outsiders, eastern alliances meant the expansion of family power and the promise of glory.

Charles IV (1347–1378) was typical of the restless **dynasts.** His grandfather, Emperor Henry VII (1308–1313), had arranged for his son, John of Luxembourg, to marry Elizabeth (d. 1330), the Premysl heiress of Bohemia, and thus acquire the Bohemian crown in 1310. John was king in name only. He spent most of his career fighting in the dynastic wars of the empire and of France. However, by mastering the intricate politics of the decaying Holy Roman Empire, he arranged the deposition of the Wittelsbach emperor Louis IV (1314–1347) and in 1346 secured the election of Charles as king of the Romans, or heir of the empire. The following year the Bohemian crown passed to Charles.

Although born in Prague and deeply committed to what he called "the sweet soil of my native land," Charles had spent most of his youth in France, where he was deeply influenced by French culture. However, upon his return to Prague in 1333 he rediscovered his Czech cultural roots. As king of Bohemia, he worked to make Prague a cultural center by combining French

Emperor Charles IV presenting sacred relics to the Church of Karlstein in Prague, built by Charles to house the crown jewels of the Holy Roman Empire.

and Czech traditions. He imported artisans, architects, and artists such as Peter Parler to transform and beautify his capital. In 1348 he founded a university in Prague, the first in the empire, modeled on the University of Paris. Keenly interested in history, Charles provided court historians with the sources necessary to write their histories of the Bohemian kingdom. Charles took a more active role in the cultural renewal than perhaps any European king since Alfred of England, fostering a literary renaissance in both Latin and Czech. He authored a number of religious texts, fostered the use of the Czech language in religious services, and initiated a Czech translation of the Bible. He even composed his own autobiography, perhaps the first lay person to do so in medieval Europe.

The effects of Charles's cultural policies were far-reaching, but in directions he never anticipated. His interests in Czech culture and religious reform bore unexpected fruit during the reign of his son Sigismund, Holy Roman Emperor (1433–1437) and king of Hungary (1387–1437), Germany (1410–1437), and Bohemia (1419–1437). During Sigismund's reign, Czech religious and political reformers came into open conflict with the powerful German-speaking minority in the University of Prague. Led by the theologian Jan Hus (ca. 1372–1415), the reform movement ultimately challenged the authority of the Roman Catholic Church and became the direct predecessor of the great reformation of the sixteenth century.

Even while building up his beloved city of Prague, Charles was dismantling the Holy Roman Empire. By the fourteenth century, the title of emperor held little political importance, although as an honorific title it was still bitterly contested by the great families of the empire. Charles sought to end such disputes and at the same time to solidify the autonomy of the kingdoms, such as Bohemia, against the threats of future imperial candidates. In 1356 he issued the **Golden Bull**, an edict that officially recognized what long had been the reality, namely, that the various German princes and kings were autonomous rulers. The bull also established the procedure by which future emperors would be elected. Thereafter, the emperor was chosen by seven great princes of the empire without the consultation or interference of the pope.

The same process that sapped the power of the emperor also reduced the significance of the princes. The empire fragmented into a number of large kingdoms and duchies such as Bohemia, Hungary, Poland, Austria, and Bavaria in the east and more than 1600 autonomous principalities, free towns, and sovereign bishoprics in the west. The inhabitants of the territories, often ruled by foreigners who had inherited sovereign powers through marriage, organized themselves into estates—political units of knights, burghers, and clergy—to present a united front in dealing with their prince. The princes in turn did not enjoy any universally recognized right to rule and were forced to negotiate with their estates for any powers they actually enjoyed.

The disintegration of the empire left political power east of the Rhine widely dispersed for more than 500 years. Although this meant that Germany did not become a nation-state until the nineteenth century, decentralization left late medieval Germany as a fertile region of cultural and constitutional creativity. In that creative process the office of emperor played no role. Rather, the office became one of the building blocks of the great multinational Habsburg Empire of central Europe, an empire that survived until 1918.

A Hundred Years of War

The political map of western Europe was no less a patchwork quilt of family holdings than was the empire. On the Iberian Peninsula, the gradual Christian reconquest bogged down as the three Christian monarchies of Castile, Aragon, and Portugal largely ignored the remaining Muslim kingdom of Granada. Instead, dynastic rivalries, expansionist adventures in Sicily and Italy, internal revolts of nobility and peasants, and futile wars against one another commanded the energy and attention of the Christian kingdoms. Only when Ferdinand of Aragon married Isabella of Castile in 1469 did something like a unified Spain begin to emerge from that world of familial rivalries.

North of the Pyrenees, the situation was even more critical. The same kinds of familial rivalries that destroyed the empire as a political entity threatened to overwhelm the feudal monarchies of France and England in the fourteenth and fifteenth centuries. In both kingdoms, weakening economic climates and demographic catastrophe exacerbated dynastic crises and fierce competition. The survival of the English and French monarchies was due to luck, to a longer tradition of bureaucratic government, and—in the minds of contemporaries—to the hand of God. Three long-simmering disputes triggered the series of campaigns collectively termed the **Hundred Years' War**. The first issue was conflicting rights to Gascony in southern France. Since the mid-thirteenth century, the kings of England had held Gascony as a fief of the French king. Neither monarchy was content with this arrangement, and for the next 75 years kings quarreled constantly over sovereignty in the region.

The second point of contention was the close relationship between England and the Flemish cloth towns. The manufacturing centers were the primary customers for English wool. Early in the fourteenth century, Flemish artisans rose up in a series of bloody revolts against the aristocratic cloth dealers who had long monopolized power. The count of Flanders and the French king supported the wealthy merchants, while the English sided with the artisans.

The third dispute concerned the royal succession in France. Charles IV (1322–1328), the son of Philip IV the Fair, died without an heir. The closest descendant of a French king was the grandson of Philip the Fair, King Edward III of England (1327–1377). Edward, however, was the son of Philip's daughter Isabella. The French aristocracy, which did not want an English king to inherit the throne and unite the two kingdoms, pretended that according to ancient Frankish law, the crown could not pass through a woman. Instead, they preferred to give the crown to a cousin of the late king, Philip VI (1328–1350), who became the first of the Valois kings of France. At first the English voiced no objection to Philip's accession, but in 1337, when the dispute over Gascony again flared up and Philip attempted to confiscate the region from his English "vassal" Edward III, the English king declared war on Philip. Edward's stated goal was not only to recover Gascony but also to claim the crown of his maternal grandfather.

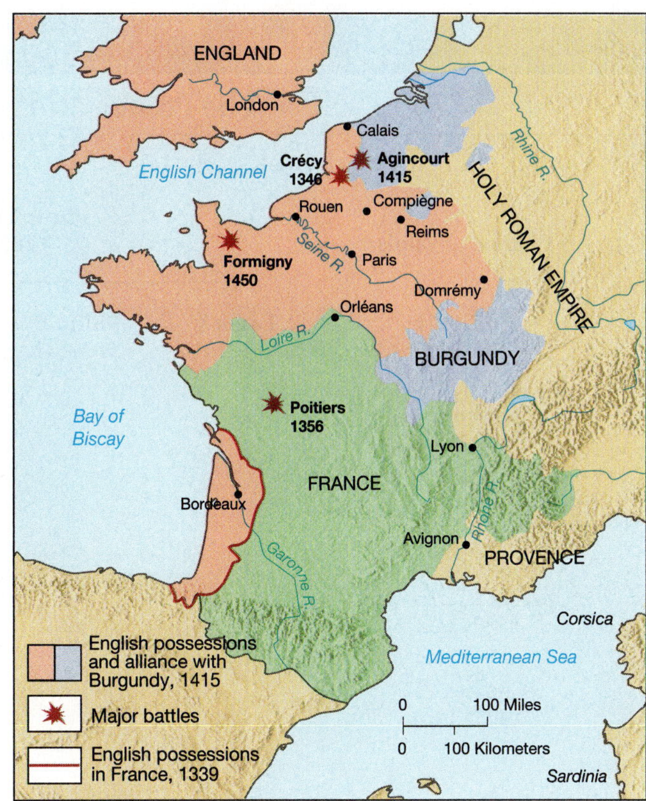

■ The Hundred Year's War. The English and their Burgundian allies almost succeeded in surrounding and conquering France in the fifteenth century.

Chivalry and Warfare. Although territorial and dynastic rivalries were the triggers that set off the war, its deeper cause was chivalry. The elites of Europe were both inspired by and trapped in a code of conduct that required them not only to maintain their honor by violence but also to cultivate violence to increase that honor. The code had been appropriate in a period of weak kingship, but by the late thirteenth century, the growth of courts and royal power in France and in England left little room for private vengeance and vendettas. Government was increasingly an affair of lawyers and bureaucrats, and war an affair of professionals. Yet kings and nobles alike still agreed with the sentiment expressed by a contemporary poet: "The glory of princes is in their pride and in undertaking great peril." By the fourteenth century, only war provided sufficient peril.

Edward III of England and his rival Philip VI of France both epitomized the chivalrous knight. Both gloried in luxurious living and conspicuous consumption. Captivated by the romantic tales of King Arthur and the Round Table, Edward created the Order of the Garter, a select group of nobles who were to embody the highest qualities of chivalry. For a ruler such as Edward, obsessed with knightly glory, war with France was the ideal way to win honor and fame.

In spite of his chivalric ideals, Edward was practical when it came to organizing and financing his campaigns. Philip shared Edward's ideals but lacked his rival's practicality and

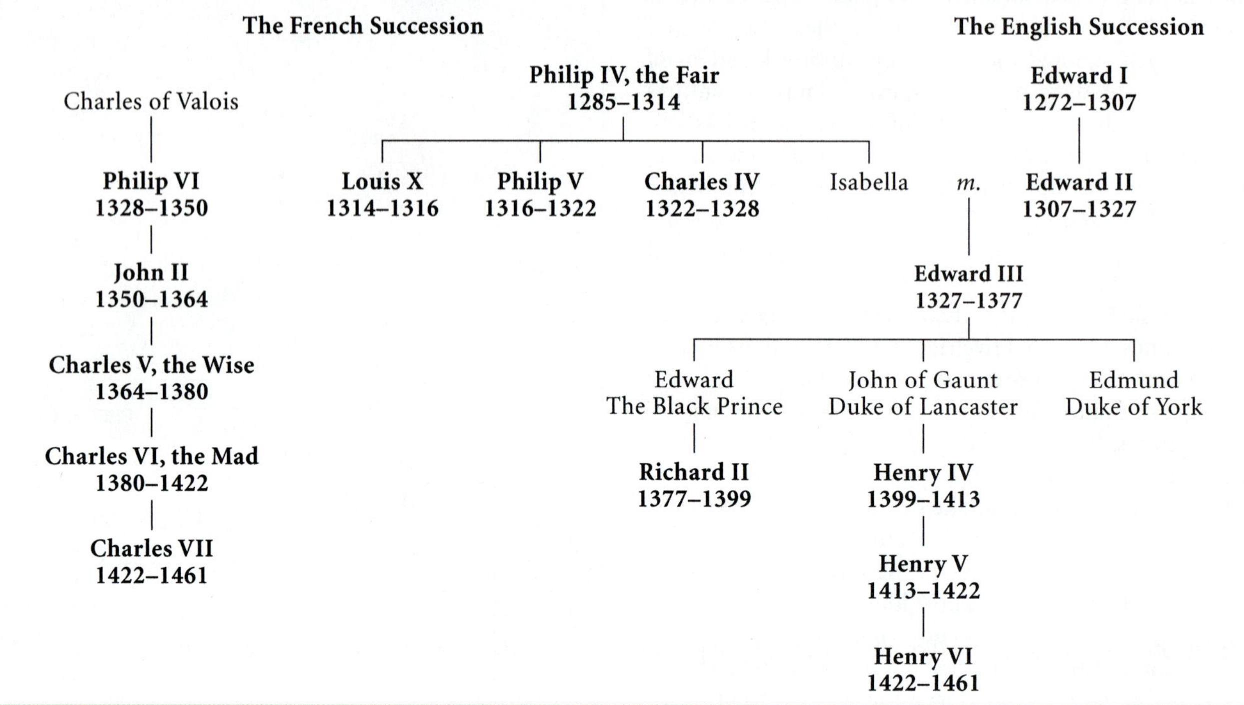

self-assurance. Before his elevation to the throne, Philip had been a valiant and successful warrior, fond of jousting, tournaments, and lavish celebrations. After his coronation he continued to act like a figure from a knightly romance, surrounding himself with aristocratic advisers who formed the most brilliant court of Europe, dispensing the royal treasure to his favorites, and dreaming of leading a great crusade to free the Holy Land. However, as the first French king in centuries elected rather than born into the right of succession, Philip treated the magnates from whose ranks he had come with excessive deference. He hesitated to press them for funds and deferred to them on matters of policy even while missing opportunities to raise other revenue from towns and merchants. Finally, although a competent warrior, Philip was no match in strategy or tactics for his English cousin.

France was far larger and wealthier than England, but the French monarch lacked the ability to tap his kingdom's resources, which the English king enjoyed by appealing to parliament. Thus, throughout the war French kings were constantly forced to extremes of taxation to fund their operations.

War was expensive. In spite of chivalrous ideals, nobles no longer fought as vassals of the king but rather as highly paid mercenaries. The nature of that service differed greatly on the two sides of the Channel. In France, tactics and personnel had changed little since the twelfth century. The core of any army was the body of heavily armored nobles who rode into battle with their lords, supported by lightly armored knights. Behind them marched infantrymen recruited from towns and armed with pikes. Although the French also hired mercenary Italian crossbowmen, the nobles despised them and never used them effectively.

In contrast, centuries of fighting against Welsh and Scottish enemies had transformed and modernized the English armies and their tactics. The great nobles continued to serve as heavily armored horsemen, but professional companies of foot soldiers raised by individual knights made up the bulk of the army. The professional companies consisted largely of pikemen and, most importantly, of longbowmen. Although not as accurate as the crossbow, the English longbow had a greater range. Moreover, when massed archers fired volleys of arrows into enemy ranks, they proved extremely effective against enemy pikemen and even lightly armored cavalry.

English Successes. The first real test of the two armies came at the Battle of Crécy in 1346. There an overwhelmingly superior French force surrounded the English army. Massing their archers on a hill, the English rained arrows down on the French cavalry, which attacked in a glorious but suicidal manner.

The English victory was total. By midnight they had repelled 16 assaults, losing only 100 men while killing more than 3000 French. The survivors, including Philip VI, fled in

■ At Crécy in 1346, a numerically inferior English force used longbows to defeat a larger but more traditional French army.

disorder. Strangely enough, the French learned nothing from the debacle. In 1356 Philip's successor, John II (1350–1364), rashly attacked an English army at Poitiers and was captured. In 1415 the French blundered in a different way at Agincourt. Then, most of the heavily armored French knights dismounted and attempted to charge the elevated English position across a soggy, muddy field. Barely able to walk and entirely unable to rise again if they fell, all were captured. Out of fear that his numerically inferior English army would be overwhelmed if the French recovered their breath, the English king ordered more than 1500 French nobles and 3000 ordinary soldiers killed. He held more than 1000 of the greatest nobles for ransom. English losses were less than 100.

Pitched battles were not the worst defeats for the French. More devastating were the constant raiding and systematic destruction of the French countryside by the English companies. The relief effort launched in 1339 by Pope Benedict XII (1334–1342) gives some idea of the scale of destruction. Papal agents, sent to aid victims of the English invasion, paid out more than 12,000 pounds—the equivalent of one-third of the English annual royal income—to peasants in just one region of northern France. The funds distributed were simple charity and far from adequate compensation. Villagers estimated that their actual losses were perhaps seven times greater than what they received.

Raiding and pillaging continued for decades, even during long truces between the French and English kings. During periods of truce, unemployed free companies of French and English mercenaries roamed the countryside, supporting themselves by banditry while awaiting the renewal of more formal hostilities. Large swaths of France were left uncultivated for years because peasants were killed or terrorized into flight. Never had the ideals of chivalric conduct been so distant from the brutal realities of warfare.

The French kings were powerless to prevent the destruction, just as they were unable to defeat the enemy in open battle. Since the kings were incapable of protecting their subjects or of leading their armies to victory, the "silken thread binding together the kingdom of France," as one observer put it, began to unravel, and the kingdom so painstakingly constructed by the Capetian monarchs began to fall apart. Not only did the English make significant territorial conquests, but the French nobles began behaving much like those in the Holy Roman Empire, carving out autonomous lordships. Private warfare and castle building, never entirely eradicated even by Louis IX and Philip IV, increased as the royal government lost its ability to control the nobility. Whole regions of the kingdom slipped entirely from royal authority. Duke Philip the Good of Burgundy (1396–1467) allied himself with England against France and profited from the war to form a far-flung lordship that included Flanders, Brabant, Luxembourg, and Hainaut. By the time of his death, he was the most powerful ruler in Europe. Much of the so-called Hundred Years' War was actually a French civil war.

During this century of war, the French economy suffered even more than the French state. Trade routes were broken and commerce declined as credit disappeared. French kings repeatedly seized the assets of Italian merchant bankers in order to finance the war. Such actions made the Italians, who had been the backbone of French commercial credit, extremely wary about extending loans in the kingdom. The kings then turned to French and Flemish merchants, extorting from them forced loans that dried up capital that might otherwise have been returned to commerce and industry. Politically and economically, France seemed doomed.

Joan of Arc and the Salvation of France. The flower of French chivalry did not save France. Instead, at the darkest moment of the long and bloody struggle, salvation came at the hands of a simple peasant girl from the county of Champagne. By 1429, the English and their Burgundian allies held virtually all of northern France, including Paris. Now they were besieging Orléans, the key to the south. The heir to the French throne, the dauphin, was the weak-willed and uncrowned Charles VII (1422–1461). To him came Joan of Arc (1412–1431), an illiterate but deeply religious girl who bore an incredible message of hope. She claimed to have heard the voices of saints ordering her to save Orléans and have the dauphin crowned according to tradition at Reims.

Charles and his advisers were more than skeptical about the brash peasant girl who announced her divinely ordained mission to save France. Finally convinced of her sincerity, if not of her ability, Charles allowed her to accompany a relief force to Orléans. The French army, its spirit buoyed by the belief that Joan's simple faith was the work of God, defeated the

■ A fifteenth-century portrait of Joan of Arc. The Maid of Orléans was tried for heresy and executed in 1431. Later, in 1456, Pope Calixtus III pronounced her innocent. Pope Benedict XV formally declared her a saint in 1920.

English and ended the siege. That victory led to others, and on 16 July 1429 Charles was crowned king at Reims.

After the coronation, Joan's luck began to fade. She failed to take Paris, and in 1431 she was captured by the Burgundians, who sold her to the English. Eager to get rid of the troublesome girl, the English had her tried as a heretic. Charles did nothing to save his savior. After all, the code of chivalry did not demand that a king intervene on behalf of a mere peasant girl, even if she had saved his kingdom. She was burned at the stake in Rouen on 30 May 1431.

Despite Joan's inglorious end, the tide had turned. The French pushed the English back toward the coast. In the final major battle of the war, fought at Formigny in 1450, the French used a new and telling weapon to defeat the English—gunpowder. Rather than charging the English directly, as they had done so often before, they mounted a cannon and pounded the English to bits. Gunpowder completed the destruction of the chivalric traditions of warfare begun by archers and pikemen. By 1452 English continental holdings had been reduced to the town of Calais. Although the English kings continued to call themselves kings of France until the eighteenth century, it was a hollow title. The continental warfare of more than a century was over.

The English Wars of the Roses. Although war on the Continent had ended, warfare in England was just beginning. In some ways, the English monarchy had suffered even more from the Hundred Years' War than had the French. At the outset, English royal administration had been more advanced than the French. The system of royal agents, courts, and parliaments had created the expectation that the king could preserve peace and provide justice at home while waging successful and profitable wars abroad. As the decades dragged on without a decisive victory, the king came to rely on the aristocracy, enlisting its financial assistance by granting the magnates greater power at home.

War created powerful and autonomous aristocratic families with their own armies. Under a series of weak kings those families fought among themselves. Ultimately, they took sides in a civil war to determine the royal succession. For 30 years, from 1455 to 1485, supporters of the house of York, whose badge was the white rose, fought the rival house of Lancaster, whose symbol was the red rose, in the sort of dynastic struggle that would not have seemed out of place in the disintegrating German Empire. The English Wars of the Roses, as the conflict came to be called, finally ended in 1485 when Henry Tudor of the Lancastrian faction defeated his opponents. He inaugurated a new era as Henry VII (1485–1509), the first king of the Tudor dynasty.

By the end of the fifteenth century, England and France had survived with their central monarchical institutions largely intact, although their aristocracies still shared an important role in the exercise of power.

LIFE AND DEATH IN THE LATER MIDDLE AGES

The violence and pageantry of late medieval warfare played out against a backdrop of extraordinary social upheaval. By the end of the thirteenth century, population growth in the West had strained available resources to the breaking point. All arable land was under cultivation, and even marginal moorland, rocky mountainsides, and arid plains were being pressed into service to feed a growing population. At the same time, kings and nobles demanded ever higher taxes and rents to finance their wars and extravagant lifestyles. The result was a precarious balance in which a late frost, a bad harvest, or hungry mercenaries could mean disaster. Part of the problem could be alleviated by importing grain from the Baltic or from Sicily, but that solution carried risks of its own. Transportation systems were too fragile to ensure regular supplies, and their rupture could initiate a cycle of famine, disease, and demographic collapse. Population began to decline slowly around 1300, and the downturn became catastrophic within the following 50 years. In the period between 1300 and 1450, Europe's population fell by more than 30 percent. It did not recover until the seventeenth century.

Dancing with Death

Between 1315 and 1317, the first great famine of the fourteenth century, triggered by crop failures and war, struck Europe. People died by the thousands. Urban workers, because they were chronically undernourished, were particularly hard hit. Although it was the greatest famine in medieval memory, it was not the last. The relatively prosperous Italian city of Pistoia, for example, recorded 16 different famines and food shortages in the fourteenth and fifteenth centuries.

Disease accompanied famine. Crowded and filthy towns, opposing armies with their massed troops, and overpopulated countrysides provided fertile ground for the spread of infectious disease. Moreover, the greatly expanded trade routes of the thirteenth and fourteenth centuries that carried goods and grain between the East and the West also provided highways for deadly microbes. At Pistoia again, local chroniclers of the fourteenth and fifteenth centuries reported 14 years of sickness, fevers, epidemic, and plague.

Between 1347 and 1352, one-third to one-half of Europe's population died from a virulent combination of bubonic, septicemic, and pneumonic plagues known to history as the **Black Death**. The disease, carried by the fleas of infected rats, traveled the caravan routes from central Asia. It arrived in Messina, Sicily, aboard a merchant vessel in October 1347. From there the Black Death spread up the boot of Italy and then into southern France, England, and Spain. By 1349 it had reached northern Germany, Portugal, and Ireland. The following year the Low Countries, Scotland, Scandinavia, and Russia fell victim.

A page from the fourteenth-century psalter and prayer book of Bonne of Luxembourg, the Duchess of Normandy. The three figures of the dead shown here contrast with the three living figures on the facing page of the psalter to illustrate a moral fable.

The plague was all the more terrifying because its cause, its manner of transmission, and its cure were totally unknown until the end of the nineteenth century. Preachers saw the plague as divine punishment for sin. Ordinary people frequently accused Jews of causing it by poisoning drinking water. The medical faculty of Paris announced that it was the result of the conjunction of the planets Saturn, Jupiter, and Mars, which caused a corruption of the surrounding air.

Responses to the plague were equally varied. Across Europe, terrified people thought that by joining penitential groups that prayed, fasted, and even whipped themselves they could turn away divine wrath through self-mortification. Others thought it best to abandon themselves to pleasure, either out of despair or in the hope that a pleasant life of eating and drinking would in some way ward off the terror of the plague. In many German towns, terrified Christian citizens looked for outside scapegoats and slaughtered the Jewish community. Cities, aware of the risk of infection although ignorant of its process, closed their gates and turned away outsiders. Individuals with means fled to country houses or locked themselves in their homes to avoid contact with others. Nothing worked. The Italian author Giovanni Boccaccio (1313–1375) remarked on the wide range of opinions on how to deal with the plague, "Of the people who held these various opinions, not all of them died. Nor, however, did they all survive."

As devastating as the first outbreak of the plague was, its aftershocks were even more catastrophic. Once established in Europe, the disease continued to return roughly once each generation. The rueful call, "Bring out your dead," resounded for centuries in European cities. The last outbreak of the plague in Europe was the 1771 epidemic in Moscow that killed 60,000.

The Black Death, along with other epidemics, famines, and war-induced shortages, affected western much more than eastern Europe. The culminating effect of the disasters was a darker, more somber vision of life than that of the previous centuries. The vision ultimately found its expression in the

THE BLACK DEATH IN FLORENCE

Giovanni Boccaccio set his Decameron *in Florence at the height of the Black Death. His eyewitness description of the plague is the most graphic account of the disease and its effects on society.*

Focus Questions

In what different ways did people try to live so as to escape the plague? What were the effects of the plague on the social fabric?

I say, then, that the sum of thirteen hundred and fifty-eight years had elapsed since the fruitful Incarnation of the Son of God, when the noble city of Florence, which for its great beauty excels all others in Italy, was visited by the deadly pestilence. Some say that it descended upon the human race through the influence of the heavenly bodies, others that it was a punishment signifying God's righteous anger at our iniquitous way of life. But whatever its cause, it had originated some years earlier in the East, where it had claimed countless lives before it unhappily spread westward, growing in strength as it swept relentlessly on from one place to the next. . . . Against these maladies, it seemed that all the advice of physicians and all the power of medicine were profitless and unavailing. . . . Some people were of the opinion that a sober and abstemious mode of living considerably reduced the risk of infection. They therefore formed themselves into groups and lived in isolation from everyone else. . . . Others took the opposite view, and maintained that an infallible way of warding off this appalling evil was to drink heavily, enjoy life to the full, go round singing and merrymaking, gratifying all of one's cravings whenever the opportunity offered, and shrug the whole thing off as one enormous joke. . . . There were many other people who steered a middle course between the two already mentioned, neither restricting their diet to the same degree as the first group, nor indulging so freely as the second in drinking and other forms of wantonness, but simply doing no more than satisfy their appetite. Instead of incarcerating themselves, these people moved about freely, holding in their hands a posy of flowers, or fragrant herbs, or one of a wide range of spices, which they applied at frequent intervals to their nostrils, thinking it an excellent idea to fortify the brain with smells of that particular sort, for the stench of dead bodies, sickness, and medicines seemed to fill and pollute the whole of the atmosphere.

Some people pursuing what was possibly the safer alternative callously maintained that there was no better or more efficacious remedy against the plague than to run away from it. . . .

Of the people who held these various opinions, not all of them died. Nor, however, did they all survive. On the contrary, many of each different persuasion fell ill here, there, and everywhere, and having themselves, when they were fit and well, set an example to those who were as yet unaffected, they languished away with virtually no one to nurse them. This scourge had implanted so great a terror in the hearts of men and women that brothers abandoned brothers, uncles their nephews, sisters their brothers, and in many cases wives deserted their husbands. But even worse, and almost incredible, was the fact that fathers and mothers refused to nurse and assist their own children, as though they did not belong to them.

From Giovanni Boccaccio, *The Decameron.*

Dance of Death, an increasingly popular image in art and literature first depicted in the murals of the Church of the Holy Innocents in Paris around 1485. Naked, rotting corpses dance with great animation before the living. The latter, depicted in the dress of all social orders, are immobile, surprised by death, reluctant but resigned.

Although no solid statistics exist from the fourteenth century, the plague certainly killed more people than all of the wars and famines of the century. It was the greatest disaster ever to befall Europe. The Black Death touched every aspect of life, hastening a process of social, economic, and cultural transformation already underway. The initial outbreak shattered social and economic structures. Fields were abandoned, workplaces stood idle, international trade was suspended. Traditional bonds of kinship, village, and even religion were broken by the horrors of death, flight, and failed expectations. "People cared no more for dead men than we care for dead goats," wrote one survivor. Brothers abandoned brothers, wives deserted husbands, and terror-stricken parents refused to nurse their own children. Nothing had prepared Europe for the catastrophe. In spite of learned Parisian professors who proclaimed it the result of the movement of the planets and the popular preachers who argued that it was punishment for human sins, no teaching of the Church or its leaders could adequately explain it. Likewise, in spite of desperate attempts by others to fix the blame on Jews or strangers, no one but God could be held responsible. Survivors stood alone and uncertain before a new world. Across Europe, moralists reported a general lapse in traditional ethics, a breakdown in the moral codes. The most troubling aspect of the breakdown was what one defender of the old order termed "the plague of insurrection" that spread across Europe. That plague was brought on by the dimming of the hopes held by the survivors of the Black Death.

The Plague of Insurrection

Initially, even that darkest cloud had a silver lining. Lucky survivors of the plague soon found other reasons to rejoice. Property owners, when they finished burying their dead, discovered that they were far richer in land and goods. At the other end of the social spectrum, the plague had eliminated the labor surplus. Peasants were suddenly in great demand. For a time at least, they were able to negotiate substantially higher wages and an improved relationship with landlords. An English thresher who before 1349 had been paid around three pence a day could hope to earn 25 percent more after the plague.

The peasants' hopes were short-lived. The rise in expectations produced by the redistribution of wealth and the labor shortage created new tensions. Landlords sought laws forcing peasants to accept preplague wages and tightened their control over serfs in order to prevent them from fleeing to cities or other lords. At the same time, governments attempted to benefit from laborers' greater prosperity by imposing new taxes. In cities, where the plague had been particularly devastating, the demographic decline sharply lowered the demand for goods and thus reduced the need for manufacturing and production of all kinds. Like rural landowners, master craftsmen sought legislation to protect their incomes. New laws reduced production by restricting access to trades and increased masters' control over the surviving urban laborers. Social mobility, once a characteristic of urban life, slowed to a halt. Membership in guilds became hereditary, and young apprentices or journeymen had little hope of ever rising to the level of independent master craftsmen.

The new tensions led to violence when kings added their demands for new war taxes to the landlords' and masters' attempts to erase the peasants' and workers' recent gains. The first revolts took place in France, where peasants and townspeople, disgusted with the incompetence of the nobility in

Spread of the Black Death and Peasant Revolts

How closely did the spread of the Black Death follow the medieval trade networks shown in the map on p. 266? What was the general direction and average annual speed of the disease's spread? Was the Black Death only a disaster to western Europe? Note the locations of peasant revolts. Based on the chapter discussion, what similarities and differences existed among the groups that revolted in the Later Middle Ages? Was there a relationship between the devastation of the plague and the outbreak of revolts?

Amid the disasters of the Hundred Years' War and the Black Death, the fourteenth century witnessed numerous peasant revolts. This manuscript illustration shows armed rioters ransacking the house of a wealthy Paris merchant.

their conduct of the war against England, feared that their new wealth would be stolen from them by corrupt and incompetent aristocrats.

The Jacquerie. In 1358, in order to ransom King John II from the English, the French government attempted to increase taxes on the peasantry. At the same time, local nobles increased their rents and demands. Peasants in the area of Beauvais, north of Paris, fearing they would lose the modest level of prosperity they had gained over the previous ten years, rebelled against their landlords. The revolt—known as the **Jacquerie** for the archetypal French peasant, Jacques Bonnehomme—was a spontaneous outburst directed against the nobility, whom the peasants saw as responsible for all their ills. Without real leadership or a program, peasants attacked as many nobles as they could find, killing them along with their wives and children and burning their homes and castles.

The peasants' brutality deeply shocked the upper classes, whose own violence was constrained by the chivalric code. One chronicler reported in horror, "Among other evil deeds, they killed a knight and quickly began to roast him before the eyes of his wife and children. After 10 or 12 had raped the noble lady, they wanted to force her to eat her husband's flesh. They then put her to death horribly." Because the Church largely supported the power structure, the uprising was also strongly anticlerical. Churches were burned and priests killed. Success bred further attacks, and the disorganized army of peasants began to march south toward Paris, killing, looting, and burning everything associated with the despised nobility.

Peasants being massacred and thrown into the Seine during the Jacquerie.

In the midst of this peasant revolt, Etienne Marcel (ca. 1316–1358), a wealthy Parisian cloth merchant, led an uprising of Parisian merchants who sought to take control of royal finances and force fiscal reforms on the dauphin, the future Charles V. Although initially the rebels were primarily members of the merchant and guild elite, Marcel soon enlisted the support of the radical townspeople against the aristocracy. He even made overtures to the leaders of the Jacquerie to join forces. For a brief time, it appeared that the aristocratic order in France might succumb. However, in the end, peasant and merchant rebels were no match for professional armies. An aristocratic force cut the peasants to pieces outside of Paris while similar armies surrounded the city and cut off its food supply. Marcel was assassinated and the dauphin Charles regained the city.

The English Peasants' Revolt. The French revolts set the pattern for similar uprisings across Europe. Rebels were usually relatively prosperous peasants or townspeople whose economic situations were threatened by aristocratic attempts to turn back the clock to the period before the Black Death. In 1381, English peasants, reacting to new and hated taxes, rose in a less violent but more coordinated revolt known as the Great Rebellion. Peasant revolts took place in the northern Spanish region of Catalonia in 1395 and in Germany throughout the fourteenth and fifteenth centuries. The largest was the great Peasant's Revolt of 1524. Although always ruthlessly suppressed, European peasant uprisings continued until the peasant rebellion of 1626 in upper Austria. The outbursts did not necessarily indicate the desperation of Europe's peasantry, but they did reflect the peasants' new belief that they could change their lives for the better through united action.

Urban Uprisings. Urban artisans imitated the example of their rural cousins. Although there had been some uprisings in the Flemish towns before the Black Death, revolts of townspeople picked up momentum in the second half of the fourteenth century. In general, the town rebels were not the destitute urban poor any more than the peasant rebels had been the landless rural poor. Instead, they were generally independent artisans and small tradesmen who wanted to break the control of the powerful guilds.

The one exception to the pattern was the **Ciompi** revolt of 1378 in Florence. There the wool workers rioted and forced recognition of two guilds of laborers alongside the powerful guilds of masters. The workers and artisans controlled city government until 1382, when mercenaries hired by the elite surrounded the workers' slums and crushed them in bloody house-to-house fighting. In spite of the brutal suppression and ultimate failure of popular revolts, they became permanent, if intermittent, features of the European social landscape.

Living and Dying in Medieval Towns

Population decline, war, and class conflict in France and the Low Countries fatally weakened the vitality of the commercial and manufacturing system of northwestern Europe. The same

The Hanseatic League. Merchant cities formed a powerful confederation that dominated northern trade from Sweden to central Europe.

events reduced the market for Italian goods and undermined the economic strength of the great Italian cities. The Hundred Years' War bankrupted many of Florence's greatest banking houses, such as the Bardi and Peruzzi, who lent to both French and English kings. Commercial activity declined as well. Whereas in the 1330s Venice had sent between four and nine trading galleys to Flanders each year, by the 1390s the city was sending only three to five. Genoa, which earlier had led in the trade with the cloth towns of the north, saw the economic activity of its port decline by roughly one-third to one-half during the same period. Although Italians did not disappear from northern cities, they no longer held a near monopoly on northern trade.

Events outside of Europe also led to the decline of Italian economic power. In the course of the fourteenth and fifteenth centuries, the Mongol Khanates gradually lost power or were absorbed into local traditions. In China, adherents of the White Lotus sect, a millenarian, messianic offshoot of Buddhism, led the revolt that established the Ming dynasty. In western Asia Tamerlane (1370–1405), a Muslim of Mongolian descent, briefly and brutally restored the Khanate, but after his death Turkish peoples divided his vast lands among tribal rulers. In Russia, Duke Ivan I of Moscow (1328–1341) rose to power by persuading the Mongols to appoint him as the sole collector of tribute from the various Slavic states. A century later his successor Prince Ivan III the Great (1462–1505) led a

WORLD TRADE CENTERS

Trade is older than civilization, and almost as old are specialized buildings where trade is carried on. When the World Trade Centers in New York City were destroyed on September 11, 2001, the terrorist attack was aimed at a symbol of American economic power. But like other trade centers throughout the centuries, these buildings contained a truly international community: citizens of eighty countries were among the victims. The tragedy struck at the United States but wounded a global community of business, finance, trade, and civilization.

Specialized buildings for international trade were well established in Asia, Europe, and Africa by the thirteenth century. Merchants needed protection from bandits, judicial organizations to settle disputes, financial organizations to manage multiple partner transactions, and secure locations to store and exchange merchandise—all functions facilitated by trade centers. Counts of Champagne, for example, constructed buildings such as the Tithe Grange whose cellar was used as a warehouse, its ground floor as a market hall, and its upper floors as residences for merchants attending the fair at Provins. In Norwegian Bergen, German Hansa merchants conducted business in a row of special buildings on the old wharf or Bryggen.

European merchants found similar buildings adapted to the specialized needs of commerce throughout the world. Across the Islamic world, caravansaries offered protection for merchants, their merchandise, and their camels when doing business. When Maffeo and Niccilo Polo traveled east in 1260, they first traveled to Sudak, where

■ The Twin Towers of the World Trade Center.

THE WEST AND THE WIDER WORLD

■ The Tithe Grange at Provins, France.

■ Merchant houses on the old wharf of Bergen, Norway.

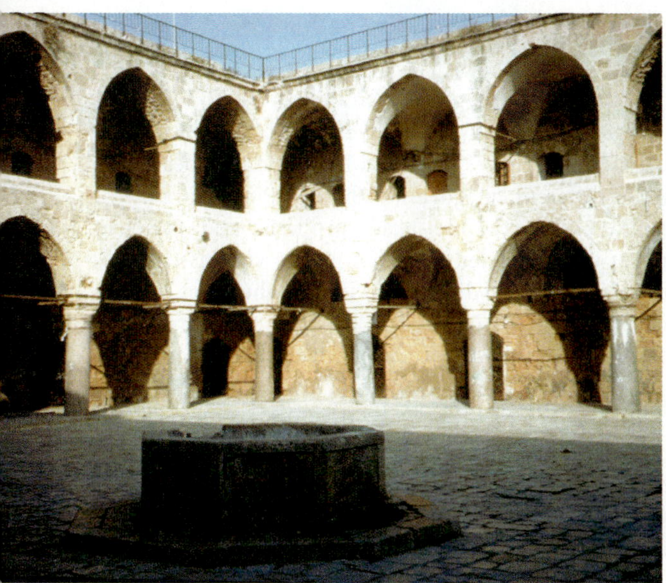

Caravansary at Akko (Acre, Israel).

Bukhara trade domes (sixteenth century).

they found an important trading center for the Crimea protected by an imposing series of fortifications. From there they traveled to Bukhara, a great trading center on the Silk Route where trade could be carried out in the protection of specially designed structures. Next they traveled to Samarkand in modern Uzbekistan before crossing the Gobi Desert and arriving in Turfan, Hami, and eventually Dunhuang on the edge of the Gobi and entering the empire of the great Emperor Kublai Khan before traveling on to the capital, Beijing.

These medieval world trade centers served merchants, but by providing security and services to traders, they fostered the development of culture as well: trade centers were often also religious and educational centers. They were nodal points for the exchange not only of goods but of ideas and artistic traditions. They were places of peace, refuge, and security that tied the West to the wider world.

The Great Wall of China

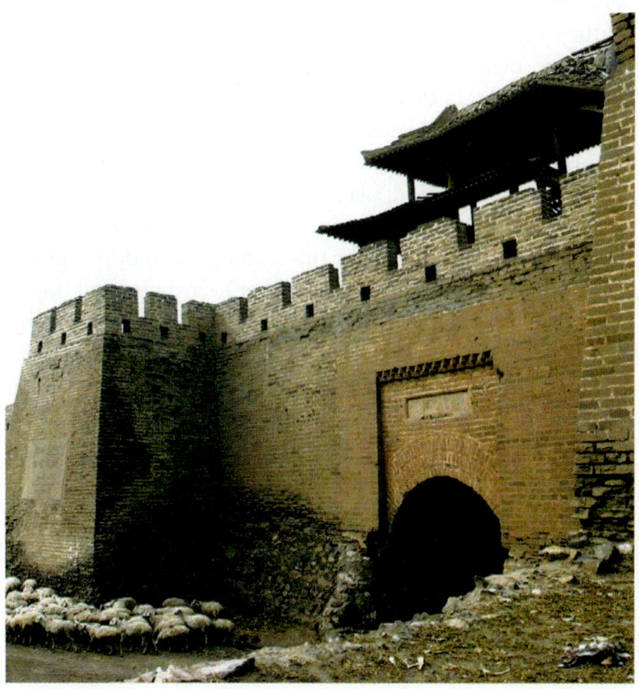

This ancient post house, 150 kilometers from Beijing, was constructed by Kublai Khan and served as a communications post and a commercial center.

successful revolt against the remnants of Mongol rule, subjugated the other Russian princes to himself, and assumed the title of tsar (or caesar). The disintegration of the Mongol Empire and the rise of new, aggressive kingdoms also caused disruptions of the Silk Route and Italian trade with China and India. Soon, Europeans would begin to look for alternative routes to the East.

Economic Shifts. The setbacks of the Italians worked to the advantage of German towns in the disintegrating empire. Along the Baltic Sea, in Scandinavia, and in northern Germany, towns such as Lübeck, Luneburg, Visby, Bremen, and Cologne formed a commercial and political alliance to control northern trade. During the second half of the fourteenth century, the **Hanseatic League**—the word *Hansa* means "company"—monopolized the northern grain trade and forced Denmark to grant its members exclusive rights to export Scandinavian fish throughout Europe. Hanseatic merchants established colonies from Novgorod to London and Bruges, and even to Venice. They carried dried and salted fish to Prague and supplied grain from Riga to England and France.

English towns also profited from the decline of Flanders and France. The population decline of the fourteenth century led many English landowners to switch from traditional farming to sheep raising. However, instead of exporting the wool to Flanders to be made into cloth, the English began to make cloth themselves. Protected by high tariffs on imports and low duties on exports, England had become a major exporter of finished cloth by the middle of the fifteenth century.

Addressing Poverty and Crime. The new social and economic circumstances of European towns accentuated the gulf between rich and poor. The streets and markets of fifteenth-century towns bustled with the sights and sounds of rich Hanseatic merchants, Italian bankers, and prosperous local tradesmen. The back alleys and squatter settlements on the edges of the towns teemed with a growing mass of desperate and despairing workers and their families. The combination of economic depression, plague, and rural crisis deepened the misery of the growing population of urban poor. Driven both by mounting compassion for the urban poor and by a growing fear of the violent potential of that ever-increasing population, medieval towns developed novel systems to deal with poverty. The first was public assistance; the second was social control and repression.

Traditionally, charity had been a religious act that focused more on the soul of the giver than on the effect on the life of the recipient. The same had been true of charitable organizations such as confraternities and hospitals. Confraternities were pious religious organizations of lay people and clergy who ministered to the poor and sick. Hospitals were all-purpose religious institutions providing lodging for pilgrims, the elderly, and the ill. By the fourteenth century, such pious institutions had become inadequate to deal with the growing numbers of poor and ill. Towns began to assume control over a centralized system of public assistance. New, specialized institutions appeared for the care of different categories of the poor, including the ill, women in childbirth, the aged, orphans, and travelers. Pesthouses were founded in which plague victims could be isolated. Hospitals also distributed food to the poor. In 1403, the hospital of the Holy Spirit in Cologne supported more than 1400 paupers per week. Seventy years later, that number had grown to almost 5000.

Although men and women who had taken religious vows staffed the institutions, city governments contributed to their budgets and oversaw their finances. Cities also attempted to rationalize the distribution of charity according to need and merit. Antwerp, for example, established a centralized relief service, which distributed badges to those deemed worthy of public assistance. Only those who presented their badges could receive food. The system spread throughout Europe in the fourteenth century.

At the same time that towns began to organize public assistance, they attempted to control more strictly the activities of the urban poor. In the fourteenth century, Nuremberg forbade begging to everyone except those who had received a special license. In Strasbourg, blind beggars organized an official "Confraternity of Strasbourg Beggars" on the model of other professional guilds, with its own officers, regulations, and membership requirements.

One consequence of poverty was increased crime. Fear of the poor led to repressive measures and harsh punishments. Traditionally, in much of Europe, crimes such as robbery, larceny, and even manslaughter had been punishable by fines and payments to the victim or the victim's heirs. Elsewhere, as in France and England, where corporal punishment had been the normal penalty for major crimes, hanging, blinding, and the loss of a hand or foot had been the most common punishments. During the Later Middle Ages, gruesome forms of mutilation and execution became common for a long list of offenses. Petty larceny was punished with whipping, cutting off ears or thumbs, branding, or expulsion. In some towns, robbery of an amount greater than three pence was punished with death. Death by hanging might be replaced by more savage punishments such as breaking on the wheel. Drowning, boiling, burning, and burial alive—a particularly common punishment for women—were other frequently used methods of execution.

The frequency of such punishments increased with their severity. In Augsburg, until the middle of the thirteenth century, executions were so rare that the city did not even have a public executioner before 1276. However, in the following two centuries, the city fathers increased executions in an attempt to control what they perceived as an ever rising crime rate, largely attributed to the growing masses of the poor. In 1452, the skulls of 250 hanged persons were found in pits on the gallows hill. At the same time, the bodies of 32 thieves twisted in the wind above.

THE SPIRIT OF THE LATER MIDDLE AGES

The Dance of Death and the gallows were not the only images of later medieval life. The constant presence of death made life more precious. Europeans celebrated life with a vigor and creativity characterized by a growing sense of individuality, independence, and variety. During the fourteenth century, the Church failed to provide unified spiritual and cultural leadership to Europe. The institutional division of the Church was paralleled by divisions over how to lead the proper Christian life. Many devout Christians developed independent lifestyles intended to bring them closer to God without reliance on the Church hierarchy. They elaborated beliefs that the Church branded as heresy. Others called into question the philosophical bases of theological speculation developed since the time of Abelard and Aquinas. Finally, the increasing pluralism of European culture gave rise to new literary traditions that both celebrated and criticized the medieval legacy of Christianity, chivalry, and social order.

Pope Boniface VIII, *Unam Sanctam*

The Crisis of the Papacy

The universal empire as well as its traditional competitor, the universal Church, declined in the Later Middle Ages. The papacy never recovered from the humiliating defeat Pope Boniface VIII suffered at the hands of King Philip the Fair in 1303. The ecclesiastical edifice created by the thirteenth-century popes was shaken to its foundations, first by becoming a virtual appendage of the French monarchy and then by a dispute that for more than 40 years gave European Christians a

IMAGE DISCOVERY

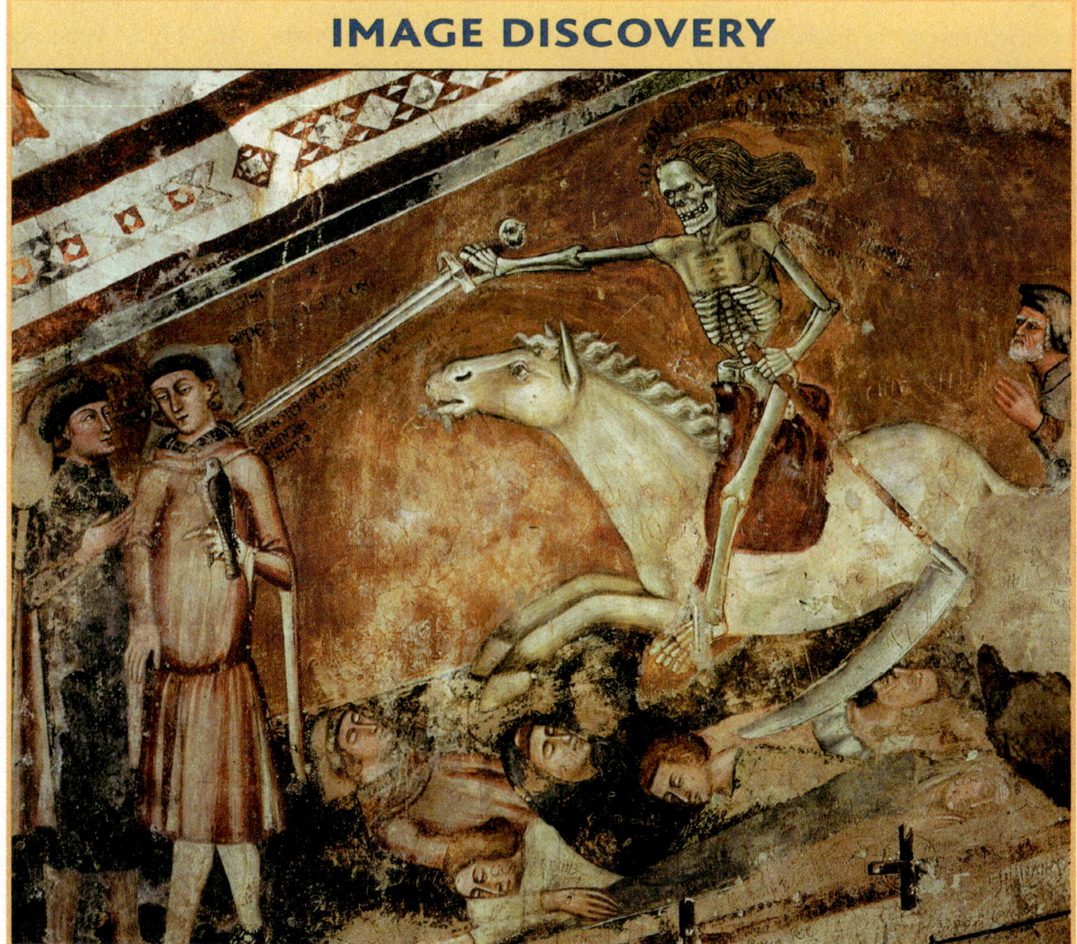

Death Against Life

The Triumph of Death is depicted in this fourteenth century fresco in the Sacro Speco, Subiaco, Italy. What message about death is being conveyed in this image? What does it proclaim about the differing orders and hierarchies of human life?

choice between two, and finally three, claimants to the chair of Saint Peter.

In 1305 the College of Cardinals elected as pope the bishop of Bordeaux. The new pope, who took the name Clement V (1305–1314), was close to Philip IV of France and had no desire to meet the fate of his predecessor, Pope Boniface VIII. Thus Clement took up residence, not in Rome, but in the papal city of Avignon on the east bank of the Rhone River. Technically, Avignon was a papal estate within the Holy Roman Empire. Actually, with France just across the river, the pope at Avignon was under French control.

The Avignon Papacy. For the next 70 years, French popes and French cardinals ruled the Church. The traditional enemies of France, as well as religious reformers who expected leadership from the papacy, looked on the situation with disgust. The Italian poet Petrarch (1304–1374) denounced what he termed the "Babylonian captivity" of the papacy in especially bitter tones:

> Now I am living in France, in the Babylon of the West. The sun in its travels sees nothing more hideous than this place on the shores of the wild Rhone. Here reign the successors of the poor fishermen of Galilee; they have strangely forgotten their origin.

Although Petrarch went on to accuse the popes and their courtiers of every possible crime and sin, the Avignon popes were no worse than any other great lords of the fourteenth century. In pursuit of political and financial rewards, they had simply lost sight of their roles as religious leaders.

The popes of Avignon were more successful in achieving their financial goals than in winning political power. Even as they developed their income sources, they lost the last remnants of political influence within the empire. In 1338 the German electors, tired of papal interference, solemnly declared that the imperial office was held directly from God and did not require papal confirmation. No longer could the popes exert any direct influence in the internal affairs of Europe's states.

Frustrated politically, the Avignon popes concentrated on perfecting the legal and fiscal systems of the Church and were enormously successful in concentrating the vast financial and legal power of the Church in the papal office. From the papal court, or curia, they created a vast and efficient central bureaucracy whose primary role was to increase papal revenues.

Revenues came from two main sources. The less lucrative but ultimately more important source was the sale of indulgences. The Church had long taught that sinners who repented might be absolved of their sins and escape the fires of hell. However, they still had to suffer temporary punishment. That punishment, called *penance,* could take the form of fasting, prayer, or performance of some good deed. Failing to do penance on earth, absolved sinners would have to endure a period in purgatory before they could be admitted to heaven. However, since the saints had done more penance than was required to make up for the temporal punishments due them, they had established a treasury of merit—a sort of spiritual bank account. The pope was the "banker" and could transfer some of the positive balance to repentant sinners in return for some pious act, such as contributing money to build a new church. The so-called **indulgences** could be purchased for one's own use or to assist the souls of family members already in purgatory. Papal "pardoners," working on commission, used high-pressure sales pitches to sell indulgences across Europe.

The second and major source of papal income was the sale of Church offices, or benefices. Popes claimed the right to appoint bishops and abbots to all benefices and to collect a hefty tax for the appointment. The system encouraged pluralism, that is, individuals could acquire numerous ecclesiastical benefices scattered across Europe in the same way that lay lords held multiple fiefs and territories from France to Poland. Like the pope, papal appointees often viewed their offices merely as sources of income, leaving pastoral duties, when they were performed at all, to hired local clergy.

The Great Schism. In 1377, Pope Gregory XI (1370–1378) returned from Avignon to Rome but died almost immediately upon arrival. Thousands of Italians, afraid that the cardinals would elect another Frenchman, surrounded the church where they were meeting and demanded an Italian pope. The terrified cardinals elected an Italian, who took the name of Urban VI (1378–1389). Once elected, Urban attempted to reform the curia, but he did so in a most undiplomatic way, insulting the cardinals and threatening to appoint sufficient non-French bishops to their number to end French control of the curia. The cardinals soon left Rome and announced that because the election had been made under duress, it was invalid and Urban should resign. When he refused, they held a second election and chose a Frenchman, Clement VII (1378–1394), who took up residence in Avignon. The Church now had two heads, both with reasonable claims to the office.

The chaos created by the so-called **Great Schism** divided Western Christendom. In every diocese, when a bishop died his successor had to be appointed by the pope. But by which pope? To whom did taxes go? Who received the income from the sale of indulgences or benefices? Did appeals in the Church courts go to Rome or to Avignon? More significantly, since each pope excommunicated the supporters of his opponent, everyone in the West was under a sentence of excommunication. Could anyone be saved?

Communities were divided. When the city of Bruges officially accepted the Avignon pope, many citizens left their homes and professions to live in cities loyal to Rome. Not surprisingly, countries tended to side with one or the other contender for political reasons. France recognized Clement. France's traditional enemies, England and the empire, recognized Urban. England's traditional enemy, Scotland, accepted Clement. Most of Italy sided with Urban, but the Angevin kingdom of Naples and Sicily recognized Clement, as did most of Spain.

The Great Schism

Consider the divisions of Europe during the Great Schism. What political considerations might have explained the varying loyalties to Rome and to Avignon? Compare this map with the map on p. 289 and speculate on the influence of princely families on the divisions. What effect might such divisions have had on the emperor's power in the Holy Roman Empire?

Nothing in Church law or tradition offered a solution to this crisis. Nor did efforts to settle the crisis politically, legally, or even militarily succeed. Moreover, the situation perpetuated itself. When Urban and Clement died, cardinals on both sides elected successors. By the end of the fourteenth century, France and the empire were exasperated with their popes and even the cardinals were determined to end the stalemate.

Conciliarism. Church lawyers argued that a general council alone could end the schism. Both popes opposed the "**conciliarism**" because it suggested that an assembly of the Church rather than the pope held supreme authority. However, in 1408 cardinals from both sides summoned a council in the Italian city of Pisa. The council deposed both rivals and elected a new pope. But the solution only made matters worse, since neither rival accepted the decision of the council. Europe now had to contend with not two popes but three, each claiming to be the true successor of Saint Peter.

Six years later the Council of Constance managed a final solution. There, under the patronage of the emperor-elect Sigismund (1410–1437), cardinals, bishops, abbots, and theologians from across Europe met to resolve the crisis. Their goal was not only to settle the schism but also to reform the Church to prevent a recurrence of such a scandal. The participants at Constance hoped to restructure the Church as a limited monarchy in which the powers of the pope would be controlled through frequent councils. The Pisan and Avignon popes were deposed. The Roman pope, abandoned by all of his supporters, abdicated. Before doing so, however, he formally convoked the council in order to preserve the tradition that a general council had to be called by the pope. Finally, the council elected as pope an Italian cardinal not aligned with any of the claimants. The election of the cardinal, who took the name Martin V (1417–1431), ended the schism.

The relief at the end of the Great Schism could not hide the very real problems left by over a century of papal weakness. The prestige of the papacy had been permanently compromised. Everywhere the Church had become more national in character. The conciliarist demand for control of the Church, which had ended the schism, lessened the power of the pope. Moreover, during the century between Boniface VIII and Martin V, new religious movements had taken root across Europe, movements that the political creatures who had occupied the papal office could neither understand nor control. The disintegration of the Church loomed ever closer as pious individuals turned away from the organized Church and sought divine help in personal piety, mysticism, or even magic.

Discerning the Spirit of God

When Joan of Arc first appeared before the dauphin in 1429, he feared that she was a witch. Only a physical examination by matrons, which determined that she was a virgin, persuaded him otherwise—witches were believed to have had intercourse with the devil. In 1431, the English burned Joan as a heretic. For the two years between 1429 and 1431 and long afterward, many venerated her as a saint. Everyone in the Later Middle Ages was familiar with witches, saints, and heretics. Distinguishing among them was often a matter of perspective.

Witchcraft. Accusations of witchcraft were relatively rare in the Middle Ages. The age of witch hunts occurred in the sixteenth and seventeenth centuries. During the Middle Ages, people believed magic existed in a wide variety of forms, but its definition was fluid and its practitioners were not always considered witches. Alchemists and astrologers held honored places in society, while simple practitioners of folk religion, medicine, and superstition were condemned—particularly when they were poor women.

Witches, believed to have made a contract with the devil, were condemned as a type of heretic and were persecuted like

A WOMAN BEFORE THE INQUISITION

In 1320, Jacques Fournier (ca. 1280–1342), bishop of Pamiers in France and the future Pope Benedict XII, interrogated the villagers of Montaillou in southern France about their involvement with the Catharsy, a dualist religion present in the region since the eleventh century. The following excerpt is from the testimony of Béatrice de Planissoles, a member of the lower nobility and a prominent inhabitant of the village.

Focus Questions

What does Béatrice mean by "good Christians"? What makes the Cathars willing to accept death?

Twenty-six years ago during the month of August, I was the wife of the late knight Bérenger de Roquefort, castellan of Montaillou. The late Raimond Roussel was the intendant and the stewart of our household which we held at the castle of Montaillou. He often asked me to leave with him and to go to Lombardy with the good Christians who are there, telling me that the Lord had said that man must quit his father, mother, wife, husband, son and daughter and follow him, and that he would give him the kingdom of heaven. When I asked him, "How could I quit my husband and my sons?" he replied that the Lord had ordered it and that it was better to leave a husband and sons whose eyes rot than to abandon him who lives for eternity and who gives the kingdom of heaven.

When I asked him, "How is it possible that God created so many men and women if many of them are not saved?" he answered that only the good Christians will be saved and no others, neither religious nor priests, nor anyone except these good Christians. Because, he said, just as it is impossible for a camel to pass through the eye of a needle, it is impossible for those who are rich to be saved. This is why the kings and princes, prelates and religious, and all those who have wealth, cannot be saved, but only the good Christians. . . . He also told me that all spirits sinned at the beginning with the sin of pride, believing that they could know more and be worth more than God, and for that they fell to earth. These spirits later take on bodies, and the world will not end before all of them have been incarnated into the bodies of men and women. Thus it is that the soul of a newborn child is as old as that of an old man.

He also said that the souls of men and women who were not good Christians, after leaving their bodies, enter the bodies of other men and women a total of nine times. If in these nine bodies they do not find the body of a good Christian, the soul is damned. If, on the contrary, they find the body of a good Christian, the soul is saved.

I asked him how the spirit of a dead man or woman could enter the mouth of a pregnant woman and from there into the mouth of the fruit that she carries in her womb. He answered that the spirit could enter the fruit of the woman's womb by any part of her body.

Thus he urged me to leave with him so that we could go together to the good Christians, mentioning various noble women who had gone there. Alesta and Serena, women of Chateauverdun, painted themselves with colors which made them appear foreign, so that they could not be recognized and went to Toulouse. When they arrived at an inn, the hostess wanted to know if they were heretics and gave them live chickens, telling them to prepare them because she had things to do in town, and left the house. [Cathars avoided killing and eating animals.] When she had returned she found the chickens still alive and asked them why they had not prepared them. They responded that if the hostess would kill them, they would prepare them but that they would not kill them. The hostess heard that and went to tell the inquisitors that two heretics were in her establishment. They were arrested and burned. When it was time to go to the stake, they asked for water to wash their faces, saying that they would not go to God painted thusly.

I told Raimond that they would have done better to abandon their heresy than to allow themselves to be burned, and he told me that the good Christians did not feel fire because fire with which they are burned cannot hurt them.

other heretics. Only at the end of the fifteenth century, with the publication of *The Witch Hammer,* a great handbook for inquisitors, did the European witch craze begin in earnest. Earlier, authorities had been more fearful of those people who sought their own pacts, not with the devil, but with God.

Lay Piety. Even as Europeans were losing respect for the institutional Church, people everywhere were seeking closer and more intimate relationships with God. Distrusting the formal institutions of the Church, lay persons and clerics turned to private devotions and mysticism to achieve union with the divine. They developed their own forms of devotion based on translations of the Bible into their native languages. They looked for a direct relationship with God, thus minimizing the importance of the Church hierarchy. Most, like the Beguines and Beghards of northern Europe, stayed within the Church. Others, among them many female mystics, maintained an ambiguous relationship with the traditional institutions of Christianity. A few, such as the Brethren of the Free Spirit, broke sharply with it.

In the fourteenth and fifteenth centuries, a great many pious lay men and women chose to live together in order to strive for spiritual perfection without entering established religious orders. The female Beguines and male Beghards of northern cities often formed miniature towns-within-towns. The Brethren of the Common Life in the Rhineland and Low Countries dedicated themselves to preaching, charity, and a pious life. In the early fifteenth century, an unknown member of the Brethren wrote the *Imitation of Christ,* a book of spiritual direction that continues to be the most widely read religious text after the Bible.

Christians of the Later Middle Ages sought to imitate Christ and venerated the Eucharist, or communion wafer, which the Church taught was the actual body of Christ. Male mystics focused on imitating Christ in his poverty, his suffering, and his humility. The Spiritual Franciscans made radical poverty the cornerstone of their belief and the yardstick by which to judge Christian action. The furor between the Spiritual Franciscans and the more moderate Conventuals led Pope John XXII to condemn radical poverty in 1323 and to begin persecuting the Spirituals as heretics. As the wealth and luxury of the Church hierarchy increased, so did the spiritual reaction against it.

Women developed their own form of piety, which focused not on wealth and power but on spiritual nourishment, particularly as provided by the Eucharist. For women mystics, radical fasting became preparation for the reception of the Eucharist, often described in highly emotional and erotic terms. After a long period of fasting, Lukardis of Oberweimar (d. 1309) had a vision in which Christ appeared to her as a handsome youth and blew into her mouth. In the words of her biographer, "She was infused with such sweetness and such inner fruition that she felt as if drunk." From the age of 23, Catherine of Siena (d. 1380) subsisted entirely on the Eucharist, cold water, and bitter herbs that she sucked and then spat out. She wrote of the importance of the Eucharist, "We must attach ourselves to the breast of Christ crucified, which is the source of charity, and by means of that flesh we draw milk." For pious women, fasting and devotion to the Eucharist did not mean rejection of the body but rather were attempts to use their senses to approach perfect union with God, who was for them both food and drink.

Heresy and Revolt

Only a thin line separated the saint's heroic search for union with God from the heretic's identification with God. The radical Brethren of the Free Spirit believed that God was all things and that all things would return to God. Such pantheism denied the possibility of sin, punishment, and the need for salvation. Members of the sect were hunted down, and many were burned as heretics. Local bishops and clergy often confused Beguines, Beghards, and Brethren of the Common Life with adherents of the Free Spirit movement. The specter of the Inquisition, the ecclesiastical court system charged with ferreting out heretics, hung over all such communities.

John Wycliffe. When unorthodox Christians were protected by secular lords, the ecclesiastical courts were powerless. Such was the case with John Wycliffe (ca. 1330–1384), an Oxford theologian who attacked the doctrinal and political bases of the Church. He taught that the value of the sacraments depended on the worthiness of the priest administering them. He also insisted that God conferred ecclesiastical authority on individuals, but that an individual who was sinful, be he priest, bishop, or pope, forfeited the right to exercise that authority. He also taught that Christ was present in the Eucharist only in spirit, that indulgences were useless, and that salvation depended on divine predestination rather than individual merit. Normally, those teachings would have led him to the stake. But he had also attacked the Church's right to wealth and luxury, an idea whose political implications pleased the English monarchy and nobility. Wycliffe's own exemplary manner of life and his teaching that the Church's role in temporal affairs should be severely limited made him an extremely popular figure in England. Thus he was allowed to live and teach in peace. Only under Henry V (1413–1422) were Wycliffe's followers, known as Lollards, vigorously suppressed by the state.

Before that condemnation took place, however, Wycliffe's teachings reached the kingdom of Bohemia through the marriage of Charles IV's daughter Anne of Bohemia to the English king Richard II. Anne took with her to England a number of Bohemian clerics, some of whom studied at Oxford and absorbed the political and religious teachings of Wycliffe, which they then took back to Bohemia. In Prague, some of Wycliffe's less radical teachings took root among the theology faculty of the new university. Wycliffe's ideas were particularly popular with Czech professors of theology, who were demanding not only a reform of religious teaching and practice but also a reduction of the influence of German professors at the University of Prague.

Jan Hus. The leading proponent of Wycliffe's teachings in Prague was Jan Hus (1373–1415), an immensely popular young master and preacher. Although Hus rejected Wycliffe's ideas about the priesthood and the sacraments, he and other Czech preachers attacked indulgences and demanded a reform of Church liturgy and morals. They grafted those religious demands onto an attack on German dominance of the Bohemian kingdom. The attacks outraged both the Pisan pope John XXIII (1410–1415) and the Bohemian king Wenceslas IV (1378–1419), who favored the German faction. The pope excommunicated Hus, and the king expelled the Czech faculty from the university. Hus believed that he was not a heretic and that a fair hearing would clear him. To defend his position, he agreed to travel to the Council of Constance under promise of safe conduct from the emperor-elect Sigismund. There he was tried on a charge of heresy, convicted, and burned at the stake.

News of Hus's execution touched off a revolt in Bohemia. Unlike the peasant revolts of the past, however, the revolt had broad popular support throughout all levels of Czech society. Peasants, nobles, and townspeople saw the attack on Hus and his followers as an attack on Czech independence and

■ In this illustration from a fifteenth-century chronicle, Jan Hus, wearing a heretic's hat, is shown being burned at the stake.

national interest by a Church and an empire controlled by Germans. The rebels slaughtered the largely German city council and defeated an army sent by emperor-elect Sigismund to crush the revolt. Soon a radical faction known as the Taborites was demanding the abolition of private property and the institution of a communal state. Although moderate **Hussites** and Bohemian Catholics combined to defeat the radicals in 1434, most of Bohemia remained Hussite throughout the fifteenth century. The sixteenth-century reformer Martin Luther declared himself a follower of Jan Hus.

Religious Persecution in Spain

A different anxiety about religious unity existed in the Iberian peninsula, where since the eleventh century Christian conquest had brought thousands of Jews and Muslims under Christian rule. These populations were the key to the economic and cultural vitality of the peninsula, and the kings of Castile, Aragon, and other Iberian monarchies initially took pains to protect their non-Christian subjects. However, in the fourteenth and fifteenth centuries, these protections disappeared in the face of rising xenophobia.

Jews had been a part of the Iberian population since Roman times and, while persecuted by the Visigoths, they had flourished under more benign Islamic rule. As the Conquest of Spain progressed, Jewish artisans, merchants, farmers, physicians, royal advisers, and moneylenders formed an important community in these new kingdoms. Because they were under direct control (and taxation) of the king rather than of local authorities, they enjoyed special royal protection and considerable rights of self-government, although they continued to be mistrusted by their Christian neighbors and were denigrated as "Christ killers" and suspected of all sorts of crimes.

Life for Muslims in Christian Spain was more difficult. Early, benign treatment by conquerors was condemned by northern clergy in their entourages, particularly by Cluniac monks. Too, Muslims under Christian rule were co-religionists of independent Muslim states in the peninsula, and Christian rulers feared subversion and revolt, such as actually did occur in Castile in 1264.

Nevertheless, through the thirteenth century, while kings of England and France expelled Jews from their kingdoms and in Germany they were subject to sporadic pogroms and massacres, Spanish Jewish and Muslim communities managed to survive. This fragile existence was shattered in the fourteenth and fifteenth centuries. The causes were complex: a declining economy, political unrest, Christian triumphalism as the reconquest moved into its last stages, and nascent nationalism all increased intercultural tensions. In 1391, mendicant friars inflamed Aragon with preaching against Jews and caused widespread violent attacks. Thereafter, in towns across Spain Christians rose up in arms against their Jewish neighbors in riots animated by both a hatred of Jews and a protest against the king. Thousands died and thousands more were forced to convert.

The Muslim population fared no better. In the fifteenth century Muslims faced conversion or expulsion, first to Granada and, after that last Muslim principality fell in 1492, to North Africa. Those who resisted were hunted down, their villages destroyed, and their populations dispersed.

In time, even Muslim and Jewish converts (termed respectively *moriscos* and *conversos*) found that Christian baptism was not necessarily a protection. Most moriscos remained secretly faithful to Islam and were ruthlessly persecuted and expelled. Many conversos also continued to practice their faith in secret for generations. However, many descendants of Jewish converts became sincere Christians: their ranks included bishops, inquisitors, and even saints (such as Teresa of Ávila). Nevertheless, Spaniards became obsessed with fears of anyone descended from Jews or Muslims and instituted legal sanctions against anyone who could not prove "purity of blood," that is, who might have Jewish or Muslim ancestors.

William of Ockham and the Spirit of Truth

The critical and individualistic approach that characterized religion during the Later Middle Ages was also typical of the philosophical thought of the period. The delicate balance between faith and reason taught by Aquinas and other intellectuals in the thirteenth century disintegrated in the fourteenth. As in other areas of life, intellectuals questioned the basic suppositions of their predecessors, directing intellectual activity away from general speculations and toward particular, observable reality.

The person primarily responsible for the new intellectual climate was the English Franciscan William of Ockham (ca.

CONVIVENCIA

By the High Middle Ages the position of Jews in western Europe was difficult. They had been expelled from England and from France. In Spain, under a system known as Convivencia, *or living together, they still enjoyed royal protection. However, as this text, known as* Las Siete Partidas, *issued in 1263 by King Alfonso X of Castile and in force through the fourteenth and fifteenth centuries shows, hostility, fueled by unfounded rumors of ritual murder, was making Jewish life increasingly precarious.*

Focus Questions

What beliefs and prejudices led to Christians' intolerance toward Jews? What protections did Jews receive from the king?

Jews should pass their lives among Christians quietly and without disorder, practicing their own religious rites, and not speaking ill of the faith of Our Lord Jesus Christ, which Christians acknowledge. Moreover, a Jew should be very careful to avoid preaching to, or converting any Christian, to the end that he may become a Jew, by exalting his own belief and disparaging ours. Whoever violates this law shall be put to death and lose all his property. And because we have heard it said that in some places Jews celebrated, and still celebrate Good Friday, which commemorates the Passion of Our Lord Jesus Christ, by way of contempt; stealing children and fastening them to crosses, and making images of wax and crucifying them, when they cannot obtain children; we order that, hereafter, if in any part of our dominions anything like this is done, and can be proved, all persons who were present when the act was committed shall be seized, arrested and brought before the king; and after the king ascertains that they are guilty, he shall cause them to be put to death in a disgraceful manner, no matter how many there may be.

We also forbid any Jew to dare to leave his house or his quarter on Good Friday, but they must all remain shut up until Saturday morning; and if they violate this regulation, we decree that they shall not be entitled to reparation for any injury or dishonor inflicted upon them by Christians.

Saturday is the day on which Jews perform their devotions, and remain quiet in their lodgings, and do not make contracts or transact any business; and for the reason that they are obliged by their religion, to keep it, no one should on that day summon them or bring them into court. Wherefore we order that no judge shall employ force or any constraint upon Jews on Saturday, in order to bring them into court on account of their debts; or arrest them; or cause them any other annoyance; for the remaining days of the week are sufficient for the purpose of employing compulsion against them, and for making demands for things which can be demanded of them, according to law. Jews are not bound to obey a summons served upon them on that day; and, moreover, we decree that any decision rendered against them on Saturday shall not be valid; but if a Jew should wound, kill, rob, steal, or commit any other offense like these for which he can be punished in person and property, then the judge can arrest him on Saturday.

We also decree that all claims that Christians have against Jews, and Jews against Christians shall be decided and determined by our judges in the district where they reside, and not by their old men. And as we forbid Christians to bring Jews into court or annoy them on Saturday; so we also decree that Jews, neither in person, nor by their attorneys, shall have the right to bring Christians into court, or annoy them on this day. And in addition we forbid any Christian, on his own responsibility, to arrest wrong any Jew either in his person or property, but where he has any complaint against him he must bring it before our judges; and if anyone be so bold as to use violence against the Jews, or rob them of anything he shall return them double the value of the same.

Las Siete Partidas, tr. Samuel Parsons Scott (Chicago: Published for the Comparative Law Bureau of the American Bar Association by Commerce Clearing House, Inc., 1931).

1300–1349). Ockham was no ivory-tower intellectual. He was a dedicated Spiritual Franciscan whose defense of radical poverty led to his excommunication by the cantankerous Pope John XXII. Excommunication drove Ockham to the court of John's enemy, the emperor Louis IV, where he became a dedicated propagandist for the imperial cause. There he developed a truly radical political philosophy. Imperial power, Ockham argued, derived not from the pope but from the people. He believed that people should be free to determine their own form of government and to elect rulers. They should be able to make their choice directly, as in the election of the emperor by electors who represent the people, or implicitly, through continuing forms of government. In either case, Ockham believed, government should be entirely secular and neither popes nor bishops nor priests should have any role. Ockham went still further. He denied the absolute authority of the pope, even in spiritual matters. Rather, Ockham argued, parishes, religious orders, and monasteries should send representatives to regional synods that in turn would elect representatives to general councils. Both laypersons and clergy would serve on the councils, which were to act rather like parliaments, tempering papal absolutism.

As radical as Ockham's political ideas were, his philosophical outlook was even more extreme and exerted a more direct and lasting influence. The Christian Aristotelianism that developed in the thirteenth century had depended on the validity of general concepts, called *universals,* that could be analyzed through the use of logic. Aquinas and others who studied the eternity of the world, the existence of God, the nature of the soul, and other philosophical questions believed that people could reach general truths by abstracting universals from particular, individual cases. Ockham argued that universals were merely names, no more than convenient tags for discussing individual things. He stated that universals had no connection with reality and could not be used to reason from particular observations to general truths. Ockham's radical **nominalism** (from the Latin *nomen,* "name") thus denied that human reason could aspire to certain truth. For Ockham and his followers, philosophical speculation was essentially a logical, linguistic exercise, not a way to certain knowledge.

Ockham died in 1349, a victim of the plague, but his political and philosophical teachings lived on. His ideas on Church governance by a general council representing the whole Christian community offered the one hope for a solution to the Great Schism that erupted shortly after his death. Conciliarists such as Pierre d'Ailly (1350–1420) and Jean de Gerson (1363–1429) drew on Ockham's attack on papal absolutism to propose an alternative church. The Council of Constance, which ended the schism, was the fruit of Ockham's political theory, as were the various organizational structures of the Protestant churches of the sixteenth century.

Just as Ockham's political theory dominated the later fourteenth century, his nominalist philosophy won over the philosophical faculties of Europe. Since he had discredited the power of Aristotelian logic to increase knowledge, the result was, on the one hand, a decline in abstract speculation, and on the other hand, a greater interest in scientific observation of individual phenomena. The next generation of Parisian professors, trained in the tradition of Ockham, laid the foundation for scientific studies of motion and the universe that led to the scientific discoveries of the sixteenth and seventeenth centuries.

Vernacular Literature and the Individual

Just as the religious and philosophical concerns of the later Middle Ages developed within national frameworks and criticized accepted authority from the perspective of individual experience, the vernacular (as opposed to Latin) literatures of the age began to explore the place of the individual within an increasingly complex society. Across Europe, authors reviewed the traditional values of society with a critical eye, reworking and transforming traditional literary genres into statements both personal and profound.

Italy. In Italy, a trio of Tuscan poets, Dante Alighieri (1265–1321), Francesco Petrarch (1304–1374), and Giovanni Boccaccio (1313–1375), not only made Italian a literary language but composed in it some of the greatest literature of all time. Dante, the first and greatest of the three, was born into a modest but respectable Florentine family, and after receiving an excellent education entered the public life of his city. At the same time, he began writing poetry and quickly acquired a reputation for his ability to express in love lyrics a new sensitivity and individual expression. In 1301, he fell victim to the viciousness of Florentine politics and was exiled from his beloved city for the remainder of his life. For two decades he traveled throughout Italy, residing in the courts of friendly princes and writing philosophical treatises and literary works, which culminated in his *Divine Comedy,* written during the last years of his life.

The Divine Comedy is a view of the whole Christian universe, populated with people from antiquity and from Dante's own day. The poem is both a sophisticated summary of philo-

■ A miniature painted by Guglielmo Giraldi to illustrate Canto VIII of Dante's *Inferno* shows Dante and Virgil being ferried across the River Styx by the boatman Phlegyas.

sophical and theological thought at the beginning of the fourteenth century and an astute political commentary on his times. The poet sets this vision within a three-part poetic journey through hell (*Inferno*), purgatory (*Purgatorio*), and heaven (*Paradiso*). In each part, Dante adopts a poetic style appropriate to the subject matter. His journey through hell to witness the sufferings of the damned is described in brutal, immediate language that lets readers almost feel the agony of the condemned, each of whom receives an eternal punishment appropriate to his or her sins. The violent conquerors Alexander the Great and Attila the Hun, for example, wallow for all eternity in boiling blood as punishment for spilling the blood of so many others.

Dante, *The Divine Comedy*

In purgatory, Dante meets sinners whose punishments will someday end. Those he described in a language of dreams and imagination, of nostalgic recollections cast in a misty landscape of the memory. On a ledge populated by hoarders and wasters, for example, the poet hears but does not see Hugh Capet, founder of the French Capetian dynasty, who describes a vision of his greedy descendants who devastate Italy to gain riches. Dante described paradise in a symbolic language that is nonphysical and nonrepresentational. In the face of transcendent perfection, human imagery and poetry fail. In his final vision of heaven, he sees the reflected light of a mystical rose in which the saints are ranked. Those include both religious leaders such as Bernard of Clairvaux and political leaders such as Emperor Henry VII, grandfather of Charles IV. *The Divine Comedy* is Dante's personal summary of all that was good and bad in medieval culture and politics.

England. English literature emerged from more than two centuries of French cultural domination with the writings of William Langland (ca. 1330–1395) and Geoffrey Chaucer (ca. 1343–1400). Both presented images of contemporary society with a critical and often ironic view. In *Piers Plowman,* Langland presents society from the perspective of the peasantry. Chaucer's work is much more sophisticated and wide-ranging, weaving together the whole spectrum of late medieval literature and life.

Chaucer was born into a London merchant family and spent a long and successful career as a courtier, serving English aristocrats and finally the king both in England and on the Continent. His travels brought him into contact with the literary and philosophical traditions of all of Europe, and he mastered every genre, always molding them with wit and imagination into something new.

Dante had set his great poem within a vision of the other world. Chaucer placed his tales in the mouths of a group of 30 pilgrims traveling to the tomb of Thomas à Becket at Canterbury. The pilgrims represent every walk of life and spectrum of medieval society: a simple knight, a vulgar miller, a lawyer, a lusty widow, a merchant, a squire, a physician, a nun, her chaplain, and a monk, among others. Each pilgrim is at once strikingly individual and representative of his or her profession or station in life. The tales that they tell are drawn from folklore, Italian literature, lives of the saints, courtly romance, and religious sermons. However, Chaucer played with the tales and their genres in the retelling. He used them to contrast or illuminate the persons and characters of their tellers, as well as to comment in subtle and complex ways on the literary, religious, and cultural traditions of which they were part. His knight, for example, tells a tale of chivalric love taken from Boccaccio. However, in Chaucer's version, the tale becomes both more real and vivid and more humorous as he plays with the traditional genre of courtly love poetry. The Wife of Bath, a forceful woman who has survived five husbands, argues for the superiority of married life over celibacy, particularly when the wife controls the marriage. Her tale, which takes a form common in religious sermons, continues her argument. It is a retelling of a fairy tale in which a woman is released from a spell by a knight. She offers him the choice of having her ugly and faithful or beautiful and free to bestow her favors where she will. The knight courteously leaves the decision to her and is rewarded by her promise to be both fair and faithful. In his mastery of the whole heritage of medieval culture and his independent use of that heritage, Chaucer proved himself the greatest English writer before Shakespeare.

France. Much of Italian and English literature drew material and inspiration from French, which continued into the fifteenth century to be the language of courtly romance. In France, literature continued to project an unreal world of allegory and nostalgia for a glorious if imaginary past. Popular literature, developed largely in the towns, often dealt with courtly themes, but with a critical and more realistic eye.

CHRONOLOGY

The Later Middle Ages, 1300–1500

1305–1377	Babylonian Captivity (Avignon papacy)
1337–1452	Hundred Years' War
1347–1352	Black Death spreads throughout Europe
1358	Jacquerie revolt of French peasants; Etienne Marcel leads revolt of Parisian merchants
1378	Ciompi revolt in Florence
1380	Death of Catherine of Siena
1378–1417	Great Schism divides Christianity
1381	Great Rebellion of English peasants
1409–1410	Council of Pisa
1414–1417	Council of Constance ends Great Schism
1415	Jan Hus executed
1431	Death of Joan of Arc
1455–1485	English Wars of the Roses

In that literary world appeared a new and extraordinary type of poet, a woman who earned her living with her pen, Christine de Pisan (1364–ca. 1430). Married at 16 and widowed at 25, de Pisan was left virtually impoverished, with the responsibility for supporting herself, her three children, her mother, and a niece. Rather than remarrying, she decided to earn her way as an author—an unheard-of decision for a woman of the fourteenth century. Beginning her education from scratch, she absorbed history and literature and began writing the sorts of conventional love poems popular with the French aristocracy. From there she moved to autobiographical poetry in which she described how fortune had changed her life. Her success was immediate and tremendous. Kings, princes, and aristocrats from England to Italy bought copies of her works and tried to attract her to their courts.

As a professional woman of letters, de Pisan fought the stereotypical medieval image of women as weak, sexually aggressive temptresses. With wit and reason she argued that women could be virtuous and showed the fallacies of traditional antifeminist preaching, poetry, and belief. She appealed to women to develop their own sense of self-worth directly from experience and not to rely on the advice of men, who, no matter how well read, could not have any direct, accurate knowledge of the meaning of being a woman. In her *Hymn to Joan of Arc,* she saluted her famous contemporary for her accomplishments: bringing dignity to women, striving for justice, and working for peace in France.

Although Christine de Pisan was the exception rather than the rule, her life and writing epitomized the new possibilities and new interests of the fifteenth century. They included an acute sense of individuality, a willingness to look for truth not in the clichés of the past but in actual experience, and a readiness to defend one's views with tenacity. Although an heir of the medieval world, de Pisan, like her contemporaries, already embodied the attitudes of a new age. That new age was reflected in a second tradition in fifteenth-century France, that of realist poetry. Around 1453, just as the English troops were enduring a final battering from the French artillery, Duke Charles of Orléans (1394–1465) organized a poetry contest. Each contestant was to write a ballad that began with the contradictory line, "I die of thirst beside the fountain." The duke, himself an outstanding poet, wrote an entry that embodied the traditional courtly themes of love and fortune:

I die of thirst beside the fountain,
Shaking from cold and the fire of love;
I am blind and yet guide the others;
I am weak of mind, a man of wisdom;
Too negligent, often cautious in vain,
I have been made a spirit,
Led by fortune for better or for worse.

An unexpected and very different entry came from the duke's prison. The prisoner-poet François Villon (1432–ca. 1464) was a child of the Paris streets, an impoverished student, a barroom brawler, a killer, and a thief who spent much of his life trying to escape the gallows. He was also the greatest realist poet of the Middle Ages. His entry read:

I die of thirst beside the fountain,
Hot as fire, my teeth clattering,
At home I am in an alien land;
I shudder beside a glowing brazier,
Naked as a worm, gloriously dressed,
I laugh and cry and wait without hope,
I take comfort and sad despair,
I rejoice and have no joy,
Powerful, I have no force and no strength,
Well received, I am expelled by all.

Christine de Pisan presenting a manuscript of her poems to Isabeau of Bavaria, the wife of King Charles VI of France.

The duke focused on the sufferings of love, the thief on the physical sufferings of the downtrodden. The two poets represent the contradictory tendencies of literature in the Later Middle Ages. From Prague to Paris, vernacular languages everywhere had come into their own. Poets used their native tongues to express a spectrum of sentiments and to describe a spectrum of emotions and values. The themes and ideas expressed ranged from the polished, traditional values of the aristocracy, trying to maintain the ideals of chivalry in a new and changed world, to the views of ordinary people, by turns reverent or sarcastic, joyful or despondent.

CONCLUSION

Late in life, Christine de Pisan relinquished her independence to enter a convent. Charles of Orléans was so moved by Villon's poetry that he released him from prison. The pope and the Hussites came to terms. King Charles VII ordered a new investigation into Joan of Arc, which absolved her—posthumously—of the charge of heresy. The religious, political, and cultural systems of the later Middle Ages remained sufficiently flexible to absorb the contradictory tendencies that they had created. The flexibility would not last. In the next century, the political, religious, and cultural landscapes of Europe would be transformed by the new impulses born in the Later Middle Ages.

The fourteenth and fifteenth centuries saw demographic collapse brought on by plague and accentuated by overpopulation and the ravages of warfare. They saw the transformation of the masses of the poor from the objects of Christian charity to the objects of fear and mistrust. During those centuries, warfare in France, England, Italy, and elsewhere evolved from elite battles to devastating professional campaigns of mass destruction capable of leaving whole countries in ruins for decades. Peasants fought for survival; aristocrats and wealthy merchants fought for greater power, prestige, and wealth on an international scale. Family alliances and merchant companies bound Europe together in a web of blood and money.

As the inherited forms of social and political organization strained to absorb those new conditions, individuals sought their own answers to the problems of life and death, using the legacy of the past, but using it in novel and creative ways. Dynasts created new principalities without regard for ancient allegiances. Mystics and heretics sought God without benefit of traditional religious hierarchies, and poets and philosophers sought personal expression outside the confines of inherited tradition.

The legacy of the Later Middle Ages was a complex and ambiguous one. The thousand years of synthesis of classical, barbarian, and Christian traditions did not disappear. The bonds holding the world together were not yet broken. But the last centuries of the Middle Ages bequeathed a critical detachment from that heritage expressed in the revolts of peasants and workers, the preaching of radical religious reformers, and the poems of mystics and visionaries.

QUESTIONS FOR REVIEW

1. What social and political forces prevented both the Holy Roman Emperors and the French kings from uniting the lands they ruled?
2. How did disease transform social relations in fourteenth-century Europe?
3. Why did a division in the papacy mean both political chaos and spiritual fear for Europeans?
4. How did the vernacular literature of Dante, Chaucer, and Christine de Pisan represent a departure from previous literary traditions?

KEY TERMS

Black Death, *p. 295*
Ciompi, *p. 299*
conciliarism, *p. 305*
dynasts, *p. 289*
Golden Bull, *p. 290*
Great Schism, *p. 304*
Hanseatic League, *p. 302*
Hundred Years' War, *p. 291*
Hussites, *p. 308*
indulgences, *p. 304*
Jacquerie, *p. 298*
nominalism, *p. 310*

DISCOVERING WESTERN CIVILIZATION ONLINE

You can obtain more information about the Later Middle Ages at the Websites listed below. See also the Companion Website that accompanies this text, www.ablongman.com/kishlansky, which contains an online study guide and additional resources.

Politics as a Family Affair

Web Gallery of Art: Bohemian School
www.kfki.hu/~arthp/tours/mini/Bohemian.html
Overview of art and architecture in Bohemia under the patronage of Charles IV.

The Hundred Years' War History Page
geocities.com/Wellesley/Veranda/1912/hundred/history.htm#top
A Web page devoted to the Hundred Years' War.

Life and Death in the Later Middle Ages

Internet Resources on the Black Death
www.historyguide.org/ancient/death.html
An annotated list of Web links to sites about the Great Plague of the fourteenth century.

The Spirit of the Later Middle Ages

Avignon: The Medieval and Papal Period
www.avignon.com/anglais/avi003.html
A brief introduction to Avignon and the papal palaces.

The World of Dante
http://www3.iath.virginia.edu/dante/
A hypermedia site for those who want to explore Dante's *Inferno* through text and image.

The Chaucer Pedagogy Page
http://hosting.uaa.alaska.edu/afdtk/pedagogy.htm
A comprehensive site for students and teachers of Chaucer.

Christine de Pisan
http://home.infionline.net/~ddisse/christin.html
A site with background and links to Christine de Pisan and her works.

SUGGESTIONS FOR FURTHER READING

General Reading

Robert Bartlett, *The Making of Europe: Conquest, Colonization, and Cultural Change, 950–1350* (Princeton, NJ: Princeton University Press, 1993). A comparative study of Europe's expansion into the Celtic, Islamic, and Slavic worlds in the Later Middle Ages.

Johan Huizinga, *The Autumn of the Middle Ages,* trans. Rodney J. Payton and Ulrich Mammitzsch (Chicago: University of Chicago Press, 1996). An important new translation of the classic interpretation of culture and society in the Burgundian court in the Later Middle Ages.

Daniel Waley, *Later Medieval Europe: From Saint Louis to Luther* (London: Longman, 1985). A brief introduction with a focus on Italy.

Politics as a Family Affair

Adrian R. Bell, *War and the Soldier in the Fourteenth Century* (Woodbridge, Suffolk and Rochester, NY: Boydell Press, 2004). Account of the ordinary soldier's experience in the Hundred Years' War.

Richard W. Kaeuper, *Chivalry and Violence in Medieval Europe* (Oxford: Oxford University Press, 1999). A fine analysis of the complex relationship between chivalric ethos and the violence of aristocratic society in the Middle Ages.

Jean W. Sedlar, *East Central Europe in the Middle Ages, 1000–1500* (Seattle: University of Washington Press, 1994). A thematic introduction to the medieval history of the region that today comprises Poland, the Czech Republic, Slovakia, Hungary, Romania, Bulgaria, Albania, and the former Yugoslavia.

Life and Death in the Later Middle Ages

P. Dollinger, *The German Hansa* (Stanford, CA: Stanford University Press, 1970). A brief history of the Hansa intended for the nonspecialist.

Bronislaw Geremek, *The Margins of Society in Late Medieval Paris,* trans. Jean Birrell (Cambridge: Cambridge University Press, 1987). A landmark study of the urban poor in the Later Middle Ages.

Edward S. Hunt and James M. Murray, *A History of Business in Medieval Europe, 1200–1550* (Cambridge: Cambridge University Press, 1995). A brief and readable history of medieval business practice.

David Nicholas, *The Growth of the Medieval City: From Late Antiquity to the Early Fourteenth Century* (London and New York: Longman, 1997). A comprehensive survey of medieval towns.

Jonathan Ray, *The Sephardic Frontier: The Reconquista and the Jewish Community in Medieval Iberia* Important new look at the Jewish community of Iberia during the Reconquista.

Teofilo F. Ruiz, *Spanish Society 1400–1600* (Harlow: Longman, 2001). A sensitive and original survey of Spanish society at the end of the Middle Ages.

Philip Zieger, *The Black Death* (New York: Sutton Publishing, 1999). A reliable introduction to the plague in the fourteenth century.

The Spirit of the Later Middle Ages

Renate Blumenfeld-Kosinski, ed., trans. Kevin Brownlee, *The Selected Writings of Christine De Pizan: New Translations, Criticism* (New York: Norton, 1997). A selection of de Pizan's works and of scholarship about her. The place to start for learning about her.

Caroline Walker Bynum, *Holy Feast and Holy Fast: The Religious Significance of Food to Medieval Women* (Berkeley: University of California Press, 1987). An imaginative and scholarly examination of the role of food in the spirituality of medieval women.

Eamon Duffy, *The Stripping of the Altars: Traditional Religion in England, 1400–1580* (New Haven: Yale University Press, 1992). A revisionist study of local religion at the end of the Middle Ages.

David A. Fein, *François Villon Reconsidered* (New York: Macmillan, 1997). Villon's poetry and his life examined by an authority.

Malcolm Lambert, *Medieval Heresy: Popular Movements from the Gregorian Reform to the Reformation,* 2nd ed. (Oxford: Blackwell Publishers, 1992). A comprehensive survey of heretical movements from the eleventh to the sixteenth centuries.

Scott L. Waugh and Peter D. Diehl, eds., *Christendom and Its Discontents: Exclusion, Persecution, and Rebellion, 1000–1500* (New York: Cambridge University Press, 1995). Important collection of essays on heresy and dissent in western Europe.

Stefano Zuffi, *European Art of the Fifteenth Century* (Los Angeles: J. Paul Getty Museum, 2005). Artistic change at the end of the Middle Ages.

For a list of additional titles related to this chapter's topics, please see http://www.ablongman.com/kishlansky.

CHAPTER 11

THE ITALIAN RENAISSANCE

DINING AL FRESCO

LEONARDO DA VINCI'S *LAST SUPPER*

No period of Western history is better known for its artwork than that of the Italian Renaissance. It was an age with a taste for opulence and a purse to satisfy its hunger. Masters competed against each other for the most lucrative commissions. Leonardo da Vinci learned his trade in Florence, but at the age of 30 he offered his services as a military engineer to the warrior Duke of Milan. Four years later he was established as a court artist.

THE VISUAL RECORD

His most important commission came in 1495 when he was instructed to decorate the wall of the new Dominican dining hall in the church of Santa Maria delle Grazie. The church was to house the tomb of the duke and his family, and Leonardo was commissioned to decorate it with a painting appropriate for the grandeur of the Sforza family and the practical purpose for which the room was to be used. He chose as his theme the Passover meal of Jesus and his Apostles.

Although *The Last Supper* was a conventional scene for a dining hall, Leonardo did not paint it conventionally. Rather than represent a group dining at leisure, he captured a moment of agitation, just after Jesus proclaimed that one of the Apostles would betray him. As you look at the picture, on the far right, you see that Matthew points back to Jesus as if to say, "Did you hear that?" At the center right, Thomas raises his finger and James sweeps his hand as if to proclaim their innocence. The three Apostles at the far left are obviously dumbstruck; Andrew holds both of his hands out as if trying to repel the thought. At the center left, Peter whispers something to John, who appears lost in concentration. Only Judas does not seem shocked by the revelation. Seated in the forefront on the left, he clutches a purse in one hand while his left hand and Jesus' right hand reach for the same bowl of wine. Every face and gesture have a story to tell, and Leonardo shows the Apostles as naturally human rather than as the idealized biblical figures of previous portrayals.

The Last Supper tells a story, but it is also designed for the contemplation of the Dominicans as they dined. Thus the painting contains much Christian symbolism, some of it deliberately ambiguous to stimulate thought. The position of the hands of Jesus, palm up and palm down, has led to centuries of speculation, while the feminine features of John have recently been the subject of a pulp-fiction sensation. The Apostles are arranged in four groups of three, the key number in the Christian doctrine of the Trinity. The groups themselves are organized in variously shaped triangles, as is the figure of Jesus in the center. The scene takes place in front of three painted windows and three decorated arches containing the arms of the dukes of Milan.

Jesus is the centerpiece of the painting in every possible way. During restoration a nail was found in the wall at the center of his right eye. It is supposed that Leonardo ran strings from that nail to determine the place of the other figures, for the lines of perspective all emanate from there. Jesus expresses serenity in contrast to the Apostles' agitation. The window directly behind his head gives the impression of surrounding him in a halo. Most interestingly, the figure of Jesus is larger than that of any of the others, though the

■ Leonardo da Vinci's *The Last Supper* (1495). A conventional scene of dining, yet one full of symbolism, in which da Vinci masterfully captures a crucial moment for Christianity.

arrangement of the group does not make this emphasis immediately obvious.

Perhaps because of all of these qualities, *The Last Supper* was an immediate sensation. But Leonardo had made a tragic mistake. In an attempt to create bolder colors, he shunned the traditional technique of fresco painting in which the paint was applied while the plaster was wet and hardened into it. Instead, using a mixture of egg whites and oil, Leonardo applied the paint to a dry surface. At first the experiment was a success and the reds, golds, and aquamarines stood out as in no other wall painting. But in less than 25 years, the paint began to crack and flake. Down through the centuries retouching and restoring were constantly necessary and very little of what remains on the wall of the church of Santa Maria delle Grazie today is what Leonardo put there more than five hundred years ago.

LOOKING AHEAD

The Last Supper is but one of many masterpieces produced on the Italian peninsula during the centuries dubbed the Renaissance. In this chapter we shall see how philosophy, art, architecture, and literature enjoyed a remarkable development in the Italian city-states and how Renaissance ideals were exported throughout the Continent and came to define the age.

CHAPTER OUTLINE

RENAISSANCE SOCIETY

Perhaps the most surprising result of the Black Death was the way in which European society revived itself in the succeeding centuries. Even at the height of the plague, a spirit of revitalization was evident in the works of artists and writers. Petrarch (1304–1374), the great humanist poet and scholar, was among the first to differentiate the new age in which he was living from two earlier ones: the **classical** world of Greece and Rome, which he admired, and the subsequent Dark Ages, which he detested. That spirit of self-awareness is one of the defining characteristics of the **Renaissance.** "It is but in our own day that men dare boast that they see the dawn of better things," wrote Matteo Palmieri (1406–1475). Like many others, Marsilio Ficino (1433–1499), a Florentine physician and philosopher who translated Plato and dabbled in astrology, dubbed his times a golden age: "This century, like a golden age, has restored to light the liberal arts, which were almost extinct: grammar, poetry, rhetoric, painting, sculpture, architecture, and music." The Renaissance was a new age by self-assertion. In that self-assertion, wave after wave of artistic celebration of the human spirit found its wellspring and created a legacy that is still vibrant 500 years later.

What was the Renaissance? A French word for an Italian phenomenon, *renaissance* literally means "rebirth." The word captures both the emphasis on humanity that characterized Renaissance thinking and the renewed fascination with the classical world. The Renaissance revered things classical, which to them meant ancient Latin and Greek history and literature. But the Renaissance was an age rather than an event. There is no moment at which the Middle Ages ended, and late medieval society was artistically creative, socially well developed, and economically diverse. Yet eventually the pace of change accelerated, and it is best to think of the Renaissance as an era of rapid transitions. Encompassing the two centuries between 1350 and 1550, it passed through three distinct phases. The first, from 1350 to 1400, was characterized by a declining population, the uncovering of classical texts, and experimentation in a variety of art forms. The second phase, from 1400 to 1500, was distinguished by the creation of a set of cultural values and artistic and literary achievements that defined Renaissance style. The large Italian city-states developed stable and coherent forms of government, and the warfare between them gradually ended. In the final period, from 1500 to 1550, invasions from France and Spain transformed Italian political life, and the ideas and techniques of Italian writers and artists radiated to all points of the Continent. Renaissance ideas and achievements spread throughout western Europe and were particularly important in Holland, but they are best studied where they first developed, on the Italian peninsula.

The Urban Environment

The Italian peninsula differed sharply from other areas of Europe in the extent to which it was urban. By the late Middle Ages nearly one in four Italians lived in a town, in contrast to one in ten elsewhere. Not even the plague did much to change that ratio. There were more Italian cities and more people in them. By 1500, seven of the ten largest cities in the West were in Italy. Naples, Venice, and Milan, each with a population of more than 100,000, led the rest. But not every city was a great metropolis, and it was the numerous smaller towns, with populations nearer to 1000, that gave the Italian peninsula its urban character. Cities also served as convenient centers of judicial and ecclesiastical power.

Cities acted as central places around which a cluster of large and small villages was organized. Urban areas, especially the small towns, provided markets for the agricultural produce of the countryside and for the manufactured goods of the urban artisans. This structure allowed for the specialization in agricultural and industrial life that increased both productivity and wages. Cities also caught the runoff of rural population, especially the surplus of younger sons and daughters who could not be accommodated on the farms. Cities grew by migration rather than by natural increase. Thus the areas surrounding a city were critical to its prosperity and survival. The urban system was a network of cities encompassed by towns and encircled by rural villages. Florence, the dominant city in the region of Tuscany, exemplifies that relationship. Although it possessed two-thirds of its region's wealth, Florence contained only 14 percent of the regional population. The surrounding countryside was agriculturally rich because marketing costs were low and demand for foodstuffs was high. Smaller cities channeled their local produce and trade to Florence.

Urban populations were organized far differently from rural ones. On the farms, the central distinctions involved ownership of land. Some farmers owned their estates outright and left them intact to their heirs. Others were involved in a

MAP DISCOVERY

Largest Cities in Western Europe, ca. 1500

Examine the locations of western Europe's largest cities at the beginning of the sixteenth century. Where were these cities concentrated? What was the least urbanized part of Europe? Based on this information, why do you suppose the Mediterranean Sea was considered the center of Europe? What was distinctive about the Holy Roman Empire?

sharecropping system by which absentee owners of land supplied working capital in return for half of the farm's produce. A great gulf in wealth separated owners from sharecroppers, but within the groups the gaps were not as great. There were gradations, but those ordinarily were temporary conditions that bad harvests, generous dowries, or divided inheritances balanced out over time.

In the city, however, distinctions were based first on occupation, which largely corresponded to social position and wealth. Cities began as markets, and the privilege to participate in the market defined citizens. City governments provided protection for consumers and producers by creating monopolies through which standards for craftsmanship were maintained and profits for craftsmen were guaranteed. The monopolies were called guilds or companies. Each large city had its own hierarchy of guilds. At the top were the important manufacturing groups—clothiers, metalworkers, and the like. Just below them were bankers, merchants, and the administrators of civic and Church holdings. At the bottom were grocers, masons, and other skilled workers. Roughly speaking, all of those within the guild structure, from bottom to top, lived comfortably. Yet the majority of urban inhabitants were not members of guilds. Many managed to eke out a living as wage laborers; many more were simply destitute. As a group, the poor constituted as much as half of the entire population. Most were dependent upon civic and private charity for their survival.

The disparities between rich and poor were overwhelming. The concentration of wealth in the hands of an ever-narrowing group of families and favored guilds characterized every large city. One reason for that was the extreme instability of economic life. Prices and wages fluctuated wildly in response to local circumstance. After an epidemic of plague, wages climbed and the prices of consumer goods tumbled. A bad harvest sent food prices skyrocketing. Only those able to even out the extreme swings by stockpiling goods in times of plenty and consuming them in times of want were safe. Capital, however initially accumulated, was the key to continued wealth. Monopolies ensured the profitability of trade and manufacturing, but only those with sufficient capital could engage in either. In Florence, for example, 10 percent of the families controlled 90 percent of the wealth, with an even more extreme concentration at the top. The combined wealth of the richest 100 Florentine families was greater than the combined wealth of 87 percent of the city's population.

Production and Consumption

The concentration of wealth and the way in which it was used defined the Renaissance economy. Economic life is bound up in the relationship between resources and desires, or, as economists would have it, supply and demand. The late medieval economy, despite the development of international banking and long-distance trade, was still an economy of primary producers: between 70 and 90 percent of Europe's population was involved in subsistence agriculture. Even in Italy, which contained the greatest concentration of urban areas in the world, agriculture predominated. The manufacture of clothing was the only other significant economic activity. Moreover, most of what was produced was for local consumption rather than for the marketplace. The relationship between supply and demand was precisely measured by the full or empty stomach. Even in good times, more than 80 percent of the population lived at subsistence level with food, clothing, and shelter their only expenses. Thus, when the market economy of the Renaissance is discussed, it actually is the circumstances of the few rather than the many that are under discussion.

The defining characteristic of the early Renaissance economy was population change. Recurring waves of plague kept population levels low for more than a century. Between 1350 and 1450, one in every six years was characterized by an unusually high mortality rate. At the end of that period, for example, Florence's population was only a quarter of what it had been at the beginning. The dramatic reduction in population depressed economic growth. Until 1460 the major sectors of the economy were stagnant. Only after the sustained population increase toward the end of the fifteenth century did the general economy revive. Until then, in both agriculture and manufacturing, supply outstripped demand.

On the farms, overabundance resulted from two related developments, the concentration of surviving farmers on the best land and the enlargement of their holdings. In the shops, finished products outnumbered the consumers who survived the epidemics. Overproduction meant lower prices for basic commodities, and the decline in population meant higher wages for labor. The result was that, at the lowest levels of society, survivors found it easier to earn their living and even to create a surplus than had their parents. For a time, the lot of the masses improved.

But for investors, such economic conditions meant that neither agriculture nor cloth making were particularly attractive. Expensive investments in land or equipment for sharecropping were paid back in inexpensive grain. High wages for the few surviving skilled workers brought a return only in cheap cloth. In such circumstances, consumption was more attractive than investment. It was not merely the perceived shortage in profitable investments that brought on the increase in conspicuous consumption during the fifteenth century. In the psychological atmosphere created by unpredictable, swift, and deadly epidemics, luxurious living seemed an appropriate response. Moreover, although tax rates increased, houses and personal property remained exempt, making luxury goods attractive investments. Even those at the lowest levels of society eagerly purchased whatever their meager means permitted.

For those reasons, the production and consumption of luxuries soared. By the middle of the fourteenth century, Florence was known for its silks and jewelry as much as for its cloth. Venice became a European center for the glass industry, especially for the finely ground glass that was used in eye-

■ Skilled workers in cities contributed greatly to European economic growth in the late medieval period. This scene shows the manufacture of cannons in a Florentine foundry.

glasses. Production of specialty crops such as sugar, saffron, fruits, and high-quality wine expanded. International trade increasingly centered on acquiring Eastern specialities, resulting in the serious outflow of gold and silver that enriched first the Byzantine and then the Ottoman emperors.

The Experience of Life

Luxury helped improve a life that for rich and poor alike was short and uncertain. Nature was still people's most potent enemy. Renaissance children who survived infancy found their lives governed by parentage and by gender. In parentage, the great divide was between those who lived with surplus and those who lived at subsistence. The first category encompassed the wealthiest bankers and merchants down to those who owned their own farms or engaged in small urban crafts. The vast majority of urban and rural dwellers comprised the second category. About the children of the poor we know very little other than that their survival was unlikely. If they did not die at birth or shortly afterward, they might be abandoned—especially if female—to the growing number of orphanages in the cities, waste away from lack of nutrition, or fall prey to ordinary childhood diseases for which there were no treatments. Eldest sons were favored; younger daughters were disadvantaged. In poor families, however, this favoritism meant little more than early apprenticeship to day labor in the city or farm labor in the countryside. Girls were frequently sent out as domestic servants far from the family home.

Childhood. Children of the wealthy had better chances for survival than did children of the poor. For children of the wealthy, childhood might begin with "milk parents," life in the home of the family of a wet nurse who would breast-feed the baby through infancy. Only the very wealthy could afford a live-in wet nurse, which would increase the child's chances of survival. Again, daughters were more likely to be sent far from home and least likely to have their nursing supervised. The use of wet nurses not only emancipated parents from the daily care of infants, it also allowed them to resume sexual relations. Nursing women refrained from sex in the belief that it affected their milk.

During the period between weaning and apprenticeship, Renaissance children lived with their families. There was no typical Renaissance family. Nuclear families—parents and their children under one roof—were probably more common than extended families, which might include grandparents and other relatives. But the composition of the family changed over the course of the life cycle and included times in which married children or grandparents were present and other times when a single parent and small children were the only members. Moreover, even nuclear families commonly contained stepparents and stepchildren as well as domestic servants or apprentices. Thus a child returning to the parental household was as likely to form emotional bonds with older siblings as with parents.

Sons inherited the family business and its most important possessions—tools of the trade or beasts of labor for the farm. Inheritance customs varied. In some places only the eldest son received the equipment of the family occupation; in others, such as Tuscany, all the sons shared it. Still, in the first 15 years of life, the most-favored children would have spent between one-third and one-half of their time outside the household in which they had been born.

Marriage and the Family. Expectations for daughters centered on their chances of marriage. For a girl, dowry was everything. If a girl's father could provide a handsome one, her future was secure; if not, the alternatives were a convent, which would take a small bequest, or a match lower down the social scale, where the quality of life deteriorated rapidly. Daughters of poor families entered domestic service in order to have a dowry provided by their masters. The dowry was taken to the household of the husband. There the couple resided until they established their own separate family. If the husband died, it was to his parental household that the widow returned.

The Office and Dutie of an Husband

Women married in late adolescence, usually around the age of 20. Among the wealthy, marriages were perceived as familial alliances and business transactions rather than love matches. The dowry was an investment on which fathers expected a return, and while the bride might have some choice, it was severely limited. Compatibility was not a central feature in matchmaking. Husbands were, on average, ten years older than their wives and likely to leave them widows. In the early fifteenth century, about one-fourth of all adult women in Florence were widows, many without prospects of remarriage.

Life experiences differed for males. Men married later—near the age of 25 on the farms, nearer the age of 30 in the cities—because of the cost of setting up in trade or on the land. Late marriage meant long supervision under the watchful eye of father or master, an extended period between adolescence and adulthood. The reputation that Renaissance cities gained for homosexuality and licentiousness must be viewed in light of the advanced age at which males married. The level of sexual frustration was high, and its outlet in ritual violence and rape was also high.

The establishment of one's own household through marriage was a late rite of passage, considering the expectations of early death. Men came of age at 30 but were thought to be old by 50. Thus for men marriage and parenthood took place in middle age rather than in youth. Valued all their lives more highly than their sisters, male heads of households were the source of all power in their domiciles, in their shops, and in the state. They were responsible for overseeing every aspect of the upbringing of their children, even choosing wet nurses for their infants and spouses for their daughters. But their wives were essential partners who governed domestic life. Women labored not only at the hearth, but in the fields and shops as well. Their economic contribution to the well-being of the family was critical, both in the dowry they brought at marriage

ON THE FAMILY

Leon Battista Alberti wrote a number of important tracts that set out the general principles of a subject, including On Architecture, *which was considered the basic text for 300 years. His writings on the family bring insight into the nature of a patriarchal, male-dominated institution.*

Focus Questions

According to Alberti, why is it important for men to look for an "honorable manner" when choosing a wife? What role would Alberti see the wife playing in a marriage?

They say that in choosing a wife one looks for beauty, parentage, and riches. . . . Among the most essential criteria of beauty in a woman is an honorable manner. Even a wild, prodigal, greasy, drunken woman may be beautiful of feature, but no one would call her a beautiful wife. A woman worthy of praise must show first of all in her conduct, modesty, and purity. Marius, the illustrious Roman, said in that first speech of his to the Roman people: "Of women we require purity, of men labor." And I certainly agree. There is nothing more disgusting than a coarse and dirty woman. Who is stupid enough not to see clearly that a woman who does not care for neatness and cleanliness in her appearance, not only in her dress and body but in all her behavior and language, is by no means well mannered? How can it be anything but obvious that a bad-mannered woman is also rarely virtuous? We shall consider elsewhere the harm that comes to a family from women who lack virtue, for I myself do not know which is the worse fate for a family, total celibacy or a single dishonored woman. In a bride, therefore, a man must first seek beauty of mind, that is, good conduct and virtue.

In her body he must seek not only loveliness, grace, and charm but must also choose a woman who is well made for bearing children, with the kind of constitution that promises to make them strong and big. There's an old proverb, "When you pick your wife, you choose your children." All her virtues will in fact shine brighter still in beautiful children. It is a well-known saying among poets: "Beautiful character dwells in a beautiful body." The natural philosophers require that a woman be neither thin nor very fat. Those laden with fat are subject to coldness and constipation and slow to conceive. They say that a woman should have a joyful nature, fresh and lively in her blood and her whole being. They have no objections to a dark girl. They do reject girls with a frowning black visage, however. They have no liking for either the undersized or the overlarge and lean. They find that a woman is most suited to bear children if she is fairly big and has limbs of ample length. They always have a preference for youth, based on a number of arguments which I need not expound here, but particularly on the point that a young girl has a more adaptable mind. Young girls are pure by virtue of their age and have not developed any spitefulness. They are by nature modest and free of vice. They quickly learn to accept affectionately and unresistingly the habits and wishes of their husbands.

From Leon Battista Alberti, *On the Family.*

and in the labor they contributed to the household. If their wives died, men with young children remarried quickly. While there were many bachelors, there were few widowers.

In most cases death came suddenly. Epidemic diseases, of which plague was the most virulent, struck with fearful regularity. Even in the absence of a serious outbreak, there were always deaths in town and country attributable to the plague. Epidemics struck harder at the young—children and adolescents, who were the majority of the population—and hardest in the summer months, when other viruses and bacteria weakened the population. Influenza must have been the second largest cause of death, although that can only be speculated in the absence of proper records. Medical treatment was more likely to hasten death than to prolong life. Lorenzo de' Medici's physician prescribed powdered pearls for the Florentine ruler's gout. After that Lorenzo complained more of stomach pains than of gout. Such remedies revealed a belief in the harmony of nature and the healing power of rare substances. The remedies were not silly or superstitious, but they were not effective either. Starvation was rare, less because of food shortage than because the seriously undernourished were more likely to succumb to disease than to famine. In urban areas, the government would intervene to provide grain from public storehouses at times of extreme shortage; in the countryside, large landholders commonly exercised the same function.

The Quality of Life

Although life may have been difficult during the Renaissance, it was not unfulfilling. Despite constant toil and frequent hardship, people of the Renaissance had reason to believe that their lives were better than those of their ancestors and that their children's lives would be better still. On the most basic

■ Double portraits of husbands and wives showed the union of individuals and of families. In this ca. 1465 diptych of Frederico da Montefeltro, the Duke of Urbino, and his wife Battista Sforza, artist Piero della Francesca shows the couple facing each other against the distant backdrop of the territory they ruled. Their union joined the Montefeltro family ruling the small duchy of Urbino in central Italy with the powerful Sforza family that ruled Milan. The wealthy couple was also a generous patron of the artist.

level, health improved and, for those who survived plague, life expectancy increased. Better health was related to better diet. Improvement came from two sources: the relative surplus of grain throughout the fifteenth century and the wider variety of foods consumed. Bread remained the most widely consumed foodstuff, but even subsistence consumers were beginning to supplement their diet with meat and dairy products. There was more pork and lamb in the diet of ordinary people in the fifteenth century than there would be for the next 400 years. At the upper levels of society, sweet wine and citrus fruits helped offset the lack of vegetables. The diversification of diet resulted from improvements in transportation and communication, which brought more goods and services to a growing number of towns in the chain that linked the regional centers to the rural countryside.

As in the Middle Ages, the Church remained the spatial, spiritual, and social center of people's lives. Though Renaissance society became more worldly in outlook, this worldliness took place within the context of an absorbing devotional life. There was not yet any separation between faith and reason. The Church provided explanations for both the mysterious and the mundane. The clergy performed the rituals of baptism, marriage, and burial that measured the passage of life. Religious symbols also adorned the flags of militia troops, the emblems of guilds, and the regalia of the city itself. The Church preserved holy relics that were venerated for their power to protect the city or to endow it with particular skills and resources. Through its holy days as much as through its rituals, the Church helped to channel leisure activities into community celebrations.

A growing sense of civic pride and individual accomplishment were underlying characteristics of the Italian Renaissance, enhanced by the development of social cohesion and community solidarity that both Church and city-state fostered. It is commonly held that the Renaissance was both elitist and male dominated, that it was an experience separate from that of the society at large. There can be no question that it was the rich who commissioned works of art and that it was the highly skilled male craftsmen who executed them. But neither lived in a social vacuum. The Renaissance was not the result of the efforts of a privileged few. Family values that permitted early apprenticeships in surrogate households and that emphasized the continuity of crafts from one generation to the next made possible the skilled artists of the Renaissance cities. The stress on the production of luxury goods placed higher value upon individual skills and therefore upon excellence in workmanship. Church and state sought to express social values through representational art. One of the chief purposes of wall murals was to instruct the unlettered in religion, to help them visualize the central episodes in Christian history and thus increase the pleasure they derived from their faith. The grandiose architecture and statuary that adorned central places were designed to enhance civic pride, nurture loyalty, and communicate the protective power of public institutions.

For ordinary people, the world of the Renaissance was not much different from the world of the Middle Ages. Although urban areas grew, providing a wider variety of occupations and a varied material life, most people continued to scratch a meager living from the soil. The crucial difference from generation to generation was the degree of infectious diseases and the rate of rising or falling population. For the lucky ones there was surplus, for the unfortunate there was dearth. Within those confines, men were privileged over women, having greater security, status, and monopolizing power. But the tightly knit organization of family life protected the weak and the poor, while the Church provided faith, hope, and charity.

RENAISSANCE ART

In every age, artistic achievement represents a combination of individual talent and predominant social ideals. Artists may be at the leading edge of the society in which they live, but it is the spirit of that society that they capture in word, song, or image. Artistic disciplines also have their own technical development. Individually, Renaissance artists were attempting to solve problems of perspective and three-dimensionality that had defeated their predecessors. But the particular techniques or experiments that interested them owed as much to the social context as they did to the artistic one. For example, the urban character of Italian government led to the need for civic architecture—public buildings on a grand scale. The celebration of individual achievement led to the explosive growth of portraiture. Not surprisingly, major technological breakthroughs were achieved in both areas. Nor should the brilliance of the artists themselves be underestimated. To deny genius is to deprecate humanity. What needs to be explained is not the existence of a Leonardo or a Michelangelo but their coexistence.

The relationship between artist and social context was all the more important in the Renaissance, when artists were closely tied to the crafts and trades of urban society and to the demands of clients who commissioned their work. Although it was the elite who patronized art, it was skilled tradesmen who produced it. Artists normally followed the pattern of any craftsman—an apprenticeship begun as a teenager and a long period of training and work in a master's shop. That form of education gave the aspiring artist a practical rather than a theoretical bent and a keen appreciation for the business side of art. Studios were identified with particular styles and competed for commissions from clients, especially the Church. Wealthy individuals commissioned art as investments, as marks of personal distinction, and as displays of public piety. They got what they paid for, usually entering into detailed contracts that stipulated the quality of materials and the amount of work done by the master. Isabella d'Este (1474–1539), one of the great patrons of Renaissance artists, wrote hundreds of letters specifying the details of the works she commissioned. She once sent an artist threads of the exact dimensions of the pictures she had ordered. Demand for art was high. The vast public works projects needed buildings, the new piazzas (public squares) and palazzos (private houses) needed statuary, and the long walls of churches needed murals.

The survival of so many Renaissance masterpieces allows us to reconstruct the stages by which the remarkable artistic achievements of the era took place. Although advances were made in a variety of fields during the Renaissance, the three outstanding areas were architecture, sculpture, and painting. Whereas modern artists would consider each a separate discipline, Renaissance artists crossed their boundaries without hesitation. Not only could the artists work with a variety of materials, their intensive and varied apprenticeships taught them to apply the technical solutions of one field to the problems of another. Few Renaissance artists confined themselves to one area of artistic expression, and many created works of enduring beauty in more than one medium. Was the greatest achievement of Michelangelo his sculpture of David, his paintings on the ceiling of the Sistine Chapel, or his design for the dome of Saint Peter's? Only a century of interdisciplinary cross-fertilization could have prepared the artistic world for such a feat.

An Architect, a Sculptor, and a Painter

The century that culminated in Michelangelo's extraordinary achievements began with the work of three Florentine masters who deeply influenced one another's development: Brunelleschi (1377–1446), Donatello (1386–1466), and Masaccio (1401–1428). In the Renaissance, the dominant artistic discipline was architecture. Buildings were the most expensive investment patrons could make, and the technical knowledge necessary for their successful construction was immense. Not only did the architect design a building, he also served as its general contractor, its construction supervisor, and its inspector. Moreover, the architect's design determined the amount and the scale of the statuary and decorative paintings to be incorporated. By 1400 the Gothic style of building had dominated western Europe for more than two centuries. Its pointed arches, vaulted ceilings, and slender spires had simplified building by removing the heavy walls formerly

IMAGE DISCOVERY

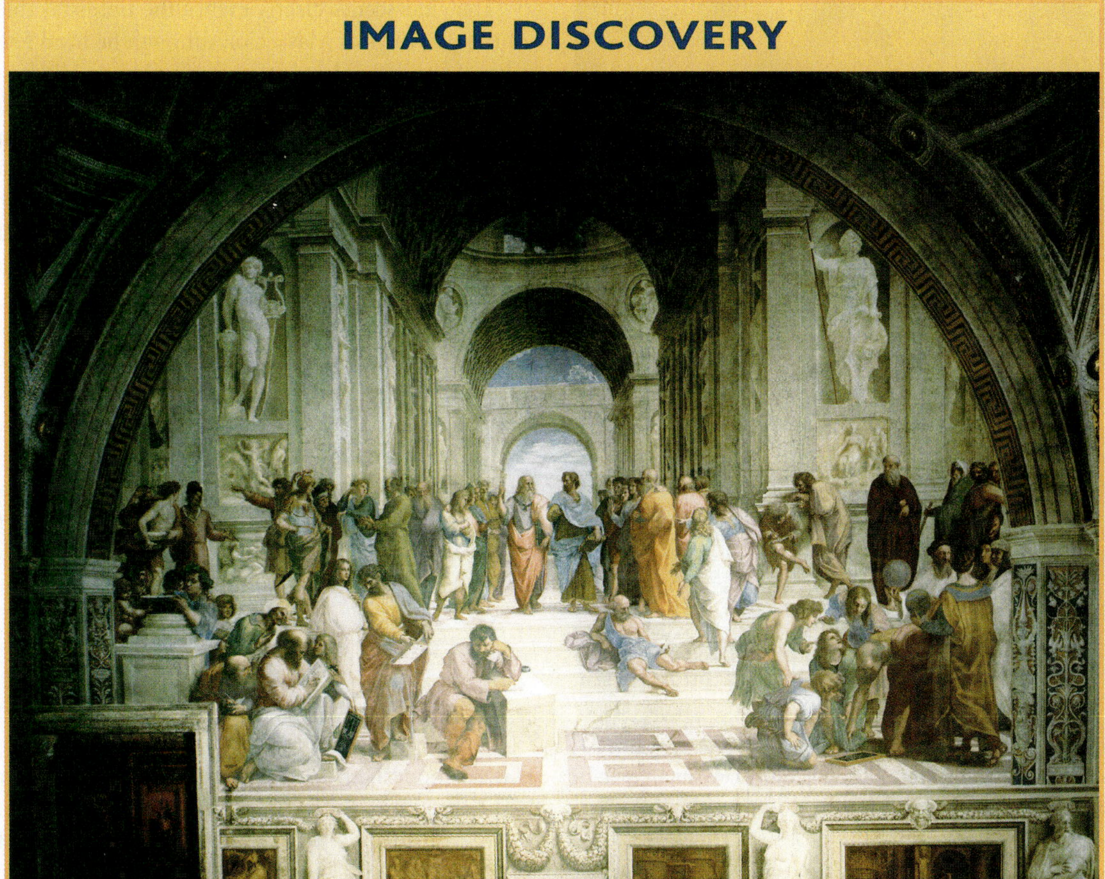

Philosophers and Painters

Raphael's fresco *The School of Athens* depicts the meeting of great minds of antiquity and of the Renaissance. The scene takes place in a dome, one of the architectural achievements of the ancient Mediterranean that was revived in the Renaissance. What might Raphael have sought to communicate by using ancient-turned-modern architecture to frame his gathering? Raphael depicts several distinct groups of learned men in active discussion. Do you think their topics differ? What can you determine about their discussions from the picture? For instance, why is the bearded man in the lower-right corner holding a globe? Which group is most important? The man with a long, white beard at the center of the painting, leading the largest group, is thought to be both Plato and Leonardo da Vinci. How would placing an ancient philosopher and a Renaissance man in the same body relate to Raphael's use of a dome as the setting for the school?

thought necessary to support great structures. Gothic construction permitted greater height, a characteristic especially desirable in cathedrals, which stretched toward the heavens. Although the buildings themselves were simplified, the techniques for erecting them became more complex. By the fifteenth century, architects had turned their techniques into an intricate style. They became obsessed by angular arches, elaborate vaultings and buttresses, and long, pointed spires.

It was Brunelleschi who decisively challenged the principles of Gothic architecture by recombining its basic elements with those of classical structures. His achievement was less an innovation than a radical synthesis of old and new. Basing his designs on geometric principles, Brunelleschi reintroduced planes and spheres as dominant motifs. His greatest work was the dome on the cathedral in Florence, begun in 1420. His design was simple but bold. The windows at the base of the dome of the cathedral illustrate Brunelleschi's geometric technique. Circular windows are set inside a square of panels, which in turn are set inside a rectangle. The facades are dominated by columns and rounded arches, proportionally spaced from a central perspective. Brunelleschi is generally credited with having been the first Renaissance artist to have understood and made use of perspective, though it was immediately put to more dramatic effect in sculpture and painting.

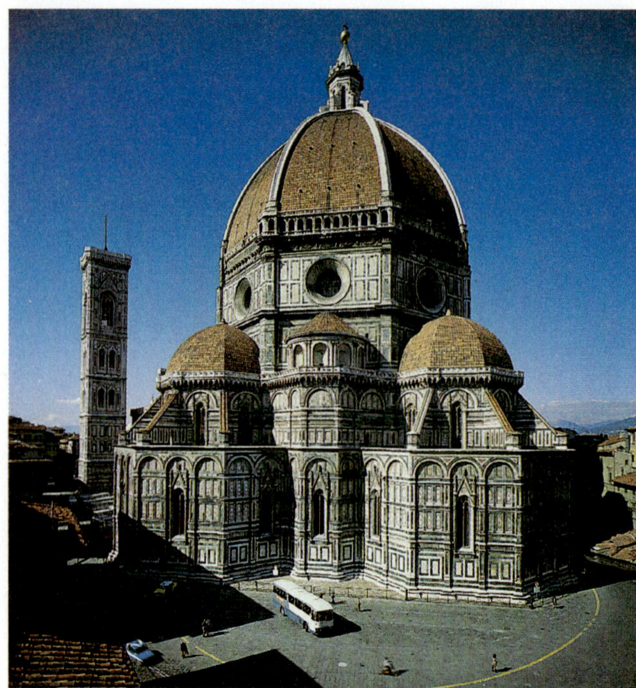

■ Florence Cathedral was begun by Arnolfo di Cambio in 1296. The nave was finished about 1350 and the dome, designed by Brunelleschi, was added in the 1420s. This view shows the dome and the apse end of the cathedral.

The sculptor's study was the human form in all of its three-dimensional complexity. The survival of Roman and Hellenistic pieces, mostly bold and muscular torsos, meant that the influence of classical art was most direct in sculpture. Donatello translated the classical styles into more naturalistic forms. His technique is evident in the long flowing robes that distinguish most of his works. Donatello sculpted the cloth, not in the stylized angularity of the past in which the creases were as sharp as sword blades, but in the natural fashion in which cloth hung. Donatello also revived the freestanding statue, which demanded greater attention to human anatomy because it was viewed from many angles. *Judith Slaying Holofernes* (1455) is an outstanding example of Donatello's use of geometric proportion and perspective. Each side of the piece captures a different vision of Judith in action. In addition, Donatello led the revival of the equestrian statue, sculpting the Venetian captain-general Gattamelata for a public square in Padua. The enormous bronze horse and rider (1445–1450) borrowed from surviving first- and second-century Roman models but relied upon the standpoint of the viewer to achieve its overpowering effect. The use of **linear perspective,** a technique applying principles of geometry to create the illusion of depth and dimension on a flat surface, was also a characteristic of Donatello's dramatic works. His breathtaking bas-relief altar scenes of the miracles of Saint Anthony in Padua, which resemble nothing so much as a canvas cast in bronze, utilize linear perspective and architectural elements to make the flattened relief panels spring to life.

The altar scenes clearly evince the unmistakable influence of the paintings of Masaccio. Although he lived fewer than 30 years, Masaccio created an enduring legacy. His frescoes in the Brancacci Chapel in Florence were studied and sketched by all the great artists of the next generation, who unreservedly praised his naturalism. What most claims the attention of the modern viewer is Masaccio's shading of light and shadow and his brilliant use of linear perspective to create the illusion that a flat surface has three dimensions. Masaccio worked with standard Christian themes, but he brought an entirely novel approach to them all. In an adoration scene he portrayed a middle-aged Madonna and a dwarfish baby Jesus; in a painting of Saint Peter paying tribute money he used his own likeness as the face of one of the Apostles. His two best-known works are *The Expulsion of Adam and Eve* (ca. 1425) and *The Holy Trinity* (1425). In *The Expulsion of Adam and Eve,* Masaccio has left an unforgettable image of the fall from grace in Eve's primeval anguish. Her deep eyes and hollow mouth are accentuated by casting the source of light downward and shading what otherwise would be lighted. In *The Holy Trinity,* Masaccio provides the classic example of the use of linear perspective. In the painting, the ceiling of a Brunelleschi-designed temple recedes to a vanishing point beyond the head of God, creating the simultaneous illusion of height and depth.

■ Donatello's bronze statue *Judith Slaying Holofernes* symbolized the Florentines' love of liberty and hatred of tyranny.

■ In this fresco, *The Expulsion of Adam and Eve* (ca. 1425), Masaccio's mastery of perspective helps create the illusion of movement, as an angel drives the grieving Adam and Eve out of paradise into the world.

Renaissance Style

By the middle of the fifteenth century, a recognizable Renaissance style had triumphed. Florence continued to lead the way, although ideas, techniques, and influences had spread throughout the Italian peninsula and even to the north and west. The outstanding architect of the period was Leon Battista Alberti (1404–1472), whose treatise *On Architecture* (1452) remained the most influential work on the subject until the eighteenth century. Alberti consecrated the geometric principles laid down by Brunelleschi and infused them with a humanist spirit. He revived the classical dictum that a building, like a body, should have an even number of supports and, like a head, an odd number of openings, which furthered precise geometric calculations in scale and design. But it was in civic architecture that Alberti made his most significant contributions. There he demonstrated how classical forms could be applied to traditional living space by being made purely decorative. His facade of the Palazzo Rucellai uses columns and arches not as building supports, but as embellishments that give geometric harmony to the building's appearance.

No sculptor challenged the preeminence of Donatello for another 50 years, but in painting there were many contenders for the garlands worn by Masaccio. The first was Piero della Francesca (ca. 1420–1492) who, though trained in the tradition of Masaccio, broke new ground in his concern for the visual unity of his paintings. From portraits to processions to his stunning fresco *The Resurrection* (ca. 1463), Piero concentrated upon the most technical aspects of composition. He was influenced by Alberti's ideas about the geometry of form, and it is said that his measurements and calculations for various parts of *The Resurrection* took more time than the painting itself. Another challenger was Sandro Botticelli (1445–1510), whose classical themes, sensitive portraits, and bright colors set him apart from the line of Florentine painters with whom he studied. His mythologies, *The Birth of Venus* and *Primavera* (both ca. 1478), depart markedly from the naturalism inspired by Masaccio. Botticelli's paintings have a dreamlike quality, an unreality highlighted by the beautiful faces and lithe figures of his characters.

Botticelli's concern with beauty and personality is also seen in the paintings of Leonardo da Vinci (1452–1519), whose creative genius embodied the Renaissance ideal of the "universal man." Leonardo's achievements in scientific, technical, and artistic endeavors read like a list of all of the subjects known during the Renaissance. His detailed anatomical drawings and the method he devised for rendering them, his botanical observations, and his engineering inventions (including models for the tank and the airplane) testify to his unrestrained curiosity. His paintings reveal the scientific application of mathematics to matters of proportion and perspective. The dramatic fresco *The Last Supper* (ca. 1495–1498), for example, takes the traditional scene of Jesus and his disciples at a long table and divides it into four groups of three, each with its

Vasari on Leonardo da Vinci

■ Botticelli's *Primavera* (Spring), also called *Garden of Venus*. Venus, in the center, is attended by the three Graces and by Cupid, Flora, Chloris, and Zephyr. Botticelli's figures have a dreamlike quality, an unreality highlighted by their beautiful faces and lithe figures.

own separate action, leaving Jesus to dominate the center of the picture by balancing its two sides. Leonardo's psychological portrait *La Gioconda* (1503–1506), popularly called the *Mona Lisa,* is quite possibly the best-known picture in the Western world.

From Brunelleschi to Alberti, from Masaccio to Leonardo da Vinci, Renaissance artists placed a unique stamp upon visual culture. By reviving classical themes, geometric principles, and a spirit of human vitality, they broke decisively from the dominant medieval traditions. Art became a source of individual and collective pride, produced by masters but consumed by all. Cities and wealthy patrons commissioned great works of art for public display. New buildings rose everywhere, adorned with the statues and murals that still stand as a testimony to generations of artists.

Michelangelo

The artistic achievements of the Renaissance culminated in the creative outpourings of Michelangelo Buonarroti (1475–1564). It is almost as if the age itself had produced a summation of how it wished to be remembered. Uncharacteristically, Michelangelo came from a family of standing in Florentine society and gained his apprenticeship over the opposition of his father. He claimed to have imbibed his love of sculpture from the milk of his wet nurse, who was the wife of a stonecutter. In 1490, Michelangelo gained a place in the household of Lorenzo de' Medici, thus avoiding the long years of apprenticeship during which someone else's style was implanted upon a young artist.

In 1496, Michelangelo moved to Rome. There his abilities as a sculptor brought him a commission from a French cardinal for a religious work in the classical style, which Michelangelo named the ***Pietà***. Although it was his first attempt at sculpting a work of religious art, Michelangelo would never surpass it in beauty or composition. The *Pietà* created a sensation in Rome, and by the time that Michelangelo returned to Florence in 1501, at the age of 26, he was already acknowledged as one of the great sculptors of his day. He was immediately commissioned to work on an enormous block of marble that had been quarried nearly a half-century before and had defeated the talents of a series of carvers. He worked continuously for three years on his *David* (1501–1504), a piece that completed the union between classical and Renaissance styles. Michelangelo's giant nude gives eloquent expression to his belief that the human body was the "mortal veil" of the soul.

Although Michelangelo always believed himself to be primarily a sculptor, his next outstanding work was in the field of painting. In 1508, Pope Julius II commissioned Michelangelo to decorate the small ceremonial chapel that had been built next to the new papal residence. The initial plan called for figures of the 12 apostles to adorn the ceiling, but Michelangelo soon launched a more ambitious scheme: to portray, in an extended narrative, human creation and those Old Testament events that foreshadowed the birth of Jesus. Everything about the execution of the Sistine Chapel paintings was extraordinary. First, Michelangelo framed his scenes within the architecture of a massive classical temple. In this way he was able to give the impression of having flattened the rounded surface ment for the grave of Saint Peter. The basework had already been laid, and drawings for the building's completion had been made 30 years earlier by Donato Bramante. Michelangelo altered the plans in an effort to bring more light inside the church and provide a more majestic facade outside. His main contribution, however, was the design of the great dome, which centered the interior of the church on Saint Peter's grave. More than the height, it is the harmony of Michelangelo's design that creates the sense of the building thrusting upward like a Gothic cathedral of old. The dome on Saint Peter's was the largest then known and provided the model, in succeeding generations, for Saint Paul's Cathedral in London and the U.S. Capitol building in Washington, DC.

Renaissance art served Renaissance society. It reflected both its concrete achievements and its visionary ideals. It was a synthesis of old and new, building upon classical models, particularly in sculpture and architecture, but adding newly discovered techniques and skills. Demanding patrons such as Pope Julius II, who commonly interrupted Michelangelo's work on the Sistine Chapel with criticisms and suggestions, fueled the remarkable growth in both the quantity and quality

■ Leonardo da Vinci's *La Gioconda*, or *Mona Lisa*.

on which he worked. Then, on the two sides of the central panels, he represented figures of Hebrew prophets and pagan Sybils as sculptured marble statues. Finally, within the center panels came his fresco scenes of the events of the creation and of human history from the Fall to the Flood. His representations were simple and compelling: the fingers of God and Adam nearly touching; Eve with one leg still emerging from Adam's side; the half-human snake in the temptation. All are majestically evocative.

The *Pietà*, the *David*, and the paintings of the Sistine Chapel were the work of youth. Michelangelo's crowning achievement—the building of Saint Peter's—was undertaken at the age of 71. The purpose of the church was to provide a suitable monu-

■ Michelangelo, *Pietà* (1498–1499). The sculptor's contract for the piece called for it to be "the most beautiful work in marble which exists today in Rome." Michelangelo made several trips to Carrara to find the highest quality marble for the *Pietà*.

The creation of Adam and Eve, a detail from Michelangelo's frescoes on the ceiling of the Sistine Chapel. The Sistine frescoes had become obscured by dirt and layers of varnish and glue applied at various times over the years. In the 1980s they were cleaned to reveal their original colors.

of Renaissance art. When Giorgio Vasari (1511–1574) came to write his *Lives of the Most Eminent Painters, Sculptors, and Architects* (1550), he found more than 200 artists worthy of distinction. But Renaissance artists did more than construct and adorn buildings and celebrate and beautify spiritual life. Inevitably their work expressed the ideals and aspirations of the society in which they lived, the new emphasis upon learning and knowledge; upon the here and now rather than the hereafter; and, most importantly, upon humanity and its capacity for growth and perfection.

RENAISSANCE IDEALS

Renaissance thought went hand in glove with Renaissance art. Scholars and philosophers searched the works of the ancients to find the principles on which to build a better life. They scoured monastic libraries for forgotten manuscripts, discovering among other things Greek poetry and history, the works of Homer and Plato, and Aristotle's *Poetics.* Their rigorous application of scholarly procedures for the collection and collation of those texts was one of the most important contributions of the Renaissance intellectuals who came to be known as **humanists.** Humanism developed in reaction to an intellectual world that was centered on the Church and dominated by otherworldly concerns. Humanism was secular in outlook, though by no means was it antireligious.

Humanists celebrated worldly achievements. Pico della Mirandola's *Oration on the Dignity of Man* (1486) is the best known of a multitude of Renaissance writings influenced by the discovery of the works of Plato. Pico believed that people could perfect their existence on earth because humans were divinely endowed with the capacity to determine their own fate: "O highest and most marvelous felicity of man! To him it is granted to have whatever he chooses, to be whatever he wills."

Thus humanists studied and taught the humanities—the skills of disciplines such as **philology,** the art of language, and **rhetoric,** the art of expression. Although they were mostly laypeople, humanists applied their learning to both religious and secular studies. Humanists were not antireligious.

THE RENAISSANCE MAN

Giorgio Vasari celebrated the creativity of the artists who made Italy the center of cultural activity in the Later Middle Ages. His commemoration of their achievements through the medium of biographies helped to create the aura that still surrounds Renaissance art.

Focus Questions

What makes Leonardo such an exemplary "Renaissance man"? Does Vasari see Leonardo as someone who excels in many separate fields, or does he see the different arts and sciences as unified?

The most heavenly gifts seem to be showered on certain human beings. Sometimes supernaturally, marvelously, they all congregate in one individual. Beauty, grace, and talent are combined in such bounty that in whatever that man undertakes, he outdistances all other men and proves himself to be specially endowed by the hand of God. He owes his pre-eminence not to human teaching or human power. This was seen and acknowledged by all men in the case of Leonardo da Vinci, who had, besides the beauty of his person (which was such that it has never been sufficiently extolled), an indescribable grace in every effortless act and deed. His talent was so rare that he mastered any subject to which he turned his attention. Extraordinary strength and remarkable facility were here combined. He had a mind of regal boldness and magnanimous daring. His gifts were such that his celebrity was worldwide, not only in his own day, but even more after his death, and so will continue until the end of time.

Leonardo was frequently occupied in the preparation of plans to remove mountains or to pierce them with tunnels from plain to plain. By means of levers, cranes, and screws, he showed how to lift or move great weights. Designing dredging machines and inventing the means of drawing water from the greatest depths were among the speculations from which he never rested. Many drawings of these projects exist which are cherished by those who practice our arts....

Leonardo, with his profound comprehension of art, began many things that he never completed, because it seemed to him that perfection must elude him. He frequently formed in his imagination enterprises so difficult and so subtle that they could not be entirely realized and worthily executed by human hands. His conceptions were varied to infinity. In natural philosophy, among other things, he examined plants and observed the stars—the movements of the planets, the variations of the moon, and the course of the sun....

From Giorgio Vasari, *Lives of the Most Eminent Painters, Sculptors, and Architects.*

Although they reacted strongly against Scholasticism (see Chapter 14), they were heavily indebted to the work of medieval churchmen, and most were devoutly religious. Nor were they hostile to the Church. Petrarch, Leonardo Bruni, and Leon Battista Alberti were all employed by the papal court at some time in their careers, as was Lorenzo Valla, the most influential of the humanists. Their interest in human achievement and human potential must be set beside their religious beliefs. As Petrarch stated quite succinctly: "Christ is my God; Cicero is the prince of the language I use."

Humanists and the Liberal Arts

The most important achievements of humanist scholars centered on ancient texts. It was the humanists' goal to discover as much as had survived from the ancient world and to provide texts of classical authors that were as full and accurate as possible.

Studying the Classical World. Although much was already known of the Latin classics, few of the central works of ancient Greece had been uncovered. Humanists preserved that heritage by reviving the study of the Greek language and by translating Greek authors into Latin. After the fall of Constantinople in 1453, Italy became the center for Greek studies as Byzantine scholars fled the Ottoman conquerors. Humanists also introduced historical methods in studying and evaluating texts, establishing principles for determining which of many manuscript copies of an ancient text was the oldest, the most accurate, and the least corrupted by copyists. That was of immense importance in studying the writings of the ancient Fathers of the Church, many of whose manuscripts had not been examined for centuries. They believed that the study of the "liberal arts" should be undertaken for its own sake. That belief gave a powerful boost to the ideal of the perfectability of the individual that appeared in so many other aspects of Renaissance culture.

Petrarch, *Letters to Cicero*

Humanists furthered the secularization of Renaissance society through their emphasis on the study of the classical world. The rediscovery of Latin texts during the Later Middle Ages spurred interest in all things ancient. Petrarch, who is rightly called the father of humanism, revered the great Roman rhetorician Cicero above all others. For Petrarch, Cicero's legacy was eloquence. He stressed that in his correspondence with the leading scholars of his day and taught it to those who would succeed him. From 1350 to 1450, Cicero was the dominant model for Renaissance poets and orators. The leading humanist in the generation after Petrarch was Leonardo Bruni (1370–1444), who was reputed to be the greatest Greek scholar of his day. He translated both Plato and Aristotle and did much to advance mastery of classical Greek and foster the ideas of Plato in the late fifteenth century.

Philology and Lorenzo Valla. The study of the origins of words, their meaning, and their proper grammatical usage may seem an unusual foundation for one of the most vital of all European intellectual movements. But philology was the humanists' chief concern and can be best illustrated by the work of Lorenzo Valla (1407–1457). Valla was brought up in Rome, where he was largely self-educated, although according to the prescriptions of the Florentine humanists. Valla entered the service of Alfonso I, king of Naples, and applied his humanistic training to affairs of state. The kingdom of Naples bordered on the Papal States, and its kings were in continual conflict with the papacy. The pope asserted the right to withhold recognition of the king, a right that was based upon the jurisdictional authority supposedly ceded to the papacy by the Emperor Constantine in the fourth century. The so-called Donation of Constantine had long been a matter of dispute, and its authenticity had been challenged frequently in the Middle Ages. But those challenges were made on political grounds, and the arguments of papal supporters were as strenuous as those of papal opponents. Valla settled the matter definitively. Applying historical and philological critiques to the text of the Donation, Valla proved that it could not have been written earlier than the eighth century, 400 years after Constantine's death. He exposed words and terms that had not existed in Roman times, such as *fief* and *satrap,* and thus proved beyond doubt that the Donation was a forgery and papal claims based upon it were without merit.

Civic Humanism. Valla's career demonstrates the impact of humanist values on practical affairs. Although humanists were scholars, they made no distinction between an active and a contemplative life. A life of scholarship was a life of public service. They saw their studies as means of improving themselves and their society: "Man is born in order to be useful to man." That **civic humanism** is best expressed in the writings of Leon Battista Alberti (1404–1472), whose treatise *On the Family* (1443) is a classic study of the new urban values, especially prudence and thrift. Alberti extolled the virtues of "the fatherland, the public good, and the benefit of all citizens." An architect, a mathematician, a poet, a playwright, a musician, and an inventor, Alberti was one of the great virtuosi of the Renaissance.

Alberti's own life might have served as a model for the most influential of all Renaissance tracts, Baldesar Castiglione's *The Courtier* (1528). While Alberti directed his lessons to the private lives of successful urban families, Castiglione (1478–1529) directed his to the public life of the aspiring elite. In Castiglione's view, the perfect courtier was as much born as made: "Besides his noble birth I would have the Courtier endowed by nature not only with talent and beauty of person and feature, but with a certain grace and air that shall make him at first sight pleasing." Everything that the courtier did was to maintain his pleasing grace and his public reputation. *The Courtier* was an etiquette book, and in it Castiglione prescribed every detail of the education necessary for the ideal state servant, from table manners to artistic attainments. Although each talent was to be acquired through careful study and application, it was to be manifested with *sprezzatura,* a natural ease and superiority that was the essence of the gentleman.

Renaissance Science

As the spirit of the Renaissance looked back to the classical world and ahead to the achievements that would come from the adaptation of ancient wisdom, so Renaissance scientific inquiry was focused in two directions. The first was text-based knowledge derived from recovered works mainly from classical Greece; the second was experiment-based knowledge achieved through observation. Texts dominated the life sciences, especially medicine and biology; experimentation enriched the physical sciences such as engineering and cartography. But it is important to realize that both ways of knowing blended together. Doctors were instructed by the classics but increasingly learned their anatomy by dissection. Navigators carried the works of Ptolemy on voyages of discovery but amended his maps and charts with what they found in practice.

The biological sciences were given new life by the recovery of the writings of Hippocrates and Galen. Medicine became a subject for learned inquiry and the medical school at Padua was considered the greatest in Europe. The work of Hippocrates concerned diagnosing common diseases and attempting to find treatments. Galen's studies of the human body, rediscovered, formed the basis for a new interest in anatomy and led to experiments in human dissection in the most advanced universities. Such experimentation improved knowledge of the skeleton and the placement of the organs, which led to medical advances in setting broken bones and treating injuries. Galen taught that the body was composed of **humors**—yellow bile, black bile, phlegm, and blood—that corresponded to the four elements of life—earth, air, water, and fire. In the healthy body the humors were well mixed together, but in the diseased body there was an imbalance. This understanding explains why doctors attempted to cure disease by the use of leeches or the practice of "bleeding," cutting open a vein and allowing blood to run out. The extraction of blood was believed to aid in restoring the balance of the humors and thus the health of the body.

Whereas the life sciences were advanced through attention to ancient texts, engineering developed through the experiences of Renaissance craftsmen and artists who were attempting to solve practical problems of proportion, stability, and height in the buildings, bridges, and ultimately domes that they built. Most of the important advances in engineering were actually made in the service of military ventures. The science of ballistics advanced through greater mathematical precision in studying the relationship between speed and trajectory in the shooting of artillery. It was Leonardo da Vinci who attempted to apply a theory of mechanics to Renaissance warfare, and he made drawings for the creation of war machines such as tanks and flying machines such as airplanes, though, of course, neither were produced during his lifetime. But he was expert in building working models of machines, in advising princes on their fortifications, and in suggesting improvements in the art of gunnery. All of his contributions were made by experimentation rather than through text-based learning. Wherever he went, Leonardo built workshops to construct models and kept careful notebooks of the results of his trials. This spirit of experimentation would ultimately lead to the birth of a recognizably scientific method in the next century.

■ Baldassare Castiglione sat for this portrait, painted by his friend Raphael, in 1515.

■ Portrait of Niccolò Machiavelli, who expounded his theory of statecraft in *The Prince*.

Machiavelli and Politics

At the same time that Castiglione was drafting a blueprint for the idealized courtier, Niccolò Machiavelli (1469–1527) was laying the foundation for the realistic sixteenth-century ruler. No Renaissance work has been more important or more controversial than Machiavelli's The Prince (1513). Its vivid prose, its epigrammatic advice—"Men must either be pampered or crushed"—and its clinical dissection of power politics have attracted generation after generation of readers. With Machiavelli began the science of politics.

Machiavelli, *The Prince*

Machiavelli came from an established Florentine family and entered state service as an assistant to one of his teachers, who then recommended him for the important office of secretary to the Council of Ten, the organ of Florentine government that had responsibility for war and diplomacy. Machiavelli devoted all his energies and his entire intellect to his career. He was a tireless correspondent, and he began to collect materials for various tracts on military matters. He also planned out a prospective history in which to celebrate the greatness of the Florentine Republic that he served.

THE LION AND THE FOX

Niccolò Machiavelli wrote The Prince *in 1513 while he was under house arrest. It is one of the classics of Western political theory in which the author separates the political from the moral.*

Focus Questions

According to Machiavelli, why is honesty not always the best policy? For a ruler, how valuable a tactic is a show of strength?

Everyone understands how praiseworthy it is in a prince to keep faith, and to live uprightly and not craftily. Nevertheless we see, from what has taken place in our own days, that princes who have set little store by their word, but have known how to overreach men by their cunning, have accomplished great things, and in the end got the better of those who trusted to honest dealing.

Be it known, then, that there are two ways of contending—one in accordance with the laws, the other by force; the first of which is proper to men, the second to beasts. But since the first method is often ineffectual, it becomes necessary to resort to the second. A prince should, therefore, understand how to use well both the man and the beast. . . . But inasmuch as a prince should know how to use the beast's nature wisely, he ought of beasts to choose both the lion and the fox; for the lion cannot guard himself from the toils, nor the fox from wolves. He must therefore be a fox to discern toils, and a lion to drive off wolves.

To rely wholly on the lion is unwise; and for this reason a prudent prince neither can nor ought to keep his word when to keep it is hurtful to him and the causes which led him to pledge it are removed. If all men were good, this would not be good advice, but since they are dishonest and do not keep faith with you, you in return need not keep faith with them.

From Niccolò Machiavelli, *The Prince.*

But as suddenly as Machiavelli rose to his position of power and influence, he fell from it. The militia that he had advocated and in part organized was soundly defeated by the Spaniards, and the Florentine Republic fell. Machiavelli was summarily dismissed from office in 1512 and was imprisoned and tortured the following year. Released and banished from the city, he retired to a small country estate and turned his restless energies to writing. Immediately he began work on what became his two greatest works, *The Prince* and the *Discourses on Livy* (1519).

Machiavelli has left a haunting portrait of his life in exile, and it is important to understand how intertwined his studies of ancient and modern politics were.

> On the coming of evening, I return to my house and enter my study; and at the door I take off the day's clothing, covered with mud and dust, and put on garments regal and courtly; and reclothed appropriately, I enter the ancient courts of ancient men, where, received by them with affection, I feed on that food which only is mine and which I was born for. For four hours of time I do not feel boredom, I forget every trouble, I do not dread poverty, I am not frightened by death; entirely I give myself over to them.

In this state of mind *The Prince* was composed.

The Prince is a handbook for a ruler who would establish a lasting government. It attempts to set down principles culled from historical examples and contemporary events to aid the prince in attaining and maintaining power. By study of those precepts and by their swift and forceful application, Machiavelli believed that the prince might even control fortune itself. *The Prince* is purely secular in content and philosophy. Where the medieval writer of a manual for princes would have stressed the divine foundations of the state, Machiavelli asserted the human bases: "The chief foundations on which all states rest are good laws and good arms." What made *The Prince* so remarkable in its day, and what continues to enliven debate over it, is that Machiavelli was able to separate all ethical considerations from his analysis. Whether that resulted from cynicism or from his own expressed desire for realism, Machiavelli uncompromisingly instructed the would-be ruler to be half man and half beast—to conquer neighbors, to murder enemies, and to deceive friends. Steeped in the humanist ideals of fame and *virtù*—a combination of virtue and virtuosity, of valor, character, and ability—he sought to reestablish Italian rule and place government upon a stable, scientific basis that would end the perpetual conflict among the Italian city-states.

The careers of both Lorenzo Valla and Niccolò Machiavelli illustrate how humanists were able to bring the study of the liberal arts into the service of the state. Valla's philological studies had a vital impact on diplomacy; Machiavelli's historical studies were directly applicable to warfare. Humanists created a demand for learning that helps account for the growth of universities, the spread of literacy, and the rise of printing. They also created a hunger for knowledge that characterized intellectual life for nearly two centuries.

MAP DISCOVERY

Italy, 1494

Notice how Italy was organized into city-states at the end of the fifteenth century. Which were the largest city-states? Which city-states seem most susceptible to foreign invasion? Which states had the best positioning for trade? When the wars of Italy began in 1494 (discussed later in this chapter), France sided with Milan against Naples, Florence, and the Papal States. Based on the positions of the combatants, what do you think would have been the likeliest route for the French invasion? Which city-states could the French avoid fighting?

THE POLITICS OF THE ITALIAN CITY-STATES

Like studs on a leather boot, **city-states** dotted the Italian peninsula. They differed in size, shape, and form. Some were large seaports, others small inland villages; some cut wide swaths across the plains, others were tiny islands. The absence of a unifying central authority in Italy, resulting from the collapse of the Holy Roman Empire and the papal schism, allowed ancient guilds and confraternities to transform themselves into self-governing societies. By the beginning of the fifteenth century the Italian city-states were the center of power, wealth, and culture in the Christian world.

That dominion rested on several conditions. First, Italy's geographical position favored the exchange of resources and goods between the East and the West. Until the fifteenth century, and despite the crusading efforts of medieval popes, the East and the West fortified each other. A great circular trade had developed, encompassing the Byzantine Empire, the North African coastal states, and the Mediterranean nations of western Europe. The Italian peninsula dominated the circumference of that circle. Its port cities, Genoa and Venice especially, became great maritime powers through their trade in spices and minerals. Second, just beyond the peninsula to the north lay the vast and populous territories of the Holy Roman Empire. There the continuous need for manufactured goods, especially cloths and metals, was filled by long caravans that traveled from Italy through the Alps. Milan specialized in metal crafts. Florence was a financial capital as well as a center for the manufacture of fine luxury goods. Finally, the city-states and their surrounding areas were agriculturally self-sufficient.

Because of their accomplishments, there has been a tendency to think of the Italian city-states as small nations. Even the term *city-state* implies national identity. Each city-state governed itself according to its own rules and customs, and each defined itself in isolation from the larger regional or tribal associations that once prevailed. Indeed, the struggles of the city-states against one another speak eloquently of their local self-identification. Italy was neither a nation nor a people.

The Five Powers

Although there were dozens of Italian city-states, by the early fifteenth century five had emerged to dominate the politics of the peninsula. In the south was the kingdom of Naples, the only city-state governed by a hereditary monarchy. Its politics were mired by conflicts over its succession, and it was not until the Spaniard Alfonso I of Aragon (1442–1458) secured the throne in 1443 that peace was restored. Bordering Naples were the Papal States, whose capital was Rome but whose territories stretched far to the north and lay on both sides of the spiny Apennine mountain chain that extends down the center of the peninsula. Throughout the fourteenth and early fifteenth centuries, the territories under the nominal control of the Church were largely independent and included such thriving city-states as Bologna, Ferrara, and Urbino. Even in Rome the weakened papacy had to contend with noble families for control of the city.

The three remaining dominant city-states were clustered together in the north. Florence, center of Renaissance culture, was one of the wealthiest cities of Europe before the devastations of the plague and the sustained economic downturn of the late fourteenth century. The city itself was inland and its main waterway, the Arno, ran to the sea through Pisa, whose subjugation in 1406 was a turning point in Florentine history. Nominally Florence was a republic, but during the fifteenth century it was ruled in effect by its principal banking family, the Medici.

To the north of Florence was the duchy of Milan, the major city in Lombardy. It too was landlocked, cut off from the sea by Genoa. But Milan's economic life was oriented northward to the Swiss and German towns beyond the Alps, and its major concern was preventing foreign invasions. The most warlike of the Italian cities, Milan was a despotism, ruled for nearly two centuries by the Visconti family.

The last of the five powers was the republic of Venice. Ideally situated at the head of the Adriatic Sea, Venice became the leading maritime power of the age. Until the fifteenth century, Venice had been less interested in securing a landed empire than in dominating a seaborne one. Its outposts along the Greek and Dalmatian coasts, and its favored position in Constantinople, were the source of vast mercantile wealth. The republic was ruled by a hereditary elite—headed by an elected **doge,** who was the chief magistrate of Venice—and a variety of small elected councils.

The political history of the Italian peninsula during the late fourteenth and early fifteenth centuries is one of unrelieved turmoil. Everywhere, the governments of the city-states were threatened by foreign invaders, internal conspiracies, or popular revolts. By the middle of the fifteenth century, however, two trends were apparent amid the political chaos. The first was the consolidation of strong centralized governments within the large city-states. The governments took different forms but yielded a similar result—internal political stability. The return of the popes to Rome after the Great Schism restored the pope to the head of his temporal estates and began a long period of papal dominance over Rome and its satellite territories. In Milan, one of the great military leaders of the day, Francesco Sforza (1401–1466), seized the reins of power. The succession of King Alfonso I in Naples ended a half century of civil war. In both Florence and Venice, the grip that the political elite held over high offices was tightened by placing greater power in small advisory councils and, in Florence, by the ascent to power of the Medici family. That process, known as the rise of signorial rule, made possible the establishment of a balance of power within the Italian peninsula.

It was the leaders of the Italian city-states who first perfected the art of diplomacy. Constant warfare necessitated continual alliances, and by the end of the fourteenth century the large city-states had begun the practice of keeping resident ambassadors at the major seats of power. That enhanced communication, a principal challenge in Renaissance diplomacy, and also provided leaders with accurate information about the conditions of potential allies and enemies. Diplomacy was both an offensive and a defensive weapon, especially because the city-states hired their soldiers as contract labor. The mercenary armies, whose leaders were known as ***condottieri*** from the name of their contract, were both expensive and dangerous to maintain. If they did not bankrupt their employers, they might desert them or, even worse, turn on them.

Venice: A Seaborne Empire

Water was the source of the prosperity of Venice. Located at the head of the Adriatic Sea, the city was formed by a web of lagoons. Through its center snaked the Grand Canal, whose banks were lined with large and small buildings that celebrated its civic and mercantile power. At the Piazza San Marco stood the vast palace of the doge, elected leader of the republic, and the Basilica of Saint Mark, a domed church built in the Byzantine style. At the Rialto were the stalls of the bankers and moneylenders, less grand perhaps but no less important. There, too, were the auction blocks for the profitable trade in European slaves, eastern European serfs, and battlefield captives who were sold into service in Egypt or Byzantium. On the eastern edge of the island city was the Arsenal, erected in the twelfth century to house the shipbuilding and arms manufacturing industries. Three centuries later it was the industrial marvel of the world, where the Venetian great galleys were constructed with assembly-line precision.

Its prosperity based on trade rather than conquest, Venice enjoyed many natural advantages. Its position at the head of the Adriatic permitted access to the raw materials of both the East and the West. The rich Alpine timberland beyond the city provided the hardwoods necessary for shipbuilding. The hinterland population were steady consumers of grain, cloth, and the new manufactured goods—glass, silk, jewelry, and cottons—that came pouring onto the market in the Later Middle Ages.

But the success of Venice owed more to its own achievements than to its rich inheritances. "It is the most triumphant city I have ever seen," wrote the Frenchman Philippe de Commynes at the end of the fifteenth century. The triumph of the Venetian state was the triumph of dedicated efficiency. The heart of its success lay in the way in which it organized its trade and its government. The key to Venetian trade was its privileged position with the Byzantine Empire. Through a treaty with the Byzantines, Venetian traders gained a competitive edge in the spice trade with the East. Venetians were the largest group of resident Europeans in Constantinople, and their personal contacts with Eastern traders were an important part of their success. The spice trade was so lucrative that special ships were built to accommodate it. The galleys were constructed at public expense and doubled as the Venetian navy in times of war. By controlling the ships, the government strictly regulated the spice trade.

Like its trade, Venetian government was also designed to disperse power. Although it was known as the Most Serene Republic, Venice was not a republic in the sense that the term is used today; rather, it was an oligarchy—a government administered by a restricted group. Political power was vested in a Great Council whose membership had been fixed at the end of the thirteenth century. All males whose fathers enjoyed the privilege of membership in the Great Council were registered at birth in the "Book of Gold" and became members of the Great Council when adults. There were no further distinctions of rank within the nobility, whose members varied widely in wealth and intermarried freely with other groups in the society. From the body of the Great Council, which numbered about 2500 at the end of the fifteenth century, was chosen the Senate—a council about one-tenth the size, whose members served a one-year term. It was from the Senate that the true officers of government were selected: the doge, who was chosen for life; and members of a number of small councils, who administered affairs and advised the doge. Members of the councils were chosen by secret ballot in an elaborate process by which nominators were selected at random. Terms of office on the councils were extremely short in order to limit factionalism and to prevent any individual from gaining too much power. Venetian-style republicanism was admired throughout Europe.

With its mercantile families firmly in control of government and trade, Venice created an overseas empire in the East during the thirteenth and fourteenth centuries. Naval supremacy, based largely on technological advances that made long-distance and winter voyages possible, allowed the Venetians to offer protection to strategic outposts in return for either privileges or tribute. But in the fifteenth century, Venice turned to the West. In a dramatic reversal of its centuries-old policy, it began a process of conquest in Italy, an empire on terra firma, as Venetian islanders called it. There were several reasons for this new policy. First, the Venetian navy was no longer the unsurpassed power that it once had been. More importantly, mainland expansion offered new opportunities for Venice. Not all Venetians were traders, and the new industries that were being developed in the city could readily benefit from control of mainland markets. So could those Venetian nobles employed to administer the conquered lands. They argued persuasively that the supply of raw materials and foodstuffs on which Venetian trade ultimately depended should be secured by the republic itself. Most decisively of all, opportunity was knocking. In Milan, Visconti rule was weakening and the Milanese territories were ripe for picking.

Venice reaped a rich harvest. For the first half of the fifteenth century, the Most Serene Republic engaged in unremitting warfare. Its successes were remarkable. It pushed out to the north to occupy all the lands between the city and the Habsburg territories; it pushed to the east until it straddled the entire head of the Adriatic; and it pushed to the west almost as far as Milan itself. Venetian victories resulted from both the traditional use of hired mercenaries and from the Venetians' own ingenuity at naval warfare. Although Venice was creating a landed empire, the course of expansion, especially in Lombardy, was along river routes. At the Arsenal were built new oared vessels armed with artillery for river sieges. Soon the captured territories were paying for continued expansion. The Western conquests in particular brought large populations under Venetian control, which, along with their potential as a market, provided a ready source of taxation. By the end of the fifteenth century, the mainland dominions of Venice were contributing nearly 40 percent of the city's revenue at a cost far smaller than that of the naval empire a century earlier. Venice had become the most powerful city-state in Italy.

Florence: Spinning Cloth into Gold

"What city, not merely in Italy, but in all the world . . . is more proud in its palazzi, more bedecked with churches, more beautiful in its architecture, more imposing in its gates, richer in piazzas, happier in its wide streets, greater in its people, more glorious in its citizenry, more inexhaustible in wealth, more fertile in its fields?" So boasted the humanist Coluccio Salutati (1331–1406) in 1403 during one of the most calamitous periods in Florentine history. Salutati's boastings were not unusual; the Florentines' mythical view of their homeland as savior of Christianity and as heir to the republican greatness of Rome was everywhere apparent. And it seemed to be most vigorously expressed in the city's darkest moments.

Florentine prosperity was built on two foundations: money and wool. Beginning in the thirteenth century, Florentine bankers were among the wealthiest and most powerful in the world. Initially their position was established through support of the papacy in its long struggle with the Holy Roman Empire. Florentine financiers established banks in all the capitals of Europe and the East, though their seats in

■ The patriarch of the great Florentine banking family, Cosimo de' Medici, portrayed here by Pontormo, was the dominant force in the city's politics from 1434 until his death in 1464.

Rome and Naples were probably most important. In the Middle Ages, bankers had served more functions than simply handling and exchanging money. Most were also tied to mercantile adventures and underwrote industrial activity. So it was in Florence, where international bankers purchased high-quality wool to be manufactured into the world's finest woven cloth. At its height before the plague, the cloth industry employed nearly 30,000 workers, providing jobs at all levels of society, from the rural women who spun the wool into yarn at piecework wages to the highly paid weavers and dyers whose skills made Florentine cloth so highly prized.

The activities of both commerce and cloth manufacture depended on external conditions, and thus the wealth of Florence was potentially unstable. In the mid-fourteenth century instability came with the plague that devastated the city. Nearly 40 percent of the entire population was lost in the single year 1348, and recurring outbreaks continued to ravage the already weakened survivors. Loss of workers and loss of markets seriously disrupted manufacturing. By 1380, cloth production had fallen to less than a quarter of pre-plague levels. On the heels of plague came wars. The property of Florentine bankers and merchants abroad was an easy target. Thirty years of warfare with Milan, interrupted by only a single decade of peace (1413–1423), resulted in total bankruptcy for many of the city's leading commercial families. More significantly, the costs of warfare, offensive and defensive, created a massive public debt. Every Florentine of means owned shares of the debt, and the republic was continually devising new methods for borrowing and staving off crises of repayment. Small wonder that the republic turned for aid to the wealthiest banking family in Europe, the Medici.

The ability of the Medici to secure a century-long dynasty in a government that did not have a head of state is just one of the mysteries surrounding the history of the remarkable family. Cosimo de' Medici (1389–1464) was one of the richest men in Christendom when he returned to the city in 1434 after a brief exile. His leading position in government rested upon supporters who were able to gain a controlling influence on the Signoria, the ruling Council in Florence's republican form of government. Cosimo built his party carefully, recruiting followers among the artisans whom he employed and even paying delinquent taxes to maintain the eligibility of his voters. Most importantly, emergency powers were invoked to reduce the number of citizens qualified to vote for the Signoria until the majority were Medici backers.

Cosimo was a practical man. He raised his children along humanist principles and was a great patron of artists and intellectuals. He collected books and paintings, endowed libraries, and spent lavishly on his own palace, the Palazzo Medici, which after his death was transformed into the very center of Florentine cultural life. Cosimo's position as an international banker brought him into contact with the heads of other Italian city-states and enabled him to negotiate peace treaties.

It was Cosimo's grandson Lorenzo (1449–1492) who linked the family's name to that of the age. Lorenzo was trained to hold office as if he had been a prince rather than a citizen of a republic. His own father ruled for five years and used his son as a diplomat in order to acquaint him with the leaders of Europe. Diplomacy was Lorenzo's greatest achievement. He held strong humanist values instilled in him by his mother, Lucrezia Tornabuoni, who organized his education. He wrote poetry and drama and even entered competitions for architectural designs. But Lorenzo's chief contribution to artistic life as it reached its height in Florence was to facilitate its production. He brought Michelangelo and other leading artists to his garden; he brought Pico della Mirandola and other leading humanists to his table. He secured commissions for Florentine artists throughout the Italian peninsula, ensuring the spread of their influence and the continued regeneration of artistic creativity in Florence itself.

Lorenzo was generally regarded as the leading citizen of Florence, and that was true in terms of both his wealth and his influence. He did not rule from high office, though he maintained the party that his grandfather had built and even extended it through wartime emergency measures. His power was based on his personality and reputation, a charisma enhanced when he survived an assassination attempt in which

A view of Florence in 1490. The Duomo of the Florence Cathedral dominates the small city, which is already built up on both sides of the Arno River.

his brother was killed. His diplomatic abilities were the key to his survival. Almost immediately after Lorenzo came to power, Naples and the papacy began a war with Florence, a war that was costly to the Florentines in both taxation and lost territory. In 1479, Lorenzo traveled to Naples and personally convinced the Neapolitan king to sign a separate treaty, which restored the Italian balance of power and ensured continued Medici rule in Florence. Soon Lorenzo even had a treaty with the pope that allowed for the recovery of lost territories and the expansion of Florentine influence. But two years after his death, the Italian peninsula was plunged into wars that turned it from the center of European civilization into one of its lesser satellites.

The End of Italian Hegemony, 1450–1527

In the course of the Renaissance, western Europe was Italianized. For a century, the city-states dominated the trade routes that connected the East and the West. Venetian and Genoese merchants exchanged spices and minerals from the Black Sea to the North Sea, enriching the material life of three continents. They brought wool from England and Spain to the skilled artisans in the Low Countries and Florence. Italian manufactures such as Milanese artillery, Florentine silk, and Venetian glass were prized above all others. The ducat and the florin, two Italian coins, were universally accepted in an age when every petty prince minted his own money. The Italian peninsula exported culture in the same way that it exported goods. Humanism quickly spread across the Alps, aided by the recent invention of printing (which the Venetians soon dominated), while Renaissance standards of artistic achievement were known worldwide and everywhere imitated. The city-states shared their technology as well. The compass and the navigational chart, projection maps, double entry bookkeeping, eyeglasses, the telescope—all profoundly influenced what could be achieved and what could be hoped for. In this spirit, Christopher Columbus—a Genoese seaman—successfully crossed the Atlantic under the Spanish flag, and Amerigo Vespucci—a Florentine merchant—gave his name to the newly discovered continents.

Political and Military Unrest. But it was not in Italy that the rewards of innovation or the satisfactions of achievement were enjoyed. There the seeds of political turmoil and military imperialism, combined with the rise of the Ottoman Turks, were to reap a not-unexpected harvest. In 1454, the five powers agreed to the Peace of Lodi, which established two balanced alliances, one between Florence and Milan, the other between Venice and Naples. The states, along with the papacy, pledged mutual nonaggression, a policy that lasted for nearly 40 years. But the Peace of Lodi did not bring peace. It only halted the long period in which the major city-states struggled against one another. Under cover of the peace, the large states continued the process of swallowing up their smaller neighbors and creating quasi-empires. It was a policy of imperialism as aggressive as that of any in the modern era. Civilian populations were overrun, local leaders exiled or exterminated, tribute monies taken, and taxes levied. Each of the five states either increased its mainland territories or strengthened its hold upon them.

■ Paolo Uccello, *Niccolò da Tolentino at the Battle of San Romano* (ca. 1435–1450). The painting represents the early stages of a 1432 battle between the Florentines and the Sienese at San Romano. The Florentine condottiere, Niccolò da Tolentino, on a white horse, dominates the center of the scene.

By the end of the fifteenth century the city-states eyed one another greedily and warily. Each expected the others to begin a peninsula-wide war for hegemony and took the steps that ultimately ensured the contest. Perhaps the most unusual aspect of the imperialism of the city-states was that it had been restricted to the Italian peninsula. Each of the major powers shared the dream of recapturing the glory that was Rome. Although the Venetians had expanded abroad, their acquisitions had not come through conquest or occupation. In their Greek and Dalmatian territories, local law and custom continued to govern under the benevolent eye of Venetian administrators. But in their mainland territories, the Venetians were as ruthless as the Florentines were in Pisa or as Cesare Borgia was in Romagna when he consolidated the Papal States by fire and sword. Long years of siege and occupation had militarized the Italian city-states. Venice and Florence balanced their budgets on the backs of their captured territories, Milan had been engaged in constant war for decades, and even the papacy was militarily aggressive.

The Italian Decline. The Italians were no longer alone. The most remarkable military leader of the age was not a Renaissance *condottieri* but an Ottoman prince, Mehmed II (1451–1481), who conquered Constantinople and Athens and threatened Rome itself. The rise of the Ottomans (whose name is derived from that of Osman, their original tribal leader) is one of the most compelling stories in world history. Little more than a warrior tribe at the beginning of the fourteenth century, 150 years later the Ottomans had replaced stagnant Byzantine rule with a virile and potent empire. First they gobbled up towns and cities in a wide arc around Constantinople. Then they fed upon the Balkans and the eastern kingdoms of Hungary and Poland. By 1400, they were a presence in all the territory that stretched from the Black Sea to the Aegean; by 1450, they were its master.

Venice was most directly affected by the Ottoman advance. Not only was its favored position in Eastern trade threatened, but during a prolonged war at the end of the fifteenth century, the Venetians lost many of their most important commercial outposts. Ottoman might closed off the markets of eastern Europe. Islands in the Aegean Sea and seaports along the Dalmatian coast fell to the Turks in alarming succession. By 1480, Venetian naval supremacy was a thing of the past. (See "A Closer Look: The Fall of Constantinople," pp. 342–343.)

The Italian city-states might have met this challenge from the East had they been able to unite in opposing it. Successive popes pleaded for holy wars to halt the advance of the Turks, which was compared in officially inspired propaganda to an

THE SIEGE OF CONSTANTINOPLE

Mehmed II (1432–1481) was one of the great military geniuses of world history. He consolidated the expansion of the Ottoman Empire in Asia Minor and in 1453 organized the siege of Constantinople. He personally directed the combined land and naval assault and brilliantly improvised the tactics that led to the fall of the city. The fall of Constantinople to the Ottomans was a watershed. Kritovoulos was a Greek who entered the service of Mehmed II, probably after the siege. Though he was not an eyewitness of the fall of Constantinople, he gathered numerous accounts together in composing his history. In this selection he refers to the defenders of the city as Romans because Constantinople was what remained of the Roman Empire.

Focus Questions

How did Mehmed get his ships into the harbor at Constantinople? Why was Mehmed's scheme for moving the ships so important in the siege of Constantinople?

Sultan Mehmed considered it necessary in preparation for his next move to get possession of the harbor and open the Horn for his own ships to sail in. So, since every effort and device of his had failed to force the entrance, he made a wise decision, and one worthy of his intellect and power. It succeeded in accomplishing his purpose and in putting an end to all uncertainties.

He ordered the commanders of the vessels to construct as quickly as possible glideways leading from the outer sea to the inner sea. . . . He brought up the ships and placed large cradles under them, with stays against each of their sides to hold them up. And having under-girded them well with ropes, he fastened long cables to the corners and gave them to the soldiers to drag, some of them by hand, and others by certain machines and capstans.

So the ships were dragged along very swiftly. And their crews, as they followed them, rejoiced at the event and boasted of it. Then they manned the ships on the land as if they were on the sea. Some of them hoisted the sails with a shout, as if they were setting sail, and the breeze caught the sails and bellied them out. Others seated themselves on the benches, holding the oars in their hands and moving them as if rowing. And the commanders, running along by the sockets of the masts with whistlings and shouting, and with their whips beating the oarsmen on the benches, ordered them to row. The ships, borne along over the land as if on the sea, were some of them being pulled up the ascent to the top of the hill while others were being hauled down the slope into the harbor, lowering the sails with shouting and great noise.

It was a strange spectacle, and unbelievable in the telling except to those who actually did see it—the sight of ships borne along on the mainland as if sailing on the sea, with their crews and their sails and all their equipment. I believe this was a much greater feat than the cutting of a canal across at Athos by Xerxes, and much stranger to see and to hear about.

The Romans, when they saw such an unheard-of thing actually happen, and warships lying at anchor in the Horn—which they never would have suspected—were astounded at the impossibility of the spectacle, and were overcome by the greatest consternation and perplexity. They did not know what to do now, but were in despair. In fact they had left unguarded the walls along the Horn for a distance of about thirty stadia, and even so they did not have enough men for the rest of the walls, either for defense or for attack, whether citizens or men from elsewhere. Instead, two or even three battlements had but a single defender.

And now, when this sea-wall also became open to attack and had to be guarded, they were compelled to strip the other battlements and bring men there. This constituted a manifest danger, since the defenders were taken away from the rest of the wall while those remaining were not enough to guard it, being so few.

From Kritovoulos, *The History of Mehmed the Conqueror.*

Two Views on the Fall of Constantinople

outbreak of plague. The fall of Constantinople in 1453 was an event of epochal proportions for Europeans, many believing that it foreshadowed the end of the world. "A thing terrible to relate and to be deplored by all who have in them any spark of humanity. The splendor and glory of the East has been captured, despoiled, ravaged and completely sacked by the most inhuman barbarians," the Venetian doge was informed. Yet it was Italians rather than Ottomans who plunged the Italian peninsula into the wars from which it never recovered.

The Wars of Italy (1494–1529) began when Naples, Florence, and the Papal States united against Milan. At first the alliance seemed little more than another shift in the balance of power. But rather than call upon Venice to redress the situation, the Milanese leader, Ludovico il Moro, sought help from the French. An army of French cavalry and Swiss mercenaries, led by Charles VIII of France (1483–1498), invaded the Italian peninsula in 1494. With Milanese support, the French swept all before them. Florence was forced to surrender Pisa, a humiliation that led to the overthrow of the

THE FALL OF CONSTANTINOPLE

The prayers of the devout were fervent on Easter Sunday in 1453. The Christians of Constantinople knew that it was only a matter of time before the last remaining stronghold of the Byzantine Empire came under siege. For decades the ring of Ottoman conquests had narrowed around the holy city until it alone stood out against the Turkish sultan. Constantinople, the bridge between Europe and Asia, was tottering. The once teeming center of Eastern Christianity had never recovered from the epidemics of the fourteenth century, and now dwindling revenues matched the dwindling population.

Perhaps it was that impoverishment that had kept the Turks at bay. Constantinople was still the best fortified city in the world. Shaped like the head of a horse, it was surrounded by water on all but one side, and that side was protected by two stout rings of walls separated by a trench lined with stones. No cannon forged in the West could dent the battlements, and no navy could hope to force its way through the narrow mouth of the Golden Horn. Thus an uneasy peace existed between sultan and emperor. It was shattered in 1451 with the accession of a new sultan, the 19-year-old Mehmed II. Mehmed's imagination was fired by the ancient prophecies that a Muslim would rule the East. Only Constantinople was a fitting capital for such an empire, and Mehmed immediately began preparations for its conquest.

A CLOSER LOOK

In 1452 Mehmed had constructed a fortress at the narrow mouth of the Bosporus and demanded tribute from all ships that entered the Golden Horn. The Byzantine emperor sent ambassadors to Mehmed to protest that aggression; Mehmed returned their severed heads. When the first Venetian convoy refused to lower its sails, Mehmed's artillery efficiently sank one of the galleys with a single shot. The Turks now controlled access to the city for trade and supplies. An attack the following spring seemed certain.

The emperor appealed far and wide for aid: to the Venetians and Genoese to protect their trade and to the pope to defend Christianity. The Europeans were willing, but as yet they were unable. They did not think that the Ottomans could assemble an army before summer. By then an Italian armada could dislodge the Ottoman fortress and reinforce the city with trained fighting men.

But they hadn't reckoned with Mehmed. While the Italians bickered over the cost of the expedition and Christians everywhere made ready to celebrate Holy Week, the Ottomans assembled a vast army of fighters and laborers and a huge train of weapons and supplies. Among them was the largest cannon ever cast, with a 26-foot barrel that shot a 1200-pound ball. Fifty teams of oxen and 200 men took two months to pull it in place.

Mehmed's forces—which eventually numbered more than 150,000, of which 60,000 were soldiers—assembled around the walls of Constantinople on 5 April. During the next week a great flotilla sailed up the Bosporus and anchored just out of reach of the Byzantine warships in the Golden Horn. A census taken inside the city revealed that there were only 7000 able-bodied defenders—about 5000 Greek residents and 2000 foreigners, mostly Genoese and Venetians. The Italians were the only true soldiers among them.

Although the defenders were vastly outnumbered, they still held the military advantage. As long as their ships controlled the entrance to the Golden Horn, they could limit the Ottoman attack to only one side of the city, where all of the best defenders could be massed. The Byzantines cast a boom—an iron chain supported by wooden floats—across the mouth of the Horn to forestall a naval attack. By the middle of April, the Turks had begun their land assault. Each day great guns pounded the walls of the city, and each night residents worked frantically to repair the damage. Everyone contributed. Old women wove baskets in which children carried stones. Monks and nuns packed mud and cut branches to shore up the breaches in the wall. The Turks suffered heavily each time they attempted to follow a cannon shot with a massed charge, but the attack took its toll among the defenders as well. No one was safe from the flaming arrows and catapulted stones flung over the city's walls. Choking black smoke filled the air as the huge cannon shook the foundations of the city and treated its stout stone walls as if they were plaster. Nevertheless, for the first month of siege the defenders held their own.

The stubborn defense of the city infuriated Mehmed. As long as there was only one point of attack, the defenders could resist indefinitely. The line of assault had to be extended, and this could only be done by sea. With the boom effectively impregnable and with Italian seamen superior to the Turks, the prospects seemed dim. But what could not be achieved by force might be achieved by intelligence. Mehmed devised a plan to carry a number of smaller ships across land and then to float them behind the Christian fleet. Protected by land forces, the ships could be used as a staging point for another line of attack. Thousands of workers built huge wooden rollers, which were greased with animal fat. Under cover of darkness and the smoke of cannon fire, 72 ships were pulled up the steep hills and pushed down into the sea. Once they were safely anchored, a pontoon bridge was built and cannons were trained on the seaward walls of the city.

By then the city had withstood siege for nearly six weeks without any significant reinforcement. At the end of May there was a sudden lull. A messenger from the sultan arrived to demand surrender. The choice was clear. If the city were taken by force, the customary three days of unrestricted pillage would be allowed; if it yielded, the sultan pledged to protect the property of all who desired to remain under his rule. The emperor replied feebly that no one who had ever laid siege to Constantinople had enjoyed a long life. He was ready to die in defense of his capital.

On 30 May the final assault began. Mehmed knew that his advantage lay in numbers. First, he sent in waves of irregular troops, mostly captured slaves and Christians, who suffered great losses and were finally driven back by the weakened defenders. Next, better-trained warriors attacked and widened the breaches made by the irregulars. Finally came the crack Janissaries, the sultan's elite warriors, disciplined from birth to fight. It was the Janissaries who found a small door left open at the base of the wall. In they rushed, quickly overwhelming the first line of defenders and battering their way through the weaker second walls. By dawn the Ottoman flag was raised over the battlements and the sack of Constantinople had begun.

There was no need for the customary three days of pillage. By the end of the first day there was nothing left worth taking. The churches and monasteries had been looted and defaced, the priests and nuns murdered or defiled, and thousands of civilians had been captured to be sold into slavery. Large areas of the city smoldered from countless fires. The bastion of Eastern Christendom was no more.

This fifteenth-century illustration shows the siege of Constantinople by the Turks.

Medici and the establishment of French sovereignty. The Papal States were next to be occupied, and within a year Charles had conquered Naples without engaging the Italians in a single significant battle. Unfortunately, the Milanese were not the only ones who could play at the game of foreign alliances. Next, it was the turn of the Venetians and the pope to unite and call upon the services of King Ferdinand of Aragon and the Holy Roman Emperor. Italy was now a battleground in what became a total European war for dynastic supremacy. The city-states used their foreign allies to settle old scores and to extend their own mainland empires. At the turn of the century Naples was dismembered. In 1509, the pope conspired to organize the most powerful combination of forces yet known against Venice. All the "terra firma" possessions of the Most Serene Republic were lost, but by a combination of good fortune and skilled diplomacy Venice itself survived. Florence was less fortunate, becoming a pawn first of the French and then of the Spanish. The final blow to Italian hegemony was the sack of Rome in 1527, when German mercenaries fulfilled the fears of what the "infidels" would do to the Holy City.

Surveying the wreckage of the Italian wars, Machiavelli ended *The Prince* with a plea for a leader to emerge to restore Italian freedom and recreate the unity of the ancient Roman Republic. He concluded with these lines from Petrarch:

Then virtue boldly shall engage
And swiftly vanquish barbarous rage,
Proving that ancient and heroic pride
In true Italian hearts had never died.

CONCLUSION

The revival of "ancient and heroic pride" fueled the Italian Renaissance. The sense of living in a new age, the spirit of human achievement, and the curiosity and wonderment of writers and artists all characterized the Renaissance. The desire to recreate the glories of Rome was not Machiavelli's alone. It could be seen in the palaces of the Italian aristocracy; in the papal rebuilding of the Holy City; and in the military ambitions of princes. But the legacy of empire, of "ancient and heroic pride," had passed out of Italian hands.

QUESTIONS FOR REVIEW

1. What social and cultural conditions were peculiar to the Italian peninsula, and how might those conditions have contributed to the Renaissance?
2. What were the principal characteristics of the Renaissance style in the visual arts?
3. What is humanism, and why was the study of languages so important to the humanists?
4. In what ways did the ideas of Niccolò Machiavelli reflect the reality of politics in the city-states of Renaissance Italy?

KEY TERMS

DISCOVERING WESTERN CIVILIZATION ONLINE

You can obtain more information about the Italian Renaissance at the Websites listed below. See also the Companion Website that accompanies this text, www.ablongman.com/kishlansky, which contains an online study guide and additional resources.

Renaissance Society

NM's Creative Impulse: Renaissance
www.history.evansville.net/renaissa.html#Resources
A site of links to a wide array of subjects relating to the era of the Renaissance. A good starting point.

The Florentine Republic
www.mega.it/eng/egui/epo/secrepu.htm
The history of the Florentine Republic with links to major tourist attractions and buildings. Brief biographies of important Florentine citizens can also be found.

The History of Costume—Index
www.siue.edu/COSTUMES/COSTUME5_INDEX.HTML
Part of a site devoted to the history of dress. This page shows examples of the clothing worn by different classes as well as in different countries during the fifteenth and sixteenth centuries.

Renaissance Art

Renaissance Art
www.anu.edu.au/ArtHistory/renart/pics.art/index_1.html
A pictorial guide to the major artists of the Italian Renaissance and their works. Thumbnail representations lead to links on specific pieces.

Leon Battista Alberti—Great Buildings Online
www.greatbuildings.com/architects/Leon_Battista_Alberti.html
A page devoted to Alberti's architecture with a brief biography and links to pictures.

Michelangelo Buonarroti
www.mega.it/eng/egui/pers/micbuon.htm
A Website devoted to Michelangelo with a variety of links to text and images of Renaissance Florence.

WebMuseum: The Italian Renaissance (1420–1600)
www.ibiblio.org/wm/paint/tl/it-ren/
Reproductions of Renaissance art, with accompanying text.

SUGGESTIONS FOR FURTHER READING

General Reading

P. Burke, *Culture and Society in Renaissance Italy* (Princeton, NJ: Princeton University Press, 1999). A good introduction to social and intellectual developments.

Paul Grendler, ed., *Encyclopedia of the Renaissance* (New York: Scribners, 1999). Reference for all aspects of the Renaissance.

Denys Hay, *The Italian Renaissance* (Cambridge, England: Cambridge University Press, 1977). The best first book to read, an elegant interpretive essay.

John M. Najemy, ed. *Italy in the Age of the Renaissance: 1300–1550* (Oxford: 2005). A collection of essays written by experts on the Italian Renaissance that provide an engaging and thorough introduction to many aspects of Renaissance Italy.

Renaissance Society

Carlo Cipolla, *Before the Industrial Revolution: European Society and Economy, 1000–1700,* 3rd ed. (New York: W. W. Norton, 1994). A sweeping survey of social and economic developments across the centuries.

J. R. Hale, *Renaissance Europe: The Individual and Society* (Berkeley: University of California Press, 1978). A lively study placing great Renaissance figures in their social context.

D. Herlihy and C. Klapisch-Zuber, *Tuscans and Their Families* (New Haven, CT: Yale University Press, 1985). A difficult but rewarding study of the social and demographic history of Florence and its environs.

Margaret L. King, *Women of the Renaissance* (Chicago: University of Chicago Press, 1991). A study by a leading women's historian.

Richard MacKenney, *Renaissances: The Cultures of Italy, c. 1300–c. 1600* (Palgrave Macmillan, 2004). A specialist argues for the diversity and plurality of cultures and experiences in Italy between the fourteenth and seventeenth centuries.

Renaissance Art

Michael Baxandall, *Painting and Experience in Fifteenth-Century Italy* (Oxford: Oxford University Press, 1972). A study of the relationship between painters and their patrons and of how and why art was produced.

Anthony Grafton, *Leon Battista Alberti: Master Builder of the Italian Renaissance* (New York: Hill and Wang, 2000). A lucid biographical study of a truly renaissance man.

Frederick Hartt, *History of Italian Renaissance Art* (Englewood Cliffs, NJ: Prentice-Hall, 1974). The most comprehensive survey, with hundreds of plates.

Howard Hibbard, *Michelangelo* (New York: Harper & Row, 1974). A compelling biography of an obsessed genius.

Lisa Jardine and Jerry Brotton, *Global Interests: Renaissance Art Between East and West* (Ithaca, NY: Cornell University Press, 2000). A bold argument about Renaissance art and its relation to Ottoman culture.

Michael Levey, *Early Renaissance* (London: Penguin, 1967). A concise survey of art, clearly written and authoritative.

Linda Murray, *High Renaissance and Mannerism* (London: Thames & Hudson, 1985). The best introduction to late Renaissance art.

Renaissance Ideals

Hans Baron, *The Crisis of the Early Italian Renaissance* (Princeton, NJ: Princeton University Press, 1966). One of the most influential intellectual histories of the period.

George Holmes, *The Florentine Enlightenment,* 2nd ed. (Oxford: Clarendon Press, 1992). A new edition of the best study of intellectual developments in Florence.

Quentin Skinner, *Machiavelli* (Oxford: Oxford University Press, 1981). A brief but brilliant biography.

The Politics of the Italian City-States

Gene Brucker, *Florence, The Golden Age 1138–1737* (Berkeley: University of California Press, 1998). The best single-volume introduction to Florentine history with excellent illustrations.

J. R. Hale, *Florence and the Medici* (London: Thames & Hudson, 1977). A compelling account of the relationship between a city and its most powerful citizens.

Frederic C. Lane, *Venice: A Maritime Republic* (Baltimore, MD: Johns Hopkins University Press, 1973). A complete history of Venice that stresses its naval and mercantile developments.

Lauro Martines, *Power and Imagination: City-States in Renaissance Italy* (New York: Alfred A. Knopf, 1979). An important interpretation of the politics of the Italian powers.

Lauro Martines, *Scourge and Fire: Savonarola in Renaissance Italy* (Jonathan Cape, 2006). An exciting new biography of the charismatic preacher Savonarola who called for religious and political reform in the 1490s.

Eugene F. Rice, Jr., *The Foundations of Early Modern Europe, 1460–1559,* 2nd ed. (New York: W. W. Norton, 1994). The best short synthetic work.

Charles Stinger, *The Renaissance in Rome* (Bloomington, IN: University of Indiana Press, 1998). A thorough account of one of the great ages in the history of Rome.

For a list of additional titles related to this chapter's topics, please see http://www.ablongman.com/kishlansky.

CHAPTER 12

THE EUROPEAN EMPIRES

ASTRIDE THE WORLD

THE AGE OF MONARCHIES

THE VISUAL RECORD

Henry VIII lived large. He was a bear of a man, famed for his ability to hunt all day while wearing out a pack of trained horses, for his prowess in wrestling bouts, including one with King Francis I of France, and, of course, for having six wives. His accomplishments as a leader were equally impressive. Bequeathed a surplus by his father, Henry spent lavishly in an attempt to restore England to European prominence. He allied with Spain to fight France and with France to fight Spain and ran an expensive but futile campaign to be elected Holy Roman Emperor. He sponsored humanist thinkers and brought them to his court from all over Europe. He also encouraged the new learning at the Universities of Oxford and Cambridge, and during his reign Sir Thomas More wrote *Utopia*, one of the classic works of English literature. Henry's generals decisively defeated the Scots, England's troublesome northern neighbor, and his ministers successfully completed the integration of Wales into the English crown.

In 1532, when his attempt to secure an annulment of his first marriage failed, Henry dissolved England's ties to the Church of Rome declaring that "this realm of England is an Empire"—the first statement of British imperial ambition. He had Parliament declare him Supreme Head of the Church in England and then helped himself to the vast holdings of the Catholic religious orders. Perhaps as much as a third of all of the land in England was forfeited to the crown when the monasteries and chantries were dissolved. Though Henry VIII shared his plunder with his loyal nobility and gentry, the lion's share was his. Henry's own religious beliefs remained shrouded in mystery, but he guided his nation toward the Protestantism that would bloom under his son Edward VI and his daughter Elizabeth I.

Henry VIII has passed through the ages as the very symbol of a monarch, an image captured by the German portrait painter Hans Holbein. Holbein was born into a family of painters and settled among the Swiss in Basel to practice his craft before being invited to the English court in the mid-1530s. His great skill was in rendering subjects true to life and his paintings of the Henrician court and its leading members such as Thomas More and Thomas Cromwell rival the works of Italian Renaissance portraiturists. But none were more memorable than the artist's numerous studies of Henry himself. Holbein was able to capture both the ferocity and the grandeur of the king.

Ironically, one of Holbein's most powerful, and most famous, portraits of Henry did not survive the seventeenth century. Part of a mural that Holbein painted in Henry's Whitehall Palace in 1537, the original work was lost when the palace burned in 1698. However, as Holbein's followers had copied the grand painting, and earlier sketches of it by Holbein himself also survived, we still have a strong visual record of Holbein's vision of the king. The image shown here is a vibrant copy of the Whitehall Palace original, painted on oak panels, likely in the mid-sixteenth century. In this portrait, Henry stands with straight legs astride suggesting the solidity of tree trunks, one arm bent at the elbow as if in defiance of all comers. There is not even a suggestion of doubt as the king thrusts out his chest and fixes the viewer with a penetrating stare. The artist represents the sumptuousness of Henry's court in the monarch's clothing. Fabric literally encases him, flowing in folds and gathers of intricate design and the costliest material. Furs drape over his doublet and

Henry VIII portrait, after Hans Holbein.

elaborately embroidered red cloak. Enormous rubies bedeck not only his great gold chain but his hat and vest, running down both sleeves, all to create an overwhelming sense of opulence. Even the protruding codpiece is meant to convey the potency of a king who had finally sired a male heir. Every detail conveys the impression of a monarch at the height of his power.

LOOKING AHEAD

This image of Henry VIII is among the most recognizable from an age of monarchy that began in the sixteenth century and coincided with the consolidations of nations in western Europe and their expansion into all corners of the globe. Everywhere small principalities and kingdoms were absorbed by their larger and more powerful neighbors, and Europe's military might was on display as far east as India and as far west as Peru. Though England played but a small part in a century dominated by Spain and France, even its monarch could believe that he bestrode the world like a colossus.

CHAPTER OUTLINE

EUROPEAN ENCOUNTERS

The sixteenth century was an age of exploration. Knowledge bequeathed from the past created curiosity about the present. Technological change made long sea voyages possible, and the demands of commerce provided incentives. Ottoman expansion on the southern and eastern frontiers of the Continent, however, threatened access to the goods of the East on which Europeans had come to rely. Spices were rare and expensive, but they were not merely luxuries. While nobles and rich merchants consumed them lavishly to enhance their reputations of wealth and generosity, spices had many practical uses. Some acted as preservatives, some as flavorings, and others were used as perfumes to battle the noxious gases that rose from urban streets and invaded homes and workplaces. The drugs of the East, the nature of which we can only guess at, helped soothe chronic ill health. The demand for all of the "spices" continued to rise at a greater rate than their supply. There was more than a fortune to be made by anyone who could participate in the trade.

Eastern spices were expensive. Most European manufactured goods had little utility in the East. Woven wool, which was the staple of Western industry, was too heavy to be worn in Eastern climes. Both silk and cotton came from the East and were more expertly spun there. Even Western jewelry relied upon imported stones. Metalwork was an attractive commodity for export, but providing Ottomans or other Muslims with weapons to wage holy wars against Christian Europe posed problems of policy and morality. And once the Ottomans began to cast great bronze cannons of their own, European arms were less eagerly sought. Western gold and silver flowed steadily east. As supplies of precious metals dwindled, economic growth in Europe slowed. Throughout the fifteenth century, ever larger amounts of Western specie were necessary to purchase ever smaller amounts of Eastern commodities. Europe faced a severe shortage of gold and silver, a shortage that threatened its standard of living and its prospects for economic growth. The search was on to discover new sources of gold.

Africa and a Passage to India

It was the Portuguese who made the first dramatic breakthroughs in exploration and colonization. Perched on the southwestern tip of Europe, Portugal was an agriculturally poor and sparsely populated nation. Among its few marketable commodities were fish and wine. The Portuguese had long been sea explorers, especially in the Atlantic Ocean, where they had established bases in the Azores and Madeira islands. Their small ships, known as **caravels**, were ideal for ocean travel, and their navigators were among the most skillful in the world. Yet they were unable to participate in the lucrative Mediterranean trade in bullion and spices until the expanding power of the Ottomans threatened the traditional eastern sea routes.

Prince Henry the Navigator. In the early fifteenth century, the Portuguese gained a foothold in northern Africa and used it to stage voyages along the continent's unexplored western coast. Like most explorers, the Portuguese were motivated by an unself-conscious mixture of faith and greed. Establishing southern bases would enable them to surround their Muslim enemies and give them access to the African bullion trade. The Portuguese navigator Bartolomeu Dias (ca. 1450–1500) summarized those goals succinctly: "To give light to those who are in darkness and to grow rich." Under the energetic leadership of Prince Henry the Navigator (1394–1460), the Portuguese pushed steadily southward. Prince Henry studied navigational techniques, accumulated detailed accounts of voyages, and encouraged the creation of accurate maps of the African coastline.

Prince Henry's systematic program paid off in the next generation. By the 1480s, Portuguese outposts had reached almost to the equator, and in 1487 Bartolomeu Dias rounded the tip of Africa and opened the eastern African shores to Portuguese traders. The aim of the enterprises was access to Asia rather than Africa. Dias might have reached India if his crew had not mutinied and forced him to return home. A decade later, Vasco da Gama (ca. 1460–1524) rounded the Cape of Good Hope and crossed into the Indian Ocean. His journey took two years, but when he returned to Lisbon in 1499 laden with the most valuable spices of the East, Portuguese ambitions were achieved. Larger expeditions followed, one of which, blown off course, touched the South American coast of Brazil. Brazil was soon subsumed within the Portuguese dominions.

Spanish and Portuguese Explorations, 1400–1600

The Beginnings of the Slave Trade. The exploration of the African coast also brought the Portuguese into contact with Muslim traders who had developed connections between North Africa and the middle of the continent. They bartered for gold, ivory, and exotic spices, exchanging colorful cloth, metalwork, and other manufactured goods. They also bartered for slaves. Slavery was a common feature of the cultures that interacted in

Africa. Europeans had used slaves in ancient times and had developed a theory that justified slavery by capture. Muslims were dependent upon them for their armies and bought many slaves from European sources. Africans enslaved those who were captured in tribal wars and sold them out of Africa, first to Muslim traders and then to the Portuguese. There was nothing new about slavery in the West, especially if the slaves were not Christians. The popes who granted Portugal a monopoly on European trade in Africa also sanctioned the trade in African slaves upon the condition that those enslaved had not converted to Christianity.

The slave trade began almost immediately. At first African slaves were imported to Europe as a curiosity and were purchased by wealthy families. But the discovery of the Azores and the Canary Islands provided a much more valuable use for the enslaved Africans. Their ability to labor in intense heat fitted them for agricultural work in the new sugar fields that were being developed in these Atlantic islands. By the 1470s it was estimated that over a thousand African slaves a year were being imported into Portugal and that a significant percentage of those were sold to Spanish masters who also saw their value in farming. Originally, the slaves were purchased either from Muslim traders or directly from African tribal leaders. As the trade became more sophisticated and more competitive, slaves could no longer be bartered for trinkets. Horses became the preferred medium of exchange, and Prince Henry the Navigator financed the trade until his death. Thereafter, the right to trade in slaves was sold to private entrepreneurs, and they were less scrupulous in their methods. Soon the Portuguese were simply conducting raids on coastal villages to capture as many Africans as they could cram on to their boats.

In these early decades, slaves were viewed as just another trading commodity and valued only in regard to their profit. Ships were still small, voyages still risky, and capital still scarce. Traders carried whatever items were most in demand, and the agricultural use of African slaves was limited by the small amount of commercial agriculture undertaken by Europeans. The Portuguese held a monopoly on transporting slaves from Africa, but the trade soon centered in Seville where Italians dominated it. This was a significant, if unplanned development. Seville would soon become the center of the Spanish overseas empire, and the Spanish colonies in America would soon become the destination for most of the African slaves bought by Europeans.

The Asian Trade. The Portuguese came to the East as traders rather than as conquerors. Building on their experi-

MAP DISCOVERY

Portuguese Explorations

Examine the routes of the Portuguese explorers. What was their strategy of exploration? How long did it take for explorers to round the tip of Africa? What was the ultimate goal of Portuguese seafarers?

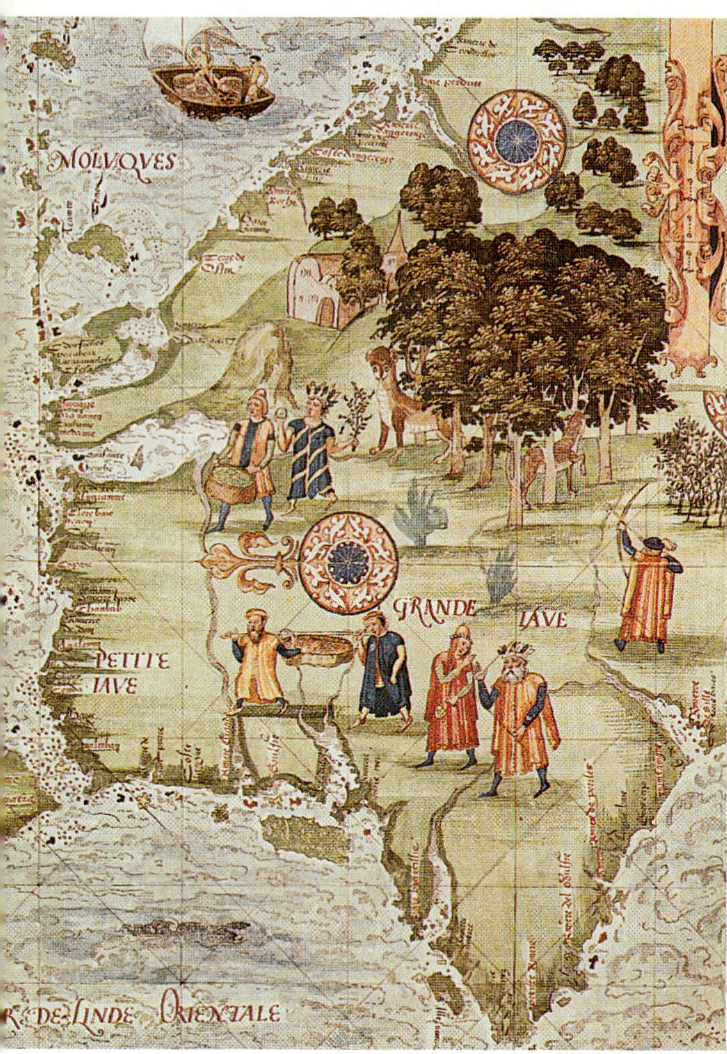

■ This sixteenth-century map of Java and the Moluccas shows European traders bartering for spices. At the upper left, a ship laden with the rich cargo sails for markets in Europe.

ence in West Africa, they developed a policy of establishing military outposts to protect their investments and subduing native populations only when necessary. Throughout the East the Portuguese took advantage of local feuds to gain allies, and they established trading compounds that were easily defensible. The Portuguese general Alfonso de Albuquerque (1453–1515) understood the need for strategically placed garrisons and conquered the vital ports of the Middle East and India. By the first decade of the sixteenth century, the Portuguese were masters of a vast empire, which spanned both the eastern and western coasts of Africa and the western shores of India. Most importantly, the Portuguese controlled Ceylon and Indonesia, the precious Spice Islands from which came cloves, cinnamon, and pepper. Almost overnight, Lisbon became one of the trading capitals of the world, tripling in population between 1500 and 1550.

It was northern Europe that was to harvest what Portugal had sown. The long voyages around Africa were costly and dangerous. Moreover, the expense of maintaining a far-flung empire ate into the profits of trade at the same time that the increased volume necessary to make the voyages worthwhile drove down spice prices. Between 1501 and 1505, more than 80 ships and 7000 men sailed from Portugal to the East. The vast commitment was underwritten by Flemish, German, and Italian bankers. Soon Antwerp replaced Lisbon as the marketplace for Asian spices. Ironically, it was in the accidental discovery of Brazil rather than in Asia that the Portuguese were rewarded for the enterprise of their explorers.

Mundus Novus

Whereas most of Portugal's resources were devoted to the Asian trade, those of the Spanish kingdom came to be concentrated in the New World. Although larger and richer than its eastern neighbor, Spain had been segmented into a number of small kingdoms and principalities and divided between Christians and Muslims. Not until the end of the fifteenth century, when the crowns of Aragon and Castile were united and the Muslims expelled from Granada, could the Spanish concentrate their resources. By then they were far behind in establishing commercial enterprises. With Portugal dominating the African route to India, Queen Isabella of Castile was persuaded to take an interest in a western route by a Genoese adventurer, Christopher Columbus ca. (1446–1506).

Christopher Columbus. Like all well-informed people of his day, Columbus believed that the world was round. By carefully calculating routes and distances, he concluded that a western track would be shorter and less expensive than the path that the Portuguese were breaking around Africa. Columbus's conclusions were based partly on conventional knowledge and partly on his own self-assurance. All were wholly erroneous. He misjudged the size of the globe by 25 percent and the distance of the journey by 400 percent. But he persevered against all odds. Columbus sailed westward into the unknown in 1492, and on 12 October he landed in the Bahamas, on an island that he named San Salvador. He had encountered a *Mundus Novus*, a New World.

Christopher Columbus, Letter from the New World

Initially, Columbus's discovery was a disappointment. He had gone in search of a western passage to the Indies, but he had failed to return to Spain laden with Eastern spices. Despite his own belief that the islands he had discovered lay just off the coast of Japan, it was soon apparent that he had found an altogether unknown landmass. Columbus's own explorations and those of his successors continued to focus on discovering a route to the Indies. That was all the more imperative once the Portuguese succeeded in finding the passage around Africa. In 1494, the **Treaty of Tordesillas** had confirmed Portugal's right to the eastern route to the Indies as well as to any undiscovered lands east of an imaginary line fixed west of the Cape Verde Islands. That entitled Portugal to Brazil; the Spanish received whatever lay west of the line. At the time few doubted that Portugal had the better end of the bargain.

But Spanish-backed explorations soon proved the value of the new lands. Using the Caribbean Islands as a staging ground, successive explorers uncovered the vast coastline of Central and South America. In 1513, Vasco Núñez de Balboa (1475–1517) crossed the land passage in Panama and became the first European to view the Pacific Ocean. The discovery of this ocean refueled Spanish ambitions to find a western passage to the Indies.

Ferdinand Magellan. In 1519, Ferdinand Magellan (ca. 1480–1521), a Portuguese mariner in the service of Spain, set sail in pursuit of Columbus's goal of reaching the Spice Islands by sailing westward. His voyage, which he did not live to complete, remains the most astounding of the age. After making the Atlantic crossing, Magellan resupplied his fleet in Brazil. Then his ships began the long southerly run toward the tip of South America, though he had no idea of the length of the continent. Suppressing mutinies and overcoming shipwrecks and desertions, Magellan finally found the straits that still bear his name. That crossing was the most difficult of all; the 300 miles took 38 terrifying days to navigate.

The Pacific voyage was equally remarkable. The sailors went nearly four months without taking on fresh food or water. Survival was miraculous. "We drank yellow water and often ate sawdust. Rats were sold for half a ducat a piece."

When Magellan finally reached land, in the Philippines, his foolhardy decision to become involved in a local war cost him his life. It was left to his navigator, Sebastian Elcano (ca. 1476–1526), to complete the journey. In 1522, three years and one month after setting out, Elcano returned to Spain with a single ship and 18 survivors of the crew of 280. But in his hold were spices of greater value than the cost of the expedition, and in his return was practical proof that the world was round.

The circumnavigation of Magellan and Elcano brought to an end the first stage of the Spanish exploration of the New World. Columbus's dreams were realized, but the vastness of

A MOMENTOUS DISCOVERY

Christopher Columbus seemingly needs no introduction. His name has forever been associated with the European discovery of the New World, although the meaning of that discovery has continually been contested. In the summer of 1492, Columbus sailed west from the Canary Islands believing that he would reach the coast of China. Instead he landed on an island in the Caribbean. This passage, from a letter addressed to the royal treasurer of Spain, contains his first impressions of the people he encountered.

Focus Questions

How do the indigenous people respond to Columbus and his men? Why is Columbus so interested in the tools and clothing of the natives?

A letter addressed to the noble Lord Raphael Sanchez, *Treasurer to their most invincible Majesties, Ferdinand and Isabella, King and Queen of Spain, by Christopher Columbus, to whom our age is greatly indebted, treating of the islands of India recently discovered beyond the Ganges, to explore which he had been sent eight months before under the auspices and at the expense of their said Majesties.*

The inhabitants of both sexes in this island, and in all the others which I have seen, or of which I have received information, go always naked as they were born, with the exception of some of the women, who use the covering of a leaf, or small bough, or an apron of cotton which they prepare for that purpose. None of them are possessed of any iron, neither have they weapons, being unacquainted with, and indeed incompetent to use them, not from any deformity of body (for they are well-formed), but because they are timid and full of fear.

They carry however in lieu of arms, canes dried in the sun, on the ends of which they fix heads of dried wood sharpened to a point, and even these they dare not use habitually; for it has often occurred when I have sent two or three of my men to any of the villages to speak with the natives, that they have come out in a disorderly troop, and have fled in such haste at the approach of our men, that the fathers forsook their children and the children their fathers. This timidity did not arise from any loss or injury that they had received from us; for, on the contrary, I gave to all I approached whatever articles I had about me, such as cloth and many other things, taking nothing of theirs in return: but they are naturally timid and fearful. As soon however as they see that they are safe, and have laid aside all fear, they are very simple and honest, and exceedingly liberal with all they have; none of them refusing any thing he may possess when he is asked for it, but on the contrary inviting us to ask them. They exhibit great love towards all others in preference to themselves: they also give objects of great value for trifles, and content themselves with very little or nothing in return.

Such are the events which I have briefly described. Farewell.

Lisbon, the 14th of March.
CHRISTOPHER COLUMBUS,
Admiral of the Fleet of the Ocean.

Christopher Columbus, *Letter from the First Voyage* (1493).

THE COLUMBIAN EXCHANGE

The encounters between Europeans and native Americans were a cultural and intellectual event of the first magnitude, likely stirring the imaginations of native tribesmen as much as those of European writers. These people had been separated for millennia, ever since the ice bridge in the Bering Sea ceased to be a conduit between North America and Asia. Their civilizations had developed along entirely different paths, and their first encounters must have mixed curiosity and fear in equal parts. The Europeans left extensive records of the differences they observed in sexual mores, attitudes toward property, and social organization. Native Americans must have made similar observations even if they were lost to posterity. Each civilization had much to teach the other though their ability to communicate with one another was limited at best.

The encounters were also a biological and ecological event and both had far reaching and long-lasting consequences. Each culture introduced the other to new diseases and to unknown plants and animals. Historians have labeled this aspect of the European discoveries the **Columbian Exchange**.

The mixing of populations that had been historically separate had effects that no one could have foreseen. First and foremost were issues of public health. Although it is believed that the Americas were originally settled by migration across a land bridge that connected Russia to Alaska, those who made the trek were few and over many generations they had lost their immunity to diseases they may have encountered in Europe. When the Spanish explorers arrived in the Caribbean islands, they carried agents of their common diseases such as measles, influenza, and especially smallpox. These diseases raged in European population centers and killed thousands each year, but those who survived them carried lifetime immunity. The native populations of the Americas endured their first exposure to these diseases all at once, and millions succumbed in the first half-century of contact. From the Caribbean to Peru, the microbes that Europeans unknowingly carried in their bodies decimated native populations.

Similarly, it was believed that Europeans first contracted the venereal disease syphilis through sexual encounters with American women. Though experts still debate whether syphilis originated in the New World it is agreed there was an epidemic of the disease in western Europe after the explorers returned home. It began in Naples in 1494 shortly after the return of Columbus's crew and spread with devastating rapidity throughout western Europe. In the first generations of infection, syphilis erupted quickly, spread rapidly, and was often fatal. In its final states it resulted in a form of mental illness that attracted the attention of numerous Renaissance physicians.

Disease was not the only unanticipated exchange that resulted from the encounters. On their ships the Spanish explorers brought horses, pigs, cows, and other domesticated animals unknown in the Americas. Native populations had no work beast sturdier than the llama, an animal barely able to carry two hundred pounds of weight and comparatively slow of foot. The lack of beasts of burden had a profound effect on the organization of Native American agriculture. Whereas European plow teams could clear trees and turn over earth with great efficiency, Americans had to accomplish these tasks by their own hands. Moreover, their range of travel was limited to what they could traverse by foot. European horses could cover many more miles at a faster speed than even the best conditioned American runners. The arrival of horses and oxen changed patterns of work among native populations almost instantly, and it eventually transformed entire cultures. Nowhere was horse culture more evident than in North America where once sedentary tribes became skilled hunters. The horses bred by North American Indians could easily outrun the herds of buffalo that roamed the Great Plains. The newly introduced animals provided hides for clothing and shelter, fat for candles and soaps, and meat that supplemented a protein-poor diet and improved the lives of generations of North Americans. Beef and pork consumption also rose dramatically in Mexico and Peru where earlier a diet of meat consisted entirely of wild turkey.

Nor was the exchange of food one-sided. Indeed, the foodstuffs of the New World proved of lasting significance to Europeans. Beginning in the 1550s, men who in later centuries would be called botanists and zoologists began to make the voyage to the Americas, hoping to discover new plants and animals that could be exported back to Europe. They catalogued thousands of unknown species, a small number of which were suited to the different climates and soils of Europe. The Jesuit missionary Jose de Acosta (1539–1600) traveled through what are now Mexico, Chile, and Peru observing the nature of the land, of the peoples who lived at altitude in the Andes, and of the many plants that were put to use as medicines and food. His book, *The Natural and Moral History of the Indies* (1590), was an immediate best seller, read for its scientific value as much as for its description of his exotic discoveries. Among these was the Aztec use of the cocoa bean to make a rich, bitter drink. Cocoa was so prized that the beans were used for exchange and to pay taxes and the Aztecs reserved the drink for their nobility. It was commonly flavored with seeds from an orchid

■ The meeting between Montezuma and Cortés in 1519. The initial encounters between Europeans and native Americans had far-reaching social, biological, and ecological consequences.

known to the natives as vanilla. Both cocoa and vanilla were exported by the Spanish back to Europe though it took several generations before they were able to master their uses. The combination of the ground bitter cocoa beans with sugar and milk made a drink called chocolate which became a European-wide fad in the eighteenth century.

If one part of the Columbian food exchanges yielded treats, another part yielded staples. One of these was a small yellow fruit that had been cultivated by the Mayans and was used in cooking in Central America. When it was exported to Europe it thrived in the hot Mediterranean climates of Spain and Italy. The Italians called it *pomodoro*—the yellow apple—but Native Americans called it tomato. Though some commentators thought it was poisonous, Italian peasants were soon using it in soups and developing sauces from its rich fruit. By the eighteenth century it was a staple of southern Italian cooking, was grown in France, and was used as a condiment in Spain. A close relative to the tomato was an even more important South American foodstuff, the potato. This was a food so nutritious that laborers could nearly survive on it alone. It could be cooked in accordance with any local custom, boiled, fried, or simply thrown into a fire. Potatoes needed little land for cultivation and little care once they were planted. Both characteristics made them perfect staples for peasant diets. They took hold quickly in central Europe where population pressure had reduced the size of farms and became a standard in German cooking. They were the most important crop in Ireland as well, where the poor survived on almost nothing else.

The Columbian Exchange was a global event that altered the nature of American and European societies. It was, of course, a much greater shock to the Native Americans who endured epidemic disease, military conquest, and occupation. Their great civilizations were ultimately obliterated, in South and Central America by the Spanish, in North America by the British and the French. The wealth they dug from the mines of the Andes financed two centuries of continental warfare as Spain vied for European supremacy. But Europeans too were changed by the encounters. Millions of them emigrated to begin new lives in the Americas and to build societies that were profoundly influenced by the natives who had preceded them.

QUESTIONS FOR DISCUSSION

Why were the diseases brought by Europeans to America so devastating? What diseases did the native peoples spread to their visitors? What was the consequence of native peoples' lack of work animals? What effect did the introduction of horses have on their societies? How did the Columbian Exchange ultimately change native and European populations?

the Pacific Ocean made a western passage to the Indies uneconomical. In 1529, the Spanish crown relinquished to the Portuguese its claims to the Spice Islands for a cash settlement. By then, trading spices was less alluring than mining gold and silver.

The Spanish Conquests

At the same moment that Magellan's voyage closed one stage of Spanish exploration, the exploits of Hernando Cortés (1485–1547) opened another. The Spanish colonized the New World along the model of their reconquest of Spain. Individuals were given control over land and the people on it in return for military service. The interests of the crown were threefold: to convert the natives to Christianity; to extend sovereignty over new dominions; and to gain some measure of profit from the venture. The colonial entrepreneurs had a singular interest—to grow rich. By and large, the colonizers came from the lower orders of Spanish society. Even the original captains and governors were drawn from groups, like younger sons of the nobility, that would have had little opportunity for rule in Castile. They undertook great risks in expectation of great rewards.

Thus many of the protective measures taken by the crown to ensure orderly colonization and fair treatment of the natives were ineffective in practice. During the first decades of the sixteenth century, Spanish captains and their followers subdued the Indian populations of the Caribbean Islands and put them to work on the agricultural haciendas that they had carved out for themselves. As early as 1498, Castilian women began arriving in the New World. Their presence helped change the character of the settlement towns from wild frontier garrisons to civilized settlements. Younger daughters of the lesser nobility, guided and guarded by chaperones, came to find husbands among the successful **conquistadores**. Some of the women ultimately inherited huge estates and participated fully in the forging of Spanish America.

Life on the hacienda, even in relative ease with a Castilian wife and family, did not always satisfy the ambitions of the Spanish colonizers. Hernando Cortés was one such conquistador. Having participated in the conquest of Cuba, Cortés sought an independent command to lead an expedition into the hinterland of Central America, where a fabulous empire was rumored to exist. Gathering a force of 600 men, Cortés sailed across the Gulf of Mexico in 1519; established a fort at Vera Cruz, where he garrisoned 200 men; and then sank his boats so that none of his company could turn back. With 400 soldiers, he began his quest. The company marched 250 miles through steamy jungles and over rugged mountains before glimpsing the first signs of the great Aztec civilization.

Cortés's Letter to Charles V

The Aztec Empire was a loose confederation of native tribes that the Aztecs had conquered during the previous century. They were ruled by the emperor Montezuma II (1502–1520) from his capital at Tenochtitlán, a marvelous city built of stone and baked clay in the middle of a lake. Invited to an audience with the Aztec emperor, Cortés and his men saw vast stores of gold and silver.

The conquest of the Aztecs took almost a year. Nearly 100,000 natives from the tribes that the Aztecs had conquered supported the Spanish assault. Cortés's cavalry terrified the Aztecs. They had never seen horses or iron armaments. Cortés also benefited from the Aztec practice of taking battlefield captives to be used in religious sacrifices. That allowed many Spanish soldiers, who would otherwise have been killed, to be rescued and to fight again.

By 1522, Cortés was master of an area larger than all of Spain. But the cost in native lives was staggering. In 30 years a population of approximately 25 million had been reduced to

■ A sixteenth-century Tenochtitlán drawing of Cortés marching on the Aztec capital at Tenochtitlán. Cortés, the bearded figure third from right, is accompanied by the Indian princess Malinche, who served as his interpreter, and the Moorish servant Estevanico. Barefoot soldiers and Indian porters bring up the rear.

THE HALLS OF MONTEZUMA

Bernal Díaz del Castillo (ca. 1492–1581) was one of the soldiers who accompanied Hernando Cortés on the conquest of the Aztecs. Díaz wrote The True History of the Conquest of New Mexico *to refute what he regarded as inaccurate accounts of the conquest. In this passage he describes the Aztec gods from a Christian point of view and shows how difficult it was for the Europeans to understand the different cultures they were encountering.*

Focus Questions

Díaz describes the Aztec gods as devils and idols. What does this view reveal about the Europeans' way of thinking? Why would Cortés want to see Montezuma's gods, and why does Montezuma show them to him?

Then Cortés said to Montezuma . . . "Your Highness is indeed a great prince, and it has delighted us to see your cities. Now that we are here in your temple, will you show us your gods?"

Montezuma replied that he would first have to consult with his priests. After he had spoken with them, he bade us enter a small tower room, a kind of hall where there were two altars with very richly painted planks on the ceiling. On each altar there were two giant figures, their bodies very tall and stout. The first one, to the right, they said was Uichilobos, their god of war. It had a very broad face with monstrous, horrible eyes, and the whole body was covered with precious stones, gold, and pearls that were stuck on with a paste they make in this country out of roots. The body was circled with great snakes made of gold and precious stones, and in one hand he held a bow and in the other some arrows. A small idol standing by him they said was his page; he held a short lance and a shield rich with gold and precious stones. Around the neck of Uichilobos were silver Indian faces and things that we took to be the hearts of these Indians, made of gold and decorated with many precious blue stones. There were braziers with copal incense, and they were burning in them the hearts of three Indians they had sacrificed that day. All the walls and floor were black with crusted blood, and the whole place stank.

To the left stood another great figure, the height of Uichilobos, with the face of a bear and glittering eyes made of their mirrors, which they call *tezcal*. It was decorated with precious stones the same as Uichilobos, for they said that the two were brothers. This Tezcatepuca was the god of hell and had charge of the souls of the Mexicans. His body was girded with figures like little devils, with snakelike tails. The walls were so crusted with blood and the floor was so bathed in it that in the slaughterhouses of Castile there was no such stink. They had offered to this idol five hearts from the day's sacrifices. . . .

Our captain said to Montezuma, half laughingly, "Lord Montezuma, I do not understand how such a great prince and wise man as yourself can have failed to come to the conclusion that these idols of yours are not gods, but evil things—devils is the term for them. . . ."

The two priests with Montezuma looked hostile, and Montezuma replied with annoyance, "Señor Malinche, if I had thought that you would so insult my gods, I would not have shown them to you. We think they are very good, for they give us health, water, good seedtimes and weather, and all the victories we desire. We must worship and make sacrifices to them. Please do not say another word to their dishonor."

From Bernal Díaz, *The True History of the Conquest of New Mexico* (1552–1568).

less than 2 million. Most of the loss was due to exposure to European diseases such as smallpox, typhoid, and measles, against which the natives were helpless. Their labor-intensive system of agriculture could not survive the rapid decrease in population, and famine followed pestilence.

This tragic sequence was repeated everywhere the Europeans appeared. In 1531, Francisco Pizarro (ca. 1475–1541) matched Cortés's feat when he conquered the Peruvian Empire of the Incas. That conquest vastly extended the territory under Spanish control and became the true source of profit for the crown when a huge silver mine was discovered in 1545 at Potosí in what is now southern Bolivia. The gold and silver that poured into Spain in the next quarter century helped support Spanish dynastic ambitions in Europe. During the course of the sixteenth century, more than 200,000 Spaniards migrated across the ocean. Perhaps one in ten was a woman who married and set up a family. In succeeding generations, the settlers created huge haciendas built on the forced labor of black African slaves, who proved better able to endure the rigors of mining and farming than did the natives.

The Legacy of the Encounters

By the seventeenth century, long-distance trade had begun to integrate the regions of the world into a single marketplace. Slaves bought in Africa mined silver in South America. The bullion was shipped to Spain, where it was distributed across Europe. Most went to Amsterdam to settle Spanish debts, Dutch bankers having replaced the Italians as the paymasters of Europe. From Holland the silver traveled east to the Baltic Sea—the Dutch lifeline where vital stores of grain and timber

MAP DISCOVERY

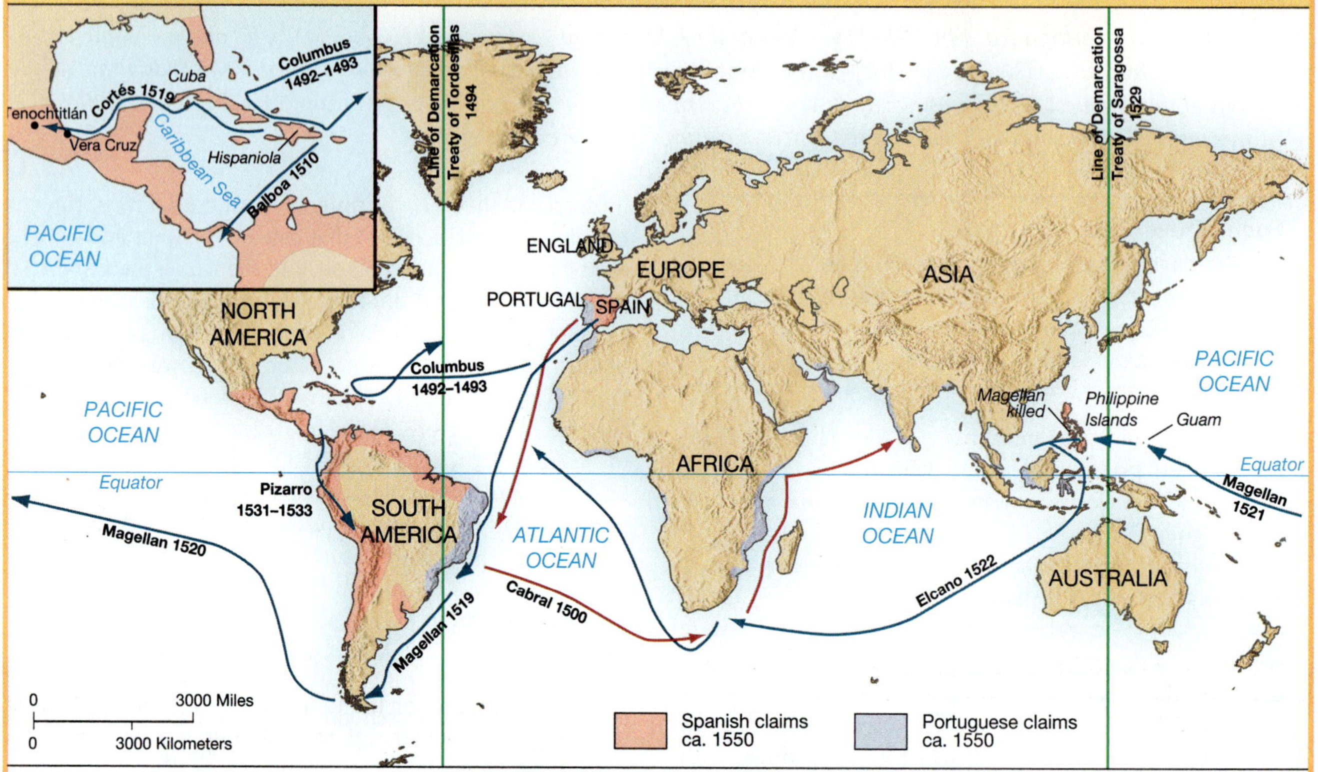

Claims of Spain and Portugal to Overseas Empires

Examine the voyages of discovery and the claims to overseas empires. How did Portuguese and Spanish explorations differ? What was the effect of the Treaty of Tordesillas on their travel and claims? Why was it believed at the time that Portugal was the more powerful empire?

were purchased for home consumption. Even more of this African-mined Spanish silver, traded by the Dutch, was carried to Asia to buy spices in the Spice Islands, cottons in India, and silk in China. Millions of ounces of silver flowed from South America to Asia via the European trading routes. On the return voyage, Indian cottons were traded in Africa to purchase slaves for the South American silver mines. (See "The West and the Wider World: The Columbian Exchange," pp. 352–353.)

Gold, God, and Glory. Gold, God, and glory neatly summarized the motives of the European explorers. Perhaps it is not necessary to delve any further. The gold of Africa and the silver of South America enriched the Western nations. Christian missions arose wherever the European empires touched down: among Africans, Asians, and Native Americans. And glory there was in plenty. The feats of the European explorers were recounted in story and song. The ***Lusiads*** (1572) by Luiz de Camões (ca. 1524–1580), one of the greatest works of Portuguese literature, celebrated the new age. "They were men of no ordinary stature, equally at home in war and in dangers of every kind: they founded a new king-

■ These engravings by Theodore de Bry accompanied a 1599 English edition of *The Destruction of the Indies* by Bartolomé de las Casas. They illustrated acts of Spanish cruelty and so bolstered Las Casas's argument by engendering sympathy for the Native American population.

dom among distant peoples, and made it great." In the achievement of exploration and conquest, the modern world had finally surpassed the ancients. "Let us hear no more then of Ulysses and Aeneas and their long journeyings, no more of Alexander and Trajan and their famous victories. My theme is the daring and renown of the Portuguese, to whom Neptune and Mars alike give homage."

The feats of exploration were worthy of celebration. In less than 50 years, tenacious European seafarers found passages to the east and continents to the west. In doing so they overcame terrors both real and imagined. Hazardous journeys in uncharted waters took their toll in men and ships. The odds of surviving a voyage of exploration were no better than those of surviving an epidemic of plague. Nearly two-thirds of da Gama's crew perished on the passage to India. The 40 men that Columbus left on Hispaniola, almost half his company, disappeared without a trace. Only one of the five ships that set out with Magellan in 1519 returned to Spain. "If you want to learn how to pray, go to sea" was a Portuguese proverb that needed no explanation.

IMAGE DISCOVERY

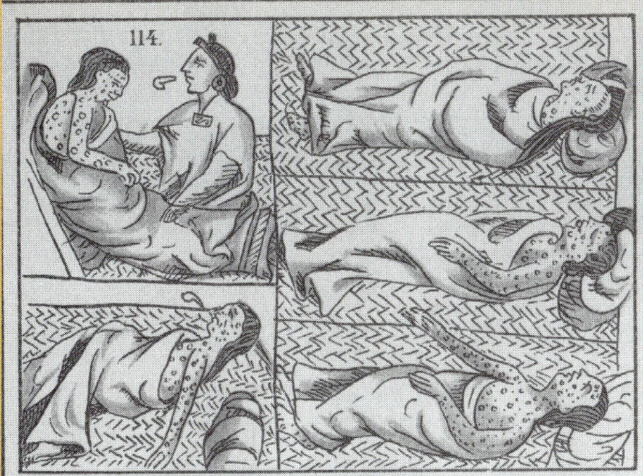

Smallpox: Death and Disease

This sixteenth-century drawing from the Aztec *Codex Florentino* depicts Native Americans suffering smallpox. Europeans often survived smallpox, but Americans had never encountered it before European contact and so had no immunity. As a result, smallpox devastated the native population. How might deaths from smallpox have affected the European conquest of America? After the conquest, Aztec survivors of the fall of Tenochtitlán developed these illustrations for a history of the conquest by Spanish church authorities. Does it seem that this image was created by Aztecs who may have lost family members to smallpox? Why, or why not? Why would the Spanish church have wanted to understand smallpox in America?

Yet all of these dangers were overcome. The expansion of Europe was a feat of technology. Advances in navigational skills, especially in dead reckoning and later in calculating latitude from the position of the sun, were essential preconditions for covering the distances that were to be traveled. So were the more sophisticated ship designs. The magnetic compass and the astrolabe were indispensable tools. New methods for the making of maps and charts, and the popular interest in them, fueled both ambitions and abilities. It was a mapmaker who named the newly found continents after Amerigo Vespucci (1451–1512), the Italian explorer who voyaged to Brazil for the Portuguese. It may have been an accident that Columbus found the New World, but it was no coincidence that he was able to land in the same place three more times.

European Reflections. Riches and converts, power and glory, all came in the wake of exploration. But in the process of exploring new lands and new cultures, Europe also discovered itself. It learned something of its own aspirations. Early Portuguese voyagers went in quest of the mythical Prester John, a saintly figure who was said to rule a heaven on earth in the middle of Africa. The first children born on Madeira were named Adam and Eve, though that slave plantation of sugar and wine was an unlikely Garden of Eden. The optimism of those who searched for the fountain of youth in the Florida swamps was not only that they would find it there, but that a long life was worth living. Contact with the cultures of the New World also forced a different kind of thinking about life in the old one. The supposed customs of strange lands also provided the setting for one of the great works of English social criticism, Sir Thomas More's *Utopia* (1516).

Europe also discovered and revealed a darker side of itself in the age of exploration. Accompanying the boundless optimism and assertive self-confidence that made so much possible was a tragic arrogance toward and callous disregard of native races. Portuguese travelers described Africans as "dog-faced, dog-toothed people, satyrs, wild men, and cannibals." Such attitudes helped justify enslavement. The European conquests were both brutal and wasteful. The Dominican priest Bartolomé de Las Casas (1474–1566) championed the cause of the native inhabitants at the court of the Spanish kings. His *Apologetic History of the Indies* (1550) highlighted the complexity of native society even as he witnessed its destruction. The German artist Albrecht Dürer (1471–1528) marveled at the "subtle ingenuity of the men in those distant lands" after viewing a display of Aztec art.

Laws on Good Treatment of the Indians

But few Europeans were so enlightened about native society. Although Europeans encountered heritages that were in some ways richer than their own, only the most farsighted Westerners could see that there was more value in the preservation of the heritages than in their demolition. The Portuguese spice trade did not depend upon the indiscriminate destruction of eastern ports. The obliteration of millions of Aztecs and Incas was not a necessary result of the fever for gold and silver. The destruction was wanton. It revealed the

■ Contact with cultures of the New World forced Europeans into a different way of thinking about the old world. In this detail from *The Cognoscenti*, a seventeenth-century Flemish painting, English scholars and navigators examine European encounters with new lands and new cultures.

rapaciousness, greed, and cruelty of the Portuguese and Spanish conquerors. Those were the impulses of the Crusades rather than of the Renaissance.

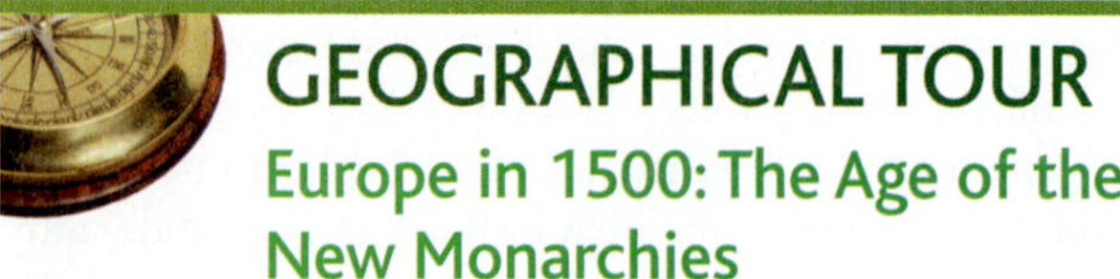

GEOGRAPHICAL TOUR

Europe in 1500: The Age of the New Monarchies

Just as the map of the world was changing as a result of the voyages of exploration, so the map of Europe was changing as a result of the activities of princes. The early sixteenth century was the age of the prince, the first great stage of nation building that would last for the next 300 years. The **New Monarchies,** as they are sometimes called, consolidated territories that were divided culturally, linguistically, and historically. The states of Europe were political units, and they were forged by political means: by diplomacy, by marriage, and, most commonly, by war. The national system that we take for granted when thinking about Europe is a relatively recent development. Before we can observe its beginnings, we must first have a picture of Europe as it existed in 1500 (see **Map A**). At that time it was composed of nearly 500 distinct political units.

Europe is a concept. Like all concepts, it is difficult to define. The vast plain that stretches from the Netherlands to the steppes of Russia presents few natural barriers to migration. Only in the south did geographical forces stem the flow of humanity. The Carpathian Mountains created a basin for the settlement of Slavic peoples that extended down to the Black Sea. The Alps provided a boundary for French, Germanic, and Italian settlements. The Pyrenees defined the Iberian Peninsula, with a mixture of African and European peoples.

Boundaries of Eastern Europe

In the East, three great empires had created the political geography that could be said to define a European boundary: the Mongol, the Ottoman, and the Russian. During the early Middle Ages, Mongol warriors had swept across the Asian steppes and conquered most of central and southern Russia. By the sixteenth century, the Mongol Empire was disintegrating, its lands divided into a number of separate states called *khanates*. The khanate of the Crimea, with lands around the northern shores of the Black Sea, created the southeastern border of Europe (see **Map B**).

The Ottoman territories defined the southern boundary. By 1450, the Ottomans controlled all of Byzantium and Greece, dominating an area from the Black Sea to the Aegean. Fifty years later, they had conquered nearly all the lands between the Aegean and the Adriatic seas. A perilous frontier was established on the Balkan Peninsula. There the principalities of Moldavia, Wallachia, Transylvania, and Hungary (see **Map B**) held out against the Ottomans for another quarter century before being overrun.

The Russian state defined the eastern boundary of Europe. Russia too had been a great territorial unit in the Middle Ages, centered at Kiev in the west and stretching eastward into Asia. The advance of the Mongols in the thirteenth century had contracted the eastern part of Russia, and its western domains had disintegrated under the practice of dividing the ruling prince's inheritance among his sons. In 1500, Europe reached as far east as the principality of Muscovy. There the heritage of East and West mingled. In some periods of history, Russia's ties with the West were more important; at other times, Russia retreated into isolation from Europe.

The northern borders of eastern Europe centered on the Baltic Sea, one of the most important trading routes of the early modern era (see **Map B**). On the northern coasts lay the Scandinavian nations of Sweden, Norway, and Denmark.

■ **Map A. Europe in 1500.** While the western part of Europe had taken on its modern features, central and eastern Europe continued to change their boundaries.

■ **Map B. Eastern Europe.** This map shows eastern Europe before the consolidation of Russia. The Duchy of Lithuania had reached the height of its power and stretched from the Baltic to the Black Sea.

These loosely confederated nations had a single king throughout the fifteenth century. Denmark, the southernmost of the three, was also the richest and most powerful. It enjoyed a favorable trading position on both the North and Baltic seas and social and economic integration with the Germanic states on its border. On the southern side of the Baltic Sea lay the dominions of the Teutonic Knights, physically divided by the large state of Poland-Lithuania. The Teutonic territories, in the valuable Baltic region of Prussia, had been colonized by German crusaders in the thirteenth century.

Poland-Lithuania comprised an enormous territory that covered the length of Europe from the Baltic to the Black Sea (see **Map B**). The crowns of the two nations had been joined at the end of the fourteenth century, and their dynastic history was tied up with the nations of Bohemia and Hungary to their west and south. Whereas Bohemia was increasingly drawn into the affairs of central Europe, Hungary remained more Eastern in orientation, partly because the Bohemians gave nominal allegiance to the Holy Roman Emperor and partly because the Ottoman conquests had engulfed a large part of the Hungarian territories. At the end of the fifteenth century, Poland, Lithuania, Bohemia, and Hungary were all ruled by the same family, the Jagiellons.

Mongols and Ottomans to the south, Russians in the east, Scandinavia in the north, Poland-Lithuania in the center, and Hungary in the west: such were the contours of the eastern portion of Europe. Its lands were, on the whole, less fertile than those farther west, and its climate was more severe. It was a sparsely populated region. Its wealth lay in the Baltic fisheries, in the Hungarian and Bohemian silver mines, and in the enormous Russian forests, where wood and its by-products were plentiful. Except in the southern portions of Poland and central Bohemia, the region was agriculturally poor.

Central Europe

The middle of the continent was defined by the Holy Roman Empire and occupied almost entirely by Germanic peoples (see **Map C**). In length, the empire covered the territory from the North and Baltic seas to the Adriatic and the Mediterranean, where the Italian city-states were located. In width, it stretched from Bohemia to Burgundy. Politically, central Europe comprised a bewildering array of principalities, Church lands, and free towns. By the end of the fifteenth century, the Holy Roman Empire was an empire in name only. The large states of Brandenburg, Bohemia, and Bavaria resembled the political units of the East. In the south, the Alps provided an effective physical boundary, which allowed the Archduchy of Austria and the Swiss Confederation to follow their own separate paths. Stretching across the center of the empire, from the Elbe River to the North Sea, was a jumble of petty states. Great cities such as Nüremberg and Ulm in the

■ **Map C. Central Europe.** This map of Central Europe shows the boundaries of the Holy Roman Empire.

south, Bremen and Hamburg in the north, and Frankfurt and Cologne in the west were free municipalities. Large sections of the northwestern part of the empire were governed by the Church through resident bishops. Farther to the west were the prosperous Low Countries: Holland and its port of Amsterdam, Brabant and its port of Antwerp. In the southwest, the empire extended in some places as far as the Rhone River and included the rich estates of Luxembourg, Lorraine, and Burgundy (see **Map C**).

The riches of the empire made it the focal point of Europe. Nearly 15 million people lived within its borders. Its agriculture varied from the olive- and wine-producing areas in the southwest to the great granaries in its center. Rich mineral deposits and large reserves of timber made the German lands industrially advanced. The European iron industry was centered there, and the empire was the arms manufacturer for the Western world. The empire was also a great commercial center, heir to the Hanseatic League of the Middle Ages. Its northern and western ports teemed with trade, and its merchants were replacing the Italians as the leading international bankers.

Like the Empire, the Italian peninsula was divided into a diverse collection of small city-states (see **Map C**). During the course of the fifteenth century, five city-states had emerged as most powerful (see Chapter 11). In the north were Florence, Venice, and the Duchy of Milan. In the south was Rome, spiritual center of Catholicism and residence of the pope. Although Roman and papal governments were separate jurisdictions, in fact their fates were bound together. Papal lands stretched far to the north of Rome, and wars to defend or expand them were Roman as well as papal ventures. The kingdom of Naples—the breadbasket of the Mediterranean—occupied the southernmost part of Italy and included the agriculturally rich island of Sicily.

Map D. Western Europe. Western Europe was already consolidated into nation-states.

Western Europe

The Iberian Peninsula, the French territories, and the British Isles formed the westernmost borders of Europe (see **Map D**). Separated from France in the north by the Pyrenees, the Iberian Peninsula is surrounded by the Atlantic Ocean and the Mediterranean Sea on the west and east. But neither its protective mountain barrier nor its ample coastline was its most significant geographical feature during its formative period. Rather, it was the fact that Iberia is separated from North Africa only by the easily navigable Strait of Gibraltar. During the Middle Ages, the peninsula was overrun by North African Muslims, whom the Spanish called Moors. From the eighth to the fifteenth centuries, Iberian history was dominated by the **reconquista**—the recapture and re-Christianization of the conquered territories. The reconquest was finally completed in 1492, when the Moors were pushed out of Granada and the Jews were expelled from Spain. At the end of the fifteenth century, the Iberian Peninsula contained several separate kingdoms. The most important were Portugal—the only Continental nation to have the same borders in 1500 as it does today—on the western coast; Aragon, with its Mediterranean ports of Barcelona and Valencia; and Castile, the largest of the Iberian states (see **Map D**). The marriage of King Ferdinand of Aragon and Queen Isabella of Castile in 1469 had joined the crowns of Aragon and Castile, but the two kingdoms remained separate.

The remnants of ancient Gaul were also favored by a maritime location. Like those of Iberia, French coasts are located along the Mediterranean Sea and the Atlantic Ocean. France's eastern boundaries touched the empire; its southern mountain border touched Spain. To the northwest, Britain was less than 30 miles from France across the English Channel. Toward the end of the fifteenth century, France was still divided into many small fiefs. The royal domain centered on Paris and extended to Champagne in the east and Normandy in the west (see **Map D**). South of this area, however, from Orléans to Brittany, were principalities that had long been contested between England and France. Nor was the rich central plain yet integrated into the royal domain. Agriculturally, French lands were the richest in Europe. France enjoyed both Mediterranean and Atlantic climates, which suited the growing of the widest variety of foodstuffs. Its population of approximately 13 million was second only to that of the empire.

Across the Channel lay Britain (composed of England, Scotland, and Wales) and Ireland (see **Map D**). Britain had been settled by an array of European colonizers—Romans, Danes, Angles, and Saxons—before being conquered in the eleventh century by the French Normans. From that time, it was protected by the rough waters of the English Channel and the North Sea and allowed to develop a distinct cultural and political heritage. Wales to the west and Scotland to the north were still separate nations at the beginning of the sixteenth century. Both were mountainous lands with harsh climates and few natural advantages. They were sparsely populated. Although Ireland, too, was sparsely populated, it contained several rich agricultural areas especially suited for dairying and grazing.

In 1500, Europe exhibited a remarkable diversity of political and geographical forms. Huge states in the east, tiny principalities in the center, emerging nations in the west, all seemingly had little in common. There was as yet no state system and no clear group of dominant powers. The western migration of the Germanic peoples appeared to be over, but their consolidation was as yet unimagined. The Iberians struggled to expel the Moors, the Hungarians to hold back the Ottomans. Everywhere one looked there was fragmentation and disarray. Yet in less than a half century the largest empire yet known in the West would be formed. States would come to be consolidated and dynasties established all over the Continent. And with the rise of the state would come the dream of dominion, an empire over all of Europe.

THE FORMATION OF STATES

It was Machiavelli who identified the prince as the agent of change in the process of state formation. He believed that the successful prince could bring unity to his lands, security to his borders, and prosperity to his subjects. The unsuccessful prince brought nothing but ruin.

A process as long and as complex as the formation of nations, however, depends on more than the will of individuals. Factors such as geography, population, and natural resources are all important. So too are the structures through which human activity is channeled. The ways in which families are organized and wealth is transmitted from generation to generation can result in large estates with similar customs or small estates with varying ones. The manner in which social groups are formed and controlled can mean that power is centralized or dispersed. The beliefs of ordinary people and the way they practice them can define who is a part of a community and who is not. All these elements and many others affected the way in which European states began to take shape at the end of the fifteenth century. Despite these complexities, we should not lose sight of the simple truth of Machiavelli's observations. In the first stages of the consolidation of European nations, the role of the prince was crucial.

Indeed, in the middle of the fifteenth century there were many factors working against the formation of large states in Europe. The most obvious involved simple things such as transportation and communication. The distance that could be covered quickly was very small. In wet and cold seasons, travel was nearly impossible. The emperor Charles V sat in Burgundy for two months awaiting a favorable wind to take him to his newly inherited kingdom of Spain. Similarly, directives from the center of the states to the localities were slow to arrive and slower still to be adopted. Large areas were difficult to control and to defend. Distinct languages or dialects also made for difficulties in communication. Only the most educated could use Latin as a common written language, and separate languages contributed to separate cultures. Customary practices, common ancestry, and shared experiences helped define a sense of community through which small states defined themselves.

To the natural forces that acted to maintain the existence of small units of government were added invented ones. To succeed, a prince had to establish supremacy over a number of rivals. For the most part, states were inherited. In some places it was customary to follow the rule of primogeniture—inheritance by the eldest son. In others, estates were split among sons, or among children of both sexes. Some traditions, like those of the French, excluded inheritance through women; others, like the Castilian, treated women's claims as equal to men's. Short lives meant prolonged disputes about inheritance. Rulers had to defend their thrones from any number of rivals with strong claims to legitimacy.

Rulers also had to defend themselves from the ambitions of their mightiest subjects. Dukes could dream only one dream. The constant warfare of the European nobility was one of the central features of the Later Middle Ages. To avoid resort to arms, princes and peers entered into all manner of alliances, using their children as pawns and the marriage bed as the chessboard. Rulers also faced independent institutions within their states, powerful organizations that had to be won over or crushed. The long process of taming the Church was well advanced by the end of the fifteenth century and about to enter a new stage. Fortified towns presented a different problem. They possessed both the manpower and wealth necessary to raise and maintain armies. They also jealously guarded their privileges. Rulers who could not tax their towns could not rule their state. Finally, most kingdoms had assemblies that represented the propertied classes, especially in matters of taxation. Some, such as the English Parliament and the Spanish Cortes, were strong; others, such as the Imperial Diet and the French Estates-General, were weak. But everywhere they posed an obstacle to the extension of the power of princes.

In combination, these factors slowed and shaped the process of state formation. But neither separately nor together were they powerful enough to overcome it. The fragmentation of Europe into so many small units of government made some consolidation inevitable; and as the first large states took shape, the position of smaller neighbors grew ever more precarious.

This consolidation was especially true by the end of the fifteenth century because of the increase in the destructive power of warfare. Technological advances in cannonry and in the skills of gunners and engineers made medieval fortifications untenable. The fall of Constantinople was as much a military watershed as it was a political one. Gunpowder decisively changed battlefield tactics. It made heavy armor obsolete and allowed for the development of a different type of warfare. Not only could lightly armored horses and riders inflict more damage upon one another, but now they were mobile enough to be used against infantry. Infantry armed with long pikes or small muskets became the crucial components of armies that were growing ever larger. Systems of supply were better, sources of small arms were more available, and the rewards of conquest were more tangible. What could not be inherited or married could be conquered.

Eastern Configurations

The interplay of factors that encouraged and inhibited the formation of states is most easily observed in the eastern parts of Europe. There the different paths taken by Muscovy and Poland-Lithuania stand in contrast. At the beginning of the sixteenth century, the principality of Muscovy was the largest European political unit. Muscovy had established itself as the heir to the ancient state of Russia through conquest, shrewd political alliances, and the good fortune of its princes to be blessed with long reigns. Muscovy's growth was phenomenal. Under Ivan III, "the Great" (1462–1505), Muscovy expanded to the north and west. During a long series of wars it annexed Novgorod and large parts of Livonia and Lithuania. Its military successes were almost unbroken, but so too were its diplomatic triumphs. Ivan the Great preferred pacification to conquest, though when necessary he could conquer with great brutality. Between 1460 and 1530, Muscovy increased its landed territory by 1.5 million square miles.

A number of factors led to the rise of Muscovy. External threats had diminished. First, the deterioration of the Mongol Empire that had dominated south-central Russia allowed Ivan to escape the yoke of Mongol rule that the Russian princes had worn for centuries. Second, the fall of Constantinople made Muscovy the heir to Eastern Christendom, successor to the Roman and Byzantine empires. Ivan's marriage to Sophia, niece of the last emperor of Byzantium, cemented the connection. Sophia brought both Italian artisans and Byzantine customs to the Russian court, helping Ivan open his contacts with the wider world.

Ivan the Terrible. What made the expansion of Muscovy so impressive was that land once gained was never lost. The military and political achievements of Ivan the Great were furthered by his son Vasili and his more famous grandson Ivan IV, "the Terrible" (1533–1584). Ivan IV defeated the Mongols on his southeastern border and incorporated the entire Volga river basin into Muscovy. But his greatest ambition was to gain a port on the Baltic Sea and establish a northern outlet for commerce. His objective was to conquer Livonia. Nearly three decades of warfare between Muscovy and Poland-Lithuania—with which Livonia had allied itself—resulted in large territorial gains, but Muscovy always fell short of the real prize. And Ivan's northern campaigns seriously weakened the defense of the south. In 1571, the Crimean Tatars advanced from their territories on Muscovy's southwestern border and inflicted a powerful psychological blow when they burned the city of Moscow. Although the Tatars were eventually driven off Muscovite soil, expansion in both north and south was at an end for the next 75 years.

By the reign of Ivan IV, Muscovite society was divided roughly into three groups: the hereditary nobility known as the *boyars*, the military service class, and the peasantry who were bound to the land. There was no large mercantile presence in Muscovy and its urban component remained small. The boyars, who were powerful landlords of great estates, owed little to the tsar. They inherited their lands and did not necessarily benefit from expansion and conquest. Members of the military service class, on the other hand, were bound to the success of the crown. Their military service was a requirement for the possession of their estates, which were granted out of lands gained through territorial expansion. Ivan IV used members of the military service class as legislative advisers and elevated them in his parliamentary council (the Zemsky Sobor), which also included representatives of the nobility, clergy, and towns.

Unlike his grandfather, Ivan IV had an abiding mistrust of the boyars. They had held power when he was a child, and it was rumored that his mother had been poisoned by them. It was in his treatment of the boyars that he earned the nickname "the Terrible." During his brutal suppression of supposed conspiracies, several thousand families were massacred by Ivan's own orders and thousands more by the violent excesses of his agents. Ivan constantly imagined plots against himself, and many of the men who served him met horrible deaths. He also forcibly relocated boyar families, stripping them of their lands in one place but granting them new lands elsewhere.

All those measures contributed to the breakdown of local networks of influence and power and to a disruption of local governance. But they also made possible a system of central administration, one of Ivan IV's most important achievements. He created departments of state to deal with the various tasks of administration, which resulted in more efficient management of revenues and of the military. Ivan IV promoted the interests of the military service class over those of the boyars, but he did not destroy the nobility. New boyars were created, especially in conquered territories, and those new families owed their positions and loyalty to the prince. Both the boyars and the military benefited from Ivan's policy of binding the great mass of people to the land. Russian peasants had few political or economic rights in comparison to those of Western peasants, but during the early sixteenth century even the meager rights Russian peasants had were curtailed. The right of peasants to move from the estate of one lord to that of another was suspended, all but binding the peasantry to the land. The serfdom made possible the prolonged absence of military leaders from their estates and contributed to the creation of the military service class. But it also made imperative the costly system of coercing agricultural and industrial labor. In the long term, serfdom retarded the development of the Muscovite economy by removing incentive from large landholders to make investments in commerce or to improve agricultural production.

Poland-Lithuania. The growth of an enlarged and centralized Muscovy stands in contrast to the experiences of Poland-Lithuania during the same period. At the end of the fifteenth century, Casimir IV (1447–1492) ruled the kingdom of Poland and the grand duchy of Lithuania. His son Vladislav II ruled Bohemia (1471–1516) and Hungary (1490–1516). Had the four states been permanently consolidated they could have become an effective barrier to Ottoman expansion in the south and Russian expansion in the east. But the union of crowns had never been the union of states. The union of crowns had taken place during the previous century by political alliances, diplomatic marriages, and the consent of the nobility. Such arrangements kept peace among the four neighbors, but they kept any one of them from becoming a dominant partner.

■ A miniature painted by a Krakow artist about 1510 depicts the final act of the coronation rite: The king in majesty is surrounded by his court while a *Te Deum* is sung. The knights in the foreground bear the standards of Poland and Lithuania.

While the Polish-Lithuanian monarchs enjoyed longevity similar to that of the Muscovites, those who ruled Hungary and Bohemia were not so fortunate: by the sixteenth century a number of claimants to both crowns existed. The competition was handled by diplomacy rather than war. The accession of Vladislav II, for example, was accompanied by large concessions, first to the Bohemian towns and later to the Hungarian nobility. The formal union of the Polish and Lithuanian crowns in 1569 also involved the decentralization of power and the strengthening of the rights of the nobility in both countries. In the end, the states split apart. The Russians took much of Lithuania, the Ottomans much of Hungary. Bohemia, which in the fifteenth century had been ruled more by its nobles than its king, was absorbed into the Habsburg territories after 1526.

There were many reasons why a unified state did not appear in east-central Europe. In the first place, external forces disrupted territorial and political arrangements, and wars with the Ottomans and the Russians absorbed resources. Second, the princes faced rivals to their crowns. Although Casimir IV was able to place his son on the thrones of both Bohemia and Hungary, he managed to do so against the powerful claims of the Habsburg princes, who continued to intrigue against the Jagiellons. The contests for power necessitated concessions to leading citizens, which decreased the ability of the princes to centralize their kingdoms or to effect real unification among them. The nobility of Hungary, Bohemia, and Poland-Lithuania all developed strong local interests that increased over time. In Bohemia, Vladislav II was king in name only, and even in Poland the nobility won confirmation of its rights and privileges from the monarchy. War, rivalries for power, and a strong nobility prevented any one prince from dominating the area as the princes of Muscovy dominated theirs.

The Western Powers

Just as in the east, there was no single pattern to the consolidation of the large western European states. They, too, were internally fragmented and externally imperiled. While England had to overcome the ruin of decades of civil war, France and Spain faced the challenges of invasion and occupation. Western European princes struggled against powerful institutions and individuals within their states. Some they conquered, others they absorbed. Each nation formed its state differently: England by administrative centralization, France by good fortune, and Spain by dynastic marriage. Yet in 1450 few imagined that any one of these states would succeed.

The Taming of England. Alone among European states, England suffered no threat of foreign invasion during the fifteenth century. The island fortress might easily have become the first consolidated European state were it not for the ambitions of the nobility and the weakness of the crown. For thirty years, the English aristocracy fought over the spoils of a helpless monarch. The Wars of the Roses (1455–1485), as they came to be called, were as much a free-for-all among the English peerage as they were a contest for the throne between the houses of Lancaster and York. At their center was an attempt by the dukes of York to wrest the crown from the mad and ineffective Lancastrian king Henry VI (1422–1461). All around the edges was the continuation of local and family feuds that had little connection to the dynastic struggle.

Three decades of intermittent warfare had predictable results. The houses of Lancaster and York were both destroyed. Edward IV (1461–1483) succeeded in gaining the crown for the House of York, but he was never able to wear it securely. When he died, his children, including his heir, Edward V (1483), were placed in the protection of their uncle Richard III (1483–1485). It was protection that they did not survive. The two boys disappeared, reputedly murdered in the Tower of London, and Richard declared himself king. Richard's usurpation led to civil war, and he was killed by the forces of Henry Tudor at the battle of Bosworth Field in 1485. By the end of the Wars of the Roses, the monarchy had lost both revenue and prestige, and the aristocracy had stored up bitter memories for the future.

It was left to Henry Tudor to pick up the pieces of the kingdom. As legend has it, he picked up the crown off a bramble bush. The two chief obstacles to his determination to consolidate the English state were the power of the nobility and the poverty of the monarchy. No English monarch had held secure title to the throne for more than a century. Henry Tudor, as Henry VII (1485–1509), put an end to the dynastic instability at once. He married Elizabeth of York, in whose heirs would rest the legitimate claim to the throne. Their children were indisputable successors to the crown. He also began the long process of taming his over-mighty subjects. Traitors were hung and turncoats rewarded. He and his son Henry VIII (1509–1547) adroitly created a new peerage, which soon was as numerous as the old feudal aristocracy. The new nobles owed their titles and loyalty to the Tudors. They were favored with offices and spoils and were relied upon to suppress both popular and aristocratic rebellions.

The financial problems of the English monarchy were not so easily overcome. In theory and practice an English king was supposed to live "of his own," that is, off the revenues from his own estates. In normal circumstances, royal revenue did not come from the king's subjects. The English landed classes had established the principle that only on extraordinary occasions were they to be required to contribute to the maintenance of government. The principle was defended through their representative institution—the Parliament. When the kings of England wanted to tax their subjects, they had first to gain the assent of Parliament. Although Parliaments did grant requests for extraordinary revenue, especially for national defense, they did so grudgingly. The English landed elites were not exempt from taxation, but they were able to control the amount of taxes they paid.

The inability of the crown to extract its living from its subjects made it more dependent on the efficient management of its own estates. Thus English state building depended upon the growth of centralized institutions that could oversee royal lands and collect royal customs. Gradually, medieval institutions such as the Exchequer were supplanted by newer organs that were better able to adjust to modern methods of accounting, record keeping, and enforcement. Henry VII sent ministers to view and value royal lands. He ordered the cataloging and collection of feudal obligations. Ship cargoes were inspected thoroughly and every last penny of customs charged. Whether Henry's reputation for greed and rapacity was warranted, it was undeniable that he squeezed as much as could be taken from a not very juicy inheritance. His financial problems limited both domestic and foreign policy.

It was not until the middle of the next reign that the English monarchy was again solvent. As a result of his dispute with the papacy over his divorce from Catherine of Aragon and marriage to Anne Boleyn, Henry VIII confiscated the enormous wealth of the Catholic Church, and with one stroke solved the crown's monetary problems (see Chapter 13). But the real contribution that Henry and his chief minister, Thomas Cromwell (ca.

■ Portrait of Anne Boleyn, the second wife of Henry VIII, by an unknown artist. Anne lost favor with Henry when she delivered a daughter instead of the son he expected. Anne made other enemies at court and in 1536 was convicted of adultery and beheaded.

LAST WORDS

Anne Boleyn was the second wife of Henry VIII and the mother of Elizabeth I. Henry's desire to have a son and his passion for Anne resulted in his divorce from Catherine of Aragon and England's formal break with the Roman Catholic Church. When Anne bore only a daughter, she too became dispensable. She was convicted of adultery and incest and executed in 1536. Here are her last words.

Focus Questions

How does Anne respond in her scaffold speech to the charges against her? What does Anne mean when she condemns "the cruel law of the land" at the same time as she praises "the King my sovereign lord"?

Good friends, I am not come here to excuse or to justify myself, for as much as I know full well that aught that I could say in my defense doth not appertain unto you, and that I could draw no hope of life from the same. But I come here only to die, and thus to yield myself humbly to the will of the King my lord. And if in my life I did ever offend the King's grace, surely with my death I do now atone for the same. And I blame not my judges, nor any other manner of person, nor anything save the cruel law of the land by which I die. But be this, and be my faults as they may, I beseech you all, good friends, to pray for the life of the King my sovereign lord and yours, who is one of the best princes on the face of the earth, and who hath always treated me so well that better could not be; wherefore I submit to death with a good will, humbly asking pardon of the world.

Anne Boleyn, scaffold speech.

1485–1540), made to forming an English state was the way in which the windfall was administered. Cromwell accelerated the process of centralizing government that had begun under Edward IV. He divided administration according to its functions by creating separate departments of state, modeled upon courts. The new departments were responsible for record keeping, revenue collection, and law enforcement. Each had a distinct jurisdiction and a permanent, trained staff. Cromwell coordinated the work of the distinct departments by expanding the power of the Privy Council, which included the heads of the administrative bodies. Through a long evolution, the Privy Council came to serve as the king's executive body. Cromwell also saw the importance of Parliament as a legislative body. Through Parliament, royal policy could be turned into statutes that had the assent of the political nation. If Parliament was well managed, issues that were potentially controversial could be defused. Laws passed by Parliament were more easily enforced locally than were proclamations issued by the king. By the end of Henry VIII's reign, the English monarchy was strong enough to withstand the succession of a child king, precisely the circumstance that had plunged the nation into civil war a century earlier.

The Unification of France. Perhaps the most remarkable thing about the unification of France is that it took place at all. The forces working against the consolidation of a French state were formidable. France was surrounded by aggressive and powerful neighbors with whom it was frequently at war. Its greatest nobles were semi-independent princes who were constant rivals for the throne and consistent opponents of the extension of royal power. The French people were deeply suspicious of the pretensions of the monarchy. **Provincialism** was not simply negative; it was a fierce pride of and loyalty to-

■ This painting by an anonymous Flemish artist of the wedding of Philip the Good, duke of Burgundy, and Isabella of Portugal evokes the courtly style and aspirations of fifteenth-century Burgundy.

ward local customs and institutions that had deep roots within communities. Furthermore, France was splintered by profound regional differences. The north and south were divided by culture and by language (*the langue d'oc* in the south and the *langue d'oïl* in the north). As late as the fifteenth century, a French king needed a translator to communicate with officials from his southern lands.

The first obstacles that were overcome were the external threats to French security. For more than a century, the throne of France had been contested by the kings of England. The so-called Hundred Years' War, which was fought intermittently between 1337 and 1453, originated in a dispute over the inheritance of the French crown and English possessions in Gascony in southern France (see Chapter 10). The war was fought on

THE KINGDOM OF FRANCE

Claude de Seyssel (ca. 1450–1519) was a legal scholar and professor at the University of Turin. He came from the duchy of Savoy, a small state that mixed French and Italian peoples and culture. Seyssel thus learned about the French monarchy as an outsider and wrote The Monarchy of France *as a book of counsel for French kings. In this passage he explains and defends the Salic law, which prohibited legitimate title to the French throne from passing through a woman. The legal documents that supposedly established Salic law were fakes.*

Focus Questions

Why is it "excellent" that the French throne cannot pass to a woman? What conditions are desirable in order for a state to be stable and prosper?

Without going too deeply into the disputes of the philosophers, we may presuppose three kinds of political rule: monarchy under a single person, aristocracy under a certain number of the better sort, and democracy the popular state. Of these, according to the true and most widespread opinion, monarchy is the best if the prince is good and has the sense, the experience, and the good will to govern justly. That rarely comes to pass, however, because with such authority and license it is hard to follow the right course and hold fairly the balance of justice. The second state seems the more reasonable and praiseworthy since it is more lasting, better founded, and easier to bear, being comprised of the persons selected by the assembly or a part of them. Such persons are, moreover, subject to corruption and change, at least to the extent that, when there are several bad and inadequate men among them, the better sort, being their superiors, can repress their boldness and thwart their unreasonable enterprises. As to the popular state, it has always been turbulent, dangerous, and hostile to the better sort. Nevertheless, the aristocratic state is often transformed into oligarchy, a monopoly by covetous and ambitious folk, who, though chosen as the wisest and most prudent of the people to rule and to govern the people well, care only for their particular profit. So when all is said, none of these states can possibly be perpetual, for ordinary in the course of time they get worse, especially when they go on growing, so that often one [by disorder] rises from the other.

The first special trait that I find good is that this realm passes by masculine succession and, by virtue of the law which the French call Salic, cannot fall into the hands of a woman. This is excellent, for by falling into the feminine line it can come into the power of a foreigner, a pernicious and dangerous thing, since a ruler from a foreign nation is of a different rearing and condition, of different customs, different language, and a different way of life from the men of the lands he comes to rule. He ordinarily, therefore, wishes to advance those of his nation, to grant them the most important authority in the handling of affairs, and to prefer them to honors and profits. Moreover, he always has more love for and faith in them and so conforms more to their customs and ways than to the customs of the land to which he has newly come, whence there always follows envy and dissension between the natives and the foreigners and indignation against the princes, as has often been seen by experience, and is seen all the time. When the succession goes from male to male, the heir is always certain and is of the same blood as those who formerly ruled, so the subjects have the very same love and reverence for him as for his predecessors. Even though he be related only distantly and the dead king have daughters, yet without deviation or scruple the people turn to him as soon as the other has ceased to be, and there is no disturbance or difficulty. So it went at the death of King Charles VIII and of King Louis XII recently deceased. Although in former times there were great quarrels and differences on such occasions, which brought great wars, persecutions, and desolations to the realm, nevertheless, these differences were not the reason for the troubles but the pretext, although well known to be frivolous and ill founded. In the end matters must have been redressed and so established that there can never again be dissensions and difficulties on this score. [In order to demonstrate what I said about the perfection of the monarchy of France I have included in this account] the state of France as it is now, joining the old laws, customs, and observances with the new and more recent.

From Claude de Seyssel, *The Monarchy of France* (1515).

French soil, and by the early fifteenth century English conquests in north-central France extended from Normandy to the borders of the Holy Roman Empire. Two of the largest French cities, Paris and Bordeaux, were in English hands.

Nor was England the only threat to the security of the French monarchy. On France's eastern border, in a long arching semicircle, were the estates of the dukes of Burgundy. The dukes of Burgundy and the kings of France shared a common ancestry—both were of the House of Valois. Still, the sons of brothers in one generation were only cousins in the next, and the two branches of the family grew apart. The original Burgundian inheritance was in the southeast, centered at Dijon. A good marriage and good fortune brought to the first duke the rich northern province of Flanders. For the next hundred years, the aim of the dukes of Burgundy was to unite their divided estates. While England and France were locked in deadly embrace, Burgundy systematically grew. It absorbed territory from both the Holy Roman Empire and France. To little pieces gained through marriages were added little pieces taken through force. As the second half of the fifteenth century began, the court of the duke of Burgundy was the glittering jewel of Europe, the heir of the Italian Renaissance. Wealthy and powerful, it stood poised to achieve what had once only been dreamed: the unification of the Burgundian lands. The conquest of Lorraine finally connected the ducal estates in one long, unbroken string.

But it was a string stretched taut. The power of Burgundy threatened its neighbors in all directions. Both France and the empire were too weak to resist its expansion, but the confederation of Swiss towns to the southwest of Burgundy was not. Fearing a Burgundian advance against them, a number of independent Swiss towns pooled their resources to raise a large army. In a series of stunning military victories, Swiss forces repelled the Burgundians from their lands and demolished their armies. Charles the Bold, the last Valois duke of Burgundy, fell at the Battle of Nancy in 1477. His estates were quickly dismembered. France recovered its ancestral territories, including Burgundy, and through no effort of its own was now secure on its eastern border.

The king most associated with the consolidation of France was Louis XI (1461–1483). He inherited an estate exhausted by warfare and civil strife. More by chance than by plan, he vastly extended the territories under the dominion of the French crown and, more importantly, subdued the nobility. Louis XI was as cunning as he was peculiar. In an age in which royalty was expressed through magnificence, Louis sported an old felt hat and a well-worn coat. His enemies constantly underestimated his abilities, which earned him the nickname "the Spider." But during the course of his reign, Louis XI gradually won back what he had been forced to give away. Years of fighting both the English and each other left the ranks of the French aris-

MAP DISCOVERY

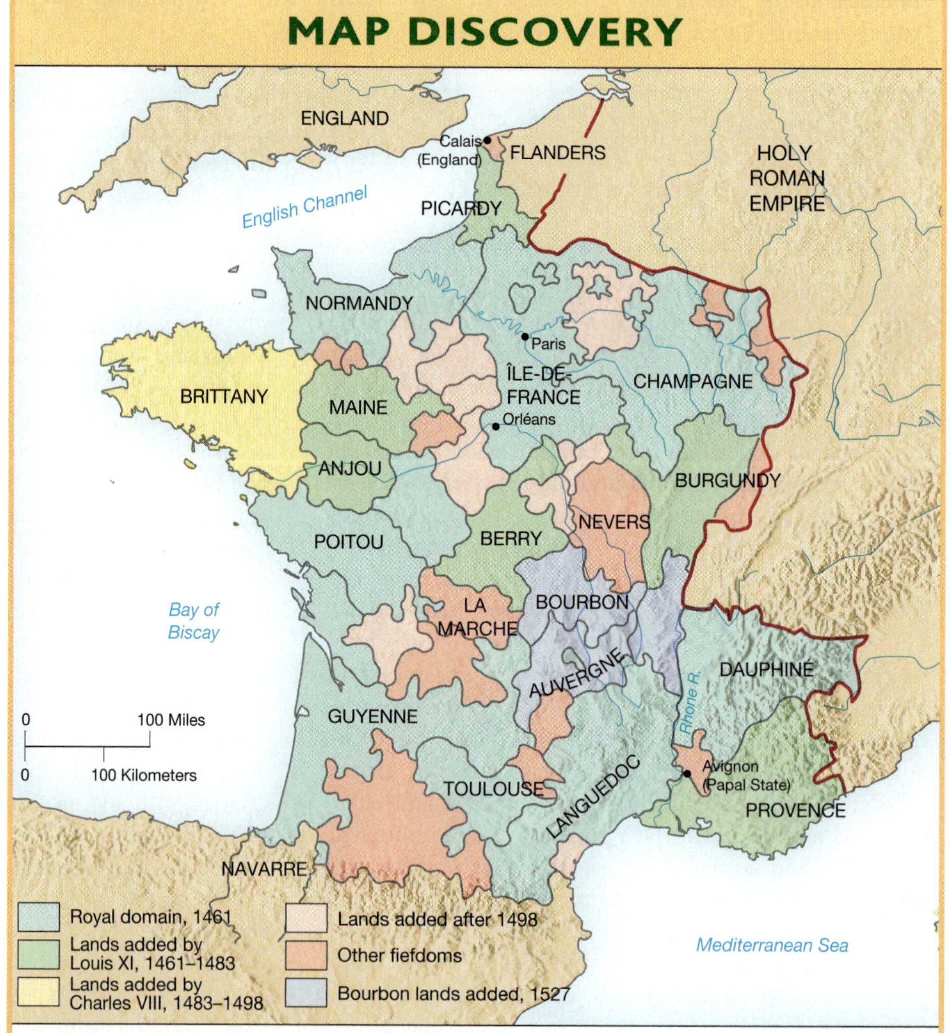

The Unification of France

Notice how France grew piecemeal rather than by acquiring large additions of adjacent estates. Which monarch added the most land to the state? Contrast the acquisitions made by Louis XI and those made by the Bourbons. Notice how France was not a unified geographical unit even after its so-called unification.

tocracy depleted. As blood spilled on the battlefields, the stocks of fathers and sons ran low. Estates, to which no male heirs existed, fell forfeit to the king. In that manner, the crown absorbed Anjou and Maine in the northwest and Provence in the south. More importantly, Louis XI ultimately obtained control of the two greatest independent fiefs, Brittany and Orléans. He managed the feat by arranging the marriage of his son Charles to the heiress of Brittany and of his daughter Jeanne to the heir of Orléans. When in 1527 the lands of the duke of Bourbon fell to the crown, the French monarch ruled a unified state.

The consolidation of France was not simply the result of the incorporation of diverse pieces of territory into the domain of the king. More than in any other state, the experience in France demonstrated how a state could be formed without the designs of a great leader. Neither Louis XI nor his son Charles VIII (1483–1498) was a nation builder. Louis's main objective was always to preserve his estate. His good fortune saved him from the consequences of many ill-conceived policies. But no amount of luck could make up for Louis's failure to obtain the Burgundian Low Countries for France after the death of Charles the Bold in 1477. The marriage of Mary of Burgundy to Maximilian of Habsburg was one of the great turning points in European history. It initiated the struggle for control of the Low Countries that endured for more than two centuries.

The long years of war established the principle of royal taxation that was so essential to the process of state building in France. It enabled the monarchy to raise money for defense and for consolidation. Because of the strength of the nobles, most taxation fell only on the commoners, the so-called third estate. The *taille* was a direct tax on property from which the nobility and clergy were exempt. The *gabelle* was a consumption tax on the purchase of salt in most parts of the kingdom, and the *aide* was a tax on a variety of commodities, including meat and wine. The consumption taxes were paid by all members of the third estate no matter how poor they might be. Although there was much complaint about taxes, the French monarchy established a broad base for taxation and a high degree of compliance long before any other European nation.

Along with money went soldiers, fighting men necessary to repel the English and to defend the crown against rebels and traitors. Again the French monarchy was the first to establish the principle of a national army, raised and directed from the center but quartered and equipped regionally. From the nobility were recruited the cavalry, from the towns and countryside the massive infantry. Fortified towns received privileges in return for military service to the king. Originally, towns were required to provide artillery, but constant troubles with the nobility had led the kings of France to establish their own store of heavy guns. The towns supplied small arms, pikes, and swords, and later pistols and muskets. By the beginning of the sixteenth century, the French monarch could raise and equip an army of his own.

The Marriages of Spain. Before the sixteenth century there was little prospect of a single nation emerging on the Iberian Peninsula. North African Muslims, called Moors, occupied the province of Granada in the south, while the stable kingdom of Portugal dominated the western coast. The Spanish peoples were divided among a number of separate states. The two most important were Castile, the largest and wealthiest kingdom, and Aragon, which was composed of a number of quasi-independent regions, each of which maintained its own laws and institutions. Three religions and four languages (not including dialects) widened the political divisions. Furthermore, the different states had different outlooks. Castile was, above all, determined to subjugate the last of Islamic Spain and to convert its large Jewish population to Christianity. Aragon played in the high-stakes game for power in the Mediterranean, claiming sovereignty over Sicily and Naples and exercising that sovereignty whenever it could.

A happy teenage marriage brought together the unhappy kingdoms of Castile and Aragon. When Ferdinand of Aragon and Isabella of Castile secretly exchanged wedding vows in 1469, both their homelands were rent by civil war. In Castile, Isabella's brother, Henry IV (1454–1474), struggled unsuccessfully against the powerful Castilian nobility. In Aragon, Ferdinand's father, John II (1458–1479), faced a revolt by the rich province of Catalonia on one side and the territorial ambitions of Louis XI of France on the other. Joining the heirs increased the resources of both kingdoms. Ferdinand took an active role in the pacification of Castile, while Castilian riches allowed him to defend Aragon from invasion. In 1479, the two crowns were united and the Catholic monarchs, as they were called, ruled the two kingdoms jointly. But the unification of the crowns of Castile and Aragon was not the same as the formation of a single state between them. Local privileges were zealously guarded, especially in Aragon, where the representative institutions of the towns—the Cortes—were aggressively independent. Their attitude is best expressed in the oath of the townspeople of Saragossa: "We accept you as our king provided you observe all our liberties and laws; and if not, not." The powerful Castilian nobility never accepted Ferdinand as their king and refused him the crown after Isabella's death.

But Ferdinand and Isabella (1479–1516) took the first steps toward forging a Spanish state. Their most notable achievement was the final recovery of the lands that had been conquered by the Moors. For centuries, the Spanish kingdoms had fought against the North African Muslims, who had conquered large areas of the southern peninsula. The reconquista was characterized by short bursts of warfare followed by long periods of wary coexistence. By the middle of the fifteenth century, the Moorish territory had been reduced to the province of Granada, but civil strife in Castile heightened the possibility of a new Moorish offensive. "We no longer mint gold, only steel," was how a Moorish ruler replied to Isabella's demand for the traditional payment of tribute money. The final stages of the reconquista began in 1482 and lasted for a decade. The struggle was waged as a holy war and was financed in part by grants from the pope and the Christian princes of Europe. It was a bloody undertaking. The Moorish population of nearly 500,000 was reduced to 100,000 before the town of Granada finally fell and the province was absorbed into Castile.

The reconquista played an important part in creating a national identity for the Christian peoples of Spain. In order to raise men and money for the war effort, Ferdinand and Isabella mobilized their nobility and town governments and created a central organization to oversee the invasion. Ferdinand was actively involved in the warfare, gaining the respect of the hostile Castilian nobles in the process. The conquered territories were used to reward those who had aided the effort, though the crown maintained control and jurisdiction over most of the province. But the idea of the holy war also had a darker side and an unanticipated consequence. The Jewish population that had lived peacefully in both Castile and Aragon became another object of hostility. Many Jews had risen to prominence in government and in skilled professions. Others, who had accepted conversion to Christianity and were known as *conversos*, had become among the most powerful figures in Church and state.

Both groups were now attacked. The conversos fell prey to a special Church tribunal created to examine their sincere devotion to Catholicism. This was the **Spanish Inquisition**, which, though it used traditional judicial practices—torture to gain confessions, public humiliation to show contrition, and burnings at the stake to maintain purity—used them on a scale never before seen. Thousands of conversos were killed, and many more families had their wealth confiscated to be used for the reconquista. In 1492, the Jews themselves were expelled from Spain. Although the reconquista and the expulsion of the Jews and the Moors inflicted great suffering upon victims and incalculable loss to the Castilian economy, both events enhanced the prestige of the Catholic monarchs.

In many ways, Ferdinand and Isabella had trodden the paths of the medieval monarchy. They relied upon personal contact with their people more than upon the use of a centralized administration. They frequently dispensed justice personally, sitting in court and accepting petitions from their subjects. Quite remarkably, they had no permanent residence and traveled the length and breadth of their kingdoms. Isabella is said to have visited every town in Castile, and it is entirely possible that a majority of the population of both kingdoms actually saw their monarchs at one time or another. Queen Isabella was venerated in Castile, where women's right to inheritance remained strong. Ferdinand's absences from Aragon were always a source of contention between him and the Cortes of the towns, yet he was careful to provide regents to preside in his absence and regularly returned to visit his native kingdom. He was not an absentee monarch.

The joint presence of Ferdinand and Isabella in the provinces of Spain was symbolic of the unity that they wanted to achieve. Despite the great obstacles, they were intent on bringing about a more permanent blending. Ferdinand made Castilian the official language of government in Aragon and even appointed Castilians to Aragonese posts. He and Isabella actively encouraged the intermarriage of the two aristocracies and the expansion of the number of wealthy nobles who held land in both kingdoms. A single coinage, stamped with the heads of both monarchs, was established for both kingdoms. Nevertheless, the measures did not unify Spain or erase the centuries' long tradition of hostility among the diverse Iberian peoples.

It was left to the heirs of Ferdinand and Isabella to forge together the Spanish kingdoms, and the process was a painful one. The hostility to a foreign monarch that both the Castilian nobility and the Aragonese towns had shown to Ferdinand and

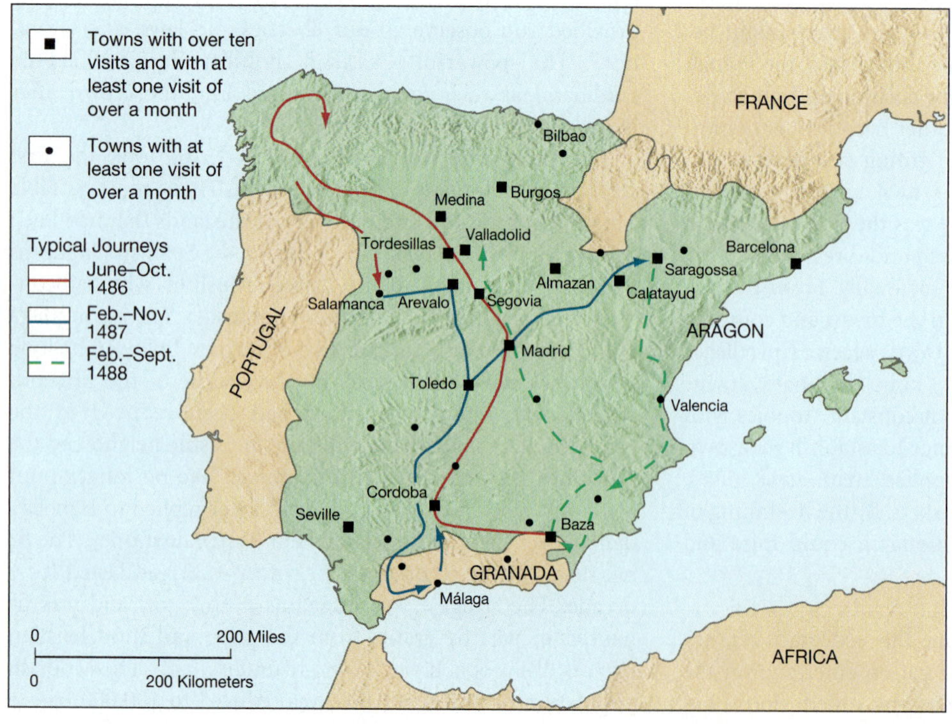

The Travels of Ferdinand and Isabella. Early modern monarchs did not reside solely in a capital city but moved around their territories to consolidate their power and ensure the loyalty of their subjects.

Isabella increased dramatically at the accession of their grandson, who became the Emperor Charles V (1516–1556). Charles had been born and raised in the Low Countries, where he ruled over Burgundy and the Netherlands. Through a series of dynastic accidents, he became heir to the Spanish crown with its possessions in the New World and to the vast Habsburg estates that included Austria. Charles established his rule in Spain gradually. For a time he was forced to share power in Castile and to suppress a disorganized aristocratic rebellion.

Because of his foreign obligations, Charles was frequently absent from Spain. During those periods he governed through regents and royal councils that did much to centralize administration. Although Castile and Aragon had separate councils, they were organized similarly and had greater contact than before. Charles V realized the importance of Spain, especially of Castile, in his empire. He learned Castilian and spent more time there than in any other part of his empire, calling it "the head of all the rest." Like Ferdinand and Isabella, he traveled throughout Castile and Aragon; unlike them, he established a more permanent bureaucratic court, modeled on that of Burgundy, and placed able Spaniards at the head of its departments. That smoothed over the long periods when Charles was abroad, especially the thirteen years between 1543 and 1556.

Yet neither his personal efforts to rule as a Spanish monarch nor those of his able administrators were the most important factor in uniting the Spanish kingdoms of Iberia. Rather it was the fact that Charles V brought Spain to the forefront of European affairs in the sixteenth century. Spanish prowess, whether in arms or in culture, became a source of national pride that helped erode regional identity. Gold and silver from the New World helped finance Charles's great empire. Whether or not he dreamed of uniting all of Europe under his rule, Charles V fulfilled nearly all of the ancient territorial ambitions of the Spanish kingdoms. In Italy, he prosecuted Aragonese claims to Sicily and Naples; in the north he held on firmly to the kingdom of Navarre, which had been annexed by Ferdinand and which secured Spain's border with France. In the south, he blocked off Ottoman and Muslim expansion. The reign of Charles V ushered in the dawn of Spain's golden age.

THE DYNASTIC STRUGGLES

The formation of large states throughout Europe led inevitably to conflicts among them. Long chains of marriages among the families of the European princes meant that sooner or later the larger powers would lay claim to the same inheritances and test the matter by force. Thus the sixteenth century was a period of almost unrelieved general warfare that took the whole of the Continent as its theater. Advances in technology made war more efficient and more expensive. They also made it more horrible. The use of artillery against infantry increased the number of deaths and maiming injuries, as did the replacement of the arrow with the bullet. As the size of armies increased, so did casualties. Nearly 60,000 men met at Marignano in 1515, where it took 30 French cavalry charges and 28 consecutive hours of battle before the Swiss infantry was driven from the field. The slaughter of French nobility at Pavia in 1525 was the largest in a century, while the Turkish sultan Suleiman the Magnificent recorded the burial of 24,000 Hungarian soldiers after the battle of Mohacs in 1526.

Power and Glory

The frequency with which offensive war was waged in the sixteenth century raises a number of questions about the militaristic values of the age. Valor remained greatly prized—a Renaissance virtue inherited from the crusading zeal and chivalric ideals of the Middle Ages. Princes saw valor as a personal attribute and sought to do great deeds. Ferdinand of Aragon and Francis I of France (1515–1547) won fame for their exploits in war. Charles the Bold and Louis II of Hungary were less fortunate: their battlefield deaths led to the breakup of their states. Wars were fought to further the interests of princes rather than the interests of national sovereignty or international

■ Titian, *Charles V on Horseback* (1548). The portrait commemorates the Emperor's victory in the Battle of Mülberg in 1547. The portrait is less that of a victorious hero, but rather that of a forceful individual girded to contend against his enemies.

Christianity. Wars certainly were not fought in the interests of their subjects. States were an extension of a prince's heritage: what rulers sought in battle was a part of the historical and familial rights that defined themselves and their subjects. The wars of the sixteenth century were dynastic wars.

The New Monarchs waged war and defended their territories in new ways. Internal security depended on locally raised forces or hired mercenaries. Both required money, which was becoming available in unprecedented quantities as a result of the increasing prosperity of the early sixteenth century and the windfall of gold and silver from the New World. Professional soldiers, of whom the Swiss and Germans were the most noteworthy, sold their services to the highest bidders. Developments in transport and supply enabled campaigns to take place far from the center of a state. Finally, communications were improving. The need for knowledge about potential rivals or allies had the effect of expanding the European system of diplomacy. Resident agents were established in all the European capitals, and they had a decisive impact upon war and peace. Their dispatches formed the most reliable source of information about the strengths of armies or the weaknesses of governments, about the birth of heirs or the death of princes.

Personality also played a part in the international warfare of the early sixteenth century. The three most consistent protagonists—Charles V, Francis I, and Henry VIII—were of similar age and outlook. Each came unexpectedly to his throne in the full flush of youth, eager for combat and glory. The three were self-consciously rivals, each jealous of the other's successes, each triumphant in the other's failures. Henry VIII and Francis I held wrestling bouts when they met in 1520. Francis I challenged Charles V to single combat after the French king's humiliating imprisonment in Madrid in 1526. As the three monarchs aged together, their youthful wars of conquest matured into strategic warfare designed to maintain a continental balance of power.

The Italian Wars

The struggle for supremacy in Europe in the sixteenth century pitted the French House of Valois against the far-flung estates of the Habsburg Empire. Yet the wars took place in Italy. The

Jean Clouet, *Francis I on Horseback* (sixteenth century). Rivalry between Francis and Charles V plunged Europe into decades of war.

rivalries among the larger Italian city-states proved fertile ground for the newly consolidated European monarchies. Both French and Spanish monarchs had remote but legitimate claims to the kingdom of Naples in southern Italy. In 1494, the French king, Charles VIII, took up an invitation from the ruler of Milan to intervene in Italian affairs. His campaign was an unqualified, if fleeting, success. He marched the length of the Italian peninsula, overthrew the Medici in Florence, forced the pope to open the gates of Rome, and finally seized the crown of Naples. The occupation was accomplished without a single great battle and lasted until the warring Italian city-states realized that they had more to fear from the French than from one another. Once that happened, Charles VIII beat a hasty retreat. But the French appetite for Italian territory was not sated. Soon a deal was struck with Ferdinand of Aragon to divide the kingdom of Naples in two. In the end, Spain wound up with all of Naples and France was left with nothing but debts and grievances.

Thus, when Francis I came to the French throne and Charles V to the Spanish, Naples was just one of several potential sources of friction. Not only had Ferdinand betrayed the French in Naples, he had also broken a long-standing peace on the Franco-Spanish border by conquering the independent but French-speaking kingdom of Navarre. Francis could be expected to avenge both slights. Charles, on the other hand, was the direct heir of the dukes of Burgundy. From his childhood he had longed for the restoration of his ancestral lands, including Burgundy itself, which had been gobbled up by Louis XI after the death of Charles the Bold. Competition between Francis and Charles became all the more ferocious when Charles's grandfather, the Holy Roman Emperor Maximilian I (1486–1519), died in 1519. Both monarchs launched a vigorous campaign for the honor of succeeding him.

For nearly a century the Holy Roman Emperor had come from the Austrian ruling family, and there was little reason to believe that Charles V, who now inherited the Habsburg lands in Austria and Germany, would not also succeed to the eminent but empty dignity. Almost as soon as he took up the imperial mantle, Charles V was determined to challenge Francis I in Italy.

The key to such a challenge was the construction of alliances among the various Italian city-states and most especially with England, whose aid both Charles and Francis sought to enlist in the early 1520s. Henry VII had found foreign alliances a ready source of cash, and he was always eager to enter into them so long as they did not involve raising armies and fighting wars. Henry VIII was made of sterner stuff. He longed to reconquer France and to cut a figure on the European scene. Despite the fact that his initial Continental adventures had emptied his treasury without fulfilling his dreams, Henry remained eager for war. He was also flattered to find himself the object of attention by both Valois and Habsburg emissaries. Charles V made two separate trips to London, while Henry crossed the Channel in 1520 to meet Francis I in one of the gaudiest displays of conspicuous consumption that the century would witness, appropriately known as the Field of the Cloth of Gold.

■ The Italian Wars with Key Battle Sites. Italy was overrun in the sixteenth century and became a battleground for the dynastic struggles of the French, the Spanish, and the Imperial forces.

The result of the diplomatic intrigues was an alliance between England and the Holy Roman Empire. English and Burgundian forces would stage an invasion of northern France while Spanish and German troops would again attempt to dislodge the French forces from Italy. The strategy worked better than anyone could have imagined. In 1523, Charles's forces gained a foothold in Milan by taking the heavily fortified town of Pavia. Two years later Francis was ready to strike back. At the head of his own royal guards, he massed Swiss mercenaries and French infantry outside Pavia and made ready for a swift assault. Instead, a large imperial army arrived to relieve the town, and in the subsequent battle the French suffered a shattering defeat. Francis I was captured.

The victory at Pavia, which occurred on Charles V's twenty-fifth birthday, seemingly made him master of all of Europe. His ally Henry VIII urged an immediate invasion and dismemberment of France and began raising an army to spearhead the attack. But Charles's position was much less secure than it appeared. The Ottomans threatened his Hungarian territories, and the Protestants threatened his German lands. He could not afford a war of conquest in France. His hope now was to reach an agreement with Francis I for a lasting European peace, and for that purpose the French king was brought in captivity to Madrid.

It is doubtful that there was ever any real chance for peace between Habsburg and Valois after the battle of Pavia.

■ The Battle of Pavia in 1525, shown in this tapestry, gave Spain a decisive victory over its French rivals. Francis I was captured and imprisoned in Madrid where he was forced to accept a humiliating peace treaty.

Francis's personal humiliation and Charles's military position were both too strong to allow for a permanent settlement in which Habsburgs ruled in Milan and Naples. But it was neither political nor personal considerations that were the source of another 30 years of continuous European warfare. Rather it was Charles's demand that Burgundy be returned to him. Although Francis was hardly in a position to bargain, he held out on this issue for as long as possible and secretly prepared a disavowal of the final agreement before it was made. By the Treaty of Madrid in 1526, Francis I yielded Burgundy and recognized the Spanish conquest of Navarre and Spanish rule in Naples. The agreement was sealed by the marriage of Francis to Charles's sister, Eleanor of Portugal. But marriage was not sufficient security for such a complete capitulation. To secure his release from Spain, Francis was required to leave behind as hostages his seven- and eight-year-old sons until the treaty was fulfilled. For three years, the children languished in Spanish captivity.

No sooner had he set foot upon French soil than Francis I renounced the Treaty of Madrid. Despite the threat that it posed to his children, Francis argued that the terms had been extracted against his will, and he even gained the approval of the pope for violating his oath. Setting France on a war footing, he began seeking new allies. Henry VIII, disappointed with the meager spoils of his last venture, switched sides. So too did a number of Italian city-states, including Rome. Most importantly, Francis I entered into an alliance with the Ottoman sultan, Suleiman the Magnificent (1520–1566), whose armies were pressing against the southeastern borders of the Holy Roman Empire. In the year following Pavia, the Ottomans secured an equally decisive triumph at Mohacs, captured Budapest, and threatened Vienna, the eastern capital of the Habsburg lands. Almost overnight Charles V had been turned from hunter into hunted. The Ottoman threat demanded immediate attention in Germany, the French and English were preparing to strike in the Low Countries, and the Italian wars continued. In 1527, Charles's unpaid German mercenaries stormed through Rome, sacked the papal capital, and captured the pope. Christian Europe was mortified.

The struggle for European mastery ground on for decades. The Treaty of Cateau-Cambrésis in 1559 brought to a close 60 years of conflict. In the end the French were no more capable of dislodging the Habsburgs from Italy than were the Habsburgs of forcing the Ottomans out of Hungary. The great stores of silver that poured into Castile from the New World were consumed in the fires of Continental warfare. In 1557, both France and Spain declared bankruptcy to avoid foreclosures by their creditors. For the French, the Italian wars were disastrous. They seriously undermined the state's financial base, eroded confidence in the monarchy, and thinned the ranks of the ruling nobility. The adventure begun by Charles VIII in search of glory brought France nearly to ruin. It ended with fitting irony. After the death of Francis I, his son Henry II (1547–1559) continued the struggle. Henry never forgave his

■ This Ottoman painting depicts the defeat of the Hungarians at the hands of the sultan's army at Mohacs in 1526. The prominence of artillery and muskets in the painting reflects the impact of technological advances on warfare.

father for abandoning him in Spain, and he sought revenge on Charles V, who had been his jailer. He regarded the Treaty of Cateau-Cambrésis as a victory and celebrated it with great pomp and pageantry. Among the feasts and festivities were athletic competitions for the king's courtiers and attendants. Henry II entered the jousting tournament and was killed there.

CONCLUSION

Charles V died in his bed. The long years of war made clear that the dream to dominate Europe could only be a dream. He split apart his empire and granted to his brother, Ferdinand I (1558–1564), the Austrian and German lands and the mantle of the Holy Roman Emperor. To his son Philip II (1556–1598) he ceded the Low Countries, Spain and the New World, Naples, and his Italian conquests. In 1555, Charles abdicated all of his titles and retired to a monastery to live out his final days. The cares of an empire that once stretched from Peru to Vienna were lifted from his shoulders. Beginning with his voyage to Castile in 1517, he had made ten trips to the Netherlands, nine to Germany, seven to Italy, six to Spain, four to France, two to England, and two to Africa. "My life has been one long journey," he told those who witnessed him relinquish his crowns. On 21 September 1558, he finally rested forever.

QUESTIONS FOR REVIEW

1. What impulses in European society were revealed by the global exploration and conquests of the Portuguese and the Spanish?
2. What qualities characterized the "New Monarchies" and what are some of the best examples of such princely states?
3. How and why did the experience of political and territorial unification differ in England, France, and Spain?
4. How did war between the great European monarchies contribute to unity within each?

KEY TERMS

caravels, *p. 348*
Columbian Exchange, *p. 352*
conquistadores, *p. 355*
Lusiads, *p. 357*
New Monarchies, *p. 359*
provincialism, *p. 367*
reconquista, *p. 362*
Spanish Inquisition, *p. 371*
Treaty of Tordesillas, *p. 350*

DISCOVERING WESTERN CIVILIZATION ONLINE

You can obtain more information about the European empires at the Websites listed below. See also the Companion Website that accompanies this text, www.ablongman.com/kishlansky, which contains an online study guide and additional resources.

European Encounters

Discoverers Web
www.win.tue.nl/cs/fm/engels/discovery/
A site devoted to all ages of discovery with maps, short biographies, and time lines. There are links to the writings of Columbus, Cortés, and other early voyagers.

The Columbus Navigation Homepage
www1.minn.net/~keithp/
Everything you ever wanted to know about Christopher Columbus.

1492: An Ongoing Voyage
www.loc.gov/exhibits/1492
A Library of Congress online exhibit on the causes and consequences of European exploration and expansion.

Christopher Columbus—A Culinary History
www.castellobanfi.com/features/story_3.html
A site devoted to the food and drink associated with a long ocean voyage in the fifteenth century.

Medieval Sourcebook: Exploration and Expansion
www.fordham.edu/halsall/sbook1z.html
Dozens of primary sources relating to the voyages of discovery.

The Formation of States

Henry VIII: Intrigue in the Tudor Court
www.archsoc.com/games/Henry.html
A board game that teaches both history and strategy.

SUGGESTIONS FOR FURTHER READING

General Reading

David Nicholas, *The Transformation of Europe 1300–1600* (New York: Oxford University Press, 1999). A comprehensive survey that emphasizes continuities between the sixteenth century and the preceding period.

Eugene Rice, *The Foundations of Early Modern Europe, 1460–1559*, 2nd ed. (New York: Norton, 1994). An outstanding synthesis.

European Encounters

C. R. Boxer, *The Portuguese Seaborne Empire, 1415–1825* (London: Hutchinson, 1968). The best history of the first of the explorer nations.

Natalie Zemon Davis. *Trickster Travels: A Sixteenth-Century Muslim Between Worlds* (New York: Hill and Wang, 2006). A gripping life of the travel writer and biographer known as Leo Africanus.

J. H. Elliott. *Empires of the Atlantic World: Britain and Spain in America 1492–1830* (New Haven: Yale, 2006). A comparative account of Spanish and British imperialism and colonization in the New World.

J. H. Elliott, *The Old World and the New, 1492–1650* (Cambridge: Cambridge University Press, 1970). A brilliant look at the reception of knowledge about the New World by Europeans.

Felipe Fernandez-Armesto, *Columbus* (Oxford: Oxford University Press, 1991). The best of the recent studies. Reliable, stimulating, and up-to-date.

Anthony Pagden, *Lords of All the World: Ideologies of Empire in Spain, Britain and France, c. 1500–c. 1800* (New Haven, CT: Yale University Press, 1995). A fresh look at the ideas behind the European encounter with the New World.

Hugh Thomas, *Rivers of Gold: The Rise of the Spanish Empire* (London: Widenfeld & Nicholson, 2004). A breathtaking retelling of Spain's New World Empire.

Geographical Tour—Europe in 1500: The Age of the New Monarchies

N. J. G. Pounds, *An Historical Geography of Europe, 1500–1800* (Cambridge: Cambridge University Press, 1990). A remarkable survey of the relationship between geography and history.

Daniel Waley, *Later Medieval Europe* (London: Longman, 1985). A good brief account.

The Formation of States

Robert Bucholz and Newton Key. *Early Modern England 1485–1714: A Narrative History* (Blackwell Publishers, 2003). The latest survey of the reigns of the Tudors and Stuarts in England.

S. B. Chrimes, *Henry VII* (Berkeley: University of California Press, 1972). A traditional biography of the first Tudor.

Robert O. Crummey, *The Formation of Muscovy, 1304–1613* (London: Longman, 1987). The best one-volume history.

Norman Davies, *God's Playground: A History of Poland, Vol. 1, The Origins to 1795* (New York: Columbia University Press, 1982). The best treatment in English of a complex history.

Bernard Guenée, *States and Rulers in Later Medieval Europe* (London: Basil Blackwell, 1985). An engaging argument about the forces that helped shape the state system in Europe.

Henry Kamen, *The Spanish Inquisition: A Historical Revision* (New Haven, CT: Yale University Press, 1998). The most recent assessment of the power and activities of the Inquisition.

Paul M. Kendall, *Louis XI: The Universal Spider* (New York: Norton, 1971). A highly entertaining account of an unusual monarch.

John Lynch, *Spain, 1516–1598: From Nation State to World Empire* (Cambridge, MA: Blackwell Publishers, 1994). The best survey.

J. H. Shennan, *The Origins of the Modern European State, 1450–1725* (London: Hutchinson, 1974). An analytic account of the rise of the state.

The Dynastic Struggles

J. R. Hale, *War and Society in Renaissance Europe* (Stroud, England: Sutton, 1998). Assesses the impact of war on the political and social history of early modern Europe.

Robert Knecht. *The Valois: Kings of France 1328–1589* (Hambledon and London, 2005). A history of the dynasty under which France was established as a major European power.

William Maltby, *The Reign of Charles V* (New York: Palgrave, 2002). The most recent study of one of Europe's great emperors.

David Potter, *A History of France, 1460–1560* (London: Macmillan, 1995). A reliable survey that connects medieval and early modern developments.

J. J. Scarisbrick, *Henry VIII* (New Haven: Yale University Press, 1997). The definitive biography.

For a list of additional titles related to this chapter's topics, please see http://www.ablongman.com/kishlansky.

CHAPTER 13

THE REFORM OF RELIGION

SOLA SCRIPTURA

THE BIBLE AND THE REFORMATION

THE VISUAL RECORD

"In the beginning was the word, and the word was with God, and the word was God." In no other period of European history was this text of the apostle John so appropriate. Men and women shared a consuming desire to hear and to read the Word of God as set down in the Bible. In the early sixteenth century, Europeans developed an insatiable appetite for the Bible. Scriptures rolled off printing presses in every shape and form, from the great vellum tomes of Gutenberg pictured here to pocket Bibles that soldiers carried into battle. They came in every imaginable language. Before 1500 there were 14 complete Bibles printed in German, 4 each in Italian, French, and Spanish, 1 in Czech, and even 1 in Flemish. There were hundreds more editions in Latin, the official Vulgate Bible first translated by Saint Jerome in the fourth century. Whole translations and editions of the Bible were only part of the story. Separate sections, especially the Psalms and the first books of the Old Testament, were printed by the thousands. There were 24 French editions of the Old Testament before an entirely new translation appeared in 1530. When Martin Luther began his own German translation of the Bible in 1522, it immediately became an international best seller. In 25 years it went into 430 editions. It is estimated that 1 million German Bibles were printed in the first half of the sixteenth century—a time when Europe had a German-speaking population of about 15 million people, 90 percent of whom were illiterate.

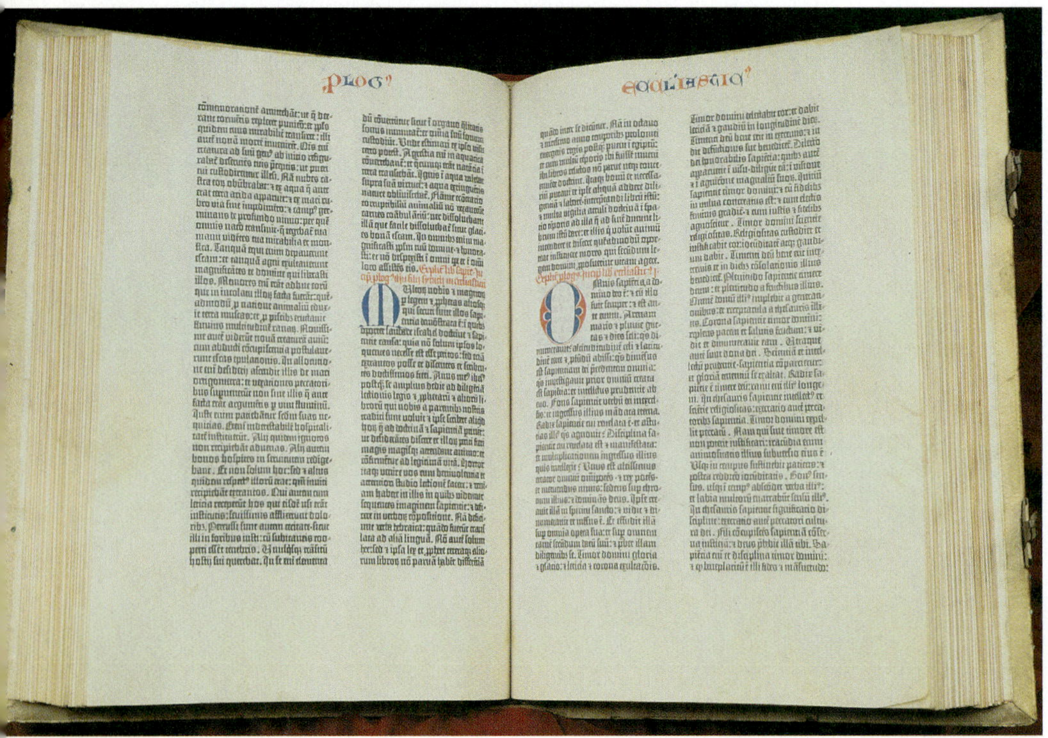

Pages from a Gutenberg Bible printed in the 1450s.

Bible owning was no fad. It was but one element in a new devotional outlook that was sweeping the Continent and that would have far-reaching consequences for European society during the next 150 years. A renewed spirituality was everywhere to be seen. It was expressed in a desire to change the traditional practices and structures of the Roman Church. It was expressed in a desire to have learned and responsible ministers to tend to the needs of their parishioners. It was expressed in a desire to establish godly families, godly cities, and godly kingdoms. Sometimes it took the form of sarcasm and bitter denunciations; sometimes it took the form of quiet devotion and pious living. The need for reform was everywhere felt; the demand for reform was everywhere heard. It came from within the Roman Church as much as from without.

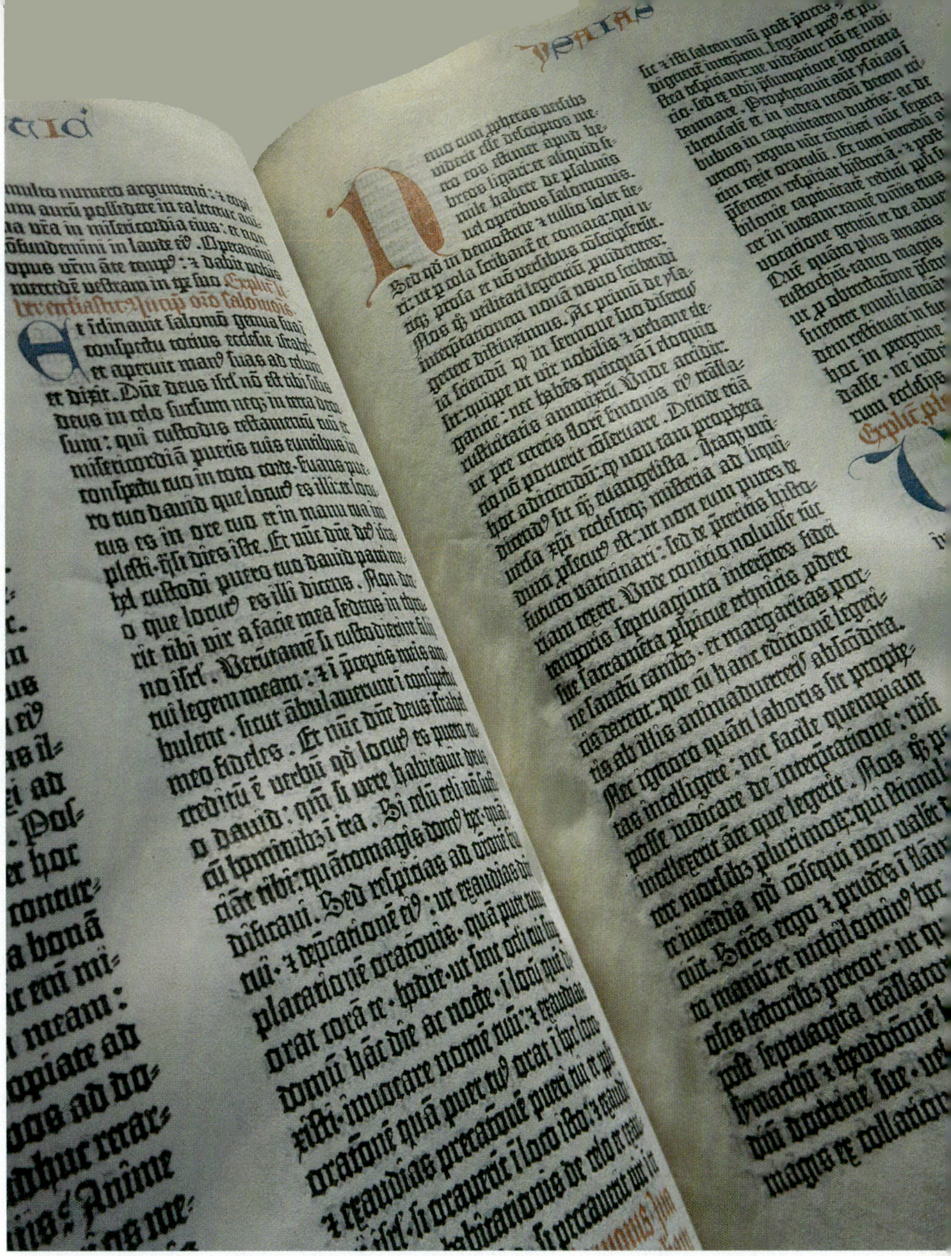

The inspiration for reform was based on the Word of God. Scholars, following humanist principles, worked on biblical translations in an attempt to bring a purer text to light. Biblical commentary dominated the writings of churchmen as never before. Woodcut pictures depicting scenes from the life of Jesus or from the Old Testament were printed in untold quantities for the edification of the unlettered. For the first time, common people could, in their own dwellings, contemplate representations of the lives of the saints. Many of the Bibles that were printed in vernacular—that is, in the languages spoken in the various European states rather than in Latin—were interleaved with illustrations of the central events of Christian history. Preachers spoke to newly aware audiences and relied on biblical texts to draw out their message. Study groups, especially in urban areas, proliferated so that the literate could read and learn together. Bible reading became a part of family life, one that mothers and fathers could share with their children and their servants.

■ Detail of pages from a Gutenberg Bible.

LOOKING AHEAD

__Sola scriptura__—by the word alone—became the battle cry of religious reform. As we will see in this chapter, in the early decades of the sixteenth century Europeans experienced one of the greatest of all religious rebirths: the Protestant Reformation. The **Reformation** *was a movement to purify the Catholic Church that resulted in the creation of new religious denominations in Europe collectively known as Protestants from their protest against Roman Catholic practices. But the Catholic Church experienced its own renewal as well. Figures such as Luther, Calvin, and Ignatius of Loyola were part of the most remarkable generation of religious leaders since the foundation of Christianity.*

CHAPTER OUTLINE

THE INTELLECTUAL REFORMATION

There is nothing as powerful as an idea whose time has come. But the coming of ideas has a history as complex as the ideas themselves. In the early sixteenth century, reformers throughout western Europe preached new ideas about religious doctrine and religious practice. At first the ideas took the form of a sustained critique of the Roman Catholic Church, but soon they developed a momentum of their own. Some reformers remained within traditional Catholicism; others moved outside and founded new Protestant churches. Whether Catholic or Protestant, wherever the movement for religious reform appeared it was fed by new ideas. But if new ideas were to supplant old ones, they had to be communicated—not only heard and repeated but accurately recorded and understood. That was made possible by the development of the technology of printing, which appeared in Germany in the late fifteenth century and rapidly spread across Europe in the succeeding decades. Yet printing was as much a result as it was a cause of the spread of ideas. The humanist call for a return to the study of the classics and for the creation of accurate texts, first heard in Italy, aroused scholars and leaders in all of the European states. Their appetite for manuscripts exhausted the abilities of the scribes and booksellers who reproduced texts. Printing responded to that demand.

The Print Revolution

The development of printing did not cause religious reform, but it is difficult to see how reform would have progressed in its absence. The campaign to change the doctrine and practice of Catholicism was waged through the press, with millions of flyers and pamphlets distributed across Europe to spread the new ideas. One-third of all books sold in Germany between 1518 and 1525 were written by Luther. But the ways in which printing came to be used by religious reformers could hardly have been foreseen by the artisans, bankers, and booksellers who together created one of the true technological revolutions in Western history.

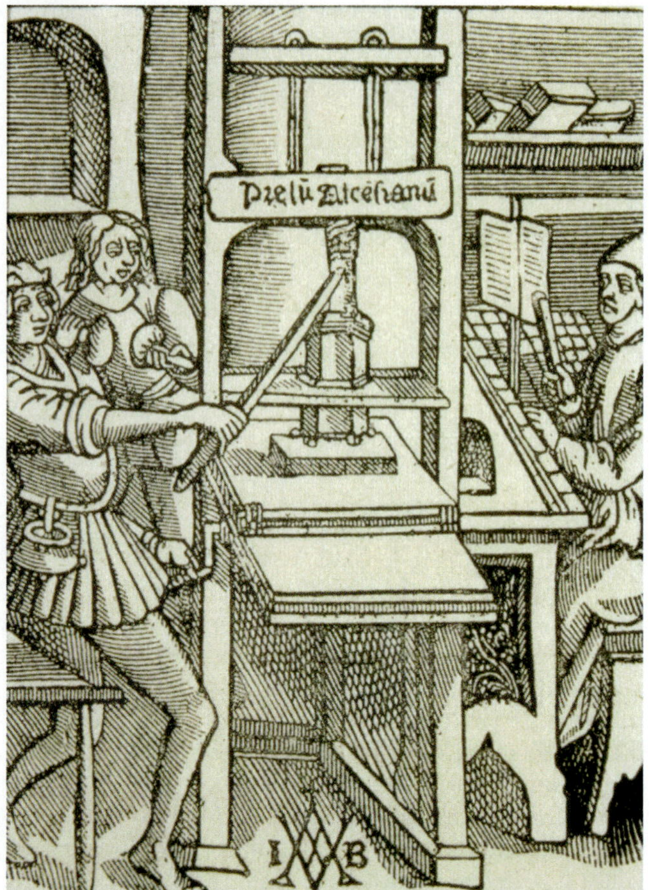

■ An early German print shop. The man at the left operates the screw press while an apprentice (right) stacks the printed sheets. The man in the back is setting type for the next impression.

Printing was not invented. It developed as a result of progress made in a number of allied industries, of which papermaking and goldsmithing were the most important. Scholars and university students needed copies of manuscripts. Their need led to the development of a trade in bookselling that flourished in almost every university town. The process of reproduction was slowed by difficulties in obtaining the sheepskins and calfskins on which the manuscripts were written. It took the skins of 300 sheep to produce a single Bible. In the early fifteenth century, copyists began to substitute paper made from linen rags for the expensive vellum skins. A number of German artisans experimented with using movable metal type to make exact reproductions of manuscripts on paper. Paper took a better impression and provided an absolutely smooth surface, which was essential for pressing the image. In the 1450s, in Mainz, Johannes Gutenberg (ca. 1400–1468) and his partners published their famous Bibles.

The association of early printing with goldsmithing resulted from the high level of technical skill that was necessary to create the hard metal stamps from which the softer metal type was produced. Printing was an expensive business. The investment in type and in paper was considerable. Only the press itself was cheap. Any corn or wine press could be used to bring the long flat sheets of paper down upon a wooden frame filled with ink-coated metal type. Booksellers initially put up the capital needed to cast the stamps, mold the type, and buy the paper. They bound the printed pages and found the markets to distribute them. At first sales were slow. Printed books were considered inferior to handwritten manuscripts. Nor at first were printed books less expensive. Bibles like those printed by Gutenberg were major investments, equivalent to purchasing a house today. Many printing shops quickly went bankrupt as they misjudged their markets and were unable to pay back their loans.

Still, once it was begun, printing spread like wildfire. By 1480, more than 110 towns had established presses, most in Italy and Germany. After that the pace quickened. By the beginning of the sixteenth century, Venice and Paris were the centers of the industry, with the Paris presses producing more than three hundred new titles annually. Most of the early printed works were either religious or classical. Bibles, church service books, and the commentaries of the Church fathers were most common. Cicero topped the list of classical authors.

What is most amazing about the printing revolution is how rapidly printing came to be a basic part of life. In the first

MAP DISCOVERY

The Spread of Printing

Examine the locations and dates of early printing. Where were the earliest printing presses concentrated? How did printing spread? Why do you think Rome had a press established before Florence?

40 years after the presses began, perhaps as many as 20 million books were produced and distributed. Printing changed the habits of teachers and students, and therefore the possibilities of education. It altered the methods by which the state conducted its business. It affected both legal training and legal proceedings. Compilations of laws could now be widely distributed and more uniformly enforced. Printing had a similar effect on the development of scientific study. The printing press popularized the discoveries of the New World and contributed to the reproduction of more accurate charts and maps, which in turn facilitated further discovery. Printing also helped standardize language—both Latin and vernacular—by frequent repetition of preferred usage and spelling. Perhaps most importantly, printing created an international intellectual community whose ideas could be dispersed the length and breadth of the Continent. The printing press enhanced the value of ideas and of thinking. Nothing could be more central to the reform of religion.

Christian Humanism

Many of the ideas that spread across Europe as the result of the printing revolution originated in Italian humanism (see Chapter 11). The revival of classical literature, with its concern for purity in language and eloquence in style, was one of the most admired achievements of the Renaissance. Students from all over Europe who descended upon Italian universities to study medicine and law came away with a strong dose of philology, rhetoric, moral philosophy, and the other liberal arts. Their heads were filled with the new learning. By the beginning of the sixteenth century, the force of humanism was felt strongly in northern and western Europe, where it was grafted on to the dominant strains of traditional theological teaching. The combination was a new and powerful intellectual movement known as **Christian humanism**.

Christian humanism was a program of reform rather than a philosophy. It aimed to make better Christians through better education. Humanists were especially interested in the education of women. "For what is more fruitful than the good education and order of women, the one half of all mankind," wrote Thomas More (1478–1535). Humanists helped found schools for girls and advocated that they be trained in the same subjects as boys. Thomas More raised his daughters to be among the educated elite of England, and they enjoyed international renown. The Spanish humanist Juan Luis Vives (1492–1540) wrote *The Instruction of a Christian Woman* (1523), a handbook for women of the elite orders commissioned by Catherine of Aragon. Renowned women scholars even held places at Italian universities. Humanist educational principles posed an implicit challenge to Roman Catholicism. Schools had once been the monopoly of the Church, which used them to train clergymen. The Church had founded them and kept them afloat in good times and in bad. Literacy itself had been preserved over the centuries so that the gospel could be propagated.

By the sixteenth century those purposes had been transformed. Schools now trained many who were not destined for careers in the Church, and literacy served the needs of the state, the aristocracy, and the merchant classes. More importantly, as the humanists perfected their techniques of scholarship, the Church continued to rely upon traditional methods of training and traditional texts. The dominant manner of teaching at the schools and universities was known as Scholasticism. Passages of biblical texts were studied through the commentaries of generations of Church fathers. Rote memorization of the opinions of others was more highly valued than critical thinking. Argument took place by formal disputation of questions on which the Church fathers disagreed. Disputed questions became more and more obscure. Even if Scholastics did not debate the question, "How many angels can dance on the head of a pin?" it seemed to many humanists that they might as well have. The Vulgate Bible was used throughout Western Christendom. It was now a thousand years old.

The Humanist Movement

Many humanist criticisms of Church teaching focused on its failure to inspire individuals to live a Christian life. Humanist writers were especially scathing about popular practices that bordered on superstition, such as pilgrimages to holy places or the worship of relics from the early history of the Church. Such beliefs became the butt of popular humor: "If the fragments [of the Lord's Cross] were joined together they would seem a full load for a freighter. And yet the Lord carried his whole cross." Christian humanists wanted to inspire Christians. As the great Dutch humanist Desiderius Erasmus observed, "To be learned is the lot of only a few; but no one is unable to be a Christian, no one is unable to be pious." The ironic strain in humanist writing is most closely associated with Erasmus, but it is also visible in the humanist social criticism of Sir Thomas More's *Utopia*. (See "A Closer Look: Utopia," pp. 384–385.)

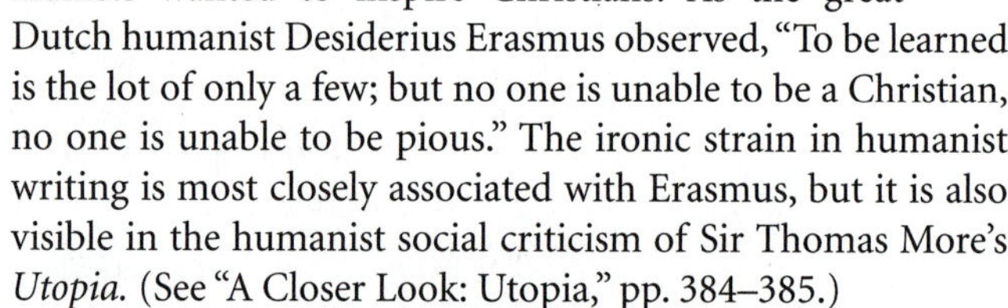

DOCUMENT

Sir Thomas More, *Utopia*

Christian humanism was an international movement. The humanists formed the elite of the intellectual world of the sixteenth century, and their services were sought by princes and peers as well as by the most distinguished universities. In fact, the New Monarchs supported the humanists and protected them from their critics. Marguerite of Navarre, sister of Francis I, was an accomplished writer who frequently interceded on behalf of the leading French humanists. Ferdinand of Aragon, Henry VIII, and the Holy Roman Emperors Maximilian I and Charles V all brought humanists to their courts and aided their projects. Maria of Hungary and Mary and Elizabeth Tudor were trained in humanist principles and participated in humanist literary achievements.

The centerpiece of humanist reforms was the translation of Christian texts. Armed with skills in Greek and Latin, informed by scholars of Hebrew and Aramaic, humanist writers prepared new editions of the books of the Bible and of the writings of the early Church fathers. Their favorite method was side-by-side translation. The Polyglot—literally "many languages"—Bible that was produced in 1522 at the University of Alcala took a team of scholars 15 years to complete. They gathered together copies of all known biblical manuscripts and rigorously compared their texts. They established the principle that inconsistencies among Latin manuscripts were to be resolved by reference to Greek texts, and difficulties in Greek texts by reference to Hebrew texts. The result was six elegantly printed volumes that allowed scholars to compare the texts. The Old Testament was printed in three parallel columns of Hebrew, Latin Vulgate, and Greek. The New Testament was printed in double columns, with the Greek text on one side and the Vulgate on the other. The Greek edition of the Bible and its establishment as a text superior to the Vulgate caused an immediate sensation throughout humanist and Church circles.

The Wit of Erasmus

Although the Polyglot Bible contained the first completed Greek edition of the New Testament, it was not the first published one. That distinction belongs to the man whose name is most closely associated with the idea of Christian humanism: Desiderius Erasmus of Rotterdam (ca. 1466–1536). Orphaned at an early age, Erasmus was educated by the Brothers of the Common Life, a lay brotherhood that specialized in schooling children and preparing them for a monastic life. Marked out early by his quick wit, pleasant though strong personality, and extraordinary intellectual gifts, Erasmus entered a monastery and was then allowed to travel to pursue his studies, first in France and then in England.

In England, Erasmus learned of new techniques for instructing children both in classical knowledge and in Christian morals, and he became particularly interested in the education of women. He dedicated a number of his later writings to women patrons who were accomplished humanist scholars. While in England, Erasmus decided to compose a short satire on the lines of his conversations with Thomas More, extolling what was silly and condemning what was wise. The result was *In Praise of Folly* (1509), a work that became one of the first best sellers in publishing history.

Before his visit to England, Erasmus had worked solely on Latin translations, but he came to realize the importance of recovering the Greek texts of the early Church fathers. At the age of 30, he began the arduous task of learning ancient Greek and devoted his energies to a study of the writings of Saint Jerome, the principal compiler of the Vulgate, and to preparing an edition of the Greek text of the Bible. Erasmus's New Testament and his edition of the writings of Saint Jerome both appeared in 1516. Coming from the pen of the most renowned intellectual in Europe, they were an immediate success.

Erasmus devoted his life to restoring the direct connection between the individual Christian and the textual basis of Christian doctrine. Although he is called the father of biblical criticism, Erasmus was not a theologian. He was more interested in the practical impact of ideas than in the ideas themselves. His scathing attacks upon the Scholastics, popular superstition, and the pretensions of the traditionalists in the Church and the universities all aimed at the same goal: to restore the experiences of

A DUTCH WIT

In Praise of Folly *(1500) was a witty satire on the abuses to be found in the Catholic Church. Desiderius Erasmus wrote it on a lark to be presented to his friend, Sir Thomas More, on whose name its Greek title puns. It was probably the first best seller of the age of printing.*

Focus Questions

How do the follies of priests and theologians differ, and how are they similar? Is this piece a satire of religion?

These various forms of foolishness so pervade the whole life of Christians that even the priests themselves find no objection to admitting, not to say fostering, them, since they do not fail to perceive how many tidy little sums accrue to them from such sources. But what if some odious philosopher should chime in and say, as is quite true: "You will not die badly if you live well. You are redeeming your sins when you add to the sum that you contribute a hearty detestation of evil doers: then you may spare yourself tears, vigils, invocations, fasts, and all that kind of life. You may rely upon any saint to aid you when once you begin to imitate his life."

As for the theologians, perhaps the less said the better on this gloomy and dangerous theme, since they are a style of man who show themselves exceeding supercilious and irritable unless they can heap up six hundred conclusions about you and force you to recant; and if you refuse, they promptly brand you as a heretic—for it is their custom to terrify by their thunderings those whom they dislike. It must be confessed that no other group of fools are so reluctant to acknowledge Folly's benefits toward them, although I have many titles to their gratitude, for I make them so in love with themselves that they seem to be happily exalted to the third heaven, whence they look down with something like pity upon all other mortals, wandering about on the earth like mere cattle.

From Erasmus, *In Praise of Folly.*

UTOPIA

"It is a general rule that the more different anything is from what people are used to, the harder it is to accept." So warned the imaginary traveler, Raphael Hythloday as he described Utopia, a fabulous society he had visited in the New World. Utopian society was different indeed. In Utopia, all property was held in common; there were no social classes; families were extended to include grandparents, in-laws, and flocks of children; and all work and most social activities were regulated by the state. Utopians were rarely tempted to sin. Everyone wore the same practical clothes to abolish vanity. "No matter how delicate the thread, they say a sheep wore it once and still was nothing but a sheep." Everyone ate the same food in large common halls to abolish jealousy. "A man would be stupid to take the trouble to prepare a worse meal at home when he had a sumptuous one near at hand in the hall." To abolish greed, Utopians scorned gold and silver. "Criminals who are to bear through life the mark of some disgraceful act are forced to wear golden rings on their ears, golden bands on their fingers, golden chains around their necks, and even golden crowns on their heads." Utopians lived harmoniously in planned cities, honored their elders, cared for their sick, and brought up their children to love learning and respect hard work. They "lead a life as free of anxiety and as full of joy as possible."

A CLOSER LOOK

There were many ways in which Christian humanists attempted to instruct their contemporaries to lead a joyful life. None has proved more enduring than the imaginary community Sir Thomas More created in *Utopia,* a social satire so convincing that a Catholic priest sought to become its bishop and sea travelers tried to learn its location. More's creation has proven so compelling that it has given its name to the entire genre of dreamworlds that followed in its wake. His vision of a carefully planned and permanently contented society has passed into our language, but in a way that would not have pleased the author. Now, utopian has a wistful ring. It is a label for impractical ideals that will never come to pass, a name for well-meaning but misguided daydreams. For More, as for his generation of humanists, the goal of teaching Christians to lead a Christian life was neither wistful nor impractical.

Sir Thomas More was a London lawyer by vocation but a humanist scholar by avocation. His father practiced law and planned a similar career for his son. But More's stay at Oxford University coincided with the first flush of humanist enthusiasm there, especially in the study of Greek. More proved so able that his father removed him to London in fear that reading Greek would turn him away from Catholicism. More was as good at law school as he had been at the university, and he was soon singled out as one of the best lawyers of his day. But in his spare time he continued to study the classics and became part of the growing humanist circle in London. There he met Erasmus, who was to become his lifelong friend.

Erasmus left a vivid portrait of More. "His complexion is fair, his face being rather blond than pale; his hair is auburn inclining to black, his eyes a bluish gray. It is a face more expressive of pleasantry than of gravity or dignity. He seems to be born and made for friendship, his extraordinary kindness and sweetness of temper are such as to cheer the dullest spirit."

More wrote *Utopia* in 1516, before he embarked upon the public career that would result in his becoming Chancellor of England, Speaker of the House of Commons, Privy Councilor and companion to Henry VIII, and finally a victim of the king's divorce and assumption of the title Supreme Head of the Church of England. More's life was ended on the chopping block, and his death was mourned by humanists throughout Europe.

The community that More described in *Utopia* combined Plato's republic with a Christian monastery and was informed by travelers' tales of the New World. But More's Utopia resembled nothing so much as England. The real and the imaginary, the serious and the absurd intermingle to disguise the author's point of view. *Utopia* is written in the form of a dialogue in which the author pretends to be one of the characters. On a visit to Antwerp, the character More is introduced to an imaginary traveler named Raphael Hythloday. During a long evening, Hythloday related a tale of a remarkable society that he encountered on his voyages. Utopia was a self-sufficient island, protected from invasion by the sea and thus able to develop its social customs without interference.

Hythloday contrasted the practices of the Utopians with those of contemporary Europeans. For example, where European peasants or craftsmen worked for fourteen hours a day, Utopians worked for only six. But all Utopians worked. There were no idle aristocrats with their marauding retainers, no priests and monks and nuns, no beggars unable to find jobs. Moreover, there was no surplus of workers in one field and shortage in another. For two years, each Utopian worked on a farm. After that, Utopians practiced a craft according to the needs of the city. Both males and females were educated to serve the community. Women were trained in less strenuous but no less essential trades such as weaving or spinning. The population of cities was strictly controlled so that there was neither poverty nor homelessness. In their spare time Utopians engaged in uplifting activities such as music, gardening, or artistic pursuits. Severe punishment awaited transgressors, but in contrast to the European practice of executing thieves, Utopian criminals were enslaved so that they could work for the restitution of the wrongs that they committed. Even as slaves they lived well, with good food and much leisure. Though they had not the benefit of Christian religion, the Utopians believed in a single divinity as well as an afterlife and their worship was simple and natural.

A woodcut of the island of Utopia by Ambrosius Holbein, from the 1518 edition of Sir Thomas More's *Utopia*.

More's *Utopia* was written in Latin, but the name of the island and its central places were all Greek words. For More's humanist friends the joke was plain. Utopia meant "nowhere" in Greek and Hythloday meant "peddler of nonsense." Humanist interest in the New World and in the strange native customs of the Amerindians made it a logical setting for an idealized community. But *Utopia* was a model for a Christian community, one in which the seven deadly sins had all been abolished and replaced by a life led according to the Golden Rule, where people did attempt to do to others what they wished done to themselves. By ironic contrast with the unfulfilling life led by Europeans, grasping for riches, the simple life of the Utopians held great attraction. By comparing the success of heathen Utopians with the failure of Christian Europeans, More called upon his contemporaries to reform their own lives. The purpose of *Utopia* was not to advocate the abolition of wealth and property but to demonstrate that a society founded upon Christian principles would become truly Christian.

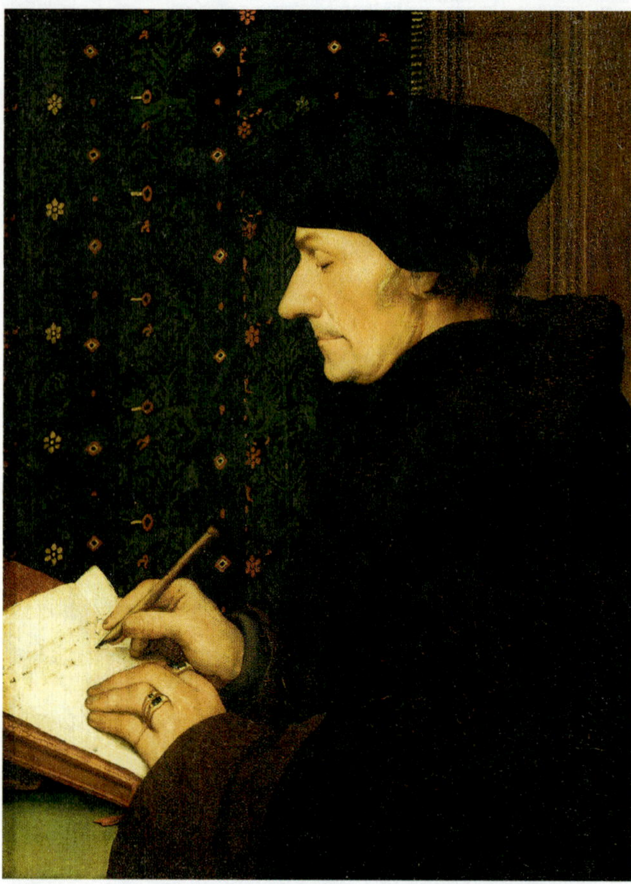

■ Hans Holbein's 1523 portrait depicts Erasmus in profile, absorbed in his work rather than looking in the direction of the viewer.

Christ to the center of Christianity. Many of Erasmus's popular writings were how-to books—how to improve one's manners, how to speak Latin properly, how to write letters—he even propounded 22 rules on how to lead a Christian life. Although his patrons were the rich and his language was Latin, Erasmus also hoped to reach men and women lower down the social order, those whom he believed the Church had failed to educate. "The doctrine of Christ casts aside no age, no sex, no fortune or position in life. It keeps no one at a distance."

THE LUTHERAN REFORMATION

On the surface, the Roman Catholic Church appeared as strong as ever at the end of the fifteenth century. The growth of universities and the spread of the new learning had helped create a better-educated clergy. The printing press proved an even greater boon to the Church than it had to the humanists by making widely available both instructional manuals for priests and up-to-date service books for congregations. The prosperity of European societies enhanced the prosperity of the Church. In Rome, successive late medieval popes had managed to protect Church interests in the wake of the disintegration of the autonomous power of the Italian city-states. That was a remarkable feat. Popes had become first diplomats and then warriors in order to repel French and Spanish invaders. Although Rome had been invaded, it had never been conquered. And it was more beautiful than ever, as the greatest artists and artisans of the Renaissance had built and adorned its churches. Pilgrims came in the hundreds of thousands to bask in its glory. On the surface all was calm.

Yet everywhere in Europe the cry was for reform. Reform the venal papacy and its money-sucking bishops. Reform the ignorant clergy and the sacrilegious priests. Raise up the fallen nuns and the wayward friars. Wherever people turned, they saw abuses. Parish livings were sold to the highest bidder to raise money. That was simony. Rich appointments were given to the kinsmen of powerful Church leaders rather than to those most qualified. That was nepotism. Individual clergymen accumulated numerous positions whose responsibilities they could not fulfill. That was pluralism. Some priests who took the vow of chastity lived openly with their concubines. Some mendicants who took the vow of poverty dressed in silk and ate from golden plates.

Yet the cry for reform that pierced the states of Europe at the beginning of the sixteenth century was a cry not so much of anguish as of hope. It came at a moment when people from all walks of life demanded greater spiritual fulfillment and held those whose vocation it was to provide such fulfillment to higher standards of achievement. It was expectation rather than experience that powered the demands for reform.

The Spark of Reform

Europe was becoming more religious. The signs of religious fervor were everywhere. Cities hired preachers to expound the gospel. Pilgrims to the shrines of saints clogged the roadways every spring and summer. It is estimated that 140,000 people visited the relics at Aachen on one day in 1496. Rome remained the greatest attraction, but pilgrims covered the Continent. The shrine of the apostle Saint James at Compostela in Spain was believed to cure the ill. Endowments of masses for the dead increased. Henry VII of England provided money for 10,000 masses to be said for his soul. Even moderately well-to-do city merchants might bequeath funds for several hundred. The chantries, where such services were performed, became overburdened by the "arithmetical piety," as there were neither enough priests nor enough altars to supply the demand.

People wanted more from the Church than the Church could possibly give them. Humanists condemned visits to the shrines as superstitious; pilgrims demanded that the relics be made more accessible. Reformers complained of pluralism; the clergy complained that they could not live on the salary of a single office. In one English diocese, 60 percent of all parish incomes were inadequate to live on. Civic authorities demanded that the established Church take greater responsibility for good works; the pope demanded that civic authorities help pay for them.

Contradiction and paradox dominated the movements for reform. Although the most vocal critics of the Church complained that its discipline was too lax, for many ordinary people its demands were too rigorous. The obligations of penance and confession weighed heavily upon them. Church doctrine held that sins had to be washed away before the souls of the dead could enter heaven. Until then they suffered in purgatory. Sins were cleansed through penance—the performance of acts of contrition assigned after confession. Despite the rule that confession must be made at least annually, it is doubtful if many Catholics entered the confessional for years on end. This is not to say that they were unconcerned about their sins or did not desire to do penance for them. Rather, it was the ordeal of the confession itself that kept many people away. "Have you skipped mass? Have you dressed proudly? Have you thought of committing adultery? Have you insulted or cursed your parents? Have you failed to offer prayers, give alms, and endow masses for departed parents?" These were just a few of the uncomfortable questions that priests were instructed to pose in confession. In towns, merchants were asked about their trading practices, shopkeepers about the quality of their goods. Magistrates were questioned about their attitudes to the clergy, intellectuals about their attitudes to the pope.

Thus it is hardly surprising that the sale of **indulgences** became a popular substitute for **penance and confession**. An indulgence was a portion of the treasury of good works performed by righteous Christians throughout the ages. They could be granted to those who desired to atone for their sins. Strictly speaking, an indulgence supplemented penance rather than substituted for it. It was effective only for the contrite—for sinners who repented of their sins. But as the practice of granting indulgences spread, the subtle distinction largely disappeared. Indulgences came to be viewed as pardons and the gift given to the Church in return as payment. "So soon as coin in coffer rings, the soul from purgatory springs." Indulgences were bought by the living to cleanse the sins of the dead, and some people even bought indulgences in anticipation of sins they had not yet committed.

By the sixteenth century, to limit abuses by local Church authorities, only the pope, through his agents, could grant indulgences. And their sale had become big business. Indulgences were one of the first items printed on Gutenberg's press. Popes used special occasions to offer an indulgence for pilgrimages to Rome or for contributions to special papal projects. Other indulgences were licensed locally, usually at the shrines of saints or at churches that contained relics—one reason why pilgrimages became increasingly popular. Frederick III, "the Wise" (1463–1525), ruler of Saxony, was one of the largest collectors of relics in Europe. At its height, his collection contained 17,000 different items, including a branch of Moses' burning bush, straw from Christ's manger, and 35 fragments of the true cross. Together, his relics

■ An anonymous caricature of Johann Tetzel, whose sale of an indulgence inspired Martin Luther's Ninety-five Theses. Tetzel answered with 122 theses of his own but was rebuked and disowned by the Catholics.

carried remission for sins that would otherwise have taken more than a quarter of a million years in purgatory to be cleansed.

The indulgence controversy was a symptom rather than a cause of the explosion of feelings that erupted in the small German town of Wittenberg in the year 1517. In that year, the pope was offering an indulgence to help finance the rebuilding of Saint Peter's Basilica in Rome. The pope chose Prince Albert of Brandenburg (1490–1545) to distribute the indulgence in Germany, and Albert hired the Dominican friar Johann Tetzel (ca. 1465–1519) to preach its benefits. Tetzel offered little warning about the theological niceties of indulgences to those who paid to mitigate their own sins or alleviate the suffering of their ancestors whose souls resided in purgatory.

Enthusiasm for the indulgence spread to the neighboring state of Saxony, where Frederick banned its sale. His great collection of relics carried their own indulgences, and Tetzel offered unwelcome competition. But Saxons flocked into Brandenburg to make their purchases. By the end of October, Tetzel was not very far from Wittenberg Castle, where Frederick's relics were housed. On All Saints' Day the relics would be opened to view and, with the harvest done, one of the largest crowds of the year would gather to see them. On the night before, Martin Luther (1483–1546), a professor of theology at Wittenberg University, posted on the door of the castle church Ninety-five Theses attacking indulgences and their sale.

Aside from the timing of Luther's action, there was nothing unusual about the posting of theses. In the Scholastic tradition of disputation, scholars presented propositions, or theses, for debate and challenged all comers to argue with them in a public forum. Luther's theses were controversial, but—as that was the whole point of offering them for discussion—they were meant to be. Only circumstance moved Luther's theses from the academic to the public sphere. Already there was growing concern among clergy and theologians about Tetzel's blatant sale of indulgences. Hordes of purchasers believed that they were buying unconditional remission of sin. In the late summer and early fall of 1517, the frenzy to buy indulgences had reached gold-rush proportions, and individual priests and monks began to sound the alarm: an indulgence without contrition was worthless.

Luther's theses focused that concern and finally communicated it beyond the walls of the Church and university. The theses were immediately translated into German and spread throughout the Holy Roman Empire by humanists who had long criticized practices such as the sale of indulgences as superstitious. Prospective buyers became wary; past purchasers became angry. They had been duped again by the Church, by the priests who took their money, and by the Italian pope who cared nothing for honest, hardworking Germans. But Prince Albert and the pope needed the income. They could not stand by while sales collapsed and anticlerical and antipapal sentiment grew. Luther and his theses would have to be challenged.

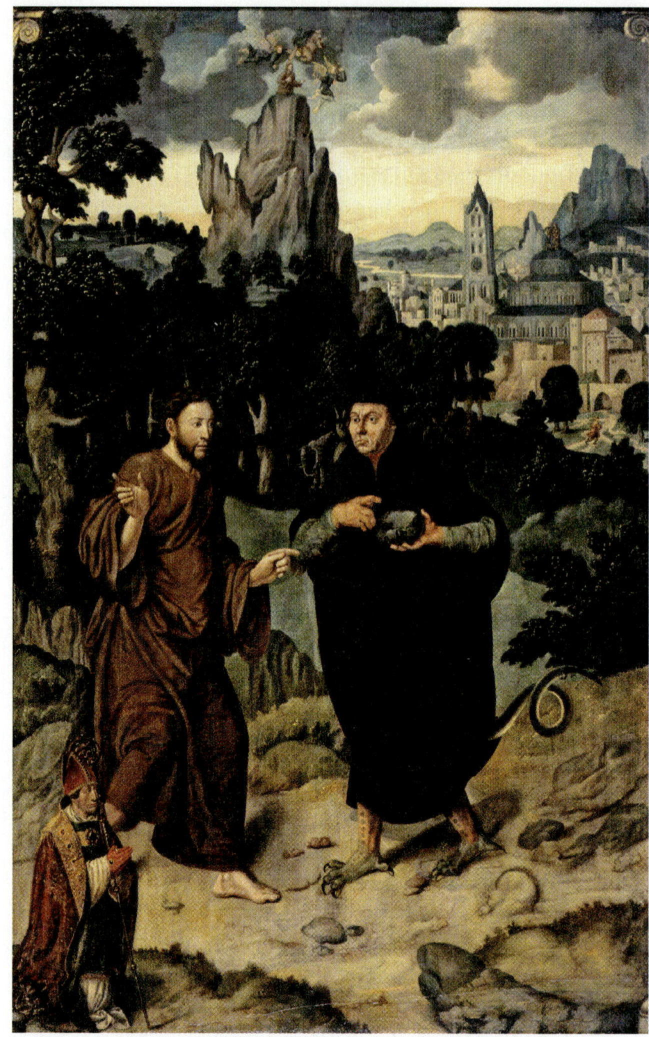

■ Catholics and Protestants alike used religious images to slander their opponents. Here Catholic propaganda portrays Martin Luther as the devil in academic disguise come to tempt Jesus.

Martin Luther's Faith

Martin Luther was not a man to challenge lightly. Although he was only an obscure German professor, he had already marked himself out to all who knew him. In his youth, Luther was an exceptionally able student whose father sent him to the best schools in preparation for a career in law. But Martin had his own ideas about his future, which were made more vivid when he was nearly struck by lightning. Against the wishes of his father, he entered an Augustinian monastery, wholeheartedly followed the strict program of his order, and was ordained a priest in 1507. Intellectually gifted, he went on to study at the university, first at Erfurt and then at Wittenberg, where he received his doctorate and was appointed to the theology faculty in 1512.

A professor at the age of 29, he also served as priest at the castle church, where he preached each week. He attracted powerful patrons in the university and gained a reputation as an outstanding teacher. He began to be picked for administrative posts and became overseer of 11 Augustinian monasteries. His skills in disputation were so widely recognized that he was sent to Rome to argue a case on behalf of his order. Each task he was given he fulfilled beyond expectation; at every step he proved himself ready to go higher.

In all outward appearances, Luther was successful and contented. But beneath this tranquil exterior lay a soul in torment. As he rose in others' estimation, he sank in his own. Through beating and fasting he mortified his flesh. Through vigil and prayer he nourished his soul. Through study and contemplation he honed his intellect. Still he could find no peace. Despite his devotion, he could not erase his sense of sin; he could not convince himself that the righteousness God demanded of him was a righteousness he could achieve. "I was one who terribly feared the last judgment and who nevertheless with all my heart wished to be saved."

Knowledge of his salvation came to Luther through study. His internal agonies led him to ponder over and over again the biblical passages that described the righteousness of God. In the intellectual tradition in which he had been trained, that righteousness was equated with law. The righteous person either followed God's law or was punished by God's wrath. It was that understanding that tormented him. "I thought that I had to perform good works till at last through them Jesus would become a friend and gracious to me." But no amount of good works could overcome Luther's feelings of guilt for his sins. Like a man caught in a net, the more he struggled the more entangled he became. For years he wrestled with his problem. Almost from the moment he began lecturing in 1512 he searched for the key to the freedom of his own soul.

Even before he wrote his Ninety-five Theses, Luther had made the first breakthrough by a unique reading of the writings of Saint Paul. "I pondered night and day until I understood the connection between the righteousness of God and the sentence 'The just shall live by faith.' Then I grasped that the justice of God is the righteousness by which through grace and pure mercy, God justifies us through faith. Immediately I felt that I had been reborn and that I had passed through wide open doors into paradise!" Finally he realized that the righteousness of God was not a burden that humans carried, but a gift that God bestowed. It could not be earned by good works but was freely given. It was this belief that fortified Luther during his years of struggle with both civil and Church powers.

Over the next several years, Luther refined his spiritual philosophy and drew out the implications of his newfound beliefs. His religion was shaped by three interconnected tenets. First came justification by faith alone—***sola fide***. An individual's everlasting salvation came from faith in God's goodness rather than from the performance of good works. Sin was ever present and inescapable. It could not be washed away by penance, and it could not be forgiven by indulgence. Second, faith in God's mercy came only through the knowledge and contemplation of the Word of God—*sola scriptura*. All that was needed to understand the justice and mercy of God was contained in the Bible, the sole authority in all things spiritual. Reading the Word, hearing the Word, expounding upon and studying the Word—that was the path to faith, and through faith to salvation. Third, all who believed in God's righteousness and had achieved their faith through the study of the Bible were equal in God's eyes. No longer was it necessary for men and women to renounce their worldly existence and take up a life consumed by spiritual works. Neither pope nor priest, neither monk nor nun, could achieve a higher level of spirituality than the most ordinary citizen. The priesthood was of all believers. Each followed his or her own calling in life and found his or her own faith through Scripture. Ministers and preachers were valuable because they could help others learn God's Word. But they could not confer faith.

Luther's spiritual rebirth and the theology that developed from it posed a fundamental challenge to the Roman Catholic Church. The doctrine of justification by faith alone called into question the Church's emphasis upon the primacy of works—that is, receiving the sacraments administered by the priests and performing acts of charity and devotion. The doctrine that faith was achieved through Scripture weakened the mediating power of the Church by making salvation an individual rather than a collective event. The doctrine of the equality of all believers struck at the vast establishment of religious houses as well as the spiritual hierarchy of the Church from the lowest priest to the pope. Although for centuries the Roman Catholic Church had met doctrinal challenges and had absorbed many seemingly unorthodox ideas, Luther's theology could not be among them. It struck too deeply at the roots of belief, practice, and structure. If Luther was right, then the Roman Catholic Church must be wrong.

Yet for all of the transforming power of the apparently simple ideas, it was not Luther alone who initiated the reform of religion. Before Luther, countless thousands strove for salvation. Justification by faith alone provided an alternative to the combination of works and faith that many Roman Catholics found too difficult to fulfill. Luther's insistence that faith comes only through the study of the Word of God was facilitated by the new learning and the invention of printing. The printing press prepared the ground for the dissemination of his thought as much as it disseminated it. That was a result of the Renaissance. Luther's hope for the creation of a spiritual elite, confirmed in their faith and confident of their salvation, readily appealed to the citizens of hundreds of German towns who had already made of themselves a social and economic elite. That was a result of the growth of towns. The idea of the equality of all believers meant that all were equally responsible for fulfilling God's commandments. That set secular rulers on an equal footing with the pope at a moment in Western history when they were already challenging papal power in matters of both Church and state. That was a result of the formation of states. For all of the painful soul-searching by which he came to his shattering insight, there was embodied in Luther the culmination of changes of which he was only dimly aware.

Lutheranism

The first to feel the seriousness of Luther's challenge to the established order was the reformer himself. The head of his order, a papal legate, and finally the Emperor Charles V all called for Luther to recant his views on indulgences. Excommunicated by Pope Leo X in 1521, Luther was ordered by Charles V to appear before the diet, or assembly, in Worms. The emperor demanded that Luther retract his teachings. Infuriatingly, Luther replied that, if he could be shown the places in the Bible that contradicted his views, he would gladly change them. "I cannot and I will not retract anything, since it is neither safe nor right to go against conscience. I cannot do otherwise." In fact, during the three years between the posting of his theses and his appearance before the emperor, Luther came to conclusions much more radical than his initial attack on indulgences. Preparing to contend with papal representatives about the pope's right to issue indulgences, Luther came to believe that the papacy was a human rather than a divine invention. Therefore he denounced both the papacy and the general councils of the Church. In his *Address to the Christian Nobility of the German Nation* (1520), he called upon the princes to take the reform of religion into their own hands. No longer was there hope of compromise. Charles V declared Luther an enemy of the empire. In both Church and state he was now an outlaw.

But Luther had attracted powerful supporters as well as powerful enemies. Prince Frederick III of Saxony consistently intervened on his behalf, and the delicate international situation forced Luther's chief antagonists to move more slowly than they might have wanted. The pope hoped first to keep Charles V off the imperial throne and then to maintain a united front with the German princes against him. Charles V, already locked in his lifelong struggle with the French, needed German military support and peace in his German territories. Those factors consistently played into Luther's hands.

While pope and emperor were otherwise occupied, Luther refined his ideas and thus was able to hold his own in the theological debates in which he won important converts. More importantly, as time passed Luther's reputation grew, not only in Germany, but all over Europe. Between 1517 and 1520 he published 30 works, all of which achieved massive sales. Yet Luther alone could not sustain what came to be called Lutheranism. The Roman Catholic Church had met heresy before and knew how to deal with it. What turned Luther's theology into a movement—which after 1529 came to be known as Protestantism—was the support he received among German princes and within German cities.

Martin Luther, The German Mass

Princes and Cities. There were many reasons that individual princes turned to Luther's theology. First and foremost was sincere religious conviction. Matters of the hereafter were a pressing concern in a world in which the average life span was 30 years and nearly all natural phenomena were inexplicable. And they were more pressing still among the educated elites inspired by the new learning and confident of their power to reason critically. Yet there were secular reasons as well. The formation of large states had provided a model for civil government. On a smaller scale, German princes worked to centralize their administration, protect themselves from predatory neighbors, and increase their revenues. They had long suffered under the burden of papal exactions. Taxes and gifts flowed south to a papacy dominated by Italians. Luther's call for civil rulers to lead their own churches meant that civil rulers could keep their own revenues.

The Reformation spread particularly well in the German cities, especially those the emperor had granted the status of freedom from the rule of any prince. Once Protestant ideas were established, entire towns adopted them. The cities had long struggled with the tension of the separate jurisdictions of state and Church. Much urban property was owned by the Church and thus exempt from taxation and law enforcement, and the clergy constituted a significant proportion of urban populations. Reformed religion stressed the equality of clergy and laity, and thus the indisputable power of civil authorities. Paradoxically, it was because the cities contained large numbers of priests that Luther's ideas reached them quickly. Many of his earliest students served urban congregations and began to develop doctrines and practices that, though based on Luther's ideas, were adapted to the circumstances of city life. The reform clergy became integrated into the life of the city in a way that the Catholic clergy had not. They married the daughters of citizens, became citizens themselves, and trained their children in the guilds. Moreover, the imperial free cities were also the center of the printing trade and home to many of the most noted humanists who were initially important in spreading Luther's ideas.

LUTHER ON MARRIAGE

Martin Luther wrote thousands of pages of theological and devotional literature in establishing a new religious movement. His simple style and everyday examples made his message accessible to hundreds of thousands of ordinary people. In this selection from his tract On Good Works *(1520), he compares the relationship of the husband and wife to that of the Christian and Christ.*

Focus Questions

Why are "good works" not of primary importance in a Christian's relationship with God? Does Luther leave a role for the Church in his ideal of the relationship between a Christian and God?

We can understand this whole matter [of good works] by an obvious human example. When husband and wife are fond of one another and live together in love and in confidence in one another, and each believes truly in the other, who shall teach them how they should act, what they should do or leave undone, say or not say, think or not think? Their own insight tells them all that need be, and more too. There is no distinction in their "works" for one another. They do the long, hard, and heavy tasks as willingly as the slight and easy things, and moreover they act with glad, peaceful, and secure hearts and are altogether free and unconstrained. But when doubt comes they begin to ask what is best, and begin to distinguish between their acts in order to gain the other's favor, and go about with troubled and heavy hearts, perhaps well-nigh in despair or driven to downright desperation.

So the Christian who lives in confidence toward God knows what things he should do, and does all gladly and freely, not with a view to accumulating merit and good works, but because it is his great joy to please God and to serve him without thought of reward, contented if he but do God's will. On the contrary, he who is not at one with God, or is in doubt, will begin to be anxious how he may satisfy God and justify himself by his works. He runs off on a pilgrimage to St. James of Compostella, to Rome, to Jerusalem—here, there, anywhere; prays to St. Bridget, or some other saint, fasts this day and that, confesses here and confesses there, asks this man and that, but finds no peace.

From Martin Luther, *On Good Works*.

Luther's message held great appeal for the middle orders in the towns. While it was necessary for the leader of a state to support reform if it was to survive, in the cities it was the petty burghers, lesser merchants, tradesmen, and artisans who led the movements that ultimately gained the approval of city governments. The groups resented the privileges given to priests and members of religious orders who paid no taxes and were exempt from the obligations of citizenship. The level of anticlericalism, always high in Germany, was especially acute in cities that were suffering economic difficulties. Pressure from ordinary people and petty traders forced town leaders into action. The evangelism of reforming ministers created converts and an atmosphere of reform. Support from members of the ruling oligarchy both mobilized the pressures and capitalized upon them. Town governments secured their own autonomy over the Church, tightening their grip upon the institutions of social control and enhancing the social and economic authority of their members. Once Protestant, city governments took over many of the religious houses, often converting them into schools or hostels for the poor. Former monks were allowed to enter trades and to become citizens. Former nuns were encouraged to marry. Luther himself married an ex-nun after the dissolution of her convent.

A portrait of Marguerite de Valois, queen of Navarre, the cultured and talented sister of King Francis I.

The Appeal for Women. Religious reform appealed to women as well as men, but it affected them differently. Noblewomen were among the most important defenders of Protestant reformers, especially in states in which the prince opposed it. Marguerite of Navarre (1492–1549), sister of Francis I, frequently intervened with her brother on behalf of individual Lutherans who fell afoul of Church authorities. She created her own court in the south of France and stocked it with both humanists and Protestants. Her devotional poem *Mirror of the Sinful Soul* (1533) inspired women reformers and was translated into English by Elizabeth I. Mary of Hungary (1505–1558) served a similar role in the Holy Roman Empire. Sister of both Charles V and Ferdinand I, queen of Hungary, and later regent of the Netherlands, she acted as patron to Hungarian reformers. Although Mary was more humanist than Protestant, Luther dedicated an edition of the Psalms to her, and she read a number of his works. Her independent religious views infuriated both of her brothers. Bona (1493–1558), wife of Sigismund I of Poland, was especially important in eastern reform. An Italian by birth, Bona was a central figure in spreading both Renaissance art and humanist learning in Poland. She became one of the largest independent landowners in the state and initiated widespread agricultural and economic reforms. Her private confessor was one of Poland's leading Protestants.

Luther's reforms also offered much to women who were not so highly placed in society. The doctrine of the equality of all believers put men and women on an equal spiritual footing, even if it did nothing to break the male monopoly of the ministry. But the most important difference that Protestantism made to ordinary women was in the private rather than the public sphere. Family life became the center of faith when salvation was removed from the control of the Church. Luther's marriage led him to a deeper appreciation of the importance of the wife and mother in the family's spirituality. "Next to God's word there is no more precious treasure than holy matrimony."

By following humanist teaching on the importance of educating women of the upper orders and by encouraging literacy, the reformers did much that was uplifting. Girls' schools were founded in a number of German cities, and townswomen could use their newly acquired skills in their roles as shopkeepers, family accountants, and teachers of their children. But there were losses as well as gains. The attack on the worship of saints, and especially of the Virgin Mary, removed female images from religion. Protestantism was male dominated in a way that Catholicism was not. Moreover, the emphasis upon reading the Bible tended to reinforce the image of women as weak and inherently sinful. The dissolution of the convents took away from women the one institution that valued their gender and allowed them to pursue a spiritual life outside marriage.

The Spread of Lutheranism

By the end of the 1520s, the Holy Roman Empire was divided between cities and states that accepted reformed religion and those that adhered to Roman Catholicism. Printing presses, traveling merchants, and hordes of students who claimed—not always accurately—to have attended Luther's lectures or sermons spread the message. Large German communities across northern Europe, mostly founded as trading outposts, became focal points for the penetration of reformist ideas. In Livonia, the Teutonic Knights established a Lutheran form of worship that soon took hold all along the shores of the Baltic. Lutheran-inspired reformers seized control of the Polish port city of Gdansk, which they held for a short time, while neighboring Prussia officially established a Lutheran church. Polish translations of Luther's writings were disseminated into Poland-Lithuania, and Protestant communities were established as far south as Krakow.

MAP DISCOVERY

The Spread of Lutheranism

Observe the extent of Lutheranism across Europe in the sixteenth century. Where was Lutheranism concentrated? Notice how Lutheranism swept through entire states. How was Europe divided between Protestants and Catholics?

Merchants and students carried Luther's ideas into Scandinavia, but there the importance of political leaders was crucial. Christian III (1534–1559) of Denmark had been present at the Diet of Worms when Luther made his famous reply to Charles V. Christian was deeply impressed by the reformer, and after a ruinous civil war, he confiscated the property of the Catholic Church in Denmark and created a reformed religion under Luther's direct supervision.

Paradoxically, Lutheranism came to Sweden as part of an effort to throw off the yoke of Danish dominance. There, too, direct connection with Luther provided the first impulses. Olaus Petri (1493–1552) had studied at Wittenberg and returned to preach Lutheran doctrine among the large German merchant community in Stockholm. He was a trained humanist who used both Erasmus's Greek New Testament and Luther's German one to prepare his Swedish translation (1526). When Gustav I Vasa (1523–1560) led a successful uprising against the Danes and became king of Sweden, he encouraged the spread of Protestant ideas and allowed Petri to continue his Swedish translations of the mass and the Lutheran service. Under the protection of the monarchy, Lutheranism flourished in Scandinavia, where it remains the dominant religion to this day.

As important as Protestant ideas were in northern and central Europe, it was in the Swiss towns of the Holy Roman Empire that they proved most fertile. Here was planted the second generation of reformers, theologians who drew radical new conclusions from Luther's insights. In the east, Huldrych Zwingli (1484–1531) brought reformed religion to the town of Zürich. Educated at the University of Basel and deeply influenced by humanist thought early in his career, Zwingli was a preacher among the Swiss mercenary troops that fought for the empire. In 1516, he met Erasmus in Basel and under his influence began a study of the Greek writings of the Church fathers and of the New Testament. Zwingli was also influenced by reports of Luther's defiance of the pope, for his own

■ Huldrych Zwingli was a scholarly humanist deeply influenced by Erasmus. He led the Reformation in Zürich, the most important Swiss town.

antipapal views were already developing. Perhaps most decisively for his early development, in 1519 Zwingli was stricken by plague. In his life-and-death struggle he came to a profoundly personal realization of the power of God's mercy.

Those experiences became the basis for the reform theology Zwingli preached in Zürich. He believed that the Church had to recover its earlier purity and to reject the innovations in practices brought in by successive popes and general councils. He stressed the equality of believers, justification by faith alone, and the sufficiency of the gospel as authority for church practice. He attacked indulgences, penance, clerical celibacy, prayers to the Virgin, statues and images in churches, and a long list of other abuses. He also stressed that the mass was to be viewed as a commemorative event rather than one that involved the real presence of Christ. He preferred to call the service the Lord's Supper. His arguments were so effective that the town council adopted them as the basis for a reform of religion.

The principles Zwingli preached quickly spread to neighboring Swiss states. He participated in formal religious disputations in both Bern and Basel. In both places, his plea for a simple, unadorned religious practice met widespread approval. Practical as well as theological, Zwingli's reforms were carried out by the civil government with which he allied himself. That was not the same as the protection that princes had given to Lutherans. Rather, in the places that came under Zwingli's influence there was an important integration of church and state. Zwingli organized a formal military alliance of the Protestant Swiss towns. For him, the Bible carried a social message, and it is fitting that he died on the battlefield defending the state. He stressed the divine origins of civil government and the importance of the magistrate as an agent of Christian reform: "A church without the magistrate is mutilated and incomplete." That theocratic idea—that the leaders of the state and the leaders of the church were linked together—became the basis for further social and political reform.

THE PROTESTANT REFORMATION

By the middle of the 1530s, Protestant reform had entered a new stage. Luther did not intend to form a new religion; his struggle had been with Rome. Before he could build, he had to tear down—his religion was one of protest. Most of his energy was expended in attack and counterattack. The second generation of reformers faced a different task. The new reformers were the church builders who had to systematize doctrine for a generation that had already accepted religious reform. Their challenge was to draw out the logic of reformed ideas and to create enduring structures for reformed churches. The problems they faced were as much institutional as doctrinal. How was the new church to be governed in the absence of the traditional hierarchy? How could discipline be enforced when members of the reformed community went astray? What was the proper relationship between the community of believers and civil authority? Whatever the failings of the Roman Catholic Church, it had ready answers to those critical questions. The first generation of reformers had thrown out the stagnant bathwater of ecclesiastical abuses; it was left to the second generation to discover if they had thrown out the baby and the bathtub as well.

Geneva and Calvin

The Reformation came late to Geneva. In the sixteenth century, Geneva was under the dual government of the Duchy of Savoy, which owned most of the surrounding rural areas, and the Catholic bishop of the town, who was frequently a Savoy client. The Genevans also had their own town council, which traditionally struggled for power against the bishop. By the 1530s the council had gained the upper hand. The council confiscated Church lands and institutions, secularized the Church's legal powers, and forced the bishop and most of his administrators to flee the city. War with Savoy inevitably followed, and Geneva would certainly have been crushed into submission had it not been for its alliance with neighboring Bern, a potent military power among the Swiss towns.

Geneva was saved and was free to follow its own course in religious matters. Under Zwingli's influence, Bern had become Protestant, and it might have been expected that Geneva

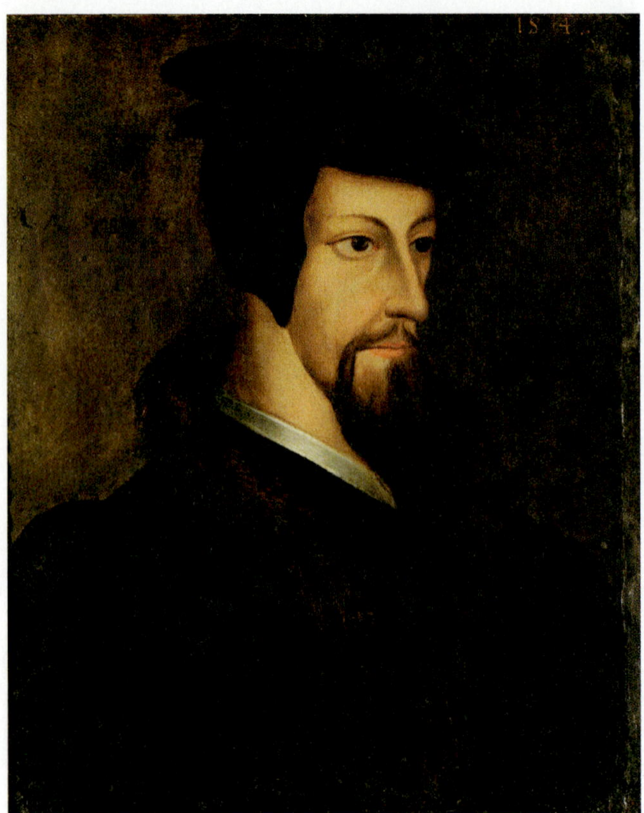

■ John Calvin, who published a major theological and political polemic and developed an alternative to Lutheranism before he turned thirty, is shown here as a young man.

would adopt that model even though French rather than German was the predominant language of the city. Some Protestant preachers arrived in Geneva to propagate reformed religion, and after a public disputation the town council abolished the mass. In 1536, the adult male citizens of the city voted to become Protestant. But as yet there was no reformer in Geneva to establish a Protestant program and no clear definition of what that program might be.

Martin Luther had started out to become a lawyer and ended up a priest. John Calvin started out to become a priest and ended up a lawyer. The difference tells much about each man. Calvin (1509–1564) was born in France, the son of a bishop's secretary. His education was based on humanist principles, and he learned Greek and Hebrew, studied theology, and received a legal degree from the University of Orléans. Around the age of 20 he converted to Lutheranism. He described the experience as "unexpected," but it had predictable results. Francis I had determined to root Protestants out of France, and Calvin fled Paris. Persecution of Protestants continued in France, and one of Calvin's close friends was burned for heresy. The events left an indelible impression upon him. In 1535, he left France for Basel, where he wrote and published the first edition of his *Institutes of the Christian Religion* (1536), a defense of French Protestants against persecution. Directed toward Francis I, it set out "the whole sum of godliness and whatever it is necessary to know of the doctrine of salvation." Calvin returned briefly to France to wind up his personal affairs and then decided to settle in Strasbourg, where he could retire from public affairs and live out his days as a scholar.

To Calvin, providence guided all human action. He could have no better evidence for that belief than what happened next. War between France and the Holy Roman Empire clogged the major highways to Strasbourg. Soldiers constantly menaced travelers, and Protestants could expect the worst from both sides. Thus Calvin and his companions detoured around the armies and passed through Geneva. How Calvin's presence there came to be known remains a mystery, but when Guillaume Farel (1489–1565), one of Geneva's leading Protestant reformers, heard of it, he quickly made his way to the inn where Calvin was staying. Farel implored Calvin to remain in Geneva and lead its reformation. Calvin was not interested. Farel tried every means of persuasion he knew until, in exasperation, Farel declared that God would curse Calvin's retirement if, Calvin wrote, "I should withdraw and refuse to help when the necessity was so urgent. By this imprecation I was so terror-struck that I gave up the journey that I had undertaken." For a quarter of a century, Calvin labored to bring order to the Genevan church.

Calvin's greatest contributions to religious reform came in church structure and discipline. He had studied the writings of the first generation of reformers and accepted without question justification by faith alone and the biblical foundation of religious authority. Like Luther and Zwingli, he believed that salvation came from God's grace. But more strongly than his predecessors he believed that the gift of faith was granted only to some and that each individual's salvation or damnation was predestined before birth. "We call predestination God's eternal decree. For all are not created in equal condition; rather, eternal life is foreordained for some, eternal damnation for others." The doctrine of **predestination** was a traditional one, but Calvin emphasized it differently and brought it to the center of the problem of faith. "Many are called but few are chosen," Calvin quoted from the Bible. Those who were predestined to salvation, "the elect," were obliged to govern; those who were predestined to damnation were obliged to be governed. Thus, for the church that Calvin erected, discipline was the central concern.

Calvin on Predestination

Calvin structured the institution of the Genevan church in four parts. First were the pastors who preached the Word to their congregations. There were fewer than 10 pastors in Geneva in the early 1540s and fewer than 20 by the time of Calvin's death—a far cry from the 500 priests who had administered the sacraments there under Catholicism. While the pastors preached, the doctors, the second element in Calvin's church, studied and wrote. The doctors were scholars who mastered the difficult portions of the Bible and who increased the stock of learned pastors by their teaching. In the beginning, Calvin was the only Genevan doctor, but after he helped to establish the University of Geneva in 1559, there was a ready supply of learned theologians.

THE ETERNAL DECREE

John Calvin was born in France but led the Reformation in the Swiss town of Geneva. He was one of the leaders of the second generation of reformers, whose task was to refine the structure of church doctrine. Calvinism was propounded in his Institutes of the Christian Religion *(1534), from which this section on the doctrine of predestination is taken.*

Focus Questions

According to Calvin, why is everyone contaminated by sin?
What power do humans have over their spiritual destiny?

We must be content with this—that such gifts as it pleased the Lord to have bestowed upon the nature of man he vested in Adam; and therefore when Adam lost them after he had received them, he lost them not only from himself but also from us all. . . . Therefore from a rotten root rose up rotten branches, which sent their rottenness into the twigs that sprang out of them; for so were the children corrupted in their father that they in turn infected their children. . . .

And the apostle Paul himself expressly witnesseth that therefore death came upon all men, because all men have sinned and are wrapped in original sin and defiled with the spots thereof. And therefore the very infants themselves, since they bring with them their own damnation from their mothers' womb, are bound not by another's but by their own fault. For although they have not as yet brought forth the fruits of their own iniquity, yet they have the seeds thereof enclosed within them; yea, their whole nature is a certain seed of sin, therefore it cannot but be hateful and abominable to God. . . .

Predestination we call the eternal decree of God, whereby he has determined with himself what he wills to become of every man. For all are not created to like estate; but to some eternal life and to some eternal damnation is foreordained. Therefore as every man is created to the one or the other end, so we say that he is predestinate either to life or to death.

From John Calvin, *Institutes of the Christian Religion.*

Pastors and doctors made up the top tier of the official church; deacons and elders the lower. Deacons, the third element in Calvin's four-part structure, were laymen chosen by the congregation to oversee the institutions of social welfare run by the church. Those institutions included the hospitals and schools that cared for the sick and the poor and instructed the young. The last element was the elders of the church, who were its governors in all moral matters. They were the most controversial part of Calvin's establishment and the most fundamental. They had the power to discipline. Chosen from among the elite of the city, the 12 elders enforced the strict Calvinist moral code that extended into all aspects of private life. The elders and the pastors met each week in a body known as the consistory to examine violations of God's laws; for them was reserved the ultimate sanction of excommunication. Offenses ranged from trivial superstitions—a woman wrapping a walnut containing a spider around the neck of her sick husband—to cases of blasphemy. Sexual offenses were the most common. Adultery and fornication were vigorously suppressed, and prostitutes, who had nearly become a recognized guild in the early sixteenth century, were expelled from Geneva.

The structure that Calvin gave to the Genevan church soon became the basis for reforms throughout the Continent. The Calvinist church was self-governing, independent of the state, and therefore capable of surviving and even flourishing in a hostile environment. Expanded in several subsequent editions, *Institutes of the Christian Religion* became the most influential work of Protestant theology. It had begun as an effort to extend Protestantism to France, and Calvin never abandoned hope that his homeland would be converted. Waves of Calvinist-educated pastors returned to France in the mid-sixteenth century and established churches along Calvinist lines. Calvinism spread north to Scotland and the Low Countries, where it became the basis for Dutch Protestantism, and east to Poland, where it flourished in Lithuania and Hungary. It reached places untouched by Luther and revitalized reform where Lutheranism had been suppressed. Perhaps its greatest impact was in Britain, where the Reformation took place not once but twice.

The English Reformation

The king of England wanted a divorce. Henry VIII had been married to Catherine of Aragon (1485–1536) as long as he had been king, and she had borne him no male heir to carry on his line. Catherine of Aragon had done her duty: in ten years she had given birth to six children and endured several miscarriages. Yet only one daughter, Mary, survived. Nothing so important as the lack of a male heir could happen by accident, and Henry came to believe that it was God's punishment for his marriage. Catherine had been married first to Henry's older brother, who had died as a teenager, and there was at least one scriptural prohibition against marrying a brother's wife. A papal dispensation had been provided for the marriage, and now Henry wanted a papal dispensation for an annulment. For three years his case ground its way through the papal courts. Catherine of Aragon was the aunt of the

An allegorical painting of Edward VI triumphing over the Pope, shown lying at the king's feet. To Edward's left is his Privy Council. His father, Henry VIII, gestures to the young king from his deathbed.

Emperor Charles V, and the emperor had taken her side in the controversy. With imperial power in Italy at its height, the pope was content to hear all of the complex legal and biblical precedents argued at leisure.

By 1533, Henry could wait no longer. He had already impregnated Anne Boleyn (ca. 1507–1536), one of the ladies-in-waiting at his court. If the child—which Henry was certain would be a boy—was to be legitimate, a marriage would have to take place at once. Legislation was prepared in Parliament to prevent papal interference in the decisions of England's courts, and Thomas Cranmer (1489–1556), archbishop of Canterbury, England's highest ecclesiastical officer, agreed to annul Henry's first marriage and celebrate his second. That was the first step in a complete break with Rome. Under the guidance of Thomas Cromwell (ca. 1485–1540), the English Parliament passed statute after statute that made Henry supreme head of the church in England and owner of its vast wealth. Monasteries were dissolved and a Lutheran service was introduced. England's first reformation came as a result of the "King's Great Matter." On 7 September 1533, Anne Boleyn gave birth not to the expected son, but to a daughter, the future Queen Elizabeth I.

The Church of England. Henry's reformation was an act of state, but the English Reformation was not. There was an English tradition of dissent from the Roman Church that stretched back to the fourteenth century and that had survived even the most determined efforts to suppress it. Anticlericalism was especially virulent in the towns, where citizens refused to pay fees to priests for performing services such as burial. And humanist ideas flourished in England, where Thomas More, John Colet, and a host of others supported both the new learning and its efforts to reform spiritual life. The English were as susceptible as other Europeans to Luther's ideas, which crossed the Channel with German merchants and English travelers. Luther's attack on ritual and the mass and his emphasis on Scripture and faith found many recruits in London and the northern port towns.

Protestantism had grown slowly in England because it had been vigorously repressed. Like Francis I and Charles V, Henry VIII had viewed actual attacks on the established church as potential attacks on the established state. The consolidation of the Tudor monarchy was too recent for him not to be concerned with its stability. Henry had earned the title "Defender of the Faith" from the pope in 1521 for authoring an attack on Luther. Bonfires of Lutheran books had lighted the English skies. Small groups of Protestants at Cambridge and Oxford universities had been sniffed out and hunted down by Henry's agents. Some had made public recantations; some had fled to the Continent; one—Thomas Bilney—went to the stake. The first published English translation of the New Testament, made by William Tyndale in 1525, had to be smuggled into England. As sensitivity to the abuses of the Church grew and Lutheran ideas spread, official censorship and persecution sharpened.

Henry's divorce unleashed a groundswell of support for religious change. The king's own religious beliefs remained a secret, but Anne Boleyn and Thomas Cromwell sponsored Lutheran reforms and Thomas Cranmer put them into practice. Religion was legislated through Parliament, and the valuable estates of the Church were sold to the gentry. The practices found favor with both the legal profession and the landed elites and made Protestantism more palatable among those conservative groups. It was in the reign of Edward VI

■ This painting depicts a Calvinist service in Lyon, France, in 1564. The men and women are segregated, and the worshipers are seated according to rank. An hourglass times the preacher's sermon.

(1547–1553), Henry's son by his third wife, that the central doctrinal and devotional changes were made. Although they were Protestant in tenor, there remained compromises and deliberate ambiguities. The chantries were abolished, and with them masses for the dead. Church service was now conducted in English, and the first two English prayer books were created. The mass was reinterpreted along Zwinglian lines and became the Lord's Supper, the altar became the communion table, and the priest became the minister. Preaching became the center of the church service, and concern over the education of learned ministers resulted in commissions to examine and reform the clergy.

Beginning in the 1530s, state repression turned against Catholics. Those who would not swear the new oaths of allegiance or recognize the legality of Henry VIII's marriage suffered for their beliefs as the early Protestants had suffered for theirs. Thomas More and more than 40 others paid with their lives for their opposition. Others took up arms against the government, marrying economic and political grievances to religious ones. An uprising in the north in 1536, known as the Pilgrimage of Grace, posed the most serious threat to the English Crown since the Wars of the Roses. Gentry and common people opposed the dissolution of the monasteries and feared for provision for their spiritual needs. Henry's ability to suppress the Pilgrimage of Grace owed more to his political power than to the conversion of his governing classes to Protestantism. Edward VI's government faced a similar uprising in 1549 when it attempted to introduce a new and more Protestant prayer book. Catholicism continued to flourish in England, surviving underground during the reigns of Henry and Edward and reemerging under Mary I (1553–1558).

The Successors of Henry VIII. Mary Tudor was her mother's child. The first woman to rule England, she held to the Catholic beliefs in which Catherine of Aragon had raised her, and she vowed to bring the nation back to her mother's church. When Edward VI died, the English ruling elite opted for political legitimacy rather than religious ideology in supporting Mary against a Protestant pretender to the throne. The new queen was as good as her word. She reestablished papal sovereignty, abolished Protestant worship, and introduced a crash program of education in the universities to train a new generation of priests. The one thing that Mary could not achieve was restoration of monastic properties and Church lands: they had been scattered irretrievably and any attempt at confiscation from the landed elite would surely have been met with insurrection. Mary had to be content with reestablishing orthodoxy. She fought fire with fire. Catholic retribution for the blood of their martyrs was not long in coming. Cranmer and three other bishops were burned for heresy, and more than 270 others, mostly commoners, were consigned to the flames.

Nearly 800 Protestants fled the country rather than suffer a similar fate. The Marian exiles, as they came to be called, settled in a number of reformed communities, Zürich, Frankfurt, and Geneva among them. There they imbibed the second generation of Protestant ideas, especially Calvinism, and from there they began a propaganda campaign to keep reformed religion alive in England. It was the Marian exiles who were chiefly responsible for the second English reformation, which began in 1558 when Mary died and her half-sister, Elizabeth I (1558–1603), came to the throne.

Under Elizabeth, England returned to Protestantism. The rapid reversals of established religion were more than disconcerting to laity and clergy alike. Imagine the experience of ordinary churchgoers. For all their lives they had prayed to the Virgin Mary for aid and comfort. One day all images of the Virgin disappeared from the church. The Latin mass was replaced by a whole new English service. Then the Latin mass returned and back came the images of the Virgin. Five years later the Virgin was gone again and the English service was restored. Imagine the plight of a clergyman who questioned the vow of chastity in the 1540s. Prohibited from marrying under Henry VIII, he was encouraged to marry under Edward VI. When Mary came to the throne, he had to put his wife aside and deny the legitimacy of his children. At Elizabeth's accession he was married again—if he could find his wife and if she had not taken another husband. The Elizabethan reforms put an end to those uncertainties.

But what was reestablished was not what had come before. Even the most advanced reforms during Edward's reign now seemed too moderate for the returning exiles. Against Elizabeth's wishes, the English church adopted the Calvinist doctrine of predestination and the simplification (but not wholesale reorganization) of the structure of the church. But it did not become a model of thoroughgoing reformation. The Thirty-nine Articles (1563) continued the English tradition of compromising points of disputed doctrine and of maintaining traditional practices wherever possible. The Calvinism that the exiles learned abroad was more demanding than the Calvinism that the queen practiced at home.

The Reformation of the Radicals

Schism breeds schism. That was the stick with which Catholic Church and civil authorities beat Luther from the beginning. By attacking the authority of the established church and flouting the authority of the established state, he was fomenting social upheaval. It was a charge to which he was particularly sensitive. He insisted that his own ideas buttressed rather than subverted authority, especially civil authority, under whose protection he had placed the Church. As early as 1525, peasants in Swabia appealed to Luther for support in their social rebellion. They based some of their most controversial demands, such as the abolition of tithes and labor service, on biblical authority. Luther offered them no comfort. "Let every person be subject to the governing authorities with fear and reverence," he quoted from the Bible while instructing rebels to lay down their arms and await their just rewards in heaven.

■ This engraving from the *Chronicle of the Peasants' War* by Abbot Murer presents a Catholic interpretation of the peasants' actions as they pillaged the Monastery of Weissenau.

■ Anabaptist leaders persecuted at Münster endured the torture of being confined in cages hung from the church belfry.

But Luther's ideas had a life of their own. He clashed with Erasmus over free will and with Zwingli over the mass. Toward the end of his life he felt he was holding back the floodgates against the second generation of Protestant thinkers. Time and again serious reformers wanted to take one or another of his doctrines further than he was willing to go himself. The water was seeping in everywhere.

The most dangerous threat to the establishment of an orthodox Protestantism came from groups who were described, not very precisely, as **Anabaptists**. *Anabaptist* was a term of abuse. Although it identified people who practiced adult baptism—literally, "baptism again"—the label was mainly used to tar religious opponents with the brush of extremism. For more than a hundred years it defined the outcast from the Protestant fold. New ideas were branded Anabaptist to discredit them; religious enthusiasts were labeled Anabaptists to expel them. Catholics and Protestants both used the term to describe what they were not, and thereby defined what they were.

Anabaptists appeared in a number of German and Swiss towns in the 1520s. Taking seriously the doctrine of justification by faith, Anabaptists argued that only believers could be members of the true church of God. Those who were not of God could not be members of his church. While Catholics, Lutherans, and Calvinists incorporated all members of society into the church, Anabaptists excluded all but true believers. Anabaptists reasoned that baptism was a sacrament for adults rather than infants. Although the practice was as much symbolic as substantive, it was a practice that horrified others. Infant baptism was a core doctrine for both Catholics and Protestants. It was one of only two sacraments that remained in reformed religion. It symbolized the acceptance of Christ, and without it eternal salvation was impossible. Luther, Zwingli, and Calvin agreed that infant baptism was biblical in origin and all wrote vigorously in its defense. It was a doctrine with practical import. Unbaptized infants who died could not be accepted in heaven, and infant mortality was appallingly common.

Thus the doctrine of Anabaptism posed a psychological as well as a doctrinal threat to the reformers. But the practice of adult baptism paled in significance to many of the other conclusions that religious radicals derived from the principle of *sola scriptura*—by the Word alone. Some groups argued the case that since true Christians were only those who had faith, all others must be cast out of the church. Those true Christians formed small separate sects. Many believed that their lives were guided by the Holy Spirit, who directed them from within. Both men and women could give testimony of revelations that appeared to them or of mystical experiences. Some went further and denied the power of civil authority over true believers. They would have nothing to do with the state, refusing to pay taxes, perform military obligations, or give oaths: "The Sword must not be used by Christians even in self-defense. Neither should Christians go to law or undertake magisterial duties." Some argued for the community of goods among believers and rejected private property. Others literally followed passages in the Old Testament that suggested polygamy and promiscuity.

Wherever they settled, the small bands of believers were persecuted to the brutal extent of the laws of heresy. Catholics burned them, Protestants drowned them, and they were stoned and clubbed out of their communities. Although Anabaptists were never a large group within the context of the

Protestant churches, they represented an alternative to mainstream views—whether Lutheran or Calvinist—that was both attractive and persistent. There was enough substance in their ideas and enough sincerity in their patient sufferings that they continued to recruit followers as they were driven from town to town, from Germany into the Swiss cities, from Switzerland into Bohemia and Hungary.

There, on the eastern edges of the Holy Roman Empire, the largest groups of Anabaptists finally settled. Although all practiced adult baptism, only some held goods in common or remained pacifist. Charismatic leaders such as Balthasar Hubmaier (1485–1528) and Jacob Hutter (d. 1536) spread Anabaptism to Moravia in southern Bohemia, where they converted a number of the nobility to their views. They procured land for their communities, which came to be known as the Moravian Brethren. The Moravian Anabaptists ultimately split on the question of pacifism when the advancing Turkish armies posed the problem starkly. Anabaptists remained a target of official persecution, and Hubmaier, Hutter, and a number of other leaders met violent deaths. But the Moravian communities were able to survive and to spread their movement throughout Hungary and Poland. Independent groups existed in England and throughout northwest Europe, where Menno Simons (1496–1561), a Dutch Anabaptist, spent his life organizing bands of followers who came to be known as Mennonites.

THE CATHOLIC REFORMATION

Like a rolling wave, Protestant reform slapped up across the face of Europe, but the rock of the Roman Catholic Church endured. Although pieces of the universal church crumbled away in northern Germany, Switzerland, Bohemia, Scandinavia, England, and Scotland, the dense mass remained in southern Germany, Italy, Poland-Lithuania, Spain, France, and Ireland. Catholics felt the same impulses toward a more

IMAGE DISCOVERY

Fishing for Souls

This allegorical painting by Adriaen van de Velde shows Protestants (on the left) and Catholics (on the right) vying for the souls of Christians. What does the painting indicate about the painter's view of the Reformation? In the water, parties from both banks try to drag men and women into their boats. What might entering a boat signify? The painter's use of fishing boats and water alludes to Jesus' promise to make his fisherman disciples "fishers of men." Would it have been unusual for an early modern painter to use biblical imagery in his work? Do you suppose Adriaen van de Velde would have used biblical imagery if he were not depicting a religious controversy?

fulfilling religious life as did Protestants and complained of the same abuses of clerical, state, and papal powers. But the Catholic response was to reform the Church from within. A new personal piety was stressed, which led to the founding of additional spiritual orders. The ecclesiastical hierarchy became more concerned with pastoral care and initiated reforms of the clergy at the parish level. The challenge of converting other races, Asians and Native Americans especially, led to the formation of missionary orders and to a new emphasis on preaching and education. Protestantism itself revitalized Catholicism. Pope and emperor met the challenge of religious reform with all of the resources at their disposal. If anything, Roman Catholicism was stronger at the end of the era of religious reformation than it had been at the beginning.

The Spiritual Revival

The quest for individual spiritual fulfillment dominated later medieval Roman Catholicism. Erasmus, Luther, and Zwingli were all influenced by a Catholic spiritual movement known as the **New Piety**. It was propagated in Germany by the Brethren of the Common Life, a lay organization that stressed the importance of personal meditation upon the life of Jesus. *The Imitation of Christ* (1427), the central text of the New Piety, commonly attributed to Thomas à Kempis (1379–1471), was among the most influential works of the later Middle Ages, with 70 editions printed before 1500. The Brethren taught that a Christian life should be lived according to Jesus' dictates as expressed in the Sermon on the Mount. They instructed their pupils to lead a simple ascetic life with personal devotion at its core. Those were the lessons that the young Erasmus found so liberating and the young Luther so stifling.

The New Piety, with its emphasis on a simple personal form of religious practice, was a central influence upon Christian humanism. It is important to realize that humanism developed within the context of Catholic education and that many churchmen embraced the new learning and supported educational reform or patronized works of humanist scholarship. The Polyglot Bible, the first new translation project of the sixteenth century, was organized by Cardinal Jiménez de Cisneros (1436–1517), Archbishop of Toledo and Primate of Spain. The greatest educational reformer in England, John Colet (1467–1519), was dean of Saint Paul's, London's cathedral church. Without any of his famed irony, Erasmus dedicated his Greek Bible to the pope. Although they set out to reform education and to provide better texts through which Christian learning could be accomplished, the leading Christian humanists remained within the Catholic Church even after many of their criticisms formed the basis of Protestant reforms.

HEAVENLY VISION

Teresa of Ávila was a Carmelite nun whose life became a model of spirituality for Spanish Catholics in the seventeenth century. She founded a number of monasteries and convents and wrote popular devotional literature. Her autobiography was published after her death.

Focus Questions

How does Teresa explain God's sympathy for humans? How does she see God's manner as different from that of earthly rulers?

My love of, and trust in, our Lord, after I had seen Him in a vision, began to grow, for my converse with Him was so continual. I saw that, though He was God, He was man also; that He is not surprised at the frailties of men; that He understands our miserable nature, liable to fall continually, because of the first sin, for the reparation of which He had come. I could speak to Him as a friend, though He is my Lord, because I do not consider Him as one of our earthly lords, who affect a power they do not possess, who give audience at fixed hours, and to whom only certain persons may speak. If a poor man have any business with these, it will cost him many goings and comings, and currying favour with others, together with much pain and labour before he can speak to them. Ah, if such a one has business with a king! Poor people, not of gentle blood, cannot approach him, for they must apply to those who are his friends; and certainly these are not persons who tread the world under their feet; for they who do this speak the truth, fear nothing, and ought to fear nothing; they are not courtiers, because it is not the custom of a court, where they must be silent about those things they dislike, must not even dare to think about them, lest they should fall into disgrace.

O my Lord! O my King! who can describe Thy Majesty? It is impossible not to see that Thou art Thyself the great Ruler of all, that the beholding of Thy Majesty fills men with awe. But I am filled with greater awe, O my Lord, when I consider Thy humility and the love Thou hast for such as I am. We can converse and speak with Thee about everything whenever we will; and when we lose our first fear and awe at the vision of Thy Majesty, we have a greater dread of offending Thee—not arising out of the fear of punishment, O my Lord, for that is as nothing in comparison with the loss of Thee!

From *The Life of St. Teresa of Ávila* (1611).

The combination of piety and humanism imbued the ecclesiastical reforms initiated by Church leaders. Archbishop Jiménez de Cisneros, who also served as Inquisitor-General of the Spanish Inquisition, undertook a wide-ranging reorganization of Spanish religious life in the late fifteenth century. Although not every project was successful, Jiménez de Cisneros's program took much of the sting out of Protestant attacks on clerical abuse, and there was never a serious Protestant movement in Spain.

The most influential reforming bishop was Gian Matteo Giberti (1495–1543) of Verona. Like Jiménez de Cisneros, Giberti believed that a bishop must be a pastor rather than an administrator. After a period of service in Rome, Giberti returned to live in his diocese and made regular visits to all of its parishes. Using his own frugal life as an example, Giberti rigorously enforced vows, residency, and the pastoral duties of the clergy. "The priests in this diocese are marked men; the unworthy are removed from their offices; the jails are full of their concubines; sermons for the people are preached incessantly and study is encouraged," came the report after one of his tours. He founded almshouses to aid the poor and orphanages to house the homeless. In Verona, Giberti established a printing press, which turned out editions of the central works of Roman Catholicism, especially the writings of Augustine.

The most important indication of the reforming spirit within the Roman Church was the foundation of new religious orders in the early sixteenth century. Devotion to a spiritual life of sacrifice was the chief characteristic of the lay and clerical orders that had flourished throughout the Middle Ages. In one French diocese, the number of clergy quadrupled in the last half of the fifteenth century, and while entrants to the traditional orders of Franciscans and Dominicans did not rise as quickly, the growth of lay communities such as the Brethren of the Common Life attested to the continuing appeal of Catholic devotionalism.

Devotionalism was particularly strong in Italy, where new orders received papal charters. The Capuchins were founded by the Italian peasant Matteo de Bascio (ca. 1495–1552). He sought to follow the strictest rule of the life of Saint Francis of Assisi, a path that even the so-called Observant Franciscans had found too arduous. Bascio won admiration for his charitable works among the poor and the victims of the plague in the late 1520s and ultimately secured approval for the establishment of a small community devoted to penance and good works.

The spiritual revival spread all over Catholic Europe and was not limited to male orders. In Spain, Saint Teresa of Ávila (1515–1582) led the reform of the Carmelites. From an early age she had had mystical visions and had entered a convent near her home. But her real spiritual awakening came when she was 40. She believed that women had to withdraw totally from the world around them in order to achieve true devotion. Against the wishes of the male superiors of her order, she founded a convent to put her beliefs into practice and began writing devotional tracts such as *The Way of Perfection* (1583). Teresa was ultimately granted the right to establish convents throughout Castile, and she supervised the organization of 16 religious houses for women. In 1535, Angela Merici (ca. 1474–1540) established another female order. The Ursulines were one of the most original of the new foundations, composed of young unmarried girls who remained with their families but lived chaste lives devoted to the instruction of other women. The group met monthly and submitted to the discipline of a superior, but otherwise they rejected both the cloistered monastic life and vows. The Ursuline movement, begun in northern Italy, spread into France and helped provide women with education and with moral role models.

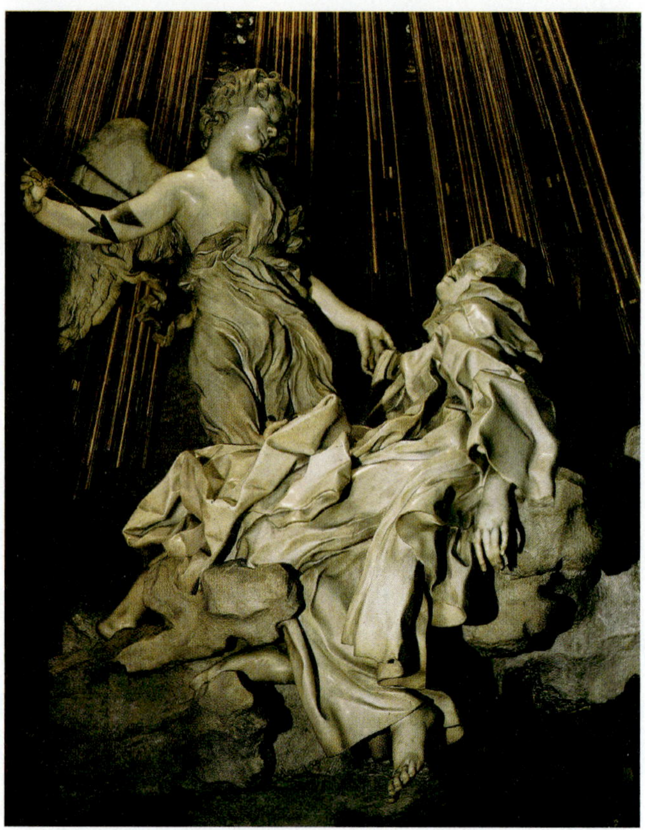

■ Gian Lorenzo Bernini, *The Ecstasy of St. Teresa*. In this work, depicting the ecstatic vision of St. Teresa of Ávila, the sixteenth-century Spanish Carmelite reformer, the saint floats toward heaven on seemingly weightless marble as an angel is about to pierce her breast with a burning arrow. The artist's creation depicts a mystic vision St. Teresa experienced and described in her writings.

Loyola's Pilgrimage

At first sight, Saint Ignatius Loyola (1491–1556) appears an unlikely candidate to lead one of the most vital movements for religious reform in the sixteenth century. The thirteenth child of a Spanish noble family, Loyola trained for a military life in the service of Castile. He began his career as an administrative official and then became a soldier. In 1521, he was one of the garrison defenders when the French besieged Pamplona. A cannonball shattered his leg, and he was carried home for a long enforced convalescence. There he slowly and carefully read the only books in the castle, a life of Jesus and a history of the saints. His reading inspired him. Before he had sought glory and renown in battle. But when he compared the truly heroic deeds of the saints to his own vainglorious exploits, he decided to give his life over to spirituality.

Loyola was not a man to do things by halves. He resolved to model his life on the sufferings of the saints about whom he had read. He renounced his worldly goods and endured a year-long regimen of physical abstinence and spiritual nourishment in the town of Manresa. He deprived himself of food and sleep for long periods and underwent a regimen of seven hours of daily prayer, supplemented by nearly continuous religious contemplation. "But when he went to bed, great enlightenment, great spiritual consolations often came to him, so that he lost much of the time he had intended for sleeping." During that period of intense concentration he first began to have visions, which later culminated in a mystical experience in which Jesus called him directly to his service.

Like Luther, Loyola was tormented by his inability to achieve grace through penance, but unlike Luther he redoubled his efforts. At Manresa, Loyola encountered *The Imitation of Christ,* which profoundly influenced his conversion. He recorded the techniques he used during this vigil in *The Spiritual Exercises,* which became a handbook for Catholic devotion. In 1523, crippled and barefoot, he made a pilgrimage to Jerusalem, where he intended to stay and battle the infidel. But he was dissuaded from that course and returned to Spain intent upon becoming a priest.

By this time, Loyola had adopted a distinctive garb that attracted both followers and suspicion. Twice the Spanish ecclesiastical authorities summoned him to be examined for heresy. In 1528, he decided to complete his studies in France. Education in France brought with it a broadening of horizons that was so important in the movement that Loyola was to found. He entered the same college that Calvin had just left, and it is more than likely that he came into contact with the Protestant and humanist ideas that were then in vogue. Given his own devotional experiences, Protestantism held little attraction. While in France, Loyola and a small group of his friends decided to form a brotherhood after they became priests. They devoted themselves to the cure of souls and took personal vows of poverty, chastity, and obedience to the pope. On a pilgrimage to Rome, Loyola and his followers again attracted the attention of ecclesiastical authorities. Loyola explained his mission to them and in 1540 won the approval of Pope Paul III to establish a new holy order, the Society of Jesus.

DOCUMENT

Ignatius Loyola, Rules for Thinking with the Church

Loyola's Society was founded at a time when the spiritual needs of the Church were being extended beyond the confines of Europe. Loyola volunteered his followers, who came to be known as Jesuits, to serve in the remotest parts of the world, and that offer was soon accepted. One disciple, Francis Xavier (1506–1552), was sent to Portugal, where he embarked on an expedition to the East. For ten years, Xavier made converts to Catholicism in the Portuguese port cities in the East, and then in India and Japan. Other Jesuits became missionaries to the New World, where they offered Christian consolation to the Native American communities. By 1556, the Society of Jesus had grown from 10 to 1000, and Loyola had become a full-time administrator in Rome.

Loyola never abandoned the military images that had dominated his youth. He thought of the world as an all-consuming struggle between the forces of God and Satan: "It is my will to conquer the whole world and all of my enemies." He enlisted his followers in military terms. The Jesuits were "soldiers of God" who served "beneath the banner of the Cross." Loyola's most fundamental innovation in those years

■ Rubens's (1577–1640) *The Miracles of Saint Ignatius Loyola*. Founder of the Society of Jesus, Loyola prepared his Jesuit recruits for an active, rather than a contemplative, life.

was the founding of schools to train recruits for his order. Jesuit training was rigorous. The period of the novitiate was extended and a second period of secular education was added. Since they were being prepared for an active rather than a contemplative life, Jesuits were not cloistered during their training. At first Loyola wanted to train only those who wanted to be missionaries. When that proved impractical, Jesuit schools were opened to the laity and lay education became one of the Jesuits' most important functions. Loyola lived to see the establishment of nearly a hundred colleges and seminaries and the spread of his order throughout the world. He died while at prayer.

The Counter-Reformation

The Jesuits were both the culmination of one wave of Catholic reform and the advance guard of another. They combined the piety and devotion that stretched from medieval mysticism through humanism, diocesan reforms, and the foundations of new spiritual orders. But they also represented an aggressive Catholic response that was determined to meet Protestantism head on and repel it—the **Counter-Reformation**. This was the Church Militant. Old instruments like the Inquisition were revived, and new weapons such as the Index of Prohibited Books were forged. But the problems of fighting Protestantism were not only those of combating Protestant ideas. Like oil and water, politics and religion failed to combine. The emperor and the hierarchy of the German church, where Protestantism was strong, demanded thoroughgoing reform of the Catholic Church; the pope and the hierarchy of the Italian church, where Protestantism was weak, resisted the call. As head of the Catholic Church, the pope was distressed by the spread of heresy in the lands of the empire. As head of a large Italian city-state, the pope was consoled by the weakening of the power of his Spanish rival. Brothers in Christ, pope and emperor were mortal enemies in everything else. Throughout the Catholic states of Germany came the urgent cry for a reforming council of the Church. But the voices were muffled as they crossed the Alps and made their way down the Italian peninsula.

At the instigation of the emperor, the first serious preparations for a general council of the Church were made in the 1530s. The papacy warded it off. The complexities of interna-

CHRONOLOGY

The Reformation and the Counter-Reformation

1517	Luther writes his Ninety-five Theses
1521	Luther is excommunicated and declared an enemy of the empire; Henry VIII receives title Defender of the Faith
1523	Zwingli expounds his faith in formal disputation
1533	Henry VIII divorces Catherine of Aragon, marries Anne Boleyn, and breaks with the church of Rome
1536	Calvin publishes *Institutes of the Christian Religion*
1540	Loyola receives papal approval for Society of Jesus
1545–1563	Council of Trent
1553	Mary I restores Catholicism in England
1563	Elizabeth I enacts the Thirty-nine Articles, which restores Protestantism to England

■ The Council of Trent met from 1545–1563 and corrected a number of abuses of the Church, including the sale of indulgences, and stressed the obligations of priests and bishops to preach to their congregations. No concessions, however, were made to Protestants. This painting is attributed to Titian.

tional diplomacy were one factor—the French king was even less anxious to bring peace to the empire than was the pope—and the complexities of papal politics were another. The powers of a general council in relation to the powers of the papacy had never been clarified. Councils were usually the product of crises, and crises were never the best times to settle constitutional matters. Hard cases make bad law. After the advent and spread of Protestantism, successive popes had little reason to believe that in that gravest crisis of all a council would be mindful of papal prerogatives. In fact, Catholic reformers were as bitter in their denunciations of papal abuses as were Protestants. The second attempt to arrange a general council of the Church occurred in the early 1540s. Again the papacy warded it off.

Those factors ensured that when a general council of the Church did finally meet, its task would not be an easy one. The emperor wanted the council in Germany; the pope wanted it in Italy. The northern churches, French and German alike, wanted reforms of the papacy; the papacy wanted a restatement of orthodox doctrine. The Spanish church wanted reform along the principles set down by Jiménez de Cisneros—for example, that bishops must be made resident in their dioceses. The papacy needed bishops to serve as administrators in Rome. Many princes whose states were divided among Catholics and Protestants wanted compromises that might accommodate both. Ferdinand I, King of Bohemia, saw the council as an opportunity to bring the Hussites back into the fold. He wanted to allow the laity

MAP DISCOVERY

The Religious Divisions of Europe, ca. 1555

Which was the largest religious denomination by the middle of the sixteenth century? Which states were most at risk of internal religious warfare? Notice the difference in the ways in which Lutheranism and Calvinism spread. Where did Catholicism remain untouched by the new religions?

to take both the bread and the wine at communion and the clergy to marry. Charles V and the German bishops wanted the leading Protestant church authorities to offer their own compromises on doctrine that might form a basis for reuniting the empire. The papacy wanted traditional Church doctrine reasserted.

The general council of the Church that finally met in Trent from 1545 to 1563 thus had nearly unlimited potential for disaster. It began in compromise—Trent was an Italian town under the government of the emperor—but ended in total victory for the views of the papacy. For all of the papacy's seeming weaknesses—the defections of England and the rich north German territories cut into papal revenues and Italy was under Spanish occupation—an Italian pope always held the upper hand at the council. Fewer than a third of the delegates came from outside Italy. The French looked upon the council suspiciously and played only a minor role, and the emperor forbade his bishops to attend after the council moved to Bologna. While 270 bishops attended one or another of the council's sessions, 187 of them were Italians.

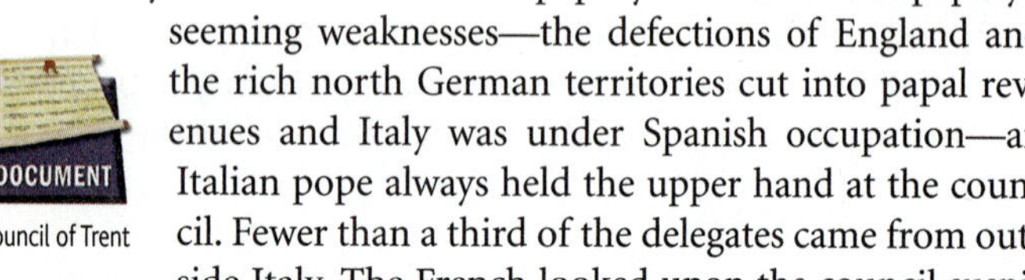

Council of Trent

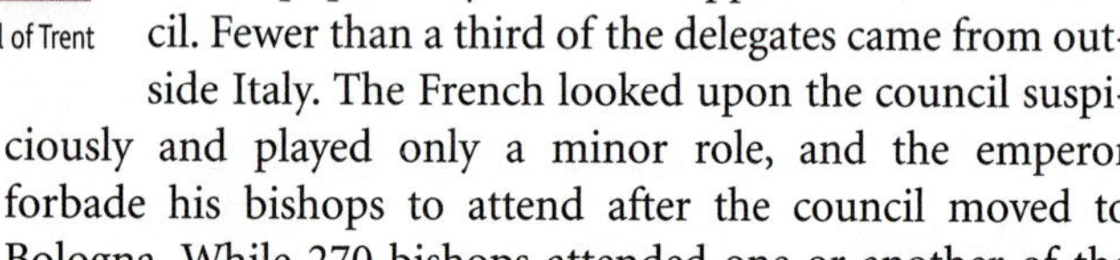

Yet for all of the difficulties, the councillors at Trent made some real progress. They corrected a number of abuses, of which the sale of indulgences was the most substantive. They formulated rules for the better regulation of parish priests and stressed the obligation of priests and bishops to preach to their congregations. Following the work of Jiménez de Cisneros and Giberti, they emphasized the pastoral function of the clergy. On the heels of the success of the Jesuits, they ordered seminaries to be founded in all dioceses where there was not already a university so that priests could receive sufficient education to perform their duties. They prepared a new modern and uniform Catholic service and centralized and updated the Index of Prohibited Books to include Protestant writings from all over the Continent.

The Council of Trent made no concessions whatever to Protestants, moderate or radical. The councillors attempted to turn back every doctrinal innovation of the previous 40 years. Although Protestant theologians attended one of the council's sessions, their views were totally repudiated and efforts at compromise, which were supported by a number of Catholics on the council, were rejected. The councillors upheld justification by faith and works over justification by faith alone. They confirmed the truth of Scripture and the traditions of the Church against Scripture alone. They declared the Vulgate the only acceptable text of the Bible and encouraged vast bonfires of Greek and Hebrew Scriptures in an effort to undo the great scholarly achievements of the humanists. They reaffirmed the seven sacraments and the doctrine of the miracle of the Eucharist. They upheld clerical celibacy. The redefinition of traditional Roman Catholicism drew the doctrinal lines clearly and ended decades of confusion. But it also meant that the differences between Catholics and Protestants could now be settled only by the sword.

The Empire Strikes Back

Warfare dominated the reform of religion almost from its beginning. The burnings, drownings, and executions by which both Catholics and Protestants attempted to maintain religious purity were but raindrops compared to the sea of blood that was shed in sieges and on battlefields beginning in the 1530s. Neither side was capable of waging an all-out war against the other, but they fought intermittently for 25 years. The Catholic divisions were clear. The Holy Roman Empire continued to be engaged in the west with its archenemy France, and in the south with the ever-expanding Ottoman Empire. Charles V needed not only peace within his own German realms, but also positive support for his offensive and defensive campaigns. He could never devote his full resources to suppressing Protestant dissent.

Yet there was never a united Protestant front to suppress. The north German towns and principalities that accepted Lutheranism in the 1520s had had a long history of warfare among themselves. Princes stored up grievances from past wars and contested inheritances; cities stored up jealousies from commercial rivalries and special privileges. Added to that was the division between Luther and Zwingli over doctrinal issues that effectively separated the German and Swiss components of the Reformation from each other. Each faction formed its own political league, and the division almost certainly cost Zwingli his life in 1531, when Zürich was left to stand by itself against imperial allies.

Although both the Protestant and the Catholic sides were internally weak, it was the greater responsibilities of Charles V that allowed for the uneasy periods of peace. Each pause gave the Protestant reformers new life. Lutheranism continued to spread in the northern part of the Holy Roman Empire, and Zwinglian reform in the south. Charles V asked the papacy to convoke a general council and the Protestants to stop evangelizing in new territories. But Protestant leaders were no more capable of halting the spread of the Reformation than were Catholics. Thus each violation of each uneasy truce seemed to prove treachery. In 1546, just after Luther's death, both sides raised armies in preparation for renewed fighting. In the first stage of war, Charles V scored a decisive victory, capturing the two leading Protestant princes and conquering Saxony and Thuringia, the homeland of Lutheran reform.

Religious Diversity in Western Europe

Charles V's greatest victories were always preludes to his gravest defeats. The remaining Protestant princes were driven into the arms of the French, who placed dynastic interests above religious concerns. Again Europe was plunged into general conflict, with the French invading the German states from the west, the Turks from the south, and the Protestant princes from the north. Charles V, now an old and broken man, was forced to flee through the Alps in the dead of winter and was brought to the bargaining table soon after. Through the Peace of Augsburg in 1555, the emperor agreed to allow the princes of Germany to establish the religion of their people. Protestant princes would govern Protestant states, Catholic princes Catholic states. The Peace of Augsburg ended 40 years of religious struggle in Germany.

CONCLUSION

In 1547, the then-victorious Charles V stood at the grave of Martin Luther. Luther had been buried in the shadow of the church in which he had been baptized, and now other shadows darkened his plot. Imperial troops were masters of all Saxony and were preparing to turn back the religious clock in Luther's homeland. The emperor was advised to have Luther's body exhumed and burned to carry out 25 years too late the Edict of Worms that had made Luther an outlaw from church and state. But Charles V was no longer the self-confident young emperor who had been faced down by the Saxon monk on that long-ago day. Popes had come and gone, and his warrior rivals Francis I and Henry VIII were both dead. He alone survived. He had little stomach for the petty revenge that he might now exact upon the man who more than any other had ruined whatever hope there might have been for a united empire dominant over all of Europe. "I do not make war on dead men," Charles declared as he turned away from the reformer's grave. But the ghosts of Luther and Zwingli, of Calvin and Ignatius of Loyola were not so easily laid to rest. For another century, they would haunt a Europe that could do nothing else but make war on dead men.

QUESTIONS FOR REVIEW

1. How did humanism prepare the way for the Protestant Reformation?
2. What motivated Martin Luther?
3. What were the differences among the reforming ideas of Luther, Zwingli, and Calvin?
4. How did the Catholic Church respond to the challenges posed by the Protestant Reformation?

KEY TERMS

Anabaptists, *p. 399*
Christian humanism, *p. 382*
Counter-Reformation, *p. 404*
indulgences, *p. 387*
New Piety, *p. 401*
penance and confession, *p. 387*
predestination, *p. 394*
Reformation, *p. 379*
sola fide, *p. 389*
sola scriptura, *p. 379*

DISCOVERING WESTERN CIVILIZATION ONLINE

You can obtain more information about the reform of religion at the Websites listed below. See also the Companion Website that accompanies this text, www.ablongman.com/kishlansky, which contains an online study guide and additional resources.

The Lutheran Reformation

Lutherstadt Wittenberg, Martin Luther
www.wittenberg.de/e/seiten/personen/luther.html
A site devoted to Martin Luther and the city of Wittenberg. Texts of the famous Ninety-five Theses and other of Luther's writings as well as pictures of locations associated with the Lutheran reformation.

The Protestant Reformation

The Reformation Guide
www.educ.msu.edu/homepages/laurence/reformation/index.htm
The Reformation guide is the best starting place for information about all aspects of the Protestant Reformation. Dozens of links to follow.

Discovery and Reformation
www.wsu.edu/~dee/REFORM/REFORM.HTM
A primarily text-based site created by Washington State University, with profiles of key individuals and explanations of the issues at stake.

Project Wittenberg
www.iclnet.org/pub/resources/text/wittenberg/wittenberg-home.html
The home page of Project Wittenberg, containing a large number of texts (including hymns) by Luther and other Reformers.

Tudor History
tudorhistory.org/
A site with links to a variety of subjects relating to England under the Tudors. Biographies of the kings and queens, bibliographies, maps, and documents.

Reformation Picture Gallery
www.mun.ca/rels/hrollmann/reform/pics/pics.html
Contemporary pictures of leading reformers and the places associated with the Protestant Reformation. Excellent reproductions, especially from woodcuts.

Internet Modern History Sourcebook: Reformation Europe
www.fordham.edu/halsall/mod/modsbook02.html
Sources for both the Reformation and Counter-Reformation with links to other valuable sites.

SUGGESTIONS FOR FURTHER READING

General Reading

Owen Chadwick, *The Reformation* (London: Penguin Books, 1972). An elegant and disarmingly simple history of religious change.

Patrick Collinson, *The Reformation: A History* (New York: Modern Library, 2004). A recent, accessible account of early modern religious upheaval.

Diarmaid MacCulloch, *The Reformation* (London: Viking, 2003). A vastly impressive survey of the Reformation from a leading scholar.

Steven Ozment, *The Age of Reform, 1250–1550* (New Haven, CT: Yale University Press, 1980). An important interpretation of an epoch of religious change.

James D. Tracy, *Europe's Reformations, 1450–1650* (Rowman and Littlefield, 2005). A leading scholar examines intellectual, religious, political, and social processes that provoked religious reform and change.

The Intellectual Reformation

E. Eisenstein, *The Printing Revolution in Early Modern Europe* (Cambridge: Cambridge University Press, 1983). An abridged edition of a larger work that examines the impact of printing upon European society.

Adrian Johns, *The Nature of the Book: Print and Knowledge in the Making* (Chicago: University of Chicago Press, 1998). A major new synthesis with an unusual interpretation.

Anthony Levi, *Renaissance and Reformation: The Intellectual Genesis* (New Haven, CT: Yale, 2004) A new interpretation of European intellectual culture in the early modern period.

R. W. Scribner, *For the Sake of Simple Folk* (Cambridge: Cambridge University Press, 1994). A study of the impact of the Reformation on common people. Especially good on the iconography of reform.

James Tracy, *Erasmus of the Low Countries* (Berkeley: University of California, 1996). A brief biography of the great Dutch humanist.

The Lutheran Reformation

Roland Bainton, *Here I Stand* (New York: New American Library, 1968). The single most compelling biography of Luther.

Bernd Moeller, *Imperial Cities and the Reformation* (Durham, NC: Labyrinth Press, 1982). A central work that defines the connection between Protestantism and urban reform.

Heiko Oberman, *Luther: Man Between God and the Devil* (New York: Doubleday, 1992). English translation of one of the best German biographies of Luther. Sets Luther within the context of late medieval spirituality.

G. R. Potter, *Huldrych Zwingli* (New York: St. Martin's Press, 1984). A difficult but important study of the great Swiss reformer.

Lyndal Roper, *The Holy Household: Women and Morals in Reformation Augsburg* (Oxford: Oxford University Press, 1991). The best work to show the impact of the Reformation on family life and women.

R. W. Scribner, *The German Reformation* (Atlantic Highlands, NJ: Humanities Press, 1986). An excellent introduction, especially to the social history of the Reformation.

The Protestant Reformation

G.W. Bernard, *The King's Reformation: Henry VIII and the Remaking of the English Church* (New Haven, CT: Yale, 2005). An account of the decisive event in early modern English history, emphasizing King Henry's personal desire for reformed religion.

William Bouwsma, *John Calvin* (Oxford: Oxford University Press, 1988). A study that places Calvin within the context of the social and intellectual movements of the sixteenth century.

Claus-Peter Clasen, *Anabaptism, A Social History, 1525–1618* (Ithaca, NY: Cornell University Press, 1972). An important study of the Anabaptist movement.

A. G. Dickens, *The English Reformation,* 2d ed. (London: Batsford, 1989). The classic study of reform in England.

Peter Marshall, *Reformation England, 1480–1642* (Hodder Arnold, 2003). A lucid and thoughtful narrative of religious change in early modern England.

J. J. Scarisbrick, *Henry VIII* (Berkeley: University of California Press, 1968). The classic biography of the larger-than-life monarch.

The Catholic Reformation

Jean Delumeau, *Catholicism Between Luther and Voltaire* (Philadelphia: Westminster Press, 1977). An important reinterpretation of the Counter-Reformation.

Carlos Eire, *From Madrid to Purgatory* (Cambridge: Cambridge University Press, 1995). A brilliant study of the Spanish culture of death during the Counter-Reformation.

W. W. Meissner, *Ignatius of Loyola: The Psychology of a Saint* (New Haven, CT: Yale University Press, 1994). A searching study of the founding spirit of the Counter-Reformation.

John W. O'Malley, *Trent and All That: Renaming Catholicism in the Early Modern Era* (Cambridge, MA: Harvard University Press, 2000). A re-examination of Catholicism in the century surrounding the Council of Trent.

A. D. Wright, *The Counter-Reformation* (New York: St. Martin's Press, 1984). A comprehensive survey.

For a list of additional titles related to this chapter's topics, please see http://www.ablongman.com/kishlansky.

CHAPTER 14

EUROPE AT WAR, 1555–1648

THE MASSACRE OF THE INNOCENTS

WAR AND EUROPEAN SOCIETY

THE VISUAL RECORD

"War is one of the scourges with which it has pleased God to afflict men," wrote Cardinal Richelieu (1585–1642), the French minister who played no small part in spreading the scourge. War was a constant of European society and penetrated to its very core. It dominated all aspects of life. It enhanced the power of the state; it defined gender roles; it consumed lives, treasure, and commodities ravenously. War affected every member of society from combatants to civilians. There were no innocent bystanders. Grain in the fields was destroyed because it was food for soldiers; houses were burned because they provided shelter for soldiers. Civilians were killed for aiding the enemy or holding out against demands for their treasure and supplies. Able-bodied men were taken forcibly to serve as conscripts, leaving women to plant and harvest as best they could.

There was nothing new about war in the middle of the sixteenth century. The early part of the century had witnessed the dynastic struggle between the Habsburgs and the House of Valois as well as the beginnings of the religious struggle between Catholics and Protestants. But the wars that dominated Europe from 1555 to 1648 brought together the worst of both of the conflicts. War was fought on a larger scale, it was more brutal and more expensive, and it claimed more victims, civilians and combatants alike. During this century, war extended throughout the Continent. Dynastic strife, rebellion, and international rivalries joined together with the ongoing struggle over religion. Ambition and faith were an explosive mixture. The French endured 40 years of civil war; the Spanish 80 years of fighting with the Dutch. The battle for hegemony in the east led to dynastic strife for decades on end as Poles, Russians, and Swedes pressed their rival claims to each other's crowns. Finally, in 1618, the separate theaters of war came together in one of the most brutal and terrifying episodes of destruction in European history: the Thirty Years' War.

Neither the ancient temple nor the Roman costume can conceal the immediacy of the picture shown here. It is as painful to look at now as it was when it was created more than 375 years ago. Painted by Nicolas Poussin (1594–1665) at the height of the Thirty Years' War, *The Massacre of the Innocents* remains a horrifying composition of power, terror, and despair. The cruel and senseless slaughter of the innocent baby that is about to take place is echoed throughout the canvas. In the background between the executioner's legs can be seen a mother clasping her own child tightly and anticipating the fall of the sword. In the background on the right, another mother turns away from the scene and carries her infant to safety. In the foreground strides a mother holding her dead child. She tears at her hair and cries in anguish. To a culture in which the image of mother and child—of Mary and Jesus—was one of sublime peacefulness and inexpressible joy, the contrast could hardly be more shocking.

The picture graphically displays the cruelty of the soldier, the helplessness of the child, and the horror of the mother. By his grip on the mother's hair and his foot on the baby's throat, the warrior shows his brute power. The mother's futile effort to stop the sword illustrates her powerlessness. She scratches uselessly at the soldier's back. Naked, the baby boy raises his hands as if to surrender to the inevitable, as if to reinforce his innocence.

To study Europe at war, we must enter into a world of politics and diplomacy, of issues and principles, of judgment and error. We must talk about armies in terms of their cost and numbers, of generals in terms of their strategy and tactics, and of battles in terms of winners and losers. There can be no doubt that the future of Europe was decisively shaped by the century of wholesale slaughter during which dynastic and religious fervor finally ran its course.

LOOKING AHEAD

As we will see in this chapter, warfare in the seventeenth century decisively reshaped power relations of families and states. Protestantism survived after nearly a century of military challenge, and the power of the great Habsburg dynasty was finally crushed. In its place rose France, England, and Holland, and a new chapter of European conflict began.

■ Nicolas Poussin, *The Massacre of the Innocents* (1632–1634).

CHAPTER OUTLINE

- THE CRISES OF THE WESTERN STATES
  The French Wars of Religion ▪ One King, Two Faiths ▪ The World of Philip II ▪ The Burgundian Inheritance ▪ The Revolt of the Netherlands
- THE STRUGGLES IN EASTERN EUROPE
  Kings and Diets in Poland ▪ Muscovy's Time of Troubles ▪ The Rise of Sweden
- THE THIRTY YEARS' WAR, 1618–1648
  Bohemia Revolts ▪ The War Widens ▪ The Long Quest for Peace

THE CRISES OF THE WESTERN STATES

"Un roi, une foi, une loi"—one king, one faith, one law. That was a prescription that members of all European states accepted without question in the sixteenth century. Society was an integrated whole, equally dependent upon monarchical, ecclesiastical, and civil authority for its effective survival. A European state could no more tolerate the presence of two churches than it could the presence of two kings. But the Reformation had created two churches.

In Germany, where the problem first arose, the Peace of Augsburg (1555) enacted the most logical solution. The religion of the ruler was to be the religion of the subjects. Princes, town governments, and bishops would determine faith. Not surprisingly, the policy was more convenient for rulers than for the ruled. Sudden conversions of princes, a hallmark of Protestantism, threw the state into disarray. Those closely identified with Catholicism and those who firmly believed in its doctrines had no choice but to move to a neighboring Catholic community and begin again. Given the dependence of ordinary people upon networks of kin and neighbors, enforced migration was devastating. Protestant minorities in Catholic states suffered the same fate. The enmity between the two groups came as much from bitter experience as from differences of belief.

Thus compromises that might have brought Protestants back into a reformed Catholic Church were doomed from the start. Doomed too was the practical solution of toleration. To the modern mind, toleration seems so logical that it is difficult to understand why it took over a century of bloodshed before it came to be grudgingly accepted by those countries most bitterly divided. But toleration was not a practical solution in a society that admitted no principle of organization other than one king, one faith. In such a world, toleration was even more threatening than warfare. Pope Clement VIII (1592–1605) described liberty of conscience as "the worst thing in the world." Those who advocated limited forms of toleration were universally despised. Those occasions during which toleration was a reluctant basis for a cease-fire were moments for catching breath before resuming the struggle for total victory. Only Poland-Lithuania, Hungary, and a few German states experimented with religious toleration during the sixteenth century.

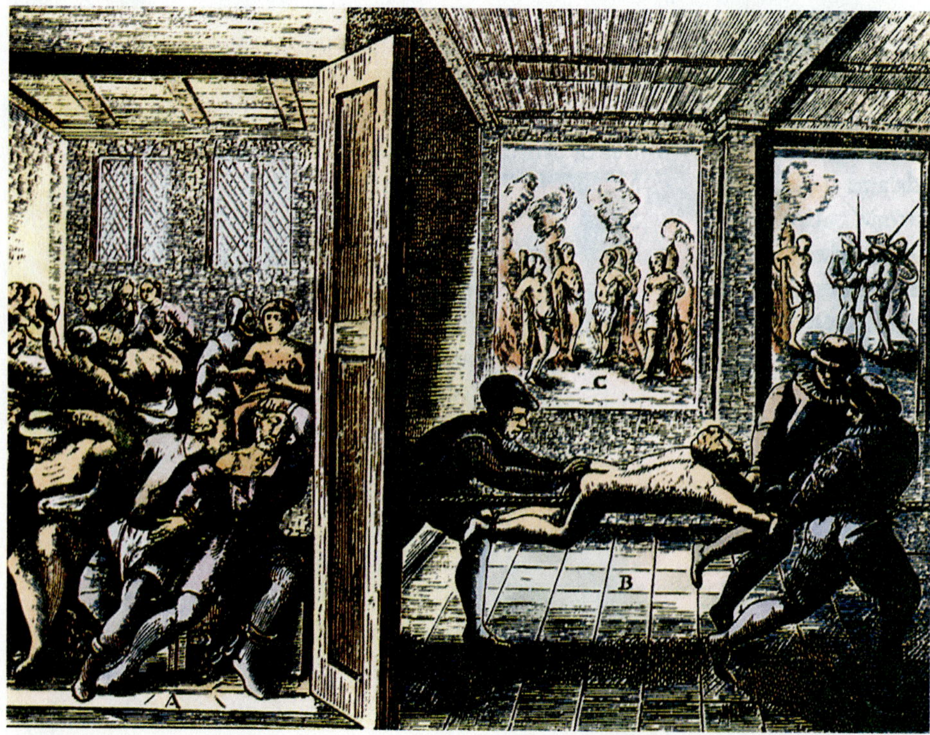

▪ This scene depicts the mistreatment of French Catholics by the Protestants in the town of Angoulême. They were deprived of all nourishment, dragged over a taut rope, and then slowly roasted at the stake.

The crises of the western European states that stretched from the middle of the sixteenth century to the middle of the seventeenth were as much internal and domestic as they were external and international. In France, a half century of religious warfare sapped the strength of both the monarchy and the nation. In Spain, the protracted revolt of the Netherlands drained men, money, and spirit from the most powerful nation in Europe. Decades of intermittent warfare turned the golden age of Spain to lead and hastened the decline of the Spanish Empire. Each crisis had its own causes and its own history. Yet it was no coincidence that they occurred together or that they starkly posed the conflict between the authority of the state and the conscience of the individual. The century between the Peace of Augsburg (1555) and the Peace of Westphalia (1648) was the century of total war.

The French Wars of Religion

No wars are more terrible than civil wars. They tear at the very fabric of society, rending its institutions and destroying the delicate web of relationships that underlie all communal life. The nation is divided; communities break into factions; families are destroyed. Civil wars are wars of passion. Issues become elevated into causes and principles that form the rallying cry of heroic self-sacrifice or wanton destruction. Civil wars feed on themselves. Each act of war becomes an outrage to be revenged, each act of revenge a new outrage. Passions run deep and, however primitive, the rules for the civilized conduct of war are quickly broken. The loss of lives and property is staggering, but the loss of communal identity is greater still. Generations pass before societies recover from their civil wars. Such was the case with the **French wars of religion.**

The Spread of Calvinism and Religious Division. Protestantism came late to France. It was not until after Calvin reformed the church in Geneva and began to export his brand of Protestantism that French society began to divide along religious lines. By 1560 there were more than 2000 Protestant congregations in France, whose membership totaled nearly 10 percent of the French population. Calvin and his successors concentrated their efforts on large provincial towns and had their greatest success among the middle ranks of urban society—merchants, traders, and artisans. They also found a receptive audience among aristocratic women, who eventually converted their husbands and their sons.

The wars of religion, however, were brought on by more than the rapid spread of Calvinism. Equally important was the vacuum of power that had been created when Henry II

CHRONOLOGY

The French Wars of Religion

1559	Death of Henry II
1560	Protestant duc de Condé sentenced to death
1562	First battle of French wars of religion
1563	Catholic duc de Guise assassinated
1572	Saint Bartholomew's Day Massacre
1574	Accession of Henry III
1576	Formation of Catholic League
1584	Death of duc d'Anjou makes Henry of Navarre heir to throne
1585	War of the three Henrys
1588	Duc de Guise murdered by order of Henry III
1589	Catherine de Médicis dies; Henry III assassinated
1594	Henry IV crowned
1598	Edict of Nantes

MAP DISCOVERY

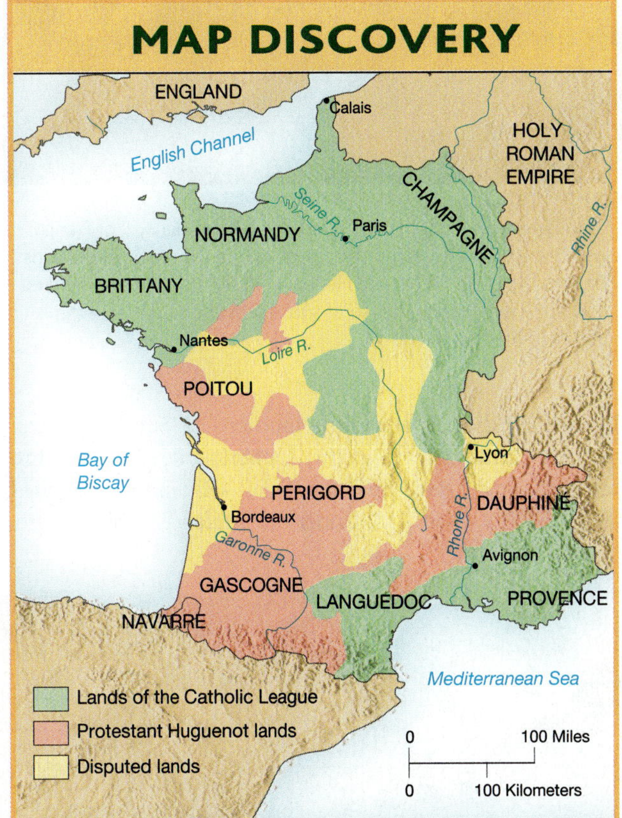

Religious Divisions in France During the Wars of Religion

What was the dominant religion of France? Notice the relationship between the location of Paris and the Huguenot strongholds. Based on region of influence, which religion controlled trade with England and in the Mediterranean?

■ Catherine de Médicis (1519–1598), the wife of Henry II of France, was the real power behind the throne during the reigns of her sons Charles IX (1560–1574) and Henry III (1574–1589). Her overriding concern was to ensure her sons' succession and to preserve the power of the monarchy.

(1547–1559) died in a jousting tournament. Surviving Henry were his extraordinary widow, Catherine de Médicis, three daughters, and four sons, the oldest of whom, Francis II (1559–1560), was only 15. Under the influence of his beautiful young wife, Mary, Queen of Scots, Francis II allowed the Guise family to dominate the great offices of state and to exclude their rivals from power. The Guises controlled the two most powerful institutions of the state, the army and the Church.

The Guises were staunchly Catholic, and among their enemies were the Bourbons, princes of the blood with a direct claim to the French throne but also a family with powerful Protestant members. The revelation of a Protestant plot to remove the king from Paris provided the Guises with an opportunity to eliminate their most potent rivals. The Bourbon duc de Condé, the leading Protestant peer of the realm, was sentenced to death. But five days before Condé's execution, Francis II died and Guise power evaporated. The new king, Charles IX (1560–1574), was only ten years old and firmly under the grip of his mother, Catherine de Médicis, who now declared herself regent of France. (See "A Closer Look: The Monstrous Regiment of Women," pp. 416–417.)

Civil War. Condé's death sentence convinced him that the Guises would stop at nothing to gain their ambitions. Force would have to be met with force. Protestants and Catholics alike raised armies, and in 1562 civil war erupted. Once the wars began, the leading Protestant peers fled the court, but the position of the Guises was not altogether secure. Henry Bourbon, king of Navarre, was the next in line to succeed to the throne should Charles IX and his two brothers die without male heirs. Henry had been raised in the Protestant faith by his mother, Jeanne d'Albret, whose own mother, Marguerite of Navarre, was among the earliest protectors of the French Protestants. The objectives of the **Huguenots,** as the French Calvinists came to be called, were less clear-cut. The townspeople wanted the right to practice their faith, the clergy wanted the right to preach and make converts, and the nobility wanted their rightful place in local government. Almost from the beginning, the Huguenots were on the defensive, fighting to preserve what they already had and to avoid annihilation.

The inconclusive nature of the early battles might have allowed for the pragmatic solution sought by Catherine de

■ Painting of the Saint Bartholomew's Day Massacre. The massacre began in Paris on 24 August 1572, and the violence soon spread throughout France.

Médicis had it not been for the assassination of the duc de Guise in 1563 by a Protestant fanatic. That act added a personal vendetta to the religious passions of the Catholic leaders. They encouraged the slaughter of Huguenot congregations and openly planned the murder of Huguenot leaders. Protestants gave as good as they got. In open defiance of Valois dynastic interests, the Guises courted support from Spain, while the Huguenots imported Swiss and German mercenaries to fight in France. Noble factions and irreconcilable religious differences were pulling the government apart.

The Saint Bartholomew's Day Massacre. By 1570 Catherine was ready to attempt another reconciliation. She announced her plans for a marriage between her daughter Margaret and Henry of Navarre, a marriage that would symbolize the spirit of conciliation between the crown and the Huguenots. The marriage was to take place in Paris during August 1572. The arrival of Huguenot leaders from all over France to attend the marriage ceremony presented an opportunity of a different kind to the Guises and their supporters. If leading Huguenots could be assassinated in Paris, the Protestant cause might collapse and the truce that the wedding signified might be turned instead into a Catholic triumph.

Massacre of St. Bartholomew

Saint Bartholomew was the apostle that Jesus described as a man without guile. Ironically, it was on his feast day that the Huguenots who had innocently come to celebrate Henry's marriage were led like lambs to the slaughter. On 24 August 1572, the streets of Paris ran red with Huguenot blood. Although frenzied, the slaughter was inefficient. Henry of Navarre and a number of other important Huguenots escaped the carnage and returned to their urban strongholds. In the following weeks, the violence spread from Paris to the countryside and thousands of Protestants paid for their beliefs with their lives. Until the French Revolution, no event in French history would evoke as much passion as the memory of the Saint Bartholomew's Day Massacre.

One King, Two Faiths

The Saint Bartholomew's Day Massacre was a transforming event in many ways. In the first place, it prolonged the wars. A whole new generation of Huguenots now had an emotional attachment to the continuation of warfare: their fathers and brothers had been mercilessly slaughtered. By itself, the event was shocking enough; in the atmosphere of anticipated reconciliation created by the wedding, it screamed out for revenge. And the target for retaliation was no longer limited to the Guises and their followers. By accepting the results of the massacre, the monarchy sanctioned it and spilled Huguenot blood on itself. For more than a decade, Catherine de Médicis had maintained a distance between the crown and the leaders of the Catholic movement. That distance no longer existed.

GENEALOGY

The Houses of Valois and Bourbon of France

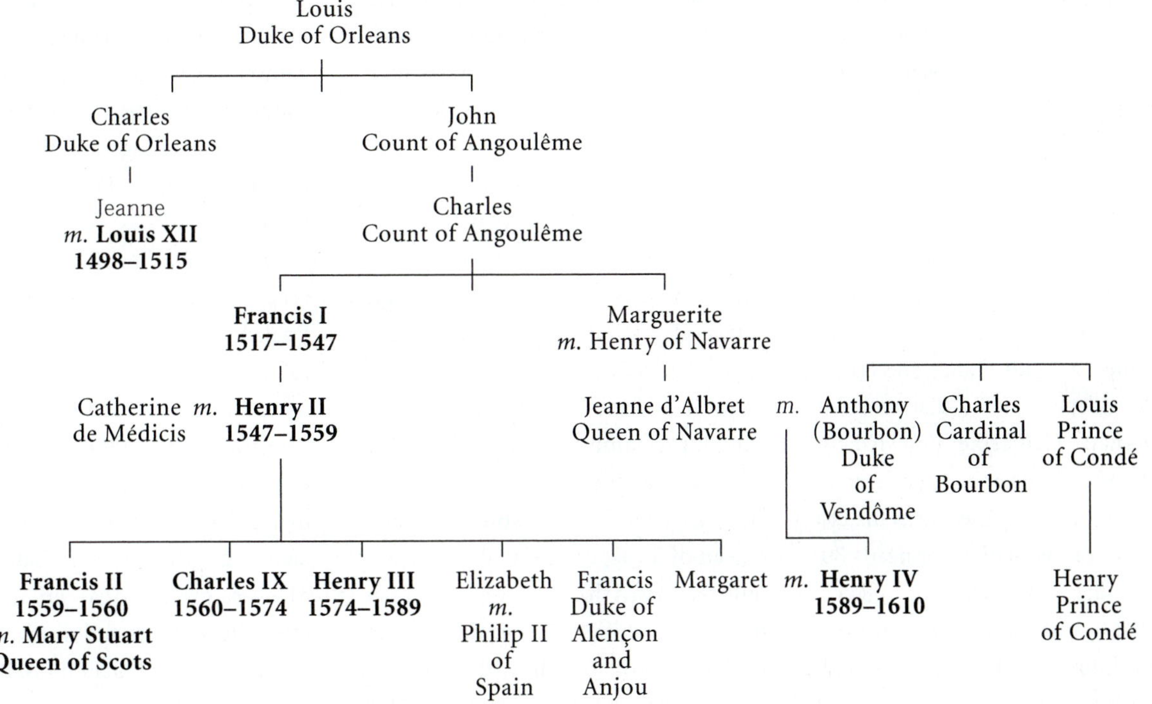

THE MONSTROUS REGIMENT OF WOMEN

A CLOSER LOOK

"To promote a woman to bear rule, superiority, dominion or empire above any realm, nation, or city is repugnant to nature, contumely to God, and the subversion of good order, of all equity and justice." So wrote the Scottish theologian John Knox (1513–1572) in *The First Blast of the Trumpet Against the Monstrous Regiment of Women* (1558). Although he made his points more emphatically than many others, Knox was only repeating the commonplace notions of his day. He could quote Aristotle and Aquinas as well as a host of secular authorities to demonstrate female inadequacies: "Nature, I say, doth paint them forth to be weak, frail, impatient, feeble, and foolish." He could quote Saint Paul along with the ancient Fathers of the Church to demonstrate the "proper" place of women—"Man is not of the woman, but the woman of the man."

But no stacking up of authorities, no matter how numerous or revered, could erase the fact that all over Europe in the sixteenth century women could and did rule. In the Netherlands, Mary, Queen of Hungary (1531–1552), and Margaret of Parma (1559–1567) were successful regents. Jeanne d'Albret (1562–1572) was queen of the tiny state of Navarre, territory claimed by both France and Spain but kept independent by that remarkable woman. Catherine de Médicis (1560–1589), wife of one king of France and mother of three others, was the effective ruler of that nation for nearly 30 years. Mary, Queen of Scots (1542–1587), was the nominal ruler of Scotland almost from her birth. England was ruled by two very different women, the Catholic Mary I (1553–1558) and her Protestant half-sister Elizabeth I (1558–1603).

The problems faced by this long list of queens and regents were more than just the ordinary cares of government. The belief that women were inherently inferior in intelligence, strength, and character was so pervasive that, for men like Knox, a woman ruler was almost a contradiction in terms. Yet this was not the view taken by everyone, and female rule had its defenders as well as its detractors. One set of objections was overcome by the traditional medieval theory of the two bodies of the monarch. That argument was developed to reconcile the divine origins and functions of monarchs with their very real human frailties. In the theory of the two bodies, there was the body natural and the body politic. Both were joined together in the person of the ruler, but the attributes of each could be separated. Rule of a woman did nothing to disrupt this notion. In fact, it made it easier to argue that the frailties of the body natural of a woman were in no way related to the strengths of the body politic of a monarch.

While such ideas might help a female ruler win the acceptance of her subjects, they did little to invigorate her own sense of her role. Female rulers often strained against the straitjacket that definitions of gender placed them in. When angered, Elizabeth I would proclaim that she had more courage than her father, Henry VIII, "though I am only a woman." Mary, Queen of Scots, once revealed that her only regret was that she "was not a man to know what life it was to lie all night in the fields or to walk with a buckler and a broadsword." Some queens assumed masculine traits, riding in armor or leading forces to battle. Elizabeth's presence in armor at the threat of the landing of the Spanish Armada was viewed as one of the heroic moments of her reign. Other women rulers combined characteristics that were usually separated by gender definitions. Margaret of Parma was considered one of the most accomplished horse riders of her day. After leading her courtiers through woods and fields at breakneck speed, she would then attend council meetings and work on her needlepoint. Mary, Queen of Scots, loved hawking, a traditional kingly sport, in the Scottish wilds. After relishing the hawk's destruction of its prey, she liked to negotiate matters of state by beginning with tears and entreaties and ending with accusations and threats. The effect was more than disconcerting.

Women were no more or less successful as rulers than were men. Women's achievements, like men's, depended upon strength of character and the circumstances of the times. All the women rulers of the sixteenth century had received outstanding educations. Whether raised Catholic or Protestant, each was trained in Latin as well as modern languages, in the liberal arts, and in fine arts. Mary and Elizabeth Tudor of England wrote poetry and played musical instruments with considerable accomplishment. Mary, Queen of Scots, who was raised at the court of France, was considered particularly apt at learning, praise not often accorded a foreigner by the French. Catherine de Médicis, orphaned as an infant, was raised in convents and instructed in the new learning by Italian nuns. It was said that her political instincts were in her blood: Machiavelli had dedicated *The Prince* to her father. Marguerite of Navarre chose one of the leading French humanists to supervise the training of her daughter, Jeanne d'Albret.

Mary, Queen of Scots, was the only one of the female rulers born to rule. She was the sole survivor of her father, who died shortly after her birth. Mary and Elizabeth Tudor came to their thrones after the death of their younger brother Edward VI; Mary of Hungary and Margaret of Parma came to theirs as princesses of the House of Habsburg. The rule of Catherine de Médicis was the most unexpected of all. Her vigorous husband, Henry II, died during a jousting tournament, and her eldest son, Francis II, husband of Mary, Queen of Scots, died the following year. Instead of retirement as a respected queen dowager (the widow of a previous king), Catherine de Médicis was forced into the vortex of French politics to protect the rights of her ten-year-old son, Charles IX.

The Latin inscription in this portrait of Mary, Queen of Scots, indicates that it was painted when she had been a prisoner in England for ten years.

For most of the queens and regents, marriage was of central importance to their position. Both Mary, Queen of Hungary, and Mary, Queen of Scots, married kings whose reigns were exceedingly brief. Lewis of Hungary died at the battle of Mohács in 1526, just four years after Mary had become his queen. Mary, Queen of Scots, was widowed even sooner, and throughout the rest of her remarkable career schemed to remarry. To strengthen her claim to the throne of England, she married the Scottish Lord Darnley. When he proved unsatisfactory to her plans, she plotted his murder and then married one of his assassins. When that husband died, she sought a match with a powerful English lord who might help her capture Elizabeth's throne. The intrigues finally led to her execution in England in 1587. Mary Tudor married Philip II of Spain in hope of reestablishing Catholicism in England through a permanent alliance with the most powerful Catholic state in Europe. Her dreams went unfulfilled when she failed to produce an heir, and the throne passed to her sister, Elizabeth, who, alone among the women rulers of the period, did not marry.

Unfortunately, the accomplishments of women rulers did little to dispel prejudices against women as a whole or to alter the definition of gender roles. Except for Mary, Queen of Scots, whose principal achievement was to provide an heir to the English throne, all the queens and regents of the sixteenth century were successful rulers. Margaret of Parma steered the careful middle course in the conflict between Spain and the Netherlands. She opposed the intervention of the Duke of Alba, and, had her advice been followed, the 80 years of war between Spain and the Netherlands might have been avoided. Catherine de Médicis held the crown of France on the heads of her sons, navigated the treacherous waters of civil war, and provided the model for religious toleration that finally was adopted in the Edict of Nantes. Elizabeth I of England became one of the most beloved rulers in that nation's history. A crafty politician who learned to balance the factions at her court and who turned the aristocracy into a service class for the crown, she brought nearly a half century of stability to England at a time when the rest of Europe was in flames.

The Theory of Resistance. The Huguenots could not continue to maintain the fiction that they were fighting against the king's evil advisers rather than against the king. After Saint Bartholomew's Day, Huguenot theorists began to develop the idea that resistance to a monarch whose actions violated divine commandments or civil rights was lawful. For the first time, Huguenot writers provided a justification for rebellion. Perhaps most importantly, a genuine revulsion against the massacres swept the nation. A number of Catholic peers now joined with the Huguenots to protest the excesses of the crown and the Guises. Those Catholics came to be called **politiques** from their desire for a practical settlement of the wars. They were led by the duc d'Anjou, next in line to the throne after Henry III (1574–1589) became king.

Against them, in Paris and a number of other towns, the **Catholic League** was formed, a society that pledged its first allegiance to religion. The League took up where the Saint Bartholomew's Day Massacre left off, and the slaughter of ordinary people who unluckily professed the wrong religion continued. Matters grew worse in 1584, when Anjou died. With each passing year it was becoming apparent that Henry III would produce no male heir. After Anjou's death, the Huguenot Henry of Navarre was the next in line for the throne. Catholic Leaguers talked openly of altering the royal succession and began to develop theories of lawful resistance to monarchical power. By 1585, when the final civil war began—the war of the three Henrys, named for Henry III, Henry Guise, and Henry of Navarre—the crown was in the weakest possible position. Paris and the Catholic towns were controlled by the League, the Protestant strongholds by Henry of Navarre. King Henry III could not abandon his capital or his religion, but neither could he gain control of the Catholic party. The extremism of the Leaguers kept the politiques away from court, and without the politiques, there could be no settlement.

In December 1588, Henry III summoned Henry Guise and Guise's brother to a meeting in the royal bedchamber. There they were murdered by the king's order. The politiques were blamed for the murders—revenge was taken on a number of them—and Henry III was forced to flee his capital. Paris was still firmly in the hands of the League, and Henry was in danger of becoming a king without a country. He made a pact with Henry of Navarre, and together royalist and Huguenot forces besieged Paris. All supplies were cut off from the city and only the arrival of a Spanish army prevented its fall. In 1589, Catherine de Médicis died, her ambition to reestablish the authority of the monarchy in shambles, and in the same year a fanatic priest gained revenge for the murder of the Guises by assassinating Henry III.

Henry IV. Now Henry of Navarre came into his inheritance. After nearly 30 years of continuous civil war, it was certain that a Huguenot could never rule France. The League had already proclaimed a Catholic rival as king, and the pope excommunicated Henry of Navarre and absolved France from loyalty to him. If Henry was to become king of all France, he would have to become a Catholic king. It is not clear when Henry made the decision to accept the Catholic faith—"Paris is worth a mass," he reportedly declared—but he did not announce his decision at once. Rather he strengthened his forces, tightened his bonds with the politiques, and urged his countrymen to expel the Spanish invaders. He finally made his conversion public and in 1594 was crowned Henry IV (1589–1610). A war-weary nation was willing to accept the sincerity of its new king rather than endure a seemingly endless struggle. Most of the leading peers on both sides were nearly bankrupt, and Henry IV was willing to pay large cash settlements to all those who would return to their estates and pledge allegiance to him.

■ Although Henry IV probably never said, "Paris is worth a mass," his conversion to Roman Catholicism, depicted here, was instrumental in securing his kingship and ending the French wars of religion.

In 1598, Henry proclaimed the **Edict of Nantes,** which granted limited toleration to the Huguenots. It was the culmination of decades of attempts to find a solution to the existence of two religions in one state. It was a compromise that satisfied no one, but it was a compromise that everyone could accept. One king, two faiths was as apt a description of Henry IV as it was of the settlement. Yet neither Henry's conversion nor the Edict of Nantes stilled the passions that had spawned and sustained the French wars of religion. Sporadic fighting between Catholics and Huguenots continued, and fanatics on both sides fanned the flames of religious hatred. Henry IV survived 18 attempts on his life before he was finally felled by an assassin's knife in 1610, but by then he had reestablished the monarchy and brought a semblance of peace to France.

The World of Philip II

By the middle of the sixteenth century, Spain was the greatest power in Europe. The dominions of Philip II (1556–1598) of Spain stretched from the Atlantic to the Pacific; his continental territories included the Netherlands in the north and Milan and Naples in Italy. In 1580, Philip became king of Portugal, uniting all the states of the Iberian peninsula. With the addition of Portugal's Atlantic ports and its sizable fleet, Spanish maritime power was now unsurpassed. Spain was also a great cultural and intellectual center. The fashions and tastes of its golden age dominated all the courts of Europe.

Great power meant great responsibilities, and few monarchs took their tasks more seriously than did Philip II. Trained from childhood for the cares of office, he exceeded all expectations. Philip II earned his reputation as "King of Paper" by maintaining a grueling work schedule. Up at eight and at mass soon afterward, he met with his advisers and visitors on official business until noon. After a brief lunch, he began the real business of the day, the study of the mountains of papers that his empire generated. Although summaries were prepared of the hundreds of documents he handled each day, Philip II frequently read and annotated the longer originals. No detail was too small to escape his attention. His workday often lasted ten hours or longer. Even when he was traveling, his secretaries carried huge chests of state papers that Philip studied in his carriage and annotated on a portable desk that always accompanied him.

There was good reason why the slightly stooped king appeared as if he had the weight of the world on his shoulders. In the Mediterranean, Spain alone stood out against the expansion of Ottoman power. The sultan's navy continually threatened to turn the Mediterranean into a Turkish lake, while his armies at-

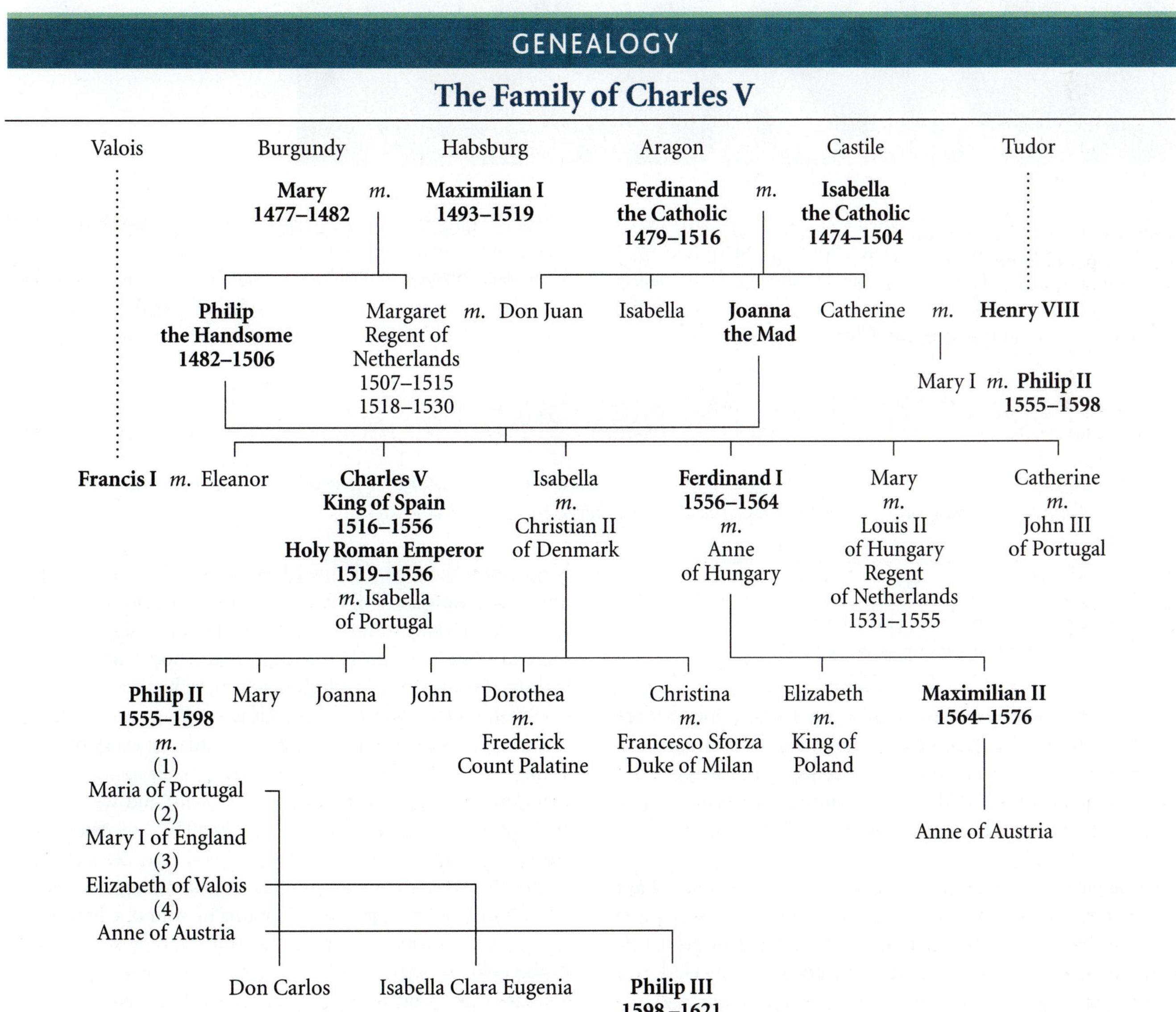

This image depicts the clash of the once-feared Spanish Armada and the English navy in 1588. The defeat of the Spanish Armada dealt a serious blow to Spain's standing in Europe.

tempted to capture and hold Italian soil. All Europe shuddered at the news of each Ottoman advance. Popes called for holy wars against the Turks, but only Philip heeded the cry. From nearly the moment that he inherited the Spanish crown, he took up the challenge of defending European Christianity. For more than a decade, Philip maintained costly coastal garrisons in North Africa and Italy and assembled large fleets and larger armies to discourage or repel Turkish invasions. The sparring could not go on indefinitely, and in 1571 both sides prepared for a decisive battle. A combined Spanish and Italian force of more than 300

THE HEART AND STOMACH OF A KING

In 1588 Queen Elizabeth rallied her subjects to oppose the invasion of England by the mighty Spanish Armada. This is part of the speech she made before the troops that were gathered in Kent.

Focus Questions

What are the images that Elizabeth uses to appeal to her people? Why does she compare herself to a king?

My loving people, we have been persuaded by some, that are careful of our safety, to take heed how we commit ourselves to armed multitudes, for fear of treachery; but I assure you, I do not desire to live to distrust my faithful and loving people. Let tyrants fear; I have always so behaved myself that, under God, I have placed my chiefest strength and safeguard in the loyal hearts and good will of my subjects. And therefore I am come amongst you at this time, not as for my recreation or sport, but being resolved, in the midst and heat of the battle, to live or die amongst you all; to lay down, for my God, and for my kingdom, and for my people, my honor and my blood, even the dust. I know I have but the body of a weak and feeble woman; but I have the heart and stomach of a king, and of a king of England, too; and think foul scorn that Parma or Spain, or any prince of Europe, should dare to invade the borders of my realms: to which, rather than any dishonor should grow by me, I myself will take up arms; I myself will be your general, judge, and rewarder of every one of your virtues in the field. I know already, by your forwardness, that you have deserved rewards and crowns; and we do assure you, on the word of a prince, they shall be duly paid you. In the mean my lieutenant general, General Leicester, shall be in my stead, than whom never prince commanded a more noble and worthy subject; not doubting by your obedience to my general, by your concord in the camp, and by your valor in the field, we shall shortly have a famous victory over the enemies of my God, of my kingdom, and of my people.

ships and 80,000 men met an even larger Ottoman flotilla off the coast of Greece. The Spanish naval victory at Lepanto was considered one of the great events of the sixteenth century, celebrated in story and song for the next 300 years. Although the Turks continued to menace the Mediterranean islands, Lepanto marked the end of Ottoman advances.

Philip was equally aggressive against the English Protestants. For a brief time he had been king in England through his marriage to Mary I (1553–1558). He encouraged Mary's efforts to restore the Catholic Church in England and supported her policies of repression. When Mary died and Elizabeth I (1558–1603) rejected his marriage proposal, his limited rule in England came to an end. From then on, England and Spain entered a long period of hostility. English pirates raided Spanish treasure ships returning to Europe, and Elizabeth covertly aided both French and Dutch Protestants. Finally, in 1588, Philip decided upon invasion. A great fleet set sail from the Portuguese coast to the Netherlands, where a large Spanish army stood waiting to be conveyed to England.

The **Spanish Armada** was composed of more than 130 ships, many of them the pride of the Spanish and Portuguese navies. They were bigger and stronger than anything possessed by the English, whose forces were largely merchant vessels hastily converted for battle. But the English ships were faster and more easily maneuverable in the unpredictable winds of the English Channel. They also contained guns that could easily be reloaded for multiple firings, while the Spanish guns were designed to discharge only one broadside before hand-to-hand combat ensued. With those advantages the English were able to prevent the Armada from reaching port in the Netherlands and to destroy many individual ships as they were blown off course. The defeat of the Spanish Armada was less a military than a psychological blow to Philip II: he could more easily replace ships than restore confidence in Spanish power.

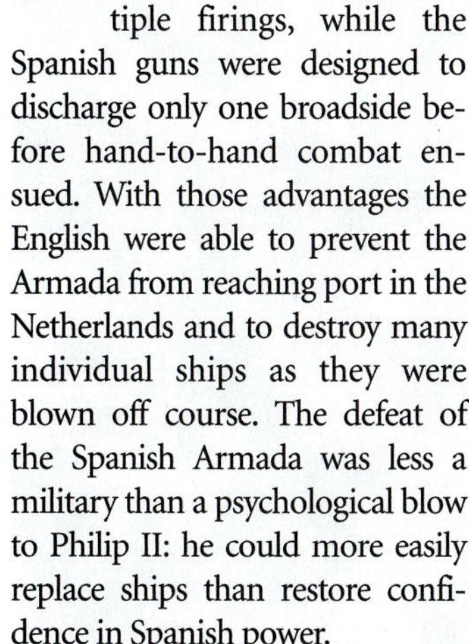

Reports on the Spanish Armada

The Burgundian Inheritance

Confidence was all the more necessary when Philip II faced the gravest crisis of his reign: the revolt of the Netherlands. Although Philip's father, Charles V, had amassed a great empire, he had begun only as the duke of Burgundy. Charles's Burgundian inheritance encompassed a diverse territory in the northwestern corner of Europe. The 17 separate provinces of the territory were called the Netherlands, or the Low Countries, because of the flooding that kept large portions of them under water. The Netherlands was one of the richest and most populous regions of Europe, an international leader in manufacturing, banking, and commerce. Antwerp and Amsterdam were bustling port cities with access to the North Sea; inland were the prosperous industrial towns of Ghent and Brussels. The preeminence of the Netherlands was all the more remarkable because the provinces themselves were divided geographically, culturally, and linguistically. Rivers, lakes, and flooded plains separated the southern provinces, where French was the background and language of the inhabitants, from the northern ones, where Germans had settled and Dutch was spoken. Charles V attempted to unify the provinces by removing them from the jurisdiction of the Holy Roman Empire and establishing a separate regency under his eldest son, Philip II. Thus the future of the Netherlands was tied to Spain and the New World when Philip II set sail for Castile in 1559 to claim the crown of Spain.

Although Philip II had every intention of returning to the Low Countries, in fact the Netherlands had seen the last of

Habsburg Lands at the Abdication of Charles V

Notice how dispersed were the states controlled by Charles V when he abdicated the throne in 1556. Why do you think he divided his empire between his son Philip II and his brother Ferdinand I? What made it possible for the Netherlands to revolt against Spanish control?

their king. Philip left his half-sister, Margaret of Parma, as regent, providing her with a talented group of Spanish administrators to carry out policies that were to be formulated in Madrid. As Philip's own grasp on the affairs of the Netherlands loosened, so did the loyalty of the native nobility to the absent monarch. The resentments that built up were traditional ones—hostility to foreigners, distrust of royal advisers, and contempt for policies that lacked understanding of local conditions. All of the discontents came together over Philip's religious policies.

The Low Countries had accepted the Peace of Augsburg in a spirit of conciliation in which it was never intended. There Catholics, Lutherans, Anabaptists, and Calvinists peaceably coexisted. As in France, the situation changed dramatically with the spread of Calvinism. The heavy concentration of urban populations in the Low Countries provided the natural habitat for Calvinist preachers, who made converts across the entire social spectrum. As Charles V, Holy Roman Emperor, he may have made his peace with Protestants, but as Charles I, king of Spain, he had not. Charles V had maintained the purity of the Spanish Catholic Church through a sensible combination of reform and repression.

Philip II intended to pursue a similar policy in the Low Countries. With papal approval he initiated a scheme to reform the hierarchy of the Church by expanding the number of bishops, and he invited the Jesuits to establish schools for orthodox learning. Simultaneously, he strengthened the power of the Inquisition and ordered the enforcement of the decrees of the Council of Trent. The Protestants sought the protection of their local nobility who—Catholic or Protestant—had their own reasons for opposing provincial nobility, and magistrates resented both the policies that were being pursued and the fact that they disregarded local autonomy. Town governors and noblemen refused to cooperate in implementing the new laws. Leading Protestants such as Prince William of Orange, one of the largest landholders in the Netherlands, and Count Egmont, an outstanding military leader, urged Margaret to adopt a policy of toleration along the lines of the Peace of Augsburg and made clear that they would resign from office rather than support anything else.

The Revolt of the Netherlands

The passive resistance of nobles and magistrates was soon matched by the active resistance of the Calvinists. Unable to enforce Philip's policy, Margaret and her advisers agreed to a limited toleration. But in the summer of 1566, before it could be put into effect, bands of Calvinists unleashed a storm of iconoclasm in the provinces, breaking stained glass windows and statues of the Virgin and the saints, which they claimed were idolatrous. Catholic churches were stormed and turned into Calvinist meeting houses. Local authorities were helpless in the face of determined Calvinists and apathetic Catholics; they could not protect Church property. Iconoclasm gave way to open revolt. Fearing social rebellion, even the leading Protestant noblemen took part in suppressing the riots.

Rebellion and War. In Spain, the events in the Netherlands were treated for what they were: open rebellion. Despite the fact that Margaret had already restored order, Philip II was determined to punish the rebels and enforce the heresy laws. A large military force under the command of the Duke of Alba (1507–1582)—whose record of success was matched only by his record of brutality—was sent from Spain as an army of occupation. As befit a warrior who had made his reputation leading imperial troops against the Lutherans, Alba gave no quarter to the Protestants of the Netherlands.

■ Portrait of Philip II by Titian (ca. 1554). Philip tried for 12 years to suppress rebellion in the Protestant Netherlands, and he sent troops to aid Catholic forces in battle with the Huguenots in France. He fared badly in his attempts to deal with England, his Spanish Armada suffering a humiliating defeat in 1588 that marked the beginning of the decline of Spanish power.

CANNIBALS

Michel de Montaigne (1533–1592) came from a wealthy family in the Bordeaux region of France and ultimately inherited the chateau from which his name derives. Before his early retirement he worked in the legal profession. His Essays *(1572–1588) combined humanist learning with the new philosophy of skepticism. The following excerpt, from "Of Cannibals," shows both his penetrating intelligence and his detached observation of the world around him. His description of the practices of cannibals was an explicit critique of his own European countrymen.*

Focus Questions

In what ways does Montaigne profess sympathy with the inhabitants of the New World? What constitutes barbarism for him?

These nations, then, seem to me barbarous in this sense, that they have been fashioned very little by the human mind, and are still very close to their original naturalness. The laws of nature still rule them, very little corrupted by ours; and they are in such a state of purity that I am sometimes vexed that they were unknown earlier, in the days when there were men able to judge them better than we. I am sorry that Lycurgus and Plato did not know of them; for it seems to me that what we actually see in these nations surpasses not only all the pictures in which poets have idealized the golden age and all their inventions in imagining a happy state of man, but also the conceptions and the very desire of philosophy. . . .

For the rest, they live in a country with a very pleasant and temperate climate, so that according to my witnesses it is rare to see a sick man there; and they have assured me that they never saw one palsied, bleary-eyed, toothless, or bent with age. They are settled along the sea and shut in on the land side by great high mountains, with a stretch about a hundred leagues wide in between. They have a great abundance of fish and flesh which bear no resemblance to ours, and they eat them with no other artifice than cooking.

They have their wars with the nations beyond the mountains, further inland, to which they go quite naked, with no other arms than bows or wooden swords ending in a sharp point, in the manner of the tongues of our boar spears. It is astonishing what firmness they show in their combats, which never end but in slaughter and bloodshed; for as to routs and terror, they know nothing of either.

Each man brings back as his trophy the head of the enemy he has killed, and sets it up at the entrance to his dwelling. After they have treated their prisoners well for a long time with all the hospitality they can think of, each man who has a prisoner calls a great assembly of his acquaintances. He ties a rope to one of the prisoner's arms by the end of which he holds him, a few steps away, for fear of being hurt, and gives his dearest friend the other arm to hold in the same way; and these two, in the presence of the whole assembly, kill him with their swords. This done, they roast him and eat him in common and send some pieces to their absent friends. This is not, as people think, for nourishment, as of old the Scythians used to do; it is to betoken an extreme revenge. And the proof of this came when they saw the Portuguese, who had joined forces with their adversaries, inflict a different kind of death on them when they took them prisoner, which was to bury them up to the waist, shoot the rest of their body full of arrows, and afterward hang them. They thought that these people from the other world, being men who had sown the knowledge of many vices among their neighbors and were much greater masters than themselves in every sort of wickedness, did not adopt this sort of vengeance without some reason, and that it must be more painful than their own; so they began to give up their old method and to follow this one.

I am not sorry that we notice the barbarous horror of such acts, but I am heartily sorry that, judging their faults rightly, we should be so blind to our own. I think there is more barbarity in eating a man alive than in eating him dead; and in tearing by tortures and the rack a body still full of feeling, in roasting a man bit by bit, in having him bitten and mangled by dogs and swine (as we have not only read but seen within fresh memory, not among ancient enemies, but among neighbors and fellow citizens, and what is worse, on the pretext of piety and religion), than in roasting and eating him after he is dead. . . .

So we may well call these people barbarians, in respect to the rules of reason, but not in respect to ourselves, who surpass them in every kind of barbarity.

Their warfare is wholly noble and generous, and as excusable and beautiful as this human disease can be; its only basis among them is their rivalry in valor. They are not fighting for the conquest of new lands, for they still enjoy that natural abundance that provides them without toil and trouble with all necessary things in such profusion that they have no wish to enlarge their boundaries. They are still in that happy state of desiring only as much as their natural needs demand; anything beyond that is superfluous to them. . . . Truly here are real savages by our standards, for either they must be thoroughly so, or we must be; there is an amazing distance between their character and ours.

From Montaigne, "Of Cannibals."

"Everyone must be made to live in constant fear of the roof breaking down over his head," he wrote.

Alba lured Count Egmont and other Protestant noblemen to Brussels, where he publicly executed them in 1568. He also established a military court to punish participants in the rebellion, a court that came to be called the Council of Blood. The Council handed down more than 9000 convictions, a thousand of which carried the death penalty. As many as 60,000 Protestants fled beyond Alba's jurisdiction. Alba next made an example of several small towns that had been implicated in the iconoclasm. He allowed his soldiers to pillage the towns at will before slaughtering their entire populations and razing them to the ground. By the end of 1568, royal policy had gained a sullen acceptance in the Netherlands, but the hostilities did not end. For the next 80 years, with only occasional truces, Spain and the Netherlands were at war.

The Protestants Rebel. Alba's policies drove the Protestants into rebellion. That forced the Spanish government to maintain its army by raising taxes from those provinces that had remained loyal. Soon the loyal provinces too were in revolt, not over religion, but over taxation and local autonomy. Tax resistance and fear of an invasion from France left Alba unprepared for the series of successful assaults Protestants launched in the northern provinces during 1572. Protestant generals established a permanent base in the northwestern provinces of Holland and Zeeland. By 1575 the Protestants had gained a stronghold that they would never relinquish. Prince William of Orange assumed

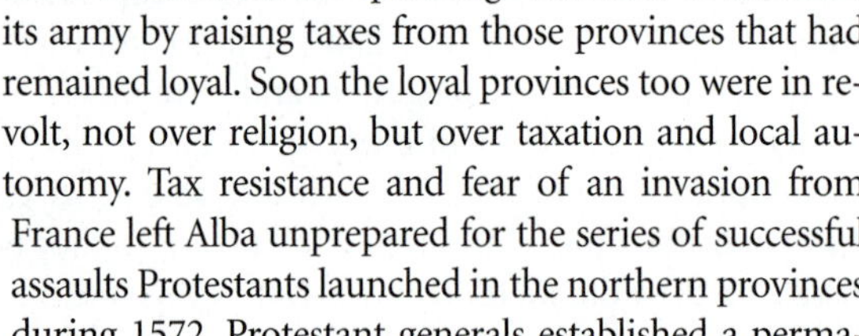

Michel de Montaigne, *Essays*

CHRONOLOGY

Revolt of the Netherlands

1559	Margaret of Parma named regent of the Netherlands
1566	Calvinist iconoclasm begins revolt
1567	Duke of Alba arrives in Netherlands and establishes Council of Blood
1568	Protestant Count Egmont executed
1572	Protestants capture Holland and Zeeland
1573	Alba relieved of his command
1576	Sack of Antwerp; pacification of Ghent
1581	Catholic and Protestant provinces split
1585	Spanish forces take Brussels and Antwerp
1609	Twelve Years' Truce

■ The Revolt of the Netherlands, 1555. The consolidation of the Low Countries under Charles V brought together lands with different languages, cultures, and forms of government.

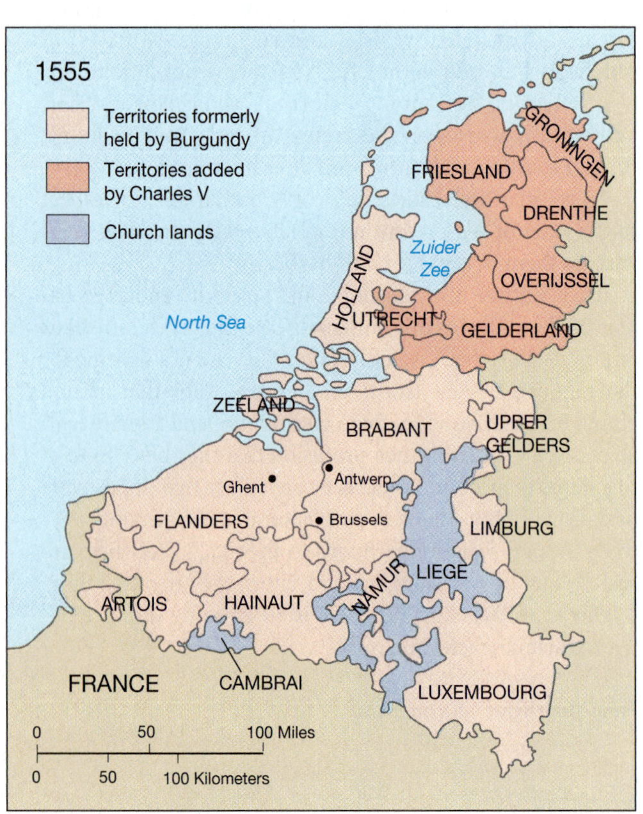

■ The Revolt of the Netherlands, 1609. By the beginning of the seventeenth century, the union had broken apart and the northern provinces had won independence from Spain.

the leadership of the two provinces that were now united against the tyranny of Philip's rule.

Spanish government was collapsing all over the Netherlands. William ruled in the north and the States-General, a parliamentary body composed of representatives from the separate provinces, ruled in the south. Margaret of Parma had resigned in disgust at Alba's tactics, and Alba had been relieved of his command when his tactics had failed. No one was in control of the Spanish army. The soldiers, who had gone years with only partial pay, now roamed the southern provinces looking for plunder. Brussels and Ghent both had been targets, and in 1576 the worst atrocities of all occurred when mutinous Spanish troops sacked Antwerp. One of the wealthiest cities in Europe, home to the most important mercantile and banking establishments in the world, Antwerp was torn apart like a roasted pig. The rampage lasted for days. When it ended, more than 7000 people had been slaughtered and nearly a third of the city burned to the ground.

The "Spanish fury" in Antwerp effectively ended Philip's rule over his Burgundian inheritance. The Protestants had established a permanent home in the north. The States-General had established its ability to rule in the south, and Spanish policy had been totally discredited. To achieve a settlement, the Pacification of Ghent of 1576, the Spanish government conceded local autonomy in taxation, the central role of the States-General in legislation, and the immediate withdrawal of all Spanish troops from the Low Countries. Five southern provinces pledged to remain Catholic and to accept the authority of the king's regent. The rift between the provinces was soon followed by a permanent split. In 1581, one group of provinces voted to depose Philip II, while a second group decided to remain loyal to him.

Philip II refused to accept the dismemberment of his inheritance and refused to recognize the independent Dutch state that now existed in Holland. Throughout the 1580s and 1590s, military expeditions attempted to reunite the southern provinces and to conquer the northern ones. But Spanish military successes in the south were outweighed by the long-term failure of Spanish objectives in the north. In 1609, Spain and the Netherlands concluded the Twelve Years' Truce, which tacitly recognized the existence of the state of Holland. By the beginning of the seventeenth century, Holland was not only an independent state, it was one of the greatest rivals of Spain and Portugal for the fruits of empire.

THE STRUGGLES IN EASTERN EUROPE

In eastern Europe, dynastic struggles outweighed the problems created by religious reform. Muscovy remained the bulwark of Eastern Orthodox Christianity, immune from the struggles over the Roman faith. Protestantism did spread into Poland-

IMAGE DISCOVERY

The Cow, as Political Symbol

This painting, *The Milch Cow,* illustrates the politics surrounding the Netherlands in the later sixteenth century. Philip II of Spain is riding on the cow. What do you think that says about Spain's relationship to the Netherlands? Why would the painter have depicted William of Orange, ruler of the Netherlands, under the cow and milking it? Elizabeth I is feeding the cow, and the King of France stands behind it, gripping its tail and collecting its droppings. Note the sizes of the figures; Philip II is smaller than Elizabeth I. Since this is not a reflection of their actual dimensions, what might this mean? What does the picture indicate about the painter's political leanings?

Lithuania, but unlike its reception in the west, its presence was tolerated by the Polish state. The spread of dissent was checked not by repression, but by a vigorous Catholic reformation led by the Jesuits. The domestic crises in the east were crises of state rather than of church. In Muscovy, the disputed succession that followed the death of Ivan the Terrible plunged the state into anarchy and civil war. Centuries of conflict between Poland-Lithuania and Muscovy came to a head with the Poles' desperate gamble to seize control of their massive eastern neighbor. War between Poland-Lithuania and Muscovy inevitably dominated the politics of the entire region. The Baltic states, of which Sweden was to become the most important, had their own ambitions for territory and economic gain. They soon joined the fray, making alliances in return for concessions and conquering small pieces of the mainland.

Kings and Diets in Poland

Until the end of the sixteenth century, Poland-Lithuania was the dominant power in the eastern part of Europe. It was economically healthy and militarily strong. Through its Baltic ports, especially Gdansk, Poland played a central role in international commerce and a dominant role in the northern grain trade. The vast size of the Polish state made defense difficult, and during the course of the sixteenth century it had lost lands to Muscovy in the east and to the Crimean Tatars in the south. But the permanent union with Lithuania in 1569 and the gradual absorption of the Baltic region of Livonia more than compensated for the losses. Matters of war and peace, of taxation and reform, were placed under the strict supervision of the **Polish Diet**, a parliamentary body that represented the

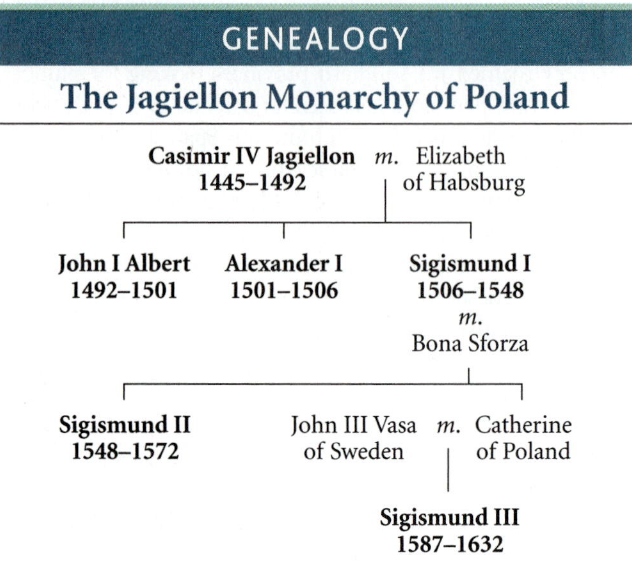

Eastern Europe (ca. 1550) after the Consolidation of Russia and the Growth of Poland. The eastern part of Europe was still sparsely populated and economically underdeveloped.

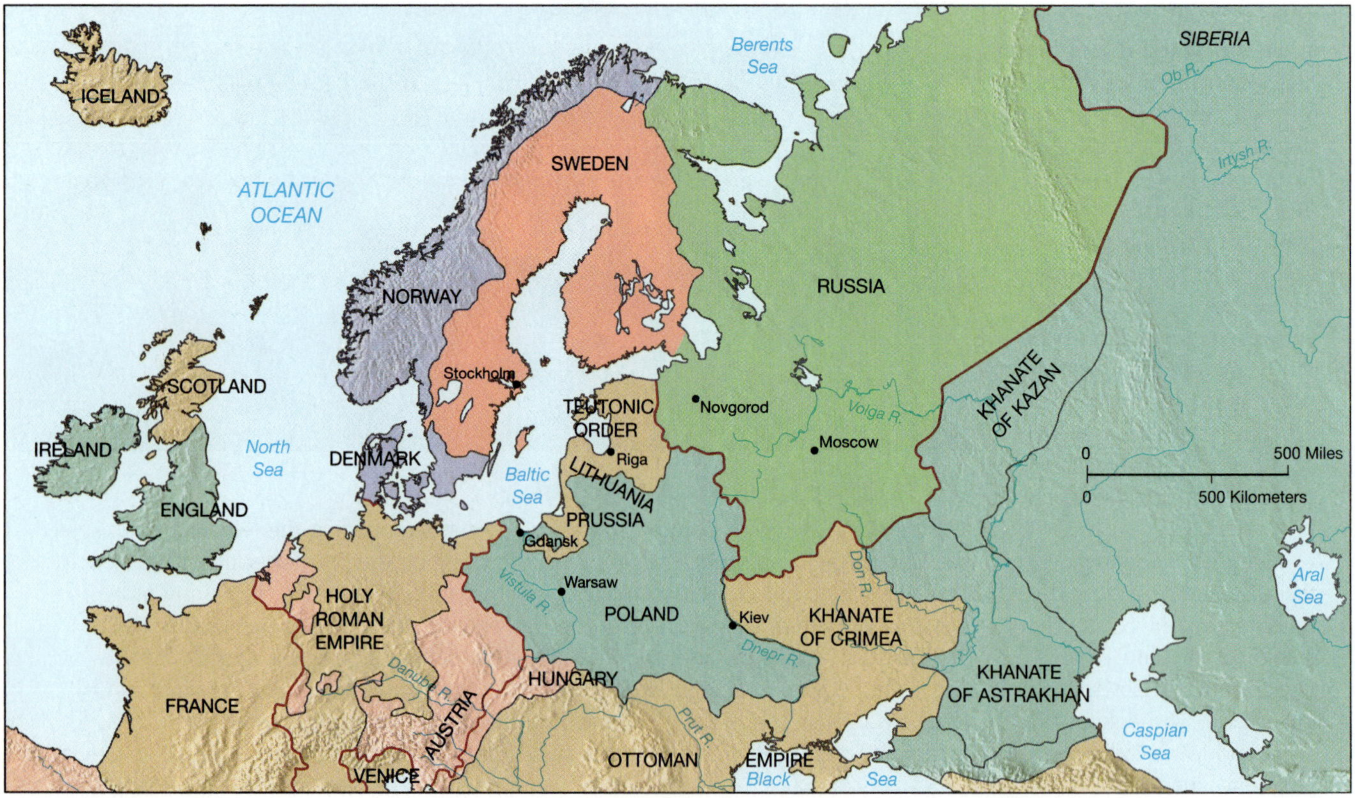

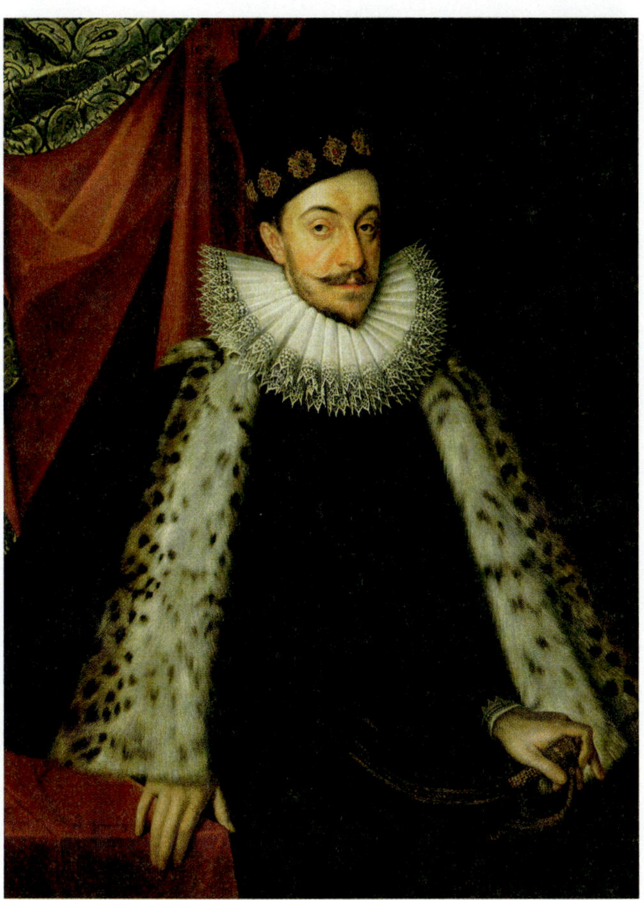

■ Portrait of Sigismund III, who was elected to the Polish throne in 1587. Also the hereditary heir to the Crown of Sweden, Sigismund brought Poland into war with Sweden in an effort to reclaim his crown.

Polish landed elite. The Diet also carefully controlled religious policy. Roman Catholicism was the principal religion in Poland, but the state tolerated numerous Protestant and Eastern creeds. In the Warsaw Confederation of 1573, the Polish gentry vowed, "We who differ in matters of religion will keep the peace among ourselves."

The biological failure of the Jagiellon monarchy in Poland ended that nation's most successful line of kings. Without a natural heir, the Polish nobility and gentry, who officially elected the monarch, had to peddle their throne among the princes of Europe. When Sigismund III (1587–1632) was elected to the Polish throne in 1587, he was also heir to the crown of Sweden. Sigismund accepted the prohibitions against religious repression that were outlined in the Warsaw Confederation, but he actively encouraged the establishment of Jesuit schools, the expansion of monastic orders, and the strengthening of the Roman Catholic Church.

All those policies enjoyed the approval of the Polish ruling classes. But the Diet would not support Sigismund's efforts to gain control of the Swedish crown, which he inherited in 1592 but from which he was deposed three years later. If Sigismund triumphed in Sweden, all Poland would get was a part-time monarch. The Polish Diet consistently refused to give the king the funds he would need to invade Sweden successfully. Nevertheless, Sigismund mounted several unsuccessful campaigns against the Swedes that sapped Polish money and manpower.

Muscovy's Time of Troubles

The wars of Ivan the Great and Ivan the Terrible in the fifteenth and sixteenth centuries were waged to secure agricultural territory in the west and a Baltic port in the north; both objectives came at the expense of Poland-Lithuania. But following the death of Ivan the Terrible in 1584, the Muscovite state began to disintegrate. For years it had been held together only by conquest and fear. Ivan's conflicts with the boyars, the hereditary nobility, had created an aristocracy unwilling and unable to come to the aid of his successors. By 1601, the crown was plunged into a crisis of legitimacy known as the **Time of Troubles.** Ivan had murdered his heir in a fit of anger and left his half-witted son to inherit the throne, which led to a vacuum of power at the center as well as a struggle for the spoils of government. Private armies ruled great swaths of the state and pretenders to the crown—all claiming to be Dimitri, the lost brother of the last legitimate tsar—appeared everywhere. Ambitious groups of boyars backed their own claimants to the throne. So, too, did ambitious foreigners who eagerly sought to carve up Muscovite possessions.

Muscovy's Time of Troubles was Poland's moment of opportunity. While anarchy and civil war raged, Poland looked to regain the territory that it had lost to Muscovy during the previous century. Sigismund abandoned war with Sweden in order to intervene in the struggle for the Russian crown. Polish forces crossed into Muscovy and Sigismund's generals backed one of the strongest of the false Dimitris, but their plan to put him on the throne failed when he was assassinated. Sigismund used the death of the last false Dimitri as a pretext to assert his own claim to the Muscovite crown. More Polish forces poured across the frontier. In 1610, they took Moscow and Sigismund proclaimed himself tsar, intending to unite the two massive states.

The Russian boyars, so long divided, now rose against the Polish enemy. The Polish garrison in Moscow was starved into submission, and a native Russian, Michael Romanov (1613–1645), was chosen tsar by an assembly of landholders, the Zemsky Sobor. He made a humiliating peace with the Swedes—who had also taken advantage of the Time of Troubles to invade Muscovy's Baltic provinces—in return for Swedish assistance against the Poles. Intermittent fighting continued for another 20 years. In the end, Poland agreed to peace and a separate Muscovite state, but only in exchange for large territorial concessions.

The Rise of Sweden

Sweden's rise to power during the seventeenth century was as startling as it was swift. Until the Reformation, Sweden had been part of the Scandinavian confederation ruled by the

Danes. Although the Swedes had a measure of autonomy, they were very much a junior partner in Baltic affairs. Denmark controlled the narrow sound that linked the Baltic with the North Sea, and its prosperity derived from the tolls it collected on imports and exports. When, in 1523, Gustav I Vasa led the uprising of the Swedish aristocracy that ended Danish domination, he won the right to rule over a poor, sparsely populated state with few towns or developed seaports. The Vasas ruled Sweden in conjunction with the aristocracy. Although the throne was hereditary, the part played by the nobility in elevating Gustav I Vasa (1523–1560) gave the nobles a powerful voice in Swedish affairs. Through the council of state, known as the Rad, the Swedish nobility exerted a strong check on the monarch. Sweden's aggressive foreign policy began accidentally. When in the 1550s the Teutonic Knights found themselves no longer capable of ruling in Livonia, the Baltic seaports that had been under their dominion scrambled for new alliances. Muscovy and Poland-Lithuania were the logical choices, but the town of Reval, an important outlet for Russian trade near the mouth of the Gulf of Finland, asked Sweden for protection. After some hesitation, since the occupation of territory on the southern shores of the Baltic would involve great expense, Sweden fortified Reval in 1560. A decade later, Swedish forces captured Narva, farther to the east, and consolidated their hold on the Livonian coast. By occupying the most important ports on the Gulf of Finland, Sweden could control a sizable portion of the Muscovite trade. As the Swedes secured the northern Livonian ports, more of the Muscovy trade moved to the south and passed through Riga, which would have to be captured or blockaded if the Swedes were to control commerce in the eastern Baltic.

■ Michael Romanov was chosen to be tsar in 1613. His father, the Patriarch Philaret of Moscow, acted as joint ruler with Michael until the patriarch's death in 1633.

■ The Rise of Russia. Russia grew through the addition of large units of territory comprising millions of square acres.

Sigismund's aggressive alliance with the Polish Jesuits persuaded the Swedish nobility that he would undermine their Lutheran church. Sigismund was deposed in favor of his uncle Charles IX (1604–1611). War with Poland resulted from Sigismund's efforts to regain the Swedish crown. The Swedes used the opportunity to blockade Riga and to occupy more Livonian territory. The Swedish navy was far superior to any force that the Poles could assemble, but on land Polish forces were masters. The Swedish invasion force suffered a crushing defeat and had to retreat to its coastal enclaves. The Poles now had an opportunity to retake all of Livonia but, as always, the Polish Diet was reluctant to finance Sigismund's wars. Furthermore, Sigismund had his eyes on a bigger prize. Rather than follow up its Swedish victory, Poland invaded Muscovy.

Meanwhile, the blockade of Riga and the assembly of a large Swedish fleet in the Baltic threatened Denmark. The Danes continued to claim sovereignty over Sweden and took the opportunity of the Polish-Swedish conflict to reassert it.

GENEALOGY

The House of Vasa of Sweden

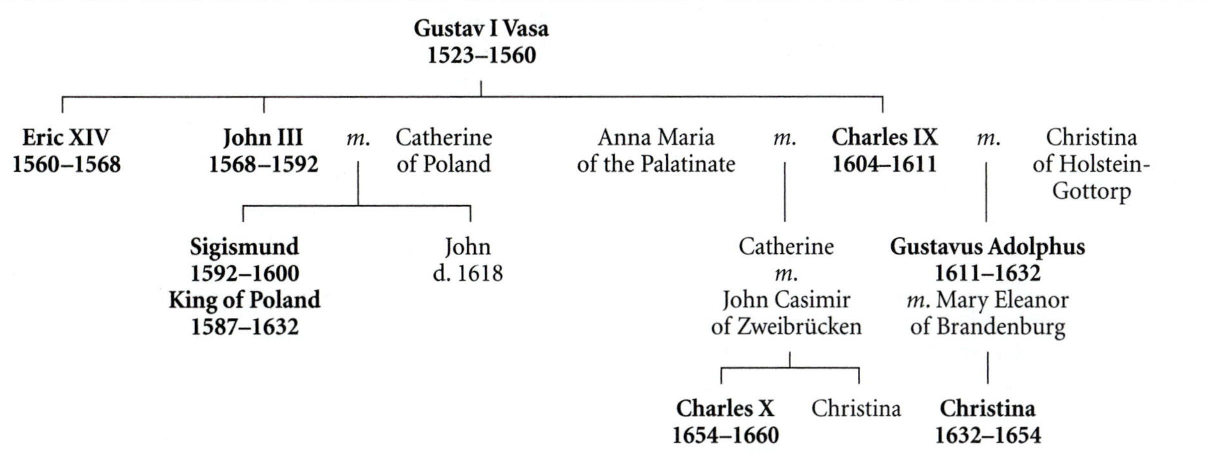

In 1611, under the energetic leadership of the Danish king Christian IV (1588–1648), Denmark invaded Sweden from both the east and the west. The Danes captured the towns of Kalmar and Alvsborg and threatened to take Stockholm. To end the Danish war, Sweden accepted humiliating terms in 1613, renouncing all claims to the northern coasts and recognizing Danish control of the Arctic trading route.

In 1611, during the middle of the Danish war, Charles IX died and was succeeded by his son Gustavus Adolphus (1611–1632). Unlike his father and cousin before him, who had come by chance to the Swedish throne, Gustavus Adolphus was raised to be king. Gruff and affable by turns, he was one of the leading Protestant princes of his day, in every way a match for Christian IV of Denmark. Gustavus's greatest skills were military, and he inherited an ample navy and an effective army. Unlike nearly every other European state, Sweden raised its forces from its own citizens. Gustavus introduced new weapons such as the light mobile gun and reshaped his army into standard-size squadrons and regiments, which were easier to administer and deploy.

The calamitous wars inherited from his father occupied Gustavus during the early years of his reign. He was forced to conclude the humiliating peace with the Danes in 1613 and to go to war with the Russians in 1614 in order to secure the Baltic coastal estates that had been promised in 1609. Gustavus's first military initiative was to resume war with Poland in order to force Sigismund to renounce his claim to the Swedish throne. In 1621, Gustavus landed in Livonia and within two weeks had captured Riga, the capstone of Sweden's Baltic ambitions. Occupation of Riga increased Swedish control of the Muscovy trade and deprived Denmark of a significant portion of its customs duties. Gustavus now claimed Riga as a Swedish port and successfully demanded that ships sailing from there pay tolls to Sweden rather than Denmark. The capture of Riga firmly established Sweden as a coequal Baltic power.

■ The Rise of Sweden. For the only time in its history, Sweden acquired territories on the European mainland.

By the mid-seventeenth century, the Sweden of Gustavus Adolphus was well on its way to international prominence. The capture of Riga gave Sweden complete control of the eastern Baltic and ended Polish pretensions to the Swedish throne. A negotiated settlement with the Danes over the collection of tolls enhanced Swedish prestige and increased Sweden's commercial prosperity. Moreover, Gustavus's marriage into the family of the Protestant rulers of Prussia gave Sweden a presence in Germany as well. For the time being, Sweden faced east. But the storm clouds of religious warfare were already bursting over the Holy Roman Empire. Gustavus Adolphus now took his place among the Protestant princes of Europe, and Sweden ranked among the leading Protestant powers.

THE THIRTY YEARS' WAR, 1618–1648

Perhaps it was just a matter of time before the isolated conflicts that dotted the corners of Europe were joined together. In 1609, Spain and the Dutch Republic had signed a truce that was to last until 1621. In more than 40 years of nearly continuous fighting, the Dutch had carved out a state in the northern Netherlands. They used the truce to consolidate their position and increase their prosperity, largely at the expense of Spain and Portugal. Thus, to the insult of rebellion was added the injury of commercial competition. Spain had reluctantly accepted Dutch independence, but Philip III (1598–1621) never abandoned the objective of recovering his Burgundian inheritance. By the start of the seventeenth century, Philip had good reasons for hope. Beginning in the 1580s, Spanish forces had reconquered the southern provinces of the Netherlands. The prosperous towns of Brussels, Antwerp, and Ghent were again under Spanish control, and they provided a springboard for another invasion.

The Twelve Years' Truce gave Spain time to prepare for the final assault. During this time, Philip III attempted to resolve all of Spain's other European conflicts so that he could then give full attention to a resumption of the Dutch war. Circumstance smiled upon his efforts. In 1603, the pacific James I (1603–1625) came to the English throne. Secure in his island state, James I desired peace among all Christian princes. He quickly concluded the war with Spain that had begun with the invasion of the Spanish Armada and entered into negotiations to marry his heir to a Spanish princess. In 1610, the bellicose Henry IV of France was felled by an assassin's knife. French plans to renew war with Spain were abandoned with the accession of the eight-year-old Louis XIII (1610–1643). As the sands of the Twelve Years' Truce ran out, Spain and the Netherlands readied for war. But not even the greatest empire in Europe could control its own destiny. War was in the air all over the Continent, and not everyone could wait until 1621. The **Thirty Years' War** was about to begin.

Bohemia Revolts

The Peace of Augsburg had served the German states well. The principle that the religion of the ruler was the religion of the state complicated the political life of the Holy Roman Empire, but it also pacified it. Although rulers had the right to enforce uniformity on their subjects, in practice many of the larger states tolerated more than one religion. By the beginning of the seventeenth century, Catholicism and Protestantism had achieved a rough equality within the German states, symbolized by the fact that of the seven electors who chose the Holy Roman Emperor, three were Catholic, three Protestant, and the seventh was the emperor himself, acting as king of Bohemia. The situation was not unwelcome to the leaders of the Austrian Habsburg family who succeeded Emperor Charles V. By necessity, the eastern Habsburgs were more tolerant than their Spanish kinfolk. Protestants fought the Ottomans with as much zeal as did Catholics, and the Ottomans were the empire's more potent enemy. The unofficial policy of toleration not only helped the Austrian Habsburgs defend their state, it allowed them to expand it. The head of their house was elected king of Bohemia and king of Hungary, both states with large Protestant populations.

A Fatal Election. In 1617, Mathias, the childless Holy Roman Emperor, began making plans for his cousin, Ferdinand Habsburg, to succeed him. In order to ensure a Catholic majority among the electors, the emperor relin-

CHRONOLOGY

The Thirty Years' War

1618	Defenestration of Prague
1619	Ferdinand Habsburg elected Holy Roman Emperor; Frederick of the Palatinate accepts the crown of Bohemia
1620	Catholic victory at Battle of the White Mountain
1621	End of Twelve Years' Truce; war between Spain and Netherlands
1626	Danes form Protestant alliance under Christian IV
1627	Spain declares bankruptcy
1630	Gustavus Adolphus leads Swedish forces into Germany
1631	Sack of Magdeburg; Protestant victory at Breitenfeld
1632	Protestant victory at Lützen; death of Gustavus Adolphus
1635	France declares war on Spain
1640	Portugal secedes from Spain
1643	Battle of Rocroi; French forces repel Spaniards
1648	Peace of Westphalia

WAR IS HELL

No source has better captured the brutality of the Thirty Years' War than the novel Simplicissimus *(1669). In a series of loosely connected episodes, the hero (whose name means "the simplest of the simple") is snatched from his village to serve in marauding armies whose confrontations with local villagers are usually more horrifying than the episode narrated here.*

Focus Questions

How do the peasants respond to the troopers' actions? What does this passage suggest about the breadth of the average villager's experience?

These troopers were even now ready to march, and had the pastor fastened by a rope to lead him away. Some cried, "Shoot him down, the rogue!" Others would have money from him. But he, lifting up his hands to heaven, begged, for the sake of the Last Judgment, for forbearance and Christian compassion, but in vain; for one of them rode down and dealt him such a blow on the head that he fell flat, and commended his soul to God. Nor did the remainder of the captured peasants fare any better. But even when it seemed these troopers, in their cruel tyranny, had clean lost their wits, came such a swarm of armed peasants out of the wood, that it seemed a wasps'-nest had been stirred. And these began to yell so frightfully and so furiously to attack with sword and musket that all my hair stood on end; and never had I been at such a merrymaking before: for the peasants of the Spessart and the Vogelsberg are as little wont as are the Hessians and men of the Sauerland and the Black Forest to let themselves be crowed over on their own dunghill. So away went the troopers, and not only left behind the cattle they had captured, but threw away bag and baggage also, and so cast all their booty to the winds lest themselves should become booty for the peasants: yet some of them fell into their hands. This sport took from me well-nigh all desire to see the world, for I thought, if 'tis all like this, then is the wilderness far more pleasant.

From Hans Von Grimmelshausen, *The Adventurous Simplicissimus.*

quished his Bohemian title and pressed for Ferdinand's election as the new king of Bohemia. Ferdinand was Catholic, very devout, and very committed. He had been educated by Jesuits and practiced what had been preached to him. On his own estates, Ferdinand abandoned the policy of toleration. Jesuit schools were founded and the precepts of the Council of Trent were enforced. Protestant preachers were barred from their offices, Protestant books were publicly burned, and thousands of common people were forced to flee, many into nearby Bohemia, where Protestants constituted the majority of the population.

Thus Ferdinand's election as king of Bohemia was no foregone conclusion. Although in the end the Protestant nobles of Bohemia could not prevent his election, they forced the new king to accept the strictest limitations upon his political and religious powers. But once elected, Ferdinand had not the slightest intention of honoring the provisions that had been thrust upon him. His opponents were equally strong willed. When Ferdinand violated Protestant religious liberties, a group of noblemen marched to the royal palace in Prague in May 1618, found two of the king's chief advisers, and hurled them out an upper-story window. The officials' lives—if not their dignity—were preserved by the pile of manure in which they landed.

The Defenestration of Prague, as the incident came to be known, initiated a Protestant counteroffensive throughout the Habsburg lands. Fear of Ferdinand's policies led to Protestant uprisings in Hungary as well as Bohemia. Those who seized control of the government declared Ferdinand deposed and the throne vacant, but they had no candidate to accept their crown. When Emperor Mathias died in 1619, the stalemate was broken. Ferdinand succeeded to the imperial title as Ferdinand II (1619–1637) and Frederick V, one of the Protestant electors, accepted the Bohemian crown.

Frederick V, the "Winter King." Frederick was a sincere but weak Calvinist whose credentials were much stronger than his abilities. His mother was a daughter of Prince William of Orange and his wife, Elizabeth, a daughter of James I of England. It was widely believed that it was Elizabeth's resolution that she would "rather eat sauerkraut with a King than roast meat with an Elector" that decided the issue. No decision could have been more disastrous for the fate of Europe. Frederick ruled a geographically divided German state known as the Palatinate. One hundred miles separated the two segments of his lands, but both were strategically important. The Lower Palatinate bordered on the Catholic Spanish Netherlands and the Upper Palatinate on Catholic Bavaria.

Once Frederick accepted the Bohemian crown, he was faced with a war on three fronts. It was over almost before it began. At the Battle of the White Mountain in 1620, Ferdinand's Catholic forces annihilated Frederick's army. Frederick and Elizabeth fled north, first to Denmark and then to Holland. Bohemia was left to face the wrath of Ferdinand, the victorious king and emperor. The retribution was horrible. Mercenaries who had fought for Ferdinand II were allowed to sack Prague for a week. Elective monarchy was abolished, and Bohemia became part of the hereditary Habsburg lands. Free peasants were enserfed and subjected to imperial law. Those nobles who had supported Frederick lost their lands and their privileges. Calvinism was repressed and thoroughly rooted out, consolidating forever the Catholic character of Bohemia. Frederick's estates were carved up and his rights as elector transferred to the Catholic duke of Bavaria. The Battle of the White Mountain was a turning point in the history of central Europe.

The War Widens

For the Habsburgs, religious and dynastic interests were inseparable. Ferdinand II and Philip III of Spain fought for their beliefs and for their patrimony. Their victory gave them more than they could have expected: Ferdinand swallowed up Bohemia and strengthened his position in the empire, and Philip gained possession of a vital link in his supply route between Italy and the Netherlands. The Habsburgs were now more dangerous than ever. Ferdinand's aggressive Catholicism threatened the Protestant princes of Germany, who prudently began to seek allies outside the empire. Spanish expansion threatened France. The occupation of the Lower Palatinate placed a ring of Spanish armies around the French borders from the Pyrenees to the Low Countries. The French too searched for allies. But French opinion remained divided over which was the greater evil: Spain or Protestantism.

The Danes Respond. Frederick, now in Holland, refused to accept the judgment of battle. He lobbied for a grand alliance to repel the Spaniards from the Lower Palatinate and to restore the religious balance in the empire. Although his personal cause met with little sympathy, his political logic was impeccable, especially after Spain again declared war upon the Dutch in 1621. A grand Protestant alliance—secretly supported by the French—brought together England, Holland, a number of German states, and Denmark. It was the Danes who led this potentially powerful coalition. In 1626, a large Danish army under the command of King Christian IV engaged imperial forces on German soil. But Danish forces could not match the superior numbers and the superior leadership of the Catholic mercenary forces under the command of the ruthless and brilliant Count Albrecht von Wallenstein (1583–1634). In 1629, the Danes withdrew from the empire and sued for peace.

If the Catholic victory at the White Mountain in 1620 threatened the well-being of German Protestantism, the Catholic triumph over the Danes threatened its survival. More powerful than ever, Ferdinand II determined to turn the religious clock back to the state of affairs that had existed when the Peace of Augsburg was concluded in 1555. He demanded that all lands that had then been Catholic but had since become Protestant be returned to the fold. He also proclaimed that as the Peace of Augsburg made no provision for the toleration of Calvinists, they would no longer be tolerated in the empire. Those policies together constituted a virtual revolution in the religious affairs of the German states, and they proved impossible to impose. Ferdinand succeeded in only one thing—he united Lutherans and Calvinists against him.

Protestant Gains. In 1630, King Gustavus Adolphus of Sweden decided to enter the German conflict. To protect Swedish interests, he reasoned, he must defend the Protestant states of northern Germany. Moreover, France was willing to pay much of the cost of a war against Ferdinand. The French

■ Gustavus Adolphus of Sweden, shown at the battle of Breitenfeld in 1631. The battle was the first important Protestant victory of the Thirty Years' War. Gustavus died on the battlefield at Lützen in the following year.

FIRE AND SWORD

No event of the Thirty Years' War had a greater effect on public opinion than the annihilation of the Protestant city of Magdeburg in 1631. Dozens of pamphlets and woodcuts, including this anonymous account, detailed the slaughter of civilians and the devastation of property. It was commonly believed that neither a human nor an animal escaped the destruction.

Focus Questions

What motivated those who destroyed Magdeburg? What is the writer trying to achieve with this account?

Thus it came about that the city and all its inhabitants fell into the hands of the enemy, whose violence and cruelty were due in part to their common hatred of the adherents of the Augsburg Confession, and in part to their being imbittered by the chain shot which had been fired at them and by the derision and insults that the Magdeburgers had heaped upon them from the ramparts.

Then was there naught but beating and burning, plundering, torture, and murder. Most especially was every one of the enemy bent on securing much booty. When a marauding party entered a house, if its master had anything to give he might thereby purchase respite and protection for himself and his family till the next man, who also wanted something, should come along. . . .

Thus in a single day this noble and famous city, the pride of the whole country, went up in fire and smoke; and the remnant of its citizens, with their wives and children, were taken prisoners and driven away by the enemy with a noise of weeping and wailing that could be heard from afar, while the cinders and ashes from the town were carried by the wind to Wanzleben, Egeln, and still more distant places. . . .

too felt the pressure of increasing imperial and Spanish power. Gustavus Adolphus had more success gaining the support of Catholic France than he did gaining the support of the Protestant German princes. Saxony and Brandenburg, the two largest states, feared the consequences of renewed war. Gustavus believed that he could defend the north German states from Ferdinand's aggression and by doing so protect Sweden's Baltic empire. "I seek not my own advantage in this war, nor any gain save the security of my Kingdom," he lectured the reluctant Germans. It was a farsighted strategy. In fact, the only thing he could not foresee when he landed in Germany early in 1630 was how successful his intervention would be.

While Gustavus Adolphus struggled to construct his alliance, imperial forces continued their triumphant progress. In 1631 they besieged, captured, and put to the torch the town of Magdeburg. In a war noted for cruelty between combatants and atrocities against civilians, the destruction of Magdeburg set new standards. Perhaps three-fourths of the 40,000 inhabitants of the town were slaughtered—"in the midst of a horrible din of heart-rending shrieks and cries they were tortured and put to death in so cruel a manner that no words would suffice to describe nor no tears to bewail it," was the report in one pamphlet. The sack of Magdeburg marked a turning point in Protestant fortunes. It gave the international Protestant community a unifying symbol that enhanced Gustavus's military efforts. Hundreds of pamphlets, woodcuts, and newspaper accounts brought the horror of Magdeburg home to Protestants throughout the Continent. Brandenburg and Saxony joined Gustavus Adolphus, not only enlarging his forces, but allowing him to open a second front in Bohemia. He would soon have 140,000 men under his command, only 13,000 of whom were Swedish. In the autumn of 1631, the combination overwhelmed the imperial armies. Gustavus won a decisive triumph at Breitenfeld, while the Saxons occupied Prague. For the first time since 1618, Protestant forces were ascendant, and they brought the war into the Catholic heartland of the empire.

Gustavus Adolphus lost no time in pressing his advantage. The Swedes marched west to the Rhine, easily conquering the richest of the Catholic cities and retaking the Lower Palatinate. In early 1632, Protestant forces plundered Bavaria. It was the Bavarian ruler Maximilian who had gained most from the years of war. His troops had occupied the Upper Palatinate, and he had received Frederick's rights as imperial elector in return for support of Ferdinand. Moreover, Maximilian had played a double game of negotiating with the French for neutrality and with the emperor for the spoils of victory. So there was poetic justice when Maximilian's state was invaded, his castles looted, and his lands plundered. But there was no justice at all for the wretched inhabitants of that stronghold of German Catholicism. Town and countryside were laid waste. Not until the winter of 1632 did the armies of Gustavus and Wallenstein finally meet. At the battle of Lützen the Swedes won the field but lost their beloved king. Wounded in the leg, the back, and the head, Gustavus Adolphus died. In less

MAP DISCOVERY

Population Loss in Germany During the Thirty Years' War

Notice the pattern of population loss during the war. Where was it heaviest? Where was it lightest? Based on the chapter discussion, how might the intervention of Sweden into the war help explain this pattern?

than two years he had decisively transformed the course of the war and the course of Europe's future. Protestant forces now occupied most of central and northern Germany. Ferdinand's ability to redraw the religious map of the empire was at an end.

The Long Quest for Peace

The Thirty Years' War was barely half over when Gustavus Adolphus fell at Lützen. But from that time forward, its central European phase receded in importance. The final stages of the war involved the resumption of the century-old struggle between France and Spain. When the Twelve Years' Truce expired in 1621, Spain again declared war upon the Dutch. Philip III's hopes of concentrating all his resources against Holland had been disappointed by the outbreak of war in central Europe. Not until after the Bohemian revolt had been repressed did the Spanish army begin the long, laborious process of besieging the well-fortified and well-defended towns of the Netherlands. The resumption of war in the Netherlands, combined with the continued successes of Habsburg forces in central Europe, convinced Louis XIII and his chief minister, Cardinal Richelieu, that the time for active French involvement in European affairs was at hand. Throughout the early stages of the war, France had secretly aided anti-Habsburg forces. The time had come to take an open stand. In 1635, France declared war on Spain.

Neither country was prepared for large-scale military action, and neither could afford it. The war resembled nothing so much as two punch-drunk fighters pounding each other, both receiving as much punishment as they inflicted. France took the offensive first, invading the Spanish Netherlands. In 1636, a Spanish army struck back, pushing to within 25 miles of Paris before it was repelled. Both sides soon began to search for a settlement, but pride prevented them from laying down their gloves. Spain toppled first. Its economy in shambles and its citizens in revolt over high prices and higher taxes, it could no longer maintain its many-fronted war. The Swedes again defeated imperial forces in Germany, the Dutch destroyed much of Spain's Atlantic fleet in 1639, and the

This painting by Jan Brueghel (1568–1625) and Sebastien Vranx (1573–1647) evokes the ravaging of the countryside by the belligerent armies between battles in the Thirty Years' War.

Portuguese rose up against the union of crowns that had brought them nothing but expense and the loss of crucial portions of their empire. In 1640, the Portuguese regained their independence. In 1643, Spain gambled once more on a knockout blow against the French. But at the battle of Rocroi, exhausted French troops held out and the Spanish invasion failed.

By then the desire for peace was universal. Most of the main combatants had long since perished: Philip III, ever optimistic, in 1621; Frederick V, an exile to the end, in 1632; Gustavus Adolphus, killed at Lützen in the same year; Wallenstein, murdered by order of Ferdinand II in 1634; Ferdinand himself in 1637; and Louis XIII in 1643, five days before the French triumph at Rocroi. Those who succeeded them had not the same passions, and after so many decades the longing for peace was the strongest emotion on the Continent. At the beginning of 1648, Spain and the Netherlands concluded their 80 years of fighting. The bilateral agreement broke the logjam. One by one, the combatants agreed to end their hostilities with one another, and soon the stage was set for a Continentwide settlement.

A series of agreements, collectively known as the Peace of Westphalia, established the outlines of the political geography of Europe for the next century. Its focus was on the Holy Roman Empire, and it reflected Protestant successes in the final two decades of war. Sweden gained further territories on the Baltic, making it master of the north German ports. France, too, gained in territory and prestige. It kept the vital towns in the Lower Palatinate through which Spanish men and material had moved, and though it did not agree to come to terms with Spain immediately, France's fear of encirclement was at an end. The Dutch gained statehood through official recognition by Spain and through the power they had displayed in building and maintaining an overseas empire.

Territorial boundaries were reestablished as they had existed in 1624, giving the Habsburgs control of both Bohemia and Hungary. The independence of the Swiss cantons was now officially recognized, as were the rights of Calvinists to the protection of the Peace of Augsburg, which again was to govern the religious affairs of the empire. Two of the larger German states were strengthened to balance the emperor's power. Bavaria was allowed to retain the Upper Palatinate, and Brandenburg, which ceded some of its coastal territory to Sweden, gained extensive territories in the east.

The emperor's political control over the German states was also weakened. German rulers were given independent authority over their states, and the imperial Diet, rather than the emperor, was empowered to settle disputes. Thus weakened, future emperors ruled in the Habsburg territorial lands with little ability to control, influence, or even arbitrate German affairs. The judgment that the Holy Roman Empire was neither holy, nor Roman, nor an empire was now irrevocably true.

CONCLUSION

The Peace of Westphalia put the pieces of the map of European states back together. Protestantism and Catholicism now coexisted and there was to be little further change in the geography of religion. The northwest of Europe—England, Holland,

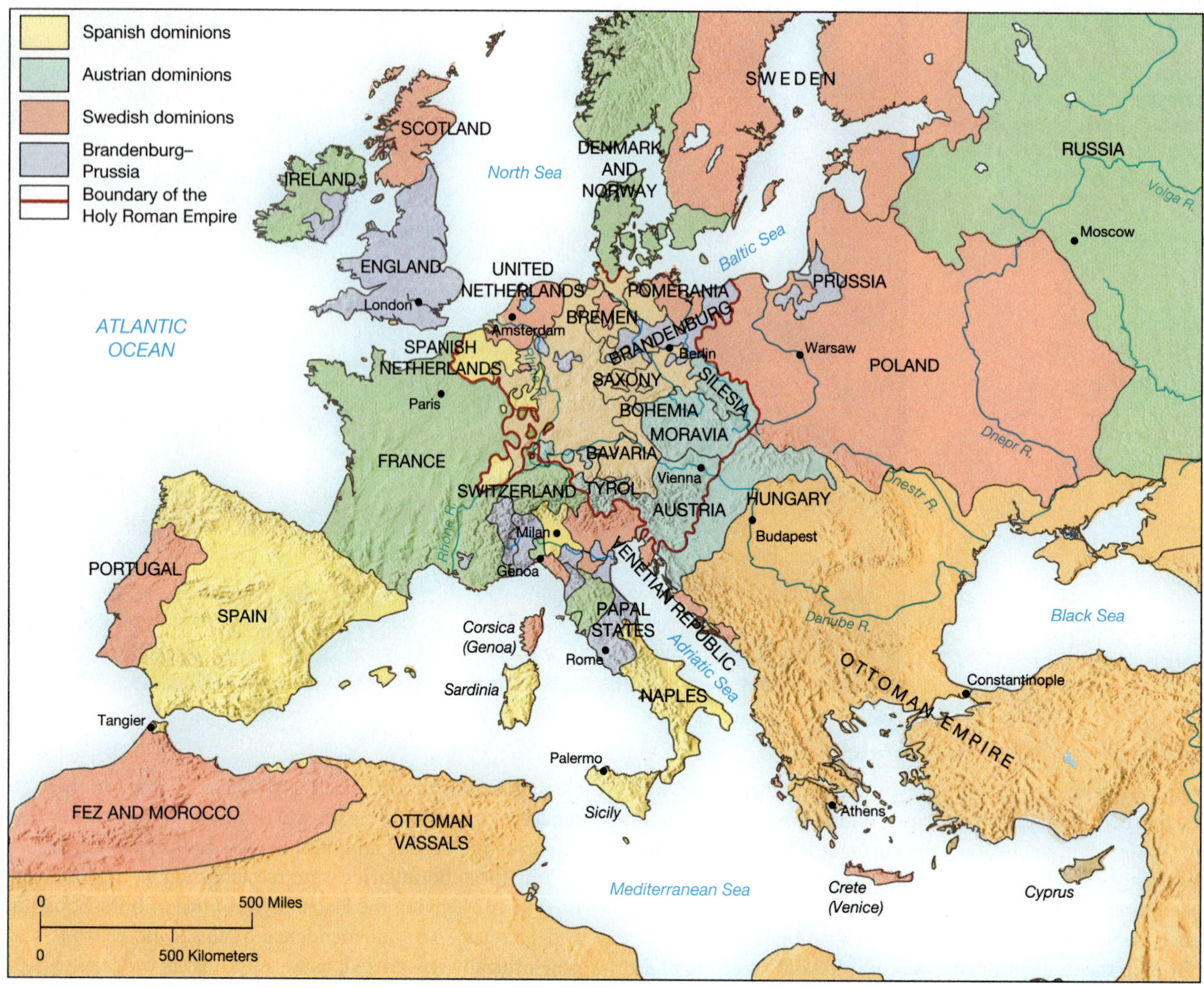

■ The Peace of Westphalia, 1648. The agreement recognized the new boundaries of European states that included an independent Portugal and the United Netherlands. It also recognized the growth of the Ottoman Empire into the Balkans.

Scandinavia, and the north German states—was Protestant, while the south was Catholic. The empire of the German peoples was at an end, the Austro-Hungarian Empire at a beginning. Holland and Sweden had become international powers; Spain and Denmark faded from prominence. Muscovy began a long period of isolation from the west, attempting to restore a semblance of government to its people. But if the negotiators at Westphalia could resolve the political and religious ambitions that gave rise to a century of nearly continuous warfare, they could do nothing to eradicate the effects of war itself. The devastation of humanity in the name of God with which the reform of religion had begun was exhausted. The costs were horrific. The population of Germany fell from 15 million in 1600 to 11 million in 1650. The armies brought destruction of all kinds in their wake. Plague again raged in Europe—the town of Augsburg lost 18,000 inhabitants in the early 1630s. Famine, too, returned to a continent that 50 years earlier had been self-sufficient in grain. The war played havoc with all of the economies that it touched. Inflation, devaluation of coinage, and huge public and private debts were all directly attributable to the years of fighting. And the toll taken on the spirit of those generations that never knew peace is incalculable.

QUESTIONS FOR REVIEW

1. How was Henry IV able to bring peace to France after decades of civil war?
2. What were the political and religious connections between the Armada launched against England by Philip II and the revolt of the Netherlands?
3. How did Sweden rise to become one of Europe's great powers in the first half of the seventeenth century?

4. How did religion help spark and spread the Thirty Years' War?
5. What were the effects of the Peace of Westphalia on political arrangements in the heart of Europe?

KEY TERMS

Catholic League, *p. 418*
Edict of Nantes, *p. 418*
French wars of religion, *p. 413*
Huguenots, *p. 414*
Polish Diet, *p. 426*
politiques, *p. 418*
Spanish Armada, *p. 421*
Thirty Years' War, *p. 430*
Time of Troubles, *p. 427*

DISCOVERING WESTERN CIVILIZATION ONLINE

You can obtain more information about Europe at war at the Websites listed below. See also the Companion Website that accompanies this text, www.ablongman.com/kishlansky, which contains an online study guide and additional resources.

The Crises of the Western States

Internet Modern History Sourcebook: Early Modern West
www.fordham.edu/halsall/mod/modsbook1.html#Conflict
Links to documents on the French wars of religion, the invasion of the Spanish Armada, and the Thirty Years' War.

WebMuseum: The Northern Renaissance (1500–1615)
www.ibiblio.org/wm/paint/tl/north-ren/
Links to pictures and portraits from the late sixteenth and early seventeenth centuries.

Pieter Bruegel the Elder: *The Triumph of Death*
www.ibiblio.org/wm/paint/auth/bruegel/death.jpg
A Web page depicting Peter Brueghel's *Triumph of Death,* one of the most evocative paintings of the destruction wrought by warfare in early modern Europe.

The Thirty Years' War, 1618–1648

The Avalon Project: Treaty of Westphalia
www.yale.edu/lawweb/avalon/westphal.htm
The full text of the Treaty of Westphalia that ended the Thirty Years' War.

SUGGESTIONS FOR FURTHER READING

General Reading

M. S. Anderson, *The Origins of the Modern European State System, 1494–1618* (London: Longman, 1998). A survey of developments stressing war and diplomacy across all of Europe.

Jan de Vries, *The European Economy in an Age of Crisis* (Cambridge: Cambridge University Press, 1976). A comprehensive study of economic development, including long-distance trade and commercial change.

J. H. Elliott, *Europe Divided, 1559–1598* (New York: Harper & Row, 1968). An outstanding synthesis of European politics in the second half of the sixteenth century.

Mark Konnert, *Early Modern Europe: The Age of Religious War, 1559–1715* (Peterborough: Ontario Broadview Press, 2006). Konnert examines political wars and their religious motivations within their social, economic, and intellectual contexts.

Geoffrey Parker, *Europe in Crisis, 1598–1648* (London: William Collins and Sons, 1979). Compelling study of European states in the early seventeenth century.

The Crises of the Western States

Susan Brigden, *New Worlds, Lost Worlds: The Rule of the Tudors, 1485–1603* (New York: Viking, 2001). The latest volume in the new Penguin History of Britain series.

J. A. Guy, *Tudor England* (Oxford: Oxford University Press, 1988). A magisterial survey by the leading scholar of Tudor England.

Mack P. Holt, *The French Wars of Religion, 1562–1629* (New York: Cambridge, 2005). An important work integrating popular and court experience during the French wars of religion.

Henry Kamen, *Spain, 1469–1714* (London: Longman, 1983). A thorough survey with valuable interpretations.

Robert Kingdon, *Myths about the St. Bartholomew's Day Massacres, 1572–1576* (Cambridge, MA: Harvard University Press, 1988). A study of the impact of a central event in the history of France.

R. J. Knecht, *The French Civil Wars, 1562–1598* (New York: Pearson Education, 2000). A compact survey of the religious, social, and political dimensions of the conflicts that raged in France through the second half of the sixteenth century.

John Lynch, *Spain, 1516–1598: From Nation State to World Empire* (Cambridge, MA: Blackwell Publishers, 1994). An up-to-date survey.

Garrett Mattingly, *The Armada* (Boston: Houghton Mifflin, 1959). Still the classic account, despite recent reinterpretations.

Geoffrey Parker, *The Dutch Revolt* (London: Penguin Books, 1977). An outstanding account of the tangle of events that comprised the revolts of the Netherlands.

Geoffrey Parker, *Philip II* (Boston: Little, Brown, 1978). The best introduction.

Michael Roberts, *Gustavus Adolphus and the Rise of Sweden* (London: English Universities Press, 1973). A highly readable account of Sweden's rise to power.

C. V. Wedgwood, *William the Silent, William of Nassau, Prince of Orange, 1533–1584* (New York: Norton, 1968). A stylish biography.

Alison Weir, *Elizabeth the Queen* (London: J. Cape, 1998). A lively biography of the great queen.

The Struggles in Eastern Europe

Robert Frost, *The Northern Wars: War, State and Society in Northeastern Europe, 1558–1721* (New York: Longman, 2000) Examining an oft-neglected sector of European political history, a noted historian explains how Sweden and Poland lost their hegemony to Russia and Prussia during the course of the seventeenth century.

David Kirby, *Northern Europe in the Early Modern Period: The Baltic World, 1492–1772* (London: Longman, 1990). The best single volume on Baltic politics.

S. F. Platonov, *The Time of Troubles* (Lawrence: University Press of Kansas, 1970). A good narrative of the disintegration of the Muscovite state.

Michael Roberts, *The Swedish Imperial Experience* (Cambridge: Cambridge University Press, 1979). Reflections on Swedish history by the preeminent historian of early modern Sweden.

The Thirty Years' War

J. H. Elliott, *Richelieu and Olivares* (Cambridge: Cambridge University Press, 1984). A comparison of statesmen and statesmanship in the early seventeenth century.

Peter Limm, *The Thirty Years' War* (London: Longman, 1984). An excellent brief survey with documents.

Geoffrey Parker, ed., *The Thirty Years' War*, 2d ed. (London: Routledge, 1997). A revised edition of the standard survey of the conflict.

Geoffrey Parker, *The World Crisis: Thirty Years of War, Famine, Plague, Regicide, and Radicalism, 1635–1665* (London: Perseus, 2007). A dynamic, broad history of a tumultuous three decades by a prize-winning military historian.

For a list of additional titles related to this chapter's topics, please see http://www.ablongman.com/kishlansky.

CHAPTER 15 THE EXPERIENCES OF LIFE IN EARLY MODERN EUROPE, 1500–1650

HAYMAKING

AGRICULTURE IN A EUROPEAN COMMUNITY

THE VISUAL RECORD

It is summer in the Low Countries. The trees are full, the meadows green; flowers rise in clumps and bushes hang heavy with fruit. The day has dawned brightly for haymaking. Yesterday the long meadow was mowed, and today the hay will be gathered and the first fruits and vegetables of the season harvested. From throughout the village families come together to labor. Twice each summer the grass is cut, dried, and stacked. Some of it will be left in the fields for the animals until autumn; some will be carried into large lofts and stored for the winter.

The scene of communal farming shown here was repeated with little variation throughout Europe in the early modern era. The village pictured is fairly prosperous with at least three horses and a large wheeled cart in view. Horses were still a luxury for farmers; they could be used for transportation as well as labor, but they were weaker than oxen and had to be fed grain rather than grass. The houses of the village also suggest comfort. The one at the far right is typical. It contains one floor for living and a loft for storage. The chimney separates a kitchen in the back from the long hall where the family works, sleeps, and entertains itself. The bed—it was not uncommon for there to be only one for the whole family—would be near the fireplace, and would be restuffed with straw after the harvest. The long end of the hall, farthest from heat and light, would be home to the family's animals once winter set in. But in summer it was a luxurious space where children could play or parents could claim a little privacy.

The church is easily distinguished by its steeple and is made of brick. The steeple has 16 windows, probably all set with expensive glass and even some stained glass. The church would have been built over several generations at considerable cost to the villagers. Even the most prosperous houses in the far meadow are made of timber and thatch. The layout of the buildings shows how the village must have grown. The original settlement was all on the rise above the church. The houses nearer the center of the picture were added later, perhaps to allow the sons of the more prosperous village farmers to begin their own families before their parents' deaths.

In the center of the scene are a large number of laborers. Four men with pitchforks load the cart while two women sweep the hay that falls back into new piles. Throughout the field, men and women, distinguished only by their clothing,

■ Detail of women laborers.

■ *Haymaking* (ca. 1565) by Pieter Brueghel.

rake hay into large stacks for successive loadings of the cart. At least 25 individuals work at these tasks. Men perform the heaviest work of loading the haycart and hammering the scythes while men and women share all the other work. Although no children appear in the scene, some are undoubtedly at work picking berries and beans.

The scenes of physical labor remind us that the life of ordinary people in the early modern period was neither romantic nor despondent, neither quaint nor primitive. It had its own joys and sorrows, its own triumphs and failures, its own measures of progress and decay. By today's standards, a sixteenth-century prince endured greater material hardships than a twentieth-century welfare recipient. There was no running water, no central heating, no lavatories, no electricity. There was no relief for toothache, headache, or numbing pain. Travel was dangerous and exhausting. There was no protection from the open air, and many nights were spent on the bare ground. Waiting for winds to sail was more tedious than waiting to board a plane. Entertainment was sparse, and the court jester would have been little match for stereo and video. Though we cannot help but be struck by the differences, we will not understand very much about the experience of life in sixteenth-century Europe if we judge it by our own standard of living.

LOOKING AHEAD

In this chapter, we will examine the social and economic conditions of early modern European society, dominated as it was by extreme change, and often, hardship. We will see how population growth put pressure on the European economy and how the rich became richer as food prices rose. We will also see how European governments were overwhelmed by changes they could only dimly perceive.

CHAPTER OUTLINE

- ECONOMIC LIFE
  Rural Life ▪ Town Life ▪ Economic Change
- SOCIAL LIFE
  Social Constructs ▪ Social Structure ▪ Social Change ▪ Peasant Revolts
- PRIVATE AND COMMUNITY LIFE
  The Family ▪ Communities ▪ Popular Beliefs and the Persecution of Witches

ECONOMIC LIFE

There was no typical sixteenth-century European. Travelers' accounts and ambassadors' reports indicate that contemporaries were constantly surprised by the habits and possessions of other Europeans. Language, custom, geography, and material conditions separated peoples in one place from those in another. Contrasts between social groups were more striking still. A Muscovite boyar had more in common with an English nobleman than either had with his country's peasants. A Spanish goldsmith and a German brass maker lived remarkably similar lives when compared to the life of a shepherd anywhere in Europe. No matter how carefully historians attempt to distinguish between country and town life, between social or occupational groups, or between men and women, they are still smoothing out edges that are very rough, still turning individuals into aggregates, still sacrificing the particular for the general. No French peasant family ever had 3.5 children even if, on average, they all did. There was no typical sixteenth-century European.

But there were experiences that most Europeans shared and common structures through which their activities were channeled that separated them from their predecessors and their successors. There was a distinctive sixteenth-century experience that we can easily discern and that they could dimly perceive. Much of it was a natural progression in which one generation improved upon the situation of another. Agriculture increased: more land was cleared, more crops were grown, and better tools were crafted. Some of the experience was natural regression. Irreplaceable resources were lost: more trees were felled, more soil was eroded, and more fresh water was polluted. But some of what was distinctive about sixteenth-century life resulted from dynamic changes in economic and social conditions. The century-long population explosion and increase in commodity prices fundamentally altered people's lives. Not since the Black Death had Europe experienced so thorough a transformation in its economic development and its social organization. Change and reactions to change became dominant themes of everyday life.

Rural Life

In the early modern era, as much as 90 percent of the European population lived on farms or in small towns in which farming was the principal occupation. Villages were small and relatively isolated, even in densely populated regions such as Italy and the Low Countries. They might range in size from 100 families, as was common in France and Spain, to fewer than 20 families, which was the average size of Hungarian villages. The villages, large or small, prosperous or poor, were the bedrock of the sixteenth-century state. A sur-

IMAGE DISCOVERY

A Rural Scene: Social or Religious?

This picture depicts the slaughtering of a hog, which required winter weather, and baking in a communal oven, which happened year-round. Why do you suppose impoverished peasants caught the blood from the slit throat of the hog? The illustration comes from a sixteenth-century calendar of religious observances and devotions. Would the readers of this calendar have participated in scenes like those pictured? Why or why not?

plus peasant population fed the insatiable appetite of towns for laborers and of crowns for soldiers. The manor, the parish, and the rural administrative district were the institutional infrastructures of Europe. Each organized the peasantry for its own purposes. Manorial rents supported the lifestyle of the nobility; parish tithes supported the works of the Church; local taxes supported the power of the state. Rents, tithes, and taxes easily absorbed more than half of the wealth produced by the land. From the remaining half, the peasants had to make provisions for their present and their future.

To survive, the village community had to be self-sufficient. In good times there was enough to eat and some to save for the future. Hard times meant hunger and starvation. Both conditions were accepted as part of the natural order, and both occurred regularly. One in every three harvests was bad; one in every five was disastrous. Bad harvests came in succession. Depending upon the soil and crop, between one-fifth and one-half of the grain harvested had to be saved as seed for the next planting season. When hunger was worst, people faced the agonizing choice of eating or saving their seed corn.

The Sixteenth-Century Household. Hunger and cold were the constant companions of the average European. In Scandinavia and Muscovy, winter posed as great a threat to survival as did starvation. There the stove and garments made from animal fur were essential requirements, as were the hearth and the woolen tunic in the south. Everywhere in Europe, homes were inadequate shelter against the cold and damp. Most were built of wood and roofed in thatch. Inside walls were patched with dried mud and sometimes covered with bark or animal skins. Windows were few and narrow. Piled leaves or straw, which could easily be replaced, covered the ground and acted as insulation. The typical house was one long room with a stone hearth at the end. The hearth provided both heat and light and belched forth soot and smoke through a brick chimney.

People had relatively few household possessions. The essential piece of furniture was the wooden chest, which was used for storage. A typical family could keep all of its belongings in the chest, which could then be buried or carried away in times of danger. The chest could also serve as a table or bench or as a sideboard on which food could be placed. Tables and stools were becoming more common during the sixteenth century, though chairs were still a great luxury. Most domestic activities, of which cooking, eating, and sleeping were dominant, took place close to the ground, and squatting, kneeling, and sitting were the usual postures of family members. All other family possessions related to food production. Iron spits and pots, or at least metal rings and clamps for wooden ones, were treasured goods that were passed from generation to generation. Most other implements were wooden. Long-handled spoons; boards known as trenchers, which were used for cutting and eating; and one large cup and bowl were the basic stock of the kitchen. The family ate from the long trencher and passed the bowl and cup. Knives were essential farm tools that doubled for kitchen and mealtime duty, but forks were still a curiosity.

Reliance on Agriculture. Peasant life centered on agriculture. Technology and technique varied little across the continent, but there were significant differences depending upon climate and soil. The lives of those who grew crops contrasted

This picture, painted in 1530, shows farmworkers threshing grain. The figure at the door seems to be an overseer. He has just sold a sack of grain, indicating the transition from a system of self-sufficient manors to a market economy.

with the experiences of those who raised animals. Across the great plain, the breadbasket that stretched from the Low Countries to Poland-Lithuania, the most common form of crop growing was still the **three-field rotation** system. In that method, winter crops such as wheat or rye were planted in one field; spring crops such as barley, peas, or beans were planted in another; and the third field was left fallow. More than 80 percent of what was grown on the farm was consumed on the farm. Most of the grain was baked into the coarse black bread that was the monotonous fare of the peasant diet. Two to three pounds a day for an adult male was an average allotment when grain was readily available. Beer and gruels of grain and skimmed milk or water flavored with fruit juice supplemented peasant fare. In one form or another, grain provided more than 75 percent of the calories in a typical diet.

The warm climate and dry weather of Mediterranean Europe favored a two-crop rotation system. With less water and stronger sunlight, half the land had to be left fallow each year to restore its nutrients. There fruit, especially grapes and olives, was an essential supplement to diet. With smaller cereal crops, wine replaced beer as a nutritious beverage. The fermentation of grapes and grain into wine and beer also provided convenient ways of storing foodstuffs, a constant problem during the winter and early spring. Wine and olive oil were also luxury products and were most commonly exchanged for meat, which was less plentiful on southern European farms.

Animal husbandry was the main occupation in the third agricultural area of Europe, the mountainous and hilly regions. Sheep were the most common animal that Europeans raised. Sheep provided the raw material for almost all clothing, their skins were used for parchment and as window coverings, and they were a ready source of inexpensive meat. They were bred in hundreds of thousands, migrating across large areas of grazing land, especially in western Europe, where their wool was the main export of both England and Spain. Pigs were domestic animals prevalent in woodland settlements. They foraged for food and were kept, like poultry, for slaughter. Cattle, on the other hand, were essential farm animals. "The fundamentals of the home," wrote the Spanish poet Luis de Leon (1527–1591), "are the woman and the ox, the ox to plow and the woman to manage things." In the dairying areas of Europe, cattle produced milk, cheese, and butter; in Hungary and Bohemia, the great breeding center of the Continent, they were raised for export; and almost everywhere else they were used as beasts of burden.

Because agriculture was the principal occupation of Europeans, land was the principal resource. Most land was owned, not by those who worked it, but by lords who let it out in various ways. The land was still divided into manors, and the manor lord, or **seigneur,** was still responsible for maintaining order, administering justice, and arbitrating disputes. Although the personal bonds between lords and tenants were gradually loosening, political and economic ties were as strong as ever. In western Europe, peasants generally owned between a third and a half of the land they worked, while eastern European peasants owned little if any land. But by the sixteenth century, almost all peasants enjoyed security of tenure on the land they worked. In return for various forms of rents, they used the land as they saw fit and could hand it down to their children. Rents were only occasionally paid in coin, although money rents became more common as the century progressed. More frequently, the lord received a fixed proportion of the yield of the land or received labor from the peasant. Labor service was being replaced by monetary payments in northern and western Europe, but it continued in the east, where it was known as the ***robot.*** German and Hungarian peasants normally owed two or three days' labor on the lord's estate each week, while Polish peasants might owe as many as

Painting of a town market by Italian painter Leandro da Ponte Bassano (1557–1622). In sixteenth-century Europe, towns were centers of commercial activity, and such scenes of bartering and buying goods were common.

LIVING BY ONE'S WITS

The Life of Lazarillo des Tormes *(1554) is among the first modern novels, one of a variety of sixteenth-century Spanish stories that are called* picaresque *after the wandering beggars that are their heroes. Although the picaresque novel was a fictional account, much of the descriptive detail accurately portrays the social conditions for the vast majority of the Spanish population in the so-called Golden Age.*

Focus Questions

Why is it so important for Lazarillo to use his cunning? Why is the reader encouraged to sympathize with the narrator?

We began our journey, and in a few days he taught me thieves' jargon, and when he saw me to be of a good wit, was well pleased, and used to say: "Gold or silver I cannot give thee, but I will show thee many pointers about life." And it was so; for after God this man gave me my life, and although blind lighted and guided me in the career of living.

He used to carry bread and everything else in a linen sack which closed at the mouth with an iron ring and a padlock and key, and when he put things in and took them out, it was with so much attention, so well counted, that the whole world wouldn't have been equal to making it a crumb less. But I would take what stingy bit he gave me, and finish it in less than two mouthfuls. After he had fastened the lock and stopped worrying about it, thinking me to be engaged in other things, by a little seam, which I unsewed and sewed up again many times in the side of the sack, I used to bleed the miserly sack, taking out bread—not measured quantities but good pieces—and slices of bacon and sausage; and thus would seek a convenient time to make good the devilish state of want which the wicked blind man left me in.

When we ate he used to put a little jug of wine near him. I would quickly seize it and give it a couple of silent kisses and return it to its place; but this plan didn't work long, for he noticed the deficiency in his draughts, and in order to keep his wine safe, he never after let go the jug, but kept hold of the handle. But there is no lode-stone that draws things to it so strongly as I with a long rye straw, which I had prepared for that purpose, and placing which in the mouth of the jug, I would suck up the wine to a fare-ye-well. But the villain was so clever that I think he heard me; and from then on he changed procedure and set his jug between his legs and covered it with his hand, and thus drank secure.

We were at Escalona, town of the Duke of that ilk, in an inn, and he gave me a piece of sausage to roast. When he had basted the sausage and eaten the basting, he took a maravedi from his purse and bade me fetch wine from the tavern. The devil put the occasion before my eyes, which, as the saying is, makes the thief; and it was this: there lay by the fire a small turnip, rather long and bad, and which must have been thrown there because it was not fit for the stew. And as nobody was there at the time but him and me alone, as I had an appetite whetted by having got the toothsome odour of the sausage inside me (the only part, as I knew, that I had to enjoy myself with), not considering what might follow, all fear set aside in order to comply with desire—while the blind man was taking the money out of his purse, I took the sausage, and quickly put the above-mentioned turnip on the spit, which my master grasped, when he had given me the money for the wine, and began to turn before the fire, trying to roast what through its demerit had escaped being boiled. I went for the wine, and on the way did not delay in despatching the sausage, and when I came back I found the sinner of a blind man holding the turnip ready between two slices of bread, for he had not yet recognized it, because he had not tried it with his hand. When he took the slices of bread and bit into them, thinking to get part of the sausage too, he found himself chilled by the chilly turnip.

From *Lazarillo des Tormes*.

four days. Labor service tied the peasants to the land they worked. Eastern European peasants were less mobile than peasants in the west, and as a result towns were fewer and smaller in the east.

Town Life

In the country, men and women worked to the natural rhythm of the day: up at the cock's crow, at work in the cooler hours, at rest in the hotter ones. Rain and cold kept them idle; sunlight kept them busy. Each season brought its own activity. In the town the bell tolled every hour. In the summer the laborers gathered at the town gates at four in the morning, in the winter at seven. The bell signaled the time for morning and afternoon meals as well as the hour to lay down tools and return home. Wages were paid for hours worked: 7 in winter, as many as 16 in June and July.

The Heart of Commerce. In all towns there was an official guild structure that organized and regulated labor. Rules laid down the requirements for training, the standards for quality, and the conditions for exchange. Only those officially sanctioned could work in trades, and each trade could perform only specified tasks. In the German town of Nüremberg, a sword maker could not make knives nor could a pin maker make thimbles. Specialization went even further in London, Paris, and other large cities.

While the life of the peasant community turned on self-sufficiency, that of the town turned on interdependence. Exchange was the medium that transformed labor and skill into food and shelter. The town was one large marketplace in which the circulation of goods dictated the survival of the residents. Men and women in towns worked as hard as did those on farms, but town dwellers received a more varied and more comfortable life in return. However, that did not mean that hunger and hardship were unknown in towns. Urban poverty was endemic and grew worse as the century wore on. In most towns, as much as a quarter of the entire population might be destitute, living from casual day labor, charity, or crime. But even for those people, food was more readily available in greater varieties than in the countryside, and the institutional network of support for the poor and homeless was stronger. In Lyon, the overseers of the poor distributed a daily ration of a pound and a half of bread, more than half of what a farm laborer would consume. The urban poor more often fell victim to disease than to starvation.

Towns were distinguished by the variety of occupations that existed within them. The preparation and exchange of food dominated small market towns. Peasants would bring in their finest produce for sale and exchange it for vital manufactured goods such as iron spits and pots for cooking or metal and leather tools for farm work. In smaller towns, there was as much barter as sale; in larger places, money was exchanged for commodities. Women dominated the food trades in most market towns, trading, buying, and selling in the shop fronts that occupied the bottom story of their houses. Because of their skills in food preparation, they were better able to obtain the best prices and advantageously display the best goods.

The Work Force. In larger towns, the specialization of labor was more intense and wage earning more essential. Large traders dominated the major occupations such as baking, brewing, and cloth manufacture, leaving distribution in the hands of the family economy, where there might still be a significant element of bartering. Piecework handicrafts became the staple for less prosperous town families, who prepared raw materials for the large manufacturers or finished products before their sale. Occupations were usually organized geographically, with metal or glassworking taking place in one quarter of the town, brewing or baking in another. There was a strong family and kin network to the occupations, as each craft required long years of technical training, which was handed down from parents to children.

Most town dwellers, however, lived by unskilled labor. The most lucrative occupations were strictly controlled, so those who flocked to towns in search of employment usually hired themselves out as day laborers, hauling and lifting goods onto carts or boats, stacking materials at building sites, or delivering water and food. After the first decades of the sixteenth century, the supply of laborers exceeded the amount of work to occupy them, and town authorities were constantly attempting to expel them. The most fortunate might succeed in becoming servants.

Domestic service was a critical source of household labor. Even families on the margins of subsistence employed ser-

Van Schwanerburg (1537–1614), *The Spinners*. Workers spinning and weaving wool. Labor in large towns was often specialized into occupations such as baking, brewing, and cloth manufacture.

MAP DISCOVERY

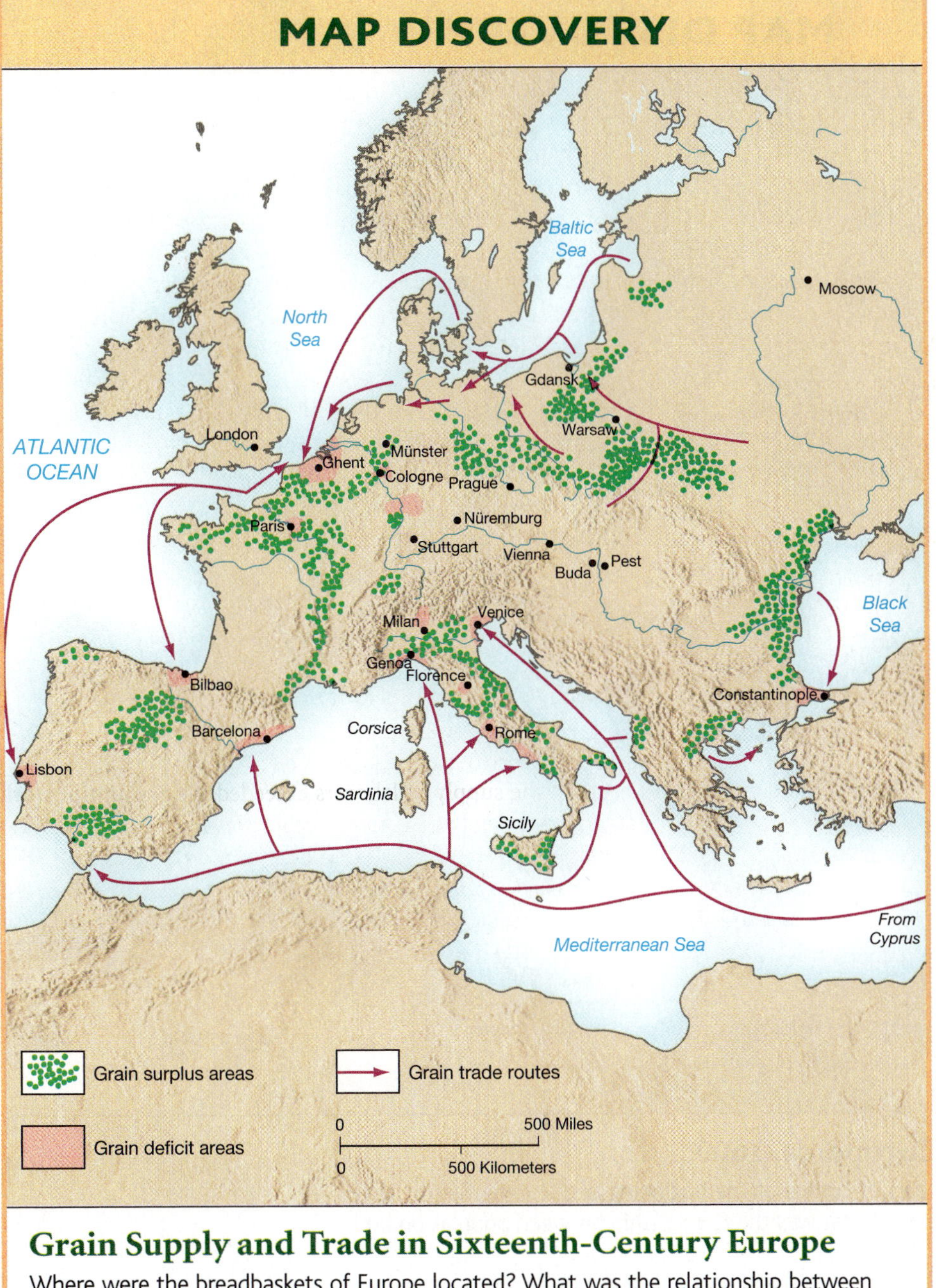

Grain Supply and Trade in Sixteenth-Century Europe

Where were the breadbaskets of Europe located? What was the relationship between urban areas and grain supply? How did grain move from suppliers to consumers?

vants to undertake the innumerable household tasks, which allowed parents to pursue their primary occupations. Everything was done by hand and on foot, and extra pairs of each were essential. In Münster at mid-century, there were 400 servants for 1000 households. Domestics were not apprentices, though they might aspire to become apprentices to the trade followed in the family with whom they lived. If they had kinship bonds in the town, apprenticeship was a likely outcome. But more commonly, domestics remained household servants, frequently changing employers in hope of more comfortable housing and better food.

Economic Change

Over the course of the sixteenth century, the European population increased by about a third, with much of the growth taking place in the first 50 years. Rough estimates suggest the rise to have been from about 80 to 105 million. Patterns of growth varied by region. The population of the eastern part of Europe seems to have increased more steadily across the century, while western Europe experienced a population explosion in the early decades. The population of France may have doubled between 1450 and 1550, from 10 to 20 million. The population of England nearly doubled between 1500 and 1600, from more than 2 million to more than 4 million. Castile, the largest region in Spain, grew 50 percent in 50 years. Europe had finally recovered from the devastation of the Black Death, and by 1600 its population was greater than it had ever been. Demographic growth was even more dramatic in the cities. In 1500, only four cities had populations greater than 100,000; in 1600, there were eight. Naples grew from 150,000 to 280,000, and both Paris and London to more than 200,000 inhabitants. Fifteen large cities more than doubled their populations, with London experiencing a phenomenal 400 percent increase.

The rise in population dramatically affected the lives of ordinary Europeans. In the early part of the century, the first phase of growth brought prosperity. The land was still not farmed to capacity, and extra hands meant increased productivity. As there was uncultivated land that could be plowed, convenient room for new housing, and enough commons and woodlands to be shared, the population increase was a welcome development. Even when rural communities began to reach their natural limits as people's needs pressed against nature's resources, opportunity still existed in the burgeoning towns and cities. At first the cycle was beneficial. Surplus on the farms led to economic growth in the towns. Growth in the towns meant more opportunities for those on the farms. More food supported more workers, and more

MAP DISCOVERY

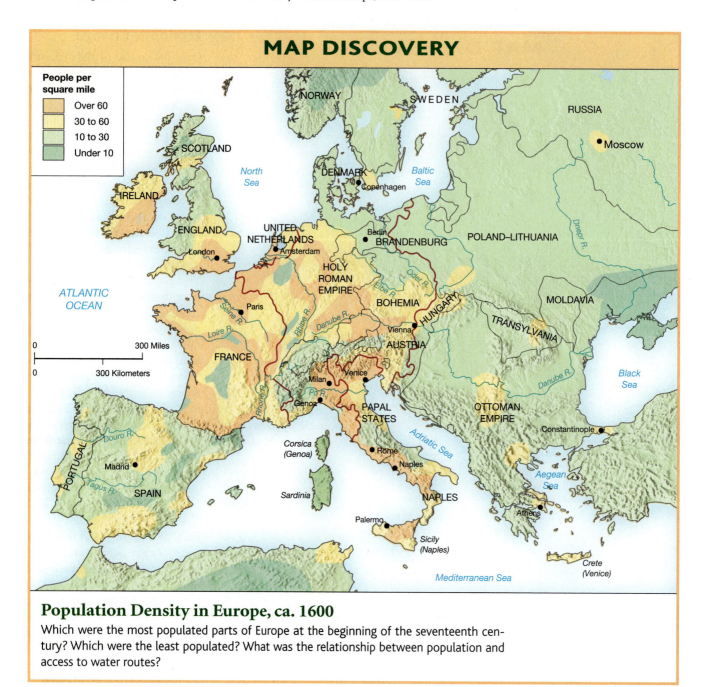

Population Density in Europe, ca. 1600

Which were the most populated parts of Europe at the beginning of the seventeenth century? Which were the least populated? What was the relationship between population and access to water routes?

workers produced more goods and services, which were exchanged for more food.

The first waves of migrants to the towns found opportunity everywhere. Even the most lucrative textile and provisioning trades were recruiting new members, and apprenticeships were easy to find. A shortage of casual labor kept wages at a decent rate. Successful migrants encouraged kin from their villages to move to the towns and sponsored their start in trade or service. For a while, rural families did not have to make elaborate preparations to provide for their younger sons and daughters: they could be sent to the towns. Instead of saving every extra penny to give their children a start in life, farmers could purchase some luxury goods or expand their landholdings.

European Population Density, c. 1600

Such an opportunity could not last. With more mouths to feed, more crops had to be planted. Since the most productive land was already under the plow, new fields were carved from less fertile areas. In some villages, land was taken from the common waste, the woodlands or scrublands that were used for animal forage and domestic fuel. The land was less suitable for crops, and it became unavailable for other important uses.

As workers continued to flood into the towns, real wages began to fall, not only among the unskilled but throughout the work force. A black market in labor developed to take advantage of the surplus population. In terms of purchasing power, the wages of a craftsman in the building trade in

The new money economy inspired this satirical portrait by Quentin Massys. It shows a moneylender counting his receipts while his wife is distracted from her Bible by the pile of coins. Many such merchants won fame and power and even titles.

England fell by one-half during the sixteenth century. A French stonemason, a highly paid skilled laborer, could buy 33 pounds of bread with his daily wage in 1480; by 1550 he could buy fewer than 10. Peasants in the French region of Languedoc who hired out for farm labor lost 56 percent of their purchasing power during the century. Only reapers, who were the physically strongest agricultural laborers, appear to have kept pace with inflation; grape pickers, among the least skilled, endured declines of up to 300 or 400 percent.

The fall in real wages took place against a backdrop of inflation that has come to be called the **Price Revolution**. Between 1500 and 1650, cereal prices increased between five- and sixfold, manufactured goods between two- and threefold. Most of the rapid increase came in the second half of the sixteenth century, a result of both population growth and the import of precious metals from the New World. Sixteenth-century governments understood little about the relationship between money supply and prices. Gold and silver from America flooded the international economy, raising commodity prices. As prices rose so did the deficits of the state, which was the largest purchaser of both agricultural and manufactured goods. With huge deficits, states began to devalue their coins in the mistaken belief that this would lower their debt. But debased coinage resulted in still higher prices, and higher prices resulted in greater debt. The Price Revolution was felt throughout the Continent and played havoc with government finances, international trade, and the lives of ordinary people.

A 500 percent inflation in agricultural products over a century is not much by modern standards. Compounded, the rate averages less than 2 percent a year. But the Price Revolution did not take place in a modern society or within a modern market economy. In the sixteenth century, that level of rising prices disrupted everything. In the Spanish town of Seville, almost all buildings were rented on 99-year leases to the families who lived and worked in them. That was a fairly common practice throughout Europe. It meant that a landlord who rented a butcher shop and living quarters in 1501 could not raise the rent until 1600! Similarly, lords frequently held the right to purchase agricultural produce at specified prices. That system, similar to today's commodity market, helped both lords and peasants plan ahead. It ensured the lord a steady supply and the peasant a steady market. But it assumed steady prices. Until the middle of the seventeenth century, the king of England had the right to purchase wheat at prices set 300 years earlier.

Thus an enduring increase in prices created profound social dislocation. Some people became destitute; others became rich beyond their dreams. The towns were particularly hard hit, for they exchanged manufactured goods for food and thus suffered when grain prices rose faster than those of other commodities. Landholders who derived their income from rents were squeezed; those who received payment in kind reaped a windfall of more valuable agricultural goods. Peasants were largely protected from the rise in food prices, but they were not insulated from its consequences. As long as they consumed what they raised, the nominal value of commodities was of no great matter. But if some part of their subsistence had to be obtained by labor, they were in grave peril.

There was now an enormous incentive to produce a surplus for market and to begin to specialize in particular grains that were in high demand. Every small scrap of land that individual peasant families could bring under cultivation would now yield foodstuffs that could be exchanged for manufactured luxury goods. The tendency for all peasants to hold roughly equivalent amounts of land abruptly ceased. The fortunate could become prosperous by selling their surplus. The unfortunate found ready purchasers for their strips and common rights. Villagers began to be divided into those who held large amounts of land and sold their surplus at a profit and those who held small amounts of land and hired themselves out as laborers to their more fortunate neighbors.

The beneficial cycle now turned vicious. Those who had sold out and left the land looking for prosperity in the towns were forced to return to the land as agrarian laborers. In western Europe, they became the landless poor, seasonal migrants without the safety net of rooted communal life. In eastern Europe, labor service enriched the landed nobility, who were able to sell stores of grain in the export market. They used the law to tie the peasants to the land in order to ensure that grain would be cultivated for the market. Poland-Lithuania became a major supplier of cereals to northern Europe, and Gdansk became the most important agricultural seaport in the world. But agricultural surplus from the east could not make up for the great shortfall in the west. By the beginning of the seventeenth century, the western European states faced a crisis of subsistence. Everyone was hungry; many were starving.

SOCIAL LIFE

Social organization combines elements of tradition, belief, and function, but the elements are so fused together that it is impossible to determine where one ends and the other begins. Society is a human construct, subject to the strengths and frailties of its creators. The basic assumption of sixteenth-century European society was inequality, and its basic form of social organization was stratification. The group, rather than the individual, was the predominant unit in society. The first level of the social order was the family and the household; then came the village or town community; and finally the gradations of ranks and orders of society at large. Elaborate rituals helped define membership in each of the groups, from the marriage ceremony to the initiation rites of citizens and to the processions and ceremonial displays of the nobility. All stressed the significance of the rights and obligations of different levels of society. Each group had its own place in the social order and each performed its own essential function. Society was the sum of its parts.

The traditional social organization was severely tested over the course of the early modern period. Economic change reshaped ideas of mobility and drew sharper distinctions between rural and urban life. The growth of towns and their domination of the countryside around them challenged beliefs about the primacy of agricultural production and the subordinate nature of trade and commerce. The rise to new wealth and prominence of some social groups challenged traditional elites' hold on power and prestige. The transformation of landholding patterns in the villages challenged the stability of rural communities. The rising numbers of both urban and rural poor challenged the institutions of charitable relief and posed the threat of crime and disorder. Eventually those developments led to bloody confrontations between social groups.

Social Constructs

Hierarchy was the dominant principle of social organization in the early modern era. Hierarchy existed at every level, from the basic distinction between lords and commoners to the fastidious complexity of the ranks of the nobility. The hierarchy of masters, journeymen, and apprentices dominated trades; trades themselves existed in a hierarchy. In the hierarchy of civic government, each official held a place in an ascending order, up to the elite of councillors and mayors. On the land was the hierarchy of freeholder, laborer, and leaseholder among the peasants. The family itself was hierarchically organized, with the wife subordinate to her husband, the children to their parents, and the apprentices and servants to their master and mistress. "All things observe degree, priority and place," Shakespeare wrote of both natural and human order in *Troilus and Cressida* (1601–1602). "Take but degree away, untune that string, and hark what discord follows."

Status, rather than wealth, determined the social hierarchy. It conferred privileges and exacted responsibilities according to rank. Status was everywhere apparent. It was confirmed in social conventions such as bowing and hat doffing. In towns and cities the clothing that people were allowed to wear—even the foods that they were allowed to eat—reflected status. Status was signified in titles: not just in the ranks of the nobility or between nobles and commoners, but even in ordinary communities masters and mistresses, goodmen and good-

Festivals disrupted the dreary routine of village life with games and feasting. The Christian or popular reason for the festival was often less important than the festival's value as a source of merriment and affirmation of solidarity.

wives, squires and ladies, adopted the English equivalents of European titles. The acceptance of status was an everyday, uncomplicated, unreflective act, similar to stopping at a red light. Inequality was a fact of European social life that was as unquestioned as it was unquestionable.

Images that people used to describe both the natural world and their social world reinforced the functional nature of hierarchy. The first, and most elaborate image, was that of the **Great Chain of Being**. The Great Chain was a description of the universe in which everything had a place, from God at the top of the chain to inanimate objects like rocks at the bottom. Complex accounts of the chain listed the seven orders of angels, the multiple ranks of humans, even the degrees of animals and plants, from which lions emerged as kings of the jungle. Spanish botanists were dispatched to the New World to help identify the unknown flora and fauna in terms of their places in the chain. Native Americans were first thought to be the lost tribes of Israel, as they were the only humans missing from traditional accounts of the chain. For ordinary people, the Great Chain of Being expressed the belief that all life was interconnected, that every link was a part of a divinely ordered universe and was as necessary as every other.

The second metaphor used to describe society stressed the notion of interdependency even more strongly. This was the image of the Body Politic, in which the head ruled, the arms protected, the stomach nourished, and the feet labored. The image described a small community as well as a large state. In the state, the king was the head, the Church the soul, the nobles the arms, the artisans the hands, and the peasants the feet. Each performed its own function, and each function was essential to the health of the body. Like the Great Chain of Being, the Body Politic was a profoundly conservative concept of social organization. Taken literally, it precluded the idea of social mobility, of people rising or falling from one group to another.

Social Structure

The Great Chain of Being and the Body Politic were static concepts of social organization. But in the early modern era, European society was in a state of dynamic change. Fundamentally, all European societies were divided into nobles and commoners. That basic distinction existed throughout the Continent, although relationships between the two orders differed from place to place.

The Nobles. Nobility was a legal status that conferred certain privileges upon its holders. The first was rank and title, a well-defined place at the top of the social order that was passed from one generation to the next. Each rank had its own privileges and each was clearly demarcated from the next by behavior, dress, and title. The escutcheon—the coat of arms—was a universally recognized symbol of rank and family connection. The coat of arms was woven in garments; emblazoned on windows, carriages, and household goods; and displayed on banners during formal processions. Although there were various systems of title in use across the Continent and the nobility of one state could not claim noble privileges in another state, the hierarchy of prince, duke, earl, count, and baron was roughly standard.

Because rulers conferred the titles on individuals, elevating some to higher ranks and others from commoner to noble, the nobility was a political order as well as a social one. Political privileges were among the nobility's most important attributes. In many countries, the highest offices of the state and the military were reserved for members of the nobility. In Poland, for example, all offices were held by noblemen. It was a privilege that could work both ways, either restricting officeholders to those already ennobled or, as in town councils in France and Spain, ennobling those who achieved certain offices. The nobility was also granted rights of political participation in the deliberative bodies of the state. In England, the peerage was defined as all those who were summoned to the House of Lords. In most parts of central Europe, the nobility alone composed the diets that advised the monarch. In the Holy Roman Empire, the rank of imperial free knights allowed the nobility to separate itself entirely from the jurisdiction of towns or individual principalities.

Finally, members of the nobility held economic privileges, a result both of their rank and of their role as lords on the lands they owned. In almost every state, the nobility was exempt from most taxation. That was an area in which the interests of the nobles conflicted directly with those of the ruler. The larger the number of tax exemptions for the nobility, the stronger was its power in relation to the monarch. Tax exemptions of the nobility were most extensive in eastern and central Europe. There the crowns were elective rather than hereditary, allowing the nobles to bargain their support. The Polish nobility was exempt from the salt tax, the alcohol tax, and all internal tolls and customs. As Polish agriculture developed into an export industry, exemption from tolls gave the nobility a competitive advantage over merchants in the marketing of goods. The Hungarian nobility was exempt from all direct taxes, including the land tax. The nobility in western Europe enjoyed fewer immunities but not necessarily less valuable ones. French nobles were exempt from the taille, Spanish nobles from the hearth tax.

Privileges implied obligations. Initially the nobility was the warrior caste of the state and its primary obligations were to raise, equip, and lead troops into battle. Much of the great wealth that nobles possessed was at the service of the ruler during times of war, and war was a perpetual activity. By the sixteenth century, the military needs of the state had far surpassed the military power of its nobility. Warfare had become a national enterprise that required central coordination. Nobles became administrators as much as warriors, though it is fair to say that many did both. The French nobility came to be divided into the nobility of the sword and the nobility of the robe—that is, warriors and officeholders. The old military nobility could hardly understand the new service nobility. "I have continually been astounded," one of them remarked, "that so many young men could thus amuse themselves in a law court, since ordinarily youthful blood is boiling." A glorious battlefield death was still an ideal for most of Europe's noblemen.

Town Elite and Gentry. The principal distinction in sixteenth-century society was between lord and commoners, but it was not the only one. In both town and countryside a new social group was emerging. It had neither the legal nor the social privileges of nobility, but it performed many of the same functions. Over the course of the century the group carved out a place that was clearly distinct from that of the commoners, even if it was not clearly identical to the lords. It was most evident in the towns, for the towns remained a separate unit of social organization in most states. Towns enjoyed many of the same political and economic privileges as the nobility. In many states, the towns sent representatives to meet with the nobles and the king and were the most important part of national deliberative assemblies such as the English Parliament, the French Estates, or the Spanish Cortes. Towns were granted legal rights to govern their own citizens, to engage in trade, and to defend themselves by raising and storing arms. Although they paid a large share of most taxes, towns also received large tax concessions.

Yet, as individuals, members of the town elite held no special status in society at large. Some were among the richest people in the state—great bankers and merchants who were wealthier than dukes—but they had to devise their own systems of honor and prestige. In Venice, the *Book of Gold* distinguished the local elite from the ranks of ordinary citizens. Members of the "Old Families," who monopolized the highest civic offices, ruled Nüremberg. In France and Spain, some of the highest officers of leading towns were granted noble status, such as the "honored citizens" of Barcelona who were ennobled by King Ferdinand of Aragon. German burghers, as prosperous townsmen were called, remained caught in a state between noble and common, despised from above because they worked with their hands, envied from below for their wealth and comfort. In Münster, many withdrew from urban affairs and sought the privileges of the lower nobility.

In rural society, the transformation of agricultural holdings in many places also created a group that fit uncomfortably between lords and commoners. The accumulation of larger and larger estates through purchase from the nobility, the state, or the Church made lords—in the sense of landowners with tenants—out of many who were not lords in rank. They received rents and dues from their tenants, admin-

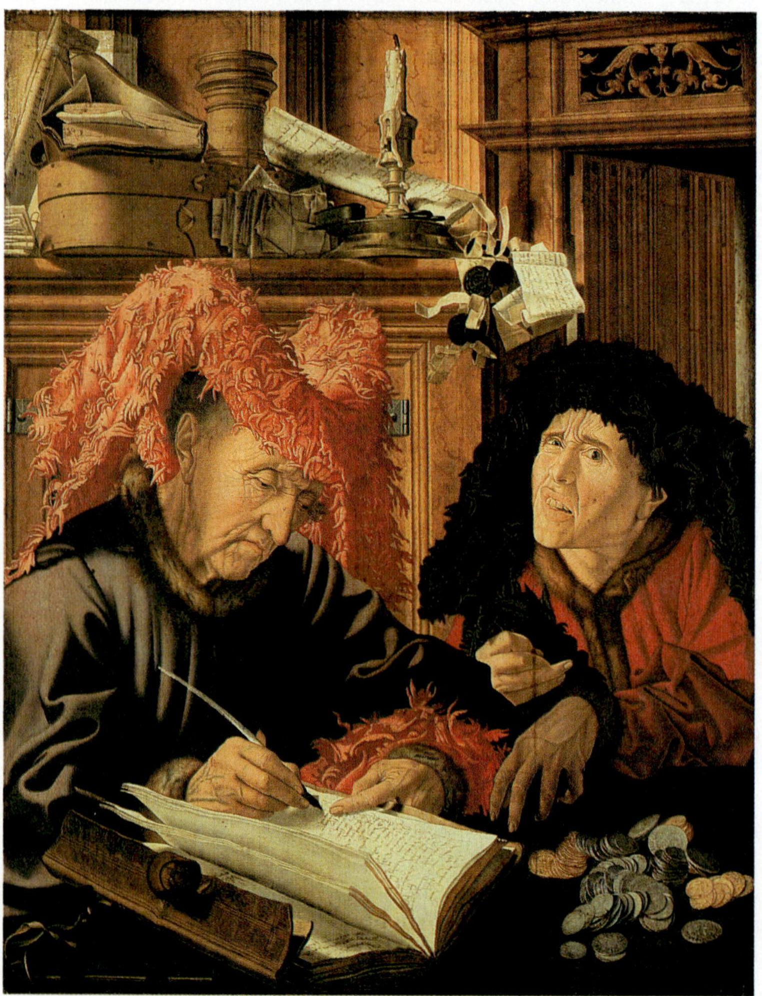

Marinus van Reymerswaele, *The Two Tax Gatherers*. The figure on the left is a city treasurer who is posting in the book an account of the city's revenues from taxes on wine, beer, fish, and other commodities. The painting is probably a satirical composition intended to expose the iniquity of covetousness, usury, or extortion.

istered their estates, and preserved the so-called moral economy that sustained the peasants during hard times. In England, the group came to be known as the gentry, and there were parallel groups in Spain, France, and the empire. The gentry aspired to the privileges of the nobility. In England, members of the gentry had the right to have a coat of arms and could be knighted. But knighthoods were not hereditary and did not confer membership in the House of Lords. In Spain, the caballeros and hidalgos gained noble privileges but were still of lower status than the grandees. The gentry aped the habits of the nobility, often outdoing nobles in lavish displays of wealth and spending.

In towns, the order of rank below the elite pertained as much to the kind of work that one performed as it did to the level at which it was undertaken. The critical division in town life was between those who had the freedom of the city—citizens—and those who did not. Citizenship was restricted to membership in certain occupations and was closely regulated. It could be purchased, especially by members of learned professions whose services were becoming vital in the early modern era, but most citizenship was earned by becoming a master in one of the guilds after a long period of apprenticeship and training. Only males could be citizens. In Germany, the feminine equivalent for the word used to denote a male citizen in good standing meant "prostitute"! But women who were married to citizens enjoyed their husbands' privileges, and widows of citizens could pass the privileges to their new husbands when they remarried. In both town and countryside, the privileges and obligations of each social group were the glue that held communities together.

Social Change

In the sixteenth century, social commentators believed that change was transforming the world in which they lived. In 1600, a Spanish observer blamed the rise of the rich commoners for the ills of the world: "They have obtained a particular status, that of a self-made group; and since they belong neither to the rich nor to the poor nor to the middle, they have thrown the state into the confusion we now see it in." An Englishman commenting on the rise of the gentry could give no better definition of its status than to say that a gentleman was one who lived like a gentleman. The challenge that the new nobility of the robe posed to the old nobility of the sword poisoned relations between the two segments of the French ruling elite. The military service class in Muscovy, who were of more use to the Muscovite princes than were the traditional landed nobility, posed an even greater threat to the privileges of the boyars.

The New Rich. Pressures on the ruling elites of European society came from above as well as below. The expansion of the state and the power of the prince frequently came as a result of direct conflict with the nobility. Only in east-central Europe—in Hungary, Bohemia, and Poland-Lithuania, where towns were small and urban elites weak—did the consolidation of the state actually enhance the privileges of the traditional noble orders.

There were many reasons why the traditional European social hierarchy was transformed during the course of the early modern era. In the first place, population increase necessitated an expansion of the ruling orders. With more people to govern, there had to be more governors who could perform the military, political, and social functions of the state. The traditional nobility grew slowly, as titles could be passed to only one son and intermarriage within the group was very high. Second, opportunities to accumulate wealth expanded dramatically with the Price Revolution. Traditionally, wealth was calculated in land and tenants rather than in the possession of liquid assets such as gold and silver. But with the increase in commodity prices, surplus producers could rapidly improve their economic position. What previously might have taken a generation or two of good fortune to amass could now be gathered seemingly overnight. Moreover, state service became a source of unlimited riches. The profits to be made from tax collecting, officeholding, or administering the law could easily surpass those to be made from landholding, especially after the economic downturn at the end of the century. The newly rich clamored for privileges, and many were in a position to lobby rulers effectively for them. Across European society the nobility grew, fed from fortunes made on the land, in trade, and in office.

The New Poor. Social change was equally apparent at the bottom of the social scale, but there it could not be so easily absorbed. The continuous population growth created a group of landless poor who squatted in villages and clogged the streets of towns and cities. Although poverty was not a new development of the early modern era, its growth created new problems. Rough estimates suggest that as many as a quarter of all Europeans were destitute. That was a staggering figure in great cities. There were tens of thousands of destitute people in London or Paris, where, it was observed, "the crowds of poor were so great that one could not pass through the streets."

Traditionally, local communities cared for their poor. Widows, orphans, and the handicapped, who would normally constitute more than half the poor in a village or town, were viewed as the "deserving poor," worthy of the care of the community through the Church or through private almsgiving. Catholic communities such as Venice created a system of private charity that paralleled the institutions of the Church. Although Protestant communities took charity out of the control of the church, they were no less concerned about the plight of the deserving poor. In England, a special tax, the poor rate, supported the poor and provided them with subsistence until they remarried or found employment. Perhaps the most elaborate system of all existed in the French town of Lyon where all the poor were registered and given identity cards. Each Sunday they would receive a week's worth of food and money. Young girls were provided with dowries, and young boys were taught crafts. Vagrants

A scene of peasant life in France during the prosperous reign of Louis XIV, by the genre painter Louis le Nain.

from the surrounding countryside were given one week's allotment to enable them to travel on. But Lyon's enlightened system was only for the deserving poor, and as the century progressed it was overwhelmed.

Charity was an obligation of the community, but as the sixteenth century progressed, the number of people who lived on the margins of subsistence grew beyond the ability of the local community to care for them. Perhaps more importantly, many of those who now begged for alms fell outside the traditional categories of the deserving poor. In England, they were called the sturdy beggars, men and women capable of working but incapable of finding more than occasional labor. To support themselves and their families, they left their native communities in search of employment and thus forfeited their claims on local charity. Most wound up in the towns and cities, where they slept and begged in the streets. Some disfigured themselves to enhance their abilities as beggars. As strangers they had no claim on local charity; as able-bodied workers they had no claim on local sympathy. Poor mothers abandoned their newborn infants on the steps of foundling hospitals or the houses of the rich. It is estimated that 10 percent of all newborn babies in the Spanish city of Valladolid were abandoned.

The problem of crime complicated the problems of poverty and vagrancy. Increasing population and increasing wealth equaled increasing crime; the addition of the poor to the equation aggravated the situation. The poor, destitute outsiders to the community, without visible means of support, were the easiest targets of official retribution. Throughout the century, numerous European states passed vagrancy laws in an effort to alleviate the problem of the wandering poor. In England, the poor were whipped from village to village until they were returned home. The sturdy beggars were branded with the letter *V* on their chests to identify them as vagrants, and therefore as potential criminals. Both Venetian and Dutch vagrants were regularly rounded up for galley service, while vagrants in Hungary were sold into slavery. Physical mutilation was used as an ineffective method of deterrence; thieves had fingers chopped off—which made it impossible for them to perform manual labor, and thus likely to steal again. Sexual offenses were criminalized—especially bastardy, since the birth of illegitimate children placed an immediate burden on the community. Prostitutes, who had long been tolerated and regulated in towns, were now persecuted. Rape increased. Capital punishment was reserved for the worst crimes—murder, incest, and grand larceny being most common—but, not surprisingly, executions were carried out mostly on outsiders to the community, with single women, the poor, and the vagrant being the most frequent victims.

Peasant Revolts

The economic and social changes of the sixteenth century bore serious consequences. Most telling was the upswing of violent confrontations between peasants and their lords. There was more than one difference between rich and poor in sixteenth-century society, but when conflict arose between them the important difference was that the wealthy controlled the means of coercion: the military and the law. Across Europe, and with alarming regularity, peasants took up arms to defend themselves from what they saw as violations of traditional rights and obligations. Peasant revolts were not hunger riots. Although they frequently occurred in periods of want, after bad harvests or marauding armies had impoverished villages, peasant revolts were not desperate attacks against warehouses or grain silos. Nor did those who took part in them form undisciplined mobs. Most revolts chose leaders, drew up peti-

Rebellious peasants gathered under a standard called the Banner of the Shoe. Here they surround a knight.

tions of grievances, and organized the rank and file into a semblance of military order. Leaders were literate—usually drawn from the lower clergy or minor gentry rather than from the peasantry—political demands were moderate, and tactics were sophisticated. But peasant revolts so profoundly threatened the social order that they were met with the severest repression. Confronted with the execution of their estate agents, rent strikes, and confiscation of their property, lords responded as if they were at war. Veteran soldiers and trained mercenaries were called out to fight peasant armies composed mostly of raw recruits. The results were horrifying.

Agrarian Changes. It is essential to realize that while peasants revolted against their lords, fundamentally their anger and frustration were products of agrarian changes that could be neither controlled nor understood. As population increased and market production expanded, many of the traditional rights and obligations of lords and peasants became oppressive. One example is that of forest rights. On most estates, the forests surrounding a village belonged to the lord. Commonly the village had its own woodlands in which animals foraged and fuel and building material were available. As the population increased, more farms came into existence. New land was put under the plow, and grain fields pressed up against the forest. There were more animals in the village, and some of them were let loose to consume the young sprouts and saplings. Soon there was not enough food for the wild game that was among the lord's most valuable property. So the game began to feed on the peasants' crops, which were now placed so appetizingly close to the forests. It was a capital crime for a peasant to kill wild game, but peasants couldn't allow the game to consume their crops.

A similar conflict arose over enclosing crop fields. An **enclosure** was a device—normally a fence or hedge that surrounded an area—to keep a parcel of land separate from the planted strips of land owned by the villagers. The parcel could be used for grazing animals or raising a specialty crop for the market. But an enclosure destroyed the traditional form of village agriculture, whereby decisions on which crops to plant were made communally. It became one of the chief grievances of the English peasants. But while enclosures broke up the old field system in many villages, they were a logical response to the transformation of land ownership that had already taken place. As more land was accumulated by fewer families, it made less sense for them to work widely scattered strips all over the village. If a family could consolidate its holdings by swaps and sales, it could gain an estate large enough to be used for both crops and grazing. An enclosed estate allowed wealthy farmers to grow more luxury crops for market or to raise only sheep on a field that had once been used for grain.

Enclosure was a process that both lord and rich peasant undertook, but it drove the smallholders from the land and was thus a source of bitter resentment for the poorer peasants. It was easy to protest the greed of the lords who, owning the most land, were the most successful enclosers. But enclosures were more a result of the process in which villages came to be characterized by a very small elite of large landholders and a very large mass of smallholders and landless poor. They were an effect rather than a cause.

From Hungary to England, peasant revolts brought social and economic change into sharp relief. A call for a crusade against Ottoman advances in 1514 provided the opportunity for Hungarian peasants to revolt against their noble landlords. Thousands dropped their plowshares and grasped the sword of a holy war. However, in fact, war against the Ottomans did not materialize. Instead, the mobilized peasants, under the leadership of disaffected army officers and clergymen, issued grievances against the labor service that they owed to their lords as well as numerous violations of customary agricultural practices. Their revolt turned into a civil war that was crushed with great brutality. In England, severe economic conditions led to a series

THE PEASANTS' REVOLT

In 1524 and 1525, a series of local protests over economic conditions coalesced into one of the largest concerted peasant uprisings in German history. The Peasants' Revolt was not a disorganized uprising of the hungry and dispossessed, but rather a carefully coordinated movement that attempted to win widespread social reforms. The Twelve Articles of the Peasants of Swabia show both the nature of the peasants' grievances and their ability to articulate them.

Focus Questions

On what grounds do the peasants base their pleas? Why are religious and economic issues so intertwined for these peasants?

The First Article. First, it is our humble petition and desire, as also our will and resolution, that in the future we should have power and authority so that each community should choose and appoint a pastor, and that we should have the right to depose him should he conduct himself improperly. The pastor thus chosen should teach us the gospel pure and simple, without any addition, doctrine, or ordinance of man.

The Second Article. According as the just tithe is established by the Old Testament and fulfilled in the New, we are ready and willing to pay the fair tithe of grain. . . . We will that for the future our church provost, whomsoever the community may appoint, shall gather and receive this tithe. . . .

The Tenth Article. In the tenth place, we are aggrieved by the appropriation by individuals of meadows and fields which at one time belonged to a community. These we will take again into our own hands. . . .

Conclusion. In the twelfth place, it is our conclusion and final resolution that if any one or more of the articles here set forth should not be in agreement with the word of God, as we think they are, such article we will willingly retract if it is proved really to be against the word of God by a clear explanation of the Scripture.

From the Twelve Articles of the Peasants of Swabia.

of revolts in 1549. Participants in the Western Rising, who succeeded in storming the town of Exeter, also combined religious and economic grievances. Cornish rebels added a social dimension with their slogan "Kill the gentlemen." In eastern England, Ket's Rebellion arose from peasant opposition to enclosure. The rebels occupied Norwich, the second largest city in the realm, but their aspirations were for reform rather than revolution. They, like the Hungarian peasants, were crushed by well-trained forces.

Uprising in Germany. The complexity of the peasants' problems is perhaps best revealed in the series of uprisings that are known collectively as the German Peasants' War. It was by far the most widespread peasant revolt of the sixteenth century, involving tens of thousands of peasants, and it combined a whole series of agrarian grievances with an awareness of the new religious spirit preached by Martin Luther. Luther condemned both lords and peasants: the lords for their rapaciousness, the peasants for their rebelliousness. Although he had a large following among the peasants, his advice that earthly oppression be passively accepted was not followed. The Peasants' War was directed against secular and ecclesiastical lords, and the rebels attacked both economic and religious abuses. Their combination of demands, such as the community's right to select its own minister and the community's right to cut wood freely, attracted a wide following in the villages and small towns of southern and central Germany. The printed demands of the peasantry, the most famous of which was the Twelve Articles of the Peasants of Swabia (1525), helped spread the movement far beyond its original bounds. The peasants organized themselves into large armies led by experienced soldiers. Initially they were able to besiege castles and abbeys and plunder lords' estates. Ultimately, those movements that refused compromise were ruthlessly crushed. By conservative estimates, more than 100,000 peasants were slaughtered during and after the war, many to serve as warning against future uprisings.

At base, the demands of the peasantry addressed the agrarian changes that were transforming German villages. Population growth was creating more poor villagers who could only hire out as laborers but who demanded a share of common grazing and woodlands. Because the presence of the poor increased the taxable wealth of the village, they were advantageous to the lord. But the strain they placed on resources was felt by both the subsistence and the surplus farmers. Tensions within the village were all the greater because the landless members were the kin of the landed—sons and daughters, brothers and sisters. If they were to be settled properly on the land, then the lord would have to let the village expand. If they were to be kept on the margins of subsistence, then the more prosperous villagers would have to be able to control their numbers and their conduct. In either case, the peasants needed more direct responsibility for governing the village than existed in their traditional relationship with their lord. Thus the grievances of the peasants of Swabia demanded release of the village peasantry from the status of serfs. They wanted to be allowed to move off the land, to marry out of the village without penalty, and to be free of the death taxes that further impoverished their children. The concessions would make it easier for the excess population to adjust to new conditions. They also wanted stable rents fixed at fair rates, a limit placed on labor service, and a return to the ancient customs that governed relations between lords and peasants. All the proposals were backed by an appeal to Christian principles of love and charity. They were profoundly conservative.

PRIVATE AND COMMUNITY LIFE

The great events of the sixteenth century—the discovery of the New World, the consolidation of states, the increasing incidence and ferocity of war, the reform of religion—all had profound impact on the lives of ordinary people. However slowly and intermittently these developments penetrated to isolated village communities, they were inextricably bound up with the experiences and the worldview of all Europeans. The states offered more protection and demanded more resources. Taxes increased, and tax collecting became more efficient. Wars took village boys and made them soldiers. Armies brought devastation to thousands of communities. The New World offered new opportunities, brought new products, and increased the wealth of the Continent. Religious reform, both Protestant and Catholic, penetrated into popular beliefs and personal piety. All the sweeping changes blurred the distinction between public and private life.

Still, the transformations wrought by political and intellectual developments were not necessarily the most important ones in people's lives. The lives of most Europeans centered on births and deaths, on the harvest, and on the social relations in their communities. For them, great events were the successful crop, the marriage of an heir, or the festivals that marked the progress of the year. Their beliefs were based as much on the customs they learned as children as on the religion they learned at church. Their strongest loyalties were to family and community rather than to church or state.

The Family

Sixteenth-century life centered on the family. The family was a crucial organizing principle for Europeans of all social ranks, and it served a variety of functions. In the most obvious sense, the family was the primary kin group. European families were predominantly nuclear, composed of a married couple and their children. In western Europe, a small number of families contained the adult siblings of the family head, uncles and aunts who had not yet established their own families. That pattern was more common in the east, especially in Hungary and Muscovy, where taxation was based on households and thus encouraged extended families. There, several nuclear families might live under the same roof. Yet however

■ Jan Vermeer's *The Milkmaid* (1658–1660) shows a domestic servant absorbed in her household tasks. Homes were sparsely furnished, though this family was rich enough to possess a table, an earthenware bowl and jug, and a footstove that held hot coals (seen on the floor behind the maid).

families were composed, kinship had a wider orbit than just parents and children. In-laws, step-relations, and cousins were considered part of the kin group and could be called upon for support in a variety of contexts, from charity to employment and business partnerships. In towns, such family connections created large and powerful clans.

A FEMININE PERSPECTIVE

Arcangela Tarabotti was born in Venice in the early seventeenth century. Her family did not have the means to provide her with a sufficient dowry, so she was sent to live in a Catholic convent, where she unhappily remained for the rest of her life. She wrote two major works. The first, Monastic Hell, *gives the flavor of her attitude toward her fate. The second was* Innocence Undone, *from which the following excerpt is taken.*

Focus Questions

What does Tarabotti point to as evidence of female superiority? Why do you think Tarabotti concentrates on the biblical account of the Creation?

Since woman is the epitome of all perfections, she is the last of the works of God, as far as material creation is concerned, but otherwise she dates from the beginning, and is the first-generated of all creatures, generated by the breath of God himself, as the Holy Spirit inferred, through the mouth of Solomon in the Ecclesiastes where he introduces the Most Holy Virgin to sing of herself: *The Lord possessed me in the beginning of his ways, before he made any thing from the beginning.*

This creature, although a woman, did not need to be made with a rib taken from man, because, so to speak, she was born before the beginning of time as well as before men, who, blinded by their ambition to dominate the world alone, astutely fail to mention this infallible truth, that the woman has existed in the Divine mind from the beginning. *I was set up from eternity, and of old before the earth was made. The depths were not as yet, and I was already conceived.*

They cannot deny the fact, although their malice prevents them from speaking it openly; but let us try to make them admit, in accordance with the Holy Scriptures rather than with some ill-informed preachers, that the woman made the man perfect and not vice versa.

After the Supreme Being created the world and all the animals (as I have said before), the text says *And God saw all the things that he had made; and they were very good.* Foreseeing that the man without woman would be the compendium of all imperfections, God said: *It is not good for man to be alone: let us make him a help like unto himself.* And therefore he created a companion for him that would be the universal glory of humanity and make him rich with merits.

Almighty God, having kept the creation of the woman as the last act of his wonderful work, desired to bestow privileges upon her, reinforce her graces and gladden the whole world with her splendour. If the supreme Architect's greatness, wisdom and love towards us shone brightly in his other works, he planned to make the woman, this excellent last addition to his splendid construction, capable of filling with wonder whoever looked at her. He therefore gave her the strength to subdue and dominate the proudest and wildest hearts and hold them in sweet captivity by a mere glance or else by the power of her pure modesty. God formed Man, who is so proud, in the field of Damascus; and from one of his ribs he formed woman in the garden of Eden.

If I were not a female, I would deduce from this that the woman, both because of her composition and because of the place in which she was created, is nobler, gentler, stronger and worthier than the man.

What is true strength anyway, if not domination over one's feelings and mastery over one's passions? And who is better at this than the female sex, always virtuous and capable of resisting every temptation to commit or even think evil things? Is there anything more fragile than your head? Compare it to the strength of a rib, the hard bone that is the material from which we were created, and you will be disappointed. Anyone knows that women show more strength than men when they conceive and give birth, by tirelessly carrying all that weight around for nine months.

But you cruel men, who always go around preaching evil for good and good for evil, you pride yourselves in your strength because, like the inhuman creatures you are, you fight and kill each other like wild beasts. . . .Thus, if strength is the ability to bear misfortunes and insults, how can you call yourselves strong when you shed other people's blood sometimes for no reason at all and take the life of innocent creatures at the slightest provocation of a word or a suspicion?

Strength is not mere violence; it requires an indomitable soul, steadfast and constant in Christian fortitude. How can you, o most inconstant ones, ever boast of such virtù? Improperly and deceitfully you have called yourselves virtuous, because only those who fill the world with people and virtù can be called strong.

And those are women. Listen to Solomon, whose words about women reinforce my argument: *Strength and dignity are her clothing.*

From Tarabotti, *Innocence Undone.*

In a different sense, family was lineage, the connections between preceding and succeeding generations. That was an important concept among the upper ranks of society, where ancient lineage, genuine or fabricated, was a valued component of nobility. That concept of family imparted a sense of stability and longevity in a world in which individual life was short. Even in peasant communities, however, lineage existed in the form of the family farm, that is, the strips in the field that were passed from generation to generation and named for the family that owned them. The village's fields and landmarks also bore the names of individual families, and membership in one of the ancient families of the village was a mark of social distinction.

The family was also an economic unit. In this sense, family overlapped with the household—all those who lived under the same roof, including servants and apprentices. In its economic functions, the family was the basic unit for the production, accumulation, and transmission of wealth. Occupation determined the organization of the economic family. Every member of the household had his or her own functions that were essential to the survival of the unit. Tasks were divided by gender and by age, but there was far more intermixture than is traditionally assumed. On farms, women worked at nearly every occupation with the exception of mowing and plowing. In towns, they were vital to the success of shops and trades, though they were denied training in the skilled crafts. As laborers, they worked in the town fields—for little more than half the wages of men performing the same tasks—and in carrying and delivering goods and materials. Children contributed to the economic vitality of the household from an early age.

Finally, the family was the primary unit of social organization. In the family, children were educated and the social values of hierarchy and discipline were taught. Authority in the family was strictly organized in a set of three overlapping categories. At the top was the husband, head of the household, who ruled over his wife, children, and servants. All members of the family owed obedience to the head. The family was like "a little commonwealth," as English writers put it, in which the adult male was the governor and all others the governed. But two other categories of relationships in the family dispersed the authority. Children owed obedience to their parents, male or female. In this role, the wife and mother was governor as well as governed. Similarly, servants owed obedience to both master and mistress. Male apprentices were under the authority of the wife, mother, and mistress of the household. The importance of the family as a social unit was underscored by the fact that people unattached to families attracted suspicion in sixteenth-century society. Single men were often viewed as potential criminals; single women as potential prostitutes. Both lived outside the discipline and social control of families.

Although the population of Europe was increasing in the early modern era, families were not large. Throughout northern and western Europe, the size of the typical family was two adults and three or four children. Late marriages and breast-feeding helped control family size: the former restricted the number of childbearing years while the latter increased the space between pregnancies. Women married around age 25, men slightly later. A woman could expect about 15 fertile years and seven or eight pregnancies if neither she nor her husband died in the interim.

In an age of high infant mortality and short life expectancy, women were expected to bear many children to ensure family continuity. This embroidery depicts a mother with her thirteen daughters.

Only three or four children were likely to survive beyond the age of ten. In her fertile years, a woman was constantly occupied with infants. She was either about to give birth or about to become pregnant. If she used a wet nurse rather than feed her own babies, as many women in the upper ranks of society did, then she was likely to have 10 or 12 pregnancies during her fertile years and correspondingly more surviving children.

Constant pregnancy and child care may help explain some of the gender roles that men and women assumed in the early modern era. Biblical injunctions and traditional stereotypes help explain others. Pregnant or not, women's labor was a vital part of the domestic economy, especially until the first surviving children were strong enough to assume their share. The woman's sphere was the household. On the farm, she was in charge of the preparation of food, the care of domestic animals, the care and education of children, and the manufacture and cleaning of the family's clothing. In towns, women supervised the shop that was part of the household. They sold goods, kept accounts, and directed the work of domestics or apprentices. Mothers trained their daughters to perform the tasks in the same way that fathers trained their sons to work the fields or ply their craft.

The Ideal Wife

L I B E R
LIBER QVARTVS.
DE VARIETATIBVS NON NA-
turalis partus, & earundem curis.
Quan-

■ A woodcut from *De Conceptu et generatione hominis* (1554), a famous sixteenth-century handbook for midwives. During the birth, astrologers cast the infant's horoscope in the background.

The man's sphere was public—the fields in rural areas, the streets in towns. Men plowed, planted, and did the heavy reaping work of farming. They made and maintained essential farm equipment and had charge of the large farm animals. They marketed surplus produce and made the few purchases of equipment or luxury goods. Men performed the labor service that was normally due the lord of the estate, attended the local courts in various capacities, and organized the affairs of the village. In towns, men engaged in heavy labor, procured materials for craft work, and marketed their product if it was not sold in the household shop. Only men could be citizens of the towns or full members of most craft guilds, and only men were involved in civic government.

The separation of men and women into the public and the domestic spheres meant that marriage was a blending of complementary skills. Each partner brought to the marriage essential knowledge and abilities that were fundamental to the economic success of the union. Except in the largest towns, nearly everyone was married for at least a part of his or her life. Remarriage was more common for men than women, however, because a man continued to control the family's property after the death of his wife, whereas a widow might have only a share of it after bequests to children and provisions for apprentices. In the French town of Nantes, a quarter of the annual weddings were remarriages.

Communities

Despite its central place in all aspects of sixteenth-century life, the family was a fragile and impermanent institution. Even without divorce—permitted in Protestant communities, though never very common—marriages were short. The early death of one of the partners abbreviated the life of the natural family. New marriage partners or social welfare to aid the indigent was sought from within the wider community. On the farm, that community was the rural village; in the town, it was the ward, quarter, or parish in which the family lived. Community life must not be romanticized. Interpersonal violence, lawsuits, and feuds were extraordinarily common in both rural and urban communities. The community was not an idyllic haven of charity and love, where everyone knew and respected neighbors and worked toward a common goal. Like every other aspect of society, the community was socially and economically stratified, gender roles were segregated, and resources were inequitably divided. But the community was the place where people found their social identity. It provided marriage partners for its families, charity for its poor, and a local culture for all of its inhabitants.

Communities were bound together by the authorities who ruled them and by their common activities. But they were also bound together by their own social customs. Early modern communities used a number of ceremonial occasions as opportunities for expressing solidarity and confirming, in one way or another, the values to which they adhered. In rural parishes there was the annual perambulation, a walk around the village fields that usually occurred before planting began. It was led by the priest, who carried with him any particularly sacred objects that the parish possessed. Behind him followed the village farmers, in some places all members of the village who were capable of walking the distance. The perambulation had many purposes. The priest blessed the fields and prayed for a bountiful crop; the farmers surveyed their own strips and any damage that had been done to the fields during the winter; the community defined its geographical space in distinction to the space of others; and all the individuals who took part reaffirmed their shared identity with others in the village.

In towns, ceremonial processions were far more elaborate. Processions might take place on saints' days in Catholic communities or on anniversaries of town liberties. The order of the march, the clothing worn by the participants, and the objects displayed reflected the strict hierarchies of the town's local organizations. In Catholic towns, the religious orders led the town governors in their robes of office. Following the governors were the members of guilds, each guild placed according to its rank of importance and each organized by masters, journeymen, and apprentices. In some towns, the wives of citizens marched in procession; in others, they were accorded special places from which to view the ceremony. Village and civic ceremonies normally ended with communal feasting and dancing, which were the most popular forms of recreation.

■ Jan van Eyck, *The Marriage of Giovanni Arnolfini and Giovanna Cenami*. This outstanding fifteenth-century painting of a nuptial scene teems with symbols, including the religious symbols of the rosary, the roundels on the mirror frame, and the post of the chair. The little dog in the foreground may represent fidelity, and the candles in the chandelier may be a symbol of marriage. The mirror reflects the image of two witnesses, who would have been standing where spectators viewing the picture would stand. The inscription on the wall, "Jan van Eyck was here, 1434," suggests that one of the figures is a self-portrait of the artist.

Weddings and Festivals. Not all ceremonial occasions were so formal. The most common ceremony was the wedding, a rite of passage that was simultaneously significant to the individual, the family, and the community. The wedding was a public event that combined a religious ceremony and a community procession with feasting and festivity. It took different forms in different parts of Europe and in different social groups. But whether eastern or western, noble or common, the wedding was celebrated as the moment when the couple entered fully into the community. Marriage involved more than just the union of bride and groom. Parents were a central feature in the event, both in arranging the economic aspects of the union—dowry and inheritance—and in approving the occasion. Many couples were engaged long before they were married, and in many places it was the engagement that was most important to the individuals and the wedding that was most important to the community. One German townsman described how he "had taken a wife but they have not held the wedding yet."

Traditional weddings involved the formal transfer of property, an important event in rural communities, where the ownership of strips of land or common rights concerned everyone. The bridal dowry and the groom's inheritance were formally exchanged during the wedding, even if both were small. The public procession—"the marriage in the streets" as it was sometimes called in towns—proclaimed the union throughout the community and was considered to be as important as the religious ceremony. It was followed by a feast as abundant as the families of bride and groom could afford. In peasant communities, gifts of food for the feast were as common as were gifts to the couple. There were always provisions made that excess food should be sent to the poor or unfortunate after the wedding.

Weddings also legitimated sexual relations. Many of the dances and ceremonies that followed the feast symbolized the sexual congress. Among German burghers it was traditional for the bride to bring the bed to her new home, and bridal beds were passed from mothers to daughters. Among the nobility, the consummation of the marriage was a vital part of the wedding, for without it the union could be annulled. Finally, the marriage inaugurated both bride and groom into new roles in the community. Their place at the wedding table next to their parents elevated them to the status of adults.

Other ceremonies were equally important in creating a shared sense of identity within the community. In both town and countryside, the year was divided by a number of festivals that defined the rhythm of toil and rest. They coincided with both the seasonal divisions of agricultural life and the central events of the Christian calendar. There was no essential difference between the popular and Christian elements in festivals, however strongly the official church insisted upon one. Christmas and Easter were probably the most widely observed Christian holidays, but **Carnival,** which preceded Lent, was a frenzied round of feasts and parties that resulted in a disproportionate number of births nine months later. The Twelve Days of Christmas, which inaugurated the slow, short days of winter, were only loosely attached to the birth of Jesus and were even abolished by some Protestant churches. The rites of May, which celebrated the rebirth of spring, were filled with sexual play among the young adults of the community. Youth groups went "a-Maying" by placing flowers at the homes of marriageable girls, electing a Queen of the May, and dancing and reveling before the hard work of planting. All Hallows' Eve was a celebration for the community's dead, whose spirits were believed to have wandered the village on that night, visiting kin and neighbors.

Festivals helped maintain the sense of community that might be weakened during the long months of increased work or enforced indoor activity. They were first and foremost celebrations in which feasting, dancing, and play were central. But they also served as safety valves for the pressures and conflicts that built up over the year. Group and individual sports, such as soccer or wrestling, frequently served to channel aggressions. Village elders would arbitrate disputes, and marriage alliances or property transactions would be arranged.

Festivals further cemented the political cohesion of the community. Seating arrangements reflected the hierarchy of the community, and public punishment of offenders reinforced deference and social and sexual mores. Youth groups, or even the village women, might band together to shame a promiscuous woman or to place horns on the head of a cuckolded husband. Sometimes a man who had been beaten or abused by his wife, or who had simply failed to enforce obedience from her, was forced to ride backward on a horse or donkey to symbolize the misrule in his family. At such processions, which the French called *charivaris* and the English *skimmingtons,* rough music was played and the offense of the individual or couple was elaborately recreated. (See "A Closer Look: Sex and the Married Man," pp. 464–465.) Such forms of community ritual worked not only to punish offenders but also to reinforce the social and sexual values of the village as a whole.

Carnivals were occasions for games and feasting. In this painting, *Struggle Between Carnival and Lent,* Pieter Brueghel the Elder depicts a contest between the fasting and other forms of self-denial during Lent (the period of fasting and penitence before Easter) and the tempting attractions of Carnival.

Popular Beliefs and the Persecution of Witches

Ceremony and festival are reminders that sixteenth-century Europe was still a preliterate society. Despite the introduction of printing and the millions of books that were produced during the period, the vast majority of Europeans conducted their affairs without the benefit of literacy. Their culture was oral and visual. They had need of an exact memory, and they developed a shorthand of adages, charms, and spells that helped them organize their activities and pass down their knowledge. It is difficult for us to recreate that mental world, in which almost all natural events were unpredictable and in which there was little certainty. Outside a small circle of intellectuals, there was little effective knowledge about either human or celestial bodies. The mysteries of the sun, moon, and stars were as deep as those of health and sickness. But ordinary people did not live in a constant state of terror and anxiety. They used the knowledge they did have to form a view of the universe that conformed to their experiences and that responded to their hopes. Although many of their beliefs seem mere superstitions, they allowed people to form a coherent explanation of the natural world and of their relationship to it.

Magical Practices. The people's beliefs blended Christian teaching and folk wisdom with a strong strain of magic. Popular belief in magic could be found everywhere in Europe, and it operated in much the same way as science does today. Only skilled

THE DEVIL'S DUE

Evidence of the supernatural world abounded for the people of premodern Europe. Natural disasters such as plague and human disasters such as war promoted fear of witchcraft. When the world seemed out of balance and the forces of good retreated before the forces of evil, people sought someone to blame for their troubles. Witches were an obvious choice. Accused witches were most commonly women on the margins of society. Once brought before the authorities, many admitted their traffic with Satan, especially under torture. The Witch Hammer *is a set of detailed instructions for the rooting out of witches, including procedures to induce their confessions.*

Focus Questions

What is the point of torture, punishment, or investigation? Is the suspected witch seen as being in control of his or her magic?

The method of beginning an examination by torture is as follows: First, the jailers prepare the implements of torture, then they strip the prisoner (if it be a woman, she has already been stripped by other women, upright and of good report). This stripping is lest some means of witchcraft may have been sewed into the clothing—such as often, taught by the Devil, they prepare from the bodies of unbaptized infants, [murdered] that they may forfeit salvation. And when the implements of torture have been prepared, the judge, both in person and through other good men zealous in the faith, tries to persuade the prisoner to confess the truth freely; but, if he will not confess, he bids attendants make the prisoner fast to the strappado or some other implement of torture. The attendants obey forthwith, yet with feigned agitation. Then, at the prayer of some of those present, the prisoner is loosed again and is taken aside and once more persuaded to confess, being led to believe that he will in that case not be put to death.

But if, neither by threats nor by promises such as these, the witch cannot be induced to speak the truth, then the jailers must carry out the sentence, and torture the prisoner according to the accepted methods, with more or less of severity as the delinquent's crime may demand. And, while he is being tortured, he must be questioned on the articles of accusation, and this frequently and persistently, beginning with the lighter charges—for he will more readily confess the lighter than the heavier. And, while this is being done, the notary must write down everything in his record of the trial—how the prisoner is tortured, on what points he is questioned, and how he answers.

And note that, if he confesses under the torture, he must afterward be conducted to another place, that he may confirm it and certify that it was not due alone to the force of the torture.

But, if the prisoner will not confess the truth satisfactorily, other sorts of tortures must be placed before him, with the statement that, unless he will confess the truth, he must endure these also. But, if not even thus he can be brought into terror and to the truth, then the next day or the next but one is to be set for a *continuation* of the tortures—not a *repetition,* for they must not be repeated unless new evidence be produced. . . .

And during the interval, before the day assigned, the judge, in person or through approved men, must in the manner above described try to persuade the prisoner to confess, promising her (if there is aught to be gained by this promise) that her life shall be spared.

The judge shall see to it, moreover, that throughout this interval guards are constantly with the prisoner, so that she may not be left alone; because she will be visited by the Devil and tempted into suicide.

From *The Witch Hammer.*

SEX AND THE MARRIED MAN

On 27 May 1618 the peace of the small hamlet of Quemerford, in the west of England, was shattered by the appearance of a large crowd from the neighboring market town of Calne. Men marched with fowling pieces and muskets to a cacophony of drums, clanging pots, whistles, and shouts. Among them, on a red horse, rode an outlandishly costumed man—a smock covering his body; on his head a nightcap with two long shoehorns tied to his ears; and on his face a false beard made from a deer's tail. The crowd escorted the rider to the home of Thomas Mills, who worked in Calne as a cutler. There they stopped. Guns were discharged into the air; an even greater clamor of rough music arose from drums, pipes, and metal objects; and when Mills opened his door, members of the crowd waved aloft the horns of goats or rams mounted on sticks. Then a few strong men entered the house; seized hold of his wife, Agnes; and dragged her to a village mud hole where she was ducked and covered in filth. She was rescued from being set on the horse and ridden to Calne.

A CLOSER LOOK

That event, known as a **skimmington** in the west of England and a charivari in France, was a shaming ritual. It was an element of popular culture that took place against the wishes of local authorities and without their connivance. Its purpose was twofold: to identify and punish sexual misconduct and to maintain the male-dominated gender system. The shaming rituals resulted from conduct that the male members of the community believed threatened local order (few women are known to have taken part in the events). In France, most charivaris were conducted against husbands who were beaten by their wives; in England, many skimmingtons were directed against husbands whose wives had been unfaithful. In both they were designed to shame men into disciplining women and to warn women to remain obedient.

Although skimmingtons and charivaris differed from place to place, all contained similar elements which were designed to invert normal behavior in one way or another. The rough music symbolized the disharmony of a household in which the woman dominated, either by her physical conduct—adultery or husband beating—or her verbal conduct—cursing or abusing her husband or other men. The music was made with everyday objects rather than instruments, and pots and pans were universally present. The "riding" of the husband was another common feature. In many rituals, the "husband," played by a neighbor, was placed facing the tail of the horse or donkey to symbolize the backwardness of his behavior. In some, a "wife," also acted by a neighbor, rode behind the man and beat him with a stick or, in England, with the long-handled ladle used to skim cream that was known as a skimmington. In the end, the real husband or wife was captured, the man to ride in shame throughout the town, the woman to be sat on a cucking stool and dunked in water.

The presence of horns on the male riding the horse and on sticks carried by members of the crowd or worn atop their heads was the universal symbol of adultery. The cuckold—a word derived from the name of a promiscuous female bird—was an object of derision throughout European society. Codes of conduct from noble to peasant stressed the importance of female sexual fidelity in maintaining the purity of bloodlines and the order of the household. The cuckold was shorn of his masculinity; he had lost his "horns," in common parlance. His personal indignity was a cause for jest and insult, but the disorderliness implicit in the conduct of his wife was a cause for community concern. In local society, reputation was equated with personal worth, and no one had less reputation than the cuckold. Among the nobility, duels were fought over the slightest suggestion of a wife's unfaithfulness, while among ordinary folks the raising of the forefinger and pinkie—the sign of horns—initiated brawls.

The skimmington or charivari combined festive play with the enforcement of social norms. It was rough justice, as the objects of shame were allowed neither explanation nor defense. They were guilty by common fame, that is, by the report of their neighbors and the gossip of the local alehouse rather than by any examination of evidence. Women who yelled at their husbands were sometimes assumed to have beaten them; women who had beaten their husbands were assumed to have cuckolded them. The crimes were all interrelated, and protestations of innocence were useless. The crowds that gathered to perform the ceremony usually had bolstered their courage at the local tavern, and among them were village toughs and those who held grudges against the targeted family. Assault, property damage, and theft occasionally accompanied a skim-

Scene of a shaming ritual, with the object of derision wearing horns and riding a donkey.

mington. But most of the crowd was there to have a bit of sport and revel in the discomfort of the victims. Their conduct was the inverse of a legal procedure, as disorderly as the conduct of those to be punished. However, their purpose was not to turn the world upside down, but to set it right side up again by restoring the dominance of husbands over wives.

While shaming rituals like the charivari and the skimmington had a long history in Europe, they seem to have exploded into prominence in the late sixteenth and early seventeenth centuries. Population pressures and economic hardship are two conventional explanations for why there were greater local tensions during that period. Skimmingtons and charivaris frequently had rough edges, with some participants motivated by hatred or revenge. But it is also likely that there were more inversion rituals because there was more inversion. Women were taking a larger role in economic affairs and were becoming increasingly literate and active in religion, especially in Protestant countries. Assertive, independent women threatened the male-dominated social order as much as demographic and social change. That the threats were most identified with sexual misconduct and with the stripping of a husband's masculinity was hardly surprising. The image of the obedient female was conventionally the image of chastity. Thus the image of the independent female had to become one of promiscuity. Through the use of skimmingtons and charivaris, men attempted to restore norms of sexual conduct and gender relations that were increasingly under attack. As one English poet put it:

Ill fares the hapless family that shows
A cock that's silent, and a Hen that crows.
I know not which live more unnatural lives,
Obedient husbands, or commanding wives.

practitioners could perform magic. It was a technical subject that combined expertise in the properties of plants and animals with theories about the composition of human and heavenly bodies. It had its own language, a mixture of ancient words and sounds with significant numbers and catchphrases. Magicians specialized: some concentrated on herbs and plants, others on the diseases of the body. Alchemists worked with rocks and minerals, astrologers with the movement of the stars. Witches were thought to understand the properties of animals especially well. The witches of Shakespeare's *Macbeth* chanted their exotic recipe for witch's gruel:

Eye of newt and toe of frog,
Wool of bat and tongue of dog,
Adder's fork and blindworm's sting,
Lizard's leg and owlet's wing,
For a charm of powerful trouble,
Like a hell-broth boil and bubble.

Magical practices appealed to people at all levels of society. The wealthy favored astrology and paid handsomely to discover which days and months were the most auspicious for marriages and investments. So-called cunning men predicted the future for those of the lower orders who would not be able to give an astrologer such vital information as the date of their birth or to pay exorbitant fees. The poorest villagers sought the aid of herbalists to help control the constant aches and pains of daily life. Sorcerers and wizards were called upon in more extreme circumstances, such as a threatened harvest or matters of life and death. The magicians competed with the remedies offered by the Church. Special prayers and visits to the shrines of particular saints were believed to have similar curative value. Magical and Christian beliefs did not oppose each other; they existed on a continuum and were practiced simultaneously. In some French villages, for example, four-leaf clovers were considered especially powerful if they were found on a particular saint's day. It was not until the end of the century, when Protestant and Catholic leaders condemned magical practices and began a campaign to root them out, that magic and religion came into conflict.

Magical practices served a variety of purposes. Healing was the most common, and many "magical" brews were effective remedies of the minor ailments for which they were prescribed. Most village magicians were women because it was believed that women had unique knowledge and understanding of the body. Women were also familiar with the properties of the herbs from which most remedies were derived. Magic was also used for predictive purposes. Certain charms and rituals were believed to have the power to affect the weather, the crops, and even human events. As always, affairs of the heart were as important as those of the stomach. Magicians advised the lovesick on potions and spells that would gain them the object of their desires. Cats were particularly associated with love spells, as were the petals of certain flowers. "He loves me, he loves me not" was more than a child's game. Magic was believed to have the power to alter the course of nature, and it could be used for both good and evil purposes.

The Witch Craze. Magic for evil was black magic, or witchcraft, which utilized beliefs in the presence of spiritual forces in nature. Witches were believed to possess special powers that put them into contact with the devil and the forces of evil, which they could then use for their own purposes. Belief in the prevalence of good and evil spirits was Christian as well as magical. But the Church had gradually consigned the operation of the devil to the afterlife and removed his direct agency from earthly affairs. Beginning in the late fifteenth century, Church authorities began to prosecute large numbers of suspected witches. By

This woodcut from the sixteenth-century *History of the Northern People* by Olaus Magnus shows a devil carrying off a witch, whose protests and gestures beseeching help go unheeded by her fellow villagers in the background.

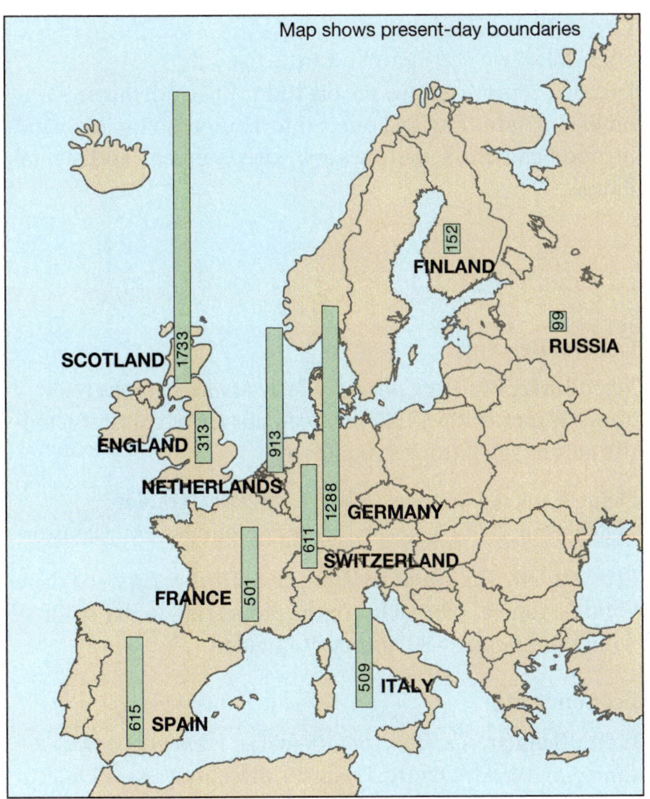

Witchcraft Persecutions. There were more trials for witchcraft in Calvinist Scotland than in all of Spain and France combined.

the end of the sixteenth century, there was a continentwide witchcraze. Unexplained misfortune or simple malice could set off accusations that might include dozens or even hundreds of suspected witches. Confessions were obtained under torture, as were further accusations. In the period from 1550 to 1650, there were more than 30,000 prosecutions in Germany alone.

Witches were usually women, most often those unmarried or widowed. Although male sorcerers and wizards were thought to have powers over evil spirits, by the sixteenth century it was females who served as the mediators between humans and the diabolical. In a sample of more than 7000 cases of witchcraft prosecuted in early modern Europe, more than 80 percent of the defendants were women. There is no clear explanation why women fulfilled this important and powerful role. Belief in women's special powers over the body through their singular ability to give birth is certainly one part of the explanation, for many stories about the origins of witches suggest that they were children fathered by the devil and left to be raised by women. The sexual element of union with the devil and the common belief that older women were sexually aggressive combined to threaten male sexual dominance. Witches were also believed to have peculiar physical characteristics. A group of Italian witches, male and female, was distinguished by having been born with a caul (a membrane around their heads that was removed after birth). Accused witches were strip-searched to find the devil's mark, which might be any bodily blemish. Another strand of explanation lies in the fact that single women existed on the fringes of society, isolated and exploited by the community at large. Their occult abilities thus became a protective mechanism that gave them a function within the community while they remained outside it.

It is difficult to know how important black magical beliefs were in ordinary communities. Most of the daily magic that was practiced was the mixture of charms, potions, and prayers that mingled magical, medical, and Christian beliefs. But as the century progressed, more and more notice was taken of black magic. Misfortunes that befell particular families or social groups were blamed upon the activities of witches. The campaign of the established churches to root out magic was largely directed against witches. The churches transposed witches' supposed abilities to communicate with the devil into the charge that they worshipped the devil. Because there was such widespread belief in the presence of diabolical spirits and in the capabilities of witches to control them, Protestant and Catholic church courts could easily find witnesses to testify in support of the charges against individual witches. Yet wherever sufficient evidence exists to understand the circumstances of witchcraft prosecutions, it is clear that the community itself was under some form of social or economic stress. Sacrificing a marginal member of the community might have been the means to restore village solidarity.

CONCLUSION

Population growth, economic diversification, and social change characterized life in early modern Europe. It was a century of extremes. The poor were getting poorer and the rich were getting richer. The early part of the century has been called the golden age of the peasantry; the later part has been called the crisis of subsistence. At all levels of the social scale, the lives of grandparents and grandchildren were dramatically different. For surplus producers, the quality of life improved throughout the century. The market economy expanded. Agricultural surplus was exchanged for more land and a wider variety of consumer goods. Children could be provided with an education, and domestic and agricultural labor was cheap and plentiful. For subsistence producers, the quality of life eroded. In the first half of the century, their diet contained more meat than it would for the next 300 years. Their children could be absorbed on new farms or sent to towns where there was a shortage of both skilled and unskilled labor. But gradually the outlook turned bleak. The land could support no more new families, and the towns needed no more labor. As wages fell and prices rose, peasants in western Europe were caught between the crushing burdens of taxation from lord, state, and church and the all-too-frequent catastrophes of poor harvests, epidemic disease, and warfare. In eastern Europe, the peasantry was tied to the land in a new serfdom that provided minimum subsistence in return for the loss of freedom and opportunity. When peasants anywhere rose up against those conditions, they were cut down and swept away like new-mown hay.

QUESTIONS FOR REVIEW

1. What physical forces and social customs shaped the everyday life of Europe's rural population?
2. What was the nature of demographic change in the sixteenth century, and what was its impact on the European economy?
3. How are the terms "stratification," "hierarchy," and "status" useful for understanding social relations in early modern Europe?
4. How were the different roles of men and women within the family reflected in the different lives of men and women in the wider community?

KEY TERMS

Carnival, *p. 462*	robot, *p. 444*
enclosure, *p. 455*	seigneur, *p. 444*
Great Chain of Being, *p. 451*	skimmington, *p. 464*
Price Revolution, *p. 449*	three-field rotation, *p. 444*

DISCOVERING WESTERN CIVILIZATION ONLINE

You can obtain more information about life in early modern Europe at the Websites listed below. See also the Companion Website that accompanies this text, www.ablongman.com/kishlansky, which contains an online study guide and additional resources.

Social Life

Internet Modern History Sourcebook: Everyday Life in Premodern Europe
www.fordham.edu/halsall/mod/modsbook04.html
A site with links to sources, pictures, and accounts of everyday life in early modern Europe. A good place to start.

Modern History Sourcebook: Social Conditions in 17th Century France
www.fordham.edu/halsall/mod/17france-soc.html
Documents illustrating social conditions in early modern France.

Private Life

Witchcraft
www2.kenyon.edu/projects/margin/witch.htm
A site with links to sources concerning European witchcraft. Also includes suggestions for further reading and a brief overview of the subject.

Witches and Witchcraft
Womenshistory.about.com/cs/witches
This site offers historical information about witches and witchcraft in Europe and America and includes links to related sites.

Life in Tudor England
englishhistory.net/tudor/tudorlife.html
Part of a comprehensive site on Tudor England, this section on life in Tudor England offers information on topics including food and drink, pastimes and entertainment, and mental illness.

SUGGESTIONS FOR FURTHER READING

General Reading

Peter Burke, *Popular Culture in Early Modern Europe* (New York: Harper & Row, 1978). A lively survey of cultural activities among the European populace.

Henry Kamen, *European Society, 1500–1700* (London: Hutchinson, 2000). A general survey of European social history.

Peter Laslett, *The World We Have Lost: Further Explored* (New York: Scribners, 1984). One of the pioneering works on the family and population history of England.

Economic Life

Judith Bennett, *Ale, Beer, and Brewsters: Women's Work in a Changing World* (Oxford: Oxford University Press, 1996). An important study of the role of women in one of the most traditional trades.

Fernand Braudel, *Civilization and Capitalism: The Structures of Everyday Life* (New York: Harper & Row, 1981). Part of a larger work filled with fascinating detail about the social behavior of humankind during the early modern period.

Emmanuel Le Roy Ladurie, *The French Peasantry, 1450–1660* (London: Scholar Press, 1987). A complex study of the lives of the French peasantry.

Peter Musgrave, *The Early Modern European Economy* (New York: St. Martin's Press, 1999). A multidimensional survey of economic life.

Merry E. Wiesner-Hanks, *Early Modern Europe, 1450–1789* (Cambridge: Cambridge University Press, 2006). A new thematic synthesis of the early modern period, emphasizing gender and social relations. This history treats the "margins" of Europe, discussing oft-neglected Scandinavia as well as the Ottoman Empire.

Social Life

Yves-Marie Bercé, *Revolt and Revolution in Early Modern Europe* (New York: St. Martin's Press, 1987). A study of the structure of uprisings throughout Europe by a leading French historian.

Natalie Zemon Davis, *Women on the Margins: Three Seventeenth-Century Lives* (Cambridge, MA: Harvard University Press, 1995). Three short and stimulating biographies of early modern European women by a leading historian of popular culture.

Jonathan Dewald, *The European Nobility 1400–1800* (Cambridge: Cambridge University Press, 1996). An outstanding survey based on a wide range of sources.

Edward Muir, *Ritual in Early Modern Europe* (Cambridge: Cambridge University Press, 2005). A new and expanded edition of a classic study examining the importance of rites and habits in early modern Europe. Muir has added material on rituals among women and argued forcefully for the persistence of traditional ritual well into the eighteenth century.

Barry Reay, *Popular Cultures in England, 1550–1750* (New York: Addison Wesley Longman, 1998). A sound and insightful thematic survey.

E. M. W. Tillyard, *The Elizabethan World Picture* (New York: Harper & Row, 1960). The classic account of the social constructs of English society.

Private Life

Roger Chartier, ed., *A History of Private Life, Vol. 3, Passions of the Renaissance* (Cambridge, MA: Harvard University Press, 1989). A lavishly illustrated study of the habits, mores, and structures of private life from the fifteenth to the eighteenth centuries.

Stuart Clark, *Thinking with Demons: The Idea of Witchcraft in Early Modern Europe* (Oxford: Oxford University Press, 1997). A sensitive reading of the sources for the study of witchcraft.

Beatrice Gottlieb, *The Family in the Western World from the Black Death to the Industrial Age* (Oxford: Oxford University Press, 1994). An outstanding introduction to the transformations in the lives of families.

R. A. Houston, *Literacy in Early Modern Europe* (London: Longman, 1988). How literacy and education became part of popular culture from 1500 to 1800.

Gary Jensen, *The Path of the Devil: A Study of Early Modern Witch Hunts* (Oxford: Rowman and Littlefield, 2006). The author compares witch hunts throughout Europe in the early modern era and analyzes them in relation to their cultural context.

Brian Levack, *The Witch-Hunt in Early Modern Europe* (New York: Longman, 2006). A study of the causes and meaning of the persecution of European witches in the sixteenth and seventeenth centuries.

R. Muchembled, *Popular Culture and Elite Culture in France, 1400–1750* (Baton Rouge: Louisiana State University Press, 1985). A detailed treatment of the practices of two conflicting cultures.

Steven Ozment, *Ancestors: The Loving Family in Old Europe* (Cambridge, MA: Harvard University Press, 2001). A brief and accessible survey by a leading historian, making a spirited defense of early modern family life against historians who have portrayed the premodern family in grim terms.

D. Underdown, *Revel, Riot, and Rebellion* (Oxford: Oxford University Press, 1985). An engaging study of popular culture and its relationship to social and economic structures in England.

Merry E. Wiesner, *Women and Gender in Early Modern Europe* (Cambridge: Cambridge University Press, 1993). The best introduction to European women's history.

For a list of additional titles related to this chapter's topics, please see http://www.ablongman.com/kishlansky.

CHAPTER 16

THE ROYAL STATE IN THE SEVENTEENTH CENTURY

FIT FOR A KING

THE GRANDEUR OF THE EUROPEAN MONARCHY

THE VISUAL RECORD

Behold Versailles: the greatest palace of the greatest king of the greatest state in seventeenth-century Europe. Everything about it was stupendous, a reflection of the grandeur of Louis XIV and of France. Sculptured gardens in dazzling geometric forms stretched for acres, scenting the air with exotic perfumes. Nearly as beautiful as the grounds were the 1400 fountains, especially the circular basins of Apollo and Latona, the sun god and his mother. The hundreds of water jets that sprayed at Versailles defied nature as well as the senses, for the locale was not well irrigated and water had to be pumped through elaborate mechanical works all the way from the Seine. Gardens and fountains provided the setting for the enormous palace with its hundreds of rooms for both use and show. Five thousand people, a tenth of whom served the king alone, inhabited the palace. Thousands of others flocked there daily. Most lived in the adjacent town, which had grown from a few hundred people to more than 40,000 in a single generation. The royal stables quartered 12,000 horses and hundreds of carriages. The cost of all that magnificence was equally astounding. Fragmentary accounts indicate that construction costs were more than 100 million French pounds. Louis XIV ordered the official receipts burned.

Like the marble of the palace, nature itself was chiseled to the requirements of the king. Forests were pared to make leafy avenues or trimmed to conform to the geometric patterns of the gardens. In spring and summer, groves of orange trees grown in tubs were everywhere; in winter and fall they were housed indoors at great expense. Life-size statues and giant carved urns lined the carefully planned walkways that led to breathtaking views or sheltered grottoes. A cross-shaped artificial canal, more than a mile long, dominated the western end of the park. Italian gondolas skimmed along its surface, carrying visitors to the zoo and aviary on one side or to the king's private chateau on the other.

But that great pile of bricks and stone, of marble and precious metals, expressed the contradictions of its age as well as its grandeur. The seventeenth century was an era in which the rich got richer and the poor got poorer. It was a time when the monarchical state expanded its power and prestige even as it faced grave challenges to its very existence. It was an epoch of unrelenting war amid a nearly universal desire for lasting peace. Thus it was fitting that the prodigious monument was uncomfortable to live in, so unpleasant that Louis had a separate chateau built on the grounds as a quiet retreat. His wife and his mistresses complained constantly of accommodations in which all interior comforts had been subordinated to the external facade of the building. Versailles was a seat of state as well as the home of the monarch, and it is revealing that the private was sacrificed to the public.

The duc de Saint-Simon, who passed much of his time at Versailles, was well aware of the contradictions: "The beautiful and the ugly were sown together, the vast and the constricted." Soldiers, artisans, and the merely curious clogged the three great avenues that led from Paris to the palace. When the king dined in public, hordes of Parisians drove out for the spectacle, filing past the monarch as if he were an exhibit at a museum. The site itself was poorly drained. "Its mud is black and stinking with a stench so penetrating that you can smell it for several leagues around." The orange groves and the stone urns filled with flower petals were more practical than beautiful: they masked the stench of sewage that was particularly noxious in the heat and the rain. Even the gardens were too vast to be enjoyed. In the planted areas, the smell of flowers was overpowering while the acres of mown lawn proved unattractive to an aristocracy little given to physical exercise. "The gardens were admired and avoided," Saint-Simon observed acidly. In those contrasts of failure amid achievement, Versailles stands as an apt symbol of its age: a gaudy mask to hide the wrinkles of the royal state.

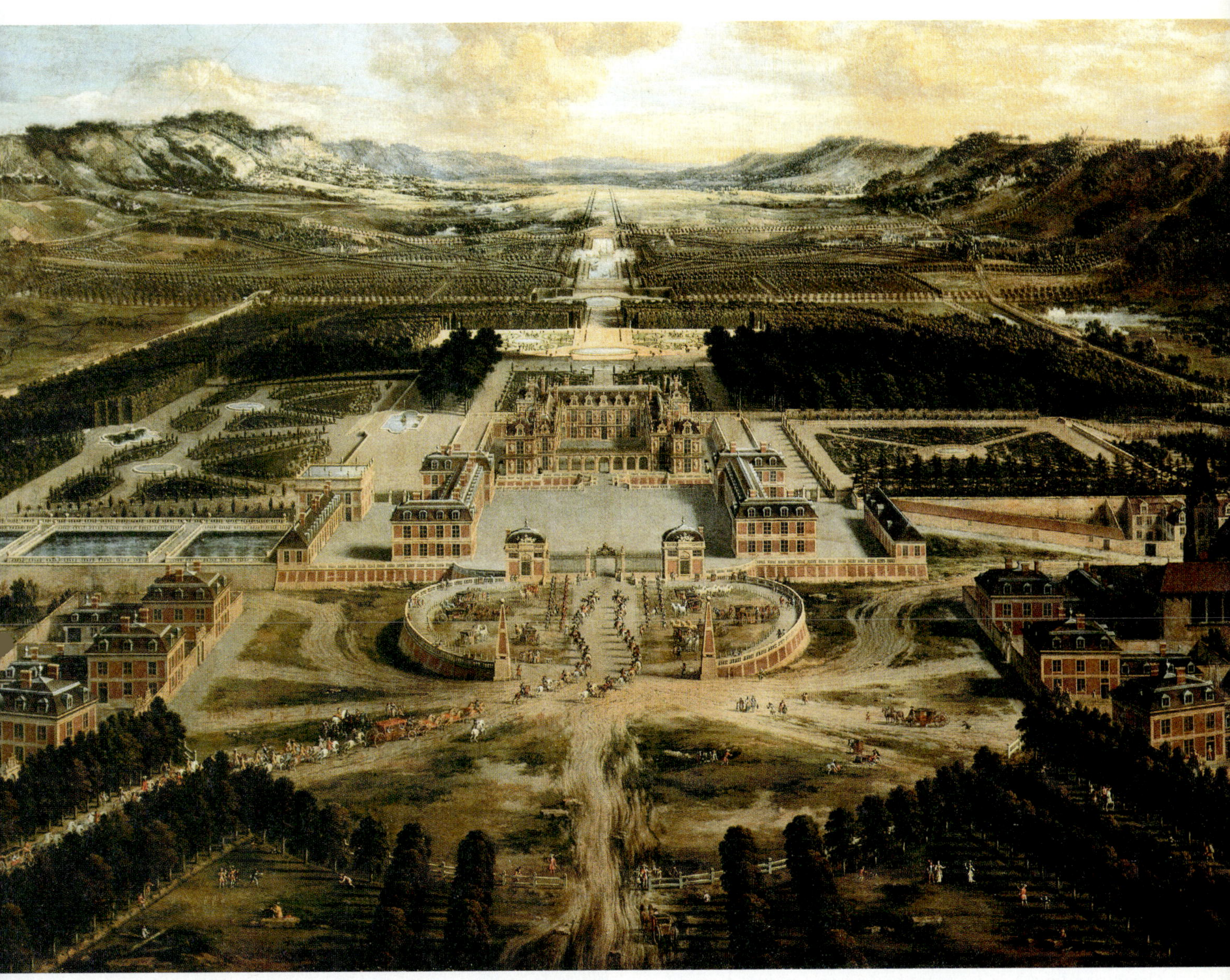

■ Pierre Patel the Elder, *View of Versailles,* 1668.

LOOKING AHEAD

The great palaces of European absolute monarchs were designed to intimidate those who visited them. They were the representation of royal power at its apex. As we will learn in this chapter, not since Rome's emperors were at the height of their glory had power been more concentrated in the hands of rulers, and what they had consolidated over centuries they now had to protect against competing dynasties or rebellious subjects.

CHAPTER OUTLINE

THE RISE OF THE ROYAL STATE

The religious and dynastic wars that dominated the early part of the seventeenth century had a profound impact upon the western European states. Not only did they cause terrible suffering and deprivation, but they also demanded efficient and better centralized states to conduct them. War was both a product of the European state system and a cause of its continued development. As armies grew in size, the resources necessary to maintain them grew in volume. As the battlefield spread from state to state, defense became government's most important function. More and more power was absorbed by the monarch and his chief advisers; more and more of the traditional privileges of aristocracy and towns were eroded. At the center of the rising states, particularly in western Europe, were the king and his court. In the provinces were tax collectors and military recruiters.

Divine Kings

"There is a divinity that doth hedge a king," wrote Shakespeare. Never was that hedge more luxuriant than in the seventeenth century. In the early sixteenth century, monarchs treated their states and their subjects as personal property. Correspondingly, rulers were praised in personal terms: for their virtue, wisdom, or strength. By the early seventeenth century, the monarchy had been transformed into an office of state. Now rulers embodied their nation and, no matter what their personal characteristics, they were held in awe because they were monarchs.

Thus, as rulers lost direct personal control over their patrimony, they gained indirect symbolic control over their nation. The symbolic power was to be seen everywhere. By the beginning of the seventeenth century, monarchs had set permanent seats of government attended by vast courts of officials, place seekers, and servants. The idea of the capital city emerged, with Madrid, London, Paris, and Vienna as the models. There the grandiose style of the ruler stood proxy for the wealth and glory of the nation. Great display bespoke great pride, and great pride was translated into great strength.

Portraits of rulers in action and repose conveyed the central message. Elizabeth I was depicted bestriding a map of England or clutching a rainbow and wearing a gown woven of eyes and ears to signify her power to see and hear her subjects. The Flemish painter Sir Anthony Van Dyck (1599–1641) created powerful images of three generations of Stuart kings of England. He was court painter to Charles I, whose qualities he portrayed with great sympathy and not a little exaggeration. Diego Velázquez (1599–1660) was court painter to Philip IV of Spain. His series of equestrian portraits of the Habsburgs—

■ Queen Elizabeth I of England. This portrait was commissioned by Sir Henry Lee to commemorate the queen's visit to his estate at Ditchley. Here the queen, shown standing on a map of England, is the very image of Gloriana—ageless and indomitable.

kings, queens, princes, and princesses—exude the spirit of the seventeenth-century monarchy, the grandeur and pomp, the power and self-assurance. Peter Paul Rubens (1577–1640) represented 21 separate episodes in the life of Marie de Médicis, queen regent of France.

The themes of writers were no different than those of artists. Monarchy was glorified in a variety of forms of literary representation. National history, particularly of recent events, enjoyed wide popularity. Its avowed purpose was to draw the connection between the past and the present glories of the state. One of the most popular French histories of the period was entitled *On the Excellence of the Kings and the Kingdom of France*. Francis Bacon (1561–1626), who is remembered more as a philosopher and scientist, wrote a laudatory history of Henry VII, founder of the Tudor dynasty.

In England it was a period of renaissance. Poets, playwrights, historians, and philosophers by the dozens gravitated to the English court. One of the most remarkable of them was Ben Jonson (1572–1637). He began life as a bricklayer, fought against the Spanish in Flanders, and then turned to acting and writing. His wit and talent brought him to court, where he made his mark by writing and staging masques, light entertainment that included music, dance, pantomime, and acting. Jonson's masques were distinguished by their lavish productions and exotic costumes and the inventive set designs of the great architect Inigo Jones (1573–1652). They were frequently staged at Christmastime and starred members of the court as players. The masques took the grandeur of England and its rulers for their themes.

Shakespeare and Kingship. The role of William Shakespeare (1564–1616) in the celebration of monarchy was more ambiguous. Like Jonson, Shakespeare came from an ordinary family, had little formal education, and began his astonishing career as an actor and producer of theater. He soon began to write as well as direct his plays, and his company, the King's Players, received royal patronage. He set many of his plays at the courts of princes, and even comedies such as *The Tempest* (1611) and *Measure for Measure* (1604) centered on the power of the ruler to dispense justice and to bring peace to his subjects. Both plays were staged at court. Shakespeare's history plays focused entirely on the character of kings. In *Richard II* (1597) and *Henry VI* (three parts, 1591–1594) Shakespeare exposed the harm that weak rulers inflicted on their states, while in *Henry IV* (two parts, 1598–1600) and *Henry V* (1599) he highlighted the benefits to be derived from strong rulers.

Shakespeare's tragedies made the point in a different way. The tragic flaw in the personality of rulers exposed the world around them to ruin. In *Macbeth* (1606), the flaw was ambition. Macbeth killed to become a king and had to keep on killing to remain one. In *Hamlet* (1602), the tragic flaw was irresolution. The inability of the Prince of Denmark to act decisively and reclaim the crown that was his by right brought his state to the brink of collapse. Shakespeare's plays were viewed in London theaters by members of all social classes, and his concentration on the affairs of rulers helped reinforce their dominating importance in the lives of all of their subjects.

Monarchy and Law. The political theory of the **divine right of kings** further enhanced the importance of monarchs. The theory held that the institution of monarchy had been created by God and that the monarch functioned as God's representative on earth. One clear statement of divine right theory was actually written by a king, James VI of Scotland, who later became James I of England (1603–1625). In *The True Law of Free Monarchies* (1598), James reasoned that God had placed kings on earth to rule and that he would judge them in heaven for their transgressions.

James I on Divine Right of Kings

The idea of the divine origin of monarchy was uncontroversial, and it was espoused not only by kings. One of the few things that the French Estates-General actually agreed upon during its meeting in 1614—the last for more than 175 years—was the statement: "The king is sovereign in France and holds his crown from God only." That sentiment echoed the commonplace view of French political theorists. The greatest writer on the subject, Jean Bodin (1530–1596), called the king "God's image on earth." In *The Six Books of the Commonwealth* (1576), Bodin defined the essence of the monarch's power: "The principal mark of sovereign majesty is essentially the right to impose laws on subjects generally without their consent."

Although at first glance the theory of the divine right of kings appears to be a blueprint for arbitrary rule, in fact it was yoked together with a number of principles that restrained the conduct of the monarch. As James I pointed out, God had charged kings with obligations: "to minister justice; to establish good laws; and to procure peace."

The Court and the Courtiers

For all of the bravura of divine right theory, far more was expected of kings than they could possibly deliver. The day-to-day affairs of government had grown beyond the capacity of any monarch to handle them. The expansion in the powers of the western states absorbed more officials than ever. At the beginning of the sixteenth century, the French court of Francis I employed 622 officers; at the beginning of the seventeenth century, the court of Henry IV employed more than 1500. Yet the difference was not only in size. Members of the seventeenth-century court were becoming servants of the state as well as of the monarch.

Like everything else in seventeenth-century government, the court revolved around the monarch. The monarch appointed, promoted, and dismissed officeholders at will. As befit that type of personal government, most monarchs chose a single individual to act as a funnel for private and public business. That person was the "favorite," whose role combined varying proportions of best friend, right-hand man, and hired gun. Some favorites, such as Cardinal Richelieu of France and Spain's Count-Duke Olivares, were able to transform themselves into chief ministers with a political philosophy and a

THE DIVINITY THAT DOTH HEDGE A KING

William Shakespeare's history play of the reign of Richard II tells the story of a rebellion against a lawful monarch. It was banned from production during Elizabeth's reign.

Focus Questions

What does Carlisle mean when he refers to the "power that made you king?" Where does Richard claim his army will come from to defeat Bolingbroke?

KING RICHARD II

Needs must I like it well: I weep for joy
To stand upon my kingdom once again.
Dear earth, I do salute thee with my hand,
Though rebels wound thee with their horses' hoofs:
As a long-parted mother with her child
Plays fondly with her tears and smiles in meeting,
So, weeping, smiling, greet I thee, my earth,
And do thee favours with my royal hands.
Feed not thy sovereign's foe, my gentle earth,
Nor with thy sweets comfort his ravenous sense;
But let thy spiders, that suck up thy venom,
And heavy-gaited toads lie in their way,
Doing annoyance to the treacherous feet
Which with usurping steps do trample thee:
Yield stinging nettles to mine enemies;
And when they from thy bosom pluck a flower,
Guard it, I pray thee, with a lurking adder
Whose double tongue may with a mortal touch
Throw death upon thy sovereign's enemies.
Mock not my senseless conjuration, lords:
This earth shall have a feeling and these stones
Prove armed soldiers, ere her native king
Shall falter under foul rebellion's arms.

BISHOP OF CARLISLE

Fear not, my lord: that Power that made you king
Hath power to keep you king in spite of all.
The means that heaven yields must be embraced,
And not neglected; else, if heaven would,
And we will not, heaven's offer we refuse,
The proffer'd means of succor and redress.

DUKE OF AUMERLE

He means, my lord, that we are too remiss;
Whilst Bolingbroke, through our security,
Grows strong and great in substance and in power.

KING RICHARD II

Discomfortable cousin! know'st thou not
That when the searching eye of heaven is hid,
Behind the globe, that lights the lower world,
Then thieves and robbers range abroad unseen
In murders and in outrage, boldly here;
But when from under this terrestrial ball
He fires the proud tops of the eastern pines
And darts his light through every guilty hole,
Then murders, treasons and detested sins,
The cloak of night being pluck'd from off their backs,
Stand bare and naked, trembling at themselves?
So when this thief, this traitor Bolingbroke,
Who all this while hath revell'd in the night
Whilst we were wandering with the antipodes,
Shall see us rising in our throne, the east,
His treasons will sit blushing in his face,
Not able to endure the sight of day,
But self-affrighted tremble at his sin.
Not all the water in the rough rude sea
Can wash the balm off from an anointed king;
The breath of worldly men cannot depose
The deputy elected by the Lord:
For every man that Bolingbroke hath press'd
To lift shrewd steel against our golden crown,
God for his Richard hath in heavenly pay
A glorious angel: then, if angels fight,
Weak men must fall, for heaven still guards the right.

From William Shakespeare, *Richard II*, Act III, scene II.

vision of government. Others, like the English duke of Buckingham, simply remained royal companions. Favorites walked a not very tight rope. They could retain their balance only as long as they retained their influence with the monarch. Richelieu claimed that it was "more difficult to dominate the four square feet of the king's study than the affairs of Europe." The parallel careers of Richelieu, Olivares, and Buckingham neatly illustrate the dangers and opportunities of the office.

Cardinal Richelieu (1585–1642) was born into a French noble family of minor importance. A younger son, he trained for the law and then for a position that his family owned in the Church; he was made a cardinal in 1622. After skillful participation in the meeting of the Estates-General of 1614, Richelieu was given a court post through the patronage of Queen Marie de Médicis, mother of Louis XIII. The two men made a good match. Louis XIII hated the work of ruling and Richelieu loved little else.

Although Richelieu received great favor from the king—he became a duke and amassed the largest private fortune in France—his position rested on his managerial abilities. Richelieu never enjoyed a close personal relationship with his

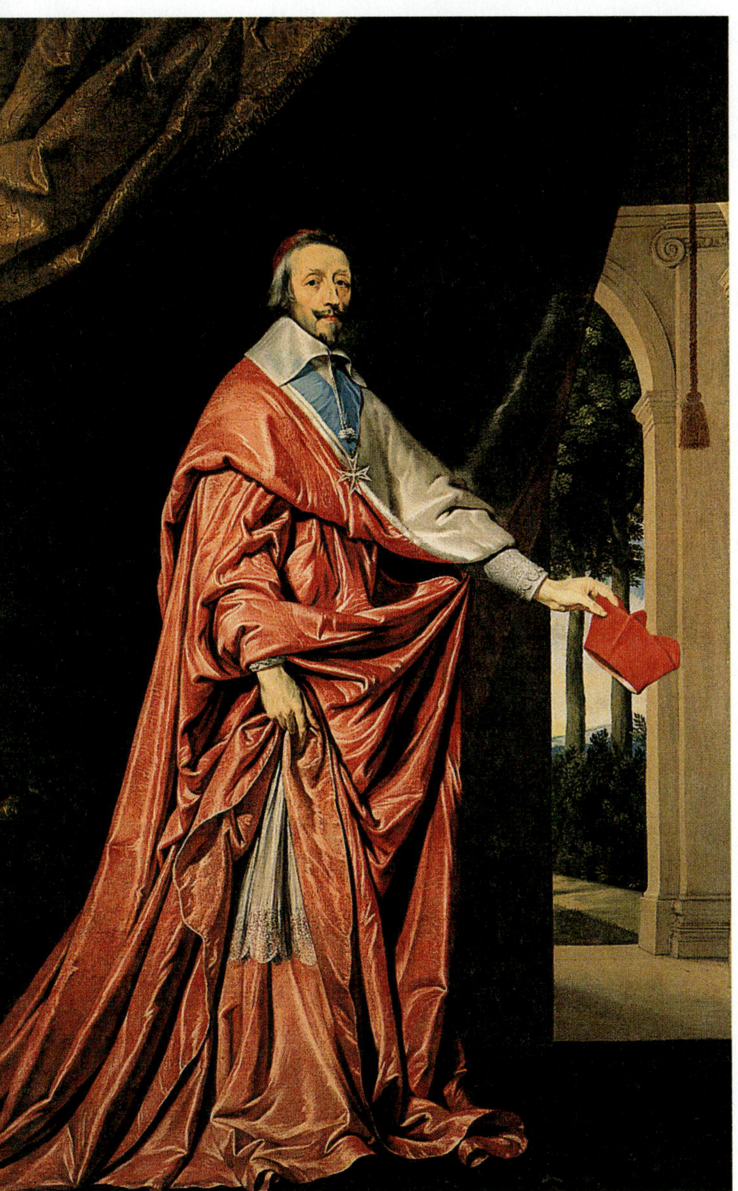

■ This portrait of Richelieu by Philippe de Champaigne shows the cardinal's intellectual power and controlled determination.

monarch, and he never felt that his position was secure. In 1630, Marie de Médicis turned against him, and he very nearly was ousted from office. His last years were filled with suppressing plots to undermine his power or to take his life.

Count-Duke Olivares (1587–1645) was a younger son of a lesser branch of a great Spanish noble family. By the time he was 20 he had become a courtier with a title, a large fortune, and, most unusually, a university education. Olivares became the favorite of King Philip IV (1621–1665). He was elevated to the highest rank of the nobility and lost no time consolidating his position.

Olivares used his closeness to the monarch to gain court appointments for his relatives and political supporters, but he was more interested in establishing political policy than in building a court faction. His objective was to maintain the greatness of Spain, whose fortunes, like his moods, waxed and waned. Like Richelieu, Olivares attempted to further the process of centralizing royal power, which was not very advanced in Spain. Olivares's plans for a nationally recruited and financed army ended in disaster. His efforts at tax reform went unrewarded. He advocated the aggressive foreign policy that mired Spain in the Thirty Years' War and 80 years of war in the Netherlands. As domestic and foreign crises mounted, Philip IV could not resist the pressure to dismiss his chief minister. In 1643, Olivares was removed from office and two years later, physically exhausted and mentally deranged, he died.

The duke of Buckingham (1592–1628) was also a younger son, but not of the English nobility. He received the aimless education of a country gentleman, spending several years in France learning the graces of fashion and dancing. Reputedly one of the most handsome men in Europe, Buckingham hung

■ The Spanish master Diego Velázquez painted this portrait of the Count-Duke Olivares.

■ George Villiers, duke of Buckingham. The royal favorite virtually ruled England between 1618 and 1628. The general rejoicing at his death embittered the king and helped bring about the 11 years' rule without Parliament.

about the fringes of the English court until his looks and charm brought him to the attention of Queen Anne, James I's wife. She recommended him for a minor office that gave him frequent access to the king. Buckingham quickly caught the eye of James I, and his rise was meteoric. In less than seven years he went from commoner to duke, the highest rank of the English nobility.

Along with his titles, Buckingham acquired political power. He assumed a large number of royal offices, among them Admiral of the Navy, and placed his relatives and dependents in many others. Buckingham took his obligations seriously. He began a reform of naval administration, for example, but his rise to power had been so sudden that he found enemies at every turn. Those increased dramatically when James I died in 1625. But Buckingham succeeded where so many others had failed by becoming the favorite and chief minister of the new king, Charles I (1625–1649). His accumulation of power and patronage proceeded unabated, as did the enmity he aroused. But Charles I stood firmly behind him. In 1628, a discontented naval officer finally accomplished what the most powerful men in England could not: Buckingham was assassinated. While Charles I wept inconsolably at the news, ordinary Londoners drank to the health of his killer.

The Taxing Demands of War

More than anything else, war propelled the consolidation of the state. Whether offensive or defensive, continuous or intermittent, successful or calamitous, war was the irresistible force of the seventeenth-century monarchy. War taxation was its immovable object. Perhaps half of all revenue of the western states went to finance war. To maintain its armies and navies, its fortresses and outposts, the state had to squeeze every penny from its subjects. Old taxes had to be collected more efficiently; new taxes had to be introduced and enforced. As one Spanish jurist observed, in a familiar refrain, "There can be no peace without arms, no arms without money, and no money without taxation." However, the unprecedented demands for money by the state were always resisted. The privileged challenged the legality of levying taxes; the unprivileged did whatever they could to avoid paying them.

The claims and counterclaims of subjects and sovereigns were very strong. Armies had grown bigger and more expensive. In 1625, Philip IV had nearly 300,000 men in arms throughout his empire. The expense of maintaining Spanish fortresses alone had quintupled since the time of Philip II. Not only were there more men to pay, equip, and supply, but the cost of war materials continued to rise with inflation. Similarly, the cost of food and fodder rose. Marauding armies might be able to plunder sufficient grain during the spring and autumn, but they still consumed massive amounts of meat and drink that could not be supplied locally.

In fact, the inability of the lower orders of European society to finance a century of warfare was clear from the beginning. In Spain and France, the principal problem was that so much of the wealth of the nation was beyond the reach of traditional royal taxation. The nobility and many of the most important towns had long achieved exemption from basic taxes on consumption and wealth. European taxation was regressive, falling most heavily on those least able to pay. Rulers and subjects alike recognized the inequities of the system. Regime after regime began with plans to overhaul the national system of taxation before settling for propping up new emergency levies against the rotting foundations of the old structure. Nevertheless, the fiscal crisis that the European wars provoked did result in an expansion of state taxation.

Fiscal Expedients. In France, for example, royal expenditures rose 60 percent during the first two decades of the seventeenth century, while the yield from the *taille*, the crown's basic commodity tax, remained constant. Thus the crown was forced to search for new revenues, the most important of which was the ***paulette***, a tax on officeholding. To raise money, especially in emergencies, the crown had been forced to sell government offices, until by the seventeenth century a majority of offices had been obtained by direct purchase. The sale of an office provided a one-time windfall for the crown, but after that the cost of salaries and benefits was a perpetual drain. Draining, too, were the administrative costs of potentially inefficient officeholders. Many purchased their posts as an investment and treated them as personal property. For an annual payment of one-sixtieth of the value of the office, the paulette allowed the current holder to sell or bequeath it as desired. Henry IV instituted the *paulette* in 1604, and it became a vital source of royal revenue as well as an acute source of aristocratic and legal complaint. In the early 1620s, revenue from the sale of offices amounted to one-third of the crown's income.

The purchase of office was inherently corrupt, but it was not necessarily inefficient. Sons who were to inherit offices could be trained for their posts, if for no other reason than to operate them profitably. The crown received money from classes in society that were generally beyond the reach of taxation, while members of those classes received power, prestige, and experience in public service. As long as profit and efficiency went hand in hand, both officeholder and monarch might be well served. Unfortunately, it was the king rather than his officers who had the greatest incentive to manipulate the system. The more offices that could be created, the larger the income from the paulette. During fiscal emergencies it was a temptation to which all French monarchs succumbed.

"Fiscal emergency" was just another name for the routine problems of the Spanish monarchy. As the greatest military power in Europe, Spain necessarily had the greatest military budget, and thus the most extensive system of taxation. The crown taxed both domestic and imperial trade and took a healthy share of the gold and silver that continued to be mined in America. But all the revenues fell short of the state's needs. In the 1590s, Philip II established an important new source of internal taxation. In an agreement with the Cortes of Castile, he introduced the *milliones*, a tax on consumption that was to yield millions of ducats a year for war costs. An extremely regressive measure, the milliones taxed the sale of meat, wine, and oil—the basic elements of diet. The tax, which hit urban areas particularly hard, was originally designed to last only six years. But the crises that the crown pleaded in the 1590s were even deeper at the turn of the century. The milliones became a permanent tax and a permanent grievance throughout Castile.

Taxation in England. By contrast, the English crown was never able to persuade Parliament to grant permanent additional revenues. Although uninvolved in European conflicts, England was not immune from military spending. War with Ireland in the 1590s and with Spain between 1588 and 1604 depleted the reserves that the crown had obtained when Henry VIII dissolved the monasteries. Disastrous wars against France and Spain in the 1620s provoked fiscal crisis for a monarchy that had few direct sources of revenue. While the great wealth of the kingdom was in land, the chief sources of revenue for the crown were in trade. In the early seventeenth century, customs duties, or *impositions*, became a lucrative source of income when the judges ruled that the king could determine which commodities could be taxed and at what rate. Impositions fell heavily upon the merchant classes and urban consumers, but unlike the milliones, impositions were placed on luxury import goods rather than on basic commodities.

Because so much of the crown's revenues derived from commerce and because foreign invasion could only come from the sea, the most pressing military need of the English monarchy was for naval defense. Even during the Armada crisis, the largest part of the English fleet had been made up of private merchant ships pressed into service through the emergency tax of Ship Money, which was a tax on each port town to hire a merchant ship and fit it out for war. In the 1630s, Charles I revived Ship Money and extended it to all English localities. His innovation aroused much opposition from the gentry, especially after his refusal to call Parliament into session to have the tax confirmed.

Still, no matter how much new revenue was provided for war finance, more was needed. New taxes and increased rates of traditional taxation created suffering and a sense of grievance throughout the western European states. Opposition to taxation was not based on greed: the state's right to tax was not yet an established principle. Monarchs received certain forms of revenue in return for grants of immunities and privileges to powerful groups in their state. The state's efforts to go beyond the restricted grants were viewed as theft of private property. In the case of Ship Money, challengers argued that the king had no right to what belonged to his subjects except in a case of national emergency. That was a claim that the king accepted, arguing that such an emergency existed in the presence of pirates who were attacking English shipping. But if Charles I did not make a convincing claim for national emergency, the monarchs of France and Spain, the princes of Germany, and the rulers of the states of eastern Europe all did.

Throughout the seventeenth century, monarchy solidified itself as a form of government. The king's authority came from God, but his power came from his people. By administering justice, assembling armies, and extracting resources through taxation, the monarch ruled as well as governed. The richer the king and the more powerful his might, the more potent was his state. Europeans began to identify themselves as citizens of a nation and to see themselves in distinction to other nations.

THE CRISES OF THE ROYAL STATE

The expansion of the functions, duties, and powers of the state in the early seventeenth century was not universally welcomed in European societies. The growth of central government came at the expense of local rights and privileges held by corporate bodies such as the Church and the towns or by

EUROPEAN POPULATION DATA (IN MILLIONS)							
Year	**1550**	**1575**	**1600**	**1625**	**1650**	**1675**	**1700**
England	3.0	—	4.0	4.5	—	5.8	5.8
France	—	20.0	—	—	—	—	19.3
Italy	11.0	13.0	13.0	13.0	12.0	11.5	12.5
Russia	9.0	—	11.0	8.0	9.5	13.0	16.0
Spain	6.3	—	7.6	—	5.2	—	7.0
All Europe	85.0	95.0	100.0	100.0	80.0	90.0	100.0

individuals such as provincial officials and aristocrats. The state proved a powerful competitor, especially in the contest for the meager surplus produced on the land. As rents and prices stabilized in the early seventeenth century after a long period of inflation, taxation increased, slowly at first and then at a pace with the gathering momentum of the Thirty Years' War. State exactions burdened all segments of society. Peasants lost the small benefit that rising prices had conferred on producers. The surplus that parents had once passed on to children was now taken by the state. Local officials, never altogether popular, came to be seen as parasites and were easy targets for peasant rebellions. Larger landholders, whose prosperity depended on rents and services from an increasingly impoverished peasantry, suffered along with their tenants. Even the great magnates were appalled by the state's insatiable appetite.

Taxation was not the only thing that aroused opposition. Social and economic regulation meant more laws. More laws meant more lawyers and agents of enforcement. State regulation may have been more efficient (though many believed it was more efficient only for the state) but it was certainly disruptive. It was also expensive at a time when the fragile European economy was in a phase of decline. The early seventeenth century was a time of hunger in most of western Europe. Subtle changes in climate reduced the length of growing seasons and the size of crops. Bad harvests in the 1620s and 1640s left disease and starvation in their wake. And the wars ground on.

By the middle of the seventeenth century, a European crisis was taking shape, though its timing and forms differed from place to place. Rural protests, such as grain riots and mob assaults on local institutions, had a long history in all of the European states. Popular revolt was not the product of mindless despair, but rather the natural form of political action for those who fell outside the institutionalized political process. Bread riots and tax revolts became increasingly common in the early seventeenth century. More significantly, as the focus of discontent moved from local institutions to the state, the forms of revolt changed. So, too, did the participants. Members of the political elite began to formulate their own grievances against the expansion of state power. A theory of resistance, first developed in the French wars of religion, came to be applied to political tyranny and posed a direct challenge to the idea of the divine right of kings. By the 1640s, all those forces had converged, and rebellion exploded across the Continent. In Spain, the ancient kingdoms of Catalonia and Portugal asserted their independence from Castilian rule; in France, members of the aristocracy rose against a child monarch and his regent. In Italy, revolts rocked Naples and Sicily. In England, a constitutional crisis gave way to civil war, and then to the first political revolution in European history.

The Need to Resist

Europeans lived more precariously in the seventeenth century than in any period since the Black Death. One benchmark of crisis was population decline. In the Mediterranean, Spain's population fell from 8.5 to 7 million and Italy's population from 13 to 11 million. The ravages of the Thirty Years' War were most clearly felt in central Europe: Germany lost nearly a third of its people, Bohemia nearly half. Northwestern Europe—England, the Netherlands, and France—was hardest hit in the first half of the century and only gradually recovered by 1700. Population decline had many causes and, rather remarkably, direct casualties from warfare were a very small component. The indirect effects of war—the disruption of agriculture and the spread of disease—were far more devastating. Spain alone lost a half million people at the turn of the century and another half million between 1647 and 1652. Severe outbreaks of plague in 1625 and in 1665 hit England, while France endured three consecutive years of epidemics, from 1629 to 1631.

All sectors of the European economy, from agriculture to trade, stagnated or declined in the early seventeenth century. Not surprisingly, peasants were hardest hit. The surplus from good harvests did not remain in rural communities to act as a buffer for bad ones. Tens of thousands died during the two great subsistence crises in the late 1620s and the late 1640s. Predictably, acute economic crisis led to rural revolt. As the

French peasants reeled from visitations of plague, frost, and floods, the French state was raising the taille, the tax that fell most heavily on the lower orders. A series of French rural revolts in the late 1630s focused on opposition to tax increases. The Nu-Pieds—"the barefooted"—rose against changes in the salt tax; others rose against new levies on wine. The revolts began in the same way: with the murder of a local tax official, the organization of a peasant militia, and the recruitment of local clergy and notables. The rebels forced temporary concessions from local authorities, but they never achieved lasting reforms. Each revolt ended with the reimposition of order by the state. In England, the largest rural protests, like the Midland Revolt of 1607, centered on opposition to the enclosure of grain fields and their conversion to pasture.

The most spectacular popular uprisings occurred in Spanish-occupied Italy. In the spring of 1647, the Sicilian city of Palermo exploded under the pressure of a disastrous harvest, rising food prices, and relentless taxation. A city of 130,000 inhabitants, Palermo imported nearly all of its foodstuffs. As grain prices rose, the city government subsidized the price of bread, running up huge debts in the process. When the town governors could no longer afford the subsidies, they decided to reduce the size of the loaf rather than increase its price. This did not fool the women of the city, who rioted when the first undersized loaves were placed on sale. Soon the entire city was in revolt. "Long live the king and down with taxes!" became the rebel slogan. Commoners who were not part of the urban power structure led the revolt in Palermo. For a time they achieved the abolition of Spanish taxes on basic foodstuffs. Their success provided the model for a similar uprising in Naples, the largest city in Europe. The Neapolitan revolt began in 1647 after the Spanish placed a tax on fruit. A crowd gathered to protest the new imposition, burned the customs house, and murdered several local officials. The protesters were led first by a fisherman and then by a blacksmith, and again the rebels achieved the temporary suspension of Spanish taxation. But neither of the Italian urban revolts could attract support from the local governors or the nobility. Both uprisings were eventually crushed.

The Right to Resist

Rural and urban revolts by members of the lower orders of European society were doomed to failure. Not only did the state control vast military resources, but it could count on the loyalty of the governing classes to suppress local disorder. It was only when local elites rebelled and joined their social and political discontent to the economic grievances of the peasants that the state faced a genuine crisis. Traditionally, aristocratic rebellion focused on the legitimacy rather than the power of the state. Claimants to the throne initiated civil wars for the prize of the crown. By the early seventeenth century, however, hereditary monarchy was too firmly entrenched to be threatened by aristocratic rebellions. When Elizabeth I of England died without an heir, the throne passed to her cousin, James I, without even a murmur of discontent. The assassination of Henry IV in 1610 left a child on the French throne, yet it provoked little more than intrigue over which aristocratic faction would advise him. The principles of hereditary monarchy and the divine right of kings laid an unshakable foundation for royal legitimacy. But if the monarch's right to rule could no longer be challenged, was the method of rule equally unassailable? Were subjects bound to their sovereign in all cases whatsoever?

Resistance Theory. Luther and Calvin had preached a doctrine of passive obedience. **Magistrates** ruled by divine

War, famine, and disease all contributed to population decline in the seventeenth century. This broadsheet shows the weekly burial of plague victims in London during a severe outbreak in 1665.

will and had to be obeyed in all things, they argued. Both left a tiny crack in the door of absolute submission, however, by recognizing the right of lesser magistrates to resist their superiors if divine law was violated. It was during the French civil wars that a broader theory of resistance began to develop. In attempting to defend themselves from accusations that they were rebels, a number of Huguenot writers responded with an argument that accepted the divine right of kings but limited royal power. They claimed that kings were placed on earth by God to uphold piety and justice. When they failed to do so, lesser magistrates were obliged to resist them. As God would not institute tyranny, oppressive monarchs could not be acting by divine right. Therefore, the king who violated divine law could be punished. In the most influential of such writings, *A Defense of Liberty Against Tyrants* (1579), Philippe Duplessis-Mornay (1549–1623) took the critical next step and argued that the king who violated the law of the land could also be resisted.

In the writings of both Huguenot and Dutch Protestants there remained strict limits to the right to resist. Those authors accepted all the premises of divine right theory and restricted resistance to other divinely ordained magistrates. Obedience tied society together at all levels, and loosening any of the knots might unravel everything. In fact, one crucial binding had already come loose when the arguments used to justify resistance in matters of religion came to be applied to matters of state. Logic soon drove the argument further. If it was the duty of lesser magistrates to resist monarchical tyranny, why was it not the duty of all citizens to do so? That was a question posed not by a Protestant rebel, but by a Jesuit professor, Juan de Mariana (1536–1624). In *The King and the Education of the King* (1598), Mariana described how human government developed from the need of individuals to have leaders to act for their convenience and well-being. The magistrates were established by the people and then legitimated by God. Magistrates were nothing other than the people's representatives, and if it was the duty of magistrates to resist the tyranny of monarchs, then it must also be the duty of every individual citizen. "If the sacred fatherland is falling into ruins, he who tries to kill the tyrant will be acting in no ways unjustly."

There remained one more vital link in the chain, which was supplied by the great English poet John Milton (1608–1674) in his defense of the English Revolution. Milton built upon traditional resistance theory as it had developed over the previous 50 years. Kings were instituted by the people to uphold piety and justice. Lesser magistrates had the right to resist monarchs. An unjust king forfeited his divine right and was to be punished as any ordinary citizen. In *The Tenure of Kings and Magistrates* (1649), Milton expanded upon the conventional idea that society was formed by a covenant, or contract, between ruler and ruled. The king in his coronation oath promised to uphold the laws of the land and rule for the benefit of his subjects. The subjects promised to obey. Failure by either side to meet obligations broke the contract.

Resistance and Rebellion. By the middle of the seventeenth century, resistance theory provided the intellectual justification for a number of different attacks on monarchical authority. In 1640, simultaneous rebellions in the ancient kingdoms of Portugal and Catalonia threatened the Spanish monarchy. The Portuguese successfully dissolved the rather artificial bonds that had been created by Philip II and resumed their separate national identity. Catalonia, the easternmost province of Spain, which Ferdinand of Aragon had brought to the union of crowns in the fifteenth century, presented a more serious challenge. Throughout the 1620s, Catalonia, with its rich Mediterranean city of Barcelona, had consistently rebuffed Olivares's attempts to consolidate the Spanish provinces. The Catalonian Cortes—the representative institution of the towns—refused to make even small contributions to the Union of Arms or to successive appeals for emergency tax increases. Catalonian leaders feared that the demands were only the thin edge of the wedge. They did not want their province to go the way of Castile, where taxation was as much an epidemic as plague.

Catalonia relied on its ancient laws to fend off demands for contributions to the Spanish military effort. But soon the province was embroiled in the French war, and Olivares was forced to bring troops into Catalonia. The presence of the soldiers and their conduct inflamed the local population. In the spring of 1640 an unconnected series of peasant uprisings took place. Soldiers and royal officials were slain, and the Spanish viceroy of the province was murdered. But the violence was not directed only against outsiders. Attacks on wealthy citizens raised the specter of social revolt.

At that point a peasant uprising broadened into a provincial rebellion. The political leaders of Barcelona not only decided to approve the rebellion but decided to lead it. They declared that Philip IV had violated the fundamental laws of Catalonia and that as a consequence their allegiance to the crown of Spain was dissolved. They turned to Louis XIII of France, offering him sovereignty if he would preserve their liberties. In fact, the Catalonians simply exchanged a devil they knew for one they did not. The French happily sent troops into Barcelona to repel a Spanish attempt to crush the rebellion, and then two armies occupied Catalonia. The Catalonian rebellion lasted for 12 years. When the Spanish finally took Barcelona in 1652, both rebels and ruler were exhausted from the struggle.

The revolt of the Catalonians posed a greater external threat to the Spanish monarchy than it did an internal one. In contrast, the French **Fronde,** an aristocratic rebellion that began in 1648, was more directly a challenge to the underlying authority of the state. It too began in response to fiscal crises brought on by war. Throughout the 1640s the French state had tottered on the edge of bankruptcy. It had used every means of creative financing that its ministers could devise, mortgaging as much of the future as anyone would buy. Still, it was necessary to raise traditional taxes and institute new ones. The first tactic revived peasant revolts, especially in the early years of the decade; the second led to the Fronde.

■ Anne of Austria acted as a regent during her son's minority, though in practice she delegated most power to her adviser Cardinal Mazarin. This painting emphasizes the piety of the royal family, as Anne, Louis, and his younger brother Philippe kneel in prayer against a backdrop of God, Jesus, and their heavenly and worldly servants.

The Fronde was a rebellion against the regency government of Louis XIV (1643–1715), who was only four years old when he inherited the French throne. His mother, Anne of Austria (1601–1666), ruled as regent with the help of her Italian adviser, Cardinal Mazarin (1602–1661). In the circumstances of war, agricultural crisis, and financial stringency, no regency government was popular, but Anne and Mazarin made the worst of a bad situation. They initiated new taxes on officeholders, Parisian landowners, and the nobility. Soon all three united against them, led by the Parlement of Paris, the highest court in the land, in which new decrees of taxation had to be registered. When the **Parlement** refused to register a number of the new taxes proposed by the government and soon insisted on the right to control the crown's financial policy, Anne and Mazarin struck back by arresting a number of leading members of the Parlement. But in 1648 barricades went up in Paris, and the court, along with the nine-year-old king, fled the capital. Quickly the Fronde—which took its name from the slingshots that children used to hurl stones at carriages—became an aristocratic revolt aimed not at the king, but at his advisers. Demands for Mazarin's resignation, removal of the new taxes, and greater participation in government by nobles and Parlement were coupled with profuse statements of loyalty to the king.

The duc de Condé, leader of the Parisian insurgents, courted Spanish aid against Mazarin's forces, and the cardinal was forced to make concessions in order to prevent a Spanish invasion of France. The leaders of the Fronde agreed that the crown must overhaul its finances and recognize the rights of the administrative nobility to participate in formulating royal policy, but they had no concrete proposals to accomplish either aim. Nor could they control the deteriorating political situation in Paris and a number of provincial capitals where urban and rural riots followed the upper-class attack upon the state. The catastrophic winter of 1652, with its combination of harvest failure, intense cold, and epidemic disease, brought the crisis to a head. Louis XIV was declared old enough to rule and his forces recaptured Paris, where he was welcomed as a savior. Born of frustration, fear, and greed, the Fronde accomplished little. It demonstrated only that the French aristocracy remained an independent force in politics. Like the Catalonian revolt, it revealed the fragility of the absolute state on the one hand, yet its underlying stability on the other.

The English Civil War

On the surface, it is difficult to understand why the most profound challenge to monarchical authority took place in England. Among the nations of Europe, England alone enjoyed peace in the early seventeenth century. Except for a brief period around 1620, the English economy sputtered along. The monarchy itself was stable. James I had succeeded his cousin Elizabeth I without challenge and already had as many children as the Tudors had produced in nearly a century.

James I. James I was not a lovable monarch, but he was capable, astute, and generous. In the eyes of his critics he had two great faults: he succeeded a legend and he was Scottish. There was little he could do about either. Elizabeth I had ruled England successfully for more than 40 years. As the economy soured and the state tilted toward bankruptcy in the 1590s, the queen remained above criticism. She sold off royal lands worth thousands of pounds and ran up huge debts at the turn of the century, yet the gleaming myth of the glorious virgin queen tarnished not the least bit. When she died, the general population wept openly and the governing elite breathed a collective sigh of relief. There was so much to be done to set things right.

At first, James I endeared himself to the English gentry and aristocracy by showering them with the gift of social elevation. On his way to London from Scotland, the first of the Stuart kings knighted thousands of gentlemen who had waited in vain for favor from the queen. He promoted peers and created new titles to meet the pent-up demands of decades of stinginess. But he showered favor equally on his own countrymen, members of his royal Scottish court who accompanied him to England. A strong strain of ethnic prejudice combined with the disappointed hopes of English courtiers to generate immediate hostility to the new regime. If Elizabeth could do no wrong, James could do little right. Although he relied upon Elizabeth's most trusted ministers to guide state business, James was soon plunged into financial and political difficulties. He never escaped from either.

IMAGE DISCOVERY

Commoner or King? Charles I at the Hunt

The artist Anthony Van Dyck painted this picture of Charles I in 1635, only a few years before his kingdoms revolted. Here, Charles is depicted in a rustic location, without crown, scepter, or other trappings of monarchy. Does he still look like a king? Charles was not, in fact, unusually fond of hunting. Why, then, would he have chosen to be painted this way? What might the drooping head of his horse have signified to seventeenth-century viewers? Remember, this was painted before anyone could have known that England, Scotland, or Ireland would revolt.

Charles I. James's financial problems resulted directly from the fact that the tax base of the English monarchy was undervalued. For decades the monarchy had staved off a crisis by selling lands that had been confiscated from the Church in the mid-sixteenth century. But that solution reduced the crown's long-term revenues and made it dependent on extraordinary grants of taxation from Parliament. Royal demands for money were met by parliamentary demands for political reform, and the differing objectives provoked unintentional political controversies in the 1620s. The most significant, in 1628, during the reign of Charles I, led to the formulation of the Petition of Right, which restated the traditional English freedoms from arbitrary arrest and imprisonment (habeas corpus), nonparliamentary taxation, and the confiscation of property by martial law.

Religious problems mounted on top of economic and political difficulties. Demands were made for thoroughgoing church reforms by groups and individuals who had little in common apart from the name given to them by their detractors: **Puritans.** One of the most contentious issues raised by

A SHORT, SHARP SHOCK

Charles I was executed at Westminster on a bitter January afternoon in 1649. This excerpt comes from an eyewitness account of his last moments. Charles, who was accompanied on the scaffold by the bishop of London, discovered that the chopping block was very short so that he could be held down if he resisted.

Focus Questions

Is Charles resigned to his execution? In what ways is the divine right of kings commented upon in this passage?

And to the executioner he said, "I shall say but very short prayers, and when I thrust out my hands—"

Then he called to the bishop for his cap, and having put it on, asked the executioner, "Does my hair trouble you?" who desired him to put it all under his cap; which, as he was doing by the help of the bishop and the executioner, he turned to the bishop, and said, "I have a good cause, and a gracious God on my side."

The bishop said, "There is but one stage more, which, though turbulent and troublesome, yet is a very short one. You may consider it will soon carry you a very great way; it will carry you from earth to heaven; and there you shall find to your great joy the prize you hasten to, a crown of glory."

The king adjoins, "I go from a corruptible to an incorruptible crown; where no disturbance can be, no disturbance in the world."

The bishop. "You are exchanged from a temporal to an eternal crown—a good exchange."

Then the king asked the executioner, "Is my hair well?" . . . and looking upon the block, said . . . "You must set it fast."

The executioner. "It is fast, sir."

King. "It might have been a little higher."

Executioner. "It can be no higher, sir."

King. "When I put out my hands this way, then—"

Then having said a few words to himself, as he stood, with hands and eyes lifted up, immediately stooping down he laid his neck upon the block; and the executioner, again putting his hair under his cap, his Majesty, thinking he had been going to strike, bade him, "Stay for the sign."

Executioner. "Yes, I will, and it please your Majesty."

After a very short pause, his Majesty stretching forth his hands, the executioner at one blow severed his head from his body; which, being held up and showed to the people, was with his body put into a coffin covered with black velvet and carried into his lodging.

His blood was taken up by divers persons for different ends: by some as trophies of their villainy; by others as relics of a martyr; and in some hath had the same effect, by the blessing of God, which was often found in his sacred touch when living.

Puritans was the survival in the Anglican church of the Catholic hierarchy of archbishops and bishops. They demanded the abolition of this episcopal form of government and its replacement with a presbyterial system similar to that in Scotland, in which congregations nominated their own representatives to a national assembly. As the king was the supreme head of the English church, an attack upon church structure was an attack upon the monarchy. "No bishop, no king," James I declared as he rejected the first formal attempts at reform. But neither James I nor his son, Charles I, opposed religious reform. They, too, wanted a better educated clergy, a plain and decorous worship service, and godly citizens. But to achieve their reforms they strengthened episcopal power. In the 1620s, Archbishop William Laud (1573–1645) rose to power in the English church by espousing a Calvinism so moderate that many denied it was Calvinism at all. Laud preached the beauty of holiness and strove to reintroduce decoration in the church and a formal decorum in the service. One of Laud's first projects after he was appointed archbishop of Canterbury was to establish a consistent divine service in England and Scotland by creating new prayer books.

It fell to the unfortunate dean of St. Giles Cathedral in Edinburgh to introduce the new Scottish prayer book in 1637. The reaction was immediate: someone threw a stool at his head and dozens of women screamed that "popery" was being brought to Scotland. There were riots by citizens and resistance to the use of the new prayer book by clergy and the nobility. To Charles I the opposition was rebellion, and he began to raise forces to suppress it. But Scottish soldiers were far more determined to preserve their religious practice than were English soldiers to impose the king's. By the end of 1640, a Scottish army had successfully invaded England.

Now the fiscal and political problems of the Stuart monarchs came into play. For 11 years, Charles I had managed to do what he was in theory supposed to do: live from his own revenues. He had accomplished that by a combination of economy and the revival of ancient feudal rights that struck hard at the governing classes. He levied fines for unheard-of offenses, expanded traditional taxes, and added a brutal efficiency to the collection of revenue. While these expedients sufficed during peacetime, they could not support an army and war. Charles I was again dependent on grants from Parliament, which he reluctantly summoned in 1640.

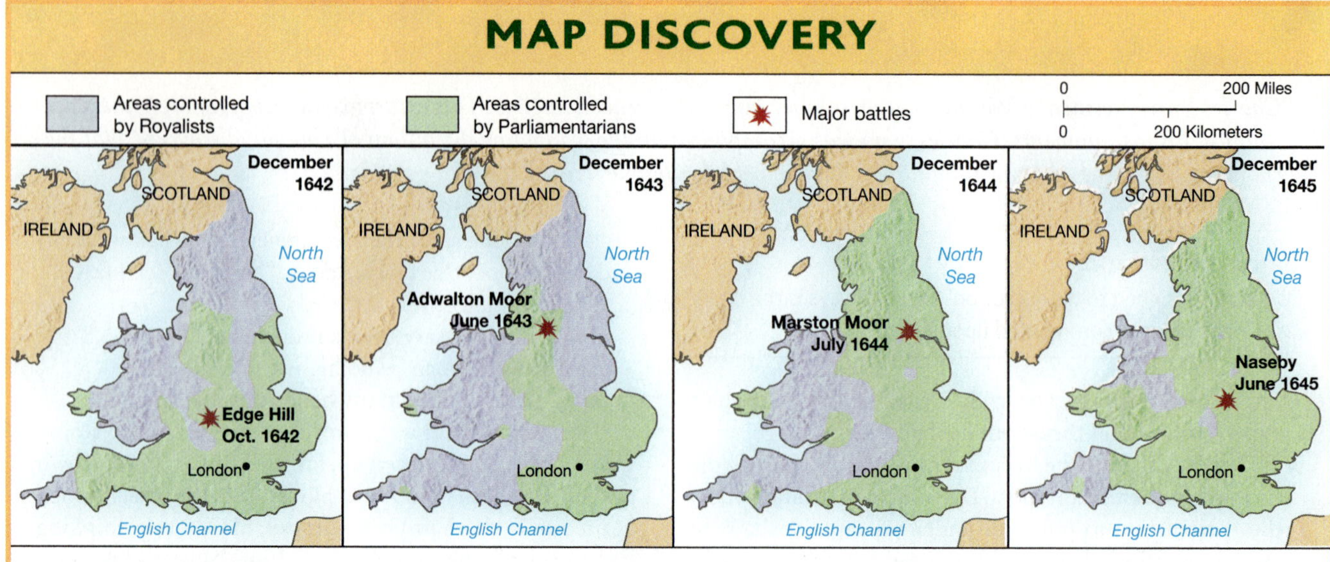

English Civil War

How would you describe the geographical divisions at the beginning of the war in 1642? Who appears to have been winning the war by December 1643? How did the war progress between 1644 and 1645?

The Long Parliament. The **Long Parliament,** which met in November 1640 and sat for 13 years, saw little urgency in levying taxes to repel the Scots. After all, the Scots were resisting Laud's religious innovations, and there were many Englishmen who believed that they should be resisted. More to the point, members of Parliament had a host of political grievances to be redressed before they granted the king his money. Parliament proposed a number of constitutional reforms that Charles I reluctantly accepted. The Long Parliament would not be dismissed without its own consent. In the future, Parliaments would be summoned once every three years. Due process in common law would be observed, and the ancient taxes that the crown had revived would be abolished. To show its seriousness of purpose, Parliament, as the highest court in the land, tried and executed Charles's leading political adviser, the Earl of Strafford, and imprisoned Archbishop Laud.

At first Charles I could do nothing but bide his time and accept the assaults on his power and authority, believing that once he had crushed the Scots he would be able to bargain from a position of strength. But as the months passed, it became clear that Parliament had no intention of providing him with money or forces. Rather, the members sought to negotiate with the Scots themselves and to continue to demand concessions from the king as long as the Scottish threat remained. By the end of 1641, Charles's patience had worn thin. He bungled an attempt to arrest the leaders of the House of Commons, but he successfully spirited his wife and children out of London. Then he too left the capital and headed north where, in the summer of 1642, he raised the royal standard and declared the leaders of Parliament rebels and traitors. England was plunged into civil war.

Parliament had finally pushed too hard, and its members now found themselves in the unprecedented situation of having to fight a war against their sovereign, a war that few of them wanted and that hardly anyone believed they could win. One of the Parliament's generals summed up the futility of the situation: "If we defeat the king ninety-nine times, yet still he is king. But if he defeat us once we will all be hanged as traitors." Nevertheless, there were strong passions on both sides. Parliamentarians believed that they were fighting to defend their religion, their liberties, and the rule of law. Royalists believed they were fighting to defend their monarch, their church, and social stability. After nearly three years of inconclusive fighting, in June 1645 Parliament won a decisive victory at Naseby and brought the war to an end the following summer. The king was in captivity, bishops had been abolished, a Presbyterian church had been established, and limitations were placed on royal power. All that remained necessary to end three years of civil war was the king's agreement to abide by the judgment of battle.

But Charles I had no intention of surrendering either his religion or his authority. Despite the rebels' successes, they could not rule without him, and he would concede nothing as long as opportunities to maneuver remained. In 1647 there were opportunities galore. The war had proved ruinously expensive to Parliament. It owed enormous sums to the Scots, to its own soldiers, and to the governors of London. Each of those elements had its own objectives in a final settlement of the war, and they were not altogether compatible. London

Print of the 1649 execution of Charles I, who was tried and found guilty of treason. As the ax fell, one witness recorded, "such a groan as I never heard before and hope never to hear again" broke forth from the crowd. With the king's execution, England was declared to be a commonwealth, and the monarchy was abolished.

feared the parliamentary army, unpaid and camped dangerously close to the capital. The Scots and the English Presbyterians in Parliament feared that the religious settlement already made would be sacrificed by those known as Independents, who desired a more decentralized church. The Independents feared that they would be persecuted just as harshly by the Presbyterians as they had been by the king. In fact, the war had settled nothing.

The English Revolutions

Charles I happily played both ends against the middle until the army decisively ended the game. In June 1647, soldiers kidnapped the king and demanded that Parliament pay their arrears, protect them from legal retribution, and recognize their service to the nation. Those in Parliament who opposed the army's intervention were impeached, and when London Presbyterians rose up against the army's show of force, troops moved in to occupy the city. The civil war, which had come so close to resolution in 1647, had now become a military revolution. Religious and political radicals flocked to the army and encouraged the soldiers to support their programs and resist disbandment. New fighting broke out in 1648 as Charles encouraged his supporters to resume the war. But forces under the command of Sir Thomas Fairfax (1612–1671) and Oliver Cromwell (1599–1658) easily crushed the royalist uprisings in England and Scotland. The army then demanded that Charles I be brought to justice for his treacherous conduct both before and during the war. When the majority in Parliament refused, still hoping against hope to reach an accommodation with the king, the soldiers again acted decisively. In December 1648, army regiments were sent to London to purge the two houses of Parliament of those who opposed the army's demands. The remaining members, contemptuously called the Rump Parliament, voted to bring the king to trial for his crimes against the liberties of his subjects. On 30 January 1649, Charles I was executed and England was declared to be a commonwealth. The monarchy and the House of Lords were abolished, and the nation was to be governed by what was left of the membership of the House of Commons.

Cromwell Abolishes Monarchy

Oliver Cromwell. For four years, the members of the Rump Parliament struggled with proposals for a new constitution while balancing the demands of moderate and radical reformers and an increasingly hostile army. It achieved little other than to raise the level of frustration. In 1653, Oliver Cromwell, with the support of the army's senior officers, forcibly dissolved the Rump and became the leader of the revolutionary government. At first he ruled along with a Parliament hand-picked from among the supporters of the commonwealth. When Cromwell's Parliament proved no more capable of governing than had the Rump, a written constitution, The Instrument of Government (1653), established a new polity. Cromwell was given the title Lord Protector, and he was to rule along with a freely elected Parliament and an administrative body known as the Council of State.

Cromwell was able to hold the revolutionary cause together through the force of his own personality. A member of the lesser landed elite who had opposed the arbitrary policies of Charles I, he was a devout Puritan who believed in a large measure of religious toleration for Christians. As both a member of Parliament and a senior officer in the army, he had been able to temper the claims of each when they conflicted.

■ The charismatic Oliver Cromwell, Lord Protector of England, wore many hats but was most comfortable under the helmet of a cavalry commander. He is pictured here in his element, armed and on horseback.

Cromwell saw God's hand directing England toward a more glorious future, and he believed that his own actions were divinely ordained: "No man climbs higher than he that knows not whither he goes." Although many urged him to accept the crown of England and begin a new monarchy, Cromwell steadfastly held out for a government in which fundamental authority resided in Parliament. Until his death he defended the achievements of the revolution and held its conflicting constituents together.

But a sense that only a single person could effectively rule a state remained too strong for the reforms of the revolutionary regimes to have much chance of success. When Cromwell died in 1658 it was only natural that his eldest son, Richard, should be proposed as the new Lord Protector despite the fact that Richard had very little experience in either military or civil affairs. Nor did he have the sense of purpose that was his father's greatest source of strength. Without an individual to hold the movement together, the revolution fell apart. In 1659, the army again intervened in civil affairs, dismissing the recently elected Parliament and calling for the restoration of the monarchy to provide stability to the state. After a period of negotiation in which the king agreed to a general amnesty with only a few exceptions, the Stuarts were restored when Charles II (1649–1685) took the throne in 1660.

Twenty years of civil war and revolution had had their effect. Parliament became a permanent part of civil government and now had to be managed rather than ignored. Royal power over taxation and religion was curtailed, although in fact Parliament proved more vigorous in suppressing religious dissent than the monarchy ever had. England was to be a reformed Protestant state, although there remained much dispute about what constituted reform. Absolute monarchy had become constitutional monarchy, with the threat of revolution behind the power of Parliament and the threat of anarchy behind the power of the crown.

The Glorious Revolution. The threats of revolution and of anarchy proved potent in 1685 when James II (1685–1688) came to the throne. A declared Catholic, James attempted to use his power of appointment to foil the constraints that Parliament imposed on him. He elevated Catholics to leading posts in the military and in the central government and began a campaign to pack a new Parliament with his supporters. That proved too much for the governing classes, who entered into negotiations with William, Prince of Orange, husband of Mary Stuart, James's eldest daughter. In 1688, William landed in England with a small force. Without support, James II fled to France, the English throne was declared vacant, and William and Mary were proclaimed king and queen of England. There was little bloodshed in England and little threat of social disorder, and the event soon came to be called the **Glorious Revolution.** Its achievements were set down in the Declaration of Rights (1689), which was presented to William and Mary before they took the throne. The

English Bill of Rights

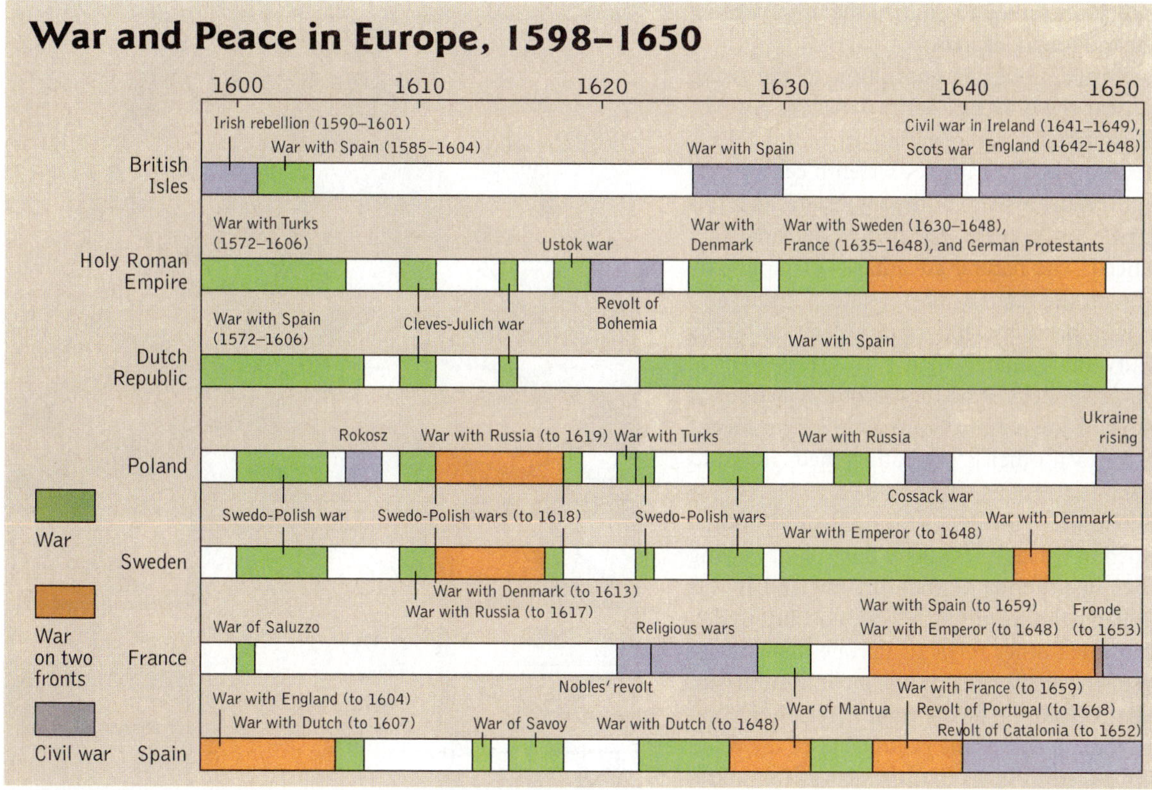

Declaration reasserted the fundamental principles of constitutional monarchy as they had developed over the previous half century. Security of property and the regularity of Parliaments were guaranteed. The Toleration Act (1689) granted religious freedom to nearly all groups of Protestants. The liberties of the subject and the rights of the sovereign were to be in balance.

The events of 1688 in England reversed a trend toward increasing power on the part of the Stuarts and resulted in the development of a unique form of government that a century later would spawn dozens of imitators. John Locke (1632–1704) was the theorist of the Revolution of 1689. He was heir to the century-old debate on resistance, and he carried the doctrine to a new plateau. In *Two Treatises on Civil Government* (1690), Locke developed the contract theory of government. Political society was a compact that individuals entered into freely for their own well-being. It was designed to maintain each person's natural rights—life, liberty, and property. Natural rights were inherent in individuals; they could not be given away. The contract between rulers and subjects was an agreement for the protection of natural rights. "Arbitrary power cannot consist with the ends of society and government. Men would not quit the freedom of the state of nature were it not to preserve their lives, liberties, and fortunes and by stated rules to secure their peace and happiness." When rulers acted arbitrarily, they were to be deposed by their subjects, preferably in the relatively peaceful manner in which James II had been replaced by William III.

The efforts of European monarchies to centralize their power came at the expense of the Church, the aristocracy, and the localities. It was a struggle that took place over decades and was not accomplished easily. In France, the Fronde was an aristocratic backlash; in Spain, the revolt of the Catalonians pitted the Castilian crown against a proud ethnic province. In England, a civil war fought to prevent the encroachments of the crown against the rights of the community gave way to a bloody revolution that combined religious and constitutional grievances—the excesses of monarchy were succeeded by the excesses of parliamentary rule. But the lesson learned by the English ruling elites was that for a nation to enjoy the benefits of a powerful central authority, it was necessary to restrain that authority. The Glorious Revolution of 1689 helped create a constitutional balance between ruler and ruled.

THE ZENITH OF THE ROYAL STATE

The crises of midcentury tested the mettle of the royal states. Over the long term, the crises had two different consequences. First, they provided a check to the exercise of royal power. Fear of recurring rebellions had a chilling effect upon policy, especially taxation. Reforms of financial administration, long overdue, were one of the themes of the later seventeenth century. Even as royal government strengthened itself, it remained concerned about the impact of its policies. Second, the memory of rebellion served to control the ambitions of factious noblemen and town oligarchs.

If nothing else, the episodes of opposition to the rising royal states made clear the universal desire for stable government, which was seen as the responsibility of both subjects and rulers. By the second half of the seventeenth century, effective government was the byword of the royal state. As Louis XIV proclaimed, rule was a trade that had to be constantly studied and practiced. The natural advantages of monarchy had to be merged with the interests of the state's citizens and their desires for wealth, safety, and honor. After so much chaos and instability, the monarchy had to be elevated above the fray of day-to-day politics; it had to become a symbol of the power and glory of the nation. Control no longer meant the greedy grasp of royal officials but rather their practiced guidance of affairs.

In England, Holland, and Sweden, a form of constitutional monarchy developed in which rulers shared power, in varying degrees, with other institutions of state. In England it was Parliament, in Holland the town oligarchies, and in Sweden the nobility. But in most other states in Europe there developed a pure form of royal government known as **absolutism.** Absolute monarchy revived the divine right theories of kingship and added to them a cult of the personality of the ruler. Absolutism was practiced in states as dissimilar as Denmark, Brandenburg-Prussia, and Russia. It reached its zenith in France under Louis XIV, the most powerful of the seventeenth-century monarchs.

■ The title page of the first edition of Thomas Hobbes's *Leviathan,* published in 1651. The huge figure, composed of many tiny human beings, symbolizes the surrender of individual human rights to those of the state.

The Nature of Absolute Monarchy

Locke's theory of contract provided one solution to the central problem of seventeenth-century government: how to balance the monarch's right to command and the subjects' duty to obey. By establishing a constitutional monarchy in which power was shared between the ruler and a representative assembly of subjects, England found one path out of this thicket. But it was not a path that many others could follow. The English solution was most suited to a state that was largely immune from invasion and land war. Constitutional government required a higher level of political participation of citizens than did an absolute monarchical one. Greater participation in turn meant greater freedom of expression, greater toleration of religious minorities, and greater openness in the institutions of government. All were dangerous. The price that England paid was a half century of governmental instability.

The alternative to constitutional monarchy was absolute monarchy. It too found its greatest theorist in England. Thomas Hobbes (1588–1679) was one of many Englishmen who went into exile in France during the course of the English civil wars. In his greatest work, *Leviathan* (1651), Hobbes argued that before civil society had been formed, humans lived in a savage state of nature, "in a war of every man against every man." That was a ghastly condition without morality or law—"the notions of right and wrong, of justice and injustice have there no place." People came together to form a government for the most basic of all purposes: self-preservation. Without government they were condemned to a life that was "solitary, poor, nasty, brutish, and short." To escape the state of nature, individuals pooled their power and granted it to a ruler. The terms of the Hobbesian contract were simple. Rulers agreed to rule; subjects agreed to obey. When the contract was intact, people ceased to live in a state of nature. When it was broken, they returned to it. With revolts, rebellions, and revolutions erupting in all parts of Europe, Hobbes's state of nature never seemed very far away.

For most states of Europe in the later seventeenth century, absolute monarchy became not only a necessity but an ideal. The consolidation of power in the hands of the divinely ordained monarch who nevertheless ruled according to principles of law and justice was seen as the perfect form of government. Absolutism was an expression of control rather than of power. If the state was sometimes pictured as a horse, the ab-

THE NATURE OF MAN

Thomas Hobbes's Leviathan *(1651) is one of the classic works of political theory in Western history. Hobbes describes the state of nature as a state of perpetual insecurity from which mankind emerged by surrendering power to a sovereign and thereby creating a political society. Writing in the context of both the English and French civil wars, Hobbes's sovereign held absolute power over life and property which he used to protect and defend his subjects.*

Focus Questions

What is the importance of security to a civilized state? What is Hobbes's view of the nature of man without government?

Whatsoever therefore is consequent to a time of war, where every man is enemy to every man, the same consequent to the time wherein men live without other security than what their own strength and their own invention shall furnish them withal. In such condition there is no place for industry, because the fruit thereof is uncertain: and consequently no culture of the earth; no navigation, nor use of the commodities that may be imported by sea; no commodious building; no instruments of moving and removing such things as require much force; no knowledge of the face of the earth; no account of time; no arts; no letters; no society; and which is worst of all, continual fear, and danger of violent death; and the life of man, solitary, poor, nasty, brutish, and short.

To this war of every man against every man, this also is consequent; that nothing can be unjust. The notions of right and wrong, justice and injustice, have there no place. Where there is no common power, there is no law; where no law, no injustice. Force and fraud are in war the two cardinal virtues. Justice and injustice are none of the faculties neither of the body nor mind. If they were, they might be in a man that were alone in the world, as well as his senses and passions. They are qualities that relate to men in society, not in solitude. It is consequent also to the same condition that there be no propriety, no dominion, no mine and thine distinct; but only that to be every man's that he can get, and for so long as he can keep it. And thus much for the ill condition which man by mere nature is actually placed in; though with a possibility to come out of it, consisting partly in the passions, partly in his reason.

From Thomas Hobbes, *Leviathan.*

solute monarch gripped the reins more tightly than the whip. "Many writers have tried to confound absolute government with arbitrary government. But no two things could be more unlike," wrote Bishop Jacques Bossuet (1627–1704), who extolled absolutism in France. The absolute ruler ruled in the interests of his people: "The prince is the public person, the whole state is included in him, the will of all the people is enclosed within his own."

The main features of absolute monarchy were designed to extend royal control. As in the early seventeenth century, the person of the monarch was revered. Courts grew larger and more lavish in an effort to enhance the glory of the monarchy, and thereby of the state. "L'état, c'est moi"—"I am the state"—Louis XIV was supposed to have said. No idea better expresses absolutism's connection between governor and governed. As the king grew in stature, his competitors for power all shrank. Large numbers of nobles were herded together at court under the watchful eye of monarchs who now ruled rather than reigned. The king shed the cloak of his favorites and rolled up his own sleeves to manage state affairs. Representative institutions, especially those that laid claim to control over taxation, were weakened or cast aside for obstructing efficient government and endangering the welfare of the state. Monarchs needed standing armies, permanent forces that could be drilled and trained in the increasingly sophisticated arts of war. Thus the military was expanded and made an integral part of the machinery of government. The military profession developed within nations, gradually replacing mercenary adventurers who had fought for booty rather than for duty.

Yet the absolute state was never as powerful in practice as it was in theory, nor did it ever exist in its ideal shape. Absolutism was always in the making, never quite made. Its success depended upon a strong monarch who knew his own will and could enforce it. It depended upon unity within the state and the absence or ruthless suppression of religious or political minorities. The absolute ruler needed to control information and ideas, to limit criticism of state policy. Ultimately, the absolute state rested upon the will of its citizens to support it.

Absolutism in the East

Frederick William, the Great Elector of Brandenburg-Prussia (1640–1688), was one of the European princes who made the most effective use of the techniques of absolutism. In 1640, he inherited a scattered and ungovernable collection of territories that had been devastated by the Thirty Years' War. Brandenburg, the richest of his possessions, had lost nearly half of its population. The war had a lasting impact on Frederick William's character. As a child, he had hidden in the woods to escape bands of marauding soldiers; as a teenager, he had followed to its burial the corpse of Gustavus Adolphus, the man he most admired and wished to emulate. A long stay in Holland during the final stages of the Dutch Revolt im-

GENEALOGY

Tsars of Russia

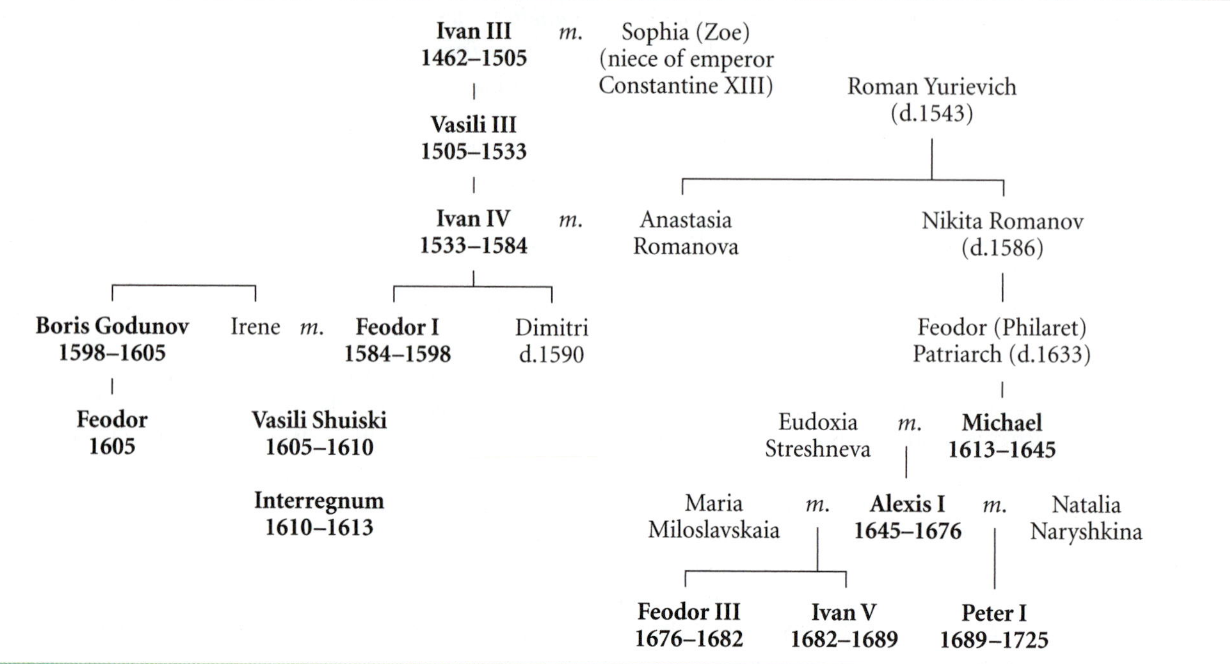

pressed on him the importance of a strong army and a strong base of revenue to support it.

Frederick William had neither. In 1640, his forces totaled no more than 2500 men, most of them, including the officers, the dregs of German society. Despite the fact that he was surrounded by powerful neighbors—Sweden and Poland both claimed sovereignty over parts of his inheritance—the territories under his control had no tradition of military taxation. The nobility, known as the Junker, enjoyed immunity from almost all forms of direct taxation, and the towns had no obligation to furnish either men or supplies for military operations beyond their walls. When Frederick William attempted to introduce an excise—the kind of commodity tax on consumption that had so successfully financed the Dutch Revolt and the English Revolution—he was initially rebuffed. But military emergency overcame legal precedents. By the 1650s Frederick William had established the excise in the towns, though not on the land.

With the excise as a steady source of revenue, the Great Elector could now create one of the most capable standing armies of the age. The strictest discipline was maintained in the new army, and the Prussian army developed into a feared and efficient fighting machine. Frederick William organized one of the first departments of war to oversee all of the details of the creation of his army, from housing and supplies to the training of young officer candidates. The department was also responsible for the collection of taxes. By integrating military and civilian government, Frederick William was able to create an efficient state bureaucracy that was particularly responsive

■ Peter I wrestled Russia into the West. Sometimes, the unusually big tsar used physical force to do so, such as when he determined that Russian nobles ought to cut off their beards and be clean-shaven in the European fashion of the period.

A CLOSE SHAVE

Peter the Great made many efforts to westernize Russia after his travels in Holland and England. He reformed the navy, built a great seaport at St. Petersburg, and instituted an array of governmental reforms. But nothing was so prominent as or affected ordinary people more than his edicts on beards and clothing. This excerpt was written by Jean Rousset de Missy, a French historian who wrote a popular account of Peter and Russia in the early eighteenth century.

Focus Questions

Why would Peter want Russians to look more like western Europeans? In dealing with his subjects, is Peter acting like Louis XIV?

The tsar labored at the reform of fashions, or, more properly speaking, of dress. Until that time the Russians had always worn long beards, which they cherished and preserved with much care, allowing them to hang down on their bosoms, without even cutting the moustache. With these long beards they wore the hair very short, except the ecclesiastics, who, to distinguish themselves, wore it very long. The tsar, in order to reform that custom, ordered that gentlemen, merchants, and other subjects, except priests and peasants, should each pay a tax of one hundred rubles a year if they wished to keep their beard; the commoners had to pay one kopeck each. Officials were stationed at the gates of the towns to collect that tax, which the Russians regarded as an enormous sin on the part of the tsar and as a thing which tended to the abolition of their religion.

These insinuations, which came from the priests, occasioned the publication of many pamphlets in Moscow, where for that reason alone the tsar was regarded as a tyrant and a pagan; and there were many old Russians who, after having their beards shaved off, saved them preciously, in order to have them placed in their coffins, fearing that they would not be allowed to enter heaven without their beards. As for the young men, they followed the new customs with the more readiness as it made them appear more agreeable to the fair sex.

From the reform in beards we may pass to that of clothes. Their garments, like those of the Orientals, were very long, reaching to the heel. The tsar issued an ordinance abolishing that costume, commanding all the boyars (nobles) and all those who had positions at the court to dress after the French fashion, and likewise to adorn their clothes with gold or silver according to their means. . . .

The same ordinance also provided that in the future women, as well as men, should be invited to entertainments, such as weddings, banquets, and the like, where both sexes should mingle in the same hall, as in Holland and England. It was likewise added that these entertainments should conclude with concerts and dances, but that only those should be admitted who were dressed in English costumes. His Majesty set the example in all these changes.

From "De Missy's Life of Peter."

in times of crisis. The creation of the Prussian army was the force that led to the creation of the Prussian state.

The same materials that forged the Prussian state led to the transformation of Russia. Soon after the young tsar Peter I (1682–1725) came to the throne, he realized that he could compete with the western states only by learning to play their game. In 1697, Peter visited the West, ostensibly to build an alliance against the Turks but actually to learn as much as he could about Western military technology. He loved novelty and introduced new agricultural products such as wine and potatoes to his subjects. When he determined that Russians should no longer wear beards, he took a hand in cutting them off. When he was persuaded of the benefits of dentistry, he practiced it himself on his terrified subjects. His campaign to westernize Russia frequently confused the momentous with the inconsequential, but it had an extraordinary impact at all levels of government and society.

Like those of Frederick William, Peter's greatest reforms were military. Peter realized that if Russia were to flourish in a world dominated by war and commerce, it would have to reestablish its hold on the Baltic ports. That meant dislodging the Swedes from the Russian mainland and creating a fleet to protect Russian trade. Neither goal seemed likely. The Swedes were one of the great powers of the age, constant innovators in battlefield tactics and military organization. Peter studied their every campaign. His first wars against the Swedes ended in humiliating defeats, but with each failure came a sharper sense of what was needed to succeed.

First Peter introduced a system of conscription that resulted in the creation of a standing army. Conscripts were branded to inhibit desertion, and a strict discipline was introduced to prepare the soldiers for battle. Peter unified the military command at the top and stratified it in the field. He established promotion based on merit. For the first time, Russian officers were given particular responsibilities to fulfill during both training and battle. Peter created military schools to train cadets for the next generation of officers.

Finally, in 1709, Peter realized his ambitions. At the battle of Poltava, the Russian army routed the Swedes, wounding King Charles XII, annihilating his infantry, and capturing dozens of his leading officers. That night Peter toasted the captured Swedish generals. He claimed that everything he

MAP DISCOVERY

Expansion of Russia Under Peter the Great

Notice the extent of the Russian Empire in 1689 and the territory added by Peter the Great. What was important about the new territory? What was the role of the battle of Poltava in expanding the empire? The route of Peter's trip to western Europe is marked here. Why did he travel where he did? Based on the chapter discussion, what impact did his trip have on the way he ruled his empire?

knew about warfare he had learned from them, and he congratulated them on their success as teachers. After the battle of Poltava, Russia gradually replaced Sweden as the dominant power in the Baltic.

Like everything else about him, Peter the Great's absolutism was uniquely his own. But though Peter's power was unlimited, it was not uncontested. He secularized the Russian Orthodox Church, subjecting it to the control of state power and confiscating much of its wealth in the process. He broke the old military service class, which attempted a coup d'état when Peter was abroad in the 1690s. By the end of his reign, the Russian monarchy was among the strongest in Europe.

The Origins of French Absolutism

Nowhere was absolutism as successfully implanted as in France. Louis XIII (1610–1643) was only eight years old when he came to the throne, and he grew slowly into his role under the tutelage of Cardinal Richelieu. It was Richelieu's vision that stabilized French government. As chief minister, Richelieu saw clearly that the prosperity and even the survival of France depended upon strengthening royal power. He preached a doctrine of ***raison d'état***—reason of state—in which he placed the needs of the nation above the privileges of its most important groups. Richelieu saw three threats to stable royal government: "The Huguenots shared the state, the nobles conducted themselves as if they were not subjects, and the most powerful governors in the provinces acted as if they were sovereign in their office."

Richelieu took measures to control all three. The power of the nobles was the most difficult to attack. The nobles' long tradition of independence from the crown had been enhanced by the wars of religion. Perhaps more importantly, the ancient aristocracy, the nobility of the sword, believed themselves to be in a particularly vulnerable position. Their world was changing and their traditional roles were becoming obsolete. Professional soldiers replaced them at war, professional administrators at government. Mercantile wealth threatened their economic superiority; the growth of the nobility of the robe—lawyers and state officials—threatened their social

■ The Battle of Poltava (1709) led to the decline of Swedish influence in Europe. Peter the Great is depicted receiving the laurel of victory.

standing. They were hardly likely to take orders from a royal minister such as Richelieu, especially when he attacked one of the great symbols of their power, the duel.

To limit the power of local officials, Richelieu used central officials, or **intendants**, to examine their conduct and to reform their administration. He made careful appointments of local governors and brought more regions under direct royal control. Against the Huguenots, Richelieu's policy was more subtle. He was less interested in challenging their religion than their autonomy. In 1627, when the English sent a force to aid the Huguenots against the government, Richelieu and Louis XIII abolished the Huguenots' privileges altogether. They were allowed to maintain their religion, but not their special status. They would have no privileges other than to be subjects of the king of France.

Richelieu's program was a vital prelude to the development of absolute monarchy in France. But the cardinal was not a king. Although it is clear that Richelieu did not act without the full support of Louis XIII and clear that the king initiated many reforms for which the cardinal received credit, there can be no doubt that Richelieu was the power behind the throne. Louis XIII hated the business of government and even neglected his principal responsibility of providing the state with an heir. For years he and his wife slept in separate palaces, and only a freak rainstorm in Paris forced him to spend a night with the queen, Anne of Austria, in 1637. It was the night Louis XIV was conceived. Louis XIII and Richelieu died within six months of each other in 1642 and 1643, and the nation again endured the turmoil of a child king. Richelieu's aggressive policy to curb the nobility and his stringent financial program in the 1630s helped precipitate the Fronde. Louis XIV (1643–1715) was never to forget the terror of the aristocratic rebellion in Paris: how he was forced to flee the capital in the dead of night, how he endured the penury of exile, how he suffered the humiliation of being bossed about by the rebels. He would never forget, and he would have a long time to remember.

Louis le Grand

Not quite five years old when he came to the throne, Louis XIV was tutored by Cardinal Jules Mazarin (1602–1661), Richelieu's successor as chief minister. If anything, Mazarin was more ruthless and less popular than his predecessor. An Italian from a modest background, Mazarin won the money to launch his career at the gaming table. Good fortune seemed to follow him everywhere. He gambled with his life and his career, and each time he raked in the stakes. He died with the largest private fortune that had ever been accumulated by a French citizen, easily surpassing the fortune of Richelieu. Like Richelieu, whom he emulated, Mazarin was an excellent administrator who had learned well the lessons of raison d'état. At the conclusion of the Thirty Years' War, for example, Mazarin refused to make peace with Spain, believing that the time was ripe to deliver a knockout blow to the Spanish Habsburgs.

The King and His Ministers. In order to pacify the rebellious nobility of the Fronde, who opposed Mazarin's power, Louis XIV was declared to have reached his majority at the age of 13. But it was not until Mazarin died ten years later in 1661 that the king began to rule. Louis was blessed with able and energetic ministers. The two central props of his state—money and might—were in the hands of dynamic men, Jean-Baptiste Colbert (1619–1683) and the Marquis de Louvois (1639–1691). Colbert—to whom credit belongs for the building of the French navy, the reform of French legal codes, and the establishment of national academies of culture—was Louis's chief minister for finance. Colbert's fiscal reforms were so successful that in less than six years a debt of 22 million French pounds had become a surplus of 29 million. Colbert achieved that astonishing feat not by raising taxes but by increasing the efficiency of their collection. Until Louis embarked on his wars, the French state was solvent.

To Louvois, Louis's minister of war, fell the task of reforming the French army. During the Fronde, royal troops were barely capable of defeating the makeshift forces of the nobil-

THE SIEGE OF VIENNA—1683

Across the Balkans, for twelve hundred miles, Muslims and Christians stared at each other. The West had seen many decisive encounters in its history, but none had larger stakes than the one at the end of the seventeenth century. Brutal wars punctuated by long periods of uneasy peace had defined relations between Ottoman sultans and Holy Roman emperors. In the eighth century it was the French who had halted the Muslim advance into Europe. In the fifteenth century fortunes had reversed, and the Ottomans had taken Constantinople. Slowly they pressed forward from Asia to the mainland of Europe. For more than a hundred years after the Ottoman victory at Mohacs in 1526, Hungary had been the battlefield, and beyond Hungary stood the imperial capital of Vienna, gateway to Germany and the West.

THE WEST AND THE WIDER WORLD

Vienna, a city of modest wealth by European standards, was thought a glittering prize by the Ottoman diplomats who visited it. Called "the golden apple," it was surely the most desirable of the territories within reach of the Ottoman armies. In 1683 Vienna was still recovering from the devastating effects of the Thirty Years' War. The forty-year-old Emperor Leopold I made it his capital and initiated a building boom and considerable conspicuous consumption. If Sultan Mehmed IV felt the pull of Vienna—his ancestor the great Suleiman had attempted to take it in the sixteenth century—it was now more attractive than ever.

In the camps of the Ottoman army, the Grand Vizier, Kara Mustafa, looked longingly toward the West. When imperial ambassadors arrived in 1682 to renew treaties of peace, Kara Mustafa made demands that were tantamount to war. Both sides anticipated the oncoming struggle. Emperor Leopold appealed to the princes of Germany for aid only to be rebuffed at every turn. The imperial states feared the French more than they feared the Turks. In desperation Leopold appealed to the young Polish king, Jan III Sobieski. Though Poland was not part of the empire, it had good reason to fear Ottoman expansion. Should Vienna fall, the heart of its state would be open to a deadly thrust. Jan Sobieski set out to raise an army. But Kara Mustafa was raising forces of his own. The Ottoman Empire was a conglomerate of conquered peoples who served the Sultan as circumstances required. Now Africans from Egypt, Tatars from the Steppes of Russia, and Sunnis from Persia all joined the Sultan's feared Janissaries to form a massive army of perhaps as many as 140,000 men. The Viennese garrison consisted of just 11,000 soldiers.

Nevertheless, Vienna was well fortified. After being besieged in 1529, successive emperors strengthened the city's walls and bulwarks. It was defended in the Italian style with a series of outworks that provided a considerable obstacle. The initial wall was built on an in-sloping angle to stop a cavalry incursion and was palisaded with long spears to prevent scaling. This glacis, as it was called, was overhung by a walkway from which defenders could establish a murderous crossfire. Beyond the glacis was a deep moat, and beyond this moat was what was known as a ravelin, an artificial mound with its own twenty-foot-high inward-facing glacis. The ravelin was criss-crossed with trenches from which defenders could emerge or disappear with alarming rapidity. Beyond the ravelin was another treacherous moat, and beyond that the forty-foot-high walls of the city itself. This series of ramparts, moats, and high thick walls gave defenders a decided advantage during the sieges of the seventeenth century. The distance between the farthest outwork and the city walls diminished the effectiveness of artillery while the narrow bottlenecks that protected each layer of defense diminished the advantage of numbers.

There were only two ways for Kara Mustafa to take Vienna. The first was to starve the city into submission by controlling the suburbs whose farms supplied it. When he brought his great army to the outskirts of Vienna in June 1683, he unleashed independent forces of Magyars and Tatars to ravish the countryside. At the news of their depredations, Emperor Leopold and his court fled the city for fear of being trapped without means of escape. They made it out just in time. By July, Kara Mustafa's tents surrounded the city on every side—his crescent flags flew in all directions. But a passive siege had its disadvantages. The garrison might eventually be starved—and it was not long before even the wealthiest citizens were reduced to eating household pets and rodents—but so, too, might the massive Ottoman army, which could store only what it could carry. Moreover, the emperor's own armies could keep up constant harrassing actions in the suburbs to deprive the Ottomans of supplies.

The second option for taking the city was more aggressive. If the Ottoman troops could not climb over the walls that defended Vienna, perhaps they could tunnel under them. This required a feat of considerable engineering skill. Tunnels had to be designed to begin in many places but to converge under the glacis. There, mines would be exploded to create a breach large enough for warriors to rush through. Additionally, the tunneling yielded mounds of earth that could be piled as high as the outwork walls. When the defenders appeared from their trenches to repel the first wave of assault, Ottoman marksmen could pepper them with shot.

This was the tactic that Kara Mustafa favored. On 26 July, after several days of bombarding the city's walls with artillery, the Grand Vizier summoned the town. He offered the defenders the choice of mercy or death. If they would surrender before the siege began, their lives would be spared. But

Jan III Sobieski at Vienna, painted by Jan Matejko.

if they held out, by the established rules of war all of the defenders would be slaughtered, Vienna's wealth would be confiscated, and its defenses would be razed to the ground. Seemingly safe behind their high walls and deep moats, the civic and military leaders of Vienna never hesitated. Kara Mustafa's offer was met with a volley from the city's own guns. The tunnelers were within range and would pay a high price for their efforts.

Meanwhile, Leopold renewed his pleas for assistance. The siege was no longer a theoretical danger and the consequences of the fall of Vienna had to be seriously contemplated. At this eleventh hour the German princes rallied to the aid of their emperor. In the first weeks of August Saxon cavalry headed south and Bavarian forces marched east. They intended to join with the powerful army that Jan Sobieski had raised in Poland. The question was whether they could arrive in time to prevent Vienna's fall. After an enormous tunnel explosion on 12 August allowed Ottoman soldiers to enter the ravelin fifty abreast, the defenders were forced to abandon the outworks and retreat inside the city's walls. From there they were able temporarily to halt the Muslim advance as every inch of the ravelin and second moat was contested. But by the first week of September mines were exploding under the walls of the city itself and buildings were ablaze in many districts. Disease ravaged soldiers and civilians alike and there were no more than 4000 able defenders left to repulse increasing Ottoman attacks. But repulse them they did. Another week passed and still the city stood.

By now Kara Mustafa was aware that a relief force was within striking distance of his encampment. Rumors exaggerated their numbers wildly, but the reality was sobering enough. The forces commanded by Sobieski numbered 60,000 while Kara Mustafa could rely upon only 28,000 fighting men to oppose them. His auxiliaries were useful for plundering and laboring but not for the life-and-death battle that ensued on 12 September, 1683. More damaging, most of his artillery was deployed against Vienna and was unavailable at the time of greatest need. The relief of Vienna was almost a foregone conclusion. Imperial forces mowed through the Ottoman battle lines as a scythe in a field of grain, and the Muslims made few stands to slow Sobieski and his allies. Kara Mustafa escaped only because of the desperate sacrifices made by his bodyguard. He carried away the Flag of the Prophet and his store of gold but left behind the myth of Ottoman invincibility. Over the course of the next two decades they would be chased entirely from the Holy Roman Empire and would never again challenge the West for military superiority.

QUESTIONS FOR DISCUSSION

What were the relations between Christians and Muslims prior to the siege of Vienna? What was the nature of the Ottoman army? Why did the Viennese believe they could defend their city? What were the reasons for Jan Sobieski's victory?

■ This Hyacinthe Rigaud portrait of Louis XIV in his coronation robes shows the splendor of *Le Roi Soleil* (the Sun King), who believed himself to be the center of France as the sun is the center of the solar system.

ity. By the end of the reign, the army had grown to 400,000 and its organization had thoroughly been reformed. Louvois introduced new ranks for the field officers who actually led their men into battle, and promotions were distributed by merit rather than purchase. He also solved one of the most serious logistical problems of the age by establishing storehouses of arms and ammunition throughout the realm. The greatest achievements of the reign were built on the backs of fiscal and military reforms, which were themselves a product of the continuing sophistication of French administration.

Louis XIV furthered the practice of relying on professional administrators to supervise the main departments of state and offer advice on matters of policy. He created a separation between courtiers and officeholders and largely excluded the nobility of the sword from the inner circles of government, which were composed of ministers of departments and small councils that handled routine affairs. The councils were connected to the central advisory body of government, the secret council of the king. Within each department, ministers furthered the process of professionalization that led to the advancement of talented clerks, secretaries, and administrators. Although there still remained a large gulf between the promulgation of policy at Versailles and its enforcement in the provinces, it was now a gulf that could be measured and ultimately bridged. Louis XIV built on the institution of the intendant that Richelieu had developed with so much success. Intendants were now a permanent part of government, and their duties expanded from their early responsibilities as coordinators and mediators into areas of policing and tax collection. It was through the intendants that the wishes of central government were made known in the provinces.

The Court of Versailles. Although Louis XIV was well served, it was the king himself who set the tone for French absolutism. "If he was not the greatest king, he was the best actor of majesty that ever filled the throne," wrote an English observer. The acting of majesty was central to Louis's rule. His residence at Versailles was the most glittering court of Europe, renowned for its beauty and splendor. It was built on a scale never before seen, and Louis took a personal interest in making sure it was fit for a king. When the court and king moved there permanently in 1682, Versailles became the envy of the Continent. But behind the imposing facade of Versailles stood a well-thought-out plan for domestic and international rule.

Louis XIV attempted to tame the French nobles by requiring their attendance at his court. Louis established a system of court etiquette so complex that constant study was necessary to prevent humiliation. While the nobility studied decorum they could not plot rebellion. At Versailles one never knocked on a door; one scratched with a fingernail. That insignificant custom had to be learned and remembered—it was useless anywhere else—and practiced if one hoped for the favor of the king. Leading noblemen of France rose at dawn so that they could watch Louis be awakened and hear him speak his first words. Dozens followed him from hall to gallery and from gallery to chamber as he washed, dressed, prayed, and ate.

That aura of court culture was equally successful in the royal art of diplomacy. During Louis's reign, France replaced Spain as the greatest nation in Europe. Massive royal patronage of art, science, and thought brought French culture to new heights.

The French language replaced Latin as the universal European tongue. It was also spoken at the court's of the Holy Roman Emperor in Vienna and the tsar in Moscow. France was the richest and most populous European state, and Louis's absolute rule finally harnessed the resources to a single purpose. France became a commercial power rivaling the Netherlands, a naval power rivaling England, and a military power without peer. It was not only for effect that Louis took the

Louis XIV Writes to His Son

LE ROY DE FRANCE.
l'Hoñe immortel Chef de la Ste Ligue.
Mon ſoleil par sa force eclaira l'heretique,
Il chassa tout d'un coup les brouillards de Calvin:
Non pas par un Zele divin,
Mais a fin de cacher ma fine Politique.

■ A symbolic drawing shows how heretics will be driven from France by the Sun King. Such a policy proved shortsighted, however, as thousands of Huguenot émigrés enriched Louis's potential enemies with their valuable skills.

image of the sun as his own. In court, in the nation, and throughout Europe, everything revolved around him.

France's rise to preeminence in Europe was undoubtedly the greatest accomplishment of the absolute monarchy of Louis XIV. But it did not come without costs. Louis XIV made his share of mistakes, which were magnified by the awe in which his opinions were held. His aggressive foreign policy ultimately bankrupted the crown. But without doubt his greatest error was to persecute the Huguenots. As an absolute ruler, Louis believed that it was necessary to have absolute conformity and obedience. The existence of the Huguenots, with their separate communities and distinct forms of worship, seemed an affront to his authority. Almost from the beginning, Louis allowed the persecution of Protestants, despite the protection provided by the Edict of Nantes. Protestant churches were pulled down, conversions to Catholicism were bought with the lure of immunities from taxation, and children were separated from their families to be brought up in Catholic schools. Finally, in 1685 Louis XIV revoked the Edict of Nantes. All forms of Protestant worship were outlawed, and the ministers who were not hunted down and killed were forced into exile. Despite a ban on Protestant emigration, more than 200,000 Huguenots fled the country, many of them carrying irreplaceable skills with them to Holland and England in the west and Brandenburg in the east.

Supporters of the monarchy celebrated the revocation of the Edict of Nantes as an act of piety. Religious toleration in seventeenth-century Europe was still a policy of expediency rather than of principle. Even the English, who prided themselves on developing the concept of toleration, and the Dutch, who welcomed Jews to Amsterdam, would not officially tolerate Catholics. But the persecution of the Huguenots was a social and political disaster for France. Those who fled to other Protestant states spread the stories of atrocities that stiffened European resolve against Louis. Those who remained became an embittered minority who pulled at the fabric of the state at every chance. Nor did the official abolition of Protestantism have much effect upon its existence. Against the policies, the Huguenots held firm to their beliefs. There were well more than a million French Protestants, undoubtedly the largest religious minority in any state. Huguenots simply went underground, practicing their religion secretly and gradually replacing their numbers. No absolutism, however powerful, could succeed in eradicating religious beliefs.

CONCLUSION

Louis XIV gave his name to the age that he and his nation dominated, but he was not its only towering figure. The Great Elector, Peter the Great, Louis the Great—so they were judged by posterity, kings who had forged nations for a new age. Their style of rule showed the royal state at its height, still revolving around the king but more and more dependent upon permanent institutions of government that followed their own imperatives. The absolute state harnessed the economic and intellectual resources of the nation to the political will of the monarch. It did so to ensure survival in a dangerous world. But while monarchs ruled as well as reigned, they did so by incorporating vital elements of the state into the process of government. In England, the importance of the landholding classes was recognized in the constitutional powers of Parliament. In Prussia, the military power of the Junker was asserted through command in the army, the most important institution of the state. In France, Louis XIV coopted many nobles at his court while making use of a talented pool of lawyers, clergymen, and administrators in his government. A delicate balance existed between the will of the king and the will of the state, a balance that would soon lead the continental powers into economic competition and military confrontation.

QUESTIONS FOR REVIEW

1. How did war in the seventeenth century contribute to the creation of more powerful monarchical states?

2. What religious and political ideas were developed to justify resistance to monarchical authority?
3. What political and religious problems combined to bring England to civil war, and what results did the conflict produce in English government?
4. How did rulers such as Frederick William of Brandenburg, Peter the Great, and Louis XIV and theorists such as Hobbes and Bossuet justify absolute monarchical power?

KEY TERMS

absolutism, *p. 488*
divine right of kings, *p. 473*
Fronde, *p. 480*
Glorious Revolution, *p. 486*
intendants, *p. 493*
Long Parliament, *p. 484*
magistrates, *p. 479*
Parlement, *p. 481*
paulette, *p. 477*
Puritans, *p. 482*
raison d'état, *p. 492*

DISCOVERING WESTERN CIVILIZATION ONLINE

You can obtain more information about the royal state in the seventeenth century at the Websites listed below. See also the Companion Website that accompanies this text, www.ablongman.com/kishlansky, which contains an online study guide and additional resources.

The Crises of the Royal State

Internet Modern History Sourcebook: Constitutional States
www.fordham.edu/halsall/mod/modsbook06.html
Links to sources relating to the reign of Charles I and the revolution against him.

The Execution of Charles I
www.baylor.edu/BIC/WCIII/Essays/charles.1.html
Excerpts from primary sources describing the execution of Charles I.

The Zenith of the Royal State

Baroque Living History Society: L'Age d'Or & Kirke's Lambs
www.kipar.org/
A site on the Golden Age of France in the seventeenth century but with extensive links to English and Dutch materials on a variety of subjects.

Chateau de Versailles
www.chateauversailles.fr/en
The Website of Versailles, with views of the gardens and rooms inside the palace. (Version of site in English.)

Creating French Culture
www.loc.gov/exhibits/bnf/bnf0005.html
The Library of Congress's exhibition on the Age of Absolutism shows manuscripts, medals, and portraits of leading figures at the French court.

Peter the Great
www.historylearningsite.co.UK/peter_the_great.htm
Follow the links for a complete history of Peter's reign, including his military and domestic reforms.

SUGGESTIONS FOR FURTHER READING

General Reading

Perry Anderson, *Lineages of the Absolutist State* (London: NLB Books, 1974). A sociological study of the role of absolutism in the development of the Western world.

Euan Cameron, ed., *Early Modern Europe: An Oxford History* (New York: Oxford University Press, 1999). Up-to-date essays by leading historians with well-chosen topics and illustrations.

Thomas Munck, *Seventeenth-Century Europe, 1598–1700* (New York: St. Martin's Press, 1990). A thorough survey.

David Sturdy, *Fractured Europe 1600–1721* (Oxford: Blackwell Publishers, 2002). A thorough survey of the complex military and political events of the long seventeenth century.

The Rise of the Royal State

Yves-Marie Bercé, *The Birth of Absolutism* (London: Macmillan, 1996). A history of France from the reign of Louis XIV to the eve of the Revolution by a leading historian of France.

J. H. Elliott, *Richelieu and Olivares* (Cambridge: Cambridge University Press, 1984). A brilliant dual portrait.

J. H. Elliott and Jonathan Brown, *A Palace for a King* (New Haven, CT: Yale University Press, 1980). An outstanding work on the building and decorating of a Spanish palace.

Alan James, *The Origins of French Absolutism, 1598–1661* (New York: Longman, 2006). A concise assessment of the development of the French government in a crucial period, directed toward college students.

Graham Parry, *The Golden Age Restor'd* (New York: St. Martin's Press, 1981). A study of English court culture in the reigns of James I and Charles I.

The Crises of the Royal State

Jonathan Israel, ed., *The Anglo-Dutch Moment* (Cambridge: Cambridge University Press, 1991). Essays by an international team of scholars on the European dimensions of the Revolution of 1688.

M. A. Kishlansky, *A Monarchy Transformed* (London: Penguin Books, 1996). The most accessible survey of a remarkable era.

G. Parker and L. Smith, eds., *The General Crisis of the Seventeenth Century* (London: Routledge & Kegan Paul, 1978). A collection of essays on the problem of the general crisis.

Quentin Skinner, *The Foundations of Modern Political Thought,* 2 vols. (Cambridge: Cambridge University Press, 1978). A seminal work on the history of ideas from Machiavelli to Calvin.

W. A. Speck, *The Revolution of 1688* (Oxford: Oxford University Press, 1988). The best single volume on the event that transformed England into a global power.

Lawrence Stone, *The Causes of the English Revolution* (New York: Harper & Row, 1972). A vigorously argued explanation of why England experienced a revolution in the mid-seventeenth century.

The Zenith of the Royal State

Martyn Bennett, *Oliver Cromwell* (London: Routledge, 2006). The most up-to-date and accessible biography of the man at the center of the English Revolution.

Joseph Bergin, *The Rise of Richelieu* (New Haven, CT: Yale University Press, 1991). A fascinating portrait of a consummate politician.

Peter Burke, *The Fabrication of Louis XIV* (New Haven, CT: Yale University Press, 1992). A compelling account of a man and a myth.

Paul Dukes, *The Making of Russian Absolutism* (London: Longman, 1982). A thorough survey of Russian history in the seventeenth and eighteenth centuries.

Nicholas Henshall, *The Myth of Absolutism: Change and Continuity in Early Modern European Monarchy* (London: Longman, 1992). A searching examination of the problem of absolutism in the western European states.

Vasili Klyuchevsky, *Peter the Great* (London: Random House, 1958). A classic work, still the best study of Peter.

H. W. Koch, *A History of Prussia* (London: Longman, 1978). A comprehensive study of Prussian history, with an excellent chapter on the Great Elector.

Anthony Levi, *Louis XIV* (New York: Carroll and Graf, 2004). An acclaimed new biography of France's most famous ruler.

Geoffrey Parker, *The Military Revolution* (Cambridge: Cambridge University Press, 1988). A lucid discussion of how power was organized and deployed in the early modern state.

John Wolf, *Louis XIV* (New York: Norton, 1968). An outstanding biography of the Sun King.

For a list of additional titles related to this chapter's topics, please see http://www.ablongman.com/kishlansky.

GLOSSARY

CREDITS

INDEX

GLOSSARY

absolutism Government in which power was consolidated in the hands of a divinely ordained monarch; typified by reverence for the monarch, weakening of representative institutions, and expansion of military.

agricultural revolution Changes in the traditional agricultural system during the eighteenth century that included enclosure, introduction of fodder crops, intensified animal husbandry, and commercial market orientation.

alchemy Study of metals in an effort to find their essence through purification. Medieval alchemists attempted to find precious metals such as silver and gold as the essence of base metals such as lead and iron.

Allies In World War I, the United States, Great Britain, France, and Russia—the alliance that opposed and defeated the Central Powers of Germany and Austria-Hungary and their allies.

Anabaptists Part of the radical Reformation, Protestant groups that varied in belief but agreed on the principle of adult baptism.

anarchism A political movement based on rejection of extant political systems; most prominent in less industrialized Western nations.

Anarcho-syndicalists Craft workers in France combined local trade union organization with anarchist principles to oppose capitalism and maintain worker solidarity from the end of the nineteenth-century to World War I.

anti-Semitism Hostility toward and discrimination against Jews.

appeasement British policy of making concessions to Germany in the 1930s in order to avoid war. It allowed Hitler to militarize the Sudetenland and eventually take all of Czechoslovakia.

April Theses Lenin's promise to the Russian people and challenge to the Provisional Government to provide peace, land, and bread. These three issues became the rallying cries for the second Russian revolution and for the withdrawal of Soviet Russia from World War I.

Arians During the early Christological controversies, followers of the Alexandrine theologian, Arius, who believed that Jesus was not equal to God the Father.

Axis Powers In World War II, the alliance of Germany, Italy, and later Japan.

Baby boom The dramatic and sustained growth in the birth rate in the United States and western Europe immediately following World War II and lasting until about 1960.

Baghdad Railway Railway Construction began at the end of the nineteenth-contury to link Constantinople with Baghdad, ad was undertaken by the Ottoman abd German Empires. The railway had geopolitical goals for Germany in the Persian Gulf and the Ottoman Empire in Arabia.

balance of power Distribution of power among nations in alliances so that any one nation is prevented from dominating the others.

Balfour Declaration The commitment by the British government issued in 1917 to support a Jewish homeland in Palestine.

Berlin Wall Barrier built by East Germany in 1961 to halt an exodus of skilled professionals to the West; opened in 1989 as a prelude to the reunification of East and West Germany.

Big Three The British, Soviet, and U.S. leaders who coordinated defeat of Germany and Japan in World War II and negotiated postwar settlements. Referred to Churchill, Stalin, and Roosevelt until 1945; Attlee, Stalin, and Truman by summer 1945.

Black Death The virulent combination of bubonic, septicemic, and pneumonic plagues that destroyed between one third and one half of the population of Europe between 1347 and 1352.

blitzkrieg "Lightning war"; the rapid advance accompanied by armored vehicles that typified the German military during World War II.

Bolsheviks Radical faction of Marxist Social Democrats following a political theory based on necessity of violent revolution. The Bolsheviks came to power with Lenin in November 1917.

bourgeoisie A French term referring to the commercial classes of Europe after the seventeenth century; primarily an urban class.

Brezhnev Doctrine Policy of Soviet leader Leonid Brezhnev that approved the use of military intervention in the internal affairs of Soviet allies to prevent counterrevolution.

broad-spectrum gathering A technique of subsistence common in the Neolithic era that preceded permanent settlement in one place and relied on the exploitation of many seasonal sources of food over a limited area.

cahiers de doléances Lists of grievances sent with representatives to the French Estates-General in 1789; demonstrated the existence of a widespread public political culture in France.

caliph The successors of Muhammad who served as political and religious leaders of the Islamic world (see Umma).

capitularies The written instructions for the implementation of royal directives at the local level produced by the clerics of the Carolingian court.

caravels Small Portuguese ships developed in the fifteenth-century that were ideal for ocean travel.

Carnival One of the traditional sixteenth-century festivals, the feasts and carousing of which preceded the onset of Lent.

Carolingian Renaissance The cultural revival of classical learning sponsored by the emperor Charlemagne. New schools and the copying of manuscripts were among its important achievements.

cartels Combinations of firms in a given industry to fix prices and establish production quotas.

Cartesianism Philosophy of René Descartes that rested on the dual existence of mind and matter, a principle that enabled the use of skepticism to create certainty.

Central Powers Germany and Austria-Hungary during World War I.

chartism An English working-class reform movement that flourished in the 1830s and 1840s and that demanded universal male suffrage (right to vote), payment for parliamentary service, equal electoral districts, and secret ballots.

chivalry The ideals of knighthood, most notably fighting, that spread from northern France across Europe in the High Middle Ages.

Christian humanism The application of the principles of humanistic education, particularly philology, to the documents of Christianity. It resulted in a program of reform through better education.

Christological controversies The debate about the Christian Trinity (Father, Son, and Holy Spirit) and the relationship between humanity and divinity within it. It caused great division and conflict in the Church and society from the third to the fifth centuries.

city-states Self-governing political units centered upon an urban area. During the fifteenth and sixteenth centuries, city-states took on various forms of government, including republics such as Venice and oligarchies such as Milan.

civic humanism The use of humanistic training and education in the service of the state. Many humanists became advisors to princes or republican governments, holding high office and helping to establish policy.

Cold War The diplomatic and ideological confrontation between the Soviet Union and the United States that began in the aftermath of World War II, dividing the world into two armed camps.

collectivization Soviet plan under Stalin to create large communal state farms to replace private farms owned by peasants.

coloni Tenant farmers who worked on the estates of wealthy landowners in the Roman Empire.

colonization Process by which colonies, or new settlements with links to a parent state, are established.

Columbian Exchange The transfer of microbes, animals, and plants in the encounters between Europeans and Native Americans during the age of exploration.

Comecon The Council for Mutual Economic Assistance established in 1949 with bilateral agreements between the Soviet Union and eastern European states. Comecon was Stalin's response to the U.S. Marshall Plan in western Europe, but rather than providing aid it sought to integrate and control the economies of eastern Europe for Soviet gain.

Communist Manifesto, The A call to arms written in 1848 by Karl Marx and Frederich Engels in which they defined in general terms the class struggle in industrializing Europe.

conciliarism The movement proposed by church lawyers in which only a general council of bishops could end the Great Schism.

condottiere A mercenary military leader who sold his services and that of his private army to the highest bidder; used in the wars between the Italian city-states.

Congress of Vienna A meeting of European powers after the Napoleonic wars in 1815; established a balance of power to preserve the status quo in post-revolutionary Europe.

conquistadores "Conquerors." Spanish adventurers who led the conquests in the Americas in the sixteenth century.

conscription Compulsory service of citizens in the army. France was the first modern state to enforce conscription. The ability to draft all able-bodied men was a key component in the Revolutionary and Napoleonic wars.

conservatism Nineteenth-century ideology that favored tradition and stability and only gradual, or "organic," growth and change.

containment Cold War policy of resisting the spread of Soviet communism.

Continental System The economic boycott of England by Napoleon during the wars beginning in 1803.

Counter-Reformation Catholic response to repel Protestantism.

Crusades Religious wars of conquest directed against non-Christians and heretics in the eleventh through the thirteenth centuries.

Crystal Palace Exhibition This international exhibition, held in London in 1851 in a specially built see-through exhibition hall, featured the greatest technological advances of the day and served as a spur for further industrialization.

culture Those shared beliefs, values, customs, and practices that humans transmit from generation to generation through learning.

cuneiform A form of writing from Mesopotamia characterized by wedge-shaped symbols pressed into wet clay tablets to record words.

Cycladic culture The artistically and economically sophisticated culture which flourished on islands in the Aegean Sea during the early and middle Greek Bronze Age (3000–1500 bce).

Cynics Followers of a Hellenistic Greek philosophy that rejected the world as the source of evil and unhappiness and advocated the reduction of possessions, connections, and pleasures to the absolute minimum.

Dawes Plan The plan crafted by international financial experts in 1924 under the leadership of the American banker Charles Dawes whose aim was to end inflation and restore economic prosperity to Germany by a reform of the reparations repayment schedule.

Dayton Peace Accords The peace agreement brokered at the end of 1995 among Bosnians, Croats and Serbs by the United States, which provided U.S. troops to support the peace. The aim was to create a unified country in Bosnia, while recognizing ethnic differences.

Declaratory Act A statute enacted in England in 1766 that stated that Parliament held sovereign jurisdiction over the North American colonies.

decolonization Withdrawal of Western nations from colonies in Africa and Asia after World War II.

decurions Members of the city councils in the Roman Empire. Initially, they were the backbone of the provincial elite but by the third and fourth centuries were crippled by their personal responsibility for provincial taxes.

deists Those who believed that God created the universe but then did not intervene in its operation.

Delian League League of Greek cities formed to drive out the Persian invaders. Its leader, Athens, turned it into its own empire.

demesne Land kept by a medieval lord for his direct profit and worked a specified number of days each week by his peasants.

democracy Form of government in which the citizens choose their leaders; began in Athens, Greece, in the fifth century b.c.e.

de-Stalinization Process initiated by Nikita Khrushchev beginning in 1956 that reversed many of Stalin's repressive policies in the Soviet Union.

détente From the French word meaning a relaxation in tension, cooperation between the two superpowers, the Soviet Union and the United States. This policy was characterized by improved U.S.-Soviet diplomatic relationships in the 1970s to lessen the possibility of nuclear war.

dictator In the Roman Republic, an official who was granted unlimited power to rule the state for a period up to six months in a time of emergency. Sulla and Caesar both used the dictatorship for political ends.

diplomas The records of royal grants and decisions produced by clerics in medieval courts.

divine rights of kings Political theory that held that the institution of monarchy had divine origin and that the monarch functioned as God's representative on earth.

doge Chief magistrate of the Venetian Republic who served for life.

Eastern Question The "question" posed by the Great Powers about the future of the Ottoman territories.

Edict of Nantes The proclamation by Henry IV of France granting limited toleration to Huguenots.

ekklesia The assembly of all free male Athenian citizens.

emirs Local military commanders who took control of provincial administration in the Islamic world at the expense of the caliphs by the tenth century.

empiricism The philosophy propounded by Aristotle which rejected Plato's idea of abstract Forms in favor of practical observation and explanation, building general theories from particular data.

enclosure In the eighteenth century, the closing off of common and public land within the open field system to foster private landholding.

Enlightenment Philosophical and intellectual movement that began in Europe during the eighteenth century. The movement was characterized by a wave of new learning, especially in the sciences and mathematics, and the application of reason to solve society's problems.

entrepôt A place where goods were brought for storage before being exchanged; a commercial concept originated by the Dutch.

Epicureans Those who adhered to a Hellenistic Greek philosophy that the world was a random collection of atoms (atheistic and materialistic), and that one must pursue pleasure, but only in moderation as excess causes pain.

equestrians In the early Roman Republic, the equestrians were one of the richest classes in the Roman army, those who could afford to maintain a horse. By the late republic, their role expanded into banking and commerce.

Estates-General An official body assembled periodically by the medieval French state, consisting of representatives from three separate groups or "estates": those who prayed (the Church), those who fought (the aristocracy), and those who worked (commoners). Long in disuse by the monarch, it was convened by Louis XVI in 1789.

ethnic cleansing Term introduced in the Balkan war of the 1990s to describe the systematic killing and forcible removal of one ethnic group by another.

ethnos Large rural territorial units in the Dark Age and Archaic Greece focused around a central religious sanctuary and dominated by a local oligarchy, such as in Aetolia.

Etruscans Peoples native to Italy who influenced the formation of the Roman state.

eugenics An ersatz scientific theory that promoted the improvement of the human race through selective breeding.

eunomia The good order and obedience to the law which was the ideal of Sparta's militaristic society.

euro Common currency of the European Union; accepted as common currency by all members of the European Union except the United Kingdom.

European Economic Community (EEC) Formed in 1957 by Belgium, the Netherlands, Luxembourg, Italy, France, and West Germany to provide a single, integrated European market. Also known as the Common Market.

European Union (EU) Formed in 1992 to succeed the European Community in terms of economic integration; members share defensive, social, and economic policies as well.

extraterritoriality Exempted all foreigners in China from Chinese legal jurisdiction; practiced within foreign "spheres of influence" in China.

Fabians Members of a late nineteenth-century socialist movement in Britain who advocated gradual reform rather than revolution and supported the Labour party.

Factory Act (1833) British Parliamentary legislation that prohibited factory work by children under age nine, provided two hours of daily education for factory children, and limited labor for adults to twelve hours each day.

fascism Rooted in mass politics of the late-nineteenth century, a totalitarian political system that glorifies the state and subordinates the individual to the state's needs. First emerging in Italy after World War I, fascism appeared in virtually all European countries, but particularly Germany.

feudalism Anachronistic term used by early modern lawyers to describe medieval relations of vassalage.

fief A parcel of productive land along with the serfs and privileges attached to it granted by a lord to a knightly follower (vassal) in return for loyalty and military service.

Final Solution The term used by the Third Reich to refer to the extermination of all people deemed unfit; resulted in the execution of 11 million men, women, and children, 6 million of them Jews.

first triumvirate Political alliance between Pompey, Crassus, and Caesar to share power in the Roman Republic.

fodder crops Crops that were grown not for human consumption but to improve the nutrients in the soil. Some, such as turnips, were also used as animal feed.

Forms In Plato's philosophy, the perfect ideal that underlies all worldly objects. In recollecting them from one's previous existence one communes with all that is good, true, and beautiful.

Fourteen Points U.S. President Woodrow Wilson's idealistic set of guidelines drawn up as part of the peace process whose goal was to create a lasting peace after World War I.

French wars of religion Violent clashes between French Catholics and Calvinists (Huguenots) from 1562–1598.

Fronde An aristocratic revolution in France beginning in 1648 during the minority of Louis XIV, which was initiated by the tax policies of the minority government under Cardinal Mazarin.

futurists Artists and intellectuals of the late nineteenth and early twentieth century who wished to create a new culture free from traditional Western civilization. Futurists lionized technology, the masses, violence, and upheaval.

general strike a central concept for anarcho-syndicalism, this strike action had as a primary purpose the symbolic promotion of worker solidarity by means of a mass protest of limited duration which could mobilize workers from a variety of sectors. Unlike a strike called by a union, general strikes were of a short and defined period of time and were not aimed at improved wages or better working conditions, but were intended to signal the end of capitalism.

generation gap The baby boom following World War II resulted in a generation that came of age in the 1960s. The gap refers to the divergence in values between a large cohort of adolescents and young adults and their parents that resulted in more liberal values and socio-cultural mores.

Geopolities Geopolitics, or the politics of geography, is based on the recognition that certain areas of the world are valuable for political reasons—for example the Suez canal was important to Great Britain because of its economic interests in India.

Girondins French revolutionary faction that was more moderate than the Jacobins.

glasnost A Russian term meaning openness; one of the programs of reform initiated by Mikhail Gorbachev in the 1980s.

Glorious Revolution Change of government in England in 1688–1689 when the Catholic monarch James II was replaced by the Dutch ruler William of Orange. Called "glorious" because it supposedly was accomplished without bloodshed.

Gnostics An early Christian group that interpreted scripture as gnosis, or secret wisdom, and believed that Jesus had no human element. They were opposed by many bishops.

Golden Bull The edict of emperor Charles IV in 1356 recognizing that German princes and kings were autonomous rulers.

Great Chain of Being A hierarchic model of social organization common in the fifteenth and sixteenth centuries in which all parts of creation held a specific place in a divinely ordered universe.

Great Depression Devastation of the global economy that began in 1929 with the U.S. stock market crash and lasted through the 1930s.

Great Fear The term refers to that period in the summer of 1789 when French peasants, gripped by fear, revolted, attacked the chateaux of French nobility and burned documents that legally bound peasants to taxes and service.

Great Patriotic War The term by which the Russian people referred to World War II, reflecting their sense of dedication, nationalism and sacrifice in waging the war.

Great Purge A series of executions between 1934 and 1938 in the Soviet Union that removed all of Joseph Stalin's political enemies.

Great Reform Bill of 1832 An extension of the right to vote in England to men of the middle class that resulted in a 50 percent increase in those eligible to vote.

Great Schism The conflict (1378–1415) between two sets of rival popes based in Rome and Avignon that divided the loyalties of states and individuals across Europe.

guilds Professional associations of merchants or artisans that offer protection of members and regulation of a particular trade or craft.

hadith The written form of the Sunnah, practices established by the prophet Muhammad that guide the interpretation of the Qur'an.

Hanseatic League A commercial and political alliance of northern German towns established in the late fourteenth century to monopolize the grain and fish trade of the Baltic Sea.

Haussmannization The radical rebuilding of the city of Paris during the Second Empire directed by the Prefect of the Seine Baron Haussmann. Wide avenues, public parks and elegant apartment buildings defined the transformation of the city of Paris from narrow medieval streets into one of the world's most beautiful cities.

Hijra In early Islam, the journey undertaken by Muhammad from Mecca to Medina in 622 in order to govern Medina and calm its internal political dissension.

Holocaust During World War II, mass extermination of Jews by the Nazis under Adolph Hitler.

Holy Alliance Prussia, Austria, and Russia, under the leadership of tsar Alexander I, agreed to protect the peace and the Christian religion following the Congress of Vienna.

honestiores The privileged classes of the later Roman Empire: senators, municipal gentry, and the military.

hoplites In Archaic Greece, armed infantry soldiers.

Huguenots French Calvinists led by Henry of Navarre. Huguenots were victims of the St. Bartholomew's Day Massacre, a slaughter of numerous Protestants in Paris in 1572 during the French wars of religion.

Humanists Scholars who studied and taught the humanities, the skills of disciplines like philology—the art of language—and rhetoric—the art of expression; concentrated on ancient texts.

humiliores The lower classes of the later Roman Empire whose status declined from the period of the *Pax Romana* and who suffered disproportionately from the tax increases of the period.

Hundred Years' War A series of military engagements between England and France (1337–1452) over territorial and dynastic rivalries.

Hussites Followers of Jan Hus who attacked the sale of indulgences and German political dominance in the kingdom of Bohemia. After his execution, they led a partially successful revolt.

iconoclasts Breakers of icons; opponents of the mediating use of icons (religious images) in worship. Most emperors supported this faction in eighth- and early ninth-century Byzantium.

iconodules Venerators of icons; the ecclesiastical faction that resisted the iconoclasts. Most of the people and lesser clergy were iconodules.

icons Sacred images.

imperium The powers conferred on magistrates by the Roman people: the supreme power to command, to execute the law, and to impose the death penalty.

indulgences Remission of temporal punishment in Purgatory due to one's sins. Originally granted for performing pious acts, but later acquired through a grant to the church treasury. In the sixteenth century, indulgences were sold to raise money for the papacy; a critical issue in the Lutheran reform.

industrialization Process by which production becomes mechanized.

Industrial Revolution Sustained period of economic growth and change brought on by technological innovations in the process of manufacturing; began in Britain in the mid-eighteenth century.

intendants Officials appointed by the central government in France to oversee the local administration of the regional aristocracy; a critical component of the centralization of the French state.

Irish Great Hunger The famine of 1845 was caused by a potato blight that resulted in the decline by 25 percent of the Irish population within five years.

iron curtain The term coined by former British Prime Minister Winston Churchill to describe the ideological divide between western and eastern Europe after World War II.

Jacobins One of the political factions of the French National Convention that seized the initiative provided by the sans-culottes to take control of the radical revolution in the late eighteenth century; led by Maximilien Robespierre.

Jacquerie The revolt of French peasants against the aristocracy and crown in 1358. It was part of the struggle for rights caused by the labor shortage after the Black Death.

jihads Holy wars waged by Muslims against their religious enemies.

jingoism Use of public opinion to stir support for one's own nation and hatred for another nation; used extensively by political leaders to justify imperial expansion.

joint-stock companies Business enterprises that raise capital by selling shares to individuals who receive dividends on their investments.

Kellogg-Briand Pact An agreement, named for the two men who devised it—the U.S. Secretary of State Frank B. Kellogg and the French Foreign Minister Aristide Briand, signed by 23 nations in 1928 whose purpose was an idealistic renunciation of war.

kouros Nude statues of young men that were a common subject in Archaic art. The stiff posture demonstrates the influence of Egyptian sculpture.

Kristallnacht "Crystal night" in German; refers to the night of 9 November 1938 when mobs directed by the Nazis destroyed the homes, businesses, and synagogues of German Jews.

Kulturkampf "Struggle for civilization"; legislation of the German Empire against the Catholic Church in the 1870s.

laissez-faire An economic theory that required government to cease interference with private economic activity; Adam Smith and the Physiocrats were its leading proponents.

latifundia The vast rural estates of the Roman patricians which were worked by slaves or free but dependent tenant farmers.

lay investiture The practice by which kings and emperors appointed bishops and invested them with the symbols of their office. It led to conflict between the Papacy and the emperors in the eleventh century.

League of Nations A global, supra-national organization formed following World War I (1919) for the purpose of promoting the peaceful resolution of disputes among member nations. Even though Germany in 1926 and the Soviet Union in 1934 were permitted to join, the failure of the United States to become a member of the League undermined its effectiveness.

Lebensraum "Living room"; one of Hitler's foreign policy objectives to extend the borders of Germany in eastern and central Europe.

lectio divina In monastic life, the process of reading and studying the Old and New Testaments that formed an important part of each day's activities.

liberalism A political philosophy based on freedom of the individual and the corruptibility of authority; associated with constitutional reform in the first half of the nineteenth century.

Linear B A syllabic form of writing from the late Greek Bronze Age which preserves the earliest known form of Greek. It was used by Mycenaean elites almost entirely for record-keeping.

linear perspective A technique developed in painting to give a flat surface the appearance of depth and dimension.

Long Parliament An English Parliament that officially met from 1640 to 1653. It forced reforms under Charles I, defeated the royal armies during the English Civil War, and tried and executed the king.

Luddites Workers who attacked machines in order to protest the loss of their skilled jobs.

Ludendorff Offensive The final German offensive of World War I, named after the general who devised it, launched against the Allies on the Western Front in March 1918. The offensive ultimately failed.

maat In Egyptian thought, the ideal state of the universe and of society which the pharaoh was supposed to uphold.

Maginot Line A system of defensive fortifications built by France along its German border in the 1920s and 1930s.

Magna Carta The "great charter" limiting royal power that King John was forced to sign in 1215.

manses Farms worked by slaves, serfs, and freemen in the Middle Ages.

March on Rome The takeover of political power in Rome by the fascists in Italy on 28 October 1922, followed by similar takeovers in Milan and Bologna.

Marchfield The assembly of all free warriors in the early Germanic kingdoms in which the king's authority was all-powerful.

Marshall Plan The U.S. economic aid program for European countries after World War II; intended to establish U.S. economic influence in European markets.

mercantilism A popular state economy of the seventeenth century; involved bullionism, protective tariffs, and monopolies.

metics The non-Athenian residents of Athens who comprised about half of the free population of the city. They were active in commerce and banking.

Minoan civilization The culture of Crete in the Middle Bronze Age (2000–1550 b.c.e.) in which elites based at great palaces, such as Knossos, dominated the island politically, economically, and religiously.

minuscule New style of handwriting developed in the Carolingian Renaissance to preserve texts; later adopted as standard script.

Mishnah In Jewish law, the oral interpretation of the Torah (scripture) which was developed by the Pharisees and later developed into an extensive written body of legal interpretation.

missi dominici Teams of counts and bishops that examined the state of each county in the Carolingian Empire on behalf of the king.

monasticism The life of monks devoted to God, from the fourth century onwards, either as part of communal organization or in solitary life. Monasticism began in Egypt as a rejection of the worldliness of civilization.

monopoly Exclusive control of a market or industry; a form of economic regulation in which special privileges are granted in return for financial considerations and an agreement to abide by the rules set out by the state.

Moujahedeen An Arabic word referring to Muslim holy warriors fighting for Islam in various countries, including the Balkans and Chechnya, in the late 20th and 21st century.

Museum The shrine to the Muses in Hellenistic Alexandria to which was added the Library containing all the great works of Greek literature and learning.

Mycenaean Late Greek Bronze Age civilization that arose ca. 1600 b.c.e. at Mycenae and that encompassed the Greek mainland and parts of Asia Minor. Myceneans developed the Linear B script.

mystery cults Religions that promised immediate, personal contact with a deity that would bring immortality.

Napoleonic Code The recodification of French law carried out during Napoleon's reign.

National Assembly That body formed on 17 June 1789 by the French Third Estate when it changed its name to the National Assembly, laying claim to being the true representatives of the French nation.

nationalities problem The existence of numerous ethnic minorities within the borders of the Soviet Union leading to demands for self-determination and political independence.

natural selection A theory advanced by Charles Darwin that accounted for evolution of species; a realist scientific approach.

Navigation Acts English economic legislation providing that colonial goods could only be shipped in English ships.

Nazism National Socialism; German variant of fascism.

Neolithic era The New Stone Age (8000–6500 b.c.e.) in which modern man developed agriculture and the first villages.

Neoplatonism Use of the writings of Plato to advance modern ideas about science, particularly mathematics and the health sciences.

New Economic Policy (NEP) A state-planned economic policy in the Soviet Union between 1921 and 1928; based on agricultural productivity, it required set payments from peasants; surpluses could be sold on the free market.

new imperialism Imperialism practiced by European countries after 1870 that was, in essence, the domination by industrial powers over the non-industrial world. Distinguished from the earlier acquisition of territory, new imperialism took a variety of forms including territorial occupations, colonization, exploitation of labor and raw materials, and development of economic spheres of influence.

New Monarchies The more centralized European governments of western Europe created in the fifteenth and sixteenth centuries.

New Piety An aspect of the Roman Catholic reform movement; originated among the Brethren of the Common Life with an emphasis on simplicity and more personalized religious practice.

nominalism The doctrine of William of Ockham that argued that human reason could not aspire to certain truth.

North Atlantic Treaty Organization (NATO) An organization founded in 1949 the members of which signed a defense pact to protect those countries bordering the North Atlantic.

nuclear club The group of nations in possession of atomic weapons, originally consisting of the United States and the Soviet Union. By 1974, the nuclear club included Great Britain, France, the People's Republic of China, and India.

Old Regime The old order; political and social system of France in the eighteenth century before the French Revolution.

oligarchy Government by an elite few.

optimates The traditionalist Roman political faction that succeeded the Gracchi and sought to preserve the senatorial oligarchy against the populares.

Orthodox Christianity The official "right-teaching" faith of Constantinople as opposed to the heterodox peoples on the margins of the Byzantine Empire.

ostracism A practice in Athenian democracy by which anyone deemed to threaten the constitution could, by popular vote, be exiled for ten years without the loss of property.

Pact of Steel A military alliance formed between Hilter's Germany and Mussolini's Italy in May 1939 pledging cooperation and military and economic coordination.

Paleolithic era The Old Stone Age (600,000–10,000 b.c.e.) in which advanced primates developed into Neanderthals and also modern man. They hunted food or collected it by gathering.

Paris Commune Created in 1871 in the aftermath of the Franco-Prussian War; crushed by the national army after a brief struggle; symbol of revolution for radical politicians, including Marxists.

parlements Provincial courts in France; the Parlement of Paris, the main law court of the state, was the most powerful of these.

parties A form of political organization in which members of the British parliament divided into groups with identifiable interests. Whigs and Tories were the first political parties.

Patent of Toleration An edict of Joseph II of Austria in 1781 that granted freedom of worship to Protestants and members of the Greek Orthodox Church, in addition to Roman Catholics.

paterfamilias The male head of household in the Roman family. His power was absolute, including the power of life and death.

patricians Leaders of the gentes, or clans, in early Roman society.

Pax Romana The two centuries of peace and stability in the early Roman Empire inaugurated by the emperor Augustus.

Peace of Paris of 1856 The peace treaty that ended the Crimean War whereby Russia relinquished its claim as protector of Christians in Turkey and ceased interference in the Ottoman Empire; the British gained the neutralization of the Black Sea; Turkish control was reestablished over the mouth of the Danube; Russia gave up a portion of Bessarabia; and the Danubian Principalities were placed under guarantee of Great Britain and France.

perestroika A Russian term meaning restructuring; part of Mikhail Gorbachev's attempts to reform the Soviet government and economy in the 1980s.

Peterloo Massacre In August 1819, the English army troops policing a political crowd gathered near Manchester, England, lost control resulting in the deaths of 11 and the injury of hundreds of others.

phalanx A tightly ordered and well-disciplined body of elite Greek warriors in heavy armor that attacked in close formation with long spears.

philology The art of language; one of the most important aspects of humanist studies, based on models of ancient texts.

philosophes A French term for the intellectuals of the eighteenth-century Enlightenment. Voltaire, Diderot, and Condorcet were leading philosophes.

phony war The period between 3 September 1939, when Great Britain and France declared war on Germany, and the spring of 1940, when the German offensive against France commenced armed combat between France and Germany. In this strange interlude, while civilian populations waited for attack, an attitude of defeatism grew in France.

Physiocrats A group of French thinkers who subscribed to the view that land was wealth and thus argued that improvements in agricultural activity should take first priority in state reforms.

pictograms The earliest form of writing in Mesopotamia, ca. 3500 b.c.e., in which pictures represented particular objects, such as animals.

Pietà A painting or sculpture of Mary mourning the dead Jesus. The most famous was carved by Michelangelo and is in St. Peter's Basilica.

plebs Families not organized into gentes, or clans, in early Roman society. The lower classes.

pogroms State-organized massacres of Jews.

polis The city-state of Archaic and Classical Greece, particularly found on the shores of the Aegean. A city formed the center of government (tyranny, oligarchy, or democracy) and of religious life with temples on its citadel (Acropolis).

politiques During the sixteenth-century French wars of religion, a group of Catholics who joined with Huguenots to demand a practical settlement of the wars.

populares The Roman political faction that succeeded the Gracchi whose leaders appealed to the masses as a source of power.

Popular Front Socialist governments established in both France and Spain in the 1930s; the French version failed to solve the Depression and was voted out of office; the creation of a socialist republic in Spain initiated a civil war.

Pragmatic Sanction The document that attempted to secure the recognition of Maria Theresa as heiress to the Habsburg possessions of Charles VI.

Prague Spring Popular uprising and reform movement in 1968 Czechoslovakia, ended by Soviet invasion in August 1968.

predestination A fundamental principle of Calvin's theology: the belief that all Christians are predestined to either heaven or hell from the act of creation.

presbyters The priests of the early Christian tradition who were subordinated to bishops as hierarchy developed in the Church.

Price Revolution The dramatic price inflation of the fifteenth and sixteenth centuries; caused by monetary debasement and the influx of bullion from the New World.

princeps "First citizen"; the title assumed by the emperor Augustus to reassure public opinion by preserving the traditional constitutional forms.

Proclamation of the German Empire The creation in 1871 of the nation-state of Germany by uniting the 38 German states into a single national entity.

proletariat The industrial working class.

pronatalism State programs implemented after the Second World War to encourage women to have larger families.

Puritans English Protestants who sought to purify the Church of England of all traces of Catholicism.

putting-out system Mobilization of the rural labor force for commercial production of large quantities of manufactured goods; raw materials put out to homes of workers where manufacture took place.

quadrivium Part of a medieval liberal arts education that included arithmetic, geometry, astronomy, and music.

Quadruple Alliance Pact signed in 1815 by the four powers who defeated Napoleon—Great Britain, Austria, Russia, and Prussia—for the purpose of protecting Europe against future French aggression.

quinine An important nineteenth-century medical advance derived from cinchona that was an effective treatment for malaria; it permitted large numbers of Europeans to travel without risking death and disease.

raison d'état Reason of state; placing the needs of the nation above the privileges of its most important groups.

realism An artistic and literary style that criticized industrialized society and rejected bourgeois concepts of morality.

Realpolitik Pragmatic political theory advanced by Otto von Bismarck; ruthless pursuit by any means, including illegal and violent ones, in the interests of the state.

reconquista The Christian reconquest of the Iberian peninsula from the Spanish Muslims or Moors; completed in 1492 under Ferdinand and Isabella.

Reformation A movement to reform and purify the Catholic Church that resulted in the creation of new religious denominations in Europe collectively known as Protestants.

Reichstag The national legislative body of the German Empire; elected by universal male suffrage.

Reign of Terror The period from 1793 to 1794 when Maximilien Robespierre assumed leadership of the Committee of Public Safety and oversaw the revolutionary tribunals that sentenced about 40,000 people to execution.

Renaissance A "rebirth" of classical learning and emphasis on humanity that characterized the period between 1350 and 1550.

revisionism A German socialist school that favored gradual reform through the parliamentary system; led by Edouard Bernstein.

rhetoric The art of expression and persuasion.

Risorgimento The nineteenth-century movement to reunite Italy.

robot Labor service that peasants owed to their lord; more typical in eastern Europe after the fifteenth century.

romanticism An artistic and literary tradition based on emotions rather than the intellect; rejection of classical traditions in favor of "nature"; often associated with nationalism.

salons Informal social gatherings during the Enlightenment, frequently organized by women, in which topics of intellectual interest were discussed.

samizdat Self-published, privately circulated manuscripts; chief vehicle for circulating information among dissidents in the Soviet Union.

sans-culottes Literally "those without knee-breeches"; working-class revolutionaries who initiated the radical stage of the French revolution in 1792.

Schlieffen Plan The strategy of the German high command at the outset of World War I, predicated on knocking France out of the war.

Scholastic method The combination of legal analysis from the new university at Bologna with Aristotelian logic; established by Peter Abelard in the twelfth century.

Schuman Plan In 1950 France and West Germany joined together to pool all their coal and steel resources. The plan is named for the French Foreign Minister Robert Schuman who was influenced by the economic vision of Jean Monney. The following year the European Coal and Steel Community, predecessor to the European Union, was formed.

scientific revolution In the sixteenth and seventeenth centuries, a period of new scientific inquiry, experimentation, and discovery that resulted in a new understanding of the universe based on mathematical principles and led to the creation of the modern sciences, particularly astronomy and physics.

scramble for Africa The colonization of Africa as part of the new imperialism. This domination of Africa by Germany, Britain, and France ended with the crisis at Fashoda.

second triumvirate Alliance of Octavian, Mark Anthony, and Lepidus following the assassination of Julius Caesar to defeat the assassins and control the Roman Empire.

seigneur Manor lord responsible for maintaining order, administering justice, and arbitrating disputes among tenants.

Semi-nomadic south A society that remains at fixed locations for extended periods but also remains migratory.

serfs Peasants of degraded status and very limited legal rights who were dependent on the lords in the High Middle Ages. They formed the great bulk of the population.

**Shi`ites** Muslims who follow the tradition that legitimate leadership of Islam can only come through the descendants of `Ali, whom they regard as the last orthodox caliph.

social Darwinists Those who applied the theory of evolutionary biology, particularly the concept of "survival of the fittest," to human society.

social question The question of how to treat poverty became a pressing issue for European societies between 1830 and 1850. The social question revolved around what the role of government and the role of private individuals should be in addressing social misery.

sola fide A fundamental principle of Luther's theology: justification of Christians by faith alone.

"Socialism in one country" The slogan employed by Joseph Stalin in the 1920s to justify his plans for rapid industrialization as a means of preserving socialism in the Soviet Union.

sola scriptura By the word alone; emphasis on scriptural authority in preference to the canons of the Church, a fundamental element of Luther's theology.

Solidarity A non-communist Polish labor organization founded by Lech Walesa in the Gdansk shipbuilding yards; legalized in 1989 as a political movement, it won a victory in the first Polish democratic elections.

Sophists Professional teachers in fifth-century Greece who traveled from city to city instructing students, for a fee, in rhetoric, the art of persuasion.

Soviets Councils of workers in Russia formed after 1905 that became one center of power after the overthrow of the tsar; source of power for Lenin and Bolsheviks.

Spanish Armada The Spanish fleet sent in 1588 to transport troops from the Low Countries for an invasion of England; defeated by the English fleets of Elizabeth I.

Spanish Inquisition An ecclesiastical tribunal utilized to combat heresy and non-Christians; used by Ferdinand and Isabella against the conversos, or converted Jews of Spain.

spheres of influence Diplomatic term used to connote territorial influence or control of weaker nations not necessarily occupied by the more powerful ones. The term was first used to explain one kind of control of western European powers in the 1800s during African imperialism, and was later used to describe European and Japanese territorial control and influence over markets in China at the end of the nineteenth century.

"Spirit of Locarno" A series of treaties, signed in Locarno, Switzerland in 1925 by Germany, France, Great Britain, Belgium and Italy, and intended to promote cooperation and respect for borders, promoted an atmosphere of good will in the international arena known as the "spirit of Locarno."

Stoics Followers of the Hellenistic Greek philosophy propounded by Zeno, which teaches that orderliness is proper to the universe and that happiness derives from embracing one's divinely ordained role and unhappiness from rejecting it.

strategoi Generals, the military commanders of themes in the Byzantine Empire. They were responsible for civil and military administration.

suffragettes Militant members of the English feminist movement led by Emmeline Pankhurst who engaged in acts of violence against private property in order to secure the vote.

sunnah In Islamic theology, the practices established by the prophet Muhammad. They were initially preserved by oral tradition.

Sunnis The majority tradition of Islam that accepts that political succession should be based on consensus, the existing political order, and a leader's merits.

synod A meeting of bishops called to debate Church policy, such as that at Whitby in 664, which established the customs of the Roman Church among Angles and Saxons.

Talmud Rabbinic discussions of the Mishna and its interpretation complied around 500 C.E.

Table of Ranks Official state hierarchy in Russia under Peter the Great that established the social position or rank of individuals according to categories of military service, civil service, and ownership of landed estates.

tetrarchy Rule by four; Diocletian's attempt to regulate the suggestion of the Roman Empire by dividing the empire into eastern and western parts, with both an augustus and a junior emperor, or caesar, ruling each part.

Taliban The fundamentalist Muslim ruling group that controlled Afghanistan for the period between 1996 to 2001, and currently waging guerilla actions against Afghanistan's democratic government. A rigid sect, the Taliban follows strict observance, denying rights to women.

Thermidorian Reaction Revolt beginning in July 1794 (the month of Thermidor) against the radicalism of the French Revolution, leading to the downfall and execution of Robespierre and the end of the Reign of Terror.

Third Estate Branch of the French Estates-General consisting of the bourgeoisie and the working classes; separated from the other estates to form the National Assembly in 1789.

Third Reich "The Third Empire"; Hitler's government, established after 1933.

third world The former colonies of European and Asian imperialism; sought to separate themselves from European economic control after independence; operated in the United Nations as a non-aligned bloc.

Thirty Years' War War lasting from 1618–1648.

three-field system An efficient agricultural system in which one-third of the land was planted in autumn with wheat or rye, one-third remained fallow, and one-third was planted in spring with a crop that added nutrients to the soil.

Time of Troubles The period of disruption within Russia following the death of Ivan the Terrible; only ended with the Polish invasion of Russia.

Torah The body of law in Hebrew scripture.

Tories Members of a political party in England that in the seventeenth century defended the principle of hereditary succession to the crown; in opposition to the Whigs. The Tories sought to preserve the traditional political structure and supported the authority of the Anglican church.

total war War that requires mobilization of the civilian population in addition to the military; typified by centralized governments with limits on economy and civil rights.

Treaty of Brest-Litovsk The Treaty between Russia and Germany signed in March 1918 whereby Soviet Russia withdrew from World War I.

Treaty of Rapallo An economic treaty signed between Weimar Germany and Soviet Russia in 1922 intended to promote economic recovery and trade.

Treaty of Tordesillas A 1494 agreement that recognized Portugal's claims to Brazil, but gave all of the remainder of the New World to Spain.

Treaty of Versailles Peace settlement with Germany at the end of World War I; included the War Guilt Clause fixing blame on Germany for the war and requiring massive reparations.

triangular trade A three-way trade system during the seventeenth century involving the shipment of calicoes to Africa for slaves who were transported to the East Indies in exchange for sugar, which was shipped to Europe.

Tripartite Pact In September 1940 Japan, Germany and Italy promised mutual support against aggression and endorsed each other's expansionist aims in Europe and Asia.

Triple Alliance An alliance founded in 1882 between Germany, Austria-Hungary, and Italy at Germany's instigation for the purpose of securing mutual support on the European continent.

Triple Entente Alliance founded in 1907 between France, Britain, and Russia. With the defection of Russia from the Three Emperors' League, it hemmed in Germany on both eastern and western borders.

trivium The basic education in cathedral schools of the Middle Ages: grammar, rhetoric, and logic.

tyrants Rulers who had seized power illegally. Tyrannies replaced oligarchies in many *poleis* in Archaic Greece, such as at Corinth and Athens. The term did not have the negative connotations it does today, as many tyrants were popular leaders welcomed by their subjects.

Umma The community of all believers in the Islamic faith. Initially, it was both a political and religious supertribe of Arabs.

universitas The guilds of students that formed the first true universities from the twelfth century onwards.

utilitarianism Jeremy Bentham's philosophical plan to ensure social harmony through measurement of pleasure and pain or the greatest happiness of the greatest number; a liberal philosophy.

vassals Knights sworn to fealty or loyalty to a lord; in return the lord granted the vassal a means of support, or fief.

Velvet revolutions the term refers to the peaceful transformations from communist rule to democratic governments that occurred in 1989 in Poland, Hungary and Czechoslovakia.

Victorian Compromise The balance between freedom and protectionism achieved by liberal parliamentary reform during the reign of Queen Victoria.

Villanovans Peoples of the first Iron Age culture in Italy (1000–800 b.c.e.), which was based in the north. They made iron tools and weapons and placed the ashes of their dead in large urns.

War Guilt Clause As part of the Treaty of Versailles of 1919, the Clause assigned sole responsibility for World War I to Germany and stated that Germany must be made to pay: "Compensation will be made by Germany for all damage done to the civilian population of the Allies and their property by the aggression of Germany by land, by sea and from the air." Reparations resulted from this assignment of guilt, which the German people considered punitive.

Warsaw Pact Defensive alliance organization formed in 1955 by Albania, Bulgaria, Romania, Czechoslovakia, Hungary, Poland, East Germany, and the Soviet Union. The alliance served as a strategic buffer zone against NATO forces.

Weimar Republic German government founded at the end of the First World War; used by German general staff as scapegoat for German defeat and harsh peace terms; overthrown in 1933.

welfare state The tendency of post–World War II states to establish safety nets for citizens in areas of birth, sickness, old age, and unemployment.

wergeld In Germanic society, the payment in reparation for crimes in place of blood vengeance. Tribal leaders used it to reduce internal hostilities.

Whigs Members of a political party in England that in the seventeenth century supported the Protestant succession and a broad-based Protestantism and advocated a constitutional monarchy that limited royal power; in opposition to the Tories. The Whigs were later identified with social and parliamentary reform.

Young Plan The plan devised by the American businessman Owen Young in 1929 that replaced the Dawes Plan and transferred $100 million to Germany to assist in reparations repayments.

zemstvos Local elected assemblies in Russia during the reign of Alexander II; representatives elected by landowners, townspeople, and peasants.

ziggurat Babylonian tiered towers (or step-pyramids) from ca. 2000 b.c.e. that were dedicated to gods and stood near temples. They were among the most important buildings of Babylonian cities.

Zimmermann note Arthur Zimmermann, the German foreign minister during World War I sent a telegram, or "note," in support of Mexico's territorial claims against the United States in New Mexico, Arizona and Texas in exchange for Mexico's support of Germany in the war. As a result of the interception and publication of this note, the United States declared war against Germany in April 1917.

Zionism A program initiated by Theodor Herzl to establish an independent Jewish state in Palestine.

Zollverein A unified trading zone created by Prussia in which member states adopted the liberal Prussian customs regulations; an attempt to overcome the fragmented nature of the German economy.

Zoroastrianism A monotheistic religion founded by Zoroaster in sixth-century b.c.e. Persia that emphasized the personal choice between good (light) and evil (darkness).

CREDITS

DOCUMENT CREDITS

Chapter 1

"The Code of Hammurabi": From James Pritchard, *Ancient Near East Texts Relating to the Old Testament, Third Edition with Supplement.* © 1950, 1955, 1969, renewed 1978 by Princeton University Press. Reprinted by permission of Princeton University Press.

"A Homesick Egyptian": From James Pritchard, *Ancient Near East Texts Relating to the Old Testament, Third Edition with Supplement.* © 1950, 1955, 1969, renewed 1978 by Princeton University Press. Reprinted by permission of Princeton University Press.

"The Kingdom of Israel": Excerpts from Samuel 8:9–10. Scripture quotations are from the Revised Standard Version of the Bible. Copyright 1946, 1952, 1971 by the Division of Christian Education of the National Council of the Churches of Christ in the United States of America. Used by permission. All rights reserved.

Chapter 2

"Race of Iron": Translated by Hugh G. Evelyn-White.

"Hector and Andromache": From *The Iliad of Homer*, translated by Richmond Lattimore. Copyright © 1951 by the University of Chicago. Reprinted by permission.

Chapter 3

"An Unexamined Life is Not Worth Living": *The Last Days of Socrates,* Plato Translated with an introduction by Hugh Tredennick (Penguin Classics 1954, Third edition 1969). Copyright © Hugh Tredennick, 1954, 1959, 1969. Reprinted with permission from Penguin Books, Ltd.

"Reconstruction Figure": From Eric William Marsden, *Greek and Roman Artillery: Historical Development*, p. 35, fig. 17. © Oxford University Press, London, 1969. Used by permission.

Chapter 4

"The Twelve Tables": From *Roman Civilization, Vol. I*, by Naphtali Lewis and Meyer Reinhold. Copyright © 1951 Columbia University Press. Used by permission.

Chapter 5

"The Reforms of Tiberius Gracchus": *From Roman Civilization, Vol. I*, by Naphtali Lewis and Meyer Reinhold. Copyright © 1951 Columbia University Press. Used by permission.

"Peter Announces the Good News": Excerpts from Acts 3:17–26. Scripture quotations are from the Revised Standard Version of the Bible. Copyright 1946, 1952, 1971 by the Division of Christian Education of the National Council of the Churches of Christ in the United States of America. Used by permission. All rights reserved.

Chapter 6

"Religious Toleration and Persecution": *From Roman Civilization, Vol. II*, by Naphtali Lewis and Meyer Reinhold. Copyright © 1951 Columbia University Press. Reprinted by permission.

"Love in the Two Cities": From Saint Augustine, *The City of God*, pp. 321–322. © 1958 Image Books. Used with permission.

Chapter 7

"A Turkish Guest in Constantinople": From Book 10 in *The Alexiad of Anna Comnena*, translated by E. R. A. Sewter (Penguin Classics 1969). Copyright © E. R. A. Sewter, 1969. Reprinted by permission of Penguin Books, Ltd.

"An Arab in Crusader Jerusalem": James Kritzack, ed., *Anthology of Islamic Literature* from *The Rise of Islam to Modern Times*, p. 194.

Chapter 8

"Two Missionaries": From *A History of the English Church and People* by Bede, translated with an introduction by Leo Sherley-Price, revised by R. E. Latham (Penguin Classics 1955, Revised Edition 1968). Copyright © Leo Sherley-Price, 1955, 1968.

Chapter 9

"Visions Like a Flame": From *Hildegard of Bingen: Mystical Writings*, edited by Fiona Bowie and Oliver Davies, new translation by Robert Carver, page 68. Copyright © 1990 by Bowie, Davies and Carver. Reprinted by permission of The Crossroad Publishing Company.

"Pope Urban II Summons a Crusade": From *The First Crusade: The Chronicle of Fulcher of Chartres and Other Source Materials,* edited by Edward Peters, pp. 30–31. Copyright © 1971 University of Pennsylvania Press. Used with permission.

Chapter 10

"A Woman Before the Inquisition": Jacques Fournier, "Inquisition Records." in Readings in Medieval History, edited by Patrick Geary, original source: Jean Duvernoy, *Le Registre d'Inquisition de Jacques Fournier* Copyright © 1978 Editions de l'Ecole des Hautes Etudes en Sciences Sociales. Reprinted by permission.

Convivencia: Excerpt from *Las Siete Partidas,* trans. by Samuel Parsons Scott (Chicago: Published for the Comparative Law Bureau of the American Bar Association by Commerce Clearing House, Inc., 1931).

Chapter 11

"On the Family": by Leon Battista Alberti in *The Family in Renaissance Florence* by Renee Watkins. Reprinted by permission of Renee Watkins.

Chapter 12

"The Halls of Montezuma": From Bernal Diaz Chronicles.

"The Kingdom of France": From Claude de Seyssel, *The Monarch of France* translated by J. H. Hexter and edited by Donald R. Kelley pp. 38–39, 48–54, 56–57. Copyright © 1981 by Yale University Press. All rights reserved.

Chapter 13

"A Dutch Wit": From *In Praise of Folly* by Erasmus.

Chapter 14

"Cannibals": Excerpts from Donald M. Frame, translator, *The Complete Essays of Montaigne.* Copyright © 1958 by the Board of Trustees of the Leland Stanford Junior University. All rights reserved.

"War Is Hell": Translated by A. T. S. Goodrick, from *The Adventurous Simplicissmus.*

Chapter 15

"The Peasants' Revolt": From Readings in European History.

"A Feminine Perspective": From Arcangela Tarabotti, "Innocence Undone," translated by Brendan Dooley. Reprinted by permission of Brendan Dooley.

"The Devil's Due": From "Medieval Witchcraft" in *Translations and Reprints from the Original Sources of European History*, Volume III. Reprinted by permission of The University of Pennsylvania Press.

PHOTO CREDITS

Unless otherwise acknowledged, all photographs are the property of Pearson Education, Inc. Page abbreviations are as follows: (T) top, (B) bottom, (L) left, (R) right.

Chapter 1

4, 5, Augustin Ochsenreiter/South Tyrol Museum of Archaeology **6** AMNH Trans. 5269 American Museum of Natural History Library **7** Kazuyoshi Nomashi/Pacific Press Service/Photo Researchers **8** (T) Javier Trueba/MSF/Science Photo Library/Photo Researchers (B) Lauros/Giraudon, Musee des Antiquites Nationale, St. Germain-en-Laye, France/ Bridgeman Art Library **11** Museum of Anatolian Civilisations Ankara/Dagli Orti /The Art Archive **13** © The Trustees of the British Museum **14** Scala/Art Resource, NY**15** Michael S. Yamashita/Corbis **17** Scala/Art Resource, NY **19** Hirmer Verlag, Munich **21** (T) Yoshio Tomil/SuperStock, Inc. (B) Réunion des Musées Nationaux/Art Resource, NY **24** Osiride Head of Hatshepusut, originally from a statue. Provenance: Thebes, Deir el Bahri. Limestone, painted. H. 64 cm. H. with crown 124.5 cm. The Metropolitan Museum of Art, Rogers Fund. 1931, (31.3.157) Photograph © 1983 The Metropolitan Museum of Art **25** Egyptian Museum Cairo/Dagli Orti/The Art Archive **26** Erich Lessing/Art Resource, NY **29** Israel Museum/Nahum Seapak **31** bpk/Art Resource, NY

Chapter 2

37 Hydria, Greece, Attica, Athens, about 520 B.C. Antiope Group, Ceramic, Black Figure; H 3 Diam: 50 x 26.1 http://diam.cm diam. cm (19 11/16 x 10 5/16 diam. in) William Francis Warden Fund (63.473). Courtesy, Museum of Fine Arts, Boston. Reproduced with permission. © 2007 The Museum of Fine Arts, Boston. All Rights Reserved. **38** © The Trustees of the British Museum (1863.2-13.1 [Sculpture A 17]) **40** The Art Archive **41** (T) Vanni/Art Resource, NY (B) Giraudon/Art Resource, NY **42** Hirmer Verlag, Munich **45** Réunion des Musées Nationaux/Art Resource, NY **47** Scala/Art Resource, NY **48** Bibliothèque Nationale de France, Paris **49** British Museum, London, UK/Bridgeman Art Library **50** bpk/Art Resource, NY **51** National Archeological Museum Athens/Dagli Orti/ The Art Archive **53** Erich Lessing/Art Resource, NY **54** Hirmer Verlag, Munich **55** Réunion des Musées Nationaux/Art Resource, NY **58** British Museum, London, UK/Bridgeman Art Library **60** Lee Boltin Picture Library/Bridgeman Art Library

Chapter 3

66 Alinari, Vatican Museums and Galleries, Vatican City, Italy/Bridgeman Art Library **67** Art Resource, NY **68** Giraudon/Persepolis, Iran/Bridgeman Art Library **69** American Museum of Classical Studies at Athens: Agora Excavation **70** Erich Lessing/Art Resource, NY **73** Réunion des Musées Nationaux/Art Resource, NY **75** © Ashmolean Museum, University of Oxford, UK/Bridgeman Art Library **77** Scala/Art Resource, NY **81** Kylix: Man and Youth. Attributed to Douris. Terra-cotta. Diameter 11 3/4 in, (29.9 cm.) J. 43/8 in. (11.1 cm.) The Metropolitan Museum of Art, Rogers Fund, 1952 (52.11.4) Photograph © 1984 The Metropolitan Museum of Art **82** Ping Amranad/SuperStock, Inc. **84** Erich Lessing/Art Resource, NY **85** Alinari/Art Resource, NY **86** Archaeological Museum of Salonika, Greece/Alinari/The Image Works **89** Scala/Art Resource, NY **92** Werner Forman/Art Resource, NY **93** (L) Bridgeman-Giraudon/Art Resource, NY (R) Veiled and Masked Dancer. Said to be from Alexandria. Bronze. H. 8 1/16 in. (20.5 cm.) The Metropolitan Museum of Art, Bequest of Walter C. Baker, 1971 (1972.118.95) Photograph © 1981 The Metropolitan Museum of Art

Chapter 4

101 Dagli Orti/The Art Archive **102** Réunion des Musées Nationaux/Art Resource, NY **105** Hirmer Verlag, Munich **106** Scala/Art Resource, NY **109** Réunion des Musées Nationaux/Art Resource, NY **110** Jan Vinchon Numismatist, Paris/Dagli Orti/The Art Archive **113** Alinari/Art Resource, NY **115** Museo Nazionale, Naples/Minestro Per I Beni E Le Attivita' Culturali **120** Vanni/Art Resource, NY **121** Alinari/Bridgeman Art Library **122** Erich Lessing/Art Resource, NY **123** Scala/Art Resource, NY

Chapter 5

128 Nimatallah/Art Resource, NY **129** Scala/Art Resource, NY **130** Museo della Civilta Romana Rome/Dagli Orti/The Art Archive **132** Giraudon, Musée d'Orsay, Paris, France/Bridgeman Art Library **134, 138** (T), **138** (B) Scala/Art Resource, NY **139** Erich Lessing/Art Resource, NY **141** Dagli Orti/The Art Archive **142** Bardo Museum Tunis/Dagli Orti/The Art Archive **144** Dagli Orti/The Art Archive **145** Scala/Art Resource, NY **147** Ronald Sheridan/Ancient Art & Architecture **148** Werner Forman/Art Resource, NY **151** Christian Baptistery. Reconstruction at Yale University. Dura-Europos Collection, Yale University Art Gallery **153** Alinari, Galleria degli Uffizi, Florence, Italy/Bridgeman Art Library **156** Biblioteca Apostolica Vaticana (Vatican) (MS VAT LAT 2057, fol. 147, recto, Math 11a NS.10) **157** Dagli Orti/The Art Archive

Chapter 6

160, 161 © The Trustees of the British Museum (MME 1866,12-29,1) **164** Archeological Museum Rabat/ Dagli Orti/The Art Archive **167, 169** Erich Lessing/Art Resource, NY **170** St. Peter's Vatican, Rome, Italy/Bridgeman Art Library **175** Jean-Louis Nou/akg-images **176** Réunion des Musées Nationaux/Art Resource, NY **178** Ronald Sheridan/Ancient Art & Architecture **180** © The Trustees of the British Museum **182** Germanisches National Museum, Nuremberg

Chapter 7

186 Hubertus Kanus/SuperStock, Inc. **187** Kurt Scholz/SuperStock, Inc. **188** Scala/Art Resource, NY **190** Vanni/Art Resource, NY **191** Norman Tellis Photo **193** Bibliothèque Nationale de France, Paris (MD Grec 74, fol. 39v) **194** National Museum of China, Beijing **195** Photo: Ann Münchow © Domkapitel Aachen **196** © British Library Board, All Rights Reserved (Add MS 19352, fol. 27v) **199** Art Resource, NY **201** Courtesy of The Freer Gallery of Art and Arthur M. Sackler Gallery, Smithsonian Institution, Washington, D.C.: Purchase, F1930.60a **202** Bildarchiv Steffens/Bridgeman Art Library **204** Bibliothèque Nationale de France, Paris (MS ARABE 5847, fol. 94v) **205** Institut Amatller d'Art Hispanic **207** Dagli Orti/The Art Archive **208** National Library, Cairo/Dagli Orti/The Art Archive **213** Topkapi Palace Museum

Chapter 8

217 Ann Münchow © Domkapital Aachen **218** Fototeca Unione, American Academy, Rome/Bridgeman Art Library **220** Ann Münchow © Domkapitel Aachen **221** The British Museum/Eileen Tweedy/ The Art Archive **223** Bodleian Library, University of Oxford (MS. Opp. 154. fol. 39v.) **226** Bibliothèque Nationale de France, Paris (RC-B-15909) **228** Osterrechische Nationalbibliothek, Vienna (E 135-C, Cod. 387, fol. 90v) **231** © The Trustees of the British Museum (1867.0120.1) **232** Louvre, Paris, France, Lauros/Giraudon Bridgeman Art Library **236** The Board of Trinity College, Dublin (TCD MS 58 fol. 32v) **237** Bibliotheek der Rijksuniversiteit, Utrecht (MS 32, fol. 13v) **239** Viking Ship Museum, Oslo, Norway/Bridgeman Art Library **242** Scala/Art Resource, NY **245** Kunsthistorisches Museum, Vienna

Chapter 9

248 Bridgeman Art Library/SuperStock, Inc. **249** Musée de la Tapisserie, Bayeux, France/Bridgeman Art Library **250** Private Collection/Bridgeman Art Library **252** Leiden University Library (ms.BPL 20, fol. 60r) **253** University Library, Heidelberg/Dagli Orti/The Art Archive **255** Church of St. Foy, Conques, France/Lauros-Giraudon/Bridgman Art Library **256** Bridgeman Art Library **257** (L) Scala/Art Resource, NY (R) Bridgeman-Giraudon/Art Resource, NY **258** Otto Müller Verlag **265** Bodleian Library, University of Oxford (MS. Bodl. 264 fol. 218r) **268** © British Library Board, All Rights Reserved (MS ROY 15 E III, fol. 269r) **269** Musée Conde, Chantilly, France, Giraudon/Bridgeman Art Library **270** bpk/Art Resource, NY **271, 272** Scala/Art Resource, NY **275** Biblioteca Apostolica Vaticana (Vatican) (MS VAT LAT 4922, fol. 49r)

Chapter 10

286, 287, 290 Erich Lessing/Art Resource, NY **293** Bibliothèque Nationale de France, Paris/The Art Archive **294** Bridgeman-Giraudon/Art Resource, NY **295** Psalter and Prayer Book of Bonne of Luxembourg, Duchess of Normandy: folio 322 recto: The Three Dead. Grisaille, color, gilt and brown ink on vellum. H. 4 15/16 in. W. 3 9/16 in. (12.5 x 9.1 cm.) The Metropolitan Museum of Art, Cloisters Collection, 1969 (69.86) Photograph © 1991 The Metropolitan Museum of Art **298** (T) © British Library Board, All Rights Reserved (MS ROY 20 CVII, fol 41v) (B) Jerome Da Cunha/akg-images **300** (T) GoodShoot/SuperStock, Inc. (B, L) French Tourist Office, Provins (B, R) Anders Blomquist/Lonely Planet Images **301** (T,L) Juergen Sorges/akg-images (T, R) Taki Zargaron, Bukhara, Uzbekistan/Bridgeman Art Library (B,L) Erich Lessing/Art Resource, NY (B,R) Zhou Wenguang/Xinhua News Agency **303** St. Benedict Sacro Speco Subiaco Italy/Dagli Orti/The Art Archive **308** Rosgarten Museum, Stadtische Museen Konstanz (Hsl, fol.58a) **310** Biblioteca Apostolica Vaticana (Vatican) (URB LAT 365, Inferno, Canto VIII, fol. 20r) **312** © British Library Board, All Rights Reserved (MS Harl. 4431, fol. 3r)

Chapter 11

317 Maria della Grazie, Milan, Italy/Bridgeman Art Library **320** Scala/Art Resource, NY **323** (L), (R) Galleria degli Uffizi, Florence/Dagli Orti/The Art Archive **325** Erich Lessing/Art Resource, NY **326** (L), (R), Scala/Art Resource, NY **327, 328, 329** (T), (B) Scala/Art Resource, NY **330** Scala/Art Resource, NY **333** (T) Scala/Art Resource, NY (B) Réunion des Musées Nationaux/Art Resource, NY **338, 339** Scala/Art Resource, NY **340** Erich Lessing/Art Resource, NY **343** Bibliothèque Nationale de France, Paris (MS Fr. 9087, fol. 207v)

Chapter 12

347 Walker Art Gallery, National Museums Liverpool **350** Bridgeman-Giraudon/Art Resource, NY **353** Mexicolore **354** Laurie Platt Winfrey, Inc. **356** Snark/Art Resource, NY **357** © 2006 Harvard University Peabody Museum, 2004.24.29636 **358** Reproduced by courtesy of the Trustees, © The National Gallery, London (NG1287) **364** Czartoyski Collection, Krakow **365** National Portrait Gallery, London (NPG668) **366** Réunion des Musées Nationaux/Art Resource, NY **371, 372** Scala/Art Resource, NY **375** Erich Lessing/Art Resource, NY **375** Topkapi Palace Museum

Chapter 13

378, 379 Library of Congress **380** Private Collection/Bridgeman Art Library **386** Erich Lessing/Art Resource, NY **387** Kunstsammlungen der Veste Coburg, Germany **388** Rheinisches LandesMuseum, Bonn **391** Bridgeman-Giraudon/Art Resource, NY **393** University Library Geneva/Dagli Orti/The Art Archive **394** Erich Lessing/Art Resource, NY **396** National Portrait Gallery, London, UK/Bridgeman Art Library **397** University Library Geneva/Dagli Orti/The Art Archive **398** Pen drawing by Jakob Murner, 1525 © Artothek **400** Collection Rijksmuseum Amsterdam **402** Scala/Art Resource, NY **403** Erich Lessing/Art Resource, NY **404** Bridgeman-Giraudon/Art Resource, NY

Chapter 14

411 Bridgeman-Giraudon/Art Resource, NY **412** Hulton Archive/Getty Images **414** (T) Art Resource, NY (B) Musée cantonal des Beaux-Arts, Lausanne **417** National Portrait Gallery, London (NPG429) **418** Bibliothèque Nationale de France, Paris, Lauros/Giraudon/Bridgeman Art Library **420** © National Maritime Museum, London **422** Palazzo Pitti. Florence/Dagli Orti/The Art Archive **425** Collection Rijksmuseum Amsterdam **427** Erich Lessing/Art Resource, NY **432** Musées de Strasbourg **435** Kunsthistorisches Museum, Vienna (Inv.Nr.GG1071)

Chapter 15

440, 441 Roudnice Lobkowicz Collection/Bridgeman Art Library **442** © British Library Board/All Rights Reserved/Bridgeman Art Library **443** Scala/Art Resource, NY **444** Museum of Art, Tula, Russia/Bridgeman Art Library **446** Erich Lessing/Art Resource, NY **449** Bridgeman-Giraudon/Art Resource, NY **450** Private Collection, Photo © Christie's Images/Bridgeman Art Library **452** Reproduced by courtesy of the Trustees, © The National Gallery, London (NG944) **454** Erich Lessing/Art Resource, NY **455** The Granger Collection, NY **457** Collection Rijksmuseum Amsterdam **459** Victoria & Albert Museum, London/Art Resource, NY **460** Philadelphia Museum of Art: Smith, Kline and French (now SmithKline Beecham) Laboratories Collection. Photo by Lynn Rosenthal, 2000 **461** Reproduced by courtesy of the Trustees, © The National Gallery, London (NG186) **462** Erich Lessing/Art Resource, NY **466** © Mary Evans Picture Library/The Image Works

Chapter 16

471 Réunion des Musées Nationaux/Art Resource, NY **472** National Portrait Gallery, London (NPG2561) **475** (L) The National Portrait Gallery, London (NPG1449) (R) Courtesy of the Hispanic Society of America, New York **476** National Portrait Gallery, London (NPG3840) **479** The Art Archive **481** Château de Versailles, France/Bridgeman Art Library **482** Peter Willi/SuperStock, Inc. **485** By permission of the Earl of Rosebury, on loan to the Scottish National Portrait Gallery. Permission of Lord Dalmeny **486** Stock Montage, Inc. **490** © Leemage **493, 495, 496** Scala/Art Resource, NY **497** Bridgeman-Giraudon/Art Resource, NY

INDEX

A boldface entry indicates a key term and the page number where its definition can be found. Terms and definitions also appear in the Glossary on pages G-1–G-7.